SCHOLASTIC Pocket

Dictionary

SCHOLASTIC REFERENCE

An imprint of

SCHOLASTIC

Content abridged from *Scholastic Children's Dictionary*
Scholastic Children's Dictionary First Edition copyright © 1994 by Usborne Publishing Ltd.

ISBN 0-439-62039-2

Art Director: Nancy Sabato
Interior design: Kristen Ekeland
Cover design: Tatiana Sperhacke
Composition: Brad Walrod/High Text Graphics, Inc.

Printed in the U.S.A.
First printing, July 2005

10 9 8 7 6 5 4 3 2 1   05 06 07 08 09

Cover photo credits: Hummingbird: Royalty-Free/Corbis; Skateboarder: RubberBall Productions/Veer; Microscope: Photodisc/PictureQuest

Contents

Pronunciation Guide

There are no strange symbols in this dictionary's pronunciation system. Instead, letters and letter combinations are used to stand for different sounds. To make our system as clear as possible, we have included more than one way to pronounce some sounds. These alternatives are indented, below. For example, the **s-** sound is given the pronunciation symbol (s) at the beginning of a word or syllable, as in (**see**) for the word **see**, but the symbol (ss) at the end of a word or syllable, as in (**layss**) for the word **lace**.

Pronunciations are not listed for some entries that consist of two or more words, such as **acid rain**, or words that are hyphenated, such as **mix-up**. The pronunciations for those words are found elsewhere in the dictionary. **Acid rain**, for example, has pronunciations indicated at the entries for **acid** and **rain**, and the words in **mix-up** are pronounced at **mix** and **up**.

Many words contain two or more syllables. In most cases, those words have one syllable that gets greater stress than any other syllable. This accented syllable is marked in boldface letters, as in (**ak**-shuhn) for the word **action**. Some words also have a syllable with a second or lighter stress. This second accented syllable is marked in italic, as in (**koh**-kuh-*nuht*) for **coconut**.

The symbol (uh) is used for both the accented vowel in the word **cup** and for almost all unaccented syllables in words, as in (uh-**bout**) for the word **about**. Here are the letters and letter combinations that stand for each sound in this dictionary.

Vowels	
a	m**a**d, p**a**t
ah	f**a**ther
air	f**air**, c**are**
ar	d**ar**k
ay	p**ay**, accl**ai**m
(a-*consonant*-e) m**ade**, n**ape**	
aw	r**aw**, c**au**ght
e	m**e**t, m**e**n
ee	b**ee**t
i	b**i**t, acc**i**dent
ihr	f**ear**, h**ere**
eye	**i**ron, rabb**i**
(i-*consonant*-e) f**ile**, r**ipe**	
(*consonant*-ie or -ye) r**ye**, l**ie**, m**y**	
o	c**o**t, d**o**t
oh	f**oe**, d**ou**gh
(o-*consonant*-e) al**one**, st**one**	
oo	p**oo**l, r**u**de
or	c**or**n, m**ore**
oi	b**oi**l, t**oy**
ou	h**ow**, **ou**ch
u	p**u**t, b**oo**k
uh	b**u**n, nat**io**n, comm**a**
ur	b**ur**n, w**orker**
yoo	m**u**sic, p**u**re

Consonants	
b	**b**ad, so**b**
ch	**ch**ip, di**tch**
d	**d**ip, re**d**
f	**f**un, cu**ff**, lau**gh**
g	**g**et, be**g**
h	**h**am
j	**j**am, e**dg**e
k	**k**eep, sa**ck**
l	**l**ap, te**ll**
m	**m**an, la**mb**
n	**n**ow, te**n**, **gn**at, **kn**ow
ng	si**ng**
p	**p**an, si**p**
r	**r**ib, pou**r**
s	**s**et
ss	mi**ss**, ra**c**e, ye**s**
sh	**sh**ip, ra**sh**
t	**t**ub, ra**t**
th	**th**in, ba**th**
TH	**th**is, ba**th**e
v	**v**an, hi**v**e
w	**w**ell, **wh**ale
y	**y**ell
z	**z**ip, ha**s**, tho**s**e
zh	mea**s**ure

Initials, Acronyms, and Abbreviations

An **initial** is a letter, usually followed by a period, that takes the place of a whole word.

An **acronym** is a group of initials that forms another word or phrase.

An **abbreviation** is a shortened form of a word, followed by a period.

AA = Alcoholics Anonymous
ACLU = American Civil Liberties Union
AM = Amplitude Modulation
anon = anonymous
ASAP = As Soon As Possible
ASPCA = American Society for the Prevention of Cruelty to Animals
Aug. = August
AWOL = Absent WithOut Leave
C = Celsius or Centigrade
CEO = Chief Executive Officer
CIA = Central Intelligence Agency
cm = centimeter
co = company
COD = cash on delivery
corp = corporation
DA = District Attorney
dB = decibel
D.C. = District of Columbia
DDS = Doctor of Dental Science
Dec. = December
dept = department
DOB = Date Of Birth
EMT = Emergency Medical Technician
EPA = Environmental Protection Agency
ERA = Equal Rights Amendment
ESL = English as a Second Language
F = Fahrenheit
FAQ = Frequently Asked Questions
FBI = Federal Bureau of Investigation
Feb. = February
FM = Frequency Modulation
Fri. = Friday
ft. = foot
FYI = For Your Information
g = gram
GCF = Greatest Common Factor
GOP = Grand Old Party (Republican Party)
HDTV = High-Definition TeleVision
HQ = HeadQuarters
hr. = hour
ID = IDentification
in. = inch
inc = incorporated
IRS = Internal Revenue Service
Jan. = January
Jr. = junior
kg = kilogram
km = kilometer
l = liter

lb. = pound

LCD = Lowest (or Least) Common Denominator

LCM = Lowest (or Least) Common Multiple

m = meter

MADD = Mothers Against Drunk Driving

MC = Master of Ceremonies

MD = *Medicinae Doctor* (Latin for "doctor of medicine")

mi. = mile

MIA = Missing In Action

min. = minute

misc. = miscellaneous

mm = millimeter

Mon. = Monday

NAACP = National Association for the Advancement of Colored People

NASA = National Aeronautics and Space Administration

NASCAR = National Association for Stock Car Auto Racing

NASDAQ = National Association of Securities Dealers Automated Quotations

NBA = National Basketball Association

NFL = National Football League

NHL = National Hockey League

no. = number

Nov. = November

NOW = National Organization for Women

Oct. = October

OPEC = Organization of Petroleum Exporting Countries

oz. = ounce

PA = Public Address

PIN = Personal Identification Number

PO = Post Office

POW = Prisoner Of War

PTA = Parent-Teacher Association

PTO = Parent-Teacher Organization

RN = Registered Nurse

RSVP = *Répondez S'il Vous Plaît* (French for "please reply")

RV = Recreational Vehicle

SADD = Students Against Drunk Driving

SASE = Self-Addressed Stamped Envelope

Sat. = Saturday

sec. = second

Sept. = September

SIDS = Sudden Infant Death Syndrome

Sr. = senior

Sun. = Sunday

t = ton

T or tbsp = tablespoon

tsp = teaspoon

TBA = To Be Announced

Thurs. = Thursday

TM = Trademark

Tues. = Tuesday

UN = United Nations

UNICEF = United Nations Children's Fund

UPC = Universal Product Code

USA = United States of America

Wac = Women's Army Corps

Wed. = Wednesday

w/o = without

WWW = World Wide Web

yd. = yard

Dictionary Entries Close Up

Syllable Breaks are indicated by small dots in most main entry words. Entries made up of two separate words or two words and a hyphen are not broken into syllables. To find their syllable breaks, look up each part of the term separately. For example, to find the syllable breaks for *table manners*, look up *table* and *manners*.

Pronunciations, given in parentheses, follow most main entry words. The "Pronunciation Guide" on p. *iv* explains which letters represent each sound. If the pronunciation of a word changes depending on its meaning, the appropriate pronunciation appears with the appropriate meaning.

Numbers appear at the beginning of each meaning when a word has more than one meaning. The most frequently used meanings generally appear first.

mouth•piece (**mouth**-*peess*) ***noun***
1. The part of a telephone that you talk into.
2. The part of a musical instrument that you blow over or into.
3. *(informal)* Someone who acts as a spokesperson for an individual or a group.

Parts of Speech labels usually appear on the first line of entries. However, if a word's part of speech changes from one meaning to the next, the part of speech label starts each new meaning. When a meaning shows the word as part of a common phrase or idiom, no part of speech is given.

Usage Guides tell you that a meaning of a word is informal or slang. Informal words are used in everyday speech but not usually in formal speech or writing. Many slang terms or meanings are very popular only for a short period of time. Like informal words, they are not appropriate in formal writing such as term papers and essays.

Definitions tell the meanings of words. When the main entry word is used within the definition, it is printed in **boldface**. In the rare occasion that a definition includes a word that is not in the dictionary, that word appears in *italics*.

Related Words and Word Forms appear at the end of an entry or at the end of a meaning. This dictionary also lists irregular plural forms with entry words that are nouns, *-er* and *-est* forms with adjectives, and *-ed*, *-ing*, and irregular forms with verbs.

rap (**rap**)
1. ***verb*** To hit something sharply and quickly.
▸ ***noun* rap**
2. ***noun*** A type of song in which the words are spoken in a rhythmical way to a musical background. ▸ ***noun* rapper** ▸ ***verb* rap**
3. ***verb*** *(slang)* To talk.
Rap sounds like **wrap.**
▸ ***verb* rapping, rapped**

Homophones, words that sound alike but have different spellings and meanings, are listed toward the ends of definitions.

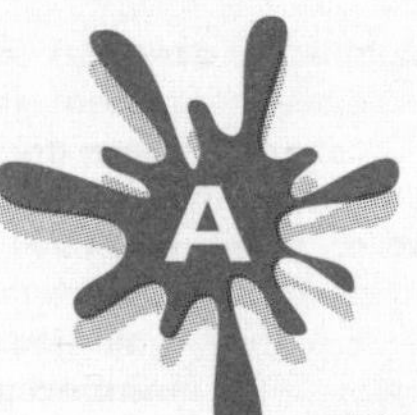

a (uh *or* **a**) ***indefinite article***
1. Any. *Pick a card.*
2. One. *I have a car.*
3. Per. *They traveled two hundred miles a day during the trip.*

aard•vark (**ard**-*vark*) ***noun*** An African mammal with a long, sticky tongue that it uses to search for insects.

ab•a•cus (**ab**-uh-kuhss) ***noun*** A frame with sliding beads on wires, used for adding, subtracting, multiplying, and dividing. ▸ ***noun, plural*** **abacuses** *or* **abaci** (**ab**-uh-sye *or* **ab**-uh-kye)

ab•a•lo•ne (*ab*-uh-**loh**-nee) ***noun*** A large sea snail with a flat shell whose meat people eat and whose shell lining is shiny like a pearl.

a•ban•don (uh-**ban**-duhn) ***verb***
1. To leave forever.
2. To give up.
▸ ***verb*** **abandoning, abandoned**

a•ban•doned (uh-**ban**-duhnd) ***adjective*** Deserted, or no longer used.

a•bate (uh-**bayt**) ***verb*** To become less intense. ▸ **abating, abated**

ab•bey (**ab**-ee) ***noun*** A group of buildings where monks or nuns live and work.

ab•bre•vi•ate (uh-**bree**-vee-*ate*) ***verb*** To make something shorter, such as a word. ▸ **abbreviating, abbreviated** ▸ ***adjective*** **abbreviated**

ab•bre•vi•a•tion (uh-*bree*-vee-**ay**-shuhn) ***noun*** A short way of writing a word.

ab•di•cate (**ab**-di-kate) ***verb*** To give up power. ▸ **abdicating, abdicated** ▸ ***noun*** **abdication**

ab•do•men (**ab**-duh-muhn) ***noun***
1. The part of your body between your chest and hips.
2. The back section of an insect's body.

ab•duct (ab-**dukt**) ***verb*** To kidnap someone. ▸ **abducting, abducted** ▸ ***noun*** **abduction**

ab•hor (ab-**hor**) ***verb*** To hate someone or something. ▸ **abhorring, abhorred** ▸ ***adjective*** **abhorrent**

a•bide (uh-**bide**) ***verb***
1. To stay or live somewhere.
2. If you **cannot abide** something, you cannot comply with it.
▸ ***verb*** **abiding, abided** *or* **abode** (uh-**bohd**)

a•bil•i•ty (uh-**bil**-i-tee) ***noun***
1. The power to do something.
2. Skill.
▸ ***noun, plural*** **abilities**

a•blaze (uh-**blaze**) ***adjective*** On fire.

a•ble (**ay**-buhl) ***adjective***
1. If you are **able** to do something, you can do it.
2. Skillful or talented.
▸ ***adjective*** **abler, ablest** ▸ ***adverb*** **ably**

able-bod•ied (**bod**-eed) ***adjective*** Someone who is **able-bodied** has a strong, healthy body.

ab•nor•mal (ab-**nor**-muhl) ***adjective*** Unusual, or not normal. ▸ ***noun*** **abnormality** (*ab*-nor-**mal**-i-tee)

a•board (uh-**bord**) ***adverb*** On or into a train, ship, or aircraft. ▸ ***preposition*** **aboard**

a•bode (uh-**bode**) ***noun*** A home.

a•bol•ish (uh-**bol**-ish) ***verb*** To put an end to something officially. ▸ **abolishes, abolishing, abolished** ▸ ***noun*** **abolition**

a•bo•li•tion•ist (*ab*-uh-**lish**-uh-nist) ***noun*** Someone who worked to abolish slavery before the Civil War.

a•bom•i•na•ble (uh-**bom**-uh-nuh-buhl) ***adjective*** Horrible, or disgusting. ▸ ***adverb*** **abominably**

Ab•o•rig•i•ne (*ab*-uh-**rij**-uh-nee) ***noun*** One of the native peoples of Australia who have lived there since before the Europeans arrived. ▸ ***adjective*** **Aboriginal**

a•bort (uh-**bort**) ***verb*** To stop something from happening in the early stages. ▸ **aborting, aborted** ▸ ***adjective*** **abortive**

a•bound (uh-**bound**) ***verb*** To have a large amount of something. ▸ **abounding, abounded**

a•bout (uh-**bout**)
1. ***preposition*** On a particular subject.
2. ***adverb*** Almost, or more or less.

a•bove (uh-**buhv**) ***preposition***
1. Higher up than, or over.
2. More than, as in *above average.*

a•bove•board (uh-**buhv**-*bord*) ***adjective*** If an action is **aboveboard,** it is completely honest and legal.

ab•ra•sive (uh-**bray**-siv) ***adjective***
1. Rough and grinding. ▸ ***noun*** **abrasive**
2. Rude.

a•breast (uh-**brest**) ***adverb*** Side by side.

a•bridged (uh-**brijd**) ***adjective*** Shortened, as in *an abridged novel.* ▸ ***verb*** **abridge**

a•broad (uh-**brawd**) ***adverb*** In or to another country. In the United States, *abroad* usually means "overseas."

a•brupt (uh-**brupt**) ***adjective***
1. Sudden and unexpected.
2. Rude and overly quick, as in *an abrupt reply.*
▸ ***adverb*** **abruptly**

ab•scess (**ab**-sess) ***noun*** A painful swelling full of a yellow substance called pus. ▸ ***noun, plural*** **abscesses**

ab•scond (ab-**skond**) ***verb*** To go away suddenly and secretly, usually after doing something wrong. ▸ **absconding, absconded**

ab•sent (**ab**-suhnt) ***adjective*** Not present. ▸ ***noun*** **absence,** ***noun*** **absentee,** ***noun*** **absenteeism**

absent-mind•ed (**mine**-duhd) ***adjective*** If you are **absent-minded,** you are forgetful and do not think about what you are doing. ▸ ***adverb*** **absent-mindedly**

ab•so•lute (**ab**-suh-loot) ***adjective***
1. Complete, or total.
2. Without any limit.
▸ ***adverb*** **absolutely**

ab•solve (ab-**zolv**) ***verb*** To pardon someone or free the person from blame. ▸ **absolving, absolved** ▸ ***noun*** **absolution**

ab•sorb (ab-**zorb**) ***verb***
1. To soak up liquid.
2. To take in information.
3. If something **absorbs** you, it takes up all your attention.
▸ ***verb*** **absorbing**, **absorbed**

ab•sorb•ent (ab-**zor**-buhnt) ***adjective*** Something that soaks up liquid, such as a washcloth, towel, or sponge, is **absorbent.**

ab•sorp•tion (ab-**zorp**-shuhn) ***noun*** The process of soaking up liquid, heat, or light.

ab•stain (ab-**stayn**) ***verb*** To stop yourself from doing something. ▸ **abstaining, abstained** ▸ ***noun*** **abstention**

ab•stract (**ab**-strakt *or* ab-**strakt**) ***adjective***
1. Based on ideas rather than things.
2. Hard to understand.

ab•surd (ab-**surd** *or* ab-**zurd**) ***adjective*** Silly, or ridiculous. ▸ **absurder, absurdest** ▸ ***noun*** **absurdity** ▸ ***adverb*** **absurdly**

a•bun•dant (uh-**bun**-duhnt) ***adjective*** If there is an **abundant** supply of something, there is plenty of it. ▸ ***noun*** **abundance** ▸ ***adverb*** **abundantly**

a•buse
1. (uh-**byooss**) ***noun*** Rude or unkind words.

A

2. (uh-**byooz**) ***verb*** To treat a person or creature cruelly. ▸ **abusing, abused** ▸ ***noun*** **abuser**
3. (uh-**byooss**) ***noun*** Wrong or harmful use of something or treatment of someone, as in *alcohol abuse* or *child abuse.* ▸ ***verb*** **abuse** (uh-**byooz**) ▸ ***adjective*** **abusive**

a•bys•mal (uh-**biz**-muhl) ***adjective*** Very bad, or terrible. ▸ ***adverb*** **abysmally**

a•byss (uh-**biss**) ***noun*** A very deep hole that seems to have no bottom. ▸ ***noun, plural*** **abysses**

a•ca•cia (uh-**kay**-shuh) ***noun*** A small tree or shrub that has feathery leaves and pleasant-smelling white or yellow flowers and grows in warm parts of the world.

ac•a•dem•ic (ak-uh-**dem**-ik)
1. ***adjective*** To do with study and learning. ▸ ***adverb*** **academically**
2. ***noun*** Someone who teaches in a university or college or someone who does research.

a•cad•e•my (uh-**kad**-uh-mee) ***noun***
1. A private junior high, middle school, or high school.
2. A school that teaches special subjects, as in *a military academy.*
▸ ***noun, plural*** **academies**

ac•cel•er•ate (ak-**sel**-uh-*rate*) ***verb*** To get faster and faster. ▸ **accelerating, accelerated** ▸ ***noun*** **acceleration**

ac•cent (**ak**-sent) ***noun***
1. The way that you pronounce words. ▸ ***verb*** **accent**
2. Some languages use an **accent mark** over, under, or next to a letter to show how it is pronounced, as in *café.*

ac•cen•tu•ate (ak-**sen**-choo-*ate*) ***verb*** To emphasize or draw attention to something. ▸ **accentuating, accentuated**

ac•cept (ak-**sept**) ***verb***
1. To take something that you are offered.
2. To agree to something.
▸ ***verb*** **accepting, accepted** ▸ ***noun*** **acceptance** ▸ ***adjective*** **acceptable**

ac•cess (**ak**-sess)
1. ***noun*** A way to enter, or an approach to a place. ▸ ***noun, plural*** **accesses** ▸ ***adjective*** **accessible**
2. ***verb*** To get information from a computer. ▸ **accesses, accessing, accessed**

ac•ces•so•ry (ak-**sess**-uh-ree) ***noun***
1. An extra part for something, as in *computer accessories.*
2. Something, such as a belt or a scarf, that goes with your clothes.
3. An **accessory** to a crime is someone who helps another person commit a crime or helps cover up a crime by not reporting it.
▸ ***noun, plural*** **accessories**

ac•ci•dent (**ak**-si-duhnt) ***noun*** Something that takes place unexpectedly and that often involves people being hurt. ▸ ***adjective*** **accidental** ▸ ***adverb*** **accidentally**

ac•claim (uh-**klaym**) ***noun*** Praise. ▸ ***verb*** **acclaim**

ac•cli•ma•tize (uh-**klye**-muh-*tize*) ***verb*** To get used to a different climate or to new surroundings. ▸ **acclimatizing, acclimatized** ▸ ***noun*** **acclimatization**

ac•com•mo•date (uh-**kom**-uh-*date*) ***verb***
1. To help out or reply to a request.
2. To provide with a place to stay.
▸ ***verb*** **accommodating, accommodated**

ac•com•pa•ny (uh-**kum**-puh-nee) ***verb***
1. To go somewhere with someone.
2. To support a musician or singer by playing along on a musical instrument.
▸ ***noun*** **accompaniment,** ***noun*** **accompanist**
▸ ***verb*** **accompanies, accompanying, accompanied**

ac•com•plice (uh-**kom**-pliss) ***noun*** Someone who helps another person commit a crime.

A

ac•com•plish (uh-**kom**-plish) ***verb*** To do something successfully. ▸ **accomplishes, accomplishing, accomplished** ▸ ***noun*** **accomplishment**

ac•com•plished (uh-**kom**-plisht) ***adjective*** Skillful, as in *an accomplished musician.*

ac•cord (uh-**kord**) ***noun***
1. Peaceful agreement.
2. If you do something **of your own accord,** you do it without being asked.

according to ***preposition***
1. As someone has said or written.
2. In a way that is suitable.
▸ ***adverb*** **accordingly**

ac•cor•di•on (uh-**kor**-dee-uhn) ***noun*** A musical instrument that you squeeze to make sound and play by pressing keys and buttons.

ac•cost (uh-**kost**) ***verb*** To approach someone and talk to the person, usually in an annoying or hostile way. ▸ **accosting, accosted**

ac•count (uh-**kount**)
1. ***noun*** A description of something that has happened, as in *an account of the accident.*
2. ***noun*** An arrangement to keep money in a bank, as in *a checking or savings account.*
3. accounts *noun, plural* Records of money earned and spent.
4. *verb* If you **account for** something, you explain it. ▸ **accounting, accounted** ▸ ***adjective*** **accountable**

ac•count•ant (uh-**koun**-tuhnt) ***noun*** An expert in money matters and keeping accounts. ▸ ***noun*** **accountancy**

ac•cu•mu•late (uh-**kyoo**-myuh-late) ***verb*** To collect things or let them pile up. ▸ **accumulating, accumulated** ▸ ***noun*** **accumulation**

ac•cu•rate (**ak**-yuh-ruht) ***adjective*** Exactly correct. ▸ ***noun*** **accuracy** ▸ ***adverb*** **accurately**

ac•cuse (uh-**kyooz**) ***verb*** To say that someone has done something wrong. ▸ **accusing, accused** ▸ ***noun*** **accusation,** ***noun*** **accuser**

ac•cus•tomed (uh-**kuss**-tuhmd) ***adjective***
1. Usual, as in *my accustomed seat.*
2. When you are **accustomed to** something, you are used to it.

ace (**ayss**) ***noun***
1. A playing card with only one symbol on it. In most card games, the ace has the highest value.
2. A serve in tennis that is not returned, or even touched, by the other player.

ache (**ake**) ***noun*** A dull pain that goes on and on. ▸ ***verb*** **ache**

a•chieve (uh-**cheev**) ***verb*** To do something successfully, especially after a lot of effort. ▸ **achieving, achieved** ▸ ***noun*** **achievement,** ***noun*** **achiever**

ac•id (**ass**-id)
1. ***noun*** A substance with a sour taste that will react with a base to form a salt. Acids turn blue litmus paper red. Strong acids can burn your skin.
2. ***adjective*** Sour, or bitter. ▸ ***adjective*** **acidic**

acid rain ***noun*** Rain that is polluted by acid in the atmosphere and damages the environment.

ac•knowl•edge (ak-**nol**-ij) ***verb***
1. To admit to something.
2. To show that you have seen and recognized somebody.
3. To let the sender know that you have received a letter or package.
▸ ***verb*** **acknowledging, acknowledged** ▸ ***noun*** **acknowledgment**

ac•ne (**ak**-nee) ***noun*** A skin condition that results from clogging up or blocking the oil glands in the skin. This causes inflammation and red pimples on the face, back, or chest.

a•corn (**ay**-korn) ***noun*** The seed of an oak tree.

a•cou•stic (uh-**koo**-stik)
1. ***adjective*** To do with sound or hearing.
2. acoustics *noun, plural* If a place has

good **acoustics,** you can hear sounds and music very clearly inside it.

acoustic guitar ***noun*** A guitar that does not need an electronic amplifier.

ac•quain•tance (uh-**kwayn**-tuhnss) ***noun*** Someone you have met but do not know very well.

ac•quire (uh-**kwire**) ***verb***
1. To obtain or get something.
2. If something is an **acquired taste,** you grow to like it slowly.
▸ ***verb*** **acquiring, acquired**

ac•quit (uh-**kwit**) ***verb*** To find someone not guilty of a crime. ▸ **acquitting, acquitted** ▸ ***noun*** **acquittal**

a•cre (**ay**-kur) ***noun*** A measurement of area equal to 43,560 square feet. An acre is almost the size of a standard football field. ▸ ***noun*** **acreage**

ac•ro•bat (**ak**-ruh-*bat*) ***noun*** A person who performs exciting gymnastic acts that require great skill. Acrobats often work with a circus.

ac•ro•bat•ics (*ak*-ruh-**bat**-iks) ***noun, plural*** Difficult gymnastic acts, often performed in the air or on a high wire. ▸ ***adjective*** **acrobatic**

ac•ro•nym (**ak**-ruh-nim) ***noun*** A word made from the first or first few letters of the words in a phrase.

a•cross (uh-**kross**) ***preposition***
1. From one side of to the other side of.
2. On the other side of.

a•cryl•ic (uh-**kril**-ik) ***noun*** A chemical substance used to make fibers and paints.

act (**akt**)
1. ***verb*** To do something. ▸ ***noun*** **act**
2. ***verb*** To perform in a play, movie, etc.
3. ***verb*** To have an effect.
4. ***noun*** A short performance, as in *a comedy act.*
5. ***noun*** One of the parts of a play.
6. ***noun*** A bill that has been passed by Congress. If signed by the president, it becomes law.
▸ ***verb*** **acting, acted**

ac•tion (**ak**-shuhn) ***noun***
1. Something that you do to achieve a result.
2. When you **take action,** you do something for a purpose.

ac•ti•vate (**ak**-tuh-*vate*) ***verb*** To turn on, or to cause to work. ▸ **activating, activated** ▸ ***noun*** **activator**

ac•tive (**ak**-tiv) ***adjective***
1. Energetic and busy, as in *an active social life.*
2. The subject of an active verb does the action, rather than having something done to it.

ac•tiv•i•ty (ak-**tiv**-uh-tee) ***noun***
1. Action, or movement.
2. Something that you do for pleasure, as in *a rainy-day activity.*
▸ ***noun, plural*** **activities**

ac•tor (**ak**-tur) ***noun*** A person who performs in the theater, movies, television, etc.

ac•tress (**ak**-triss) ***noun*** A girl or a woman who performs in the theater, movies, television, etc.

ac•tu•al (**ak**-choo-uhl) ***adjective*** Real, or true. ▸ ***adverb*** **actually**

ac•u•punc•ture (**ak**-yoo-*pungk*-chur) ***noun*** A way of treating illness by pricking parts of the body with small needles.

a•cute (uh-**kyoot**) ***adjective***
1. Sharp, or severe, as in *an acute pain.*
2. Able to detect things easily, as in *an acute sense of smell.* ▸ ***noun*** **acuteness** ▸ ***adverb*** **acutely**
3. An **acute** angle is an angle of less than 90 degrees.
▸ ***adjective*** **acuter, acutest**

A.D. (**ay dee**) The initials of the Latin phrase *Anno Domini,* which means "in the year of the Lord." A.D. is used to show that a date comes after the birth of Jesus.

ad (**ad**) ***noun*** A short term for **advertisement** or **advertising**, as in *ad agency.*

ad•age (**ad**-ij) ***noun*** An old saying that people generally believe is true.

A

A

a·dapt (uh-**dapt**) ***verb***
1. To make something suitable for a different purpose.
2. To change because you are in a new situation.
▸ ***verb*** **adapting, adapted** ▸ ***adjective*** **adaptable**

ad·ap·ta·tion (ad-ap-**tay**-shuhn) ***noun***
1. The act of adjusting.
2. A change that a living thing goes through so it fits in better with its environment.

a·dapt·er *or* **a·dap·tor** (uh-**dap**-tur) ***noun*** A device that connects two parts that are of slightly different shapes or sizes.

add (**ad**) ***verb***
1. To find the sum of two or more numbers.
2. To put one thing with another.
▸ ***verb*** **adding, added**

ad·dend (**ad**-end) ***noun*** Any number that is added to another to form a sum.

ad·der (**ad**-ur) ***noun***
1. A small, poisonous European snake, sometimes called a viper.
2. A harmless North American snake that hisses and swells up its head when annoyed.

ad·dict (**ad**-ikt) ***noun*** A person who cannot give up doing or using something, as in *a drug addict.* ▸ ***noun*** **addiction** ▸ ***adjective*** **addicted**

ad·dic·tive (uh-**dik**-tiv) ***adjective*** If something, such as a drug, is **addictive,** people find it very hard to give it up.

ad·di·tion (uh-**dish**-uhn) ***noun***
1. In math, **addition** is the adding together of two or more numbers to come up with a sum.
2. A part of a building that is added on to the original.
3. Anything or anyone new.

ad·di·tion·al (uh-**dish**-uh-nuhl) ***adjective*** Extra, or more.

ad·di·tive (**ad**-uh-tiv) ***noun*** Something added to a substance to change it in some way.

ad·dress (uh-**dress** *or* **ad**-ress)
1. ***noun*** The street, number, etc., of a business or residence.
2. ***verb*** To write an address on a letter, card, or package.
3. ***verb*** To give a speech to. ▸ ***noun*** **address**
4. ***verb*** When you **address** a problem, you tackle it or deal with it.
▸ ***verb*** **addresses, addressing, addressed** ▸ ***noun*** **addressee** (*ad*-ress-**ee**)

ad·e·noid (**ad**-uh-*noyd*) ***noun*** A spongy lump of flesh at the back of your nose that can become swollen, making it hard to breathe.

a·dept (uh-**dept**) ***adjective*** Able to do something well.

ad·e·quate (**ad**-uh-kwit) ***adjective*** Just enough, or good enough. ▸ ***adverb*** **adequately**

ADHD (*ay*-dee-**aych**-dee) or **ADD** (*ay*-dee-**dee**) ***noun*** A set of behaviors including overactivity and poor concentration, defined by many as a medical disorder, and that may interfere with learning. ADHD stands for *Attention Deficit Hyperactivity Disorder.* ADD stands for *Attention Deficit Disorder.*

ad·here (ad-**hihr**) ***verb***
1. To stick very tightly to something.
2. To stick with an idea or plan.
▸ ***verb*** **adhering, adhered**

ad·he·sive (ad-**hee**-siv) ***noun*** A substance, such as glue, that makes things stick together. ▸ ***adjective*** **adhesive**

a·di·os (ah-dee-**ohss**) ***interjection*** The Spanish word for good-bye.

ad·ja·cent (uh-**jay**-suhnt) ***adjective*** Close or next to something or someone.

ad·jec·tive (**aj**-ik-tiv) ***noun*** A word that describes a noun or pronoun.

ad·journ (uh-**jurn**) ***verb*** To close or end something, especially a court session or government meeting. ▸ **adjourning, adjourned**

ad•just (uh-**juhst**) ***verb***
1. To move or change something slightly. ▸ ***adjective*** **adjustable**
2. To get used to something new and different.
▸ ***verb*** **adjusting, adjusted** ▸ ***noun*** **adjustment**

ad lib (**ad lib**) ***verb*** To speak in public without preparing first. ▸ **ad libbing, ad libbed** ▸ ***adverb*** **ad lib**

ad•min•is•ter (ad-**min**-uh-stur) ***verb***
1. To govern or control something. ▸ ***noun*** **administrator**
2. To give something to someone.
▸ ***verb*** **administering, administered** ▸ ***noun*** **administration**

ad•mi•ral (**ad**-muh-ruhl) ***noun*** An officer who ranks above a vice admiral in the navy or coast guard.

ad•mire (ad-**mire**) ***verb***
1. To like and respect someone.
2. To look at something and enjoy it.
▸ ***verb*** **admiring, admired** ▸ ***noun*** **admiration**

ad•mit (ad-**mit**) ***verb***
1. To confess to something, or agree that something is true, often reluctantly.
2. To allow someone or something to enter.
▸ ***verb*** **admitting, admitted** ▸ ***noun*** **admission,** ***noun*** **admittance**

ad•mon•ish (ad-**mon**-ish) ***verb*** To warn or advise someone of his or her faults. ▸ **admonishes, admonishing, admonished** ▸ ***noun*** **admonishment**

a•do•be (uh-**doh**-bee) ***noun***
1. A brick made of clay mixed with straw and dried in the sun.
2. A building made with these bricks.

ad•o•les•cent (ad-uh-**less**-uhnt) ***noun*** A young person who is more grown-up than a child but is not yet an adult.
▸ ***noun*** **adolescence** ▸ ***adjective*** **adolescent**

a•dopt (uh-**dopt**) ***verb***
1. When adults **adopt** a child, they take the child into their family and become his or her legal parents. ▸ ***adjective*** **adopted**
2. To accept an idea or a way of doing things.
▸ ***verb*** **adopting, adopted** ▸ ***noun*** **adoption**

a•dor•a•ble (uh-**dor**-uh-buhl) ***adjective*** Very sweet and lovable.

a•dore (uh-**dor**) ***verb*** To be very fond of someone or something. ▸ **adoring, adored** ▸ ***noun*** **adoration** (a-dor-**ay**-shuhn)

a•dorned (uh-**dornd**) ***adjective*** Decorated. ▸ ***verb*** **adorn**

ad•ren•a•line (uh-**dren**-uh-lin) ***noun***
1. A chemical produced by your body when you are excited, frightened, or angry.
2. Adrenalin is a trademark for a manufactured substance that speeds up a person's heartbeat, decreases tiredness, and increases energy.

a•drift (uh-**drift**) ***adverb*** Drifting or floating freely through water or air.
▸ ***adjective*** **adrift**

a•dult (uh-**duhlt** *or* **ah**-duhlt) ***noun*** A fully grown person or animal. ▸ ***noun*** **adulthood** ▸ ***adjective*** **adult**

a•dul•ter•ate (uh-**dul**-tuh-*rate*) ***verb*** To spoil something by adding something less good to it. ▸ **adulterating, adulterated**

ad•vance (ad-**vanss**)
1. ***verb*** To move forward, or to make progress. ▸ ***noun*** **advancement**
2. ***adjective*** Happening before something else, as in *advance warning.*
3. ***verb*** To lend money. ▸ ***noun*** **advance**
4. ***noun*** A movement forward made by a group of soldiers.
▸ ***verb*** **advancing, advanced**

ad•vanced (ad-**vanst**) ***adjective***
1. If something has reached an **advanced** stage, it is nearly finished or fully developed.
2. Advanced work is not elementary or easy, as in *advanced math.*

A

A

ad•van•tage (ad-**van**-tij)
1. ***noun*** Something that helps you or is useful to you. ▸ ***adjective*** **advantageous** (*ad*-vuhn-**tay**-juhss)
2. ***noun*** The first point in a tennis game after the score of deuce.
3. If you **take advantage of** a person or situation, you use it for your own benefit.

ad•vent (**ad**-vent) ***noun***
1. The beginning of something important, as in *the advent of the computer age.*
2. Advent The period leading up to Christmas in the Christian church's year.

ad•ven•ture (ad-**ven**-chur) ***noun*** An exciting or dangerous experience. ▸ ***adjective*** **adventurous**

ad•verb (**ad**-verb) ***noun*** A word usually used to describe a verb or adjective. Adverbs tell how, when, where, how often, or how much something happens.

ad•ver•sar•y (**ad**-ver-ser-ee) ***noun*** Someone who fights or argues against you. ▸ ***noun, plural*** **adversaries**

ad•verse (ad-**verss**) ***adjective*** Unfavorable, or difficult, as in *adverse weather conditions.* ▸ ***adverb*** **adversely**

ad•ver•si•ty (ad-**vur**-suh-tee) ***noun*** Hardship, or misfortune. ▸ ***noun, plural*** **adversities**

ad•ver•tise (**ad**-ver-tize) ***verb*** To give information about something that you want to sell. ▸ **advertising, advertised** ▸ ***noun*** **advertiser**

ad•ver•tise•ment (*ad*-ver-**tize**-muhnt *or* ad-**vuhr**-tiss-muhnt) ***noun*** A public notice, usually published in the press or broadcast over the air, that calls attention to something, such as a product or an event.

ad•vice (ad-**vice**) ***noun*** A suggestion about what someone should do.

ad•vis•a•ble (ad-**vye**-zuh-buhl) ***adjective*** If something is **advisable,** it is sensible and worth doing. ▸ ***adverb*** **advisably**

ad•vise (ad-**vize**) ***verb*** To give someone information or suggestions. ▸ **advising, advised** ▸ ***noun*** **adviser, *noun*** **advisor** ▸ ***adjective*** **advisory**

ad•vo•cate
1. ***verb*** (**ad**-vuh-kate) To support or call for an idea or a plan. ▸ **advocating, advocated**
2. ***noun*** (ad-vuh-**kit**) A person who supports an idea or plan, as in *a women's rights advocate.*

aer•i•al (**air**-ee-uhl)
1. ***noun*** A piece of wire that receives television or radio signals.
2. ***adjective*** Happening in the air, as in *aerial refueling.*

aer•o•bat•ics (*air*-uh-**bat**-iks) ***noun, plural*** Skillful or dangerous movements performed by aircraft in the sky. ▸ ***adjective*** **aerobatic**

aer•o•bics (air-**oh**-biks) ***noun, plural*** Energetic exercises that strengthen the heart and improve respiration. Aerobics are often performed to music. ▸ ***adjective*** **aerobic**

aer•o•dy•nam•ic (*air*-oh-dye-**nam**-mik) ***adjective*** Designed to move through the air very easily and quickly.

aer•o•nau•tics (*air*-uh-**naw**-tiks) ***noun*** The science and practice of designing, building, and fixing aircraft. ▸ ***adjective*** **aeronautical**

aer•o•sol (**air**-uh-sol) ***noun***
1. A mass of tiny solid or liquid particles suspended in air or another gas.
2. A product, such as a deodorant or insecticide, that is sold in a pressurized container. When you press the nozzle, the substance comes out in a spray. ▸ ***adjective*** **aerosol**

aer•o•space (**air**-oh-spayss)
1. ***noun*** The earth's atmosphere and all the space beyond it.
2. ***adjective*** To do with the science and technology of jet flight or space travel.

af•fa•ble (**af**-uh-buhl) ***adjective*** Friendly, or pleasant.

af•fair (uh-**fair**)
1. ***noun*** A special event.

2. **affairs *noun, plural*** Matters connected with private or public life, as in *personal affairs* or *business affairs.*

af•fect (uh-**fekt**) ***verb*** To influence or change someone or something. ▸ **affecting, affected**

af•fect•ed (uh-**fek**-tid) ***adjective*** False and unnatural.

af•fec•tion (uh-**fek**-shuhn) ***noun*** A great liking for someone or something.

af•fec•tion•ate (uh-**fek**-shuh-nuht) ***adjective*** Very loving. ▸ ***adverb*** **affectionately**

af•fil•i•ate (uh-**fil**-ee-*ate*) ***verb*** To join or connect closely with something. ▸ **affiliating, affiliated** ▸ ***noun*** **affiliate** (uh-**fil**-ee-it)

af•fin•i•ty (uh-**fin**-i-tee) ***noun*** If you have an **affinity** for something, you like it and feel a natural attraction to it. ▸ ***noun, plural*** **affinities**

af•firm•a•tive (uh-**fur**-muh-tiv) ***adjective*** Giving the answer "yes," or stating that something is true.

affirmative action ***noun*** A program that promotes increased opportunities for minorities and women in order to make up for past discrimination.

af•flic•tion (uh-**flik**-shuhn) ***noun*** Illness, or suffering. ▸ ***verb*** **afflict**

af•flu•ent (**af**-loo-uhnt) ***adjective*** If you are **affluent**, you have plenty of money. ▸ ***noun*** **affluence**

af•ford (uh-**ford**) ***verb***
1. If you can **afford** something, you have enough money to buy it.
2. To have enough time or ability to do something.
▸ ***verb*** **affording, afforded**

af•ghan (**af**-gan) ***noun*** A crocheted or knitted blanket.

a•float (uh-**flote**) ***adjective*** Floating on water.

a•fraid (uh-**frayd**) ***adjective***
1. Frightened, or worried.
2. Sorry, as in *I'm afraid I can't come to your party.*

a•fresh (uh-**fresh**) ***adverb*** When you start **afresh,** you begin something again.

Af•ri•can American (**af**-ruh-kuhn) ***noun*** Someone who was born in the United States or who became a U.S. citizen and can trace his or her ancestors back to Africa. ▸ ***adjective*** **African-American**

Af•ro (**af**-roh) ***noun*** An African-American hairstyle with tight curls in a full, rounded shape.

aft (**aft**) ***adverb*** Toward the back of a ship or an airplane.

af•ter (**af**-tur) ***preposition***
1. Later than, as in *after lunch.*
2. Following behind.
3. Trying to catch someone or something.

af•ter•noon (*af*-tur-**noon**) ***noun*** The time of day between noon and evening.

af•ter•shock (**af**-tuhr-*shok*) ***noun*** An earthquake that comes soon after a stronger earthquake in the same general location.

af•ter•ward (**af**-tur-*wurd*) *or* **af•ter•wards** (**af**-tur-*wurdz*) ***adverb*** Later.

a•gain (uh-**gen**) ***adverb*** One more time.

a•gainst (uh-**genst**) ***preposition***
1. Next to and touching.
2. Competing with.
3. Opposed to.

ag•ate (**ag**-it) ***noun*** A hard, semiprecious stone with bands of color.

age (**aje**)
1. ***noun*** The number of years that someone has lived or that something has existed.
2. ***noun*** A period of time in history, as in *the Stone Age.*
3. ***verb*** To become or seem older. ▸ **aging** *or* **ageing, aged**
4. When you **come of age,** you become an adult in the eyes of the law.

a•ged ***adjective***
1. (**ayjd**) Being a particular number of years old.
2. (**ay**-jid) Someone who is **aged** is very old. ▸ ***noun, plural*** **the aged**

A

A

age•ism (**aje**-iz-uhm) ***noun*** Prejudice or discrimination because of age.
▸ ***adjective*** **ageist**

age•ist (**ay**-jist) ***adjective*** Someone who is **ageist** discriminates against young or old people. ▸ ***noun*** **ageism** ▸ ***noun*** **ageist**

a•gen•cy (**ay**-juhn-see) ***noun*** An office or a business that provides a service to the public. ▸ ***noun, plural*** **agencies**

a•gen•da (uh-**jen**-duh) ***noun*** A list of things that need to be done or discussed.

a•gent (**ay**-juhnt) ***noun***
1. Someone who arranges things for other people, as in *a travel agent.*
2. A spy, as in *a secret agent.*

ag•gra•vate (**ag**-ruh-*vate*) ***verb*** To make something even worse. ▸ ***verb*** **aggravating, aggravated** ▸ ***noun*** **aggravation** ▸ ***adjective*** **aggravating**

ag•gre•gate (**ag**-ri-guht) ***noun*** A total created by adding together lots of smaller amounts.

ag•gres•sion (uh-**gresh**-uhn) ***noun*** Fierce or threatening behavior.
▸ ***adjective*** **aggressive** ▸ ***adverb*** **aggressively**

ag•ile (**aj**-il *or* **aj**-ile) ***adjective***
1. If you are **agile**, you can move fast and easily.
2. Someone with an **agile** mind can think quickly and cleverly.
▸ ***noun*** **agility**

ag•ing (**ay**-jing) ***adjective*** Growing older.

ag•i•tate (**aj**-uh-*tate*) ***verb***
1. To make someone nervous and worried. ▸ ***noun*** **agitation** ▸ ***adjective*** **agitated**
2. To stir or shake up.
▸ ***verb*** **agitating, agitated**

ag•nos•tic (ag-**nos**-tik) ***noun*** Someone who believes that it is impossible to prove if God exists. ▸ ***adjective*** **agnostic**

a•go (uh-**goh**) ***adverb*** Before now, or in the past, as in *three days ago.*

ag•o•ny (**ag**-uh-nee) ***noun*** Great pain or suffering. ▸ ***noun, plural*** **agonies**
▸ ***adjective*** **agonizing**

a•gree (uh-**gree**) ***verb***
1. To say yes to something.
2. To share the same opinions.
3. If something **agrees with** you, it suits you, or is good for you.
▸ ***verb*** **agreeing, agreed**

a•gree•a•ble (uh-**gree**-uh-buhl) ***adjective***
1. Pleasing or likable.
2. Willing or ready to say yes.

a•gree•ment (uh-**gree**-muhnt) ***noun***
1. If you are **in agreement** with someone, you think the same way about a particular topic.
2. An arrangement.

ag•ri•cul•ture (**ag**-ruh-*kul*-chur) ***noun*** Farming. ▸ ***adjective*** **agricultural** *See* **farm.**

a•ground (uh-**ground**) ***adverb*** If a boat runs **aground,** it gets stuck on the bottom in shallow water.

a•head (uh-**hed**) ***adverb***
1. In front.
2. In the future.

a•hoy (uh-**hoi**) ***interjection*** An exclamation used by sailors to call other ships or attract attention.

AI Short for **artificial intelligence**.

aid (**ayd**)
1. ***verb*** To help someone. ▸ **aiding, aided** ▸ ***noun*** **aid**
2. ***noun*** Money or equipment for people in need, as in *foreign aid.*

aide (**ayd**) ***noun*** A person who works along with others to help them do their jobs.

AIDS (**aydz**) ***noun*** A fatal illness in which the body's ability to protect itself against disease is destroyed. AIDS stands for *Acquired Immune Deficiency Syndrome.*

ai•ki•do (eye-**kee**-doh) ***noun*** A Japanese art of self-defense in which you use wrist, joint, and elbow grips to stop or throw your opponent.

ail (**ayl**) ***verb***
1. To give pain or trouble to.
2. To have poor health.
▸ ***verb*** **ailing, ailed**

ai•le•ron (**ay**-luh-*ron*) ***noun*** A hinged piece on an aircraft wing, used to control balance. *See* **aircraft.**

ail•ment (**ayl**-muhnt) ***noun*** An illness, though not usually a serious one.

aim (**aym**) ***verb***
1. To hit, throw, or shoot something in a particular direction.
2. To intend to achieve something.
▶ ***verb*** **aiming, aimed** ▶ ***noun*** **aim**

aim•less (**aym**-luhss) ***adjective*** Without direction or purpose. ▶ ***adverb*** **aimlessly**

ain't (**aynt**) ***contraction*** (*informal*) A short form of *am not, is not, are not, has not,* or *have not.*

air (**air**)
1. *noun* The invisible mixture of gases around you that you need to breathe.
2. *verb* To let air into a room. ▶ **airing, aired**
3. *noun* An appearance, or a manner.

air bag ***noun*** A large bag in some automobiles and trucks that automatically inflates rapidly during an accident to protect a driver or passenger.

air-conditioning ***noun*** A system for keeping the air inside cool and clean when it is hot outside.

air•craft (**air**-*kraft*) ***noun*** A vehicle that can fly. ▶ ***noun, plural*** **aircraft**

aircraft car•ri•er (**ka**-ree-ur) ***noun*** A warship with a large, flat deck where aircraft take off and land.

air•field (**air**-*feeld*) ***noun***
1. A large area that includes a runway for airplanes to take off and land.
2. An airport.

air force ***noun*** The part of a country's fighting force that can attack or defend from the air.

air•line (**air**-*line*) ***noun*** A company that owns and flies aircraft, carrying passengers and freight by air.

air•mail (**air**-*mayl*) ***noun*** A postal service by which letters, packages, etc., are carried by aircraft.

air•plane (**air**-*plane*) ***noun*** A machine with wings and an engine that flies through the air. *See* **aircraft.**

air•port (**air**-*port*) ***noun*** A place where aircraft take off and land and where people get on and off them.

air pressure ***noun*** The density or weight of the air, which is greater near the earth than it is at high altitudes.

air•ship (**air**-*ship*) ***noun*** A large air balloon with engines and a passenger compartment hanging underneath it. Blimps and zeppelins are airships.

air•sick (**air**-*sik*) ***adjective*** If you are **airsick,** you feel ill while flying in a plane, with symptoms that include nausea and dizziness.

air•tight (**air**-*tite*) ***adjective*** If a container is **airtight,** it is so well sealed that no air can get in or out.

air•y (**air**-ee) ***adjective***
1. An **airy** room is full of fresh air.
2. Lighthearted, or casual.
▶ ***adjective*** **airier, airiest** ▶ ***adverb*** **airily**

aisle (**ile**) ***noun*** The passage that runs between the rows of seats in a theater, house of worship, aircraft, etc. **Aisle** sounds like **isle** or **I'll.**

a•jar (uh-**jar**) ***adjective*** If a door is **ajar,** it is partly open. ▶ ***adverb*** **ajar**

a•kim•bo (uh-**kim**-boh) ***adjective*** If you have your arms **akimbo,** your hands or knuckles are on your hips and your elbows are turned outward. ▶ ***adverb*** **akimbo**

a•kin (uh-**kin**) ***adjective***
1. Belonging to the same family.
2. Similar.

a•la•bas•ter (**al**-uh-*bass*-tur)
1. *noun* A smooth, white piece of stone, often used to make sculpture.
2. *adjective* Smooth, pale, and almost see-through.

A

a•larm (uh-**larm**)
1. ***noun*** A device with a bell, buzzer, or siren that wakes people or warns them of danger.
2. ***noun*** A sudden fear that something bad will happen.
3. ***verb*** To make someone afraid that something bad might happen.
▸ **alarming, alarmed**
▸ ***adjective*** **alarming** ▸ ***adverb*** **alarmingly**

alarm clock ***noun*** A type of clock that can be set to ring or buzz at a particular time.

a•las (uh-**lass**) ***interjection*** Unfortunately, or sadly.

al•ba•tross (**al**-buh-*tross*) ***noun***
1. A large seabird with webbed feet and long wings that can fly for a long time.
2. If something is an **albatross around your neck,** it is a burden.
▸ ***noun, plural*** **albatrosses**

al•bi•no (al-**bye**-noh) ***noun*** A person or animal born without any natural coloring in the skin, hair, or eyes.

al•bum (**al**-buhm) ***noun***
1. A book in which you keep photographs, stamps, etc.
2. A collection of music recorded on a CD, tape, or record.

al•co•hol (**al**-kuh-*hol*) ***noun***
1. A colorless liquid found in drinks such as wine, whiskey, and beer that can make people drunk.
2. A liquid used in making medicines, chemicals, and fuels.

al•co•hol•ic (*al*-kuh-**hol**-ik)
1. ***adjective*** Containing alcohol.
2. ***noun*** An **alcoholic** has a disease that makes it difficult not to drink alcohol even when drinking hurts his or her body, mind, or ability to function. ▸ ***noun*** **alcoholism**

al•cove (**al**-kove) ***noun*** A part of a room that is set back from the main area.

al•der (**awl**-dur) ***noun*** A tree or bush with rough bark and jagged leaves that grows in cool, moist places.

ale (**ayl**) ***noun*** An alcoholic drink that is similar to beer but has a more bitter taste.

a•lert (uh-**lurt**)
1. ***adjective*** If you are **alert,** you pay attention to what is happening and are ready for action.
2. ***verb*** To warn someone that there might be danger. ▸ **alerting, alerted**
3. ***noun*** A warning of danger, as in *a nuclear alert.*

al•fal•fa (al-**fal**-fuh) ***noun*** A type of grain that is used mostly as feed for farm animals.

al•gae (**al**-jee) ***noun, plural*** Small plants without roots or stems that grow in water or on damp surfaces.

al•ge•bra (**al**-juh-bruh) ***noun*** A type of mathematics in which symbols and letters are used to represent unknown numbers; for example, $2x + y = 7$.

a•li•as (**ay**-lee-uhss) ***noun*** A false name, especially one used by a criminal.
▸ ***noun, plural*** **aliases**

al•i•bi (**al**-i-*bye*) ***noun*** A claim that a person accused of a crime was somewhere else when the crime was committed.

al•ien (**ay**-lee-uhn *or* **ay**-lyuhn)
1. ***noun*** A creature from another planet.
2. ***noun*** A foreigner.
3. ***adjective*** Different and strange.

a•lign (uh-**line**) ***verb*** To put a series of things in a straight line. ▸ **aligning, aligned** ▸ ***noun*** **alignment**

a•like (uh-**like**)
1. ***adjective*** Looking or acting the same.
2. ***adverb*** In a similar way

al•i•men•ta•ry canal (al-uh-**men**-tuh-ree) ***noun*** The path that food follows as it is digested by the body. It includes the esophagus, stomach, small intestine, and large intestine.

a•live (uh-**live**) ***adjective***
1. Living.
2. Full of life.

al•ka•li (**al**-kuh-*lye*) ***noun*** A strong base, such as lye or ammonia, that dissolves in water and reacts with an acid to form a

salt. Strong alkalis can burn your skin.
▸ ***adjective*** **alkaline** (**al**-kuh-*line*)

all (**awl**)
1. ***adjective*** **All** of a group or thing is the whole of it.
2. ***pronoun*** Everyone.
3. ***adverb*** Completely.
4. ***adverb*** For each side.
5. ***noun*** Everything.
All sounds like **awl.**

Al·lah (**al**-uh) ***noun*** The Muslim name for God.

al·lege (uh-**lej**) ***verb*** To say that something is true without offering proof.
▸ **alleging, alleged**

al·leged (uh-**lejd** *or* uh-**lej**-uhd) ***adjective*** If a newspaper reports that someone is an **alleged** jewel thief, he or she has been accused of stealing but has not yet been convicted. ▸ ***adverb*** **allegedly**

al·le·giance (uh-**lee**-junss) ***noun*** Loyal support for someone or something.

al·ler·gic (uh-**lur**-jik) ***adjective*** If you are **allergic** to something, it causes you to sneeze, develop a rash, or have another unpleasant reaction. People can be allergic to dust, pollen, foods, and other things. ▸ ***noun*** **allergy** (**al**-er-jee)

al·ley (**al**-ee) ***noun***
1. A narrow passageway between or behind buildings or backyards.
2. **bowling alley** A long, narrow lane down which you roll bowling balls. Also the building where you go to bowl.
▸ ***noun, plural*** **alleys**

al·li·ance (uh-**lye**-uhnss) ***noun*** A friendly agreement to work together.

al·lied (**al**-ide) ***adjective***
1. People or groups that join together for a common cause are **allied.**
2. Similar or related.

al·li·ga·tor (**al**-i-*gay*-tuhr) ***noun*** A large reptile with strong jaws and very sharp teeth, related to the crocodile. Alligators live in parts of North and South America and China.

al·lit·er·a·tion (uh-lit-uh-**ray**-shuhn) ***noun*** Repeated use of the same sound at the beginning of a group of words; for example, "The gruesome ghost gave a ghastly groan." ▸ ***adjective*** **alliterative**

al·lo·cate (**al**-uh-kate) ***verb*** To decide that something should be used for a particular purpose. ▸ **allocating, allocated** ▸ ***noun*** **allocation**

al·lot (uh-**lot**) ***verb***
1. To give out something in equal shares or parts.
2. To set aside for a particular purpose.
▸ ***verb*** **allotting, allotted** ▸ ***noun*** **allotment**

al·low (uh-**lou**) ***verb*** To let someone have or do something. ▸ **allowing, allowed**

al·low·ance (uh-**lou**-uhnss) ***noun*** Money given to someone regularly.

al·loy (**al**-oi) ***noun*** A mixture of two or more metals.

all right
1. ***adjective*** Good enough, or acceptable.
2. ***adjective*** Not hurt, or not ill.
3. ***adverb*** You say **all right** when you agree to do something.

all-star ***adjective*** Made up of the best people in a particular sport or skill.
▸ ***noun*** **all-star**

al·lude (uh-**lood**) ***verb*** To hint at or mention briefly. ▸ **alluding, alluded**

al·ly (**al**-eye) ***noun*** A person or country that gives support to another. ▸ ***noun, plural*** **allies**

al·ma·nac (**awl**-muh-nak) ***noun*** A book published once a year with facts and statistics about a large variety of subjects.

al·might·y (awl-**mye**-tee) ***adjective***
1. Possessing total power.
2. Very big, as in *an almighty crash.*

al·mond (**ah**-muhnd *or* **ahl**-muhnd) ***noun*** A sweet, oval-shaped nut that is used in cooking or baking or eaten alone.

al·most (**awl**-most) ***adverb*** Very nearly.

A

A

al•oe (**a**-loh) ***noun*** An African plant whose juice can be used to help heal burns and cuts. Aloe is often used in creams to soften skin.

a•loft (uh-**loft**) ***adjective*** High up in the air. ▸ ***adverb* aloft**

a•lo•ha (uh-**loh**-ha) ***interjection*** In Hawaiian, a term used to say hello or good-bye.

a•lone (uh-**lone**) ***adjective*** Without anyone else. ▸ ***adverb* alone**

a•long (uh-**lawng**) ***preposition***
1. Following the length or direction of.
2. all along All the time.

a•long•side (uh-**lawng-side**)
1. ***adverb*** Near to the side.
2. ***preposition*** Parallel to.

a•loof (uh-**loof**)
1. ***adverb*** When you remain **aloof** from someone or something, you keep yourself apart and don't get involved.
2. ***adjective*** Distant or not friendly.

a•loud (uh-**loud**) ***adverb*** In a voice that other people can hear, as in *reading aloud.*

al•pha•bet (**al**-fuh-bet) ***noun*** All the letters of a language arranged in order. ▸ ***adjective* alphabetical**

al•pha•bet•ize (**al**-fah-buh-*tize*) ***verb*** To arrange a series of things so that they follow the order of the letters of the alphabet, from *A* to *Z.* ▸ **alphabetizing, alphabetized**

al•read•y (awl-**red**-ee) ***adverb*** Before now.

al•so (**awl**-soh) ***adverb*** As well.

al•tar (**awl**-tur) ***noun*** A large table in a house of worship, used for religious ceremonies.

al•ter (**awl**-tur) ***verb*** To change something. ▸ **altering, altered** ▸ ***noun* alteration**

al•ter•nate
1. ***adjective*** (**awl**-tur-nit) If something happens on **alternate** days, it happens every second day.
2. ***verb*** (**awl**-tuhr-*nate*) To take turns. ▸ **alternating, alternated**

al•ter•na•tive (awl-**tur**-nuh-tiv)
1. ***noun*** Something that you can choose to have or do instead of something else. ▸ ***adjective* alternative** ▸ ***adverb* alternatively**
2. ***adjective*** Different from what is usual, as in *alternative medicine.*

alternative energy ***noun*** Energy from natural sources that are renewable and don't harm the environment, such as the sun, ocean waves, and wind. *See* **solar energy, wind turbine.**

al•though (*awl*-**THoh**) ***conjunction***
1. In spite of the fact that.
2. But.

al•tim•e•ter (al-**tim**-uh-tur) ***noun*** An instrument that measures how high something is above the ground. Airplane pilots use altimeters when they fly.

al•ti•tude (**al**-ti-tood) ***noun*** The height of something above the ground.

al•to (**al**-toh) ***noun***
1. A singing voice that is high for a male and low for a female.
2. A singer with an alto voice.

al•to•geth•er (awl-tuh-**ge**-THur) ***adverb***
1. In total.
2. Completely, or entirely.
3. On the whole.

a•lu•mi•num (uh-**loo**-mi-nuhm) ***noun*** A light, silver-colored metal.

al•ways (**awl**-*waze*) ***adverb*** If something is **always** happening, it happens all the time or very many times.

Alz•hei•mer's disease (**awlts**-hye-muhrz) ***noun*** A disease of the nervous system that damages brain cells, making it increasingly hard to remember even simple things, to speak, and eventually to move.

A.M. (**ay em**) The initials of the Latin phrase *ante meridiem,* which means "before midday."

am•a•teur (**am**-uh-chur *or* **am**-uh-tur) ***noun*** Someone who takes part in a sport or other activity for pleasure rather than for money. ▸ ***adjective* amateur**

a•maze (uh-**maze**) ***verb*** To make someone feel very surprised. ▸ **amazing, amazed** ▸ ***noun*** **amazement** ▸ ***adjective*** **amazing** ▸ ***adverb*** **amazingly**

am•bas•sa•dor (am-**bass**-uh-dur) ***noun*** The top person sent by a government to represent it in another country.

am•ber (**am**-bur) ***noun***
1. A yellowish brown substance formed from fossilized tree sap and used for making ornaments and jewelry.
2. A yellowish brown color. ▸ ***adjective*** **amber**

am•bi•dex•trous (*am*-bi-**dek**-struhss) ***adjective*** If you are **ambidextrous,** you can use both hands equally well, especially for writing.

am•big•u•ous (am-**big**-yoo-uhss) ***adjective*** If something is **ambiguous,** it can be understood in more than one way. ▸ ***noun*** **ambiguity** (*am*-buh-**gyoo**-uh-tee) ▸ ***adverb*** **ambiguously**

am•bi•tion (am-**bish**-uhn) ***noun***
1. Something you really want to do.
2. A strong wish to be successful.
▸ ***adjective*** **ambitious**

am•biv•a•lent (am-**biv**-uh-luhnt) ***adjective*** If you feel **ambivalent** about something, you have two different opinions about it at the same time. ▸ ***noun*** **ambivalence**

am•ble (**am**-buhl) ***verb*** To walk slowly because you are not in a hurry. ▸ **ambling, ambled**

am•bu•lance (**am**-byuh-luhnss) ***noun*** A vehicle that takes ill or injured people to the hospital.

am•bush (**am**-bush) ***verb*** To hide and then attack someone. ▸ **ambushes, ambushing, ambushed** ▸ ***noun*** **ambush**

a•men (ay-**men** *or* ah-**men**) ***interjection***
1. People say **amen** after a prayer to mean "May it be so."
2. **Amen** also shows agreement with a statement.

a•mend (uh-**mend**)
1. ***verb*** To change a legal document or a law. ▸ **amending, amended**
2. ***noun, plural*** When you make **amends,** you do something to make up for a wrong or a mistake.

a•mend•ment (uh-**mend**-muhnt) ***noun*** A change that is made to a law or a legal document.

A•mer•i•can (uh-**mer**-uh-kuhn)
1. ***adjective*** To do with the United States, as in *American government.*
2. ***adjective*** To do with North, Central, or South America, as in *the American continents.*
3. ***noun*** Someone born or living in the United States.
4. ***noun*** Someone born or living in either North, Central, or South America.

American Indian ***noun*** One of the original inhabitants of North, Central, or South America, or a descendant. American Indians are sometimes called Native Americans. ▸ ***adjective*** **American Indian**

am•e•thyst (**am**-uh-thist) ***noun***
1. A type of quartz crystal that is purple or violet and often is used as a gemstone in jewelry.
2. A shade of purple.

a•mi•a•ble (**ay**-mee-uh-bul) ***adjective*** Friendly and easygoing.

a•mid (uh-**mid**) ***preposition*** In the middle of or surrounded by.

a•mi•go (uh-**mee**-goh) ***noun*** The Spanish word for "male friend." The Spanish word for "female friend" is **amiga** (uh-**mee**-guh).

am•mo•nia (uh-**moh**-nyuh) ***noun*** A gas or solution with a strong smell. Some cleaning liquids contain ammonia.

am•mu•ni•tion (am-yuh-**nish**-uhn) ***noun***
1. Things that can be fired from weapons, such as bullets or arrows.
2. Information that you can use against somebody else.

A

A

am•ne•sia (am-**nee**-zhuh) ***noun*** A partial or total loss of memory that can be temporary or permanent.

am•nes•ty (**am**-nuh-stee) ***noun***
1. An official promise by a government to release prisoners and pardon crimes.
2. A chance to hand in something you should not possess, without being punished. ▸ ***noun, plural*** **amnesties**

a•moe•ba (uh-**mee**-buh) ***noun*** A microscopic creature made of only one cell. ▸ ***noun, plural*** **amoebas** *or* **amoebae** (uh-**mee**-bee)

a•mong *or* **a•mongst** (uh-**mung** *or* uh-**mungst**) ***preposition***
1. In the middle of, or surrounded by.
2. If you share something **among** several people, you divide it between them.

a•mount (uh-**mount**)
1. *noun* The **amount** of something is how much of it there is.
2. *verb* If something **amounts to** a total, it adds up to that total.
▸ **amounting, amounted**

amp (**amp**) ***noun*** A unit used to measure the strength of an electrical current. Amp is short for *ampere* (**am**-pihr).

am•per•sand (**am**-pur-*sand*) ***noun*** A symbol (&) that stands for the word "and."

am•phi•bi•an (am-**fib**-ee-uhn) ***noun***
1. A cold-blooded animal with a backbone that lives in water and breathes with gills when young. As an adult, it develops lungs and lives on land. Frogs, toads, and salamanders are amphibians.
2. A vehicle that can travel on land and in water.
▸ ***adjective*** **amphibious**

am•phi•the•a•ter (**am**-fi-*thee*-uh-tur) ***noun*** A large, open-air building with rows of seats in a high circle around an arena. In ancient Roman times, amphitheaters were used for public entertainment, such as gladiator and animal fights.

am•ple (**am**-puhl) ***adjective***
1. More than enough. ▸ ***adverb*** **amply**
2. Large.
▸ ***adjective*** **ampler, amplest**

am•pli•fi•er (**am**-pluh-fye-ur) ***noun*** A piece of equipment that makes sound louder. ▸ ***noun*** **amplification**

am•pli•fy (**am**-pli-*fye*) ***verb*** To make something louder or stronger.
▸ **amplifies, amplifying, amplified**

am•pu•tate (**am**-pyuh-*tate*) ***verb*** To cut off someone's arm, leg, finger, etc., usually because it is damaged or diseased. ▸ **amputating, amputated**
▸ ***noun*** **amputation**

a•muse (uh-**myooz**) ***verb***
1. To make someone laugh or smile.
▸ ***adjective*** **amusing**
2. To keep someone happy and stop him or her from being bored.
▸ ***verb*** **amusing, amused** ▸ ***noun*** **amusement**

amusement park ***noun*** A place where people pay to go on rides, play games of skill, and enjoy other forms of entertainment.

an (**uhn** *or* **an**) ***indefinite article*** A form of **a** used before a word that is pronounced with a vowel as its first sound, as in *an onion*.

an•a•con•da (an-uh-**kon**-duh) ***noun*** A very long, nonpoisonous South American snake that wraps itself tightly around its prey to kill it.

an•a•gram (**an**-uh-gram) ***noun*** A word or phrase made by rearranging the letters in another word or phrase.

an•a•log (**an**-uh-log) ***adjective*** Using moving parts to show changing information.

an•a•lyze (**an**-uh-lize) ***verb*** To examine something carefully in order to understand it. ▸ **analyzing, analyzed**
▸ ***noun*** **analysis** (uh-**nal**-uh-siss)
▸ ***adjective*** **analytical**

an•ar•chy (**an**-ur-kee) ***noun*** A situation with no order and no one in control.
▸ ***noun*** **anarchist**

a•nat•o•my (uh-**nat**-uh-mee) ***noun***
1. The **anatomy** of a person or an animal is the structure of its body.

2. The scientific study of the structure of living things.
▸ ***noun, plural* anatomies** ▸ ***adjective* anatomical** (*an*-uh-**tom**-i-kuhl)

an•ces•tor (**an**-sess-tur) ***noun*** Your **ancestors** are members of your family who lived a long time ago, usually before your grandparents. ▸ ***noun* ancestry** ▸ ***adjective* ancestral**

an•chor (**ang**-kur) ***noun*** A heavy metal hook that is lowered from a ship or boat to stop it from drifting.

an•chor•per•son (**ang**-kur-*pur*-suhn) ***noun*** The main person who reports the news on a television news show.

an•cho•vy (**an**-choh-vee) ***noun*** A small, edible fish. Anchovies have a salty taste. ▸ ***noun, plural* anchovies**

an•cient (**ayn**-shunt) ***adjective***
1. Very old.
2. Belonging to a time long ago, as in *an ancient monument* or *ancient Rome.*

and (**and**) ***conjunction***
1. As well as.
2. Added to, or plus.
3. As a result.
4. (*informal*) To.

an•droid (**an**-droid) ***noun*** A robot that acts and looks like a human being. ▸ ***adjective* android**

an•ec•dote (**an**-ik-dote) ***noun*** A short, often funny story about something that has happened. ▸ ***adjective* anecdotal**

a•ne•mic (uh-**nee**-mik) ***adjective*** If you are **anemic,** you feel weak and become easily tired because your blood does not contain enough iron. ▸ ***noun* anemia**

an•e•mom•et•er (an-i-**mom**-uh-tur) ***noun*** A scientific instrument used to measure the wind's speed.

a•nem•o•ne (uh-**nem**-uh-nee) ***noun*** A plant with purple, red, white, or pink flowers.

an•es•thet•ic (an-iss-**thet**-ik) ***noun*** A drug or a gas given to people before an operation to prevent them from feeling pain.

a•nes•the•tist (uh-**ness**-thuh-tist) ***noun*** A medical professional who specializes in giving people drugs or gas to prevent pain during operations.

a•new (uh-**noo**) ***adverb*** Again, or once more.

an•gel (**ayn**-juhl) ***noun***
1. In religion, a messenger of God.
2. A very kind, gentle person.
▸ ***adjective* angelic**

an•ger (**ang**-gur) ***noun*** The strong feeling of being very annoyed.

an•gle (**ang**-guhl) ***noun***
1. The figure formed by two lines that start at the same point. Angles are measured in degrees.
2. A way of looking at something.
3. If something is **at an angle,** it is sloping and not straight.

an•gling (**ang**-gling) ***noun*** The sport of fishing with a fishing rod rather than a net. ▸ ***noun* angler** ▸ ***verb* angle**

an•go•ra (ang-**gor**-uh) ***noun***
1. A long-haired variety of rabbit, goat, or cat.
2. Fluffy wool made from the hair of angora rabbits or goats mixed with sheep's wool.

an•gry (**ang**-gree) ***adjective*** If you are **angry,** you feel that you want to argue or fight with someone. ▸ **angrier, angriest** ▸ ***adverb* angrily**

an•guish (**ang**-gwish) ***noun*** A strong feeling of misery or distress. ▸ ***adjective* anguished**

an•gu•lar (**ang**-gyu-lur) ***adjective*** Something that is **angular** has straight lines and sharp turns or corners.

an•i•mal (**an**-uh-muhl) ***noun*** Any living creature that can breathe and move about.

animal rights ***noun*** A movement for the fair and humane treatment of animals. Some of the people who support animal rights object to the wearing of fur coats and the use of animals for scientific experiments. ▸ ***adjective* animal rights**

A

an•i•mat•ed (**an**-i-may-tid) ***adjective***
1. Lively, as in *an animated conversation.* ▸ ***noun*** **animation** ▸ ***adverb*** **animatedly**
2. An **animated film** is made by projecting a series of drawings very quickly, one after the other, so that the characters in the drawings seem to move. ▸ ***noun*** **animation,** ***noun*** **animator** ▸ ***verb*** **animate**

an•i•mos•i•ty (an-i-**moss**-uh-tee) ***noun*** A strong dislike for someone.

an•kle (**ang**-kuhl) ***noun*** The joint that connects your foot to your leg.

an•klet (**ang**-klit) ***noun***
1. A band worn around the ankle as a piece of jewelry.
2. A short sock that covers the ankle.

an•nex
1. (an-**eks** *or* **an**-eks) ***verb*** When one country **annexes** another, it takes control of it by force. ▸ **annexes, annexing, annexed**
2. (**an**-eks) ***noun*** An extra building that is joined onto or placed near a main building.
▸ ***noun*** **annexation**

an•ni•hi•late (uh-**nye**-uh-late) ***verb*** To destroy something completely.
▸ **annihilating, annihilated** ▸ ***noun*** **annihilation**

an•ni•ver•sa•ry (an-uh-**vur**-suh-ree) ***noun*** A date that people remember because something important happened on that date in the past, as in *a wedding anniversary.* ▸ ***noun, plural*** **anniversaries**

an•no•tate (**an**-oh-tate) ***verb*** To write notes explaining a piece of writing.
▸ **annotating, annotated** ▸ ***noun*** **annotation** ▸ ***adjective*** **annotated**

an•nounce (uh-**nounss**) ***verb*** To say something officially or publicly.
▸ **announcing, announced** ▸ ***noun*** **announcement**

an•nounc•er (uh-**noun**-sur) ***noun***
1. Someone who introduces programs on television or radio.
2. Someone who describes the action during a sports event.

an•noy (uh-**noi**) ***verb*** To make someone lose patience or feel angry. ▸ **annoying, annoyed** ▸ ***noun*** **annoyance**
▸ ***adjective*** **annoying** ▸ ***adverb*** **annoyingly**

an•nu•al (**an**-yoo-uhl)
1. ***adjective*** Happening once every year or over a period of one year, as in *the annual Labor Day parade* or *an annual magazine subscription.*
▸ ***adverb*** **annually**
2. ***noun*** A book published once a year.
3. ***noun*** A plant that lives for only one year.

a•noint (uh-**noint**) ***verb*** To honor someone during a religious ceremony by rubbing oil on his or her head.
▸ **anointing, anointed**

a•non•y•mous (uh-**non**-uh-muhss) ***adjective*** Written, done, or given by a person whose name is not known or made public, as in *an anonymous letter.* ▸ ***noun*** **anonymity** (*an*-o-**nim**-i-tee) ▸ ***adverb*** **anonymously**

an•o•rex•ic (*an*-uh-**rek**-sik) ***adjective*** When people are **anorexic**, they think they are too fat, so they eat very little and become dangerously thin. ▸ ***noun*** **anorexic,** ***noun*** **anorexia** (*an*-uh-**rek**-see-uh)

an•oth•er (uh-**nuTH**-ur)
1. ***adjective*** One more of the same kind of thing.
2. ***pronoun*** A different one.

an•swer (**an**-sur)
1. ***verb*** To say or write something as a reply, as in *to answer a question.* ▸ ***noun*** **answer**
2. ***noun*** The solution to a problem.
3. ***verb*** If you **answer back,** you make a rude reply.
4. If someone **has a lot to answer for,** he or she has caused a lot of trouble.
▸ ***verb*** **answering, answered**

answering machine ***noun*** A machine connected to or built into a telephone that records messages from people who telephone while you are out.

ant (**ant**) ***noun*** A small insect that lives in a large group called a colony. Ants are very strong for their size. They can carry 27 times their own weight.

ant·ac·id (ant-**ass**-id) ***noun*** A medicine that reduces the amount of acid in your stomach to soothe an upset stomach.

an·tag·o·nize (an-**tag**-uh-nize) ***verb*** If you **antagonize** a person or an animal, you make it very angry.
▸ **antagonizing, antagonized** ▸ ***noun*** **antagonism,** ***noun*** **antagonist**

Ant·arc·tic (ant-**ark**-tik) ***noun*** The area around the South Pole. ▸ ***adjective*** **Antarctic**

ant·eat·er (**ant**-ee-tur) ***noun*** A South American mammal with a very long tongue that it uses to search for ants and other small insects.

an·te·ced·ent (*an*-tuh-**see**-duhnt) ***noun*** In grammar, the word or phrase to which a pronoun refers.

an·te·lope (**an**-tuh-lope) ***noun*** An animal that looks like a large deer and runs very fast. Antelopes have long horns without branches and are found in Africa and parts of Asia.

an·ten·na (an-**ten**-uh) ***noun***
1. A feeler on the head of an insect.
2. A wire that receives radio and television signals.
▸ ***noun, plural*** **antennas** *or* **antennae** (an-**ten**-ee)

an·them (**an**-thuhm) ***noun*** A religious or national song, often sung by a choir, as in *a national anthem.*

an·ther (**an**-thur) ***noun*** The part of a flower at the tip of the stamen that contains its pollen.

an·thol·o·gy (an-**thol**-uh-jee) ***noun*** A collection of poems or stories by different writers that are all printed in the same book. ▸ ***noun, plural*** **anthologies**

an·thra·cite (**an**-thruh-*site*) ***noun*** A type of shiny, hard coal that doesn't give off much smoke when it is burned.

an·thro·pol·o·gy (*an*-thruh-**pol**-uh-jee) ***noun*** The study of the beliefs and ways of life of different people around the world. ▸ ***noun*** **anthropologist**

an·ti·bi·ot·ic (*an*-ti-bye-**ot**-ik) ***noun*** A drug, such as penicillin, that kills bacteria and is used to cure infections and diseases.

an·ti·bod·y (**an**-ti-*bod*-ee) ***noun*** Your blood makes **antibodies** to fight against infection and disease.
▸ ***noun, plural*** **antibodies**

an·tic·i·pate (an-**tiss**-i-*pate*) ***verb*** To expect something to happen and be prepared for it. ▸ **anticipating, anticipated** ▸ ***noun*** **anticipation**

an·ti·cli·max (*an*-ti-**klye**-maks) ***noun*** If something is an **anticlimax,** it is not as exciting as you had expected. ▸ ***noun, plural*** **anticlimaxes**

an·ti·dote (**an**-ti-dote) ***noun*** Something that stops a poison from working.

an·ti·freeze (**an**-tee-*freez*) ***noun*** A chemical substance that is added to liquid to stop it from freezing. Antifreeze is mixed with the water in a car's radiator to keep the car running in cold weather.

an·ti·per·spi·rant (*an*-tee-**pur**-spuh-ruhnt) ***noun*** A substance that you put on your skin to stop you from sweating too much.

an·tique (an-**teek**)
1. ***noun*** A very old object that is valuable because it is rare or beautiful.
2. ***adjective*** Very old, as in *antique jewelry.*

an·ti·sep·tic (an-ti-**sep**-tik) ***noun*** A substance that kills germs and prevents infection by stopping the growth of germs.

an·ti·so·cial (an-tee-**soh**-shuhl) ***adjective***
1. If somebody is **antisocial,** he or she does not enjoy being with others.
2. When people behave in an **antisocial** way, they do something that upsets or harms other people.

A

ant•ler (**ant**-lur) ***noun*** One of the two large, branching, bony structures on the head of a deer, moose, or elk. These animals grow and shed new antlers each year.

an•to•nym (**an**-toh-nim) ***noun*** A word that means the opposite of another word. **Hot** and **cold** are antonyms; so are **weak** and **strong; up** and **down; over** and **under.**

anx•i•e•ty (ang-**zye**-uh-tee) ***noun*** A feeling of worry or fear. ▸ ***noun, plural*** **anxieties**

anx•ious (**angk**-shuhss) ***adjective***
1. Worried. ▸ ***adverb*** **anxiously**
2. Very eager to do something.

an•y (**en**-ee)
1. ***adjective*** One or more.
2. ***adjective*** Every.
3. ***pronoun*** A way of suggesting people or things without naming them.
4. ***adverb*** At all.

an•y•bod•y (**en**-ee-*bod*-ee) ***pronoun*** Any person.

an•y•how (**en**-ee-*hou*) ***adverb*** In any case.

an•y•more (*en*-ee-**mor**) ***adverb*** Now, or from now on.

an•y•one (**en**-ee-*wuhn*) ***pronoun*** Any person.

an•y•place (**en**-ee-playss) ***adverb*** Anywhere.

an•y•thing (**en**-ee-*thing*)
1. ***pronoun*** Any thing or item of any kind.
2. ***adverb*** At all.

an•y•time (**en**-ee-*time*) ***adverb*** At any hour or date, or whenever.

an•y•way (**en**-ee-*way*) ***adverb*** In any case.

an•y•where (**en**-ee-*wair*) ***adverb*** In or to any place.

a•or•ta (ay-**or**-tuh) ***noun*** The main tube that carries blood away from the heart to the rest of the body, except the lungs. *See* **circulation, heart.**

A•pach•e (uh-**pa**-chee) ***noun*** One of a group of American Indians that lives primarily in the southwestern United States. ▸ ***noun, plural*** **Apache** *or* **Apaches**

a•part (uh-**part**) ***adverb*** If two people or things are **apart**, they are separated from each other.

a•part•heid (uh-**part**-hate *or* uh-**part**-hite) ***noun*** A political policy in which people of different races are kept apart from each other.

a•part•ment (uh-**part**-muhnt) ***noun*** A set of rooms to live in, usually on one floor of a building.

ap•a•thet•ic (ap-uh-**thet**-ik) ***adjective*** If you are **apathetic**, you do not care about anything or want to do anything. ▸ ***noun*** **apathy**

ape (**ape**)
1. ***noun*** A large animal related to a monkey, but with no tail. Gorillas, gibbons, orangutans, and chimpanzees are kinds of apes.
2. ***verb*** To copy the way another person behaves or speaks. ▸ **aping, aped**

ap•er•ture (**ap**-ur-chur) ***noun*** A hole behind a camera lens that can be opened or closed to control the amount of light that shines onto the film.

a•pex (**ay**-peks) ***noun*** The highest point of something, as in *the apex of a mountain.* ▸ ***noun, plural*** **apexes**

a•phid (**ay**-fid) ***noun*** A tiny insect that feeds by sucking the juices from plants.

a•piece (uh-**peess**) ***adverb*** Each.

a•pol•o•gize (uh-**pol**-uh-jize) ***verb*** To say that you are sorry about something. ▸ **apologizing, apologized** ▸ ***noun*** **apology** ▸ ***adjective*** **apologetic**

a•pos•tle (uh-**poss**-uhl) ***noun***
1. A close follower of another person or cause.
2. In Christianity, one of the 12 men chosen by Jesus to spread his teaching, plus St. Paul.

a•pos•tro•phe (uh-**poss**-truh-fee) ***noun*** A punctuation mark (') used to show ownership; for example, "Jane's bag"; or to show that letters have been left out; for example, "can't."

ap•pall•ing (uh-**paw**-ling) ***adjective*** Horrifying and shocking. ▸ ***adverb*** **appallingly**

ap•pa•rat•us (ap-uh-**rat**-uhss) ***noun***
1. Equipment used for performing sports, especially gymnastics.
2. Equipment or machines used to do a job or laboratory experiment.
▸ ***noun, plural*** **apparatus** *or* **apparatuses**

ap•par•el (uh-**pa**-ruhl) ***noun*** Clothing.

ap•par•ent (uh-**pa**-ruhnt) ***adjective***
1. Obvious, or clear.
2. Seeming real or true.
▸ ***adverb*** **apparently**

ap•peal (uh-**peel**) ***verb***
1. To ask for something urgently.
2. To ask for a decision made by a court of law to be changed. ▸ ***noun*** **appeal**
3. If something **appeals to** you, you like it or find it interesting.
▸ ***verb*** **appealing, appealed**

ap•pear (uh-**pihr**) ***verb***
1. To come into view.
2. To seem.
▸ ***verb*** **appearing, appeared** ▸ ***noun*** **appearance**

ap•pease (uh-**peez**) ***verb***
1. To make someone content or calm.
2. To give someone what is needed, or to satisfy someone.
▸ ***verb*** **appeasing, appeased**

ap•pen•di•ci•tis (uh-*pen*-duh-**sye**-tiss) ***noun*** A person with **appendicitis** has an infected appendix and is in pain.

ap•pen•dix (uh-**pen**-diks) ***noun***
1. A small, closed tube leading from the large intestine.
2. Extra information at the end of a book.
▸ ***noun, plural*** **appendixes** *or* **appendices** (uh-**pen**-di-seez)

ap•pe•tite (**ap**-uh-*tite*) ***noun***
1. Desire for food.
2. Great enjoyment of something.

ap•pe•tiz•er (**ap**-uh-*tye*-zur) ***noun*** A small portion of food eaten before a meal or at the start of a meal.

ap•pe•tiz•ing (**ap**-uh-*tye*-zing) ***adjective*** Food that is **appetizing** looks and smells good to eat.

ap•plaud (uh-**plawd**) ***verb*** To show that you like something, usually by clapping your hands. ▸ **applauding, applauded** ▸ ***noun*** **applause**

ap•ple (**ap**-uhl) ***noun*** A round, usually crisp fruit.

ap•pli•ance (uh-**plye**-uhnss) ***noun*** A machine designed to do a particular job.

ap•pli•cant (**ap**-luh-kuhnt) ***noun*** Someone who has written formally asking for something, such as a job, a loan, or entrance to a school.

ap•pli•ca•tion (ap-luh-**kay**-shuhn) ***noun***
1. A written request for something, such as a job, as in *a job application.*
2. A way of using something.
3. A computer program that performs a certain task.

ap•ply (uh-**plye**) ***verb***
1. To bring something into direct contact with something else, as in *to apply makeup.*
2. To ask for something in writing, as in *to apply for a loan.*
3. To be relevant.
4. If you **apply yourself** to something, you work hard at it.
▸ ***verb*** **applies, applying, applied**

ap•point (uh-**point**) ***verb***
1. To choose someone for a job.
2. To arrange something officially.
▸ ***verb*** **appointing, appointed**

ap•point•ment (uh-**point**-muhnt) ***noun***
1. The act of naming or choosing someone for a job.
2. The job itself.
3. The arrangement to meet someone at a certain time, as in *a dentist appointment.*

ap•praise (uh-**praze**) ***verb*** To decide on something's value by inspecting it closely. ▸ **appraising, appraised**

ap•pre•cia•ble (uh-**pree**-shuh-buhl) ***adjective*** Enough to be noticed.

ap•pre•ci•ate (uh-**pree**-shee-*ate*) ***verb***
1. To enjoy or value somebody or something. ▸ ***adjective* appreciative** ▸ ***adverb* appreciatively**
2. To understand something.
3. To increase in worth.
▸ ***verb* appreciating, appreciated**
▸ ***noun* appreciation**

ap•pre•hend (ap-ri-**hend**) ***verb***
1. To capture and arrest someone.
2. To understand, or to capture the meaning of something.
▸ ***verb* apprehending, apprehended**

ap•pre•hen•sive (*ap*-ri-**hen**-siv) ***adjective*** Worried and slightly afraid.
▸ ***noun* apprehension** ▸ ***adverb* apprehensively**

ap•pren•tice (uh-**pren**-tiss) ***noun*** Someone who learns a trade or craft by working with a skilled person. ▸ ***noun* apprenticeship**

ap•proach (uh-**prohch**) ***verb***
1. To move nearer.
2. If you **approach** somebody, you go up to the person and talk to him or her.
3. When you **approach** a problem, you think of ways of tackling it.
▸ ***verb* approaches, approaching, approached** ▸ ***noun* approach**

ap•proach•a•ble (uh-**proh**-chuh-buhl) ***adjective*** If people are **approachable,** they are friendly and easy to talk to.

ap•pro•pri•ate
1. (uh-**proh**-pree-uht) ***adjective*** Suitable, or right, as in *appropriate attire.* ▸ ***adverb* appropriately**
2. (uh-**proh**-pree-***ate***) ***verb*** To take something that is not yours. ▸ ***verb* appropriating, appropriated**

ap•prove (uh-**proov**) ***verb***
1. If you **approve of** someone or something, you think that he or she is acceptable or good.
2. To officially accept a plan or an idea.
▸ ***verb* approving, approved** ▸ ***noun* approval**

ap•prox•i•mate (uh-**prok**-si-muht) ***adjective*** More or less accurate or correct, as in *an approximate price.*
▸ ***noun* approximation** ▸ ***adverb* approximately**

a•pri•cot (**ay**-pri-*kot* or **ap**-ri-*kot*) ***noun*** A small, soft fruit with an orange skin.

A•pril (**ay**-pruhl) ***noun*** The fourth month on the calendar, after March and before May. April has 30 days.

April Fools' Day April 1, a day when it is customary to play practical jokes on people.

a•pron (**ay**-pruhn) ***noun***
1. An article of clothing that you wear to protect your clothes when you are cooking, painting, etc.
2. The part of a stage in front of the curtain.

apt (**apt**) ***adjective***
1. Very suitable, as in *an apt reply.*
2. Quick to learn things, as in *an apt student.*
3. If you are **apt** to do something, you are likely to do it.

ap•ti•tude (**ap**-ti-tood) ***noun*** A natural ability to do something well, as in *an aptitude for drawing.*

Aq•ua-Lung (**ak**-wuh-*lung*) ***noun*** Trademark for a breathing apparatus for diving. An Aqua-Lung consists of an air tank with a tube leading to a mouthpiece.

a•quar•i•um (uh-**kwair**-ee-uhm) ***noun*** A glass tank in which you can keep fish.
▸ ***noun, plural* aquariums** *or* **aquaria** (uh-**kwair**-ee-uh)

a•quat•ic (uh-**kwat**-ik *or* uh-**kwot**-ik) ***adjective***
1. Living or growing in water, as in *aquatic plants.*
2. Performed in or on water, as in *aquatic sports.*

aq•ue•duct (**ak**-wuh-*duhkt*) ***noun*** A large bridge built to carry water across a valley.

Ar•a•bic (**a**-ruh-bik) ***noun*** A language spoken by many people in the Middle East and North Africa.

Arabic numerals ***noun, plural*** The figures 0, 1, 2, 3, 4, 5, 6, 7, 8, and 9 that we use today. These numerals were first taught to Europeans by Arab scholars.

ar•a•ble (**a**-ruh-buhl) ***adjective*** **Arable** land is fit for growing crops.

ar•bi•trar•y (**ar**-buh-*trer*-ee) ***adjective*** Based on personal feelings or opinions rather than on law or logic.

ar•bi•trate (**ar**-bi-*trate*) ***verb*** To help two sides reach an agreement in a dispute. ▸ **arbitrating, arbitrated** ▸ ***noun*** **arbitration,** ***noun*** **arbitrator**

ar•bor (**ar**-bur) ***noun***
1. A place that is surrounded by trees, shrubs, vines, or other plants.
2. **Arbor Day** is a day in spring that is set aside for planting trees. The actual date varies.

arc (**ark**) ***noun***
1. A curved line.
2. In math, an **arc** is a curved line between two points.
Arc sounds like **ark.**

ar•cade (ar-**kade**) ***noun***
1. A row of arches in a building.
2. **penny arcade** A covered area with machines for amusement, such as pinball games, that you pay to use.
3. **shopping arcade** A covered passageway with stores or stalls.

arch (**arch**)
1. ***noun*** A curved structure. Arches often help support a building or bridge.
2. ***verb*** To curve. ▸ **arches, arching, arched** ▸ ***adjective*** **arched**
3. ***adjective*** Main or chief.

ar•chae•o•lo•gy *or* **archeology** (ar-kee-**ol**-uh-jee) ***noun*** If you study **archaeology,** you learn about the past by digging up old buildings and objects and examining them carefully.
▸ ***noun*** **archeologist** ▸ ***adjective*** **archeological**

ar•cha•ic (ar-**kay**-ik) ***adjective*** Very old-fashioned and not used anymore, as in *archaic customs.*

arch•bish•op (*arch*-**bish**-uhp) ***noun*** The supervisor of bishops in some Christian denominations.

ar•che•o•lo•gy *See* **archaeology.**

arch•er•y (**ar**-chuh-ree) ***noun*** The sport of shooting at targets using a bow and arrow. ▸ ***noun*** **archer**

ar•chi•pel•a•go (*ar*-kuh-**pel**-uh-goh) ***noun*** A group of small islands.

ar•chi•tect (**ar**-ki-tekt) ***noun*** Someone who designs buildings and checks that they are built properly.

ar•chi•tec•ture (**ar**-ki-tek-chur) ***noun***
1. The activity of designing buildings.
2. The style in which buildings are designed.
▸ ***adjective*** **architectural**

arc•tic (**ark**-tik)
1. ***adjective*** Extremely cold and wintry, as in *arctic weather conditions.*
2. **The Arctic** ***noun*** The frozen area around the North Pole. ▸ ***adjective*** **Arctic**

ar•dent (**ar**-duhnt) ***adjective*** If you are **ardent** about something, you feel very strongly about it, as in *an ardent supporter of animal rights.* ▸ ***adverb*** **ardently**

ar•du•ous (**ar**-joo-uhss) ***adjective*** Very difficult and demanding a lot of effort, as in *an arduous task.*

ar•e•a (**air**-ee-uh) ***noun***
1. The amount of surface within a given boundary, measured in square units.
2. A part of a place, as in *a poor area of town.*

area code ***noun*** A three-digit number that indicates the telephone service area in which you live. When telephoning from one area to another, you dial 1 plus the area code, followed by the seven-digit local number.

a•re•na (uh-**ree**-nuh) ***noun*** A large area that is used for sports or entertainment.

aren't (**arnt** *or* **ar**-ent) ***contraction*** A short form of *are not.*

ar•gue (**ar**-gyoo) ***verb***
1. To give your opinion about something.
▸ ***noun*** **argument**
2. To disagree with someone forcefully.
▸ ***adjective*** **argumentative** (*ar*-gyoo-**men**-tuh-tiv) ▸ ***verb*** **arguing, argued**

A

ar•id (**a**-rid) ***adjective*** Land that is **arid** is extremely dry because very little rain has fallen on it.

a•rise (uh-**rize**) ***verb***
1. To get up.
2. To come into being.
▸ ***verb* arising, arose** (uh-**rohz**), **arisen** (uh-**riz**-in)

a•ris•to•crat (uh-**riss**-tuh-krat) ***noun*** A member of a group of people thought to be the best in some way, usually based on how much money they have, how well-known they are, or how much they are respected. In history, a member of the highest social rank, or nobility.
▸ ***noun* aristocracy** (*a*-ruh-***stok***-ruh-see) ▸ ***adjective* aristocratic**

a•rith•me•tic (uh-**rith**-muh-tik) ***noun*** The science of numbers and computation. Addition, subtraction, multiplication, and division are the four basic operations of arithmetic.

ark (**ark**) ***noun***
1. In the Bible, a boat built by Noah to carry his family and two of every kind of animal during the great flood.
2. In a synagogue, the cabinet in which the Torah scrolls are kept.
Ark sounds like **arc.**

arm (**arm**)
1. ***noun*** The part of your body between your shoulder and your hand.
2. ***verb*** If a country **arms** itself, it gets ready for war by taking up weapons.
▸ **arming, armed**
3. arms *noun, plural* Weapons.

ar•ma•da (ar-**mah**-duh) ***noun*** A large group of warships.

ar•ma•dil•lo (ar-muh-**dil**-oh) ***noun*** A mammal covered by hard, bony plates.

ar•ma•ments (**ar**-muh-muhnts) ***noun, plural*** Weapons and other equipment used for fighting wars.

arm•chair (**arm**-*chair*) ***noun*** A comfortable chair with supports for your arms.

armed forces ***noun, plural*** All of the branches of a country's military. In the United States, the armed forces include the Army, Navy, Air Force, Marine Corps, and Coast Guard.

ar•mis•tice (**arm**-iss-tiss) ***noun*** A temporary agreement to stop fighting a war.

ar•mor (**ar**-mur) ***noun***
1. Metal covering worn by soldiers to protect them in battle.
2. Strong metal protection for tanks and other military vehicles.
3. Protective scales, spines, etc., that cover some animals, such as an armadillo.

armored vehicle ***noun*** A tank or other military vehicle with a strong metal covering.

ar•mor•y (**ar**-mur-ee) ***noun*** A place where weapons are stored or soldiers are trained. ▸ ***noun, plural* armories**

arm•pit (**arm**-*pit*) ***noun*** The area under your arm where it joins your shoulder.

ar•my (**ar**-mee) ***noun*** A large group of people trained to fight on land. ▸ ***noun, plural* armies**

a•ro•ma (uh-**roh**-muh) ***noun*** A smell that is usually pleasant. ▸ ***adjective* aromatic** (*a*-ruh-**mat**-ik)

a•round (uh-**round**)
1. ***preposition*** Surrounding.
2. ***adverb*** In many different parts of a place.
3. ***adverb*** More or less.

a•rouse (uh-**rouz**) ***verb***
1. To stir up a feeling.
2. To wake up someone.
▸ ***verb* arousing, aroused** ▸ ***noun* arousal**

ar•range (uh-**raynj**) ***verb***
1. To make plans for something to happen.
2. To place things so that they look attractive, as in *to arrange flowers.*
3. To change a piece of music slightly, so that it can be played on different instruments, as in *to arrange music.*
4. If you have an **arranged marriage,** your parents choose a husband or wife for you.

▸ ***verb*** **arranging, arranged** ▸ ***noun*** **arrangement**

ar•ray (uh-**ray**) ***noun***
1. A large number of things.
2. An orderly arrangement.
▸ ***verb*** **array**

ar•rest (uh-**rest**) ***verb***
1. To stop and hold someone by the power of law.
2. To stop something from developing or happening anymore.
▸ ***verb*** **arresting, arrested** ▸ ***noun*** **arrest**

ar•ri•val (uh-**rye**-vuhl) ***noun***
1. The act of getting to a place.
2. Someone or something that has gotten to a place.

ar•rive (uh-**rive**) ***verb***
1. To reach a place.
2. To come.
▸ ***verb*** **arriving, arrived**

ar•ro•gant (**a**-ruh-guhnt) ***adjective*** Conceited and too proud. ▸ ***noun*** **arrogance** ▸ ***adverb*** **arrogantly**

ar•row (**a**-roh) ***noun***
1. A pointed stick shot from a bow.
2. A sign (→) showing a direction on maps, road signs, etc.

ar•row•head (**a**-roh-*hed*) ***noun*** The sharp tip of an arrow.

ar•se•nal (**ar**-suh-nuhl) ***noun*** A place where weapons and ammunition are made or stored.

ar•se•nic (**ar**-suh-nik) ***noun*** A chemical element that usually appears as a gray-white powder and is poisonous if swallowed.

ar•son (**ar**-suhn) ***noun*** If someone commits **arson,** he or she deliberately and wrongly sets fire to something.
▸ ***noun*** **arsonist**

art (**art**)
1. ***noun*** The skill of creating something beautiful by drawing, painting, or making things with your hands.
2. ***noun*** Something that requires a lot of skill, as in *the art of Chinese cooking.*
3. **the arts *noun, plural*** Forms of entertainment, such as music, theater, and film.

ar•ter•y (**ar**-tuh-ree) ***noun***
1. One of the tubes that carry blood from your heart to all the other parts of your body.
2. A main road.
▸ ***noun, plural*** **arteries** ▸ ***adjective*** **arterial**

ar•thri•tis (ar-**thrye**-tiss) ***noun*** A disease that makes people's joints swollen and painful. ▸ ***adjective*** **arthritic**

ar•thro•pod (**ar**-thruh-*pod*) ***noun*** An animal without a backbone that has a hard outer skeleton and three or more pairs of legs that can bend. Insects, spiders, lobsters, and shrimp are all arthropods.

ar•ti•cle (**ar**-ti-kuhl) ***noun***
1. An object, or a thing, as in *an article of clothing.*
2. A piece of writing published in a newspaper or magazine.
3. A word, such as *a, an,* or *the,* that goes in front of a noun.

ar•tic•u•late (ar-**tik**-yuh-luht) ***adjective*** If you are **articulate**, you can express yourself clearly in words. ▸ ***verb*** **articulate** (ar-**tik**-yuh-late)
▸ ***adverb*** **articulately**

ar•ti•fact (**art**-uh-fakt) ***noun*** An object made or changed by human beings, especially a tool or weapon used in the past.

ar•ti•fi•cial (*ar*-ti-**fish**-uhl) ***adjective*** False, not real, or not natural, as in *artificial flowers.* ▸ ***adverb*** **artificially**

artificial intelligence ***noun*** The science of making computers do things that previously needed human intelligence, such as understanding language. Abbreviated AI.

artificial respiration ***noun*** A method of starting breathing after it has stopped by forcing air into and out of somebody's lungs.

A

ar•til•ler•y (ar-**til**-uh-ree) ***noun***
1. Large, powerful guns that are mounted on wheels or tracks.
2. The part of an army that uses large guns.

ar•ti•san (**ar**-tuh-zuhn) ***noun*** Someone who is skilled at working with his or her hands at a particular craft. Carpenters and quiltmakers are artisans.

art•ist (**ar**-tist) ***noun*** Someone very skilled at painting, making things, or performing in the arts. ▸ ***adjective*** **artistic** ▸ ***adverb*** **artistically**

as (**az**)
1. ***conjunction*** In comparison with.
2. ***adverb*** To the same degree.
3. ***conjunction*** In the same way that.
4. ***conjunction*** While or when.
5. ***conjunction*** Since or because.
6. ***preposition*** In the manner of, or in the role of.

as•bes•tos (ass-**bess**-tuhss) ***noun*** A grayish mineral whose fibers can be woven into a fireproof fabric. Asbestos is rarely used today, even though it was once a popular building material, because breathing its fibers is now known to cause serious illness.

as•cend (uh-**send**) ***verb*** To move or go up. ▸ **ascending, ascended** ▸ ***noun*** **ascent**

ash (**ash**) ***noun***
1. The powder that remains after something has been burned.
2. A tree with long, thin leaves.
▸ ***noun, plural*** **ashes**

a•shamed (uh-**shamed**) ***adjective*** If you are **ashamed,** you feel embarrassed and guilty.

a•shore (uh-**shor**) ***adverb*** On or to the shore or land.

A•sian American (**ay**-zhuhn) ***noun*** Someone who was born in the United States or became a U.S. citizen and can trace his or her ancestors back to Asia.
▸ ***adjective*** **Asian-American**

a•side (uh-**side**)
1. ***adverb*** To one side, or out of the way.
2. ***noun*** A remark made quietly so that not everyone can hear it.

ask (**ask**) ***verb***
1. To make a request or put a question to someone.
2. To invite someone to do something.
▸ ***verb*** **asking, asked**

a•skew (uh-**skyoo**) ***adverb*** Crooked, or off center. ▸ ***adjective*** **askew**

a•sleep (uh-**sleep**) ***adjective*** Sleeping.

as•par•a•gus (uh-**spar**-uh-guhss) ***noun*** A green plant whose spear-shaped stalks can be cooked and eaten as a vegetable.

as•pect (**ass**-pekt) ***noun*** One feature or characteristic of something.

as•pen (**ass**-puhn) ***noun*** A kind of poplar tree with white wood that is used to make paper. Aspens are well-known for their leaves, which flutter in the slightest breeze.

as•phalt (**ass**-fawlt) ***noun*** A black, tarlike substance that is mixed with sand and gravel and then rolled flat to make roads.

as•phyx•i•ate (ass-**fik**-see-*ate*) ***verb*** To suffocate. ▸ **asphyxiating, asphyxiated** ▸ ***noun*** **asphyxiation**

as•pi•ra•tion (ass-pi-**ray**-shuhn) ***noun*** A strong desire to do something great or important. ▸ ***verb*** **aspire**

as•pi•rin (**ass**-pi-rin) ***noun*** A drug that relieves pain and reduces fever.

ass (**ass**) ***noun***
1. A donkey.
2. (*informal*) A silly or stupid person.
▸ ***noun, plural*** **asses**

as•sas•si•nate (uh-**sass**-uh-nate) ***verb*** To murder someone who is well-known or important, such as a president.
▸ **assassinating, assassinated** ▸ ***noun*** **assassin,** ***noun*** **assassination**

as•sault (uh-**sawlt**) ***verb*** To attack someone or something violently.
▸ **assaulting, assaulted** ▸ ***noun*** **assault**

as•sem•ble (uh-**sem**-buhl) ***verb***
1. To gather together in one place.

A

2. To put all the parts of something together.
▸ ***verb*** **assembling, assembled**

as•sem•bly (uh-**sem**-blee) ***noun***
1. A meeting of lots of people.
2. assembly line An arrangement of machines and workers in a factory, where work passes from one person or machine to the next until it is complete.

as•sent (uh-**sent**) ***verb*** To agree to something. ▸ **assenting, assented** ▸ ***noun*** **assent**

as•sert (uh-**surt**) ***verb*** If you **assert yourself,** you behave in a strong, confident way so that people take notice of you. ▸ **asserting, asserted**

as•ser•tive (uh-**sur**-tiv) ***adjective*** If you are **assertive**, you are able to stand up for yourself and tell other people what you think or want. ▸ ***noun*** **assertiveness** ▸ ***adverb*** **assertively**

as•sess (uh-**sess**) ***verb*** To judge how good or bad something is. ▸ **assesses, assessing, assessed** ▸ ***noun*** **assessment,** ***noun*** **assessor**

as•set (**ass**-et) ***noun*** Something or somebody who is helpful or useful.

as•sign•ment (uh-**sine**-muhnt) ***noun*** A specific job that is given to somebody. ▸ ***verb*** **assign**

as•sist•ance (uh-**siss**-tuhnss) ***noun*** If someone gives you **assistance**, he or she does something to help you or to make things easier for you. ▸ ***verb*** **assist**

as•sist•ant (uh-**siss**-tuhnt) ***noun*** A person who helps someone else do a task or job.

as•so•ci•a•tion (uh-*soh*-see-**ay**-shuhn) ***noun***
1. An organization, a club, or a society.
2. A connection that you make in your mind between thoughts and feelings and a person or thing. ▸ ***verb*** **associate**

as•so•nance (**ass**-uh-nuhnss) ***noun*** Repeated use of the same vowel sound in words that are close together; for example, "How now, brown cow?"

as•sort•ment (uh-**sort**-muhnt) ***noun*** A mixture of different things. ▸ ***adjective*** **assorted**

as•sume (uh-**soom**) ***verb***
1. To suppose that something is true, without checking it. ▸ ***noun*** **assumption** (uh-**suhmp**-shuhn)
2. If you **assume** responsibility for something, you agree to look after it.
3. An **assumed name** is a false name.
▸ ***verb*** **assuming, assumed**

as•sur•ance (uh-**shur**-uhnss) ***noun***
1. A firm promise.
2. Self-assurance is confidence in yourself and in what you can do.

as•sure (uh-**shur**) ***verb***
1. To promise something, or say something positively.
2. If you **assure yourself** about something, you make certain of it.
▸ ***verb*** **assuring, assured**

as•ter (**ass**-tur) ***noun*** A plant with flowers that have white, pink, yellow, or purple petals around a yellow center. Asters resemble daisies.

as•ter•isk (**ass**-tuh-risk) ***noun*** The mark (*) used in printing and writing to tell readers to look elsewhere on the page for more information.

as•ter•oid (**ass**-tuh-roid) ***noun*** A very small planet that travels around the sun.

asth•ma (**az**-muh) ***noun*** If you have **asthma,** you have a condition that sometimes causes you to wheeze and have difficulty breathing. ▸ ***noun*** **asthmatic** (*az*-**mat**-ik) ▸ ***adjective*** **asthmatic**

as•ton•ish (uh-**ston**-ish) ***verb*** To make someone feel very surprised.
▸ **astonishes, astonishing, astonished** ▸ ***noun*** **astonishment** ▸ ***adjective*** **astonishing** ▸ ***adverb*** **astonishingly**

as•tound (uh-**stound**) ***verb*** To amaze or astonish someone. ▸ **astounding, astounded**

A

a•stray (uh-**stray**) ***adverb***
1. If something has gone **astray,** it has been lost.
2. If someone **leads you astray,** the person encourages you to do something wrong.

a•stride (uh-**stride**) ***preposition*** If you sit **astride** something, such as a horse or a bicycle, you sit with a leg on either side of it.

as•trol•o•gy (uh-**strol**-uh-jee) ***noun*** The study of how the positions of stars and planets supposedly affect people's lives. ▸ ***noun* astrologer** ▸ ***adjective* astrological** (ass-truh-**loj**-i-kuhl)

as•tro•naut (**ass**-truh-*nawt*) ***noun*** Someone who travels in space.

as•tro•nom•i•cal (*ass*-truh-**nom**-uh-kuhl) ***adjective***
1. To do with astronomy
2. Very large, as in *an astronomical amount of money.* ▸ ***adverb* astronomically**

as•tron•o•my (uh-**stron**-uh-mee) ***noun*** The study of stars, planets, and space. ▸ ***noun* astronomer**

as•tute (uh-**stoot**) ***adjective*** If someone is **astute,** he or she understands situations and people clearly and quickly.

a•sun•der (uh-**sun**-dur) ***adverb*** In or into pieces, as in *torn asunder.*

a•sy•lum (uh-**sye**-luhm) ***noun***
1. Protection given by a country to people escaping from danger in their own country.
2. A hospital for people who are mentally ill and cannot live independently.

a•sym•met•ri•cal (*ay*-si-**met**-ruh-kuhl) ***adjective*** A shape that is **asymmetrical** cannot be divided so both pieces match exactly in shape and size.

at (**at**) ***preposition***
1. In a place or position. *We were at the movies.*
2. Describing a time. *We'll meet at noon.*
3. In the direction of. *Look at all those books!*
4. In a state or condition of. *The two countries were at war.*
5. For the amount or price of. *The store sells apples at $1 per pound.*

a•the•ist (**ay**-thee-ist) ***noun*** Someone who does not believe that there is a God. ▸ ***noun* atheism**

ath•lete (**ath**-leet) ***noun*** Someone who is trained in or very good at sports or games that require strength, speed, and/or skill. ▸ ***adjective* athletic** (*ath*-**let**-ik)

athlete's foot ***noun*** An itchy rash that can develop on your feet and between your toes. Athlete's foot is caused by a fungus and is usually treated by applying special creams or ointments to the rash.

ath•let•ics (ath-**let**-iks) ***noun, plural***
1. Competitive sports that involve running, jumping, or throwing.
2. All competitive sports. ▸ ***adjective* athletic**

at•las (**at**-luhss) ***noun*** A book of maps.

ATM (*ay*-tee-**em**) ***noun*** A machine linked to a bank that lets you put money into your account or take it out without actually going into the bank. ATM stands for *Automatic Teller Machine* or *Automated Teller Machine.*

at•mos•phere (**at**-muhss-fihr) ***noun***
1. The mixture of gases that surrounds a planet.
2. The air in a particular place.
3. A mood or feeling created by a place or a work of art.
▸ ***adjective* atmospheric**

at•oll (**a**-tol) ***noun*** A chain of tiny coral islands that forms a ring around a lagoon.

at•om (**at**-uhm) ***noun*** The tiniest part of an element that has all the properties of that element. Everything is made up of atoms.

a•tom•ic (uh-**tom**-ik) ***adjective***
1. To do with atoms, as in *atomic research.*
2. Using the power created when atoms are split.

atomic bomb ***noun*** A powerful bomb that explodes with great force, heat, and bright light. The explosion results from the energy that is released by splitting atoms. It destroys large areas and leaves behind dangerous radiation.

atomic energy ***noun*** The energy released when atoms are split apart or forced together. Atomic energy is also called nuclear energy. It can be used to power submarines, heat homes, and treat certain diseases.

a·tone (uh-**tone**) ***verb*** If you **atone** for something, you make up for it.
▸ **atoning, atoned**

a·tri·um (**ay**-tree-uhm) ***noun***
1. Either of two sections of the heart that receive blood from the veins.
2. A patio or courtyard around which a building is built.
▸ ***noun, plural*** **atriums** *or* **atria** (**ay**-tree-uh)

a·tro·cious (uh-**troh**-shuhss) ***adjective*** Very cruel, or terrible, as in *an atrocious accident.*

a·troc·i·ty (uh-**tross**-uh-tee) ***noun*** A very wicked or cruel act, often involving killing. ▸ ***noun, plural*** **atrocities**

at·tach (uh-**tach**) ***verb***
1. To join or fix one thing to another.
2. If you are **attached to** someone, you are very fond of that person.
▸ ***verb*** **attaches, attaching, attached**
▸ ***noun*** **attachment**

at·tack (uh-**tak**)
1. ***verb*** To try to hurt someone or something.
2. ***verb*** To criticize someone strongly.
3. ***verb*** To try to defeat an enemy or capture a place where the enemy is.
4. ***noun*** A sudden period of illness, as in *a bad attack of flu.*
▸ ***verb*** **attacking, attacked** ▸ ***noun*** **attack,** ***noun*** **attacker**

at·tain·ment (uh-**tayn**-muhnt) ***noun*** An achievement. ▸ ***verb*** **attain**
▸ ***adjective*** **attainable**

at·tempt (uh-**tempt**) ***verb*** To try to do something. ▸ **attempting, attempted**
▸ ***noun*** **attempt**

at·tend (uh-**tend**) ***verb***
1. To be present in a place or at an event. ▸ ***noun*** **attendance**
2. If you **attend to** something, you deal with it. ▸ ***verb*** **attending, attended**

at·ten·dant (uh-**ten**-duhnt) ***noun*** Someone who looks after a person or place, as in *a parking lot attendant.*

at·ten·tion (uh-**ten**-shuhn) ***noun***
1. Concentration and careful thought, as in *attention to detail.*
2. If you **pay attention,** you concentrate on something.
3. If something needs **attention,** it needs you to do something to it.
4. When soldiers **stand at attention,** they stand up straight, with their feet together and their arms by their sides.

at·ten·tive (uh-**ten**-tiv) ***adjective*** If you are **attentive,** you are alert and are paying close attention to something or someone. ▸ ***adverb*** **attentively**

at·test (uh-**test**) ***verb***
1. To declare that something is true.
2. To be proof of something.
▸ ***verb*** **attesting, attested**

at·tic (**at**-ik) ***noun*** A space in a building just under the roof.

at·tire (uh-**tire**) ***noun*** Clothing. ▸ ***verb*** **attire**

at·ti·tude (**at**-i-tood) ***noun***
1. Your opinions and feelings about someone or something.
2. The position in which you are standing or sitting.

at·tor·ney (uh-**tur**-nee) ***noun*** A lawyer.

at·tract (uh-**trakt**) ***verb***
1. If something **attracts** you, you are interested in it.
2. If a person **attracts** you, you like him or her.
3. If something **attracts** objects or people to itself, it pulls them toward itself.
▸ ***verb*** **attracting, attracted** ▸ ***noun*** **attraction**

A

at•trac•tive (uh-**trak**-tiv) ***adjective***
1. Pleasant or pretty to look at.
2. Interesting or exciting, as in *an attractive idea.* ▸ ***noun*** **attractiveness**
▸ ***adverb*** **attractively**

at•trib•ute
1. (**at**-ruh-*byoot*) ***noun*** A quality or characteristic that belongs to or describes a person or thing.
2. (uh-**trib**-yoot) ***verb*** When you **attribute** something to someone, you give him or her credit for it.
▸ **attributing, attributed**

ATV (*ay-tee*-**vee**) ***noun*** A vehicle with three or more large wheels, ridden like a motorcycle, that can travel over rough ground. ATV stands for *All-Terrain Vehicle.*

au•burn (**aw**-burn) ***noun*** A reddish brown color. ▸ ***adjective*** **auburn**

auc•tion (**awk**-shuhn) ***noun*** A sale where goods are sold to the person who offers the most money for them. ▸ ***noun*** **auctioneer** (*awk*-shuh-**neer**)

au•di•ble (**aw**-duh-buhl) ***adjective*** Loud enough to be heard.

au•di•ence (**aw**-dee-uhnss) ***noun***
1. The people who watch or listen to a performance, speech, or movie.
2. A formal meeting with an important or powerful person, as in *an audience with the pope.*

au•di•o (**aw**-dee-oh)
1. ***adjective*** To do with how sound is heard, recorded, and played back.
2. ***noun*** Sound, especially the sound portion of a television or motion picture.

au•di•o•book (**aw**-dee-oh-*buk*) ***noun*** A sound recording of a book being read that can be listened to on a CD, audiotape, or computer.

au•di•o•tape (**aw**-dee-oh-*tape*) ***noun*** Magnetic tape that records sound.

au•di•o•vis•u•al (*aw*-dee-oh-**vizh**-oo-uhl) ***adjective*** **Audiovisual** equipment uses sound and pictures, often to teach people something.

au•di•tion (aw-**dish**-uhn) ***noun*** A short performance by an actor, singer, musician, or dancer to see whether he or she is suitable for a part in a play, concert, etc. ▸ ***verb*** **audition**

au•di•to•ri•um (aw-di-**tor**-ee-uhm) ***noun*** A building or large room where people gather for meetings, plays, concerts, or other events.

aug•ment (awg-**ment**) ***verb*** You **augment** something when you add to it or make it larger. ▸ **augmenting, augmented**

Au•gust (**aw**-guhst) ***noun*** The eighth month on the calendar, after July and before September. August has 31 days.

aunt (**ant** *or* **ahnt**) ***noun*** The sister of your father or mother, or the wife of your uncle.

au pair (**oh pair**) ***noun*** A young person from another country who lives with a family and helps them, in order to learn that country's language.

au•ral (**or**-uhl) ***adjective*** To do with listening. **Aural** sounds like **oral.**

au•ri•cle (**or**-uh-kuhl) ***noun***
1. The outer part of the ear.
2. Either of two sections of the heart that receive blood from the veins. Also called **atrium.**

au•ro•ra bo•re•al•is (uh-**ror**-uh *bor*-ee-**al**-iss) ***noun*** Colorful bands of flashing lights that sometimes can be seen at night, especially near the Arctic Circle. Also called the **northern lights.**

aus•tere (aw-**stihr**) ***adjective*** Severe or cold in manner or appearance.

aus•ter•i•ty (aw-**stair**-uh-tee) ***noun*** A way of living without extras or comforts. ▸ ***noun, plural*** **austerities**

au•then•tic (aw-**then**-tik) ***adjective*** Real, or genuine.

au•thor (**aw**-thur) ***noun*** The writer of a book, play, article, or poem. ▸ ***noun*** **authorship**

au•thor•i•ta•tive (uh-**thor**-uh-tay-tiv) ***adjective***
1. Official, or coming from someone who has the power to give orders.
2. Expert.

au•thor•i•ty (uh-**thor**-uh-tee) ***noun***
1. The right to do something or to tell

other people what to do.
2. A group of people with power in a certain area.
3. Someone who knows a lot about a particular subject.
▸ ***noun, plural*** **authorities**

au•thor•ize (**aw**-thuh-*rize*) ***verb*** To give official permission for something to happen. ▸ **authorizing, authorized** ▸ ***noun*** **authorization**

au•tis•tic (aw-**tiss**-tik) ***adjective*** People who are **autistic** have a condition that causes them to have trouble communicating and forming relationships with people. They may have difficulty with language. ▸ ***noun*** **autism**

au•to•bi•og•ra•phy (*aw*-toh-bye-**og**-ruh-fee) ***noun*** A book in which the author tells the story of his or her life. ▸ ***noun, plural*** **autobiographies** ▸ ***adjective*** **autobiographical**

au•to•graph (**aw**-tuh-*graf*) ***noun*** A person's handwritten signature.

au•to•mat•ic (aw-tuh-**mat**-ik) ***adjective***
1. An **automatic** machine can perform its functions without anyone operating it.
2. An **automatic** action happens without your thinking about it.
▸ ***adverb*** **automatically**

au•to•ma•tion (aw-tuh-**may**-shuhn) ***noun*** The use of machines rather than people to do jobs, especially in factories. ▸ ***verb*** **automate**

au•to•mo•bile (**aw**-tuh-muh-*beel*) ***noun*** A passenger vehicle that usually has four wheels and is powered by an engine. *See also* **car.**

au•top•sy (**aw**-top-see) ***noun*** An examination performed on a dead person to find the cause of death. ▸ ***noun, plural*** **autopsies**

au•tumn (**aw**-tuhm) ***noun*** The season between summer and winter, from late September to late December in the Northern Hemisphere. It is also called **fall.** ▸ ***adjective*** **autumnal** (aw-**tuhm**-nuhl)

aux•il•ia•ry (awg-**zil**-yur-ee) ***adjective*** Helping, or giving extra support. ▸ ***noun*** **auxiliary**

a•vail•a•ble (uh-**vay**-luh-buhl) ***adjective***
1. Ready to be used or bought.
2. Not busy, and therefore free to talk to people.
▸ ***noun*** **availability**

av•a•lanche (**av**-uh-lanch) ***noun*** A large mass of snow, ice, or earth that suddenly moves down the side of a mountain.

av•e•nue (**av**-uh-noo) ***noun*** A wide road in a town or city.

av•er•age (**av**-uh-rij)
1. ***noun*** In math, you find an **average** by adding a group of figures together and then dividing the sum by the number of figures you have added. ▸ ***verb*** **average**
2. ***adjective*** Usual, or ordinary.

a•vert (uh-**vurt**) ***verb*** To turn away from something or avoid it. ▸ **averting, averted** ▸ ***noun*** **aversion** (uh-**vur**-zhuhn)

a•vi•ar•y (**ay**-vee-*air*-ee) ***noun*** A large cage or other enclosed area for birds. ▸ ***noun, plural*** **aviaries**

a•vi•a•tion (*ay*-vee-**ay**-shuhn) ***noun*** The science of building and flying aircraft. ▸ ***noun*** **aviator**

av•id (**av**-id) ***adjective*** Very eager or committed. ▸ ***adverb*** **avidly**

av•o•ca•do (av-uh-**kah**-doh) ***noun*** A green or black pear-shaped fruit with a tough skin and a creamy, light green pulp. ▸ ***noun, plural*** **avocados**

av•o•ca•tion (a-voh-**kay**-shun) ***noun*** If you have an **avocation**, you have a hobby or pastime that is different from your regular job.

a•void (uh-**void**) ***verb***
1. To stay away from a person or place.
2. To try to prevent something from happening.
▸ ***verb*** **avoiding, avoided** ▸ ***noun*** **avoidance** ▸ ***adjective*** **avoidable**

A

a•wait (uh-**wayt**) ***verb*** To wait for or expect someone or something.
▸ **awaiting, awaited**

a•wake (uh-**wake**)
1. ***adjective*** Not asleep.
2. ***verb*** To wake up. ▸ **awaking, awoke** (uh-**wohk**), **awoken** (uh-**woh**-ken)
▸ ***noun*** **awakening**

a•ward (uh-**word**) ***verb*** To give someone something officially, such as a prize. ▸ **awarding, awarded** ▸ ***noun*** **award**

a•ware (uh-**wair**) ***adjective*** If you are **aware** of something, you know that it exists. ▸ ***noun*** **awareness**

a•way (uh-**way**)
1. ***adverb*** Moving from a place, person, or thing.
2. ***adverb*** Distant from a place.
4. ***adverb*** In a safe place.
5. ***adjective*** An **away** game in sports is one you play at your opponent's home field or court.

awe (**aw**) ***noun*** A feeling of admiration and respect, mixed with a little fear.
▸ ***adjective*** **awesome** (**aw**-*suhm*)

aw•ful (**aw**-fuhl) ***adjective***
1. Terrible, or horrible.
2. (*informal*) Very great. ▸ ***adverb*** **awfully**

a•while (uh-**wile**) ***adverb*** For a short time.

awk•ward (**awk**-wurd) ***adjective***
1. Difficult or embarrassing.
2. Not able to relax and talk to people easily.
▸ ***noun*** **awkwardness** ▸ ***adverb*** **awkwardly**

awl (**awl**) ***noun*** A sharp metal tool for making holes in leather or wood. **Awl** sounds like **all**.

aw•ning (**aw**-ning) ***noun*** A piece of cloth, metal, or wood that is fastened to the top of a window or to the front roof of a building to shade it from sun and help keep out rain.

ax *or* **axe** (**aks**)
1. ***noun*** A tool with a sharp blade on the end of a handle, used for chopping wood.
▸ ***noun, plural*** **axes**
2. ***verb*** To bring something to an end.
▸ **axing, axed**

ax•is (**ak**-siss) ***noun***
1. An imaginary line through the middle of an object, around which that object spins, as in *the earth's axis*.
2. A line at the side or the bottom of a graph. ▸ ***noun, plural*** **axes** (**ak**-seez)

ax•le (**ak**-suhl) ***noun*** A rod in the center of a wheel, around which the wheel turns.

aye (**eye**) ***noun*** A vote of "yes."
▸ ***adverb*** **aye**

a•za•lea (uh-**zayl**-yuh) ***noun*** A shrub with funnel-shaped pink, orange, or white flowers and dark green leaves.

Az•tec (**az**-tek) ***noun*** A member of a Mexican Indian people who built a great civilization before the conquest of Mexico by Hernán Cortés in the 16th century.
▸ ***adjective*** **Aztec**

az•ure (**azh**-ur) ***noun*** A deep, clear blue, such as the color of a cloudless sky or deep, still water. ▸ ***adjective*** **azure**

B

bab•ble (**bab**-uhl) ***verb***
1. To talk in an excited way, without making any sense.
2. To make sounds like a baby.
▸ ***verb* babbling, babbled**

babe (**babe**) ***noun*** A baby.

ba•boon (ba-**boon**) ***noun*** A large monkey that lives in Africa. Baboons have long, doglike snouts and large teeth.

ba•by (**bay**-bee) ***noun*** A newly born or very young child or animal. ▸ ***noun, plural* babies** ▸ ***adjective* babyish**

baby boom ***noun*** A noticeable increase in the number of babies born in a nation, as in *the U.S. baby boom* between 1946 and 1964. ▸ ***noun* baby boomer**

baby-sit•ter (**sit**-ur) ***noun*** Someone who is paid to stay with and look after children. ▸ ***verb* baby-sit**

baby tooth ***noun*** A first tooth in infants and baby mammals. Baby teeth fall out and are replaced by permanent teeth.
▸ ***noun, plural* baby teeth**

bach•e•lor (**bach**-uh-lur) ***noun*** A man who has never been married.

back (**bak**)
1. *noun* The rear part of your body between your neck and the end of your spine.
2. *noun* The opposite end or side from the front, as in *the back of the room.*
▸ ***adjective* back**
3. *adverb* Where someone or something was before.
4. *verb* To support someone. ▸ ***noun* backer**
5. back down *verb* To stop arguing for something.
6. back out *verb* To decide not to do something that you had agreed to do.
▸ ***verb* backing, backed**

back•board (**bak**-*bord*) ***noun*** The wood or plastic surface attached to a basketball hoop and net.

back•bone (**bak**-*bohn*) ***noun*** A set of connected bones that run down the middle of the back. The backbone is also called the **spine** and the **spinal column.**

back•fire (**bak**-*fire*) ***verb***
1. If an action **backfires,** it does not work out as you planned it.
2. If a car **backfires,** there is a small explosion inside its exhaust pipe.
▸ ***verb* backfiring, backfired**

back•ground (**bak**-*ground*) ***noun***
1. The part of a picture that is behind the main subject.
2. A person's past experience.
▸ ***adjective* background**

back•hand (**bak**-*hand*) ***noun*** A stroke in tennis that you play with your arm across your body and the back of your hand facing outward.

back•hoe (**bak**-*hoh*) ***noun*** A digging machine that has a bucket with teeth. The bucket is pulled down and backward through the earth.

back•pack (**bak**-*pak*)
1. *noun* A large bag that you carry on your back when you are walking or climbing.
2. *verb* If you **backpack,** you go on a long walk or hike carrying a backpack.

back•stroke (**bak**-*stroke*) ***noun*** A style of swimming in which you lie on your back.

back•ward (**bak**-wurd) *or* **back•wards** (**bak**-wurdz) ***adverb***
1. In the reverse direction.
2. In the opposite to the usual way.
▸ ***adjective* backward**

B

back•yard (**bak**-**yard**) ***noun*** An open area behind a house.

ba•con (**bay**-kuhn) ***noun*** Smoked or salted meat from the back or sides of a pig.

bac•te•ri•a (bak-**tihr**-ee-uh) ***noun, plural*** Microscopic living things that exist all around you and inside you. Many bacteria are useful, but some cause disease. ▸ ***noun, singular*** **bacterium** (bak-**tihr**-ee-uhm)

bad (**bad**) ***adjective***
1. Not good, as in *bad news.*
2. Serious, as in *a bad mistake.*
3. Not fit to eat.
4. Sorry.
▸ ***adjective*** **worse, worst**

badge (**baj**) ***noun*** A small sign with a picture, name, or message on it that you pin to your clothes.

badg•er (**baj**-ur)
1. ***noun*** A mammal with a gray body and a black and white head that lives in a burrow and comes out at night to eat.
2. ***verb*** To keep asking someone to do something. ▸ **badgering, badgered**

bad•ly (**bad**-lee) ***adverb***
1. Urgently.
2. Not well, or not skillfully.

bad•min•ton (**bad**-min-tuhn) ***noun*** A game similar to tennis in which players use rackets to hit a shuttlecock back and forth over a high net.

bad•mouth (**bad**-*mouth*) ***verb*** To say negative things about someone or something. ▸ **badmouthing, badmouthed**

baf•fle (**baf**-uhl) ***verb*** To puzzle or confuse someone. ▸ **baffling, baffled** ▸ ***adjective*** **baffling**

bag (**bag**) ***noun*** A usually flexible container for carrying things. ▸ ***verb*** **bag**

ba•gel (**bay**-guhl) ***noun*** A round, chewy roll with a hole in the middle. A bagel looks like a doughnut but is made of bread.

bag•gage (**bag**-ij) ***noun*** Travelers' suitcases, bags, and trunks.

bag•gy (**bag**-ee) ***adjective*** Hanging in loose folds, as in *baggy shorts.* ▸ **baggier, baggiest**

bag•pipes (**bag**-*pipes*) ***noun, plural*** A musical instrument. To play the bagpipes, you blow air through a pipe into a bag and squeeze it out through the drones and the chanter.

bail (**bayl**) ***noun*** A sum of money paid to a court to allow someone accused of a crime to be set free until his or her trial.

bail•iff (**bay**-lif) ***noun*** A law officer who has charge of prisoners in court.

bail out ***verb***
1. To jump out of an aircraft using a parachute.
2. To scoop water out of a boat.
3. If you **bail someone out,** you pay his or her bail or help him or her out of a difficult situation.
▸ ***verb*** **bailing out, bailed out**

bait (**bayt**) ***noun*** A small amount of food used to attract a fish or an animal so you can catch it.

bake (**bayk**) ***verb***
1. To cook food in an oven, especially bread or cake. ▸ ***noun*** **baker,** ***noun*** **bakery**
2. To heat something in order to make it hard.
▸ ***verb*** **baking, baked**

bak•ing powder (**bayk**-ing) ***noun*** A white powder used in baking to make dough or batter rise.

baking soda ***noun*** A white powder used to make dough rise, or to soothe an upset stomach. Also called **sodium bicarbonate**.

bal•ance (**bal**-uhnss)
1. ***noun*** Your **balance** is your ability to keep steady and not fall over.
2. ***verb*** If you **balance** something, you keep it steady and do not let it fall.
3. ***verb*** When two things **balance** in a pair of scales, they weigh the same and do not tip the scales either way.
4. ***noun*** An instrument used for weighing things.

B

5. ***noun*** Remainder.
▸ ***verb*** **balancing, balanced**

balance beam ***noun*** A narrow, horizontal beam, usually about four feet off the floor, used in gymnastics for doing various tumbling and dance movements.

balanced diet ***noun*** A diet that contains the proper kinds and amounts of food.

bal•co•ny (**bal**-kuh-nee) ***noun***
1. A platform with railings on the outside of a building, usually on an upper level.
2. The upstairs seating in a theater.

bald (**bawld**) ***adjective***
1. Someone who is **bald** has very little or no hair on his or her head. ▸ ***noun*** **baldness** ▸ ***adjective*** **balding**
2. Without any natural covering.
▸ ***adjective*** **balder, baldest**

bald eagle ***noun*** An eagle with a brown body and a white head that appears bald from a distance. The bald eagle is the national symbol of the United States.

bale (**bale**)
1. ***noun*** A large bundle of things, such as straw or hay, that is tied tightly together.
2. ***verb*** To put hay or some other substance into a tightly packed bundle.
▸ **baling, baled**

balk (**bawk**) ***verb*** To stop and refuse to go on. ▸ **balking, balked**

ball (**bawl**) ***noun***
1. A round object used in games.
2. Something made into a round shape, as in *a ball of wool.*
3. A formal party where people dance.
4. In baseball, a pitch that a batter does not swing at and that does not cross home plate between the batter's shoulders and knees.
5. (*informal*) If you are **on the ball,** you are quick at understanding things.
Ball sounds like **bawl.**

bal•lad (**bal**-uhd) ***noun*** A song or poem that tells a story.

bal•last (**bal**-uhst) ***noun***
1. Heavy material, such as water or sand, that is carried by a ship to make it more stable.
2. **ballast tank** A large tank in a submarine that is filled with water to make the submarine sink or with air to make it come to the surface.

ball bearings ***noun, plural*** Small metal balls used to help parts of machinery move more smoothly against each other.

bal•le•ri•na (bal-uh-**ree**-nuh) ***noun*** A female ballet dancer.

bal•let (**bal**-lay *or* bal-**lay**) ***noun***
1. A style of dance with set movements.
2. A performance that uses dance and music, often to tell a story.

bal•loon (buh-**loon**) ***noun***
1. A small bag made of thin rubber that is blown up and used as a decoration.
2. A **hot-air balloon** is an aircraft consisting of a very large bag filled with hot air or gas, with a basket for carrying passengers and equipment.

bal•lot (**bal**-uht) ***noun***
1. A secret way of voting, such as on a machine or on a slip of paper.
2. **ballot box** A box with a slit in the top into which votes are put.

ball•point (**bawl**-*point*) ***noun*** A pen with a tiny ball at its tip that lets ink flow as you write.

ball•room (**bawl**-*room*) ***noun*** A very large room where parties and dances are held.

bal•sa (**bawl**-suh) ***noun*** A very light wood used for making models.

bal•sam fir (**bawl**-suhm) ***noun*** A type of fragrant evergreen tree found in North America.

bam•boo (bam-**boo**) ***noun*** A tropical plant with a hard, hollow stem, often used for making furniture.

ban (**ban**) ***verb*** To forbid something.
▸ **banning, banned** ▸ ***noun*** **ban**

ba•nan•a (buh-**na**-nuh) ***noun*** A tropical fruit that is long, curved, and yellow.

banana split ***noun*** A dessert of ice cream served between two halves of a banana with nuts, syrup, and other flavorings on top.

B

band (**band**)
1. ***noun*** A narrow ring of rubber, paper, or other material that is put around something, sometimes to hold it together.
2. ***noun*** A group of people who play music together.
3. ***noun*** A group of people who do something together, as in *a band of robbers.*
4. ***noun*** A stripe of color or material.
5. ***verb*** When people **band** together, they join together in a group in order to do something. ▸ **banding, banded**

band•age (**ban**-dij) ***noun*** A piece of cloth or material that is wrapped around an injured part of the body to protect it. ▸ ***verb*** **bandage**

ban•dan•na (ban-**dan**-uh) ***noun*** A large, brightly colored handkerchief.

ban•dit (**ban**-dit) ***noun*** An armed robber, usually a member of a gang.

bang (**bang**)
1. ***noun*** A sudden loud noise.
2. ***verb*** To knock hard against something. ▸ **banging, banged**

bang•le (**bang**-guhl) ***noun*** A band of metal, plastic, etc., worn as jewelry around the wrist.

bangs (**bangz**) ***noun, plural*** The hair that hangs over your forehead.

ban•ish (**ban**-ish) ***verb*** To send someone away from a place and order the person not to return. ▸ **banishing, banished** ▸ ***noun*** **banishment**

ban•is•ter (**ban**-iss-tur) ***noun*** A railing that runs along the side of a flight of stairs.

ban•jo (**ban**-joh) ***noun*** A musical instrument similar to a guitar, with a small, round body and a long neck. ▸ ***noun, plural*** **banjos** *or* **banjoes**

bank (**bangk**)
1. ***noun*** A place where people keep their money. Banks also lend money and offer other financial services. ▸ ***noun*** **banker** ▸ ***verb*** **bank**
2. ***noun*** The land along the side of a river or a canal.
3. ***noun*** A place where something is collected and stored, as in *a blood bank.*
4. If you **bank on** something, you rely on it.

bank•rupt (**bangk**-*ruhpt*) ***adjective*** If people or companies are **bankrupt,** they cannot pay their debts. ▸ ***noun*** **bankruptcy** ▸ ***verb*** **bankrupt**

ban•ner (**ban**-ur) ***noun*** A long piece of material with writing, pictures, or designs on it, hung from a pole or displayed at sporting events or parades.

ban•quet (**bang**-kwit) ***noun*** A formal meal for a large number of people, usually on a special occasion.

ban•ter (**ban**-tur) ***verb*** To tease someone in a friendly way. ▸ **bantering, bantered** ▸ ***noun*** **banter**

bap•tize (**bap**-tize) ***verb*** To pour water on someone's head or to immerse someone in water, as a sign that he or she has become a Christian. ▸ **baptizing, baptized** ▸ ***noun*** **baptism**

bar (**bar**)
1. ***noun*** A long stick of metal, as in *an iron bar.*
2. ***noun*** A long, flat block of something hard, as in *a chocolate bar.*
3. ***noun*** A place where drinks, especially alcoholic drinks, are sold.
4. ***noun*** One of the groups of notes into which a piece of music is divided.
5. ***verb*** To block someone, or to keep someone out. ▸ **barring, barred**

barb (**barb**) ***noun*** A sharp point that sticks out and backward, as on a hook or arrowhead. ▸ ***adjective*** **barbed**

bar•bar•i•an (bar-**bair**-ee-uhn) ***noun*** Anyone who is savage or uncivilized.

bar•bar•ic (bar-**ba**-rik) ***adjective*** Very cruel.

bar•be•cue (**bar**-buh-kyoo) ***noun***
1. A charcoal grill used for cooking meat and other food outdoors. ▸ ***verb*** **barbecue**

2. An outdoor meal or party in which food is cooked using a barbecue.

barbed wire (**barbd**) ***noun*** Wire with small spikes along it, used for fences.

bar•ber (**bar**-bur) ***noun*** Someone who cuts hair and trims or shaves beards.

bar code ***noun*** A band of thick and thin lines printed on goods sold in stores. When read electronically, the bar code gives the price and other information about the product.

bare (**bair**)
1. ***adjective*** Wearing no clothes, or not covered.
2. ***adjective*** Empty.
3. ***verb*** To uncover or reveal something.
▸ **baring, bared**
4. ***adjective*** Plain and simple.
Bare sounds like **bear.**
▸ ***adjective*** **barer, barest**

bare•faced (**bair**-*fayst*) ***adjective*** Open and not disguised, as in *a barefaced lie.*

bare•foot (**bair**-*fut*) ***adjective*** Without shoes or socks. ▸ ***adverb*** **barefoot**

bare•ly (**bair**-lee) ***adverb*** Hardly, or almost not.

bar•gain (**bar**-guhn)
1. ***noun*** Something that you buy for less than the usual price.
2. ***verb*** When you **bargain** with someone, you discuss the price of something or the terms of an agreement.
▸ **bargaining, bargained**

barge (**barj**)
1. ***noun*** A long boat with a flat bottom, used on canals.
2. ***verb*** If you **barge** into a room, you enter it rudely or abruptly. ▸ **barging, barged**

bar graph ***noun*** A chart that shows the comparison of information by the lengths of rectangular bars.

bar•i•tone (**ba**-ruh-*tone*) ***noun***
1. The second-lowest singing voice for a man. ▸ ***adjective*** **baritone**
2. A singer with such a voice.

bar•i•um (**bair**-ee-uhm) ***noun*** A silver-colored chemical element used in paints and ceramics to make them white. When a patient drinks a liquid containing barium, the digestive system can be seen better in X rays.

bark (**bark**)
1. ***verb*** When a dog **barks,** it makes a short, loud sound. ▸ ***noun*** **bark**
2. ***noun*** The hard covering on the outside of a tree.
3. ***verb*** To shout at someone gruffly.
▸ ***verb*** **barking, barked**

bar•ley (**bar**-lee) ***noun*** A common cereal plant.

bar mitz•vah (**bar mits**-vuh) ***noun*** A ceremony and celebration that takes place on or close to a Jewish boy's 13th birthday, after which he can take part in his religion as an adult.

barn (**barn**) ***noun*** A farm building where crops, animals, and equipment are kept.

bar•na•cle (**bar**-nuh-kuhl) ***noun*** A small shellfish that attaches itself firmly to the sides of boats, rocks, and other shellfish.

barn•yard (**bahrn**-*yard*) ***noun*** The area near a barn, usually surrounded by a fence.

ba•rom•e•ter (buh-**rom**-uh-tur) ***noun*** An instrument that measures changes in air pressure and shows how the weather is going to change.

bar•on (**ba**-ruhn) ***noun*** A nobleman of the lowest rank. ▸ ***adjective*** **baronial** (ba-**rohn**-ee-uhl)

bar•on•ess (**ba**-ruhn-iss) ***noun*** A noblewoman of the lowest rank. ▸ ***noun, plural*** **baronesses**

bar•racks (**ba**-ruhks) ***noun, plural*** The building or buildings where soldiers live.

bar•ra•cu•da (ba-ruh-**koo**-duh) ***noun*** A fish with a long, narrow body and many sharp teeth.

bar•rage (buh-**rahzh**) ***noun***
1. Concentrated gunfire.
2. A large amount of something that all comes at the same time, as in *a barrage of complaints.*

B

bar•rel (**ba**-ruhl) ***noun***
1. A large container that has curved sides and a flat top and bottom.
2. The long part of a gun that looks like a tube.
3. If someone has you **over a barrel,** he or she has made you powerless.

bar•ren (**ba**-ruhn) ***adjective*** If land is **barren,** farmers cannot grow crops on it.

bar•rette (buh-**ret**) ***noun*** A plastic or metal clip used to hold the hair in place.

bar•ri•cade (**ba**-ruh-*kade*)
1. ***noun*** A barrier to stop people from getting past a certain point.
2. ***verb*** If people **barricade** themselves into a place, they build walls or put up obstacles to stop other people from reaching them. ▸ **barricading, barricaded**

bar•ri•er (**ba**-ree-ur) ***noun***
1. A bar, fence, or wall that prevents people, traffic, or other things from going past it.
2. Anything that prevents you from communicating properly with someone else, as in *a language barrier.*

bar•ring (**bar**-ing) ***preposition*** Except for.

bar•ri•o (**ba**-ree-oh) ***noun*** A neighborhood where Spanish is the main language. Barrio means "neighborhood" in Spanish.

bar•row (**ba**-roh) ***noun*** A mound of earth made to cover a grave in prehistoric times.

bar•ten•der (**bar**-*ten*-dur) ***noun*** Someone who mixes and serves drinks at a bar or tavern.

bar•ter (**bar**-tur) ***verb*** To trade by exchanging food or other goods or services, rather than by using money.
▸ **bartering, bartered** ▸ ***noun*** **barter**

base (**bayss**)
1. ***noun*** The lowest part of something, or the part that it stands on, as in *the base of a lamp.*
2. ***verb*** To use something as the starting point for something else. ▸ **basing, based**
3. ***noun*** The place from which a business, an army, etc., is controlled, as in *a base of operations.*
4. ***noun*** In baseball, a **base** is one of the four corners of the diamond to which you must run in order to score.
5. ***noun*** In chemistry, a **base** is a substance that will react with an acid to form a salt.
6. ***noun*** In mathematics, a **base** is the starting point for a counting system. For example, ten is the base of the decimal system.
7. ***adjective*** Selfish or mean, as in *a base trick.* ▸ **baser, basest**

base•ball (**bayss**-*bawl*) ***noun***
1. A game played with a bat and ball and two teams of nine players each.
2. The ball used in this game.

base•ment (**bayss**-muhnt) ***noun*** An area or room in a building below ground level.

bash (**bash**)
1. ***verb*** To hit something hard.
▸ **bashes, bashing, bashed**
2. ***noun*** (*informal*) A very large party.

bash•ful (**bash**-fuhl) ***adjective*** Shy.
▸ ***adverb*** **bashfully**

BA•SIC (**bay**-sik) ***noun*** A computer programming language that is easy to learn. BASIC is an acronym for *Beginner's All-purpose Symbolic Instruction Code.*

ba•sic (**bay**-sik)
1. ***adjective*** Essential and fundamental.
2. **basics** ***noun, plural*** The most important things to know about a subject.

ba•sin (**bay**-suhn) ***noun***
1. A large bowl used for washing, usually fixed to a wall.
2. An area of land around a river from which water drains into the river.

ba•sis (**bay**-siss) ***noun*** The idea or reason behind something, as in *the basis of a plan.*

B

bask (**bask**) ***verb***
1. To lie or sit in the sunshine and enjoy it.
2. If you **bask in** someone's praise, admiration, etc., you enjoy it.
▸ ***verb*** **basking, basked**

bas•ket (**bass**-kit) ***noun*** A container, often with handles, made of cane, wire, etc.

bas•ket•ball (**bass**-kit-*bawl*) ***noun***
1. A game played by two teams of five players each that try to score points by throwing a ball through a high net at the end of a court.
2. The large, round ball used in this game.

bass ***noun***
1. (**bayss**) The lowest singing voice for a man.
2. (**bayss**) A singer with such a voice.
3. (**bayss**) A stringed instrument that makes a low sound, as in *a bass guitar.*
4. (**bass**) Any of several freshwater or saltwater fish found in North America.
▸ ***noun, plural*** **bass** *or* **basses**

bass drum ***noun*** A very large drum that makes a deep, loud noise.

bas•soon (buh-**soon**) ***noun*** A musical instrument with keys, holes, and a small curved mouthpiece. The bassoon makes a very deep sound.

baste (**bayst**) ***verb***
1. To pour juices from the pan over food while it is cooking in an oven.
2. To sew something with loose stitches to hold it in place temporarily.
▸ ***verb*** **basting, basted**

bat (**bat**)
1. ***noun*** A small, flying mammal that comes out at night to feed. Bats find their way around by making squeaks. These noises send back echoes that are picked up by their sensitive ears.
2. ***noun*** A piece of wood or aluminum used for hitting the ball in baseball and softball.
3. ***verb*** To take a turn at trying to hit the ball and score a run or runs in baseball or softball. ▸ **batting, batted**

batch (**bach**) ***noun*** A group of things that arrive together or are made together, as in *a batch of cookies.* ▸ ***noun, plural*** **batches**

bath (**bath**) ***noun***
1. The act of washing something in water.
2. The water used in bathing, as in *a warm bath.*
3. A bathroom.

bathe (**bayTH**) ***verb***
1. To take a bath.
2. To give someone a bath, as in *to bathe a baby.*
3. To go swimming. ▸ ***noun*** **bather**
▸ ***verb*** **bathing, bathed**

bathing suit ***noun*** A piece of clothing that people wear to go swimming; a swimsuit.

bath•robe (**bath**-*robe*) ***noun*** A long, loose piece of clothing that people wear after bathing or while relaxing.

bath•room (**bath**-*room* or **bath**-*rum*) ***noun*** A room that contains a sink and a toilet and often a bathtub or a shower.

bath•tub (**bath**-*tuhb*) ***noun*** A large, open container for water in which you sit and wash your whole body.

ba•tik (buh-**teek**) ***noun*** A method of printing designs on cloth, started in Indonesia. Parts of the cloth are covered with wax so that when it is put into the dye these parts are not colored.

bat mitz•vah (**baht mits**-vuh) ***noun*** A ceremony and celebration that takes place on or close to a Jewish girl's 13th birthday, after which she can take part in her religion as an adult. Also called **bas mitzvah** (**bahss mits**-vuh).

ba•ton (buh-**ton**) ***noun***
1. A short, thin stick used by a conductor to beat time for an orchestra.
2. A short stick passed from one runner to another in a relay race.

bat•tal•ion (buh-**tal**-yun) ***noun*** A large unit of soldiers.

B

bat•ter (**bat**-ur)
1. ***verb*** To injure someone by hitting him or her over and over. ▸ **battering, battered** ▸ ***noun*** **battering** ▸ ***adjective*** **battered**
2. ***noun*** A mixture consisting mainly of milk, eggs, and flour used to make cakes or other baked goods or used to coat food that you fry.
3. ***noun*** The player whose turn it is to bat in baseball or softball.

battering ram ***noun*** A heavy wooden beam, sometimes protected by a hut on wheels, that is rammed against an enemy's walls or gates.

bat•ter•y (**bat**-uh-ree) ***noun***
1. A container filled with chemicals that produces electrical power.
2. A group of machines, devices, or heavy guns that are all used together.
▸ ***noun, plural*** **batteries**

bat•tle (**bat**-uhl) ***noun***
1. A fight between two armies.
2. A struggle with someone.
▸ ***verb*** **battle**

bat•tle•ground (**bat**-uhl-*ground*) ***noun*** A field or an area where a battle is fought.

bat•tle•ment (**bat**-uhl-muhnt) ***noun*** A low wall at the top of a tower or other wall, with openings along it for soldiers to shoot through.

bat•tle•ship (**bat**-uhl-*ship*) ***noun*** A warship armed with powerful guns.

bawl (**bawl**) ***verb***
1. To cry out loud like a baby.
2. To shout in a harsh voice.
3. When you **bawl** someone **out,** you scold him or her.
Bawl sounds like **ball.**
▸ ***verb*** **bawling, bawled**

bay (**bay**) ***noun***
1. A portion of the ocean that is partly enclosed by land.
2. If you keep someone or something **at bay,** you fight it off.
3. bay window A window that sticks out from the wall of a house.

bay•o•net (**bay**-uh-net) ***noun*** A long knife that can be fastened to the end of a rifle.

bay•ou (**bye**-oo) ***noun*** A stream that runs slowly through a swamp and leads to or from a lake or river. Bayous are most common in Louisiana and Mississippi.

ba•zaar (buh-**zar**) ***noun***
1. A sale held to raise money for charity.
2. A street market.

B.C. (**bee cee**) The initials of the phrase "before Christ." B.C. is used to show that a date comes before the birth of Jesus.

be (**bee**) ***verb***
1. To exist. *There* ***is*** *time left to play.*
2. To happen. *The start of our vacation* ***was*** *last week.*
3. To take up space. *The cat* ***was*** *on the couch.*
4. To come or go. *I've* ***been*** *to the store many times today.*
5. To stay or continue. *They've* ***been*** *in class for over an hour.*
6. Be can connect the subject of a sentence to a noun, adjective, or pronoun. *Roses* ***are*** *beautiful.*
7. Be can support the main verb in a sentence. *We* ***are*** *eating dinner together tonight.*
Be sounds like **bee.**

beach (**beech**) ***noun*** A strip of sand or pebbles where land meets water. **Beach** sounds like **beech.** ▸ ***noun, plural*** **beaches**

bea•con (**bee**-kuhn) ***noun*** A light or fire used as a signal or warning.

bead (**beed**) ***noun***
1. A small piece of glass, wood, or plastic with a hole through the middle that can be threaded onto a string.
2. A drop of liquid.

bea•gle (**bee**-guhl) ***noun*** A medium-sized dog with short legs, long ears, and a smooth coat. Beagles are often kept as pets or used as hunting dogs.

beak (**beek**) ***noun*** The hard, horny part of a bird's mouth.

B

beak•er (**bee**-kur) ***noun*** A plastic or glass jar with a spout for pouring, used in chemistry.

beam (**beem**)
1. *noun* A ray or band of light from a flashlight, a car headlight, or the sun.
2. *noun* A long, thick piece of wood, concrete, or metal used to support the roof or floors of a building.
3. *verb* To shine.
4. *verb* To smile widely.
▸ ***verb*** **beaming, beamed**

bean (**been**)
1. *noun* **Beans** are large seeds or pods that you can eat or that can be used to make a drink, as in *baked beans* and *coffee beans.*
2. *verb* To hit someone on the head with something you throw, such as a baseball.
▸ **beaning, beaned**

bear (**bair**)
1. *verb* To support or carry something.
2. *verb* When a tree or plant **bears** fruit, flowers, or leaves, it produces them.
3. *verb* If you cannot **bear** something, you cannot put up with it, either because it upsets you or because you do not like it at all. ▸ ***adjective*** **bearable**
4. *verb* If you **bear** a resemblance to someone, you look somewhat like the person.
5. *noun* A large, heavy mammal with thick fur.
Bear sounds like **bare.**
▸ ***verb*** **bearing, bore** (**bor**), **borne** (**born**)

beard (**bihrd**) ***noun*** The hair on a man's chin and cheeks. ▸ ***adjective*** **bearded**

bear•ing (**bair**-ing) ***noun***
1. The way someone acts, stands, or walks.
2. A connection to something else.
3. In machinery, a part that allows moving parts to work with as little friction as possible.
4. *noun, plural* Your **bearings** are your sense of direction in relation to where things are.

beast (**beest**) ***noun***
1. A wild animal.
2. A horrible or unkind person. ▸ ***noun*** **beastliness** ▸ ***adjective*** **beastly**

beat (**beet**)
1. *verb* To hit someone or something many times. ▸ ***noun*** **beating**
2. *verb* To defeat someone in a game or contest.
3. *noun* The regular rhythm of a piece of music or of your heart.
4. *verb* In cooking, if you **beat** a mixture, you stir it up quickly with a machine, spoon, or fork.
5. *noun* A regular route, as in *a police officer's beat.*
Beat sounds like **beet.**
▸ ***verb*** **beating, beat, beaten** (**beet**-in)

beau•ti•ful (**byoo**-ti-fuhl) ***adjective*** Very pleasant to look at or listen to.
▸ ***noun*** **beauty** (**byoo**-tee) ▸ ***verb*** **beautify** (**byoo**-ti-*fye*) ▸ ***adverb*** **beautifully**

bea•ver (**bee**-vur) ***noun*** An animal similar to a large rat with a wide, flat tail that lives both on land and in water. By gnawing down trees, beavers build dams across streams to create safe areas for their lodges.

be•cause (bi-**kawz**) ***conjunction*** For the reason that.

beck•on (**bek**-uhn) ***verb*** To make a sign to someone, asking the person to come.
▸ **beckoning, beckoned**

be•come (bi-**kuhm**) ***verb***
1. To start to be.
2. To suit, or to look good on.
▸ ***verb*** **becoming, became** (bi-***kaym***)

be•com•ing (bi-**kuhm**-ing) ***adjective*** Flattering or attractive.

bed (**bed**) ***noun***
1. A piece of furniture that you sleep on.
▸ ***verb*** **bed**
2. A place in a garden where flowers are planted.
3. The bottom of a body of water, as in *an ocean bed.*

bed•ding (**bed**-ing) ***noun*** Sheets, blankets, comforters, quilts, etc.

B

be•drag•gled (bi-**drag**-uhld) ***adjective*** Wet, limp, or soiled; messy.

bed•rid•den (**bed**-*rid*-uhn) ***adjective*** If you are **bedridden,** you must stay in bed, usually because of illness.

bed•rock (**bed**-*rok*) ***noun*** The solid layer of rock under the soil and loose rock.

bed•room (**bed**-*room or* **bed**-*rum*) ***noun*** A room used for sleeping.

bed•side (**bed**-*side*)
1. ***noun*** The area next to a bed.
2. ***adjective*** To do with something that sits by a bed.

bed•spread (**bed**-*spred*) ***noun*** A decorative quilt or other cover for a bed.

bed•time (**bed**-*time*) ***noun*** The time when someone usually goes to bed.

bee (**bee**) ***noun*** A flying insect with four wings that collects pollen to make honey.

beech (**beech**) ***noun*** A tree with smooth, gray bark and small nuts that are eaten as food. **Beech** sounds like **beach.**
▸ ***noun, plural*** **beeches**

beef (**beef**) ***noun*** The meat from a steer, bull, or cow.

bee•hive (**bee**-*hive*) ***noun*** A nest or house for a swarm of bees. *See* **hive.**

beep (**beep**) ***noun*** A short, high sound, as made by a horn or machine. ▸ ***noun*** **beeper** ▸ ***verb*** **beep** ▸ ***adjective*** **beeping**

beer (**bihr**) ***noun*** An alcoholic drink made from malt, barley, and hops.

bees•wax (**beez**-*waks*) ***noun*** A waxy substance produced and used by bees to make their honeycombs. Beeswax is used to make candles, crayons, and furniture polish.

beet (**beet**) ***noun*** A dark red root vegetable. **Beet** sounds like **beat.**

bee•tle (**bee**-tuhl) ***noun*** An insect with two pairs of wings. A pair of hard wings in front protects a pair of soft flying wings that are folded underneath.

be•fall (bi-**fawl**) ***verb*** To happen to someone. ▸ **befalling, befell, befallen**

be•fore (bi-**for**)
1. ***preposition*** Sooner, or earlier than, as in *the time before last.*
2. ***preposition*** In front of.
3. ***adverb*** Earlier.
4. ***conjunction*** Rather than.

be•fore•hand (bi-**for**-hand) ***adverb*** Ahead of time. ▸ ***adjective*** **beforehand**

be•friend (bi-**frend**) ***verb*** To make friends with someone. ▸ **befriending, befriended**

beg (**beg**) ***verb***
1. To ask someone in the street for help, especially for money or food. ▸ ***noun*** **beggar**
2. To plead with someone to do something.
▸ ***verb*** **begging, begged**

be•gin (bi-**gin**) ***verb*** To start.
▸ **beginning, began** (bi-**gan**), **begun** (bi-**guhn**) ▸ ***noun*** **beginner,** ***noun*** **beginning**

be•go•ni•a (bi-**goh**-nyuh) ***noun*** A tropical plant with white, yellow, red, purple, or pink flowers.

be•half (bi-**haf**) ***noun*** If you do something **on behalf** of someone else, you do it for that person or in his or her place.

be•have (bi-**hayv**) ***verb***
1. To act properly.
2. To do and say things in a particular way.
▸ ***verb*** **behaving, behaved** ▸ ***noun*** **behavior** (bi-**hayv**-yuhr)

be•head (bi-**hed**) ***verb*** To chop off someone's head. ▸ **beheading, beheaded**

be•hind (bi-**hinde**)
1. ***preposition*** On the other side, or toward the back of something.
2. ***preposition*** Further back, or in a lower position.
3. ***preposition*** Later than, as in *behind schedule.*
4. ***preposition*** In support of.
5. ***adverb*** Not making good progress.

be•hold (bi-**hohld**) ***verb*** To look at something with great interest, or to see.
▸ **beholding, beheld**

beige (**bayzh**) ***noun*** A pale brown color.
▸ ***adjective*** **beige**

B

be•ing (**bee**-ing) ***noun***
1. The state of existing.
2. A person or creature that is alive.

be•lat•ed (bi-**lay**-tuhd) ***adjective*** Delayed, or late. ▸ ***adverb*** **belatedly**

belch (**belch**) ***verb***
1. To let out gases from your stomach through your mouth with a loud noise. ▸ ***noun*** **belch**
2. To send out fire and smoke.
▸ ***verb*** **belches, belching, belched**

bel•fry (**bel**-free) ***noun*** The tower, or room in a tower, where a large bell is hung. ▸ ***noun, plural*** **belfries**

be•lieve (bi-**leev**) ***verb***
1. To feel sure that something is true. ▸ ***noun*** **belief** (bi-**leef**) ▸ ***adjective*** **believable**
2. To support someone or something.
▸ ***verb*** **believing, believed** ▸ ***noun*** **believer**

bell (**bel**) ***noun***
1. An instrument that makes a ringing sound. Bells are often cone-shaped and have clappers hanging inside them.
2. (*informal*) If something **rings a bell,** you think you have heard it somewhere before.
3. Something that is shaped like a bell, especially on a musical instrument.

bel•lig•er•ent (buh-**lij**-ur-uhnt) ***adjective***
1. Eager to fight, or hostile.
2. Warlike, as in *belligerent nations.*
▸ ***adverb*** **belligerently**

bel•low (**bel**-oh)
1. ***verb*** To shout or to roar.
▸ **bellowing, bellowed** ▸ ***noun*** **bellow**
2. bellows ***noun, plural*** An instrument or a device whose sides are squeezed to pump air into something such as an organ or a fire.

bel•ly (**bel**-ee) ***noun***
1. The stomach, or the part of a human's or animal's body that contains the stomach and intestines.
2. belly flop A dive into water in which you hit the water hard with the front of your body. ▸ ***noun, plural*** **bellies**

belly button ***noun*** The navel; a hollow or raised dimple in the center of your stomach where your umbilical cord was attached to your mother before you were born.

be•long (bi-**long**) ***verb***
1. If something **belongs** to you, you own it. ▸ ***noun, plural*** **belongings**
2. If you **belong** to a group, you are a member of it.
3. If something **belongs** somewhere, that is its proper place.
▸ ***verb*** **belonging, belonged**

be•lov•ed (bi-**luhv**-id)
1. ***adjective*** Greatly loved or dear to someone's heart.
2. ***noun*** Someone who is greatly loved.

be•low (bi-**loh**)
1. ***preposition*** Lower than.
2. ***adverb*** In or to a lower place than.

belt (**belt**)
1. ***noun*** A strip of leather or other material that you wear around your waist. ▸ ***verb*** **belt**
2. ***noun*** A moving band of rubber used for transporting objects or for driving machinery, as in *a conveyor belt.*
3. ***verb*** (*informal*) To hit someone hard.
▸ **belting, belted**
4. ***noun*** An area or strip, as in *the corn belt.*

bench (**bench**) ***noun***
1. A long, narrow seat for several people, usually made of wood or plastic.
2. A table in a workshop or laboratory, as in *a carpenter's bench.*
3. The place where a judge sits in a court of law. Judges ask lawyers to "approach the bench" to discuss issues in private during a trial.

bend (**bend**) ***verb***
1. If you **bend** or **bend over,** you lean forward from your waist.
2. If something **bends,** it changes direction by turning to one side. ▸ ***noun*** **bend**
3. To change the shape of something so that it is no longer straight.
▸ ***verb*** **bending, bent** (**bent**)

B

be•neath (bi-**neeth**) ***preposition***
1. Lower than, or not worthy of.
2. Underneath. ▸ ***adverb*** **beneath**

ben•e•fi•cial (ben-uh-**fish**-uhl) ***adjective*** Something that is **beneficial** is good for you. ▸ ***adverb*** **beneficially**

ben•e•fit (**ben**-uh-fit)
1. ***verb*** If you **benefit** from something, you get an advantage from it or are helped by it. ▸ **benefiting, benefited** ▸ ***noun*** **benefit**
2. benefits ***noun, plural*** Money paid by a government, employer, or insurance company to people in time of need, as in *unemployment benefits.*

be•nev•o•lent (buh-**nev**-uh-luhnt) ***adjective*** Kind and helpful. ▸ ***noun*** **benevolence** ▸ ***adverb*** **benevolently**

be•nign (bi-**nine**) ***adjective*** Harmless.

bent (**bent**) ***adjective***
1. Crooked or curved.
2. Determined.

be•queath (bi-**kweeth**) ***verb*** To leave something to somebody in a will. ▸ **bequeathing, bequeathed** ▸ ***noun*** **bequest** (bi-**kwest**)

be•reaved (bi-**reevd**) ***adjective*** A **bereaved** person feels sad because someone very close to him or her has died. ▸ ***noun*** **bereavement**

be•ret (buh-**ray**) ***noun*** A round, flat cap made of felt, wool, or some other soft material.

ber•ry (**ber**-ee) ***noun*** A small, often brightly colored fruit found on bushes or trees. **Berry** sounds like **bury.** ▸ ***noun, plural*** **berries**

berth (**burth**)
1. ***noun*** A bed in a ship, a train, or an airplane.
2. ***noun*** A place in a harbor where a boat is tied up.
3. ***verb*** When a boat **berths,** it comes into a harbor and is tied up. ▸ **berthing, berthed**
Berth sounds like **birth.**

be•seech (bi-**seech**) ***verb*** To ask someone in a very serious way; to beg. ▸ **beseeching, besought** (bi-**sawt**), **beseeched**

be•set (bi-**set**) ***verb*** To attack on all sides. ▸ **besetting, beset**

be•side (bi-**side**) ***preposition***
1. Next to.
2. Apart from.
3. If you are **beside yourself,** you are overcome with emotion.

be•sides (bi-**sidez**)
1. ***preposition*** As well as, or apart from.
2. ***adverb*** Also, or in addition to this.

be•siege (bi-**seej**) ***verb***
1. To surround a place to make it surrender.
2. To crowd around.
▸ ***verb*** **besieging, besieged**

best (**best**) ***adjective***
1. Better than everything else.
2. When you **do your best,** you try as hard as you can to do something.
3. best man The friend or relative of a bridegroom who helps him at his wedding.
▸ ***noun*** **best** ▸ ***verb*** **best** ▸ ***adverb*** **best**

be•stow (bi-**stoh**) ***verb*** To give someone a gift or a prize. ▸ **bestowing, bestowed**

bet (**bet**) ***verb***
1. To risk a sum of money on the result of something, such as a horse race. If you guess the result correctly, you win some money; if not, you lose money. ▸ ***noun*** **bet,** ***noun*** **betting**
2. If you **bet** someone that he or she cannot do something, you dare the person to do it.
3. (*informal*) If you **bet** that someone will do something, you predict that he or she will do it.
▸ ***verb*** **betting, bet**

be•tray (bi-**tray**) ***verb***
1. If you **betray** someone, you are not loyal to that person or do something to hurt him or her. ▸ ***noun*** **betrayal**
2. If you **betray** your feelings, you are

not able to keep them hidden.
▸ ***verb*** **betraying, betrayed**

bet•ter (**bet**-ur)
1. ***adjective*** More suitable, or higher in quality, as in *a better job.*
2. ***adjective*** No longer ill or hurting.
3. **better off** Richer, or in an improved condition.
4. ***adverb*** More efficiently, more completely, or more suitably.
▸ ***verb*** **better**

be•tween (bi-**tween**) ***preposition***
1. If something is **between** two things, it has them on either side of it.
2. From one to the other of.
3. Somewhere within the limits of.
4. By comparing.

bev•er•age (**bev**-rij) ***noun*** A drink.

be•ware (bi-**wair**) ***verb*** If a person or a sign tells you to **beware of** something, it warns you to look out for something dangerous or harmful.

be•wil•der (bi-**wil**-dur) ***verb*** To confuse someone. ▸ **bewildering, bewildered** ▸ ***noun*** **bewilderment** ▸ ***adjective*** **bewildered**

be•witch (bi-**wich**) ***verb*** To cast a spell on. ▸ **bewitching, bewitched**

be•yond (bi-**yond**) ***preposition***
1. On the far side of something.
▸ ***adverb*** **beyond**
2. If something is **beyond** you, you cannot understand it.

bi•ased (**bye**-uhst) ***adjective*** Prejudiced, or favoring one person or point of view more than another. ▸ ***noun*** **bias** ▸ ***verb*** **bias**

bi•ath•lon (bye-**ath**-lon) ***noun*** A sport in which the participants carry a rifle as they ski on a course and stop to shoot at targets along the way.

Bi•ble (**bye**-buhl) ***noun***
1. The sacred book of the Christian religion that contains the Old and New Testaments.
2. The sacred book in the Jewish religion consisting of the Old Testament.

bib•li•og•ra•phy (*bib*-lee-**og**-ruh-fee) ***noun*** A list of writings on a subject.
▸ ***noun, plural*** **bibliographies**
▸ ***adjective*** **bibliographical** (*bib*-lee-uh-**graf**-i-kuhl)

bi•ceps (**bye**-seps) ***noun, plural*** The large muscle on the front of your arm between your shoulder and inner elbow.

bick•er (**bik**-ur) ***verb*** To argue about small things. ▸ **bickering, bickered**

bi•coast•al (bye-**kohss**-tuhl) ***adjective*** Living and working on both the east and west coasts of the United States.

bi•cus•pid (bye-**kuss**-pid) ***noun*** A tooth with two points located just beside the front sets of upper and lower teeth.

bi•cy•cle (**bye**-si-kuhl) ***noun*** A vehicle with two wheels that you ride by steering with handlebars and by pedaling. ▸ ***verb*** **bicycle**

bid (**bid**)
1. ***verb*** To offer a certain amount of money for something, as at an auction.
▸ ***noun*** **bid,** ***noun*** **bidder**
2. ***verb*** To order someone to do something.
3. ***verb*** To say, as in *to bid someone hello.*
4. ***noun*** An attempt to do or win something.
▸ ***verb*** **bidding, bid** *or* **bade** (**bayd**)

bide (**bide**) ***verb*** To wait for the right moment. ▸ **biding, bided**

bi•en•ni•al (bye-**en**-ee-uhl)
1. ***adjective*** Happening every two years or over a period of two years.
2. ***noun*** A plant that lives for two years.

bi•fo•cals (**bye**-*foh*-kuhlz) ***noun, plural*** Glasses or lenses that have two sections, for seeing up close and farther away.

big (**big**) ***adjective***
1. Large in size.
2. Of great importance.
▸ ***adjective*** **bigger, biggest**

big•horn (**big**-*horn*) ***noun*** A type of sheep with large, rounded horns, found in the western mountains of North America.

B

B

big•ot (**big**-uht) ***noun*** Someone who has a strong and unreasonable dislike for a certain other group of people, especially people of a different race, nationality, or religion. ▸ ***noun*** **bigotry** ▸ ***adjective*** **bigoted**

bike (**bike**)
1. ***noun*** A bicycle, or a motorcycle.
2. ***verb*** To ride a bicycle or motorcycle.
▸ **biking, biked** ▸ ***noun*** **biker**

bi•ki•ni (bi-**kee**-nee) ***noun*** A two-piece bathing suit worn by women and girls.

bile (**bile**) ***noun*** A green liquid that is made by the liver and helps digest food.

bi•lin•gual (bye-**ling**-gwuhl) ***adjective*** If someone is **bilingual**, the person can speak two languages well.

bill (**bil**) ***noun***
1. A piece of paper telling you how much money you owe for something that you have bought. ▸ ***verb*** **bill**
2. A written plan for a new law, to be debated in Congress.
3. The beak of a bird.
4. A piece of paper money, as in *a ten-dollar bill.*

bill•board (**bil**-*bord*) ***noun*** A large outdoor sign used to advertise products or services.

bill•fold (**bil**-*fohld*) ***noun*** A small folding wallet for paper money.

bil•liards (**bil**-yurdz) ***noun, plural*** A game in which you use a stick, called a cue, to hit balls around a table.

bil•lion (**bil**-yuhn) ***noun*** One thousand times one million, written 1,000,000,000.
▸ ***adjective*** **billion**

bil•low (**bil**-oh)
1. ***verb*** When a curtain, sail, or sheet **billows,** it is pushed outward by the wind.
2. ***verb*** If smoke or fog **billows,** it rises up in large clouds.
3. ***noun*** A large ocean wave.
▸ ***verb*** **billowing, billowed**

bin (**bin**) ***noun*** A large covered container or box for storing things, as in *a trash bin.*

bi•na•ry (**bye**-nuh-ree *or* **bye**-ner-ee) ***adjective***
1. Made up of two parts or units.
2. In mathematics, the **binary** number system uses only two digits, 1 and 0.

bind (**binde**) ***verb***
1. To tie something up.
2. To wrap a piece of material tightly around something, as in *to bind a wound.*
3. If you **bind** a book, you fasten its pages together and put a cover on it.
▸ ***noun*** **binding**
4. To oblige. ▸ ***adjective*** **binding**
▸ ***verb*** **binding, bound** (**bound**)

bind•er (**bine**-dur) ***noun*** A detachable cover used for holding papers.

binge (**binj**)
1. ***verb*** To overdo some activity such as eating or drinking. ▸ **bingeing** *or* **binging, binged**
2. ***noun*** A period of overdoing something; a spree.

bin•go (**bing**-goh) ***noun*** A game in which you cross out numbers on a card as they are called out.

bin•oc•u•lars (buh-**nok**-yuh-lurz) ***noun, plural*** An instrument that you look through with both eyes to make distant things seem nearer.

bi•o•de•grad•a•ble (*bye*-oh-di-**gray**-duh-buhl) ***adjective*** Something that is **biodegradable** can be broken down naturally by bacteria.

bi•o•di•ver•si•ty (*bye*-oh-duh-**vurs**-it-ee) ***noun*** The condition of nature in which a wide variety of species live in a single area.

bi•og•ra•phy (bye-**og**-ruh-fee) ***noun*** A book that tells someone's life story.
▸ ***noun, plural*** **biographies** ▸ ***noun*** **biographer** ▸ ***adjective*** **biographical** (bye-*oh*-**graf**-i-kuhl)

bi•ol•o•gy (bye-**ol**-uh-jee) ***noun*** The scientific study of living things. ▸ ***noun*** **biologist** ▸ ***adjective*** **biological** (bye-oh-**log**-i-kuhl) ▸ ***adverb*** **biologically**

bi•o•mass (**bye**-oh-*mass*) ***noun*** The amount or weight of living matter in a certain area or volume of a habitat.

bi•o•rhythm (**bye**-oh-*riTH*-uhm) ***noun*** The natural rhythm of the human body.

bi•o•tech•nol•o•gy (*bye*-oh-tek-**nol**-uh-jee) ***noun*** The use of biological materials and processes in industry.

bi•plane (**bye**-*plane*) ***noun*** An airplane with two sets of wings, one above the other.

birch (**burch**) ***noun*** A type of tree with hard wood and smooth bark that peels off easily in long strips.

bird (**burd**) ***noun*** A warm-blooded creature with two legs, wings, feathers, and a beak. All birds lay eggs and most birds can fly.

birth (**burth**) ***noun***
1. The event of being born.
2. The beginning of something, as in *the birth of television.*
3. When a woman **gives birth,** she has a baby.
Birth sounds like **berth.**

birth•day (**burth**-*day*) ***noun*** The day that someone was born, or the yearly celebration in its honor.

birth•mark (**burth**-*mark*) ***noun*** A mark on the skin that was there from birth.

birth•place (**burth**-*playss*) ***noun*** The place where someone was born, or where something began.

birth•right (**burth**-*rite*) ***noun*** A right or an object given to someone because the person is born into a specific family or group.

bis•cuit (**biss**-kit) ***noun*** A small, round bread, often made with baking soda.

bi•sect (**bye**-*sekt*) ***verb*** To divide a line, an angle, or a shape into two equal parts. ▸ **bisecting, bisected** ▸ ***noun*** **bisection**

bish•op (**bish**-uhp) ***noun***
1. A senior priest in the Christian church who is in charge of priests and churches in a large area called a **diocese.**
2. A chess piece that can move diagonally across the board.

bi•son (**bye**-suhn) ***noun*** A large animal with a big, shaggy head, a humped back, and short horns, found in North America; a buffalo. ▸ ***noun, plural*** **bison**

bit (**bit**) ***noun***
1. A small piece or amount of something.
2. The smallest unit of information in a computer's memory.
3. The metal bar that goes in a horse's mouth and is attached to the reins.
4. The end part of a drill.

bite (**bite**) ***verb***
1. To close your teeth around something.
2. If an insect or snake **bites** you, it makes a wound in your skin with its stinger or its teeth.
Bite sounds like **byte.**
▸ ***verb*** **biting, bit** (**bit**), **bitten** (**bit**-in)
▸ ***noun*** **bite**

bit•ter (**bit**-ur) ***adjective***
1. Tasting sharp and harsh, like aspirin.
2. If you feel **bitter,** you are upset and angry about something.
3. If the weather is **bitter,** it is very cold.
▸ ***adjective*** **bitterest** ▸ ***noun*** **bitterness**

bi•zarre (bi-**zar**) ***adjective*** Very strange or odd.

black (**blak**) ***noun*** The color of coal or of the sky at night. ▸ ***adjective*** **black**

black•ber•ry (**blak**-*ber*-ee) ***noun*** A small, juicy, black fruit that grows on brambles. ▸ ***noun, plural*** **blackberries**

black•bird (**blak**-*burd*) ***noun*** One of a large number of birds with black feathers. Crows and grackles are types of blackbirds.

black•board (**blak**-*bord*) ***noun*** A hard, smooth surface, often made of slate, that people write on with chalk.

black•en (**blak**-uhn) ***verb***
1. To make black or become black.
2. To damage or ruin.
▸ **blackening, blackened**

black eye ***noun*** A bruise on the skin around the eye, caused by broken blood vessels.

Black•foot (**blak**-*fut*) ***noun*** One of a group of American Indians that lives principally in Montana and in the Canadian provinces of Alberta and Saskatchewan. ▸ ***noun, plural*** **Blackfoot** *or* **Blackfeet**

B

black hole ***noun*** The area in space around a collapsed star whose gravity sucks in everything around it, even light.

black•mail (**blak**-*mayl*) ***noun*** The crime of threatening to reveal a secret about someone unless the person pays a sum of money or grants a favor. ▸ ***verb*** **blackmail**

black•out (**blak**-*out*) ***noun***
1. If someone has a **blackout,** he or she becomes unconscious for a short time.
2. If a town or city suffers a **blackout,** the lights go off because the electricity has failed.
▸ ***verb*** **black out**

black•smith (**blak**-*smith*) ***noun*** Someone who makes and fits horseshoes and mends things made of iron.

black•top (**blak**-*top*) ***noun*** Asphalt that covers many roadways, parking lots, and playgrounds.

blad•der (**blad**-ur) ***noun*** The organ where waste liquid is stored before it leaves your body.

blade (**blayd**) ***noun***
1. The cutting part on a knife, sword, dagger, etc.
2. The long, thin part of an oar or propeller.
3. A single piece of grass.
4. The metal runner on an ice skate.

blame (**blaym**) ***verb*** If you **blame** someone for something, you say that it is his or her fault. ▸ **blaming, blamed** ▸ ***noun*** **blame**

bland (**bland**) ***adjective*** Mild and rather dull, as in *bland food.* ▸ **blander, blandest**

blank (**blangk**)
1. ***adjective*** If something is **blank,** it has nothing on it, as in *a blank cassette.* ▸ **blanker, blankest**
2. ***noun*** An empty line or space.
3. ***noun*** A cartridge for a gun that makes a noise but does not fire a bullet.
4. If you **go blank,** you suddenly cannot think of anything.
5. blank verse A type of poetry that does not rhyme.

blan•ket (**blang**-kit) ***noun***
1. A thick cover for a bed.
2. A thick covering of something, such as snow or flowers. ▸ ***verb*** **blanket**

blare (**blair**) ***verb*** To make a very loud and unpleasant noise. **blaring, blared**

blas•phe•my (**blass**-fuh-mee) ***noun*** The act of saying offensive things about God or a religion. ▸ ***verb*** **blaspheme** (**blass**-feem) ▸ ***adjective*** **blasphemous** (**blass**-fuh-muhss)

blast (**blast**)
1. ***noun*** A loud noise or an explosion.
2. ***noun*** A sudden rush of air.
3. ***verb*** To blow up with explosives. ▸ **blasting, blasted**
4. When a rocket or spaceship **blasts off,** it leaves the ground.

blast•off (**blast**-*awf*) ***noun*** The launching into space of a rocket, missile, or spaceship.

bla•tant (**blay**-tuhnt) ***adjective*** Obvious and shameless, as in *a blatant lie.* ▸ ***adverb*** **blatantly**

blaze (**blayz**)
1. ***verb*** To burn fiercely. ▸ **blazing, blazed**
2. ***noun*** A large fire.

blaz•er (**blay**-zur) ***noun*** An informal jacket.

bleach (**bleech**)
1. ***noun*** A chemical that takes color, dirt, and stains out of materials.
2. ***verb*** To make something cleaner or lighter in color by using a bleach or the sun. ▸ **bleaching, bleached**

bleach•ers (**blee**-churz) ***noun, plural*** Raised seats or benches arranged in rows. Bleachers are usually found in stadiums or along a parade route.

bleak (**bleek**) ***adjective***
1. A **bleak** place is cold, empty, and depressing.
2. Without hope. ▸ ***adjective*** **bleaker, bleakest**

bleat (**bleet**) ***noun*** The cry made by a sheep or goat. ▸ ***verb*** **bleat**

B

bleed (**bleed**) ***verb***
1. To lose blood.
2. If your heart **bleeds** for someone, you feel sorrow or pity for the person.
▸ ***verb*** **bleeding, bled** (**bled**)
▸ ***adjective*** **bleeding**

bleep (**bleep**) ***verb*** To make a short, high sound. ▸ **bleeping, bleeped**
▸ ***noun*** **bleep**

blem•ish (**blem**-ish) ***noun*** A mark or spot that makes something less than perfect; a flaw. ▸ ***verb*** **blemish**

blend (**blend**) ***verb*** To mix two or more things together. ▸ **blending, blended**
▸ ***noun*** **blend**

blend•er (**blen**-dur) ***noun*** An electrical machine that grinds and mixes food.

bless (**bless**) ***verb***
1. To make sacred.
2. To ask God to look after someone or something.
3. You say **bless you** when a person sneezes, or as a way of thanking someone.
▸ ***verb*** **blesses, blessing, blessed**
▸ ***noun*** **blessing**

blight (**blite**) ***noun***
1. A disease that destroys plants.
2. Something that can hurt or destroy the health or beauty of something.

blimp (**blimp**) ***noun*** An airship, or dirigible, whose body does not have a rigid frame.

blind (**blinde**)
1. ***adjective*** Someone who is **blind** cannot see. ▸ ***noun*** **blindness**
2. ***adjective*** A **blind** corner is so sharp that drivers cannot see around it.
3. ***noun*** A covering for a window that can be pulled down over it or across it.
4. A driver's **blind spot** is the area slightly behind the vehicle that cannot be seen either in the side or rear mirror.
5. ***verb*** To cause to lose judgment.
▸ **blinding, blinded**

blind•fold (**blinde**-*fohld*)
1. ***verb*** To cover someone's eyes with a strip of material so that he or she cannot see. ▸ **blindfolding, blindfolded**
2. ***noun*** Something that is put over the eyes and tied around the head, designed to keep the wearer from seeing anything.

blink (**blingk**) ***verb***
1. To move your eyelids up and down very quickly.
2. To flash on and off.
▸ ***verb*** **blinking, blinked** ▸ ***noun*** **blink**

bliss (**bliss**) ***noun*** Great happiness.
▸ ***adjective*** **blissful** ▸ ***adverb*** **blissfully**

blis•ter (**bliss**-tur) ***noun*** A sore bubble of skin, filled with liquid, that is caused by something burning the skin or rubbing against it. ▸ ***verb*** **blister**

bliz•zard (**bliz**-urd) ***noun*** A heavy snowstorm.

bloat•ed (**bloh**-tid) ***adjective*** Swollen, often as a result of eating too much.

blob (**blob**) ***noun*** A small lump of something soft, wet, or thick; a drop.

block (**blok**)
1. ***noun*** A piece of something hard, as in *a block of wood.*
2. ***verb*** To stop something from getting past or from happening. ▸ **blocking, blocked** ▸ ***noun*** **block**
3. ***noun*** The distance or area from one street to another.
4. ***noun*** The area or section in a city surrounded by four streets.

block•ade (blok-**ade**) ***noun*** A closing off of an area to keep people or supplies from going in or out.

block•house (**blok**-*houss*) ***noun***
1. A small fort or building designed as a defense against attack.
2. A strong concrete building used to protect the observers of a rocket launch or an explosion.

blond (**blond**) ***adjective*** Having golden or pale yellow hair. A girl or woman with such hair is usually referred to as *blonde.*
▸ ***noun*** **blond** *or* **blonde**

blood (**bluhd**) ***noun*** The red liquid that is pumped through your body by your heart.

B

blood bank ***noun*** A place where blood is donated and stored. Hospitals use this stored blood to replace blood lost by someone during an operation or in an accident.

blood donor ***noun*** A person who lets some blood be taken out of his or her body to be stored and given to somebody else.

blood•hound (**bluhd**-*hound*) ***noun*** A large dog with a wrinkled face, drooping ears, and a very good sense of smell.

blood•shed (**bluhd**-*shed*) ***noun*** The killing that happens in a battle or war.

blood•shot (**bluhd**-*shot*) ***adjective*** Red and irritated, as in *bloodshot eyes.*

blood•stream (**bluhd**-*streem*) ***noun*** Blood circulating through the body.

blood•thirst•y (**bluhd**-*thur*-stee) ***adjective*** Someone who is **bloodthirsty** enjoys violence or killing.

blood vessel ***noun*** One of the narrow tubes in your body through which your blood flows.

blood•y (**bluhd**-ee) ***adjective***
1. Full of blood, or covered with blood.
2. Violent, or showing blood.
▸ ***adjective*** **bloodier, bloodiest**

bloom (**bloom**)
1. ***noun*** A flower on a plant.
2. ***verb*** When a plant **blooms,** its flowers appear.
3. ***verb*** To flourish.
▸ ***verb*** **blooming, bloomed**
▸ ***adjective*** **blooming**

blos•som (**bloss**-uhm)
1. ***noun*** A flower on a fruit tree or other plant, as in *apple blossoms.*
2. ***verb*** To grow or to improve.
▸ **blossoming, blossomed**

blot (**blot**)
1. ***noun*** A stain of ink, paint, etc.
2. ***verb*** To dry by soaking up excess liquid. ▸ **blotting, blotted**

blotch (**bloch**) ***noun*** An area of reddened skin, or a stain. ▸ ***noun, plural*** **blotches** ▸ ***adjective*** **blotchy**

blot•ter (**blot**-ur) ***noun*** A pad or piece of thick paper that absorbs extra ink.

blouse (**blouss**) ***noun*** A loose shirt worn by women and girls.

blow (**bloh**)
1. ***verb*** To make air come out of your mouth.
2. ***verb*** To move in the wind.
3. ***noun*** A punch or hit on the body.
4. ***noun*** A shock or a disappointment.
5. **blow up** ***verb*** To destroy something with an explosion.
▸ ***verb*** **blowing, blew** (**bloo**), **blown** (**blohn**)

blow•torch (**bloh**-*torch*) ***noun*** A small torch with an intense flame that is used to melt metal or take off paint. ▸ ***noun, plural*** **blowtorches**

blub•ber (**bluh**-bur)
1. ***noun*** The fat under the skin of a whale or seal.
2. ***verb*** To cry noisily. ▸ **blubbering, blubbered**

blue (**bloo**)
1. ***noun*** The color of the sky on a sunny day. ▸ ***adjective*** **blue**
2. ***adjective*** Sad and depressed. ▸ **bluer, bluest**
3. **out of the blue** Suddenly and unexpectedly.

blue•ber•ry (**bloo**-*ber*-ee) ***noun*** A round, dark blue berry that grows on bushes. ▸ ***noun, plural*** **blueberries**

blue•bird (**bloo**-*burd*) ***noun*** A small songbird that has blue feathers on its back and wings. It is found in North America.

blue•fish (**bloo**-*fish*) ***noun*** A silver-blue ocean fish. ▸ ***noun, plural*** **bluefish** *or* **bluefishes**

blue•grass (**bloo**-*grass*) ***noun***
1. A grass with a slightly blue tinge, used for lawns and for cattle and horse feed.
2. A type of country music. ▸ ***adjective*** **bluegrass**

blue jay (**jay**) ***noun*** A blue and white bird with a crest of feathers that is found in North America.

blue jeans ***noun, plural*** Pants made of blue denim; dungarees.

blue•print (**bloo**-*print*) ***noun*** A detailed plan for a project or an idea.

blues (**blooz**) ***noun, plural***
1. A type of slow, sad jazz music first sung by African Americans.
2. Low spirits.

blue whale ***noun*** A type of whale that can weigh up to 100 tons.

bluff (**bluhf**)
1. ***verb*** To pretend to be in a stronger position than you really are or to know more about something than you really do. ▸ **bluffing, bluffed** ▸ ***noun*** **bluff**
2. If you **call someone's bluff,** you challenge the person to do what he or she says he or she can do.

blun•der (**bluhn**-dur)
1. ***noun*** A stupid mistake.
2. ***verb*** To make a stupid mistake.
3. ***verb*** To move in an awkward and clumsy way, usually because you cannot see where you are going.
▸ ***verb*** **blundering, blundered**

blunt (**bluhnt**)
1. ***adjective*** Not sharp, as in *a blunt instrument.*
2. ***verb*** To make or become less sharp.
▸ **blunting, blunted**
3. ***adjective*** Direct and straightforward in what you say.
▸ ***adjective*** **blunter, bluntest** ▸ ***noun*** **bluntness** ▸ ***adverb*** **bluntly**

blur (**blur**)
1. ***verb*** To make something smeared and unclear. ▸ **blurring, blurred**
2. ***noun*** A shape that is unclear because it has no outline or is moving too fast.
▸ ***adjective*** **blurred**

blurb (**blurb**) ***noun*** A short piece written about a person or a product in order to get people interested in buying it.

blurt (**blurt**) ***verb*** If you **blurt** something out, you say it suddenly, without thinking. ▸ **blurting, blurted**

blush (**bluhsh**) ***verb*** When you **blush,** your face turns red because you are embarrassed or ashamed. ▸ **blushes, blushing, blushed** ▸ ***noun*** **blush**

blus•ter (**bluhss**-tur) ***verb***
1. To blow in gusts. ▸ ***adjective*** **blustery**
2. To act or speak in an aggressive and overconfident way.
▸ ***verb*** **blustering, blustered** ▸ ***noun*** **bluster**

bo•a con•stric•tor (**boh**-uh kuhn-**strik**-tur) ***noun*** A large, nonpoisonous tropical snake that kills its prey by coiling around it and squeezing. ▸ ***noun, plural*** **boa constrictors**

boar (**bor**) ***noun***
1. A male pig.
2. A type of wild pig.
Boar sounds like **bore.**

board (**bord**)
1. ***noun*** A flat piece of wood or a stiff card.
2. ***verb*** To get on a train, an airplane, a bus, or a ship. ▸ **boarding, boarded**
3. ***noun*** The **board** of a company is the group of people who control it.
4. ***noun*** Meals provided to paying guests.

board•er (**bor**-dur) ***noun*** A person who pays to live somewhere and receive meals.

board•ing (**bord**-ing) ***noun*** The sport of riding a skateboard or snowboard.

boarding school ***noun*** A school that students may live in during the school year.

boast (**bohst**) ***verb***
1. To talk proudly about what you can do or what you own in order to impress people.
2. If a place **boasts** something good, it possesses it.
▸ ***verb*** **boasting, boasted** ▸ ***noun*** **boast** ▸ ***adjective*** **boastful** ▸ ***adverb*** **boastfully**

boat (**bote**) ***noun*** A vehicle used for traveling on water. ▸ ***verb*** **boat**

boat•house (**boht**-*houss*) ***noun*** A building where small boats are sheltered or stored.

boat people ***noun, plural*** People who are forced to leave their country in boats, usually because of a war.

B

bob (**bob**)
1. ***verb*** To keep moving up and down on water. ▸ **bobbing, bobbed**
2. ***noun*** A short haircut in which the hair is all one length. ▸ ***verb*** **bob**

bob•bin (**bob**-in) ***noun*** A spool inside a sewing machine or on a loom that holds the thread.

bob•by pin (**bob**-ee) ***noun*** A piece of bent wire with sides that press together to hold hair in place.

bob•cat (**bob**-*kat*) ***noun*** A small, wild cat with reddish brown fur, black spots, and a short tail. A bobcat is a type of lynx.

bob•o•link (**bob**-uh-*link*) ***noun*** A North and South American songbird that lives in fields.

bob•sled (**bob**-*sled*) ***noun*** A sled with a steering wheel and brakes, used for racing down a steep, ice-covered run. ▸ ***verb*** **bobsled**

bob•white (**bob-wite**) ***noun*** A common North American songbird with a reddish brown body and white, black, and tan markings. A bobwhite is a type of quail. Its call sounds like its name. ▸ ***noun, plural*** **bobwhite** *or* **bobwhites**

bode (**bohd**) ***verb*** To be a sign of something. ▸ **boding, boded**

bod•y (**bod**-ee) ***noun***
1. All the parts that a person or an animal is made of, as in *the human body.*
2. The main part of something, especially a car or an aircraft.
3. A dead person.
4. A group of people working together, as in *the student body.*
5. A separate mass of matter, as in *a heavenly body.*

bod•y•guard (**bod**-ee-*gard*) ***noun*** A man or woman who protects someone.

bog (**bog**)
1. ***noun*** An area of wet, spongy land. ▸ ***adjective*** **boggy**
2. ***verb*** To make or become stuck. ▸ **bogging, bogged**

bo•gus (**boh**-guhss) ***adjective*** False.

boil (**boil**)
1. ***verb*** To heat a liquid until it starts to bubble and give off steam. ▸ ***noun*** **boil** ▸ ***adjective*** **boiling**
2. ***verb*** To cook something in boiling water.
3. ***noun*** An infected lump under the skin. ▸ ***verb*** **boiling, boiled**

boil•er (**boi**-lur) ***noun*** A tank that heats water for a house or other building.

boiling point ***noun*** The temperature at which a liquid that has been heated turns to a gas. The boiling point of water is 212 degrees Fahrenheit or 100 degrees Celsius.

bois•ter•ous (**boi**-stur-uhss) ***adjective*** If you are **boisterous,** you behave in a wild and noisy way. ▸ ***noun*** **boisterousness** ▸ ***adverb*** **boisterously**

bold (**bohld**) ***adjective***
1. Someone who is **bold** is very confident and shows no fear of danger. ▸ ***noun*** **boldness**
2. **Bold** colors stand out clearly. ▸ ***adjective*** **bolder, boldest** ▸ ***adverb*** **boldly**

boll wee•vil (**bohl wee**-vuhl) ***noun*** A beetle that lays eggs in cotton plants.

bol•ster (**bohl**-stur)
1. ***verb*** To support someone or something. ▸ **bolstering, bolstered**
2. ***noun*** A long pillow.

bolt (**bohlt**)
1. ***noun*** A metal bar that slides into place and locks something. ▸ ***verb*** **bolt**
2. ***noun*** A strong metal pin with spiral grooves, used with a metal nut to hold things together.
3. ***verb*** To run away suddenly. ▸ **bolting, bolted**
4. ***noun*** A flash of lightning or crack of thunder.
5. ***noun*** A roll of something, such as cloth.

bomb (**bom**)
1. ***noun*** A container filled with explosives, used in war or to blow up buildings, vehicles, etc.

2. ***verb*** To attack a place with bombs.
▸ **bombing, bombed**

bom•bard (bom-**bahrd**) ***verb***
1. To attack a place with heavy gunfire.
2. If you **bombard** someone with questions, you ask the person lots of questions in a short time.
▸ ***verb*** **bombarding, bombarded**
▸ ***noun*** **bombardment**

bomb•er (**bom**-ur) ***noun***
1. A large airplane that drops bombs on targets.
2. Someone who sets off bombs.

bomb•shell (**bom**-*shel*) ***noun***
1. A bomb.
2. Something that shocks and surprises you.

bo•na fide (**bone**-uh *fide*) ***adjective***
1. Genuine or sincere, as in *a bona fide friendship.*
2. In good faith, or without fraud, as in *a bona fide agreement.*

bond (**bond**)
1. ***noun*** A close friendship or connection with someone.
2. ***verb*** When you **bond** two things, you cause them to stick together. ▸ **bonding, bonded** ▸ ***noun*** **bond**
3. bonds ***noun, plural*** Ropes, chains, etc., used to tie someone up.

bond•age (**bon**-dij) ***noun*** If people are held in **bondage,** they are held against their will or kept as slaves.

bone (**bohn**) ***noun*** One of the hard, white parts that make up the skeleton of a person or an animal.

bon•fire (**bon**-*fire*) ***noun*** A large outdoor fire.

bon•go drum (**bong**-goh) ***noun*** Either of a pair of small connected drums, held between the knees and struck with the fingers.

bon•net (**bon**-it) ***noun*** A baby's or woman's hat, tied with strings under the chin.

bon•sai (**bon**-sye) ***noun*** A miniature tree or shrub, grown in a pot for decoration.
▸ ***noun, plural*** **bonsai**

bo•nus (**boh**-nuhss) ***noun***
1. An extra reward that you get for doing something well.
2. A good thing that is more than you expected.
▸ ***noun, plural*** **bonuses** ▸ ***adjective*** **bonus**

bon•y (**boh**-nee) ***adjective***
1. Extremely thin or full of bones.
2. Made of bone.

boo•by trap (**boo**-bee) ***noun*** A hidden trap or explosive device that is set off when someone or something touches it.
▸ ***verb*** **booby-trap**

book (**buk**)
1. ***noun*** A set of pages that are bound together in a cover.
2. ***verb*** To arrange for something ahead of time. ▸ **booking, booked** ▸ ***noun*** **booking**

book•case (**buk**-*kayss*) ***noun*** A cabinet or piece of furniture with shelves that hold books.

book•keep•er (**buk**-*kee*-pur) ***noun*** Someone who keeps financial records for a business. ▸ ***noun*** **bookkeeping**

book•let (**buk**-luht) ***noun*** A book with a paper cover and a small number of pages.

book•mark (**buk**-*mark*) ***noun*** A piece of ribbon, paper, or other material used to mark a place in a book.

book•mo•bile (**buk**-muh-beel) ***noun*** A van or truck that is used as a small, mobile library.

book•worm (**buk**-*wurm*) ***noun*** Someone who loves reading books.

boom (**boom**)
1. ***noun*** A very loud, deep sound, such as an explosion.
2. ***verb*** To speak in a loud, deep voice.
▸ **booming, boomed**
3. ***noun*** A rapid increase in something, as in *a building boom.*
4. If you **lower the boom** on someone, you punish the person.

boo•mer•ang (**boo**-muh-rang) ***noun*** A curved stick that can be thrown through the air so that it returns to the thrower.

B

boon (**boon**) ***noun*** Something that makes life easier.

boost (**boost**)
1. ***verb*** To lift someone or something by pushing from below.
2. ***verb*** To increase the power or amount of something, as in *to boost profits.*
3. ***noun*** If something gives you a **boost,** it cheers you up.
▸ ***noun*** **boost** ▸ ***verb*** **boosting, boosted**

boost·er (**boo**-stur) ***noun***
1. A rocket that gives extra power to a spacecraft. *See* **space shuttle.**
2. A **booster shot** is an injection of a drug given to increase the effect of an earlier injection.

boot (**boot**)
1. ***noun*** A heavy shoe that covers your ankle and sometimes part of your leg.
2. ***verb*** When you **boot up** a computer, you turn it on and get it ready to work.
3. ***verb*** To kick the ball in football.
▸ ***verb*** **booting, booted**

boot·ee *or* **boot·ie** (**boot**-ee *or* boo-**tee**) ***noun*** A knitted sock for a baby.

booth (**booth**) ***noun***
1. A temporary display area that is used to sell or show a product.
2. A small enclosed place, such as *a voting booth, a ticket booth,* or *a telephone booth.*

boo·ty (**boo**-tee) ***noun*** Valuable objects that are taken away by force, as by an army after a battle.

bor·der (**bor**-dur)
1. ***noun*** The dividing line between one country or region and another.
2. ***verb*** If two countries **border** one another, their boundaries meet.
▸ **bordering, bordered**
3. ***noun*** A decorative strip around the edge of something.

bore (**bor**)
1. ***verb*** If something or someone **bores** you, you find the thing or person very dull and not interesting. ▸ ***noun*** **bore,** ***noun*** **boredom**
2. ***verb*** To make a hole in something with a drill.
3. ***noun*** The hole inside a gun barrel.
Bore sounds like **boar.**
▸ ***verb*** **boring, bored**

born (**born**) ***adjective***
1. Brought into life.
2. Naturally gifted at something.

bor·ough (**bur**-oh) ***noun***
1. In some states, a town or village that has its own local government.
2. One of the five political divisions of New York City.
Borough sounds like **burro** and **burrow.**

bor·row (**bor**-oh) ***verb*** To use something that belongs to someone else, with permission. ▸ **borrowing, borrowed**

bos·om (**buz**-uhm *or* **boo**-zuhm)
1. ***noun*** The front part of a person's chest.
2. ***adjective*** Close and dear.

boss (**bawss**)
1. ***noun*** Someone in charge of a company, or someone for whom people work. ▸ ***noun, plural*** **bosses** ▸ ***verb*** **boss**
2. **boss around** ***verb*** To keep telling somebody what to do. ▸ **bosses, bossing, bossed**

bos·sy (**bawss**-ee) ***adjective*** A **bossy** person likes telling other people what to do. ▸ **bossier, bossiest** ▸ ***noun*** **bossiness**

bot·a·ny (**bot**-uh-nee) ***noun*** The scientific study of plants. ▸ ***noun*** **botanist** ▸ ***adjective*** **botanical** (buh-**tan**-i-kuhl)

both (**bohth**)
1. ***pronoun*** Two things or people.
2. ***adjective*** Referring to the one and the other.
3. ***conjunction*** Equally, or as well.

both·er (**boTH**-ur)
1. ***verb*** If something **bothers** you, it disturbs or annoys you.
2. ***noun*** Something that annoys you.

3. ***verb*** To make an effort to do something.
▸ ***verb*** **bothering, bothered**

bot•tle (**bot**-uhl)
1. ***noun*** A glass or plastic container with a narrow neck and mouth and no handle.
2. ***verb*** To put things into bottles.
3. ***verb*** If you **bottle up** your feelings, you keep them to yourself.
▸ ***verb*** **bottling, bottled**

bot•tle•neck (**bot**-uhl-*nek*) ***noun*** A narrow part of a road that causes traffic jams.

bot•tom (**bot**-uhm) ***noun***
1. The lowest part of something, as in *the bottom of the sea.* ▸ ***adjective*** **bottom**
2. The part of your body that you sit on.
3. The most basic part of something.

bough (**bou**) ***noun*** A thick branch on a tree.

boul•der (**bohl**-dur) ***noun*** A large, rounded rock.

bou•le•vard (**bul**-uh-vard) ***noun*** A wide city street that often has grass, trees, or flowers planted down the middle or along either side.

bounce (**bounss**)
1. ***verb*** To spring back after hitting something. ▸ **bouncing, bounced**
▸ ***noun*** **bounce**
2. ***noun*** If someone has lots of **bounce,** he or she is very cheerful.
▸ ***adjective*** **bouncy**

bound (**bound**)
1. ***verb*** To move forward quickly with leaps and jumps. ▸ **bounding, bounded**
▸ ***noun*** **bound**
2. ***adjective*** If something is **bound** to happen, it will certainly or almost certainly take place.
3. If a place is **out of bounds,** you are not allowed to go there. In sports, **out of bounds** means out of the field of play.

bound•a•ry (**boun**-duh-ree) ***noun*** The line, fence, etc., that separates one area from another. ▸ ***noun, plural*** **boundaries**

boun•ti•ful (**boun**-tuh-fuhl) ***adjective*** More than enough; generous; plentiful.

boun•ty (**boun**-tee) ***noun***
1. Goodness or generosity.
2. A reward offered for the capture of a criminal or a harmful animal.

bou•quet (boh-**kay**) *or* (boo-**kay**) ***noun*** A bunch of picked or cut flowers.

bout (**bout**) ***noun***
1. An attack or a spell.
2. A boxing match.

bou•tique (boo-**teek**) ***noun*** A small shop that sells fashionable clothes or other specialty items.

bow
1. (**bou**) ***verb*** To bend low as a sign of respect or to accept applause.
▸ **bowing, bowed** ▸ ***noun*** **bow**
2. (**boh**) ***noun*** A knot with loops.
3. (**bou**) ***noun*** The front of a ship.
4. (**boh**) ***noun*** A long, flat piece of wood with strings stretched along it, used for playing stringed instruments.
5. (**boh**) ***noun*** A curved piece of wood with a stretched string attached to it, used for shooting arrows.

bow•els (**boulz**) ***noun, plural*** Intestines.

bowl (**bohl**)
1. ***noun*** A deep dish.
2. ***verb*** When you **bowl,** you roll a heavy ball down an alley to knock over wooden pins. ▸ **bowling, bowled**
▸ ***noun*** **bowler**
3. When something **bowls you over,** it greatly surprises you.

bow•leg•ged (**boh**-*leg*-id) ***adjective*** If someone is **bowlegged,** he or she has legs that are curved outward so that the knees do not touch when the ankles are together.

bowl•ing (**boh**-ling) ***noun*** A game played by rolling a heavy ball down an alley at wooden pins.

bow tie ***noun*** A necktie in the shape of a bow, often worn on formal occasions.

B

B

box (**boks**)
1. ***noun*** A container, especially one with four flat sides. ▸ ***verb* box**
2. ***verb*** To fight with your fists as a sport. ▸ ***noun* boxer, *noun* boxing**
3. ***verb*** If you **box** someone **in,** you surround the person so that he or she cannot escape.
▸ ***noun, plural* boxes** ▸ ***verb* boxes, boxing, boxed**

box•car (**boks**-*kar*) ***noun*** An enclosed railway car with a sliding door on one side to load and unload freight.

box office ***noun*** The ticket office at a theater.

boy (**boi**) ***noun*** A male child. ▸ ***adjective* boyish**

boy•cott (**boi**-kot) ***verb*** To refuse to buy something or to take part in something as a way of making a protest.
▸ **boycotting, boycotted** ▸ ***noun* boycott**

boy•friend (**boi**-*frend*) ***noun***
1. The man or boy with whom someone is having a romantic relationship.
2. A male friend.

boy•hood (**boi**-*hud*) ***noun*** The time during which someone is a boy.

bra (**brah**) ***noun*** An undergarment that covers and supports a woman's breasts. Bra is short for *brassiere.*

brace (**brayss**)
1. ***noun*** An object fastened to another object to support it. ▸ ***verb* brace**
2. **braces *noun, plural*** A device with wires worn inside your mouth to straighten your teeth.
3. ***verb*** If you **brace** yourself, you prepare yourself for a shock or for the force of something hitting you.
▸ **bracing, braced**

brace•let (**brayss**-lit) ***noun*** A band worn around the wrist as a piece of jewelry.

brack•et (**brak**-it) ***noun***
1. A support, made of metal or wood, used to hold up a shelf or cupboard.
2. A grouping.
3. ***noun, plural*** **Brackets** are the two symbols [ ] that are used to separate some material from the main written text. ▸ ***verb* bracket**

brag (**brag**) ***verb*** To talk in a boastful way about how good you are at something. ▸ **bragging, bragged**

braid (**brayd**) ***noun*** A piece of hair or other material that has been divided into three or more parts and woven together.
▸ ***verb* braid**

Braille (**brayl**) ***noun*** A system of writing and printing for blind people. Braille uses raised dots that are read by feeling with the fingertips.

brain (**brayn**) ***noun***
1. The organ inside your head that controls your body and allows you to think and have feelings.
2. Your mind or intelligence.

brain•storm (**brayn**-*storm*)
1. ***verb*** When people **brainstorm,** they get together to share ideas on a topic or to solve a problem. ▸ **brainstorming, brainstormed** ▸ ***noun* brainstorming**
2. ***noun*** A sudden idea.

brain•wash (**brayn**-*wahsh*) ***verb*** To make someone accept and believe something by saying it over and over again. ▸ **brainwashes, brainwashing, brainwashed** ▸ ***noun* brainwashing**

brain•y (**bray**-nee) ***adjective*** Clever, or intelligent. ▸ **brainier, brainiest**

brake (**brayk**)
1. ***noun*** A device to slow down or stop a vehicle.
2. ***verb*** To slow down or stop by using a brake. ▸ **braking, braked**
Brake sounds like **break.**

brake•man (**brake**-muhn) ***noun***
1. A worker on a train who helps the conductor. Originally, the brakeman worked the brakes on the train. ▸ ***noun, plural* brakemen**
2. The end person on a bobsled team who operates the brakes.

bram•ble (**bram**-buhl) ***noun*** A thorny bush or shrub. Blackberries grow on a type of bramble.

bran (**bran**) ***noun*** The outer covering of wheat or other grains that is sifted out when flour is made. Bran is used in baked goods and cereals.

branch (**branch**)
1. ***noun*** A part of a tree that grows out of its trunk like an arm.
2. ***verb*** When a road, river, etc., **branches,** it splits into two or more parts that go in different directions.
▸ ***noun*** **branch**
3. ***noun*** A **branch** of a company or organization is one of its stores, offices, etc., in a particular area.
4. ***verb*** If you **branch out,** you start doing something new.
▸ ***noun, plural*** **branches** ▸ ***verb*** **branches, branching, branched**

brand (**brand**)
1. ***noun*** A particular make of a product, as in *a brand of toothpaste.*
2. ***verb*** If someone **brands** an animal, the person burns a mark onto its skin to show that the animal belongs to him or her. ▸ ***noun*** **brand**
3. ***verb*** To call by a shameful name.
▸ ***verb*** **branding, branded**

bran·dish (**bran**-dish) ***verb*** To hold up something, such as a weapon, and wave it around. ▸ **brandishes, brandishing, brandished**

brand-new ***adjective*** Never used before; completely new, or recently purchased.

brand·y (**bran**-dee) ***noun*** A strong alcoholic drink made from wine.

brass (**brass**)
1. ***noun*** A yellow metal made from copper and zinc.
2. ***adjective*** The **brass** section in an orchestra contains musical instruments that are made of brass and usually have a funnel-shaped mouthpiece.

brass rubbing ***noun*** A copy of a picture carved on a brass plate. Brass rubbings are made by rubbing with a wax crayon on a piece of paper placed over the plate.

brat (**brat**) ***noun*** An unpleasant or spoiled child who misbehaves or has bad manners.

bra·va·do (bruh-**vah**-doh) ***noun*** If you are full of **bravado,** you pretend to be braver and more confident than you really are.

brave (**brave**)
1. ***adjective*** If you are **brave,** you show courage and are willing to do difficult things. ▸ **braver, bravest** ▸ ***noun*** **bravery** ▸ ***adverb*** **bravely**
2. ***verb*** If you **brave** something unpleasant and difficult, you face it with determination. ▸ **braving, braved**
3. ***noun*** In history, an American Indian warrior.

bra·vo (brah-**voh** *or* **brah**-voh) ***interjection*** Well done!

brawl (**brawl**) ***noun*** A rough fight.
▸ ***verb*** **brawl**

bray (**bray**) ***verb***
1. When a donkey **brays,** it makes a loud, harsh noise. ▸ ***noun*** **bray**
2. When a person **brays,** he or she makes a harsh noise like a donkey.
▸ ***verb*** **braying, brayed**

braz·en (**bray**-zuhn) ***adjective***
1. Shameless. ▸ ***adverb*** **brazenly**
2. Harsh sounding, or loud.

breach (**breech**)
1. ***verb*** To break through something; to make a hole in something.
▸ **breaches, breaching, breached**
2. ***noun*** A failure to live up to a law or promise, as in *a breach of contract.*
3. ***noun*** A break in a relationship.
▸ ***noun, plural*** **breaches**

bread (**bred**) ***noun***
1. A baked food made from flour, water, and often yeast.
2. (*slang*) Money.

breadth (**bredth**) ***noun***
1. The distance from one side of something to the other.
2. A wide range.

bread·win·ner (**bred**-*win*-ur) ***noun*** Someone who earns money for a family.

B

break (**brayk**)
1. ***verb*** To damage something so that it is in pieces or no longer works. ▸ ***noun*** **break,** ***noun*** **breakage** ▸ ***adjective*** **breakable,** ***adjective*** **broken**
2. ***noun*** A rest from working or studying.
3. ***verb*** To stop, as in *to break a bad habit.*
4. ***verb*** To do better than, as in *to break a record.*
5. ***verb*** If someone **breaks** the rules or the law, the person does something that is not allowed.
6. ***verb*** **break in** To get into a building by force.
7. ***verb*** **break out** To begin suddenly.
▸ ***verb*** **breaking, broke** (**brohk**), **broken** (**brohk**-in)

break dancing ***noun*** A very energetic and acrobatic form of dance in which dancers touch the ground with their hands, heads, etc. ▸ ***noun*** **break-dancer** ▸ ***verb*** **break-dance**

break·down (**brayk**-*down*) ***noun***
1. If you have a **breakdown** while you are traveling, your vehicle stops moving because something has gone wrong.
2. If someone has a **breakdown,** the person is so worried or depressed about something that he or she becomes ill.

break·er (**bray**-kur) ***noun*** A big sea wave that breaks into foam when it reaches the shore.

break·fast (**brek**-fuhst) ***noun*** The first meal of the day.

break-in (**brake**-*in*) ***noun*** The act of forcibly entering a building or house in order to steal things.

break·through (**brayk**-*throo*) ***noun*** An important step toward achieving something. ▸ ***adjective*** **breakthrough**

break·wa·ter (**brayk**-*wah*-tur) ***noun*** A wall built to protect a harbor or beach from the force of ocean waves.

breast (**brest**) ***noun***
1. One of the glands in a female mammal that can produce milk to feed her young.
2. A man's or a woman's chest.

breast·bone (**brest**-*bohn*) ***noun*** The flat bone in your chest that is attached to your ribs.

breast·stroke (**brest**-*stroke*) ***noun*** A style of swimming face down in which you move your arms forward and out from your chest and kick your legs like a frog.

breath (**breth**) ***noun***
1. The air that you take into your lungs and breathe out again.
2. If you are **out of breath,** you have difficulty breathing.
3. When you say something **under your breath,** you say it very quietly.

breathe (**breeTH**) ***verb***
1. To take air in and out of your lungs.
2. To whisper.
▸ ***verb*** **breathing, breathed**

breath·er (**bree**-THur) ***noun*** A short rest.

breath·less (**breth**-liss) ***adjective***
1. Out of breath.
2. Very fast.

breath·tak·ing (**breth**-*tay*-king) ***adjective*** Very beautiful or impressive. ▸ ***adverb*** **breathtakingly**

breech·es (**brich**-iz) ***noun, plural*** Knee-length pants that are tight at the bottom.

breed (**breed**)
1. ***verb*** To keep animals or plants so that you can produce more of them and control their quality. ▸ ***noun*** **breeder**
2. ***verb*** When animals **breed,** they mate and produce young.
3. ***noun*** A particular type of animal, as in *a popular breed of dog.*
▸ ***verb*** **breeding, bred** (**bred**)

breeze (**breez**)
1. ***noun*** A gentle wind. ▸ ***adjective*** **breezy**
2. ***verb*** To move quickly and easily.
▸ **breezing, breezed**

brew (**broo**) ***verb***
1. To make tea or coffee.
2. To make beer.
3. If something is **brewing,** it is about to start.
▸ ***verb*** **brewing, brewed** ▸ ***noun*** **brew**

brew•er•y (**broo**-ur-ee) ***noun*** A place where beer is made. ▸ ***noun, plural*** **breweries**

bri•ar (**brye**-ur) *See* **brier.**

bribe (**bribe**)
1. ***noun*** Money or a gift that you offer to someone to persuade the person to do something for you, especially something wrong.
2. ***verb*** To offer someone a bribe.
▸ **bribing, bribed** ▸ ***noun*** **bribery**

bric-a-brac (**brik**-uh-*brak*) ***noun, plural*** Various objects that are used as ornaments.

brick (**brik**) ***noun*** A block of hard-baked clay, used for building.

bride (**bride**) ***noun*** A woman who is about to get married or has just gotten married. ▸ ***adjective*** **bridal**

bride•groom (**bride**-*groom*) ***noun*** A man who is about to get married or has just gotten married.

brides•maid (**bridez**-*mayd*) ***noun*** A girl or woman who helps a bride on her wedding day.

bridge (**brij**)
1. ***noun*** A structure built over a river, railway, etc., so that people or vehicles can get to the other side. ▸ ***verb*** **bridge**
2. ***noun*** A card game for four players.
3. ***noun*** The bony part of your nose between your eyes.
4. If something **bridges a gap,** it provides a connection between two different things.
5. ***noun*** An upright piece of wood on a guitar, violin, etc., over which the strings are stretched.

bri•dle (**brye**-duhl) ***noun*** The straps that fit around a horse's head and mouth and are used to control it. ▸ ***verb*** **bridle**

bridle path ***noun*** A track or path for riding or walking horses.

brief (**breef**)
1. ***adjective*** Lasting only a short time, as in *a brief visit.*
2. ***adjective*** Using only a few words.
3. ***verb*** To give someone information so that the person can carry out a task.
▸ **briefing, briefed**
4. ***noun*** An outline of the main information and arguments of a legal case.
▸ ***adjective*** **briefer, briefest** ▸ ***adverb*** **briefly**

brief•case (**breef**-*kayss*) ***noun*** A bag with a handle, used for carrying papers.

bri•er (**brye**-ur) ***noun*** A prickly twig or the shrub on which it grows.

brig (**brig**) ***noun***
1. A military prison, usually on a ship.
2. A sailing ship with two masts and square sails.

bri•gade (bri-**gayd**) ***noun***
1. A unit of an army.
2. An organized group of workers, as in *the fire brigade.*

brig•and (**bri**-gund) ***noun*** (*old-fashioned*) A member of a gang of robbers.

bright (**brite**) ***adjective***
1. A **bright** light or color is strong and can be seen clearly. ▸ ***adverb*** **brightly**
2. Smart.
▸ ***adjective*** **brighter, brightest** ▸ ***noun*** **brightness**

bril•liant (**bril**-yuhnt) ***adjective***
1. Shining very brightly, as in *a brilliant diamond.*
2. Very smart.
3. Splendid, or terrific, as in *a brilliant performance.*
▸ ***noun*** **brilliance** ▸ ***adverb*** **brilliantly**

brim (**brim**) ***noun***
1. The wide part that sticks out around the bottom of a hat.
2. The edge of a cup or glass.

brine (**brine**) ***noun*** Salty water.

bring (**bring**) ***verb***
1. To take something or someone with you.
2. To make something happen or appear.
3. To sell for.
4. If a company **brings out** a product, it starts selling it.
5. **bring up** To look after and guide a child as he or she grows up.
▸ ***verb*** **bringing, brought** (**brawt**)

B

brink (**bringk**) ***noun***
1. The edge of something, such as a cliff or the bank of a river.
2. If you are **on the brink** of something, you are just about to do it.

brisk (**brisk**) ***adjective*** Quick and energetic, as in *a brisk walk.* ▸ **brisker, briskest** ▸ ***adverb*** **briskly**

bris•tle (**briss**-uhl)
1. ***noun*** One of the long, wiry hairs used to make brushes.
2. **bristles** ***noun, plural*** The short, stiff hairs that start to grow on a man's chin if he does not shave.
3. ***verb*** To show anger. ▸ **bristling, bristled**
▸ ***adjective*** **bristly**

brit•tle (**brit**-uhl) ***adjective*** Easily snapped or broken. ▸ **brittler, brittlest**

broach (**brohch**) ***verb*** When you **broach** a subject with someone, you start to talk or ask about it. ▸ **broaches, broaching, broached**

broad (**brawd**) ***adjective***
1. Wide.
2. Covering the most important points, but not the details. ▸ ***adjective*** **broader, broadest** ▸ ***adverb*** **broadly**

broad•cast (**brawd**-*kast*)
1. ***verb*** To send out a program on television or radio. ▸ **broadcasting, broadcasted** ▸ ***noun*** **broadcaster,** ***noun*** **broadcasting**
2. ***noun*** A television or radio program.

broad•en (**brawd**-uhn) ***verb*** To make something broader or more liberal.
▸ **broadening, broadened**

broad-mind•ed (**minde**-id) ***adjective*** If you are **broad-minded,** you are open to new ideas and other people's views.

bro•cade (broh-**kayd**) ***noun*** Fabric woven with a raised overall pattern.

broc•co•li (**brok**-uh-lee) ***noun*** A green vegetable with rounded heads on stalks.

bro•chure (broh-**shur**) ***noun*** A booklet, usually with pictures, that gives information about a product or service, as in *a vacation brochure.*

broil•er (**broi**-lur) ***noun*** The part of a stove that heats food from above.

broke (**brohk**) ***adjective*** (*informal*) If you are **broke,** you have no money.

bron•chi•al tubes (**brong**-kee-uhl) ***noun, plural*** Small tubes in your lungs through which air passes.

bron•chi•tis (brong-**kye**-tiss) ***noun*** An illness of the throat and lungs that makes you cough a lot.

bron•co (**brong**-ko) ***noun*** A type of wild horse found in the western United States.
▸ ***noun, plural*** **broncos**

bron•to•saur•us (**bron**-tuh-*sor*-uhss) ***noun*** A large, plant-eating dinosaur with a long neck and tail and a small head, from the Jurassic period. The brontosaurus is now called an apatosaurus.

bronze (**bronz**) ***noun***
1. A hard, reddish brown metal that is a mixture of copper and tin.
2. A reddish brown color. ▸ ***adjective*** **bronze** ▸ ***verb*** **bronze**

Bronze Age ***noun*** A period of history, before the introduction of iron, when bronze was commonly used to make tools and weapons. Different parts of the world experienced a Bronze Age at different times.

brooch (**brohch** *or* **brooch**) ***noun*** A piece of jewelry that can be pinned to your clothes.

brood (**brood**)
1. ***verb*** To keep worrying or thinking about something. ▸ **brooding, brooded**
2. ***noun*** A family of young birds.
3. ***noun*** All the children in one family.

brook (**bruk**) ***noun*** A small stream.

broom (**broom**) ***noun*** A large brush with a long handle, used for sweeping floors.

broth (**brawth**) ***noun*** The clear liquid that remains after meat or vegetables have been cooked.

broth•er (**bruhTH**-ur) ***noun*** A boy or man who has the same parents as another person. ▸ ***adjective*** **brotherly**

broth•er•hood (**bruhTH**-ur-hud) ***noun***
1. Warm feelings and good will among people.
2. A group that works or lives together in a brotherly way.

brother-in-law ***noun*** Someone's **brother-in-law** is the brother of his or her spouse or the husband of his or her sister. ▸ ***noun, plural*** **brothers-in-law**

brow (**brou**) ***noun***
1. Forehead, as in *a wrinkled brow.*
2. The top of a hill.

brown (**broun**)
1. ***noun*** The color of wood, chocolate, leather, or coffee. ▸ ***adjective*** **brown**
2. ***verb*** To make something brown, as by cooking it. ▸ **browning, browned**

brown•ie (**brou**-nee) ***noun*** A small, flat chocolate cake, usually with nuts in it.

brown•out (**broun**-*out*) ***noun*** A partial loss of electrical power that causes the lights to dim.

browse (**brouz**) ***verb***
1. To eat by nibbling on twigs, leaves, or shoots.
2. To look casually at something.
▸ **browsing, browsed**

brows•er (**brou**-zur) ***noun***
1. An animal that eats by browsing.
2. A computer program that lets you find and look through Web pages or other data.

bruise (**brooz**) ***noun*** A dark mark that you get on your skin when you fall or are hit by something. ▸ ***verb*** **bruise** ▸ ***adjective*** **bruised**

bru•nette (broo-**net**) ***adjective*** Having dark brown hair. ▸ ***noun*** **brunette**

brush (**bruhsh**)
1. ***noun*** An object with bristles and a handle, used for sweeping, painting, or smoothing hair.
2. ***verb*** To use a brush.
3. ***verb*** To touch something lightly.
4. ***noun*** An area of land where small trees and shrubs grow.
▸ ***noun, plural*** **brushes** ▸ ***verb*** **brushes, brushing, brushed**

Brus•sels sprout (**bruss**-uhlz sprout) ***noun*** A vegetable that looks like a small head of cabbage. ▸ ***noun, plural*** **Brussels sprouts**

bru•tal (**broo**-tuhl) ***adjective*** Cruel and violent. ▸ ***noun*** **brutality** (broo-**tal**-i-tee) ▸ ***adverb*** **brutally**

brute (**broot**)
1. ***noun*** A rough and violent person.
2. If you do something by **brute force,** you use a lot of strength instead of skill or intelligence.

bub•ble (**buh**-buhl)
1. ***noun*** One of the tiny balls of gas in fizzy drinks, boiling water, etc.
2. ***verb*** To make bubbles. ▸ **bubbling, bubbled**

bub•bly (**buhb**-lee) ***adjective***
1. If a liquid is **bubbly,** it is full of balls of gas.
2. If a person is **bubbly,** he or she is very lively and talkative.

buc•ca•neer (buhk-uh-**nihr**) ***noun*** A pirate.

buck (**buhk**)
1. ***noun*** A male deer, antelope, or rabbit.
2. ***verb*** If a horse **bucks,** it jumps in the air with its head down and all four feet off the ground.
3. If you **pass the buck,** you pass on the responsibility for something to someone else.
4. ***noun*** (*slang*) A dollar.
5. ***verb*** To work against.
▸ ***verb*** **bucking, bucked**

buck•et (**buh**-kit) ***noun*** A plastic, wooden, or metal container with a handle, used for carrying liquids or other things.

buck•le (**buhk**-uhl)
1. ***noun*** A metal fastening on shoes, belts, or straps. ▸ ***verb*** **buckle**
2. ***verb*** To crumple.
3. When someone **buckles down,** he or she works very hard.
▸ ***verb*** **buckling, buckled**

buck•skin (**buhk**-*skin*) ***noun*** A strong, soft material made from the skin of a deer or sheep.

B

buck•tooth (**buhk**-**tooth**) ***noun*** A longer front tooth that sticks out. ▸ ***noun, plural*** **buckteeth**

buck•wheat (**buhk**-weet) ***noun*** A plant with small seeds, used as cattle feed or made into flour.

bud (**buhd**) ***noun*** A small shoot on a plant that grows into a leaf or flower. ▸ ***verb*** **bud**

Bud•dha (**boo**-duh) ***noun***
1. The name given to Siddhartha Gautama, the Indian teacher who founded the religion of Buddhism.
2. A statue or picture of Buddha.

Bud•dhism (**boo**-diz-uhm) ***noun*** A religion based on the teachings of Buddha and practiced mainly in eastern and central Asia. Buddhists believe that you should not become too attached to material things and that you live many lives in different bodies. ▸ ***noun*** **Buddhist** ▸ ***adjective*** **Buddhist**

bud•ding (**buhd**-ing) ***adjective*** In the early stages of maturity, or gaining skill.

bud•dy (**buhd**-ee) ***noun*** A close friend; a pal. ▸ ***noun, plural*** **buddies**

budge (**buhj**) ***verb*** If you cannot **budge** something, you are not able to move it. ▸ **budging, budged**

budg•et (**buhj**-it)
1. ***noun*** A plan for how money will be earned and spent. ▸ ***adjective*** **budgetary**
2. ***verb*** If you **budget** your money, you plan how you will spend it. ▸ **budgeting, budgeted**

buff (**buhf**)
1. ***noun*** A pale, yellow-brown color. ▸ ***adjective*** **buff**
2. ***noun*** (*informal*) Someone who knows a lot about a particular subject.
3. ***verb*** To polish something. ▸ **buffing, buffed**

buf•fa•lo (**buhf**-uh-loh) ***noun***
1. A type of ox with heavy horns found in Europe, Africa, and Asia.
2. A bison.
▸ ***noun, plural*** **buffaloes** *or* **buffalos** *or* **buffalo**

buff•er (**buhf**-ur) ***noun*** Something that softens a blow. ▸ ***verb*** **buffer**

buf•fet
1. (**buh**-fit) ***verb*** To strike and shake something or someone. ▸ **buffeting, buffeted**
2. (buf-**ay**) ***noun*** A meal in which many foods are laid out on a table and people serve themselves.
3. (buf-**ay**) ***noun*** A piece of furniture with a flat top for serving food and drawers for storing dishes and silverware.

bug (**buhg**)
1. ***noun*** An insect.
2. ***noun*** A minor illness caused by germs, as in *a stomach bug.*
3. ***noun*** An error in a computer program or system that prevents it from working properly.
4. ***verb*** If someone **bugs** a room, the person hides microphones there so that he or she can listen to what people are saying. ▸ ***noun*** **bug**
5. ***verb*** (*informal*) If people or things **bug** you, they annoy you.
▸ ***verb*** **bugging, bugged**

bug•gy (**buhg**-ee) ***noun***
1. A light carriage with two wheels pulled by a horse.
2. A baby carriage.
▸ ***noun, plural*** **buggies**

bu•gle (**byoo**-guhl) ***noun*** A musical instrument shaped like a trumpet but without keys. Bugles are often used in the army to send signals to the troops. ▸ ***noun*** **bugler**

build (**bild**)
1. ***verb*** To make something by putting different parts together.
2. ***noun*** The size and shape of a person's body.
3. **build up** ***verb*** To increase or make stronger.
▸ ***verb*** **building, built** (**bilt**)

build•ing (**bil**-ding) ***noun*** A structure with walls and a roof.

built-in ***adjective*** Built as a permanent part of something.

bulb (**buhlb**) ***noun***
1. The onion-shaped underground plant part from which some plants grow. Tulips and lilies grow from bulbs.
2. The glass part of an electric light or flashlight that lights up when you switch it on.

bulge (**buhlj**) ***verb*** To swell out like a lump. ▸ **bulging, bulged** ▸ ***noun*** **bulge**

bulk (**buhlk**) ***noun***
1. Large size.
2. The **bulk** of something is the main part of it.
3. When you buy **in bulk,** you buy in large quantities.

bulk·y (**buhl**-kee) ***adjective***
1. Large and difficult to handle, as in *a bulky package.*
2. Taking up a lot of space, as in *a bulky sweater.* ▸ ***adjective*** **bulkier, bulkiest**

bull (**bul**) ***noun***
1. The male of the cattle family.
2. A male elephant, seal, moose, or whale.

bull·dog (**bul**-*dawg*) ***noun*** A strong dog with a round head, powerful jaws, and short legs.

bull·doz·er (**bul**-*doh*-zur) ***noun*** A powerful tractor with a wide blade at the front, used for moving earth and rocks.

bul·let (**bul**-it) ***noun*** A small, pointed metal object fired from a gun.

bul·le·tin (**bul**-uh-tuhn) ***noun*** A short, important news report on television or the radio.

bul·let·proof (**bul**-uht-*proof*) ***adjective*** Something that is **bulletproof** is made to protect people from bullets, as in *bulletproof glass.*

bull·fight (**bul**-*fite*) ***noun*** A public entertainment in which people fight against bulls. ▸ ***noun*** **bullfighter**

bull·frog (**bul**-*frawg*) ***noun*** A large frog with a deep croak.

bul·lion (**bul**-yuhn) ***noun*** Gold or silver shaped into bars.

bull's-eye ***noun*** The center of a target that is usually round and is used for archery or darts.

bul·ly (**bul**-ee) ***verb*** To frighten or pick on people who are weaker than you.
▸ **bullies, bullying, bullied** ▸ ***noun*** **bully**

bum·ble·bee (**buhm**-buhl-*bee*) ***noun*** A large, hairy bee with yellow and black stripes that hums when it flies.

bump (**buhmp**)
1. ***verb*** To knock into something. ▸ ***noun*** **bump**
2. ***noun*** A heavy knock or collision.
3. ***noun*** A round lump or swelling.
4. ***verb*** If you **bump into** someone, you meet the person by chance.
5. ***verb*** To move with jolts and jerks.
▸ ***verb*** **bumping, bumped**

bump·er (**buhm**-pur)
1. ***noun*** The heavy metal bar on the front or back of a car or truck that helps protect the vehicle in an accident.
2. ***adjective*** Very large.

bump·tious (**buhmp**-shuhss) ***adjective*** Loud and conceited.

bump·y (**buhm**-pee) ***adjective*** Very uneven, as in *a bumpy road.* ▸ **bumpier, bumpiest**

bun (**buhn**) ***noun***
1. A small, round cake or roll.
2. Hair fastened in a round shape at the back of the head.

bunch (**buhnch**) ***noun*** A group of people or things. ▸ ***noun, plural*** **bunches**
▸ ***verb*** **bunch**

bun·dle (**buhn**-duhl) ***verb***
1. To tie or wrap things together. ▸ ***noun*** **bundle**
2. To hurry someone.
▸ ***verb*** **bundling, bundled**

bun·ga·low (**buhng**-guh-loh) ***noun*** A small house, usually with only one floor.

bun·gee jumping (**buhn**-jee) ***noun*** A sport in which someone jumps from a high place and is stopped from hitting the ground by a long elastic cord attached to his or her legs.

bun·gle (**buhng**-guhl) ***verb*** To do something badly or clumsily.
▸ **bungling, bungled**

B

bunk (**buhngk**) ***noun***
1. A narrow bed.
2. bunk bed A bed stacked on top of or below another.
▸ ***verb*** **bunk**

bun•ker (**buhngk**-ur) ***noun***
1. An underground shelter from bomb attacks and gunfire.
2. A large, sand-filled hollow on a golf course.

bun•ny (**buhn**-ee) ***noun*** A rabbit.
▸ ***noun, plural*** **bunnies**

Bun•sen burner (**buhn**-suhn) ***noun*** A device consisting of a metal pipe through which gas flows and is mixed with air to make a very hot flame. It is often used in laboratories.

bunt (**buhnt**) ***verb*** To tap a baseball lightly with a bat, so that the ball doesn't go very far. ▸ **bunting, bunted**

bun•ting (**buhn**-ting) ***noun***
1. A light cloth used for making flags.
2. Small flags joined by a string and used for decorations.

buoy (**boi** *or* **boo**-ee) ***noun*** A floating marker in the ocean or in a river.

buoy•ant (**boi**-uhnt *or* **boo**-yuhnt) ***adjective***
1. Able to keep afloat. ▸ ***noun*** **buoyancy**
2. Cheerful, as in *a buoyant personality.*
▸ ***adverb*** **buoyantly**

bur *or* **burr** (**bur**) ***noun***
1. A prickly pod that sticks to the clothing of people or the fur of animals.
2. The bush that produces these pods.

bur•den (**bur**-duhn)
1. *noun* A heavy load that someone has to carry.
2. *verb* To weigh someone down with something heavy. ▸ **burdening, burdened**
3. *noun* A serious task or responsibility.
▸ ***adjective*** **burdensome**

bu•reau (**byur**-oh) ***noun***
1. A chest of drawers.
2. An office that provides information or some other service, as in *a travel bureau.*

burg•er (**bur**-gur) ***noun*** A round, flat piece of cooked meat, usually served on a bun. Burger is short for **hamburger.**

bur•glar (**burg**-lur) ***noun*** Someone who breaks into a building and steals things.
▸ ***noun*** **burglary**

bur•i•al (**ber**-ee-uhl) ***noun*** The placing of a dead body in the earth or sea.

bur•lap (**bur**-lap) ***noun*** A tough, coarse material used to make bags that will hold heavy objects during shipping.

bur•ly (**bur**-lee) ***adjective*** Husky; strong and with large muscles. ▸ **burlier, burliest**

burn (**burn**)
1. *verb* To hurt or damage someone or something by means of heat, a chemical, or radiation.
2. *noun* A sore area on the skin or a mark on something, caused by burning.
3. *verb* To feel very hot.
4. *verb* To feel strong emotion.
▸ ***verb*** **burning, burned** *or* **burnt** (**burnt**) ▸ ***adjective*** **burnt**

burn•er (**bur**-nur) ***noun*** The circular, flat area on a stove where flame or heat is used to cook things.

burp (**burp**) ***verb*** To make a noise in your throat because gases have been forced up from your stomach, usually after eating and drinking. ▸ **burping, burped** ▸ ***noun*** **burp**

bur•ro (**bur**-oh) ***noun*** A small donkey. **Burro** sounds like **borough** and **burrow.** ▸ ***noun, plural*** **burros**

bur•row (**bur**-oh)
1. *noun* A tunnel or hole in the ground made or used by a rabbit or other animal.
2. *verb* To dig or live in such a tunnel or hole. ▸ **burrowing, burrowed**
Burrow sounds like **borough** and **burro.**

burst (**burst**)
1. *verb* To explode or break apart suddenly.
2. *noun* A short, concentrated outbreak of something, such as speed, gunfire, or applause.

3. ***verb*** To start doing something suddenly.
4. ***verb*** To be very full.
▸ ***verb*** **bursting, burst**

bur•y (**ber**-ee) ***verb***
1. To put a dead body into a grave.
2. To hide something in the ground or under a pile of things.
Bury sounds like **berry.**
▸ ***verb*** **buries, burying, buried**

bus (**buhss**) ***noun*** A large vehicle used for carrying passengers. ▸ ***noun, plural*** **buses** ▸ ***verb*** **bus**

bush (**bush**) ***noun***
1. A large plant with many branches.
2. If you **beat around the bush,** you talk a lot but don't come to the point.
▸ ***noun, plural*** **bushes**

bush•el (**bush**-uhl) ***noun*** A unit of dry measure that tells how much a container holds. A bushel equals 32 quarts.

bush•whack (**bush**-*wak*) ***verb***
1. To make a path, usually in the jungle, by cutting away at the underbrush with a machete or other sharp tool.
2. To ambush someone from a hiding place.
▸ ***verb*** **bushwhacking, bushwhacked**
▸ ***noun*** **bushwhacker**

bush•y (**bush**-ee) ***adjective*** Thick and spreading, as in *bushy eyebrows.*
▸ **bushier, bushiest**

busi•ness (**biz**-niss) ***noun***
1. The buying and selling of goods and services.
2. The type of work that someone does.
3. A company that makes or sells things or provides a service.
4. If something is **none of your business,** it has nothing to do with you.
▸ ***noun, plural*** **businesses**

busi•ness•like (**biz**-niss-*like*) ***adjective*** Efficient and practical.

bust (**buhst**)
1. ***noun*** A sculpture of a person's head and shoulders.
2. ***verb*** To break something. ▸ **busting, busted** *or* **bust** ▸ ***adjective*** **bust** *or* **busted**

bus•tle (**buh**-suhl) ***verb*** To rush around being busy. ▸ **bustling, bustled** ▸ ***noun*** **bustle**

bus•y (**biz**-ee) ***adjective***
1. If you are **busy,** you have a lot of things to do. ▸ ***verb*** **busy** ▸ ***adverb*** **busily**
2. A **busy** place has a lot of people in it and is full of activity.
3. In use. ▸ ***adjective*** **busier, busiest**

bus•y•bod•y (**biz**-ee-*bod*-ee) ***noun*** Someone who likes to know other people's business. ▸ ***noun, plural*** **busybodies**

but (**buht**)
1. ***conjunction*** On the other hand.
2. ***preposition*** Other than.
3. ***preposition*** With the exception of.
4. ***adverb*** Only, or just.
But sounds like **butt.**

butch•er (**buch**-ur) ***noun*** Someone who prepares and sells meat.

but•ler (**buht**-lur) ***noun*** The chief male servant in a house.

butt (**buht**)
1. ***noun*** Someone whom people make fun of.
2. ***verb*** To hit with the head or horns.
▸ **butting, butted**
3. ***noun*** The thicker end, as in *a rifle butt.*
Butt sounds like **but.**

butte (**byoot**) ***noun*** A large mountain with steep sides and a flat top that stands by itself, mostly found in the western United States.

but•ter (**buht**-ur) ***noun*** A yellow fat made from cream, used in cooking and for spreading on bread.

but•ter•cup (**buht**-ur-*kuhp*) ***noun*** A small, yellow wildflower.

but•ter•fly (**buht**-ur-*flye*) ***noun*** A thin insect with large, often brightly colored wings. ▸ ***noun, plural*** **butterflies**

but•ter•milk (**buht**-ur-*milk*) ***noun*** The sour liquid left over after butter has been churned from cream.

but•ter•scotch (**buht**-ur-*skoch*) ***noun*** A flavor or candy made by mixing brown sugar, butter, and vanilla extract.

B

but•tock (**buht**-uhk) ***noun*** The back of your hip that forms the fleshy part on which you sit.

but•ton (**buht**-uhn) ***noun***
1. A round piece of plastic, metal, etc., that is sewn onto clothing and used as a fastener. ▸ ***verb*** **button**
2. A small knob on a machine that you turn or press to make it work.

but•ton•hole (**buht**-uhn-*hole*) ***noun*** The small hole that you push a button through in order to close a garment.

but•tress (**buh**-truhss)
1. ***noun*** A structure built against a wall to help support it.
2. ***verb*** To give support or make stronger. ▸ ***verb*** **buttresses, buttressing, buttressed**

buy (**bye**)
1. ***verb*** To get something by paying money for it.
▸ **buying, bought** (**bawt**) ▸ ***noun*** **buyer**
2. ***noun*** A bargain.
Buy sounds like **by.**

buzz (**buhz**) ***verb*** To make a noise like a bee or a wasp. ▸ **buzzes, buzzing, buzzed** ▸ ***noun*** **buzz,** ***noun*** **buzzer**

buz•zard (**buz**-urd) ***noun*** A large bird of prey, similar to a vulture, with a hooked beak and long, sharp claws.

by (**bye**)
1. ***preposition*** Next to, or beside, as in *a phone by the door.*
2. ***adverb*** Near, or close at hand. *They just stood by and laughed.*
3. ***preposition*** Through the work of. *It was painted by my father.*
4. ***preposition*** Through the means of. *We went home by bus.*
5. ***preposition*** Beyond, or past. *They drove by the accident.*
6. ***adverb*** Past. *Time goes by slowly.*
7. by and by After a while; soon. *We'll do the work by and by.*
By sounds like **buy.**

by•gone (**bye**-*gon*) ***adjective*** Past or former.

by•pass (**bye**-*pass*)
1. ***noun*** A main road that goes around a town rather than through it. ▸ ***noun, plural*** **bypasses**
2. ***verb*** To avoid something by going around it. ▸ **bypasses, bypassing, bypassed**
▸ ***adjective*** **bypass**

by-product (**bye**-*prod*-uhkt) ***noun*** Something that is left over after you make or do something.

by•stand•er (**bye**-*stan*-dur) ***noun*** Someone who is at a place where something happens to someone else; a spectator.

byte (**bite**) ***noun*** A unit of information that is contained in a computer's memory. **Byte** sounds like **bite.**

Byz•an•tine (**biz**-uhn-teen) ***adjective***
1. To do with Byzantium (biz-**an**-tee-uhm), the ancient eastern Roman Empire.
2. In the style of art or architecture used in the Byzantine Empire, especially in the fifth and sixth centuries. Byzantine buildings have large domes and rounded arches and are highly decorated, often with mosaics.

cab (**kab**) ***noun***
1. A car that takes people from one place to another for a fee.
2. The driver's area of a large truck or machine, such as a bulldozer.

cab•bage (**kab**-ij) ***noun*** A large vegetable with green or purple leaves shaped into a round head.

cab•in (**kab**-in) ***noun***
1. A small, simple house, often built of wood.
2. A private room for passengers or members of the crew to sleep in on a ship.
3. A section of an airplane for the passengers, crew, or cargo.

cab•i•net (**kab**-in-it) ***noun***
1. A piece of furniture with shelves or drawers.
2. A group of advisors for the head of a government.

ca•ble (**kay**-buhl) ***noun***
1. A thick wire or rope.
2. A tight bundle of wires used for carrying electricity, television signals, etc.
3. A message sent by an underwater cable. ▸ ***verb*** **cable**
4. cable car A vehicle pulled along by a moving cable, used for carrying people along city streets or up mountains.
5. cable television A television service in which signals from broadcasting stations are sent by cable to the homes of paying customers.

ca•boose (kuh-**booss**) ***noun*** The last car on a freight train, used by the crew.

ca•ca•o (kuh-**kaw**) ***noun*** An evergreen tree found in warm climates that produces a seed from which cocoa and chocolate are made.

cack•le (**kak**-uhl) ***verb*** To laugh in a sharp, loud way. ▸ **cackling, cackled** ▸ ***noun*** **cackle**

ca•coph•o•ny (kuh-**ka**-fuh-*nee*) ***noun*** A harsh, unpleasant sound or combination of sounds. ▸ ***noun, plural*** **cacophonies** ▸ ***adjective*** **cacophonous**

cac•tus (**kak**-tuhss) ***noun*** A plant with a thick trunk and sharp spikes in place of leaves that grows in hot, dry areas. ▸ ***noun, plural*** **cacti** (**kak**-tye) *or* **cactuses**

CAD (**see ay dee**) ***noun*** Short for **computer-aided design.**

ca•det (kuh-**det**) ***noun*** A young person who is training to become a member of the armed forces or a police force.

ca•fé (kaf-**ay**) ***noun*** A small restaurant.

caf•e•te•ri•a (kaf-uh-**tihr**-ee-uh) ***noun*** A self-service restaurant.

caf•feine (**kaf**-een *or* kaf-**een**) ***noun*** A chemical found in tea, coffee, and some soft drinks that acts as a stimulant.

caf•tan (**kaf**-tuhn) ***noun*** An ankle-length, loose piece of clothing with long sleeves, often worn by men in Arabic countries.

cage (**kayj**) ***noun*** A container in which birds or other kinds of animals are kept, made of wires or bars. ▸ ***verb*** **cage** ▸ ***adjective*** **caged**

ca•gey (**kay**-jee) ***adjective*** Cautious or wary.

ca•jole (kuh-**johl**) ***verb*** To persuade someone to do something by flattering or coaxing the person. ▸ **cajoling, cajoled**

C

Ca•jun (**kay**-juhn)
1. ***noun*** Someone who is a descendant of the French-speaking people who left eastern Canada for Louisiana in the 1700s.
2. ***adjective*** To do with a style of spicy cooking invented by the Cajuns, as in *Cajun rice.*

cake (kayk)
1. ***noun*** A sweet food made by baking flour, butter, eggs, and sugar together.
2. ***noun*** A shaped mass of something, as in *a cake of soap.*
3. ***adjective*** If you are **caked** in something, you are covered with it.

ca•lam•i•ty (kuh-**lam**-it-ee) ***noun*** A terrible disaster. ▸ ***noun, plural*** **calamities** ▸ ***adjective*** **calamitous**

cal•ci•um (**kal**-see-uhm) ***noun*** A soft, silver-white chemical element found in teeth and bones.

cal•cu•late (**kal**-kyuh-late) ***verb*** To work out by using arithmetic. ▸ **calculating, calculated** ▸ ***noun*** **calculation**

cal•cu•lat•ing (**kal**-kyuh-*lay*-ting) ***adjective*** A **calculating** person schemes to make sure things work out the way he or she wants.

cal•cu•la•tor (**kal**-kyuh-*lay*-tur) ***noun*** An electronic machine used for figuring out math problems.

cal•en•dar (**kal**-uhn-dur) ***noun*** A chart showing all the days, weeks, and months in a year.

calf (**kaf**) ***noun***
1. A young cow, seal, elephant, giraffe, or whale.
2. The fleshy part at the back of your leg, below your knee.
▸ ***noun, plural*** **calves**

cal•i•co (**kal**-i-koh)
1. ***noun*** Plain cotton cloth printed with a colorful pattern, as in *a dress made of calico.* ▸ ***noun, plural*** **calicoes** *or* **calicos** ▸ ***adjective*** **calico**
2. ***adjective*** Having spotted colors, as in *a calico cat.*

call (**kawl**) ***verb***
1. To give someone or something a name.
2. To shout something out, especially someone's name.
3. To telephone someone. ▸ ***noun*** **caller**
4. If you **call on** someone, you visit the person.
5. If something is **called off,** it is canceled.
6. call collect To reverse telephone charges from the person who is making the call to the person who is receiving it.
▸ ***verb*** **calling, called** ▸ ***noun*** **call**

call•er ID (**kaw**-lur *eye*-**dee**) ***noun*** A telephone company service that shows you the telephone number of the person who is calling before you answer the telephone.

cal•lig•ra•phy (kuh-**lig**-ruh-fee) ***noun*** The art of beautiful handwriting.

call number ***noun*** The numbers and letters used in a system of organization that indicates where an item is kept.

cal•lous (**kal**-uhss) ***adjective*** Having no tender feelings; cruel. ▸ ***noun*** **callousness** ▸ ***adverb*** **callously**

calm (**kahm**)
1. ***adjective*** Peaceful and not troubled. ▸ **calmer, calmest** ▸ ***noun*** **calmness** ▸ ***adverb*** **calmly**
2. ***verb*** To soothe. ▸ **calming, calmed**
3. ***noun*** Peacefulness.
4. ***noun*** A lack of wind or motion.

cal•o•rie (**kal**-uh-ree) ***noun*** A measurement of the amount of energy that a food gives you.

ca•lyp•so (kuh-**lip**-soh) ***noun*** A style of Caribbean music with a strong rhythm.

cam•cord•er (**kam**-*kor*-dur) ***noun*** A video camera with a sound recorder that you can carry around with you.

cam•el (**kam**-uhl) ***noun*** A mammal with one or two humps on its back. Camels are used for carrying people and goods across the desert.

cam•e•o (**kam**-ee-oh) ***noun***
1. A piece of colored stone with a figure carved into it.
2. A small character part taken in a play or a movie, usually by a famous actor.

cam•er•a (**kam**-ur-uh) ***noun***
1. A machine for taking photographs or making films.
2. A device for transmitting images of a television broadcast.

cam•ou•flage (**kam**-uh-flahzh)
1. ***noun*** Coloring or covering that makes animals, people, and objects look like their surroundings.
2. ***verb*** To disguise something so that it blends in with its surroundings.
▸ **camouflaging, camouflaged**

camp (**kamp**)
1. ***noun*** An outdoor area, usually with tents or cabins, where people stay for a while.
2. ***verb*** To live or stay in a camp.
▸ **camping, camped** ▸ ***noun*** **camping**

cam•paign (kam-**payn**) ***noun*** A series of actions organized over a period of time in order to achieve or win something, as in *an election campaign.*
▸ ***verb*** **campaign**

camp•er (**kam**-pur) ***noun***
1. Someone who stays or vacations at a camp.
2. A large vehicle in which you can sleep and cook meals.

camp•fire (**kamp**-*fire*) ***noun*** A fire lit at the site of a camp for warmth and for cooking.

camp•ground (**kamp**-*ground*) ***noun*** A place where people camp.

camp•us (**kam**-puhss) ***noun*** The land and buildings of a school, college, or university.

can (**kan**)
1. ***verb*** To be able to.
2. ***verb*** (*informal*) To be allowed to do something.
3. ***noun*** A metal container.
4. ***verb*** To put in a jar or can; to preserve. ▸ **canning, canned**
▸ ***adjective*** **canned**
▸ ***verb*** **could**

ca•nal (kuh-**nal**) ***noun*** A channel that is dug across land. Canals connect bodies of water so that ships can travel between them.

ca•nar•y (kuh-**nair**-ee) ***noun***
1. A bright yellow bird noted for its singing ability. ▸ ***noun, plural*** **canaries**
2. A bright yellow color.

can•cel (**kan**-suhl) ***verb***
1. If someone **cancels** something that has been arranged, he or she has decided that it is not going to happen.
2. cancel out If two things **cancel** each other **out,** they stop the effect of one another.
3. If you **cancel** a postage stamp, you mark it so that it cannot be used again.
▸ ***verb*** **canceling, canceled** ▸ ***noun*** **cancel**

can•cer (**kan**-sur) ***noun*** A serious disease in which some cells in the body grow faster than normal cells and destroy healthy organs and tissues.
▸ ***adjective*** **cancerous**

can•did (**kan**-did) ***adjective*** Honest and open in what you are saying. ▸ ***noun*** **candor** ▸ ***adverb*** **candidly**

can•di•date (**kan**-duh-date) ***noun*** Someone who is applying for a job or running in an election. ▸ ***noun*** **candidacy**

can•dle (**kan**-duhl) ***noun*** A stick of wax or tallow with a string or wick running through it that you burn to give light.
▸ ***noun*** **candlelight**

can•dy (**kan**-dee)
1. ***noun*** A small piece of food made with sugar or syrup and often chocolate, nuts, or other flavorings. ▸ ***noun, plural*** **candies**
2. ***verb*** To coat with sugar, as in *to candy yams.* ▸ **candies, candying, candied**
▸ ***adjective*** **candied**

C

cane (**kane**)
1. ***noun*** The woody, sometimes hollow, stem of a plant such as bamboo or sugarcane.
2. ***noun*** A plant or grass having such a woody, jointed stem.
3. ***noun*** A stick, especially a walking stick or a stick used for beating someone.
4. ***verb*** To beat someone with a cane or a stick as a punishment. ▸ **caning, caned**

ca•nine (**kay**-nine)
1. ***adjective*** To do with dogs. ▸ ***noun*** **canine**
2. ***noun*** One of the pointed teeth on each side of your upper and lower jaws. There are four canines.

can•ni•bal (**kan**-uh-buhl) ***noun*** Someone who eats human flesh. ▸ ***noun*** **cannibalism**

can•non (**kan**-uhn) ***noun*** A heavy gun that fires large metal balls.

can•not (**kan**-ot *or* ka-**not**) ***verb*** To be unable to do something.

ca•noe (kuh-**noo**) ***noun*** A narrow boat that you move through the water by paddling.

can•o•py (**kan**-uh-pee) ***noun***
1. A piece of cloth or other material suspended as a cover over an entrance, bed, etc.
2. A shelter over something.
3. A cover over an airplane cockpit.
▸ ***noun, plural*** **canopies**

can't (**kant**) ***contraction*** A short form of *can not.*

can•ta•loupe (**kan**-tuh-lope) ***noun*** A melon with a rough skin and sweet, juicy, orange fruit.

can•teen (kan-**teen**) ***noun*** A small portable metal container for holding water or other liquids.

can•ter (**kan**-tur) ***verb*** When a horse **canters,** it runs at a speed between a trot and a gallop. ▸ **cantering, cantered** ▸ ***noun*** **canter**

can•tor (**kan**-tur) ***noun*** A member of the clergy who sings and leads prayers in a synagogue.

can•vas (**kan**-vuhss) ***noun***
1. A type of coarse, strong cloth used for tents, sails, and clothing.
2. A surface for painting made from canvas cloth stretched over a wooden frame. ▸ ***noun, plural*** **canvases**

can•vass (**kan**-vuhss) ***verb*** To ask people for their opinions or votes.
▸ **canvasses, canvassing, canvassed**
▸ ***noun*** **canvasser**

can•yon (**kan**-yuhn) ***noun*** A deep, narrow river valley with steep sides.

cap (**kap**) ***noun***
1. A soft, flat hat with a peak at the front.
2. The top of a bottle, jar, or pen. ▸ ***verb*** **cap**
3. A small amount of explosive on a piece of paper that makes a bang when fired in a toy gun.

ca•pa•ble (**kay**-puh-buhl) ***adjective***
1. If you are **capable** of doing something, you are able to do it. ▸ ***noun*** **capability**
2. Adept and skillful. ▸ ***adverb*** **capably**

ca•pac•i•ty (kuh-**pass**-uh-tee) ***noun***
1. The amount that a container can hold.
2. An ability to do something.
3. A role or job.
▸ ***noun, plural*** **capacities**

cape (**kape**) ***noun***
1. A sleeveless coat that you wear over your shoulders.
2. A part of the coastline that sticks out into the sea.

ca•per (**kay**-pur) ***noun***
1. A trick or prank.
2. (*slang*) A criminal act, as in *a bank caper.*

cap•il•lar•y (**kap**-uh-ler-ee) ***noun*** A small tube in your body that carries blood between the arteries and veins.
▸ ***noun, plural*** **capillaries**

cap•i•tal (kap-**uh**-tuhl) ***noun***
1. A large letter.

2. The city in a country or state where the government is based.
3. An amount of money used to start a business.
4. capital punishment Punishment by death.
▸ ***adjective* capital**

cap•i•tal•ism (**kap**-uh-tuh-*liz*-uhm) ***noun*** A way of organizing a country's economy so that all the land, houses, factories, etc., belong to private individuals rather than the government. ▸ ***noun* capitalist** ▸ ***adjective* capitalist**

Cap•lets (**kap**-luhts) ***noun, plural*** Trademark for medicine tablets shaped like capsules.

cap•puc•ci•no (*kap*-uh-**chee**-noh) ***noun*** Coffee made with frothy milk and often flavored with cinnamon.

ca•pri•cious (kuh-**prish**-uhss) ***adjective*** Someone who is **capricious** is unpredictable and tends to change his or her mind without any obvious reason.

cap•size (**kap**-size) ***verb*** If a boat or ship **capsizes,** it turns over in the water. ▸ **capsizing, capsized**

cap•sule (**kap**-suhl) ***noun***
1. A small container you can swallow that holds one dose of medicine.
2. The part of a rocket or spacecraft in which the crew travels.

cap•tain (**kap**-tuhn) ***noun***
1. The person in charge of a ship or an aircraft.
2. The leader of a sports team.
3. An officer in the armed forces.
▸ ***verb* captain**

cap•tion (**kap**-shuhn) ***noun*** A short title or description printed below a cartoon, drawing, or photograph.

cap•ti•vate (**kap**-ti-vate) ***verb*** To delight someone. ▸ **captivating, captivated**

cap•tive (**kap**-tiv) ***noun*** A person or an animal that has been taken prisoner.
▸ ***noun* captivity** ▸ ***adjective* captive**

cap•ture (**kap**-chur) ***verb***
1. To take a person, an animal, or a place by force.
2. To attract and hold.
▸ ***verb* capturing, captured** ▸ ***noun* capture**

car (**kar**) ***noun***
1. A type of passenger motor vehicle.
2. A vehicle on wheels that carries passengers and freight, such as a unit of a train.
3. The part of an elevator or balloon that carries people or freight.

car•a•mel (**ka**-ruh-muhl *or* **kar**-muhl) ***noun***
1. Burnt sugar.
2. A candy made from burnt sugar, butter, and milk.
3. A light brown color.
▸ ***adjective* caramel**

car•at (**ka**-ruht) ***noun*** A unit for measuring the weight of precious gems and metals. **Carat** sounds like **carrot.**

car•a•van (**ka**-ruh-*van*) ***noun*** A group of people or vehicles traveling together.

car•bo•hy•drate (*kar*-boh-**hye**-drate) ***noun*** One of the substances in foods such as bread, rice, and potatoes that give you energy. Carbohydrates are made up of carbon, hydrogen, and oxygen and are produced by green plants.

car•bon (**kar**-buhn) ***noun***
1. A chemical element found in coal and diamonds and in all plants and animals.
2. carbon di•o•xide (dye-**ok**-side) A gas that is a mixture of carbon and oxygen, with no color or odor. People and animals breathe this gas out, while plants absorb it during the day.
3. carbon mon•ox•ide (muh-**nok**-side) A poisonous gas produced by the engines of vehicles.

car•bu•re•tor (**kar**-buh-ray-tur) ***noun*** The part of an engine where air and gasoline mix.

car•cass (**kar**-kuhss) ***noun*** The body of a dead animal. ▸ ***noun, plural* carcasses**

C

card (**kard**) ***noun***
1. Stiff paper.
2. A folded piece of card sent on birthdays and special occasions.
3. One of a set of rectangular pieces of card, used in games such as poker and bridge.

card•board (**kard**-*bord*) ***noun*** Very thick, stiff paper used for making boxes and other things.

car•di•ac (**kar**-dee-ak) ***adjective*** To do with the heart.

car•di•gan (**kar**-duh-guhn) ***noun*** A knitted sweater that fastens down the front.

car•di•nal (**kar**-duh-nuhl)
1. *noun* A songbird with black coloring around the beak and a crest of feathers on its head. The male is bright red.
2. *noun* One of the officials in the Roman Catholic church, ranking just below the pope.
3. *adjective* Most important, as in *a cardinal rule.*

cardinal number ***noun*** A number, such as one, two, three, four, etc., used to show the amount of something.

care (**kair**)
1. *verb* If you **care** about something, you are very concerned about what happens to it. ▸ **caring, cared** ▸ ***noun*** **care** ▸ ***adjective*** **caring**
2. *noun* Concern or attention.
3. If you **take care of** someone, you look after him or her.
4. *noun* A worry or a fear about something.

ca•reer (kuh-**rihr**) ***noun*** The work or the series of jobs that a person has.

care•free (**kair**-*free*) ***adjective*** Someone who is **carefree** has no worries.

care•ful (**kair**-fuhl) ***adjective*** Someone who is **careful** takes trouble over what he or she is doing and does not take risks. ▸ ***adverb*** **carefully**

care•giv•er (**kair**-*giv*-ur) ***noun*** Someone who takes care of children or very sick people.

care•less (**kair**-luhss) ***adjective*** Someone who is **careless** does not take much trouble over things and often makes mistakes. ▸ ***noun*** **carelessness** ▸ ***adverb*** **carelessly**

ca•ress (kuh-**ress**) ***verb*** To touch gently. ▸ **caresses, caressing, caressed** ▸ ***noun*** **caress**

care•tak•er (**kair**-*tay*-kur) ***noun*** Someone whose job is to look after a building, property, or other people.

car•fare (**kar**-*fair*) ***noun*** The money used to pay for a ride on a bus, subway, etc.

car•go (**kar**-goh) ***noun*** Freight that is carried by a ship or an aircraft. ▸ ***noun, plural*** **cargoes**

Ca•rib•be•an (kuh-**rib**-ee-uhn *or* ka-ri-**bee**-uhn) ***noun*** The sea near the Atlantic Ocean, between North and South America. The Caribbean is dotted with many small islands. ▸ ***adjective*** **Caribbean**

car•i•bou (**ka**-ri-boo) ***noun*** A large North American mammal of the deer family. Caribou are related to reindeer. ▸ ***noun, plural*** **caribou** *or* **caribous**

car•i•ca•ture (**ka**-ri-kuh-chur) ***noun*** An exaggerated drawing of someone.

car•jack (**kar**-*jak*) ***verb*** To steal a car by threat of force against the driver. ▸ **carjacking, carjacked** ▸ ***noun*** **carjacking**

car•na•tion (kar-**nay**-shuhn) ***noun***
1. A fragrant flower, usually pink, white, or red.
2. A pink color.

car•ni•val (**kar**-nuh-vuhl) ***noun*** A public celebration, often with rides, games, and parades.

car•ni•vore (**kar**-nuh-*vor*) ***noun*** An animal that eats meat.

car•niv•o•rous (kar-**niv**-ur-uhss) ***adjective*** Eating meat. Wolves, lions, dogs, and cats are carnivorous animals.

car•ob (**kar**-ruhb) ***noun***
1. An evergreen tree whose beans are used to make a food something like chocolate.
2. A food similar to chocolate.

car•ol (**kar**-ruhl) ***noun*** A joyful song, especially one that people sing at Christmas. ▸ ***verb* carol**

carp (**karp**)
1. ***noun*** A large fish that lives in fresh water and is used as food. ▸ ***noun, plural* carp** *or* **carps**
2. ***verb*** To find fault with someone or something. ▸ **carping, carped**

car•pen•ter (**kahr**-puhn-tur) ***noun*** Someone who works with wood or builds and repairs the wooden parts of buildings. ▸ ***noun* carpentry**

car•pet (**kar**-pit) ***noun***
1. A thick floor covering made of a woven fabric.
2. A thick layer of something, as in *a carpet of flowers.*
▸ ***verb* carpet**

car pool ***noun***
1. A system in which a group of people travel together, often taking turns driving their own cars.
2. A group of people involved in such a system.

car•riage (**ka**-rij) ***noun***
1. A vehicle with wheels, sometimes pulled by horses.
2. Your **carriage** is the way you stand, sit, and walk.

car•rot (**kar**-ruht) ***noun***
1. An orange root vegetable.
2. If someone holds out a **carrot** to you, the person promises you something nice in order to persuade you to do something.
Carrot sounds like **carat.**

car•ry (**ka**-ree) ***verb***
1. To hold on to something and take it somewhere.
2. If a sound **carries,** it can be heard some distance away.
3. To offer something for sale.
4. To continue or to extend.
5. To sing, as in *to carry a tune.*
6. When you **carry on** with something, you continue to do it.
7. If you **carry out** a plan or an idea, you put it into practice.
▸ ***verb* carries, carrying, carried**

car•sick (**kar**-*sik*) ***adjective*** Having a dizzy, nauseated feeling from the motion of a moving vehicle such as a car, train, or bus.

cart (**kart**) ***noun***
1. A small wagon with two wheels, often pulled by an animal.
2. A light wagon that is pushed by someone and used to carry heavy items such as groceries.

car•ti•lage (**kar**-tuh-lij) ***noun*** A strong, elastic tissue that connects bones in human beings and animals. The outside of your ear is also mostly cartilage.

car•tog•ra•phy (kar-**tog**-ruh-fee) ***noun*** The art of making maps. ▸ ***noun* cartographer**

car•ton (**kar**-tuhn) ***noun*** A cardboard or plastic box or container used for holding or shipping goods.

car•toon (kar-**toon**) ***noun***
1. A short, animated film.
2. A funny drawing or series of drawings.
▸ ***noun* cartoonist**

car•tridge (**kar**-trij) ***noun***
1. A container that holds a bullet or pellets and the explosive that fires them.
2. Any small container that holds something, as in *an ink cartridge for a fountain pen.*

cart•wheel (**kart**-*weel*) ***noun*** A circular, sideways handstand.

carve (**karv**) ***verb***
1. To cut slices from a piece of meat.
2. To cut a shape out of a piece of wood, stone, or other substance.
▸ ***verb* carving, carved** ▸ ***noun* carver, *noun* carving**

cas•cade (kass-**kade**)
1. ***noun*** A waterfall.
2. ***noun*** Anything arranged in a downward pattern, such as streamers or flowers in a bouquet.
3. ***verb*** To fall like water over rocks.
▸ **cascading, cascaded**

C

C

case (**kayss**) ***noun***
1. An example of something.
2. A trial in a court of law.
3. A crime that the police are investigating.
4. A box or container that holds something, as in *a camera case.*

cash (**kash**)
1. ***noun*** Money in the form of bills and coins.
2. ***verb*** If someone **cashes** a check, the person exchanges it for money.
3. ***verb*** If you **cash in** on something, you take advantage of it.
▸ ***verb*** **cashes, cashing, cashed**

cash•ew (**kash**-oo) ***noun*** A sweet nut that is shaped like a bean. Cashews grow on evergreen trees in tropical countries.

cash•ier (ka-**shihr**) ***noun*** Someone who takes in or pays out money in a store or bank.

cash machine ***noun*** A machine usually found outside a bank that allows customers to take out or put in money, using a special card; also called an ATM, which stands for *Automated Teller Machine.*

cask (**kask**) ***noun*** A large, wooden barrel, usually used to make and store wine.

cas•ket (**kass**-kit) ***noun***
1. A long, wooden or metal container into which a dead person is placed for burial; a coffin.
2. A jewelry box.

cas•se•role (**kass**-uh-role) ***noun***
1. A dish with a lid that is used for cooking and serving.
2. Food that is cooked in such a dish.

cas•sette (ka-**set** *or* kuh-**set**) ***noun*** A flat, plastic box that contains recording tape, used to record and play sound or sound and pictures.

cast (**kast**)
1. ***noun*** The actors in a play, movie, or television program.
2. ***noun*** A hard plaster covering that supports a broken arm or leg.
3. ***verb*** When people who fish **cast** their fishing lines or nets, they throw them into the water. ▸ ***noun*** **cast**
4. ***verb*** When you **cast** a ballot in an election, you formally include your vote.
5. ***verb*** To form something by pouring soft material into a mold.
▸ ***verb*** **casting, cast**

cast•a•way (**kass**-tuh-*way*) ***noun*** Someone left on a deserted island after a shipwreck.

cast iron ***noun*** A hard and brittle form of iron made by melting iron with other metals. The mixture is poured into a mold to make something.

cas•tle (**kass**-uhl) ***noun***
1. A large building, often surrounded by a wall and a moat. In the Middle Ages, noble families stayed in castles and soldiers defended them from attack. *See also* **portcullis.**
2. A piece used in chess, also known as a rook, that moves in straight lines across the board.

cas•u•al (**kazh**-oo-uhl) ***adjective***
1. Not formal, as in *casual dress.*
2. Not planned, as in *a casual meeting.*
▸ ***adverb*** **casually**

cas•u•al•ty (**kazh**-oo-uhl-tee) ***noun*** Someone who is injured or killed in an accident, a disaster, or a war.
▸ ***noun, plural*** **casualties**

cat (**kat**) ***noun***
1. A small, furry animal with sharp claws and whiskers, often kept as a pet.
2. Any member of the cat family, including lions, tigers, and cheetahs.

cat•a•log *or* **cat•a•logue** (**kat**-uh-log) ***noun***
1. A book or pamphlet listing things you can buy from a company or works of art in an exhibition.
2. A list of all the books in a library.
▸ ***verb*** **catalog** *or* **catalogue**

cat•a•lyst (**kat**-uh-list) ***noun***
1. A substance that causes or speeds up a chemical reaction, without itself changing.

2. A person or thing that causes something to happen.

cat•a•ma•ran (*kat*-uh-muh-**ran**) ***noun*** A boat with two hulls that are joined together.

cat•a•pult (**kat**-uh-*puhlt*) ***noun***
1. A hydraulic device used to launch airplanes from the deck of a ship.
2. A weapon, similar to a large slingshot, used in the past for firing rocks over castle walls.
▸ ***verb*** **catapult**

cat•a•ract (**kat**-uh-*rakt*) ***noun***
1. A cloudy film that sometimes grows on the lens of a person's eye, causing blindness or partial blindness.
2. A steep waterfall.

ca•tas•tro•phe (kuh-**tass**-truh-fee) ***noun*** A terrible and sudden disaster. ▸ ***adjective*** **catastrophic** (kat-uh-**strof**-ik)

cat•bird (**kat**-*burd*) ***noun*** A gray North American songbird with a call that sounds like a cat meowing.

catch (**kach**)
1. ***verb*** To grab hold of something moving through the air, as in *to catch a ball.* ▸ ***noun*** **catch**
2. ***verb*** To get something or someone you are chasing.
3. ***verb*** If you **catch** a bus or train, you get on it.
4. ***verb*** If you **catch** someone doing something wrong, you see him or her doing it.
5. ***noun*** A fastening on a door, box, etc.
6. ***noun*** A game in which two or more people throw a ball to one another.
7. ***verb*** To attend or to watch.
8. ***verb*** If something **catches on,** it becomes very popular.
▸ ***noun, plural*** **catches** ▸ ***verb*** **catches, catching, caught** (**kawt**)

catch•er (**ka**-chur) ***noun*** Someone who catches; the baseball player behind home plate who catches the balls thrown by the pitcher.

cat•e•gor•i•cal (*kat*-uh-**gor**-i-kuhl) ***adjective*** Clear and plain. ▸ ***adverb*** **categorically**

cat•e•go•ry (**kat**-uh-*gor*-ee) ***noun*** A class or group of things that has something in common. ▸ ***noun, plural*** **categories**

ca•ter (**kay**-tur) ***verb***
1. To provide food for a lot of people, as at a large party. ▸ ***noun*** **caterer,** ***noun*** **catering**
2. To provide people with the things they need.
▸ ***verb*** **catering, catered**

cat•er•pil•lar (**kat**-ur-pil-ur) ***noun*** A larva that changes into a butterfly or moth. It looks like a worm and is sometimes hairy.

cat•fish (**kat**-*fish*) ***noun*** A freshwater fish with long tendrils around its mouth that look like cat whiskers.

ca•the•dral (kuh-**thee**-druhl) ***noun*** A large and important church with a bishop or an archbishop as its main priest.

cath•ode-ray tube (**kath**-ode) ***noun*** A glass tube with no air inside it, through which rays travel to produce an image on a screen.

Cath•o•lic (**kath**-uh-lik) ***noun*** A member of the Roman Catholic church. ▸ ***noun*** **Catholicism** ▸ ***adjective*** **Catholic**

CAT scan (**kat**) ***noun*** An X-ray image made by computer from a series of cross-sectional images, resulting in a single three-dimensional image. CAT is an acronym for *Computerized Axial Tomography.*

cat•sup (**kat**-suhp *or* **kech**-uhp) *See* **ketchup.**

cat•tail (**kat**-*tayl*) ***noun*** A tall, thin plant with long, brown, furry pods at the top and narrow leaves. Cattails grow in large groups in marshes.

cat•tle (**kat**-uhl) ***noun, plural*** Cows, bulls, and steers that are raised for food or for their hides.

C

Cau•ca•sian (kaw-**kay**-zhuhn) ***noun*** A member of a race of peoples with light or tan skin. It refers to many people from Europe, America, northern Africa, India, and other regions. ▸ ***adjective*** **Caucasian**

caul•dron (**kawl**-druhn) ***noun*** A large, rounded cooking pot.

cau•li•flow•er (**kaw**-luh-*flou*-ur) ***noun*** A vegetable with a large, rounded, white head surrounded by leaves.

caulk (**kawk**)
1. ***noun*** A waterproof paste that is applied to edges that need to be watertight.
2. ***verb*** To apply a waterproof material to something in order to prevent water from leaking in or out. ▸ **caulking, caulked**

cause (**kawz**)
1. ***verb*** To make something happen. ▸ **causing, caused**
2. ***noun*** The reason that something happens.
3. ***noun*** An aim or a principle for which people fight, raise money, etc.

cause•way (**kawz**-*way*) ***noun*** A raised road built across water or low ground.

cau•tion (**kaw**-shun)
1. ***noun*** Carefulness or watchfulness.
2. ***verb*** To warn about something or someone. ▸ **cautioning, cautioned**

cau•tious (**kaw**-shuhss) ***adjective*** If you are **cautious,** you try hard to avoid mistakes or danger. ▸ ***noun*** **caution** ▸ ***adverb*** **cautiously**

cav•al•ry (**kav**-uhl-ree) ***noun***
1. Soldiers who fight on horseback.
2. Soldiers who fight in armored vehicles. ▸ ***noun, plural*** **cavalries**

cave (**kayv**)
1. ***noun*** A large hole underground or in the side of a hill or cliff.
2. ***verb*** If something **caves in,** it collapses. ▸ **caving, caved**

cave-in ***noun*** The collapse of a structure such as a mine or tunnel.

cave•man (**kayv**-*man*) ***noun*** A man who lived in a cave in prehistoric times. ▸ ***noun, plural*** **cavemen**

cave painting ***noun*** A picture painted by a cave dweller on a cave wall in prehistoric times.

cav•ern (**kav**-ern) ***noun*** A large cave. ▸ ***adjective*** **cavernous**

cave•wom•an (**kayv**-*wum*-uhn) ***noun*** A woman who lived in a cave in prehistoric times. ▸ ***noun, plural*** **cavewomen**

cav•i•ty (**kav**-uh-tee) ***noun*** A hole or hollow space in something solid, such as a tooth. ▸ ***noun, plural*** **cavities**

CB (**see bee**) ***noun*** A radio system that people use to talk to each other over short distances. The initials stand for *citizens band.*

CD (**see dee**) Short for *compact disk.*

CD-ROM (**see dee rom**) ***noun*** A compact disk that produces text and pictures that can be read by a computer. The initials stand for *compact disk read-only memory.*

cease (**seess**) ***verb*** To stop. ▸ **ceasing, ceased**

cease-fire ***noun*** A period during a war when both sides agree to stop fighting.

ce•dar (**see**-dur) ***noun*** A type of evergreen tree with leaves shaped like needles and red bark, often used for making closet or trunk linings. ▸ ***adjective*** **cedar**

ceil•ing (**see**-ling) ***noun***
1. The upper surface inside a room.
2. The upper limit that something can reach, as in *a price ceiling.*

cel•e•brate (**sel**-uh-brate) ***verb*** To do something enjoyable on a special occasion, such as having a party. ▸ **celebrating, celebrated** ▸ ***adjective*** **celebratory** (**sel**-uh-bra-*tor*-ee)

cel•e•bra•tion (sel-uh-**bray**-shuhn) ***noun*** A joyous ceremony or gathering, usually to mark a major event.

ce•leb•ri•ty (suh-**leb**-ruh-tee) ***noun*** A famous person, especially an entertainer

C

or a movie star. ▸ ***noun, plural*** **celebrities**

cel•e•ry (**sel**-uh-ree) ***noun*** A vegetable with white or green crisp stalks, often eaten raw in salads.

ce•les•tial (suh-**less**-chuhl) ***adjective*** To do with the sky or the heavens.
▸ ***adverb*** **celestially**

cell (**sel**) ***noun***
1. A room in a prison or a police station for locking up people.
2. A basic, microscopic part of an animal or a plant.
Cell sounds like **sell.**

cel•lar (**sel**-ur) ***noun*** A room below ground level in a house, often used for storage.

cel•lo (**chel**-oh) ***noun*** A large stringed instrument that rests on the floor. It is played with a bow like a violin but is held between the knees. The cello has a deep, resonant sound.

cel•lo•phane (**sel**-uh-fayn) ***noun*** Clear plastic material made from cellulose and used to wrap food and make clear tape.

cell phone ***noun*** A cellular telephone.

cel•lu•lar (**sel**-yuh-lur) ***adjective*** Made of or to do with cells, as in *cellular tissue.*

cellular telephone ***noun*** A portable telephone that uses signals sent over radio channels.

cel•lu•loid (**sel**-yuh-loid) ***noun***
1. A substance similar to plastic once used to make motion picture film.
2. Motion picture film.
▸ ***adjective*** **celluloid**

cel•lu•lose (**sel**-yuh-lohss) ***noun*** The substance from which the cell walls of plants are made. Cellulose is used to make paper, cloth, and plastics.

Cel•si•us (**sel**-see-uhss) ***adjective*** A measurement of temperature using a scale on which water boils at 100 degrees and freezes at 0 degrees. It is also called **centigrade.**

ce•ment (suh-**ment**) ***noun***
1. A gray powder made from crushed limestone that is used in building and that becomes hard when you mix it with water and let it dry. Cement is used to make concrete.
2. A substance that joins two things together.
▸ ***verb*** **cement**

cem•e•ter•y (**sem**-uh-*ter*-ee) ***noun*** A place where dead people are buried.
▸ ***noun, plural*** **cemeteries**

cen•sor (**sen**-sur)
1. ***verb*** To remove parts of a book, film, play, etc., thought to be harmful or offensive to the public. ▸ **censoring, censored** ▸ ***noun*** **censorship**
2. ***noun*** Someone whose job is to examine books, films, plays, etc., for objectionable parts.

cen•sus (**sen**-suhss) ***noun*** An official count of all the people living in a country or district.

cent (**sent**) ***noun*** A unit of money in the United States, Canada, Australia, and New Zealand. One hundred cents are equal to one dollar. **Cent** sounds like **scent** and **sent.**

cen•taur (**sen**-tor) ***noun*** A creature found in Greek and Roman myths that has the body and legs of a horse but the chest, arms, and head of a man.

cen•ten•ar•y (sen-**ten**-uh-ree) ***noun*** The 100th anniversary of something.
▸ ***noun, plural*** **centenaries** ▸ ***adjective*** **centenary**

cen•ten•ni•al (sen-**ten**-ee-uhl) ***noun*** The 100th-year celebration of an event.
▸ ***adjective*** **centennial**

cen•ter (**sen**-tur)
1. ***noun*** The middle of something.
2. ***noun*** A place where people go to do a particular activity, as in *an arts center.*
3. ***verb*** To concentrate on something.
▸ **centering, centered**
4. center of gravity ***noun*** The point on an object at which it can balance.

cen•ti•grade (**sen**-tuh-grayd) ***adjective*** *See* **Celsius.**

C

cen•ti•me•ter (**sent**-uh-*mee*-tur) ***noun*** A unit of length in the metric system. A centimeter is equal to 1/100 of a meter. A pencil is approximately one centimeter wide.

cen•ti•pede (**sen**-ti-peed) ***noun*** A small creature with a very long body and lots of legs.

cen•tral (**sen**-truhl)
1. ***adjective*** In the middle. ▸ ***adverb*** **centrally**
2. ***adjective*** Most important, as in *the central problem.*
3. central heating ***noun*** A system for heating a building in which water or air is heated in one place and then carried in pipes all over the building.

cen•tri•fu•gal (sen-**trif**-yuh-guhl) ***adjective*** To do with a physical force that causes a body rotating around a center to move away from the center.

cen•trip•e•tal (sen-**trip**-uh-tuhl) ***adjective*** To do with the physical force that pulls a body toward a center it is rotating around.

cen•tu•ri•on (sen-**tur**-ee-uhn) ***noun*** An officer in the ancient Roman army who was in command of 100 soldiers.

cen•tu•ry (**sen**-chuh-ree) ***noun*** A period of 100 years. ▸ ***noun, plural*** **centuries**

ce•ram•ics (suh-**ram**-iks)
1. ***noun*** The craft of making objects out of clay.
2. ***noun, plural*** Objects made of clay.
▸ ***adjective*** **ceramic**

ce•re•al (**sihr**-ee-uhl) ***noun***
1. A grain crop grown for food, such as wheat, corn, rice, oats, and barley.
2. A breakfast food usually made from grain and eaten with milk.
Cereal sounds like **serial.**

cer•e•mo•ny (**ser**-uh-*moh*-nee) ***noun*** Formal actions, words, and often music performed to mark an important occasion, as in *a wedding ceremony.*
▸ ***noun, plural*** **ceremonies** ▸ ***adjective*** **ceremonial** ▸ ***adverb*** **ceremonially**

cer•tain (**sur**-tuhn) ***adjective***
1. If you are **certain** about something, you are sure of it. ▸ ***noun*** **certainty** ▸ ***adverb*** **certainly**
2. Particular.

cer•tif•i•cate (sur-**tif**-uh-kit) ***noun*** A piece of paper that officially states that something is a fact.

chad (**chad**) ***noun*** A small piece of paper made by punching a hole in a card, ballot, or paper.

chafe (**chayf**) ***verb***
1. To make something raw or sore by rubbing.
2. To annoy.
▸ ***verb*** **chafing, chafed**

chain (**chayn**) ***noun***
1. A series of metal rings, called links, joined together.
2. A series of connected things, as in *a chain of events.*
3. chain store One of a group of stores in different towns that is owned by the same company and sells similar products.
▸ ***verb*** **chain**

chair (**chair**)
1. ***noun*** A piece of furniture that you sit on, with a seat, legs, and a back.
2. ***noun*** A chairman or a chairwoman.
3. ***verb*** To take charge of a meeting.
▸ **chairing, chaired**

chair•lift (**chair**-*lift*) ***noun*** A line of chairs attached to a moving cable, used for carrying people up mountains, usually to ski.

chair•man (**chair**-*man*) ***noun*** Someone, especially a man, who is in charge of a committee, company, or department in a school. ▸ ***noun, plural*** **chairmen**

chair•per•son (**chair**-*pur*-suhn) ***noun*** A chairman or a chairwoman.

chair•woman (**chair**-*wum*-uhn) ***noun*** A woman who is in charge of a committee, company, or department in a school. ▸ ***noun, plural*** **chairwomen**

cha•let (**shal**-ay *or* shal-**ay**) ***noun*** A small, wooden house with a sloping roof.

chalk (**chawk**) ***noun***
1. A soft, white rock.
2. A stick of this material, used for writing on blackboards. ▸ ***verb*** **chalk**

chalk•board (**chawk**-*bord*) ***noun*** A hard, smooth, slate surface on which chalk is used; a blackboard.

chal•lenge (**chal**-uhnj)
1. ***noun*** Something difficult that requires extra work or effort to do. ▸ ***adjective*** **challenging**
2. ***verb*** If you **challenge** someone, you invite the person to fight or to try to do something.
3. ***verb*** If you **challenge** something, you question whether it is right or not.
▸ ***noun*** **challenge**
▸ ***verb*** **challenging, challenged**

cham•ber (**chaym**-bur) ***noun***
1. A large room.
2. An enclosed space in a machine or an animal's body, as in *the four chambers of the human heart.*
3. chamber music Classical music for a small number of instruments.

cha•me•le•on (kuh-**mee**-lee-uhn) ***noun*** A lizard that can change color, sometimes matching its surroundings.

cham•pagne (sham-**payn**) ***noun*** A fine white wine that has small bubbles.

cham•pi•on (**cham**-pee-uhn)
1. ***noun*** The winner of a competition or a tournament. ▸ ***noun*** **championship**
2. ***verb*** If someone **champions** a cause, he or she supports it. ▸ **championing, championed** ▸ ***noun*** **champion**

cham•pi•on•ship (**cham**-pee-uhn-*ship*) ***noun*** A contest or final game of a series that determines which team or player will be the overall winner.

chance (**chanss**) ***noun***
1. The possibility of something happening.
2. An opportunity to do something.
3. If you **take a chance,** you try something even though it is risky.
4. If something happens **by chance,** it happens accidentally.

chan•cel•lor (**chan**-suh-lur) ***noun*** A title for the leader of a country or a university.

chan•de•lier (*shan*-duh-**lihr**) ***noun*** A light fixture that hangs from the ceiling and is usually lit by many small lights.

change (**chaynj**)
1. ***verb*** To become different or to make different. ▸ ***noun*** **change**
2. ***noun*** If you pay more money than something costs, the money you get back is called **change**.
3. ***noun*** Coins rather than bills.
4. ***verb*** To exchange.
▸ ***verb*** **changing, changed**

chan•nel (**chan**-uhl) ***noun***
1. A narrow stretch of water between two areas of land.
2. A television or radio station.

channel surf ***verb*** To change television channels rapidly to find something of interest. ▸ **channel surfing, channel surfed**

chant (**chant**) ***verb*** To say or sing a phrase over and over again. ▸ **chanting, chanted** ▸ ***noun*** **chant**

Cha•nu•kah (**hah**-nuh-kuh) *See* **Hanukkah.**

cha•os (**kay**-oss) ***noun*** Total confusion.
▸ ***adjective*** **chaotic** (kay-**ot**-ik)
▸ ***adverb*** **chaotically**

chap (**chap**)
1. ***verb*** To become rough or dry to the point of cracking, especially skin.
▸ **chapping, chapped** ▸ ***adjective*** **chapped**
2. ***noun*** A man or boy; a fellow.

chap•el (**chap**-uhl) ***noun***
1. A small church.
2. A small, separate section of a large church or synagogue.
3. A place in a college, prison, etc., where religious services are held.

chap•e•ron *or* **chap•e•rone** (**shap**-uh-*rohn*) ***noun*** An adult who protects the safety of young people at an event such as a dance or a class trip and who makes sure they behave well. ▸ ***verb*** **chaperon, chaperone**

chap•lain (**chap**-lin) ***noun*** A priest, minister, or rabbi who works in the military, or in a school or prison. A chaplain leads religious services and counsels people.

C

chaps (**chaps**) ***noun, plural*** Leather leggings that fit over jeans or other pants and protect the legs of people riding on horseback.

chap•ter (**chap**-tur) ***noun***
1. One of the parts into which a book is divided.
2. A branch of an organization.

char•ac•ter (**ka**-rik-tur) ***noun***
1. Your **character** is what sort of person you are.
2. One of the people in a story, book, play, movie, or television program.
3. A letter, figure, or other mark used in printing. All the letters of the alphabet are characters.

char•ac•ter•is•tic (*ka*-rik-tuh-**riss**-tik)
1. ***noun*** A typical quality or feature.
2. ***adjective*** Typical.
▸ ***adverb*** **characteristically**

char•ac•ter•ize (**ka**-rik-tuh-rize) ***verb***
1. To describe the individual qualities of something or someone.
2. To mark or identify the important qualities of someone or something.
▸ ***verb*** **characterizing, characterized**

char•coal (**char**-kole) ***noun*** A form of carbon made from incompletely burned wood. Charcoal is used in drawing pencils and as barbecue fuel.

charge (**charj**)
1. ***verb*** To ask someone to pay a particular price for something.
2. ***noun*** The cost or price.
3. ***verb*** To rush at in order to attack.
4. ***noun*** An attack.
5. ***verb*** To put off paying for something by using a credit card or signing an agreement.
6. ***verb*** To accuse.
7. ***noun*** An accusation or statement of blame, as in *a charge of murder.*
8. ***verb*** When you **charge** a battery, you pass an electric current through it so that it stores electricity.
9. If someone is **in charge** of something, he or she has to manage it or take control of it.
▸ ***verb*** **charging, charged**

char•i•ot (**cha**-ree-uht) ***noun*** A small vehicle pulled by a horse, used in ancient times in battles or for racing.

cha•ris•ma (kuh-**riz**-muh) ***noun*** A powerful personal appeal that attracts a great number of people, as in *the charisma of a popular politician.*
▸ ***adjective*** **charismatic** (ka-riz-**mat**-ik)

char•i•ty (**cha**-ruh-tee) ***noun***
1. An organization that raises money to help people in need.
2. Money or other help that is given to people in need.
▸ ***noun, plural*** **charities** ▸ ***adjective*** **charitable**

charm (**charm**)
1. ***noun*** If someone has **charm,** he or she behaves in a pleasing and attractive way. ▸ ***noun*** **charmer**
2. ***verb*** To please someone and make the person like you. ▸ **charming, charmed**
3. ***noun*** A small object that some people believe will bring them good luck.

charm•ing (**charm**-ing) ***adjective*** Attractive, full of charm, or delightful.

chart (**chart**)
1. ***noun*** A drawing that shows information in the form of a table, graph, or picture.
2. ***noun*** A map of the stars or the oceans.
3. ***verb*** To show information in the form of a chart. ▸ **charting, charted**

char•ter (**char**-tur)
1. ***noun*** A formal document that states the rights or duties of a group of people.
2. ***verb*** To hire a bus, plane, etc., for private use. ▸ **chartering, chartered**

chase (**chayss**) ***verb*** To run after someone in order to catch the person or make him or her go away. ▸ **chasing, chased** ▸ ***noun*** **chase**

chasm (**kaz**-uhm) ***noun*** A deep crack in the surface of the earth.

chas•sis (**chass**-ee *or* **shass**-ee) ***noun*** The frame on which the body of a vehicle is built. ▸ ***noun, plural*** **chassis**

C

chat (**chat**) ***verb***
1. To talk in a friendly and informal way.
2. To communicate using a chat room.
▸ **chatting, chatted** ▸ ***noun* chat**

châ•teau (sha-**toh**)
noun A castle or large country house in France. ▸ ***noun, plural* châteaux** (sha-**toh** *or* sha-**tohz**)

chat room ***noun*** An Internet or Web site where people can type messages back and forth quickly.

chat•ter (**chat**-ur) ***verb***
1. To talk about unimportant things.
▸ ***noun* chatter**
2. When your teeth **chatter,** they knock together because you are cold.
▸ ***verb* chattering, chattered**

chauf•feur (**shoh**-fur) ***noun*** Someone whose job is to drive a car for somebody else. ▸ ***verb* chauffeur**

chau•vin•ist (**shoh**-vuh-nist) ***noun*** Someone who is overly proud of his or her nationality, gender, ethnic background, etc. ▸ ***noun* chauvinism** ▸ ***adjective* chauvinistic**

cheap (**cheep**) ***adjective***
1. Not costing or worth very much.
▸ ***noun* cheapness** ▸ ***adverb* cheaply**
2. Unkind and mean.
▸ ***adjective* cheaper, cheapest**

cheat (**cheet**)
1. ***verb*** To act dishonestly in order to win a game or get what you want.
▸ **cheating, cheated**
2. ***noun*** A person who acts dishonestly.

check (**chek**)
1. ***verb*** To look at something in order to make sure that it is all right.
2. ***verb*** To stop something from moving or growing.
3. ***noun*** A pattern of squares of different colors. ▸ ***adjective* checked**
4. ***noun*** A printed piece of paper on which someone writes to tell the bank to pay money from his or her account.
5. ***noun*** A mark (✓) used to show that a thing has been looked at or verified.
▸ ***verb* check**
6. ***verb*** If you **check in,** you register for a room at a motel or hotel.
7. ***verb*** If you **check out,** you pay your bill at a motel or hotel and leave.
8. ***verb*** If you **check** your coat in a public place, you leave it with someone whose job is to guard it.
▸ ***verb* checking, checked**

check•ers (**chek**-urz) ***noun*** A game for two people with 12 round pieces each, played on a board marked with squares of alternating colors.

check•out (**chek**-*out*) ***noun*** The place in a supermarket where you pay for your purchases.

check•up (**chek**-*uhp*) ***noun*** A medical examination to make sure that there is nothing wrong with you.

cheek (**cheek**) ***noun***
1. Either side of your face below your eyes.
2. Rude and disrespectful behavior or speech. ▸ ***adjective* cheeky** ▸ ***adverb* cheekily**

cheer (**chihr**)
1. ***verb*** To shout encouragement or approval.
2. ***noun*** A shout of encouragement.
3. ***verb*** If you **cheer up,** you begin to feel better.
4. ***noun*** Happiness.
5. If you **are of good cheer,** you are happy.
▸ ***verb* cheering, cheered**

cheer•ful (**chihr**-fuhl) ***adjective*** Happy and lively. ▸ ***noun* cheerfulness** ▸ ***adverb* cheerfully**

cheese (**cheez**) ***noun*** A food made from the solid parts of milk after the milk has turned sour.

cheese•bur•ger (**cheez**-*bur*-gur) ***noun*** A hamburger with cheese melted on top of the meat.

chee•tah (**chee**-tuh) ***noun*** A wild cat with a spotted coat that is found in Africa and southern Asia. Cheetahs can run faster than any other land animal in short bursts.

chef (**shef**) ***noun*** The chief cook in a restaurant.

C

chem•i•cal (**kem**-uh-kuhl)
1. ***noun*** A substance used in chemistry, as in *dangerous chemicals.*
2. ***adjective*** To do with or made by chemistry, as in *a chemical reaction.*
▸ ***adverb*** **chemically**

chem•ist (**kem**-ist) ***noun*** A person trained in chemistry.

chem•is•try (**kem**-is-tree) ***noun*** The scientific study of substances, what they are composed of, and how they react with each other.

che•mo•ther•a•py (*kee*-moh-**ther**-uh-pee) ***noun*** The use of chemicals to kill diseased cells in cancer patients. ▸ ***noun*** **chemotherapist**

cher•ish (**cher**-ish) ***verb*** To care for someone or something in a kind and loving way. ▸ **cherishes, cherishing, cherished**

Cher•o•kee (**cher**-uh-kee) ***noun*** A member of an American Indian nation that lives primarily in Oklahoma and North Carolina.

cher•ry (**cher**-ee) ***noun*** A small, sweet, red fruit with a pit inside. ▸ ***noun, plural*** **cherries**

chess (**chess**) ***noun*** A game for two people with 16 pieces each, played on a board marked with squares of alternating colors.

chest (**chest**) ***noun***
1. The front part of your body between your neck and waist.
2. A large, strong box.

chest•nut (**chess**-*nuht*) ***noun***
1. A large, reddish brown nut that grows in a prickly case.
2. A tree that produces chestnuts.
3. A reddish brown color.
▸ ***adjective*** **chestnut**

chest of drawers ***noun*** A piece of furniture with drawers, usually used for storing clothes. ▸ ***noun, plural*** **chests of drawers**

chew (**choo**) ***verb*** To grind food between your teeth. ▸ **chewing, chewed**

chewing gum ***noun*** A sweet, flavored substance that you chew for a long time but do not swallow.

Chey•enne (shye-**en**) ***noun*** A member of an American Indian nation that lives primarily in Montana and Oklahoma.

Chi•ca•na (chi-**kah**-nuh) ***noun***
1. An American girl or woman born of Mexican parents; a Mexican American.
2. A Mexican woman living and working in the United States.
▸ ***noun, plural*** **Chicanas**

Chi•ca•no (chi-**kah**-noh) ***noun***
1. An American boy or man born of Mexican parents; a Mexican American.
2. A Mexican man living and working in the United States.
▸ ***noun, plural*** **Chicanos**

chick (**chik**) ***noun*** A very young bird, especially a very young chicken, or a small lobster.

chick•a•dee (**chik**-uh-dee) ***noun*** One of a group of small birds with a black head and throat, gray wings, and white feathers on its underside. The call of the chickadee sounds like its name.

chick•en (**chik**-uhn) ***noun***
1. A common type of fowl that is raised on farms for its meat and eggs.
2. The meat from this bird, used as food, as in *roast chicken.*
3. (*slang*) Someone who is too scared to do something.

chicken pox (**poks**) ***noun*** A common, contagious disease, especially among children, that causes red, itchy spots on the skin.

chick•pea (**chick**-*pea*) ***noun*** The edible seed of a plant originally grown in Asia. Chickpeas resemble peas in size and shape.

chide (**chide**) ***verb*** To scold or to find fault with someone. ▸ **chiding, chided**

chief (**cheef**)
1. ***noun*** The leader of a group of people, as in *a chief of police.*
2. ***adjective*** Main, or most important.
▸ ***adverb*** **chiefly**

chief•tain (**cheef**-tuhn) ***noun*** The chief or leader of a tribe, clan, or community.

chig•ger (**chig**-ur) ***noun*** A tiny insect that burrows under the skin, causing a rash and severe itching.

child (**childe**) ***noun***
1. A young boy or girl.
2. A son or daughter.
▸ ***noun, plural*** **children** (**chil**-drin)

child•birth (**childe**-*burth*) ***noun*** The act or process of giving birth to a baby.

child•hood (**childe**-hud) ***noun*** The time when you are a child.

child•ish (**chile**-dish) ***adjective*** Immature and silly, as in *childish behavior.*
▸ ***noun*** **childishness** ▸ ***adverb*** **childishly**

chil•i (**chil**-ee) ***noun***
1. Any of several types of peppers with red skin used to make foods spicy.
2. A spicy food made with chilies, and often with beans and meat.
▸ ***noun, plural*** **chilies**

chill (**chil**)
1. ***verb*** To make something cold.
▸ **chilling, chilled**
2. ***noun*** A feeling of slight coldness.
▸ ***adjective*** **chilly**
3. ***noun*** A shiver you feel in your body, often related to fear. ▸ ***adjective*** **chilling**
4. ***adjective*** Cool or cold. ▸ **chillier, chilliest**

chime (**chime**) ***verb*** When a bell or clock **chimes,** it makes a ringing sound.
▸ **chiming, chimed** ▸ ***noun*** **chime**

chim•ney (**chim**-nee) ***noun*** An upright pipe or hollow structure that carries smoke away from a fire.

chim•pan•zee (*chim*-pan-**zee** *or* chim-**pan**-zee) ***noun*** A small ape with dark fur that comes from Africa.

chin (**chin**) ***noun*** The part of your face below your mouth.

chi•na (**chye**-nuh) ***noun***
1. Very thin, delicate pottery.
2. Cups, plates, and dishes made of china.

chin•chil•la (chin-**chil**-uh) ***noun*** A small South American rodent with silvery-gray fur.

chink (**chingk**) ***noun*** A narrow opening.

chip (**chip**)
1. ***noun*** A small piece of something that is cut or broken off.
2. ***verb*** To break a small piece off something. ▸ ***noun*** **chip**
3. If you have a **chip on your shoulder,** you feel angry because you think you have been treated unfairly.
4. ***verb*** If you **chip in** with others to buy something, you give some money for it.
5. ***noun*** A very thin slice of potato cooked in oil.
6. ***noun*** A tiny piece of silicon with electronic circuits printed on it, used in computers and electronic equipment.
▸ ***verb*** **chipping, chipped**

chip•munk (**chip**-*muhnk*) ***noun*** A small animal related to the squirrel that is found in North America. Chipmunks have brown fur and dark stripes on their backs and tails.

Chip•pe•wa (**chip**-uh-wah) *See* **Ojibwa.**

chi•ro•prac•tor (**kye**-roh-prak-tur) ***noun*** A person who treats back pain and other illnesses by adjusting the spine.

chirp (**churp**)
1. ***noun*** The twittering sound a bird makes; the high sound an insect makes.
2. ***verb*** To make such a sound.
▸ **chirping, chirped**

chis•el (**chiz**-uhl)
1. ***noun*** A tool with a flat, sharp end used to cut or shape wood, stone, or metal.
2. ***verb*** To chip away at something and form it into a desired shape. ▸ **chiseling, chiseled**

chiv•al•ry (**shiv**-uhl-ree) ***noun***
1. Very polite and helpful behavior, especially by a man toward a woman.
2. A code of noble and polite behavior that was expected of a medieval knight.
▸ ***adjective*** **chivalrous**

C

C

chlo•rine (**klor**-een) ***noun*** A gas with a strong smell that is added to water to kill harmful germs. ▸ ***verb* chlorinate** (**klor**-i-*nate*)

chlo•ro•phyll (**klor**-uh-fil) ***noun*** The green substance in plants that uses light to manufacture food from carbon dioxide and water.

choc•o•late (**chok**-uh-lit *or* **chok**-lit) ***noun*** A food, especially a candy, made from beans that grow on the tropical cacao tree. ▸ ***adjective* chocolate, *adjective* chocolaty**

Choc•taw (**chok**-taw) ***noun*** A member of an American Indian nation that lives primarily in Oklahoma, Mississippi, and Louisiana. ▸ ***noun, plural* Choctaw** *or* **Choctaws**

choice (**choiss**)
1. ***noun*** The thing or person that has been selected.
2. ***noun*** All the things that you can choose from.
3. ***noun*** The chance to choose.
4. ***adjective*** Of very good quality, as in *choice fruits and vegetables.*

choir (**kwire**) ***noun*** A group of people who sing together.

choke (**chohk**) ***verb***
1. To struggle to breathe because something is blocking your breathing passages.
2. To cause someone to stop breathing by squeezing his or her neck.
3. To block something.
4. To hold back.

▸ ***verb* choking, choked**

chol•e•ra (**kol**-ur-uh) ***noun*** A dangerous disease that causes severe sickness and diarrhea.

cho•les•ter•ol (kuh-**less**-tuh-*rol*) ***noun*** A fatty substance that humans and animals need to digest food and produce certain vitamins and hormones. Too much cholesterol in the blood can increase the possibility of heart disease.

choose (**chooz**) ***verb***
1. To pick out one person or thing from several.
2. If you **choose** to do something, you decide to do it.

▸ ***verb* choosing, chose** (**chohz**), **chosen** (**chohz**-in)

chop (**chop**)
1. ***verb*** To cut something with a knife or an axe. ▸ **chopping, chopped** ▸ ***noun* chop**
2. ***noun*** A small piece of lamb, veal, or pork with a rib bone attached.

chop•py (**chop**-ee) ***adjective***
1. When the sea is **choppy,** it is quite rough.
2. A **choppy** sentence is expressed in a jerky, unclear style.

▸ ***adjective* choppier, choppiest**

chop•sticks (**chop**-*stiks*) ***noun, plural*** Narrow sticks for eating food, used primarily by people in Asian countries.

cho•ral (**kor**-uhl) ***adjective*** Sung by a choir, as in *choral music.* **Choral** sounds like **coral.**

chord (**kord**) ***noun***
1. A combination of musical notes played at the same time.
2. A straight line that joins two points on a curve.

Chord sounds like **cord.**

chore (**chor**) ***noun*** A job that has to be done regularly, such as washing dishes or cleaning.

cho•re•og•ra•pher (*kor*-ee-**og**-ruh-fur) ***noun*** Someone who arranges dance steps and movements for a ballet or show. ▸ ***noun* choreography** ▸ ***verb* choreograph** (**kor**-ee-uh-*graph*)

cho•rus (**kor**-uhss) ***noun***
1. The part of a song that is repeated after each verse.
2. A large group of people who sing or speak together. ▸ ***noun, plural* choruses**

chow•der (**chou**-dur) ***noun*** A thick soup made with clams or fish and vegetables.

Christ (**kriste**) ***noun*** Jesus, the figure that Christians worship as the son of God.

chris•ten•ing (**kriss**-uhn-ing) ***noun*** A ceremony in which a baby is given a name and accepted into the Christian religion. ▸ ***verb*** **christen**

Chris•ti•an•i•ty (*kriss*-chee-**an**-uh-tee) ***noun*** The religion based on the life and teachings of Jesus. Christians believe that Jesus is the son of God and that he died so that, after death, their souls would go to heaven. ▸ ***noun*** **Christian** ▸ ***adjective*** **Christian**

Christ•mas (**kriss**-muhss) ***noun*** The Christian festival on December 25 that celebrates the birth of Jesus. ▸ ***noun, plural*** **Christmases**

chro•ma•to•gra•phy (*kroh*-muh-**tog**-ruh-fee) ***noun*** The process of separating parts of a mixture by letting it travel through a material that absorbs each part at a different rate.

chro•mo•some (**kroh**-muh-*sohm*) ***noun*** The part of a cell that carries the genes that give living things their special characteristics. Chromosomes determine your hair color, eye color, size, etc., which you inherit from your parents.

chron•ic (**kron**-ik) ***adjective*** If something is **chronic,** it does not get better for a long time. ▸ ***adverb*** **chronically**

chron•i•cle (**kron**-uh-kuhl) ***verb*** To record historical events in a careful, detailed way. ▸ **chronicling, chronicled** ▸ ***noun*** **chronicle**

chron•o•log•i•cal (*kron*-uh-**loj**-uh-kuhl) ***adjective*** Arranged in the order in which events happened. ▸ ***noun*** **chronology** (kruh-**nol**-uh-jee) ▸ ***adverb*** **chronologically**

chrys•a•lis (**kriss**-uh-liss) ***noun*** A butterfly at the stage of development between a caterpillar and an adult. A chrysalis is covered by a hard outer shell. ▸ ***noun, plural*** **chrysalises**

chry•san•the•mum (kruh-**san**-thuh-muhm) ***noun*** A flower of various shapes and colors that has many usually small petals.

chub•by (**chuhb**-ee) ***adjective*** Slightly fat or plump. ▸ **chubbier, chubbiest**

chuck•le (**chuh**-kuhl) ***verb*** To laugh quietly. ▸ **chuckling, chuckled** ▸ ***noun*** **chuckle**

chuck•wag•on (**chuhk**-*wag*-uhn) ***noun*** A covered wagon that serves as a portable kitchen.

chug (**chuhg**) ***verb*** To make a heavy, regular, thumping sound while moving along. ▸ **chugging, chugged**

chum (**chuhm**) ***noun*** A friend, buddy, or pal.

chunk (**chuhngk**) ***noun*** A thick piece of something.

chunk•y (**chuhng**-kee) ***adjective***
1. Full of chunks or pieces.
2. Short and solid in build; stocky.
▸ ***adjective*** **chunkier, chunkiest**

church (**church**) ***noun***
1. A building used by Christians for worship.
2. A group of Christians.
3. Christian religious services.
▸ ***noun, plural*** **churches**

churn (**churn**)
1. ***noun*** A machine or device in which milk is made into butter. ▸ ***verb*** **churn**
2. ***verb*** To move roughly. ▸ **churning, churned**

chute (**shoot**) ***noun*** A narrow, tilted passage for goods, garbage, laundry, grain, or coal. **Chute** sounds like **shoot.**

chut•ney (**chut**-nee) ***noun*** A relish of vegetables, fruit, and spices.

ci•der (**sye**-dur) ***noun*** A beverage made by pressing apples.

ci•gar (si-**gar**) ***noun*** A thick, brown roll of tobacco that people smoke.

cig•a•rette *or* **cig•a•ret** (sig-uh-**ret**) ***noun*** A thin roll of tobacco covered with paper that people smoke.

cin•der (**sin**-dur) ***noun*** A small piece of wood or coal that has been partly burned.

cin•e•ma (**sin**-uh-muh) ***noun***
1. A movie theater.
2. The film industry. ▸ ***adjective*** **cinematic**

C

C

cin•na•mon (**sin**-uh-muhn) ***noun***
1. A spice that comes from the inner bark of a tropical tree.
2. A light reddish brown color.

cir•ca (**sur**-kuh) ***preposition*** The Latin word for "about." You can also write circa as "c." or "ca."

cir•cle (**sur**-kuhl)
1. ***noun*** A flat, perfectly round shape. ▸ ***adjective*** **circular** (**sur**-kyuh-lur)
2. ***verb*** To draw or make a circle around something. ▸ **circling, circled**
3. ***noun*** A group of people who all know each other.

cir•cuit (**sur**-kit) ***noun***
1. A circular route.
2. The complete path that an electrical current can flow around.

circuit breaker ***noun*** A device that switches the electricity off when there is too much current in the system.

cir•cu•late (**sur**-kyuh-late) ***verb***
1. To move in a circle or pattern.
2. To follow a course from place to place or person to person.
▸ ***verb*** **circulating, circulated**

cir•cu•la•tion (*sur*-kyuh-**lay**-shuhn) ***noun***
1. The movement of blood in blood vessels through the body.
▸ ***adjective*** **circulatory** (**sur**-kyuh-luh-*tor*-ee)
2. The number of copies of a newspaper, magazine, etc., that are bought each day, week, etc.

cir•cum•fer•ence (sur-**kuhm**-fur-uhnss) ***noun***
1. The outer edge of a circle or the length of this edge.
2. The distance around something.

cir•cum•spect (**sur**-kuhm-*spekt*) ***adjective*** Cautious or careful, as in *a circumspect reply.* ▸ ***noun*** **circumspection** ▸ ***adverb*** **circumspectly**

cir•cum•stance (**sur**-kuhm-stanss) ***noun*** The **circumstances** of an event are the facts or conditions that are connected to it.

cir•cus (**sur**-kuhss) ***noun*** A traveling show in which clowns, acrobats, and animals perform. ▸ ***noun, plural*** **circuses**

cis•tern (**siss**-turn) ***noun*** A reservoir or tank for storing water.

cite (**site**) ***verb***
1. To quote from a written work.
2. To give someone a commendation or medal.
3. To use a thing or an event as proof of an argument.
▸ ***verb*** **citing, cited**
Cite sounds like **site** and **sight.**

cit•i•zen (**sit**-i-zuhn) ***noun***
1. A member of a particular country who has the right to live there.
2. A resident of a particular town or city.

cit•i•zen•ship (**sit**-uh-zuhn-ship) ***noun*** The rights, privileges, and duties that come with being a citizen of a certain country.

cit•rus fruit (**sit**-ruhss) ***noun*** An acidic, juicy fruit such as an orange, a lemon, or a grapefruit.

cit•y (**sit**-ee) ***noun*** A very large or important town.
▸ ***noun, plural*** **cities**

civ•ic (**siv**-ik) ***adjective*** To do with a city or the people who live in it, as in *civic pride.*

civ•ics (**siv**-iks) ***noun*** The study of being a good citizen of a community or country.

civ•il (**siv**-il)
1. ***adjective*** To do with the government or people of a country, rather than its army or religion, as in *civil service.*
2. ***adjective*** Polite. ▸ ***noun*** **civility** (si-**vil**-i-tee)
3. civil rights ***noun, plural*** The individual rights that all members of a society have to freedom and equal treatment under the law.
4. civil servant ***noun*** Someone who works in a government department.

ci•vil•ian (si-**vil**-yuhn) ***noun*** Someone who is not a member of the armed forces.

civ•i•li•za•tion (*siv*-i-luh-**zay**-shuhn) ***noun***
1. An advanced stage of human organization, technology, and culture.
2. A highly developed and organized society, as in *the ancient civilizations of Greece and Rome.*

civ•i•lize (**siv**-i-lize) ***verb***
1. To improve someone's manners and education.
2. To improve a society so that it is better organized and its people have a higher standard of living.
▸ ***verb*** **civilizing, civilized** ▸ ***adjective*** **civilized**

civil war ***noun***
1. A war between different groups of people within the same country.
2. Civil War The U.S. war between the Confederacy, or southern states, and the Union, or northern states, that lasted from 1861 to 1865.

clad (**klad**) ***verb*** A past tense and past participle of **clothe**.

claim (**klaym**) ***verb***
1. To say that something belongs to you or that you have a right to have it.
2. To say that something is true.
▸ ***verb*** **claiming, claimed** ▸ ***noun*** **claim**

clam (**klam**) ***noun*** A shellfish with two tightly closed shells that are hinged together. The soft meat inside the shells can be eaten.

clam•bake (**klam**-*bake*) ***noun*** A party, often held at the beach, where clams are cooked on heated stones.

clamb•er (**klam**-bur) ***verb*** To climb quickly and awkwardly by using the hands and feet. ▸ **clambering, clambered**

clam•my (**klam**-ee) ***adjective*** Unpleasantly damp, as in *clammy hands.* ▸ **clammier, clammiest**

clam•or (**klam**-ur) ***verb*** To demand something noisily. ▸ **clamoring, clamored** ▸ ***noun*** **clamor**

clamp (**klamp**)
1. ***noun*** A tool for holding things firmly in place.
2. ***verb*** To fasten something with a clamp.
3. ***verb*** When you **clamp down** on something, you control it more firmly.
▸ ***verb*** **clamping, clamped**

clan (**klan**) ***noun*** A large group of families, especially in Scotland, that believe they all are descended from a common ancestor.

clap (**klap**)
1. ***verb*** To hit your hands together to show that you have enjoyed something or to get someone's attention.
▸ **clapping, clapped** ▸ ***noun*** **clap**
2. ***noun*** A loud bang of thunder.

clar•i•fy (**kla**-ruh-fye) ***verb*** To make something clear. ▸ **clarifies, clarifying, clarified** ▸ ***noun*** **clarification**

clar•i•net (klair-uh-**net**) ***noun*** A long, hollow woodwind instrument. A clarinet is played by blowing into a mouthpiece and pressing keys or covering holes with the fingers to change the pitch.

clar•i•ty (**kla**-ruh-tee) ***noun*** Clearness.

clash (**klash**) ***verb***
1. To fight or argue vehemently.
2. If colors **clash,** they look unpleasant together.
3. To make a loud, crashing noise.
▸ ***verb*** **clashes, clashing, clashed**
▸ ***noun*** **clash**

clasp (**klasp**)
1. ***verb*** To hold firmly and tightly.
▸ **clasping, clasped**
2. ***noun*** A small fastener.

class (**klass**) ***noun***
1. A group of people who are taught together, as in *a fifth grade class.*
2. A group of people or things that are similar, as in *a class of automobiles.*
3. A group of people in society with a similar way of life or range of income, as in *the middle class.*
4. (*informal*) Attractiveness and style.
▸ ***noun, plural*** **classes**

C

clas·sic (**klass**-ik)
1. ***adjective*** Of very good quality and likely to remain popular for a long time, as in *a classic movie.*
2. ***adjective*** Typical.
3. **classics *noun, plural*** The languages and literature of ancient Greece and Rome.

clas·si·cal (**klass**-uh-kuhl) ***adjective***
1. In the style of ancient Greece or Rome, as in *classical architecture.*
2. Traditional or accepted.
3. **Classical** music is timeless, serious music in the European tradition, such as opera, chamber music, and symphony.

clas·si·fied (**klass**-uh-fide) ***adjective***
1. Declared secret by the government, as in *classified information.*
2. A **classified** advertisement in a newspaper is a small ad for a job or item on sale listed in columns according to the subject.

clas·si·fy (**klass**-uh-fye) ***verb*** To put things into groups according to their characteristics. ▸ **classifies, classifying, classified** ▸ ***noun*** **classification**

class·mate (**klass**-*mate*) ***noun*** Someone who is in the same class as another.

class·room (**klass**-*room*) ***noun*** A room in a school in which classes take place.

clas·sy (**klass**-ee) ***adjective*** (*informal*) Attractive and stylish.

clat·ter (**klat**-ur) ***verb*** When things **clatter,** they bang together noisily. ▸ **clattering, clattered** ▸ ***noun*** **clatter**

clause (**klawz**) ***noun***
1. A group of words that contains a subject and a predicate and forms a sentence or one part of a sentence.
2. One section of a formal legal document.

claus·tro·pho·bi·a (*klawss*-truh-**foh**-bee-uh) ***noun*** The fear of being in small, enclosed places. ▸ ***adjective*** **claustrophobic**

claw (**klaw**)
1. ***noun*** A hard, curved nail on the foot of an animal or a bird.
2. ***verb*** To scratch with nails or claws. ▸ **clawing, clawed**

clay (**klay**) ***noun*** A kind of earth that can be shaped when wet and baked to make bricks or pottery.

clean (**kleen**)
1. ***adjective*** Not dirty or messy. ▸ ***noun*** **cleanness** ▸ ***adverb*** **cleanly**
2. ***adjective*** Fair, or obeying the rules.
3. ***verb*** To remove the dirt from something. ▸ **cleaning, cleaned** ▸ ***noun*** **cleaner** ▸ ***adjective*** **cleaner, cleanest**

clean·li·ness (**klen**-lee-niss) ***noun*** Cleanness.

cleanse (**klenz**) ***verb*** To make something clean or pure. ▸ **cleansing, cleansed**

cleans·er (**klen**-zur) ***noun*** A powder or liquid used to clean or scrub things.

clear (**klihr**)
1. ***adjective*** Easy to see through.
2. ***verb*** To make or become bright.
3. ***adjective*** Bright; not dark or cloudy, as in *clear skies.*
4. ***adjective*** Easy to understand, as in *clear instructions.*
5. ***verb*** To remove things that are covering or blocking a place.
6. ***verb*** To jump over something without touching it.
7. ***verb*** To declare that someone is not guilty of a crime.
8. ***adjective*** Free from worry or guilt, as in *a clear conscience.*
9. ***adverb*** In a clear way; distinctly. ▸ ***verb*** **clearing, cleared** ▸ ***noun*** **clearness** ▸ ***adjective*** **clearer, clearest** ▸ ***adverb*** **clearly**

clear·ance (**klihr**-uhnss) ***noun***
1. The act of clearing.
2. Permission to do something.
3. The space between two objects such that neither object will touch the other.

clear·ing (**klihr**-ing) ***noun*** An area of a forest or woods from which trees have been removed.

clef (**klef**) ***noun*** A symbol written at the beginning of a line of music to show the pitch of the notes, as in *bass clef; treble clef.*

cleft (**kleft**) ***noun***
1. A split or division.
2. An indentation something like a dimple.

clench (**klench**) ***verb*** To hold or squeeze something tightly. ▸ **clenches, clenching, clenched**

cler•gy (**klur**-jee) ***noun*** A group of people trained to conduct religious services, such as priests, ministers, and rabbis. ▸ ***noun, plural*** **clergies**

cl•er•i•cal (**kler**-i-kuhl) ***adjective***
1. To do with the clergy.
2. Clerical work is general office work, such as filing.

clerk (**klurk**) ***noun***
1. A salesperson in a store.
2. Someone who keeps records in an office, a bank, or a law court.

clev•er (**klev**-ur) ***adjective***
1. Able to understand things or do things quickly and easily.
2. Intelligently and carefully thought out, as in *a clever plan.*
▸ ***adjective*** **cleverer, cleverest** ▸ ***noun*** **cleverness** ▸ ***adverb*** **cleverly**

cli•ché (klee-**shay**) ***noun*** An idea or a phrase that is used so often that it no longer has very much meaning.

click (**klik**) ***verb***
1. To make a short, sharp sound. ▸ ***noun*** **click**
2. (*informal*) If an idea **clicks,** it suddenly becomes clear to you.
3. To instruct a computer to do something by pressing the mouse button when the cursor is over or pointing to the desired choice.
▸ ***verb*** **clicking, clicked**

cli•ent (**klye**-uhnt) ***noun*** Someone who uses the services of a professional person such as a lawyer or an accountant.

cliff (**klif**) ***noun*** A high, steep rock face.

cliff-hang•er (*hang*-ur) ***noun*** A story, movie, or television program presented in several parts that is exciting because each part ends at a moment of suspense.

cli•mate (**klye**-mit) ***noun***
1. The usual weather in a place, as in *a warm climate.* ▸ ***adjective*** **climatic** (klye-**mat**-ik)
2. The general situation or mood at a particular time, as in *a positive climate for change.*

cli•max (**klye**-maks) ***noun*** The most exciting part of a story or an event, usually happening near the end. ▸ ***noun, plural*** **climaxes**

climb (**klime**)
1. *verb* To move upward. ▸ ***noun*** **climber**
2. *noun* An upward movement or slope.
3. *verb* To go in various directions using your hands to support and help you.
▸ ***verb*** **climbing, climbed**

clinch (**klinch**) ***verb*** To settle a matter once and for all. ▸ ***verb*** **clinches, clinching, clinched**

cling (**kling**) ***verb*** To stick to or hold on to something or someone very tightly. ▸ **clinging, clung** (kluhng)

clin•ic (**klin**-ik) ***noun*** A room or building where people can go for medical treatment or advice, as in *a dental clinic* or *an emergency clinic.*

clip (**klip**)
1. *verb* To attach things together with a small fastener.
2. *noun* A small metal or plastic fastener.
3. *verb* To trim something, as in *to clip the hedges.*
4. *noun* A short piece of a movie or television program shown by itself.
▸ ***verb*** **clipping, clipped**

clip art ***noun*** Images or pictures that are stored on disk in a computer for use in illustrating a document.

clip•board (**klip**-*bord*) ***noun*** A board with a clip at the top for holding papers.

clip•per (**klip**-ur) ***noun***
1. A tool that clips something, such as hedges or fingernails.
2. A fast sailing ship with three masts, built in the United States in the 1800s and used to carry cargo.

C

C

clip•ping (**klip**-ing) ***noun*** Something clipped or cut from something else, as in *a magazine clipping* or *grass clippings.*

clique (**kleek**) ***noun*** A small group of people who are very friendly with each other and do not easily accept others into their group. ▸ ***adjective*** **cliquish**

cloak (**klohk**) ***noun***
1. A loose coat with no sleeves that you wrap around your shoulders and fasten at the neck.
2. cloakroom (**klohk**-*room*) A room where you can hang coats and store umbrellas, hats, and bags.

clock (**klok**)
1. ***noun*** An instrument that tells the time.
2. ***verb*** To measure the time or speed of something, as in *to clock a race.*

clock•wise (**klok**-wize) ***adverb*** In the direction that the hands of a clock move. ▸ ***adjective*** **clockwise**

clock•work (**klok**-wurk) ***noun***
1. A mechanism with gears, springs, and wheels that makes things such as clocks and toys work. ▸ ***adjective*** **clockwork**
2. If things go **like clockwork,** there are no problems.

clod (**klod**) ***noun***
1. A lump of earth or clay.
2. A dull or awkward person.

clog (**klog**)
1. ***verb*** To block something. ▸ **clogging, clogged**
2. ***noun*** A heavy wooden shoe, often worn in the Netherlands.

clois•ter (**kloi**-stur) ***noun***
1. A place where nuns and monks live; a convent or monastery.
2. A covered walk with columns along the wall of a convent, monastery, or other building.

clone (**klohn**) ***verb*** To grow a plant or an animal from the cells of a parent plant or animal so that it is identical to the parent. ▸ **cloning, cloned** ▸ ***noun*** **clone**

close
1. (**klohz**) ***verb*** To shut something.
2. (**klohz**) ***verb*** To end something. ▸ ***noun*** **close**
3. (**klohss**) ***adverb*** Near. ▸ ***adjective*** **close**
4. (**klohss**) ***adjective*** Careful. ▸ ***adverb*** **closely**
5. (**klohss**) ***adjective*** When the weather is **close,** it is very hot and humid.
6. (**klohss**) ***adjective*** Almost even.
▸ ***verb*** **closing, closed** ▸ ***adjective*** **closer, closest,** ***adjective*** **closed** ▸ ***adverb*** **closer, closest**

closed-circuit television ***noun*** A television system that shows images or pictures to a limited number of television screens.

clos•et (**kloz**-it) ***noun*** A small room used for storing things, especially clothes.

close-up (**klohss**) ***noun*** A very detailed view of something, especially a camera shot taken at close range. ▸ ***adjective*** **close-up**

clot (**klot**) ***verb*** When a liquid, such as blood, **clots,** it becomes thicker and more solid. ▸ **clotting, clotted** ▸ ***noun*** **clot**

cloth (**kloth** *or* **klawth**) ***noun***
1. Material made from wool, cotton, etc.
2. A small piece of material used for cleaning or some other purpose.

clothe (**klohTH**) ***verb*** To dress or provide with clothing. ▸ **clothing, clothed**

clothes (**klohz**) ***noun, plural*** Things that you wear; for example, shirts, pants, and dresses.

clothes•pin (**klohz**-*pin*) ***noun*** A wood or plastic clip used to hold freshly washed or wet clothes on a line while they dry.

cloth•ing (**kloh**-THing) ***noun*** Garments worn to cover the body; clothes.

cloud (**kloud**)
1. ***noun*** A white or gray mass of water drops or ice crystals suspended in the air.
2. ***noun*** A mass of smoke or dust.

3. ***verb*** If something **clouds over,** it becomes less easy to see through.
▸ **clouding, clouded**

cloud•burst (**kloud**-*burst*) ***noun*** A sudden, heavy rain shower.

cloud•y (**kloud**-ee) ***adjective***
1. Covered with clouds.
2. Not clear.
▸ ***adjective*** **cloudier, cloudiest**

clove (**klove**) ***noun***
1. The dried flower bud of a tropical tree, used whole or ground up as a spice in cooking.
2. One of the sections of a bulb of garlic.

clo•ver (**kloh**-vur) ***noun*** A small plant with pink or white flowers and leaves usually divided into three parts.

clown (**kloun**)
1. ***noun*** An entertainer who wears funny clothes, has a painted face, and tries to make people laugh.
2. ***noun*** Someone who does silly or foolish things.
3. ***verb*** To do silly things in order to make people laugh.
▸ **clowning, clowned**

club (**kluhb**) ***noun***
1. A group of people who meet regularly to enjoy a common interest.
2. The place where a group meets to share a common interest.
3. A stick with a metal or wooden head used in the game of golf.
4. A thick, heavy stick used as a weapon.
▸ ***verb*** **club**
5. clubs ***noun, plural*** One of the four suits in a deck of cards, with a black symbol having three leaves.

clue (**kloo**) ***noun*** Something that helps you find an answer to a question or a mystery.

clump (**kluhmp**)
1. ***noun*** A group of trees, other plants, or dirt.
2. ***verb*** To walk slowly, with clumsy, noisy footsteps. ▸ **clumping, clumped**
▸ ***noun*** **clump**

clum•sy (**kluhm**-zee) ***adjective*** Careless and awkward in the way that you move or behave. ▸ **clumsier, clumsiest**
▸ ***noun*** **clumsiness** ▸ ***adverb*** **clumsily**

clus•ter (**kluhss**-tur) ***verb*** To stand or grow close together. ▸ **clustering, clustered** ▸ ***noun*** **cluster**

clutch (**kluhch**)
1. ***verb*** To hold on to something tightly.
▸ **clutches, clutching, clutched** ▸ ***noun*** **clutch**
2. ***noun*** The pedal or lever of some cars and other vehicles that you press to change gears in a motor.

clut•ter (**kluht**-ur) ***verb*** To fill up a place and make it messy. ▸ **cluttering, cluttered** ▸ ***noun*** **clutter**

co. Short for **company.**

coach (**kohch**)
1. ***verb*** To train someone in a subject or a sport. ▸ **coaches, coaching, coached**
▸ ***noun*** **coach**
2. ***noun*** A large carriage pulled by horses.
3. ***noun*** A section of passenger seats on a bus, a train, or an airplane that are less expensive than first class.
4. ***noun*** A bus or railroad passenger car.
▸ ***noun, plural*** **coaches**

coal (**kohl**) ***noun***
1. A black mineral formed from the remains of ancient plants. Coal is mined underground and burned as a fuel.
2. A small piece of coal.
3. A piece of burned wood.

co•a•li•tion (koh-uh-**lish**-uhn) ***noun*** When two or more groups form a **coalition,** they join together for a common purpose.

coarse (**korss**) ***adjective***
1. If something is **coarse,** it has a rough texture or surface.
2. If a person is **coarse,** he or she is rude and has bad manners.
3. Having large particles; not fine.
Coarse sounds like **course.**
▸ ***adjective*** **coarser, coarsest** ▸ ***noun*** **coarseness** ▸ ***adverb*** **coarsely**

C

coast (**kohst**)
1. ***noun*** The land that is next to the sea. ▸ ***adjective*** **coastal**
2. ***verb*** To move along in a car or other vehicle without using any power.
3. ***verb*** To make progress without much effort.
▸ ***verb*** **coasting, coasted**

coast guard (**kohst** *gard*) ***noun*** The branch of a nation's armed forces that watches the sea for ships in danger and protects the coastline.

coast·line (**kohst**-*line*) ***noun*** The place where the land and the ocean meet; the outline of the coast.

coat (**koht**)
1. ***noun*** A piece of clothing that you wear over other clothes to keep yourself warm.
2. ***noun*** An animal's fur or wool.
3. ***noun*** A thin layer.
4. ***verb*** To cover a surface with a thin layer of something. ▸ **coating, coated**

coat·ing (**koht**-ing) ***noun*** A layer that is covering something, as in *a coating of dust.*

coat of arms ***noun*** A design in the shape of a shield that is used as the special sign of a family, a city, or an organization. ▸ ***noun, plural*** **coats of arms**

coax (**kohks**) ***verb*** To persuade someone gently and patiently to do something.
▸ **coaxes, coaxing, coaxed**
▸ ***adjective*** **coaxing** ▸ ***adverb*** **coaxingly**

cob (**kob**) ***noun*** The center part of an ear of corn on which the kernels grow.

co·balt (**koh**-bahlt) ***noun***
1. A silver-white chemical element used to make alloys and paints.
2. A deep blue color. ▸ ***adjective*** **cobalt**

cob·bler (**kob**-lur) ***noun***
1. Someone who makes or repairs shoes.
2. A dessert made of fruit, with a top crust.

cob·ble·stone (**kob**-uhl-*stone*) ***noun*** A flat, round, gray rock once used to pave roads and driveways. ▸ ***adjective*** **cobbled**

co·bra (**koh**-bruh) ***noun*** A large, poisonous snake that when excited rears up and spreads its skin so that its head and neck look like a hood. It can be as long as seven feet.

cob·web (**kob**-*web*) ***noun*** A very fine net of sticky threads made by a spider to catch flies and other insects.

co·caine (koh-**kayn**) ***noun*** A powerful drug used medically to block pain. Cocaine is dangerous and is used illegally by some people.

cock (**kok**)
1. ***noun*** A fully grown male chicken.
2. ***noun*** A male bird.
3. ***verb*** To turn up to one side.
▸ **cocking, cocked**

cock·a·too (**kok**-uh-too) ***noun*** A white parrot with a crest of feathers, found in Asia and Australia.

cock·er spaniel (**kok**-ur) ***noun*** A popular breed of small dog, with a long, silky coat and long ears.

cock·le (**kok**-uhl) ***noun*** An edible shellfish shaped like a heart.

cock·pit (**kok**-*pit*) ***noun*** The area in the front of a plane or boat where the pilot sits.

cock·roach (**kok**-*rohch*) ***noun*** A brown or black insect that lives in warm, dark places and is a household pest.

cock·tail (**kok**-*tayl*) ***noun***
1. A drink made by mixing several different kinds of liquids together. Cocktails are usually alcoholic.
2. Seafood or fruit served at the start of a meal, as in *a shrimp cocktail.*

cock·y (**kok**-ee) ***adjective*** (*informal*) Too sure of oneself; self-confident to the point of being unpleasant. ▸ **cockier, cockiest**

co·coa (**koh**-koh) ***noun***
1. A brown powder made from the roasted beans of the cacao tree and used to make chocolate.
2. A hot drink made with cocoa powder, sugar, and milk or water.

co•co•nut (**koh**-kuh-*nuht*) ***noun*** A very large nut with a hard, hairy shell and sweet, white meat that is often shredded for use as food.

co•coon (kuh-**koon**) ***noun*** A covering made from silky threads produced by some animals to protect themselves or their eggs.

COD (**cee oh dee**) An abbreviation meaning *cash on delivery;* a way to send packages so that the receiver must pay for the merchandise when it is delivered.

cod (**kod**) ***noun*** A fish that is found in the northern Atlantic Ocean and that has white meat that you can eat. ▸ ***noun, plural*** **cod**

code (**kode**) ***noun***
1. A system of words, letters, symbols, or numbers used instead of ordinary words to send messages or store information, as in *a secret code.* ▸ ***verb*** **code** ▸ ***adjective*** **coded**
2. A set of rules, as in *a safety code.*

co•ed•u•ca•tion (*koh*-ej-uh-**kay**-shuhn) ***noun*** The system of teaching boys and girls together in the same school. ▸ ***adjective*** **coeducational**

co•erce (koh-**urss**) ***verb*** To force someone to do something. ▸ **coercing, coerced** ▸ ***noun*** **coercion**

cof•fee (**kaw**-fee *or* **kof**-ee) ***noun***
1. A hot drink made from the roasted and ground beans of the coffee shrub.
2. Ground coffee beans used to make coffee.

cof•fin (**kawf**-in) ***noun*** A long container into which a dead person is placed for burial.

cog (**kog**) ***noun***
1. One of the teeth on the edge of a wheel that turns machinery.
2. **cog-wheel** (**kog**-*weel*) A wheel with teeth that turns machinery.

co•her•ent (koh-**hihr**-uhnt) ***adjective*** Clear and logical, as in *a coherent argument.*

coil (**koil**)
1. ***verb*** To wind something around and around into a series of loops.
2. ***noun*** A loop or series of loops.
3. ***verb*** To wind or wrap around something.
▸ ***verb*** **coiling, coiled**

coin (**koin**)
1. ***noun*** A small piece of metal stamped with a design and used as money. ▸ ***verb*** **coin**
2. ***verb*** To invent a new word or a new meaning of a word. ▸ **coining, coined** ▸ ***noun*** **coinage**

co•in•cide (koh-in-**side**) ***verb*** If two things **coincide,** they happen at the same time. ▸ **coinciding, coincided**

co•in•ci•dence (koh-**in**-si-duhnss) ***noun*** A chance happening or meeting. ▸ ***adjective*** **coincidental** (*koh*-in-si-**den**-tuhl) ▸ ***adverb*** **coincidentally**

col•an•der (**kol**-uhn-dur) ***noun*** A kitchen utensil with holes, used for draining liquid off foods.

cold (**kohld**)
1. ***adjective*** Having a low temperature. ▸ ***noun*** **cold**
2. ***noun*** A common mild illness that causes sneezes, a sore throat, and sometimes a cough and a slight fever.
3. ***adjective*** Unfriendly. ▸ ***noun*** **coldness** ▸ ***adverb*** **coldly** ▸ ***adjective*** **colder, coldest**

cold-blood•ed (**bluhd**-id) ***adjective***
1. **Cold-blooded** animals have body temperatures that change according to the temperature of their surroundings.
2. A **cold-blooded** act is done deliberately and cruelly.

cole•slaw (**kohl**-*slaw*) ***noun*** A salad made up of shredded cabbage mixed with a dressing of vinegar and other ingredients.

col•i•se•um (kol-i-**see**-uhm) ***noun*** A large stadium or auditorium for sports or other events.

col•lab•o•rate (kuh-**lab**-uh-rate) ***verb*** To work together to do something. ▸ **collaborating, collaborated** ▸ ***noun*** **collaboration,** ***noun*** **collaborator**

C

col·lage (kuh-**lahzh**) ***noun*** A picture made by fixing different things onto a surface, such as pieces of cloth onto paper.

col·lapse (kuh-**laps**) ***verb***
1. To fall down suddenly from weakness or illness.
2. To fail suddenly and completely.
▸ ***verb*** **collapsing, collapsed** ▸ ***noun*** **collapse**

col·lar (**kol**-ur)
1. ***noun*** The part of a shirt, blouse, coat, etc., that fits around your neck and is usually folded down.
2. ***noun*** A thin band of material worn around the neck of a dog or cat.
3. ***verb*** To catch someone. ▸ **collaring, collared**

col·lards (**kol**-urdz) ***noun, plural*** The green leaves of a vegetable related to cabbage, popular in the southern United States.

col·league (**kol**-eeg) ***noun*** Someone who works with you.

col·lect (kuh-**lekt**) ***verb***
1. To gather things together.
2. To ask for payment for something bought or delivered.
▸ ***verb*** **collecting, collected**

col·lec·tion (kuh-**lek**-shuhn) ***noun***
1. A group of things gathered over a long time, as in *a shell collection.*
2. If you **take up a collection** for something, you gather money for it.

col·lege (**kol**-ij) ***noun*** A place of higher learning where students can continue to study after they have finished high school.

col·lide (kuh-**lide**) ***verb*** To crash together forcefully, often at high speed.
▸ **colliding, collided** ▸ ***noun*** **collision**

col·lie (**kol**-ee) ***noun*** A breed of large dog with a long nose, a narrow head, and a thick coat.

col·lier·y (**kol**-yur-ee) ***noun*** A coal mine. ▸ ***noun, plural*** **collieries**

col·lo·qui·al (kuh-**loh**-kwee-uhl) ***adjective*** **Colloquial** language is used in everyday informal conversation.

co·lon (**koh**-luhn) ***noun***
1. The punctuation mark (:) used to introduce a list of things.
2. The part of your large intestine where partially digested food is broken down by bacteria and has water removed from it.

colo·nel (**kur**-nuhl) ***noun*** An officer in the army, air force, or Marine Corps ranking below a general.

col·o·nist (**kol**-uh-nist) ***noun*** Someone who lives in a newly settled area.

col·o·nize (**kol**-uh-nize) ***verb*** To establish a new colony in. ▸ **colonizing, colonized**

col·o·ny (**kol**-uh-nee) ***noun***
1. A group of people who leave their country to settle in a new area.
2. A territory that has been settled by people from another country and is controlled by that country. ▸ ***adjective*** **colonial** (kuh-**loh**-nee-uhl)
3. A large group of insects that live together, as in *a colony of ants.*
▸ ***noun, plural*** **colonies**

col·or (**kuhl**-ur)
1. ***noun*** A property of an object that reflects light of a certain wavelength. The eye perceives such light as being red, yellow, blue, etc. ▸ ***adjective*** **colorful,** ***adjective*** **colorless**
2. ***verb*** To make something red, yellow, black, etc. ▸ **coloring, colored**
3. ***noun*** The appearance of a person's skin.
4. ***adjective*** If you are **color-blind,** you are unable to see the difference between certain colors.

col·or·ing (**kuhl**-ur-ing) ***noun***
1. The way in which something is colored.
2. Something used to color something else.

col·or·ize (**kuhl**-ur-ize) ***verb*** To add color, usually to motion pictures, using a computer. ▸ **colorizing, colorized**
▸ ***noun*** **colorization**

co·los·sal (kuh-**loss**-uhl) ***adjective*** Extremely large.

colt (**kohlt**) ***noun*** A young horse, donkey, or zebra, especially a male.

col•um•bine (**kol**-uhm-bine) ***noun*** A tall flower with long, narrow petals.

Co•lum•bus Day (kuh-**luhm**-buhss) ***noun*** A holiday, the second Monday in October, celebrating Christopher Columbus's arrival in North America in 1492.

col•umn (**kol**-uhm) ***noun***
1. A tall, upright pillar that helps support a building or statue.
2. A row of numbers or words running down a page.
3. A piece of writing by the same person, or on the same subject, that appears regularly in a newspaper or magazine.
▸ ***noun*** **columnist**

co•ma (**koh**-muh) ***noun*** A state of deep unconsciousness from which it is very hard to wake up.

comb (**kohm**)
1. ***noun*** A flat piece of metal or plastic with a row of teeth, used for making your hair smooth and neat.
2. ***verb*** To use a comb to make your hair smooth and neat.
3. ***verb*** To search a place thoroughly.
4. ***noun*** The brightly colored crest on the head of a rooster or a related bird.
▸ ***verb*** **combing, combed**

com•bat (**kom**-bat)
1. ***noun*** Fighting between people or armies.
2. ***verb*** To fight against something.
▸ **combating, combated** *or* **combatting, combatted**

com•bine (kuhm-**bine**) ***verb*** To join or mix two or more things together.
▸ **combining, combined** ▸ ***noun*** **combination**

com•bus•ti•ble (kuhm-**buhss**-tuh-buhl) ***adjective*** Capable of catching fire.

com•bus•tion (kuhm-**buss**-chuhn) ***noun*** The process of catching fire and burning.

come (**kuhm**) ***verb***
1. To move toward a place.
2. To arrive.
3. If you **come from** a particular place, you were born in that place.
4. If something **comes about,** it happens.
5. If you **come across** something, you find it by chance.
6. If you **come down with** something, you become sick with it.
7. If you **come into** money, you inherit it.
8. If you **come to,** you become conscious again.
▸ ***verb*** **coming, came** (**kaym**)**, come**

co•me•di•an (kuh-**mee**-dee-uhn) ***noun*** An entertainer who tells jokes and funny stories to make people laugh.

com•e•dy (**kom**-uh-dee) ***noun***
1. A funny play or film.
2. Anything that makes people laugh.
▸ ***noun, plural*** **comedies**

com•et (**kom**-it) ***noun*** A bright heavenly body with a long tail of light. A comet travels around the sun in a long, slow path.

com•fort (**kuhm**-furt)
1. ***verb*** To make someone feel less worried or upset. ▸ **comforting, comforted** ▸ ***adjective*** **comforting** ▸ ***adverb*** **comfortingly**
2. ***noun*** The feeling of being relaxed and free from pain or worries.
3. ***noun*** Something that makes your life more pleasant and enjoyable, as in *the comforts of home.*

com•fort•a•ble (**kuhm**-fur-tuh-buhl) ***adjective***
1. If you are **comfortable,** you feel relaxed in your body or your mind.
2. If something is **comfortable,** it allows you to relax and feel pleasure, as in *a comfortable chair.* ▸ ***adverb*** **comfortably**

com•ic (**kom**-ik)
1. ***noun*** Someone who tells jokes and funny stories.
2. ***adjective*** Funny or amusing.
3. **comics** ***noun, plural*** A group of comic strips.

C

com•i•cal (**kom**-i-kuhl) ***adjective*** Causing amusement or laughter. ▸ ***adverb*** **comically**

comic book ***noun*** A booklet with stories told in cartoons.

comic strip ***noun*** A story told in a sequence of panels or cartoons, found in a newspaper or comic book.

com•ma (**kom**-uh) ***noun*** The punctuation mark (,) used for separating parts of a sentence or words in a list.

com•mand (kuh-**mand**)
1. ***verb*** To order someone to do something.
2. ***verb*** To have control over a group of people in the armed forces. ▸ ***noun*** **commander**
3. ***noun*** Your **command** of something is your knowledge of it and your skill in using it.
▸ ***verb*** **commanding, commanded**
▸ ***noun*** **command**

com•mand•ment (kuh-**mand**-muhnt) ***noun*** A law or order from someone in power.

com•mem•o•rate (kuh-**mem**-uh-rate) ***verb*** When you **commemorate** an event or the life of an important person, you do something special to honor and remember it. ▸ **commemorating, commemorated** ▸ ***noun*** **commemoration** ▸ ***adjective*** **commemorative**

com•mence (kuh-**menss**) ***verb*** To begin something. ▸ **commencing, commenced**

com•mence•ment (kuh-**menss**-ment) ***noun***
1. The start or beginning of something.
2. Graduation day, or a graduation ceremony.

com•mend (kuh-**mend**) ***verb*** To praise. ▸ **commending, commended** ▸ ***noun*** **commendation** ▸ ***adjective*** **commendable**

com•ment (**kom**-ent)
1. ***noun*** A remark or note that expresses your opinion or gives an explanation.
2. ***verb*** If you **comment** on something, you give an explanation or an opinion about it. ▸ **commenting, commented**

com•men•tar•y (**kom**-uhn-*ter*-ee) ***noun***
1. A description of and comments about an event, as in *political commentary.*
▸ ***noun*** **commentator**
2. Something that serves as an example or an illustration.
▸ ***noun, plural*** **commentaries**

com•merce (**kom**-urss) ***noun*** The buying and selling of things in order to make money.

com•mer•cial (kuh-**mur**-shuhl)
1. ***adjective*** To do with buying and selling things, as in *commercial activities.*
2. ***noun*** A television or radio advertisement.
3. ***adjective*** Having profit as a main aim, as in *a commercial idea.*

com•mer•cial•ized (kuh-**mur**-shuh-lized) ***adjective*** If something is **commercialized,** it has been changed in order to make a profit. ▸ ***noun*** **commercialization**

com•mis•er•ate (kuh-**miz**-ur-ate) ***verb*** To share someone else's sadness or disappointment. ▸ **commiserating, commiserated** ▸ ***noun*** **commiseration**

com•mis•sion (kuh-**mish**-uhn)
1. ***noun*** A group of people who meet to solve a particular problem or do certain tasks.
2. ***noun*** Money for work done.
3. ***noun*** A written order giving rank in the armed services.
4. ***noun*** The act of committing.
5. ***noun*** Working order or condition.
6. ***verb*** To give someone the power to do something.
7. ***verb*** To put a ship into service.
▸ ***verb*** **commissioning, commissioned**

com•mit (kuh-**mit**) ***verb***
1. To do something wrong or illegal, as in *to commit murder.*

2. If you **commit** yourself to something, you promise that you will do it or support it.
▸ ***verb*** **committing, committed**
▸ ***noun*** **commitment** ▸ ***adjective*** **committed**

com•mit•tee (kuh-**mit**-ee) ***noun*** A group of people chosen to discuss things and make decisions for a larger group.

com•mod•i•ty (kuh-**mod**-uh-tee) ***noun*** A product that is bought and sold.
▸ ***noun, plural*** **commodities**

com•mon (**kom**-uhn) ***adjective***
1. Existing in large numbers.
2. Happening often, as in *a common problem.*
3. Ordinary and not special in any way.
4. Shared by two or more people or things.
▸ ***adjective*** **commoner, commonest**

common denominator ***noun***
1. A denominator shared by several fractions. In the fractions ¼ and ¾, the common denominator is the number 4.
2. A trait or belief held in common by many people.

Common Market ***noun*** Former name for the **European Economic Community,** a European trade group.

common noun ***noun*** A noun that refers to a class of people, places, or things and is generally not spelled with a capital. The words *boy* and *island* are common nouns in the sentence *The boy lives on an island. See* **proper noun.**

com•mon•place (**kom**-uhn-*playss*) ***adjective*** Ordinary, or not new.

common sense ***noun*** **Common sense** is the ability to think and behave sensibly.

com•mon•wealth (**kom**-uhn-*welth*) ***noun***
1. A nation or state that is governed by the people who live there.
2. The people who live in and make up a nation.

com•mo•tion (kuh-**moh**-shuhn) ***noun*** A lot of noisy, excited activity.

com•mu•nal (kuh-**myoo**-nuhl) ***adjective*** Shared by several people, as in *a communal bathroom.* ▸ ***adverb*** **communally**

com•mune (**kom**-yoon) ***noun*** A group of people who live together and share things with each other.

com•mu•ni•ca•ble (kuh-**myoo**-nuh-kuh-buhl) ***adjective*** Easily passed from one person to another.

com•mu•ni•cate (kuh-**myoo**-nuh-kate) ***verb*** To share information, ideas, or feelings with another person by talking, writing, etc. ▸ **communicating, communicated** ▸ ***noun*** **communication** ▸ ***adjective*** **communicative** (kuh-**myoo**-nuh-kuh-tiv)

Com•mun•ion (kuh-**myoo**-nyuhn) ***noun*** A Christian service in which people eat bread and drink wine or grape juice to remember the last meal of Jesus.

com•mu•ni•qué (kuh-myoo-nuh-**kay**) ***noun*** An official report or statement.

com•mun•ism *or* **Com•mun•ism** (**kom**-yuh-*niz*-uhm) ***noun*** A way of organizing a country so that all the land, houses, factories, etc., belong to the government or community, and the profits are shared by all. ▸ ***noun*** **communist** ▸ ***adjective*** **communist**

Communist party ***noun*** The main political party of the former Soviet Union, which advocated the principles of communism.

com•mu•ni•ty (kuh-**myoo**-nuh-tee) ***noun*** A group of people who live in the same area or who have something in common with each other. ▸ ***noun, plural*** **communities**

com•mut•er (kuh-**myoo**-tur) ***noun*** Someone who travels a relatively long distance to work or school each day, usually by car, bus, or train. ▸ ***verb*** **commute**

C

C

com•pact
1. (kuhm-**pakt**) ***adjective*** Designed to take up very little space. ▸ ***noun*** **compactness**
2. (**kom**-pakt) ***noun*** A small, flat case containing face powder and a mirror.
3. (**kom**-pakt) ***noun*** An agreement between people or groups.

compact disk ***noun*** A disk with music or information stored on it that can be read by using a laser beam.

com•pan•ion (kuhm-**pan**-yuhn) ***noun***
1. Someone with whom you spend time; a friend.
2. A person hired to spend time with another person.
▸ ***noun*** **companionship**

com•pa•ny (**kuhm**-puh-nee) ***noun***
1. A group of people who work together to produce or sell products or services.
2. One or more guests.
3. An army unit under the command of a captain.
4. A group of performers, as in *a ballet company.*
5. Companionship.
▸ ***noun, plural*** **companies**

com•par•a•tive (kuhm-**pa**-ruh-tiv) ***adjective***
1. Judged against other similar things.
▸ ***adverb*** **comparatively**
2. Comparative forms of adjectives and adverbs are used when you compare two things or actions. ▸ ***noun*** **comparative**

com•pare (kuhm-**pair**) ***verb***
1. To judge one thing against another and notice similarities and differences.
▸ ***noun*** **comparison**
2. To be as good as something or somebody else.
▸ ***verb*** **comparing, compared**

com•part•ment (kuhm-**part**-muhnt) ***noun*** A separate part of a container, used for keeping certain things, as in *a wallet compartment.*

com•pass (**kuhm**-puhss) ***noun***
1. An instrument for finding directions, with a magnetic needle that always points north.
2. An instrument that has two legs connected by a flexible joint, used for drawing circles.
▸ ***noun, plural*** **compasses**

com•pas•sion (kuhm-**pash**-uhn) ***noun*** A feeling of sympathy for and a desire to help someone who is suffering.
▸ ***adjective*** **compassionate** ▸ ***adverb*** **compassionately**

com•pat•i•ble (kuhm-**pat**-uh-buhl) ***adjective*** If people or objects are **compatible,** they can live together or be used together without difficulty.
▸ ***noun*** **compatibility**

com•pel (kuhm-**pel**) ***verb*** To make someone do something by giving him or her orders or by using force.
▸ **compelling, compelled**

com•pen•sate (**kom**-puhn-sate) ***verb***
1. To make up for something.
2. To pay.
▸ ***noun*** **compensation** ▸ ***verb*** **compensating, compensated**

com•pete (kuhm-**peet**) ***verb*** To try hard to outdo others at a task, race, or contest. ▸ **competing, competed**

com•pe•tent (**kom**-puh-tuhnt) ***adjective*** If you are **competent** at something, you have the skill or ability to do it well. ▸ ***noun*** **competence**
▸ ***adverb*** **competently**

com•pe•ti•tion (*kom*-puh-**tish**-uhn) ***noun***
1. A situation in which two or more people are trying to get the same thing.
2. A contest of some kind, as in *a swimming competition.* ▸ ***noun*** **competitor** (kuhm-**pet**-i-tur)

com•pet•i•tive (kuhm-**pet**-uh-tiv) ***adjective***
1. A **competitive** sport or game is one in which the players try to win.
2. Very eager to win.
3. If a store offers **competitive** prices, its prices are at least as low as in most other stores.

com•pile (kuhm-**pile**) ***verb*** If you **compile** a list, you bring together many pieces of information. ▸ **compiling, compiled** ▸ ***noun*** **compilation** (*kom*-puh-**lay**-shun)

com•pla•cent (kuhm-**play**-suhnt) ***adjective*** Overly satisfied or happy with one's situation in life.

com•plain (kuhm-**playn**) ***verb***
1. To say that you are unhappy about something.
2. To report, or to make an accusation.
▸ **complaining, complained**

com•plaint (kuhm-**playnt**) ***noun***
1. A statement saying that you are unhappy about something.
2. A cause for complaining, such as an illness.
3. A formal charge against someone.

com•ple•ment (**kom**-pluh-muhnt) ***noun*** Something that completes something or makes a thing whole and perfect. **Complement** sounds like **compliment.**

com•plete (kuhm-**pleet**)
1. ***adjective*** If something is **complete,** it has all the parts that are needed or wanted, as in *a complete deck of cards.*
2. ***verb*** To finish something.
▸ **completing, completed** ▸ ***noun*** **completion**
3. ***adjective*** In every way. ▸ ***adverb*** **completely**

com•plex
1. (kuhm-**pleks** *or* **kom**-pleks) ***adjective*** Very complicated, as in *complex instructions.* ▸ ***noun*** **complexity**
2. (kuhm-**pleks** *or* **kom**-pleks) ***adjective*** Having a large number of parts.
3. (**kom**-pleks) ***noun*** A set of strong feelings that you cannot control or forget about and that causes problems for you.
4. (**kom**-pleks) ***noun*** A group of buildings that are close together and are used for a particular purpose, as in *a sports complex.*
▸ ***noun, plural*** **complexes**

com•plex•ion (kuhm-**plek**-shuhn) ***noun*** The color and look of the skin, especially that on your face.

com•pli•cat•ed (**kom**-pli-kay-tid) ***adjective*** Something that is **complicated** contains lots of different parts or ideas and so is difficult to use or understand. ▸ ***noun*** **complication** ▸ ***verb*** **complicate**

com•pli•ment (**kom**-pluh-ment) ***verb*** When you **compliment** someone, you tell the person that you admire him or her or think that he or she has done something well. **Compliment** sounds like **complement.** ▸ **complimenting, complimented** ▸ ***noun*** **compliment**

com•pli•men•ta•ry (kom-pli-**men**-tuh-ree) ***adjective***
1. If someone is **complimentary** about a person or thing, the person praises it.
2. Free or without cost, as in *complimentary tickets.*

com•ply (kuhm-**plye**) ***verb*** To act in agreement with rules or requests.
▸ **complies, complying, complied**

com•po•nent (kuhm-**poh**-nuhnt) ***noun*** A part of a machine or system.

com•pose (kuhm-**poze**) ***verb***
1. To write a piece of music, a poem, etc.
▸ ***noun*** **composer**
2. If something is **composed** of certain things, it is made from those things.
▸ ***verb*** **composing, composed**

com•pos•ite (kuhm-**poz**-it) ***adjective*** Made up of many parts from different sources.

com•po•si•tion (kom-puh-**zish**-uhn) ***noun***
1. The combining of parts to form a whole.
2. What something is made of.
3. Something that is created, especially a written work.

com•post (**kom**-pohst) ***noun*** A mixture of rotted leaves, vegetables, manure, etc., that is added to soil to make it richer.

com•po•sure (kuhm-**poh**-zhur) ***noun*** A calm state; self-control.

C

com•pound
1. (**kom**-pound) ***noun*** An area of land, usually fenced in.
2. (**kom**-pound) ***noun*** Something formed by combining two or more parts.
3. (**kom**-pound) ***adjective*** Having two or more parts.
4. (kom-**pound**) ***verb*** To add to, as in *to compound the problem.* ▸ **compounding, compounded**

com•pre•hend (kom-pri-**hend**) ***verb*** To understand. ▸ **comprehending, comprehended**

com•pre•hen•sion (kom-pri-**hen**-shuhn) ***noun*** Understanding, or the power to understand.

com•pre•hen•sive (kom-pri-**hen**-siv) ***adjective*** Complete and inclusive, as in *a comprehensive list of supplies.* ▸ ***adverb*** **comprehensively**

com•press
1. (kuhm-**press**) ***verb*** To press or to squeeze something so that it will fit into a small space. ▸ **compresses, compressing, compressed** ▸ ***noun*** **compression**
2. (**kom**-press) ***noun*** A small cloth pad placed on a part of the body for warmth, cold, or pressure. ▸ ***noun, plural*** **compresses**

com•prise (kuhm-**prize**) ***verb*** To include or to contain. ▸ **comprising, comprised**

com•pro•mise (**kom**-pruh-mize)
1. ***verb*** To agree to accept something that is not exactly what you wanted. ▸ **compromising, compromised**
2. ***noun*** An agreement that is reached after people with opposing views each give up some of their demands.

com•pul•so•ry (kuhm-**puhl**-suh-ree) ***adjective*** If something is **compulsory,** there is a law or rule that says you must do it.

com•pute (kuhm-**pyoot**) ***verb*** To find an answer by using mathematics; to calculate. ▸ ***noun*** **computation**

com•put•er (kuhm-**pyoo**-tur) ***noun*** An electronic machine that can store and retrieve large amounts of information and do very quick and complicated calculations. ▸ ***noun*** **computing**

computer-aided design ***noun*** The process of using plans and drawings displayed on a computer screen to develop vehicles, buildings, etc. It is sometimes shortened to CAD.

computer graphics ***noun, plural*** The pictures or images that can be made on a computer.

computer language ***noun*** The words and symbols used in computer programs that tell the computer how to perform certain processes.

computer science ***noun*** The study of computers and how they work.

com•rade (**kom**-rad) ***noun***
1. A good friend or a colleague. ▸ ***noun*** **comradeship**
2. A companion in combat, as in *comrades in arms.*

con•cave (kon-**kayv** *or* kong-**kayv**) ***adjective*** Curved inward, like the inside surface of a dish.

con•ceal (kuhn-**seel**) ***verb*** To hide something. ▸ **concealing, concealed** ▸ ***noun*** **concealment**

con•cede (kuhn-**seed**) ***verb*** To admit something unwillingly. ▸ **conceding, conceded**

con•ceit•ed (kuhn-**see**-tid) ***adjective*** If you are **conceited,** you are too proud of yourself and what you can do. ▸ ***noun*** **conceit**

con•ceive (kuhn-**seev**) ***verb***
1. To come up with an idea.
2. To become pregnant.
▸ ***verb*** **conceiving, conceived**

con•cen•trate (**kon**-suhn-trate) ***verb***
1. To focus your thoughts and attention on something.
2. To come together in one place.
3. To make a liquid thicker and stronger by removing water from it.
▸ ***verb*** **concentrating, concentrated**
▸ ***noun*** **concentrate,** ***noun***

concentration ▸ ***adjective*** **concentrated**

con•cen•tric (kuhn-**sen**-trik) ***adjective*** **Concentric** circles all have their center at the same point.

con•cept (**kon**-sept) ***noun*** A general idea or understanding of something.

con•cep•tion (kuhn-**sep**-shuhn) ***noun***
1. A general idea.
2. The process of becoming pregnant.

con•cern (kuhn-**surn**) ***verb***
1. To involve someone or be of interest to him or her.
2. To be about a particular subject.
3. To worry.
▸ ***verb*** **concerning, concerned** ▸ ***noun*** **concern**

con•cerned (kuhn-**surnd**) ***adjective*** If you are **concerned** about something, you are anxious and worried about it.

con•cern•ing (kuhn-**sern**-ing) ***preposition*** Having to do with; about.

con•cert (**kon**-surt) ***noun*** A performance by musicians or singers.

con•cer•to (kuhn-**cher**-toh) ***noun*** A piece of music for one or more solo instruments playing with an orchestra.
▸ ***noun, plural*** **concertos** *or* **concerti** (kuhn-**chur**-tee)

con•cess•ion (kuhn-**sesh**-uhn) ***noun***
1. An agreement to allow something that would not normally be permitted.
2. Permission to sell something, especially food, granted by a governing body to the seller.

conch (**kongk** *or* **konch**) ***noun***
1. A marine animal that lives in a spiral shell.
2. The shell of this animal.

con•cise (kuhn-**sisse**) ***adjective*** Saying a lot in a few words. ▸ ***adverb*** **concisely**

con•clude (kuhn-**klood**) ***verb***
1. To arrive at a decision or realization based on the facts that you have.
2. To finish or end something.
▸ ***verb*** **concluding, concluded** ▸ ***noun*** **conclusion**

con•coct (kon-**kokt** *or* kuhn-**kokt**) ***verb***
1. To create something by mixing several different things together. ▸ ***noun*** **concoction**
2. If you **concoct** an excuse, you invent it.
▸ ***verb*** **concocting, concocted**

con•cord (**kon**-kord) ***noun***
1. A state of harmony and peace, especially between two people or groups.
2. A treaty or an agreement.

con•crete (**kon**-kreet *or* kon-**kreet**)
1. *noun* A building material made from a mixture of sand, gravel, cement, and water.
2. *adjective* Real or definite.

con•cur (kuhn-**kur**) ***verb*** To agree.
▸ **concurring, concurred**

con•cus•sion (kuhn-**kush**-uhn) ***noun*** An injury to the brain caused by a heavy blow to the head. A concussion can result in unconsciousness, dizziness, or sickness. ▸ ***adjective*** **concussed**

con•demn (kuhn-**dem**) ***verb***
1. To say very strongly that you do not approve of something. ▸ ***noun*** **condemnation** (*kon*-dem-**nay**-shuhn)
2. To force someone to suffer something unpleasant.
3. To state that something is unsafe.
▸ ***verb*** **condemning, condemned**

con•den•sa•tion ***noun*** (*kon*-den-**say**-shuhn)
1. The act or process of condensing something.
2. Something that has been condensed.

con•dense (kuhn-**denss**) ***verb***
1. When a gas **condenses,** it turns into a liquid, usually as a result of cooling.
2. To make a piece of writing shorter by taking out unnecessary parts.
3. To make something thicker by boiling away liquid.
▸ ***verb*** **condensing, condensed**
▸ ***adjective*** **condensed**

con•de•scend•ing (*kon*-di-**sen**-ding) ***adjective*** If you are **condescending,** you behave as though you are better or more important than other people.
▸ ***noun*** **condescension** ▸ ***verb*** **condescend**

con·di·tion (kuhn-**dish**-uhn)
1. ***noun*** The general state of a person, an animal, or a thing.
2. ***noun*** General health or physical fitness.
3. ***verb*** To get into good health.
4. ***noun*** A medical problem that continues over a long period of time, as in *a heart condition.*
5. ***noun*** Something that is needed before another thing can happen or be allowed.
6. ***verb*** To train someone to believe certain things or to behave in certain ways. ▸ ***noun* conditioning**
▸ ***verb* conditioning, conditioned**

con·di·tion·al (kuhn-**dish**-uh-nuhl) ***adjective*** Requiring something else to happen first. ▸ ***adverb* conditionally**

con·di·tion·er (kuhn-**dish**-uh-nur) ***noun*** A thick liquid that you rub into your hair after washing it to make it strong and shiny.

con·do·lence (kuhn-**doh**-luhnss) ***noun*** An expression of sympathy for a person who is upset because a friend or relative has just died.

con·do·min·i·um (*kon*-duh-**min**-ee-uhm) ***noun*** An apartment house or other development in which each unit is owned by the person who lives in it.

con·dor (**kon**-dur) ***noun*** A large vulture. Condors are the largest flying birds in the Western Hemisphere.

con·duct
1. (kuhn-**duhkt**) ***verb*** To organize something and carry it out.
2. (kuhn-**duhkt**) ***verb*** To stand in front of a group of musicians and direct their playing.
3. (kuhn-**duhkt**) ***verb*** If something **conducts** heat, electricity, or sound, it allows it to pass through. ▸ ***noun* conduction**
4. (**kon**-duhkt) ***noun*** Behavior. ▸ ***verb* conduct** (kuhn-**duhkt**)
▸ ***verb* conducting, conducted**

con·duc·tor (kuhn-**duhk**-tur) ***noun***
1. Someone who stands in front of a group of musicians and directs it as it plays.
2. Someone who collects railroad fares.
3. A substance that allows heat, electricity, or sound to travel through it.

cone (**kohn**) ***noun***
1. An object or a shape with a round base and a point at the top. ▸ ***adjective* conical** (**kon**-i-kuhl)
2. The hard, woody fruit of a pine or fir tree.

con·fed·er·a·cy (kuhn-**fed**-ur-uh-see) ***noun***
1. A union of states, provinces, tribes, towns, or people with a common goal.
2. The Confederacy The group of 11 states that declared it was independent from the rest of the United States just before the Civil War. ▸ ***noun, plural* confederacies**

con·fed·er·ate (kuhn-**fed**-ur-uht)
1. ***adjective*** Belonging to a confederacy or union.
2. Confederate *adjective* Having to do with the Confederacy before and during the Civil War.
3. ***noun*** Someone who bands together with others for a common purpose.

con·fed·er·a·tion (kuhn-*fed*-er-**ay**-shun) ***noun*** A union or confederacy.

con·fer (kuhn-**fur**) ***verb***
1. To give someone something, such as a gift, an honor, or a reward.
2. To hold a meeting with someone; to seek someone's advice.
▸ ***verb* conferring, conferred**

con·fer·ence (**kon**-fur-uhnss *or* **kon**-fruhnss) ***noun*** A formal meeting for discussing ideas and opinions.

con·fess (kuhn-**fess**) ***verb*** To admit that you have done something wrong.
▸ **confesses, confessing, confessed**
▸ ***noun* confession**

con·fet·ti (kuhn-**fet**-ee) ***noun, plural*** Small pieces of colored paper that are thrown over the bride and groom after a wedding or at parades, carnivals, and other celebrations.

con•fide (kuhn-**fide**) ***verb*** If you **confide** in someone, you tell the person a secret. ▸ **confiding, confided**

con•fi•dent (**kon**-fuh-duhnt) ***adjective***
1. Having a strong belief in your own abilities.
2. Certain that things will happen in the way you want.
▸ ***noun*** **confidence** ▸ ***adverb*** **confidently**

con•fi•den•tial (*kon*-fuh-**den**-shuhl) ***adjective*** Secret. ▸ ***adverb*** **confidentially**

con•fine (kuhn-**fine**) ***verb***
1. To keep within certain bounds; to limit.
2. To shut or keep in or prevent from leaving a place.
▸ ***verb*** **confining, confined** ▸ ***noun*** **confinement**

con•firm (kuhn-**furm**) ***verb***
1. To say that something is definitely true or will definitely happen.
2. When someone is **confirmed,** the person is accepted as a full member of a church or synagogue in a special ceremony.
▸ ***verb*** **confirming, confirmed** ▸ ***noun*** **confirmation**

con•fis•cate (**kon**-fuh-skate) ***verb*** To take something away from someone as a punishment or because that thing is not allowed. ▸ **confiscating, confiscated** ▸ ***noun*** **confiscation**

con•flict
1. (**kon**-flict) ***noun*** A serious disagreement.
2. (**kon**-flict) ***noun*** A war or a period of fighting.
3. (kuhn-**flict**) ***verb*** To clash or to disagree. ▸ **conflicting, conflicted**

con•form (kuhn-**form**) ***verb***
1. If you **conform,** you behave in the same way as everyone else or in a way that is expected of you. ▸ ***noun*** **conformist,** ***noun*** **conformity**
2. If something **conforms** to a rule or law, it does what the rule or law requires.
▸ ***verb*** **conforming, conformed**

con•front (kuhn-**fruhnt**) ***verb***
1. To meet or face someone in a threatening or accusing way. ▸ ***noun*** **confrontation**
2. To come face to face with something.
▸ ***verb*** **confronting, confronted**

Con•fu•cius (kuhn-**fyoo**-shuhss) ***noun*** A Chinese philosopher who lived from 551 to 479 B.C. His teachings are called Confucianism, an important system of ethics. ▸ ***adjective*** **Confucian**

con•fuse (kuhn-**fyooz**) ***verb***
1. If someone or something **confuses** you, you do not understand it or know what to do. ▸ ***adjective*** **confusing,** ***adjective*** **confused**
2. To mistake one thing for another.
▸ ***verb*** **confusing, confused** ▸ ***noun*** **confusion**

con•geal (kuhn-**jeel**) ***verb*** When a liquid **congeals,** it becomes thick or solid. ▸ **congealing, congealed**

con•ges•ted (kuhn-**jess**-tid) ***adjective*** Blocked up and not allowing movement, as in *congested roads; congested sinuses.* ▸ ***noun*** **congestion**

con•grat•u•late (kuhn-**grach**-uh-late) ***verb*** To tell someone that you are pleased because something good has happened to the person or he or she has done something well. ▸ **congratulating, congratulated** ▸ ***noun*** **congratulation**

con•gre•gate (**kon**-gri-gate) ***verb*** To gather together for a common activity. ▸ **congregating, congregated**

con•gre•ga•tion (*kong*-gruh-**gay**-shuhn) ***noun*** A group of people gathered together for worship.

Con•gress (**kong**-griss) ***noun*** The government body of the United States that makes laws, made up of the Senate and the House of Representatives. ▸ ***adjective*** **congressional**

con•gru•ent (kuhn-**groo**-ent) ***adjective*** Equal in shape or size, as in *congruent triangles.*

C

con•i•fer (**kon**-uh-fur *or* **koh**-nuh-fur) ***noun*** An evergreen tree that produces cones. ▸ ***adjective*** **coniferous** (kuh-**nif**-ur-uhss)

con•junc•tion (kuhn-**juhngk**-shuhn) ***noun*** A word that connects words, phrases, or sentences. The words *and, but,* and *if* are all conjunctions.

con•jur•er *or* **con•jur•or** (**kon**-juh-rur) ***noun*** A person who performs magic tricks to entertain people. ▸ ***noun*** **conjuring** ▸ ***verb*** **conjure**

con•nect (kuh-**nekt**) ***verb*** To join together two or more things, ideas, or places. ▸ **connecting, connected**

con•nec•tion (kuh-**nek**-shuhn) ***noun***
1. A link between objects, people, ideas, etc.
2. A train, plane, or bus scheduled so that people getting off other trains, planes, or buses can use it to continue their journey.
3. **connections *noun, plural*** People you know, especially people who might be useful to you in your career.

con•nois•seur (kon-uh-**sur**) ***noun*** Someone who knows a lot about a subject and appreciates things that are of good quality.

con•quer (**kong**-kur) ***verb*** To defeat and take control of an enemy.
▸ **conquering, conquered** ▸ ***noun*** **conqueror**

con•quest (**kon**-kwest) ***noun***
1. Something that is won, such as land, treasure, or buildings.
2. The act of conquering.

con•science (**kon**-shuhnss) ***noun*** Your knowledge of what is right and wrong that makes you feel guilty when you have done something wrong.

con•sci•en•tious (kon-shee-**en**-shuhss) ***adjective***
1. If you are **conscientious,** you make sure that you do things well and thoroughly. ▸ ***adverb*** **conscientiously**
2. A **conscientious objector** is someone who refuses to fight in a war because he or she believes that it is wrong to fight and kill.

con•scious (**kon**-shuhss) ***adjective***
1. Awake and able to think and perceive.
2. Aware of something.
3. Deliberate.
▸ ***noun*** **consciousness** ▸ ***adverb*** **consciously**

con•sec•u•tive (kuhn-**sek**-yuh-tiv) ***adjective*** Happening or following one after the other. ▸ ***adverb*** **consecutively**

con•sen•sus (kuhn-**sen**-suhss) ***noun*** An agreement among all the people in a discussion or meeting.

con•sent (kuhn-**sent**) ***verb*** If you **consent** to something, you agree to it.
▸ **consenting, consented** ▸ ***noun*** **consent**

con•se•quence (**kon**-suh-kwenss) ***noun*** The result of an action. ▸ ***adjective*** **consequent** ▸ ***adverb*** **consequently**

con•ser•va•tion (*kon*-sur-**vay**-shuhn) ***noun*** The protection of valuable things, especially forests, wildlife, and natural resources. ▸ ***noun*** **conservationist**

con•serv•a•tive (kuhn-**sur**-vuh-tiv)
1. ***adjective*** Moderate, cautious, and not extreme.
2. ***noun*** Someone who opposes radical change and likes things to stay as they are or used to be.
▸ ***adjective*** **conservatively**

con•serv•a•to•ry (kuhn-**sur**-vuh-*tor*-ee) ***noun***
1. A school for music or the arts.
2. A greenhouse, or a glass room attached to a house and used for growing plants.
▸ ***noun, plural*** **conservatories**

con•serve (kuhn-**surv**) ***verb*** To save something from loss, decay, or waste; to preserve. ▸ **conserving, conserved**

con•sid•er (kuhn-**sid**-ur) ***verb***
1. To think about something carefully before deciding what to do.
2. To believe that something is true.
3. To take something into account.
▸ ***verb*** **considering, considered**

con•sid•er•a•ble (kuhn-**sid**-uh-ruh-buhl) ***adjective*** A **considerable** amount is a fairly large amount. ▸ ***adverb*** **considerably**

con•sid•er•ate (kuhn-**sid**-uh-rit) ***adjective*** If you are **considerate,** you think about other people's needs and feelings when you do something. ▸ ***adverb*** **considerately**

con•sid•er•a•tion (kuhn-sid-uh-**ray**-shuhn) ***noun***
1. If you show **consideration,** you show you care about other people's needs and feelings.
2. Careful thought that you give to something before making a decision.
3. A fact that needs to be taken into account before a decision can be made.

con•sign•ment (kuhn-**sine**-muhnt) ***noun*** A number of things that are delivered together.

con•sist (kuhn-**sist**) ***verb*** If something **consists** of different things, it is made up of those things. ▸ **consisting, consisted**

con•sis•tent (kuhn-**siss**-tuhnt) ***adjective*** If you are **consistent,** you always behave in the same way or support the same ideas or principles. ▸ ***noun*** **consistency** ▸ ***adverb*** **consistently**

con•sole
1. (kuhn-**sole**) ***verb*** To cheer up or comfort someone. ▸ **consoling, consoled** ▸ ***noun*** **consolation** (*kon*-suh-**lay**-shun)
2. (**kon**-sole) ***noun*** A cabinet for a television, radio, etc., designed to stand on the floor.

con•sol•i•date (kuhn-**sol**-uh-date) ***verb*** To bring several different parts together into one. ▸ **consolidating, consolidated** ▸ ***noun*** **consolidation**

con•so•nant (**kon**-suh-nuhnt) ***noun*** A speech sound that is not a vowel. Consonants are represented by the written letters *b, m, r,* etc.

con•spic•u•ous (kuhn-**spik**-yoo-uhss) ***adjective*** Something that is **conspicuous** stands out and can be seen easily. ▸ ***adverb*** **conspicuously**

con•spir•a•cy (kuhn-**spihr**-uh-see) ***noun*** A secret, illegal plan made by two or more people. ▸ ***noun, plural*** **conspiracies** ▸ ***noun*** **conspirator** ▸ ***verb*** **conspire** (kuhn-**spire**) ▸ ***adjective*** **conspiratorial** (kuhn-*spihr*-uh-**tor**-ee-uhl)

con•sta•ble (**kon**-stuh-buhl) ***noun*** A police officer, especially in a rural area of Great Britain.

con•stant (**kon**-stuhnt) ***adjective***
1. Happening all the time and never stopping. ▸ ***adverb*** **constantly**
2. Staying at the same rate or level all the time, as in *a constant speed.*

con•stel•la•tion (*kon*-stuh-**lay**-shuhn) ***noun*** A group of stars that forms a shape or pattern.

con•sti•pat•ed (**kon**-sti-*pay*-tid) ***adjective*** If someone is **constipated,** the person cannot move his or her bowels frequently or easily. ▸ ***noun*** **constipation**

con•stit•u•ent (kuhn-**stich**-oo-uhnt) ***noun*** A voter represented by an elected official.

con•sti•tute (**kon**-stuh-toot) ***verb***
1. To form or to compose; to make up.
2. To set up or form legally, as in *to constitute a set of laws.*
▸ ***verb*** **constituting, constituted**

con•sti•tu•tion (*kon*-stuh-**too**-shuhn) ***noun***
1. The system of laws in a country that state the rights of the people and the powers of the government.
2. Constitution The written document containing the governmental principles by which the United States is governed. It went into effect in 1789.
3. Your general health and strength.
▸ ***adjective*** **constitutional**

con•straint (kuhn-**straynt**) ***noun*** Something that limits what you are able or allowed to do. ▸ ***verb*** **constrain**

C

con•strict (kuhn-**strikt**) ***verb*** To slow or stop a natural flow; to squeeze. ▸ **constricting, constricted**

con•struct (kuhn-**struhkt**) ***verb*** To build or make something. ▸ **constructing, constructed** ▸ ***noun*** **construction**

con•struc•tive (kuhn-**struhk**-tiv) ***adjective*** Helpful and useful, as in *constructive criticism.* ▸ ***adverb*** **constructively**

con•sul (**kon**-suhl) ***noun*** Someone appointed by the government of a country to live and work in another country. A consul's job is to protect fellow citizens who are working or traveling abroad.

con•sult (kuhn-**suhlt**) ***verb***
1. To go to a person for advice. ▸ ***noun*** **consultation**
2. If you **consult** a book or map, you use it to find information.
▸ ***verb*** **consulting, consulted**

con•sul•tant (kuhn-**suhl**-tuhnt) ***noun*** A person with a lot of knowledge and experience who gives professional advice to others.

con•sume (kuhn-**soom**) ***verb***
1. To eat or drink something.
2. To use something up.
3. If a fire **consumes** something, it destroys it.
▸ ***verb*** **consuming, consumed** ▸ ***noun*** **consumption**

con•sum•er (kuhn-**soo**-mur) ***noun*** Someone who buys and uses products and services.

con•tact (**kon**-takt)
1. ***noun*** When things are in **contact,** they touch each other.
2. ***noun*** If you are in **contact** with someone, you write or talk to the person.
3. ***verb*** To get in touch with someone. ▸ **contacting, contacted**

contact lens ***noun*** A small plastic lens that fits closely over your eyeball to improve your eyesight. ▸ ***noun, plural*** **contact lenses**

con•ta•gious (kuhn-**tay**-juhss) ***adjective*** A **contagious** disease can be spread by direct contact with someone or something already infected with it.

con•tain (kuhn-**tayn**) ***verb***
1. When an object **contains** something, it holds that thing inside itself, or that thing forms a part of it.
2. To keep an emotion under control.
▸ ***verb*** **containing, contained**

con•tain•er (kuhn-**tayn**-er) ***noun*** A box, jar, barrel, etc., that is used to hold something.

con•tam•i•nat•ed (kuhn-**tam**-uh-nay-tid) ***adjective*** If something is **contaminated,** it has been made dirty or unfit for use, as in *contaminated drinking water.* ▸ ***noun*** **contamination** ▸ ***verb*** **contaminate**

con•tem•plate (**kon**-tuhm-plate) ***verb***
1. To think seriously about something.
2. To look at something thoughtfully.
▸ ***verb*** **contemplating, contemplated**
▸ ***noun*** **contemplation**

con•tem•po•rar•y (kuhn-**tem**-puh-rer-ee)
1. ***adjective*** Up-to-date or modern.
2. ***adjective*** If an event is **contemporary** with another event, it happened at about the same time.
3. ***noun*** A **contemporary** is a person of about the same age as you. ▸ ***noun, plural*** **contemporaries**

con•tempt (kuhn-**tempt**) ***noun*** Total lack of respect. ▸ ***adjective*** **contemptuous** ▸ ***adverb*** **contemptuously**

con•tend (kuhn-**tend**) ***verb***
1. To compete. ▸ ***noun*** **contender**
2. To argue.
3. To try to deal with a difficulty.
▸ ***verb*** **contending, contended**

con•tent (kuhn-**tent**)
1. ***adjective*** Happy and satisfied. ▸ ***noun*** **content,** ***noun*** **contentment**
▸ ***adjective*** **contented** ▸ ***adverb*** **contentedly**
2. ***verb*** If you **content yourself** with

something, you are satisfied with it. ▸ **contenting, contented**

con·tents (**kon**-tentss) ***noun, plural*** The things that are inside something or that make it up.

con·test
1. (**kon**-test) ***noun*** A competition.
2. (kuhn-**test**) ***verb*** To compete or fight for something. ▸ ***noun*** **contestant**
3. (kuhn-**test**) ***verb*** To claim that something is wrong.
▸ ***verb*** **contesting, contested**

con·text (**kon**-tekst) ***noun***
1. The **context** of a word or phrase is the language around it that helps you understand its meaning.
2. If you put an event or an action **in context,** you take into account all the things that affect it.

con·ti·nent (**kon**-tuh-nuhnt) ***noun***
1. One of the seven large land masses of the earth. They are Asia, Africa, Europe, North America, South America, Australia, and Antarctica.
2. **the Continent** The mainland of Europe. ▸ ***adjective*** **continental**

continental shelf ***noun*** A shallow, gently sloping area of the sea floor near a coastline.

con·tin·u·al (kuhn-**tin**-yoo-uhl) ***adjective***
1. Happening again and again; frequent.
2. Happening without a pause; continuous. ▸ ***adverb*** **continually**

con·tin·ue (kuhn-**tin**-yoo) ***verb*** To go on doing something. ▸ **continuing, continued** ▸ ***noun*** **continuation**

con·tin·u·ous (kuhn-**tin**-yoo-uhss) ***adjective*** When something is **continuous,** it does not stop, as in *a continuous noise.* ▸ ***adverb*** **continuously**

con·tort (kuhn-**tort**) ***verb*** To twist something out of its usual shape. ▸ **contorting, contorted** ▸ ***noun*** **contortion** ▸ ***adjective*** **contorted**

con·tour (**kon**-toor) ***noun*** The outline of a curving figure or object.

con·tra·band (**kon**-truh-*band*) ***noun*** Goods that are brought illegally from one place to another. ▸ ***adjective*** **contraband**

con·tract
1. (**kon**-trakt) ***noun*** A legal agreement between people or companies stating the terms by which one will work for the other or sell to the other.
2. (kuhn-**trakt**) ***verb*** To become smaller.
3. (kuhn-**trakt**) ***verb*** To get.
▸ ***verb*** **contracting, contracted**

con·trac·tion (kuhn-**trak**-shuhn) ***noun***
1. A shortening of something.
2. Two words combined with an apostrophe, such as *can't, wouldn't, I'd, won't.*

con·tra·dict (*kon*-truh-**dikt**) ***verb*** To say the opposite of what has been said. ▸ **contradicting, contradicted** ▸ ***noun*** **contradiction**

con·tra·dic·tor·y (*kon*-truh-**dik**-tur-ee) ***adjective*** Opposite, contrary, or not consistent.

con·trap·tion (kuhn-**trap**-shuhn) ***noun*** A strange or odd device or machine.

con·trar·y ***adjective***
1. (**kon**-trer-ee) Opposite. ▸ ***noun*** **contrary**
2. (kuhn-**trair**-ee) Deliberately stubborn and difficult.

con·trast (kuhn-**trast**) ***verb***
1. To be very different from something else.
2. To identify the differences between things.
▸ ***verb*** **contrasting, contrasted**
▸ ***noun*** **contrast** (**kon**-trast)

con·tri·bute (kuhn-**trib**-yoot) ***verb***
1. To give help or money to a person or an organization.
2. To write for a magazine or newspaper.
▸ ***verb*** **contributing, contributed**
▸ ***noun*** **contribution,** ***noun*** **contributor**

con·trive (kuhn-**trive**) ***verb***
1. To form an intelligent plan; to scheme.
2. To make something up.
▸ ***verb*** **contriving, contrived**

C

con•trol (kuhn-**trohl**)
1. ***verb*** To make something or someone do what you want. ▸ ***noun*** **control**
2. ***noun*** Power or authority over people or a situation.
3. ***noun, plural*** The **controls** of a machine are the levers and switches that make it work.
4. ***verb*** To hold back.
▸ ***verb*** **controlling, controlled**

con•tro•ver•sial (*kon*-truh-**vur**-shuhl) ***adjective*** If something is **controversial,** it causes a lot of argument. ▸ ***noun*** **controversy**

con•va•les•cence (*kon*-vuh-**less**-uhnss) ***noun*** The time during which someone recovers from an illness. ▸ ***verb*** **convalesce**

con•va•les•cent (*kon*-vuh-**less**-uhnt)
1. ***noun*** A person recovering from an illness.
2. ***adjective*** To do with a person recovering from an illness or with a period of convalescence.

con•vec•tion (kuhn-**vek**-shuhn) ***noun*** The movement of heat through liquids and gases.

con•vene (kuhn-**veen**) ***verb*** To gather together. ▸ **convening, convened**

con•ven•ience (kuhn-**vee**-nyuhnss)
1. ***noun*** Something that is useful and easy to use. ▸ ***adjective*** **convenient** ▸ ***adverb*** **conveniently**
2. ***adjective*** **Convenience food** is food that is quick and easy to prepare, such as a frozen dinner.

con•ven•ient (kuhn-**vee**-nyuhnt) ***adjective*** If something is **convenient,** it is useful or easy to use. ▸ ***adverb*** **conveniently**

con•vent (**kon**-vent) ***noun*** A building where nuns live and work.

con•ven•tion (kuhn-**ven**-shuhn) ***noun***
1. A large gathering of people who have the same interests, such as a political meeting where party candidates are chosen.
2. A custom or accepted way to behave.

con•ven•tion•al (kuhn-**ven**-shuh-nuhl) ***adjective*** A **conventional** person does things in a traditional or accepted way. ▸ ***adverb*** **conventionally**

con•verge (kuhn-**verj**) ***verb*** To come together and form a single unit. ▸ **converging, converged**

con•ver•sa•tion (kon-vur-**say**-shuhn) ***noun*** If you have a **conversation** with someone, you talk with the person for a while.

con•verse
1. (kon-**vurss**) ***verb*** To talk with someone. ▸ **conversing, conversed**
2. (**kon**-vurss) ***noun*** The opposite. ▸ ***adverb*** **conversely**

con•vert
1. (kuhn-**vurt**) ***verb*** To make something into something else. ▸ **converting, converted**
2. (**kon**-vert) ***noun*** A person who has changed his or her religion or other beliefs.
▸ ***noun*** **conversion**

con•vert•i•ble (kuhn-**vur**-tuh-buhl)
1. ***adjective*** Able to be changed into something else.
2. ***noun*** A car with a top that can be put down or removed.

con•vex (**kon**-veks *or* kuhn-**veks**) ***adjective*** Curved outward, like the outer side of a ball.

con•vey (kuhn-**vay**) ***verb***
1. To carry or take from one place to another.
2. To tell or to communicate.
▸ ***verb*** **conveying, conveyed**

con•vey•or belt (kuhn-**vay**-ur) ***noun*** A moving belt that carries objects from one place to another in a factory.

con•vict
1. (kuhn-**vikt**) ***verb*** To find or prove that someone is guilty of a crime. ▸ **convicting, convicted**
2. (**kon**-vikt) ***noun*** Someone who is in prison because he or she has committed a crime.

con•vic•tion (kuhn-**vik**-shuhn) ***noun***
1. A strong belief in something.

2. If you have a **conviction** for a crime, you have been found guilty of committing it.

con•vince (kuhn-**vinss**) ***verb*** If you **convince** somebody, you make the person believe you. ▸ **convincing, convinced** ▸ ***adjective*** **convincing** ▸ ***adverb*** **convincingly**

con•voy (**kon**-voi) ***noun*** A group of ships, military vehicles, trucks, etc., traveling together for convenience or safety.

con•vul•sion (kuhn-**vul**-shuhn) ***noun*** An involuntary jerking movement of the muscles or the whole body; a spasm.

cook (**kuk**)
1. ***verb*** To prepare and heat food for a meal. ▸ **cooking, cooked** ▸ ***noun*** **cooking**
2. ***noun*** Someone whose job is to prepare food.

cook•book (**kuk**-*buk*) ***noun*** A book filled with recipes, cooking directions, and information about food.

cook•ie (**kuk**-ee) ***noun*** A small, sweetened, usually flat cake.

cool (**kool**)
1. ***adjective*** Rather cold. ▸ ***noun*** **coolness**
2. ***verb*** To lower the temperature of something. ▸ **cooling, cooled**
3. ***adjective*** Unfriendly and distant. ▸ ***adverb*** **coolly** *or* **cooly**
4. ***adjective*** (*informal*) Fashionable and trendy.
▸ ***adjective*** **cooler, coolest**

coop (**koop**) ***noun*** A small building or pen used to house chickens or other small animals.

co-op (**koh**-op) ***noun*** A store, society, or building in which the members own shares in the organization.

co•op•er•ate (koh-**op**-uh-rate) ***verb*** To work together. ▸ **cooperating, cooperated** ▸ ***noun*** **cooperation**

co•op•er•a•tive (koh-**op**-ur-uh-tiv)
1. ***adjective*** If you are **cooperative,** you work well with other people. ▸ ***noun*** **cooperativeness**
2. ***noun*** A business owned by all the people who work in it.

co•or•di•nate
1. (koh-**or**-duh-*nate*) ***verb*** To organize activities or people so that they all work together. ▸ **coordinating, coordinated** ▸ ***noun*** **coordination,** ***noun*** **coordinator**
2. (koh-**or**-duh-nit) ***noun*** One of a set of numbers used to show the position of a point on a line, graph, or map.

co•or•di•nat•ed (koh-**or**-duh-nay-tid) ***adjective*** If you are **coordinated,** you have good control in moving your arms and legs.

cope (**kope**) ***verb*** To deal with something successfully. ▸ **coping, coped**

cop•i•er (**kop**-ee-ur) ***noun*** A machine that copies printed material.

co•pi•lot (**koh**-*pye*-luht) ***noun*** The assistant pilot of an airplane.

cop•per (**kop**-ur) ***noun***
1. A reddish brown metal that conducts heat and electricity well.
2. A reddish brown color. ▸ ***adjective*** **copper,** ***adjective*** **coppery**

cop•per•head (**kop**-ur-*hed*) ***noun*** A poisonous snake with a light brown body and dark brown markings. Copperheads are found in the eastern part of the United States.

cop•y (**kop**-ee)
1. ***verb*** To do the same as someone else.
2. ***noun*** A **copy** of something is made to look or sound exactly the same as the original.
3. ***verb*** To make a copy of something.
▸ ***noun, plural*** **copies** ▸ ***verb*** **copies, copying, copied**

cop•y•right (**kop**-ee-*rite*) ***noun*** The right to produce, publish, or sell a song, book, etc., such that others must obtain permission to copy or perform the material.

cor•al (**kor**-uhl) ***noun***
1. A substance found underwater, made up of the skeletons of tiny sea creatures.
2. A pink-red color.

C

C

coral reef ***noun*** A reef made of coral and other materials that have solidified into rock.

coral snake ***noun*** A poisonous snake with red, black, and yellow bands on its body.

cord (**kord**) ***noun***
1. A length of string or rope.
2. Covered wire that connects an electrical appliance to an outlet.
3. A pile of cut wood four feet wide, four feet high, and eight feet long.
Cord sounds like **chord.**

cor·dial (**kor**-juhl) ***adjective*** Friendly, as in *a cordial visit.* ▸ ***adverb*** **cordially**

cor·du·roy (**kor**-duh-roi) ***noun*** A heavy cotton material with many rows of close ribs.

core (**kor**) ***noun***
1. The hard center part of an apple, pear, etc., which often contains seeds. ▸ ***verb*** **core**
2. The intensely hot, most inner part of the earth.
3. The most important part of something.
4. The place in a nuclear reactor where fission occurs.

cork (**kork**) ***noun*** Soft bark used as a stopper in bottles or to make mats, etc. ▸ ***verb*** **cork**

cork·screw (**kork**-*skroo*)
1. ***noun*** A tool for pulling corks out of bottles.
2. ***adjective*** Spiraling or turning in circles, as in *corkscrew pasta.*

corn (**korn**) ***noun***
1. The sweet seeds that grow in rows on the large ears of a tall grass plant, eaten as a vegetable.
2. A small patch of hard skin on your foot.

cor·ne·a (**kor**-nee-uh) ***noun*** The transparent outer layer of the eyeball. The cornea covers the iris and pupil.

cor·ner (**kor**-nur)
1. ***noun*** The place where two sides of something meet. ▸ ***adjective*** **corner**
2. ***verb*** To get a person or an animal into a situation or position that is a trap. ▸ **cornering, cornered**

cor·net (kor-**net**) ***noun*** A brass musical instrument that is similar to but shorter than a trumpet.

corn·meal (**korn**-*meel*) ***noun*** Ground corn.

corn·row (**korn**-*roh*) ***noun*** A flat braid arranged close to the scalp. ▸ ***verb*** **cornrow**

cor·o·nar·y (**kor**-uh-ner-ee)
1. ***adjective*** To do with the heart, as in *a coronary disease.*
2. ***noun*** A heart attack. ▸ ***noun, plural*** **coronaries**

cor·o·na·tion (kor-uh-**nay**-shun) ***noun*** The ceremony in which a king or queen is crowned.

cor·o·ner (**kor**-uh-nur) ***noun*** A medical official who investigates sudden or unnatural deaths.

cor·po·ral (**kor**-pur-uhl) ***noun*** A soldier who ranks below a sergeant.

corporal punishment ***noun*** Physical punishment, such as spanking.

cor·po·ra·tion (kor-puh-**ray**-shuhn) ***noun*** A group of people who are allowed by law to run a company, college, or town as a single person. Like an individual, a corporation can enter into contracts and buy and sell property.

corps (**kor**) ***noun***
1. A group of people acting together or doing the same thing.
2. A company of military officers and enlisted personnel. ▸ ***noun, plural*** **corps** (**kors**)

corpse (**korps**) ***noun*** A dead body, especially of a human.

cor·pus·cle (**kor**-puhss-uhl) ***noun*** A red or white blood cell.

cor·ral (kuh-**ral**)
1. ***noun*** A fenced area that holds horses, cattle, or other animals.
2. ***verb*** To gather people, animals, or things in an enclosed area. ▸ **corralling, corralled**

C

cor•rect (kuh-**rekt**)
1. ***adjective*** True, or right. ▸ ***adverb*** **correctly**
2. ***verb*** To make something right.
▸ **correcting, corrected** ▸ ***noun*** **correction**

cor•res•pond (kor-uh-**spond**) ***verb***
1. When you **correspond** with someone, you write letters to each other.
2. If two things **correspond,** they match in some way.
▸ ***verb*** **corresponding, corresponded**
▸ ***noun*** **correspondence**

cor•res•pond•ent (kor-uh-**spon**-duhnt) ***noun***
1. Someone who reports for television, radio, or newspapers about a special subject or place, as in *a war correspondent.*
2. Someone who writes letters.

cor•ri•dor (**kor**-uh-dur) ***noun*** A long hallway or passage in a building or train.

cor•rode (kuh-**rode**) ***verb*** To destroy or eat away at something little by little.
▸ **corroding, corroded** ▸ ***noun*** **corrosion** ▸ ***adjective*** **corrosive**

cor•ru•gated (**kor**-uh-*gay*-tid) ***adjective*** Shaped into ridges or ripples, as in *corrugated iron.*

cor•rupt (kuh-**ruhpt**)
1. ***verb*** To make someone bad or dishonest. ▸ **corrupting, corrupted**
▸ ***adjective*** **corrupt**
2. ***adjective*** If computer data is **corrupt,** it contains errors. ▸ ***verb*** **corrupt**

cor•sage (kor-**sahj**) ***noun*** A small flower bouquet worn on clothing or strapped to the wrist.

cos•met•ic (koz-**met**-ik)
1. **cosmetics** ***noun, plural*** Beauty products such as lipstick and mascara.
2. ***adjective*** Done to change the way a person or thing looks, as in *cosmetic surgery.*

cos•mic (**koz**-mik) ***adjective*** To do with the universe, as in *cosmic laws.* ▸ ***adverb*** **cosmically**

cos•mo•naut (**koz**-muh-*nawt*) ***noun*** A Russian astronaut.

cos•mo•pol•i•tan (koz-muh-**pol**-uh-tuhn) ***adjective*** If you are **cosmopolitan,** you feel at home in more than one country. ▸ ***noun*** **cosmopolitan**

cos•mos (**koz**-muhss) ***noun*** The universe.

cost (**kost** *or* **kawst**)
1. ***verb*** To have a certain price.
2. ***verb*** To make someone give up or lose something.
3. **cost of living** ***noun*** The amount of money you need to spend on food, housing, clothing, etc.
▸ ***noun*** **cost** ▸ ***verb*** **costing, cost**

co-star (**koh**-*star*) ***noun*** An actor who appears in a movie, play, or television show with another actor of equal importance. ▸ ***verb*** **co-star**

cost•ly (**kost**-lee) ***adjective*** Expensive, as in *costly gifts.* ▸ **costlier, costliest**

cos•tume (**koss**-toom) ***noun***
1. Clothes worn by actors or people dressing in disguise.
2. Clothes worn by people at a particular time or in a particular place.

cot (**kot**) ***noun*** A small, narrow bed that can be folded up and put away.

cot•tage (**kot**-ij) ***noun*** A small house, especially in a beach or country setting.

cottage cheese ***noun*** Soft, white cheese made from curdled skim milk.

cot•ton (**kot**-uhn) ***noun***
1. Cloth made from the fluffy white fibers surrounding the seed pods of a certain plant.
2. The plant that produces such fibers.
3. Thread from these fibers, used for sewing.
▸ ***adjective*** **cotton**

cot•ton•mouth (**kot**-uhn-*mouth*) ***noun*** A poisonous snake that lives near water and in swamps in the southeastern part of the United States. It is also called a water moccasin.

cot•ton•tail (**kot**-uhn-*tale*) ***noun*** A rabbit with a short, fluffy, white tail.

C

couch (**kouch**) ***noun***
1. A long, soft piece of furniture that two or more people can sit on at the same time. ▸ ***noun, plural* couches**
2. couch potato (*informal*) Someone who spends most of his or her time watching television rather than being active.

cou•gar (**koo**-gur) ***noun*** A member of the cat family with a small head, long legs, and a strong body. Cougars lived in the mountains of North and South America, but are now mostly extinct; also called **mountain lions**, **panthers**, or **pumas**.

cough (**kawf**)
1. ***verb*** To make a sudden, harsh noise as you force air out of your lungs. ▸ **coughing, coughed** ▸ ***noun* cough**
2. ***noun*** An illness that makes you cough.

could (**kud**) ***verb*** Past tense of **can.**

could•n't (**kud**-uhnt) ***contraction*** A short form of *could not.*

coun•cil (**koun**-suhl) ***noun*** A group of people chosen to look after the interests of a town, a county, or an organization, as in *the city council.* **Council** sounds like **counsel.**

coun•sel (**koun**-suhl)
1. ***verb*** To listen to people's problems and give advice. ▸ **counseling, counseled**
2. ***noun*** Advice.
Counsel sounds like **council.**
▸ ***noun* counseling**

coun•sel•or (**koun**-suh-lur) ***noun***
1. Someone trained to help with problems or give advice.
2. A lawyer.

count (**kount**) ***verb***
1. To say numbers in order. ▸ ***noun* counting**
2. To work out how many there are of something. ▸ ***noun* count**
3. To be worth something.
4. If you can **count on** something or someone, you rely on that thing or person.
5. To think of as.
▸ ***verb* counting, counted**

count•down (**kount**-*down*) ***noun*** A backward counting from a certain number down to zero, as at a missile launch.

coun•ter (**koun**-tur)
1. ***noun*** A long, flat surface, as in *a counter in a department store.*
2. ***noun*** A small, flat, round playing piece used in some games or to do math.
3. ***adjective*** Opposite. ▸ ***adverb* counter**

coun•ter•act (*koun*-tur-**akt**) ***verb*** To act against something so that it is less effective. ▸ **counteracting, counteracted**

coun•ter•clock•wise (*koun*-tur-**klok**-wize) ***adverb*** In a direction opposite to the hands of a clock. ▸ ***adjective* counterclockwise**

coun•ter•feit (**koun**-tur-fit) ***adjective*** Something that has been made to look like the real thing but is a fake, as in *counterfeit money.* ▸ ***noun* counterfeit** ▸ ***verb* counterfeit**

coun•ter•part (**koun**-tur-*part*) ***noun***
1. Someone or something that closely resembles another in some way.
2. One of two parts that complete each other.

count•less (**kount**-liss) ***adjective*** So many that you cannot count them.

coun•try (**kuhn**-tree) ***noun***
1. A part of the world with its own borders and government.
2. Undeveloped land away from towns or cities. ▸ ***adjective* country**
3. The people of a nation.
▸ ***noun, plural* countries**

coun•try•side (**kuhn**-tree-*side*) ***noun*** Undeveloped land away from towns or cities.

coun•ty (**koun**-tee) ***noun*** A division or part of a state with its own local government. ▸ ***noun, plural* counties** ▸ ***adjective* county**

cou•ple (**kuhp**-uhl) ***noun***
1. Two of something.
2. Two people paired together.

cou•pon (**koo**-pon) ***noun***
1. A small piece of paper that gives you a discount on something.
2. A small form that you fill out to get information about something.

cour•age (**kur**-ij) ***noun*** Bravery, or fearlessness. ▸ ***adjective* courageous** (kuh-**ray**-juhss) ▸ ***adverb* courageously**

cour•i•er (**kur**-ee-ur *or* **koor**-ee-ur) ***noun*** Someone who carries messages or parcels for somebody else.

course (**korss**) ***noun***
1. A part of a meal served by itself.
2. A series of lessons.
3. An area where a sport is played, as in *a golf course.*
4. A route.
Course sounds like **coarse.**

court (**kort**)
1. ***noun*** A place where legal cases are heard and decided.
2. ***noun*** An area where games such as basketball, tennis, and racquetball are played.
3. ***noun*** A place closed in by walls or buildings.
4. ***verb*** To try to win the love of someone, especially so as to marry.
5. ***verb*** To try to attract.
6. ***verb*** To tempt.
▸ ***verb* courting, courted**

cour•te•ous (**kur**-tee-uhss) ***adjective*** Polite and respectful. ▸ ***noun* courteousness** ▸ ***adverb* courteously**

cour•te•sy (**kur**-tuh-see)
1. ***noun*** Behaving in a way that shows good manners and behavior.
2. ***noun*** A thoughtful act; a favor.
▸ ***noun, plural* courtesies**

court•house (**kort**-*houss*) ***noun*** A building where trials and government business are conducted.

court•ship (**kort**-ship) ***noun*** Attempts by one person to win the love and affection of another.

court•yard (**kort**-*yard*) ***noun*** An open area surrounded by walls; a court.

cous•cous (**koos**-koos) ***noun*** A steamed dish made from the centers of grains of wheat.

cous•in (**kuhz**-uhn) ***noun*** Your **cousin** is the child of your uncle or aunt.

cove (**kove**) ***noun*** A small, sheltered inlet along a coast.

cov•er (**kuhv**-ur) ***verb***
1. To put something over something else. ▸ ***noun* cover**
2. To teach or study something thoroughly. ▸ ***noun* coverage**
3. To travel a certain distance.
4. To include or to provide for.
▸ ***verb* covering, covered**

covered wagon ***noun*** A large, wooden wagon with a canvas cover spread over metal hoops, used by pioneers crossing the country during the United States' westward expansion.

cov•et (**kuhv**-it) ***verb*** To want something very much even though it belongs to someone else. ▸ **coveting, coveted**

cow (**kou**) ***noun***
1. An adult female of cattle, raised especially for her milk.
2. An adult female of some other large mammals, including seals and whales.

cow•ard (**kou**-urd) ***noun*** Someone who is easily scared and runs away from frightening situations. ▸ ***adjective* cowardly**

cow•ard•ice (**kou**-ur-diss) ***noun*** Lack of bravery.

cow•boy (**kou**-*boi*) ***noun*** A man or boy who herds and looks after cattle.

cow•girl (**kou**-*gurl*) ***noun*** A woman or girl who herds and looks after cattle.

cow•hand (**kou**-*hand*) ***noun*** Someone who works on a ranch.

cow•hide (**kou**-*hide*) ***noun*** The skin of a cow, used to make leather goods.

coy•o•te (kye-**oh**-tee *or* **kye**-oht) ***noun*** An animal that looks like a small wolf and is native to the western United States. ▸ ***noun, plural* coyote** *or* **coyotes**

C

C

co•zy (**koh**-zee) ***adjective*** Comfortable or snug. ▸ **cozier, coziest** ▸ ***noun*** **coziness** ▸ ***adverb*** **cozily**

CPR ***noun*** (**see pee ar**) A method of reviving heart attack victims using mouth-to-mouth breathing and rhythmical compressing of the chest. CPR stands for *cardiopulmonary resuscitation.*

crab (**krab**) ***noun*** A creature that lives in water and has a hard shell, eight legs, and two claws, or pincers.

crab apple ***noun*** A small, sour apple used to make jelly.

crack (**krak**)
1. ***verb*** To break or split, often with a loud, sharp noise. ▸ ***noun*** **crack**
2. ***verb*** To find the answer to something.
3. ***noun*** A break or a narrow opening.
4. ***noun*** (*informal*) A nasty or sarcastic remark.
5. ***noun*** (*slang*) A form of the drug cocaine.
6. (*informal*) When you **take a crack at** something, you try to do it.
▸ ***verb*** **cracking, cracked**

crack•er (**krak**-ur) ***noun*** A thin, plain biscuit or wafer.

crack•le (**krak**-uhl) ***verb*** To make a lot of quick, sharp sounds. ▸ **crackling, crackled** ▸ ***noun*** **crackle**

cra•dle (**kray**-duhl)
1. ***noun*** A small bed for a young baby.
2. ***verb*** To hold something or someone in or as if in a cradle. ▸ **cradling, cradled**
3. ***noun*** The place where something starts, as in *the cradle of democracy.*

craft (**kraft**) ***noun***
1. Work or a hobby in which you make things with your hands. ▸ ***verb*** **craft**
2. A vehicle such as a boat, spaceship, or plane.

crafts•per•son (**krafts**-*per*-suhn) ***noun*** Someone skilled at making things with his or her hands. ▸ ***noun, plural*** **craftsmen** ▸ ***noun*** **craftsmanship**

craft•y (**kraf**-tee) ***adjective*** A **crafty** person is skilled at tricking other people. ▸ **craftier, craftiest** ▸ ***adverb*** **craftily**

crag (**krag**) ***noun*** A steep, sharp rock or cliff. ▸ ***adjective*** **craggy**

cram (**kram**) ***verb***
1. To fit things into a small space.
2. To study very hard over a short period of time, as in *to cram for an exam.*
▸ ***verb*** **cramming, crammed**

cramp (**kramp**)
1. ***noun*** Pain caused by a muscle tightening suddenly. ▸ ***verb*** **cramp**
2. ***verb*** (*informal*) If someone or something **cramps your style,** it does not allow you to express yourself freely.
▸ **cramping, cramped**
3. ***noun, plural*** **Cramps** are sharp pains in your abdomen.

cramped (**krampt**) ***adjective*** If a place is **cramped,** there is not enough room in it for everyone or everything.

cran•ber•ry (**kran**-*ber*-ee) ***noun*** A small, red, tart berry that grows on low bushes in bogs and in swamps.

crane (**krane**)
1. ***noun*** A large wading bird with long legs and a long neck and bill.
2. ***noun*** A machine with a long arm used to lift and move heavy objects.
3. ***verb*** To stretch your neck so that you can see over or around something better.
▸ **craning, craned**

crank (**krangk**)
1. ***noun*** A handle that is attached at a right angle to a shaft and is turned to make a machine work.
2. ***verb*** To start something, such as an old-fashioned car, by turning a crank.
▸ **cranking, cranked**
3. ***noun*** (*informal*) Someone with strange ideas. ▸ ***adjective*** **crank**

crank•y (**krang**-kee) ***adjective*** Acting in an annoyed way; grouchy. ▸ ***adjective*** **crankier, crankiest**

crash (**krash**)
1. ***verb*** To make a loud noise like thunder.
▸ ***noun*** **crash**
2. ***noun*** An accident in which a vehicle hits something at high speed. ▸ ***verb*** **crash** ▸ ***noun, plural*** **crashes**
3. ***verb*** When a computer system or

program **crashes,** it fails completely.
▸ ***verb*** **crashes, crashing, crashed**

crate (**krate**) ***noun*** A large, usually wooden box, as in *a crate of oranges.*
▸ ***verb*** **crate**

cra•ter (**kray**-tur) ***noun***
1. The mouth of a volcano or geyser.
2. A large hole in the ground caused by something such as a bomb or meteorite.

crave (**krave**) ***verb*** To want something desperately. ▸ **craving, craved** ▸ ***noun*** **craving**

crawl (**krawl**)
1. ***verb*** To move on your hands and knees.
2. ***verb*** To move slowly.
3. ***noun*** A style of swimming face down in which you use your arms in turn while kicking your legs.
▸ ***noun*** **crawl** ▸ ***verb*** **crawling, crawled**

cray•fish (**kray**-*fish*) ***noun*** A small animal related to the lobster that lives in fresh water and is used for food. ▸ ***noun, plural*** **crayfish** *or* **crayfishes**

cray•on (**kray**-uhn *or* **kray**-on)
1. ***noun*** A colored wax stick used for drawing and coloring.
2. ***verb*** To draw or color with a crayon.
▸ **crayoning, crayoned**

craze (**kraze**) ***noun*** A very popular fashion or pastime that usually does not stay popular very long.

cra•zy (**kray**-zee) ***adjective***
1. Insane or foolish.
2. (*informal*) Very enthusiastic.
▸ ***adjective*** **crazier, craziest** ▸ ***noun*** **craziness** ▸ ***adverb*** **crazily**

creak (**kreek**) ***verb*** To make a squeaky, grating noise. **Creak** sounds like **creek.**
▸ **creaking, creaked** ▸ ***noun*** **creak**
▸ ***adjective*** **creaky** ▸ ***adverb*** **creakily**

cream (**kreem**) ***noun***
1. A thick, fatty liquid found in whole milk. When cream is churned, butter forms. ▸ ***verb*** **cream**
2. A thick, smooth substance like cream that you put on your skin, as in *hand cream.*
3. A yellow-white color, or the color of cream. ▸ ***adjective*** **cream**
4. The best part, as in *the cream of the crop.*
▸ ***noun*** **creaminess** ▸ ***adjective*** **creamy**

crease (**kreess**) ***verb*** To make lines or folds in something, especially fabric or paper. ▸ **creasing, creased** ▸ ***noun*** **crease**

cre•ate (kree-**ate**) ***verb*** To make or design something. ▸ **creating, created**
▸ ***noun*** **creator**

cre•a•tion (kree-**ay**-shuhn) ***noun***
1. Something that has been made.
2. The act of making something.

cre•a•tive (kree-**ay**-tiv) ***adjective*** If you are **creative,** you use your imagination and are good at thinking of new ideas.
▸ ***noun*** **creativity** ▸ ***adverb*** **creatively**

crea•ture (**kree**-chur) ***noun*** A living being, human or animal.

crèche (**kresh**) ***noun*** A model of the baby Jesus with his parents, visitors, animals, etc., in the stable where he was born.

cre•den•tials (kri-**den**-shuhlz) ***noun, plural*** Written proof of someone's background, experience, or certification, such as a diploma or certificate.

cred•i•ble (**kred**-uh-buhl) ***adjective*** Believable, as in *a credible witness.*
▸ ***noun*** **credibility**

cred•it (**kred**-it) ***noun***
1. If you buy something **on credit,** you pay for it later.
2. The balance in your favor in an account.
3. Praise or acknowledgement.
4. ***noun, plural*** The **credits** at the end of a movie or television program tell you who made it.
▸ ***verb*** **credit**

credit card ***noun*** A small, plastic card used in stores and restaurants to pay for products. Later, a bill is sent by the credit card company for all purchases made that month.

C

creed (**kreed**) ***noun*** A system of beliefs; a guiding belief.

creek (**kreek**) ***noun*** A small stream, usually one that is larger than a brook and smaller than a river. **Creek** sounds like **creak.**

creep (**kreep**)
1. ***verb*** To move very slowly and quietly. ▸ ***noun*** **creep**
2. ***verb*** To crawl along the ground.
3. ***noun*** (*slang*) An unpleasant person.
4. (*informal*) If something or someone **gives you the creeps,** that thing or person is unpleasant and frightening.
▸ ***noun*** **creep** ▸ ***verb*** **creeping, crept** (**krept**) ▸ ***adjective*** **creepy**

cre•mate (**kree**-mate) ***verb*** To burn a dead body to ashes. ▸ **cremating, cremated** ▸ ***noun*** **cremation**

Cre•ole (**kree**-ohl)
1. ***noun*** Someone of European descent born in the West Indies or South America.
2. ***noun*** Someone of French or Spanish descent living in Louisiana or Texas.
3. ***noun*** The French language spoken in Louisiana and Haiti.
4. **creole** *or* **Creole** ***adjective*** Prepared with a spicy sauce of tomatoes, peppers, okra, etc.

crepe (**krape**) ***noun*** A very thin pancake that is sometimes rolled up around a filling.

crepe paper ***noun*** A thin paper with a crinkled texture, often used as a party decoration.

cres•cent (**kress**-uhnt) ***noun*** A curved shape similar to that of the moon when it is just a sliver in the sky.

crest (**krest**)
1. ***noun*** The top of something such as a wave or a hill.
2. ***noun*** A comb or tuft of feathers on a bird's head. ▸ ***adjective*** **crested**
3. ***verb*** To reach the highest point. ▸ **cresting, crested**
4. ***noun*** Part of a coat of arms.

crev•ice (**krev**-iss) ***noun*** A crack or split in something, such as a rock.

crew (**kroo**) ***noun*** A team of people who work together on a ship, an aircraft, or a specific job.

crib (**krib**)
1. ***noun*** A small bed for a baby.
2. ***noun*** A small farm building in which grain is stored.
3. ***verb*** (*informal*) To copy someone else's work and pretend it is your own. ▸ **cribbing, cribbed**

crick•et (**krik**-it) ***noun***
1. A jumping insect similar to a grasshopper.
2. An outdoor game played by two teams of 11 players with smooth, flat bats; a small, hard ball; and two wickets. It is popular in England.

crime (**krime**) ***noun*** Something that is against the law.

crim•i•nal (**krim**-uh-nuhl)
1. ***noun*** Someone who commits a crime.
2. ***adjective*** To do with crime, as in *a criminal investigation.* ▸ ***adverb*** **criminally**

crim•son (**krim**-zuhn) ***noun*** A deep red color. ▸ ***adjective*** **crimson**

crin•kle (**kring**-kuhl) ***verb***
1. To wrinkle or to crumple. ▸ ***adjective*** **crinkled**
2. To make a soft, slight, rustling sound.
▸ ***verb*** **crinkling, crinkled** ▸ ***noun*** **crinkle**

crip•ple (**krip**-uhl)
1. ***noun*** Someone who is not able to walk normally due to disease or injury. ▸ ***verb*** **cripple**
2. ***verb*** To stop someone or something from moving or working properly. ▸ **crippling, crippled** ▸ ***adjective*** **crippled**

cri•sis (**krye**-siss) ***noun***
1. A time of danger and difficulty.
2. A turning point or decision point.
▸ ***noun, plural*** **crises** (**krye**-seez)

crisp (**krisp**) ***adjective***
1. Firm and easily broken, as in *a crisp piece of toast.* ▸ ***adjective*** **crispy**
2. Fresh, dry, and cool, as in *a crisp winter morning.*

▸ ***adverb*** **crisply** ▸ ***adjective*** **crisper, crispest**

criss•cross (**kriss**-*krawss*) ***verb*** To form or move in a pattern of intersecting lines. ▸ **crisscrossing, crisscrossed** ▸ ***noun*** **crisscross** ▸ ***adjective*** **crisscross**

crit•ic (**krit**-ik) ***noun***
1. Someone who finds something wrong with people or things.
2. Someone whose job is to write a review of a book, movie, play, television program, etc.

crit•i•cal (**krit**-uh-kuhl) ***adjective***
1. If you are **critical** of something, you find fault with it.
2. Dangerous or serious, as in *a critical operation.* ▸ ***adverb*** **critically**

crit•i•cize (**krit**-uh-size) ***verb***
1. To tell someone what he or she has done wrong.
2. To point out the good and bad parts in a book, movie, play, television program, etc.
▸ ***verb*** **criticizing, criticized** ▸ ***noun*** **criticism**

croak (**krohk**) ***verb***
1. When a frog **croaks,** it makes a deep, hoarse sound.
2. If you **croak,** you speak with a deep, hoarse voice. ▸ ***adjective*** **croaky**
3. (*slang*) To die.
▸ ***verb*** **croaking, croaked** ▸ ***noun*** **croak**

cro•chet (croh-**shay**) ***verb*** To make a kind of needlework from thread or yarn using a hooked needle. ▸ **crocheting, crocheted** ▸ ***noun*** **crochet,** ***noun*** **crocheting**

crock•er•y (**krok**-ur-ee) ***noun*** Pottery that you use for food, such as plates, cups, and saucers.

croc•o•dile (**krok**-uh-dile) ***noun*** A large, scaly reptile with short legs and strong jaws, related to the alligator.

cro•cus (**kroh**-kuhss) ***noun*** A small plant with purple, yellow, or white flowers and thin leaves like blades of grass. Crocuses bloom early in the spring. ▸ ***noun, plural*** **crocuses, crocus** *or* **croci**

crook (**kruk**) ***noun***
1. A bent or curved part of something, as in *the crook of your arm.* ▸ ***verb*** **crook**
2. A dishonest person or a criminal.
3. A long stick with a hook at one end used by shepherds.

crook•ed (**kruk**-id) ***adjective***
1. Not straight, as in *a crooked path.*
2. Dishonest, as in *a crooked deal.*

crop (**krop**)
1. ***noun*** A plant grown in large amounts, usually for food.
2. ***noun*** The amount of food produced in a single harvest, as in *a big tomato crop.*
3. ***verb*** If an animal **crops** grass, it eats the top part of it.
4. ***verb*** To cut off or remove the tops or edges from something, as in *to crop a photograph.*
5. ***noun*** The pouch in a bird's gullet where food is stored and softened before being digested.
▸ ***verb*** **cropping, cropped**

cro•quet (kroh-**kay**) ***noun*** An outdoor game played by hitting wooden balls with sticks through wire hoops that are stuck into the ground.

cross (**krawss**)
1. ***verb*** To go from one side to the other.
2. ***adjective*** Angry and not pleased.
3. ***noun*** The shape × is a **cross.** So is +.
4. ***noun*** An upright post with a horizontal bar that crosses it, or a pendant shaped this way. The cross is the symbol of Christianity.
5. ***verb*** To draw a line through.
6. ***verb*** To intersect.
7. ***verb*** If someone **crosses** you, the person opposes you.
8. ***verb*** To make the sign of a cross on.
▸ ***verb*** **crosses, crossing, crossed**

cross•bow (**krawss**-*boh*) ***noun*** A weapon with a bow mounted across a piece of wood. Crossbows were first used in the Middle Ages.

cross-country ***adjective*** A **cross-country** race is run through the countryside instead of on a track.

C

C

cross-examine ***verb*** To question somebody very closely.
▸ **cross-examining, cross-examined**
▸ ***noun*** **cross-examination**

cross-eyed ***adjective*** Having eyes that turn inward, toward each other, so that they are difficult to focus and the person cannot see clearly.

cross-reference ***noun*** A mention in one part of a book that tells you where to find more information in another part. A cross-reference can be in the index or in the text of the book.

cross•roads (**krawss**-*rohdz*)
1. A place where one road crosses another.
2. A point where an important decision must be made.
▸ ***noun, plural*** **crossroads**

cross section ***noun***
1. A diagram that shows the inside of something, as if it had been cut through.
2. A **cross section** of the public is a selection of different types of people.
▸ ***adjective*** **cross-sectional**

cross•walk (**krawss**-*wawk*) ***noun*** A place where pedestrians can safely cross a street, often marked with painted lines.

cross•word puzzle (**krawss**-*wurd*) ***noun*** A puzzle in which you answer clues in order to fill blank squares with words, writing one letter in each square.

crotch (**krotch**) ***noun*** The area of the body below the abdomen and between the legs.

crouch (**krouch**) ***verb*** When you **crouch,** you bend your legs and lower your body. ▸ **crouches, crouching, crouched** ▸ ***noun*** **crouch**

croup (**kroop**) ***noun*** A children's disease that causes frequent coughing and difficulty in breathing.

crow (**kroh**)
1. ***noun*** A large, black bird.
2. ***verb*** When a rooster **crows,** it makes a loud, crying noise. ▸ ***noun*** **crow**
3. ***verb*** To boast about something.
▸ ***verb*** **crowing, crowed**

crow•bar (**kroh**-*bar*) ***noun*** A heavy steel or iron bar with a flat end that can be used to lift heavy things or as a lever to pry something open.

crowd (**kroud**)
1. ***noun*** A lot of people packed together.
▸ ***adjective*** **crowded**
2. ***verb*** If you **crowd** someone, you do not give the person enough room.
▸ **crowding, crowded**

crown (**kroun**)
1. ***noun*** A headdress worn by a king or queen made from gold or silver and jewels.
2. ***verb*** To make someone king or queen by placing a crown on his or her head.
3. ***noun*** The top of something.
4. ***verb*** To declare someone to be the winner.
5. ***noun*** A wreath or headdress given to the winner of a competition.
▸ ***noun*** **crowning** ▸ ***verb*** **crowning, crowned**

crow's nest ***noun*** A small platform used for a lookout, found on top of the mast of a sailing ship.

cru•cial (**kroo**-shuhl) ***adjective*** Extremely important or vital. ▸ ***adverb*** **crucially**

crude (**krood**) ***adjective***
1. Rough and poorly made.
2. A **crude** joke is rude and in poor taste.
▸ ***noun*** **crudity**
▸ ***adjective*** **cruder, crudest** ▸ ***adverb*** **crudely**

cru•el (**kroo-uhl**) ***adjective*** A **cruel** person deliberately causes pain to others or is happy to see them suffer. ▸ **crueler, cruelest** ▸ ***noun*** **cruelty** ▸ ***adverb*** **cruelly**

cruise (**krooz**)
1. ***noun*** If you go on a **cruise,** you take a vacation on a ship that docks at several places. ▸ ***verb*** **cruise**
2. ***verb*** To travel smoothly and easily.
▸ **cruising, cruised**

cruis•er (**kroo**-zur) ***noun***
1. A boat with a cabin that is used for short cruises.
2. A warship that is faster than a battleship and has fewer guns.

crumb (**kruhm**) ***noun*** A tiny piece of bread or cake.

crum•ble (**kruhm**-buhl) ***verb*** To break into small pieces. ▸ **crumbling, crumbled** ▸ ***adjective*** **crumbly**

crum•ple (**kruhm**-puhl) ***verb***
1. If you **crumple** a piece of paper, you crush it into wrinkles and folds.
2. To collapse.
▸ ***verb*** **crumpling, crumpled**
▸ ***adjective*** **crumpled**

crunch (**kruhnch**) ***verb*** If you **crunch** something, you crush or chew it noisily.
▸ **crunches, crunching, crunched**
▸ ***noun*** **crunch** ▸ ***adjective*** **crunchy**

cru•sade (kroo-**sade**) ***noun***
1. A battle or fight for which someone feels a great deal of emotion.
2. One of the battles fought in the 11th, 12th, and 13th centuries by European Christians attempting to capture Biblical lands from the Muslims.

crush (**kruhsh**)
1. ***verb*** To squash something under a heavy weight.
2. ***noun*** If you have a **crush** on someone, you have strong, romantic feelings toward him or her.
3. ***verb*** To put down or to dash.
▸ ***verb*** **crushes, crushing, crushed**

crust (**kruhst**) ***noun***
1. The crisp, outer layer of bread or pastry. ▸ ***adjective*** **crusty**
2. The earth's **crust** is its hard outer layer.

crus•ta•cean (kruhss-**tay**-shuhn) ***noun*** A sea creature that has an outer skeleton, such as a crab, lobster, or shrimp.

crutch (**kruhch**) ***noun*** A long stick with a padded top, used to help support someone with a leg injury. ▸ ***noun, plural*** **crutches**

cry (**krye**) ***verb***
1. To weep tears.
2. To shout out.
▸ ***verb*** **cries, crying, cried** ▸ ***noun*** **cry**

crys•tal (**kriss**-tuhl) ***noun***
1. A clear or nearly clear mineral or rock, such as quartz.
2. A body that forms a pattern of many flat surfaces when it becomes a solid. Salt and snowflakes are crystals.
3. Glass of superior quality, used to make fine glasses for drinking, vases, etc.
▸ ***adjective*** **crystal,** ***adjective*** **crystalline** (**kriss**-tuh-lin)

crys•tal•lize (**kriss**-tuh-lize) ***verb***
1. To form crystals.
2. To take form.
▸ ***verb*** **crystallizing, crystallized**

cub (**kuhb**) ***noun*** A young lion, wolf, bear, etc.

cube (**kyoob**)
1. ***noun*** A three-dimensional shape with six square faces. Dice are cubes.
▸ ***verb*** **cube** ▸ ***adjective*** **cubic**
2. ***verb*** To multiply a number by itself twice. ▸ **cubing, cubed** ▸ ***noun*** **cube**

cu•bi•cle (**kyoo**-buh-kuhl) ***noun*** A small office or area surrounded by partitions.

cu•bit (**kyoo**-bit) ***noun*** An ancient form of measurement based on the length of the forearm, measured from the elbow to the tip of the middle finger (usually 17 to 22 inches).

cuck•oo (**koo**-koo)
1. ***noun*** A bird with a distinct call and long tail that lays its eggs in other birds' nests. ▸ ***noun, plural*** **cuckoos**
2. ***adjective*** (*informal*) Silly, or acting in a scatterbrained manner.

cu•cum•ber (**kyoo**-*kuhm*-bur) ***noun*** A long, green vegetable with a soft center filled with seeds.

cud (**kuhd**) ***noun*** Food that has not been digested that cows bring up from the first part of their stomachs to chew again.

cud•dle (**kudh**-uhl) ***verb*** To hold someone closely and lovingly in your arms. ▸ **cuddling, cuddled**

C

cue (**kyoo**) ***noun***
1. The signal to say some lines or do some specific thing in a play.
2. Any signal to do something.
3. A long stick used to hit the ball in billiards and pool.
Cue sounds like **queue.** ▸ ***verb* cue**

cuff (**kuhf**) ***noun***
1. The folded part of the sleeve of a shirt or blouse that goes around your wrist.
2. The band at the bottom of a trouser leg.
3. If you speak **off the cuff,** you give a speech or an answer without preparing it first.

cui•sine (kwi-**zeen**) ***noun*** A style or manner of cooking or presenting food.

cul-de-sac (**kuhl**-duh-**sak**) ***noun*** A road that is closed at one end; a dead end.

cul•mi•nate (**kuhl**-mi-*nate*) ***verb*** To reach the highest or final point.
▸ **culminating, culminated** ▸ ***noun* culmination**

cul•prit (**kuhl**-prit) ***noun*** A person who is guilty of doing something wrong or of committing a crime.

cult (**kuhlt**) ***noun***
1. A particular form of religious worship.
2. A strong, almost religious devotion to a person, a thing, an idea, or a way of life, as in *a cult of sun lovers.*
3. A **cult hero** is someone who is very popular with his or her devoted followers.

cul•ti•vate (**kuhl**-tuh-*vate*) ***verb***
1. If you **cultivate** land, you grow crops on it.
2. To develop by studying.
▸ ***verb* cultivating, cultivated** ▸ ***noun* cultivation**

cul•ture (**kuhl**-chur) ***noun***
1. An appreciation for the arts, such as music, literature, painting, etc.
2. The **culture** of a group of people is their way of life, ideas, customs, and traditions.
▸ ***adjective* cultural**

cul•tured (**kuhl**-churd) ***adjective*** Well-educated or refined.

cum•ber•some (**kum**-bur-suhm) ***adjective*** Heavy or bulky and difficult to move around.

cun•ning (**kuhn**-ing) ***adjective*** A **cunning** person is clever at tricking people. ▸ ***noun* cunning** ▸ ***adverb* cunningly**

cup (**kuhp**) ***noun***
1. A small container for holding liquids, often with a handle.
2. A unit of measurement equal to eight fluid ounces.
3. Any ornament shaped like a cup.

cup•board (**kuhb**-urd) ***noun*** A cabinet or closet for storing dishes, food, etc.

cup•cake (**kuhp**-*kake*) ***noun*** A small, round cake made in a baking pan that has individual cups.

cup•ful (**kuhp**-ful) ***noun***
1. The amount a cup can hold.
2. An amount equal to eight fluid ounces; half a pint.

cu•ra•tor (**kyoo**-ray-tur *or* kyoo-**ray**-tur) ***noun*** The person in charge of a museum or an art gallery.

curb (**kurb**)
1. ***noun*** A raised border along the edge of a paved street.
2. ***verb*** To control or hold back something. ▸ **curbing, curbed**

curd (**kurd**) ***noun*** The solid part of sour milk, often used to make cheese.

cur•dle (**kur**-duhl) ***verb*** When milk **curdles,** it goes sour and breaks up into curds and whey. ▸ **curdling, curdled** ▸ ***adjective* curdled**

cure (**kyur**)
1. ***verb*** To make someone better when he or she has been sick. ▸ **curing, cured**
2. ***noun*** A drug or course of treatment that makes someone better.

cur•few (**kur**-fyoo) ***noun*** A rule or an order that prevents people from traveling around freely, especially after dark.

cu•ri•ous (**kyur**-ee-uhss) ***adjective***
1. Eager to find out.
2. Strange, as in *a curious creature.*
▸ ***noun* curiosity** (*kyur*-ee-**ahss**-i-tee)
▸ ***adverb* curiously**

curl (**kurl**)
1. ***noun*** A curved lock of hair.
2. ***verb*** To bend or move into a spiral shape.
▸ **curling, curled**

cur•ly (**kur**-lee) ***adjective*** Having curls; twisted. ▸ **curlier, curliest**

cur•rant (**kur**-uhnt) ***noun***
1. A small raisin used in cooking and baking.
2. A small, sour berry, used in making jelly.
Currant sounds like **current.**

cur•ren•cy (**kur**-uhn-see) ***noun*** The form of money used in a country.
▸ ***noun, plural*** **currencies**

cur•rent (**kur**-uhnt)
1. ***noun*** The movement of water in a river or an ocean, or of electricity through a wire.
2. ***adjective*** Happening now. ▸ ***adverb*** **currently**
Current sounds like **currant.**

current affairs ***noun, plural*** Important events that are happening now and are often discussed on television or in newspapers.

cur•ric•u•lum (kuh-**rik**-yuh-luhm) ***noun*** A program of study for a school or college, as in *the science curriculum.*
▸ ***noun, plural*** **curricula** (kuh-**rik**-yuh-luh)

cur•ry (**kuh**-ree) ***noun***
1. A powder with a hot, pungent taste, made from grinding various spices.
2. A dish made with curry and meat, fish, or vegetables. ▸ ***noun, plural*** **curries**
▸ ***adjective*** **curried**

curse (**kurss**)
1. ***noun*** An evil spell intended to harm someone. ▸ ***verb*** **curse**
2. ***verb*** To swear. ▸ **cursing, cursed**

cur•sor (**kur**-sur) ***noun*** A small indicator, often a flashing rectangle, that shows your position on a computer screen.

curt (**kurt**) ***adjective*** Short and abrupt; delivered in a rude manner, as in *a curt answer.* ▸ **curter, curtest**

cur•tain (**kurt**-uhn) ***noun*** A piece of fabric pulled across a window or stage to cover it.

curt•sy (**kurt**-see) ***verb*** To bend slightly at the knee, with one leg crossed behind the other. Women and girls curtsy, while men and boys bow, to show respect or to accept applause. ▸ **curtsies, curtsying, curtsied** ▸ ***noun*** **curtsy**

curve (**kurv**)
1. ***verb*** To bend or turn gently and continuously. ▸ **curving, curved**
2. ***noun*** A continuous bend in something.
3. A **curve ball** is a baseball or softball pitch that spins away from a straight path as it approaches the batter.
▸ ***adjective*** **curved,** ***adjective*** **curvy**

cush•ion (**kush**-uhn)
1. ***noun*** A type of pillow used to make chairs or sofas more comfortable.
2. ***verb*** To soften the effect of something.
▸ **cushioning, cushioned** ▸ ***noun*** **cushion**

cus•tard (**kuhss**-turd) ***noun*** A sweet, yellow dessert made from milk, eggs, and sugar.

cus•to•di•an (kuhss-**toh**-dee-uhn) ***noun***
1. Someone who takes care of someone.
2. A person whose job is to clean and maintain a large building or institution, as in *a school custodian.*

cus•to•dy (**kuhss**-tuh-dee) ***noun***
1. If someone has **custody** of a child, he or she has the legal right to look after the child.
2. If someone is taken into **custody,** he or she is arrested by the police.
▸ ***noun, plural*** **custodies** ▸ ***adjective*** **custodial** (kuhss-**toh**-dee-uhl)

cus•tom (**kuhss**-tuhm) ***noun***
1. A tradition in a culture or society.
2. Something that you do regularly, as in *a family custom.*
3. customs ***noun, plural*** A checkpoint at a country's borders, ports, or airports where officials make sure that you are not carrying anything illegal.

C

cus•tom•ar•y (**kuss**-tuh-*mer*-ee) ***adjective*** Happening regularly by habit or custom; usual.

cus•tom•er (**kuhss**-tuh-mur) ***noun*** A store's **customers** are the people who buy things from it.

cus•tom•ize (**kuhss**-tuh-mize) ***verb*** To change something to suit an individual's needs, as in *to customize a car.* ▸ **customizing, customized**

cut (**kuht**)
1. ***verb*** To use a sharp instrument, such as scissors or a knife, to divide, shorten, or shape something.
2. ***verb*** To reduce something.
3. ***noun*** A skin wound.
4. ***verb*** To shorten or trim, as in *to cut the grass.*
5. ***verb*** To stop or interrupt.
6. ***verb*** If you are **cut off** from other people, you are isolated from them.
7. ***verb*** If you **cut down** on something such as caffeine, you have it less often.
8. ***verb*** If a person or an organization **cuts back,** it reduces the amount of money that it spends.
9. If you **cut and paste** words or images on a computer document, you move them from one place to another.
▸ ***noun*** **cutback,** ***noun*** **cut** ▸ ***verb*** **cutting, cut**

cute (**kyoot**) ***adjective*** Charming, pretty, or attractive. ▸ **cuter, cutest**

cu•ti•cle (**kyoo**-tuh-kuhl) ***noun*** The tough layer of dead skin around the edges of a fingernail or a toenail.

cut•le•ry (**kuht**-luh-ree) ***noun*** Knives, forks, and spoons.

cut•ting (**kuht**-ing)
1. ***noun*** A small part of a plant taken off to put in the ground and grow a new plant.
2. ***adjective*** If you make a **cutting** remark, you say something hurtful.

cy•ber•space (**sye**-bur-*spayss*) ***noun***
1. The total communications universe available to computer networks.
2. The environment of virtual reality.

cy•cle (**sye**-kuhl)
1. ***verb*** To ride a bicycle. ▸ **cycling, cycled** ▸ ***noun*** **cyclist**
2. ***noun*** A bicycle.
3. ***noun*** A series of events that are repeated over and over again, as in *the cycle of the seasons.*

cy•clone (**sye**-klone) ***noun*** A storm with very strong, destructive winds that blow around a quiet center; a tornado.

cyg•net (**sig**-nit) ***noun*** A young swan.

cyl•in•der (**sil**-uhn-dur) ***noun***
1. A shape with flat, circular ends and sides shaped like the outside of a tube.
▸ ***adjective*** **cylindrical**
2. A chamber in an engine that is shaped like a tube.

cym•bal (**sim**-buhl) ***noun*** A musical instrument made of brass and shaped like a plate. It is played by striking it with a stick or another cymbal. **Cymbal** sounds like **symbol.**

cyn•i•cal (**sin**-uh-kuhl) ***adjective*** Someone who is **cynical** always expects the worst to happen and thinks that anything people do is for selfish reasons.
▸ ***noun*** **cynic,** ***noun*** **cynicism** ▸ ***adverb*** **cynically**

cy•press (**sye**-pruhss) ***noun*** An evergreen tree with small, dark green leaves that resemble scales. ▸ ***noun, plural*** **cypresses**

cyst (**sist**) ***noun*** A small sac of tissue inside the skin that fills with fluid and is sometimes removed by surgery.

cy•to•plasm (**sye**-tuh-*plaz*-uhm) ***noun*** The contents of a cell, apart from its nucleus.

czar *or* **tsar** (zar) ***noun*** An emperor of Russia before the revolution of 1917.

cza•ri•na *or* **tsa•ri•na** (zar-**ee**-nuh) ***noun*** A former empress of Russia or wife of a czar.

dab (**dab**)
1. ***verb*** To touch a surface gently with something soft.
2. ***verb*** To apply.
3. ***noun*** A little bit, as in *a dab of mustard.*
▸ ***verb*** **dabbing, dabbed**

dab•ble (**dab**-uhl) ***verb***
1. If you **dabble** in something, you do not do it very seriously or very thoroughly. ▸ ***noun*** **dabbler**
2. To dip something playfully in and out of water.
▸ ***verb*** **dabbling, dabbled**

dachs•hund (**dahks**-*hunt*) ***noun*** A breed of dog with a long body, brown or red hair, very short legs, and drooping ears.

dad (**dad**) *or* **dad•dy** (**dad**-ee) ***noun*** *(informal)* Father.

daddy-long•legs (**long**-*legz*) ***noun*** An animal that looks like a spider but has a small, rounded body and very long, spindly legs. ▸ ***noun, plural*** **daddy-longlegs**

daf•fo•dil (**daf**-uh-dil) ***noun*** A plant that has yellow, bell-like flowers and long, narrow leaves.

daft (**daft**) ***adjective*** *(informal)* Silly or foolish, as in *a daft idea.* ▸ **dafter, daftest**

dag•ger (**dag**-ur) ***noun*** A short, pointed weapon that is used for stabbing.

dai•ly (**day**-lee) ***adjective*** Produced or happening every day, as in *a daily newspaper.* ▸ ***noun*** **daily** ▸ ***adverb*** **daily**

dain•ty (**dayn**-tee) ***adjective*** Small and delicate. ▸ **daintier, daintiest** ▸ ***noun*** **daintiness** ▸ ***adverb*** **daintily**

dair•y (**dair**-ee)
1. ***noun*** A place where milk is bottled and milk products, such as cheese and yogurt, are made. ▸ ***noun, plural*** **dairies**
2. ***adjective*** If something is a **dairy** product, it is made with milk.

dais (**day**-iss) ***noun*** A raised platform at the end of a meeting room or banquet hall, used to seat special guests or to speak from. ▸ ***noun, plural*** **daises**

dai•sy (**day**-zee) ***noun*** A flower with white, pink, or yellow petals and a yellow center. ▸ ***noun, plural*** **daisies**

dale (**dayl**) ***noun*** A valley.

dal•ma•tian (dal-**may**-shuhn) ***noun*** A breed of large dog with a white coat and black or brown spots. Dalmatians are often mascots at firehouses.

dam (**dam**) ***noun*** A strong barrier built across a stream or river to hold back water.

dam•age (**dam**-ij)
1. ***verb*** To harm something.
▸ **damaging, damaged**
2. ***noun*** The harm that something does, as in *flood damage.*
3. damages ***noun, plural*** Money given to individuals by a court of law to try to make up for an injury or a loss that they have suffered.
▸ ***adjective*** **damaging**

damp (**damp**) ***adjective*** Slightly wet, or moist. ▸ **damper, dampest** ▸ ***noun*** **dampness**

damp•en (**dam**-puhn) ***verb***
1. To make something moist or slightly wet.
2. To make dull or depressed.
▸ ***verb*** **dampening, dampened**

dam•sel (**dam**-zuhl) ***noun*** A young woman.

D

dance (**danss**)
1. ***verb*** To move in time to music.
▸ **dancing, danced**
2. ***noun*** A place or event where people dance.
3. ***noun*** A particular set of steps, such as a waltz, square dance, etc.
▸ ***noun*** **dancer,** ***noun*** **dancing**

dan•de•li•on (**dan**-duh-*lye*-uhn) ***noun*** A plant with bright yellow flowers that is often found on lawns. Dandelion leaves can be eaten in salads.

dan•druff (**dan**-druhf) ***noun*** Small, white flakes of dead skin from the scalp, sometimes found in hair.

dan•dy (**dan**-dee)
1. ***noun*** A **dandy** is a man who pays too much attention to his appearance or clothing. ▸ ***noun, plural*** **dandies**
2. ***adjective*** Great, or fine. ▸ **dandier, dandiest**

dan•ger (**dayn**-jur)
1. ***noun*** A situation that is not safe.
2. ***noun*** Something or someone that may cause harm or injury.

dan•ger•ous (**dayn**-jur-uhss) ***adjective*** Likely to cause harm or injury; not safe; risky. ▸ ***adverb*** **dangerously**

dan•gle (**dang**-guhl) ***verb*** To swing or hang down loosely. ▸ **dangling, dangled**

dank (**dangk**) ***adjective*** Unpleasantly wet or damp, as in *a dank cellar.*
▸ **danker, dankest**

dap•pled (**dap**-uhld) ***adjective*** Marked with spots or patches of light and dark, as in *a dappled pony.*

dare (**dair**) ***verb***
1. To challenge someone to do something.
2. To be brave enough to do something.
▸ ***verb*** **daring, dared** ▸ ***noun*** **dare**
▸ ***adjective*** **daring** ▸ ***adverb*** **daringly**

dare•dev•il (**dair**-*dev*-il) ***noun*** Someone who takes risks and does dangerous things.

dark (**dark**)
1. ***adjective*** Without light, as in *a dark night.*
2. ***adjective*** Containing more black than white, as in *dark blue.*
3. ***noun*** Nightfall.
4. ***noun*** Lack or absence of light.
5. ***adjective*** Bad, or evil, as in *a dark secret.*
6. ***adjective*** Gloomy, or dismal.
▸ ***adjective*** **darker, darkest** ▸ ***noun*** **darkness**

dark•en (**dar**-kuhn) ***verb*** To make or become darker. ▸ **darkening, darkened**
▸ ***adjective*** **darkened**

dark•room (**dark**-*room*) ***noun*** A room with special equipment and chemicals where you can develop photographs.

dar•ling (**dar**-ling)
1. ***noun*** Someone who is dearly loved.
2. ***adjective*** Beloved, or cherished, as in *my darling daughter.*
3. ***adjective*** Charming, or adorable.

darn (**darn**) ***verb*** To fix or mend a hole in a piece of cloth by sewing back and forth across it. ▸ **darning, darned**
▸ ***noun*** **darning**

dart (**dart**)
1. ***noun*** A pointed object that you throw at a target in the game of darts.
2. **darts** ***noun*** A game in which players score points by throwing darts at a target that usually has concentric circles and a bull's-eye in the center.
3. ***verb*** To move suddenly and quickly.
▸ **darting, darted**
4. ***noun*** A kind of pleat in a piece of clothing that makes it fit better.

dash (**dash**)
1. ***noun*** A very small amount of something.
2. ***noun*** A horizontal line (—) used as a punctuation mark to show a pause in a sentence.
3. ***verb*** To move quickly.
4. ***noun*** A short race, as in *a 50-yard dash.*
5. ***verb*** To destroy or crush.
▸ ***noun, plural*** **dashes** ▸ ***verb*** **dashes, dashing, dashed**

dash•board (**dash**-*bord*) ***noun*** The instrument panel of a car or truck where the gauges and warning lights are located.

da•ta (**day**-tuh) ***noun*** Information, or facts.

da•ta•base (**day**-tuh-*bayss*) ***noun*** The information that is organized and stored in a computer.

date (**dayt**)
1. ***noun*** A particular day, month, or year.
2. ***noun*** An appointment to meet someone, especially a girlfriend or boyfriend.
3. ***verb*** To go out with on a date.
4. ***verb*** If something **dates** from a certain time, it was made then.
5. ***noun*** A sticky, brown fruit with a long, thin pit inside it.
6. ***adjective*** If something is **dated** or **out of date,** it is no longer fashionable.
7. If something is **up to date,** it is modern.
▸ ***verb*** **dating, dated**

daub (**dawb**) ***verb*** To smear or coat with a substance such as plaster, paint, or mud.
▸ **daubing, daubed**

daugh•ter (**daw**-tur) ***noun*** Someone's **daughter** is his or her female child.

daughter-in-law ***noun*** Someone's **daughter-in-law** is his or her son's wife.
▸ ***noun, plural*** **daughters-in-law**

daunt (**dawnt**) ***verb*** If something **daunts** you, it frightens and discourages you. ▸ **daunting, daunted**

daw•dle (**daw**-duhl) ***verb*** To do something slowly, or to waste time.
▸ **dawdling, dawdled** ▸ ***noun*** **dawdler**

dawn (**dawn**)
1. ***noun*** The beginning of the day; sunrise.
2. ***noun*** The start of something new, as in *the dawn of a new age.*
3. ***verb*** If something **dawns** on you, you begin to understand it. ▸ **dawning, dawned**

day (**day**) ***noun***
1. A 24-hour period, from midnight to midnight.
2. The period of light between sunrise and sunset.
3. The part of the day spent at work, as in *a five-day work schedule.*
4. A certain period of time.

day•break (**day**-*brayk*) ***noun*** Dawn, or the time when the first rays of sunlight appear.

day care ***noun***
1. Care given by adults to young children away from their homes during the day.
2. The place where care is provided.
▸ ***adjective*** **day-care**

day•dream (**day**-*dreem*)
1. ***noun*** A pleasant dream you have while you are awake.
2. ***verb*** To let your mind wander.
▸ **daydreaming, daydreamed** ▸ ***noun*** **daydreamer**

day•light (**day**-*lite*) ***noun*** The light of the sun during daytime hours.

day•time (**day**-*time*) ***noun*** The hours of daylight, from dawn till dusk.

daze (**dayz**)
1. ***noun*** If you are in a **daze,** you are stunned and unable to think clearly.
2. ***verb*** To confuse or bewilder someone.
▸ **dazing, dazed**

daz•zle (**daz**-uhl) ***verb***
1. To blind someone for a short time with a bright light.
2. To amaze someone.
▸ ***verb*** **dazzling, dazzled** ▸ ***adjective*** **dazzling**

dea•con (**dee**-kuhn) ***noun*** In the Christian church, a person who helps a minister or preacher.

dead (**ded**)
1. ***adjective*** No longer alive.
2. ***adjective*** Without activity or excitement.
3. ***adverb*** Completely, as in *dead tired.*
4. **the dead** ***noun, plural*** All those who are no longer alive

D

dead•en (**ded**-uhn) ***verb*** To weaken or make less sharp. ▸ **deadening, deadened**

dead end
1. ***noun*** A street that is closed to traffic at one end.
2. dead-end ***adjective*** Leading nowhere.

dead•line (**ded**-*line*) ***noun*** A time by which a piece of work or a job must be finished.

dead•lock (**ded**-*lok*) ***noun*** A situation where nothing can be agreed upon.

dead•ly (**ded**-lee) ***adjective***
1. Capable of killing, or likely to kill, as in *a deadly explosion.*
2. Aiming to kill or destroy someone, as in *deadly enemies.*
▸ ***adjective*** **deadlier, deadliest**

deaf (**def**) ***adjective***
1. If someone is **deaf,** he or she cannot hear anything or can hear very little.
▸ **deafer, deafest**
2. If you are **deaf to** something, you choose not to hear it.
▸ ***noun*** **deafness**

deaf•en•ing (**def**-uh-ning) ***adjective*** Very loud, as in *a deafening crash.*
▸ ***adverb*** **deafeningly**

deal (**deel**)
1. ***verb*** To cover a subject or an area.
2. ***verb*** To do business.
3. ***noun*** An agreement.
4. ***verb*** To give or to deliver, as in *to deal the cards* or *to deal a blow.*
5. ***verb*** When you **deal with** something, you take some sort of action about it.
▸ ***verb*** **dealing, dealt** (**delt**)

deal•er (**dee**-lur) ***noun***
1. Someone who buys and sells things.
2. Someone who gives out cards during a card game.

dear (**dihr**)
1. ***adjective*** Highly valued or much loved, as in *a dear friend.*
2. ***noun*** A kind or sweet person.
3. ***adjective*** You use the word **dear** when you write to someone, as in *Dear Sir.*
4. ***adjective*** Expensive.
Dear sounds like **deer.**
▸ ***adjective*** **dearer, dearest** ▸ ***adverb*** **dearly**

death (**deth**) ***noun***
1. The end of life.
2. The destruction or end of something.

death•ly (**deth**-lee) ***adjective*** Very pale, or very quiet.

death•trap (**deth**-*trap*) ***noun*** A place or a vehicle that is very dangerous.

de•bate (di-**bate**)
1. ***noun*** A discussion between sides with different views.
2. ***verb*** To consider or discuss something.
▸ **debating, debated** ▸ ***adjective*** **debatable**

deb•it (**deb**-it)
1. ***noun*** An entry of money that is owed.
2. ***verb*** If a bank **debits** your account, the bank removes a certain amount of money from the account. ▸ **debiting, debited**

de•bris (duh-**bree**) ***noun*** The scattered pieces of something that has been broken or destroyed.

debt (**det**) ***noun***
1. An amount of money or something else that you owe.
2. If you are **in debt** to someone, you owe the person money or a favor.

debt•or (**det**-ur) ***noun*** Someone who owes money.

de•bug (dee-**buhg**) ***verb***
1. To remove the defects or errors in a computer program.
2. To remove secret listening devices from a place.
▸ ***verb*** **debugging, debugged**

de•but (**day**-byoo *or* day-**byoo**)
1. ***noun*** A first public appearance, as in *an acting debut.*
2. ***verb*** To perform something for the first time. ▸ **debuting, debuted**

dec•ade (**dek**-ayd) ***noun*** A period of 10 years.

de•caf•fein•at•ed (dee-**kaf**-uh-nay-tid) ***adjective*** If a drink, such as coffee or tea, is **decaffeinated,** it has had most of its caffeine removed. ▸ ***verb*** **decaffeinate**

de•cal (**dee**-kal) ***noun*** A picture or label on specially treated paper that can be transferred to glass, metal, or other hard surfaces.

de•cant•er (di-**kan**-tur) ***noun*** A fancy glass bottle with a stopper, used to hold and serve liquids, especially wine.

de•cap•i•tate (di-**kap**-uh-*tate*) ***verb*** To remove the head of a person or creature. ▸ **decapitating, decapitated** ▸ ***noun*** **decapitation**

de•cath•lon (di-**kath**-lon) ***noun*** A track-and-field contest made up of 10 athletic events.

de•cay (di-**kay**)
1. ***verb*** To rot or break down.
2. ***verb*** To decline in quality.
3. ***noun*** The breaking down of plant or animal matter by natural causes, as in *tooth decay.*
4. ***noun*** A decline in quality.
▸ ***verb*** **decaying, decayed**

de•ceased (di-**seest**) ***adjective*** Dead.

de•ceit (di-**seet**) ***noun*** The act of lying to or deceiving someone.

de•ceit•ful (di-**seet**-fuhl) ***adjective*** If someone is **deceitful,** that person might lie to you or deceive you. ▸ ***adverb*** **deceitfully**

de•ceive (di-**seev**) ***verb*** If someone **deceives** you, that person tricks you into believing something that is not true. ▸ **deceiving, deceived**

De•cem•ber (di-**sem**-bur) ***noun*** The 12th month on the calendar. December follows November and has 31 days.

de•cent (**dee**-suhnt) ***adjective***
1. Good or satisfactory, as in *decent quality.*
2. Respectable and proper, as in *decent behavior.*
3. Thoughtful or kind.
▸ ***noun*** **decency** ▸ ***adverb*** **decently**

de•cep•tion (di-**sep**-shuhn) ***noun*** A trick that makes people believe something that is not true; a lie.

de•cep•tive (di-**sep**-tiv) ***adjective*** Misleading, or not telling the true situation. ▸ ***adverb*** **deceptively**

dec•i•bel (**dess**-uh-bel) ***noun*** A unit for measuring the volume of sounds.

de•cide (di-**side**) ***verb***
1. To make up your mind about something.
2. To settle something.
▸ ***verb*** **deciding, decided**

de•cid•u•ous (di-**sij**-oo-uhss) ***adjective*** Trees that are **deciduous** shed their leaves every year.

dec•i•mal (**dess**-uh-muhl)
1. ***adjective*** A **decimal** system is a system of counting and computation that has 10 as its base.
2. ***noun*** A fraction, or a whole number and a fraction, written with a decimal point.

decimal point ***noun*** A period used in a number to show that all the numbers to its right are less than 1. The number 3.14 combines the whole number 3 and the fraction .14, or 14 hundredths.

de•ci•pher (di-**sye**-fur) ***verb*** To figure out something that is written in code or is hard to understand. ▸ **deciphering, deciphered** ▸ ***adjective*** **decipherable**

de•ci•sion (di-**sizh**-uhn) ***noun*** If you make a **decision,** you make up your mind about something.

de•ci•sive (di-**sye**-siv) ***adjective*** If you are **decisive,** you make choices quickly and easily. ▸ ***adverb*** **decisively**

deck (**dek**) ***noun***
1. The floor of a boat or ship.
2. A platform with railings on the outside of a building.
3. A full set of playing cards.

dec•la•ra•tion (dek-luh-**ray**-shuhn) ***noun*** The act of announcing something, or the announcement made, as in *a declaration of war.*

Declaration of Independence ***noun*** A document declaring the freedom of the 13 American colonies from British rule. It was adopted on July 4, 1776.

D

de•clare (di-**klair**) ***verb***
1. To say something firmly.
2. To announce something formally.
▸ ***verb*** **declaring, declared**

de•cline (di-**kline**) ***verb***
1. To turn something down or refuse something.
2. To get worse, or to get smaller.
3. To bend or slope downward.
▸ ***verb*** **declining, declined** ▸ ***noun*** **decline**

de•code (dee-**kode**) ***verb*** To turn something that is written in code into ordinary language. ▸ **decoding, decoded** ▸ ***noun*** **decoder**

de•com•pose (dee-kuhm-**poze**) ***verb*** To rot or decay. ▸ **decomposing, decomposed** ▸ ***noun*** **decomposition,** ***noun*** **decomposer**

de•con•ges•tant (dee-kuhn-**jess**-tuhnt) ***noun*** A drug or treatment that unblocks your nose, chest, etc., when you have a cold. ▸ ***noun*** **decongestion** ▸ ***verb*** **decongest**

de•con•tam•i•nate (dee-kuhn-**tam**-uh-nate) ***verb*** To remove radioactive or other harmful substances from something or someplace.
▸ **decontaminating, decontaminated** ▸ ***noun*** **decontamination**

dec•o•rate (**dek**-uh-rate) ***verb***
1. If you **decorate** something, you add things to it to make it prettier. ▸ ***noun*** **decorator** ▸ ***adjective*** **decorative** (**dek**-ur-uh-tiv)
2. To give a medal or badge to someone.
▸ ***verb*** **decorating, decorated** ▸ ***noun*** **decorating,** ***noun*** **decoration**

de•cou•page (day-koo-**pahzh**) ***noun*** The art of decorating a surface by pasting on pieces of paper and then covering the whole object with layers of varnish.

de•coy (**dee**-koi)
1. ***noun*** A carved model of a bird used by hunters to attract real birds.
2. ***noun*** Someone who lures a person into a trap or draws attention away from something.
3. (di-**koi** *or* **dee**-koi) ***verb*** To lure someone or something into a trap.
▸ **decoying, decoyed**

de•crease (**dee**-kreess *or* di-**kreess**)
1. ***verb*** To become less, smaller, or fewer.
▸ **decreasing, decreased** ▸ ***adjective*** **decreasing** ▸ ***adverb*** **decreasingly**
2. ***noun*** A loss, or the amount by which something grows less, as in *a decrease in your allowance.*

de•cree (di-**kree**)
1. ***verb*** To give an order or proclaim officially. ▸ **decreeing, decreed**
2. ***noun*** An official decision or order, as in *a divorce decree.*

de•crep•it (di-**krep**-it) ***adjective*** Weakened by old age or too much use, as in *a decrepit building.*

ded•i•cate (**ded**-uh-kate) ***verb***
1. If you **dedicate** yourself to something, you give a lot of time and energy to it.
2. If you **dedicate** a book to someone, you put that person's name at the front of it, usually to say thanks or show appreciation.
▸ ***verb*** **dedicating, dedicated**

ded•i•ca•tion (*ded*-uh-**kay**-shun) ***noun***
1. Devotion or concentration of effort.
2. The inscription written in a book.
3. The opening of a new bridge, hospital, etc., with a special ceremony.

de•duce (di-**dooss**) ***verb*** To figure something out from clues or from what you know already. ▸ **deducing, deduced**

de•duct (di-**duhkt**) ***verb*** To take away or subtract something. ▸ **deducting, deducted** ▸ ***adjective*** **deductible**

de•duc•tion (di-**duhk**-shuhn) ***noun***
1. An amount that is taken away or subtracted from a larger amount.
2. Something that is figured out from clues, as in *a logical deduction.*

deed (**deed**) ***noun***
1. Something that is done, as in *a good deed.*
2. A legal document saying who owns a house or a piece of land.

deep (**deep**) ***adjective***
1. Going a long way down, as in *a deep well.*
2. Very intense and strong, as in *deep sorrow.*
3. Very low in pitch, as in *a deep voice.*
4. Not easy to understand.
▸ ***adjective* deeper, deepest** ▸ ***noun* deep** ▸ ***verb* deepen** ▸ ***adverb* deeply**

deep-sea ***adjective*** Living or happening in the deeper part of an ocean.

deer (**dihr**) ***noun*** An animal with hooves that runs very fast and eats plants. Male deer grow bony, branching antlers. **Deer** sounds like **dear.** ▸ ***noun, plural* deer**

de•face (di-**fayss**) ***verb*** To spoil the way something looks by writing on it, scratching it, etc. ▸ **defacing, defaced**

de•feat (di-**feet**)
1. ***verb*** To beat someone in a war or a competition. ▸ **defeating, defeated**
2. ***noun*** If you suffer a **defeat,** you are beaten.

de•fect
1. (**dee**-fekt *or* di-**fekt**) ***noun*** A fault or weakness in something or someone.
▸ ***adjective* defective**
2. (di-**fekt**) ***verb*** To leave your country or political party and join another one. ▸ **defecting, defected** ▸ ***noun* defector, *noun* defection**

de•fend (di-**fend**) ***verb***
1. To protect something or someone from harm.
2. To support someone or some idea by arguing.
3. To try to stop points being scored in football, hockey, soccer, basketball, etc.
▸ ***verb* defending, defended** ▸ ***noun* defense, *noun* defender**

de•fend•ant (di-**fen**-duhnt) ***noun*** The person in a court case who has been accused of a crime or who is being sued.

de•fen•sive (di-**fen**-siv) ***adjective***
1. Serving to defend yourself or others, as in *defensive action* or *defensive plans.*
2. If you are **defensive** or **on the defensive,** you feel and act as if you are being attacked or criticized. ▸ ***noun* defensiveness** ▸ ***adverb* defensively**

de•fer (di-**fur**) ***verb***
1. To put something off until later.
2. To give in to another's wishes or opinions.
▸ ***verb* deferring, deferred** ▸ ***noun* deferment**

de•fi•ant (di-**fye**-uhnt) ***adjective*** If you are **defiant,** you stand up to someone or to some organization and refuse to obey. ▸ ***noun* defiance** ▸ ***adverb* defiantly**

de•fi•cient (di-**fish**-uhnt) ***adjective*** Lacking something necessary. ▸ ***noun* deficiency**

def•i•cit (**def**-uh-sit) ***noun***
1. If a **deficit** exists, more money has been spent than has come in.
2. A lessening in quality or amount.

de•fine (di-**fine**) ***verb*** To explain or describe something exactly. ▸ **defining, defined** ▸ ***noun* definer**

def•i•nite (**def**-uh-nit) ***adjective***
1. Certain. ▸ ***adverb* definitely**
2. Clear, as in *a definite writing style.*

definite article ***noun*** The term for the article *the.* A definite article is used before a noun when the noun refers to something specific.

def•i•ni•tion (def-uh-**nish**-uhn) ***noun*** An explanation of the meaning of a word or phrase.

de•flate (di-**flate**) ***verb***
1. To let the air out of something such as a tire or a balloon.
2. To reduce in size or importance.
▸ ***verb* deflating, deflated** ▸ ***noun* deflation**

de•flect (di-**flekt**) ***verb*** To make something go in a different direction.
▸ **deflecting, deflected** ▸ ***noun* deflection**

de•for•est (dee-**far**-ist *or* dee-**for**-ist) ***verb*** To remove or cut down forests.
▸ **deforesting, deforested** ▸ ***noun* deforestation**

D

de•formed (di-**formd**) ***adjective*** Twisted, bent, or disfigured. ▸ ***noun*** **deformity** ▸ ***verb*** **deform**

de•fraud (di-**frawd**) ***verb*** To cheat someone out of something that belongs to him or her, such as money or property, as in *to defraud the government of taxes.* ▸ **defrauding, defrauded**

de•frost (di-**frawst**) ***verb***
1. To completely thaw out an item that is frozen, as in *to defrost a steak.*
2. To remove ice from something, such as a refrigerator or freezer.
▸ ***verb*** **defrosting, defrosted**

deft (**deft**) ***adjective*** Skillful, quick, and neat. ▸ **defter, deftest** ▸ ***noun*** **deftness** ▸ ***adverb*** **deftly**

de•fuse (dee-**fyooz**) ***verb***
1. When someone **defuses** a bomb, he or she makes it safe so it cannot explode.
2. If a situation is **defused,** it is made calmer.
▸ ***verb*** **defusing, defused**

de•fy (di-**fye**) ***verb***
1. If you **defy** a person or a rule, you refuse to obey.
2. To challenge or dare someone to do something.
▸ ***verb*** **defies, defying, defied**

de•gen•er•ate (di-**gen**-uh-rate) ***verb*** To become worse or inferior in quality.
▸ **degenerating, degenerated**

de•grad•ing (di-**gray**-ding) ***adjective*** If a situation or an activity is **degrading,** it makes you feel worthless or disgraced.
▸ ***noun*** **degradation** (*deg*-ruh-**day**-shuhn) ▸ ***verb*** **degrade**

de•gree (di-**gree**) ***noun***
1. A step in a series.
2. A unit for measuring temperature. The symbol for a degree is °, as in *85° Fahrenheit.*
3. A unit for measuring arcs and angles.
4. A title given by a college or university, as in *a degree in medicine.*

de•hy•drat•ed (dee-**hye**-dray-tid) ***adjective***
1. Dehydrated food has had the water removed from it.
2. If you are **dehydrated,** you do not have enough water in your body.
▸ ***noun*** **dehydration** ▸ ***verb*** **dehydrate**

de•ice (dee-**eyess**) ***verb*** To remove or keep free of ice. ▸ **deicing, deiced**
▸ ***noun*** **deicer**

de•i•ty (**dee**-uh-tee) ***noun***
1. A god or a goddess.
2. the Deity God.
▸ ***noun, plural*** **deities**

de•ject•ed (di-**jek**-tid) ***adjective*** Sad and depressed. ▸ ***noun*** **dejection**
▸ ***adverb*** **dejectedly**

de•lay (di-**lay**) ***verb***
1. To be late.
2. To make someone or something late.
3. To put something off until later.
▸ ***verb*** **delaying, delayed** ▸ ***noun*** **delay**

del•e•gate
1. (**del**-uh-gate) ***verb*** To give someone responsibility for doing a part of your job.
▸ **delegating, delegated**
2. (**del**-uh-guht) ***noun*** Someone who represents other people at a meeting.

del•e•ga•tion (del-uh-**gay**-shuhn) ***noun*** A group of people that represents an organization or a government at meetings.

de•lete (di-**leet**) ***verb*** To remove something from a piece of writing or computer text. ▸ **deleting, deleted**
▸ ***noun*** **deletion**

de•lib•er•ate
1. (duh-**lib**-ur-uht) ***adjective*** Planned or intended. ▸ ***adverb*** **deliberately**
2. (duh-**lib**-ur-uht) ***adjective*** Careful and slow.
3. (duh-**lib**-uh-rate) ***verb*** To consider something carefully.
▸ **deliberating, deliberated**
▸ ***noun*** **deliberation**

del•i•cate (**del**-uh-kuht) ***adjective***
1. Very pleasant to the senses, as in *a delicate flavor.*
2. Finely made or sensitive, as in *a delicate instrument.*

3. If a person is **delicate,** he or she is not very strong and can easily become ill. ▸ ***adverb* delicately**

del·i·ca·tes·sen (del-uh-kuh-**tess**-uhn) ***noun*** A store that sells different kinds of food already prepared.

de·li·cious (di-**lish**-uhss) ***adjective*** Very pleasing to taste or smell. ▸ ***adverb* deliciously**

de·light (di-**lite**)
1. ***noun*** Great pleasure. ▸ ***adjective* delightful** ▸ ***adverb* delightfully**
2. ***verb*** If something **delights** you, it pleases you very much. ▸ **delighting, delighted** ▸ ***adjective* delighted**

de·lin·quent (di-**ling**-kwuhnt)
1. ***noun*** A person who is often in trouble with the police. ▸ ***adjective* delinquent**
2. ***adjective*** Overdue for payment, as in *a delinquent account.*
▸ ***noun* delinquency**

de·lir·i·ous (di-**lihr**-ee-uhss) ***adjective*** If you are **delirious,** you cannot think straight either because you have a high fever or you are extremely happy.
▸ ***adverb* deliriously**

de·liv·er (di-**liv**-ur) ***verb***
1. To take something to someone.
2. To say.
3. When someone **delivers** a baby, he or she helps it to be born.
4. To rescue someone from something.
▸ ***noun* deliverance**
▸ ***verb* delivering, delivered** ▸ ***noun* delivery**

del·ta (**del**-tuh) ***noun***
1. An area of land shaped like a triangle where a river deposits mud, sand, or pebbles as it enters the sea.
2. The fourth letter of the Greek alphabet.

del·uge (**del**-yooj)
1. ***noun*** Heavy rain, or a flood.
2. ***verb*** If a river or storm **deluges** a place, it floods it.
3. ***verb*** If people **deluge** you with letters, presents, etc., they send you lots of them. ▸ ***noun* deluge**
▸ ***verb* deluging, deluged**

de·lu·sion (di-**loo**-zhuhn) ***noun*** A false idea or a hallucination. ▸ ***verb* delude**

de·mand (di-**mand**)
1. ***verb*** To claim something, or to ask for something firmly.
2. ***verb*** To require.
3. ***noun*** If there is a **demand** for something, many people want it.
▸ ***verb* demanding, demanded**

de·mand·ing (di-**man**-ding) ***adjective*** Requiring a lot of time, attention, or effort.

de·mer·it (di-**mer**-it) ***noun*** A mark against someone, usually given for doing something wrong.

dem·o (**dem**-oh) ***noun*** *(informal)* A recording made to demonstrate a new performer or piece of music.

de·moc·ra·cy (di-**mok**-ruh-see) ***noun***
1. A way of governing a country in which the people choose their leaders in elections.
2. A country that has an elected government. ▸ ***noun, plural* democracies**

dem·o·crat (**dem**-uh-krat) ***noun***
1. Someone who agrees with the system of democracy.
2. Democrat A member of the Democratic Party.

dem·o·crat·ic (dem-uh-**krat**-ik) ***adjective***
1. To do with or in favor of democracy.
2. A **democratic** system is one where all people have equal rights. ▸ ***adverb* democratically**

Democratic Party ***noun*** One of the main political parties in the United States.

de·mo·graph·ics (dee-moh-**gra**-fiks) ***noun, plural*** Population statistics, including data on age and income. Companies often use demographics to decide how and where to sell their products. ▸ ***adjective* demographic**

de·mol·ish (di-**mol**-ish) ***verb*** To knock down or destroy something.
▸ **demolishes, demolishing, demolished** ▸ ***noun* demolition** (dem-oh-**lish**-uhn)

D

D

de•mon (**dee**-muhn) ***noun***
1. A devil, or an evil spirit.
2. If you work **like a demon,** you are very energetic.
▸ ***adjective*** **demonic** (dee-**mon**-ik)

dem•on•strate (**dem**-uhn-strate) ***verb***
1. To show other people how to do something or use something.
2. To show something clearly.
3. To join together with other people to protest something.
▸ ***verb*** **demonstrating, demonstrated**
▸ ***noun*** **demonstration**

dem•on•stra•tive (duh-**mon**-struh-tiv) ***adjective*** Showing affection freely; affectionate.

de•mor•al•ized (di-**mor**-uh-lized) ***adjective*** If you are **demoralized,** you feel depressed and hopeless.

den (**den**) ***noun***
1. The home of a wild animal, such as a lion.
2. A small, comfortable room where you can work or play.

den•im (**den**-im) ***noun*** Strong cotton material used to make jeans and other articles of clothing. ▸ ***adjective*** **denim**

de•nom•i•na•tion (di-nom-uh-**nay**-shuhn) ***noun***
1. An organized religion.
2. A value or unit in a system of measurement.

de•nom•i•na•tor (di-**nom**-uh-nay-tur) ***noun*** In fractions, the **denominator** is the number under the line that shows how many equal parts the whole number can be divided into.

de•note (di-**note**) ***verb***
1. To show or be a sign of something.
2. To mean.
▸ ***verb*** **denoting, denoted** ▸ ***noun*** **denotation**

de•nounce (di-**nounss**) ***verb*** To say in public that someone has done something wrong. ▸ **denouncing, denounced**

dense (**denss**) ***adjective***
1. Crowded, or thick, as in *dense fog.*
2. *(informal)* Slow to understand.
▸ ***adjective*** **denser, densest** ▸ ***noun*** **denseness** ▸ ***adverb*** **densely**

den•si•ty (**den**-si-tee) ***noun***
1. The **density** of an object is how heavy or light it is for its size. Density is measured by dividing an object's mass by its volume.
2. The amount of something per unit.

dent (**dent**) ***verb*** To damage something by making a hollow in it. ▸ **denting, dented** ▸ ***noun*** **dent**

den•tal (**den**-tuhl) ***adjective*** To do with your teeth, as in *dental hygiene.*

dental floss *See* **floss.**

den•tist (**den**-tist) ***noun*** Someone who is trained to examine, clean, and treat teeth. ▸ ***noun*** **dentistry**

den•ture (**den**-chur) ***noun***
1. A device that fits into someone's mouth, with a false tooth or false teeth attached to it.
2. dentures ***noun, plural*** A set of false teeth.

de•ny (di-**nye**) ***verb***
1. To say that something is not true.
2. To stop someone from having something or going somewhere.
▸ ***verb*** **denies, denying, denied**
▸ ***noun*** **denial**

de•o•dor•ant (dee-**oh**-duh-ruhnt) ***noun*** A substance used to cover up or get rid of unpleasant smells.

de•part (di-**part**) ***verb***
1. To leave, especially to go on a journey.
2. To change a course of action.
▸ ***verb*** **departing, departed** ▸ ***noun*** **departure**

de•part•ment (di-**part**-muhnt) ***noun*** A part of a store, hospital, university, etc., that has a particular function or purpose.
▸ ***adjective*** **departmental**

department store ***noun*** A large store with sections or departments for the different kinds of things sold.

de•pend (di-**pend**) ***verb***
1. To rely on someone or something.
▸ ***adjective*** **dependable**

2. If a thing **depends on** something else, it is determined or influenced by it.
▸ ***verb*** **depending, depended** ▸ ***noun*** **dependence**

de•pend•ent (di-**pen**-duhnt)
1. ***noun*** A person who is looked after and supported by somebody else.
2. ***adjective*** Depending on or controlled by something or someone else.
3. A **dependent clause** is a part of a sentence that cannot stand on its own. *See* **independent clause.**

de•pict (di-**pikt**) ***verb*** To show something in a picture or by using words.
▸ **depicting, depicted**

de•plete (di-**pleet**) ***verb*** To empty, or to use up. ▸ **depleting, depleted** ▸ ***noun*** **depletion** (di-**plee**-shuhn)

de•plor•a•ble (di-**plor**-uh-buhl) ***adjective*** Very bad, as in *deplorable conditions.* ▸ ***verb*** **deplore** ▸ ***adverb*** **deplorably**

de•port (di-**port**) ***verb*** To send people back to their own country. ▸ **deporting, deported** ▸ ***noun*** **deportation**

de•port•ment (di-**port**-muhnt) ***noun*** The way that you behave.

de•pose (di-**poze**) ***verb***
1. If kings or queens are **deposed,** they have their power taken from them.
2. To declare under oath or in writing.
▸ ***verb*** **deposing, deposed** ▸ ***noun*** **deposition** (*dep*-uh-**zish**-uhn)

de•pos•it (di-**poz**-it)
1. ***noun*** A sum of money given as the first part of a payment or as a promise to pay for something.
2. ***noun*** A natural layer of rock, sand, or minerals found in the ground.
3. ***verb*** To place, or to lay down.
4. ***verb*** To put money into a bank account.
▸ ***verb*** **depositing, deposited**

de•pot (**dee**-poh) ***noun*** A bus station or railroad station.

de•pre•ci•ate (di-**pree**-shee-ate) ***verb*** To lose value. ▸ **depreciating, depreciated** ▸ ***noun*** **depreciation**

de•pressed (di-**prest**) ***adjective*** If you feel **depressed,** you feel sad or gloomy.
▸ ***adjective*** **depressing** ▸ ***verb*** **depress**

de•pres•sion (di-**presh**-uhn) ***noun***
1. Sadness or gloominess.
2. A time when businesses do badly and many people become poor.
3. A hollow place.

de•prive (di-**prive**) ***verb*** To prevent a person from having something, or to take a thing away from someone.
▸ **depriving, deprived** ▸ ***noun*** **deprivation** (*dep*-ri-**vay**-shuhn)
▸ ***adjective*** **deprived**

depth (**depth**) ***noun***
1. Deepness, or a measurement of deepness.
2. If you study something **in depth,** you study it thoroughly.
3. If you are **out of your depth,** you cannot understand what is going on.

dep•u•ty (**dep**-yuh-tee) ***noun*** A person who helps or acts for somebody else, as in *a sheriff's deputy.* ▸ ***noun, plural*** **deputies** ▸ ***verb*** **deputize**

de•ranged (di-**raynjd**) ***adjective*** Insane.

der•by (**dur**-bee) ***noun***
1. A stiff hat with a narrow brim and a round top.
2. A race or contest, especially one involving horses.
▸ ***noun, plural*** **derbies**

der•e•lict (**der**-uh-likt)
1. ***adjective*** Neglected and in ruins.
2. ***noun*** A wandering homeless person.

de•rive (di-**rive**) ***verb***
1. To take or receive something.
2. If a word is **derived** from another word, it has developed from it.
▸ ***verb*** **deriving, derived** ▸ ***noun*** **derivation** (der-i-**vay**-shuhn)

der•rick (**der**-ik) ***noun***
1. A tall crane with a long, movable arm that can raise or lower heavy objects.
2. A tall framework that holds the machines used to drill oil wells.

D

D

de•scend (di-**send**) ***verb***
1. To climb down or go down to a lower level.
2. If you are **descended** from someone, you belong to a later generation of the same family. ▸ ***verb*** **descending, descended** ▸ ***noun*** **descent**

de•scend•ant (di-**send**-uhnt) ***noun*** Your **descendants** are your children, their children, and so on into the future.

de•scribe (di-**skribe**) ***verb*** To create a picture of something in words. ▸ **describing, described** ▸ ***noun*** **description** (di-**skrip**-shuhn) ▸ ***adjective*** **descriptive** (di-**skrip**-tiv)

de•seg•re•gate (dee-**seg**-ruh-gate) ***verb*** To do away with the practice of separating people of different races in schools, restaurants, and other public places. ▸ **desegregating, desegregated** ▸ ***noun*** **desegregation**

des•ert
1. (di-**zurt**) ***verb*** To abandon someone or something, or to run away from the army. ▸ **deserting, deserted** ▸ ***noun*** **deserter,** ***noun*** **desertion**
2. (**dez**-urt) ***noun*** A dry, often sandy area where hardly any plants grow because there is so little rain. ▸ ***adjective*** **desert**

de•serve (di-**zurv**) ***verb*** To earn something because of the way you behave. ▸ **deserving, deserved** ▸ ***adjective*** **deserving**

de•sign (di-**zine**)
1. ***verb*** To draw something that could be built or made. ▸ **designing, designed** ▸ ***noun*** **designer**
2. ***noun*** The shape or style of something.

des•ig•nate (**dez**-ig-nate) ***verb***
1. To name or mark something.
2. To call or name something.
3. To choose someone for an office or duty.
▸ ***verb*** **designating, designated** ▸ ***noun*** **designation**

designated hitter ***noun*** In baseball, a player who is named at the start of the game to bat in the pitcher's place without causing the pitcher to be taken out of the game.

de•sire (di-**zire**) ***noun*** A strong wish or need for something or someone. ▸ ***verb*** **desire** ▸ ***adjective*** **desirable**

desk (**desk**) ***noun*** A table, often with drawers, used for working at or writing on.

desk•top publishing (**desk**-*top*) ***noun*** The process of writing, editing, and designing a book or a newsletter on a computer so that the pages are ready to be printed.

des•o•late (**dess**-uh-luht) ***adjective***
1. Deserted or uninhabited, as in *a desolate village.*
2. Sad and lonely.
▸ ***noun*** **desolation** ▸ ***adverb*** **desolately**

de•spair (di-**spair**) ***verb*** To lose hope completely. ▸ **despairing, despaired** ▸ ***noun*** **despair** ▸ ***adjective*** **despairing** ▸ ***adverb*** **despairingly**

des•per•a•do (dess-puh-**rah**-doh) ***noun*** A bold, reckless criminal; a bandit. ▸ ***noun, plural*** **desperadoes** *or* **desperados**

des•per•ate (**dess**-pur-it) ***adjective***
1. If you are **desperate,** you will do anything to change your situation. ▸ ***noun*** **desperation**
2. Dangerous or difficult, as in *a desperate act.*
▸ ***adverb*** **desperately**

de•spise (di-**spize**) ***verb*** If you **despise** something or someone, you dislike that thing or that person greatly. ▸ **despising, despised** ▸ ***adjective*** **despicable**

de•spite (di-**spite**) ***preposition*** In spite of.

de•spond•ent (di-**spon**-duhnt) ***adjective*** Miserable and depressed. ▸ ***adverb*** **despondently**

des•sert (di-**zurt**) ***noun*** A food, such as ice cream, fruit, or cake, usually served at the end of a meal.

des•ti•na•tion (dess-tuh-**nay**-shuhn) ***noun*** The place that a person or vehicle is traveling to.

des•tined (**dess**-tuhnd) ***adjective***
1. Having a certain fate.
2. Bound for a certain place.

des•ti•ny (**dess**-tuh-nee) ***noun*** Your **destiny** is your fate or the future events in your life. ▸ ***noun, plural*** **destinies**

des•ti•tute (**dess**-tuh-toot) ***adjective*** A **destitute** person lacks food, shelter, and clothing. ▸ ***noun*** **destitution**

de•stroy (di-**stroi**) ***verb*** To ruin something or someone completely. ▸ **destroying, destroyed** ▸ ***noun*** **destruction** (di-**struhk**-shuhn)

de•stroy•er (di-**stroi**-ur) ***noun*** A small, very fast warship that uses guns, missiles, and torpedoes to protect other ships from submarines.

de•struc•tive (di-**struhk**-tiv) ***adjective*** Causing lots of damage and unhappiness. ▸ ***adverb*** **destructively**

de•tach (di-**tach**) ***verb*** To separate one part of something from the rest of it. ▸ **detaches, detaching, detached** ▸ ***adjective*** **detachable**

de•tached (di-**tacht**) ***adjective***
1. If you are **detached,** you are able to stand back from a situation and not get too involved in it. ▸ ***noun*** **detachment**
2. If a house is **detached,** it is separate and not connected to another building.

de•tail (di-**tayl** *or* **dee**-tayl) ***noun***
1. A small part of a whole item, as in *a detail of a painting.*
2. The treatment of something item by item. ▸ ***adjective*** **detailed**
3. ***noun, plural*** If you ask for **details** about something, you want information about it. ▸ ***verb*** **detail**

de•tain (di-**tayn**) ***verb*** To hold somebody back when he or she wants to go. ▸ **detaining, detained**

de•tect (di-**tekt**) ***verb*** To notice or discover something. ▸ **detecting, detected** ▸ ***noun*** **detection** ▸ ***adjective*** **detectable**

de•tec•tive (di-**tek**-tiv) ***noun*** One who investigates crimes, usually for or with the police.

de•tec•tor (di-**tek**-tur) ***noun*** A machine used to reveal the presence of something, such as smoke, metal, or radioactivity, as in *a smoke detector.*

de•ten•tion (di-**ten**-shuhn) ***noun***
1. A punishment in which a student has to report early to or stay after school.
2. If people are held **in detention,** they are kept as prisoners until their trial date.

de•ter (di-**tur**) ***verb*** To prevent or discourage something. ▸ **deterring, deterred**

de•ter•gent (di-**tur**-juhnt) ***noun*** Liquid or powder used for cleaning things.

de•te•ri•o•rate (di-**tihr**-ee-uh-rate) ***verb*** To get worse. ▸ **deteriorating, deteriorated** ▸ ***noun*** **deterioration**

de•ter•mine (di-**tur**-min) ***verb***
1. To have an effect on.
2. To make a discovery or to find out.
3. If you **determine** the solution to a problem, you are able to settle or resolve it.

de•ter•mined (di-**tur**-mind) ***adjective*** If you are **determined** to do something, you have made a firm decision to do it. ▸ ***noun*** **determination** ▸ ***adverb*** **determinedly**

de•ter•rent (di-**tur**-uhnt) ***noun*** A thing that stops something else from happening.

de•test (di-**test**) ***verb*** If you **detest** something or somebody, you dislike that thing or person very much. ▸ **detesting, detested** ▸ ***adjective*** **detestable**

det•o•nate (**det**-uh-nate) ***verb*** To set off an explosion. ▸ **detonating, detonated** ▸ ***noun*** **detonator**

de•tour (**dee**-toor) ***noun*** A longer alternative route usually taken when the direct route is closed for repairs.

de•tract (di-**trakt**) ***verb*** To take away something enjoyable or valuable. ▸ **detracting, detracted**

det•ri•men•tal (det-ri-**men**-tuhl) ***adjective*** Harmful. ▸ ***noun*** **detriment**

D

de•val•ue (dee-**val**-yoo) ***verb*** To reduce the value of a currency in relation to another currency or to gold.
▸ **devaluing, devalued** ▸ ***noun*** **devaluation**

dev•as•tat•ed (**dev**-uh-stay-tid) ***adjective***
1. Very badly damaged, or destroyed.
▸ ***noun*** **devastation**
2. Shocked and distressed.
▸ ***adjective*** **devastating** ▸ ***verb*** **devastate**

de•vel•op (di-**vel**-uhp) ***verb***
1. To grow.
2. To build on something, or to make something grow.
3. When film is **developed,** it is treated with chemicals to bring out the pictures that have been taken.
▸ ***verb*** **developing, developed** ▸ ***noun*** **developer,** ***noun*** **development**

developing nation ***noun*** A nation in which most people are poor and there is not yet much industry.

de•vi•ate (**dee**-vee-ate) ***verb*** To do something differently from the usual way. ▸ **deviating, deviated** ▸ ***noun*** **deviation**

de•vice (di-**visse**) ***noun***
1. A piece of equipment that does a particular job.
2. If you are **left to your own devices,** you can do what you want.

dev•il (**dev**-uhl) ***noun***
1. **Devil** *or* **devil** In many religions, the primary spirit of evil.
2. If you call someone a **devil,** you mean that the person is full of mischief or is wicked. ▸ ***adjective*** **devilish**

de•vi•ous (**dee**-vee-uhss) ***adjective*** **Devious** people keep their thoughts and actions secret and cannot be trusted.
▸ ***noun*** **deviousness** ▸ ***adverb*** **deviously**

de•vise (di-**vize**) ***verb*** To think something up, or to invent something.
▸ **devising, devised**

de•void (di-**void**) ***adjective*** Without something, or empty of something.

de•vote (di-**voht**) ***verb*** To give your time, effort, or attention to some purpose. ▸ **devoting, devoted**

de•vot•ed (di-**voh**-tid) ***adjective*** Loyal and loving. ▸ ***noun*** **devotion** ▸ ***adverb*** **devotedly**

de•vour (di-**vour**) ***verb*** To eat something quickly and hungrily.
▸ **devouring, devoured**

de•vout (di-**vout**) ***adjective*** Deeply religious, as in *devout church members.*
▸ ***noun*** **devoutness** ▸ ***adverb*** **devoutly**

dew (**doo**) ***noun*** Moisture in the form of small drops that collects overnight on cool surfaces outside. **Dew** sounds like **do** and **due.** ▸ ***adjective*** **dewy**

dew•lap (**doo**-*lap*) ***noun*** The loose skin that hangs under an animal's chin or neck.

dex•ter•i•ty (dek-**ster**-uh-tee) ***noun*** Skill, especially in using your hands.
▸ ***adjective*** **dexterous**

di•a•be•tes (*dye*-uh-**bee**-tuhss *or dye*-uh-**bee**-teez) ***noun*** A disease in which there is too much sugar in the blood.
▸ ***adjective*** **diabetic** (*dye*-uh-**bet**-ik)

di•a•bol•ic (*dye*-uh-**bol**-ik) ***adjective***
1. Extremely wicked, as in *a diabolic plan.*
2. To do with the devil. ▸ ***adjective*** **diabolical** ▸ ***adverb*** **diabolically**

di•ag•nose (dye-uhg-**nohss**) ***verb*** To determine what disease a patient has or what the cause of a problem is.
▸ **diagnosing, diagnosed** ▸ ***noun*** **diagnosis**

di•ag•o•nal (dye-**ag**-uh-nuhl) ***adjective*** A **diagonal** line is a straight line joining opposite corners of a square or rectangle. ▸ ***noun*** **diagonal** ▸ ***adverb*** **diagonally**

di•a•gram (**dye**-uh-gram) ***noun*** A drawing or plan that explains something.
▸ ***adjective*** **diagrammatic**

di•al (**dye**-uhl)
1. ***noun*** The face on a clock, watch, or other measuring instrument.

2. ***noun*** A disk on certain devices, such as a television set or telephone, that is moved to operate the device.
3. ***verb*** To enter a telephone number by pressing buttons or, on older phones, turning a **dial**.
▸ **dialing, dialed**

di•a•lect (**dye**-uh-lekt) ***noun*** A way a language is spoken in a particular place or among a particular group of people.

di•a•logue (**dye**-uh-lawg) ***noun*** Conversation, especially in a play, movie, television program, or book.

dial tone ***noun*** The sound that you should hear when you first pick up a telephone receiver.

di•am•e•ter (dye-**am**-uh-tur) ***noun*** A straight line through the center of a circle, from one side to another.

dia•mond (**dye**-muhnd *or* **dye**-uh-muhnd) ***noun***
1. A very hard, clear, precious stone.
2. A shape with four equal sides, like a square standing on one of its corners.
3. diamonds *noun, plural* One of the four suits in a deck of cards.
4. The area of a baseball field enclosed by first, second, and third base, plus home plate.

di•a•per (**dye**-pur *or* **dye**-uh-pur) ***noun*** A piece of soft, absorbent clothing worn as underwear by babies and young children.

di•a•phragm (**dye**-uh-fram) ***noun*** The wall of muscle between your chest and your abdomen.

di•ar•rhe•a (*dye*-uh-**ree**-uh) ***noun*** A condition in which normally solid waste becomes runny and frequent.

di•a•ry (**dye**-uh-ree) ***noun*** A book in which people write down things that happen each day, either to use as a record or to plan ahead. ▸ ***noun, plural*** **diaries**

dice (**disse**)
1. ***noun, plural*** Cubes with a different number of dots on each face, used in games. The singular of *dice* is *die,* although some people use dice as the singular.
2. ***verb*** To cut something, such as vegetables, into cubes, as in *to dice the carrots.* ▸ **dicing, diced** ▸ ***adjective*** **diced**

dic•tate (**dik**-tate) ***verb***
1. To talk aloud so that someone can write down what you say. ▸ ***noun*** **dictation**
2. To control.
▸ ***verb*** **dictating, dictated**

dic•ta•tor (**dik**-tay-tur) ***noun*** Someone who has complete control of a country, often ruling it unjustly. ▸ ***noun*** **dictatorship**

dic•tion•ar•y (**dik**-shuh-ner-ee) ***noun*** A book such as this one that lists words in a language in alphabetical order and explains what they mean. ▸ ***noun, plural*** **dictionaries**

did•n't (**did**-uhnt) ***contraction*** A short form of *did not.*

die (**dye**)
1. ***verb*** To stop living, or to come to an end.
2. ***verb*** If you are **dying** to do something, you really want to do it.
3. ***noun*** The singular form of the word *dice.*
Die sounds like **dye.**
▸ ***verb*** **dying, died**

die•sel (**dee**-zuhl) ***noun*** A fuel used in diesel engines that is heavier than gasoline.

diesel engine ***noun*** A type of engine that burns fuel oil using heat produced by compressing air. By contrast, a gasoline engine uses an electric spark to start the burning process.

di•et (**dye**-uht)
1. ***noun*** Your **diet** is what you usually eat. ▸ ***adjective*** **dietary**
2. ***noun*** A prescribed or selected eating plan, usually for losing weight.
3. ***verb*** When you **diet,** you choose what you eat in order to lose weight, gain weight, or improve your health.
▸ **dieting, dieted** ▸ ***noun*** **dieter**

D

dif•fer•ence (**dif**-ur-uhnss or **dif**-ruhnss) ***noun***
1. The way in which things are not like each other. ▸ ***verb*** **differ**
2. The **difference** between two numbers is the amount by which one is less or more than the other.

dif•fer•ent (**dif**-ur-uhnt *or* **dif**-ruhnt) ***adjective*** Not the same. ▸ ***adverb*** **differently**

dif•fi•cult (**dif**-uh-*kuhlt*) ***adjective***
1. Not easy, as in *a difficult exam.*
2. A **difficult** person is not easy to get along with.

dif•fi•cul•ty (**dif**-uh-*kuhl*-tee) ***noun*** A problem. ▸ ***noun, plural*** **difficulties**

dig (**dig**)
1. ***verb*** To use a shovel or spade to move earth.
2. ***verb*** To look very hard for information.
3. ***noun*** A push or a poke, as in *a dig in the ribs.*
4. ***noun*** An unkind remark.
5. ***noun*** An archaeological excavation.
▸ ***verb*** **digging, dug** (**duhg**)

di•gest
1. (dye-**jest**) ***verb*** To break down food in the organs of digestion so that it can be absorbed into the blood and used by the body. ▸ **digesting, digested**
2. (**dye**-jest) ***noun*** A shortened form of a book or other written work, or a collection of such shortened forms.

di•ges•tion (duh-**jess**-chuhn) ***noun*** The process of breaking down food in the stomach and other organs so that it can be absorbed into the blood. ▸ ***adjective*** **digestive**

dig•it (**dij**-it) ***noun***
1. Any one of the Arabic numerals from 1 to 9, and sometimes 0.
2. A finger or toe.

dig•it•al (**dij**-uh-tuhl) ***adjective***
1. A **digital** display shows time, speed, etc., in numerals.
2. Using the binary number system for recording text, images, or sound in a form that can be used on a computer.

dig•i•tize (**dij**-uh-tize) ***verb*** To convert or change data or graphic images to digital form, usable by a computer.
▸ **digitizing, digitized**

dig•ni•fied (**dig**-nuh-fide) ***adjective*** Calm, proud, and in control; noble; stately.

dig•ni•ty (**dig**-nuh-tee) ***noun*** A person who has **dignity** has a quality or manner that makes him or her worthy of honor or respect.

dike (**dike**) ***noun*** A high wall or dam that is built to hold back water and prevent flooding.

di•lap•i•dat•ed (duh-**lap**-uh-day-tid) ***adjective*** Shabby and falling to pieces, as in *a dilapidated old barn.* ▸ ***noun*** **dilapidation**

di•lem•ma (duh-**lem**-uh) ***noun*** If you are **in a dilemma,** you have to make a choice between two difficult alternatives.

dil•i•gent (**dil**-uh-juhnt) ***adjective*** Working hard and carefully. ▸ ***noun*** **diligence** ▸ ***adverb*** **diligently**

di•lute (duh-**lute** *or* dye-**lute**) ***verb*** When you **dilute** something, you make it weaker by adding water or other liquid. ▸ **diluting, diluted** ▸ ***noun*** **dilution**

dim (**dim**)
1. ***adjective*** Somewhat dark, as in *a dim corner of the room.*
2. ***adjective*** Formless, or hard to see.
3. ***verb*** To make less bright. ▸ **dimming, dimmed**

dime (**dime**) ***noun*** A small coin of the United States and Canada that is worth 10 cents.

di•men•sion (duh-**men**-shuhn) ***noun*** The **dimensions** of an object are its measurements or its size. All objects have three dimensions: length, width, and height. ▸ ***adjective*** **dimensional**

di•min•ish (duh-**min**-ish) ***verb*** If something **diminishes,** it becomes smaller or weaker. ▸ **diminishes, diminishing, diminished**

di•min•u•tive (duh-**min**-yuh-tiv) ***adjective*** Tiny, or very small.

dim•ple (**dim**-puhl) ***noun*** A small hollow in a person's cheek or chin. ▸ ***adjective*** **dimpled**

din (**din**) ***noun*** A great deal of noise.

dine (**dine**) ***verb*** To have a meal, especially dinner, in a formal way. ▸ **dining, dined**

din•er (**dye**-nur) ***noun***
1. A person eating in a restaurant, hotel, etc.
2. A restaurant with a long counter and small eating areas or booths.

di•nette (dye-**net**) ***noun***
1. A small space, usually next to a kitchen, for eating meals.
2. A **dinette set** is a table and chairs used for eating in such an area.

din•ghy (**ding**-ee) ***noun*** A small, open boat. ▸ ***noun, plural*** **dinghies**

din•gy (**din**-jee) ***adjective*** Dull and dirty, as in *a dingy room.* ▸ **dingier, dingiest**

dining room ***noun*** A room where meals are served.

din•ner (**din**-ur) ***noun***
1. The main meal of the day.
2. A formal banquet.

di•no•saur (**dye**-nuh-sor) ***noun*** Any of a group of large reptiles that lived on land in prehistoric times.

di•o•cese (**dye**-uh-siss *or* **dye**-uh-seess) ***noun*** A church district that is presided over by a bishop. ▸ ***noun, plural*** **dioceses** (**dye**-uh-seess *or* **dye**-uh-siss-iz)

dip (**dip**)
1. ***verb*** To put something briefly into a liquid.
2. ***verb*** To slope downward. ▸ ***noun*** **dip**
3. ***noun*** If you **take a dip,** you go for a short swim.
4. ***noun*** A thick, tasty sauce into which you dip raw vegetables, chips, etc.
▸ ***verb*** **dipping, dipped**

di•plo•ma (duh-**ploh**-muh) ***noun*** A certificate from a school showing that you have finished a course of study.

dip•lo•mat (**dip**-luh-mat) ***noun*** A person who represents his or her country's government in a foreign country.

dip•lo•mat•ic (**dip**-luh-**mat**-ik) ***adjective***
1. To do with being a diplomat, as in *the diplomatic service.*
2. If you are **diplomatic,** you are tactful and good at dealing with people. ▸ ***noun*** **diplomacy** (di-**ploh**-muh-see)

dip•per (**dip**-ur) ***noun*** A cup with a long handle used to scoop liquid out of a large container.

dire (**dire**) ***adjective*** Dreadful or urgent, as in *dire need.* ▸ **direr, direst**

di•rect (duh-**rekt** *or* dye-**rekt**)
1. ***adjective*** In a straight line, or by the shortest route.
2. ***verb*** To supervise people, especially in a play, movie, or television program.
3. ***verb*** To tell someone the way to go.
4. ***adjective*** If someone is **direct,** he or she has a very straightforward manner.
▸ ***verb*** **directing, directed** ▸ ***adverb*** **directly**

di•rec•tion (duh-**rek**-shuhn) ***noun***
1. The way that someone or something is moving or pointing.
2. Guidance or supervision.
3. directions *noun, plural* Instructions.

di•rec•tor (duh-**rek**-tur) ***noun***
1. The person in charge of making a play, a movie, or a radio or television program.
2. One of a group of people responsible for directing the affairs of a company.

di•rec•to•ry (duh-**rek**-tuh-ree) ***noun*** A book that gives addresses, phone numbers, etc., in alphabetical order. ▸ ***noun, plural*** **directories**

di•ri•gi•ble (dihr-**uh**-juh-buhl) ***noun*** An aircraft that is shaped like a cigar, filled with a gas that makes it rise, and powered by a motor.

dirt (**durt**) ***noun***
1. Earth, or soil.
2. Mud, dust, and other unclean substances.

D

dir•ty (**durt**-ee) ***adjective***
1. Not clean.
2. Unfair, as in *a dirty trick.*
3. Showing bad feeling toward someone, as in *dirty looks.*
▸ ***adjective*** **dirtier, dirtiest**

dis (**diss**) ***verb*** *(slang)* To show disrespect for someone. ▸ ***verb*** **disses, dissing, dissed**

dis•a•ble (diss-**ay**-buhl) ***verb*** To take away the ability to do something.
▸ **disabling, disabled**

dis•a•bled (diss-**ay**-buhld) ***adjective*** People who are **disabled** are restricted in what they can do, usually because of an illness or injury or from a condition present from birth. ▸ ***noun*** **disability**

dis•ad•van•tage (diss-uhd-**van**-tij) ***noun***
1. Something that causes a problem or makes life more difficult.
2. Loss or damage.
3. disadvantaged ***adjective*** People who are **disadvantaged** are very poor and lack many opportunities.

dis•a•gree (diss-uh-**gree**) ***verb***
1. If you **disagree** with someone, you have different opinions. ▸ ***noun*** **disagreement**
2. To cause discomfort.
▸ ***verb*** **disagreeing, disagreed**

dis•ap•pear (diss-uh-**pihr**) ***verb*** To go out of sight. ▸ **disappearing, disappeared** ▸ ***noun*** **disappearance**

dis•ap•point (diss-uh-**point**) ***verb*** To let someone down by failing to do what he or she expected. ▸ **disappointing, disappointed** ▸ ***noun*** **disappointment**
▸ ***adjective*** **disappointed,** ***adjective*** **disappointing**

dis•ap•prove (diss-uh-**proov**) ***verb*** If you **disapprove** of something, you do not think it is a good thing.
▸ **disapproving, disapproved** ▸ ***noun*** **disapproval**

dis•arm (diss-**arm**) ***verb***
1. To take weapons away from somebody.
2. If a country **disarms,** it gives up its weapons. ▸ ***noun*** **disarmament**
3. If someone **disarms** you, the person makes you feel friendly or forget your suspicions. ▸ ***adjective*** **disarming**
▸ ***verb*** **disarming, disarmed**

dis•as•ter (duh-**zass**-tur) ***noun***
1. An event that causes great damage, loss, or suffering, such as a flood or a serious train wreck.
2. If something is a **disaster,** it turns out completely wrong.
▸ ***adjective*** **disastrous** ▸ ***adverb*** **disastrously**

dis•be•lief (diss-bi-**leef**) ***noun*** Refusal to believe something.

dis•be•lieve (diss-bi-**leev**) ***verb*** If you **disbelieve** something, you do not think it is true. ▸ **disbelieving, disbelieved**

disc (**disk**) ***noun*** Another spelling of **disk.**

dis•card (diss-**kard**) ***verb*** To throw something away. ▸ **discarding, discarded**

dis•charge (diss-**charj**) ***verb***
1. To tell someone officially that he or she can go or leave.
2. To release a substance into the open.
▸ ***verb*** **discharging, discharged**
▸ ***noun*** **discharge** (**diss**-*charj*)

dis•ci•ple (duh-**sye**-puhl) ***noun*** Someone who follows the teachings of a leader.

dis•ci•pline (**diss**-uh-plin) ***noun***
1. Control over the way that you or other people behave. ▸ ***verb*** **discipline**
▸ ***adjective*** **disciplinary**
2. An area of study.

disc jockey ***noun*** Someone who plays music on the radio or at a party or club.
▸ ***noun, plural*** **disc jockeys**

dis•close (diss-**klohz**) ***verb*** To reveal something. ▸ ***noun*** **disclosure** (diss-**kloh**-zhur)

dis•co (**diss**-koh)
1. ***noun*** A club where music is played for dancing. ▸ ***noun, plural*** **discos**
2. ***adjective*** A type of music played at clubs.

dis•com•fort (diss-**kuhm**-furt) ***noun*** A feeling of pain or uneasiness that keeps you from relaxing.

dis•con•nect (*diss*-kuh-**nekt**) ***verb***
1. To separate things that are joined together.
2. If something such as the electrical supply or a telephone line is **disconnected,** it is cut off.
▸ ***verb*** **disconnecting, disconnected**
▸ ***noun*** **disconnection**

dis•con•tent•ed (*diss*-kuhn-**ten**-tid) ***adjective*** Not satisfied. ▸ ***noun*** **discontent** ▸ ***adverb*** **discontentedly**

dis•con•tin•ue (*diss*-kuhn-**tin**-yoo) ***verb*** To stop something that is done regularly. ▸ **discontinuing, discontinued**

dis•cord (**diss**-kord) ***noun***
1. Disagreement between two or more people.
2. A mixture of musical notes that sounds unpleasant. ▸ ***adjective*** **discordant** (diss-**kord**-uhnt)

dis•count (**diss**-kount) ***noun***
1. A price cut.
2. A **discount store** sells things at reduced prices.

dis•cour•age (diss-**kur**-ij)
1. ***verb*** If you **discourage** people from doing something, you persuade them not to do it. ▸ **discouraging, discouraged**
2. ***adjective*** If you are **discouraged,** you lose your enthusiasm or confidence.
▸ ***noun*** **discouragement**

dis•cov•er (diss-**kuh**-vur) ***verb***
1. To find something.
2. To find out about something.
▸ ***verb*** **discovering, discovered**
▸ ***noun*** **discovery,** ***noun*** **discoverer**

dis•creet (diss-**kreet**) ***adjective*** If you are **discreet,** you know the right thing to say and can be trusted to keep a secret. ▸ ***noun*** **discretion** (diss-**kre**-shuhn) ▸ ***adverb*** **discreetly**

dis•crim•i•nate (diss-**krim**-uh-nate) ***verb***
1. If you **discriminate** against people, you are prejudiced against them and treat them unfairly. ▸ **discriminating, discriminated** ▸ ***adjective*** **discriminatory**
2. To recognize differences between things or people. ▸ ***adjective*** **discriminating**

dis•crim•i•na•tion (*diss*-krim-i-**nay**-shuhn) ***noun***
1. Prejudice or unjust behavior to others based on differences in age, race, gender, etc.
2. The ability to recognize small differences.

dis•cus (**diss**-kuhss) ***noun*** A large heavy disk that is thrown in a track-and-field event. ▸ ***noun, plural*** **discuses**

dis•cuss (diss-**kuhss**) ***verb*** To talk over something. ▸ **discusses, discussing, discussed** ▸ ***noun*** **discussion**

dis•ease (duh-**zeez**) ***noun***
1. A specific illness.
2. Sickness in general. ▸ ***adjective*** **diseased**

dis•fig•ure (diss-**fig**-yur) ***verb*** To spoil the way something looks. ▸ **disfiguring, disfigured** ▸ ***noun*** **disfigurement**
▸ ***adjective*** **disfigured**

dis•grace (diss-**grayss**)
1. ***verb*** If you **disgrace** yourself, you do something that other people disapprove of and that makes you feel ashamed.
▸ **disgracing, disgraced**
2. ***noun*** If something is a **disgrace,** it causes shame or disapproval.
▸ ***adjective*** **disgraceful**

dis•grun•tled (diss-**grunt**-uhld) ***adjective*** Unhappy, or dissatisfied.

dis•guise (diss-**gize**)
1. ***verb*** To hide something. ▸ **disguising, disguised**
2. ***noun*** If you put on a **disguise,** you dress in a way that hides your identity.

dis•gust•ing (diss-**guhss**-ting) ***adjective*** Very unpleasant and offensive to others. ▸ ***noun*** **disgust** ▸ ***verb*** **disgust** ▸ ***adverb*** **disgustingly**

D

dish (**dish**)
1. ***noun*** A container, such as a plate or bowl, used for serving food.
2. ***noun*** Food made in a certain way, as in *a chicken dish.*
3. ***verb*** If you **dish up** food, you put or serve it in a dish. ▸ **dishes, dishing, dished**
▸ ***noun, plural*** **dishes**

di•shev•eled (di-**shev**-uhld) ***adjective*** Very messy.

dis•hon•est (diss-**on**-ist) ***adjective*** Not honest or fair. ▸ ***noun*** **dishonesty** ▸ ***adverb*** **dishonestly**

dis•hon•or (diss-**on**-ur) ***verb*** To bring shame or disgrace upon yourself or others. ▸ **dishonoring, dishonored** ▸ ***noun*** **dishonor** ▸ ***adjective*** **dishonorable**

dish•wash•er (**dish**-*wah*-shur) ***noun***
1. A machine for washing dishes.
2. Someone whose job is to wash dishes.

dis•il•lu•sion (diss-i-**loo**-zhuhn) ***verb*** If you **disillusion** someone, you destroy his or her mistaken ideas or unrealistic hopes about something.
▸ **disillusioning, disillusioned** ▸ ***noun*** **disillusionment**

dis•in•fect•ant (diss-in-**fek**-tuhnt) ***noun*** A chemical used to kill germs, as on a cut or on a household surface. ▸ ***verb*** **disinfect**

dis•in•te•grate (diss-**in**-tuh-grate) ***verb***
1. To break into small pieces.
2. To break up.
▸ ***verb*** **disintegrating, disintegrated**
▸ ***noun*** **disintegration**

dis•in•ter•est•ed (diss-**in**-tuh-*ress*-tid) ***adjective*** Impartial, or without personal feelings for either side of a contest or an argument.

dis•joint•ed (diss-**join**-tid) ***adjective*** Not connected, or not flowing smoothly.

disk *or* **disc** (**disk**) ***noun***
1. A flat, circular object.
2. A piece of plastic, used for recording music or computer information, as in *a floppy disk.*

disk drive ***noun*** The part of a computer that reads information from, or saves information onto, a disk.

dis•like (diss-**like**) ***verb*** If you **dislike** someone or something, you have a feeling of displeasure about that person or thing. ▸ **disliking, disliked** ▸ ***noun*** **dislike**

dis•lo•cate (diss-**loh**-kate or **diss**-loh-*kate*) ***verb*** If you **dislocate** a bone, it comes out of its usual place, as in *to dislocate a shoulder.* ▸ **dislocating, dislocated** ▸ ***noun*** **dislocation** ▸ ***adjective*** **dislocated**

dis•lodge (diss-**loj**) ***verb*** To force something out of position. ▸ **dislodging, dislodged**

dis•mal (**diz**-muhl) ***adjective***
1. Gloomy and sad.
2. Dreadful, as in *a dismal failure.*

dis•man•tle (diss-**man**-tuhl) ***verb*** To take something apart, as in *to dismantle a store display.* ▸ **dismantling, dismantled**

dis•mayed (diss-**made**) ***adjective*** If you are **dismayed,** you are upset and worried about something. ▸ ***noun*** **dismay**

dis•miss (diss-**miss**) ***verb***
1. To allow to leave.
2. To fire someone from a job.
3. To put something out of your mind.
▸ ***verb*** **dismisses, dismissing, dismissed** ▸ ***noun*** **dismissal**

dis•mount (diss-**mount**) ***verb*** If you **dismount** from something, you get off it. ▸ **dismounting, dismounted** ▸ ***noun*** **dismount**

dis•o•be•di•ent (diss-uh-**bee**-dee-uhnt) ***adjective*** If you are **disobedient,** you do not do as you are told. ▸ ***noun*** **disobedience** ▸ ***adverb*** **disobediently**

dis•o•bey (diss-oh-**bay**) ***verb*** To go against the rules or someone's wishes.
▸ **disobeying, disobeyed**

dis•or•der (diss-**or**-dur) ***noun***
1. Lack of order.
2. A physical or mental illness.

dis•or•der•ly (diss-**or**-dur-lee)
adjective
1. Untidy and disorganized, as in *a disorderly desk.*
2. A **disorderly** mob of people is uncontrolled and possibly violent.
▸ ***noun*** **disorderliness**

dis•or•gan•i•zed (diss-**or**-guh-nized) ***adjective*** Confused and not in order.
▸ ***noun*** **disorganization**

dis•own (diss-**ohn**) ***verb*** If you **disown** someone, you refuse to accept the person as a relative any longer.
▸ **disowning, disowned**

dis•patch (diss-**pach**)
1. ***noun*** A message or a report. ▸ ***noun, plural*** **dispatches**
2. ***verb*** To send something or somebody off. ▸ **dispatches, dispatching, dispatched**

dis•pel (diss-**pel**) ***verb*** To put an end to something, as in *to dispel a rumor.*
▸ **dispelling, dispelled**

dis•perse (diss-**purss**) ***verb*** To scatter.
▸ **dispersing, dispersed** ▸ ***noun*** **dispersal**

dis•place (diss-**playss**) ***verb***
1. To move someone or something from its usual place.
2. To take the place of something or somebody else.
▸ ***verb*** **displacing, displaced** ▸ ***noun*** **displacement**

dis•play (diss-**play**)
1. ***verb*** To show something.
▸ **displaying, displayed**
2. ***noun*** A public show or exhibition.
3. ***noun*** A screen or panel on electronic equipment that shows information, as in *the video display terminal of a computer.*
4. ***noun*** Special behavior by an animal to attract a mate.

dis•please (diss-**pleez**) ***verb*** If you **displease** someone, you annoy the person or cause him or her to be dissatisfied. ▸ **displeasing, displeased**
▸ ***noun*** **displeasure** (diss-**plezh**-ur)
▸ ***adjective*** **displeased**

dis•pos•a•ble (diss-**poh**-zuh-buhl) ***adjective*** Made to be thrown away after use, as in *disposable diapers.* ▸ ***verb*** **dispose**

dis•pos•al (diss-**poze**-uhl) ***noun***
1. The act of throwing away or recycling something.
2. A **garbage disposal** is a small machine under a sink that grinds up leftover food and sends it into the sewer system.

dis•po•si•tion (diss-puh-**zish**-uhn) ***noun***
1. A person's general attitude or temperament.
2. A tendency or inclination to behave a certain way.

dis•prove (diss-**proov**) ***verb*** If you **disprove** something, you show that it cannot be true. ▸ **disproving, disproved**

dis•pute (diss-**pyoot**)
1. ***noun*** A disagreement.
2. ***verb*** If you **dispute** what someone says, you say that you think it is wrong.
▸ **disputing, disputed**

dis•qual•i•fy (diss-**kwol**-uh-fye) ***verb*** To prevent someone from taking part in an activity, often because the person has broken a rule. ▸ **disqualifies, disqualifying, disqualified** ▸ ***noun*** **disqualification**

dis•re•gard (diss-ri-**gard**) ***verb*** To take no notice of someone or something.
▸ **disregarding, disregarded** ▸ ***noun*** **disregard**

dis•rep•u•ta•ble (diss-**rep**-yuh-tuh-buhl) ***adjective*** If someone or something is **disreputable,** that person or thing has a bad reputation. ▸ ***noun*** **disrepute** (diss-ri-**pyoot**)

dis•res•pect (diss-ri-**spekt**) ***noun*** A lack of respect, or rudeness. ▸ ***adjective*** **disrespectful** ▸ ***adverb*** **disrespectfully**

dis•rupt (diss-**ruhpt**) ***verb*** To disturb or break up something that is happening.
▸ **disrupting, disrupted** ▸ ***noun*** **disruption** ▸ ***adjective*** **disruptive**

D

dis•sat•is•fied (diss-**sat**-uhss-fide) ***adjective*** Unhappy or discontented. ▸ ***noun*** **dissatisfaction** ▸ ***verb*** **dissatisfy**

dis•sect (di-**sekt** *or* dye-**sekt**) ***verb***
1. To cut apart an animal or a human body so as to examine it.
2. To examine and analyze something very carefully, as in *to dissect an argument.*
▸ ***verb*** **dissecting, dissected** ▸ ***noun*** **dissection**

dis•sent (di-**sent**)
1. ***verb*** To disagree with an idea or opinion. ▸ **dissenting, dissented**
2. ***noun*** Disagreement with an opinion or idea.
▸ ***noun*** **dissension**

dis•si•dent (**diss**-uh-duhnt) ***noun*** Someone who disagrees with the laws of a country or an organization, as in *a political dissident.* ▸ ***noun*** **dissidence**

dis•solve (di-**zolv**) ***verb***
1. To seem to disappear when mixed with liquid.
2. If a partnership is **dissolved,** it is officially ended.
▸ ***verb*** **dissolving, dissolved** ▸ ***noun*** **dissolution** (diss-uh-**loo**-shuhn)

dis•tance (**diss**-tuhnss) ***noun***
1. The amount of space between two places.
2. If you see something **in the distance,** it is far away.
3. If you **keep your distance** from somebody, you keep away from the person.

dis•tant (**diss**-tuhnt) ***adjective***
1. Not close in space or time, as in *a distant land* or *the distant future.*
2. Not closely related, as in *a distant cousin.*
3. Not warm or friendly.

dis•taste (diss-**tayst**) ***noun*** A feeling of not liking.

dis•taste•ful (diss-**tayst**-fuhl) ***adjective*** Unpleasant or not to a person's taste; offensive.

dis•tem•per (diss-**temp**-ur) ***noun*** An often deadly disease common among dogs and some other animals. It is caused by a virus and has symptoms including fever and loss of appetite.

dis•till (di-**stil**) ***verb*** To purify a liquid by heating it until it turns into a gas and then letting the gas cool to form a liquid again. ▸ **distilling, distilled** ▸ ***noun*** **distillation,** ***noun*** **distiller** ▸ ***adjective*** **distilled**

dis•tinct (diss-**tingkt**) ***adjective***
1. Very clear. ▸ ***adverb*** **distinctly**
2. Clearly different.

dis•tinc•tion (diss-**tingk**-shuhn) ***noun***
1. A clear difference.
2. Excellence, as in *an actor of distinction.*
3. Something that makes an object or a person unusual or different.

dis•tinc•tive (diss-**tingk**-tiv) ***adjective*** Making a person or thing different from all others.

dis•tin•guish (diss-**ting**-gwish) ***verb***
1. To tell the difference between things.
2. To see or hear clearly.
▸ ***verb*** **distinguishes, distinguishing, distinguished** ▸ ***adjective*** **distinguishable**

dis•tin•guished (diss-**ting**-gwisht) ***adjective*** A **distinguished** person is noted for the important things that he or she has done.

dis•tort (diss-**tort**) ***verb***
1. To twist something out of shape.
2. To change the facts in order to mislead someone.
▸ ***verb*** **distorting, distorted** ▸ ***noun*** **distortion** ▸ ***adjective*** **distorted**

dis•tract (diss-**trakt**) ***verb*** If someone or something **distracts** you, that person or thing weakens your concentration on what you are doing. ▸ **distracting, distracted** ▸ ***noun*** **distraction**

dis•tress (diss-**tress**) ***noun***
1. A feeling of great pain or sadness.
▸ ***verb*** **distress** ▸ ***adjective*** **distressed,** ***adjective*** **distressing**
2. in distress In need of help.

dis•trib•ute (diss-**trib**-yoot) ***verb***
1. To give things out.
2. To deliver products to various places.
▸ ***verb*** **distributing, distributed**
▸ ***noun*** **distribution** (diss-tri-**byoo**-shuhn)

dis•trib•u•tor (diss-**trib**-yuh-tur) ***noun***
1. A person or company that delivers products to various places.
2. The part of a car engine that sends electricity from the ignition system to the spark plugs.

dis•trict (**diss**-trikt) ***noun*** An area or a region.

dis•trust (diss-**trust**) ***verb*** If you **distrust** someone, you think that the person may do you harm. ▸ **distrusting, distrusted** ▸ ***noun*** **distrust** ▸ ***adjective*** **distrustful** ▸ ***adverb*** **distrustfully**

dis•turb (diss-**turb**) ***verb***
1. To interrupt somebody when he or she is doing something.
2. To worry or upset someone.
▸ ***adjective*** **disturbing**
▸ ***verb*** **disturbing, disturbed**

dis•use (diss-**yooss**) ***noun*** If something is in **disuse,** it is no longer used.
▸ ***adjective*** **disused**

ditch (**dich**)
1. ***noun*** A long, narrow trench that drains water away. ▸ ***noun, plural*** **ditches**
2. ***verb*** If a pilot **ditches** a plane, he or she makes an emergency landing in water.
3. ***verb*** *(slang)* If one person **ditches** another, he or she leaves the person suddenly.
▸ ***verb*** **ditches, ditching, ditched**

dit•to (**dit**-oh) ***noun*** **Ditto** marks (") are used in lists to show that what is written above is repeated on the line with the marks. ▸ ***noun, plural*** **dittos**

dive (**dive**) ***verb***
1. To plunge with your head first into water with your arms stretched out in front of you.
2. To drop down suddenly.
▸ ***verb*** **diving, dived** *or* **dove** (**dohv**)
▸ ***noun*** **dive**

div•er (**dye**-vur) ***noun***
1. Someone who dives underwater.
2. Someone who uses breathing apparatus to swim or explore underwater. *See* **scuba diving.**

di•verse (duh-**vurss** *or* dye-**vurss**) ***adjective*** Varied or assorted.

di•ver•sion (duh-**vur**-zhuhn *or* dye-**vur**-zhuhn) ***noun*** Something that takes your mind off other things.

di•ver•si•ty (di-**vur**-suh-tee) ***noun*** A variety.

di•vert (duh-**vurt** *or* dye-**vurt**) ***verb***
1. If someone **diverts** the traffic, he or she makes it take a different route.
2. When you **divert** someone's attention from something, you stop the person from thinking about it.
▸ ***verb*** **diverting, diverted** ▸ ***adjective*** **diverting**

di•vide (duh-**vide**) ***verb***
1. To split into parts.
2. In math, if you **divide** one number by a second number, you figure out how many times the second number will go into the first.
3. To share something.
4. To split into opposing groups.
▸ ***verb*** **dividing, divided**

div•i•dend (**div**-i-*dend*) ***noun***
1. In a division problem, the number that is divided.
2. A share of the money earned by an investment or a business.

di•vine (duh-**vine**)
1. ***adjective*** To do with or from God or a god, as in *divine worship* or *divine love.*
2. ***verb*** To discover something by instinct, magic, or guessing. ▸ **divining, divined**
3. ***adjective*** Wonderful.

diving board ***noun*** A long wooden or plastic board that juts out over the deep end of a swimming pool, allowing people to jump or dive into the water.

di•vis•i•ble (di-**viz**-uh-buhl) ***adjective*** Able to be divided.

D

di•vi•sion (di-**vizh**-uhn) ***noun***
1. The act of dividing one number by another, as in *long division.*
2. One of the parts into which something large has been divided, as in *the research division of a chemical company.*
3. Part of an army made up of several regiments.
4. Something that separates.

di•vi•sor (di-**vye**-zur) ***noun*** In a division problem, the number that you divide by.

di•vorce (di-**vorss**)
1. *noun* The ending of a marriage by a court of law. ▸ ***verb* divorce**
2. *verb* Totally separated from something. ▸ **divorcing, divorced**
▸ ***adjective* divorced**

di•vulge (di-**vulj**) ***verb*** To reveal information that was secret or unknown.
▸ **divulging, divulged**

diz•zy (**diz**-ee) ***adjective***
1. If you are **dizzy,** you feel very unsteady on your feet, and your head seems to be spinning.
2. Bewildered and confused.
▸ ***adjective* dizzier, dizziest, *adjective* dizzying**

DJ (**dee** *jay*) ***noun*** Short for **disc jockey.**

DNA (dee en **ay**) ***noun*** The molecule that carries the genetic code that gives living things their special characteristics. The letters stand for *DeoxyriboNucleic Acid.*

do (**doo**) ***verb***
1. To perform an action.
2. To complete.
3. To be acceptable.
4. To get along.
5. To behave or act in a certain way.
6. To create.
7. To bring about an effect.
Do sounds like **dew** and **due.**
▸ ***verb* does (duhz), doing, did (did), done (duhn)**

Do•ber•man pin•scher (**doh**-bur-muhn **pin**-chur) ***noun*** A breed of dog with a long head; a large, muscular body; and a short, black or brown coat.

doc•ile (**doss**-uhl) ***adjective*** Calm and easy to manage or train, as in *a docile pet.*

dock (**dok**) ***noun*** A place where ships load and unload cargo. ▸ ***verb* dock**

doc•tor (**dok**-tur) ***noun***
1. Someone trained and licensed to treat sick and injured people.
2. Someone who has the highest degree given by universities.

doc•trine (**dok**-trin) ***noun*** A belief or teaching of a religion or other group of people.

doc•u•dra•ma (**dok**-yuh-*drah*-muh) ***noun*** A television show, movie, or play that presents a retelling of actual events, especially recent events surrounded by scandal or controversy.

doc•u•ment (**dok**-yuh-muhnt) ***noun*** A piece of paper containing important information. ▸ ***verb* document (dok**-yuh-ment)

doc•u•men•ta•ry (dok-yuh-**men**-tuh-ree) ***noun*** A movie or television program made about real situations and people.
▸ ***noun, plural* documentaries**

do•dec•a•he•dron (doh-*dek*-uh-**hee**-dron) ***noun*** A solid shape with 12 faces.

dodge (**doj**) ***verb***
1. To avoid something or somebody by moving quickly, as in *to dodge a thrown ball.*
2. To avoid.
▸ ***verb* dodging, dodged** ▸ ***noun* dodge**

do•do (**doh**-doh) ***noun***
1. An extinct bird that had a large body and wings so small it was unable to fly. Dodos lived on an island in the Indian Ocean.
2. *(slang)* A stupid person.
▸ ***noun, plural* dodos *or* dodoes**

doe (**doh**) ***noun*** A female deer; the female of any mammal where the male is called a buck. **Doe** sounds like **dough.**

does•n't (**duhz**-uhnt) ***contraction*** A short form of *does not.*

doff (**dof**) ***verb***
1. If you **doff** a coat, jacket, or another article of clothing, you remove it.
2. If you **doff your hat** or **cap,** you tip it as a sign of greeting.
▸ ***verb*** **doffing, doffed**

dog (**dawg** *or* **dog**)
1. ***noun*** A domestic mammal with four legs that is often kept as a pet or as a work animal. Dogs are related to wolves, coyotes, and foxes.
2. ***verb*** To follow someone closely.
▸ **dogging, dogged**

dog•mat•ic (dawg-**mat**-ik) ***adjective*** If you are **dogmatic,** you insist very strongly that you are right about things.

dog•wood (**dawg**-*wud*) ***noun*** A tree or shrub that has small, green flowers surrounded by pink or white leaves that look like petals.

doi•ly (**doi**-lee) ***noun*** A small piece of lace or cut paper placed under a plate or other item as a decoration or on furniture to protect it. ▸ ***noun, plural*** **doilies**

do-it-yourself ***adjective*** To do with home improvements, repairs, or projects that you do yourself.

dole (**dohl**) ***verb*** If you **dole out** something, such as food or money, you give it out in small quantities. ▸ **doling, doled**

doll (**dol**) ***noun*** A small model of a human being used as a child's toy.

dol•lar (**dol**-ur) ***noun*** The main unit of money in the United States, Canada, Australia, and New Zealand.

doll•house (**dol**-*houss*) ***noun*** A small toy house.

dol•phin (**dol**-fin) ***noun*** An intelligent water mammal with a long snout, related to whales, but smaller.

do•main (doh-**mayn**) ***noun***
1. A region or place controlled by a government or person.
2. A **domain name** is a computer address for a site on the Internet, as in *www.whitehouse.gov.*

dome (**dohm**) ***noun*** A roof shaped like half of a sphere.

do•mes•tic (duh-**mess**-tik) ***adjective***
1. To do with the home, as in *domestic chores.*
2. Domestic animals are no longer wild but are kept for food, as work animals, or as pets.
3. To do with your own country, as in *the domestic market.*

do•mes•ti•cate (duh-**mess**-tuh-kate) ***verb*** To tame something so it can live with or be used by human beings.
▸ **domesticating, domesticated**
▸ ***adjective*** **domesticated**

dom•i•nant (**dom**-uh-nuhnt) ***adjective*** Most influential or powerful.

dom•i•nate (**dom**-uh-nate) ***verb***
1. To control, or to rule. ▸ ***noun*** **domination**
2. To be the main feature of a situation.
▸ ***verb*** **dominating, dominated**

do•min•ion (duh-**min**-yuhn) ***noun***
1. A large area of land controlled by a single ruler or government.
2. Power to rule over something.

dom•i•no (**dom**-uh-noh) ***noun***
1. A small rectangular tile that is divided into two halves that are blank or contain dots.
2. dominoes A game played with a number of these tiles. ▸ ***noun, plural*** **dominoes**

don (**don**) ***verb*** If you **don** clothing, you put it on. ▸ **donning, donned**

do•nate (**doh**-nate) ***verb*** To give something as a present. ▸ **donating, donated** ▸ ***noun*** **donation**

don•key (**dong**-kee) ***noun*** A mammal with long ears, related to the horse, but smaller.

do•nor (**doh**-nur) ***noun***
1. Someone who gives something, usually to an organization or a charity.
2. Someone who agrees to give his or her body, or a part of it, to medical science to help sick people.

don't (**dohnt**) ***contraction*** A short form of *do not.*

D

D

do•nut (**doh**-nuht) *See* **doughnut.**

doo•dle (**doo**-duhl) ***verb*** To draw absentmindedly while you are concentrating on something else. ▸ **doodling, doodled** ▸ ***noun*** **doodle**

doom (**doom**) ***noun*** If you meet your **doom,** you suffer a terrible fate, usually ending in death. ▸ ***verb*** **doom** ▸ ***adjective*** **doomed**

door (**dor**) ***noun***
1. A barrier that opens and closes at the entrance or exit of a building, room, etc.
2. A house or a building.

door•bell (**dor**-*bel*) ***noun*** A bell or buzzer outside a door that is rung by someone who wants the door to be opened.

door•knob (**dor**-*nob*) ***noun*** A handle that you turn to open a door.

door•step (**dor**-*step*) ***noun*** A step or steps on the outside doorway of a building.

door•way (**dor**-*way*) ***noun*** An area between two rooms, or between the inside and outside of a building, that can be closed by a door.

dope (**dohp**) ***noun***
1. *(informal)* A stupid person.
2. *(informal)* An illegal or addictive drug.
3. A thick varnish.

dor•mant (**dor**-muhnt) ***adjective***
1. Animals become **dormant** when they hibernate. They show no signs of action, as if they were asleep.
2. A **dormant** volcano is not active at present but could erupt again.
3. When plants or seeds are **dormant,** they are alive but not growing.

dor•mi•to•ry (**dor**-muh-tor-ee) ***noun*** A building with many separate sleeping rooms, as in *a college dormitory.* ▸ ***noun, plural*** **dormitories**

dor•mouse (**dor**-*mouss*) ***noun*** A European, African, or Asian rodent that looks like a small squirrel, with black or gray fur and a furry tail. ▸ ***noun, plural*** **dormice** (**dor**-misse)

DOS (**doss**) ***noun*** A system of commands and codes that make it possible to run and use a computer. DOS stands for *Disk Operating System.*

dose (**dohss**) ***noun***
1. A prescribed amount of medicine.
2. A small amount, especially of something unpleasant, as in *a dose of hard work.*

dot (**dot**)
1. ***noun*** A small, round point. ▸ ***verb*** **dot**
2. ***verb*** To be here and there around an area. ▸ **dotting, dotted**

dote (**doht**) ***verb*** To pay too much attention to, or to show too much fondness for. ▸ **doting, doted**

dou•ble (**duh**-buhl)
1. ***adjective*** Twice the amount, the number, or the strength.
2. ***adverb*** Twice as much.
3. ***verb*** To make something twice as big.
4. ***noun*** If you have a **double,** there is another person who looks just like you.
5. **doubles** ***noun, plural*** When you play **doubles** in badminton, tennis, etc., there are two players on each side.
6. ***noun*** A hit in baseball that allows the player to get to second base.
7. ***verb*** To bend or fold in two.
8. ***verb*** To serve more than one purpose.
▸ ***verb*** **doubling, doubled**

double-cross ***verb*** When you **double-cross** someone, you betray him or her. ▸ **double-crosses, double-crossing, double-crossed** ▸ ***noun*** **double cross**

double-head•er (**hed**-ur) ***noun*** Two baseball games played one right after the other. ▸ ***noun, plural*** **double-headers**

doubt (dout)
1. ***noun*** Uncertainty.
2. ***verb*** If you **doubt** something, you are uncertain about it. ▸ **doubting, doubted** ▸ ***adjective*** **doubtful** ▸ ***adverb*** **doubtfully**

dough (doh) ***noun***
1. A thick, sticky mixture of flour, water, etc., used to make bread, cookies, muffins, and other foods.

2. *(slang)* Money.
Dough sounds like **doe.**

dough•nut (**doh**-nuht) ***noun*** A cake fried in fat. A doughnut is round and usually has a hole in the middle. Also spelled **donut.**

dove (**duhv**) ***noun*** A plump bird that makes a gentle cooing sound.

down (**doun**)
1. ***preposition*** From a higher to a lower place. ▸ ***adjective*** **downward** (**doun**-wurd) ▸ ***adverb*** **downward** *or* **downwards**
2. ***noun*** The soft feathers of a bird. ▸ ***adjective*** **downy**
3. ***adjective*** If you feel **down,** you feel sad or depressed.
4. ***noun*** In football, one of a series of four attempts to advance the ball ten yards.
5. ***adverb*** To a lower place or condition.
6. ***preposition*** In a direction lower or farther away, as in *down the ladder* or *down the road.*

down•cast (**down**-*kast*) ***adjective*** Very sad.

down•load (**doun**-*lohd*) ***verb*** To transfer information from a computer or network to a disk or the memory of another computer. ▸ **downloading, downloaded**

down•pour (**doun**-*por*) ***noun*** A very heavy rain.

down•right (**doun**-*rite*)
1. ***adjective*** Total, or complete.
2. ***adverb*** Absolutely, or completely.

downs (**dounz**) ***noun, plural*** An area of rolling hills, especially in England.

down•size (**doun**-*size*) ***verb*** To reduce the size of something, such as the scale of an automobile or the number of employees in a company. ▸ **downsizing, downsized**

down•stairs
1. (**doun-stairz**) ***adverb*** Down the stairs or to a lower floor.
2. ***adjective*** (**doun**-stairz) On a lower level of a house. ▸ ***noun*** **downstairs**

down•stream (**doun-streem**) ***adverb*** In the direction of the flowing current in a river or stream. ▸ ***adjective*** **downstream**

Down syndrome ***noun*** A genetic condition in which a person is born mentally retarded and with eyes that appear to slant, a broad skull, and shorter fingers than normal. Also called *Down's syndrome.*

down•town (**doun-toun**) ***adverb*** To or in a city's main business district. ▸ ***adjective*** **downtown**

dow•ry (**dou**-ree) ***noun*** The money or property that women in some cultures bring with them when they marry. ▸ ***noun, plural*** **dowries**

doze (**dohz**) ***verb*** To sleep lightly for a short time. ▸ **dozing, dozed** ▸ ***noun*** **doze**

doz•en (**duhz**-uhn) ***noun*** A group of 12.

Dr. Short for **Doctor.**

drab (**drab**) ***adjective*** Very dull and dreary. ▸ ***noun*** **drabness**

draft (**draft**)
1. ***noun*** A flow of cold air. ▸ ***adjective*** **drafty**
2. ***adjective*** Drawn out of a barrel or keg, as in *draft beer.*
3. ***verb*** When you **draft** something, such as a letter, you make a first rough copy of it.
4. ***verb*** If someone is **drafted,** the person is made to join the armed forces. ▸ ***noun*** **draft** ▸ ***verb*** **drafting, drafted**

drag (**drag**)
1. ***verb*** To pull something along the ground.
2. ***verb*** If something **drags,** it seems to go slowly.
3. ***noun*** *(informal)* If something is a **drag,** it is boring. ▸ ***verb*** **dragging, dragged**

drag•on (**drag**-uhn) ***noun*** A mythical monster that breathes fire.

drag•on•fly (**drag**-uhn-*flye*) ***noun*** A large insect with two sets of wings and a long, slender body.

D

drain (**drayn**)
1. ***verb*** To remove the liquid from something.
2. ***noun*** A pipe or channel that takes away water or sewage.
3. ***verb*** To tire, or to use up.
▸ ***verb*** **draining, drained**

drain•age (**dray**-nij) ***noun*** The act or process of removing liquid from an area.

drained (**draynd**) ***adjective*** If you feel **drained,** you have no energy left.

dra•ma (**drah**-muh) ***noun***
1. A play.
2. If you study **drama,** you learn about acting and the theater.
3. Something that affects people seriously.

dra•mat•ic (druh-**mat**-ik) ***adjective***
1. To do with acting and the theater.
2. Very noticeable, as in *a dramatic change.*
3. If someone is being **dramatic,** the person is making too much fuss about something. ▸ ***adverb*** **dramatically**

dram•a•tist (**dram**-uh-tist) ***noun*** Someone who writes plays.

dram•a•tize (**dram**-uh-tize) ***verb***
1. To adapt a story into a play.
2. If you **dramatize** an event, you make it seem more exciting than it really was.
▸ ***verb*** **dramatizing, dramatized**

drape (**drayp**) ***noun***
1. A piece of material placed across a window or stage to cover it. ▸ ***noun*** **drapery**
2. ***verb*** To cover with a loosely hanging cloth.

dras•tic (**drass**-tik) ***adjective*** If you do something **drastic,** you take sudden, severe, or violent action. ▸ ***adverb*** **drastically**

draw (**draw**)
1. ***verb*** To make a picture with a pencil, pen, etc. ▸ ***noun*** **drawing**
2. ***verb*** To pull something.
3. ***verb*** To attract, as in *to draw a crowd.*
4. ***verb*** To figure out by using your power of reason, as in *to draw conclusions.*
5. ***verb*** To inhale, as in *to draw a deep breath.*
6. ***noun*** If a competition ends in a **draw,** both sides are even.
▸ ***verb*** **drawing, drew** (**droo**), **drawn** (**drawn**)

draw•back (**draw**-*bak*) ***noun*** A problem or disadvantage.

draw•bridge (**draw**-*brij*) ***noun*** A bridge that can be raised or moved to let boats pass underneath.

draw•er (**dror**) ***noun*** A sliding box in a piece of furniture, used for storing things.

drawing room ***noun*** A formal room where guests are entertained.

drawl (**drawl**)
1. ***verb*** To speak in a slow manner, stretching out the vowel sounds.
▸ **drawling, drawled**
2. ***noun*** A slow manner of speaking.

draw•string (**draw**-*string*) ***noun*** A string or cord that closes or tightens a bag or piece of clothing when you pull the ends.

dread (**dred**) ***verb*** If you **dread** something, you are very afraid of it.
▸ **dreading, dreaded** ▸ ***noun*** **dread**
▸ ***adjective*** **dreaded**

dread•ful (**dred**-fuhl) ***adjective***
1. Very frightening; awful, as in *a dreadful storm.*
2. Very bad, as in *a dreadful movie.*
▸ ***adverb*** **dreadfully**

dread•locks (**dred**-loks) ***noun, plural*** A hairstyle in which the hair is grown long and worn in thick, ropelike strands.

dream (**dreem**) ***verb***
1. To imagine events while you are asleep.
2. If you **dream** of doing something, you really want to do it.
▸ ***verb*** **dreaming, dreamed** *or* **dreamt** (**dremt**) ▸ ***noun*** **dream,** ***noun*** **dreamer**

dream•y (**dree**-mee) ***adjective***
1. If you are **dreamy,** you are always daydreaming.
2. Vague or soft, as in *dreamy music.*
▸ ***adjective*** **dreamier, dreamiest**
▸ ***adverb*** **dreamily**

D

drear•y (**drihr**-ee) ***adjective*** Dull and miserable. ▸ **drearier, dreariest** ▸ ***adverb* drearily**

dredge (**drej**) ***verb*** To scrape sand, mud, etc., from the bottom of a river or harbor. ▸ **dredging, dredged** ▸ ***noun* dredger**

dregs (**dregz**) ***noun, plural*** The solid bits that drop to the bottom of some liquids, such as coffee.

drench (**drench**) ***verb*** To make something completely wet. ▸ **drenches, drenching, drenched**

dress (**dress**)
1. ***verb*** To put clothes on.
2. ***noun*** A piece of clothing worn by women and girls that covers the body from shoulders to legs. ▸ ***noun, plural* dresses**
3. ***noun*** Clothes in general, as in *formal dress.*
4. ***verb*** If you **dress a wound,** you put an ointment on it and bandage it.
▸ ***verb* dresses, dressing, dressed**

dress•er (**dress**-ur) ***noun*** A piece of furniture with drawers, used for storing clothes.

dress•ing (**dress**-ing) ***noun***
1. A covering for a wound.
2. A type of sauce for salads.
3. A mixture used to stuff a chicken or turkey before it is roasted.

dressing table ***noun*** A piece of bedroom furniture, often with a mirror and drawers.

dress rehearsal ***noun*** The last rehearsal of a play, in full costume.

drib•ble (**drib**-uhl) ***verb***
1. To let liquid trickle from your mouth.
2. When you **dribble** in basketball, you bounce the ball while running, keeping it under your control.
▸ ***verb* dribbling, dribbled**

drift (**drift**)
1. ***verb*** When something **drifts,** it moves wherever the water or wind takes it.
2. ***verb*** To move or act without any sense of purpose. ▸ ***noun* drifter**
3. ***noun*** A pile of sand or snow created by the wind.
4. If you **get someone's drift,** you understand what the person is saying.
▸ ***verb* drifting, drifted**

drift•wood (**drift**-*wud*) ***noun*** Wood that floats ashore or is floating on water.

drill (**dril**)
1. ***noun*** A tool used for making holes.
2. ***verb*** To use a drill.
3. ***verb*** To teach someone how to do something by having the person do it over and over again. ▸ ***noun* drill** ▸ ***verb* drilling, drilled**

drink (**dringk**)
1. ***noun*** A liquid that you swallow.
2. ***verb*** To swallow liquid. ▸ **drinking, drank** (**drangk**), **drunk** (**druhngk**)
3. ***noun*** An alcoholic liquid.
▸ ***noun* drinker**

drip (**drip**)
1. ***verb*** When a liquid **drips,** it falls slowly, drop by drop. ▸ **dripping, dripped** ▸ ***noun* drip**
2. ***noun*** *(informal)* A silly and boring person.

drip•pings (**drip**-ingz) ***noun, plural*** Fat and liquid or juice obtained from meat while it is cooking, which can often be used again.

drive (**drive**)
1. ***verb*** To operate and control a vehicle.
▸ ***noun* driver, *noun* driving**
2. ***verb*** To carry someone somewhere in a vehicle. ▸ ***noun* drive**
3. ***verb*** To hit something hard and far.
4. ***verb*** To force someone into a desperate state.
5. ***noun*** A private road leading to a house.
6. ***noun*** Energy and determination.
7. ***noun*** An organized campaign to do something.
▸ ***verb* driving, drove, driven** (**driv**-in)

drive-in ***adjective*** Designed so that customers may be served or entertained in their cars. ▸ ***noun* drive-in**

driv•el (**driv**-uhl) ***noun*** If someone talks **drivel,** what he or she says is nonsense.

D

drive•way (**drive**-*way*) ***noun*** A private road that leads from the street to a house or garage.

driz•zle (**driz**-uhl) ***noun*** Light rain. ▸ ***verb*** **drizzle**

drom•e•dar•y (**drom**-uh-*der*-ee) ***noun*** A camel with one hump, found in the Middle East and northern Africa. ▸ ***noun, plural*** **dromedaries**

drone (**drohn**)
1. ***verb*** To make a steady, dull sound.
2. ***verb*** To talk in a dull, monotonous way.
3. ***noun*** A male insect such as a bee whose function is to mate with the queen. ▸ ***verb*** **droning, droned**

drool (**drool**) ***verb***
1. To let saliva trickle from your mouth.
2. If you **drool over** something, you really like it and want it.
▸ ***verb*** **drooling, drooled**

droop (**droop**) ***verb***
1. To hang down, or to sag. ▸ ***adjective*** **drooping**
2. When people **droop,** they run out of energy.
▸ ***verb*** **drooping, drooped**

drop (**drop**)
1. ***verb*** To let something fall.
2. ***verb*** To fall down. ▸ ***noun*** **drop**
3. ***noun*** A small quantity of liquid, as in *a drop of water.*
4. ***noun*** Any small amount, as in *a drop of kindness.*
5. ***verb*** If you **drop out,** you stop doing something. ▸ ***noun*** **dropout**
6. ***verb*** When players are **dropped,** they are not kept on a team.
7. **A drop in the bucket** is a very small amount.
8. ***noun*** A small piece of candy or medication for the throat, as in *lemon drops* and *cough drops.*
9. ***verb*** To leave out.
10. **drop off** ***verb*** To deliver.
11. **drop by** ***verb*** To pay a short visit.
▸ ***verb*** **dropping, dropped**

drought (**drout**) ***noun*** A long spell of very dry weather.

drove (**drove**)
1. ***noun*** A large herd of animals being moved as a group.
2. ***noun*** A large crowd of people.
3. ***verb*** Past tense of *drive.*

drown (**droun**) ***verb***
1. To die from lack of air when under water or another liquid.
2. **drown out** To make a louder noise than something else.
▸ ***verb*** **drowning, drowned**

drow•sy (**drou**-zee) ***adjective*** Sleepy. ▸ **drowsier, drowsiest** ▸ ***noun*** **drowsiness** ▸ ***verb*** **drowse** ▸ ***adverb*** **drowsily**

drudg•er•y (**druhj**-ur-ee) ***noun*** Difficult, boring, or unpleasant work, as in *household drudgery.*

drug (**druhg**)
1. ***noun*** A substance, either natural or synthetic, used to treat illness.
2. ***noun*** A chemical substance that people take because of its effect on them. Drugs are dangerous and usually cause addiction.
3. ***verb*** To make someone unconscious by giving him or her a drug. ▸ **drugging, drugged** ▸ ***adjective*** **drugged**
4. **drug addict** ***noun*** Someone who cannot give up using drugs.

drug•gist (**druhg**-ist) ***noun*** A person who is trained to prepare and sell drug prescriptions; a pharmacist.

drug•store (**druhg**-*stor*) ***noun*** A store where medicines and other items are sold.

drum (**druhm**)
1. ***noun*** A musical instrument with a hollow body covered with a stretched skin that makes a loud noise when you hit it.
2. ***verb*** To beat a drum or other surface with drumsticks or with your fingers. ▸ **drumming, drummed** ▸ ***noun*** **drummer**
3. ***noun*** A container shaped like a drum.

drum•stick (**druhm**-*stik*) ***noun***
1. A stick used to hit a drum.

D

2. The leg portion of a chicken, turkey, etc.

drunk (**druhngk**)
1. ***adjective*** If people are **drunk,** they have had too much alcohol to drink and cannot control their actions or emotions.
2. ***noun*** A person who often gets drunk. ▸ ***noun*** **drunkard** ▸ ***adjective*** **drunken**
3. ***verb*** Past participle of **drink**.

dry (**drye**)
1. ***verb*** To take the moisture out of something. ▸ **dries, drying, dried**
2. ***adjective*** Not wet.
3. ***adjective*** Dull and boring, as in *a dry speech.*
4. ***adjective*** Without butter or margarine, as in *dry toast.*
▸ ***adjective*** **drier, driest** ▸ ***adverb*** **drily**

dry cell ***noun*** A container in which chemicals that produce electricity are stored in paste form so that they cannot spill. Dry cells are used in toys and other small appliances.

dry-clean ***verb*** To clean clothes with special chemicals in order to remove stains. ▸ **dry-cleaning, dry-cleaned** ▸ ***noun*** **dry cleaner**

dry•er (**drye**-ur) ***noun*** A machine that dries something.

dry goods ***noun, plural*** Fabric, clothing, and related materials, such as threads and ribbons.

du•al (**doo**-uhl) ***adjective***
1. Double.
2. Made up of two parts.
Dual sounds like **duel.**

du•bi•ous (**doo**-bee-uhss) ***adjective*** If you are **dubious** about something, you are not sure about it. ▸ ***adverb*** **dubiously**

du•chess (**duhch**-iss) ***noun*** The wife or widow of a duke, or a woman with the rank that is equal to that of a duke.

duck (**duhk**)
1. ***noun*** A bird with webbed feet that swims and feeds in water.
2. ***verb*** To bend low to avoid something.
3. ***verb*** To avoid or to evade.
▸ ***verb*** **ducking, ducked**

duct (**duhkt**) ***noun*** A tube that carries air or liquid from one place to another, as in *air-conditioning ducts.*

dud (**duhd**) ***noun*** Something that does not work as it should. ▸ ***adjective*** **dud**

due (**doo**) ***adjective***
1. If someone or something is **due,** it is expected to arrive or happen.
2. Suitable. ▸ ***adverb*** **duly**
3. If something happens **due to** something else, it happens because of it.
4. Owed.
Due sounds like **dew** and **do.**

du•el (**doo**-uhl) ***noun*** A fight between two people using swords or guns, fought according to strict rules. **Duel** sounds like **dual.**

du•et (doo-**et**) ***noun*** A piece of music that is played or a song that is sung by two people.

dug•out (**duhg**-*out*) ***noun***
1. A long, low shelter where baseball players sit when they are not at bat or in the field.
2. A rough shelter dug out of the ground or in the side of a hill.
3. A canoe made from the outer portion of a large log.

duke (**dook**) ***noun*** A nobleman. In Britain, a duke holds the rank just below that of a prince.

dull (**duhl**) ***adjective***
1. Not bright; dim.
2. Not perceptive or intelligent.
3. Boring.
4. Not shiny, as in *a dull finish.*
5. Not sharp, as in *a dull blade.*
6. Slow or sluggish.
▸ ***adjective*** **duller, dullest** ▸ ***verb*** **dull** ▸ ***adverb*** **dully**

dumb (**duhm**) ***adjective*** Stupid. ▸ **dumber, dumbest**

dumb•bell (**duhm**-*bel*) ***noun***
1. A short bar with heavy weights at each end, used to exercise and strengthen the muscles.
2. *(slang)* A stupid person.

D

dumb•found•ed (**duhm**-*found*-id) ***adjective*** So amazed that you cannot speak.

dum•my (**duhm**-ee) ***noun***
1. An imitation person or object, as in *a crash-test dummy.*
2. *(informal)* A stupid person.
▸ ***noun, plural*** **dummies**

dump (**duhmp**)
1. ***verb*** To put something down thoughtlessly or roughly.
2. ***noun*** A place where unwanted things can be left, as in *a garbage dump.*
3. ***verb*** *(informal)* To end a friendship with someone.
▸ ***verb*** **dumping, dumped**

dump•ling (**duhm**-pling) ***noun*** Dough that has been boiled, fried, or steamed, sometimes with meat, vegetables, or fruit wrapped inside.

dune (**doon**) ***noun*** A sand hill made by the wind near the ocean or a large lake or in a desert.

dun•ga•ree (*duhng*-guh-**ree**) ***noun***
1. Blue denim; a heavy cotton cloth used to make work clothes.
2. **dungarees** ***noun, plural*** Blue jeans.

dun•geon (**duhn**-juhn) ***noun*** A prison, usually underground.

du•pli•cate
1. (**doo**-pluh-*kate*) ***verb*** To make an exact copy of something. ▸ **duplicating, duplicated** ▸ ***noun*** **duplication,** ***noun*** **duplicator**
2. (**doo**-pluh-kit) ***noun*** An exact copy.

du•ra•ble (**dur**-uh-buhl) ***adjective*** Tough and lasting for a long time, as in *a durable material.* ▸ ***noun*** **durability**

du•ra•tion (du-**ray**-shuhn) ***noun*** The period of time during which something lasts.

dur•ing (**du**-ring) ***preposition*** Within a particular time.

dusk (**duhsk**) ***noun*** The time of day after sunset when it is nearly dark.

dust (**duhst**)
1. ***noun*** Tiny particles of dirt, fluff, etc., that gather on surfaces or in the air.
2. ***verb*** To remove dirt from surfaces.
▸ **dusting, dusted** ▸ ***noun*** **duster**

dust•bin (**duhst**-*bin*) ***noun*** A large container for rubbish.

du•ti•ful (**doo**-ti-fuhl) ***adjective*** If you are **dutiful,** you are obedient and aware of what you should or must do.
▸ ***adverb*** **dutifully**

du•ty (**doo**-tee) ***noun***
1. A thing a person must do or ought to do.
2. Tax charged on goods brought into a country.
3. If you are **on duty,** you are at work.
▸ ***noun, plural*** **duties**

DVD (*dee-vee*-**dee**) ***noun*** A disk the size of a compact disk but that can hold much more information. A DVD can contain computer data or recordings of movies or music. DVD stands for *Digital Versatile Disk* or *Digital VideoDisk.*

dwarf (**dworf**)
1. ***noun*** A very small person, animal, or plant. ▸ ***noun, plural*** **dwarfs** *or* **dwarves** (**dworvz**) ▸ ***adjective*** **dwarf**
2. ***verb*** To make something else seem very small. ▸ **dwarfing, dwarfed**

dwell (**dwel**) ***verb*** To live in a place.
▸ **dwelling, dwelt** (**dwelt**) *or* **dwelled**

dwell•ing (**dwel**-ing) ***noun*** The place where someone lives, such as a house or an apartment.

dwin•dle (**dwin**-duhl) ***verb*** To become smaller or less. ▸ **dwindling, dwindled**

dye (**dye**)
1. ***noun*** A substance used to change the color of something.
2. ***verb*** If someone **dyes** something, he or she changes its color by soaking it in dye. ▸ **dying, dyed** ▸ ***adjective*** **dyed**
Dye sounds like **die.**

dy•nam•ic (dye-**nam**-ik) ***adjective*** If someone is **dynamic,** he or she is very energetic and good at getting things done. ▸ ***noun*** **dynamism**

dy•na•mite (**dye**-nuh-mite) ***noun*** A very powerful explosive.

dy•na•mo (**dye**-nuh-moh) ***noun***
1. A machine for converting the power

of a turning wheel into electricity; a generator
2. A forceful person who works very hard. ▸ ***noun, plural* dynamos**

dy•nas•ty (**dye**-nuh-stee) ***noun***
1. A series of rulers belonging to the same family, as in *the Ming dynasty.*
2. A group or family that succeeds for a long time. ▸ ***noun, plural* dynasties**

dys•lex•i•a (diss-**lek**-see-uh) ***noun*** If someone has **dyslexia**, the person finds reading extremely difficult. He or she may often see letters and symbols in the wrong order or in mirror image. Another word for *reading disorders.* ▸ ***adjective* dyslexic**

each (**eech**)
1. ***adjective*** Every one of two or more.
2. ***pronoun*** Every one.
3. ***adverb*** Apiece.

ea•ger (**ee**-gur) ***adjective*** Very interested in doing something; enthusiastic. ▸ ***noun* eagerness** ▸ ***adverb* eagerly**

ea•gle (**ee**-guhl) ***noun*** A large bird of prey that often nests on mountains.

ear (**ihr**) ***noun***
1. The part of the body used for hearing.
2. The outer part of the ear, formed of skin and cartilage.
3. The part of some plants on which grain or seeds grow, as in *an ear of corn.*

ear•ache (**ihr**-*ake*) ***noun*** A pain inside the ear.

ear•drum (**ihr**-*druhm*) ***noun*** A membrane inside the ear that vibrates as sound strikes it.

ear•ly (**ur**-lee)
1. ***adverb*** At or near the beginning.
2. ***adjective*** Before the usual time.
3. ***adjective*** Near the beginning of a period of time, as in *an early-20th-century house.*
▸ ***adjective* earlier, earliest**

ear•muffs (**ihr**-*muhfss*) ***noun, plural*** Pads that fit over the ears to keep them warm in cold weather.

earn (**urn**) ***verb***
1. To receive payment for work done.
▸ ***noun* earner** ▸ ***noun, plural* earnings**
2. To work to achieve a result.
Earn sounds like **urn.**
▸ ***verb* earning, earned**

ear•nest (**ur**-nist) ***adjective*** Serious and eager. ▸ ***adverb* earnestly**

ear•ring (**ihr**-ing) ***noun*** A piece of jewelry worn on or through the ear.

earth (**urth**) ***noun***
1. The planet on which we live. Earth is the third planet from the sun, between Venus and Mars. In cases where it is described as a part of the solar system, Earth is often capitalized.
2. Soil.
3. The ground; dry land.
4. If someone is **down to earth,** he or she does not pretend to be someone important. ▸ ***adjective* earthly**

earth•quake (**urth**-*kwayk*) ***noun*** A sudden, violent shaking of the earth, caused by a shifting of the earth's crust.

earth•worm (**urth**-*wurm*) ***noun*** A gray, pink, red, or brown worm that digs through the ground and eats the nutrients in dirt.

E

ease (**eez**)
1. ***noun*** Freedom from hard work, pain, or discomfort.
2. ***noun*** A calm state of mind.
3. ***verb*** To make less difficult.
4. ***verb*** To lessen, as in *to ease a person's fear.*
5. ***verb*** To maneuver something into a tight space.
▸ ***verb*** **easing, eased**

ea•sel (**ee**-zuhl) ***noun*** A folding wooden stand used to support a painting, sign, etc.

east (**eest**)
1. ***noun*** One of the four main points of the compass. ▸ ***adverb*** **east**
2. **East** ***noun*** Any area or region lying in this direction.
3. **the East** ***noun*** In the United States, the states lying along the Atlantic coast, especially those east of the Allegheny Mountains and north of Maryland.
4. ***adjective*** To do with or existing in the east, as in *the east side of the city.*
▸ ***adjective*** **eastern** ▸ ***adjective*** **Eastern**

Eas•ter (**ee**-stur) ***noun*** The Christian holiday on which people celebrate the resurrection of Jesus.

Eastern Hemisphere ***noun*** The half of the world east of the Atlantic Ocean. It includes Europe, Africa, Asia, and Australia and surrounding waters.

east•ward (**eest**-wurd) ***adverb*** To or toward the east. ▸ ***adjective*** **eastward**

eas•y (**ee**-zee) ***adjective***
1. If something is **easy,** it does not require much effort, ability, or training.
▸ ***noun*** **easiness** ▸ ***adverb*** **easily**
2. Comfortable and relaxing, as in *an easy chair.*
3. Not strict or hard to please, as in *an easy teacher.*
▸ ***adjective*** **easier, easiest**

eat (**eet**) ***verb***
1. To take in food through your mouth.
2. To have a meal.
3. If something is being **eaten away,** it is being destroyed slowly.
▸ ***verb*** **eating, ate** (**ayt**), **eaten** (**ee**-tin)

eaves (**eevz**) ***noun, plural*** The part of a roof that hangs over the side of a building.

eaves•drop (**eevz**-*drop*) ***verb*** To listen in secret to someone's conversation.
▸ **eavesdropping, eavesdropped**
▸ ***noun*** **eavesdropper**

ebb (**eb**) ***verb***
1. When the tide **ebbs,** it goes down and back out to sea. ▸ ***noun*** **ebb**
2. To fade or to get weaker.
▸ ***verb*** **ebbing, ebbed**

eb•on•y (**eb**-uh-nee) ***noun***
1. A very hard, black wood.
2. A deep black color.
▸ ***adjective*** **ebony**

ec•cen•tric (ek-**sen**-trik)
1. ***adjective*** Acting odd or strange, but in a harmless or charming way.
▸ ***adverb*** **eccentrically**
2. ***noun*** Someone with odd habits.

ech•o (**ek**-oh) ***verb*** When a sound **echoes,** it repeats because its sound waves have met a large surface and have bounced back. ▸ **echoes, echoing, echoed** ▸ ***noun*** **echo**

e•clec•tic (i-**klek**-tik) ***adjective*** If you have **eclectic** taste, you like a wide range of things.

e•clipse (i-**klips**)
1. ***noun*** In an **eclipse of the moon,** the earth comes between the sun and the moon so that all or part of the moon's light is blocked out.
2. ***noun*** In an **eclipse of the sun,** the moon comes between the sun and the earth so that all or part of the sun's light is blocked out.
3. ***verb*** To do a great deal better than, as in *eclipse other teams.* ▸ **eclipsing, eclipsed**
▸ ***verb*** **eclipse**

e•col•o•gy (ee-**kol**-uh-jee) ***noun***
1. The study of the relationship between plants, animals, and their environment.
2. The study of how human activity

E

affects the earth. This is also known as *human ecology*. ▸ ***noun*** **ecologist** ▸ ***adjective*** **ecological** (*ek*-uh-**loj**-i-kuhl) ▸ ***adverb*** **ecologically**

e•com•merce (**ee**-*kom*-urss) ***noun*** Buying and selling things over the Internet.

ec•o•nom•i•cal (ee-kuh-**nom**-uh-kuhl *or* ek-uh-**nom**-uh-kuhl) ***adjective*** Not wasteful. ▸ ***adverb*** **economically**

ec•o•nom•ics (ee-kuh-**nom**-iks *or* ek-uh-**nom**-iks) ***noun*** The study of the way money, goods, and services are made and used in a society; the study of wealth. ▸ ***noun*** **economist** (ee-**kon**-i-mist) ▸ ***adjective*** **economic**

e•con•o•mize (i-**kon**-uh-mize) ***verb*** To cut down on spending in order to save money. ▸ **economizing, economized**

e•con•o•my (i-**kon**-uh-mee) ***noun***
1. The way a country runs its industry, trade, and finance.
2. The careful use of money and other things to cut down on waste.
▸ ***noun, plural*** **economies**

ec•o•sys•tem (**ee**-koh-*siss*-tuhm *or* **ek**-oh-*siss*-tuhm) ***noun*** A community of animals and plants interacting with their environment.

ec•sta•sy (**ek**-stuh-see) ***noun*** A feeling of great happiness; extreme joy. ▸ ***noun, plural*** **ecstasies** ▸ ***adjective*** **ecstatic** ▸ ***adverb*** **ecstatically**

ec•ze•ma (**ek**-suh-muh *or* eg-**zee**-muh) ***noun*** A skin disease that makes the skin dry, rough, and itchy.

ed•dy (**ed**-ee) ***noun*** A circular current in water or air. ▸ ***noun, plural*** **eddies** ▸ ***verb*** **eddy** ▸ ***adjective*** **eddying**

edge (**ej**)
1. ***noun*** A boundary.
2. ***verb*** To move very slowly and carefully. ▸ **edging, edged**
3. ***noun*** The sharp side of a cutting tool, as in *a razor's edge.*
4. ***noun*** An advantage.
5. If you are **on edge,** you are nervous or anxious. ▸ ***adjective*** **edgy**

edge•wise (**ej**-*wize*) ***adverb***
1. Sideways.
2. If you cannot **get a word in edgewise** in a discussion, other people do not give you a chance to speak.

ed•i•ble (**ed**-uh-buhl) ***adjective*** Able to be eaten.

ed•it (**ed**-it) ***verb***
1. To check a piece of writing for spelling, grammatical, stylistic, and factual mistakes and shorten it if it is too long.
2. To cut and rearrange pieces of film, audiotape, or videotape to make a movie, television program, etc.
▸ ***verb*** **editing, edited**

e•di•tion (i-**dish**-uhn) ***noun***
1. The form or version of a book or newspaper that is printed at a particular time, as in *a new paperback edition.*
2. The number of copies of a newspaper, book, or magazine that are printed at the same time.

ed•i•tor (**ed**-uh-tur) ***noun***
1. Someone who checks the contents of a book and gets it ready to be published.
2. The person in charge of a newspaper or a magazine.

ed•i•to•ri•al (*ed*-uh-**tor**-ee-uhl)
1. ***adjective*** To do with putting together a publication, as in *an editorial department.*
2. ***noun*** An article or a statement that reflects the opinions of a newspaper or magazine editor or the managers of a television or radio station.

ed•u•cate (**ej**-u-kate) ***verb***
1. To give knowledge or a skill.
2. To send someone to school, as in *to educate a child.*
▸ ***verb*** **educating, educated** ▸ ***noun*** **educator**

ed•u•ca•tion (ej-uh-**kay**-shuhn) ***noun***
1. The process of gaining or giving knowledge and skills.
2. The knowledge, skills, and abilities gained from schooling.
▸ ***adjective*** **educational**

eel (**eel**) ***noun*** A long, snakelike fish.

E

ee•rie (**ihr**-ee) ***adjective*** Strange and frightening, as in *an eerie sight.* ▸ **eerier, eeriest** ▸ ***adverb*** **eerily**

ef•fect (uh-**fekt**)
1. ***noun*** The result or consequence of something, as in *the effect of the explosion.*
2. ***noun*** Influence, or the power to make something happen.
3. ***noun*** When something **goes into effect,** it starts to happen.
4. ***verb*** To cause to happen, as in *to effect a change.*▸ **effecting, effected**

ef•fec•tive (uh-**fek**-tiv) ***adjective***
1. Working very well, or getting the job done. ▸ ***adverb*** **effectively**
2. In force.

ef•fer•ves•cent (*ef*-ur-**vess**-uhnt) ***adjective***
1. An **effervescent** liquid is very bubbly.
2. An **effervescent** person is very lively. ▸ ***noun*** **effervescence**

ef•fi•cient (uh-**fish**-uhnt) ***adjective*** If people or things are **efficient,** they work very well and do not waste time or energy. ▸ ***noun*** **efficiency** ▸ ***adverb*** **efficiently**

ef•flu•ent (**ef**-loo-uhnt) ***noun***
1. Something that flows out. ▸ ***adjective*** **effluent**
2. Waste water and sewage.

ef•fort (**ef**-urt) ***noun*** If you make an **effort,** you try hard.

e.g. (**eee jee**)The initials of the Latin phrase *exempli gratia,* which means "for example."

egg (eg) ***noun***
1. An oval or round object with a covering or shell, produced by female birds, reptiles, and fish, in which their young develop.
2. A cell created within the body of a woman or female animal that, when fertilized, grows into a new individual.

egg•plant (**eg**-*plant*) ***noun*** A large purple vegetable shaped like a pear.

e•go•cen•tric (ee-goh-**sen**-trik) ***adjective*** If you are **egocentric,** you are far more interested in yourself than in others. ▸ ***noun*** **egocentricity**

e•gret (**ee**-grit) ***noun*** A tall heron with white feathers.

ei•der (**eye**-dur) ***noun*** A sea duck that lives in northern waters.

ei•der•down (**eye**-dur-*doun*) ***noun***
1. The soft feathers of an eider duck.
2. A warm comforter filled with eiderdown.

eight (**ate**) ***noun*** The whole number, written 8, that comes after seven and before nine. ▸ ***adjective*** **eight**

ei•ther (ee-THur *or* **eye**-THur)
1. ***conjunction*** **Either** can be used to indicate a choice.
2. ***pronoun*** One of two.
3. ***adverb*** Also, or similarly.
4. ***adjective*** One or the other of two, as in *either glove.*
5. ***adjective*** Each of two.

e•ject (i-**jekt**) ***verb***
1. To push something out.
2. To throw someone out.
3. When fighter pilots **eject** in an emergency, they are hurled out of the cockpit by a special seat.
▸ ***verb*** **ejecting, ejected**

e•lab•o•rate
1. (i-**lab**-ur-it) ***adjective*** Complicated and detailed, as in *an elaborate pattern.*
▸ ***adverb*** **elaborately**
2. (i-**lab**-uh-rate) ***verb*** To give more details. ▸ **elaborating, elaborated**

e•lapse (i-**laps**) ***verb*** When time **elapses,** it passes. ▸ **elapsing, elapsed**

e•las•tic (i-**lass**-tik) ***noun*** A rubbery material that stretches. ▸ ***noun*** **elasticity** ▸ ***adjective*** **elastic**

e•lat•ed (i-**lay**-tid) ***adjective*** Very pleased and excited. ▸ ***noun*** **elation**

el•bow (**el**-boh) ***noun*** The joint that connects the upper and lower parts of your arm.

el•der (**el**-dur) ***adjective*** Older.

el•der•ly (**el**-dur-lee) ***adjective*** Old.

el•dest (**el**-duhst) ***adjective*** The oldest in a group, as in *my eldest child.*

e•lect (i-**lekt**) ***verb*** To choose someone or decide something by voting.
▸ **electing, elected**

e•lec•tion (i-**lek**-shuhn) ***noun*** The act or process of choosing someone or deciding something by voting.

electric eel ***noun*** A long, snakelike fish that can give off electric shocks to protect itself and stun its prey.

e•lec•tri•cian (i-lek-**trish**-uhn) ***noun*** Someone who installs electrical systems and fixes electrical equipment.

e•lec•tric•i•ty (i-lek-**triss**-uh-tee) ***noun***
1. A form of energy caused by the motion of electrons and protons. It can be produced by rotating a magnet within a coil of wire. ▸ ***adjective*** **electric,** ***adjective*** **electrical**
2. Electrical power or an electric current.

e•lec•tro•cute (i-**lek**-truh-*kyoot*) ***verb*** To injure or kill yourself or someone else with a severe electric shock.
▸ **electrocuting, electrocuted** ▸ ***noun*** **electrocution**

e•lec•trode (i-**lek**-trode) ***noun*** A point through which an electric current can flow into or out of a device or substance.

e•lec•tro•lyte (i-**lek**-truh-*lite*) ***noun*** A soluble substance that conducts electricity.

e•lec•tro•mag•net (i-*lek*-troh-**mag**-nit) ***noun*** A temporary magnet formed when electricity flows through a coil of wire. ▸ ***adjective*** **electromagnetic**

e•lec•tron (i-**lek**-tron) ***noun*** A tiny particle that moves around the nucleus of an atom. Electrons carry a negative electrical charge.

e•lec•tron•ic (i-lek-**tron**-ik) ***adjective*** **Electronic** devices are powered by minute amounts of electricity produced by electrons. They contain transistors, silicon chips, or valves that control an electric current. ▸ ***adverb*** **electronically**

electronic mail *See* **E-mail.**

e•lec•tron•ics (i-lek-**tron**-iks) ***noun***
1. The scientific study of the behavior of electrons.
2. The technology that makes electronic machines work.

el•e•gant (**el**-uh-guhnt) ***adjective*** Graceful and stylish, as in *an elegant wedding.* ▸ ***noun*** **elegance** ▸ ***adverb*** **elegantly**

el•e•gy (**el**-uh-jee) ***noun*** A sad poem or speech in memory of someone who has died. ▸ ***noun, plural*** **elegies**

el•e•ment (**el**-uh-muhnt) ***noun***
1. One of the simple, basic parts of something.
2. In chemistry, an **element** is a substance that cannot be split into a simpler substance.
3. A wire or coil in an electric heater or toaster that heats up when electricity passes through it.
4. the elements ***noun, plural*** The weather.

el•e•men•ta•ry (el-uh-**men**-tuh-ree) ***adjective*** Simple or basic, as in *elementary arithmetic.*

elementary school ***noun*** A school that children attend from kindergarten through sixth or eighth grade.

el•e•phant (**el**-uh-fuhnt) ***noun*** A large mammal with a long trunk and ivory tusks that lives in Africa and India.

el•e•vate (**el**-uh-vate) ***verb***
1. To lift something up.
2. To promote someone to an important job or status.
▸ ***verb*** **elevating, elevated** ▸ ***adjective*** **elevated**

e•le•va•tion (el-uh-**vay**-shuhn) ***noun***
1. A high place or a hill.
2. The height above sea level.

el•e•va•tor (**el**-uh-vay-tur) ***noun***
1. A machine that carries people or goods up and down between different levels of a building.
2. A very large, hollow building used for storing grain after it is harvested.

e•lev•en (i-**lev**-uhn) ***noun*** The whole number, written 11, that comes after ten and before twelve. ▸ ***adjective*** **eleven**

E

elf (**elf**) ***noun*** A small, magical, mischievous person described in legends and fairy tales. ▸ ***noun, plural*** **elves** (**elvz**) ▸ ***adjective*** **elfin**

el•i•gi•ble (**el**-uh-juh-buhl) ***adjective***
1. If you are **eligible** for something, such as a job, you have the right qualifications for it.
2. An **eligible** man or woman is a suitable person for someone to marry.
▸ ***noun*** **eligibility**

e•lim•i•nate (i-**lim**-uh-nate) ***verb***
1. To leave out, or to get rid of.
2. To remove from a competition by a defeat.
▸ ***verb*** **eliminating, eliminated** ▸ ***noun*** **elimination**

e•lite (i-**leet** *or* ay-**leet**) ***noun*** A group of people who have special advantages and privileges. ▸ ***noun*** **elitism** ▸ ***adjective*** **elite**

elk (**elk**) ***noun*** A type of large deer similar to, but smaller than, the moose.

el•lipse (i-**lips**) ***noun*** An oval shape.
▸ ***adjective*** **elliptical**

elm (**elm**) ***noun*** A tall tree with spreading branches.

El Ni•ño (el-**neen**-yoh) ***noun*** Warm water temperatures, currents, and wind conditions in the Pacific Ocean that combine to affect weather conditions over much of the earth.

e•lon•gate (i-**lawng**-gate)
1. ***verb*** To make something longer or more stretched out. ▸ **elongating, elongated**
2. elongated ***adjective*** Long and thin.

e•lope (i-**lope**) ***verb*** When a man and woman **elope,** they run away to get married without others knowing about it.
▸ **eloping, eloped** ▸ ***noun*** **elopement**

el•o•quent (**el**-uh-kwuhnt) ***adjective*** An **eloquent** person expresses him- or herself smoothly and clearly. ▸ ***noun*** **eloquence** ▸ ***adverb*** **eloquently**

else (**elss**) ***adverb***
1. Other, or different.
2. More.

else•where (**elss**-*wair*) ***adverb*** Somewhere else.

e•lude (i-**lude**) ***verb*** To escape or get away from someone. ▸ **eluding, eluded**

e•lu•sive (i-**loo**-siv) ***adjective*** Very hard to find or catch. ▸ ***noun*** **elusiveness**
▸ ***adverb*** **elusively**

E-mail (**ee**-*mayl*) ***noun*** Electronic messages that are sent between computer terminals linked by phone lines. Short for *electronic mail.* ▸ ***verb*** **E-mail** ▸ ***adjective*** **E-mail**

e•man•ci•pate (i-**man**-si-pate) ***verb*** To free a person or group from slavery or control. ▸ **emancipating, emancipated**
▸ ***noun*** **emancipation**

em•bank•ment (em-**bangk**-muhnt) ***noun***
1. A long, low, earthen structure built to carry a railroad, road, etc.
2. A high bank at the sides of a river built to keep it from flooding.

em•bar•go (em-**bar**-goh) ***noun*** An official order forbidding something from happening, especially trade. ▸ ***noun, plural*** **embargoes**

em•bark (em-**bark**) ***verb***
1. To go on board a ship or an airplane, ready for a journey.
2. To start something that will take a long time to finish.
▸ ***verb*** **embarking, embarked**

em•bar•rass (em-**ba**-ruhss) ***verb*** If something **embarrasses** you, it makes you feel awkward and uncomfortable.
▸ **embarrasses, embarrassing, embarrassed** ▸ ***noun*** **embarrassment**
▸ ***adjective*** **embarrassing,** ***adjective*** **embarrassed**

em•bas•sy (**em**-buh-see) ***noun*** The official place in a foreign country where an ambassador lives and works. ▸ ***noun, plural*** **embassies**

em•bers (**em**-burz) ***noun, plural*** The hot, glowing remains of a fire.

em•bez•zle (em-**bez**-uhl) ***verb*** To steal money secretly from the organization that you work for. ▸ **embezzling,**

embezzled ▸ ***noun*** **embezzler,** ***noun*** **embezzlement**

em•blem (**em**-bluhm) ***noun*** A symbol or a sign.

em•boss (em-**boss**) ***verb*** To create raised lettering or designs on a flat piece of paper or metal. ▸ **embosses, embossing, embossed**

em•brace (em-**brayss**) ***verb***
1. To hug. ▸ ***noun*** **embrace**
2. To take up eagerly; to welcome.
3. To include.
4. To cherish or to love.
▸ ***verb*** **embracing, embraced**

em•broi•der (em-**broi**-dur) ***verb*** To sew a picture or a design onto cloth. ▸ **embroidering, embroidered** ▸ ***noun*** **embroiderer,** ***noun*** **embroidery**

em•bry•o (**em**-bree-oh) ***noun***
1. A fetus in its earliest stage of development.
2. A plant in its first stage of development, contained within a seed.
▸ ***noun, plural*** **embryos**

em•er•ald (**em**-ur-uhld) ***noun***
1. A bright green precious stone.
2. A bright green color.
▸ ***adjective*** **emerald**

e•merge (i-**murj**) ***verb***
1. If you **emerge** from somewhere, you come out into the open.
2. To become known.
▸ ***verb*** **emerging, emerged** ▸ ***noun*** **emergence**

e•mer•gen•cy (i-**mur**-juhn-see) ***noun*** A sudden and dangerous situation that must be dealt with quickly. ▸ ***noun, plural*** **emergencies**

em•er•y (**em**-ur-ee) ***noun*** A mineral used for grinding or polishing.

em•i•grate (**em**-uh-grate) ***verb*** To leave your own country in order to live in another one. ▸ **emigrating, emigrated** ▸ ***noun*** **emigrant,** ***noun*** **emigration**

em•i•nent (**em**-uh-nuhnt) ***adjective*** Well-known and respected, as in *an eminent professor.* ▸ ***noun*** **eminence** ▸ ***adverb*** **eminently**

e•mis•sion (i-**mish**-uhn) ***noun***
1. The release of something such as chemicals into the atmosphere.
2. emissions ***noun, plural*** Substances released into the air.

e•mit (i-**mit**) ***verb*** To release or send out something such as heat, light, or sound. ▸ **emitting, emitted**

e•mo•tion (i-**moh**-shuhn) ***noun*** A strong feeling, such as happiness, love, anger, or grief.

e•mo•tion•al (i-**moh**-shuh-nuhl) ***adjective***
1. To do with your feelings, as in *emotional problems.*
2. When someone becomes **emotional,** the person shows his or her feelings.
▸ ***adverb*** **emotionally**

em•per•or (**em**-pur-ur) ***noun*** The male ruler of an empire.

em•pha•sis (**em**-fuh-siss) ***noun*** Importance given to something. ▸ ***noun, plural*** **emphases** (**em**-fuh-*seez*)

em•pha•size (**em**-fuh-size) ***verb*** If you **emphasize** something, you make it stand out clearly because you think it is important. ▸ **emphasizing, emphasized** ▸ ***adjective*** **emphatic** (em-**fat**-ik)

em•pire (**em**-pire) ***noun***
1. A group of countries that have the same ruler, as in *the Roman Empire.*
2. A country that is ruled over by an emperor or empress.
3. A large group of companies controlled by one person, as in *a communications empire.*

em•ploy (em-**ploi**) ***verb***
1. To pay someone to work for you.
▸ ***noun*** **employer,** ***noun*** **employment**
2. To use something.
▸ ***verb*** **employing, employed**

em•ploy•ee (em-**ploi**-ee *or* em-ploi-**ee**) ***noun*** A person who works for and is paid by another person or business.

em•press (**em**-priss) ***noun*** The female ruler of an empire, or the wife of an emperor.

E

E

em•pty (**emp**-tee)
1. ***adjective*** If a container is **empty,** there is nothing inside it.
2. ***verb*** To take the contents out of a container. ▸ **empties, emptying, emptied**
3. ***noun*** An empty bottle or can. ▸ ***noun, plural*** **empties**
4. ***adjective*** Without meaning or purpose, as in *an empty promise.*
▸ ***noun*** **emptiness** ▸ ***adjective*** **emptier, emptiest**

e•mu (**ee**-myoo) ***noun*** A large bird from Australia that is related to the ostrich. It runs fast but does not fly.

e•mul•sion (i-**muhl**-shuhn) ***noun***
1. A mixture of two liquids in which the particles of one liquid mix with the other liquid but do not dissolve.
2. A light-sensitive chemical coating on camera film.

en•a•ble (en-**ay**-buhl) ***verb*** To make it possible for someone to do something.
▸ **enabling, enabled** ▸ ***noun*** **enabler**

e•nam•el (i-**nam**-uhl) ***noun***
1. A shiny substance similar to glass that is used to coat and protect metal, pottery, and other materials.
2. Paint that dries to a hard, shiny surface.
3. The hard, white surface of your teeth.
▸ ***verb*** **enamel** ▸ ***adjective*** **enameled**

en•chant (en-**chant**) ***verb*** To delight or charm someone. ▸ **enchanting, enchanted**

en•chant•ed (en-**chan**-tid) ***adjective*** A place or thing that is **enchanted** has been put under a magic spell or seems magical, as in *an enchanted castle.*

en•chant•ing (en-**chan**-ting) ***adjective*** Delightful and charming. ▸ ***adverb*** **enchantingly**

en•close (en-**kloze**) ***verb***
1. To put a fence or a wall around an area.
2. To put something in with a letter or a package that you are sending.
▸ ***verb*** **enclosing, enclosed** ▸ ***adjective*** **enclosed**

en•clo•sure (en-**kloh**-zhur) ***noun***
1. An area closed in by a fence, walls, etc.
2. Something put in with a letter or a package.

en•com•pass (en-**kuhm**-puhss) ***verb***
1. To form a circle around something.
2. To include something.
▸ ***verb*** **encompasses, encompassing, encompassed**

en•core (**ong**-kor *or* **on**-kor)
1. ***noun*** An extra song or musical selection added to the end of a performance because the audience has been cheering for more or applauding so much.
2. ***interjection*** Again, please!

en•coun•ter (en-**koun**-tur) ***noun*** An unexpected or difficult meeting. ▸ ***verb*** **encounter**

en•cour•age (en-**kur**-ij) ***verb*** To give someone confidence by praising or supporting the person. ▸ **encouraging, encouraged** ▸ ***noun*** **encouragement**
▸ ***adjective*** **encouraging** ▸ ***adverb*** **encouragingly**

en•cy•clo•pe•di•a (en-*sye*-kloh-**pee**-dee-uh) ***noun*** A book or set of books with information about many different subjects, usually arranged in alphabetical order. ▸ ***adjective*** **encyclopedic**

end (**end**)
1. ***noun*** The last part of something.
2. ***noun*** One of the two points farthest from the middle of an object.
3. ***verb*** To finish. ▸ **ending, ended**

en•dan•ger (en-**dayn**-jur) ***verb*** To put in a dangerous situation; to threaten.
▸ **endangering, endangered**
▸ ***adjective*** **endangered**

endangered species ***noun*** A species or type of plant or animal that is in danger of becoming extinct.

en•deav•or (en-**dev**-ur)
1. ***verb*** To try very hard to do something. ▸ **endeavoring, endeavored**
2. ***noun*** A serious attempt or effort.

end•less (**end**-liss) ***adjective*** Something **endless** has no end or seems to have no end. ▸ ***adverb*** **endlessly**

en•dor•phin (en-**dor**-fuhn) ***noun*** A substance created by the brain that reduces pain.

en•dorse (en-**dorss**) ***verb***
1. To support or approve of someone or something.
2. To sign one's name on the reverse side of an official document.
▸ ***verb*** **endorsing, endorsed** ▸ ***noun*** **endorsement**

en•dow (en-**dou**) ***verb***
1. If you are **endowed** with a gift or a talent, you are given it or enriched by it.
2. To give money or property.
▸ ***verb*** **endowing, endowed** ▸ ***noun*** **endowment**

en•dure (en-**dur**) ***verb***
1. If you **endure** something unpleasant or painful, you put up with it.
2. If something **endures,** it lasts for a long time.
▸ ***verb*** **enduring, endured** ▸ ***adjective*** **enduring** ▸ ***noun*** **endurance**

en•e•my (**en**-uh-mee) ***noun***
1. Someone who hates and wants to harm or destroy another.
2. The country or army that you are fighting against in a war.
▸ ***noun, plural*** **enemies**

en•er•get•ic (en-ur-**jet**-ik) ***adjective*** Strong and active, as in *an energetic workout.* ▸ ***adverb*** **energetically**

en•er•gy (**en**-ur-jee) ***noun***
1. The strength to do active things without getting tired.
2. Power from coal, electricity, or other sources that makes machines work and produces heat.
3. In physics, **energy** is the ability of something to do work. It is measured in **joules**.

en•force (en-**forss**) ***verb*** To make sure that a law or rule is obeyed.
▸ **enforcing, enforced** ▸ ***noun*** **enforcement**

en•gaged (en-**gayjd**) ***adjective***
1. If two people are **engaged,** they have decided that they will get married.
2. If someone is **engaged** in doing something, the person is busy and occupied doing it.
▸ ***noun*** **engagement**

en•gine (**en**-juhn) ***noun***
1. A machine that changes an energy source such as gasoline into movement.
2. The front part of a train that pulls the cars.

en•gi•neer (en-juh-**nihr**)
1. ***noun*** Someone who is trained to design and build machines, vehicles, bridges, roads, or other structures.
▸ ***noun*** **engineering**
2. ***verb*** To make something happen by using a clever plan. ▸ **engineering, engineered**

Eng•lish (**ing**-glish)
1. ***adjective*** From England, or to do with England.
2. ***noun*** The main language spoken in the United States, Canada, Great Britain, Australia, and many other countries.
3. ***adjective*** To do with the English language.

en•grave (en-**grayv**) ***verb*** To cut a design or letters into a metal, wood, or glass surface. ▸ **engraving, engraved** ▸ ***noun*** **engraver,** ***noun*** **engraving** ▸ ***adjective*** **engraved**

en•grossed (en-**grohst**) ***adjective*** If you are **engrossed** in something, you give it all your attention. ▸ ***adjective*** **engrossing**

en•gulf (en-**guhlf**) ***verb*** To cover or swallow up someone or something.
▸ **engulfing, engulfed**

en•hance (en-**hanss**) ***verb*** To make something better or greater.
▸ **enhancing, enhanced** ▸ ***noun*** **enhancement**

e•nig•ma (i-**nig**-muh) ***noun*** A mystery or a puzzle. ▸ ***adjective*** **enigmatic**

E

en•joy (en-**joi**) ***verb***
1. To get pleasure from doing something.
2. To have the benefit of.
▸ ***verb*** **enjoying, enjoyed** ▸ ***noun*** **enjoyment** ▸ ***adjective*** **enjoyable** ▸ ***adverb*** **enjoyably**

en•large (en-**larj**) ***verb*** To make bigger. ▸ **enlarging, enlarged** ▸ ***noun*** **enlarger,** ***noun*** **enlargement**

en•light•en (en-**lite**-uhn) ***verb*** To teach or give understanding to. ▸ **enlightening, enlightened** ▸ ***noun*** **enlightenment**

en•list (en-**list**) ***verb***
1. To join or get someone to join the army, navy, or one of the other armed forces.
2. If you **enlist** someone's help, you get the person to assist you.
▸ ***verb*** **enlisting, enlisted**

e•nor•mous (i-**nor**-muhss) ***adjective*** Extremely large. ▸ ***noun*** **enormity,** ***noun*** **enormousness** ▸ ***adverb*** **enormously**

e•nough (i-**nuf**) ***adjective*** As much as is needed. ▸ ***noun*** **enough** ▸ ***pronoun*** **enough** ▸ ***adverb*** **enough**

en•rage (en-**rayj**) ***verb*** To make someone angry. ▸ **enraging, enraged**

en•rich (en-**rich**) ***verb***
1. To make richer.
2. To improve the quality of something by adding good things to it.
3. To fertilize.
▸ ***verb*** **enriches, enriching, enriched** ▸ ***noun*** **enrichment** ▸ ***adjective*** **enriching,** ***adjective*** **enriched**

en•roll (en-**rohl**) ***verb*** When you **enroll** in a club, class, or school, you put your name on a list because you want to join. ▸ **enrolling, enrolled** ▸ ***noun*** **enrollment**

en route (on **root**) ***adverb*** On the way. ▸ ***adjective*** **en route**

en•sem•ble (on-**som**-buhl) ***noun*** A group of musicians or actors who perform together.

en•sue (en-**soo**) ***verb*** To happen next. ▸ **ensuing, ensued** ▸ ***adjective*** **ensuing**

en•sure (en-**shur**) ***verb*** To make certain that something happens. ▸ **ensuring, ensured**

en•tan•gle (en-**tang**-guhl) ***verb***
1. To become twisted or trapped.
2. To get into a difficult situation.
▸ ***verb*** **entangling, entangled** ▸ ***noun*** **entanglement**

en•ter (**en**-tur) ***verb***
1. To go into a place.
2. To sign up for a competition, a race, or an exam.
3. To type information into a computer or write it in a book.
▸ ***verb*** **entering, entered**

en•ter•prise (**en**-tur-*prize*) ***noun*** Something that you do or plan to do that is very important, dangerous, or difficult. Explorations, research, and starting up a business are all enterprises.

en•ter•pris•ing (**en**-tur-*prize*-ing) ***adjective*** Someone who is **enterprising** has a lot of good ideas and is brave enough to try things that are new and difficult.

en•ter•tain (en-tur-**tayn**) ***verb***
1. To amuse and interest someone. ▸ ***noun*** **entertainer,** ***noun*** **entertainment** ▸ ***adjective*** **entertaining**
2. To invite people to your home for a party, a visit, or a meal, as in *to entertain friends.*
▸ ***verb*** **entertaining, entertained**

en•thrall (en-**thrawl**) ***verb*** To excite or charm someone. ▸ **enthralling, enthralled**

en•thu•si•asm (en-**thoo**-zee-*az*-uhm) ***noun*** Great excitement or interest.

en•thu•si•as•tic (en-*thoo*-zee-**ass**-tik) ***adjective*** If you are **enthusiastic** about something, you are very excited about it or interested in it. ▸ ***noun*** **enthusiast** ▸ ***adverb*** **enthusiastically**

en•tice (en-**tisse**) ***verb*** To tempt someone to do something. ▸ **enticing,**

enticed ▸ ***noun*** **enticement**
▸ ***adjective*** **enticing**

en•tire (en-**tire**) ***adjective*** Whole.
▸ ***adverb*** **entirely**

en•ti•tle (en-**tye**-tuhl) ***verb***
1. To give a right or a privilege to someone. ▸ ***noun*** **entitlement**
2. To put a name on a book or other work.
▸ ***verb*** **entitling, entitled**

en•trance
1. (**en**-truhnss) ***noun*** The way into a place.
2. (en-**transs**) ***verb*** To give someone a feeling of wonder and pleasure.
▸ **entrancing, entranced** ▸ ***adjective*** **entrancing**

en•trant (**en**-truhnt) ***noun*** Someone who takes part in a contest, competition, or race.

en•tre•pre•neur (*on*-truh-pruh-**nur**) ***noun*** Someone who starts businesses and is good at finding new ways to make money. ▸ ***adjective*** **entrepreneurial**

en•trust (en-**truhst**) ***verb*** If you **entrust** someone with something valuable or important, you give it to the person to look after for you. ▸ **entrusting, entrusted**

en•try (**en**-tree) ***noun***
1. A way into a place.
2. A picture, a story, an answer, etc., that you send in to a competition.
3. A piece of information in a dictionary, diary, computer, etc.
▸ ***noun, plural*** **entries**

e•nun•ci•ate (i-**nuhn**-see-ate) ***verb*** To speak or pronounce words.
▸ **enunciating, enunciated** ▸ ***noun*** **enunciation**

en•vel•op (en-**vel**-uhp) ***verb*** To cover or surround something completely.
▸ **enveloping, enveloped**

en•ve•lope (**en**-vuh-lope *or* **on**-vuh-lope) ***noun*** A paper container for a letter or anything flat that is to be mailed.

en•vi•a•ble (**en**-vee-uh-buhl) ***adjective*** Very desirable or much wanted.

en•vi•ous (**en**-vee-uhss) ***adjective*** If you are **envious,** you wish that you could have something that someone else has.
▸ ***adverb*** **enviously**

en•vi•ron•ment (en-**vye**-ruhn-muhnt) ***noun***
1. All the things that influence your life, such as the area where you live, your family, and the things that happen to you.
2. The natural world of the land, sea, and air.
▸ ***noun*** **environmentalist** ▸ ***adjective*** **environmental** ▸ ***adverb*** **environmentally**

environmentally friendly ***adjective*** Products are **environmentally friendly** if they are made of substances that do not damage the natural environment and if they are reusable or can be recycled easily.

en•vy (**en**-vee) ***verb*** When you **envy** someone, you wish that you could have something that the person has or do something that he or she has done.
▸ **envies, envying, envied** ▸ ***noun*** **envy**

en•zyme (**en**-zime) ***noun*** A protein in the bodies of humans and animals that causes chemical reactions to occur.

e•on (**ee**-on) ***noun*** A very long period of time.

ep•ic (**ep**-ik)
1. ***noun*** A long story, poem, or movie about heroic adventures and great battles. An epic is usually historical in subject matter.
2. ***adjective*** Heroic or impressive, as in *an epic voyage of exploration.*
3. ***adjective*** Very large.

ep•i•cen•ter (**ep**-uh-*sent*-ur) ***noun*** The area directly above the place where an earthquake occurs.

ep•i•dem•ic (ep-uh-**dem**-ik) ***noun*** When there is an **epidemic,** an infectious disease spreads quickly through a population.

ep•i•gram (**ep**-uh-*gram*) ***noun*** A short, witty saying. ▸ ***adjective*** **epigrammatic**

E

ep•i•lep•sy (**ep**-uh-*lep*-see) ***noun*** A disease of the brain that causes a person to have sudden blackouts or convulsions. ▸ ***noun*** **epileptic** ▸ ***adjective*** **epileptic**

ep•i•logue (**ep**-uh-*log*) ***noun*** A short speech or piece of writing added to the end of a play, story, or poem.

ep•i•sode (**ep**-uh-*sode*) ***noun***
1. An event or set of events in your life.
2. One of the programs in a television or radio series.

ep•i•taph (**ep**-uh-*taf*) ***noun*** A short description of someone who has died, written on the person's gravestone.

e•poch (**ep**-uhk) ***noun*** A period of history marked by important events.

e•qual (**ee**-kwuhl)
1. ***adjective*** The same as something else in size, value, or amount. ▸ ***adverb*** **equally**
2. ***adjective*** The same for each member of a group, as in *equal housing opportunities.*
3. ***noun*** A person of equal ability or position, or a thing of equal quality, as in *a jury of one's equals.*
4. ***verb*** If you **equal** what someone else has done, you do as well as that person. ▸ **equaling, equaled**

e•qual•i•ty (i-**kwol**-uh-tee) ***noun*** The same rights for everyone.

e•qua•tion (i-**kway**-zhuhn *or* i-**kway**-shuhn) ***noun*** A mathematical statement that one set of numbers or values is equal to another set of numbers or values. For example, $4 \times 4 = 16$ and $3x + 2y = 13$ are equations.

e•qua•tor (i-**kway**-tur) ***noun*** An imaginary line around the middle of the earth, halfway between the North and South Poles. ▸ ***adjective*** **equatorial** (*ek*-wuh-**tor**-ee-uhl)

e•ques•tri•an (i-**kwess**-tree-uhn) ***adjective*** To do with horseback riding. ▸ ***noun*** **equestrian**

e•qui•lat•er•al (*ee*-kwuh-**lat**-ur-uhl) ***adjective*** Having sides of equal length.

e•qui•lib•ri•um (ee-kwuh-**lib**-ree-uhm) ***noun*** Balance.

e•qui•nox (**ee**-kwuh-*noks*) ***noun*** One of the two days in the year when day and night last exactly the same length of time all over the world. ▸ ***noun, plural*** **equinoxes**

e•quip (i-**kwip**) ***verb*** To provide with the things that are needed. ▸ **equipping, equipped**

e•quip•ment (i-**kwip**-muhnt) ***noun*** The tools and machines needed for a particular purpose.

e•quiv•a•lent (i-**kwiv**-uh-luhnt) ***adjective*** If one thing is **equivalent** to another, it is the same as the other in amount, value, or importance. ▸ ***noun*** **equivalent,** ***noun*** **equivalence**

e•ra (**ihr**-uh) ***noun*** A period of time in history.

e•rad•i•cate (i-**rad**-uh-kate) ***verb*** To get rid of something completely, especially something bad such as disease, crime, or poverty. ▸ **eradicating, eradicated** ▸ ***noun*** **eradication,** ***noun*** **eradicator**

e•rase (i-**rayss**) ***verb***
1. To rub something out with an eraser.
2. To wipe out something stored in a computer or recorded on a tape.
3. To get rid of completely.
▸ ***verb*** **erasing, erased** ▸ ***noun*** **erasure**

e•ras•er (i-**ray**-sur) ***noun*** Something used for rubbing off pencil or pen marks from paper, or chalk marks from a blackboard, etc.

e•rect (i-**rekt**)
1. ***adjective*** Standing upright. ▸ ***adverb*** **erectly**
2. ***verb*** To put up a structure. ▸ **erecting, erected** ▸ ***noun*** **erection**

er•mine (**ur**-muhn) ***noun*** A kind of weasel. Its brown fur turns white in winter.

e•rode (i-**rode**) ***verb*** When something is **eroded,** it is gradually worn away by water or wind. ▸ **eroding, eroded**

E

e·ro·sion (i-**roh**-zhuhn) ***noun*** The gradual wearing away of a substance by water or wind, as in *soil erosion.*

er·rand (**er**-uhnd) ***noun*** If someone sends you on an **errand,** the person asks you to take a message or to deliver or pick up something.

er·rat·ic (i-**rat**-ik) ***adjective*** If something is **erratic,** it does not follow a regular pattern, as in *erratic behavior.* ▸ ***adverb*** **erratically**

er·ror (**er**-ur) ***noun*** A mistake.

e·rupt (i-**ruhpt**) ***verb***
1. When a volcano **erupts,** it throws out rocks, hot ashes, and lava with great force. ▸ ***noun*** **eruption**
2. To start happening suddenly.
3. If someone **erupts,** the person suddenly becomes very angry.
▸ ***verb*** **erupting, erupted**

es·ca·la·tor (**ess**-kuh-lay-tur) ***noun*** A moving staircase.

es·cape (ess-**kape**)
1. ***verb*** To break free from a place where you have been kept against your will.
2. ***noun*** The act of breaking free from a place.
3. ***noun*** A way of escaping.
4. ***verb*** To avoid something.
5. ***verb*** To leak out.
▸ ***verb*** **escaping, escaped**

es·cort (ess-**kort**) ***verb*** To accompany someone, especially to protect the person. ▸ **escorting, escorted** ▸ ***noun*** **escort** (**ess**-kort)

Es·ki·mo (**ess**-kuh-moh) ***noun*** A member of a group of native peoples of the Arctic, the area around the North Pole. *See* **Inuit.** ▸ ***noun, plural*** **Eskimo** *or* **Eskimos**

e·soph·a·gus (i-**sof**-uh-guhss) ***noun*** The tube that carries food from the throat to the stomach.

es·pe·cial·ly (ess-**pesh**-uh-lee) ***adverb***
1. More than usually; particularly.
2. Mainly.

Es·pe·ran·to (ess-puh-**ron**-toh) ***noun*** A language invented in the 19th century and intended to be a world language.

es·pi·o·nage (**ess**-pee-uh-*nahzh*) ***noun*** The act of spying or the work of a spy in trying to gain national or economic secret information.

es·say (**ess**-ay) ***noun*** A piece of writing about a particular subject.

es·sence (**ess**-uhnss) ***noun***
1. The most important quality of something that makes it what it is.
2. A plant substance used to make perfume.

es·sen·tial (i-**sen**-shuhl)
1. ***adjective*** Vital and important.
2. ***noun*** Something you really need and cannot do without.
▸ ***adverb*** **essentially**

es·tab·lish (ess-**tab**-lish) ***verb***
1. To set up a business, a society, or an organization. ▸ ***noun*** **establishment**
2. To settle somewhere.
3. To confirm that something is true or correct.
▸ ***verb*** **establishes, establishing, established**

es·tate (ess-**tate**) ***noun***
1. A large area of land, usually with a house on it.
2. All the money, property, and other assets that someone leaves behind when he or she dies.

es·teem (ess-**teem**) ***noun*** If you hold someone in **esteem,** you respect and admire the person. ▸ ***verb*** **esteem** ▸ ***adjective*** **esteemed**

es·ti·mate
1. (**ess**-ti-muht) ***noun*** A rough guess or calculation about an amount, distance, cost, etc, as in *an estimate of the room's length.*
2. (**ess**-ti-mate) ***verb*** To form an opinion about something. ▸ **estimating, estimated** ▸ ***noun*** **estimator**

es·tu·ar·y (**ess**-chu-er-ee) ***noun*** The wide part of a river where it joins a sea. ▸ ***noun, plural*** **estuaries**

E

etc. (**et set**-uh-ruh) An abbreviation of the Latin phrase *et cetera*, which means "and the rest." *Etc.* is used at the end of a list to mean that the list is not complete.

etch (**ech**) ***verb*** To engrave or draw on metal or glass, using a sharp object and acid to cut through the surface. ▸ **etches, etching, etched** ▸ ***adjective*** **etched**

etch ***noun*** A picture or print that is made from an etched plate.

e•ter•nal (i-**tur**-nuhl) ***adjective*** Lasting forever. ▸ ***adverb*** **eternally**

e•ter•ni•ty (i-**tur**-nuh-tee) ***noun***
1. Time without beginning or end.
2. A seemingly endless time period.
▸ ***noun, plural*** **eternities**

e•ther (**ee**-thur) ***noun*** A clear liquid with a strong smell. Ether is used to put a person to sleep before an operation.

eth•nic (**eth**-nik) ***adjective*** To do with a group of people sharing the same national origins, language, or culture. ▸ ***adverb*** **ethnically**

et•i•quette (**et**-uh-ket) ***noun*** Rules of polite behavior, such as the proper way to introduce people to each other or to eat.

é•tude (ay-**tood**) ***noun*** A piece of music designed to teach a particular technique.

et•y•mol•o•gy (*et*-uh-**mol**-uh-jee) ***noun*** The history of a word, tracing it back to its earlier form and meaning and including changes it has undergone along the way. ▸ ***noun, plural*** **etymologies**

eu•ca•lyp•tus (*yoo*-kuh-**lip**-tuhss) ***noun*** A fragrant evergreen tree that grows in dry climates. ▸ ***noun, plural*** **eucalyptuses**

Eu•ro•pe•an (*yu*-ruh-**pee**-uhn) ***adjective*** From Europe or to do with Europe. ▸ ***noun*** **European**

European Economic Community ***noun*** A group of European countries that have joined together to encourage trade among them.

eu•tha•na•sia (*yoo*-thuh-**nay**-zhuh) ***noun*** The ending of a life so as to release an animal or a person from an incurable disease or intolerable suffering.

e•vac•u•ate (i-**vak**-yoo-ate) ***verb*** To move away from an area because it is dangerous there. ▸ **evacuating, evacuated** ▸ ***noun*** **evacuation**

e•vade (i-**vade**) ***verb***
1. To keep away from someone, or to keep out of someone's way.
2. To avoid something that you should do or respond to.
▸ ***verb*** **evading, evaded** ▸ ***noun*** **evasion** ▸ ***adjective*** **evasive**

e•val•u•ate (i-**val**-yoo-*ate*) ***verb*** To decide how good or how valuable something is after thinking carefully about it. ▸ **evaluating, evaluated** ▸ ***noun*** **evaluation,** ***noun*** **evaluator**

e•van•gel•i•cal (ev-uhn-**jel**-uh-kuhl) ***adjective*** An **evangelical** Christian tells people about the Christian gospel.
▸ ***noun*** **evangelism** (ee-**van**-jel-izm)
▸ ***noun*** **evangelist** (ee-**van**-jel-ist)

e•vap•o•rate (i-**vap**-uh-rate) ***verb***
1. When a liquid **evaporates,** it changes into a vapor or gas. ▸ ***noun*** **evaporation**
2. To become less and then disappear completely.
▸ ***verb*** **evaporating, evaporated**

eve (**eev**) ***noun*** The evening or day before an important or special day, as in *New Year's Eve.*

e•ven (**ee**-vuhn)
1. ***adjective*** Staying about the same, as in *an even speed* or *an even temperature.*
2. ***adjective*** An **even** number can be divided exactly by two.
3. ***adjective*** Equal, as in *an even score.*
4. ***adjective*** Smooth and level, as in *an even surface.*
5. ***verb*** If you **even** something, you make it smooth, level, or equal.
▸ **evening, evened**
6. ***adverb*** Indeed.
7. ***adverb*** Surprisingly.
▸ ***adverb*** **evenly**

eve•ning (**eev**-ning) ***noun*** The time of day between the late afternoon and the early part of the night.

e•vent (i-**vent**) ***noun***
1. Something that happens, especially something interesting or important.
▸ ***adjective*** **eventful**
2. One of the activities, such as a race, that is held during a sports competition.

e•ven•tu•al (i-**ven**-choo-uhl) ***adjective*** Final, or happening at the end.

e•ven•tu•al•ly (i-**ven**-choo-uh-lee) ***adverb*** Finally or at last.

ev•er (**ev**-ur) ***adverb***
1. At any time.
2. All the time, as in *ever grateful.*
3. In any way.

ev•er•glade (**ev**-ur-*glade*) ***noun*** An area of swampy land with tall grasses and many slow streams.

ev•er•green (**ev**-ur-*green*) ***noun*** A bush or tree that has green leaves throughout the year. ▸ ***adjective*** **evergreen**

ev•er•last•ing (*ev*-ur-**lass**-ting) ***adjective*** Lasting forever or for a very long time.

eve•ry (**ev**-ree) ***adjective*** Each of the people or things in a group, as in *every day of the week.*

eve•ry•bod•y (**ev**-ree-*buh*-dee) ***pronoun*** Each and every person.

eve•ry•day (**ev**-ree-*day*) ***adjective***
1. Happening every day, as in *everyday events.*
2. All right for ordinary days, as in *everyday clothing.*

eve•ry•one (**ev**-ree-*wuhn*) ***pronoun*** Every person; everybody.

eve•ry•thing (**ev**-ree-*thing*) ***pronoun***
1. Each and every thing.
2. A very important thing.

eve•ry•where (**ev**-ree-wair) ***adverb*** In all places.

e•vict (i-**vikt**) ***verb*** To force someone to move out of a home, building, or occupied land. ▸ **evicting, evicted** ▸ ***noun*** **eviction**

ev•i•dence (**ev**-uh-duhnss) ***noun*** Information and facts that help prove something or make you believe that something is true.

ev•i•dent (**ev**-uh-duhnt) ***adjective*** Clear and obvious. ▸ ***adverb*** **evidently**

e•vil (**ee**-vuhl) ***adjective*** Wicked and cruel. ▸ ***noun*** **evil**

ev•o•lu•tion (ev-uh-**loo**-shuhn) ***noun***
1. The gradual change of living things over thousands of years.
2. Gradual change into a different form.
▸ ***adjective*** **evolutionary**

e•volve (i-**volv**) ***verb***
1. To change slowly, sometimes over many years.
2. To develop an idea or a plan by making small changes.
▸ ***verb*** **evolving, evolved**

ewe (**yoo**) ***noun*** A female sheep. **Ewe** sounds like **you** and **yew.**

ex•act (eg-**zakt**) ***adjective*** Perfectly correct and accurate. ▸ ***noun*** **exactness** ▸ ***adverb*** **exactly**

ex•ag•ger•ate (eg-**zaj**-uh-rate) ***verb*** To make something seem bigger, better, more important, etc., than it really is. ▸ **exaggerating, exaggerated** ▸ ***noun*** **exaggeration** ▸ ***adjective*** **exaggerated**

ex•am (eg-**zam**) ***noun*** An official test that you take to show how much you know about a subject. Exam is short for *examination.*

ex•am•i•na•tion (eg-*zam*-uh-**nay**-shuhn) ***noun***
1. *See* **exam.**
2. A careful check or inspection, as in *a medical examination.*

ex•am•ine (eg-**zam**-uhn) ***verb***
1. To look carefully at something.
2. When doctors **examine** you, they check your body carefully to see if anything is wrong with you.
▸ ***verb*** **examining, examined** ▸ ***noun*** **examiner**

E

E

ex•am•ple (eg-**zam**-puhl) ***noun***
1. Something typical of a larger group of things.
2. A model for others to follow.
3. A question or a problem, given with its answer.
4. If you **make an example** of someone, you punish the person as a warning to others.

ex•as•per•ate (eg-**zass**-puh-rate) ***verb*** If someone or something **exasperates** you, you become very annoyed. ▸ **exasperating, exasperated** ▸ ***noun*** **exasperation** ▸ ***adjective*** **exasperating,** ***adjective*** **exasperated**

ex•ca•vate (**ek**-skuh-vate) ***verb*** To dig in the earth, either to put up a building or to search for ancient remains. ▸ **excavating, excavated** ▸ ***noun*** **excavation,** ***noun*** **excavator**

ex•ceed (ek-**seed**) ***verb***
1. To be greater or better than something else.
2. To do more than is allowed or expected.
▸ ***verb*** **exceeding, exceeded**

ex•cel (ek-**sel**) ***verb*** If you **excel** at something, you do it extremely well. ▸ **excelling, excelled**

ex•cel•lent (**ek**-suh-luhnt) ***adjective*** Very good. ▸ ***noun*** **excellence** ▸ ***adverb*** **excellently**

ex•cept (ek-**sept**)
1. ***preposition*** Apart from.
2. ***conjunction*** But for the fact that.

ex•cep•tion (ek-**sep**-shuhn) ***noun***
1. Something that is not included in a general rule or statement.
2. If someone **takes exception** to something, the person is offended or annoyed by it.

ex•cep•tion•al (ek-**sep**-shuh-nuhl) ***adjective*** Outstanding or rare.

ex•cerpt (**ek**-surpt) ***noun*** A short piece taken from a longer piece of writing, music, or film. ▸ ***verb*** **excerpt** (ek-**surpt**)

ex•cess (**ek**-sess *or* ek-**sess**) ***noun***
1. Too much of something. ▸ ***adjective*** **excess**
2. in excess of More than.
3. If you do something **to excess,** you do it too much.
▸ ***noun, plural*** **excesses**

ex•ces•sive (ek-**sess**-iv) ***adjective*** Too much. ▸ ***adverb*** **excessively**

ex•change (eks-**chaynj**)
1. ***verb*** To give one thing and receive another. ▸ **exchanging, exchanged** ▸ ***noun*** **exchange**
2. ***noun*** A place where people meet to buy and sell things such as stock, merchandise, etc., as in *a stock exchange.*
3. exchange rate ***noun*** A comparison of the worth of currency in different countries. You use the exchange rate to calculate how much money you will get when you exchange one currency for another.

ex•cite (ek-**site**) ***verb*** If something **excites** you, it makes you eager and interested. ▸ **exciting, excited** ▸ ***noun*** **excitement** ▸ ***adjective*** **exciting,** ***adjective*** **excited**

ex•claim (ek-**sklaym**) ***verb*** To say something suddenly or with force, especially because you are surprised or excited. ▸ **exclaiming, exclaimed** ▸ ***noun*** **exclamation** (ek-skluh-**may**-shuhn)

exclamation mark ***noun*** The punctuation mark (!) used after an expression of surprise, excitement, or another strong feeling.

ex•clude (ek-**sklood**) ***verb***
1. If you **exclude** something, you leave it out. ▸ ***preposition*** **excluding**
2. To keep someone from joining or taking part in something.
▸ ***verb*** **excluding, excluded** ▸ ***noun*** **exclusion**

ex•clu•sive (ek-**skloo**-siv)
1. ***adjective*** If a group or club is **exclusive,** only certain people are welcome to join it.
2. ***adjective*** Complete or whole.
3. ***noun*** A story that appears in one place only.

ex•crete (ek-**skreet**) ***verb*** To pass waste matter out of the body. ▸ **excreting, excreted** ▸ ***noun*** **excretion** ▸ ***adjective*** **excretory** (**ek**-skruh-*tor*-ee)

ex•cru•ci•a•ting (ek-**skroo**-shee-*ay*-ting) ***adjective*** Extremely painful, as in *an excruciating headache.* ▸ ***adverb*** **excruciatingly**

ex•cur•sion (ek-**skur**-zhuhn) ***noun***
1. A short journey, often to a place of interest.
2. A trip on a train, plane, bus, etc., at a reduced fare.

ex•cuse
1. ***noun*** (ek-**skyooss**) A reason you give to explain why you have done something wrong.
2. ***verb*** (ek-**skyooz**) To give someone permission not to do something.
3. ***verb*** (ek-**skyooz**) If you **excuse** someone for doing something, you forgive the person.
▸ ***verb*** **excusing, excused** ▸ ***adjective*** **excusable**

ex•e•cute (**ek**-suh-*kyoot*) ***verb***
1. If you **execute** a plan or an order, you put it into action.
2. To kill someone as a punishment for a crime.
▸ ***verb*** **executing, executed** ▸ ***noun*** **execution**

ex•ec•u•tive (eg-**zek**-yuh-tiv)
1. ***noun*** Someone who has a senior job in a company and is involved in planning its future. ▸ ***adjective*** **executive**
2. ***adjective*** To do with the branch of government that executes the laws of the United States or any state.

ex•empt (eg-**zempt**) ***adjective*** If you are **exempt** from something, you do not have to take part in it. ▸ ***noun*** **exemption** ▸ ***verb*** **exempt**

ex•er•cise (**ek**-sur-*size*)
1. ***noun*** Physical activity that you do to keep fit and healthy.
2. ***verb*** To make your body work hard through vigorous activity, such as sports, in order to keep fit and healthy.
3. ***noun*** A piece of work that you do in order to practice a skill, as in *piano exercises.*
4. ***verb*** To put into practice.
▸ ***verb*** **exercising, exercised**

ex•ert (eg-**zurt**) ***verb*** To make an effort to do something. ▸ **exerting, exerted** ▸ ***noun*** **exertion**

ex•hale (eks-**hale**) ***verb*** To breathe out. ▸ **exhaling, exhaled** ▸ ***noun*** **exhalation**

ex•haust (eg-**zawst**)
1. ***verb*** If something **exhausts** you, it makes you very tired. ▸ ***noun*** **exhaustion** ▸ ***adjective*** **exhausting,** ***adjective*** **exhausted**
2. ***verb*** To use something up completely.
3. ***noun*** The waste gases produced by the engine of a motor vehicle.
4. ***noun*** The pipe found at the back of a motor vehicle from which waste gases from the engine escape.
▸ ***verb*** **exhausting, exhausted**

ex•hib•it (eg-**zib**-it) ***verb*** To show something to the public. ▸ **exhibiting, exhibited** ▸ ***noun*** **exhibit,** ***noun*** **exhibitor**

ex•hi•bi•tion (ek-suh-**bish**-uhn) ***noun*** A public display of works of art, historical objects, etc.

ex•hil•a•rat•ing (eg-**zil**-uh-ray-ting) ***adjective*** Very exciting and thrilling, as in *an exhilarating ride on the roller coaster.* ▸ ***noun*** **exhilaration** ▸ ***verb*** **exhilarate**

ex•ile (**eg**-zile *or* **ek**-sile) ***verb*** To send someone away from his or her own country and order the person not to return. ▸ **exiling, exiled** ▸ ***noun*** **exile**

ex•ist (eg-**zist**) ***verb***
1. To live, or to have reality.
2. To have just enough food to stay alive.
▸ ***verb*** **existing, existed** ▸ ***noun*** **existence**

ex•it (**eg**-zit *or* **ek**-sit)
1. ***verb*** To leave or to go out. ▸ **exiting, exited** ▸ ***noun*** **exit**
2. ***noun*** The way out of a place.

ex•o•dus (**ek**-suh-duhss) ***noun*** A departure of a large number of people at one time.

E

ex•o•skel•e•ton (*eks*-oh-**skel**-uht-uhn) ***noun*** A bony structure on the outside of an animal, such as the shell of a lobster or a crab.

ex•o•tic (eg-**zot**-ik) ***adjective***
1. Strange and fascinating, as in *an exotic perfume.*
2. From a faraway country, as in *an exotic plant.*

ex•pand (ek-**spand**) ***verb*** To increase in size. ▸ **expanding, expanded** ▸ ***noun*** **expansion** ▸ ***adjective*** **expandable**

ex•panse (ek-**spanss**) ***noun*** A broad, open area.

ex•pect (ek-**spekt**) ***verb***
1. To wait for someone to arrive.
2. To think that something ought to happen. ▸ ***noun*** **expectation**
3. If a woman is **expecting,** she is pregnant.
▸ ***verb*** **expecting, expected**

ex•pe•di•tion (ek-spuh-**dish**-uhn) ***noun***
1. A long journey for a special purpose, such as exploring.
2. A short trip to do something enjoyable, as in *a shopping expedition.*

ex•pel (ek-**spel**) ***verb***
1. If someone is **expelled** from a school, the person has to leave because he or she has behaved badly.
2. To send or force something out.
▸ ***verb*** **expelling, expelled** ▸ ***noun*** **expulsion** (ek-**spuhl**-shuhn)

ex•pend•i•ture (ek-**spen**-duh-chur) ***noun***
1. The spending or using up of time, money, or materials in order to do something.
2. The amount of money that a person, company, or country spends.

ex•pense (ek-**spenss**) ***noun***
1. The spending of money, time, energy, etc.
2. Money spent on a particular job or task, as in *business expenses.*

ex•pen•sive (ek-**spen**-siv) ***adjective*** Costing a lot of money. ▸ ***adverb*** **expensively**

ex•pe•ri•ence (ek-**spihr**-ee-uhnss)
1. ***noun*** Something that happens to you.
2. ***verb*** If you **experience** something, it happens to you. ▸ **experiencing, experienced**
3. ***noun*** The knowledge and skill that you gain by doing something.
▸ ***adjective*** **experienced**

ex•per•i•ment (ek-**sper**-uh-ment)
1. ***noun*** A scientific test to try out a theory or to see the effect of something.
▸ ***verb*** **experiment**
2. ***verb*** To try something new.
▸ **experimenting, experimented**
▸ ***noun*** **experiment**

ex•per•i•men•tal (ek-*sper*-uh-**men**-tuhl) ***adjective*** If something is **experimental,** it has not yet been tested thoroughly.

ex•pert (**ek**-spurt) ***noun*** Someone who is very skilled at something or knows a lot about a particular subject.
▸ ***adjective*** **expert** (ek-**spurt** *or* **ek**-spurt)

ex•pire (ek-**spire**) ***verb***
1. When a ticket, license, etc., **expires,** it reaches the end of the time when it can be used. ▸ ***noun*** **expiration**
2. To die.
▸ ***verb*** **expiring, expired**

ex•plain (ek-**splayn**) ***verb***
1. To make something clear so that it is easier to understand. ▸ ***adjective*** **explanatory** (ek-**splan**-uh-*tor*-ee)
2. To give a reason for something.
▸ ***verb*** **explaining, explained** ▸ ***noun*** **explanation** (ek-spluh-**nay**-shuhn)

ex•plic•it (ek-**spliss**-it) ***adjective*** Very clearly stated.

ex•plode (ek-**splode**) ***verb*** If something **explodes,** it blows apart with a loud bang and great force. ▸ **exploding, exploded**

ex•ploit
1. (**ek**-sploit) ***noun*** A brave or daring deed.
2. (ek-**sploit**) ***verb*** To treat someone unfairly, usually by not paying the

person enough for his or her work. ▸ **exploiting, exploited** ▸ ***noun*** **exploitation**

ex•plo•ra•tion (ek-spluh-**ray**-shuhn) ***noun*** The act of looking into or studying something or someplace unknown.

ex•plore (ek-**splor**) ***verb***
1. To travel in order to discover what a place is like. ▸ ***noun*** **explorer**
2. If you **explore** an idea or a possibility, you discuss it or think about it carefully.
▸ ***verb*** **exploring, explored**
▸ ***adjective*** **exploratory**

ex•plo•sion (ek-**sploh**-zhuhn) ***noun***
1. A sudden and noisy release of energy.
2. A sudden increase or growth, as in *a population explosion.*

ex•plo•sive (ek-**sploh**-siv)
1. ***noun*** A substance that can blow up.
2. ***adjective*** Able or likely to explode.
▸ ***adverb*** **explosively**
3. ***adjective*** If a situation is **explosive,** it is very dangerous.

ex•po•nent (ek-**spoh**-nuhnt) ***noun*** A number placed next to and above another to show how many times that number is to be multiplied by itself. In 4^3, 3 is the exponent.

ex•port
1. ***verb*** (ek-**sport** *or* **ek**-sport) To send products to another country to be sold there. ▸ **exporting, exported**
2. ***noun*** (**ek**-sport) The act of selling something to another country, or a product thus sold.
▸ ***noun*** **exporter**

ex•pose (ek-**spoze**) ***verb***
1. To uncover something so it can be seen.
2. To reveal the truth about someone or something. ▸ ***noun*** **exposé**
3. To let light fall on photographic film.
4. To leave without protection.
▸ ***verb*** **exposing, exposed**

ex•po•sure (ek-**spoh**-zhur) ***noun***
1. The harmful effect of severe weather on someone's body.
2. A piece of film that produces a photograph when it is exposed to light.
3. The length of time that a photographic film is exposed to the light.

ex•press (ek-**spress**)
1. ***verb*** To show what you feel or think by saying, doing, or writing something.
▸ **expresses, expressing, expressed**
2. ***noun*** A fast train or bus that stops at only a few stations. ▸ ***noun, plural*** **expresses**
3. ***adjective*** Very fast, as in *express delivery.*

ex•pres•sion (ek-**spresh**-uhn) ***noun***
1. A phrase that has a particular meaning, as in *the expression "lock, stock, and barrel."*
2. The look on someone's face, as in *a puzzled expression.*
3. The act of showing your feelings, as in *the expression of our concern.*

ex•pres•sive (ek-**spress**-iv) ***adjective*** Filled with meaning or feeling. ▸ ***adverb*** **expressively**

ex•press•way (ek-**spress**-*way*) ***noun*** A wide highway on which cars, trucks, etc., can go long distances without traffic lights or stop signs.

ex•quis•ite (ek-**swiz**-it *or* **ek**-swi-zit) ***adjective*** Very beautiful and delicate, as in *an exquisite piece of embroidery.*
▸ ***adverb*** **exquisitely**

ex•tend (ek-**stend**) ***verb***
1. To make something longer or bigger.
2. To stretch out.
3. To offer, as in *to extend help to flood victims.*
▸ ***verb*** **extending, extended** ▸ ***noun*** **extension**

ex•ten•sive (ek-**sten**-siv) ***adjective***
1. Spreading over a wide area.
2. Including a lot of things, as in *an extensive choice of desserts.*

ex•tent (ek-**stent**) ***noun*** The size, level, or scale of something.

ex•te•ri•or (ek-**stihr**-ee-ur) ***noun*** The outside of something, especially a building. ▸ ***adjective*** **exterior**

E

E

ex•ter•mi•nate (ek-**stur**-muh-nate) ***verb*** To kill large numbers of people or animals. ▸ **exterminating, exterminated** ▸ ***noun*** **extermination,** ***noun*** **exterminator**

ex•ter•nal (ek-**stur**-nuhl) ***adjective*** On the outside. ▸ ***adverb*** **externally**

ex•tinct (ek-**stingkt**) ***adjective***
1. If a type of animal or plant is **extinct,** it has died out. ▸ ***noun*** **extinction**
2. If a volcano is **extinct,** it has stopped erupting.

ex•tin•guish (ek-**sting**-gwish) ***verb***
1. To put out a flame, a fire, or a light. ▸ ***noun*** **extinguisher**
2. To put an end to a feeling or a belief.
▸ ***verb*** **extinguishes, extinguishing, extinguished**

ex•tra (**ek**-struh)
1. ***adjective*** More than the usual amount, as in *an extra helping of potatoes.*
2. ***adverb*** Extremely, or more than usual, as in *extra large.*
3. ***noun*** Something that is added to the usual or the normal.

ex•tract
1. (ek-**strakt**) ***verb*** To take or pull something out. ▸ **extracting, extracted** ▸ ***noun*** **extraction**
2. (**ek**-strakt) ***noun*** A short section taken from a book, speech, piece of music, etc.

ex•traor•di•nar•y (ek-**stror**-duh-ner-ee) ***adjective*** Very unusual or remarkable, as in *an extraordinary skill.* ▸ ***adverb*** **extraordinarily**

ex•tra•ter•res•tri•al (*ek*-struh-tuh-**ress**-tree-uhl)
1. ***adjective*** Coming from outer space, as in *extraterrestrial messages in a science fiction story.*
2. ***noun*** A creature from outer space.

ex•trav•a•gant (ek-**strav**-uh-guhnt) ***adjective*** If you are **extravagant,** you spend too much money or are wasteful in the way you use things. ▸ ***adverb*** **extravagantly**

ex•treme (ek-**streem**)
1. ***adjective*** Very great, as in *extreme happiness.* ▸ ***adverb*** **extremely**
2. ***adjective*** Farthest.
3. ***noun*** One of two ends or opposites, as in *extremes of love and hate.*
4. ***adjective*** Exciting and very dangerous.

ex•tro•vert (**ek**-struh-vurt) ***noun*** Someone who enjoys being with other people and is lively and talkative. ▸ ***adjective*** **extrovert,** ***adjective*** **extroverted**

ex•trem•i•ty (ek-**strem**-i-tee) ***noun***
1. The extreme point or end of something.
2. Your **extremities** are your hands and feet.
▸ ***noun, plural*** **extremities**

ex•u•ber•ant (eg-**zoo**-bur-uhnt) ***adjective*** Very cheerful and lively, as in *an exuberant mood.* ▸ ***noun*** **exuberance** ▸ ***adverb*** **exuberantly**

eye (**eye**)
1. ***noun*** One of the two organs in your head that you use to see with.
2. ***noun*** The small hole in a needle.
3. If you **have an eye for** something, you can judge how good it is.
4. ***verb*** To look carefully at someone or something. ▸ **eyeing, eyed**
5. ***noun*** The calm, clear zone at the very center of a hurricane.

eye•ball (**eye**-*bawl*)
1. ***noun*** The globe or spherical part of the eye.
2. ***verb*** To take a close look at something. ▸ **eyeballing, eyeballed**

eye•brow (**eye**-*brou*) ***noun*** The line of hair that grows above each of your eyes.

eye•glass•es (**eye**-*glass*-uhz) ***noun, plural*** A pair of lenses in a frame that helps a person see better.

eye•lash (**eye**-*lash*) ***noun*** One of the short, curved hairs that grows on the edge of eyelids. ▸ ***noun, plural*** **eyelashes**

eye•lid (**eye**-*lid*) ***noun*** The upper or lower fold of skin that covers the eye when it is closed.

eye•sight (**eye**-*site*) ***noun*** The ability to see.

eye•tooth (**eye**-*tooth*) ***noun*** A pointed tooth found on the front of the upper jaw. Each person has two eyeteeth.
▸ ***noun, plural*** **eyeteeth**

eye•wit•ness (**eye-wit**-niss) ***noun*** Someone who has seen something take place and can describe what happened.
▸ ***noun, plural*** **eyewitnesses**

F

fa•ble (**fay**-buhl) ***noun***
1. A story that teaches a lesson. Fables often have animal characters that talk and act like people.
2. A lie or an untrue story.

fab•ric (**fab**-rik) ***noun*** Cloth or material.

fab•u•lous (**fab**-yuh-luhss) ***adjective***
1. Wonderful or marvelous. ▸ ***adverb*** **fabulously**
2. Amazing or hard to believe.

fa•cade (fuh-**sahd**) ***noun***
1. The front of a building.
2. A person's **facade** is the way he or she wants to be seen or thought of.

face (**fayss**)
1. ***noun*** The front of your head, from your forehead to your chin. ▸ ***adjective*** **facial**
2. ***noun*** An expression or look on the face.
3. ***noun*** The front, outer, or upper surface of something, as in *a mountain face* or *a clock face.*
4. ***verb*** To look toward something.
▸ ***adjective*** **facing**
5. ***verb*** To deal with something boldly or bravely.
▸ ***verb*** **facing, faced**

fac•et (**fass**-it) ***noun***
1. A flat, polished surface of a cut gem.
2. A part or side of something.

fa•cil•i•tate (fuh-**sil**-uh-tate) ***verb*** To make something easier. ▸ **facilitating, facilitated** ▸ ***noun*** **facilitator**

fa•cil•i•ty (fuh-**sil**-uh-tee) ***noun***
1. The ability to do something easily or skillfully.
2. A service provided for people to use and enjoy, such as a sports recreation center, park, etc.
▸ ***noun, plural*** **facilities**

fac•sim•i•le (fak-**sim**-uh-lee) ***noun***
1. An exact copy of something written or of a work of art.
2. A fax.

fact (**fakt**) ***noun***
1. A piece of information that is true.
▸ ***adjective*** **factual** ▸ ***adverb*** **factually**
2. **in fact** Actually.

fac•tor (**fak**-tur) ***noun***
1. One of the things that help produce a result.
2. A whole number that can be divided exactly into a larger number.
▸ ***verb*** **factor**

fac•to•ry (**fak**-tuh-ree) ***noun*** A building where products, such as cars or chemicals, are made in large numbers, often using machines. A factory is also called a **plant.** ▸ ***noun, plural*** **factories**

fac•ul•ty (**fak**-uhl-tee) ***noun***
1. A group of teachers and professors at a school, college, or university, as in *the history faculty.*
2. One of the powers of the body or mind, such as memory, reason, sight, or speech.
3. A unique talent or ability.
▸ ***noun, plural*** **faculties**

F

fad (**fad**) ***noun*** Something that is very popular for a short time.

fade (**fayd**) ***verb***
1. To become paler in color.
2. To lose freshness.
3. To become gradually weaker.
▸ ***verb*** **fading, faded**

Fahr•en•heit (**fa**-ren-*hite*) ***adjective*** A measurement of temperature using a scale on which water boils at 212 degrees and freezes at 32 degrees.

fail (**fayl**) ***verb***
1. If you **fail** to do something, you do not do it.
2. If you **fail** an exam or a test, you do not pass it.
3. To disappoint.
4. To break down or stop working.
5. To lose power or strength.
6. To go bankrupt.
7. without fail Definitely, or every single time.
▸ ***verb*** **failing, failed**

fail•ure (**fayl**-yur) ***noun***
1. Someone or something that is not successful.
2. Lack of favorable results.
3. A weakening or loss of ability, as in *heart failure.*
4. Neglect.

faint (**faynt**)
1. ***adjective*** Not clear or strong.
2. ***adjective*** Dizzy and weak.
3. ***verb*** To become dizzy and lose consciousness for a short time.
▸ **fainting, fainted** ▸ ***noun*** **faint**
4. ***adjective*** A **faint** chance is a very slight one.
5. faint-hearted (**hart**-id) ***adjective*** Timid and not at all confident.
Faint sounds like **feint.**
▸ ***noun*** **faintness** ▸ ***adjective*** **fainter, faintest** ▸ ***adverb*** **faintly**

fair (**fair**)
1. ***adjective*** Reasonable and just, as in *fair treatment.* ▸ ***noun*** **fairness** ▸ ***adverb*** **fairly**
2. ***adjective*** **Fair** hair is light yellow.
3. ***adjective*** Neither good nor bad.
▸ ***adverb*** **fairly**
4. ***adjective*** **Fair** weather is clear and sunny.
5. ***noun*** An outdoor show of farm products and animals, often with entertainment, amusements, and rides.
6. ***adverb*** By the rules. ▸ ***adverb*** **fairer, fairest**
Fair sounds like **fare.**
▸ ***adjective*** **fairer, fairest**

fair•ground (**fair**-*ground*) ***noun*** A large outdoor area where fairs are held.

fair•y (**fair**-ee) ***noun***
1. A magical creature such as a tiny person with wings, found in fairy tales.
2. fairy tale A children's story about magic, fairies, giants, witches, etc.
▸ ***noun, plural*** **fairies**

faith (**fayth**) ***noun***
1. Trust and confidence in someone or something.
2. Belief in God.
3. A religion.

faith•ful (**fayth**-fuhl) ***adjective*** Loyal and trustworthy. ▸ ***noun*** **faithfulness** ▸ ***adverb*** **faithfully**

fake (**fayk**)
1. ***verb*** To pretend that something is genuine. ▸ **faking, faked**
2. ***noun*** Someone or something that is not what it seems to be.
3. ***verb*** To make a fake of something.
▸ ***noun*** **faker** ▸ ***adjective*** **fake**

fa•la•fel (fuh-**lah**-fuhl) ***noun*** A spicy mixture of ground vegetables, such as chickpeas, that is shaped into a ball or a patty and fried.

fal•con (**fawl**-kuhn *or* **fal**-kuhn) ***noun*** A bird of prey with long wings and hooked claws that catches small birds in flight. Falcons can be trained to return with their prey to their owner. ▸ ***noun*** **falconry,** ***noun*** **falconer**

fall (**fawl**)
1. ***verb*** To drop down to the ground.
2. ***verb*** To decrease or become lower.
3. ***verb*** To become.
4. ***verb*** To happen.
5. ***noun*** The season between summer

F

and winter, when it gets colder, the days get shorter, and the leaves fall from the trees.
6. *verb* To be defeated, captured, or overthrown.
7. *verb* If two people **fall out,** they quarrel with each other.
8. *verb* If something **falls through,** it fails to happen.
▸ ***verb* falling, fell** (**fel**), **fallen** (**fawl**-in) ▸ ***noun* fall**

fall•out (**fawl**-*out*) ***noun***
1. Radioactive dust from a nuclear explosion.
2. The result of an action.

fal•low (**fal**-oh) ***adjective*** Land that is **fallow** has not been planted with crops. It remains out of use so that its nutrients can be restored.

false (**fawlss**) ***adjective***
1. Not true or correct, as in *false information.* ▸ ***adverb* falsely**
2. Not faithful or loyal.
3. Not real, as in *false eyelashes.*

false•hood (**fawlss**-hud) ***noun*** A lie.

fal•ter (**fawl**-tur) ***verb***
1. To act or move in an unsteady way.
2. To pause while speaking because you are unsure or confused.
▸ ***verb* faltering, faltered**

fame (**faym**) ***noun*** Being well-known.
▸ ***adjective* famed**

fa•mil•iar (fuh-**mil**-yur) ***adjective***
1. If something is **familiar,** it is well-known or easily recognized, as in *a familiar saying.*
2. If you are **familiar** with something, you know it well.
3. Friendly.

fam•i•ly (**fam**-uh-lee) ***noun***
1. A group of people related to one another, especially parents or guardians and their children.
2. A group of related animals or plants.
3. family tree A chart that shows how the members of a family are related over many generations.
▸ ***noun, plural* families**
4. family room A room in a house that is used for relaxing, watching television, etc.

fam•ine (**fam**-uhn) ***noun*** A serious lack of food.

fam•ished (**fam**-isht) ***adjective*** If you are **famished,** you are very hungry.

fa•mous (**fay**-muhss) ***adjective*** If you are **famous,** you are well-known to many people.

fan (**fan**) ***noun***
1. A person who is very interested in or enthusiastic about something.
2. A machine or an object that you use to blow or wave air onto you in order to keep cool. ▸ ***verb* fan**

fa•nat•ic (fuh-**nat**-ik) ***noun*** Someone who is wildly enthusiastic about a belief, a cause, or an interest. ▸ ***adjective* fanatical** ▸ ***adverb* fanatically**

fan•cy (**fan**-see)
1. *adjective* Highly decorated or elaborate. ▸ **fancier, fanciest**
2. *noun* Imagination.
3. *noun* A great liking.
4. *verb* To imagine. ▸ **fancies, fancying, fancied**
▸ ***noun, plural* fancies**

fang (**fang**) ***noun*** A long, pointed tooth.

fan•ny pack (**fan**-ee) ***noun*** A small bag on a belt. It is worn around the waist and used to carry personal items.

fan•tas•tic (fan-**tass**-tik) ***adjective***
1. Too strange to be believable.
2. Terrific or wonderful.
▸ ***adverb* fantastically**

fan•ta•sy (**fan**-tuh-see *or* **fan**-tuh-zee) ***noun***
1. Something you imagine happening that is not likely to happen in real life.
▸ ***verb* fantasize**
2. A story with very strange characters, places, or events.
▸ ***noun, plural* fantasies**

far (**far**)
1. *adverb* A great distance.
2. *adverb* Very much.
3. *adjective* Distant or not near.
▸ ***adjective* and *adverb* farther, farthest** *or* **further, furthest**

F

far•a•way (**far**-uh-**way**) ***adjective***
1. Distant or remote.
2. Dreamy or lost in thought.

farce (**farss**) ***noun***
1. A funny play in which there are many silly misunderstandings.
2. A ridiculous situation. ▸ ***adjective*** **farcical**

fare (**fair**)
1. ***noun*** The cost of traveling on a bus, subway, train, plane, etc.
2. ***verb*** To get along.
Fare sounds like **fair.**

Far East ***noun*** The countries in eastern Asia, such as China, Japan, and Korea.

fare•well (fair-**wel**) ***interjection*** Good-bye and good luck. ▸ ***noun*** **farewell**

far-fetched ***adjective*** Hard to believe.

farm (**farm**)
1. ***verb*** To grow crops and raise animals. ▸ **farming, farmed** ▸ ***noun*** **farmer,** ***noun*** **farming**
2. ***noun*** An area of land with buildings on it used for growing crops or raising animals. ▸ ***adjective*** **farm**

far•sight•ed (**far**-**site**-uhd) ***adjective***
1. Able to see things in the distance more clearly than things that are close.
2. Able to imagine and plan for the future.

far•ther (**far**-THur)
1. ***adjective*** *and* ***adverb*** A comparative of **far.**
2. ***adverb*** At greater distance than something else.
3. ***adjective*** More distant or remote.

fas•ci•nate (**fass**-uh-nate) ***verb*** To attract and hold the attention of. ▸ **fascinating, fascinated** ▸ ***noun*** **fascination**

fas•cism (**fash**-iz-uhm) ***noun*** A form of government in which a dictator and the dictator's political party have complete power over a country. ▸ ***noun*** **fascist**

fash•ion (**fash**-uhn)
1. ***noun*** A style of clothing that is popular at a certain time. ▸ ***adjective*** **fashionable**
2. ***noun*** A way of doing things.
3. ***verb*** To make or shape something. ▸ **fashioning, fashioned**

fast (**fast**)
1. ***adjective*** Moving in a hurry, or quick. ▸ ***adverb*** **fast**
2. ***verb*** To give up eating food for a time. ▸ **fasting, fasted** ▸ ***noun*** **fast**
3. ***adjective*** **Fast** colors or dyes do not run or fade when you wash them.
4. ***adjective*** Ahead of the right time. ▸ ***adjective*** **faster, fastest**

fas•ten (**fass**-uhn) ***verb*** To tie, attach, or close firmly. ▸ **fastening, fastened** ▸ ***noun*** **fastening**

fas•ten•er (**fass**-uhn-ur) ***noun*** An object such as a button, buckle, or clip that is used to hold things together.

fast food ***noun*** Food such as hamburgers, fried chicken, and pizza that is prepared and served quickly by restaurants.

fat (**fat**)
1. ***adjective*** Heavy or plump. ▸ ***noun*** **fatness** ▸ ***verb*** **fatten**
2. ***noun*** An oily substance found in the body tissues of animals and some plants. Fats are found in foods such as meat, milk, nuts, and avocados. They give you energy and are stored in your body to keep you warm. ▸ ***adjective*** **fatty**
3. ***adjective*** Big or thick, as in *a fat dictionary.* ▸ ***adjective*** **fatter, fattest**

fa•tal (**fay**-tuhl) ***adjective***
1. Causing death, as in *a fatal accident.* ▸ ***adverb*** **fatally**
2. Likely to have very bad or harmful results, as in *a fatal mistake.*

fa•tal•i•ty (fay-**tal**-uh-tee *or* fuh-**tal**-uh-tee) ***noun*** A death caused by an accident, a war, or other form of violence. ▸ ***noun, plural*** **fatalities**

fate (**fayt**) ***noun***
1. The force that some people believe controls events and decides what happens to people.
2. Your **fate** is what will happen to you.

F

fate•ful (**fayt**-fuhl) ***adjective*** Important because it has a strong and usually unpleasant effect on future events.
▸ ***adverb*** **fatefully**

fa•ther (**fah**-THur) ***noun***
1. A male parent. ▸ ***noun*** **fatherhood**
▸ ***adjective*** **fatherly**
2. A priest.

father-in-law ***noun*** Someone's **father-in-law** is the father of his or her spouse.
▸ ***noun, plural*** **fathers-in-law**

Father's Day ***noun*** A holiday that honors fathers, celebrated on the third Sunday in June.

fath•om (**faTH**-uhm)
1. ***noun*** A unit for measuring the depth of water. One fathom equals six feet.
2. ***verb*** If you cannot **fathom** something, you cannot understand it.
▸ **fathoming, fathomed**

fa•tigue (fuh-**teeg**) ***noun*** Great tiredness. ▸ ***verb*** **fatigue**

fau•cet (**faw**-sit) ***noun*** A device with a valve used to turn the flow of a liquid on or off.

fault (**fawlt**)
1. ***noun*** If something is your **fault,** you are to blame for it.
2. ***noun*** Something wrong that keeps another thing from being perfect.
3. ***noun*** A weakness in someone's character.
4. ***verb*** To criticize or find a mistake in something. ▸ **faulting, faulted**
5. ***noun*** A large crack in the earth's surface that can cause earthquakes.

fau•na (**faw**-nuh) ***noun*** The animal life of a particular area.

fa•vor (**fay**-vur)
1. ***noun*** Something helpful or kind that you do for someone.
2. ***verb*** To like one thing or person best.
3. ***verb*** To look like someone else.
4. ***noun*** A small gift.
5. If you are **in favor of** something, you agree with it or support it.
▸ ***verb*** **favoring, favored**

fa•vor•a•ble (**fay**-vur-uh-buhl) ***adjective***
1. Helpful.
2. Approving, as in *a favorable review.*
3. Pleasing, as in *a favorable impression.*

fa•vor•ite (**fay**-vuh-rit) ***noun***
1. The person or thing that you like best.
2. The person, team, or animal that is expected to win a race.
▸ ***adjective*** **favorite**

fa•vor•it•ism (**fay**-vur-i-*tiz*-uhm) ***noun*** Unfair advantage shown to one person more than others.

fawn (**fawn**) ***noun***
1. A young deer.
2. A light brown color. ▸ ***adjective*** **fawn**

fax (**faks**) ***noun*** A copy of a letter, document, etc., sent along a telephone line using a special machine. Fax is short for *facsimile.* ▸ ***noun, plural*** **faxes**
▸ ***verb*** **fax**

fear (**fihr**)
1. ***noun*** The feeling you have when you are in danger or you expect something bad to happen. ▸ ***adjective*** **fearful**
2. ***verb*** To be afraid of something or someone.
3. ***verb*** To be worried about something.
▸ ***verb*** **fearing, feared**

fear•less (**fihr**-liss) ***adjective*** Very brave and not afraid, as in *a fearless knight.*
▸ ***adverb*** **fearlessly**

fear•some (**fihr**-suhm) ***adjective*** Frightening, as in *a fearsome monster.*

fea•si•ble (**fee**-zuh-buhl) ***adjective*** If something is **feasible,** it can be done.
▸ ***noun*** **feasibility** ▸ ***adverb*** **feasibly**

feast (**feest**) ***noun*** A large, fancy meal for a lot of people on a special occasion.
▸ ***verb*** **feast**

feat (**feet**) ***noun*** An achievement that shows great courage, strength, or skill.

feath•er (**feTH**-ur) ***noun*** One of the light, fluffy parts that cover a bird's body.
▸ ***adjective*** **feathered,** ***adjective*** **feathery**

F

fea•ture (**fee**-chur) ***noun***
1. An important part or quality of something. ▸ ***verb*** **feature**
2. Your **features** are the different parts of your face.
3. A full-length movie.
4. A newspaper article or part of a television program that deals with a particular subject.

Feb•ru•ar•y (**feb**-roo-er-ee *or* **feb**-yoo-er-ee) ***noun*** The second month on the calendar, after January and before March. February has 28 days except in a leap year, when it has 29.

fed•er•al (**fed**-ur-uhl) ***adjective*** In a **federal** government, several states are united under and controlled by one central power or authority. However, each state also has its own government and can make its own laws. ▸ ***noun*** **federalism,** ***noun*** **federalist**

fed•er•a•tion (*fed*-uh-**ray**-shuhn) ***noun*** A union of states, nations, or other groups joined together by an agreement.

fed up ***adjective*** *(informal)* If you are **fed up,** you are annoyed, bored, or disgusted about something.

fee (**fee**) ***noun*** The amount of money that someone charges for a service.

fee•ble (**fee**-buhl) ***adjective*** Very weak. ▸ **feebler, feeblest**

feed (**feed**)
1. ***verb*** To give food to a person or an animal.
2. ***verb*** When animals **feed,** they eat.
3. ***noun*** Food for animals.
4. ***verb*** To supply, or to put in.
▸ ***verb*** **feeding, fed** (**fed**)

feed•back (**feed**-*bak*) ***noun***
1. Comments and reactions to something.
2. The loud, piercing noise made when sounds produced by an amplifier go back into it.

feel (**feel**) ***verb***
1. To touch something with your fingers, or to experience something touching you. ▸ ***noun*** **feel**
2. To have a certain emotion or sensation.
3. To think or to have an opinion.
4. To seem to be.
▸ ***verb*** **feeling, felt** (**felt**) ▸ ***noun*** **feeling**

feign (**fayn**) ***verb*** To pretend. ▸ **feigning, feigned**

feint (**faynt**) ***noun*** A blow or movement meant to take attention away from the real point of attack. **Feint** sounds like **faint.** ▸ ***verb*** **feint**

feist•y (**fye**-stee) ***adjective***
1. Easily angered or likely to quarrel.
2. Very lively or frisky, as in a *feisty puppy.*

fe•line (**fee**-line)
1. ***adjective*** To do with cats.
2. ***noun*** Any animal of the cat family.
3. ***adjective*** Like a cat.

fell (**fel**) ***verb*** To cut something down or to make something fall. ▸ **felling, felled**

fel•low (**fel**-oh)
1. ***noun*** A man or a boy.
2. ***adjective*** Belonging to the same class or group. ▸ ***noun*** **fellow**

fel•low•ship (**fel**-oh-*ship*) ***noun***
1. A group of people sharing an interest.
2. A friendly feeling among people who share an interest or do something together.

fel•on (**fel**-uhn) ***noun*** Someone who has committed a serious crime, such as murder or burglary. ▸ ***noun*** **felony**

felt (**felt**) ***noun*** A thick cloth made of wool or other fibers that are pressed together in layers.

fe•male (**fee**-male) ***noun*** A person or an animal of the sex that can give birth to young animals or lay eggs. ▸ ***adjective*** **female**

fem•i•nine (**fem**-uh-nuhn) ***adjective***
1. To do with women.
2. Having qualities that are supposed to be typical of women. ▸ ***noun*** **femininity**

fem•i•nist (**fem**-uh-nist) ***noun*** Someone who believes strongly that women ought to have the same opportunities and rights that men have. ▸ ***noun*** **feminism** ▸ ***adjective*** **feminist**

fence (**fenss**)
1. ***noun*** A structure, often made of wood or wire, used to surround, protect, or mark off an area. ▸ ***verb*** **fence**
2. ***verb*** To fight with long, thin swords, or foils, as a sport. ▸ **fencing, fenced** ▸ ***noun*** **fencer**
3. If you are **on the fence,** you are undecided about which side to take in an argument.

fenc•ing (**fen**-sing) ***noun***
1. The sport of fighting with long, thin swords called foils.
2. Fences, or the material used to make them.

fend (**fend**) ***verb***
1. If you **fend** for yourself, you take care of yourself.
2. If you **fend off** someone who is attacking you, you defend yourself.
▸ ***verb*** **fending, fended**

fend•er (**fen**-dur) ***noun*** A metal cover over the wheel of a car or bicycle that protects the wheel against damage and reduces splashing.

fer•ment (fur-**ment**) ***verb*** When a drink, such as beer or wine, **ferments,** a chemical change takes place that makes the sugar in it turn into alcohol.
▸ **fermenting, fermented** ▸ ***noun*** **fermentation**

fern (**furn**) ***noun*** A plant with feathery leaves, or fronds, and no flowers. Ferns usually grow in damp places. They reproduce by spores instead of seeds.

fe•ro•cious (fuh-**roh**-shuhss) ***adjective*** Very fierce and savage, as in *a ferocious lion.* ▸ ***noun*** **ferocity** (fuh-**rah**-si-tee) ▸ ***adverb*** **ferociously**

fer•ret (**fer**-it)
1. ***noun*** A long, thin animal that is related to the weasel.
2. ***verb*** To search. ▸ **ferreting, ferreted**

Fer•ris wheel (**fer**-iss) ***noun*** A large, spinning wheel with seats hung on its side, used as a ride in a carnival or amusement park.

fer•ry (**fer**-ee)
1. ***noun*** A boat or ship that regularly carries people across a stretch of water.
▸ ***noun, plural*** **ferries**
2. ***verb*** To carry people or things from one place to another. ▸ **ferries, ferrying, ferried**

fer•tile (**fur**-tuhl) ***adjective***
1. Land that is **fertile** is good for growing lots of crops and plants.
2. Able to have babies.
3. Having a lot of ideas, as in *a fertile imagination.*
▸ ***noun*** **fertility**

fer•ti•lize (**fur**-tuh-lize) ***verb***
1. To put a substance such as manure on land to make it richer and to make crops grow better. ▸ ***noun*** **fertilizer**
2. To begin reproduction in an egg or a plant by causing sperm to join with the egg or pollen to come into contact with the reproductive part of the plant.
▸ ***verb*** **fertilizing, fertilized** ▸ ***noun*** **fertilization**

fer•vent (**fur**-vuhnt) ***adjective*** Showing strong or intense feeling. ▸ ***noun*** **fervor** ▸ ***adverb*** **fervently**

fes•ti•val (**fess**-tuh-vuhl) ***noun***
1. A celebration or holiday.
2. An organized set of artistic or musical events, often held at the same time each year.

fes•tive (**fess**-tiv) ***adjective*** Cheerful and lively, as in *a festive mood.*

fes•tiv•i•ty (fess-**tiv**-uh-tee) ***noun*** An activity that is part of a celebration.
▸ ***noun, plural*** **festivities**

fes•toon (fess-**toon**) ***verb*** To cover something with flowers, ribbons, or other decorations. ▸ **festooning, festooned**

fetch (**fech**) ***verb***
1. To go after and bring back something or somebody.
2. To be sold for a particular price.
▸ ***verb*** **fetches, fetching, fetched**

fetch•ing (**fech**-ing) ***adjective*** Attractive or pretty.

fet•tuc•ci•ne (fet-uh-**chee**-nee) ***noun*** A narrow strip of pasta that is shaped like a ribbon. ▸ ***noun, plural*** **fettuccini** (fet-uh-**chee**-nee)

F

fe•tus (**fee**-tuhss) ***noun*** A baby or an animal before it is born, at the stage when it is developing in its mother's womb. *See* **pregnant.**

feud (**fyood**) ***noun*** A bitter quarrel between two people, families, or groups that lasts for a long time. ▸ ***verb*** **feud**

feu•dal•ism (**fyoo**-duh-li-zuhm) ***noun*** The medieval system in which people were given land and protection by the owner of the land, or lord, and in return worked and fought for him. ▸ ***adjective*** **feudal**

fe•ver (**fee**-vur) ***noun***
1. A body temperature that is higher than normal. Most people have a fever if their temperature is more than 98.6 degrees Fahrenheit.
2. Great excitement or activity.
▸ ***adjective*** **feverish**

few (**fyoo**) ***adjective*** Not many. ▸ ***noun*** **few**

fez (**fez**) ***noun*** A round, red felt cap with no brim. Fezzes are worn by men, mainly in the Middle East. ▸ ***noun, plural*** **fezzes**

fi•an•cé (fee-ahn-**say** *or* fee-**ahn**-say) ***noun*** If a man and woman are engaged to be married, he is her **fiancé.**

fi•an•cée (fee-ahn-**say** *or* fee-**ahn**-say) ***noun*** If a man and woman are engaged to be married, she is his **fiancée.**

fi•as•co (fee-**ass**-koh) ***noun*** A complete failure. ▸ ***noun, plural*** **fiascoes**

fib (**fib**) ***verb*** To tell a small lie. ▸ **fibbing, fibbed** ▸ ***noun*** **fib,** ***noun*** **fibber**

fi•ber (**fye**-bur) ***noun***
1. A long, thin thread of material such as cotton, wool, hemp, or nylon.
2. A part of foods such as bran, fruits, and vegetables that passes through the body but is not digested. Fiber helps food move through the intestines. ▸ ***adjective*** **fibrous**

fi•ber•glass (**fye**-bur-*glass*) ***noun*** A strong insulating material made from fine threads of glass, used in buildings, cars, boats, etc.

fiber op•tics (**op**-tiks) ***noun, plural*** Bundles of extremely thin glass or plastic tubes, or fibers through which light passes. Fiber optics are used in medical operations and for sending telephone signals.

fick•le (**fik**-uhl) ***adjective*** Someone who is **fickle** changes his or her mind often. ▸ ***noun*** **fickleness**

fic•tion (**fik**-shuhn) ***noun*** Stories about characters and events that are not real. ▸ ***adjective*** **fictional,** ***adjective*** **fictitious** (fik-**tish**-uhss)

fid•dle (**fid**-uhl)
1. ***noun*** *(informal)* A violin. ▸ ***noun*** **fiddler**
2. ***verb*** To touch or play nervously with something, as in *to fiddle with a pencil.*
3. ***verb*** To waste.
▸ ***verb*** **fiddling, fiddled**

fidg•et (**fij**-it) ***verb*** To keep moving because you are bored, nervous, or uneasy. ▸ **fidgeting, fidgeted** ▸ ***adjective*** **fidgety**

field (**feeld**)
1. ***noun*** A piece of open land, sometimes used for growing crops or playing sports.
2. ***verb*** In baseball, to catch or stop a ball that has been hit. ▸ **fielding, fielded**
3. ***noun*** An area of study or interest.

field•er (**feel**-dur) ***noun*** A baseball player who has a position in the outfield.

field goal ***noun***
1. In football, a play in which the ball is kicked from the field, scoring three points.
2. In basketball, a basket made when the ball is in play, scoring two or three points.

field hockey ***noun*** A team game played on a rectangular field using curved sticks and a small ball. Players attempt to hit the ball along the ground and into the opposition's goal.

field trip ***noun*** If you go on a **field trip,** you travel somewhere with a group to see things and learn.

fiend (**feend**) ***noun***
1. An evil spirit.
2. An evil or cruel person.
▸ ***adjective*** **fiendish** ▸ ***adverb*** **fiendishly**

fierce (**fihrss**) ***adjective***
1. Violent or dangerous.
2. Very strong or extreme.
▸ ***adjective*** **fiercer, fiercest** ▸ ***noun*** **fierceness** ▸ ***adverb*** **fiercely**

fier•y (**fye**-ree *or* **fye**-uh-ree) ***adjective***
1. Like fire, or to do with fire.
2. Very emotional, as in *a fiery speech.*
▸ ***adjective*** **fierier, fieriest**

fi•es•ta (fee-**ess**-tuh) ***noun*** A holiday or religious festival, especially in Spain and Latin America.

fife (**fife**) ***noun*** A small instrument, similar to a flute, that has a high pitch and is often played with drums in a band.

fifth (**fifth**)
1. ***adjective*** That which comes after fourth and before sixth.
2. ***noun*** One part of something that has been divided into five equal parts, written $\frac{1}{5}$.

fig (**fig**) ***noun*** A small, sweet fruit with tiny seeds, often eaten dried.

fight (**fite**)
1. ***noun*** A battle between animals, persons, or groups in which each side tries to hurt the other. ▸ ***verb*** **fight**
2. ***verb*** To have an argument or a quarrel. ▸ **fighting, fought** (**fawt**) ▸ ***noun*** **fight**
3. ***noun*** A hard struggle to gain a goal. ▸ ***noun*** **fighter**

fig•ure (**fig**-yur)
1. ***noun*** A written number.
2. **figures** ***noun, plural*** Arithmetic.
3. ***noun*** An amount given in numbers, as in *a population figure.*
4. ***noun*** A shape or an outline.
5. ***noun*** A person's shape.
6. ***noun*** A well-known person, as in *a public figure.*
7. **figure out** ***verb*** To understand or solve something. ▸ **figuring, figured**

fig•ure•head (**fig**-yur-*hed*) ***noun***
1. Someone who holds an important position or office but has no real power.
2. A carved statue found on the bow of a ship.

figure of speech ***noun*** An expression, such as a metaphor, in which words are used in a poetic way. Authors often use figures of speech to make their writing more colorful. "He is as strong as an ox" is a figure of speech that means "He is very strong." ▸ ***noun, plural*** **figures of speech**

fil•a•ment (**fil**-uh-muhnt) ***noun*** A very fine wire or thread. In a lightbulb, the filament is a fine thread of tungsten that glows and produces light.

file (**file**)
1. ***noun*** A box or folder for papers or documents.
2. ***verb*** To put papers or documents away in a file. ▸ **filing, filed**
3. ***noun*** A tool used to make things smooth. ▸ ***verb*** **file**
4. ***noun*** A set of data held in a computer.
5. ***noun*** A line of people one behind the other.

fill (**fil**) ***verb***
1. To make or become full.
2. To take up the whole space of.
3. To stop or plug up, as in *to fill a hole.*
4. If you **fill in** a form, you answer all the questions on it.
5. If you **fill in** for someone, you do the person's job while he or she is away.
▸ ***verb*** **filling, filled**

fil•let (fil-**ay** *or* **fil**-ay) ***noun*** A piece of meat or fish with the bones taken out. ▸ ***verb*** **fillet**

fill•ing (**fil**-ing) ***noun***
1. A substance that a dentist puts into holes in your teeth to prevent more decay.
2. The food inside a sandwich, pie, cake, etc.

fil•ly (**fil**-ee) ***noun*** A young female horse. ▸ ***noun, plural*** **fillies**

F

F

film (**film**)
1. ***noun*** A very thin layer of something, as in *a film of dirt.*
2. ***noun*** A roll of thin plastic that you put in a camera so you can take photographs or motion pictures.
3. ***verb*** To record something with a camera or a camcorder. ▸ **filming, filmed**
4. ***noun*** A movie.

fil·ter (**fil**-tur)
1. ***noun*** A device that cleans liquids or gases as they pass through it.
2. ***verb*** To put something through a filter.
3. ***verb*** To go through very slowly or sparsely.
▸ ***verb*** **filtering, filtered**

filth (**filth**) ***noun***
1. Dirt.
2. Foul or obscene language.
▸ ***noun*** **filthiness** ▸ ***adjective*** **filthy**

fin (**fin**) ***noun***
1. A part on the body of a fish shaped like a flap that is used for moving and steering through the water.
2. A small, triangular structure on an airplane, boat, etc., used to help with steering.
3. One of two long, flat attachments worn on the feet to help you swim underwater.

fi·nal (**fye**-nuhl)
1. ***adjective*** Last. ▸ ***adverb*** **finally**
2. ***adjective*** Not to be changed or discussed.
3. ***noun*** The last and usually most important examination in a school term.

fi·na·le (fuh-**nal**-ee) ***noun*** The last part of a show or piece of music.

fi·nal·ist (**fye**-nuh-list) ***noun*** Someone who has reached the last part of a competition.

fi·nal·ize (**fye**-nuh-lize) ***verb*** To finish making arrangements. ▸ **finalizing, finalized**

fi·nance (fuh-**nanss** *or* **fye**-nanss)
1. ***noun*** The management and use of money by businesses, banks, and governments. ▸ ***adjective*** **financial** ▸ ***adverb*** **financially**
2. ***verb*** To provide money for something. ▸ **financing, financed**
3. **finances** ***noun, plural*** The amount of money that an individual or a company has.

finch (**finch**) ***noun*** A small songbird with a strong, thick bill used for cracking seeds. ▸ ***noun, plural*** **finches**

find (**finde**)
1. ***verb*** To discover or come across something.
2. ***verb*** To come to and state a decision.
3. **find out** ***verb*** To learn about something or someone.
4. ***noun*** A valuable or important discovery.
▸ ***verb*** **finding, found** (**found**)

finding ***noun*** One of the results of an investigation or a study.

fine (**fine**)
1. ***adjective*** Very good or excellent, as in *a fine painting.*
2. ***adjective*** Not cloudy or rainy, as in *a fine day.*
3. ***adjective*** Thin or delicate.
4. ***noun*** A sum of money paid as a punishment for doing something wrong. ▸ ***verb*** **fine**
▸ ***noun*** **fineness** ▸ ***adjective*** **finer, finest**

fin·ger (**fing**-gur)
1. ***noun*** One of the long parts of your hands that you can move.
2. ***verb*** To touch something lightly with your fingers. ▸ **fingering, fingered**

fin·ger·nail (**fing**-gur-*nale*) ***noun*** The hard layer of material at the tip of each finger.

fin·ger·print (**fing**-gur-*print*) ***noun*** The print made by the pattern of curved ridges on the tips of your fingers.

fin·ick·y (**fin**-uh-kee) ***adjective*** Fussy, especially about food, as in *a finicky eater.*

F

fin•ish (**fin**-ish)
1. ***verb*** To end or complete something.
▸ **finishes, finishing, finished**
2. ***noun*** The end of something, such as a race.
3. ***noun*** A coating on the surface of metal, wood, etc. ▸ ***verb*** **finish**
▸ ***noun, plural*** **finishes**

fi•nite (**fye**-nite) ***adjective*** Limited, or with an end.

fiord (**fyord**) ***noun*** *See* **fjord.**

fir (**fur**) ***noun*** A pointed evergreen tree with thin, flat needles and cones that grow erect on the branches. **Fir** sounds like **fur.**

fire (**fire**)
1. ***noun*** Flames, heat, and light produced by burning.
2. ***verb*** To shoot a gun or other weapon.
▸ ***noun*** **fire**
3. ***noun*** Strong emotion.
4. ***verb*** To dismiss someone from his or her job.
▸ ***verb*** **firing, fired**

fire•arm (**fire**-*arm*) ***noun*** A weapon that shoots bullets. Rifles, pistols, and shotguns are firearms.

fire•crack•er (**fire**-*krak*-ur) ***noun*** A paper tube containing gunpowder and a fuse. Firecrackers make a loud popping noise when they explode.

fire engine ***noun*** A large truck that carries powerful pumps, hoses, ladders, and firefighters to a fire.

fire escape ***noun*** A set of metal stairs on the outside of a building, designed to allow people to escape in case of fire.

fire extinguisher ***noun*** A metal container with chemicals and water inside it that you use to put out a fire.

fire•fight•er (**fire**-*fite*-ur) ***noun*** Someone who is trained to put out fires.

fire•fly (**fire**-*flye*) ***noun*** A small beetle that flies at night and gives off flashes of chemically produced light from the rear part of its body. Also called **lightning bug.** ▸ ***noun, plural*** **fireflies**

fire•house (**fire**-*houss*) ***noun*** A building where fire engines are kept and where firefighters wait until they are needed to put out fires.

fire•man (**fire**-muhn) ***noun*** A male firefighter. ▸ ***noun, plural*** **firemen**

fire•place (**fire**-*playss*) ***noun*** A structure, usually made of brick or stone, in which a fire can burn safely.

fire•proof (**fire**-*proof*) ***adjective*** If something is **fireproof,** it is made from material that will not burn easily.

fire•side (**fire**-*side*) ***noun*** The area around a fireplace.

fire station ***noun*** Another term for **firehouse.**

fire•trap (**fire**-*trap*) ***noun*** A building that is likely to catch on fire, or one that would be hard to escape from if it caught fire.

fire•wood (**fire**-*wud*) ***noun*** Logs or other pieces of wood that are burned as fuel.

fire•works (**fire**-*wurks*) ***noun, plural*** Devices that make very loud noises and colorful lights when they are burned or exploded.

firm (**furm**)
1. ***adjective*** Strong and solid, as in *a firm mattress.*
2. ***adjective*** Definite and not easily changed, as in *a firm belief.*
3. ***adjective*** Steady, as in *a firm voice.*
4. ***noun*** A business or a company.
▸ ***adjective*** **firmer, firmest** ▸ ***adverb*** **firmly**

first (**furst**)
1. ***adjective*** That which comes before second.
2. ***noun*** A person or thing that acts or happens earliest.
3. ***adjective*** Earliest in time.
4. ***adverb*** Before something else.
5. ***adjective*** Best, or most important, as in *the first team.*

first aid ***noun*** Emergency care given to an injured or sick person before he or she is examined by a doctor.

F

first class
1. ***noun*** The most expensive level of service offered to travelers on trains, ships, and airplanes.
2. ***noun*** A level of mail service used for letters, postcards, and bills that usually is faster than other levels of service, except for express delivery.
3. **first-class *adjective*** Of the highest quality.
▸ ***adjective* first-class** ▸ ***adverb* first-class**

first·hand (**furst-hand**) ***adjective*** Direct from the original source. ▸ ***adverb* firsthand**

first-rate ***adjective*** Excellent.

fish (**fish**)
1. ***noun*** A cold-blooded animal that lives in water and has scales, fins, and gills.
▸ ***noun, plural* fish** *or* **fishes**
2. ***verb*** To try to catch fish. ▸ ***noun* fishing**
3. ***verb*** If you **fish** for information, you try to discover something in a sly or indirect way.
▸ ***verb* fishes, fishing, fished**

fish·er·man (**fish**-ur-muhn) ***noun*** Someone who catches fish for a job or as a sport. ▸ ***noun, plural* fishermen**

fish·er·y (**fish**-ur-ee) ***noun***
1. A place where fish are bred commercially.
2. A place where fish are caught.
▸ ***noun, plural* fisheries**

fishing rod ***noun*** A long, flexible pole used with a hook, line, and reel to catch fish.

fish·y (**fish**-ee) ***adjective***
1. Tasting or smelling of fish.
2. *(informal)* Unlikely or suspicious, as in *a fishy story.*
▸ ***adjective* fishier, fishiest**

fis·sion (**fish**-uhn) ***noun***
1. The act of splitting into parts, as in *cell fission.*
2. **nuclear fission *noun*** The splitting of the nucleus of an atom, which creates energy.

fist (**fist**) ***noun*** A tightly closed hand.

fit (**fit**)
1. ***verb*** To be the right size or shape.
2. ***verb*** To be right for, as in *fit for a king.*
3. ***adjective*** Healthy and strong. ▸ ***noun* fitness**
4. ***noun*** A sudden attack of something that cannot be controlled, as in *a fit of giggles.*
5. ***adjective*** Good enough, as in *fit to eat.*
▸ ***verb* fitting, fitted,** *or* **fit** ▸ ***adjective* fitter, fittest**

fit·ting (**fit**-ing)
1. ***adjective*** Right or suitable.
2. ***noun*** A small metal or plastic part that connects things, as in *pipe fittings.*

five (**five**) ***noun*** The whole number, written 5, that comes after four and before six. ▸ ***adjective* five**

fix (**fiks**)
1. ***verb*** To repair something.
2. ***verb*** To decide on something.
3. ***verb*** To get something ready to eat.
4. ***verb*** To place or fasten firmly.
5. ***noun*** If you are in a **fix,** you are in an awkward or difficult situation. ▸ ***noun, plural* fixes**
▸ ***verb* fixes, fixing, fixed**

fix·a·tion (fik-**say**-shuhn) ***noun*** An overly strong attachment to a person, idea, or thing. ▸ ***verb* fixate** (**fik**-sate)

fix·ture (**fiks**-chur) ***noun*** Something that is fixed firmly and permanently in place.

fizz (**fiz**) ***verb*** To bubble and hiss.
▸ **fizzes, fizzing, fizzed** ▸ ***adjective* fizzy**

fiz·zle (**fiz**-uhl) ***verb***
1. To make a hissing or sputtering sound.
2. *(informal)* To fail or die out, especially after a good start.
▸ ***verb* fizzling, fizzled**

fjord (**fyord**) ***noun*** A long, narrow inlet of the ocean between high cliffs. Fjords were formed by glaciers during the Ice Age.

flab (**flab**) ***noun*** Extra fat on your body.
▸ ***noun* flabbiness** ▸ ***adjective* flabby**

flab•ber•gast•ed (**flab**-ur-*gass*-tid) ***adjective*** *(informal)* Stunned and surprised.

flac•cid (**flass**-id *or* **flak**-sid) ***adjective*** Soft and limp, as in *flaccid muscles.*

flag (**flag**)
1. ***noun*** A piece of cloth with a pattern on it that is a symbol of a country, an organization, etc.
2. ***verb*** To stop, or to signal. ▸ **flagging, flagged**

Flag Day ***noun*** A holiday that celebrates the day in 1777 when the Stars and Stripes became the official flag of the United States. It is celebrated on June 14.

flag•pole (**flag**-*pohl*) ***noun*** A tall pole made of wood or metal for raising and flying a flag.

flair (**flair**) ***noun*** Natural skill or ability. **Flair** sounds like **flare.**

flak (**flak**) ***noun***
1. Shots fired against aircraft.
2. *(informal)* Opposition and criticism.

flake (**flayk**)
1. ***noun*** A small, thin piece of something. ▸ ***adjective*** **flaky**
2. ***verb*** If something **flakes,** small, thin pieces of it peel off. ▸ **flaking, flaked**

flam•boy•ant (flam-**boi**-uhnt) ***adjective*** Bold, showy, or brightly colored, as in *a flamboyant shirt.*

flame (**flaym**)
1. ***noun*** A tongue of heat and light given off by a fire. ▸ ***adjective*** **flaming**
2. **flame-colored** ***adjective*** Deep orange-red.

fla•min•go (fluh-**ming**-goh) ***noun*** A pink bird with a long neck, long legs, and webbed feet. ▸ ***noun, plural*** **flamingos** *or* **flamingoes**

flam•ma•ble (**flam**-uh-buhl) ***adjective*** Likely to catch fire.

flank (**flangk**)
1. ***noun*** The side of an animal, between its ribs and hips.
2. ***verb*** To guard or be at the side of something or someone. ▸ **flanking, flanked**
3. ***noun*** The far left or right side of a group of soldiers, a fort, or a naval fleet.

flan•nel (**flan**-uhl) ***noun*** A soft, woven cloth, usually made of cotton or wool.

flap (**flap**)
1. ***verb*** To move up and down.
2. ***verb*** To swing loosely.
3. ***noun*** A hanging part attached on the side of something, as in *the flap of an envelope.*
4. ***noun*** A hinged part on an airplane wing, used to control the way the plane rises and falls.
▸ ***verb*** **flapping, flapped**

flap•jack (**flap**-*jak*) ***noun*** A pancake.

flare (**flair**) ***verb***
1. To burn with a sudden, very bright light.
2. To break out in sudden or violent feeling.
3. To spread out in a bell shape at the bottom.
4. If something **flares up,** it suddenly becomes stronger or more violent.
Flare sounds like **flair.**
▸ ***verb*** **flaring, flared**

flash (**flash**)
1. ***noun*** A short burst of light, as in *a flash of lightning.*
2. ***noun*** A very brief period of time.
3. ***verb*** To move rapidly. ▸ **flashes, flashing, flashed**
4. ***noun*** A sudden outburst, as in *a flash of anger.*
5. ***noun*** A brief report of very recent or important news.
▸ ***noun, plural*** **flashes**

flash•back (**flash**-*bak*) ***noun***
1. A part of a book or movie that tells you what happened earlier in the story.
2. A sudden memory of something that happened and was forgotten.

flash•light (**flash**-*lite*) ***noun*** A portable light that is powered by a battery.

flash•y (**flash**-ee) ***adjective*** If something is **flashy,** it is showy and very bright. ▸ **flashier, flashiest**

flask (**flask**) ***noun***
1. A small, flat bottle made to be carried in the pocket.
2. A bottle with a narrow neck used in science laboratories.

F

flat (**flat**) ***adjective***
1. Smooth and even, as in *flat land.*
2. Lying or stretched at full length.
3. Not very deep or thick, as in *a flat tray.*
4. Very definite, as in *a flat refusal.*
5. Emptied of air, as in *a flat tire.*
6. Dull or lifeless, as in *a flat performance.*
7. In music, a **flat** note is lower in pitch than the usual note.
8. In a musical score, a **flat** sign shows that the next note is flat.
▸ ***adjective*** **flatter, flattest** ▸ ***noun*** **flat** ▸ ***verb*** **flatten**

flat•bed (**flat**-*bed*) ***noun*** A truck with a large, flat cargo area in the back, designed to carry a heavy load.

flat•car (**flat**-*kar*) ***noun*** A railroad car that has no roof or sides and is used to carry freight.

flat•fish (**flat**-*fish*) ***noun*** A fish with a flat body and both eyes on its upper side, such as halibut, sole, or flounder. ▸ ***noun, plural*** **flatfish** *or* **flatfishes**

flat•ter (**flat**-ur)
1. ***verb*** To praise too much or insincerely, especially when you want a favor. ▸ **flattering, flattered** ▸ ***noun*** **flatterer,** ***noun*** **flattery**
2. ***adjective*** If something, such as a piece of clothing, is **flattering,** it makes you look good.

flaunt (**flawnt**) ***verb*** To show off in order to impress others. ▸ **flaunting, flaunted**

fla•vor (**flay**-vur)
1. ***noun*** Taste. ▸ ***adjective*** **flavored,** ***adjective*** **flavorless**
2. ***verb*** To add taste to food.
▸ **flavoring, flavored** ▸ ***noun*** **flavoring**

flaw (**flaw**) ***noun*** A fault or a weakness.
▸ ***adjective*** **flawed,** ***adjective*** **flawless**

flax (**flaks**) ***noun***
1. A plant with blue flowers and long leaves that produces oil and fiber.
2. The fiber of the flax, which can be woven into thread that is used to make linen.

flea (**flee**) ***noun***
1. A small, wingless insect that lives on the blood of people and other animals.
2. flea market An indoor or outdoor market selling old clothes and other secondhand items.
Flea sounds like **flee.**

fleck (**flek**) ***noun*** A spot or tiny patch of something. ▸ ***adjective*** **flecked**

fledg•ling (**flej**-ling) ***noun*** A young bird.

flee (**flee**) ***verb*** To run away from danger. **Flee** sounds like **flea.** ▸ **fleeing, fled** (**fled**)

fleece (**fleess**)
1. ***noun*** A sheep's woolly coat.
▸ ***adjective*** **fleecy**
2. ***verb*** To rob someone, especially in a tricky way. ▸ **fleecing, fleeced**

fleet (**fleet**)
1. ***noun*** A group of warships under one command.
2. ***noun*** A number of ships, planes, or cars that form a group, as in *a fleet of taxis.*
3. ***adjective*** Swift or fast.

fleet•ing (**fleet**-ing) ***adjective*** Not lasting long, as in *a fleeting glance.*
▸ ***adverb*** **fleetingly**

flesh (**flesh**) ***noun***
1. The soft part of your body that covers your bones. Flesh is made up of fat and muscle.
2. The meat of an animal, or the part of a fruit or vegetable that you can eat.
▸ ***adjective*** **fleshy**

flex (**fleks**) ***verb*** To bend or stretch something. ▸ **flexes, flexing, flexed**

flex•i•ble (**flek**-suh-buhl) ***adjective***
1. Able to bend.
2. Able to change.
▸ ***noun*** **flexibility** ▸ ***adverb*** **flexibly**

flex•time (**fleks**-*time*) ***noun*** A system of adjusting the hours of work so that employees may select their own starting and finishing times.

F

flick (**flik**) ***verb*** To move with a quick, sudden movement. ▸ **flicking, flicked** ▸ ***noun*** **flick**

flick•er (**flik**-ur) ***verb*** If something **flickers,** it moves unsteadily. ▸ **flickering, flickered** ▸ ***noun*** **flicker**

flight (**flite**) ***noun***
1. The act or manner of flying, or the ability to fly.
2. A journey by aircraft.
3. A set of stairs or steps between floors or landings of a building.
4. If you **take flight,** you run away.

flight attendant ***noun*** Someone who helps passengers and serves food and beverages on an airplane.

flim•sy (**flim**-zee) ***adjective*** Thin, or weak, as in *flimsy material.* ▸ **flimsier, flimsiest** ▸ ***noun*** **flimsiness** ▸ ***adverb*** **flimsily**

flinch (**flinch**) ***verb*** To make a quick movement away from the source of a pain or fear. ▸ **flinches, flinching, flinched** ▸ ***noun*** **flinch**

fling (**fling**) ***verb*** To throw something violently. ▸ **flinging, flung** (**fluhng**)

flint (**flint**) ***noun*** A very hard, gray stone that makes sparks when steel is struck against it.

flip (**flip**)
1. ***verb*** To toss or move something quickly.
2. ***noun*** A somersault.
3. ***verb*** *(informal)* If someone **flips,** he or she suddenly becomes angry or delighted.
▸ ***verb*** **flipping, flipped**

flip•pant (**flip**-uhnt) ***adjective*** Lacking respect or seriousness, as in *a flippant comment.* ▸ ***noun*** **flippancy** ▸ ***adverb*** **flippantly**

flip•per (**flip**-ur) ***noun***
1. One of the broad, flat limbs of a sea creature such as a seal or a dolphin that help it swim.
2. One of the two long, flat rubber attachments that you wear on your feet to help you swim.

flirt (**flurt**) ***verb***
1. If you **flirt** with someone, you play at being in love with that person. ▸ ***noun*** **flirt**
2. If you **flirt** with an idea, you consider it, but not very seriously.
▸ ***verb*** **flirting, flirted**

float (**floht**)
1. ***verb*** To rest on water or air.
2. ***verb*** To move lightly and easily.
3. ***noun*** A small floating object attached to the end of a fishing line that holds the line up.
4. ***noun*** A decorated truck or flat platform that forms part of a parade.
▸ ***verb*** **floating, floated**

flock (**flok**)
1. ***noun*** A group of animals of one kind that live, travel, or feed together.
2. ***verb*** To gather in a crowd. ▸ **flocking, flocked**

flog (**flog**) ***verb*** To beat with a whip or a stick. ▸ **flogging, flogged** ▸ ***noun*** **flogging**

flood (**fluhd**) ***verb***
1. When something, such as a river, **floods,** it overflows with water beyond its normal limits.
2. To overwhelm, or to come in large amounts.
▸ ***verb*** **flooding, flooded** ▸ ***noun*** **flood**

flood•light (**fluhd**-*lite*) ***noun*** A lamp that produces a broad and very bright beam of light.

flood plain ***noun*** An area of low land near a stream or river that becomes flooded during heavy rains.

floor (**flor**)
1. ***noun*** The flat surface that you walk or stand on inside a building. ▸ ***noun*** **flooring**
2. ***noun*** A story in a building.
3. ***verb*** *(informal)* To surprise.
▸ **flooring, floored**

flop (**flop**) ***verb***
1. To fall or drop heavily.
2. To flap or move about. ▸ ***adjective*** **floppy**
3. *(informal)* To fail. ▸ ***noun*** **flop**
▸ ***verb*** **flopping, flopped**

F

floppy disk ***noun*** A small, thin piece of flexible plastic coated with magnetic particles used for storing information from a computer.

flo•ra (**flor**-uh) ***noun*** The plant life of a particular area, as in *desert flora.*

flo•ral (**flor**-uhl) ***adjective*** Of, relating to, or showing flowers, as in *a floral arrangement* or *floral curtains.*

flo•rist (**flor**-ist) ***noun*** Someone who sells flowers and plants.

floss (**flawss** *or* **floss**) ***noun*** A thin strand of thread used to clean between the teeth. Also called *dental floss.*

flot•sam (**flot**-suhm) ***noun*** Objects from a shipwreck that float in the sea or are washed up on the shore.

floun•der (**floun**-dur)
1. ***verb*** To struggle through water, snow, mud, etc.
2. ***verb*** To have difficulties coping with something.
3. ***noun*** A flat ocean fish used for food.
▸ ***verb*** **floundering, floundered**

flour (**flou**-ur) ***noun*** Ground wheat or other grain that you use for baking. **Flour** sounds like **flower.** ▸ ***adjective*** **floury**

flour•ish (**flur**-ish) ***verb***
1. To grow and succeed.
2. To wave something around in order to show it off. ▸ ***noun*** **flourish**
▸ ***verb*** **flourishes, flourishing, flourished**

flout (**flout**) ***verb*** If you **flout** the rules, you break them deliberately. ▸ **flouting, flouted**

flow (**floh**) ***verb*** To move along smoothly, like a river. ▸ **flowing, flowed**
▸ ***noun*** **flow**

flow•chart (**floh**-*chart*) ***noun*** A diagram that shows how something develops and progresses, step by step.

flow•er (**flou**-ur)
1. ***noun*** The colored part of a plant that produces seeds or fruit.
2. ***verb*** To produce flowers. ▸ **flowering, flowered**
3. ***noun*** A plant that has flowers.
Flour sounds like **flower.**

flu (**floo**) ***noun*** An illness that is like a bad cold, with fever and muscle pains. Flu is short for influenza. It is caused by a virus.

fluc•tu•ate (**fluhk**-choo-ate) ***verb*** To change back and forth or up and down.
▸ **fluctuating, fluctuated** ▸ ***noun*** **fluctuation**

flue (**floo**) ***noun*** A hollow part or passage, such as the pipe inside a chimney that carries smoke away from a fire.

flu•ent (**floo**-uhnt) ***adjective*** Able to speak smoothly and clearly, especially in another language. ▸ ***noun*** **fluency**
▸ ***adverb*** **fluently**

fluff (**fluhf**)
1. ***noun*** A light, soft, downy substance.
2. ***verb*** When a bird **fluffs** its feathers, it shakes them out.
3. ***verb*** To make a mistake in speaking or reading something.
▸ ***verb*** **fluffing, fluffed**

fluff•y (**fluhf**-ee) ***adjective***
1. Light and airy, as in *a fluffy pillow.*
2. Covered with soft, fine hair or feathers, as in *a fluffy rabbit.*
▸ ***adjective*** **fluffier, fluffiest**

flu•id (**floo**-id)
1. ***noun*** A flowing substance, either a liquid or a gas.
2. ***adjective*** Flowing, or liquid. ▸ ***noun*** **fluidity**

fluke (**flook**) ***noun***
1. A lucky accident.
2. Part of the tail of a sea creature such as a whale or dolphin.

fluo•res•cent (flu-**ress**-uhnt) ***adjective***
1. Giving out a bright light by using a certain type of energy, such as ultraviolet light or X rays, as in *fluorescent lighting.*
▸ ***noun*** **fluorescence**
2. A **fluorescent** color is so bright that it seems to give out light when a light is shone on it.

fluor•i•date (**flawr**-uh-date) ***verb*** To add fluoride in order to fight decay in teeth. ▸ **fluoridating, fluoridated**

fluor•ide (**flawr**-ide) ***noun*** A chemical compound put in toothpaste and water to prevent tooth decay.

fluo•rine (**flawr**-een) ***noun*** A green or yellow gaseous element that easily combines with other elements to form compounds.

flur•ry (**flur**-ee) ***noun***
1. A confusion or a commotion, as in *a flurry of activity.*
2. A brief snow shower.
▸ ***noun, plural*** **flurries**

flush (**fluhsh**)
1. ***verb*** To turn red or to blush.
2. ***verb*** To flood something with water as a way of cleaning it. ▸ ***noun*** **flush**
3. ***adjective*** Exactly even.
▸ ***verb*** **flushes, flushing, flushed**

flushed (**fluhsht**) ***adjective*** If you are **flushed,** your face has become red.
▸ ***noun*** **flush**

flus•ter (**fluhss**-tur) ***verb*** To confuse or rush someone. ▸ **flustering, flustered**

flute (**floot**) ***noun*** A long, cylindrical musical instrument played by blowing air across a hole at one end and fingering keys to change notes.

flut•ter (**fluht**-ur)
1. ***verb*** To wave or flap rapidly.
▸ **fluttering, fluttered**
2. ***noun*** If you are in a **flutter** about something, you are excited and nervous about it.

fly (**flye**)
1. ***verb*** To travel through the air.
2. ***noun*** An insect with two wings.
3. ***noun*** A flap on trousers covering a zipper or buttons.
4. ***verb*** To move or pass quickly.
5. ***noun*** A baseball hit high in the air.
▸ ***noun, plural*** **flies** ▸ ***verb*** **flies, flying, flew** (**floo**), **flown** (**flohn**)

fly•catch•er (**flye**-*kach*-ur) ***noun*** A songbird that feeds on insects caught in the air.

fly fishing ***noun*** A type of fishing using fake flies made from fur, feathers, etc., attached to a hook that the fish swallows.

flying fish ***noun*** A type of fish with large fins that spread open like wings, allowing it to jump out of the water and glide in the air for a short time.

flying saucer ***noun*** Any of various flying objects shaped like disks, reportedly seen by some people and believed to be spacecraft from other planets.

foal (**fohl**)
1. ***noun*** A young horse, donkey, or zebra.
2. ***verb*** To give birth to a young horse or similar animal. ▸ **foaling, foaled**

foam (**fohm**)
1. ***noun*** A mass of small bubbles.
2. ***verb*** To make bubbles. ▸ **foaming, foamed**

foam rubber ***noun*** A soft, spongy material often used to stuff toys and furniture.

fo•cus (**foh**-kuhss)
1. ***noun*** The point where rays of light meet after being bent by a lens. ▸ ***verb*** **focus**
2. ***verb*** To adjust your eyes or a camera lens so that you can see something clearly.
3. ***verb*** To concentrate on something or somebody.
4. ***noun*** The center of activity, interest, or attention.
▸ ***noun, plural*** **focuses** *or* **foci** (**foh**-*sye*)
▸ ***verb*** **focuses, focusing, focused**
▸ ***adjective*** **focal**

fod•der (**fod**-ur) ***noun*** Food for cattle and horses.

foe (**foh**) ***noun*** An enemy.

fog (**fog** *or* **fawg**) ***noun***
1. A very thick mist of water vapor in the air.
2. A daze or a state of confusion.
▸ ***verb*** **fog, fogging, fogged**
▸ ***adjective*** **foggy**

fog•horn (**fog**-*horn*) ***noun*** A loud horn used to warn ships in foggy weather.

F

F

foil (**foil**)
1. ***noun*** Thin, silvery sheets of metal.
2. ***verb*** To prevent someone from doing something. ▸ **foiling, foiled**
3. ***noun*** A long, thin sword used in fencing.

fold (**fohld**)
1. ***verb*** To bend something over on itself.
2. ***noun*** A line or crease made by folding.
3. ***verb*** To bring together, or to bend close to the body, as in *to fold one's arms.*
4. ***noun*** A small, enclosed area for sheep.
5. ***verb*** If a company **folds,** it collapses.
▸ ***verb*** **folding, folded**

fold•er (**fohl**-dur) ***noun*** A cardboard holder used for keeping papers.

fo•li•age (**foh**-lee-ij) ***noun*** Leaves.

folk (**fohk**)
1. ***noun*** People. ▸ ***noun, plural*** **folk** *or* **folks**
2. folks ***noun, plural*** Family members, especially parents.
3. ***adjective*** Traditional and belonging to ordinary people, as in *folk music.*

folk dance ***noun*** A kind of dance that is native to a particular area or group.

folk•lore (**fohk**-*lor*) ***noun*** The stories, customs, and beliefs of ordinary people that are passed down to their children.

folk music ***noun*** Traditional music of an area that is often handed down from one generation to the next.

folk singer ***noun*** Someone who sings folk music.

folk song ***noun*** A traditional song with music and words, usually with a simple melody.

folk•tale (**fohk**-*tale*) ***noun*** A story that is passed down orally from generation to generation.

fol•low (**fol**-oh) ***verb***
1. To be guided by someone or something.
2. To go behind someone.
3. To come after.
4. To obey, as in *to follow orders.*
5. If you **follow up** on something, you return to something that you started.
▸ ***verb*** **following, followed** ▸ ***noun*** **follower**

following
1. ***preposition*** Next, after, or coming after.
2. ***adjective*** Next in time or order of occurrence, as in *the following year.*
3. ***noun*** If someone has a **following,** the person has many supporters or admirers.

fol•ly (**fol**-ee) ***noun*** Foolishness. ▸ ***noun, plural*** **follies**

fond (**fond**) ***adjective*** If you are **fond** of something, you like it very much.
▸ **fonder, fondest** ▸ ***noun*** **fondness**
▸ ***adverb*** **fondly**

fon•dle (**fon**-duhl) ***verb*** To touch or stroke lovingly or tenderly. ▸ **fondling, fondled**

font (**font**) ***noun***
1. A large, stone bowl used in a church to hold the water for baptisms.
2. A set of type of one size and style.

food (**food**) ***noun*** Substances that people, animals, and plants eat to stay alive and grow.

food chain ***noun*** An ordered arrangement of animals and plants in which each feeds on the one below it in the chain.

food pro•ces•sor (**pross**-ess-ur) ***noun*** A machine that cuts up, purees, or liquefies food.

food web ***noun*** The complex network of food chains in an ecosystem.

fool (**fool**)
1. ***noun*** A person who lacks good sense.
2. ***verb*** To trick someone. ▸ **fooling, fooled**

fool•ish (**fool**-ish) ***adjective*** Not showing good sense; not wise. ▸ ***noun*** **foolishness**

fool•proof (**fool**-*proof*) ***adjective*** Something that is **foolproof** is very simple to use and cannot easily go wrong.

foot (**fut**) ***noun***
1. The part of your body at the end of your leg.

2. The bottom or lower end of something, as in *the foot of the bed.*
3. A unit of length that equals 12 inches.
4. If you **put your foot down,** you insist on something and act firmly.
▸ ***noun, plural* feet (feet)**

foot•ball (**fut**-*bal*) ***noun***
1. A game played by two teams of 11 players each on a long field with goals at each end. Each team tries to score points by getting the ball across the opponent's goal line.
2. The ball used in this game.

foot•hill (**fut**-*hil*) ***noun*** A low hill at the base of a mountain or mountain range.

foot•ing (**fut**-ing) ***noun***
1. A secure place on which to stand.
2. In architecture, the **footing** of a building is the bottom of its foundation.

foot•lights (**fut**-*lites*) ***noun, plural*** Lights arranged along the front floor of a stage that allow the audience to see the actors.

foot•note (**fut**-*noht*) ***noun*** A note at the bottom of a page that explains something in the text.

foot•print (**fut**-*print*) ***noun*** A mark made by a foot or shoe.

foot•step (**fut**-*step*) ***noun***
1. The act of placing the foot on the ground or floor.
2. The sound that the foot makes when it hits the ground or floor.

for (**for**)
1. ***preposition*** Intended to be used on or with. *These markers are for posters.*
2. ***preposition*** Meeting the needs of. *I take vitamins for my health.*
3. ***preposition*** Over the time or distance of. *We marched for miles.*
4. ***preposition*** Due to. *She has to travel for her job.*
5. ***preposition*** In honor of, or on behalf of. *He picked the flowers for me.*
6. ***preposition*** Worth the amount of. *I bought a pack of gum for 50 cents.*
7. ***preposition*** Intended for, or sent to. *This is for you.*
8. ***preposition*** In place of. *In the recipe, we substituted honey for sugar.*
9. ***conjunction*** Because. *We must rejoice, for life is good.*

for•age (**for**-ij)
1. ***noun*** Hay, grain, and other food for horses, cattle, and similar animals.
2. ***verb*** To go in search of food.
▸ **foraging, foraged**

for•bid (fur-**bid**) ***verb*** To order someone not to do something. ▸ **forbidding, forbade** (fur-**bayd**), **forbidden** (fur-**bid**-in) ▸ ***adjective* forbidden**

for•bid•ding (fur-**bid**-ing) ***adjective*** Looking unfriendly or dangerous.
▸ ***adverb* forbiddingly**

force (**forss**)
1. ***noun*** Strength or power. ▸ ***adjective* forceful** ▸ ***adverb* forcefully**
2. ***verb*** If you **force** someone to do something, you make the person do it.
▸ **forcing, forced**
3. ***noun*** In physics, a **force** is any action that changes the shape or the movement of an object.
4. ***noun*** An army or other team of people who work together, as in *the police force.*

for•ceps (**for**-seps) ***noun, plural*** Tongs used for grasping, holding, or pulling, especially by dentists or surgeons.

ford (**ford**)
1. ***noun*** A shallow part of a stream or river where you can cross.
2. ***verb*** To cross at a ford. ▸ **fording, forded**

fore•arm (**for**-arm) ***noun*** The part of your arm from your wrist to your elbow.

fore•cast (**for**-kast) ***verb*** To say what you think will happen in the future.
▸ **forecasting, forecast** *or* **forecasted**
▸ ***noun* forecast, *noun* forecaster**

fore•fa•ther (**for**-*fah*-THur) ***noun*** An ancestor.

fore•fin•ger (**for**-*fing*-gur) ***noun*** The finger used for pointing; the index finger.

fore•gone (**for**-*gon*) ***adjective*** Decided in advance.

F

fore•ground (**for**-*ground*) ***noun*** The part of a picture that is or seems to be nearest to the person looking at it.

fore•head (**for**-id *or* **for**-hed) ***noun*** The top part of your face between your hair and your eyes.

for•eign (**for**-uhn) ***adjective***
1. To do with or coming from another country. ▸ ***noun*** **foreigner**
2. If something is **foreign** to you, it is strange or unnatural.

fore•leg (**for**-*leg*) ***noun*** One of the front legs of an animal with four legs.

fore•man (**for**-muhn) ***noun***
1. Someone who leads a group of people who work together.
2. The lead man or woman on a jury.
▸ ***noun, plural*** **foremen**

fore•most (**for**-*mohst*) ***adjective*** First in rank, position, or importance.

fo•ren•sic (fuh-**ren**-sik) ***adjective*** Using science to help investigate or solve crimes. A forensic investigation uses fingerprints, blood tests, handwriting analysis, etc.

fore•per•son (**for**-*pur*-suhn) ***noun*** A foreman or a forewoman.

fore•run•ner (**for**-*ruhn*-ur) ***noun***
1. Someone who has come before, such as an ancestor or a predecessor.
2. A sign of something to come.

fore•see (for-**see**) ***verb*** To expect or predict that something will happen.
▸ **foreseeing, foresaw, foreseen**
▸ ***adjective*** **foreseeable**

fore•sight (**for**-*site*) ***noun*** The ability to see into or plan for the future.

for•est (**far**-ist *or* **for**-ist) ***noun*** A large area thickly covered with trees and plants. ▸ ***adjective*** **forested**

forest ranger ***noun*** A person who manages and protects the land in a forest.

fore•tell (for-**tel**) ***verb*** To forecast or predict something. ▸ **foretelling, foretold**

for•ev•er (fur-**ev**-ur) ***adverb***
1. For all time.
2. Always or continually.

fore•wom•an (**for**-wum-an) ***noun***
1. A woman who leads a group of people who work together.
2. The lead woman on a jury.
▸ ***noun, plural*** **forewomen**

for•feit (**for**-fit)
1. ***noun*** A penalty for something not done or badly done.
2. ***verb*** To give up the right to something. ▸ ***noun*** **forfeiture**
▸ **forfeiting, forfeited**

forge (**forj**)
1. ***verb*** To make illegal copies of paintings, money, etc. ▸ ***noun*** **forger,** ***noun*** **forgery**
2. ***verb*** If you **forge ahead,** you move forward or make progress.
3. ***verb*** To make or to form.
4. ***noun*** A blacksmith's shop.
▸ ***verb*** **forging, forged**

for•get (fur-**get**) ***verb*** If you **forget** something, you do not remember it.
▸ **forgetting, forgot, forgotten**
▸ ***noun*** **forgetfulness** ▸ ***adjective*** **forgetful**

forget-me-not ***noun*** A plant with clusters of small, blue flowers, often used as a symbol of friendship.

for•give (fur-**giv**) ***verb*** To pardon someone, or to stop blaming the person for something. ▸ **forgiving, forgave, forgiven** ▸ ***noun*** **forgiveness**
▸ ***adjective*** **forgiving**

fork (**fork**)
1. ***noun*** An instrument with prongs used for eating or for lifting hay.
2. ***noun*** A place where a road, river, tree, etc., branches into two or more directions. ▸ ***verb*** **fork** ▸ ***adjective*** **forked**
3. ***verb*** If you **fork out** for something, you pay for it reluctantly. ▸ **forking, forked**

fork•lift (**fork**-*lift*) ***noun*** A vehicle with two prongs or forks at the front, used for lifting and carrying loads.

for•lorn (for-**lorn**) ***adjective*** Sad or lonely. ▸ ***adverb*** **forlornly**

F

for·mu·late (**for**-myuh-late) ***verb*** If you **formulate** a theory, you work out an idea and then state it clearly.
▸ **formulating, formulated**

form (**form**)
1. ***noun*** Type or kind.
2. ***noun*** Shape. ▸ ***adjective*** **formless**
3. ***verb*** To make up or create something.
4. ***noun*** A piece of paper with questions to be filled in.
5. ***verb*** To make or to organize.
6. ***noun*** In grammar, one of the ways a word appears, depending on how it is used.
▸ ***verb*** **forming, formed**

for·mal (**for**-muhl) ***adjective***
1. Proper and not casual, as in *formal clothes.* ▸ ***noun*** **formal**
2. Official.
▸ ***adverb*** **formally**

for·mat (**for**-mat)
1. ***noun*** The shape or style of something.
2. ***verb*** To prepare a computer disk to be used.
▸ **formatting, formatted**

for·ma·tion (for-**may**-shuhn) ***noun***
1. The process of making something.
2. A pattern or a shape.
3. The way in which the members of a group are arranged.

for·mer (**for**-mur)
1. ***noun*** The first of two things that you have been talking about.
2. ***adjective*** Previous or earlier, as in *my former wife.*

for·mer·ly (**for**-mur-lee) ***adverb*** In the past, or at an earlier time.

for·mi·da·ble (**for**-muh-duh-buhl) ***adjective*** Frightening, as in *a formidable opponent.* ▸ ***adverb*** **formidably**

for·mu·la (**for**-myuh-luh) ***noun***
1. A rule in science or math that is written with numbers and symbols.
2. A suggested set of actions.
3. A liquid substitute for mother's milk.
▸ ***noun, plural*** **formulas** *or* **formulae** (**for**-myuh-lee *or* **for**-myuh-lye)

for·mu·late (**for**-myuh-late) ***verb*** If you **formulate** a theory, you work out an idea and then state it clearly.
▸ **formulating, formulated**

for·sake (for-**sayk**) ***verb*** To give up, leave, or abandon. ▸ **forsaking, forsook** (for-**suk**), **forsaken**

for·sak·en (for-**say**-kuhn) ***adjective*** Abandoned or left, as in *a forsaken building.*

for·syth·i·a (for-**sith**-ee-uh) ***noun*** A bush with brilliant yellow flowers that bloom in the spring.

fort (**fort**) ***noun***
1. A building that is strongly built to survive attacks.
2. If you **hold the fort,** you look after things for someone else while the person is away.

forte
1. (**fort** *or* **for**-tay) ***noun*** Your **forte** is your strong point.
2. (**for**-tay) ***adverb*** **Forte** is the Italian word for loud. It is used in music.

forth (**forth**) ***adverb***
1. Forward, or onward.
2. Out from hiding.
3. Away, or abroad.

forth·com·ing (**forth**-*kum*-ing) ***adjective***
1. Coming soon.
2. If someone is not very **forthcoming,** he or she does not tell the entire truth.

for·ti·fy (**for**-tuh-fye) ***verb***
1. To make a place stronger against attack. ▸ ***noun*** **fortification**
2. If you **fortify** yourself, you make yourself feel better and stronger.
3. To improve or to enrich.
▸ ***verb*** **fortifies, fortifying, fortified**

fort·night (**fort**-*nite*) ***noun*** A period of two weeks. ▸ ***adjective*** **fortnightly**
▸ ***adverb*** **fortnightly**

for·tress (**for**-triss) ***noun*** A place that is strengthened against attack. ▸ ***noun, plural*** **fortresses**

for·tu·nate (**for**-chuh-nit) ***adjective*** Lucky. ▸ ***adverb*** **fortunately**

for·tune (**for**-chuhn) ***noun***
1. Fate or destiny.
2. Chance or good luck.
3. A large amount of money.

F

fo•rum (**for**-uhm) ***noun***
1. The town square of an ancient Roman city.
2. A public discussion of an issue.

for•ward (**for**-wurd)
1. ***adverb*** Toward the front, or ahead. ▸ ***adjective*** **forward** ▸ ***adverb*** **forwards**
2. ***adjective*** Toward the future.
3. ***noun*** A player in basketball, hockey, or soccer who plays in an attacking position and tries to score goals.
4. ***adjective*** Bold or rude.

fos•sil (**foss**-uhl) ***noun*** The remains or traces of an animal or a plant from millions of years ago, preserved as rock. ▸ ***verb*** **fossilize** ▸ ***adjective*** **fossilized**

fossil fuel ***noun*** Coal, oil, or natural gas, formed from the remains of prehistoric plants and animals.

fos•ter (**fawss**-tur *or* **foss**-tur) ***verb***
1. To look after a child who is not your own, without becoming the legal parent. ▸ ***adjective*** **foster**
2. To help the growth and development of.
▸ ***verb*** **fostering, fostered**

foul (**foul**)
1. ***adjective*** Very dirty or disgusting. ▸ ***noun*** **foulness** ▸ ***adverb*** **foully**
2. ***verb*** To make something dirty or unpleasant. ▸ **fouling, fouled**
3. ***adjective*** Cloudy, rainy, or stormy, as in *foul weather*.
4. ***noun*** An action in sports that is against the rules. ▸ ***verb*** **foul**
Foul sounds like **fowl**.
▸ ***adjective*** **fouler, foulest**

foul line ***noun***
1. In baseball, either of the two lines drawn from home plate to first and third bases. A ball hit outside of the foul lines is a *foul ball*.
2. In basketball, the line on either side of the court from which a player shoots a penalty shot.

found (**found**) ***verb*** To set up or start something, such as a school. ▸ **founding, founded** ▸ ***noun*** **founder**

foun•da•tion (foun-**day**-shuhn) ***noun***
1. A solid structure on which a building is built.
2. The base or basis of something.
3. An organization that gives money to worthwhile causes.

found•ry (**foun**-dree) ***noun*** A factory for melting and shaping metal.

foun•tain (**foun**-tuhn) ***noun***
1. A stream or jet of water used for drinking or for decoration.
2. A rich or abundant source.

fountain pen ***noun*** A pen with a point that is supplied with ink from a container inside the pen.

four (**for**) ***noun*** The whole number, written 4, that comes after three and before five. ▸ ***adjective*** **four**

Four-H Club ***noun*** A rural club for young people that teaches community values through farming and other useful skills. The four Hs stand for head, heart, hands, and health.

fourth (**forth**)
1. ***adjective*** That which comes after third and before fifth.
2. ***noun*** One part of something that has been divided into four equal parts, written ¼.

Fourth of July ***noun*** A U.S. holiday that celebrates the signing of the Declaration of Independence on July 4, 1776.

fowl (**foul**) ***noun*** A bird, such as a chicken, turkey, duck, etc., often raised for its eggs or its meat. **Fowl** sounds like **foul**. ▸ ***noun, plural*** **fowl** *or* **fowls**

fox (**foks**) ***noun*** A wild animal related to the dog, with thick fur, a pointed nose and ears, and a bushy tail. ▸ ***noun, plural*** **foxes**

fox•hound (**foks**-*hound*) ***noun*** A breed of dog of medium size trained to hunt foxes.

foy•er (**foi**-ur *or* foi-**ay**) ***noun*** An entrance hall, especially of a theater, an apartment building, or a hotel.

frac•tal (**frak**-tuhl) ***noun*** A shape, often drawn on a computer, that repeats itself in a pattern over and over again.

frac•tion (**frak**-shuhn) ***noun***
1. A part of a whole number. For example, ½, ¾, and ⅞ are all fractions.
2. A part of a whole.
3. A small amount. ▸ ***adjective*** **fractional** ▸ ***adverb*** **fractionally**

frac•ture (**frak**-chur) ***verb*** To break or crack something, especially a bone. ▸ **fracturing, fractured** ▸ ***noun*** **fracture**

frag•ile (**fraj**-il) ***adjective*** Delicate, or easily broken.

frag•ment (**frag**-muhnt) ***noun*** A small piece or a part that is broken off. ▸ ***verb*** **fragment** (frag-**ment**)

fra•grant (**fray**-gruhnt) ***adjective*** Having a sweet smell. ▸ ***noun*** **fragrance**

frail (**frayl**) ***adjective*** Weak. ▸ **frailer, frailest** ▸ ***noun*** **frailty**

frame (**fraym**)
1. ***noun*** A basic structure over which something is built.
2. ***noun*** A border that surrounds and holds something, as in *a picture frame.* ▸ ***verb*** **frame**
3. ***noun*** The way in which a person's body is built.
4. ***verb*** *(informal)* If someone **frames** an innocent person, he or she makes the person seem guilty by giving false information or evidence. ▸ **framing, framed**

frame•work (**fraym**-*wurk*) ***noun*** A structure that gives shape or support to something.

franc (**frangk**) ***noun*** The main unit of money in Switzerland and many African countries. **Franc** sounds like **frank.**

fran•chise (**fran**-chize)
1. ***noun*** The right to vote.
2. ***noun*** Permission given by a company to sell its services or distribute its products in a certain area.
3. ***verb*** To give the right to someone to sell a product or service in a certain area. ▸ **franchising, franchised** ▸ ***noun*** **franchiser**

frank (**frangk**) ***adjective*** Open and honest. **Frank** sounds like **franc.** ▸ **franker, frankest** ▸ ***noun*** **frankness** ▸ ***adverb*** **frankly**

frank•fur•ter (**frangk**-fur-tur) ***noun*** A hot dog or small smoked sausage made of beef, pork, chicken, etc.

fran•tic (**fran**-tik) ***adjective*** Wildly excited by worry or fear. ▸ ***adverb*** **frantically**

fraud (**frawd**) ***noun***
1. If you practice **fraud,** you cheat or trick people. ▸ ***adjective*** **fraudulent** (**fraw**-juh-luhnt) ▸ ***adverb*** **fraudulently**
2. If someone is a **fraud,** the person pretends to be something he or she is not.

fray (**fray**)
1. ***verb*** To unravel. ▸ **fraying, frayed**
2. ***noun*** A noisy quarrel or battle.

freak (**freek**)
1. ***noun*** A person, an animal, or a plant that has not developed normally.
2. ***adjective*** Very odd or unusual, as in *freak weather conditions.*
3. ***noun*** *(informal)* Someone who is very enthusiastic about something, as in *an exercise freak.*
▸ ***adjective*** **freakish**

freck•le (**frek**-uhl) ***noun*** A small, light brown spot on your skin. ▸ ***adjective*** **freckled,** ***adjective*** **freckly**

free (**free**)
1. ***adjective*** If something is **free,** it does not cost anything.
2. ***adjective*** If a person or an animal is **free,** it can do what it likes. ▸ ***adverb*** **freely**
3. ***verb*** If you **free** a person or an animal, you let it go from a prison or cage. ▸ **freeing, freed**
4. ***adjective*** Not held back, as in *a free discussion.*
5. ***adjective*** Not affected by something, as in *free of disease.*
▸ ***adjective*** **freer, freest**

F

free•dom (**free**-duhm) ***noun*** The right to do and say what you like.

free•lance (**free**-lanss) ***adjective*** If you are a **freelance** worker, you do not earn a salary but are paid for each job that you do. ▸ ***noun*** **freelancer**

free-range ***adjective*** **Free-range** animals are allowed to feed and wander freely outside cages or pens.

free•way (**free**-*way*) ***noun*** A wide highway that you can travel on without paying tolls.

freeze (**freez**) ***verb***
1. To become solid or icy at a very low temperature. ▸ ***adjective*** **freezing**
2. To make or become very cold.
3. To stop still because you are frightened.
4. To be damaged or killed from the cold.
5. To keep from rising.

Freeze sounds like **frieze.**
▸ ***verb*** **freezing, froze** (**frohz**), **frozen**

freez•er (**free**-zur) ***noun*** A refrigerator or part of a refrigerator that freezes food quickly and keeps it from spoiling.

freezing point ***noun*** The temperature at which a liquid turns solid or freezes. The freezing point of water is 32 degrees Fahrenheit or 0 degrees Celsius.

freight (**frayt**) ***noun*** Goods or cargo carried by trains, ships, planes, trucks, etc.

freight•er (**fray**-tur) ***noun*** A ship that carries cargo.

French fries ***noun, plural*** Strips of potato that are fried in deep fat or oil.

French horn ***noun*** A brass instrument made of a coiled tube that flares into a bell at the end.

fren•zy (**fren**-zee) ***noun*** If you are in a **frenzy,** you are wildly excited about something. ▸ ***noun, plural*** **frenzies** ▸ ***adjective*** **frenzied**

fre•quen•cy (**free**-kwuhn-see) ***noun***
1. If something happens with **frequency,** it happens again and again.
2. The number of times that something happens.
3. The number of cycles per second of a radio wave.
4. The number of vibrations per second in a light wave.
▸ ***noun, plural*** **frequencies**

fre•quent
1. (**free**-kwent) ***adjective*** Common, or happening often. ▸ ***adverb*** **frequently**
2. (free-**kwent**) ***verb*** To visit somewhere often or regularly. ▸ **frequenting, frequented**

fres•co (**fress**-koh) ***noun*** A painting made on a wall or ceiling while the plaster is still wet. ▸ ***noun, plural*** **frescoes** *or* **frescos**

fresh (**fresh**) ***adjective***
1. Clean or new, as in *a fresh piece of paper.* ▸ ***adverb*** **freshly**
2. Not frozen or canned, as in *fresh fruit.*
3. Cool or refreshing, as in *a fresh sea breeze.*
4. Not salty, as in *fresh water.*
5. Rude.
▸ ***adjective*** **fresher, freshest**

fresh•man (**fresh**-muhn) ***noun*** Someone in the first year of high school or college.

fresh•wa•ter (**fresh**-*wa*-tur) ***adjective*** To do with or living in water that does not contain salt, as in *freshwater fish.* ▸ ***noun*** **freshwater**

fret (**fret**)
1. ***verb*** To worry or get upset about something. ▸ **fretting, fretted** ▸ ***noun*** **fretfulness** ▸ ***adjective*** **fretful** ▸ ***adverb*** **fretfully**
2. ***noun*** One of the bars or ridges on the neck of a stringed musical instrument, such as a guitar.

fric•tion (**frik**-shuhn) ***noun***
1. Rubbing.
2. The force that slows down objects when they rub against each other.
3. Disagreement or anger.

Fri•day (**frye**-*day or* **frye**-dee) ***noun*** The sixth day of the week, after Thursday and before Saturday.

fridge (**frij**) *Short for* **refrigerator.**

friend (**frend**) ***noun***
1. Someone whom you enjoy being with and know well. ▸ ***noun*** **friendship**
2. Someone who supports a group or cause.

friend•ly (**frend**-lee) ***adjective***
1. Kind and helpful.
2. Not angry or hostile, as in *friendly relations between nations.*
▸ ***adjective*** **friendlier, friendliest**
▸ ***noun*** **friendliness**

frieze (**freez**) ***noun*** A decorated or painted strip, usually along the top of a wall. **Frieze** sounds like **freeze.**

fright (**frite**) ***noun*** A sudden feeling of fear.

fright•en (**frite**-uhn) ***verb***
1. To scare someone. ▸ ***adjective*** **frightening**
2. To drive away by scaring.
▸ ***verb*** **frightening, frightened**

fright•ful (**frite**-fuhl) ***adjective*** Terrible or shocking. ▸ ***adverb*** **frightfully**

frig•id (**frij**-id) ***adjective***
1. Extremely cold.
2. Unfriendly.

frill (**fril**) ***noun*** A ruffled strip of material or paper used as decoration. ▸ ***adjective*** **frilly**

fringe (**frinj**)
1. ***noun*** A border of cords or threads attached to something.
2. ***noun*** Any border or edge.
3. ***verb*** To form an edge or a border.
▸ **fringing, fringed**

Fris•bee (**friz**-bee) ***noun*** A trademark for a plastic disk tossed from person to person in any of various games.

frisk (**frisk**) ***verb***
1. *(informal)* To search someone for weapons, drugs, etc.
2. To play in a lively way.
▸ ***verb*** **frisking, frisked**

frisk•y (**friss**-kee) ***adjective*** Playful and full of energy. ▸ ***adverb*** **friskily**

frit•ta•ta (free-**tah**-tuh) ***noun*** A flat omelet filled with chopped vegetables, cheese, meat, etc.

frit•ter (**frit**-ur)
1. ***verb*** To use up in a careless, wasteful way. ▸ **frittering, frittered**
2. ***noun*** A small fried cake containing corn, clams, fruit, or other ingredients.

friv•o•lous (**friv**-uh-luhss) ***adjective***
1. Silly. ▸ ***adverb*** **frivolously**
2. Not important.

frog (**frog** *or* **frawg**) ***noun*** A small, green or brown animal with webbed feet and long back legs that it uses for jumping. Frogs are amphibians and live in or near water.

frog•man (**frog**-muhn) ***noun*** An investigator or military person who swims underwater using diving equipment. ▸ ***noun, plural*** **frogmen**

frol•ic (**frol**-ik) ***verb*** To play happily.
▸ **frolicking, frolicked** ▸ ***noun*** **frolic**

from (**fruhm**) ***preposition***
1. Starting at. *The train headed north from Washington to New York.*
2. In relative distance to. *The garage is not far from the house.*
3. The source. *The hurricane came from the south.*
4. As opposed to. *I can't tell him from his twin brother.*
5. Out of. *The first little pig's house was made from straw.*
6. Because of. *I became sick from food poisoning.*
7. At. *I got this sundae from the ice-cream shop.*

frond (**frond**) ***noun*** A large, divided leaf on a plant such as a fern or palm.

front (**fruhnt**) ***noun***
1. The part of something that comes first, as in *the front of a book.*
2. The part of something that faces forward.
3. The place where armies are fighting.
4. The edge of a mass of cold or warm air.
5. If you **put up a front,** you pretend to feel or think something.
▸ ***adjective*** **front**

F

fron•tier (fruhn-**tihr** *or* **fruhn**-tihr) ***noun***
1. The far edge of a country, where few people live.
2. The border between two countries.
3. A subject or an area of study that is just beginning to be understood, as in *the frontiers of medicine.*

frost (**frawst**)
1. ***noun*** Powdery ice that forms on things in freezing weather.
2. ***verb*** If something **frosts up,** it becomes covered with frost.
3. ***noun*** Weather with a temperature below the freezing point.
4. ***verb*** To put frosting on, as in *to frost a cake.*
▸ ***verb*** **frosting, frosted**

frost•bite (**frawst**-*bite*) ***noun*** If someone suffers from **frostbite,** parts of the body, such as fingers, toes, or ears, are damaged by extreme cold.
▸ ***adjective*** **frostbitten**

frost•ing (**frawst**-ing) ***noun*** A sweet sugar coating used to decorate cakes and pastries.

frost•y (**fraw**-stee) ***adjective***
1. Covered with powdery ice.
2. Very cold, as in *frosty weather.*
3. If someone is **frosty,** he or she is unfriendly.
▸ ***adjective*** **frostier, frostiest** ▸ ***noun*** **frostiness** ▸ ***adverb*** **frostily**

froth (**frawth**) ***noun*** Lots of small bubbles in or on top of a liquid. ▸ ***verb*** **froth** ▸ ***adjective*** **frothy**

frown (**froun**) ***verb***
1. To move your eyebrows together and wrinkle your forehead, usually as a sign that you are annoyed or unhappy.
▸ ***noun*** **frown**
2. To disapprove or to be against.
▸ ***verb*** **frowning, frowned**

fro•zen (**froh**-zuhn) ***adjective***
1. If water is **frozen,** it has been made so cold that it has turned into ice.
2. Extremely cold.
3. Chilled until hard, then stored in a freezer, as in *frozen food.*
4. Plugged up with ice, as in *frozen pipes.*
5. Too frightened to move, as in *frozen with terror.*

fru•gal (**froo**-guhl) ***adjective*** If you are **frugal,** you are very careful not to waste things. ▸ ***noun*** **frugality** ▸ ***adverb*** **frugally**

fruit (**froot**) ***noun***
1. The fleshy, juicy product of a plant that contains one or more seeds and is usually edible. ▸ ***adjective*** **fruity**
2. The part of a flowering plant that contains seeds, such as a nut or a pod.
3. The result of something.
▸ ***noun plural*** **fruit** ***or*** **fruits**

fruit•ful (**froot**-fuhl) ***adjective*** Successful or useful, as in *a fruitful discussion.* ▸ ***noun*** **fruitfulness** ▸ ***adverb*** **fruitfully**

fruit•less (**froot**-liss) ***adjective*** Unsuccessful or useless. ▸ ***adverb*** **fruitlessly**

frus•trate (**fruhss**-trate) ***verb***
1. If something **frustrates** you, it prevents you from doing something.
▸ ***noun*** **frustration**
2. To make someone feel helpless or discouraged.
▸ ***verb*** **frustrating, frustrated**
▸ ***adjective*** **frustrated,** ***adjective*** **frustrating**

fry (**frye**) ***verb*** To cook food in hot fat or oil. ▸ **fries, frying, fried** ▸ ***adjective*** **fried**

fudge (**fuhj**) ***noun*** A sweet, rich candy made with butter, sugar, milk, and usually chocolate.

fu•el (**fyoo**-uhl) ***noun*** Something that is used as a source of heat or energy, such as coal, wood, gasoline, natural gas, etc.
▸ ***verb*** **fuel**

fu•gi•tive (**fyoo**-juh-tiv) ***noun*** Someone who is running away, especially from the police. ▸ ***adjective*** **fugitive**

ful•crum (**ful**-kruhm) ***noun*** The point on which a lever rests or turns. The support on which a seesaw balances acts as a fulcrum. ▸ ***noun, plural*** **fulcrums** *or* **fulcra** (**ful**-kruh)

ful•fill (ful-**fil**) ***verb***
1. To perform or to do what is needed.
2. If you **fulfill** a need, a wish, or an ambition, you satisfy it.
▸ ***verb*** **fulfilling, fulfilled** ▸ ***noun*** **fulfillment**

full (**ful**) ***adjective***
1. If something is **full,** there is no room left inside it.
2. Whole or complete. ▸ ***adverb*** **fully**
3. Having a large number.
▸ ***adjective*** **fuller, fullest**

full moon ***noun*** The phase of the moon when the side turned toward the earth is entirely lit.

fum•ble (**fuhm**-buhl) ***verb***
1. To look for something in a clumsy way.
2. To drop something or to handle it clumsily. ▸ ***noun*** **fumble**
▸ ***verb*** **fumbling, fumbled**

fume (**fyoom**)
1. fumes *noun, plural* Unpleasant or harmful gas, smoke, or vapor given off by something burning or by chemicals.
2. *verb* To be very angry. ▸ **fuming, fumed**

fun (**fuhn**) ***noun*** A good time, or something that provides enjoyment.

func•tion (**fuhngk**-shuhn)
1. *verb* If something **functions,** it works. ▸ **functioning, functioned**
2. *noun* A purpose, role, or job.
3. *noun* A formal social gathering, such as a wedding.

func•tion•al (**fuhngk**-shuh-nuhl) ***adjective*** If something is **functional,** it works well or is designed to work well.

fund (**fuhnd**)
1. *noun* Money kept for a special purpose, as in *a college fund.*
2. *noun* A supply.
3. funds *noun, plural* Money that is ready to use.
4. *verb* If someone **funds** something, the person gives money to support it.
▸ **funding, funded**

fun•da•men•tal (fuhn-duh-**men**-tuhl) ***adjective*** Basic and necessary. ▸ ***noun, plural*** **fundamentals** ▸ ***adverb*** **fundamentally**

fu•ner•al (**fyoo**-nuh-ruhl) ***noun*** The ceremony held after someone has died, after which the body is buried or cremated.

fun•gus (**fuhn**-guhss) ***noun*** A plantlike organism that has no leaves, flowers, roots, or chlorophyll. ▸ ***noun, plural*** fungi (**fuhn**-jye *or* **fuhng**-gye)

fun•nel (**fuhn**-uhl)
1. *noun* An open cone that narrows to a tube, used for pouring something into a container with a narrow neck.
2. *noun* A smokestack on a ship or locomotive.
3. *verb* To pour something through a funnel. ▸ **funneling, funneled**

fun•ny (**fuh**-nee) ***adjective***
1. Amusing or humorous, as in *a funny joke.*
2. Strange. ▸ ***adjective*** **funnier, funniest** ▸ ***adverb*** **funnily**
3. *noun* **The funnies** are the comic strips or the comic section of a newspaper.

fur (**fur**) ***noun*** The soft, thick, hairy coat of an animal. **Fur** sounds like **fir.**
▸ ***adjective*** **furry**

fu•ri•ous (**fyu**-ree-uhss) ***adjective***
1. Extremely angry.
2. Fierce or violent, as in *a furious storm.*
▸ ***adverb*** **furiously**

fur•long (**fur**-long) ***noun*** A distance of 220 yards.

fur•lough (**fur**-loh) ***noun*** Time off from duty for military people.

fur•nace (**fur**-niss) ***noun*** A large enclosed metal chamber in which fuel is burned to produce heat. Furnaces are used to heat buildings or melt metals.

F

fur•nish (**fur**-nish) ***verb***
1. To equip a room or a house with furniture. ▸ ***noun, plural*** **furnishings**
2. To supply something.
▸ ***verb*** **furnishes, furnishing, furnished**

fur•ni•ture (**fur**-nuh-chur) ***noun*** The movable things such as chairs, tables, and beds that are needed in a home or an office.

fur•row (**fur**-oh) ***noun*** The groove cut by a plow when it turns over the soil.

fur•ther (**fur**-THur)
1. ***adjective*** *or* ***adverb*** A comparative of **far.**
2. ***adverb*** To a greater degree or extent.
3. ***adjective*** Additional, as in *further information.*
4. ***adverb*** At a greater distance; farther.
5. ***adjective*** More distant or remote, as in *the further shore.*
6. ***verb*** To help advance or go forward.

fur•ther•more (**fur**-THur-*mor*) ***adverb*** In addition, or as well.

fur•tive (**fur**-tiv) ***adjective*** Sly or sneaky, as in *a furtive glance.* ▸ ***noun*** **furtiveness** ▸ ***adverb*** **furtively**

fu•ry (**fyoo**-ree) ***noun*** Violent anger or rage. ▸ ***noun, plural*** **furies**

fuse (**fyooz**)
1. ***noun*** A safety device in electrical equipment that cuts off the power if something goes wrong.
2. ***verb*** To join two pieces of metal, plastic, etc., by heating them. ▸ **fusing, fused**
3. ***noun*** A cord or wick leading from a bomb that is lit to make the bomb explode.

fu•se•lage (**fyoo**-suh-lahzh *or* **fyoo**-suh-lij) ***noun*** The main body of an aircraft where the passengers, crew, and cargo are carried.

fu•sion (**fyoo**-zhuhn) ***noun*** The joining together of two pieces of metal, plastic, etc., caused by heating.

fuss (**fuhss**)
1. ***verb*** To be unnecessarily worried or excited about something. ▸ **fusses, fussing, fussed**
2. ***noun*** More talk or activity than is necessary. ▸ ***noun, plural*** **fusses**

fuss•y (**fuhss**-ee) ***adjective***
1. Overly concerned with small details.
2. If you are a **fussy** eater, you are very particular about what you eat.
▸ ***adjective*** **fussier, fussiest**

fu•tile (**fyoo**-tuhl *or* **fyoo**-tile) ***adjective*** If an action is **futile,** it is useless and a waste of time. ▸ ***noun*** **futility**

fu•ton (**foo**-ton) ***noun*** A small mattress that is filled with cotton or similar material and is used on the floor or in a bed frame.

fu•ture (**fyoo**-chur) ***noun***
1. The time to come.
2. The **future tense.**
▸ ***adjective*** **future**

future tense ***noun*** A form of a verb using "will," "be going to," or "shall" to indicate future time, as in *I will go home tomorrow.*

fuzz (**fuhz**) ***noun*** Short, soft hair or fiber. ▸ ***adjective*** **fuzzy**

fuzz•y (**fuhz**-ee) ***adjective***
1. Like fuzz, or covered with fuzz.
2. Not clear or distinct, as in *a fuzzy idea.*
▸ ***adjective*** **fuzzier, fuzziest**

gab (**gab**) ***verb*** *(slang)* To chat or to gossip.

gad•get (**gaj**-it) ***noun*** A small tool that does a particular job.

gag (**gag**)
1. ***verb*** To tie a piece of cloth around someone's mouth in order to stop the person from talking or crying out.
2. ***noun*** Something put over the mouth to stop someone from making a noise.
3. ***verb*** If you **gag,** you feel as though you are about to choke or throw up.
4. ***noun*** *(informal)* A joke.
▸ ***verb*** **gagging, gagged**

gain (**gayn**)
1. ***verb*** To get or win something.
2. ***noun*** A profit, or an increase.
3. ***verb*** If you **gain on** someone, you start to catch up with the person.
▸ ***verb*** **gaining, gained**

gait (**gate**) ***noun*** A way of walking. **Gait** sounds like **gate.**

ga•la (**gay**-luh *or* **gal**-uh) ***noun*** A special event. ▸ ***adjective*** **gala**

gal•ax•y (**gal**-uhk-see) ***noun*** A very large group of stars and planets. ▸ ***noun, plural*** **galaxies** ▸ ***adjective*** **galactic**

gale (**gale**) ***noun***
1. A very strong wind.
2. A noisy outburst, as in *gales of laughter.*

gal•lant (**gal**-uhnt) ***adjective***
1. Brave and fearless.
2. Courteous and attentive.
▸ ***adverb*** **gallantly**

gall•blad•der (**gawl**-*blad*-ur) ***noun*** The organ in your body that stores a liquid called bile, or gall, that helps you digest food.

gal•le•on (**gal**-ee-uhn) ***noun*** A sailing ship with three masts used in the 15th to early 18th centuries for trading and warfare.

gal•ler•y (**gal**-uh-ree) ***noun***
1. A place where paintings, sculpture, photographs, etc., are exhibited and sometimes sold.
2. An upstairs seating area or balcony, especially in large halls and theaters.
▸ ***noun, plural*** **galleries**

gal•ley (**gal**-ee) ***noun***
1. The kitchen on a boat or an airplane.
2. A long boat with oars, used in ancient times.

gal•lon (**gal**-uhn) ***noun*** A liquid measure equal to four quarts. If you run a shower for one minute, you use about five gallons of water.

gal•lop (**gal**-uhp) ***verb*** When a horse **gallops,** it runs as fast as it can with all four feet leaving the ground at once.
▸ **galloping, galloped** ▸ ***noun*** **gallop**

gal•lows (**gal**-ohz) ***noun*** A wooden frame used in the past for hanging criminals.

ga•loot (guh-**loot**) ***noun*** *(slang)* An awkward or silly person.

gal•ore (guh-**lor**) ***adjective*** In large numbers.

ga•losh•es (guh-**losh**-iz) ***noun, plural*** Waterproof shoes that fit over your ordinary shoes and protect them from rain and snow.

gal•va•nize (**gal**-vuh-nize) ***verb***
1. To coat steel or iron with zinc to keep it from rusting.
2. If you **galvanize** someone into action, you shock the person into doing something.
▸ ***verb*** **galvanizing, galvanized**

G

gam•ble (**gam**-buhl) ***verb***
1. To bet money on the outcome of a race, a game, or something that might happen.
2. To take a risk.
▸ ***verb*** **gambling, gambled** ▸ ***noun*** **gambler**

game (**game**)
1. ***noun*** An activity with rules that can be played by one or more people, as in *a game of tennis* or *a computer game.*
2. ***noun*** Wild animals, including birds, that are hunted for sport and food.
3. ***adjective*** If you are **game** to do something, you are willing to go ahead with it.
4. ***adjective*** Spirited and determined.
▸ ***adverb*** **gamely**

gan•der (**gan**-dur) ***noun*** A male goose.

gang (**gang**)
1. ***noun*** A group of people with similar interests or goals. A gang usually has a leader.
2. ***noun*** An organized group of criminals.
3. ***verb*** If several people **gang up** on you, they all turn against you.
▸ **ganging, ganged**

gang•plank (**gang**-*plangk*) ***noun*** A short bridge or piece of wood used for walking onto and off of a ship.

gan•grene (gang-**green** *or* **gang**-green) ***noun*** If someone has **gangrene,** his or her flesh decays, usually because the blood supply has been cut off to that part of the body.

gang•ster (**gang**-stur) ***noun*** A member of a criminal gang.

gang•way (**gang**-*way*) ***noun***
1. A passageway on a ship or between buildings.
2. A gangplank.

gap (**gap**) ***noun*** A space between things.

gape (**gape**)
1. ***verb*** To open your mouth wide, usually with surprise.
2. ***verb*** To open widely.
3. ***noun*** A large opening.
4. ***noun*** The part of a beak that opens.
▸ ***verb*** **gaping, gaped** ▸ ***noun*** **gape**

ga•rage (guh-**rahzh** *or* guh-**rahj**) ***noun***
1. A building used for storing vehicles.
2. A place where cars and other vehicles are fixed.

gar•bage (**gar**-bij) ***noun*** Food or things thrown away.

gar•bled (**gar**-buhld) ***adjective*** A **garbled** message is mixed up and does not make sense.

gar•den (**gard**-uhn) ***noun*** A place where flowers, vegetables, and shrubs are grown. ▸ ***noun*** **gardener,** ***noun*** **gardening** ▸ ***verb*** **garden**

gar•de•nia (gar-**deen**-yuh) ***noun*** A tropical evergreen tree or bush with fragrant flowers.

gar•gle (**gar**-guhl) ***verb*** To move a liquid around your mouth without swallowing it. ▸ **gargling, gargled** ▸ ***noun*** **gargle**

gar•goyle (**gar**-goil) ***noun*** A grotesque stone head or figure carved below the roof of old buildings such as churches. Gargoyles were often used as spouts to drain water from roofs.

gar•ish (**ga**-rish) ***adjective*** Too brightly colored and overly decorated. ▸ ***adverb*** **garishly**

gar•land (**gar**-luhnd) ***noun*** A ring of flowers, often worn on the head.

gar•lic (**gar**-lik) ***noun***
1. A strong-smelling plant related to an onion.
2. The strong-tasting bulb of the garlic plant, used in cooking to add flavor.

gar•ment (**gar**-muhnt) ***noun*** A piece of clothing.

gar•net (**gar**-nit) ***noun*** A dark red stone worn as jewelry or used as an abrasive.

gar•nish (**gar**-nish) ***verb*** To decorate food with small amounts of other food or spices. ▸ **garnishes, garnishing, garnished** ▸ ***noun*** **garnish**

gar•ri•son (**ga**-ruh-suhn) ***noun*** A group of soldiers based in a town and ready to defend it. ▸ ***verb*** **garrison**

gar•ter (**gar**-tur) ***noun*** A piece of elastic worn around the top of a sock or stocking to keep it from slipping down.

garter snake ***noun*** A small, brown or green snake with yellow stripes on its back. A garter snake is not poisonous.

gas (**gass**) ***noun***
1. A substance, such as air, that will spread to fill any space that contains it. ▸ ***adjective*** **gaseous** (**gass**-ee-uhss *or* **gash**-uhss)
2. A substance that is used as a source of energy. Gas can be made from coal and can also be found underground.
3. A liquid fuel used in many vehicles. **Gas** is short for **gasoline.**

▸ ***noun, plural*** **gases**

gash (**gash**) ***noun*** A long, deep cut. ▸ ***noun, plural*** **gashes** ▸ ***verb*** **gash**

gas mask ***noun*** A mask that fits over the whole face to keep a person from breathing poisonous gas.

gas•o•hol (**gass**-uh-*hawl*) ***noun*** A motor-vehicle fuel made of about 90 percent gasoline and ten percent grain alcohol.

gas•o•line (gass-uh-**leen**) ***noun*** A liquid fuel made from oil, which is used in many vehicles. Also called **gas.**

gasp (**gasp**) ***verb***
1. To take in breath suddenly because you are surprised, in pain, or have exercised heavily. ▸ ***noun*** **gasp**
2. To speak while out of breath.

▸ ***verb*** **gasping, gasped**

gas station ***noun*** A place that sells gasoline, oil, and other things needed to keep motor vehicles running. Most gas stations also have mechanics who do repairs.

gas•tric (**gass**-trik) ***adjective*** To do with the stomach, as in *gastric juices.*

gate (**gate**) ***noun***
1. A frame or barrier that can be opened and closed.
2. The number of people paying to see a game, a sporting event, or a performance, such as a concert.

Gate sounds like **gait.**

gate-crash•er (**krash**-ur) ***noun*** Someone who goes to a party he or she was not invited to or to a performance without paying for a ticket. ▸ ***verb*** **gate-crash**

gate•way (**gate**-*way*) ***noun***
1. An opening through which you can enter by a gate.
2. A way to get something you want.
3. A place where people enter a country.

gath•er (**gaTH**-ur) ***verb***
1. To collect or pick things.
2. To come together in a group.
3. To discover or learn something.
4. To gain little by little.

▸ ***verb*** **gathering, gathered**

gaud•y (**gaw**-dee) ***adjective*** If someone's clothing is **gaudy,** it is too brightly colored, and if someone's jewelry is **gaudy,** it is too showy. ▸ **gaudier, gaudiest**

gauge (**gayj**)
1. ***verb*** To judge something or make a guess about it. ▸ **gauging, gauged**
2. ***noun*** An instrument for measuring something, as in *a pressure gauge.* ▸ ***verb*** **gauge**
3. ***noun*** A set measurement, such as the distance between two rails of a railroad track.

gaunt (**gawnt**) ***adjective*** Very thin and bony.

gaunt•let (**gawnt**-lit) ***noun*** A long, protective glove. In the past, gauntlets were worn by soldiers to prevent injury from weapons.

gauze (**gawz**) ***noun*** A very thin woven cloth used as a bandage.

gav•el (**gav**-uhl) ***noun*** A small, wooden mallet used to signal the beginning of a meeting or to call for quiet. A gavel is used by an auctioneer or a judge.

gay (**gay**) ***adjective***
1. Happy and lively.
2. Decorated with bright colors.

▸ ***adjective*** **gayer, gayest** ▸ ***adverb*** **gaily**

gaze (**gayz**) ***verb*** To look at something steadily. ▸ **gazing, gazed** ▸ ***noun*** **gaze**

ga•zelle (guh-**zel**) ***noun*** A graceful antelope found in Africa and Asia. The gazelle can run very fast.

G

ga•zet•teer (*gaz*-uh-**tihr**) ***noun*** A dictionary that lists names of places, rivers, oceans, and mountains alphabetically; a geographical dictionary.

gear (**gihr**)
1. gears *noun, plural* A set of wheels with teeth that fit together and pass on or change the movement of a machine.
2. *noun* Equipment or clothing, as in *hiking gear.*
3. *verb* To make suitable. ▸ **gearing, geared**

gear•shift (**gihr**-*shift*) ***noun*** A handle used to change gears in the transmission of a vehicle.

Gei•ger counter (**gye**-gur) ***noun*** An instrument that finds and measures radioactivity.

gel (**jel**) ***noun*** A thick, jellylike substance, as in *hair gel.* **Gel** sounds like **jell.**

gel•a•tin *or* **gel•a•tine** (**jel**-uh-tuhn) ***noun*** A clear substance used in making jelly, desserts, and glue that is obtained from bones and other animal tissues.

gem (**jem**) ***noun*** A precious stone, such as a diamond, a ruby, or an emerald.

gen•der (**jen**-dur) ***noun***
1. The sex of a person or creature.
2. A **gender** is a category of nouns. In English we show the gender of a noun mainly by the kind of pronoun that can refer to it. Feminine nouns such as *girl* use *she,* masculine nouns such as *boy* use *he,* neuter nouns such as *table* use *it,* and common nouns such as *children* use *they.*

gene (**jeen**) ***noun*** One of the parts of the cells of all living things. Genes are passed from parents to children and determine how you look and the way you grow.
▸ ***adjective*** **genetic**

ge•ne•al•o•gy (*jee*-nee-**al**-uh-jee *or jee*-nee-**ol**-uh-jee) ***noun***
1. The study of family history. ▸ ***noun*** **genealogist**
2. The history of a family.
▸ ***noun, plural*** **genealogies**

gen•e•ral (**jen**-ur-uhl)
1. *adjective* To do with everybody or everything.
2. *adjective* Not detailed or specialized.
3. *noun* A very high-ranking officer in the army, air force, or marines.
▸ ***adverb*** **generally**

gen•er•al•ize (**jen**-ur-uh-lize) ***verb***
1. To create a general rule from a small number of specific examples.
2. To discuss something in a vague or general way.
▸ ***verb*** **generalizing, generalized**
▸ ***noun*** **generalization**

gen•er•ate (**jen**-uh-rate) ***verb*** To produce something. ▸ **generating, generated**

gen•er•a•tion (*jen*-uh-**ray**-shuhn) ***noun***
1. All the people born around the same time, as in *the younger generation.*
2. The average amount of time between the birth of parents and that of their children. A generation is said to be about 30 years.
3. The descendants from a shared ancestor.
4. The process of bringing something into being, as in *the generation of heat by the sun.*

gen•er•a•tor (**jen**-uh-*ray*-tur) ***noun*** A machine that produces electricity by turning a magnet inside a coil of wire.

gen•er•ic (juh-**ner**-ik) ***adjective***
1. To do with a whole group or class of something.
2. To do with a product not sold under a trademark or copyright, as in *a generic drug.*

gen•er•ous (**jen**-ur-uhss) ***adjective*** People who are **generous** are happy to use their time and money to help others.
▸ ***noun*** **generosity** (*jen*-u-**ross**-i-tee)
▸ ***adverb*** **generously**

gene therapy ***noun*** The treatment of genetic disorders by inserting healthy genes inside the cells, replacing defective genes.

ge•net•ics (juh-**net**-iks) ***noun*** The study of the ways that personal characteristics are passed from one generation to another through genes. ▸ ***adjective*** **genetic** ▸ ***adverb*** **genetically**

ge•nial (**jeen**-yuhl *or* **jeen**-ee-uhl) ***adjective*** Friendly and welcoming, as in *a genial conversation.* ▸ ***noun*** **geniality** ▸ ***adverb*** **genially**

ge•nie (**jee**-nee) ***noun*** In tales from the Middle East, a **genie** is a spirit who obeys the person who summons it and grants the person's wishes.

gen•ius (**jee**-nee-uhss *or* **jeen**-yuhss) ***noun*** An unusually intelligent or talented person. ▸ ***noun, plural*** **geniuses**

ge•nome (**jee**-nohm) ***noun*** A full set of chromosomes in an organism.

gen•teel (jen-**teel**) ***adjective*** Extremely polite and careful in your behavior. ▸ ***noun*** **gentility**

gen•tile *or* **Gen•tile** (**jen**-tile) ***noun***
1. A person who is not Jewish.
2. In the Mormon church, a person who is not Mormon.

gen•tle (**jen**-tuhl) ***adjective***
1. Not rough.
2. Kind and sensitive.
3. Not extreme, as in *a gentle slope.*
▸ ***adjective*** **gentler, gentlest** ▸ ***noun*** **gentleness** ▸ ***adverb*** **gently**

gen•tle•man (**jen**-tuhl-muhn) ***noun***
1. A polite term for a man.
2. A man with good manners.
3. A man who belongs to a high social class.
▸ ***noun, plural*** **gentlemen**

gen•tle•wom•an (**jen**-tuhl-*wu*-muhn) ***noun***
1. A woman with good manners.
2. A woman who belongs to a high social class.
▸ ***noun, plural*** **gentlewomen**

gen•tri•fi•ca•tion (**jen**-truh-fuh-**kay**-shuhn) ***noun*** The rebuilding of decaying neighborhoods to attract wealthier residents.

gen•u•ine (**jen**-yoo-uhn) ***adjective***
1. Real and not fake, as in *a genuine diamond.*
2. Honest or true, as in *genuine love.*
▸ ***adverb*** **genuinely**

ge•nus (**jee**-nuhss) ***noun*** A group of related plants or animals. A genus usually consists of many species. ▸ ***noun, plural*** **genera** (**jen**-ur-uh) *or* **genuses**

ge•o•de•sic (*jee*-uh-**dess**-ik) ***adjective*** To do with the geometry of curved surfaces, as in *a geodesic dome.*

ge•og•ra•phy (jee-**og**-ruh-fee) ***noun*** The study of the earth, including its people, resources, climate, and physical features. ▸ ***noun*** **geographer** ▸ ***adjective*** **geographical**

ge•ol•o•gy (jee-**ol**-uh-jee) ***noun*** The study of the earth's layers of soil and rock. ▸ ***noun*** **geologist** ▸ ***adjective*** **geological**

ge•o•met•ric (jee-uh-**met**-rik) ***adjective***
1. To do with geometry.
2. A **geometric** shape is the outside edge or surface of a figure, such as a circle, a triangle, a rectangle, a square, or a sphere.

ge•om•e•try (jee-**om**-uh-tree) ***noun*** The branch of mathematics that deals with lines, angles, shapes, etc.

ge•o•ther•mal (jee-oh-**thur**-muhl) ***adjective*** To do with the intense heat of the internal part of the earth and its commercial use, as in *geothermal steam* or *geothermal electricity.*

ge•ra•ni•um (juh-**ray**-nee-uhm) ***noun*** A garden plant with thick stems and red, pink, white, or purple clusters of flowers.

ger•bil (**jur**-buhl) ***noun*** A small, furry rodent with long feet and a long, tufted tail. Gerbils are often kept as pets.

ger•i•at•ric (jer-ee-**at**-rik) ***adjective*** To do with very old people, as in *a geriatric hospital.*

germ (**jurm**) ***noun***
1. A very small living organism that can cause disease.
2. The very beginning of something, as in *the germ of an idea.*

G

Ger•man•ic (jer-**man**-ik) ***noun*** A language that scholars suppose was the parent of modern English, German, Dutch, and other related languages. ▸ ***adjective*** **Germanic**

German measles ***noun*** A contagious illness that gives you a rash and a slight fever.

German shepherd ***noun*** A breed of large dog with pointed ears, a narrow nose, and black, brown, or gray fur.

ger•mi•nate (**jur**-muh-nate) ***verb*** When seeds or beans **germinate,** they start to grow shoots and roots. ▸ **germinating, germinated**

ges•tic•u•late (jess-**tik**-yuh-late) ***verb*** To indicate something by waving your hands about in an excited or angry way. ▸ **gesticulating, gesticulated** ▸ ***noun*** **gesticulation**

ges•ture (**jess**-chur)
1. ***verb*** To move your head or hands in order to communicate a feeling or an idea. ▸ **gesturing, gestured** ▸ ***noun*** **gesture**
2. ***noun*** An action that shows a feeling.

get (**get**) ***verb***
1. To obtain something.
2. To capture.
3. To become.
4. To arrive somewhere.
5. get by To manage with very little money.
6. To become sick with.
▸ ***verb*** **getting, got** (**got**) *or* **gotten** (**got**-in)

get•a•way (**get**-uh-*way*) ***noun*** A fast escape from a situation, especially a crime.

gey•ser (**gye**-zur) ***noun*** A hole in the ground through which hot water and steam shoot up in bursts.

ghast•ly (**gast**-lee) ***adjective***
1. Horrible, as in *a ghastly crime.*
2. *(informal)* Very bad or unpleasant, as in *a ghastly party.*
3. If you feel or look **ghastly,** you feel or look very ill.
▸ ***adjective*** **ghastlier, ghastliest**

ghet•to (**get**-oh) ***noun*** A usually poor neighborhood in a city where people of the same race, religion, or ethnic background live. ▸ ***noun, plural*** **ghettos** *or* **ghettoes**

ghost (**gohst**) ***noun*** A spirit of a dead person believed to haunt people or places.

ghost•ly (**gohst**-lee) ***adjective*** To do with ghosts, as in *a ghostly figure.*

ghost town ***noun*** A deserted town. There were many ghost towns in the American West after nearby gold and silver mines closed down.

GI (**gee eye**) ***noun*** An American soldier. GI is short for *Government Issue.*

gi•ant (**jye**-uhnt)
1. ***noun*** In folktales and fairy tales, a **giant** is a very large and strong creature.
2. ***adjective*** Very large, as in *giant size.*

gib•ber•ish (**jib**-ur-ish) ***noun*** Uncontrolled speech that does not make sense.

gid•dy (**gid**-ee) ***adjective*** If you feel **giddy,** you feel dizzy and unsteady, either because you are ill or because you are excited. ▸ **giddier, giddiest** ▸ ***noun*** **giddiness** ▸ ***adverb*** **giddily**

gift (**gift**) ***noun***
1. A present.
2. A special talent. ▸ ***adjective*** **gifted**

gig (**gig**) ***noun*** *(informal)* A booking for a musician or a band to play rock, jazz, etc., in public; a job.

gig•a•byte (**gig**-uh-*bite*) ***noun*** A unit for measuring the amount of data in a computer memory or file. A gigabyte is about 1 billion bytes.

gi•gan•tic (jye-**gan**-tik) ***adjective*** Huge, or enormous. ▸ ***adverb*** **gigantically**

gig•gle (**gig**-uhl) ***verb*** To laugh in a nervous or silly way. ▸ **giggling, giggled** ▸ ***noun*** **giggle** ▸ ***adjective*** **giggly**

gild (**gild**) ***verb*** To coat something with a thin layer of gold or gold paint. ▸ **gilding, gilded**

gill (**gil**) ***noun*** The organ on a fish's side through which it breathes.

gilt (**gilt**) ***adjective*** A **gilt** object is decorated with a thin coating of gold or gold paint. **Gilt** sounds like **guilt.**

gim·mick (**gim**-ik) ***noun*** A clever gadget, trick, or idea used to get people's attention.

gin·ger (**jin**-jur) ***noun***
1. A plant root used to give a hot, spicy flavor to food and drink.
2. A reddish brown color.
▸ ***adjective* ginger, *adjective* gingery**

gin·ger·bread (**jin**-jur-*bred*) ***noun*** A cake or cookie flavored with ginger and other spices.

gin·ger·ly (**jin**-jur-lee) ***adverb*** Cautiously and carefully.

ging·ham (**ging**-uhm) ***noun*** Checked cotton cloth.

gi·raffe (juh-**raf**) ***noun*** An African mammal with a very long neck and legs and dark spots on its coat. The giraffe is the tallest animal in the world.

gird·er (**gur**-dur) ***noun*** A large, heavy beam made of steel or concrete, used in construction.

girl (**gurl**) ***noun*** A female child or young woman.

girl·friend (**gurl**-*frend*) ***noun***
1. The girl or woman with whom someone is having a romantic relationship.
2. A female friend.

girl·hood (**gurl**-*hud*) ***noun*** The time during which someone is a girl.

girth (**gurth**) ***noun*** The measurement around something.

gist (**jist**) ***noun*** The main part of something.

give (**giv**) ***verb***
1. To hand something to another person.
2. To pay.
3. To supply.
4. To offer.
5. To cause to happen.
▸ ***verb* giving, gave** (**gayv**), **given** (**giv**-in)

gla·cier (**glay**-shur) ***noun*** A huge sheet of ice found in mountain valleys or polar regions. A glacier is formed when snow falls and does not melt because the temperature remains below freezing.

glad (**glad**) ***adjective*** Pleased or happy.
▸ **gladder, gladdest** ▸ ***noun* gladness** ▸ ***verb* gladden** ▸ ***adverb* gladly**

glade (**glade**) ***noun*** An open, grassy space in the middle of a wood or forest.

glad·i·a·tor (**glad**-ee-ay-tur) ***noun*** A warrior of ancient Rome who fought against other warriors or fierce animals in order to entertain the public.

glad·i·o·lus (*glad*-ee-**oh**-luhss) ***noun*** A plant with a long, leafy stalk and white or brightly colored flowers. ▸ ***noun, plural* gladioli** (*glad*-ee-**oh**-lye)

glam·or·ous (**glam**-ur-uhss) ***adjective*** Attractive and exciting.

glam·our *or* **glam·or** (**glam**-ur) ***noun*** Fashion, charm, or appeal.

glance (**glanss**) ***verb***
1. To look at something very briefly.
▸ ***noun* glance**
2. To hit something and slide off at an angle.
▸ ***verb* glancing, glanced** ▸ ***adjective* glancing**

gland (**gland**) ***noun*** An organ in the body that either produces natural chemicals or allows substances to leave the body, as in *sweat glands.* ▸ ***adjective* glandular** (**glan**-juh-lur)

glare (**glair**)
1. ***noun*** Very bright light that dazzles.
▸ ***verb* glare**
2. ***verb*** To look at someone in a very angry way. ▸ **glaring, glared** ▸ ***noun* glare**

glar·ing (**glair**-ing) ***adjective***
1. Very bright and gaudy, as in *glaring colors.*
2. Very obvious, as in *a glaring error.*
▸ ***adverb* glaringly**

glass (**glass**) ***noun***
1. A transparent material made from melted sand, used in windows, bottles, and lenses.
2. A container for drinking, made from glass or plastic. ▸ ***noun, plural* glasses**

G

glass•es (**glass**-iz) ***noun, plural*** Lenses set in frames, worn to improve a person's eyesight.

glaze (**glayz**)
1. *noun* A thin coat of liquid painted on pottery before it is fired to give it a shiny finish.
2. *verb* To put glass into a window.
3. *verb* If your eyes **glaze over,** they look fixed and vacant because you are tired or bored.
▸ ***verb* glazing, glazed** ▸ ***adjective* glazed**

gla•zier (**glay**-zhur) ***noun*** A person who puts glass into windows.

gleam (**gleem**)
1. *verb* To shine. ▸ **gleaming, gleamed** ▸ ***noun* gleam**
2. *noun* A beam of light.

glee (**glee**) ***noun*** Enjoyment and delight. ▸ ***adjective* gleeful** ▸ ***adverb* gleefully**

glen (**glen**) ***noun*** A narrow valley.

glide (**glide**) ***verb*** To move smoothly and easily. ▸ **gliding, glided** ▸ ***noun* glide**

glid•er (**glye**-dur) ***noun*** A very light aircraft that flies by floating and rising on air currents instead of by engine power.

glim•mer (**glim**-ur)
1. *verb* To shine faintly. ▸ **glimmering, glimmered** ▸ ***noun* glimmer**
2. *noun* A trace, as in *a glimmer of hope.*

glimpse (**glimps**) ***verb*** To see something very briefly. ▸ **glimpsing, glimpsed** ▸ ***noun* glimpse**

glint (**glint**)
1. *verb* To sparkle, or to flash. ▸ **glinting, glinted**
2. *noun* If you have a **glint in your eye,** you are secretly amused or excited about something.

glis•ten (**gliss**-uhn) ***verb*** To shine in a sparkling way. ▸ **glistening, glistened**

glitch (**glich**) ***noun*** *(informal)* Any sudden thing that goes wrong or causes a problem, usually with machinery, as in *a computer glitch.*

glit•ter (**glit**-ur) ***verb*** To sparkle with many tiny lights or reflections. ▸ **glittering, glittered**

gloat (**gloht**) ***verb*** To delight in your own good luck or someone else's bad luck. ▸ **gloating, gloated**

global warming ***noun*** An apparent gradual rise in the temperature of the earth's atmosphere, caused by the greenhouse effect.

globe (**glohb**) ***noun***
1. The world. ▸ ***adjective* global**
2. A round model of the world.
3. Anything shaped like a round ball.
▸ ***adjective* globular** (**glob**-yuh-lur)

glock•en•spiel (**glok**-uhn-speel) ***noun*** A musical instrument with metal plates of different sizes on a frame, which are struck to give different notes.

gloom (**gloom**) ***noun***
1. A sense of hopelessness.
2. A dark and depressing atmosphere.

gloom•y (**gloo**-mee) ***adjective***
1. Dull and dark, as in *a gloomy dungeon.*
2. If you are **gloomy,** you feel sad and pessimistic.
▸ ***adjective* gloomier, gloomiest**

glo•ri•fy (**glor**-uh-fye) ***verb***
1. To praise or treat as very important or splendid.
2. To honor or promote the glory of.
▸ ***verb* glorifies, glorifying, glorified**

glo•ry (**glor**-ee) ***noun***
1. Great fame or honor, as in *the glory of victory.*
2. Something that brings great fame or honor.
3. Splendor or magnificence, as in *the glory of sunrise.*
▸ ***noun, plural* glories** ▸ ***adjective* glorious**

gloss (**gloss** *or* **glawss**) ***noun*** A shine on a surface. ▸ ***noun, plural* glosses** ▸ ***adjective* glossy**

glos•sa•ry (**gloss**-uh-ree) ***noun*** A **glossary** explains the meaning of technical or specialized words and phrases used in a book. ▸ ***noun, plural* glossaries**

glove (**gluhv**) ***noun***
1. A warm or protective hand covering

that has separate parts for the thumb and fingers.
2. A leather covering for the hand worn by players of sports such as boxing and baseball.

glow (**gloh**)
1. ***verb*** If something **glows,** it gives off a steady, low light, often because it is hot.
2. ***noun*** A light from something that glows.
3. ***verb*** To show a color suggesting brightness, warmth, or health.
4. ***noun*** A bright, warm, or healthy color.
5. ***verb*** To show a warm feeling.
▸ ***verb*** **glowing, glowed** ▸ ***adjective*** **glowing**

glow•er (**glou**-ur) ***verb*** To stare angrily at someone. ▸ **glowering, glowered** ▸ ***noun*** **glower**

glow•worm (**gloh**-*wurm*) ***noun*** The larva of a firefly, or an adult firefly that does not have wings.

glu•cose (**gloo**-kose) ***noun*** A natural sugar found in plants that gives energy to living things.

glue (**gloo**) ***noun*** A substance used to make one surface stick to another. ▸ ***verb*** **glue**

glum (**gluhm**) ***adjective*** Gloomy and miserable. ▸ **glummer, glummest** ▸ ***adverb*** **glumly**

glut (**gluht**) ***noun*** If there is a **glut** of something, there is too much of it.

glut•ton (**gluht**-uhn) ***noun*** A person who is greedy, especially for food. ▸ ***noun*** **gluttony** ▸ ***adjective*** **gluttonous**

gnarled (**narld**) ***adjective*** Twisted and lumpy with age, as in *a gnarled oak tree.*

gnash (**nash**) ***verb*** If you **gnash** your teeth, you grind them together in anger or grief. ▸ **gnashes, gnashing, gnashed**

gnat (**nat**) ***noun*** A small insect with two wings that bites.

gnaw (**naw**) ***verb*** To keep biting on something. ▸ **gnawing, gnawed**

gnome (**nome**) ***noun*** In folktales and fairy tales, **gnomes** are dwarflike old men.

gnu (**noo**) ***noun*** A kind of antelope that has a large head like an ox, curved horns, and a long tail. The gnu lives in Africa. **Gnu** sounds like **new.** ▸ ***noun, plural*** **gnus** *or* **gnu**

go (**goh**)
1. ***verb*** To move away from or toward a place.
2. ***verb*** To work properly.
3. ***verb*** To pass.
4. ***verb*** To have a certain place.
5. ***verb*** If you are **going to** do something, you will do it in the future.
6. ***verb*** To be suitable.
7. ***verb*** To turn out.
8. ***adjective*** Ready to happen.
▸ ***verb*** **goes, going, went (went), gone (gon)**

goad (**gohd**) ***verb*** To tease or urge someone into doing something. ▸ **goading, goaded**

goal (**gohl**) ***noun***
1. A frame with a net into which you aim a ball in sports such as soccer and hockey.
2. When you score a **goal** in a game, you send a ball or puck into or through a goal.
3. Something that you aim for.

goal•ie (**goh**-lee) ***noun*** Someone who guards the goal in soccer or hockey to keep the other team from scoring.

goal•keep•er (**gohl**-*keep*-ur) ***noun*** A goalie.

goat (**goht**) ***noun*** An animal with horns and a beard. Some goats are raised on farms for their milk.

goa•tee (goh-**tee**) ***noun*** A beard grown around the mouth and chin.

gob•ble (**gob**-uhl) ***verb***
1. To eat food quickly and greedily.
2. To make the sound a turkey makes.
▸ ***verb*** **gobbling, gobbled**

gob•let (**gob**-lit) ***noun*** A tall drinking container with a stem and a base.

G

G

gob•lin (**gob**-luhn) ***noun*** In fairy tales, **goblins** are small, unpleasant, ugly creatures.

go-cart ***noun*** A very low, small, open vehicle built for racing.

God (**god**) ***noun***
1. In Christianity, Islam, and Judaism, **God** is the creator and ruler of the universe.
2. god A supernatural being who is worshiped.

god•dess (**god**-iss) ***noun*** A female supernatural being who is worshiped.

god•par•ent (**god**-*pair*-uhnt) ***noun*** Someone who promises his or her support for a child when the child is baptized into the Christian religion.

gog•gles (**gog**-uhlz) ***noun, plural*** Special glasses that fit tightly around your eyes to protect them.

gold (**gohld**) ***noun***
1. A precious metal used in jewelry and sometimes for money.
2. A warm, yellow color.
▸ ***adjective*** **gold,** ***adjective*** **golden**

gold•en•rod (**gohld**-uhn-*rod*) ***noun*** A tall, wild plant with many small, yellow flowers. Goldenrods bloom in late summer and in the fall.

gold•finch (**gohld**-*finch*) ***noun*** A small bird that looks very much like a canary. The male goldfinch is yellow with black markings. ▸ ***noun, plural*** **goldfinches**

gold•fish (**gohld**-*fish*) ***noun*** An orange-colored fish often kept in ponds and aquariums. ▸ ***noun, plural*** **goldfish** *or* **goldfishes**

golf (**golf**) ***noun*** A game in which players use clubs to hit a small white ball around a special course and into a hole. ▸ ***noun*** **golfer,** ***noun*** **golfing** ▸ ***verb*** **golf**

gon•do•la (**gon**-duh-luh) ***noun***
1. A light boat with high, pointed ends, used on the canals of Venice, Italy. Gondolas are moved through the water using a single oar.
2. A railroad freight car with low sides and no roof.
3. A compartment under a hot-air balloon or a blimp.

gong (**gong**) ***noun*** A disk of metal that makes a hollow, echoing sound when it is hit with a hammer.

good (**gud**) ***adjective***
1. Well-behaved.
2. Fit and well.
3. Of high quality, as in *a good piece of furniture.*
4. Useful.
5. Clever or skillful, as in *a good hitter.*
6. Kind or helpful, as in *good to animals.*
7. If you **make good** at something, you are doing well at it.
▸ ***adjective*** **better, best** ▸ ***noun*** **good**

good-bye *or* **good-by** ***interjection*** A word said to someone who is leaving.

Good Friday ***noun*** A date commemorated by Christian religions as the day Jesus died on the cross; the Friday before Easter.

good-na•tured (**nay**-churd) ***adjective*** Pleasant and generally warm and kind.

good•ness (**gud**-niss) ***noun*** Generosity or kindness.

goods (**gudz**) ***noun, plural*** Things that are sold, or things that someone owns, as in *leather goods* or *household goods.*

good•will (*gud*-**wil**) ***noun***
1. Kindness or cheerfulness.
2. The value a business has because of a good relationship with its customers.

goo•ey (**goo**-ee) ***adjective*** *(informal)* Sticky. ▸ **gooier, gooiest** ▸ ***noun*** **gooeyness**

goose (**gooss**) ***noun*** A large bird with a long neck and webbed feet. ▸ ***noun, plural*** **geese** (**geess**)

goose bumps ***noun, plural*** Tiny bumps on your skin that appear when you are cold or frightened.

go•pher (**goh**-fur) ***noun*** A small, furry animal related to the squirrel that lives underground. The gopher can be found throughout North America.

gore (**gor**)
1. ***noun*** Clotted blood.
2. ***verb*** If someone is **gored** by a bull,

the person is pierced by its horns.
▸ **goring, gored**

gorge (**gorj**)
1. ***noun*** A deep valley with steep, rocky sides.
2. ***verb*** If you **gorge** yourself, you stuff yourself with food. ▸ **gorging, gorged**

gor•geous (**gor**-juhss) ***adjective*** Really beautiful or attractive.

go•ril•la (guh-**ril**-uh) ***noun*** A very large, strong ape with dark fur found in Africa. **Gorilla** sounds like **guerrilla.**

gor•y (**gor**-ee) ***adjective*** If something is **gory,** it involves a lot of blood. ▸ **gorier, goriest**

gos•pel (**goss**-puhl) ***noun***
1. The teachings of Jesus.
2. Gospel One of the first four books in the New Testament of the Bible. The gospels describe the life and teachings of Jesus.
3. If you **take something as gospel,** you believe it to be completely true.

gos•sa•mer (**goss**-uh-mur) ***noun*** A very delicate film of spiders' webs.

gos•sip (**goss**-ip) ***noun***
1. A person who likes to talk about other people's personal business.
2. Idle talk about other people's personal business.
▸ ***verb*** **gossip**

Goth•ic (**goth**-ik) ***adjective*** In the style of art or architecture used in western Europe between the 12th and 16th centuries. Gothic buildings have pointed arches and windows.

gouge (**gouj**)
1. ***noun*** A tool used to make deep impressions in wood or other hard materials.
2. ***noun*** A deep cut caused by such a tool or other object.
3. ***verb*** To cut something deeply with a tool that has a sharp edge.
4. ***verb*** To cheat or steal from someone.
▸ ***verb*** **gouging, gouged**

gourd (**gord**) ***noun*** A fruit with a rounded shape similar to that of a squash or pumpkin. Gourds are sometimes used for decoration and to make bowls or jugs.

gour•met (gor-**may**) ***noun*** An expert on food and wine. ▸ ***adjective*** **gourmet**

gov•ern (**guhv**-urn) ***verb*** To control a country, organization, etc., using laws.
▸ **governing, governed** ▸ ***noun*** **governor**

gov•ern•ment (**guhv**-urn-muhnt) ***noun***
1. The control and administration of a country, state, or organization.
2. The people who rule or govern a country or state.
▸ ***adjective*** **governmental**

gown (**goun**) ***noun***
1. A woman's dress, as in *a wedding gown.*
2. A loose robe worn by judges and surgeons and by students at their graduation ceremonies.

GP (**jee pee**) ***noun*** A family doctor who treats common illnesses and refers patients to specialists if necessary. GP is short for *general practitioner.*

grab (**grab**) ***verb*** To take hold of something suddenly and roughly.
▸ **grabbing, grabbed**

grace (**grayss**) ***noun***
1. An elegant way of moving.
▸ ***adjective*** **graceful** ▸ ***adverb*** **gracefully**
2. Pleasant behavior. ▸ ***adjective*** **gracious** (**gray**-shuhss) ▸ ***adverb*** **graciously**
3. A short prayer of thanks that is said before a meal.

grack•le (**grak**-uhl) ***noun*** A bird with a long tail and shiny black feathers; a type of blackbird.

grade (**grayd**)
1. ***noun*** A mark given for work done in school. ▸ ***verb*** **grade**
2. ***noun*** Quality.
3. ***noun*** A class or year in a school.
4. ***verb*** To make more level, as in *to grade a side street.* ▸ **grading, graded**
5. ***noun*** The amount of slope on a road, as in *a steep grade.*

grade school ***noun*** An elementary school or a grammar school.

gra·di·ent (**gray**-dee-uhnt) ***noun*** A slope, or the steepness of a slope; a sloping surface.

G

grad·u·al (**graj**-yoo-uhl) ***adjective*** If an event is **gradual,** it takes place slowly but steadily. ▸ ***adverb*** **gradually**

grad·u·ate
1. (**graj**-oo-it) ***noun*** Someone who has completed the last year in a school and has received a diploma.
2. (**graj**-oo-ate) ***verb*** To finish a course of study in a school and receive a diploma.
3. (**graj**-oo-ate) ***verb*** To mark something such as a cup or a stick with lines so that you can measure with it.
▸ ***verb*** **graduating, graduated** ▸ ***noun*** **graduation**

graf·fi·ti (gruh-**fee**-tee) ***noun, plural*** Pictures drawn or words written on the walls of buildings, on subway cars, or on other surfaces.

graft (**graft**)
1. ***noun*** The taking of money dishonestly as a member of a government.
2. ***noun*** Money taken dishonestly.
3. ***verb*** To take the skin from one part of the body to help repair an injury to another part.
4. ***verb*** To plant a shoot from one plant into a slit in another so that they grow as one.
▸ ***noun*** **graft** ▸ ***verb*** **grafting, grafted**

grain (**grayn**) ***noun***
1. A very small particle, as in *a grain of salt.*
2. Cereal plants.
3. The seed of a cereal plant.

gram (**grahm**) ***noun*** A unit of measurement equal to one thousandth of a kilogram. A nickel weighs about five grams.

gram·mar (**gram**-ur) ***noun*** The rules of speaking or writing a language.
▸ ***adjective*** **grammatical**

grammar school ***noun*** A school that children attend from kindergarten through fifth or sixth grade.

gra·na·ry (**gray**-nuh-ree *or* **gran**-uh-ree) ***noun*** A building for storing grain.
▸ ***noun, plural*** **granaries**

grand (**grand**) ***adjective***
1. Large and impressive, as in *the grand ballroom.*
2. Very worthy or dignified, as in *the grand lady.*
3. *(informal)* Wonderful.
4. Complete.
▸ ***adjective*** **grander, grandest**
▸ ***adverb*** **grandly**

grand·child (**grand**-*childe*) ***noun*** You are the **grandchild** of your parents' parents. ▸ ***noun, plural*** **grandchildren**

grand·fa·ther (**grand**-*fah*-THur) ***noun*** The father of your mother or father.

grandfather clock ***noun*** A clock built into the top of a tall, narrow, usually wooden cabinet.

grand jury ***noun*** A group of people that meet to decide if there is enough evidence to try someone for a crime.
▸ ***noun, plural*** **grand juries**

grand·moth·er (**grand**-*muh*-THur) ***noun*** The mother of your mother or father.

grand·pa·rent (**grand**-*pa*-ruhnt) ***noun*** The parent of one of your parents.

grand·stand (**grand**-*stand*) ***noun*** The main area at a ballpark or stadium with seats for spectators.

gran·ite (**gran**-it) ***noun*** A hard, gray rock used in the construction of buildings.

gra·no·la (gruh-**noh**-luh) ***noun*** A food made with grains, nuts, and dried fruit and often eaten as a breakfast cereal.

grant (**grant**)
1. ***verb*** To give something, or to allow something.
2. ***noun*** A sum of money given by the government or another organization for a special purpose, as in *a study grant.*
3. ***verb*** To accept something for the sake of argument.
4. If you **take** something **for granted,**

G

you do not appreciate it, or you assume that you will get it.
▸ ***verb*** **granting, granted**

gran•u•la•ted sugar (**gran**-yuh-lay-tid) ***noun*** Sugar that is in the form of grains or tiny particles.

grape (**grayp**) ***noun*** A small fruit that grows on a vine that can be eaten fresh, dried to make currants or raisins, or crushed to make wine.

grape•fruit (**grayp**-*froot*) ***noun*** A large, yellow citrus fruit.

grape•vine (**grayp**-*vine*) ***noun***
1. A climbing plant on which grapes grow.
2. If you hear information **through the grapevine,** you hear it unofficially or as a rumor.

graph (**graf**) ***noun*** A diagram that shows the relationship between numbers or amounts. Common graphs use bars, lines, or parts of a circle to display data.

graph•ic (**graf**-ik) ***adjective***
1. Very realistic.
2. To do with art and design.
3. To do with handwriting, as in *graphic symbols.*

graph•ics (**graf**-iks) ***noun, plural*** Images such as drawings, maps, or graphs.

graph•ite (**graf**-ite) ***noun*** A common black or gray mineral used as lead in pencils.

grap•ple (**grap**-uhl) ***verb***
1. To wrestle with someone.
2. If you **grapple** with a problem, you think hard about all the ways it can be solved.
▸ ***verb*** **grappling, grappled**

grasp (**grasp**) ***verb***
1. To seize something and hold it tightly.
2. To understand something completely.
▸ ***verb*** **grasping, grasped** ▸ ***noun*** **grasp**

grass (**grass**) ***noun***
1. A green plant with long, thin, erect leaves that grows wild and is used for lawns.
2. Any of several other plants, such as grains, bamboo, and sugarcane.
▸ ***noun, plural*** **grasses** ▸ ***adjective*** **grassy**

grass•hop•per (**grass**-*hop*-ur) ***noun*** An insect that eats plants and has long back legs adapted for leaping.

grass•land (**grass**-*land*) ***noun*** A large, open area of grass, often used as pasture for animals.

grate (**grayt**)
1. ***verb*** To shred food, such as cheese, into small, thin pieces.
2. ***verb*** If something **grates** on you, it annoys you.
3. ***noun*** A grid of metal bars in the base of a furnace or fireplace.
Grate sounds like **great.**
▸ ***verb*** **grating, grated**

grate•ful (**grayt**-fuhl) ***adjective*** If you are **grateful** for something that you are given, you appreciate it and are thankful for it. ▸ ***adverb*** **gratefully**

grat•i•fy (**grat**-i-fye) ***verb*** To give pleasure to someone by fulfilling his or her needs or desires. ▸ **gratifies, gratifying, gratified** ▸ ***noun*** **gratification**

grat•i•tude (**grat**-uh-tood) ***noun*** A feeling of being grateful and thankful.

grave (**grayv**)
1. ***noun*** A place where a dead person is buried.
2. ***adjective*** Very serious, as in *grave danger.* ▸ **graver, gravest** ▸ ***adverb*** **gravely**

grav•el (**grav**-uhl) ***noun*** Small, loose stones used for paths and roads.

grave•stone (**grayv**-*stohn*) ***noun*** A piece of carved stone that marks someone's grave.

grave•yard (**grayv**-*yard*) ***noun*** A piece of land, often near a church, where dead people are buried; a cemetery.

grav•i•ty (**grav**-uh-tee) ***noun***
1. The force that pulls things down toward the surface of the earth and keeps them from floating away into space.
2. Seriousness.
▸ ***noun, plural*** **gravities**

G

gra•vy (**gray**-vee) ***noun*** A flavored sauce served with meat and usually made from the juices of cooked meat.
▸ ***noun, plural*** **gravies**

gray (**gray**) ***noun*** The color between black and white, such as the color of the sky on a rainy day. ▸ ***adjective*** **gray**

graze (**grayz**) ***verb***
1. When animals **graze,** they eat grass that is growing in a field.
2. To scrape the surface off your skin.
▸ ***noun*** **graze**
3. To touch just barely.
▸ ***verb*** **grazing, grazed**

grease (**greess**) ***noun***
1. A thick, oily substance used on machines to help the parts move easily.
2. An oily substance found in animal fat and in hair and skin.
▸ ***verb*** **grease** ▸ ***adjective*** **greasy**

great (**grayt**) ***adjective***
1. Very big or large. ▸ ***adverb*** **greatly**
2. Very important and famous. ▸ ***noun*** **greatness**
3. Very good, or wonderful.
Great sounds like **grate.**
▸ ***adjective*** **greater, greatest**

Great Dane (**dayn**) ***noun*** A very large, powerful dog with a short coat and long legs.

great-grandchild ***noun*** The son or daughter of your grandchild.

great-grandparent ***noun*** The father or mother of one of your grandparents.

greed (**greed**) ***noun*** Extreme selfishness; wanting everything for oneself.

greed•y (**gree**-dee) ***adjective*** If you are **greedy,** you want more of something than you need. ▸ **greedier, greediest**
▸ ***adverb*** **greedily**

green (**green**)
1. ***noun*** The color of grass or leaves.
▸ ***adjective*** **green**
2. ***adjective*** Not ripe, as in *green apples.*
3. ***noun*** An area of grass in a public place, as in *the village green.*
4. ***noun*** An area of ground used for an activity or sport, as in *a putting green.*
5. **greens** ***noun, plural*** Green leaves or stems used as food, as in *salad greens.*
6. ***adjective*** Having little experience.
▸ ***adjective*** **greener, greenest**

green card ***noun*** A permit or identification card that allows someone who is not a citizen to live and work in the United States.

green•horn (**green**-*horn*) ***noun*** *(informal)* Someone who is new to and unfamiliar with an organization, activity, or area.

green•house (**green**-*houss*) ***noun*** An enclosed structure used for the growth and protection of tender plants. Temperature and light are controlled in a greenhouse so that all plants can grow out of season.

greenhouse effect ***noun*** The warming of the atmosphere around the earth caused by gases such as carbon dioxide that collect in the atmosphere and prevent the sun's heat from escaping.

greenhouse gases ***noun, plural*** Gases such as carbon dioxide and methane that are found in the earth's atmosphere and help hold heat in.

green thumb ***noun*** A talent for making plants grow.

greet (**greet**) ***verb***
1. To say something friendly or welcoming to someone when you meet him or her. ▸ ***noun*** **greeting,** ***noun*** **greeter**
2. To react to something in a particular way.
▸ ***verb*** **greeting, greeted**

gre•nade (gruh-**nade**) ***noun*** A small bomb that is thrown by hand or fired from a rifle.

grey (**gray**) ***noun*** Another spelling of **gray.** ▸ ***adjective*** **grey**

grey•hound (**gray**-*hound*) ***noun*** A thin dog with a smooth coat. A greyhound can run very fast.

grid (**grid**) ***noun*** A set of straight lines that cross each other at right angles to form a regular pattern of squares.

G

grid•dle (**grid**-uhl) ***noun*** A large, flat pan with a handle, used for frying food.

grid•i•ron (**grid**-eye-urn) ***noun***
1. A griddle.
2. A playing field marked out for football.

grid•lock (**grid**-*lok*) ***noun*** A severe traffic jam that results in blocking all intersections in a grid of streets so that vehicles cannot move in any direction.

grief (**greef**) ***noun*** A feeling of great sadness.

griev•ance (**gree**-vuhnss) ***noun*** If you have a **grievance,** you have a real or imagined reason to feel angry or annoyed about something.

grieve (**greev**) ***verb*** To feel very sad, usually because someone whom you love has died. ▸ **grieving, grieved**

grill (**gril**)
1. ***noun*** A cooking utensil or device used outdoors that heats or cooks food.
2. ***verb*** To cook food on a **grill.**
3. ***verb*** *(informal)* To ask someone a lot of detailed questions in order to find out information.
▸ ***verb*** **grilling, grilled**

grim (**grim**) ***adjective*** Gloomy, stern, and unpleasant, as in *a grim expression.* ▸ **grimmer, grimmest** ▸ ***adverb*** **grimly**

gri•mace (**grim**-iss) ***noun*** A facial expression usually indicating a negative reaction to something. ▸ ***verb*** **grimace**

grime (**grime**) ***noun*** Dirt or soot that accumulates on a surface. ▸ ***adjective*** **grimy**

grin (**grin**) ***verb*** To give a large, cheerful smile. ▸ **grinning, grinned** ▸ ***noun*** **grin**

grind (**grinde**)
1. ***verb*** To crush something into a powder.
2. ***verb*** To sharpen a blade on a rough, hard surface.
3. ***noun*** A period of very hard work or study.
▸ ***verb*** **grinding, ground** (**ground**)

grind•stone (**grinde**-*stone*) ***noun***
1. A rotating stone used to sharpen or shape something.
2. If you **keep your nose to the grindstone,** you do not let anything distract you from your work.

grip (**grip**) ***verb***
1. To hold something very tightly.
▸ ***noun*** **grip**
2. If something **grips** you, it holds your attention completely because it is so exciting. ▸ ***adjective*** **gripping**
▸ ***verb*** **gripping, gripped**

gris•tle (**griss**-uhl) ***noun*** A tough substance sometimes found in meat. Gristle is cartilage tissue.

grit (**grit**)
1. ***noun*** A sandy or grainy material on an otherwise smooth surface.
▸ ***adjective*** **gritty**
2. ***noun*** The ability to keep on doing something even though it is very difficult.
3. ***verb*** To grind your teeth together.
▸ **gritting, gritted**

grits (**grits**) ***noun, plural*** Coarsely ground grain, especially white corn, boiled and eaten as a cereal or side dish.

griz•zly bear (**griz**-lee) ***noun*** A large, brown or gray bear of western North America.

groan (**grohn**) ***verb*** To make a long, low sound showing that you are in pain or are unhappy. ▸ **groaning, groaned** ▸ ***noun*** **groan**

gro•cer (**groh**-sur) ***noun*** Someone who owns or runs a store selling food and household goods. ▸ ***noun*** **grocery**

grog•gy (**grog**-ee) ***adjective*** Sleepy or dizzy. ▸ **groggier, groggiest**

groin (**groin**) ***noun*** The hollow that marks the meeting of the inner part of your thigh and your stomach.

groom (**groom**)
1. ***noun*** A man who is about to get married or has just gotten married.
2. ***verb*** To take care of your appearance and your clothing.
3. ***noun*** Someone who takes care of horses.
4. ***verb*** To brush and clean an animal such as a horse. ▸ ***noun*** **grooming**
▸ ***verb*** **grooming, groomed**

G

groove (**groov**) ***noun***
1. A long cut in the surface of something.
2. A habitual or routine way of doing something.

grope (**grohp**) ***verb***
1. To feel about with your hands for something that you cannot see.
2. To look for or think about in an uncertain way.
▸ ***verb*** **groping, groped**

gross (**grohss**)
1. ***adjective*** Very large, as in *a gross error.*
2. ***adjective*** Very rude and improper, as in *gross behavior.*
3. ***adjective*** Unpleasantly big and ugly.
4. ***noun*** A group of 12 dozen, or 144, things, as in *a gross of pens.*
5. ***adjective*** The **gross** amount is the total amount, with nothing taken away.
▸ ***adjective*** **grosser, grossest** ▸ ***adverb*** **grossly**

gro•tesque (groh-**tesk**) ***adjective*** Very strange or ugly. ▸ ***adverb*** **grotesquely**

grouch (**grouch**) ***noun*** Someone who is in a bad mood. ▸ ***noun, plural*** **grouches**

grouch•y (**grou**-chee) ***adjective*** Mean, nasty, or cross.

ground (**ground**)
1. ***noun*** The surface of the earth.
2. ***noun*** Land used for a certain activity, as in *a parade ground.*
3. ***verb*** In baseball, to hit a ball that bounces along the ground. ▸ **grounding, grounded**
4. ground ball ***noun*** In baseball, a ball hit along the ground by a batter.
5. grounds ***noun, plural*** Reason or cause.
6. grounds ***noun, plural*** The land surrounding a large building or group of buildings.

ground•ed (**groun**-did) ***adjective***
1. If an aircraft is **grounded,** it cannot fly.
2. *(informal)* If you are **grounded,** you are not allowed to go out.
3. If an electrical appliance is **grounded,** it is connected directly to the earth and is safe to use.

ground•hog (**ground**-*hog*) ***noun*** A small, furry, burrowing animal with large front teeth. Also called a **woodchuck.**

Groundhog Day ***noun*** A day, February 2, said to forecast the coming of spring. If the groundhog sees its shadow, the forecast is for six more weeks of winter, but if the groundhog does not see its shadow, the forecast is for an early spring.

group (**groop**)
1. ***noun*** A number of things that go together or are similar in some way.
2. ***verb*** To put things into groups, or to make a group. ▸ **grouping, grouped**
3. ***noun*** A number of people who gather together or share a common purpose, as in *a musical group.*

grouse (**grouss**)
1. ***noun*** A small, plump game bird.
2. ***verb*** To complain loudly about something.
▸ **grousing, groused**

grove (**grohv**) ***noun*** A group of trees growing or planted near one another, as in *an olive grove.*

grov•el (**gruhv**-uhl *or* **grov**-uhl) ***verb*** To be unnaturally humble and polite to someone because you are afraid of the person or because you think he or she is very important. ▸ **groveling, groveled**

grow (**groh**) ***verb***
1. To increase in size, length, or amount.
2. To plant something and look after it so that it lives and gets bigger.
3. To become.
4. If something **grows on** you, you gradually start to like it.
▸ ***verb*** **growing, grew** (**groo**), **grown** (**grohn**)

growl (**groul**) ***verb*** When an animal **growls,** it makes a low, deep noise, usually because it is angry. ▸ **growling, growled** ▸ ***noun*** **growl**

grown-up ***noun*** An adult. ▸ ***adjective*** **grown-up**

G

growth (**grohth**) ***noun***
1. The process of growing.
2. A lump of body tissue either on or inside someone's body.

grub (**gruhb**) ***noun***
1. The young form of some insects that looks like a short, white worm.
2. *(slang)* Food.

grub•by (**gruhb**-ee) ***adjective*** Dirty or sloppy. ▸ **grubbier, grubbiest** ▸ ***noun*** **grubbiness**

grudge (**gruhj**) ***noun*** A feeling of resentment toward someone who has hurt or insulted you in the past. ▸ ***verb*** **grudge**

gru•el•ing (**groo**-uh-ling) ***adjective*** Very demanding and tiring, as in *a grueling job.*

grue•some (**groo**-suhm) ***adjective*** Something that is **gruesome** is disgusting and horrible.

gruff (**gruhf**) ***adjective*** Rough or rude. ▸ **gruffer, gruffest** ▸ ***adverb*** **gruffly**

grum•ble (**gruhm**-buhl) ***verb*** To complain about something in a grouchy way. ▸ **grumbling, grumbled**

grump•y (**gruhm**-pee) ***adjective*** Grouchy or cross. ▸ **grumpier, grumpiest** ▸ ***adverb*** **grumpily**

grunge (**gruhnj**) ***noun*** A type of rock music influenced by heavy metal and punk. ▸ ***adjective*** **grunge**

grunt (**gruhnt**) ***verb*** To make a deep, gruff sound like a pig. ▸ **grunting, grunted** ▸ ***noun*** **grunt**

gua•ca•mo•le (gwah-kuh-**moh**-lee) ***noun*** A dip made of avocado, tomatoes, onions, and seasonings.

guar•an•tee (ga-ruhn-**tee**) ***noun***
1. A promise made by manufacturers that if their product breaks within a certain time or is defective, they will repair or replace it.
2. A promise that something will definitely happen.
▸ ***verb*** **guarantee**

guard (**gard**)
1. ***verb*** To protect a person or place from attack.
2. ***verb*** To watch a person carefully to prevent him or her from escaping.
3. ***noun*** Someone who protects or keeps watch over a person or place.
4. ***noun*** A football player whose job is often to protect the quarterback or tackle the opposition's quarterback.
5. ***noun*** A basketball player whose job is often to initiate plays.
6. ***noun*** An object placed near another object to provide protection, as in *a shin guard.*
7. ***verb*** If you **guard against** something, you try to keep it from happening.
▸ ***verb*** **guarding, guarded**

guard•i•an (**gar**-dee-uhn) ***noun***
1. Someone who is not the parent of a child but who has the legal responsibility to look after him or her.
2. Someone who guards or protects something. ▸ ***adjective*** **guardian**

gua•va (**gwah**-vuh) ***noun*** A tropical tree bearing a large yellow fruit.

guer•ril•la (guh-**ril**-uh) ***noun*** A member of a small group of fighters or soldiers that often launches surprise attacks against an official army. **Guerrilla** sounds like **gorilla.** ▸ ***adjective*** **guerrilla**

guess (**gess**) ***verb***
1. To give an answer that may be right but that you cannot be sure of. ▸ ***noun*** **guess**
2. To suppose or believe something.
▸ ***verb*** **guesses, guessing, guessed**

guest (**gest**) ***noun***
1. Someone who has been invited to visit or to stay in another's home.
2. Someone staying in a hotel, a motel, or an inn.

gui•dance (**gye**-duhnss) ***noun***
1. Advice or counsel, especially about a student's future plans, as in *career guidance.*
2. Direction or supervision.

G

guide (**gide**) ***verb*** To help someone, usually by showing the person around a place or by leading the person across difficult country. ▸ **guiding, guided** ▸ ***noun*** **guide**

guide•book (**gide**-*buk*) ***noun*** A book containing maps and information about a place.

guided missile ***noun*** A missile that can be aimed directly at its target and guided during flight.

guide dog ***noun*** A dog trained to lead a visually impaired person.

guide word ***noun*** One of the words at the top of a page in a dictionary or encyclopedia that show the part of the alphabet included on that page.

guild (**gild**) ***noun*** A group or organization of people who do the same kind of work or have the same interests.

guile (**gile**) ***noun*** Cunning or artful deception.

guil•lo•tine (**gil**-uh-*teen or* **gee**-uh-*teen*) ***noun*** A large machine with a sharp blade used in the past to sever the heads of criminals.

guilt (**gilt**) ***noun***
1. The fact of having committed a crime or done something wrong.
2. A feeling of shame or remorse for having done something wrong or having failed to do something.
Guilt sounds like **gilt.**

guilt•y (**gil**-tee) ***adjective***
1. If you are **guilty,** you have committed a crime or done something wrong.
2. If you feel **guilty,** you feel bad because you have done something wrong or have failed to do something.
▸ ***adjective*** **guiltier, guiltiest** ▸ ***adverb*** **guiltily**

guin•ea pig (**gin**-ee) ***noun***
1. A small mammal with smooth fur, short ears, and a very short tail, often kept as a pet.
2. A person who is used in an experiment.

gui•tar (guh-**tar**) ***noun*** A musical instrument with strings that you pluck or strum.

gulch (**guhlch**) ***noun*** A deep ravine or valley that fills with water when it rains. ▸ ***noun, plural*** **gulches**

gulf (**guhlf**) ***noun***
1. A large area of sea that is partly surrounded by land, as in *the Gulf of Mexico.*
2. A difference or gap between people.

gull (**guhl**) ***noun*** Short for **seagull.**

gul•li•ble (**guhl**-uh-buhl) ***adjective*** If you are **gullible,** you believe anything you are told and you are easily tricked. ▸ ***noun*** **gullibility**

gul•ly (**guhl**-ee) ***noun*** A long, narrow ravine or ditch. ▸ ***noun, plural*** **gullies**

gulp (**guhlp**)
1. ***verb*** To swallow something quickly and noisily. ▸ **gulping, gulped**
2. ***noun*** A mouthful of something that is swallowed.

gum (**guhm**) ***noun***
1. Your **gums** are the areas of firm, pink flesh around the base of your teeth.
2. A thick liquid from any of various plants.
3. A sticky substance made from such a liquid and used as glue.
4. A sweet substance used for chewing. Also called **chewing gum.**

gum•drop (**guhm**-*drop*) ***noun*** A small, chewy candy covered with sugar.

gun (**guhn**)
1. ***noun*** A weapon that fires bullets through a long metal tube.
2. gun down ***verb*** To shoot someone with a gun.
3. ***verb*** To speed up something quickly, as in *to gun an engine.*
▸ ***verb*** **gunning, gunned**

gun•fire (**guhn**-*fire*) ***noun*** The firing of guns.

gun•pow•der (**guhn**-*pou*-dur) ***noun*** A powder that explodes easily. Gunpowder is used in large naval guns, in fireworks, and in blasting.

gun•smith (**guhn**-*smith*) ***noun*** Someone who makes and repairs guns.

gup•py (**guhp**-ee) ***noun*** A tiny freshwater fish popular in home aquariums. ▸ ***noun, plural*** **guppies**

gur•gle (**gur**-guhl) ***verb***
1. When water **gurgles,** it makes a low, bubbling sound.
2. To make a low, bubbling sound like gurgling water.
▸ ***verb*** **gurgling, gurgled** ▸ ***noun*** **gurgle**

gush (**guhsh**) ***verb***
1. When liquid **gushes,** it flows quickly in large amounts. ▸ ***noun*** **gush**
2. When a person **gushes,** he or she is embarrassingly sentimental or emotional.
▸ ***verb*** **gushes, gushing, gushed**
▸ ***adjective*** **gushing**

gust (**guhst**) ***noun*** A sudden, strong blast of wind. ▸ ***adjective*** **gusty**

gus•to (**guhss**-toh) ***noun*** If you do something with **gusto,** you do it with energy and enthusiasm.

gut (**guht**)
1. ***noun*** The alimentary canal in your body.
2. guts ***noun, plural*** Intestines.
3. ***verb*** To destroy the inside of a building. ▸ **gutting, gutted**
4. guts ***noun, plural*** *(informal)* Courage.

gut•ter (**guht**-ur) ***noun*** A channel or length of tubing through which rain is drained away from a road or from the roof of a building.

guy (**gye**) ***noun*** *(informal)* A man or a boy.

guz•zle (**guh**-zuhl) ***verb*** To eat or drink something quickly and noisily.
▸ **guzzling, guzzled**

gym (**jim**) ***noun***
1. A large room or building with special equipment for doing exercises and physical training. Gym is short for *gymnasium.*
2. A class or course in physical education.

gym•na•si•um (jim-**nay**-zee-uhm) ***noun*** A gym.

gym•nast (**jim**-nast) ***noun*** Someone who practices gymnastics.

gym•nas•tics (jim-**nass**-tiks) ***noun*** Physical exercises, often performed on apparatus, that involve difficult and carefully controlled body movements.
▸ ***adjective*** **gymnastic**

Gypsy (**jip**-see) ***noun*** A term sometimes used for one of the Romany people. *See* **Rom.** ▸ ***noun, plural*** **Gypsies**

gy•rate (**jye**-rate) ***verb*** To move around and around in a circle. ▸ **gyrating, gyrated**

gy•ro•scope (**jye**-ruh-*skope*) ***noun*** A wheel that spins inside a frame and causes the frame to balance in any position. Gyroscopes are used to help keep ships and aircraft steady.

H

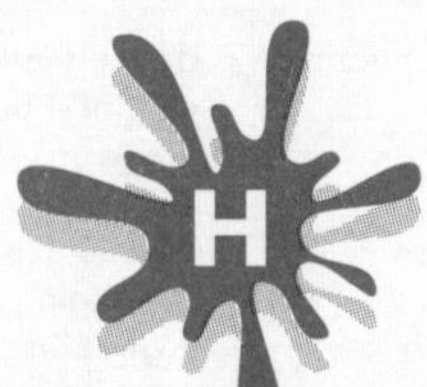

ha (**hah**) *interjection*
1. A word used to express joy, surprise, or triumph.
2. A word used to express laughter.

hab•it (**hab**-it) ***noun***
1. Something that you do regularly, often without thinking about it.
2. A piece of clothing that looks like a long, loose dress, worn by monks and nuns.
3. Clothing worn for a particular activity, as in *a riding habit.*

hab•it•a•ble (**hab**-uh-tuh-buhl) ***adjective*** If a building is **habitable,** it is safe, comfortable, and clean enough to live in.

hab•i•tat (**hab**-uh-*tat*) ***noun*** The place and natural conditions in which a plant or an animal lives.

ha•bit•u•al (huh-**bich**-oo-uhl) ***adjective***
1. Behaving from habit, as in *a habitual smoker.*
2. Done over and over again.
3. Regular or usual.

ha•bit•u•al•ly (huh-**bich**-oo-uh-lee) ***adverb*** Usually or normally.

ha•ci•en•da (hah-see-**en**-duh) ***noun*** A large ranch or estate found in the southwestern part of the United States or in Mexico or other Spanish-speaking countries.

hack (**hak**)
1. ***verb*** To chop or cut something roughly. ▸ **hacking, hacked**
2. ***noun*** A short, dry cough. ▸ ***verb* hack**
3. ***noun*** *(informal)* A taxi.

hack•er (**hak**-ur) ***noun*** Someone who is expert at getting into a computer system illegally.

had•n't (**had**-uhnt) ***contraction*** A short form of *had not.*

hag•gard (**hag**-urd) ***adjective*** Someone who is **haggard** looks thin, tired, and worried.

hag•gle (**hag**-uhl) ***verb*** To argue, usually about the price of something.
▸ **haggling, haggled**

hai•ku (**hye**-*koo*) ***noun*** A short Japanese poem in 3 lines containing a total of 17 syllables.

hail (**hayl**) ***verb***
1. When it **hails,** small balls of ice fall from the sky. ▸ ***noun* hail**
2. To attract someone's attention.
▸ ***verb* hailing, hailed**

hair (**hair**) ***noun*** The mass of fine, soft strands that grow on your head or body or on the body of an animal. **Hair** sounds like **hare.**

hair•cut (**hair**-*kuht*) ***noun*** When you get a **haircut,** someone cuts and styles your hair.

hair•do (**hair**-*doo*) ***noun*** The way hair is styled or arranged.

hair•dress•er (**hair**-*dress*-ur) ***noun*** Someone who cuts and styles people's hair.

hair•pin (**hair**-*pin*)
1. ***noun*** A piece of bent wire with sides that press together to hold hair in place.
2. ***adjective*** Shaped like a hairpin, as in *a hairpin turn.*

hair-rais•ing (**hair**-*ray*-zing) ***adjective*** Extremely frightening.

hair•y (**hair**-ee) ***adjective***
1. Covered with hair.
2. *(slang)* Dangerous and frightening.
▸ ***adjective* hairier, hairiest**

half (**haf**)
1. ***noun*** One of two equal parts of something. ▸ ***adjective*** **half**
2. ***adverb*** Partly or not completely.
3. ***noun*** One of two equal lengths of time played in games.
▸ ***noun, plural*** **halves** (**havz**)

half brother ***noun*** A brother who shares only one parent with someone else.

half•heart•ed (**haf-har**-tid) ***adjective*** Without much enthusiasm or interest.
▸ ***adverb*** **halfheartedly**

half-mast ***noun*** The position halfway between the top and bottom of a flagpole or mast. Flags are flown at this position as a sign of respect for someone who has just died.

half sister ***noun*** A sister who shares only one parent with someone else.

half•time (**haf**-*time*) ***noun*** A short break in the middle of a game such as football, basketball, or hockey.

half•way (**haf-way**)
1. ***adjective*** Half the distance from one point to another.
2. ***adjective*** Not thorough or complete.
3. ***adverb*** To or at half the distance.

hal•i•but (**hal**-uh-buht) ***noun*** A type of fish found in both the Atlantic and Pacific oceans and used as food. ▸ ***noun, plural*** **halibut** *or* **halibuts**

hall (**hawl**) ***noun***
1. An area of a house just inside the front door.
2. A large room used for meetings or other public events.
3. A corridor or a passageway.
Hall sounds like **haul.**

hal•le•lu•jah (hal-uh-**loo**-yuh) ***interjection*** A word used to express joy and thanks.

hal•lowed (**hal**-ohd *or* **hal**-oh-id) ***adjective*** Sacred or holy. ▸ ***verb*** **hallow**

Hal•low•een *or* **Hallowe'en** (*hal*-oh-**een**) ***noun*** The evening of October 31, believed in the past to be the night when witches and ghosts were active. On Halloween, children dress up in costumes and go out to trick-or-treat.

hal•lu•ci•nate (huh-**loo**-suh-*nate*) ***verb*** To see something in your mind that is not really there. ▸ **hallucinating, hallucinated** ▸ ***noun*** **hallucination**

ha•lo (**hay**-loh) ***noun***
1. A ring of light around an object.
2. A circle of light shown in pictures around the heads of angels and sacred people.

halt (**hawlt**) ***verb*** To stop. ▸ **halting, halted** ▸ ***noun*** **halt**

hal•ter (**hawl**-tur) ***noun***
1. A rope or strap used to lead or tie an animal such as a horse. A halter fits over the animal's nose and behind its ears.
2. A woman's top with a band that ties behind the neck, leaving the back and shoulders bare.

halve (**hav**) ***verb***
1. To cut or divide something into two equal parts.
2. To reduce something so that there is only half as much as there was.
Halve sounds like **have.**
▸ ***verb*** **halving, halved**

ham (**ham**) ***noun*** The meat from the upper part of a pig's hind leg that has been salted and sometimes smoked.

ham•burg•er (**ham**-*bur*-gur) ***noun***
1. A round, flat piece of cooked beef, usually served on a bun.
2. Ground beef.

ham•let (**ham**-lit) ***noun*** A very small village.

ham•mer (**ham**-ur)
1. ***noun*** A tool with a metal head on a handle, used for hitting things such as nails. ▸ ***verb*** **hammer**
2. ***verb*** To hit something hard.
▸ **hammering, hammered**

ham•mock (**ham**-uhk) ***noun*** A piece of strong cloth or net that is hung up by each end and used as a bed or as a place to relax.

H

ham•per (**ham**-pur)
1. ***noun*** A large box or basket used for carrying food or for storing dirty clothing, as in *a picnic hamper* or *a laundry hamper.*
2. ***verb*** To make it difficult for someone to do something. ▸ **hampering, hampered**

ham•ster (**ham**-stur) ***noun*** A small animal like a mouse, often kept as a pet.

hand (**hand**)
1. ***noun*** The part of your body on the end of your arm. The hand includes your wrist, palm, fingers, and thumb.
2. ***verb*** To pass or give something to someone. ▸ **handing, handed**
3. ***noun*** A set of cards that you hold during a game of cards.
4. ***noun*** One of the pointers on a clock, as in *the minute hand.*
5. If you **give** or **lend a hand** to someone, you help the person.
6. ***noun*** One of a ship's crew.
7. ***noun*** A laborer, as in *a hired hand.*
8. If something is **at hand,** it is nearby and handy to use, or its time has come.
9. If you **have your hands full** with something, you are very busy with it.
10. If things are **out of hand,** they are not under control.
11. If you **wash your hands of** something, you refuse to have anything more to do with it.
12. If you are **in good hands,** you are well taken care of.

hand•bag (**hand**-*bag*) ***noun*** A bag in which a woman carries her wallet and other small things.

hand•ball (**hand**-*bawl*) ***noun***
1. A game played in a large room or outdoors in which two or four players take turns hitting a small, hard rubber ball against a wall with their hands.
2. The rubber ball used for playing **handball.**

hand•book (**hand**-*buk*) ***noun*** A book that gives you information or advice.

hand•cuffs (**hand**-*kuhfs*) ***noun, plural*** Metal rings joined by a chain that are locked around a prisoner's wrists to prevent escape. ▸ ***verb*** **handcuff**

hand•ful (**hand**-ful) ***noun***
1. The amount of something that you can hold in your hand.
2. A small number of people or things.
3. *(informal)* If someone is a **handful,** he or she is difficult to cope with.

hand•i•cap (**han**-dee-*kap*)
1. ***noun*** If someone has a **handicap,** the person has a physical disability. ▸ ***adjective*** **handicapped**
2. ***noun*** A disadvantage that makes it difficult for you to do something.
3. ***noun*** A disadvantage given to skilled competitors in a sport in order to make the competition more equal, as in *a golf handicap.*
4. ***verb*** To state the chances that each horse in a race has of winning the race. ▸ **handicapping, handicapped** ▸ ***noun*** **handicapper**

hand•i•craft (**han**-dee-*kraft*) ***noun*** A skill, such as pottery or sewing, that involves making things with your hands.

hand•ker•chief (**hang**-kur-chif) ***noun*** A small square of cloth that you use for wiping off your face or hands or blowing your nose.

han•dle (**han**-duhl)
1. ***noun*** The part of an object that you use to carry, move, or hold that object, as in *a door handle.*
2. ***verb*** To pick something up and hold it in your hands in order to look at it carefully.
3. ***verb*** To deal with someone or something.
▸ ***verb*** **handling, handled**

han•dle•bars (**han**-duhl-*barz*) ***noun, plural*** The bar at the front of a bicycle or motorcycle that you use for steering.

hand•made (**hand-made**) ***adjective*** Made by hand, not by machine.

hand-me-down ***noun*** An article of clothing or another item passed along for someone else's use. ▸ ***noun, plural*** **hand-me-downs**

hand•out (**hand**-*out*) ***noun***
1. Money, food, or clothing that is given to a needy person.
2. A pamphlet or leaflet that is given out for free.

hand•rail (**hand**-*rail*) ***noun*** A narrow rail that can be held by the hand for support, usually used on stairways.

hand•shake (**hand**-*shayk*) ***noun*** A way of greeting or saying good-bye to someone by taking the person's hand and shaking it.

hand•some (**han**-suhm) ***adjective***
1. Attractive in appearance.
2. Generous, as in *a handsome contribution.*

hand•spring (**hand**-*spring*) ***noun*** A gymnastic movement in which you spring forward or backward onto both hands, then flip all the way over to land back on your feet.

hand•stand (**hand**-*stand*) ***noun*** When you do a **handstand,** you balance on your hands with your feet in the air.

hand•writ•ing (**hand**-*rye*-ting) ***noun***
1. The style you use for forming letters and words when you write.
2. Writing done by a person, not a machine.
▸ ***adjective*** **handwritten**

hand•y (**han**-dee) ***adjective***
1. Useful and easy to use.
2. Skillful.
3. Close by.
▸ ***adjective*** **handier, handiest**

hang (**hang**) ***verb***
1. To fasten something somewhere by attaching the top of it and leaving the bottom free.
2. To kill someone by putting a rope around the person's neck and then taking the support from under the feet. The past tense and past participle of this sense of the verb is *hanged.*
3. hang up To end a telephone conversation by putting down the receiver.
4. hang out *(informal)* To spend a lot of time in a place. ▸ ***noun*** **hangout**
▸ ***verb*** **hanging, hung** (**huhng**) *or* **hanged**

han•gar (**hang**-ur) ***noun*** A large building where aircraft are kept. **Hangar** sounds like **hanger.**

hang•er (**hang**-ur) ***noun*** A piece of specially shaped wood, metal, or plastic used for hanging clothes. **Hanger** sounds like **hangar.**

hang glider ***noun*** An aircraft like a giant kite with a harness for a pilot hanging below it. ▸ ***noun*** **hang gliding**

hang•over (**hang**-*oh*-vur) ***noun*** A headache and a sick feeling that someone gets after drinking too much alcohol.

hang-up ***noun*** *(informal)* If you have a **hang-up** about something, it bothers you.

han•ker (**hang**-kur) ***verb*** To wish or long for something. ▸ **hankering, hankered** ▸ ***noun*** **hankering**

Ha•nuk•kah *or* **Chanukah** (**hah**-nuh-kuh) ***noun*** An eight-day Jewish festival that usually falls in December. Also called the Feast or Festival of Lights.

hap•haz•ard (hap-**haz**-urd) ***adjective*** Disorganized. ▸ ***adverb*** **haphazardly**

hap•less (**hap**-luhss) ***adjective*** Unlucky or unfortunate. ▸ ***adverb*** **haplessly** ▸ ***noun*** **haplessness**

hap•pen (**hap**-uhn) ***verb***
1. To take place or to occur.
2. If you **happen** to do something, you have the chance or luck to do it.
▸ ***verb*** **happening, happened**

hap•py (**hap**-ee) ***adjective***
1. Pleased and contented. ▸ ***noun*** **happiness**
2. Lucky or fortunate.
▸ ***adjective*** **happier, happiest**
▸ ***adverb*** **happily**

happy-go-lucky ***adjective*** Without any worries or troubles.

H

har•ass (huh-**rass** *or* **ha**-ruhss) ***verb*** To pester or annoy someone. ▸ **harasses, harassing, harassed** ▸ ***noun*** **harassment**

har•bor (**har**-bur)
1. ***noun*** A place where ships shelter or unload their cargo.
2. ***verb*** To take care of someone or something, as in *to harbor a wounded bird.*
3. ***verb*** To hide someone, as in *to harbor a fugitive.*
▸ ***verb*** **harboring, harbored**

hard (**hard**)
1. ***adjective*** Firm and solid, as in *a hard bed.*
2. ***adjective*** Difficult, as in *a hard exam.*
3. ***adjective*** Strong and powerful enough to cause addiction, as in *hard drugs.*
4. ***adjective*** Energetic, as in *a hard worker.*
5. ***adverb*** Energetically, as in *to work hard.*
6. ***adjective*** Not gentle; severe, as in *a hard winter.*
▸ ***noun*** **hardness** ▸ ***adjective*** **harder, hardest**

hard-boiled ***adjective***
1. Cooked by boiling until firm, as in *a hard-boiled egg.*
2. Tough and not sympathetic, as in *a hard-boiled detective.*

hard copy ***noun*** A printed version of a document created by a computer.

hard disk ***noun*** A disk inside a computer used for storing large amounts of data.

hard drive ***noun*** A device fixed inside a computer containing a disk for storing large amounts of data.

hard•en (**hard**-uhn) ***verb***
1. To become harder, or to make something harder.
2. To make or become tough and indifferent.
▸ ***verb*** **hardening, hardened**
▸ ***adjective*** **hardened**

hard•ly (**hard**-lee) ***adverb***
1. Scarcely or only just.
2. Surely not.

hard•ship (**hard**-ship) ***noun*** Difficulty or suffering.

hard•ware (**hard**-*wair*) ***noun***
1. Tools and other household equipment.
2. Computer equipment, such as a printer, a monitor, or a keyboard.

hard•wood (**hard**-*wud*) ***noun*** Strong, hard wood from various trees, such as oak, beech, or ash.

har•dy (**har**-dee) ***adjective*** If a person, an animal, or a plant is **hardy,** it is tough and can survive under very difficult conditions. ▸ **hardier, hardiest**

hare (**hair**) ***noun*** A mammal like a large rabbit with long, strong back legs. **Hare** sounds like **hair.**

harm (**harm**) ***verb*** To injure or hurt someone or something. ▸ **harming, harmed** ▸ ***noun*** **harm** ▸ ***adjective*** **harmful**

harm•less (**harm**-liss) ***adjective*** Not able to cause injury or damage, as in *a harmless joke.* ▸ ***noun*** **harmlessness** ▸ ***adverb*** **harmlessly**

har•mon•i•ca (har-**mon**-uh-kuh) ***noun*** A small musical instrument played by blowing out and drawing in your breath through the mouthpiece.

har•mo•nize (**har**-muh-nize) ***verb***
1. To sing or play music using harmony.
2. To go together in a pleasing or agreeable way.
▸ ***verb*** **harmonizing, harmonized**

har•mo•ny (**har**-muh-nee) ***noun***
1. Agreement.
2. A set of musical notes played at the same time that are part of a chord.
▸ ***noun, plural*** **harmonies** ▸ ***adjective*** **harmonious**

har•ness (**har**-niss)
1. ***noun*** A set of leather straps and metal pieces that connect a horse or another animal to a plow, cart, or wagon.
2. ***noun*** An arrangement of straps used to keep someone safe, as in *a parachute harness.*

H

3. ***verb*** To control and use something.
▸ **harnesses, harnessing, harnessed**
▸ ***noun, plural*** **harnesses**

harp (**harp**)
1. ***noun*** A large, triangular musical instrument with strings that you play by plucking. ▸ ***noun*** **harpist**
2. ***verb*** If you **harp on** something, you keep talking about it. ▸ **harping, harped**

har•poon (har-**poon**)
1. ***noun*** A long spear with an attached rope that can be thrown or shot out of a special gun. It is usually used for hunting large fish or whales.
2. ***verb*** To hit or kill with a harpoon.
▸ **harpooning, harpooned**

harp•si•chord (**harp**-suh-*kord*) ***noun*** A keyboard instrument that looks like a small piano. A harpsichord has wire strings that are plucked rather than being struck like the strings in a piano.

harsh (**harsh**) ***adjective***
1. Cruel or rough, as in *a harsh punishment.*
2. Unpleasant or hard on the body or senses, as in *a harsh light* or *a harsh voice.*
▸ ***adjective*** **harsher, harshest**
▸ ***adverb*** **harshly**

har•vest (**har**-vist)
1. ***noun*** The gathering in of crops that are ripe, or the crops gathered in.
2. ***verb*** To collect or gather up crops.
▸ **harvesting, harvested**

har•vest•er (**har**-vi-stur) ***noun*** A machine used to harvest crops.

hash (**hash**) ***noun***
1. Small pieces of meat and vegetables cooked together.
2. A mess.
▸ ***noun, plural*** **hashes**

has•n't (**haz**-uhnt) ***contraction*** A short form of *has not.*

has•sle (**hass**-uhl)
1. ***verb*** *(informal)* If someone **hassles** you, the person annoys you persistently about something. ▸ **hassling, hassled**
2. ***noun*** *(informal)* A troublesome nuisance.

haste (**hayst**) ***noun*** Speed or quickness in moving or acting.

has•ten (**hayss**-uhn) ***verb***
1. To move quickly.
2. To make someone or something move or happen faster.
▸ ***verb*** **hastening, hastened**

has•ty (**hay**-stee) ***adjective*** Too quick or hurried, as in *a hasty decision.* ▸ **hastier, hastiest** ▸ ***adverb*** **hastily**

hat (**hat**) ***noun***
1. An item of clothing that you wear on your head.
2. **hat trick** Three successes in a row, such as three goals in a single game by a hockey player.

hatch (**hach**)
1. ***verb*** When an egg **hatches,** a baby bird or reptile breaks out of it.
2. ***noun*** A group of young birds or reptiles that have hatched.
3. ***verb*** To devise a plot.
4. ***noun*** A covered hole in a floor, deck, door, wall, or ceiling.
▸ ***noun, plural*** **hatches** ▸ ***verb*** **hatches, hatching, hatched**

hatch•back (**hach**-*bak*) ***noun*** A car with a rear window that opens upward.

hatch•er•y (**hach**-er-ee) ***noun*** A place where eggs, especially chicken or fish eggs, are hatched. ▸ ***noun, plural*** **hatcheries**

hatch•et (**hach**-it) ***noun*** A small ax.

hatch•ling (**hach**-ling) ***noun*** A recently hatched animal.

hate (**hate**) ***verb*** To dislike or detest someone or something. ▸ **hating, hated**
▸ ***noun*** **hate,** ***noun*** **hatred**

hate•ful (**hate**-fuhl) ***adjective*** Horrible.
▸ ***adverb*** **hatefully**

haugh•ty (**haw**-tee) ***adjective*** If you are **haughty,** you are very proud and look down on other people.
▸ **haughtier, haughtiest** ▸ ***noun*** **haughtiness** ▸ ***adverb*** **haughtily**

H

haul (**hawl**)
1. ***verb*** To pull something with difficulty.
2. ***verb*** To transport with a vehicle, as in *to haul grain to the mill.*
3. ***noun*** A quantity of something that is caught, as in *a big haul of fish.*
4. ***noun*** A distance to be traveled.
Haul sounds like **hall.**
▸ ***verb*** **hauling, hauled**

haunch (**hawnch**) ***noun*** The hip, buttock, and upper thigh of an animal or a person. ▸ ***noun, plural*** **haunches**

haunt (**hawnt**)
1. ***verb*** If a ghost **haunts** a place, it visits it often. ▸ ***adjective*** **haunted**
2. ***verb*** If something **haunts** you, it stays on your mind. ▸ ***adjective*** **haunting**
3. ***noun*** A place you visit often.
▸ ***verb*** **haunting, haunted**

have (**hav**) ***verb***
1. To own or possess something.
2. To experience or enjoy something.
3. To receive or get something.
4. To contain or consist of.
5. To be the parent or parents of.
6. To arrange for.
Have sounds like **halve.**
▸ ***verb*** **has** (**haz**), **having, had** (**had**)

ha•ven (**hay**-vuhn) ***noun***
1. A harbor.
2. A safe place.

have•n't (**hav**-uhnt) ***contraction*** A short form of *have not.*

hav•oc (**hav**-uhk) ***noun*** Great damage and chaos.

hawk (**hawk**)
1. ***noun*** A bird of prey with a hooked beak and sharp claws that eats other birds and small animals.
2. ***verb*** To offer goods for sale by shouting in the street. ▸ **hawking, hawked**

hay (**hay**) ***noun*** Grass that is dried and fed to farm animals. **Hay** sounds like **hey.**

hay fever ***noun*** An allergy to pollen or grass that makes you sneeze, makes your eyes water, and can make you wheeze.

hay•loft (**hay**-*loft*) ***noun*** A platform high above the floor of a barn where hay is stored.

hay•stack (**hay**-*stak*) ***noun*** A large pile of hay.

hay•wire (**hay**-*wire*) ***adjective***
1. Out of order or proper working condition.
2. Acting wildly or out of control.

haz•ard (**haz**-urd)
1. ***noun*** A danger or a risk.
2. ***verb*** To risk or take a chance on something, as in *hazard a guess.*
▸ **hazarding, hazarded**

haz•ard•ous (**haz**-ur-duhss) ***adjective*** Dangerous or risky.

hazardous waste ***noun*** Dangerous materials that should not be thrown away without some sort of protective covering.

haze (**hayz**) ***noun*** Smoke, dust, or moisture in the air that prevents you from seeing very far.

ha•zel (**hay**-zuhl) ***noun***
1. A small tree or shrub that produces nuts.
2. A green-brown color. ▸ ***adjective*** **hazel**

haz•y (**hay**-zee) ***adjective***
1. Misty, as in *a hazy morning.*
2. If you have a **hazy** memory of something, it is vague and unclear in your mind.
▸ ***adjective*** **hazier, haziest** ▸ ***adverb*** **hazily**

H-bomb (**aych**) *See* **hydrogen bomb.**

he (**hee**) ***pronoun***
1. The male person or animal mentioned before.
2. That person.

head (**hed**)
1. ***noun*** The top part of your body where your brain, eyes, nose, and mouth are.
2. ***noun*** The person in charge.
▸ ***adjective*** **head**

3. ***noun*** The top or front of something, as in *the head of the line* or *the head of a pin.*
4. ***verb*** To lead.
5. ***verb*** To move toward something.
6. ***noun*** A single person or animal, as in *a head of cattle.*
7. ***noun*** A cluster of leaves or flowers, as in *a head of lettuce.*
8. If something **goes to your head,** it makes you dizzy.
9. If a compliment **goes to your head,** it makes you conceited.
10. If you **keep a cool head** in an emergency, you remain calm and relaxed.
▸ ***verb*** **heading, headed**

head•ache (**hed**-*ayk*) ***noun*** A pain in your head.

head•band (**hed**-*band*) ***noun*** A strip of cloth worn around the head to soak up sweat or keep hair out of the face.

head•dress (**hed**-*dress*) ***noun*** A covering, often decorative, for the head. ▸ ***noun, plural*** **headdresses**

head•first (**hed-furst**) ***adverb*** With the head first, or leading with the head.

head•ing (**hed**-ing) ***noun*** Words written as a title at the top of a page or over a section of writing in a magazine, newspaper, or book.

head•light (**hed**-*lite*) ***noun*** A bright light on the front of a vehicle that allows the driver or pilot to see ahead in the dark.

head•line (**hed**-*line*) ***noun*** The title of a newspaper article, printed in large, usually bold type. ▸ ***verb*** **headline**

head•long (**hed**-*lawng*) ***adverb***
1. With the head first.
2. Rashly, or with little thought.

head•mas•ter (**hed**-*mass*-tuhr) ***noun*** A man who is in charge of a private day or boarding school.

head•mis•tress (**hed**-*miss*-triss) ***noun*** A woman who is in charge of a private day or boarding school. ▸ ***noun, plural*** **headmistresses**

head-on (**hed-on**) ***adjective*** With the head or front end first. ▸ ***adverb*** **head-on**

head•phones (**hed**-*fohnz*) ***noun, plural*** Small speakers that you wear in or over your ears.

head•quar•ters (**hed**-*kwor*-turz) ***noun*** The place from which an organization is run. ▸ ***noun, plural*** **headquarters**

head start ***noun*** An advantage, usually in a race when one runner is allowed to start first.

head•strong (**hed**-*strong*) ***adjective*** Determined to have one's own way.

head•way (**hed**-*way*) ***noun*** Progress or forward movement.

heal (**heel**) ***verb***
1. To cure someone or make the person healthy. ▸ ***noun*** **healer,** ***noun*** **healing**
2. To get better.
Heal sounds like **heel.**
▸ ***verb*** **healing, healed**

health (**helth**) ***noun***
1. Strength and fitness.
2. The state or condition of your body.

health food ***noun*** Food that is grown organically, using natural fertilizers, and prepared without preservatives.

health•y (**hel**-thee) ***adjective***
1. If you are **healthy,** you are fit and well.
2. Something that is **healthy** makes you fit, as in *a healthy diet.*
▸ ***adjective*** **healthier, healthiest**
▸ ***adverb*** **healthily**

heap (**heep**)
1. ***noun*** A pile.
2. ***verb*** To pile up. ▸ **heaping, heaped**
3. ***noun*** *(informal)* A great deal of something.

hear (**hihr**) ***verb***
1. To sense sounds through your ears. ▸ ***noun*** **hearing**
2. To get news.
3. To listen to.
Hear sounds like **here.**
▸ ***verb*** **hearing, heard** (**hurd**)

H

hearing aid ***noun*** A small piece of electronic equipment that people wear in or behind one or both ears to help them hear better.

hear•say (**hihr**-*say*) ***noun*** Things that you are told but have not actually seen or experienced; rumor.

hearse (**hurss**) ***noun*** A car that carries a coffin to a funeral and burial.

heart (**hart**) ***noun***
1. The organ in your chest that pumps blood all through your body.
2. Courage or enthusiasm.
3. Love and affection.
4. The center of something, as in *the heart of the city.*
5. If you learn something **by heart,** you memorize it.
6. **hearts *noun, plural*** One of the four suits in a deck of cards. Hearts have a red symbol shaped like a heart.
7. If you **take something to heart,** you think about it seriously.

heart attack ***noun*** If someone has a **heart attack,** the person's heart is not pumping blood properly to the rest of the body. The result can be extreme chest pain, collapse, or, in very severe cases, death.

heart•beat (**hart**-*beet*) ***noun*** One complete pumping movement of the heart.

heart•bro•ken (**hart**-*broh*-kuhn) ***adjective*** If you are **heartbroken,** you are sad or filled with grief.

hearth (**harth**) ***noun*** The area in front of a fireplace.

heart•less (**hart**-liss) ***adjective*** Cruel and unkind. ▸ ***noun*** **heartlessness** ▸ ***adverb*** **heartlessly**

heart•y (**har**-tee) ***adjective***
1. Enthusiastic or sincere. ▸ ***adverb*** **heartily**
2. A **hearty** meal is large and filling. ▸ ***adjective*** **heartier, heartiest** ▸ ***noun*** **heartiness**

heat (**heet**)
1. ***noun*** Great warmth.
2. ***verb*** To warm or cook something. ▸ **heating, heated**
3. ***noun*** A trial run in a race.
4. ***noun*** Passion. ▸ ***adjective*** **heated** ▸ ***adverb*** **heatedly**
5. ***noun*** In physics, energy that comes from the motion of molecules passing from one substance to another, which increases temperature.
6. **heat wave *noun*** Unusually hot weather that lasts for several days.

heat•er (**hee**-tur) ***noun*** A device that produces heat, such as a radiator or a furnace.

heath (**heeth**) ***noun*** A large, wild area of grasses, ferns, and heather.

hea•then (**hee**-THuhn) ***noun***
1. Someone who does not believe in the God of Christianity, Judaism, or Islam.
2. *(informal)* Someone who is uncivilized.

heath•er (**heTH**-ur) ***noun*** A small bush with pink, purple, or white flowers.

heave (**heev**)
1. ***verb*** To lift, pull, push, or throw something with great effort.
2. ***verb*** To go up and down.
3. ***noun*** The act of lifting or pulling. ▸ ***verb*** **heaving, heaved**

heav•en (**hev**-uhn) ***noun***
1. In Christianity and some other religions, a glorious place where God is believed to live and where good people are believed to go after they die.
2. A wonderful place, thing, or state.
3. **the heavens *noun, plural*** The sky.

heav•en•ly (**hev**-uhn-lee) ***adjective***
1. To do with heaven; divine.
2. To do with the sky or outer space, as in *heavenly bodies.*
3. Delightful or wonderful.

heav•y (**hev**-ee) ***adjective***
1. Weighing a lot.
2. Great in amount or force, as in *heavy fighting* or *heavy rain.*
3. Slow or difficult, as in *heavy work.*
4. Difficult to digest, as in *heavy, greasy food.*
5. *(slang)* Serious and hard to cope with, as in *a heavy film.*

▸ ***adjective*** **heavier, heaviest** ▸ ***noun*** **heaviness** ▸ ***adverb*** **heavily**

heavy metal ***noun*** A type of rock-and-roll music with a strong beat and loud electric guitars.

He•brew (**hee**-broo)
1. ***noun*** A member of or descendant from one of the Jewish tribes of ancient times.
2. ***noun*** The language of the ancient Hebrews, used today as a language of prayer and by the people who live in Israel.
3. ***adjective*** To do with the Hebrews or their language.

heck•le (**hek**-uhl) ***verb*** To interrupt a speaker by making rude comments.
▸ **heckling, heckled** ▸ ***noun*** **heckler**

hect•are (**hek**-tair) ***noun*** A unit of area in the metric system. One hectare is equal to 10,000 square meters. It takes about 15 school soccer fields to make one hectare. A hectare is about 2½ acres.

hec•tic (**hek**-tik) ***adjective*** Very busy.
▸ ***adverb*** **hectically**

hedge (**hej**)
1. ***noun*** A border of bushes.
2. ***verb*** To avoid giving a direct answer.
▸ **hedging, hedged**

heed (**heed**) ***verb*** To pay close attention to someone or something. ▸ **heeding, heeded** ▸ ***noun*** **heed**

heel (**heel**) ***noun***
1. The back part of your foot.
2. Something that supports or is worn on the back part of your foot.
3. If you **kick up your heels,** you are having a very good time.
Heel sounds like **heal.**

hef•ty (**hef**-tee) ***adjective*** *(informal)* Large or powerful. ▸ **heftier, heftiest**
▸ ***noun*** **heftiness** ▸ ***adverb*** **heftily**

heif•er (**hef**-ur) ***noun*** A young cow that has not had a calf.

height (**hite**) ***noun***
1. A measurement of how high something is.
2. The most important or greatest point of something.

height•en (**hite**-uhn) ***verb*** To make something higher or stronger, as in *to heighten suspense.*

Heim•lich maneuver (**hime**-lik) ***noun*** An emergency action done to dislodge food from the windpipe, performed by squeezing the person from behind, below the ribs.

heir (**air**) ***noun*** Someone who has been, or will be, left money, property, or a title, as in *the heir to a fortune.* **Heir** sounds like **air.**

heir•ess (**air**-uhss) ***noun*** A girl or woman who has been, or will be, left money, property, or a title. ▸ ***noun, plural*** **heiresses**

heir•loom (**air**-*loom*) ***noun*** Something precious that is owned by a family member and handed down from one generation to the next.

hel•i•cop•ter (**hel**-uh-*kop*-tur) ***noun*** An aircraft with large rotating blades on top that can take off and land in a small space.

he•li•um (**hee**-lee-uhm) ***noun*** A light, colorless gas that does not burn. It is used in airships and balloons.

hell (**hel**) ***noun***
1. In Christianity and some other religions, a place of suffering and misery where evil people are believed to go when they die.
2. A very unpleasant place, thing, or state.
▸ ***adjective*** **hellish**

hel•lo (hel-**oh** *or* huh-**loh**) ***interjection*** A word said in greeting when you meet a person or speak on the telephone.

helm (**helm**) ***noun***
1. The wheel or handle used to steer a boat.
2. If someone is **at the helm** of something, such as a company, the person is in charge of it.

hel•met (**hel**-mit) ***noun*** A hard hat that protects your head during sports or dangerous activities.

H

help (**help**)
1. ***verb*** To assist. ▸ ***noun*** **helper**
2. ***noun*** Assistance.
3. ***verb*** To make feel better.
4. ***verb*** To avoid.
▸ ***verb*** **helping, helped**

help•ful (**help**-fuhl) ***adjective*** Friendly and willing to help. ▸ ***noun*** **helpfulness** ▸ ***adverb*** **helpfully**

help•ing (**help**-ing) ***noun*** A portion of food.

helping verb ***noun*** A verb, such as *may* or a form of *be*, that is used together with another verb to complete the meaning of that verb, as in "may marry" or "is married." A helping verb is also called an **auxiliary** *verb*.

help•less (**help**-liss) ***adjective*** If you are **helpless,** you cannot look after yourself. ▸ ***noun*** **helplessness** ▸ ***adverb*** **helplessly**

hem (**hem**) ***verb***
1. To fold over an edge of material and sew it down. ▸ ***noun*** **hem**
2. If you are **hemmed in,** you are surrounded and cannot get out.
▸ ***verb*** **hemming, hemmed**

hem•i•sphere (**hem**-uhss-*fihr*) ***noun*** One half of a sphere, especially of the earth.

hem•lock (**hem**-lok) ***noun***
1. An evergreen tree similar to the pine. It has flat needles, small cones, and reddish bark.
2. A poisonous plant of the carrot family.

he•mo•glo•bin (**hee**-muh-*gloh*-buhn) ***noun*** A substance in your red blood cells that carries oxygen to all parts of your body.

he•mo•phil•i•a (*hee*-muh-**fil**-ee-uh) ***noun*** If people suffer from **hemophilia,** their blood does not clot properly, so they bleed severely if cut or bruised.

hem•or•rhage (**hem**-ur-ij) ***noun*** Severe bleeding from a torn or cut blood vessel.

hemp (**hemp**) ***noun*** A plant whose fibers are used to make rope and sacks.

hen (**hen**) ***noun***
1. Any of various female birds.
2. A female bird raised for its eggs and its meat.

hep•tath•lon (hep-**tath**-luhn) ***noun*** A competition made up of seven athletic events.

her (**hur**)
1. ***pronoun*** The form of **she** used as a grammatical object.
2. ***adjective*** Belonging to or to do with her.

her•ald•ry (**her**-uhl-dree) ***noun*** The study of coats of arms and family histories.

herb (**urb**) ***noun*** A plant used in cooking or medicine. ▸ ***noun*** **herbalist** ▸ ***adjective*** **herbal**

her•bi•vore (**hur**-buh-*vor*) ***noun*** An animal that eats plants rather than other animals. ▸ ***adjective*** **herbivorous** (hur-**biv**-uh-ruhss)

herd (**hurd**)
1. ***noun*** A large group of animals, as in *a herd of cattle.*
2. ***verb*** To make people or animals move together as a group. ▸ **herding, herded** ▸ ***noun*** **herder**
Herd sounds like **heard.**

here (**hihr**)
1. ***adverb*** At or in this place.
2. ***adverb*** At this point or time.
3. ***interjection*** A word used to answer a roll call.
4. ***noun*** This place.
Here sounds like **hear.**

here•af•ter (*hihr*-**af**-tur) ***adverb*** From now on.

here•by (**hihr**-*bye or hihr*-**bye**) ***adverb*** By means of this.

he•red•i•tar•y (huh-**red**-uh-*ter*-ee) ***adjective*** If something is **hereditary,** it is passed from parent to child, as in *a hereditary disease.*

he•red•i•ty (huh-**red**-uh-tee) ***noun***
1. The passing on of traits from parents to children through the genes.

2. All of the traits that are passed on in this way.

her•e•tic (**her**-uh-tik) ***noun*** Someone whose views are different from those of a particular religion or unacceptable to people in authority. ▸ ***noun* heresy** ▸ ***adjective* heretical**

her•i•tage (**her**-uh-tij) ***noun*** Valuable or important traditions handed down from generation to generation.

her•mit (**hur**-mit) ***noun*** Someone who lives totally alone and isolated from other people.

he•ro (**hihr**-oh) ***noun***
1. A brave or good person. ▸ ***noun* heroism**
2. The main character in a book, play, movie, or any kind of story.
▸ ***noun, plural* heroes**

he•ro•ic (hi-**roh**-ik) ***adjective***
1. Very brave or daring.
2. To do with the deeds and actions of heroes.
▸ ***adverb* heroically**

her•o•in (**her**-oh-uhn) ***noun*** A powerful, illegal, addictive drug. **Heroin** sounds like **heroine.**

her•o•ine (**her**-oh-uhn) ***noun***
1. A brave girl or woman.
2. The main female character in a book, play, movie, or any kind of story. **Heroine** sounds like **heroin.**

her•on (**her**-uhn) ***noun*** A bird with a long, thin beak and long legs that lives near water.

her•pes (**hur**-peez) ***noun*** Any of several diseases that cause painful blisters at various places on the body. Herpes is caused by any one of several related viruses.

her•ring (**her**-ing) ***noun*** A bony fish that swims in the northern Atlantic and Pacific oceans and is used for food.

hers (**hurz**) ***pronoun*** The one or ones belonging to or to do with her.

her•self (hur-**self**) ***pronoun*** Her and no one else.

hertz (**hurts**) ***noun*** A unit for measuring the frequency of vibrations and waves, equal to one cycle per second. The abbreviation for *hertz* is *Hz.* ▸ ***noun, plural* hertz**

hes•i•tate (**hez**-uh-tate) ***verb*** To pause before you do something. ▸ **hesitating, hesitated** ▸ ***noun* hesitation** ▸ ***adjective* hesitant**

hex•a•gon (**hek**-suh-*gon*) ***noun*** A shape with six straight sides. *See* **shape.** ▸ ***adjective* hexagonal**

hey (**hay**) ***interjection*** A word used to get someone's attention or to express surprise or joy. **Hey** sounds like **hay.**

hey•day (**hay**-*day*) ***noun*** Your **heyday** is the best or most successful period in your life.

hi (**hye**) ***interjection*** A word used as a greeting; hello. **Hi** sounds like **high.**

hi•ber•nate (**hye**-bur-nate) ***verb*** When animals **hibernate,** they spend the winter in a deep sleep. Animals hibernate to survive low temperatures and a lack of food. ▸ **hibernating, hibernated** ▸ ***noun* hibernation**

hic•cup (**hik**-uhp) ***noun***
1. A sudden sound in your throat caused by a spasm in your chest.
2. hiccups *noun, plural* The condition of having these spasms for a period of time. Sometimes called **the hiccups.**

hick•o•ry (**hik**-ur-ee) ***noun*** A tall tree of North America with hard wood and an edible nut. ▸ ***noun, plural* hickories** ▸ ***adjective* hickory**

hide (**hide**)
1. *verb* To go where you cannot be seen.
2. *verb* To keep something secret or concealed.
3. *noun* An animal's skin used to make leather.
4. If something stays **in hiding,** it remains out of sight.
▸ ***verb* hiding, hid** (**hid**), **hidden** (**hid**-in)

hide-and-seek ***noun*** A game in which people hide while one person, who is "it," looks for—or seeks—them.

H

hid•e•ous (**hid**-ee-uhss) ***adjective*** Ugly or horrible. ▸ ***noun*** **hideousness** ▸ ***adverb*** **hideously**

hide•out (**hide**-*out*) ***noun*** A place where someone can hide, especially a criminal trying to escape from the police.

hi•er•o•glyph•ics (*hye*-ur-uh-**glif**-iks) ***noun, plural*** Writing used by ancient Egyptians, made up of pictures and symbols.

high (**hye**) ***adjective***
1. Something that is **high** is a great distance from the ground, as in *a high mountain.* ▸ ***adverb*** **high**
2. Measuring from top to bottom.
3. More than the normal level or amount, as in *high prices.* ▸ ***noun*** **high** ▸ ***adverb*** **highly**
High sounds like **hi.**
▸ ***adjective*** **higher, highest**

higher education ***noun*** Education at a college or university.

high jump ***noun*** An event in a track-and-field competition in which the athlete must jump over a bar without knocking it down. ▸ ***noun*** **high jumper**

high•land (**hye**-luhnd) ***noun*** An area with mountains or hills. ▸ ***adjective*** **highland**

high•light (**hye**-*lite*)
1. ***verb*** To draw attention to something.
2. ***noun*** The best or most interesting part of something, as in *the highlight of our trip.*
3. ***verb*** To mark important words using a pen with brightly colored ink.
4. **highlights** ***noun, plural*** Streaks of a light color in hair.
▸ ***verb*** **highlighting, highlighted**

high-rise ***noun*** A very tall building. ▸ ***adjective*** **high-rise**

high seas ***noun, plural*** The open waters of an ocean or a sea that are beyond the boundaries or control of any country.

high-strung ***adjective*** Very nervous or excitable.

high tech (**tek**) ***noun*** The latest technology based on advanced electronics, computers, etc. ▸ ***adjective*** **high-tech**

high tide ***noun*** The time at which the water level in an ocean, a gulf, or a bay is at its highest point.

high•way (**hye**-*way*) ***noun*** A main public road.

hi•jack (**hye**-*jak*) ***verb*** If someone **hijacks** a plane or other vehicle, the person takes illegal control of it and forces its pilot or driver to go somewhere. ▸ **hijacking, hijacked** ▸ ***noun*** **hijacker,** ***noun*** **hijacking**

hike (**hike**) ***noun*** A long walk, especially in the country. ▸ ***noun*** **hiker,** ***noun*** **hiking** ▸ ***verb*** **hike**

hi•lar•i•ous (huh-**lair**-ee-uhss *or* hi-**lair**-ee-uhss) ***adjective*** Very funny. ▸ ***noun*** **hilarity**

hill (**hil**) ***noun*** A raised area of land that is smaller than a mountain. ▸ ***adjective*** **hilly**

hill•side (**hil**-*side*) ***noun*** The sloping side of a hill.

hill•top (**hil**-*top*) ***noun*** The highest part of a hill.

hilt (**hilt**) ***noun***
1. The handle of a sword or dagger.
2. to the hilt To the limit; completely.

him (**him**) ***pronoun*** The form of **he** used as a grammatical object. **Him** sounds like **hymn.**

him•self (him-**self**) ***pronoun*** Him and no one else.

hind (**hinde**) ***adjective*** At the back or rear.

hin•der (**hin**-dur) ***verb*** If someone or something **hinders** you, it makes things difficult for you. ▸ **hindering, hindered**

Hin•du•ism (**hin**-doo-*iz*-uhm) ***noun*** A religion and philosophy practiced mainly in India. Hindus believe that they must act in harmony with universal laws and that various gods are different forms of the Supreme Deity. ▸ ***noun*** **Hindu** ▸ ***adjective*** **Hindu**

hinge (**hinj**)
1. ***noun*** A movable metal joint on a

window or a door. ▸ ***adjective*** **hinged**
2. ***verb*** To depend on something.
▸ **hinging, hinged**

hint (**hint**) ***noun***
1. A clue or helpful tip. ▸ ***verb*** **hint**
2. A tiny amount; a trace.

hip (**hip**) ***noun*** The part of your body below your waist that sticks out on either side, covering the joint where the thigh joins the pelvis.

hip-hop ***noun*** A style of dancing, art, music, and dress that originated in urban areas and became popular through break dancing, graffiti, and rap music.

hip•pie (**hip**-ee) ***noun*** A member of a cultural movement that began in the United States during the 1960s. Hippies opposed the war in Vietnam and rebelled against society by developing their own style of dress and behavior. ▸ ***noun, plural*** **hippies**

hip•po•pot•a•mus (*hip*-uh-**pot**-uh-muhss) ***noun*** A large African mammal with short legs and thick skin that lives in or near water. ▸ ***noun, plural*** **hippopotamuses** *or* **hippopotami** (*hip*-uh-**pot**-uh-*mye or hip*-uh-**pot**-uh-*mee*)

hire (**hire**) ***verb*** To employ someone.
▸ **hiring, hired**

his (**hiz**)
1. ***adjective*** Belonging to or to do with him.
2. ***pronoun*** The one or ones belonging to or to do with him.

His•pan•ic (hiss-**pan**-ik) ***adjective*** Coming from or to do with countries where Spanish is spoken. ▸ ***noun*** **Hispanic**

hiss (**hiss**) ***verb*** To make a "ssss" noise like a snake, especially to show that you do not like something or someone.
▸ **hisses, hissing, hissed** ▸ ***noun*** **hiss**

his•tor•ic (hiss-**tor**-ik) ***adjective*** If an event is **historic,** it was important in the past or will be seen as important in the future, as in *the historic first landing on the moon.*

his•tor•ic•al (hi-**stor**-uh-kuhl) ***adjective*** To do with people or events of the past, as in *an historical novel.* ▸ ***adverb*** **historically**

his•to•ry (**hiss**-tuh-ree) ***noun***
1. The study of past events. ▸ ***noun*** **historian**
2. A description of past events.
▸ ***noun, plural*** **histories**

hit (**hit**)
1. ***verb*** To smack or strike something with your hand or with an object such as a bat or a hammer. ▸ ***noun*** **hit,** ***noun*** **hitter**
2. ***verb*** To knock or bump into something.
3. ***verb*** To have a bad effect on someone or something.
4. ***noun*** A successful song, play, or any type of presentation.
5. ***verb*** *(informal)* If you **hit it off** with someone, you get along well with the person.
▸ ***verb*** **hitting, hit**

hitch (**hich**)
1. ***verb*** To fasten with a rope, etc., as in *to hitch a horse to a post.*
2. ***noun*** A problem.
3. ***verb*** To join something to a vehicle.
4. *(slang)* If you **get hitched,** you marry someone.
▸ ***noun, plural*** **hitches** ▸ ***verb*** **hitches, hitching, hitched**

hitch•hike (**hich**-*hike*) ***verb*** To travel by getting rides in other people's vehicles.
▸ **hitchhiking, hitchhiked** ▸ ***noun*** **hitchhiker**

hith•er (**hiTH**-ur) ***adverb*** To or toward this place.

HIV (**aych eye vee**) ***noun***
1. A virus that can lead to AIDS. HIV stands for *Human Immunodeficiency Virus.*
2. If someone is **HIV positive,** the person has the HIV virus and his or her immune system is weak. People who are HIV positive can develop AIDS.

H

hive (**hive**) ***noun***
1. A natural structure in which bees build a honeycomb.
2. A box for keeping bees so that their honey can be collected.
3. hives *noun, plural* A rash that appears on the skin, usually from an allergic reaction.

hoard (**hord**) ***verb***
1. To collect and store things.
2. To buy up a lot of supplies because you think there will be a shortage.
Hoard sounds like **horde.**
▸ ***verb* hoarding, hoarded** ▸ ***noun* hoard, *noun* hoarder**

hoarse (**horss**) ***adjective*** A **hoarse** voice is rough and sore. **Hoarse** sounds like **horse.**

hoax (**hohks**) ***noun*** A trick or a practical joke. ▸ ***noun, plural* hoaxes**

hob•ble (**hob**-uhl) ***verb*** To walk with difficulty because you are in pain or are injured. ▸ **hobbling, hobbled**

hob•by (**hob**-ee) ***noun*** Something that you enjoy doing in your spare time.
▸ ***noun, plural* hobbies**

hock•ey (**hok**-ee) *See* **ice hockey**, **field hockey.**

Hodg•kin's disease (**hoj**-kinz) ***noun*** A disease in which the lymph glands, spleen, and liver become increasingly enlarged.

hoe (**hoh**) ***noun*** A gardening tool with a long handle and a thin blade, used for weeding and loosening earth. ▸ ***verb* hoe**

hog (**hog**)
1. *noun* A fully grown pig.
2. *noun* *(informal)* A selfish person who takes more than his or her fair share, as in *a road hog.*
3. *verb* *(informal)* To take more than one's fair share. ▸ **hogging, hogged**

ho•gan (**hoh**-guhn) ***noun*** A Navajo house made with logs and branches and covered with earth.

hoist (**hoist**)
1. *verb* To lift something heavy, usually with a piece of equipment. ▸ **hoisting, hoisted**
2. *noun* A piece of equipment used for lifting heavy objects.

hold (**hohld**)
1. *verb* To carry, support, or keep something. ▸ ***noun* holder**
2. *verb* To contain something or be able to contain it.
3. *verb* To have.
4. *noun* The part of a ship where the cargo is stored.
5. If you **hold out** in a difficult situation, you continue with what you are doing.
6. If someone is **held up,** the person is robbed by someone with a weapon.
▸ ***verb* holding, held** (**held**)

hold•up (**hohld**-*uhp*) ***noun***
1. A robbery by someone who has a weapon.
2. A delay in activity.

hole (**hohl**) ***noun***
1. A hollow place, or a gap.
2. An animal's den.
3. *(informal)* An unpleasant or dirty place.

hol•i•day (**hol**-uh-*day*) ***noun***
1. A day on which work, school, or any regular activities are officially suspended. Labor Day and Memorial Day are holidays.
2. A religious festival or holy time, such as Passover, Christmas, or the month of Ramadan.

ho•lis•tic (hoh-**liss**-tik) ***adjective*** To do with the whole of anything rather than with its individual parts. Holistic medicine deals with the whole patient, the mind and the body, not just an isolated physical pain or symptom.

hol•low (**hol**-oh)
1. *adjective* If something is **hollow,** it has an empty space inside it. ▸ ***noun* hollow**
2. hollow out *verb* If you **hollow**

something **out,** you take its insides out. ▸ **hollowing, hollowed**

hol•ly (**hol**-ee) ***noun*** An evergreen tree or bush with prickly leaves and red berries.

hol•ly•hock (**hol**-ee-*hok*) A tall garden plant grown for its showy spikes of large, brightly colored flowers.

ho•lo•caust (**hol**-uh-*kost*) ***noun***

1. Total destruction and great loss of life, especially by fire, as in *a nuclear holocaust.*

2. the Holocaust The killing of millions of European Jews and others by the Nazis during World War II.

ho•lo•gram (**hol**-uh-*gram*) ***noun*** An image made by laser beams that looks three-dimensional. ▸ ***noun*** **holography** (huh-**log**-ruh-fee)

hol•ster (**hohl**-stur) ***noun*** A holder for a gun worn on a belt.

ho•ly (**hoh**-lee) ***adjective*** To do with or belonging to God or a higher being. ▸ **holier, holiest**

Holy Communion ***noun*** A Christian service in which people eat bread and drink wine or grape juice to symbolize the death and resurrection of Jesus.

home (**home**) ***noun***

1. Your **home** is where you live or belong. ▸ ***adverb*** **home**

2. A place where you are likely to find something.

3. A place where the ill, the aged, or the homeless can receive proper care, as in *a nursing home.*

4. If you **feel at home** with someone, you feel comfortable with the person.

home•less (**home**-liss)

1. ***adjective*** Without a permanent home or place to sleep.

2. the homeless ***noun, plural*** People who have no permanent home or place to sleep.

home•ly (**home**-lee) ***adjective***

1. Not attractive in appearance; plain.

2. Not fancy or pretentious; simple. ▸ ***adjective*** **homelier, homeliest**

home•made (**home-made**) ***adjective*** Made at home or by hand, as in *homemade soup.*

home•mak•er (**home**-*may*-kur) ***noun*** Someone who takes care of a house and family. ▸ ***noun*** **homemaking** ▸ ***adjective*** **homemaking**

home page ***noun*** The first Web page found on a Web site, usually with links to other Web pages or Web sites.

home plate ***noun*** In baseball, the base next to which a batter stands to hit the ball. The batter must run to all the bases and cross home plate to score a run.

home•room (**home**-*room or* **home**-*rum*) ***noun*** A classroom in which students meet with their teacher before studying begins.

home run ***noun*** In baseball, a hit that allows the batter to run all the way around the bases and score a run.

home•school (**home**-*skool*) ***verb*** To educate someone at home rather than at a school. ▸ ***verb*** **homeschooling, homeschooled** ▸ ***noun*** **homeschooler**

home•sick (**hohm**-*sik*) ***adjective*** If you are **homesick,** you miss your home and family.

home•spun (**hohm**-*spuhn*) ***adjective***

1. Spun or made at home, especially fabric.

2. Plain and simple, as in *homespun humor.*

home•stead (**home**-sted) ***noun***

1. A house, especially a farmhouse, with its buildings and land.

2. In the American West, a piece of land measuring 160 acres (65 hectares) given to a settler by the U.S. government. ▸ ***noun*** **homesteader** ▸ ***verb*** **homestead**

home•work (**home**-*wurk*) ***noun*** Work assigned in school that is to be done at home.

ho•mi•cide (**hom**-uh-*side or* **hoh**-muh-*side*) ***noun*** Murder. ▸ ***adjective*** **homicidal**

H

H

ho•mog•e•nize (huh-**moj**-uh-nize) ***verb*** To mix the cream in milk so that it is spread evenly through the liquid and does not rise to the top.
▸ **homogenizing, homogenized**
▸ ***noun*** **homogenization**

hom•o•graph (**hom**-uh-*graf*) ***noun*** One of two or more words that have the same spelling but different meanings and possibly different pronunciations. A *bowl*, meaning "a kind of dish," and to *bowl*, meaning "to play a game of bowling," are homographs, as are *wind*, "a current of air," and *wind*, or "to coil something."

hom•o•nym (**hom**-uh-nim) ***noun*** One of two or more words that have the same pronunciation and often the same spelling but different meanings. *Lock* meaning "a tuft of hair" and *lock* meaning "a part of a door that you open and shut with a key" are homonyms.

hom•o•phone (**home**-uh-*fone*) ***noun*** One of two or more words that have the same pronunciation but different spellings and different meanings. *To, too,* and *two* are homophones.

hon•est (**on**-ist) ***adjective*** An **honest** person is truthful and will not lie or steal or cheat anyone. ▸ ***noun*** **honesty**
▸ ***adverb*** **honestly**

hon•ey (**huhn**-ee) ***noun*** A sweet, sticky, golden-brown substance made by bees.

hon•ey•comb (**huhn**-ee-*kohm*) ***noun*** A wax structure made by bees and used by them to store honey, pollen, and eggs. A honeycomb consists of many rows of cells with six sides.

hon•ey•moon (**huhn**-ee-*moon*) ***noun*** A trip that a bride and groom take together after their wedding.

hon•ey•suck•le (**huhn**-ee-*suhk*-uhl) ***noun*** A climbing vine or shrub with fragrant white, red, or yellow flowers shaped like small tubes.

honk (**hongk**)
1. ***noun*** The sound a goose makes.
2. ***noun*** The sound a car horn makes.
3. ***verb*** To make the sound of a goose or a car horn. ▸ **honking, honked**

hon•or (**on**-ur)
1. ***noun*** Someone's **honor** is his or her good reputation and the respect that other people have for the person.
2. ***verb*** To give praise or an award.
▸ ***noun*** **honor**
3. ***verb*** To keep an agreement.
4. ***noun*** A special privilege.
▸ ***verb*** **honoring, honored**

hon•or•a•ble (**on**-ur-uh-buhl) ***adjective***
1. An **honorable** action is good and deserves praise.
2. If someone is **honorable,** the person keeps his or her promises.

hon•or•ar•y (**on**-uh-rer-ee) ***adjective*** Given as an honor without the usual requirements or duties.

hood (**hud**) ***noun***
1. The part of a jacket or coat that goes over your head. ▸ ***adjective*** **hooded**
2. The cover for a car's engine.

hood•lum (**hood**-luhm) ***noun***
1. A gangster or a thug.
2. A young person who is rough, mean, or violent.

hoof (**huf** *or* **hoof**) ***noun***
1. The hard covering over the foot of a horse, deer, etc.
2. The entire foot of a horse, deer, etc.
▸ ***noun, plural*** **hoofs** *or* **hooves**
▸ ***adjective*** **hoofed** *or* **hooved**

hook (**huk**) ***noun***
1. A curved piece of metal or plastic used to fasten or hold something.
2. A curved piece of metal with a barb at one end, used to catch fish.
3. A punch in boxing made with the elbow bent, as in *a right hook.*
▸ ***verb*** **hook**

hooked (**hukt**) ***adjective***
1. Curved, as in *a hooked nose.*
2. If you are **hooked** on something, you like it a lot or are addicted to it.

hoo•li•gan (**hoo**-luh-guhn) ***noun*** A noisy, violent person who makes trouble.
▸ ***noun*** **hooliganism**

H

hoop (**hoop** *or* **hup**) ***noun***
1. A large ring, as in *the hoops of a barrel.*
▸ ***adjective*** **hooped**
2. A ring with a net attached, used as a goal in basketball.
3. hoops *noun, plural* *(informal)* Basketball.

hoo•ray *See* **hurray.**

hoot (**hoot**) ***verb***
1. To make a sound like an owl.
2. To show dislike or disapproval by making a loud shout.
▸ ***verb*** **hooting, hooted** ▸ ***noun*** **hoot**

hop (**hop**)
1. *verb* To move with short jumps or leaps.
2. *verb* To jump on one foot.
3. *verb* To jump over, as in *to hop a fence.*
4. hops *noun, plural* The dried seed cases of hop plants, which are used to make beer.
▸ ***verb*** **hopping, hopped** ▸ ***noun*** **hop**

hope (**hope**)
1. *verb* To wish for or expect something.
▸ **hoping, hoped**
2. *noun* A feeling of expectation or confidence.
▸ ***noun*** **hopefulness** ▸ ***adjective*** **hopeful** ▸ ***adverb*** **hopefully**

hope•less (**hope**-liss) ***adjective***
1. Without hope.
2. Bad, or lacking in skill.
▸ ***noun*** **hopelessness** ▸ ***adverb*** **hopelessly**

Ho•pi (**hoh**-pee) ***noun*** One of a group of American Indians that lives primarily in northeastern Arizona. ▸ ***noun, plural*** **Hopi** *or* **Hopis**

hop•scotch (**hop**-*skoch*) ***noun*** A game in which players throw a stone or other object into a pattern of numbered shapes drawn on the ground. The players hop into the shapes in a certain order and try to pick up the stone.

horde (**hord**) ***noun*** A large, noisy, moving crowd of people or animals. **Horde** sounds like **hoard.**

ho•ri•zon (huh-**rye**-zuhn) ***noun***
1. The line where the sky and the earth or sea seem to meet.
2. The limit of your experience or opportunities.

hor•i•zon•tal (hor-uh-**zon**-tuhl) ***adjective*** Flat and parallel to the ground, as in *a horizontal line.* ▸ ***adverb*** **horizontally**

hor•mone (**hor**-mohn) ***noun*** Your **hormones** are chemicals made by certain glands in your body that affect the way you grow and develop.
▸ ***adjective*** **hormonal**

horn (**horn**) ***noun***
1. A hard, bony, permanent growth on the heads of some animals. ▸ ***adjective*** **horned**
2. The hard, bony substance that horns and hoofs are made from. ▸ ***adjective*** **horny**
3. A brass musical instrument that you blow, as in *a French horn.*
4. A machine that gives a signal by making a loud sound, as in *a car horn.*

hor•net (**hor**-nit) ***noun*** A large, stinging wasp that lives in colonies and builds a large nest.

hor•o•scope (**hor**-uh-*skope*) ***noun*** A diagram of the stars and planets on the day when you were born, used by astrologers to try to tell your character and predict events in your life.

hor•ri•ble (**hor**-uh-buhl) ***adjective***
1. Causing horror or fear, as in *a horrible crime.*
2. Very bad, as in *a horrible cold.*
▸ ***adverb*** **horribly**

hor•rid (**hor**-id) ***adjective*** Nasty or horrible.

hor•rif•ic (hor-**if**-ik) ***adjective*** Shocking.

hor•ri•fy (**hor**-uh-fye) ***verb*** If something **horrifies** you, it shocks and disgusts you. ▸ **horrifies, horrifying, horrified** ▸ ***adjective*** **horrifying**

H

hor•ror (**hor**-ur)
1. ***noun*** Great fear, terror, or shock.
2. ***noun*** Something that brings on such a feeling.
3. ***adjective*** Intended to cause great fear or terror, as in *a horror story.*

horse (**horss**)
1. ***noun*** A large, strong animal with hoofs that people ride or use to pull coaches, carriages, plows, etc.
2. ***noun*** A piece of gymnastics apparatus that you jump over.
3. ***verb*** If you **horse around,** you get into mischief. ▸ **horsing, horsed**
Horse sounds like **hoarse.**
See also **mustang.**

horse•back (**horss**-*bak*)
1. ***noun*** The back of a horse.
2. ***adverb*** On the back of a horse.

horse•fly (**horss**-*flye*) ***noun*** A large fly. The female bites and sucks the blood of humans, horses, cattle, and other animals. ▸ ***noun, plural*** **horseflies**

horse•play (**horss**-*play*) ***noun*** Rough and noisy play or fun.

horse•pow•er (**horss**-*pou*-ur) ***noun*** A unit for measuring the power of an engine.

horse•shoe (**horss**-*shoo*) ***noun***
1. A piece of metal shaped like a U and nailed to the bottom of a horse's hoof to protect it.
2. horseshoes *noun, plural* A game in which horseshoes are thrown around a metal stake.
▸ ***verb*** **horseshoe**

hor•ti•cul•ture (**hor**-tuh-*kuhl*-chur) ***noun*** The growing of fruits, vegetables, and flowers. ▸ ***adjective*** **horticultural**

hose (**hohz**)
1. ***noun*** A long, rubber or plastic tube through which liquids or gases travel.
2. ***noun*** Stockings or socks.
3. ***verb*** To wash or water something with a hose. ▸ **hosing, hosed**

ho•sier•y (**hoh**-zhur-ee) ***noun*** Stockings and socks.

hos•pice (**hoss**-piss) ***noun*** A place that provides care for people who are dying and comfort for their families.

hos•pi•tal (**hoss**-pi-tuhl) ***noun*** A place where you receive medical treatment and are looked after when you are sick or injured.

hos•pi•tal•i•ty (*hoss*-puh-**tal**-uh-tee) ***noun*** A generous and friendly way of treating people, especially guests, so that they feel comfortable and at home.
▸ ***noun, plural*** **hospitalities**
▸ ***adjective*** **hospitable** (**hoss**-pi-tuh-buhl *or* hoss-**pit**-uh-buhl)

host (**hohst**) ***noun***
1. A person who entertains guests.
2. A large number.
3. A person who is in charge of a TV show that offers conversation, music, etc., with celebrities and other guests.
4. An animal or plant from which a parasite or another organism gets nutrition.
▸ ***verb*** **host**

hos•tage (**hoss**-tij) ***noun*** Someone taken and held prisoner as a way of demanding money or other conditions.

hos•tel (**hoss**-tuhl) ***noun*** A building that provides inexpensive lodging or shelter for travelers, especially young people who are hiking or biking. **Hostel** sounds like **hostile.**

host•ess (**hoh**-stuhss) ***noun***
1. A woman who entertains guests.
2. A woman who greets people in a restaurant or serves food on an airplane.
▸ ***noun, plural*** **hostesses**

hos•tile (**hoss**-tuhl) ***adjective*** Unfriendly or angry, as in *a hostile crowd.* **Hostile** sounds like **hostel.**

hos•til•i•ty (hoss-**til**-uh-tee)
1. ***noun*** A strong hatred or dislike.
2. hostilities *noun, plural* Acts of war.

hot (**hot**) ***adjective***
1. Having a high temperature.
2. Very spicy and strong in taste.
3. Fiery.
4. Eager.

H

5. Recent or exciting, as in *hot news.*
▸ ***adjective*** **hotter, hottest**

hot-air balloon *See* **balloon.**

hot dog ***noun*** A long sausage usually eaten in a bun.

ho•tel (hoh-**tel**) ***noun*** A place where you pay to stay overnight. Many hotels serve meals.

hot spring ***noun*** A natural source of water heated by the earth's interior.

hot-water bottle ***noun*** A rubber container for hot water, used to warm a bed or soothe an ache.

hound (**hound**)
1. ***noun*** Any of various kinds of dog that have been bred to hunt by sight or scent.
2. ***verb*** To chase or pester somebody.
▸ **hounding, hounded**

hour (**our**) ***noun*** A unit of time equal to 60 minutes; 1/24 of the time it takes the earth to make one turn on its axis. **Hour** sounds like **our.** ▸ ***adverb*** **hourly**

hour•glass (**our**-*glass*) ***noun*** An instrument for measuring time. It is made of two glass bulbs joined in the middle by a thin glass tube. A quantity of sand falls from the upper bulb into the lower one in exactly one hour.

house (**houss**)
1. ***noun*** A building where people live.
2. ***noun*** People who live in a house.
3. If something in a restaurant is **on the house,** it is free.
4. ***verb*** (**houz**) If you **house** someone, you provide the person with a place to stay or live. ▸ **housing, housed**

house•boat (**houss**-*boht*) ***noun*** A boat that people live on, with cooking and sleeping areas.

house•fly (**houss**-*flye*) ***noun*** A common fly found in most parts of the world. It feeds on food and garbage and spreads diseases among humans.

house•hold (**houss**-*hohld*)
1. ***noun*** All the people who live together in a house.
2. ***adjective*** Belonging to or to do with a house or a family.

House of Representatives ***noun*** One of the two houses of the U.S. Congress that makes laws. In this body, members are elected for two-year terms, and the number of members from each state is based on population.

house-sit ***verb*** To live in or take care of a home while the owners or regular residents are away. ▸ **house-sitting, house-sat** ▸ ***noun*** **house sitter**

house•work (**houss**-*wurk*) ***noun*** Work done to keep a house clean and tidy.

hous•ing (**hou**-zing) ***noun***
1. Buildings or other shelters where people live, as in *student housing.*
2. A frame or cover that protects a machine's moving parts.

hov•el (**huhv**-uhl *or* **hov**-uhl) ***noun*** A small, dirty house or hut.

hov•er (**huhv**-ur) ***verb***
1. To remain in one place in the air.
2. To stay attentively nearby.
3. To linger, or to be uncertain.
▸ ***verb*** **hovering, hovered**

hov•er•craft (**huhv**-ur-*kraft*) ***noun*** A vehicle that can travel over land and water, supported by a cushion of air.

how (**hou**) ***adverb***
1. In what way, or by what means.
2. In what condition.
3. To what extent, amount, or degree.
4. For what reason, or why.

how•ev•er (hou-**ev**-ur)
1. ***conjunction*** In spite of that.
2. ***adverb*** In whatever way, or to whatever extent.

howl (**houl**) ***verb***
1. To cry out in pain like a dog or a wolf.
2. To yell out with laughter.
3. To make a loud, sad noise.
▸ ***verb*** **howling, howled** ▸ ***noun*** **howl**

HTML (*aych-tee-em*-**el**) ***noun*** The set of computer codes that is used to make basic Web pages. HTML stands for *HyperText Markup Language.*

hub (**huhb**) ***noun***
1. The center of a wheel.
2. The center of an organization or activity.

H

huck•le•ber•ry (**huhk**-uhl-*ber*-ee) ***noun*** A shiny, dark blue or black berry, similar to a blueberry that grows on a low shrub. Huckleberry can mean both the berry and the bush it grows on. ▸ ***noun, plural*** **huckleberries**

hud•dle (**huhd**-uhl)
1. ***verb*** To crowd together in a tight group. ▸ **huddling, huddled** ▸ ***noun*** **huddle**
2. ***noun*** A grouping of the offensive team in football to prepare for the next play. ▸ ***verb*** **huddle**

hue (**hyoo**) ***noun*** A color, or a variety of a color.

huff (**huhf**) ***noun*** If you are **in a huff,** you are upset or very annoyed.

hug (**huhg**) ***verb*** To hold someone or something tightly in a loving or caring way. ▸ **hugging, hugged** ▸ ***noun*** **hug**

huge (**hyooj**) ***adjective*** Enormous or gigantic, as in *a huge amount of money.* ▸ **huger, hugest**

hulk (**huhlk**) ***noun***
1. The remains of a wrecked ship.
2. A large, heavy person. ▸ ***adjective*** **hulking**

hull (**huhl**)
1. ***noun*** The frame or body of a boat or ship.
2. ***noun*** The outer covering of certain fruits, seeds, or nuts.
3. ***verb*** To remove the outer skin of a seed or nut. ▸ **hulling, hulled**
4. ***noun*** The small leaves around the stem of a strawberry and some other fruits. ▸ ***verb*** **hull**

hum (**huhm**) ***verb***
1. To sing a melody with your mouth closed.
2. To make a steady, buzzing noise. ▸ ***verb*** **humming, hummed** ▸ ***noun*** **hum**

hu•man (**hyoo**-muhn)
1. human *or* **human being *noun*** A person. ▸ ***adjective*** **human**
2. ***adjective*** Natural and understandable.
3. human rights *noun, plural* Everyone's right to justice, fair treatment, and free speech.

hu•mane (hyoo-**mayn**) ***adjective*** Someone who is **humane** is kind and charitable. ▸ ***adverb*** **humanely**

hu•man•i•tar•i•an (hyoo-*man*-uh-**ter**-ee-uhn) ***adjective*** To do with helping people and relieving suffering.

hu•man•i•ty (hyoo-**man**-uh-tee) ***noun***
1. All human beings.
2. Kindness and sympathy.
3. the humanities *noun, plural* Subjects outside the sciences, such as literature, history, and art.

hum•ble (**huhm**-buhl) ***adjective*** Modest and not proud. ▸ **humbler, humblest** ▸ ***adverb*** **humbly**

hum•drum (**huhm**-*druhm*) ***adjective*** A **humdrum** life is dull and filled with routine events.

hu•mid (**hyoo**-mid) ***adjective*** Damp and moist. ▸ ***noun*** **humidity**

hu•mil•i•ate (hyoo-**mil**-ee-ate) ***verb*** To make someone look or feel foolish or embarrassed. ▸ **humiliating, humiliated** ▸ ***noun*** **humiliation**

hu•mil•i•ty (hyoo-**mil**-uh-tee) ***noun*** If you show **humility,** you are not too proud, and you recognize your own faults.

hum•ming•bird (**huhm**-ing-*burd*) ***noun*** A very small, brightly colored bird that makes a humming sound when it flaps its wings rapidly.

hum•mus (**huhm**-uhss) ***noun*** A dip or sandwich spread made of chickpeas and sesame paste.

hu•mor (**hyoo**-mur)
1. ***noun*** The funny or amusing aspect of something.
2. ***noun*** If you have a **sense of humor,** you are quick to appreciate the funny side of life.
3. ***noun*** Mood or state of mind, as in *a good humor.*
4. ***verb*** If you **humor** someone, you keep the person happy by agreeing with

him or her or doing what he or she wants. ▸ **humoring, humored**

hu•mor•ous (**hyoo**-mur-uhss) ***adjective*** Amusing.

hump (**huhmp**) ***noun*** A large lump that sticks out or up from something. ▸ ***adjective*** **humped**

hump•back (**huhmp**-*bak*) ***noun***
1. A humped or severely crooked back. Another term for a humpback is a **hunchback.**
2. A type of large whale that is black with a white underside.

hu•mus (**hyoo**-muhss) ***noun*** Rich, dark earth made from rotting vegetable and animal matter.

hunch (**huhnch**)
1. ***verb*** To lower your head into your shoulders and lean forward. ▸ **hunches, hunching, hunched**
2. ***noun*** An idea that is not backed by proof but comes from intuition. ▸ ***noun, plural*** **hunches**

hunch•back (huhnch-**bak**) ***noun***
1. A humpback.
2. A person having a humpback.

hun•dred (**huhn**-druhd) ***noun*** The whole number, written 100, that is equal to 10 × 10. ▸ ***adjective*** **hundred**

hun•dredth (**huhn**-dredth)
1. ***noun*** One part of something that has been divided into 100 equal parts, written 1⁄100.
2. ***noun*** In decimal notation, the position of the second number to the right of the decimal point, known as *the hundredths place.* In the number 4.0129, the digit 1 is in the hundredths place.

hun•gry (**huhng**-gree) ***adjective*** Wanting food. ▸ **hungrier, hungriest** ▸ ***noun*** **hunger** ▸ ***adverb*** **hungrily**

hunk (**huhngk**) ***noun*** A large piece of something, such as bread, cheese, or meat.

hunt (**huhnt**) ***verb***
1. To search for something.
2. To chase and kill deer, geese, or other wild animals for food or sport. ▸ ***verb*** **hunting, hunted** ▸ ***noun*** **hunt,** ***noun*** **hunting**

hunt•er (**huhnt**-ur) ***noun***
1. Someone who hunts.
2. A horse or a dog that you use to help during hunting.

hur•dle (**hur**-duhl)
1. ***noun*** A small fence that you jump over in a running event. ▸ ***noun*** **hurdler**
2. ***verb*** To jump over something. ▸ **hurdling, hurdled**
3. ***noun*** An obstacle.

hurl (**hurl**) ***verb*** To throw something with great effort. ▸ **hurling, hurled**

hur•ray *or* **hooray** (huh-**ray**) *or* **hurrah** (huh-**rah**) ***interjection*** A word used when people cheer.

hur•ri•cane (**hur**-uh-*kane*) ***noun*** A violent storm with high winds that starts in the regions of the Atlantic Ocean or the Caribbean Sea near the equator and then travels north, northeast, or northwest.

hur•ry (**hur**-ee)
1. ***verb*** To do things as fast as possible. ▸ **hurries, hurrying, hurried**
2. When you are **in a hurry,** you do everything very quickly and often impatiently. ▸ ***adjective*** **hurried**

hurt (**hurt**) ***verb***
1. To cause physical or emotional pain. ▸ ***adjective*** **hurtful**
2. To be in pain. ▸ ***verb*** **hurting, hurt**

hur•tle (**hur**-tuhl) ***verb*** To move at great speed. ▸ **hurtling, hurtled**

hus•band (**huhz**-buhnd) ***noun*** The male partner in a marriage.

hush (**huhsh**)
1. ***noun*** A sudden period of quietness. ▸ ***verb*** **hush** ▸ ***noun, plural*** **hushes**
2. ***interjection*** Be quiet!
3. **hush up** ***verb*** To keep something secret. ▸ **hushes, hushing, hushed**
4. **hush-hush** ***adjective*** *(informal)* Very secret and confidential.

H

H

husk (**huhsk**) ***noun*** The outer casing of seeds or grains.

husk•y (**huhss**-kee)
1. ***adjective*** A **husky** voice sounds low and hoarse.
2. ***adjective*** Large and powerful.
3. ***noun*** A strong dog with a thick coat, bred to pull sleds in the far North.
▸ ***noun, plural*** **huskies** ▸ ***adjective*** **huskier, huskiest** ▸ ***noun*** **huskiness**

hus•tle (**huhss**-uhl) ***verb***
1. To push someone roughly in order to make the person move.
2. To work rapidly and energetically.
▸ ***noun*** **hustler** ▸ ***verb*** **hustling, hustled**

hut (**huht**) ***noun***
1. A small, primitive house.
2. A wooden shed.

hutch (**huhch**) ***noun***
1. A pen or coop for rabbits or other small pets.
2. A wooden cupboard having open shelves on top to hold dishes.
▸ ***noun, plural*** **hutches**

hy•a•cinth (**hye**-uh-sinth) ***noun*** A plant related to the lily that grows from a bulb. It has a thick stem with small flowers that grow in long clusters.

hy•brid (**hye**-brid) ***noun*** A plant or an animal that has been bred from two different species or varieties. ▸ ***adjective*** **hybrid**

hy•drant (**hye**-druhnt) ***noun*** A large outdoor pipe connected to a water supply for use against fires and in other emergencies.

hy•drau•lic (hye-**draw**-lik) ***adjective*** **Hydraulic** machines work on power created by liquid being forced under pressure through pipes. ▸ ***noun*** **hydraulics**

hy•dro•e•lec•tric (*hye*-droh-i-**lek**-trik) ***adjective*** To do with the production of electricity by water power that is used to turn a generator. Hydroelectric power plants are often built at dams.

hy•dro•e•lec•tric•i•ty (*hye*-droh-i-lek-**triss**-uh-tee) ***noun*** Electricity made from energy produced by running water.

hy•dro•foil (**hye**-druh-*foil*) ***noun*** A boat with skilike attachments at the front and back used to lift the hull out of the water once the boat is traveling fast.

hy•dro•gen (**hye**-druh-juhn) ***noun*** A colorless gas that is lighter than air and catches fire easily.

hydrogen bomb ***noun*** An extremely powerful bomb, more powerful than the atomic bomb. Its tremendous force comes from the energy that is released when hydrogen atoms combine to form helium atoms. Also called **H-bomb.**

hy•drom•e•ter (hye-**drom**-uh-tur) ***noun*** An instrument used to measure the density of a liquid.

hy•dro•pon•ics (*hye*-druh-**pon**-iks) ***noun*** The science of growing plants in a solution of water and chemicals rather than in soil. ▸ ***adjective*** **hydroponic**

hy•e•na (hye-**ee**-nuh) ***noun*** A wild animal that looks somewhat like a dog. It eats meat and has a shrieking howl.

hy•giene (**hye**-jeen) ***noun*** Actions taken by people to stay healthy and keep clean. ▸ ***adjective*** **hygienic** (**hye**-gee-*en*-ik *or* hye-**jen**-ik) ▸ ***adverb*** **hygienically**

hy•gien•ist (hye-**jee**-nist) ***noun*** Someone trained to know how to keep people healthy and clean.

hymn (**him**) ***noun*** A song of praise to God. **Hymn** sounds like **him.**

hym•nal (**him**-nuhl) ***noun*** A book of religious songs used in religious services.

hype (**hipe**) ***noun*** Exaggerated claims made about something in order to promote it. Hype is short for *hyperbole.* ▸ ***verb*** **hype**

hy•per•ac•tive (*hye*-pur-**ak**-tiv) ***adjective*** If someone is **hyperactive,** the person is unusually restless and has difficulty sitting quietly. ▸ ***noun*** **hyperactivity**

hy•phen (**hye**-fuhn) ***noun*** The punctuation mark (-) used in a word made of two or more parts or words. Words such as *half-mast, middle-aged,* and *ice-skate* use hyphens. ▸ ***noun*** **hyphenation** ▸ ***verb*** **hyphenate**

hyp•no•tize (**hip**-nuh-tize) ***verb*** To put someone into a trance. ▸ **hypnotizing, hypnotized** ▸ ***noun*** **hypnotism,** ***noun*** **hypnotist**

hy•po•chon•dri•ac (*hye*-puh-**kon**-dree-ak) ***noun*** Someone who continually thinks that he or she is ill or will become ill. ▸ ***noun*** **hypochondria**

hyp•o•crite (**hip**-uh-krit) ***noun*** Someone who pretends to be loyal, honest, or good. ▸ ***noun*** **hypocrisy** (hi-**pok**-ri-see) ▸ ***adjective*** **hypocritical** ▸ ***adverb*** **hypocritically**

hy•po•der•mic (*hye*-puh-**dur**-mik) ***noun*** A hollow needle used for giving injections.

hy•pot•e•nuse (hye-**pot**-uhn-*ooss*) ***noun*** The side opposite the right angle in a right triangle.

hy•po•ther•mi•a (*hye*-puh-**thur**-mee-uh) ***noun*** If someone is suffering from **hypothermia,** the person's body temperature has become dangerously low.

hy•poth•e•sis (hye-**poth**-uh-siss) ***noun*** A temporary prediction that can be tested about how a scientific investigation or experiment will turn out. ▸ ***noun, plural*** **hypotheses**

hys•ter•i•cal (hi-**ster**-uh-kuhl) ***adjective*** If someone is **hysterical,** the person laughs or cries a lot because he or she is very excited, frightened, or angry. ▸ ***noun*** **hysteria** ▸ ***adverb*** **hysterically**

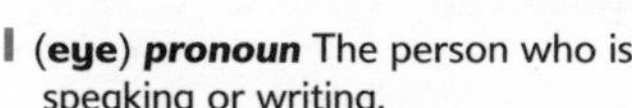

I

I (**eye**) ***pronoun*** The person who is speaking or writing.

ice (**eyess**)
1. ***noun*** Frozen water.
2. ***verb*** To turn into ice.
3. ***verb*** To cool with ice.
4. ***noun*** A frozen dessert made from fruit juice and sweetened water.
5. ***verb*** If someone **ices** a cake, the person covers it with icing. ▸ **icing, iced**

Ice Age *or* **ice age** ***noun*** A period of time in history when a large part of the earth was covered with ice.

ice•berg (**eyess**-*berg*) ***noun*** A huge mass of ice floating in the sea. Icebergs break off from glaciers.

ice•box (**eyess**-*boks*) ***noun***
1. A box or chest kept cool with blocks of ice.
2. A refrigerator.

▸ ***noun, plural*** **iceboxes**

ice•break•er (**eyess**-*bray*-kur) ***noun***
1. A ship designed to clear away ice in frozen waters so that other ships can pass through.
2. An event or comment that relieves the tension at a social gathering.

ice•cap (**eyess**-*kap*) ***noun*** A mound of ice that covers an area of land and gets bigger as snow falls, melts, and freezes.

ice cream ***noun*** A sweet, frozen dessert made from milk products, various flavors, and sweeteners.

I

ice hockey ***noun*** A team game played on ice with sticks and a flat disk called a puck that skaters try to hit into their opponents' net.

ice-skate ***verb*** To move around on ice wearing high, laced boots with blades on the bottom. ▸ **ice-skating, ice-skated** ▸ ***noun*** **ice-skater**

ice skate ***noun*** A shoe or boot with a blade on the bottom that makes it easy for the wearer to glide on ice. ▸ ***noun*** **ice-skating**

i•ci•cle (**eye**-si-kuhl) ***noun*** A long, thin stem of ice formed from dripping water that has frozen.

ic•ing (**eye**-sing) ***noun*** A sugar coating used to decorate cakes.

i•con (**eye**-kon) ***noun***
1. One of several small pictures on a computer screen representing available programs or functions.
2. A picture of a holy figure that is present in some churches.

i•cy (**eye**-see) ***adjective***
1. Very cold, or covered with ice.
2. Unfriendly, as in *an icy stare.*
▸ ***adjective*** **icier, iciest**

I'd (**eyed**) ***contraction*** A short form of *I had, I would,* or *I should.*

I.D. (**eye dee**) Short for **identification.**

i•de•a (eye-**dee**-uh) ***noun*** A thought, a plan, or an opinion.

i•de•al (eye-**dee**-uhl)
1. ***adjective*** Very suitable or perfect.
2. ***noun*** Someone or something considered perfect.
3. ***noun*** A standard of excellence.
▸ ***adjective*** **idealistic**

i•den•ti•cal (eye-**den**-ti-kuhl) ***adjective*** Exactly alike, as in *identical twins.* ▸ ***adverb*** **identically**

i•den•ti•fi•ca•tion (*eye*-den-tuh-fuh-**kay**-shuhn) ***noun*** Something that proves who you are.

i•den•ti•fy (eye-**den**-tuh-fye) ***verb*** To recognize or tell what something is or who someone is. ▸ **identifies, identifying, identified**

i•den•ti•ty (eye-**den**-ti-tee) ***noun*** Your **identity** is who you are. ▸ ***noun, plural*** **identities**

id•i•om (**id**-ee-uhm) ***noun*** A commonly used expression or phrase that means something different from what it appears to mean. For example, if a homework assignment is "a piece of cake," it means that it is easy. ▸ ***adjective*** **idiomatic**

id•i•ot (**id**-ee-uht) ***noun*** A stupid or foolish person. ▸ ***adjective*** **idiotic** (*id*-ee-**ot**-ik) ▸ ***adverb*** **idiotically**

i•dle (**eye**-duhl)
1. ***adjective*** Not busy, or not working. ▸ ***verb*** **idle** ▸ ***adverb*** **idly**
2. ***adjective*** Not active, or not in use.
3. ***verb*** To run slowly without being connected to the transmission.
Idle sounds like **idol.**
▸ ***verb*** **idling, idled** ▸ ***noun*** **idleness,** ***noun*** **idler** ▸ ***adjective*** **idler, idlest**

i•dol (**eye**-duhl) ***noun***
1. An image or statue worshipped as a god.
2. Someone whom people love and admire, as in *a pop idol.*
Idol sounds like **idle.**

i.e. (**eye ee**) An abbreviation of the Latin phrase *id est,* which means "that is" and is used to explain something further.

if (**if**) ***conjunction*** A word used to show that something will happen on condition that another thing happens first.

ig•loo (**ig**-loo) ***noun*** The traditional house of the Eskimo, or Inuit people, made in the shape of a dome out of sod, wood, stone, blocks of ice, or hard snow.

ig•ne•ous (**ig**-nee-uhss) ***adjective*** Produced by great heat or by a volcano, as in *igneous rock.*

ig•nite (ig-**nite**) ***verb*** To set fire to something, or to catch fire. ▸ **igniting, ignited**

ig•ni•tion (ig-**nish**-uhn) ***noun***
1. The electrical system of a vehicle that uses power from the battery to start the engine.
2. The firing or blasting off of a rocket.

ig•no•rant (**ig**-nur-uhnt) ***adjective***
1. Not aware of something.
2. Not educated, or not knowing about many things.
▸ ***noun*** **ignorance** ▸ ***adverb*** **ignorantly**

ig•nore (ig-**nor**) ***verb*** To take no notice of something. ▸ **ignoring, ignored**

i•gua•na (i-**gwan**-uh) ***noun*** A large tropical American lizard. An iguana has a ridge down its back and can grow to more than five feet in length.

ill (**il**) ***adjective***
1. Sick. ▸ ***noun*** **illness**
2. Bad. ▸ ***adverb*** **ill**

I'll (**eye**-uhl) ***contraction*** A short form of *I will* or *I shall.* **I'll** sounds like **aisle** and **isle.**

il•le•gal (i-**lee**-guhl) ***adjective*** Against the law. ▸ ***adverb*** **illegally**

il•leg•i•ble (i-**lej**-uh-buhl) ***adjective*** If your handwriting is **illegible,** it is difficult to read.

il•lit•er•ate (i-**lit**-ur-it) ***adjective*** Not able to read or write. ▸ ***noun*** **illiteracy**

il•log•i•cal (i-**loj**-uh-kuhl) ***adjective*** Something **illogical** does not make sense. ▸ ***adverb*** **illogically**

il•lu•mi•nate (i-**loo**-muh-nate) ***verb***
1. To light up something, such as a building.
2. To make something clearer and easier to understand. ▸ ***adjective*** **illuminating**
3. In the Middle Ages, manuscripts were **illuminated** by adding pictures and decoration to the text.
▸ ***verb*** **illuminating, illuminated**
▸ ***noun*** **illumination** ▸ ***adjective*** **illuminated**

il•lu•sion (i-**loo**-zhuhn) ***noun*** Something that appears to exist but does not.
▸ ***adjective*** **illusory** (i-**loo**-suh-ree)

il•lus•trate (**il**-uh-*strate*) ***verb***
1. To draw pictures, by hand or by computer, for a book, magazine, or other publication. ▸ ***adjective*** **illustrated**
2. To make clear or explain by using examples or comparisons.
▸ ***verb*** **illustrating, illustrated** ▸ ***noun*** **illustrator**

il•lus•tra•tion (il-uh-**stray**-shuhn) ***noun***
1. A picture in a book, magazine, etc.
2. An example. ▸ ***adjective*** **illustrative** (i-**luhss**-truh-tiv)

ill will ***noun*** Unfriendly feeling or hatred.

I'm (**eyem**) ***contraction*** A short form of *I am.*

im•age (**im**-ij) ***noun***
1. A picture you have in your mind.
2. A representation, such as a picture or a statue.
3. Your **image** is the way that you appear to other people.
4. A picture formed in a lens or mirror.

im•age•ry (**im**-ij-ree) ***noun*** Descriptive language used by writers in poems, stories, etc.

i•mag•i•nar•y (i-**maj**-uh-*ner*-ee) ***adjective*** Existing in the imagination and not the real world.

i•mag•i•na•tion (i-*maj*-uh-**nay**-shuhn) ***noun***
1. The ability to form pictures in your mind of things that are not present or real.
2. The ability to create new images or ideas of things you have never experienced.

i•mag•i•na•tive (i-**maj**-uh-nuh-tiv) ***adjective***
1. Creative or having great imagination, as in *an imaginative child.*
2. Showing imagination.
▸ ***adverb*** **imaginatively**

im•ag•ine (i-**maj**-uhn) ***verb*** To picture something in your mind. ▸ **imagining, imagined**

im•be•cile (**im**-buh-suhl) ***noun*** A stupid person.

im•i•tate (**im**-uh-tate) ***verb*** To copy or mimic someone or something.
▸ **imitating, imitated** ▸ ***noun*** **imitation**

im•mac•u•late (i-**mak**-yuh-lit) ***adjective*** Very clean or neat. ▸ ***adverb*** **immaculately**

im•ma•ture (im-uh-**chur** *or* im-uh-**tur**) ***adjective***
1. Young and not fully developed.
2. If someone is **immature,** he or she behaves in a silly, childish way.
▸ ***noun*** **immaturity** ▸ ***adverb*** **immaturely**

im•mea•sur•a•ble (im-**ezh**-ur-uh-buhl) ***adjective*** Too great or vast to be measured. ▸ ***adverb*** **immeasurably**

im•me•di•ate (i-**mee**-dee-it) ***adjective***
1. Happening or done at once, as in *an immediate reply.*
2. Close or near.

im•me•di•ate•ly (i-**mee**-dee-it-lee) ***adverb***
1. Now or at once.
2. Closely, or next.

im•mense (i-**menss**) ***adjective*** Huge, or enormous. ▸ ***noun*** **immensity** ▸ ***adverb*** **immensely**

im•merse (i-**murss**) ***verb***
1. To cover something completely in a liquid.
2. In some religions, to baptize someone by completely placing the person under water for a moment.
3. If you **immerse** yourself in something, you involve yourself in it completely.
▸ ***verb*** **immersing, immersed** ▸ ***noun*** **immersion** (i-**mur**-zhuhn)

im•mi•grant (**im**-uh-gruhnt) ***noun*** Someone who comes from abroad to live permanently in a country. ▸ ***noun*** **immigration** ▸ ***verb*** **immigrate**

im•mi•nent (**im**-uh-nuhnt) ***adjective*** About to happen, as in *imminent danger.* ▸ ***adverb*** **imminently**

im•mo•bi•lize (i-**moh**-buh-lize) ***verb*** To make it impossible for something or someone to move. ▸ **immobilizing, immobilized**

im•mor•al (i-**mor**-uhl) ***adjective*** Unfair, or without a sense of right and wrong.
▸ ***noun*** **immorality** ▸ ***adverb*** **immorally**

im•mor•tal (i-**mor**-tuhl)
1. ***adjective*** Living or lasting forever.
2. ***adjective*** Famous or remembered forever.
3. ***noun*** Someone or something that lives or is famous forever.
▸ ***noun*** **immortality**

im•mune (i-**myoon**) ***adjective***
1. Protected against a disease.
2. Protected from physical or emotional harm.
▸ ***noun*** **immunity**

immune system ***noun*** The system that protects your body against disease and infection. It includes white blood cells and antibodies.

im•mu•nize (**im**-yuh-*nize*) ***verb*** To make someone immune to a disease.
▸ **immunizing, immunized** ▸ ***noun*** **immunization**

im•pact (**im**-pakt) ***noun***
1. The striking of one thing against another.
2. The effect that something has on a person or a thing.

im•pair (im-**pair**) ***verb*** To damage something or make it less effective.
▸ **impairing, impaired** ▸ ***noun*** **impairment**

im•pal•a (im-**pal**-uh) ***noun*** A small African antelope that has curved horns and a reddish brown coat. The impala can leap great distances. ▸ ***noun, plural*** **impala** *or* **impalas**

im•par•tial (im-**par**-shuhl) ***adjective*** Fair and not favoring one person or point of view over another. ▸ ***noun*** **impartiality** ▸ ***adverb*** **impartially**

im•pa•tient (im-**pay**-shuhnt) ***adjective***
1. In a hurry and unable to wait.
2. Easily annoyed.
▸ ***noun*** **impatience** ▸ ***adverb*** **impatiently**

im•peach (im-**peech**) ***verb*** To bring formal charges against a public official who may have committed a crime or done something wrong while in office.
▸ **impeaches, impeaching, impeached** ▸ ***noun*** **impeachment**

im•per•a•tive (im-**per**-uh-tiv) ***adjective***
1. Extremely important.

2. Expressing a command, an order, or a request, as in *an imperative sentence.* ▸ ***noun*** **imperative**

im•per•fect (im-**pur**-fikt) ***adjective*** Faulty or not perfect. ▸ ***noun*** **imperfection** ▸ ***adverb*** **imperfectly**

im•pe•ri•al (im-**pihr**-ee-uhl) ***adjective***
1. To do with an empire.
2. To do with an emperor or empress, as in *the imperial palace.*

im•per•son•al (im-**pur**-suh-nuhl) ***adjective***
1. Lacking in warmth and feeling.
2. To do with people generally rather than with one particular person.
▸ ***adverb*** **impersonally**

im•per•son•ate (im-**pur**-suh-nate) ***verb*** To pretend to be someone else, either seriously or for fun.
▸ **impersonating, impersonated**
▸ ***noun*** **impersonation,** ***noun*** **impersonator**

im•per•ti•nent (im-**pur**-tuh-nuhnt) ***adjective*** Rude and impudent, as in *impertinent behavior.* ▸ ***noun*** **impertinence** ▸ ***adverb*** **impertinently**

im•pet•u•ous (im-**pech**-oo-uhss) ***adjective*** Someone who is **impetuous** does things suddenly, without thinking first. ▸ ***adverb*** **impetuously**

im•plant (im-**plant**) ***verb***
1. To establish or instill firmly and deeply.
2. To put an organ or a device into the body by surgery.
▸ ***verb*** **implanting, implanted** ▸ ***noun*** **implant** (**im**-plant)

im•ple•ment
1. (**im**-pluh-muhnt) ***noun*** A tool or a utensil.
2. (**im**-pluh-ment) ***verb*** To put something such as a plan or an idea into action. ▸ **implementing, implemented**
▸ ***noun*** **implementation**

im•pli•ca•tion (im-pluh-**kay**-shuhn) ***noun***
1. The meaning or significance of something.
2. Something suggested but not actually said.

im•ply (im-**plye**) ***verb*** To suggest or mean something without actually saying it. ▸ **implies, implying, implied**

im•po•lite (im-puh-**lite**) ***adjective*** If someone is **impolite,** he or she behaves in a rude manner. ▸ ***adverb*** **impolitely**

im•port (im-**port** *or* **im**-port) ***verb*** To bring into a place or country from elsewhere. ▸ **importing, imported**
▸ ***noun*** **import** (**im**-port)**,** ***noun*** **importer**

im•por•tant (im-**port**-uhnt) ***adjective***
1. Something **important** is worth taking seriously and can have a great impact, as in *an important discovery.* ▸ ***adverb*** **importantly**
2. An **important** person is powerful and holds a high position.
▸ ***noun*** **importance**

im•pose (im-**poze**) ***verb***
1. To force to accept by legal means, as in *to impose taxes* or *to impose a prison sentence.*
2. To take advantage of someone or make unfair demands.
▸ ***verb*** **imposing, imposed** ▸ ***noun*** **imposition**

im•pos•si•ble (im-**poss**-uh-buhl) ***adjective*** If something is **impossible,** it cannot be done or cannot be true.
▸ ***noun*** **impossibility** ▸ ***adverb*** **impossibly**

im•pos•tor (im-**poss**-tur) ***noun*** Someone who pretends to be something that he or she is not.

im•prac•ti•cal (im-**prak**-tuh-kuhl) ***adjective*** Not sensible, or not useful, as in *an impractical plan.*

im•press (im-**press**) ***verb***
1. To make people think highly of you.
2. To have an effect on someone's mind.
▸ ***verb*** **impresses, impressing, impressed** ▸ ***adjective*** **impressive**

im•pres•sion (im-**presh**-uhn) ***noun***
1. An idea or a feeling.
2. An imitation of someone.
3. If something **makes an impression** on you, it has a strong effect on you.

I

im•pres•sion•a•ble (im-**presh**-uh-nuh-buhl) ***adjective*** If someone is **impressionable,** the person is easily influenced.

im•print
1. (**im**-print) ***noun*** A mark made by pressing or stamping something on a surface. ▸ ***verb*** **imprint** (im-**print**)
2. (**im**-print) ***noun*** A strong influence.
3. (im-**print**) ***verb*** To fix firmly in the mind or memory. ▸ **imprinting, imprinted**

im•pris•on (im-**priz**-uhn) ***verb*** To put someone in prison, or to lock the person up. ▸ **imprisoning, imprisoned** ▸ ***noun*** **imprisonment**

im•prop•er (im-**prop**-ur) ***adjective***
1. Incorrect, as in *an improper response.*
2. Showing bad manners or bad taste.
3. An **improper fraction** is a fraction whose numerator is greater than its denominator, as in $\frac{5}{4}$ or $\frac{11}{8}$.
▸ ***adverb*** **improperly**

im•prove (im-**proov**) ***verb*** To get better, or to make something better.
▸ **improving, improved** ▸ ***noun*** **improvement** ▸ ***adjective*** **improved**

im•pro•vise (**im**-pruh-vize) ***verb***
1. To do the best you can with what is available.
2. When actors or musicians **improvise,** they make up material on the spot.
▸ ***noun*** **improvisation** (im-*prov*-uh-**zay**-shuhn)
▸ ***verb*** **improvising, improvised**
▸ ***noun*** **improviser**

im•pu•dent (**im**-pyuh-duhnt) ***adjective*** Rude, bold, and outspoken, as in *an impudent remark.* ▸ ***noun*** **impudence** ▸ ***adverb*** **impudently**

im•pulse (**im**-puhlss) ***noun***
1. A sudden desire to do something.
2. A sudden push or thrust.
3. A pulse of energy, as in *an electrical impulse.*

im•pul•sive (im-**puhl**-siv) ***adjective*** Acting on impulse, or done on impulse, as in *an impulsive person.* ▸ ***adverb*** **impulsively**

im•pure (im-**pyoor**) ***adjective***
1. Unclean or contaminated, as in *impure water.*
2. Mixed with foreign substances, as in *an impure metal.*
▸ ***adverb*** **impurely**

in (**in**)
1. ***preposition*** Inside.
2. ***preposition*** Into.
3. ***preposition*** During, as in *in the autumn.*
4. ***adverb*** In or into some condition, relation, or place, as in *to join in* or *to fall in.*
5. ***adverb*** Inside a certain place.
In sounds like **inn.**

in•a•bil•i•ty (in-uh-**bil**-uh-tee) ***noun*** Lack of power or ability to do something.

in•ac•cu•rate (in-**ak**-yuh-rit) ***adjective***
1. Not very precise or correct.
2. Off the mark; not on target.
▸ ***noun*** **inaccuracy** ▸ ***adverb*** **inaccurately**

in•ad•e•quate (in-**ad**-uh-kwit) ***adjective*** Not enough or not good enough. ▸ ***adverb*** **inadequately**

in•ap•pro•pri•ate (in-uh-**proh**-pree-it) ***adjective*** Unsuitable for the time, place, etc. ▸ ***adverb*** **inappropriately**

in•ar•tic•u•late (in-ar-**tik**-yuh-lit) ***adjective*** Not able to express oneself very clearly in words.

in•au•di•ble (in-**aw**-duh-buhl) ***adjective*** Not loud enough to be heard. ▸ ***noun*** **inaudibility** ▸ ***adverb*** **inaudibly**

in•au•gu•rate (in-**aw**-gyuh-*rate*) ***verb***
1. To swear a public official into office with a formal ceremony, as in *to inaugurate the president of the United States.*
2. To formally open, or to begin to use publicly, as in *to inaugurate a new plan.*
▸ ***verb*** **inaugurating, inaugurated**

in•au•gu•ra•tion (in-aw-gyuh-**ray**-shuhn) ***noun*** The ceremony of swearing in a public official.

in•born (**in**-*born*) ***adjective*** If you have an **inborn** skill or quality, you have it from birth and it is natural to you.

in•can•des•cent (in-kan-**dess**-uhnt) ***adjective***
1. Glowing with intense light and heat, as in *an incandescent bulb.*
2. Radiant or brightly shining, as in *an incandescent smile.*

in•ca•pa•ble (in-**kay**-puh-buhl) ***adjective*** If someone is **incapable** of doing something, he or she is unable to do it.

in•cense
1. (**in**-senss) ***noun*** A substance that is burned to give off a sweet smell.
2. (in-**senss**) ***verb*** To make very angry. ▸ **incensing, incensed**

in•cen•tive (in-**sen**-tiv) ***noun*** Something that encourages you to make an effort.

in•ces•sant (in-**sess**-uhnt) ***adjective*** Nonstop or continuous, as in *incessant noise.* ▸ ***adverb*** **incessantly**

inch (**inch**)
1. ***noun*** A unit of length equal to of a foot. The diameter of a quarter measures about an inch.
2. ***noun*** A very small amount or distance.
3. ***verb*** To move very slowly. ▸ **inches, inching, inched** ▸ ***noun, plural*** **inches**

inch•worm (**inch**-*wurm*) ***noun*** A caterpillar that moves by arching and stretching its body.

in•ci•dent (**in**-suh-duhnt) ***noun*** Something that happens; an event.

in•ci•den•tal•ly (in-suh-**dent**-uh-lee) ***adverb*** By the way.

in•cin•er•a•tor (in-**sin**-uh-ray-tur) ***noun*** A furnace for burning garbage and other waste materials.

in•ci•sion (in-**sizh**-uhn) ***noun*** A clean cut made by a knife or blade.

in•cite (in-**site**) ***verb*** If you **incite** someone to do something, you provoke the person or urge him or her to do it. ▸ **inciting, incited**

in•cline (in-**kline**) ***verb*** To lean, or to slope. ▸ **inclining, inclined** ▸ ***noun*** **incline** (**in**-kline)

in•clined (in-**klinde**) ***adjective***
1. Leaning, or sloping.
2. If you are **inclined to** do something, you like to do it or tend to do it. ▸ ***noun*** **inclination** (in-kluh-**nay**-shuhn)

in•clude (in-**klood**) ***verb*** To contain something or someone as part of something else. ▸ **including, included**

in•clu•sive (in-**kloo**-siv) ***adjective*** Including and covering everything.

in•co•her•ent (*in*-koh-**hihr**-uhnt) ***adjective*** Not clear, or not logical. ▸ ***adverb*** **incoherently**

in•come (**in**-kuhm) ***noun*** The money that someone earns or receives regularly.

income tax ***noun*** A payment made to the government based on the amount of money a person makes. ▸ ***noun, plural*** **income taxes**

in•com•pat•i•ble (*in*-kuhm-**pat**-uh-buhl) ***adjective*** If people are **incompatible,** they cannot get along, and if objects are **incompatible,** they cannot be used together. ▸ ***noun*** **incompatibility**

in•com•pe•tent (in-**kom**-puh-tuhnt) ***adjective*** If someone is **incompetent** at something, she or he cannot do it well or effectively. ▸ ***noun*** **incompetence** ▸ ***adverb*** **incompetently**

in•com•plete (*in*-kuhm-**pleet**) ***adjective*** Not finished or not complete. ▸ ***adverb*** **incompletely**

in•com•pre•hen•si•ble (*in*-kom-pri-**hen**-suh-buhl) ***adjective*** Impossible to understand.

in•con•ceiv•a•ble (*in*-kuhn-**see**-vuh-buhl) ***adjective*** Impossible to believe or imagine. ▸ ***adverb*** **inconceivably**

in•con•clu•sive (*in*-kuhn-**kloo**-siv) ***adjective*** Not clear, or not certain, as in *inconclusive results.* ▸ ***adverb*** **inconclusively**

in•con•sid•er•ate (*in*-kuhn-**sid**-ur-it) ***adjective*** Someone who is **inconsiderate** does not think about other people's needs or feelings. ▸ ***adverb*** **inconsiderately**

I

in•con•spic•u•ous (*in*-kuhn-**spik**-yoo-uhss) ***adjective*** Something that is **inconspicuous** cannot be seen easily or does not attract attention. ▸ ***adverb*** **inconspicuously**

in•con•ven•ience (*in*-kuhn-**vee**-nyuhnss) ***noun***
1. Trouble or difficulty.
2. Something that causes trouble or difficulty.
▸ ***verb*** **inconvenience**

in•con•ven•ient (*in*-kuhn-**vee**-nyuhnt) ***adjective*** If something is **inconvenient,** it causes trouble or difficulty. ▸ ***adverb*** **inconveniently**

in•cor•po•rate (in-**kor**-puh-*rate*) ***verb***
1. When you **incorporate** something into another thing, you make it a part of that thing.
2. To make or become a corporation.
▸ ***verb*** **incorporating, incorporated** ▸ ***noun*** **incorporation** ▸ ***adjective*** **incorporated**

in•cor•rect (*in*-kuh-**rekt**) ***adjective*** Wrong. ▸ ***adverb*** **incorrectly**

in•crease (in-**kreess**) ***verb*** To grow in size or number. ▸ **increasing, increased** ▸ ***noun*** **increase** (**in**-kreess) ▸ ***adverb*** **increasingly**

in•cred•i•ble (in-**kred**-uh-buhl) ***adjective*** Unbelievable or amazing. ▸ ***adverb*** **incredibly**

in•cred•u•lous (in-**krej**-uh-luhss) ***adjective*** Not able to believe something or accept that something is true. ▸ ***adverb*** **incredulously**

in•crim•i•nate (in-**krim**-uh-*nate*) ***verb*** To show that someone is guilty of a crime or another wrong action. ▸ **incriminating, incriminated** ▸ ***noun*** **incrimination**

in•cu•bate (**ing**-kyuh-bate) ***verb***
1. To keep eggs warm before they hatch.
2. To keep a premature or sick baby safe and warm in a specially heated apparatus.
3. To nurture, or to allow to develop, as in *to incubate an idea.*
▸ ***verb*** **incubating, incubated** ▸ ***noun*** **incubation**

in•cu•ba•tor (**ing**-kyuh-*bay*-tur) ***noun***
1. A heated apparatus in which premature or sick babies are kept safe and warm.
2. A container in which eggs are kept warm until they hatch.

in•cur•a•ble (in-**kyur**-uh-buhl) ***adjective*** If someone has an **incurable** disease, the person cannot be made well.

in•debt•ed (in-**det**-id) ***adjective***
1. Owing thanks or gratitude to someone for a favor.
2. Owing money; in debt.
▸ ***noun*** **indebtedness**

in•de•cent (in-**dee**-suhnt) ***adjective*** Unpleasant, rude, or shocking, as in *indecent language.* ▸ ***noun*** **indecency** ▸ ***adverb*** **indecently**

in•deed (in-**deed**) ***adverb*** Certainly.

in•def•i•nite (in-**def**-uh-nit)
1. ***adjective*** Not clear, or not certain, as in *an indefinite amount of time.* ▸ ***adverb*** **indefinitely**
2. indefinite article ***noun*** The grammatical term for *a* or *an,* used before a noun when it refers to something general or not specific, as in *a baseball* or *an orange.*

in•dent (in-**dent**) ***verb*** To start a line of writing or typing a few spaces in from the margin. ▸ **indenting, indented** ▸ ***noun*** **indent** (**in**-dent) ***noun*** **indentation**

in•de•pen•dence (in-di-**pen**-duhnss) ***noun*** Freedom; the condition of being independent.

Independence Day ***noun*** A U.S. holiday, celebrated on July 4th, to commemorate the signing of the Declaration of Independence in 1776. Also known as *the Fourth of July.*

in•de•pend•ent (in-di-**pen**-duhnt)
1. ***adjective*** Free from the control of other people or things.

2. ***adjective*** If someone is **independent,** the person does not want or need much help from other people.
3. independent clause *noun* A sentence that can stand alone and be grammatical, as the sentence *"He likes to swim." See* **dependent clause.**
▸ ***adverb* independently**

in•de•struc•ti•ble (in-di-**struhk**-tuh-buhl) ***adjective*** If something is **indestructible,** it cannot be destroyed.
▸ ***adverb* indestructibly**

in•dex (**in**-deks)
1. ***noun*** An alphabetical list that shows you where to find things in a book.
▸ ***noun, plural* indexes** *or* **indices** (**in**-di-*seez*)
2. ***verb*** To supply with an index.
▸ **indexes, indexing, indexed** ▸ ***noun* indexer**

index finger ***noun*** The finger next to the thumb, used for pointing.

In•di•an (**in**-dee-uhn)
1. ***noun*** Someone who is from India.
2. ***adjective*** To do with India, its people, or its culture.
3. ***noun*** A Native American. *See* **American Indian.**
4. ***adjective*** To do with American Indians.

in•di•cate (**in**-duh-kate) ***verb***
1. To show or prove something.
▸ ***adjective* indicative** (in-**dik**-uh-tiv)
2. To point something out clearly.
▸ ***verb* indicating, indicated** ▸ ***noun* indicator**

in•di•ca•tion (in-di-**kay**-shuhn) ***noun*** Something that indicates or points out.

in•dict (in-**dite**) ***verb*** To officially charge someone with a crime. ▸ **indicting, indicted** ▸ ***noun* indictment**

in•dif•fer•ent (in-**dif**-uhr-uhnt) ***adjective***
1. If someone is **indifferent** to something, the person is not interested in it. ▸ ***noun* indifference** ▸ ***adverb* indifferently**
2. Poor in quality.

in•di•ges•tion (in-duh-**jess**-chuhn) ***noun*** If you have **indigestion,** your stomach is uncomfortable and you are having difficulty digesting food.

in•dig•nant (in-**dig**-nuhnt) ***adjective*** If you are **indignant,** you are upset and annoyed because you feel that something is not fair. ▸ ***noun* indignation** ▸ ***adverb* indignantly**

in•di•go (**in**-duh-goh) ***noun***
1. A plant with dark purple berries from which a dark blue dye can be made.
2. A dark violet-blue color or dye.

in•di•rect (*in*-dye-**rekt** *or in*-duh-**rekt**) ***adjective***
1. Not in a straight line, as in *an indirect route.*
2. Not directly connected.
3. Not to the point.
▸ ***adverb* indirectly**

in•dis•pen•sa•ble (*in*-diss-**pen**-suh-buhl) ***adjective*** If someone or something is **indispensable** to an organization, the person or thing is absolutely necessary to its smooth running. ▸ ***adverb* indispensably**

in•dis•tin•guish•a•ble (*in*-diss-**ting**-gwi-shuh-buhl) ***adjective*** When two people or things are **indistinguishable,** you cannot tell the difference between them. ▸ ***adverb* indistinguishably**

in•di•vid•u•al (*in*-duh-**vij**-oo-uhl)
1. ***adjective*** Single and separate.
2. ***noun*** A person, as in *a strange individual.*
3. ***adjective*** Unusual or different.
▸ ***adverb* individually**

in•di•vid•u•al•i•ty (*in*-duh-*vij*-oo-**al**-uh-tee) ***noun*** The qualities that set a person apart from all others.

in•di•vis•i•ble (in-duh-**viz**-uh-buhl) ***adjective*** Not able to be divided or broken into pieces. ▸ ***adverb* indivisibly**

in•door (**in**-*dor*) ***adjective*** Used, done, or built inside.

in•doors (**in**-**dorz**) ***adverb*** Inside a building.

I

in•dulge (in-**duhlj**) ***verb***
1. To let someone have his or her own way. ▸ ***adjective*** **indulgent**
2. If you **indulge in** something, you allow yourself to enjoy it.
▸ ***verb*** **indulging, indulged** ▸ ***noun*** **indulgence**

in•dus•tri•al (in-**duhss**-tree-uhl) ***adjective*** To do with businesses and factories. ▸ ***adverb*** **industrially**

in•dus•tri•al•ize (in-**duhss**-tree-uh-*lize*) ***verb*** To set up businesses and factories in an area. ▸ **industrializing, industrialized** ▸ ***noun*** **industrialization**

in•dus•try (**in**-duh-stree) ***noun***
1. Manufacturing companies and other businesses, taken together.
2. A single branch of business or trade, as in *the tourist industry.*
3. Hard work or effort.
▸ ***noun, plural*** **industries**

in•ef•fi•cient (in-uh-**fish**-uhnt) ***adjective*** If someone or something is **inefficient,** the person or thing does not work very well and wastes time and energy. ▸ ***noun*** **inefficiency** ▸ ***adverb*** **inefficiently**

in•e•qual•i•ty (*in*-i-**kwol**-uh-tee) ***noun*** The treatment of people or things in an unequal and unfair way. ▸ ***noun, plural*** **inequalities**

in•ert (in-**urt**) ***adjective***
1. Lifeless or not moving.
2. An **inert** gas is characterized by great stability and extremely low reaction rates.

in•er•tia (in-**ur**-shuh) ***noun***
1. A lazy, tired feeling.
2. The **inertia** of an object is its resistance to any change in motion.

in•ev•i•ta•ble (in-**ev**-uh-tuh-buhl) ***adjective*** If something is **inevitable,** it is sure to happen. ▸ ***noun*** **inevitability** ▸ ***adverb*** **inevitably**

in•ex•pen•sive (in-ik-**spen**-siv) ***adjective*** Not costing a lot of money. ▸ ***adverb*** **inexpensively**

in•ex•pe•ri•enced (*in*-ik-**spihr**-ee-uhnst) ***adjective*** An **inexperienced** person has had little practice in doing something.

in•ex•pli•ca•ble (in-ik-**splik**-uh-buhl *or* in-**ek**-spluh-kuh-buhl) ***adjective*** If something is **inexplicable,** it cannot be explained. ▸ ***adverb*** **inexplicably**

in•fa•mous (**in**-fuh-muhss) ***adjective*** If someone or something is **infamous,** the person or thing has a very bad reputation.

in•fant (**in**-fuhnt) ***noun*** A newborn child. Babies are considered infants until the time they can walk. ▸ ***noun*** **infancy** ▸ ***adjective*** **infant**

in•fan•try (**in**-fuhn-tree) ***noun*** The part of an army that fights on foot.

in•fat•u•at•ed (in-**fach**-yoo-ay-tid) ***adjective*** If you are **infatuated** with someone or something, you like the person or thing so much that you stop thinking clearly and sensibly. ▸ ***noun*** **infatuation**

in•fect (in-**fekt**) ***verb*** To cause disease or contaminate by introducing germs or viruses. ▸ **infecting, infected** ▸ ***adjective*** **infected**

in•fec•tion (in-**fek**-shuhn) ***noun*** An illness caused by germs or viruses.

in•fec•tious (in-**fek**-shuhss) ***adjective***
1. An **infectious** disease can spread from one person to another by germs or viruses in the air or on objects.
2. If a mood is **infectious,** it spreads easily, as in *infectious laughter.*

in•fer (in-**fur**) ***verb*** To draw a conclusion after considering all the facts. ▸ **inferring, inferred** ▸ ***noun*** **inference**

in•fe•ri•or (in-**fihr**-ee-ur) ***adjective*** If something is **inferior** to something else, it is not as good. ▸ ***noun*** **inferiority**

in•fer•tile (in-**fur**-tuhl) ***adjective***
1. Land that is **infertile** is useless for growing crops and plants.
2. Unable to reproduce or have offspring.
▸ ***noun*** **infertility**

in•fes•ted (in-**fess**-tid) ***adjective*** If an object or a place is **infested,** it is full of animal or insect pests. ▸ ***noun*** **infestation** ▸ ***verb*** **infest**

in•fil•trate (**in**-fil-*trate*) ***verb*** To join an enemy's side secretly in order to spy or cause some sort of damage.
▸ **infiltrating, infiltrated** ▸ ***noun*** **infiltration**

in•fi•nite (**in**-fuh-nit) ***adjective*** Endless.
▸ ***noun*** **infinity** ▸ ***adverb*** **infinitely**

in•fin•i•tive (in-**fin**-uh-tiv) ***noun*** The basic form of a verb, often preceded by *to;* for example, *to run, to be, to write.*

in•firm (in-**furm**) ***adjective*** Weak or ill.
▸ ***noun*** **infirmity**

in•fir•ma•ry (in-**fur**-mur-ee) ***noun*** A place where sick people are cared for.

in•flame (in-**flame**) ***verb***
1. To make hot, red, or swollen, usually as the result of an infection or injury.
2. To stir up or excite the emotions of a person or group.
▸ ***verb*** **inflaming, inflamed**

in•flam•ma•ble (in-**flam**-uh-buhl) ***adjective*** An **inflammable** substance can catch fire easily.

in•flam•ma•tion (in-fluh-**may**-shuhn) ***noun*** Redness, swelling, heat, and pain, usually caused by an infection or injury.

in•flat•a•ble (in-**flay**-tuh-buhl) ***adjective*** An **inflatable** object can be filled with air and expanded. ▸ ***noun*** **inflatable**

in•flate (in-**flate**) ***verb*** To make something expand by blowing or pumping air into it. ▸ **inflating, inflated**

in•fla•tion (in-**flay**-shuhn) ***noun***
1. A general increase in prices.
▸ ***adjective*** **inflationary**
2. The act of making something expand by blowing air into it.

in•flex•i•ble (in-**flek**-suh-buhl) ***adjective*** Not able to bend or change; rigid. ▸ ***noun*** **inflexibility** ▸ ***adverb*** **inflexibly**

in•flict (in-**flikt**) ***verb*** To cause suffering to someone or something, as in *to inflict damage.* ▸ **inflicting, inflicted** ▸ ***noun*** **infliction**

in•flu•ence (**in**-floo-uhnss) ***verb*** To have an effect on someone or something.
▸ **influencing, influenced** ▸ ***noun*** **influence**

in•flu•en•tial (in-floo-**en**-shuhl) ***adjective*** Having the power to change or affect someone or something, as in *an influential senator.*

in•flu•en•za (*in*-floo-**en**-zuh) *See* **flu.**

in•fo•mer•cial (in-foh-**mur**-shuhl) ***noun*** A program-length television commercial with demonstrations, interviews, and detailed information about a service or product.

in•form (in-**form**) ***verb***
1. To tell someone something.
2. If you **inform on** a criminal, you give the police information about the person.
▸ ***verb*** **informing, informed** ▸ ***noun*** **informer,** ***noun*** **informant**

in•for•mal (in-**for**-muhl) ***adjective***
1. Relaxed and casual, as in *an informal party.* ▸ ***noun*** **informality**
2. Informal language is used in everyday speech but not usually in formal speaking or in writing.
▸ ***adverb*** **informally**

in•for•ma•tion (in-fur-**may**-shuhn) ***noun*** Facts and knowledge.

information su•per•high•way (*soo*-pur-**hye**-way) ***noun*** A vast network of information available to a computer user with a modem.

information technology ***noun*** The use of computers and other electronic equipment to find, create, store, or communicate information.

in•for•ma•tive (in-**for**-muh-tiv) ***adjective*** If something or someone is **informative,** the thing or person provides useful information.

in•fre•quent (in-**free**-kwuhnt) ***adjective*** Not happening very often.
▸ ***adverb*** **infrequently**

I

in•fu•ri•ate (in-**fyur**-ee-*ate*) ***verb*** If someone or something **infuriates** you, the person or thing makes you extremely angry. ▸ **infuriating, infuriated** ▸ ***adjective*** **infuriating** ▸ ***adverb*** **infuriatingly**

in•gen•ious (in-**jee**-nee-uhss) ***adjective*** Inventive and original, as in *an ingenious plan.* ▸ ***noun*** **ingenuity** (in-ji-**noo**-i-tee) ▸ ***adverb*** **ingeniously**

in•got (**ing**-uht) ***noun*** A mass of metal that has been shaped into a block or bar.

in•gre•di•ent (in-**gree**-dee-uhnt) ***noun*** One of the items that something is made from, such as an item of food in a recipe.

in•hab•it (in-**hab**-it) ***verb*** If you **inhabit** a place, you live there. ▸ **inhabiting, inhabited** ▸ ***noun*** **inhabitant**

in•hale (in-**hayl**) ***verb*** To breathe in. ▸ **inhaling, inhaled** ▸ ***noun*** **inhalation** (in-huh-**lay**-shuhn)

in•hal•er (in-**hay**-lur) ***noun*** A small device from which you may inhale medicine through your mouth.

in•her•it (in-**her**-it) ***verb***
1. To receive money, property, or a title from someone who has died. ▸ ***noun*** **inheritance**
2. If you **inherit** a particular characteristic, it is passed down to you from your parents.
▸ ***verb*** **inheriting, inherited**

in•hu•man (in-**hyoo**-muhn) ***adjective*** Cruel and brutal, as in *inhuman treatment.* ▸ ***noun*** **inhumanity** ▸ ***adverb*** **inhumanly**

in•i•tial (i-**nish**-uhl)
1. ***noun*** The first letter of a name or word.
2. ***adjective*** First, or at the beginning. ▸ ***adverb*** **initially**
3. ***verb*** To write your initials on. ▸ **initialing, initialed**

i•ni•ti•ate (i-**nish**-ee-ate) ***verb***
1. To introduce or start something new.
2. To bring someone into a club or group, often with a ceremony.
▸ ***verb*** **initiating, initiated** ▸ ***noun*** **initiation**

in•i•tia•tive (i-**nish**-ee-uh-tiv) ***noun*** If you take the **initiative,** you do what is necessary without other people telling you to do it.

in•ject (in-**jekt**) ***verb*** To use a needle and syringe to put medicine or nourishment into someone's body. ▸ **injecting, injected** ▸ ***noun*** **injection**

in•jure (**in**-jur) ***verb*** To hurt or harm yourself or someone else. ▸ **injuring, injured**

in•ju•ry (**in**-juh-ree) ***noun*** Damage or harm. ▸ ***noun, plural*** **injuries** ▸ ***adjective*** **injurious** (in-**jur**-ee-uhss)

in•jus•tice (in-**juhss**-tiss) ***noun***
1. Unfairness or lack of justice.
2. An unfair situation or action.

ink (**ingk**) ***noun*** A colored liquid used for writing and printing. ▸ ***adjective*** **inky**

in•land (**in**-luhnd) ***adjective*** Away from the sea. ▸ ***adverb*** **inland**

in•let (**in**-let) ***noun*** A narrow body of water that leads inland from a larger body of water, such as an ocean.

in-line skate (**in**-*line*) ***noun*** A skate whose wheels are in a straight line.

in•mate (**in**-*mayt*) ***noun*** Someone who has been sentenced to live in a prison or other institution where one is under supervision.

inn (**in**) ***noun*** A small hotel that often includes a restaurant. **Inn** sounds like **in.**

in•ner (**in**-ur) ***adjective***
1. Inside, or near the center.
2. Private.

in•ning (**in**-ing) ***noun*** A part of a baseball game in which each team gets a turn at bat.

in•no•cent (**in**-uh-suhnt) ***adjective***
1. Not guilty.
2. Not knowing about something.
▸ ***noun*** **innocence** ▸ ***adverb*** **innocently**

in•no•va•tion (in-uh-**vay**-shuhn) ***noun*** A new idea or invention. ▸ ***verb*** **innovate** ▸ ***adjective*** **innovative**

in•nu•mer•ate (in-**noo**-mur-uht) ***adjective*** Unable to do basic math problems or understand the concepts behind them. ▸ ***noun*** **innumeracy**

in•oc•u•late (in-**ok**-yuh-*late*) ***verb*** To inject a weakened form of a disease into someone's body so that the person becomes protected against it. ▸ **inoculating, inoculated** ▸ ***noun*** **inoculation**

in•pa•tient (**in**-*pay*-shuhnt) ***noun*** Someone who stays in the hospital while being treated.

in•put (**in**-*put*) ***noun***
1. Advice.
2. Information fed into a computer. ▸ ***verb*** **input**
3. Something that is put in, as energy to be used by a machine.

in•quire (in-**kwire**) ***verb*** To ask about someone or something. ▸ **inquiring, inquired** ▸ ***adjective*** **inquiring** ▸ ***adverb*** **inquiringly**

in•quir•y (in-**kwye**-ree *or* **in**-kwuh-ree) ***noun*** A study or an investigation, especially an official or scientific one. ▸ ***noun, plural*** **inquiries**

in•quis•i•tive (in-**kwiz**-uh-tiv) ***adjective*** Questioning or curious. ▸ ***noun*** **inquisitiveness** ▸ ***adverb*** **inquisitively**

in•sane (in-**sayn**) ***adjective***
1. Mentally ill.
2. Very foolish.
▸ ***noun*** **insanity** (in-**san**-i-tee) ▸ ***adverb*** **insanely**

in•san•i•tar•y (in-**san**-uh-*ter*-ee) ***adjective*** Dirty and unhealthy.

in•scribe (in-**skribe**) ***verb***
1. To carve or engrave letters on a surface.
2. To write a special message or dedication in a book.
▸ ***verb*** **inscribing, inscribed** ▸ ***adjective*** **inscribed**

in•scrip•tion (in-**skrip**-shuhn) ***noun*** A carved, engraved, or specially written message.

in•sect (**in**-sekt) ***noun*** A small creature with three pairs of legs, one or two pairs of wings, three main sections to its body, an exoskeleton, and no backbone.

in•sec•ti•cide (in-**sek**-tuh-*side*) ***noun*** A chemical used to kill insects.

in•se•cure (*in*-si-**kyoor**) ***adjective***
1. Unsafe, or not fastened tightly.
2. Anxious and not confident. ▸ ***noun*** **insecurity** ▸ ***adverb*** **insecurely**

in•sen•si•tive (in-**sen**-suh-tiv) ***adjective*** Thoughtless and unsympathetic to other people's feelings. ▸ ***noun*** **insensitivity** ▸ ***adverb*** **insensitively**

in•sert
1. ***verb*** (in-**surt**) To put something inside something else. ▸ **inserting, inserted** ▸ ***noun*** **insertion**
2. ***noun*** (**in**-surt) Something that is put inside something else.

in•side (*in*-**side** *or* **in**-*side*)
1. ***noun*** The interior or inner part of something. ▸ ***adjective*** **inside** (**in**-**side**)
2. ***preposition*** In less than.
3. ***preposition*** Within.
4. ***adverb*** (*in*-**side**) Into.

in•sid•i•ous (in-**sid**-ee-uhss) ***adjective***
1. Quietly harmful or deceitful, as in *an insidious enemy.*
2. Working in a hidden but harmful way, as in *an insidious disease.*

in•sight (**in**-site) ***noun*** If you have **insight** into something or someone, you understand something about that matter or person that is not obvious.

in•sig•ni•a (in-**sig**-nee-uh) ***noun*** A badge, emblem, or design that shows someone's rank or membership in an organization.

in•sig•nif•i•cant (in-sig-**nif**-uh-kuhnt) ***adjective*** Unimportant. ▸ ***noun*** **insignificance** ▸ ***adverb*** **insignificantly**

in•sin•cere (*in*-sin-**sihr**) ***adjective*** Someone who is **insincere** is not genuine or honest. ▸ ***noun*** **insincerity** ▸ ***adverb*** **insincerely**

in•sip•id (in-**sip**-id) ***adjective*** Dull or tasteless, as in *an insipid television program.*

in•sist (in-**sist**) ***verb*** If you **insist** on something, you demand it very firmly. ▸ **insisting, insisted** ▸ ***noun*** **insistence** ▸ ***adjective*** **insistent**

in•so•lent (**in**-suh-luhnt) ***adjective*** Insulting and outspoken. ▸ ***noun*** **insolence** ▸ ***adverb*** **insolently**

in•sol•u•ble (in-**sol**-yuh-buhl) ***adjective***
1. A substance that is **insoluble** will not dissolve in water or other liquid.
2. A problem that is **insoluble** cannot be solved.

in•som•ni•a (in-**som**-nee-uh) ***noun*** If you have **insomnia,** you often find it very hard to fall asleep or stay asleep. ▸ ***noun*** **insomniac** (in-**som**-nee-ak)

in•spect (in-**spekt**) ***verb*** To look at something very carefully. ▸ **inspecting, inspected** ▸ ***noun*** **inspection**

in•spec•tor (in-**spek**-tur) ***noun***
1. Someone who checks or examines things.
2. A senior police officer.

in•spire (in-**spire**) ***verb***
1. To fill someone with an emotion, an idea, or an attitude.
2. To influence and encourage someone to do something.
▸ ***verb*** **inspiring, inspired** ▸ ***noun*** **inspiration** (*in*-spihr-**ay**-shuhn) ▸ ***adjective*** **inspiring,** ***adjective*** **inspirational** (*in*-spihr-**ay**-shuhn-uhl)

in•stall (in-**stawl**) ***verb*** To put something in place, ready to be used. ▸ **installing, installed** ▸ ***noun*** **installation** (*in*-stuhl-**lay**-shuhn)

in•stall•ment (in-**stawl**-muhnt) ***noun***
1. If you pay for something in **installments,** you pay for it in regular, small amounts over a period of time.
2. One part of a story printed or shown in separate parts.

in•stance (**in**-stuhnss) ***noun***
1. An example.
2. for instance As an example.

in•stant (**in**-stuhnt)
1. ***adjective*** Happening right away, as in *instant results.* ▸ ***adverb*** **instantly**
2. ***noun*** A moment. ▸ ***adjective*** **instantaneous** (*in*-stuhn-**tay**-nee-uhss) ▸ ***adverb*** **instantaneously**
3. ***adjective*** Already mixed and prepared, needing only to be heated with added liquid, as in *instant pudding.*

in•stead (in-**sted**) ***adverb*** In place of another.

in•step (**in**-*step*) ***noun*** The top part of your foot, between your toes and your ankle.

in•still (in-**stil**) ***verb*** To put into a person's mind slowly, over a period of time. ▸ **instilling, instilled**

in•stinct (**in**-stingkt) ***noun***
1. Behavior that is natural rather than learned. ▸ ***adjective*** **instinctual** (in-**stingk**-choo-uhl)
2. If you have an **instinct** about something, you know or feel something without being told about it.
▸ ***adjective*** **instinctive** ▸ ***adverb*** **instinctively**

in•sti•tute (**in**-stuh-toot)
1. ***noun*** An organization set up to promote or represent the interests of a particular cause or group of people.
2. ***verb*** To begin, to set up, or to found. ▸ **instituting, instituted**

in•sti•tu•tion (*in*-stuh-**too**-shuhn) ***noun***
1. A large organization where people live or work together, such as a hospital or a college. ▸ ***adjective*** **institutional**
2. A well-established custom or tradition.

in•struct (in-**struhkt**) ***verb***
1. To teach a subject or a skill. ▸ ***noun*** **instructor**
2. To give an order.
▸ ***verb*** **instructing, instructed**

in•struc•tion (in-**struhk**-shuhn) ***noun***
1. The act of teaching or giving lessons.
2. instructions ***noun, plural*** Directions on how to do something, or orders on what to do, as in *to follow instructions.*

in•stru•ment (**in**-struh-muhnt) ***noun***
1. An object that you use to make music. ▸ ***noun*** **instrumentalist** ▸ ***adjective*** **instrumental**
2. A tool or apparatus for delicate or scientific work, as in *surgical instruments.*

I

in•suf•fi•cient (in-suh-**fish**-uhnt) ***adjective*** Not enough or inadequate. ▸ ***adverb*** **insufficiently**

in•su•late (**in**-suh-late) ***verb*** To cover something with material in order to stop heat or electricity from escaping. ▸ **insulating, insulated** ▸ ***noun*** **insulation,** ***noun*** **insulator** ▸ ***adjective*** **insulating**

in•su•lin (**in**-suh-luhn) ***noun*** A hormone produced in the pancreas that regulates the amount of sugar that you have in your body. People who have diabetes need to be given insulin.

in•sult (in-**suhlt**) ***verb*** To say or do something rude and upsetting to somebody. ▸ **insulting, insulted** ▸ ***noun*** **insult** (**in**-suhlt) ▸ ***adjective*** **insulting**

in•sur•ance (in-**shu**-ruhnss) ***noun*** When you take out **insurance,** you pay money to a company that agrees to pay you in the event of sickness, fire, accident, or other loss.

in•sure (in-**shur**) ***verb*** To take out insurance on something. ▸ **insuring, insured** ▸ ***adjective*** **insured**

in•tact (in-**takt**) ***adjective*** Not broken or harmed; complete.

in•take (**in**-*take*) ***noun***
1. The amount of something taken in.
2. The act of taking something in, as in *a sharp intake of breath.*

in•te•ger (**in**-tuh-jur) ***noun*** The whole numbers and their opposites. Examples of integers include –3, –2, –1, 0, 1, 2, and 3.

in•te•grate (**in**-tuh-*grate*) ***verb***
1. To combine several things or people into one whole.
2. To include people of all races.
▸ ***verb*** **integrating, integrated**
▸ ***adjective*** **integrated**

in•te•gra•tion (in-tuh-**gray**-shuhn) ***noun*** The act or practice of making facilities or an organization open to people of all races and ethnic groups.

in•teg•ri•ty (in-**teg**-ruh-tee) ***noun*** If someone has **integrity,** the person is honest and sticks to his or her principles.

in•tel•lect (**in**-tuhl-*ekt*) ***noun*** The power of the mind to think, reason, understand, and learn.

in•tel•lec•tu•al (in-tuh-**lek**-choo-uhl)
1. ***adjective*** Involving thought and reason.
2. ***noun*** Someone who spends most of his or her time thinking and studying.
▸ ***adverb*** **intellectually**

in•tel•li•gent (in-**tel**-uh-juhnt) ***adjective*** Someone who is **intelligent** is quick to understand, think, and learn. ▸ ***noun*** **intelligence** ▸ ***adverb*** **intelligently**

in•tel•li•gi•ble (in-**tel**-uh-juh-buhl) ***adjective*** If something is **intelligible,** it can be understood. ▸ ***adverb*** **intelligibly**

in•tend (in-**tend**) ***verb***
1. If you **intend** to do something, you mean to do it. ▸ **intending, intended**
2. If something is **intended** for you, it is meant to be yours.

in•tense (in-**tenss**) ***adjective***
1. Very strong, as in *intense heat* or *intense happiness.*
2. Showing strong feelings about something.
▸ ***noun*** **intensity** ▸ ***adverb*** **intensely**

in•ten•si•fy (in-**ten**-suh-*fye*) ***verb*** To make something more powerful or concentrated. ▸ **intensifies, intensifying, intensified**

in•tent (in-**tent**)
1. ***adjective*** If you are **intent on** doing something, you are determined to do it.
2. ***noun*** An aim or a purpose.
▸ ***adverb*** **intently**

in•ten•tion (in-**ten**-shuhn) ***noun*** A thing that you mean to do. ▸ ***adjective*** **intentional**

in•ter•ac•tive (*in*-tur-**ak**-tiv) ***adjective***
1. Describing action between people, groups, or things.
2. An **interactive** computer program allows users to make choices in order to control and change it in some ways.
▸ ***verb*** **interact**

I

in•ter•cept (*in*-tur-**sept**) ***verb*** To stop the movement of someone or something. ▸ **intercepting, intercepted** ▸ ***noun*** **interception**

in•ter•change•a•ble (*in*-tur-**chaynj**-uh-buhl) ***adjective*** Easily switched with someone or something else. ▸ ***adverb*** **interchangeably**

in•ter•com (**in**-tur-*kom*) ***noun*** A microphone-and-speaker system that allows you to listen and talk to someone in another room or building. **Intercom** is short for *intercommunication system.*

in•ter•est (**in**-tur-ist *or* **in**-trist)
1. ***verb*** If something **interests** you, you want to know more about it. ▸ **interesting, interested**
2. ***noun*** A feeling of curiosity or concern, as in *an interest in sports.*
3. ***noun*** The power to cause such curiosity or concern.
4. ***noun*** A legal share, as in a business.
5. ***noun*** A fee paid for borrowing money.
6. If it is **in your interest** to do something, it will help you.

▸ ***adjective*** **interested,** ***adjective*** **interesting**

in•ter•face (**in**-tur-*fayss*) ***noun*** The point at which two different things meet. ▸ ***verb*** **interface**

in•ter•fere (*in*-tur-**fihr**) ***verb***
1. To involve yourself in a situation that has nothing to do with you.
2. To hinder.

▸ ***verb*** **interfering, interfered** ▸ ***adjective*** **interfering**

in•ter•fer•ence (*in*-tur-**fihr**-uhnss) ***noun***
1. An unwelcome involvement in the affairs of others.
2. When you get **interference** on your television or radio, something interrupts the signal so that you cannot see or hear the program properly.
3. In sports, the illegal obstruction of an opponent.

in•ter•ga•lac•tic (*in*-tur-guh-**lak**-tik) ***adjective*** Between galaxies, as in *intergalactic space travel.*

in•te•ri•or (in-**tihr**-ee-ur) ***noun*** The inside of something, especially a building. ▸ ***adjective*** **interior**

in•ter•jec•tion (in-tur-**jek**-shuhn) ***noun*** A word spoken suddenly and used to express surprise, pain, or delight.

in•ter•me•di•ate (*in*-tur-**mee**-dee-*it*) ***adjective*** In between two things, or in the middle.

in•ter•mis•sion (*in*-tur-**mish**-uhn) ***noun*** A short break in a play or concert.

in•ter•mit•tent (*in*-tur-**mit**-uhnt) ***adjective*** Stopping and starting, as in *intermittent rain.* ▸ ***adverb*** **intermittently**

in•tern (**in**-turn) ***noun***
1. Someone who is learning a skill or job by working with an expert in that field.
2. A newly graduated doctor of medicine who is working at a hospital to get practical experience.

▸ ***noun*** **internship** ▸ ***verb*** **intern**

in•ter•nal (in-**tur**-nuhl) ***adjective***
1. Happening or existing inside someone or something, as in *internal bleeding.* ▸ ***adverb*** **internally**
2. To do with matters inside a country, as in *internal affairs.*

in•ter•na•tion•al (*in*-tur-**nash**-uh-nuhl) ***adjective*** Involving different countries, as in *international trade.* ▸ ***adverb*** **internationally**

In•ter•net (**in**-tur-*net*) ***noun*** The electronic network that allows millions of computers around the world to connect together.

in•ter•plan•e•tar•y (*in*-tur-**plan**-uh-ter-ee) ***adjective*** Between planets.

in•ter•pret (in-**tur**-prit) ***verb***
1. If someone **interprets** for people speaking different languages, the person translates for them. ▸ ***noun*** **interpreter**
2. To decide what something means.

▸ ***verb*** **interpreting, interpreted** ▸ ***noun*** **interpretation**

in•ter•ro•gate (in-**ter**-uh-*gate*) ***verb*** To question someone in detail.

▸ **interrogating, interrogated** ▸ ***noun*** **interrogation**

in•ter•rupt (*in*-tuh-**ruhpt**) ***verb***
1. To stop or hinder for a short time.
2. To start talking before someone else has finished talking.
▸ ***verb*** **interrupting, interrupted**
▸ ***noun*** **interruption** ▸ ***adjective*** **interruptive**

in•ter•sect (in-tur-**sekt**) ***verb*** To meet or cross something. ▸ **intersecting, intersected**

in•ter•sec•tion (*in*-tur-**sek**-shuhn or **in**-tur-*sek*-shuhn) ***noun*** The point at which two things meet and cross each other.

in•ter•state (*in*-tur-**state**) ***adjective*** Connecting, between, or having to do with two or more states, as in *an interstate highway.*

in•ter•val (**in**-tur-vuhl) ***noun*** A time between two events, or a space between two objects.

in•ter•vene (*in*-tur-**veen**) ***verb***
1. If you **intervene** in a situation, you get involved in it in order to change what is happening. ▸ ***noun*** **intervention** (*in*-tur-**ven**-shuhn)
2. If a period of time **intervenes** between events, it comes between them.
▸ ***verb*** **intervening, intervened**

in•ter•view (**in**-tur-*vyoo*) ***noun*** A meeting at which someone is asked questions, as in *a job interview* or *a radio interview.* ▸ ***verb*** **interview**

in•tes•tine (in-**tess**-tin) ***noun*** A long tube extending below the stomach that digests food and absorbs liquids and salts. It consists of the **small intestine** and the **large intestine.**

in•ti•mate (**in**-tuh-mit) ***adjective*** Friends who are **intimate** are very close and share their feelings with one another.
▸ ***noun*** **intimacy** (**in**-tuh-muh-see)
▸ ***adverb*** **intimately**

in•tim•i•date (in-**tim**-uh-*date*) ***verb*** To frighten. ▸ **intimidating, intimidated**
▸ ***noun*** **intimidation** ▸ ***adjective*** **intimidating**

in•to (**in**-too *or* **in**-tuh) ***preposition***
1. To the inside of.
2. To the occupation of.
3. To the condition or form of.
4. Against.
5. Toward.

in•tol•er•a•ble (in-**tol**-ur-uh-buhl) ***adjective*** If something is **intolerable,** it is difficult to endure. ▸ ***adverb*** **intolerably**

in•tol•er•ant (in-**tol**-ur-uhnt) ***adjective*** People who are **intolerant** get unreasonably angry when others think or behave differently from them.
▸ ***noun*** **intolerance** ▸ ***adverb*** **intolerantly**

in•tox•i•cate (in-**tok**-suh-*kate*) ***verb***
1. To make drunk, especially with alcohol.
2. To excite or to make enthusiastic, as in *an intoxicating aroma.*
▸ ***verb*** **intoxicating, intoxicated**
▸ ***noun*** **intoxication**

in•tran•si•tive (in-**tran**-suh-tiv) ***adjective*** **Intransitive** verbs stand on their own and do not need an object. *See* **transitive.**

in•trep•id (in-**trep**-id) ***adjective*** An **intrepid** person is courageous and bold.

in•tri•cate (**in**-truh-kit) ***adjective*** Detailed and complicated, as in *an intricate pattern.* ▸ ***noun*** **intricacy**
▸ ***adverb*** **intricately**

in•trigue
1. (in-**treeg**) ***verb*** To fascinate or interest someone very much.
▸ **intriguing, intrigued** ▸ ***adjective*** **intriguing**
2. (**in**-treeg *or* in-**treeg**) ***noun*** A secret plot or scheme. ▸ ***verb*** **intrigue** (in-**treeg**)

in•tro•duce (in-truh-**dooss**) ***verb***
1. To bring in something new.
2. To cause to be known by name.
3. To start.
▸ ***verb*** **introducing, introduced**

I

in•tro•duc•tion (in-truh-**duhk**-shuhn) ***noun***
1. Your **introduction** to something is your first experience of it.
2. The act of introducing one person to another.
3. The opening words of a book, speech, etc. ▸ ***adjective*** **introductory**

in•tro•vert (**in**-truh-vurt) ***noun*** A shy person who keeps his or her thoughts and feelings to himself or herself.
▸ ***adjective*** **introverted**

in•trude (in-**trood**) ***verb*** To force your way into a place or situation where you are not wanted or invited. ▸ **intruding, intruded** ▸ ***noun*** **intruder,** ***noun*** **intrusion** ▸ ***adjective*** **intrusive**

in•tu•i•tion (*in*-too-**ish**-uhn) ***noun*** A feeling about something that cannot be explained logically. ▸ ***verb*** **intuit**
▸ ***adjective*** **intuitive**

In•u•it (**in**-oo-it *or* **in**-yoo-it) ***noun*** A person, or a group of people, from the Arctic north of Canada, Alaska, and Greenland. Inuits are also known as **Eskimos.** ▸ ***adjective*** **Inuit**

in•un•date (**in**-uhn-*date*) ***verb***
1. To flood.
2. To overwhelm someone with a large quantity of something.
▸ ***verb*** **inundating, inundated** ▸ ***noun*** **inundation**

in•vade (in-**vade**) ***verb*** To send armed forces into another country in order to take it over. ▸ **invading, invaded**
▸ ***noun*** **invader,** ***noun*** **invasion**

in•va•lid
1. (**in**-vuh-lid) ***noun*** Someone who is bedridden or must limit his or her activity because he or she is seriously ill.
2. (in-**val**-id) ***adjective*** If a ticket, library card, etc., is **invalid,** it cannot be used for some reason.

in•val•u•a•ble (in-**val**-yuh-buhl) ***adjective*** Very useful or precious.
▸ ***adverb*** **invaluably**

in•vent (in-**vent**) ***verb***
1. To think up and create something new.
▸ ***noun*** **inventor**
2. To make something up.
▸ ***verb*** **inventing, invented** ▸ ***noun*** **invention**

in•ven•tive (in-**ven**-tiv) ***adjective*** Good at thinking up new ideas or ways of doing things; creative.

in•ven•to•ry (**in**-vuhn-*tor*-ee)
1. ***noun*** A complete list of items someone owns.
2. ***noun*** All the items on hand for sale in a store. ▸ ***noun, plural*** **inventories**
3. ***verb*** To count and list the items available for sale in a store.
▸ **inventories, inventorying, inventoried**

in•vert (in-**vurt**) ***verb***
1. To turn something upside down.
2. To reverse the order of something.
▸ ***verb*** **inverting, inverted**

in•ver•te•brate (in-**vur**-tuh-brit) ***noun*** A creature without a backbone.
▸ ***adjective*** **invertebrate**

in•vest (in-**vest**) ***verb***
1. To give or lend money to something, such as a company, in the belief that you will get more money back in the future.
▸ ***noun*** **investment,** ***noun*** **investor**
2. To give time or effort to something.
▸ ***verb*** **investing, invested**

in•ves•ti•gate (in-**vess**-tuh-gate) ***verb*** If you **investigate** something, such as a crime, you find out as much as possible about it. ▸ **investigating, investigated**
▸ ***noun*** **investigation,** ***noun*** **investigator** ▸ ***adjective*** **investigative**

in•vin•ci•ble (in-**vin**-suh-buhl) ***adjective*** If someone is **invincible,** that person cannot be beaten or defeated. ▸ ***adverb*** **invincibly**

in•vis•i•ble (in-**viz**-uh-buhl) ***adjective*** Something that is **invisible** cannot be seen. ▸ ***noun*** **invisibility** ▸ ***adverb*** **invisibly**

in•vite (in-**vite**) ***verb*** To ask someone to do something or to go somewhere.

▸ **inviting, invited** ▸ ***noun*** **invitation** (in-vi-**tay**-shuhn)

in•voice (**in**-voiss) ***noun*** An itemized bill for goods shipped to a customer or for work done or to be done for a customer. ▸ ***verb*** **invoice**

in•vol•un•tar•y (in-**vol**-uhn-*ter*-ee) ***adjective***
1. Not done willingly or by choice.
2. Done without a person's control.

in•volve (in-**volv**) ***verb*** To include something as a necessary part. ▸ **involving, involved** ▸ ***noun*** **involvement**

in•volved (in-**volvd**) ***adjective***
1. If you are **involved** in or with something, you take a part in it or are mixed up in it.
2. Complicated, as in *an involved story.*

in•ward (**in**-wurd) ***adverb*** Toward the inside. ▸ ***adjective*** **inward**

i•o•dine (**eye**-uh-*dine*) ***noun***
1. A chemical element found in seaweed and saltwater that is used in medicine and photography.
2. A brown medicine containing iodine and alcohol that is used to kill germs on wounds.

i•on (**eye**-uhn *or* **eye**-on) ***noun*** An electrically charged atomic particle. Ions are either positive or negative.

IQ (**eye kyoo**) ***noun*** A measure of a person's intelligence. IQ stands for *Intelligence Quotient.*

i•rate (**eye**-rate *or* eye-**rate**) ***adjective*** Extremely angry or annoyed. ▸ ***adverb*** **irately**

i•ris (**eye**-riss) ***noun***
1. The round, colored part of the eye around the pupil.
2. A plant with long, thin leaves and large purple, white, or yellow flowers.

I•rish set•ter (**eye**-rish **set**-ur) ***noun*** A large hunting dog with a silky, red coat. These dogs originally were bred in Ireland.

i•ron (**eye**-urn)
1. ***noun*** A strong, hard metal used to make such things as gates and railings. It is also found in some foods as well as in your body's red blood cells. ▸ ***adjective*** **iron**
2. ***noun*** A piece of electrical equipment with a handle and a heated surface, used to smooth creases out of clothing. ▸ ***verb*** **iron**
3. ***verb*** If you **iron out** a problem, you solve it. ▸ **ironing, ironed**

Iron Age ***noun*** A period of history when iron was commonly used to make tools and weapons. Different parts of the world experienced an Iron Age at different times.

i•ron•ic (eye-**ron**-ik) ***adjective***
1. If a situation is **ironic,** the actual result differs from the expected result.
2. Mildly sarcastic. ▸ ***adverb*** **ironically**

i•ro•ny (**eye**-ruh-nee) ***noun*** A way of speaking or writing that means the opposite of what the words say. Saying *"Beautiful weather, isn't it?"* when it is raining is an example of irony.

I•ro•quois (**ihr**-uh-kwoi) ***noun*** A member of a confederation of American Indian tribes originally of New York. ▸ ***noun, plural*** **Iroquois**

ir•ra•tio•nal (i-**rash**-uh-nuhl) ***adjective*** Not sensible, or not logical. ▸ ***adverb*** **irrationally**

ir•reg•u•lar (i-**reg**-yuh-luhr) ***adjective***
1. Not standard in shape, timing, size, etc., as in *irregular bus service.*
2. Not following the normal pattern. ▸ ***noun*** **irregularity**
3. An **irregular** verb is one whose main parts are not formed according to a regular pattern. *Sink* is irregular because its past tense is *sank* rather than *sinked.* ▸ ***adverb*** **irregularly**

ir•rel•e•vant (i-**rel**-uh-vuhnt) ***adjective*** If something is **irrelevant,** it has nothing to do with a particular subject. ▸ ***noun*** **irrelevance** ▸ ***adverb*** **irrelevantly**

I

ir•re•sist•i•ble (ihr-i-**ziss**-tuh-buhl) ***adjective*** Too tempting to resist. ▸ ***adverb*** **irresistibly**

ir•re•spon•si•ble (ihr-i-**spon**-suh-buhl) ***adjective*** Reckless and lacking a sense of responsibility. ▸ ***noun*** **irresponsibility** ▸ ***adverb*** **irresponsibly**

ir•re•vers•i•ble (ihr-uh-**ver**-suh-buhl) ***adjective*** Unable to be changed or undone.

ir•ri•gate (**ihr**-uh-*gate*) ***verb*** To supply water to crops by artificial means, such as channels and pipes. ▸ **irrigating, irrigated** ▸ ***noun*** **irrigation**

ir•ri•ta•ble (**ihr**-uh-tuh-buhl) ***adjective*** Someone who is **irritable** is cross and grumpy. ▸ ***adverb*** **irritably**

ir•ri•tate (**ihr**-uh-tate) ***verb***
1. If something **irritates** you, it annoys you.
2. To make sore or sensitive.
▸ ***verb*** **irritating, irritated** ▸ ***noun*** **irritation** ▸ ***adjective*** **irritating** ▸ ***adverb*** **irritatingly**

Is•lam (**iss**-luhm *or* i-**slahm**) ***noun*** The religion based on the teachings of Muhammad. Muslims believe that Allah is God and that Muhammad is Allah's prophet. The religion is based on prayer, fasting, charity, and pilgrimage, as taught through the Koran. ▸ ***adjective*** **Islamic**

is•land (**eye**-luhnd) ***noun*** A piece of land surrounded by water.

isle (**eye**-uhl) ***noun*** A small island. **Isle** sounds like **aisle** and **I'll.**

is•n't (**iz**-uhnt) ***contraction*** A short form of *is not.*

i•so•late (**eye**-suh-*late*) ***verb***
1. To keep something or someone separate. ▸ ***noun*** **isolation**
2. To discover and identify something.
▸ ***verb*** **isolating, isolated**

i•so•met•rics (*eye*-suh-**met**-riks) ***noun*** A system of physical exercises that strengthens muscles by using pressure against an unmoving object such as a wall or your own hand. Two hands pushing against each other create an isometric exercise. ▸ ***adjective*** **isometric**

i•sos•ce•les (eye-**soss**-uh-leez) ***adjective*** An **isosceles** triangle has two equal sides.

is•sue (**ish**-oo)
1. ***noun*** The main topic for debate or decision.
2. ***noun*** An edition of a newspaper or magazine.
3. ***verb*** To send out, or to give out.
4. ***verb*** To come out of.
▸ ***verb*** **issuing, issued**

isth•mus (**iss**-muhss) ***noun*** A narrow strip of land that lies between two bodies of water and connects two larger land masses.

it (**it**)
1. ***pronoun*** A thing, part, person, or situation mentioned earlier or later. *You can't see it, but there's a squirrel on the other side of that tree.*
2. ***pronoun*** The subject of some verbs that shows an action or condition. *It is snowing. It is hot today.*
3. ***noun*** The player in a game who has to perform the main action, such as trying to find others in hide-and-seek.

i•tal•ic (i-**tal**-ik *or* eye-**tal**-ik) ***noun*** A sloping form of print used to emphasize certain words or to make them stand out. ▸ ***verb*** **italicize** ▸ ***adjective*** **italic**

itch (**ich**) ***verb*** If your skin **itches,** it is uncomfortable and you want to scratch it. ▸ **itches, itching, itched** ▸ ***noun*** **itch** ▸ ***adjective*** **itchy**

i•tem (**eye**-tuhm) ***noun*** One of a number of things, as in *an item of clothing.*

i•tem•ize (**eye**-tuh-*mize*) ***verb*** To list the individual units or parts of something. ▸ **itemizing, itemized** ▸ ***adjective*** **itemized**

i•tin•er•ant (eye-**tin**-uh-ruhnt) ***adjective*** Traveling from place to place, usually to find or do work.

i•tin•er•ar•y (eye-**tin**-uh-rer-ee) ***noun*** A detailed plan of a journey. ▸ ***noun, plural*** **itineraries**

its (**its**) ***adjective*** Related to or belonging to something.

it's (**its**) ***contraction*** A short form of *it is* or *it has.*

it•self (it-**self**) ***pronoun*** It and nothing else.

I've (**eyev**) ***contraction*** A short form of *I have.*

i•vo•ry (**eye**-vur-ee) ***noun***
1. The natural substance from which the tusks of elephants and some other animals are made.
2. A creamy-white color.
▸ ***adjective*** **ivory**

i•vy (**eye**-vee) ***noun*** An evergreen climbing or trailing plant that has pointed leaves.

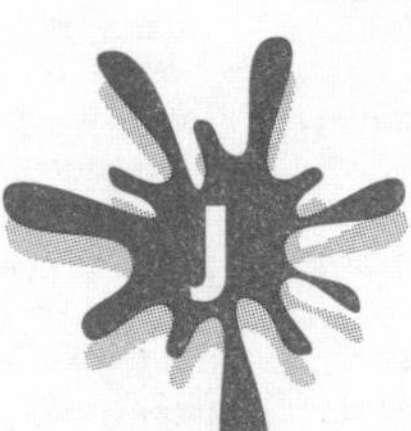

jab (**jab**)
1. ***verb*** To poke somebody with something sharp. ▸ **jabbing, jabbed**
2. ***noun*** A short, quick punch.

jab•ber (**jab**-ur) ***verb*** To talk in a fast, confused, or foolish way that is hard to understand. ▸ **jabbering, jabbered**
▸ ***noun*** **jabber**

jack (**jak**) ***noun***
1. A tool used to raise a vehicle off the ground for repair. ▸ ***verb*** **jack**
2. A picture playing card with a value between that of a 10 and a queen.
3. A small, metal piece with six points used in the game of jacks.
4. **jacks** A game played with jacks and a rubber ball.

jack•al (**jak**-uhl) ***noun*** A kind of wild dog of Africa and Asia that feeds off dead animals.

jack•et (**jak**-it) ***noun***
1. A short coat.
2. An outer covering for a book or record.

jack•ham•mer (**jak**-*ham*-ur) ***noun*** A machine that is operated by air that is compressed. It is used to drill rock, concrete, and similar hard materials.

jack-in-the-box ***noun*** A toy box with a clown's head that pops out when the lid is opened. ▸ ***noun, plural*** **jack-in-the-boxes**

jack•knife (**jak**-*nife*)
1. ***noun*** A large knife with a blade that folds into a handle.
2. ***noun*** A type of dive in which a diver bends the body double in the air, then straightens out before striking the water headfirst.
3. ***verb*** To fold in like a jackknife.
▸ **jackknifing, jackknifed**
▸ ***noun, plural*** **jackknives**

jack-o'-lan•tern (**jak**-uh-*lan*-turn) ***noun*** A pumpkin with a face carved into it and a candle inside, used at Halloween.

jack•pot (**jak**-*pot*) ***noun*** The top prize in a game or contest.

jack•rab•bit (**jak**-*rab*-it) ***noun*** A large hare, common in the western part of the United States. The jackrabbit has very long ears and strong back legs for leaping.

Ja•cuz•zi (ja-**koo**-zee) ***noun*** Trademark for a large bath with underwater jets of water that massage your skin.

jade (**jayd**) ***noun***
1. A hard, green stone used for making ornaments and jewelry.
2. A green color.
▸ ***adjective*** **jade**

jag•ged (**jag**-id) ***adjective*** Uneven and sharp, as in *a jagged edge.*

jag•uar (**jag**-wahr) ***noun*** A large wildcat, similar to a leopard, found in the southwestern United States, Mexico, and South and Central America.

jail (**jayl**)
1. ***noun*** A building for keeping people who are awaiting trial or who have been found guilty of minor crimes. ▸ ***noun*** **jailer**
2. ***verb*** To put someone in jail. ▸ **jailing, jailed**

jam (**jam**)
1. ***noun*** A sweet, thick food made from boiled fruit and sugar.
2. ***noun*** A situation in which things or people cannot move, as in *a traffic jam.*
3. ***verb*** To squeeze or wedge something into a tight space.
4. ***noun*** *(informal)* A difficult situation.
5. ***verb*** To become stuck and not work.
6. ***verb*** To bruise or crush by squeezing.
7. *(informal)* When musicians have a **jam** or **jam session,** they play together without any planning. ▸ ***verb*** **jam**
▸ ***verb*** **jamming, jammed**

jan•gle (**jang**-guhl) ***verb*** To make a loud, unpleasant, ringing sound. ▸ **jangling, jangled**

jan•i•tor (**jan**-uh-tur) ***noun*** Someone whose job is to look after and clean a school or some other building.

Jan•u•ar•y (**jan**-yoo-er-ee) ***noun*** The first month on the calendar. January is followed by February and has 31 days.

Jap•a•nese beetle (*jap*-uh-**neez**) ***noun*** An insect that eats leaves and can destroy plants, brought to the United States from Japan.

jar (**jar**)
1. ***noun*** A container with a wide mouth.
2. ***verb*** To jolt or shake something or someone.
3. ***verb*** If something **jars** you, it makes you feel uncomfortable or annoyed.
4. ***verb*** If something **jars** with the facts, it conflicts with them.
▸ ***verb*** **jarring, jarred**

jar•gon (**jar**-guhn) ***noun*** Words used by people in a particular business or activity that others cannot easily understand, as in *computer jargon.*

jaun•dice (**jawn**-diss) ***noun*** A disease, usually of the liver, that turns the skin yellow.

jaunt (**jawnt**) ***noun*** A short pleasure trip or outing.

jaun•ty (**jawn**-tee) ***adjective*** Giving a carefree and self-confident impression.
▸ **jauntier, jauntiest** ▸ ***adverb*** **jauntily**

jave•lin (**jav**-uh-luhn) ***noun*** A light, metal spear that is thrown for distance in a track-and-field event.

jaw (**jaw**)
1. ***noun*** Either of two bones between your nose and your chin that hold your teeth.
2. ***noun*** The lower part of your face.
3. jaws ***noun, plural*** The parts of a tool that close to grip an object, as in *the jaws of a clamp.*
4. ***verb*** *(slang)* To talk for a long time in a boring way. ▸ **jawing, jawed**

jay•walk (**jay**-*wawk*) ***verb*** To cross a street carelessly, taking no notice of traffic or signals. ▸ **jaywalking, jaywalked** ▸ ***noun*** **jaywalker**

jazz (**jaz**) ***noun*** A lively, rhythmical type of music in which players often improvise, or make up their own tunes and add new notes in unexpected places. Jazz was started by African Americans between 1900 and 1905 in New Orleans, Louisiana. ▸ ***adjective*** **jazzy**

jeal•ous (**jel**-uhss) ***adjective***
1. If you are **jealous** of someone, you want what he or she has.
2. Afraid that a person you love cares more for someone else than for you.
▸ ***noun*** **jealousy** ▸ ***adverb*** **jealously**

jeans (**jeenz**) ***noun, plural*** Pants for casual wear made of denim or similar strong cloth.

J

Jeep (**jeep**) ***noun*** Trademark for a small, powerful vehicle used for driving over rough country.

jeer (**jihr**) ***verb*** To scorn someone in a loud, unpleasant way. ▸ **jeering, jeered** ▸ ***noun*** **jeer** ▸ ***adverb*** **jeeringly**

Je•ho•vah (ji-**hoh**-vuh) ***noun*** A name for God in the Old Testament.

Jell-O (**jel**-oh) ***noun*** Trademark for a dessert made with gelatin and a flavoring, which is boiled and then allowed to set.

jel•ly (**jel**-ee) ***noun*** A sweet, thick food made from boiled fruit and sugar. ▸ ***noun, plural*** **jellies**

jel•ly•fish (**jel**-ee-*fish*) ***noun*** A sea creature with a body that is soft and quivering like jelly and has trailing tentacles. ▸ ***noun, plural*** **jellyfish** *or* **jellyfishes**

jeop•ard•y (**jep**-ur-dee) ***noun*** If someone's job or life is **in jeopardy,** it is in danger or is threatened in some way. ▸ ***verb*** **jeopardize**

jerk (**jurk**)
1. ***verb*** To move or pull something very suddenly and sharply. ▸ **jerking, jerked**
2. ***noun*** A sudden movement as something starts up.
3. ***noun*** An annoyingly stupid or foolish person.

▸ ***adjective*** **jerky** ▸ ***adverb*** **jerkily**

jest (**jest**) ***noun*** A joke or something said in fun. ▸ ***verb*** **jest**

jest•er (**jes**-tur) ***noun*** An entertainer at a court in the Middle Ages.

Je•sus (**jee**-zuhss) ***noun*** The founder of Christianity. Also called *Jesus Christ.* See **Christ.**

jet (**jet**) ***noun***
1. A stream of liquid or gas forced through a small opening with great pressure.
2. An aircraft powered by jet engines.

▸ ***verb*** **jet**

jet engine ***noun*** An engine that is powered by a stream of gases made by burning a mixture of fuel and air inside the engine itself.

jet lag ***noun*** A feeling of tiredness or confusion after a long plane flight from a different time zone.

jet propulsion ***noun*** A way of moving an aircraft in one direction by using a stream of hot gas propelled in the opposite direction.

jet•sam (**jet**-suhm) ***noun*** Part of a ship's cargo that is thrown or lost overboard.

jet stream ***noun*** A very strong current of wind, usually found between seven and nine miles above the earth's surface. Jet streams usually move west to east at speeds reaching over 200 miles per hour.

jet•ti•son (**jet**-uh-suhn) ***verb*** To throw overboard, or to throw out something that you no longer need. ▸ **jettisoning, jettisoned**

jet•ty (**jet**-ee) ***noun*** A wall built out into the sea to give an area shelter from the waves. Boats moor and unload beside jetties. ▸ ***noun, plural*** **jetties**

Jew (**joo**) ***noun***
1. Someone who is descended from the ancient Hebrew tribes of Israel.
2. Someone who practices the religion of Judaism.

jew•el (**joo**-uhl) ***noun***
1. A precious stone, such as a diamond, a ruby, or an emerald.
2. A person or thing that is greatly admired or valued.

jew•el•er (**joo**-uh-lur) ***noun*** A person who designs, makes, repairs, or sells jewelry.

jew•el•ry (**joo**-uhl-ree) ***noun*** Ornaments that you wear, such as rings, bracelets, and necklaces, often made of jewels, gold, etc.

Jew•ish (**joo**-ish) ***adjective*** To do with Jews, their religion, or their culture.

jib (**jib**) ***noun*** A triangular sail that is set in front of the mast and attached to the bow of a ship.

jif•fy (**jif**-ee) ***noun*** A very short time; a moment. ▸ ***noun, plural*** **jiffies**

J

jig (**jig**) ***noun***
1. A fast, lively dance, or the music played during this dance. ▸ ***verb*** **jig**
2. *(informal)* If **the jig is up,** the trick you are playing or the secret you are keeping is over because someone has caught on to you.

jig•saw puzzle (**jig**-*saw*) ***noun*** A wooden or cardboard puzzle made up of pieces of a picture that have to be put together.

jin•gle (**jing**-guhl) ***noun***
1. A tinkling or ringing sound made by the movement of small bells, keys, etc. ▸ ***verb*** **jingle**
2. A simple, upbeat song used to advertise a product.

jinx (**jingks**) ***noun*** A person or thing that is supposed to bring bad luck. ▸ ***noun, plural*** **jinxes** ▸ ***verb*** **jinx**

job (**job**) ***noun***
1. A task or a chore.
2. The work that someone does for a living.

jock•ey (**jok**-ee)
1. ***noun*** Someone who rides horses in races. ▸ ***verb*** **jockey**
2. ***verb*** If you **jockey for position** with someone, you try to beat him or her at something, often by unfair actions. ▸ **jockeying, jockeyed**

joc•u•lar (**jok**-yuh-lur) ***adjective*** Joking, or liking to make jokes.

jodh•purs (**jod**-purz) ***noun, plural*** Pants worn for horseback riding. Jodhpurs are loose around the top part of the leg and fit tightly below the knee.

jog (**jog**) ***verb***
1. To run at a slow, steady pace. ▸ ***noun*** **jogger**
2. To shake or to push.
3. If something **jogs your memory,** it reminds you of something.
▸ ***verb*** **jogging, jogged** ▸ ***noun*** **jogging**

join (**join**) ***verb***
1. To fasten two things together. ▸ ***noun*** **join**
2. To come together with something or someone.
3. To become a member of a club or group.
4. join up To become a member of the armed forces.
▸ ***verb*** **joining, joined**

join•er (**joi**-nur) ***noun***
1. Someone who makes wooden furniture and house fittings such as door frames. ▸ ***noun*** **joinery**
2. A person who enjoys joining a lot of clubs or groups.

joint (**joint**)
1. ***noun*** A place where two bones meet; for example, your knee or elbow. There are four main types of joints in your body: fixed, sliding, hinge, and ball-and-socket.
2. ***noun*** A place where two or more things meet or come together.
▸ ***adjective*** **jointed**
3. ***adjective*** Done or shared by two or more people, as in *a joint effort.* ▸ ***adverb*** **jointly**
4. ***noun*** *(informal)* A cheap, unattractive place to eat, drink, or spend the night.

jo•jo•ba (hoh-**hoh**-buh) ***noun*** A large evergreen shrub or small tree that grows in the southwestern part of the United States and Mexico. Jojoba oil is used in products such as shampoos and lotions.

joke (**joke**) ***verb*** To say funny things or play tricks on people in order to make them laugh. ▸ **joking, joked** ▸ ***noun*** **joke**

jol•ly (**jol**-ee) ***adjective*** Happy and cheerful. ▸ **jollier, jolliest**

jolt (**johlt**)
1. ***verb*** To move with sudden, rough jerks. ▸ **jolting, jolted** ▸ ***noun*** **jolt**
2. ***noun*** A sudden surprise or shock.

jon•quil (**jon**-kwil) ***noun*** A plant that grows from bulbs and has long, narrow leaves and fragrant, white or yellow flowers. The jonquil is a kind of daffodil.

jos•tle (**joss**-uhl) ***verb*** To bump or push roughly. ▸ **jostling, jostled**

J

jot (**jot**) ***verb*** To write something down quickly. ▸ **jotting, jotted**

joule (**jool**) ***noun*** A unit for measuring energy or work done. Joule is a term used by physicists.

jour•nal (**jur**-nuhl) ***noun***
1. A diary in which you regularly write down your thoughts and experiences.
2. A magazine or newspaper.

jour•na•lism (**jur**-nuhl-iz-uhm) ***noun*** The work of gathering and reporting news for newspapers, magazines, and other media.

jour•nal•ist (**jur**-nuhl-ist) ***noun*** Someone who collects information and writes articles for newspapers, magazines, television, or radio. ▸ ***adjective*** **journalistic**

jour•ney (**jur**-nee) ***noun*** A long trip. ▸ ***verb*** **journey**

joust (**joust** *or* **juhst**) ***noun*** A battle between two knights riding horses and armed with lances. ▸ ***verb*** **joust**

jo•vi•al (**joh**-vee-uhl) ***adjective*** Someone who is **jovial** is cheerful and enjoys talking and laughing with other people. ▸ ***noun*** **joviality** ▸ ***adverb*** **jovially**

jowl (**joul**) ***noun*** A layer of loose flesh that hangs down around the throat or lower jaw.

joy (**joi**) ***noun***
1. A feeling of great happiness.
2. A person or thing that brings great happiness to someone. ▸ ***adjective*** **joyous**

joy•ful (**joi**-fuhl) ***adjective*** Very happy. ▸ ***noun*** **joyfulness** ▸ ***adverb*** **joyfully**

joy•stick (**joi**-*stik*) ***noun*** A lever used to control movement in a computer game or in an aircraft.

ju•bi•lant (**joo**-buh-luhnt) ***adjective*** Very happy and delighted. ▸ ***noun*** **jubilation** ▸ ***adverb*** **jubilantly**

ju•bi•lee (**joo**-buh-lee) ***noun*** A big celebration to mark the anniversary of a special event.

Ju•da•ism (**joo**-dee-iz-uhm) ***noun*** The religion of the Jewish people, based chiefly on a belief in one God and the teachings of the Torah, the first five books of the Old Testament.

judge (**juhj**)
1. ***noun*** A person who listens to cases before a court and decides how a guilty person should be punished. ▸ ***verb*** **judge**
2. ***verb*** To decide who is the winner of a competition. ▸ ***noun*** **judge**
3. ***verb*** To form an opinion about something or someone.
▸ ***verb*** **judging, judged**

judg•ment *or* **judge•ment** (**juhj**-muhnt) ***noun***
1. An opinion of something or someone.
2. A decision made by a judge.
3. The ability to decide or form opinions wisely.

ju•di•cial (joo-**dish**-uhl) ***adjective*** To do with a court of law or a judge. ▸ ***adverb*** **judicially**

ju•di•cious (joo-**dish**-uhss) ***adjective*** Sensible and wise, as in *a judicious decision.* ▸ ***adverb*** **judiciously**

ju•do (**joo**-doh) ***noun*** A sport in which two people fight each other using quick, controlled movements, each trying to throw the other to the ground.

jug (**juhg**) ***noun*** A container with a narrow neck and a small handle.

jug•ger•naut (**juhg**-ur-*nawt*) ***noun*** A very powerful force that can destroy anything in its path.

jug•gle (**juhg**-uhl) ***verb*** To keep a set of balls, clubs, or other objects moving through the air by repeatedly throwing them up and catching them again, one after another. ▸ **juggling, juggled** ▸ ***noun*** **juggler**

juice (**joos**) ***noun*** Liquid that comes out of fruit, vegetables, or meat. ▸ ***adjective*** **juicy**

juke•box (**jook**-*boks*) ***noun*** A machine that plays music or records when you put coins into it. ▸ ***noun, plural*** **jukeboxes**

Ju•ly (juh-**lye** *or* joo-**lye**) ***noun*** The seventh month on the calendar, after June and before August. July has 31 days.

J

jum•ble (**juhm**-buhl) ***verb*** To mix things up so that they are messy and not well organized. ▸ **jumbling, jumbled** ▸ ***noun*** **jumble**

jum•bo (**juhm**-boh)
1. ***adjective*** Very large, as in *jumbo shrimp.*
2. jumbo jet ***noun*** *(informal)* A very large jet airplane that can carry hundreds of passengers.

jump (**juhmp**)
1. ***verb*** To push off with your legs and feet and move through or into the air.
2. ***noun*** The distance covered by a jump, as in *a long jump.*
3. ***verb*** To move or get up suddenly, as in *to jump in surprise.*
4. ***noun*** A sudden rise or increase, as in *a jump in prices.*
5. ***verb*** If you **jump at** something, you accept it eagerly.
▸ ***verb*** **jumping, jumped**

jum•per (**juhm**-pur) ***noun*** A sleeveless dress, usually worn over a shirt or sweater.

jumper cables ***noun, plural*** Thick wires that are used to connect the batteries of two cars so that one can be started using the other's battery.

jump rope ***noun***
1. A rope used for exercise and children's games. The jump rope is swung over the head and under the feet as the player jumps up to let it pass.
2. A game in which this rope is used.

junc•tion (**juhngk**-shuhn) ***noun*** A place where roads or railroad lines meet or join.

June (**joon**) ***noun*** The sixth month on the calendar, after May and before July. June has 30 days.

jun•gle (**juhng**-guhl) ***noun*** Land in warm, tropical areas near the equator that is thickly covered with trees, vines, and bushes.

jun•ior (**joo**-nyur)
1. ***adjective*** **Junior** is used after the name of a son who has the same name as his father. It means "the younger of two," as in *John Smith, Jr.*
2. ***adjective*** Not very important in rank or position, as in *a junior manager.*
3. ***adjective*** For young children, as in *a junior encyclopedia.*
4. ***noun*** A third-year high school or college student.

junior high school ***noun*** A school between elementary school and high school. It usually includes the seventh and eighth grades and sometimes includes the ninth grade.

ju•ni•per (**joo**-nuh-pur) ***noun*** An evergreen bush or tree similar to a pine. It bears purple fruit that look like berries.

junk (**juhngk**) ***noun***
1. Old metal, wood, rags, or other items that are thrown away.
2. Things that are worthless or useless.
3. A Chinese sailing boat with square sails and a flat bottom.

junk food ***noun*** Food that is not good for you because it contains a lot of calories, fat, sugar, salt, and/or chemical additives. Potato chips, candy, and cookies are all considered junk food.

junk mail ***noun*** Advertisements, catalogs, and other mail that you receive without having asked for them.

junk•yard (**juhnk**-*yard*) ***noun*** An area used to collect, store, and sometimes sell discarded materials, such as old or wrecked cars.

Ju•pi•ter (**joo**-puh-tur) ***noun*** The fifth planet from the sun. Jupiter is the largest planet in our solar system.

ju•ror (**jur**-ur) ***noun*** A member of a jury.

ju•ry (**ju**-ree) ***noun*** A group of people at a trial that listens to the facts and decides whether the person accused of a crime is innocent or guilty. ▸ ***noun, plural*** **juries**

just (**juhst**)
1. ***adjective*** Fair and right, as in *a just decision.* ▸ ***adverb*** **justly**
2. ***adverb*** Exactly.

K

3. ***adverb*** A very little while ago.
4. ***adverb*** Barely.
5. ***adverb*** Nothing more than.

jus•tice (**juhss**-tiss) ***noun***
1. Fair and impartial behavior or treatment.
2. The system of laws and judgment in a country.
3. A judge.
4. **justice of the peace** Someone who hears cases in local courts of law and marries couples.

jus•ti•fy (**juhss**-tuh-fye) ***verb*** If you **justify** an action, you give a reason or explanation to show that it is fair or reasonable. ▸ **justifies, justifying, justified** ▸ ***noun*** **justification**

jut (**juht**) ***verb*** To stick out. ▸ **jutting, jutted**

jute (**joot**) ***noun*** A strong fiber that is woven to make rope and a coarse material called burlap. Jute comes from a plant that grows in tropical Asia.

ju•ve•nile (**joo**-vuh-nuhl *or* **joo**-vuh-*nile*)
1. ***noun*** A young person who is not yet an adult according to the law.
2. ***adjective*** Of or for young people, as in *juvenile books.*
3. ***adjective*** Childish or immature, as in *juvenile behavior.*
4. **juvenile delinquent** ***noun*** A young person who breaks the law. ▸ ***noun*** **juvenile delinquency**

jux•ta•pose (*juhk*-stuh-**poze**) ***verb*** To place things side by side, especially to compare or contrast them.
▸ **juxtaposing, juxtaposed** ▸ ***noun*** **juxtaposition** (*juhk*-stuh-puh-**zi**-shuhn)

ka•bob *or* **ke•bob** (kuh-**bob**) ***noun*** Small pieces of meat or vegetables cooked on a skewer.

Ka•bu•ki (kuh-**boo**-kee) ***noun*** A type of Japanese drama traditionally performed by men in elaborate costumes.

ka•lei•do•scope (kuh-**lye**-duh-*skope*) ***noun*** A tube that you twist or turn as you look into it to see changing patterns made by mirrors and pieces of colored glass. ▸ ***adjective*** **kaleidoscopic**

kan•ga•roo (*kang*-guh-**roo**) ***noun*** An animal of Australia with short front legs and long, powerful back legs that are used for leaping. The female carries her young in a pouch for about six months after birth.

kar•a•o•ke (kah-ree-**oh**-kee) ***noun*** A form of entertainment that originated in Japan in which people sing the words of popular songs while a machine plays the background music.

ka•ra•te (kah-**rah**-tee) ***noun*** A form of self-defense in which people fight each other using controlled kicks and punches.

ka•ty•did (**kay**-tee-did) ***noun*** A large, green insect that is related to the grasshopper. The male rubs its front wings together to make a shrill noise that sounds like its name.

kay•ak (**kye**-ak) ***noun*** A covered, narrow boat in which you sit and move through water by paddling. Kayaks were first used by the Inuit.

keel (**keel**)
1. ***noun*** A long beam along the bottom of a boat or ship that holds it together.
2. **keel over** ***verb*** *(informal)* To fall over in one smooth, steady movement.
▸ **keeling, keeled**

K

keen (**keen**) ***adjective***
1. Very sharp, as in *a keen blade.*
2. Able to notice things easily, as in *a keen sense of smell.*
3. Quick or alert, as in *a keen mind.*
4. Eager or enthusiastic.
▸ ***adjective* keener, keenest**

keep (**keep**) ***verb***
1. To have something and not get rid of it.
2. To stay the same.
3. To continue doing something.
4. To store.
5. To hold back or to stop.
6. To carry out or to fulfill, as in *to keep a promise.*
▸ ***verb* keeping, kept** (**kept**)

keep·er (**kee**-pur) ***noun*** Someone who looks after or guards something.

keg (**keg**) ***noun*** A small barrel.

kelp (**kelp**) ***noun*** A large, edible, brown seaweed. When kelp is burned, the ashes can be used to produce iodine, fertilizer, and other products. ▸ ***noun, plural* kelp**

ken·nel (**ken**-uhl) ***noun***
1. A shelter where dogs and cats are kept.
2. A place where dogs and cats are raised and trained or looked after while their owners are away.

ker·chief (**kur**-chif) ***noun*** A piece of cloth, usually square, worn around the head or neck.

ker·nel (**kur**-nuhl) ***noun***
1. A grain or seed of corn, wheat, or other cereal plant.
2. The soft part inside the shell of a nut that is good to eat.
3. The central or most important part of something, as in *a kernel of truth.*

ker·o·sene (**ker**-uh-*seen*) ***noun*** A thin, colorless fuel that is made from petroleum.

ketch·up (**kech**-uhp) ***noun*** A thick, red sauce made with tomatoes, onions, salt, sugar, and spices.

ket·tle (**ket**-uhl) ***noun*** A metal pot used for boiling liquids or cooking foods.

ket·tle·drum (**ket**-uhl-*druhm*) ***noun*** A large drum with a metal body shaped like a bowl and that makes a deep, booming sound.

key (**kee**)
1. ***noun*** A piece of metal shaped to fit into a lock to open it or to start an engine.
2. ***noun*** Something that provides a solution or an explanation, as in *the key to the mystery.*
3. ***noun*** One of the buttons on a computer or typewriter.
4. ***noun*** One of the black or white bars that you press on a piano.
5. ***adjective*** Very important, as in *a key decision.*
6. ***noun*** A list or chart that explains the symbols on a map.
7. ***noun*** A group of musical notes based around one particular note, as in *a song in the key of F.*
Key sounds like **quay.**

key·board (**kee**-*bord*) ***noun***
1. The set of keys on a computer, typewriter, piano, etc.
2. An **electronic keyboard** has keys like a piano and buttons that produce other sounds. It is worked by electricity.

key·hole (**kee**-*hole*) ***noun*** The hole in a lock where a key fits.

key·pad (**kee**-*pad*) ***noun*** A small panel of keys or buttons used for operating an electronic machine such as a calculator.

kha·ki (**kak**-ee *or* **kah**-kee) ***noun***
1. A yellow-brown color.
2. A strong cotton cloth of this color, often used for soldiers' uniforms.
▸ ***adjective* khaki**

kib·butz (ki-**buts**) ***noun*** A small community in Israel in which all the people live and work together. ▸ ***noun, plural* kibbutzim** (ki-but-**seem**)

kick (**kik**)
1. ***verb*** To hit something with your foot.
▸ **kicking, kicked** ▸ ***noun* kick**
2. ***noun*** *(informal)* A feeling of excitement or pleasure.

kick•box•ing (**kik**-*bok*-sing) ***noun*** A sport in which two contestants hit each other with their hands and feet. ▸ ***verb*** **kickbox**

kick•off (**kik**-*of*) ***noun*** A kick of the ball that begins the action in a game of football or soccer.

kid (**kid**)
1. ***noun*** *(informal)* A child.
2. ***noun*** A young goat.
3. ***verb*** To make fun of or tease someone. ▸ **kidding, kidded**

kid•nap (**kid**-*nap*) ***verb*** The illegal activity of capturing someone and keeping the person as a prisoner, usually until certain demands are met.
▸ **kidnapping** *or* **kidnaping, kidnapped** *or* **kidnaped** ▸ ***noun*** **kidnapper** *or* **kidnaper**

kid•ney (**kid**-nee) ***noun*** One of a pair of organs in your body that remove waste matter from your blood and turn it into urine.

kill (**kil**) ***verb***
1. To end the life of a person, an animal, or a plant. ▸ ***noun*** **killer**
2. To end or to destroy.
3. To hurt very much.
▸ ***verb*** **killing, killed**

kiln (**kil** *or* **kiln**) ***noun*** A very hot oven used to bake objects made of clay until they are hard.

kil•o•byte (**kil**-uh-*bite*) ***noun*** A unit for measuring the amount of data in a computer memory or file. A kilobyte is 1,024 bytes.

ki•lo•gram (**kil**-uh-*gram*) ***noun*** A unit of mass or weight in the metric system equal to 1,000 grams or 2.2 pounds.

ki•lo•hertz (**kil**-uh-*hurts*) ***noun*** A unit for measuring the frequency of radio waves. One kilohertz is equal to 1,000 vibrations per second. ▸ ***noun, plural*** **kilohertz**

ki•lo•joule (**kil**-uh-*jool*) ***noun*** A unit for measuring energy or work done. One kilojoule is equal to 1,000 joules.

ki•lo•me•ter (kuh-**lom**-uh-tur *or* **kil**-uh-*mee*-tur) ***noun*** A unit of length in the metric system equal to 1,000 meters, or about 0.6 miles. The Golden Gate Bridge in San Francisco, California, is about one kilometer long.

ki•lo•watt (**kil**-uh-*waht*) ***noun*** A unit for measuring electrical power. One kilowatt equals 1,000 watts.

kilt (**kilt**) ***noun*** A pleated, plaid skirt worn by Scottish men as part of a traditional costume.

ki•mo•no (kuh-**moh**-nuh) ***noun*** A long, loose robe with wide sleeves and a sash, worn in Japan.

kin (**kin**) ***noun*** A person or people related to you.

kind (**kinde**)
1. ***adjective*** Friendly, helpful, and generous. ▸ **kinder, kindest** ▸ ***noun*** **kindness** ▸ ***adverb*** **kindly**
2. ***noun*** A group of the same or similar things; a category.
3. ***noun*** A type or sort.

kin•der•gar•ten (**kin**-dur-*gart*-uhn) ***noun*** A class for children ages four to six.

kin•dle (**kin**-duhl) ***verb***
1. To make something start to burn.
2. To stir up or to excite.
▸ ***verb*** **kindling, kindled**

kin•dling (**kind**-ling) ***noun*** Small, thin pieces of wood used for starting fires.

ki•net•ic (ki-**net**-ik) ***adjective*** To do with movement, or caused by movement, as in *kinetic energy.* ▸ ***adverb*** **kinetically**

king (**king**) ***noun***
1. A man from a royal family who is the ruler of his country.
2. A chess piece that can move one square in any direction.
3. A playing card with a picture of a king on it.

king•dom (**king**-duhm) ***noun***
1. A country that has a king or queen as its ruler.
2. One of the main groups into which all living things are divided, such as the animal kingdom and the plant kingdom.

K

K

king•fish•er (**king**-*fish*-ur) ***noun*** A small bird with bright feathers and a long bill that lives near water and catches fish for food.

kink (**kingk**) ***noun***
1. A tight curl or twist in a rope, wire, hose, chain, or hair. ▸ ***adjective*** **kinky**
2. A painful or stiff feeling in a neck or back muscle.
3. An imperfection that is likely to cause problems.

kin•ship (**kin**-ship) ***noun***
1. A family relationship.
2. Any close connection.

ki•osk (**kee**-osk) ***noun*** A small structure with one or more open sides, often used as a stand for selling newspapers.

kiss (**kiss**) ***verb*** To touch someone with your lips to greet the person or to show that you like or love him or her. ▸ **kisses, kissing, kissed** ▸ ***noun*** **kiss**

kit (**kit**) ***noun***
1. A set of parts that you put together to make something, as in *a model airplane kit.*
2. A set of tools and materials for a certain purpose, as in *a sewing kit* or *a first-aid kit.*

kitch•en (**kich**-uhn) ***noun*** A room in which food is prepared and cooked.

kite (**kite**) ***noun*** A frame covered with paper or material that is attached to a long piece of string and flown in the wind.

kit•ty (**kit**-ee) ***noun***
1. A kitten.
2. An amount of money contributed by everyone in a group and then used to buy something.
▸ ***noun, plural*** **kitties**

ki•wi (**kee**-wee) ***noun***
1. A bird from New Zealand that cannot fly.
2. A small, round fruit with brown, fuzzy skin and green flesh. Kiwis are grown in New Zealand. Also called **kiwifruit.**

Klee•nex (**klee**-neks) ***noun*** A trademark for a soft tissue paper that can be used as a handkerchief.

klutz (**kluhts**) ***noun*** *(slang)* A clumsy person.

knack (**nak**) ***noun*** An ability to do something difficult or tricky.

knap•sack (**nap**-*sak*) ***noun*** A canvas or leather bag used to carry books or supplies on your back.

knave (**nayv**) ***noun*** *(old-fashioned)* A dishonest man or boy.

knead (**need**) ***verb*** When you **knead** dough, you press, fold, and stretch it to make it smooth. **Knead** sounds like **need.** ▸ **kneading, kneaded**

knee (**nee**) ***noun*** The joint between your upper and lower leg that you bend when you walk.

knee•cap (**nee**-*kap*) ***noun*** The round bone at the front of the knee.

kneel (**neel**) ***verb*** To bend your legs and put your knees on the ground.
▸ **kneeling, knelt** (**nelt**)

knick•ers (**nik**-urz) ***noun, plural*** Loose, short pants that end just below the knee.

knick•knack (**nik**-*nak*) ***noun*** A small object used as a decoration.

knife (**nife**)
1. ***noun*** A tool with a sharp blade used for cutting things. ▸ ***noun, plural*** **knives**
2. ***verb*** To stab someone with a knife.
▸ **knifing, knifed**

knight (**nite**) ***noun***
1. In medieval times, a **knight** was a warrior who fought on horseback. A king or noble would give a knight land, and in return the knight would fight for him.
▸ ***adjective*** **knightly**
2. In Great Britain, a man who has been given the title "Sir" as a reward for service to his country. ▸ ***noun*** **knighthood** ▸ ***verb*** **knight**
3. A chess piece with a horse's head that always has to move three squares at a time.
Knight sounds like **night.**

knit (**nit**) ***verb***
1. To make cloth or clothing by looping yarn together either by hand with long, pointed needles or by machine. ▸ ***noun*** **knitting**
2. When a bone **knits,** it heals after it has been broken.
▸ ***verb*** **knitting, knitted** *or* **knit**

knob (**nob**) ***noun***
1. A small, round handle on a drawer or door.
2. A control button on a radio, television, or other device.
3. A roundish lump.

knock (**nok**) ***verb***
1. To bang or hit something or someone. ▸ ***noun*** **knock**
2. To hit and cause to fall.
3. To criticize harshly.
4. knock out To make someone unconscious.
▸ ***verb*** **knocking, knocked**

knock•er (**nok**-ur) ***noun*** A piece of metal attached to a door that you use to knock on the door.

knoll (**nohl**) ***noun*** A small hill.

knot (**not**)
1. ***noun*** A fastening made by looping and twisting one or more pieces of string or rope.
2. ***verb*** To make a knot in. ▸ **knotting, knotted**
3. ***noun*** A small, hard spot in a piece of wood where a branch once joined the main trunk.
4. ***noun*** A unit for measuring the speed of a ship or an aircraft, equal to 6,076 feet per hour.
Knot sounds like **not.**

knot•ty (**not**-ee) ***adjective***
1. Having many knots, as in *knotty pine.*
2. Difficult to understand or solve, as in *a knotty problem.*
▸ ***adjective*** **knottier, knottiest**

know (**noh**) ***verb*** To be familiar with a person, place, or piece of information. **Know** sounds like **no.** ▸ **knowing, knew** (**noo**), **known** (**nohn**)

know-how ***noun*** The knowledge and skill needed to complete a task or job correctly.

know•ledge (**nol**-ij) ***noun***
1. The things that someone knows; information.
2. Awareness or a clear idea.

knowl•edge•a•ble (**nol**-ij-uh-buhl) ***adjective*** If you are **knowledgeable,** you know a lot.

knuck•le (**nuhk**-uhl) ***noun*** One of the joints in a finger.

ko•a•la (koh-**ah**-luh) ***noun*** An Australian animal that looks like a small bear and lives in eucalyptus trees.

kook (**kook**) ***noun*** *(slang)* Someone who acts in a silly or strange way or who has crazy ideas. ▸ ***adjective*** **kooky**

kook•a•bur•ra (**kuk**-uh-*bur*-uh) ***noun*** An Australian bird that makes a loud, cackling sound like the sound of someone laughing.

Ko•ran *or* **Qur'an** (kor-**ahn** *or* kor-**an**) ***noun*** The holy book of the Muslim religion.

ko•sher (**koh**-shur) ***adjective*** **Kosher** food is food that has been prepared according to the laws of the Jewish religion.

kung fu (**kuhng foo**) ***noun*** One of the Chinese martial arts in which a person uses punches, kicks, and blocks for self-defense. Kung fu is similiar to karate.

Kwan•za *or* **Kwan•zaa** (**kwahn**-zuh) ***noun*** An African-American holiday based on a traditional African harvest festival. Kwanza is celebrated for seven days beginning on December 26 and ending on New Year's Day, January 1. Each day is devoted to a different principle, such as faith, creativity, unity, and purpose.

L

lab (**lab**) Short for **laboratory**.

la•bel (**lay**-buhl)
1. ***noun*** A piece of paper, cloth, or plastic that is attached to something and gives information about it.
2. ***noun*** A word or phrase that describes something.
3. ***verb*** To attach a label to something or to give something a label. ▸ **labeling, labeled**

la•bor (**lay**-bur)
1. ***verb*** To work hard. ▸ **laboring, labored** ▸ ***noun*** **labor,** ***noun*** **laborer**
2. ***noun*** The work of giving birth to a baby.
3. ***noun*** People employed to do work, especially physical work.

lab•o•ra•tor•y (**lab**-ruh-*tor*-ee) ***noun*** A room, building, or institute containing special equipment for people to use in scientific experiments. ▸ ***noun, plural*** **laboratories**

Labor Day ***noun*** A legal holiday in the United States to honor people who work. It is celebrated on the first Monday in September.

labor union ***noun*** An organized group of workers set up to help improve working conditions and pay.

lace (**layss**)
1. ***noun*** Thin material made from cotton or silk with a pattern of small holes and delicate stitches. ▸ ***adjective*** **lacy**
2. ***noun*** A long piece of thin string, cord, or leather used to tie shoes.
3. ***verb*** To tie something together with a lace. ▸ **lacing, laced**

lack (**lak**)
1. ***verb*** To be without something that you need. ▸ **lacking, lacked**
2. ***noun*** If there is a **lack** of something, there is not enough of it, as in *a lack of rain.*
3. ***noun*** Something that is needed or is missing.

lac•quer (**lak**-ur)
1. ***noun*** A liquid coating that is put on wood or metal to give it a shiny finish and protect it.
2. ***verb*** To coat with this liquid. ▸ **lacquering, lacquered**

la•crosse (luh-**krawss**) ***noun*** A ball game for two teams in which each player has a long stick with a small net on the end. The players use the net to run with the ball, pass it or throw it to one another, and aim to score goals.

lad (**lad**) ***noun*** A boy or a young man.

lad•der (**lad**-ur) ***noun*** A metal, wooden, or rope structure that is used to climb up and down. Ladders are made from two long, upright pieces linked by a series of horizontal pieces called rungs.

lad•en (**layd**-uhn) ***adjective*** Carrying a lot of things.

la•dle (**lay**-duhl) ***noun*** A large, deep spoon with a long handle, used for serving soup, casseroles, etc. ▸ ***verb*** **ladle**

la•dy (**lay**-dee) ***noun***
1. A woman.
2. A girl or woman who has good manners.
3. Lady In Great Britain, a title used by a woman who has either earned the title herself as a reward for service to her country or who is married to a lord or a man with the title "Sir."
▸ ***noun, plural*** **ladies**

la•dy•bug (**lay**-dee-*buhg*) ***noun*** A small, round beetle that usually has red or orange wings and black spots. Ladybugs eat insects, such as aphids, that are harmful to plants.

lag (**lag**)
1. ***verb*** To move so slowly that you fall behind the others.
2. ***noun*** A delay.
3. ***verb*** To drop, or to lessen. ▸ ***noun*** **lag** ▸ ***verb*** **lagging, lagged**

la•goon (luh-**goon**) ***noun*** A shallow pool of seawater separated from the sea by a narrow strip of land.

laid-back ***adjective*** *(informal)* Very relaxed and calm.

lair (**lair**) ***noun*** A place where a wild animal rests and sleeps.

lake (**lake**) ***noun*** A large body of fresh water surrounded by land.

lamb (**lam**) ***noun***
1. A young sheep.
2. Meat from a young sheep.

lame (**laym**) ***adjective***
1. Someone who is **lame** has an injured leg and so is unable to walk freely. ▸ ***noun*** **lameness**
2. Weak or unconvincing, as in *a lame excuse.* ▸ ***adverb*** **lamely**

la•ment (luh-**ment**)
1. ***verb*** To feel or show great sadness. ▸ **lamenting, lamented**
2. ***noun*** A sad song, especially one about someone's death.

lamp (**lamp**) ***noun*** A light that uses gas, oil, or electricity.

LAN (**lan**) ***noun*** A system of computers in a small area that are linked by cables so that users can share information and equipment. LAN stands for *Local Area Network.*

lance (**lanss**)
1. ***noun*** A long spear used in the past by soldiers riding horses.
2. ***verb*** To cut open with a sharp knife. ▸ **lancing, lanced**

land (**land**)
1. ***noun*** The part of the earth's surface that is not covered by water.
2. ***noun*** Earth or soil.
3. ***verb*** To come down from the air to the land or water.
4. ***noun*** A country.
5. ***verb*** To succeed in getting something.
6. ***verb*** To cause you to end up somewhere.
▸ ***verb*** **landing, landed**

land•fill (**land**-*fil*) ***noun***
1. Garbage that is stacked and covered with earth.
2. **landfill site** A large area where garbage is buried.

land•ing (**land**-ing) ***noun***
1. The act of coming to land or coming ashore after a flight or voyage, as in *a rough landing.*
2. The place on a dock or pier where boats load and unload.
3. A level area of floor at the top of a staircase.
4. **landing strip** A level area of ground that aircraft use for taking off and landing.

land•la•dy (**land**-*lay*-dee) ***noun*** A woman who owns and rents out an apartment, a room, a house, or other property. ▸ ***noun, plural*** **landladies**

land•lord (**land**-*lord*) ***noun*** A man who owns and rents out an apartment, a room, a house, or other property.

land•mark (**land**-*mark*) ***noun***
1. An object in a landscape that can be seen from far away.
2. An important event.
3. A building or place selected and pointed out as important, as in *a historical landmark.*

land•scape (**land**-*skape*) ***noun***
1. A large area of land that you can view from one place.
2. A painting, drawing, or photograph that shows such a stretch of land.
3. **landscape gardening** The designing, shaping, and planting of a garden in an attractive way.

L

land•slide (**land**-*slide*) ***noun***
1. A sudden slide of earth and rocks down the side of a mountain or a hill.
2. An election victory in which the winner gets many more votes than anyone else.

lane (**layn**) ***noun***
1. A narrow road or street.
2. One of the strips marked on a main road that is wide enough for a single line of vehicles.
3. One of the strips, each wide enough for one person, into which a track or swimming pool is divided.
4. A narrow wooden path on which bowling balls are rolled.

lan•guage (**lang**-gwij) ***noun***
1. The words and grammar that people use to talk and write to each other.
2. Speech used by one country or group of people, as in *the Spanish language.*
3. A set of signs, symbols, or movements used to express meaning, as in *sign language.*

lank•y (**lang**-kee) ***adjective*** Someone who is **lanky** is very tall and thin.
▸ **lankier, lankiest**

lan•tern (**lan**-turn) ***noun*** A light with a protective frame around it.

lan•yard (**lan**-yurd) ***noun*** A cord worn around the neck to which you can attach a knife or a whistle.

lap (**lap**)
1. *noun* The flat area formed by the top part of your legs when you are sitting down.
2. *noun* One time over or around something.
3. *verb* To lie partly over something else.
4. *verb* When water **laps** against something, it moves gently against it.
5. *verb* When an animal **laps up** a drink, it flicks the liquid up into its mouth with its tongue.
▸ ***verb*** **lapping, lapped**

la•pel (luh-**pel**) ***noun*** The part of the collar of a coat or jacket that folds back over itself.

lapse (**laps**)
1. *noun* A small mistake or failure, as in *a lapse of memory.* ▸ ***verb*** **lapse**
2. *noun* The passing of time.
3. *verb* To drop or fall off little by little.
4. *verb* To come to an end.
▸ ***verb*** **lapsing, lapsed**

lap•top (**lap**-*top*) ***noun*** A portable computer that is so small and light that you can use it on your lap.

larch (**larch**) ***noun*** A tall tree with small cones and needles that drop off in the fall. The larch is related to the pine.

lard (**lard**) ***noun*** A solid, white grease made from the melted-down fat of pigs and hogs. Lard is used in cooking.

lar•der (**lar**-dur) ***noun*** A small room or pantry in which food is stored.

large (**larj**)
1. *adjective* Great in size or amount.
▸ **larger, largest** ▸ ***noun*** **largeness**
2. If a person or an animal is **at large,** it is free.

large intestine ***noun*** The thick, lower end of the digestive system, containing the appendix, colon, and rectum.

large•ly (**larj**-lee) ***adverb*** Mostly.

la•ri•at (**la**-ree-uht) ***noun*** A lasso.

lark (**lark**) ***noun***
1. A small, brown bird that flies very high in the sky and has a beautiful song.
2. Something silly that you do for fun or as a joke.

lark•spur (**lark**-spur) ***noun*** A tall plant that has long stalks of blue, purple, or white flowers.

lar•va (**lar**-vuh) ***noun*** An insect at the stage of development between an egg and a pupa when it looks like a worm. A caterpillar is the larva of a moth or a butterfly. ▸ ***noun, plural*** **larvae** (**lar**-vee)

lar•yn•gi•tis (la-rin-**jye**-tiss) ***noun*** A swelling of the throat caused by an infection. It causes hoarseness.

lar•ynx (**la**-ringks) ***noun*** The upper part of the windpipe. The larynx holds your vocal cords.

la·sa·gna *or* **la·sa·gne** (luh-**zah**-nyuh) ***noun*** An Italian dish made with layers of wide noodles, chopped meat or vegetables, tomato sauce, and cheese.

la·ser (**lay**-zur) ***noun***
1. A device that makes a very narrow, powerful beam of light that can be used for light shows, for cutting things, or for medical operations. Laser stands for *Light Amplification by Stimulated Emission of Radiation.*
2. **laser beam** A concentrated beam of light made by a laser. Laser beams are used to read compact disks.

laser printer ***noun*** A computer printer that reproduces high-quality images using a laser.

lash (**lash**)
1. ***noun*** One of the small hairs that grow around your eyelid.
2. ***noun*** A stroke with a whip. ▸ ***verb*** **lash**
3. ***verb*** To tie things together very firmly using rope or cord.
4. ***verb*** To whip back and forth.
5. **lash out** ***verb*** To hit or to speak out against someone suddenly and angrily.
▸ ***verb*** **lashes, lashing, lashed** ▸ ***noun, plural*** **lashes**

lass (**lass**) ***noun*** A girl or a young woman. ▸ ***noun, plural*** **lasses**

las·so (**lass**-oh *or* lass-**oo**) ***noun*** A length of rope with a large loop at one end that can be thrown over an animal to catch it. Also called a lariat. ▸ ***noun, plural*** **lassos** *or* **lassoes** ▸ ***verb*** **lasso**

last (**last**)
1. ***adjective*** Coming at the end or after everything else. ▸ ***adverb*** **lastly**
2. ***adjective*** Being the only one left.
3. ***adjective*** Most recent.
4. ***noun*** The last person or thing.
5. ***verb*** To go on for a particular length of time.
6. ***verb*** To stay in good condition.
▸ ***verb*** **lasting, lasted**

last·ing (**last**-ing) ***adjective*** Something that is **lasting** keeps going for a long time.

latch (**lach**)
1. ***noun*** A lock or fastening for a door.
▸ ***noun, plural*** **latches** ▸ ***verb*** **latch**
2. ***verb*** If you **latch on to** someone or something, you become very attached to and dependent on it. ▸ **latches, latching, latched**

latch·key (**lach**-*kee*) ***noun***
1. A key that opens a door with a latch.
2. **Latchkey children** have to let themselves in when they return from school because there is nobody else at home yet.

late (**late**) ***adjective***
1. When someone or something is **late,** it comes after the expected time. ▸ ***noun*** **lateness** ▸ ***adverb*** **late**
2. Near the end of a period of time, as in *the late 20th century.*
3. No longer alive, as in *the late Elvis Presley.*
▸ ***adjective*** **later, latest**

late·com·er (**late**-*kuhm*-ur) ***noun*** Someone who arrives late.

late·ly (**late**-lee) ***adverb*** Recently.

la·tent (**late**-uhnt) ***adjective*** Present but not very obvious or strong, as in *latent fingerprints* or *a latent talent.*

lat·er·al (**lat**-ur-uhl) ***adjective*** On, from, or to the side.

la·tex (**lay**-teks) ***noun***
1. A milky liquid that comes from certain plants. This natural liquid is used to make rubber.
2. A similar liquid that is produced artificially and is used to make rubber, paints, and chewing gum.
▸ ***noun, plural*** **latexes**

lathe (**layTH**) ***noun*** A machine that holds a piece of wood or metal while turning it against a cutting tool that shapes it.

lath·er (**laTH**-ur) ***noun*** A thick, creamy foam formed when soap is mixed with water. ▸ ***verb*** **lather**

Lat·in (**lat**-uhn) ***noun*** The language of the ancient Romans.

L

La•ti•na (lah-**tee**-nuh *or* luh-**tee**-nuh) ***noun***
1. A woman or girl who was born in or lives in Latin America.
2. A woman or girl born in Latin America who lives in the United States.
▸ ***adjective*** **Latina**

Latin America ***noun*** All of the Americas found south of the United States where the languages spoken are based on Latin. Latin America includes Mexico as well as the countries of Central America and South America.

Latin-American ***adjective*** To do with the people, cultures, and countries of Mexico, Central America, and South America. ▸ ***noun*** **Latin American**

La•ti•no (lah-**tee**-noh *or* luh-**tee**-noh) ***noun***
1. A person who was born in or lives in Latin America.
2. A person born in Latin America who lives in the United States.
▸ ***adjective*** **Latino**

lat•i•tude (**lat**-uh-tood) ***noun*** The position of a place, measured in degrees north or south of the equator.
▸ ***adjective*** **latitudinal**

lat•ter (**lat**-ur)
1. ***noun*** The second of two things just mentioned.
2. ***adjective*** Later.

lat•tice (**lat**-iss) ***noun*** A structure made from strips of wood, metal, etc., that cross each other, often diagonally, forming a pattern of diamond shapes.
▸ ***adjective*** **latticed**

laugh (**laf**) ***verb*** When you **laugh,** you make a sound to show that you think that something is funny. ▸ **laughing, laughed** ▸ ***noun*** **laugh,** ***noun*** **laughter**

laugh•a•ble (**laf**-uh-buhl) ***adjective*** If something is **laughable,** it is ridiculous and cannot be taken seriously.

laugh track ***noun*** Previously recorded laughter of a studio audience that is added to the sound track of a television program.

launch (**lawnch**)
1. ***verb*** To put a boat or ship into the water.
2. ***verb*** To send a rocket up into space.
3. ***verb*** To start or introduce something new.
4. ***noun*** A type of boat that is often used for sightseeing. ▸ ***noun, plural*** **launches**
5. **launching pad** *or* **launch pad** ***noun*** A place where rockets leave the ground to go into space.
▸ ***verb*** **launches, launching, launched**
▸ ***noun*** **launch**

laun•der (**lawn**-dur) ***verb*** To wash and iron clothes. ▸ **laundering, laundered**

Laun•dro•mat (**lawn**-druh-*mat*) ***noun*** Trademark for a place where you pay to use washing machines and clothes dryers.

laun•dry (**lawn**-dree) ***noun***
1. Clothes, towels, sheets, and other such items that are being washed or are about to be washed.
2. A place where washing is done.
▸ ***noun, plural*** **laundries**

lau•rel (**lor**-uhl) ***noun***
1. An evergreen bush or tree with smooth, shiny leaves.
2. A wreath made from laurel leaves, given to heroes and poets in ancient Rome.
3. If you **rest on your laurels,** you rely on your past achievements and do not try anymore.

la•va (**lah**-vuh *or* **la**-vuh) ***noun***
1. The hot, liquid rock that pours out of a volcano when it erupts.
2. The rock formed when this liquid has cooled and hardened.

lav•a•to•ry (**lav**-uh-*tor*-ee) ***noun*** A bathroom. ▸ ***noun, plural*** **lavatories**

lav•en•der (**lav**-uhn-dur) ***noun***
1. A plant with pale purple flowers that have a pleasant smell.
2. A pale purple color, the color of lavender flowers.
▸ ***adjective*** **lavender**

lav•ish (**lav**-ish)
1. ***adjective*** Generous or extravagant, as in *lavish gifts.* ▸ ***adverb*** **lavishly**
2. ***verb*** If you **lavish** attention, money, care, etc., on someone, you give the person a lot of it. ▸ **lavishes, lavishing, lavished**

law (**law**) ***noun***
1. A rule made by the government that must be obeyed.
2. A statement in science or math about what always happens whenever certain events take place, as in *the law of gravity.*
3. The profession and work of a lawyer, as in *a career in law.*

law-a•bid•ing (uh-**bye**-ding) ***adjective*** If you are **law-abiding,** you obey the laws of a government.

law•ful (**law**-fuhl) ***adjective*** Permitted by the law, as in *a lawful agreement.* ▸ ***noun*** **lawfulness** ▸ ***adverb*** **lawfully**

lawn (**lawn**) ***noun*** An area covered with grass, usually next to a house.

lawn mow•er (**moh**-ur) ***noun*** A machine that people use to cut grass.

law•suit (**law**-*soot*) ***noun*** A legal action or case brought against a person or a group in a court of law.

law•yer (**law**-yur *or* **loi**-ur) ***noun*** A person who is trained to advise people about the law and who acts and speaks for them in court.

lax (**laks**) ***adjective*** Relaxed or not strict, as in *lax discipline.* ▸ ***noun*** **laxity,** ***noun*** **laxness** ▸ ***adverb*** **laxly**

lay (**lay**) ***verb***
1. To put or to place.
2. To produce an egg or eggs.
3. If a person has been **laid off,** he or she has been dismissed from a job, often for a short period of time.
4. If you are **laid up,** you are in bed with an injury or illness.
Lay sounds like **lei.** ▸ ***verb*** **laying, laid (layd)**

lay•er (**lay**-ur) ***noun*** A thickness or coating of something, as in *a layer of dust.* ▸ ***verb*** **layer** ▸ ***adjective*** **layered**

lay•off (**lay**-*of*) ***noun*** A period in which people are temporarily dismissed from work because there is not enough for them to do.

lay•out (**lay**-*out*) ***noun*** The pattern or design of something, as in *the layout of a book.*

la•zy (**lay**-zee) ***adjective*** If you are **lazy,** you do not want to work or be active. ▸ **lazier, laziest** ▸ ***noun*** **laziness** ▸ ***verb*** **laze** ▸ ***adverb*** **lazily**

lead
1. (**leed**) ***verb*** To show someone the way, usually by going in front of the person.
2. (**leed**) ***verb*** To be in charge, as in *to lead a discussion.* ▸ ***noun*** **leadership**
3. (**leed**) ***noun*** A person's position at the front.
4. (**leed**) ***noun*** A piece of helpful advice or information.
5. (**leed**) ***noun*** The main actor or role in a play, movie, etc.
6. (**led**) ***noun*** A soft, gray metal.
7. (**led**) ***noun*** The black or gray material used in pencils; graphite.
8. (**leed**) ***noun*** A leash.
▸ ***verb*** **leading, led (led)** ▸ ***noun*** **leader**

leaf (**leef**)
1. ***noun*** A flat and usually green part of a plant or tree that grows out from a stem, twig, branch, etc. Leaves make food by the process of photosynthesis, giving off oxygen as a by-product. ▸ ***adjective*** **leafy**
2. ***noun*** A page of a book.
3. ***verb*** To turn pages and glance at them quickly. ▸ **leafing, leafed**
4. ***noun*** A flat, removable part of a table. ▸ ***noun, plural*** **leaves**

leaf•let (**leef**-lit) ***noun***
1. A single sheet of paper giving information or advertising something.
2. A small or young leaf.

L

league (**leeg**) ***noun***
1. A group of people with a common interest or activity, such as a group of sports teams or a political organization.
2. A measure of distance equal to about three miles.

leak (**leek**) ***verb***
1. If a container **leaks,** water, gas, or another fluid escapes from it. ▸ ***adjective*** **leaky**
2. If a liquid or gas **leaks,** it escapes through a hole or crack in a container.
3. If someone **leaks** a story or information, the person tells it to someone else who is not meant to know it.
Leak sounds like **leek.**
▸ ***verb*** **leaking, leaked** ▸ ***noun*** **leak**

lean (**leen**)
1. ***verb*** To bend toward or over something.
2. ***verb*** To rest your body against something for support.
3. ***verb*** To rely on for help.
4. ***adjective*** Slim and muscular.
5. ***adjective*** If meat is **lean,** it has very little or no fat. ▸ ***noun*** **lean**
▸ ***verb*** **leaning, leaned** ▸ ***adjective*** **leaner, leanest**

leaning ***noun*** If you have a **leaning** toward something, you are interested in it or tend to like it.

leap (**leep**) ***verb*** To jump or jump over something. ▸ **leaping, leaped** *or* **leapt** (**leept** *or* **lept**) ▸ ***noun*** **leap**

leap•frog (**leep**-*frog*) ***noun*** A game in which one player bends over and another jumps over his or her back, using the hands for support. ▸ ***verb*** **leapfrog**

leap year ***noun*** A year that has 366 days, caused by adding an extra day in February. A leap year comes every fourth year.

learn (**lurn**) ***verb***
1. To gain knowledge or a skill.
2. To memorize.
3. To discover some news.
▸ ***verb*** **learning, learned** *or* **learnt**

learn•ed (**lur**-nid) ***adjective*** Having much knowledge or education, as in *a learned scholar.*

learning disabled ***adjective*** Having difficulty in learning a basic skill, such as reading, because of a physical condition, such as dyslexia. Abbreviated *LD.* ▸ ***noun*** **learning disability**

lease (**leess**) ***noun*** An agreement that a landlord and tenant sign when renting an apartment, a house, or other property.
▸ ***verb*** **lease**

leash (**leesh**) ***noun*** A strap, cord, or chain that you use to hold and control an animal. ▸ ***noun, plural*** **leashes**

least (**leest**)
1. ***noun*** The smallest amount.
▸ ***adjective*** **least**
2. ***adverb*** Less than anything else.
3. **at least** Not less or fewer than.

leath•er (**leTH**-ur) ***noun*** Animal skin that is treated with chemicals and used to make shoes, bags, and other goods.
▸ ***adjective*** **leathery**

leave (**leev**)
1. ***verb*** To go away, as in *to leave for a vacation.*
2. ***verb*** To let something stay or remain.
3. ***verb*** To give property to someone through a will, after death.
4. ***verb*** To quit.
5. ***noun*** Time away from work, as in *maternity leave.*
6. ***verb*** To have remaining.
7. **leave behind** ***verb*** If you **leave** something **behind,** you forget to bring it.
8. **leave out** ***verb*** If you **leave** something **out,** you do not include it.
▸ ***verb*** **leaving, left** (**left**)

lec•ture (**lek**-chur) ***noun***
1. A talk given to a class or an audience in order to teach something. ▸ ***noun*** **lecturer**
2. A scolding that lasts a long time.
▸ ***verb*** **lecture**

ledge (**lej**) ***noun***
1. A narrow shelf that sticks out from a wall, as in *a window ledge.*

L

2. A narrow, flat shelf on the side of a mountain or cliff.

lee (**lee**) ***noun*** The side of something such as a ship or mountain that is away from the wind; shelter. ▸ ***adjective* lee**

leech (**leech**) ***noun***
1. A worm that lives in water or wet earth and survives by sucking blood from animals. In the past, doctors often used leeches to take blood from patients. Leeches are still used for that purpose in some parts of the world.
2. A person who clings to others, hoping to get something from them.
▸ ***noun, plural* leeches**

leek (**leek**) ***noun*** A long, white vegetable with green leaves at one end. It tastes like a mild onion. **Leek** sounds like **leak.**

leer (**lihr**) ***noun*** A sly or evil grin. ▸ ***verb* leer**

left (**left**) ***noun***
1. The side you begin to read from in a line of English writing. ▸ ***adjective* left** ▸ ***adverb* left**
2. In politics, people **on the left** have liberal or radical views.

left-hand•ed (**han**-did) ***adjective*** If you are **left-handed,** you use your left hand more easily than your right hand.
▸ ***noun* left-hander**

left•o•vers (**left**-*oh*-vurz) ***noun, plural*** The part of a meal that has not been eaten and can be used for another meal.

leg (**leg**) ***noun***
1. The part of your body between your hip and your foot.
2. The part of a pair of pants that covers a leg.
3. A part of a chair, table, etc., on which it stands.
4. A **leg** of a journey is one part or stage of it.
5. Either of two sides of a triangle besides the base.
6. *(informal)* If you **pull** someone's **leg,** you make fun of the person by telling him or her something untrue.
7. If something is **on its last legs,** it is about to collapse or die.

leg•a•cy (**leg**-uh-see) ***noun***
1. Money or property that has been left to someone in a will.
2. Something handed down from one generation to another.
▸ ***noun, plural* legacies**

le•gal (**lee**-guhl) ***adjective***
1. To do with the law, as in *legal documents.*
2. Lawful, or allowed by law. ▸ ***verb* legalize** ▸ ***adverb* legally**

leg•end (**lej**-uhnd) ***noun***
1. A story handed down from earlier times. Legends are often based on fact, but they are not entirely true.
▸ ***adjective* legendary**
2. The words written beneath or beside a map or chart to explain it.

leg•gings (**leg**-ingz) ***noun, plural*** A covering for the legs that fits like tights.

leg•i•ble (**lej**-uh-buhl) ***adjective*** If handwriting or print is **legible,** it can be read fairly easily. ▸ ***noun* legibility** ▸ ***adverb* legibly**

le•gion (**lee**-juhn)
1. ***noun*** A unit in the Roman army.
2. ***noun*** A large body of soldiers or former soldiers.
3. ***adjective*** Very many, or numerous.

leg•is•la•tion (lej-uh-**slay**-shuhn) ***noun*** Laws that have been proposed or made.
▸ ***noun* legislator** ▸ ***verb* legislate**

leg•is•la•ture (**lej**-iss-*lay*-chur) ***noun*** A group of people who have the power to make or change laws for a country or state.

le•git•i•mate (luh-**jit**-uh-mit) ***adjective***
1. Lawful or rightful.
2. Reasonable, as in *a legitimate complaint.*
▸ ***adverb* legitimately**

le•gume (**leg**-yoom) ***noun*** A plant with seeds that grow in pods. Peas, beans, lentils, and peanuts are legumes.

lei (**lay**) ***noun*** A necklace of leaves or flowers, often given as a gift of welcome in Hawaii. **Lei** sounds like **lay.**

L

leis•ure (**lee**-zhur *or* **lezh**-ur) ***noun*** Free time, when you do not have to work or study. ▸ ***adjective*** **leisure**

lei•sure•ly (**lee**-zhur-lee *or* **lezh**-ur-lee) ***adjective*** Not hurried or not rushed.

lem•on (**lem**-uhn) ***noun*** A yellow citrus fruit with a thick skin and a sour taste.

lem•on•ade (lem-uh-**nade**) ***noun*** A drink made from lemon juice, water, and sugar.

lend (**lend**) ***verb*** To let someone have something that you expect to get back. ▸ **lending, lent** (**lent**)

length (**lengkth**) ***noun***
1. The distance from one end of something to the other.
2. The amount or extent from beginning to end, as in *the length of a vacation* or *the length of a book.* ▸ ***adjective*** **lengthy**
3. A piece of something, as in *a length of rope.*

length•en (**lengk**-thuhn) ***verb*** To make something longer. ▸ **lengthening, lengthened**

length•wise (**lengkth**-*wize*) ***adverb*** In the direction of the longest side. ▸ ***adjective*** **lengthwise**

le•ni•ent (**lee**-nyuhnt *or* **lee**-nee-uhnt) ***adjective*** Gentle and not strict. ▸ ***adverb*** **leniently**

lens (**lenz**) ***noun***
1. A piece of curved glass or plastic in a pair of glasses or in a camera, telescope, etc. Lenses bend light rays so that you can focus a camera or see things magnified through a telescope or microscope.
2. The clear part of your eye that focuses light on the retina.
▸ ***noun, plural*** **lenses**

Lent (**lent**) ***noun*** The 40 days before Easter, not including Sundays, in the Christian Church's year.

len•til (**len**-tuhl) ***noun*** The flat, round seed of a plant related to beans and peas. Lentils are often cooked in soups.

leop•ard (**lep**-urd) ***noun*** A large wildcat with a spotted coat found in Africa, India, and eastern Asia.

le•o•tard (**lee**-uh-*tard*) ***noun*** A tight, one-piece garment worn for dancing or exercise.

lep•re•chaun (**lep**-ri-*kon*, **lep**-ri-*kawn*) ***noun*** A playful and annoying elf in Irish folklore.

lep•ro•sy (**lep**-ruh-see) ***noun*** A disease caused by a bacterium that attacks the skin, nerves, and muscles. Leprosy can cause a person to lose feeling or become paralyzed in the areas that are affected.

less (**less**)
1. ***adjective*** Smaller, or in smaller quantities. ▸ ***adverb*** **less**
2. ***adjective*** Made up of a smaller number than wanted, needed, or expected.
3. ***preposition*** Minus.

les•sen (**less**-uhn) ***verb*** To get smaller in size, strength, importance, etc. **Lessen** sounds like **lesson.** ▸ **lessening, lessened**

les•son (**less**-uhn) ***noun***
1. Some information or skill that you need to learn or study.
2. A set period in school when pupils are taught, or a session when a skill is taught.
3. An experience that teaches you something.
Lesson sounds like **lessen.**

let (**let**) ***verb***
1. To allow or permit something.
2. To allow to pass or go.
3. To rent out a house or an apartment.
4. If you are **let down** by someone, you are disappointed by the person because the person did not do something that he or she promised.
▸ ***verb*** **letting, let**

le•thal (**lee**-thuhl) ***adjective*** If something is **lethal,** it can kill, as in *a lethal poison.* ▸ ***adverb*** **lethally**

let's (**lets**) ***contraction*** A short form of *let us.*

let•ter (**let**-ur) ***noun***
1. A mark that is part of an alphabet. A letter stands for a sound or sounds and is used in writing, as in *the letter A.* ▸ ***verb*** **letter**
2. A message that you write to someone or that someone writes to you.

letter car•ri•er (**kar**-ee-ur) *See* **mail carrier.**

let•ter•ing (**let**-ur-ing) ***noun*** Letters that have been drawn, painted, or printed on something, such as a sign or a greeting card.

let•tuce (**let**-iss) ***noun*** A green, leafy salad vegetable.

leu•ke•mi•a (loo-**kee**-mee-uh) ***noun*** A serious disease in which the blood makes too many white cells.

lev•ee (**lev**-ee) ***noun***
1. A bank built up near a river to prevent flooding.
2. A place for boats or ships to land.
Levee sounds like **levy.**

lev•el (**lev**-uhl)
1. ***adjective*** Flat and smooth, as in *a level surface.*
2. ***adjective*** At the same height.
3. ***noun*** A floor or story of a structure.
4. ***noun*** A height, as in *sea level.*
5. ***noun*** A position or rank in a series.
6. ***verb*** To flatten.
7. ***verb*** If something **levels off,** it stops rising or falling and stays the same.
8. ***noun*** A tool used to show if a surface is flat.
▸ ***verb*** **leveling, leveled**

lev•er (**lev**-ur *or* **lee**-vur) ***noun***
1. A bar that you use to lift an object by placing one end under the object and pushing down on the other end. ▸ ***verb*** **lever**
2. A bar or a handle that you use to work or control a machine.

lev•i•tate (**lev**-i-tate) ***verb***
1. To rise in the air and float, in seeming defiance of gravity.
2. To cause to rise in the air and float.
▸ ***noun*** **levitation**

lev•y (**lev**-ee)
1. ***verb*** To impose or collect by lawful actions or by force. ▸ **levies, levying, levied**
2. ***noun*** A tax. ▸ ***noun, plural*** **levies**
Levy sounds like **levee.**

li•a•ble (**lye**-uh-buhl) ***adjective***
1. Likely.
2. If you are **liable** for something you have done, you are responsible for it by law. ▸ ***noun*** **liability**

li•ar (**lye**-ur) ***noun*** Someone who tells lies.

lib•er•al (**lib**-ur-uhl) ***adjective***
1. Generous, as in *a liberal donation.*
2. More than enough, as in *a liberal helping of food.*
3. Broad-minded and tolerant, especially of other people's ideas.
4. In favor of political change and reform.
▸ ***noun*** **liberal,** ***noun*** **liberalism**

lib•er•ate (**lib**-uh-*rate*) ***verb*** To set someone free. ▸ **liberating, liberated**
▸ ***noun*** **liberation,** ***noun*** **liberator**

lib•er•at•ed (**lib**-uh-*ray*-tid) ***adjective*** Someone who is **liberated** has been set free or feels free.

lib•er•ty (**lib**-ur-tee) ***noun*** Freedom.
▸ ***noun, plural*** **liberties**

li•brar•y (**lye**-brer-ee) ***noun*** A place where books, magazines, newspapers, records, and videos are kept for reading or borrowing. ▸ ***noun, plural*** **libraries,**
▸ ***noun*** **librarian**

lice (**lisse**) ***noun, plural*** Small insects without wings that live on animals or people. *Lice* is the plural form of **louse.**

li•cense (**lye**-suhnss)
1. ***noun*** A document giving permission for you to do something or own something, as in *a driver's license.*
2. ***verb*** If someone is **licensed** to do something, such as practice medicine, he or she has official permission to do it.
▸ **licensing, licensed**

li•chen (**lye**-ken) ***noun*** A flat, mosslike growth on rocks, trees, etc. Lichen is made up of a kind of algae and a fungus that grow together.

L

lick (**lik**) ***verb***
1. To pass your tongue over something. ▸ ***noun*** **lick**
2. To touch something lightly.
3. To defeat. ▸ ***noun*** **licking**
▸ ***verb*** **licking, licked**

lic•o•rice (**lik**-ur-ish *or* **lik**-ur-iss) ***noun***
1. A plant with a sweet, edible root that is used to flavor medicine and candy.
2. A candy flavored with licorice.

lid (**lid**) ***noun***
1. A top or a cover, as in *a lid on a jar.*
2. An eyelid.

lie (**lye**)
1. ***verb*** To get into or be in a flat, horizontal position.
2. ***verb*** To be or be placed somewhere.
3. ***verb*** To stay in a certain place or condition, as in *to lie hidden.*
4. ***noun*** A statement that is not true.
5. ***verb*** To say something that is not true. The past tense of this sense of the verb is *lied.*
Lie sounds like **lye.**
▸ ***verb*** **lying, lay** (**lay**), **lain** (**layn**) *or* **lying, lied**

lieu•ten•ant (loo-**ten**-uhnt) ***noun*** An officer of low rank in the armed forces.

life (**life**) ***noun***
1. The quality that separates people, animals, and plants from things such as rocks and machines that are not alive. Life is the quality that makes it possible for things to grow and reproduce.
2. Your **life** is the time from your birth until your death.
3. A living person.
4. Living things.
5. Energy, or a feeling of being alive.
▸ ***noun, plural*** **lives** (**livez**)

life•boat (**life**-*boht*) ***noun*** A strong boat usually carried on a larger ship that is used to save lives during shipwrecks or other emergencies.

life cycle ***noun*** The series of changes each living thing goes through from birth to death.

life•guard (**life**-*gard*) ***noun*** Someone who is trained to save swimmers in danger.

life jacket ***noun*** A jacket that will keep you afloat if you fall into the water.

life•less (**life**-liss) ***adjective***
1. Dead or without life, as in *a lifeless body* or *a lifeless planet.*
2. Boring or dull, as in *a lifeless party.*
▸ ***noun*** **lifelessness** ▸ ***adverb*** **lifelessly**

life•like (**life**-*like*) ***adjective*** Looking alive or real, as in *a lifelike drawing.*

life•long (**life**-*long*) ***adjective*** Lasting for a lifetime, as in *lifelong friends.*

life pre•serv•er (pri-**zurv**-er) ***noun*** A belt, vest, or ring that can be filled with air and used to keep a person afloat in water.

life span ***noun*** The period of time a person, an animal, a plant, or an object is expected to live or last. ▸ ***noun, plural*** **life spans**

life•style (**life**-*stile*) ***noun*** A way of living.

life•time (**life**-*time*) ***noun*** The period of time that a person lives or an object lasts.

lift (**lift**)
1. ***verb*** To raise something or someone.
2. ***verb*** To rise into the air. ▸ ***noun*** **lift**
3. ***verb*** To rise and disappear.
4. ***noun*** A ride, especially in a car.
5. ***noun*** A happy feeling.
▸ ***verb*** **lifting, lifted**

lift•off (**lift**-*of*) ***noun*** The movement of a rocket or spacecraft as it rises from its launching pad.

lig•a•ment (**lig**-uh-muhnt) ***noun*** A tough band of tissue that connects bones and holds some organs in place.

light (**lite**)
1. ***verb*** To start something burning. ▸ ***noun*** **light**
2. ***verb*** To make something bright and visible.

3. ***noun*** Brightness, as from the sun or a lamp.
4. ***adjective*** Pale in color, as in *light blue.*
5. ***noun*** An object that gives out light, such as a flashlight or lamp.
6. ***adjective*** Gentle, as in *a light rain.*
7. ***adjective*** Weighing little. ▸ ***noun*** **lightness**
8. ***adjective*** Moving easily or gracefully.
9. ***adjective*** Not serious, as in *a light novel.*
10. ***adjective*** Low in calories or fat, as in *a diet of light foods.*
11. If you **shed light** or **throw light on** something, you make it clear.
▸ ***verb*** **lighting, lighted** *or* **lit** (**lit**)
▸ ***adjective*** **lighter, lightest**

light•en (**lite**-uhn) ***verb***
1. To make brighter or lighter.
2. To make or become lighter in color.
3. To make or become lighter in weight or quantity.
4. To make or become more cheerful.
▸ ***verb*** **lightening, lightened**

light•heart•ed (**lite**-*hart*-id) ***adjective*** Funny and not very serious; cheerful.

light•house (**lite**-*houss*) ***noun*** A tower set in or near the sea. A lighthouse has a flashing light at the top that guides ships or warns them of danger.

light•ning (**lite**-ning) ***noun*** A flash of light in the sky when electricity moves between clouds or between a cloud and the ground.

lightning bug *See* **firefly**.

light pen ***noun*** A penlike device used to draw or to change or move information or images on a computer screen.

light•weight (**lite**-*wayt*) ***adjective***
1. Not heavy, as in *a lightweight coat.*
2. Not important or not serious.

light-year ***noun*** A unit for measuring distance in space. A light-year is the distance that light travels in one year.

lik•a•ble (**lye**-kuh-buhl) ***adjective*** Easy to like, as in *a likable person.*

like (**like**)
1. ***verb*** To enjoy or be pleased by something or someone. ▸ ***noun*** **liking**
2. ***verb*** To wish for or want something.
3. ***preposition*** Similar to.
4. ***preposition*** Typical of.
5. ***preposition*** Such as.
6. ***adjective*** Similar or equal, as in *a like amount.*
7. ***conjunction*** *(informal)* As if.
▸ ***verb*** **liking, liked**

like•ly (**like**-lee) ***adjective*** Probable.
▸ **likelier, likeliest** ▸ ***noun*** **likelihood**

like•wise (**like**-*wize*) ***adverb*** Also, or in the same way.

li•lac (**lye**-luhk *or* **lye**-lak) ***noun***
1. A shrub or tree with large clusters of fragrant purple, pink, or white flowers.
2. A pale purple color.

lil•y (**lil**-ee) ***noun*** Any of several plants that grow from bulbs and have flowers that are shaped like trumpets. ▸ ***noun, plural*** **lilies**

lily of the valley ***noun*** A plant of the lily family with broad leaves and a stem covered with small, white flowers shaped like bells. ▸ ***noun, plural*** **lilies of the valley**

li•ma bean (**lye**-muh **been**) ***noun*** A bean plant with flat, light green, edible seeds.

limb (**lim**) ***noun***
1. A part of a body used in moving or grasping. Arms, legs, wings, and flippers are limbs.
2. A branch of a tree.

lim•ber (**lim**-bur)
1. ***adjective*** Bending or moving easily.
2. ***verb*** When you **limber up,** you stretch your muscles before exercising.
▸ **limbering, limbered**

lime (**lime**) ***noun***
1. A small, green citrus fruit shaped like a lemon.
2. A white substance or powder that is made up of calcium and oxygen. Lime is used to make cement and as a fertilizer.

lime•light (**lime**-*lite*) ***noun*** If you are **in the limelight,** you are the center of attention.

L

lim•er•ick (**lim**-ur-ik) ***noun*** A funny poem made up of five lines that rhyme in a particular pattern.

lime•stone (**lime**-*stohn*) ***noun*** A hard rock used in building and in making lime and cement. Limestone is formed from the remains of shells or coral.

lim•it (**lim**-it)
1. ***noun*** A point beyond which someone or something cannot or should not go, as in *the speed limit.* ▸ ***adjective* limitless** ▸ ***adverb* limitlessly**
2. ***verb*** To keep within a certain area or amount. ▸ **limiting, limited** ▸ ***noun* limitation**
3. limits *noun, plural* Boundaries.

lim•it•ed (**lim**-uh-tid) ***adjective*** Small and unable to increase, as in *limited shelf space.*

limp (**limp**)
1. ***verb*** To walk in an uneven way, usually because of an injury. ▸ **limping, limped** ▸ ***noun* limp**
2. ***adjective*** Floppy and not firm, as in *a limp handshake.* ▸ **limper, limpest** ▸ ***adverb* limply**

Lin•coln's Birthday (**ling**-kinz) ***noun*** A holiday on February 12 when some states celebrate the birth of Abraham Lincoln (1809–1865), 16th president of the United States. The holiday is observed in some states on Presidents' Day, the third Monday in February.

line (**line**)
1. ***noun*** A long, thin mark made by a pen, pencil, or other tool.
2. ***noun*** A row of people or words.
3. ***noun*** A long, thin rope, string, or cord, as in *a fishing line.*
4. ***noun*** A boundary, as in *the state line.*
5. ***noun*** A short letter.
6. ***noun*** A wire or set of wires that connect points in a telephone or telegraph system.
7. ***noun*** A transportation system that runs on a specific route.
8. lines *noun, plural* Words that you speak in a play.
9. ***noun*** In mathematics, a set of points extending in a straight path without end in either direction.
10. ***verb*** To make a lining for something.
11. ***noun*** An attitude or approach to something.
12. ***verb*** To form a straight line.
▸ ***verb* lining, lined**

lin•e•ar (**lin**-ee-ur) ***adjective***
1. Using or having to do with lines, as in *a linear drawing.*
2. To do with length. Feet, miles, centimeters, and kilometers are linear measures.

lin•en (**lin**-uhn) ***noun***
1. Cloth made from the flax plant.
2. Household items, such as tablecloths and sheets, that were once made of linen.

lines•per•son (**linez**-*per*-suhn) ***noun*** An official who decides whether the ball has gone over the boundary line in games such as football, soccer, hockey, and tennis.

lin•ger (**ling**-gur) ***verb*** To stay or wait around. ▸ **lingering, lingered** ▸ ***adjective* lingering**

lin•gui•ne (ling-**gwee**-nee) ***noun*** Pasta cut into long, thin strips.

lin•guist (**ling**-gwist) ***noun*** Someone who studies languages or speaks them well.

lin•ing (**lye**-ning) ***noun*** The layer or coating that covers the inside of something, as in *the stomach lining* or *the lining of a coat.*

link (**lingk**)
1. ***noun*** One of the separate rings that make up a chain.
2. ***noun*** A connection between things or people.
3. ***noun*** A connection between one Web page or Web site and another.
4. ***verb*** To join objects, ideas, or people together. ▸ **linking, linked**

li•no•le•um (luh-**noh**-lee-uhm) ***noun*** A material with a strong, shiny surface and a canvas or cloth back. Linoleum is used as a floor covering, most commonly in kitchens.

lin•seed oil (**lin**-*seed*) ***noun*** Oil from the seed of certain flax plants used to make paints, varnishes, printing inks, patent leather, and linoleum.

lint (**lint**) ***noun*** Very small bits of thread or fluff from cloth.

li•on (**lye**-uhn) ***noun*** A large, light brown wildcat found in Africa and southern Asia. Male lions have manes.

li•on•ess (**lye**-uh-ness) ***noun*** A female lion.

lip (**lip**) ***noun***

1. Your **lips** are the fleshy edges of your mouth.

2. The edge or rim of a container or hole.

lip-read ***verb*** When deaf or hearing impaired people **lip-read,** they watch someone's lips while the person is talking in order to understand what the person is saying. ▸ **lip-reading, lip-read** ▸ ***noun*** **lipreading**

lip•stick (**lip**-*stik*) ***noun*** A small, crayonlike stick used to color the lips.

liq•ue•fy (**lik**-wuh-*fye*) ***verb*** To make something solid into a liquid. ▸ **liquefies, liquefying, liquefied**

liq•uid (**lik**-wid) ***noun*** A wet substance that you can pour. ▸ ***adjective*** **liquid**

liquid crystal display ***noun*** A way of showing numbers and letters on clocks, calculators, etc. Different parts of a grid of liquid crystals reflect light as electronic signals are sent to them. Abbreviated *LCD.*

liq•uor (**lik**-ur) ***noun*** A strong alcoholic drink, such as whiskey, gin, or vodka.

li•ra (**lihr**-uh) ***noun*** The main unit of money in Turkey and Malta. ▸ ***noun, plural*** **lire** (**lihr**-uh)

lisp (**lisp**) ***noun*** A way of talking in which you say "th" instead of "s." ▸ ***verb*** **lisp**

list (**list**)

1. ***noun*** A series of items, names, numbers, etc., often written in a particular order.

2. ***verb*** To put into a list.

3. ***verb*** When a ship **lists,** it leans to one side.

▸ ***verb*** **listing, listed**

lis•ten (**liss**-uhn) ***verb*** To pay attention so that you can hear something. ▸ **listening, listened** ▸ ***noun*** **listener**

li•ter (**lee**-tur) ***noun*** A unit of measurement in the metric system. A liter is the amount held by a rectangular container 10 centimeters by 10 centimeters by 10 centimeters. A liter is about 1.1 quarts.

lit•er•a•cy (**lit**-ur-uh-see) ***noun*** The ability to read and write.

lit•er•al•ly (**lit**-ur-uh-lee) ***adverb***

1. Word for word.

2. Actually.

3. If you **take** someone **literally,** you believe the person's exact words.

lit•er•ate (**lit**-ur-it) ***adjective***

1. Able to read and write.

2. Highly educated.

lit•er•a•ture (**lit**-ur-uh-chur) ***noun*** Written works that have lasting value or interest. Literature includes novels, plays, short stories, essays, and poems. ▸ ***adjective*** **literary**

lit•mus paper (**lit**-muhss) ***noun*** Paper soaked in a dye that changes from red to blue in a base solution and from blue to red in an acid solution.

lit•ter (**lit**-ur) ***noun***

1. Bits or scraps of paper or other garbage scattered around carelessly. ▸ ***verb*** **litter**

2. A group of kittens, puppies, baby pigs, etc., born at the same time to one mother.

3. A stretcher for carrying a sick or wounded person.

lit•tle (**lit**-uhl)

1. ***adjective*** Small in size or amount.

2. ***noun*** A small amount of something.

3. ***adjective*** Not much.

▸ ***adjective*** **littler** *or* **less, littlest** *or* **least**

L

live
1. **(liv)** ***verb*** To be alive.
2. **(live)** ***adjective*** Alive or living.
3. **(liv)** ***verb*** To have your home somewhere.
4. **(liv)** ***verb*** To support oneself.
5. **(live)** ***adjective*** Broadcast or televised as it is happening.
6. **(live)** ***adjective*** Burning, as in *live coals.*
7. **(live)** ***adjective*** If an electrical wire is **live,** it is carrying electricity that can give you a shock.
8. **(live)** ***adjective*** Unexploded, as in *a live bomb.*
9. If you **live and let live,** you are tolerant and able to accept or respect the behavior, customs, beliefs, or opinions of others.
10. If you can **live with** a difficult situation, you can put up with it or bear it.
▸ ***verb*** **living, lived**

live•li•hood (**live**-lee-*hud*) ***noun*** The way that you make money to support yourself.

live•ly (**live**-lee) ***adjective***
1. Active and full of life, as in *a lively dance step.*
2. Bright.
3. Exciting, as in *a lively debate.*
4. Creative, as in *a lively imagination.*
▸ ***adjective*** **livelier, liveliest** ▸ ***noun*** **liveliness**

liv•er (**liv**-ur) ***noun***
1. The organ in a human or animal body that cleans the blood. The liver also produces bile, which helps digest food.
2. A food prepared from the liver of a calf, pig, or other animal.

liv•er•y (**liv**-ur-ee) ***noun***
1. A uniform worn by servants or members of a profession.
2. A stable where horses are taken care of for a fee.

live•stock (**live**-*stok*) ***noun*** Animals raised on a farm or ranch, such as horses, sheep, and cows.

liv•id (**liv**-id) ***adjective***
1. Having a pale, usually white or somewhat blue color.
2. Very angry.
3. Purple or dark in color because of a bruise.

liv•ing (**liv**-ing)
1. ***adjective*** Alive now; not dead.
2. ***noun*** Money to live on.
3. ***adjective*** Still active or in use.

living room ***noun*** A lounge or sitting room in a house.

liz•ard (**liz**-urd) ***noun*** A reptile with a scaly body, four legs, and a long tail.

lla•ma (**lah**-muh) ***noun*** A large South American mammal raised for its wool and used to carry loads. The llama is related to the camel.

load (**lohd**)
1. ***noun*** Something that is carried, especially something heavy.
2. ***noun*** The amount carried at one time.
3. ***verb*** To put things onto or into something.
4. ***verb*** To put a bullet into a gun, film into a camera, or a program into a computer.
5. ***noun, plural*** *(informal)* If you have **loads** of something, you have lots of it.
▸ ***verb*** **loading, loaded**

loaf (**lohf**)
1. ***noun*** Bread baked in one piece.
2. ***noun*** Food in the shape of a loaf of bread, as in *meat loaf.*
3. ***verb*** To spend time doing little or nothing. ▸ **loafing, loafed**
▸ ***noun, plural*** **loaves** (**lohvz**)

loaf•er (**loh**-fur) ***noun***
1. Someone who is lazy and does not do much.
2. **Loafer** A trademark for a flat, casual shoe.

loam (**lohm**) ***noun*** Loose, rich soil made of sand, clay, and decayed leaves and plants. ▸ ***adjective*** **loamy**

loan (**lohn**)
1. ***noun*** The act of lending something to someone.

2. ***noun*** Something borrowed, especially money.
3. ***verb*** To lend something to someone.
▸ **loaning, loaned**
Loan sounds like **lone.**

loathe (**lohTH**) ***verb*** To hate or dislike someone or something. ▸ **loathing, loathed** ▸ ***noun*** **loathing**

loath•some (**lohTH**-suhm) ***adjective*** Very unpleasant or disgusting, as in *a loathsome disease.*

lob (**lob**) ***verb*** To throw or hit a ball high into the air. ▸ **lobbing, lobbed** ▸ ***noun*** **lob**

lob•by (**lob**-ee) ***noun***
1. A hall or room at the entrance to a building.
2. A group of people who try to persuade politicians to act or vote in a certain way. ▸ ***verb*** **lobby**
▸ ***noun, plural*** **lobbies**

lob•ster (**lob**-stur) ***noun*** A sea creature with a hard shell and five pairs of legs. The front pair are large, heavy claws. Lobsters can be eaten and turn red when they are cooked.

lo•cal (**loh**-kuhl)
1. ***adjective*** Near your house, or to do with the area where you live, as in *a local newspaper.* ▸ ***adverb*** **locally**
2. ***noun*** A train, subway, or bus that makes all the stops on a route.
▸ ***adjective*** **local**
3. ***adjective*** Affecting only a part of the body, as in *a local anesthetic.*

lo•cal•i•ty (loh-**kal**-uh-tee) ***noun*** An area or a neighborhood. ▸ ***noun, plural*** **localities**

lo•cate (**loh**-kate) ***verb***
1. To find out where something is.
2. To put or place somewhere.
3. To settle in a particular place.
▸ ***verb*** **locating, located**

lo•ca•tion (loh-**kay**-shuhn) ***noun***
1. The place or position where someone or something is.
2. If a movie or television program is made **on location,** it is filmed out of the studio.

lock (**lok**)
1. ***verb*** To fasten something with a key.
2. ***noun*** A part of a door, box, etc., that you can open and shut with a key.
3. ***verb*** To join or link together.
4. ***noun*** A part of a canal with gates at each end where boats are raised or lowered to different water levels.
5. ***noun*** A tuft of hair.
▸ ***verb*** **locking, locked**

lock•er (**lok**-ur) ***noun*** A small chest or closet that can be locked and where you can leave your belongings.

lock•et (**lok**-it) ***noun*** A piece of jewelry that women wear on a chain around their necks and that often contains a photograph, lock of hair, or other memento.

lock•jaw (**lok**-*jaw*) *See* **tetanus.**

lock•smith (**lok**-*smith*) ***noun*** Someone who makes and repairs locks and keys.

lo•co•mo•tion (*loh*-kuh-**moh**-shuhn) ***noun*** The act of moving from one place to another, or the ability to do so.

lo•co•mo•tive (*loh*-kuh-**moh**-tiv) ***noun*** An engine used to push or pull railroad cars.

lo•cust (**loh**-kuhst) ***noun*** A type of grasshopper that eats and destroys crops. Locusts fly in large swarms of up to two billion.

lode•stone (**lohd**-*stohn*) ***noun*** A stone with iron in it that acts as a magnet.

lodge (**loj**)
1. ***noun*** A small house, cottage, or cabin, often used for a short stay, as in *a ski lodge.*
2. ***verb*** If you **lodge** with someone, you stay in the person's house and usually pay him or her money.
3. ***verb*** If something **lodges** somewhere, it gets stuck there.
4. ***noun*** A beaver's home.
5. ***verb*** To bring to someone in authority, as in *to lodge a complaint.*
▸ ***verb*** **lodging, lodged**

lodg•er (**loj**-ur) ***noun*** Somebody who pays to live in a room in someone else's house. ▸ ***noun*** **lodgings**

L

loft (**loft**) ***noun***
1. A room or space under the roof of a building.
2. An upper story in a business building used for living or as an artist's studio.

loft•y (**lof**-tee) ***adjective***
1. Very tall and imposing, as in *a lofty skyscraper.*
2. Thinking of oneself as better than other people, as in *a lofty manner.*
▸ ***adjective*** **loftier, loftiest**

log (**log**)
1. ***noun*** A part of a tree that has been chopped down or has fallen down.
2. ***verb*** To cut down trees. ▸ ***noun*** **logger**
3. ***noun*** A written record kept by the captain of a ship.
4. ***noun*** A written record of something.
▸ ***verb*** **log**
5. ***verb*** When you **log on** or **log in** to a computer, you begin to use it; for example, by entering a name or a password.
6. ***verb*** When you have finished using a computer, you **log off** or **log out.**
▸ ***verb*** **logging, logged**

lo•gan•ber•ry (**loh**-guhn-*ber*-ee) ***noun*** A large, dark red berry that grows on a prickly shrub. The loganberry is a cross between the blackberry and the raspberry.

log•ic (**loj**-ik) ***noun***
1. Careful and correct reasoning or thinking.
2. The study of the rules for forming careful reasoning.
3. A particular way of thinking.
▸ ***adjective*** **logical** ▸ ***adverb*** **logically**

lo•go (**loh**-goh) ***noun*** A symbol that represents a particular company or organization.

loin (**loin**) ***noun***
1. In people or animals, the part of the sides and back of the body between the ribs and the hip.
2. A cut of meat from this part of an animal.

loi•ter (**loi**-ter) ***verb*** To stand around, usually because you have nothing to do.
▸ **loitering, loitered** ▸ ***noun*** **loiterer**

loll (**lol**) ***verb***
1. To sit or stand in a lazy or relaxed way.
2. To hang loosely.
▸ ***verb*** **lolling, lolled**

lol•li•pop (**lol**-ee-*pop*) ***noun*** A piece of hard candy on a stick.

lone (**lohn**) ***adjective***
1. Alone or solitary.
2. Only or single, as in *the lone survivor of a plane crash.*
Lone sounds like **loan.**

lone•ly (**lone**-lee) ***adjective***
1. If you are **lonely,** you are sad because you are by yourself. ▸ ***noun*** **loneliness**
2. Far from other people or things, as in *a lonely cabin.*
▸ ***adjective*** **lonelier, loneliest**

lone•some (**lohn**-suhm) ***adjective***
1. If you are **lonesome,** you are sad because you feel alone.
2. Not often visited or used by people, as in *a lonesome road.*

long (**lawng**)
1. ***adjective*** More than the average length, distance, time, etc., as in *a long walk.*
2. ***adjective*** From one end to the other.
3. ***adjective*** Taking a lot of time.
4. ***adverb*** For a long time.
5. ***adverb*** Throughout the length or duration of, as in *all week long.*
6. ***noun*** A long time.
7. ***verb*** If you **long for** something, you want it very much. ▸ **longing, longed**
▸ ***noun*** **longing** ▸ ***adjective*** **longer, longest**

long-distance ***adjective***
1. Covering or able to cover a long distance, as in *a long-distance runner.*
2. Connecting distant places, as in *a long-distance telephone call.*
▸ ***adverb*** **long-distance**

long•hand (**lawng**-*hand*) ***noun*** Ordinary writing in which you use a pencil or pen to write the words out in full, without abbreviations.

lon•gi•tude (**lon**-juh-*tood*) ***noun*** The position of a place, measured in degrees east or west of a line that runs through the Greenwich Observatory in London, England. On a map or globe, lines of longitude are drawn from the North Pole to the South Pole. ▸ ***adjective*** **longitudinal**

long-range ***adjective***
1. To do with the future, as in *long-range plans.*
2. Designed to travel a long way, as in *long-range missiles.*

long•ship (**long**-*ship*) ***noun*** A long, narrow ship with many oars and a sail, used especially by the Vikings.

long-term ***adjective*** To do with a long period of time, as in *long-term plans.*

long-wind•ed (**win**-did) ***adjective*** Unnecessarily long and boring, as in *a long-winded speech.*

loo•fah (**loo**-fuh) ***noun*** A rough sponge that you use to wash yourself with in the bath.

look (**luk**)
1. ***verb*** To use your eyes to see things.
2. ***verb*** To turn your eyes or attention.
3. ***noun*** A glance or expression on someone's face, as in *an angry look.*
4. ***verb*** To seem or to appear.
5. ***noun*** Appearance.
6. ***verb*** To face in a certain direction.
7. ***verb*** If you **look after** someone or something, you take care of him, her, or it.
8. ***verb*** If you **look down on** someone, you think that you are better than the person.
9. ***verb*** If you **look forward to** something, you wait for it eagerly.
10. ***verb*** If you **look** something **up,** you try to find out about it in a book or other reference.
11. ***verb*** If you **look up to** a person, you respect him or her.
▸ ***verb*** **looking, looked**

looking glass ***noun*** A mirror.

look•out (**luk**-*out*) ***noun*** Someone who keeps watch over something.

loom (**loom**)
1. ***verb*** To appear in a sudden or frightening way. ▸ **looming, loomed**
2. ***noun*** A machine used for weaving cloth.

loon (**loon**) ***noun*** A large diving bird with webbed feet, short legs, and a speckled back. The cry of the loon sounds like wild laughter.

loop (**loop**) ***noun*** A curve or circle in a piece of string, rope, etc. ▸ ***verb*** **loop**

loose (**looss**) ***adjective***
1. Not fastened or attached firmly.
2. Free.
3. Not fitting tightly, as in *loose pants.*
4. Not contained or bound together, as in *loose papers.*
5. Not placed or packed tightly together, as in *loose gravel* or *a loose weave.*
▸ ***adjective*** **looser, loosest** ▸ ***adverb*** **loosely**

loose-leaf ***adjective*** Holding or made to hold pages that have holes and are easily removed, as in *a loose-leaf notebook.*

loos•en (**loo**-suhn) ***verb***
1. To make something less tight.
2. To set free.
3. If you **loosen up,** you become more relaxed and often less shy.
▸ ***verb*** **loosening, loosened**

loot (**loot**)
1. ***verb*** To steal from stores or houses in a riot or a war. ▸ **looting, looted** ▸ ***noun*** **looter**
2. ***noun*** Stolen money or valuables.
Loot sounds like **lute.**

lop•sid•ed (**lop-sye**-did) ***adjective*** Unbalanced, with one side heavier, larger, or higher than the other.

L

lord (**lord**) ***noun***
1. A person who has great power or authority over others. In the Middle Ages, a lord lived in a castle and had many people under his rule. ▸ ***adjective*** **lordly**
2. Lord A name for God.
3. Lord In Great Britain, a title for a man of noble birth. Some British men earn this title as a reward for service to their country.

lose (**looz**) ***verb***
1. If you **lose** something, you do not have it anymore.
2. To fail to keep or hold on to something.
3. To be beaten or defeated in a game, argument, etc. ▸ ***noun*** **loser**
4. To waste.
▸ ***verb*** **losing, lost** (**lost**)

loss (**loss**) ***noun***
1. The losing of something, as in *the loss of a race* or *a memory loss.*
2. Something that is lost.
▸ ***noun, plural*** **losses**

lot (**lot**)
1. ***noun*** A large number or amount.
2. ***noun*** A piece of land, as in *a vacant lot.*
3. a lot *or* **lots** ***adverb*** Much.
4. ***noun*** A group of objects or people.
5. If you and other people **draw lots,** everyone in the group picks objects, such as straws, to decide who will do or get something.

lo•tion (**loh**-shuhn) ***noun*** A thin cream that is used to clean, soften, or heal the skin.

lot•ter•y (**lot**-ur-ee) ***noun*** A way of raising money in which people buy tickets with the aim of winning a prize.
▸ ***noun, plural*** **lotteries**

lo•tus (**loh**-tuhss) ***noun*** A water plant with pink, yellow, or white flowers.
▸ ***noun, plural*** **lotuses**

loud (**loud**) ***adjective***
1. Noisy, or producing a lot of sound.
▸ ***adverb*** **loud,** ***adverb*** **loudly**
2. Very bright and colorful, as in *a loud tie.*
▸ ***adjective*** **louder, loudest**

loud•speak•er (**loud**-*spee*-kur) ***noun*** A machine that turns electrical signals into sounds that are loud enough to be heard in a large room or area.

lounge (**lounj**)
1. ***verb*** To stand, sit, or lie in a lazy or relaxed way. ▸ **lounging, lounged**
2. ***noun*** A comfortable room where people can sit and relax.

louse (**louss**) ***noun*** A small, wingless insect that often lives on people or animals and sucks their blood. Lice can spread some diseases. ▸ ***noun, plural*** **lice**

lov•a•ble (**luhv**-uh-buhl) ***adjective*** Easy to love, as in *a lovable kitten.* ▸ ***adverb*** **lovably**

love (**luhv**)
1. ***verb*** To like someone or something very much. ▸ **loving, loved**
2. ***noun*** A strong liking for something, as in *a love of music.*
3. If you are **in love** with someone, you are passionately fond of him or her.

love•ly (**luhv**-lee) ***adjective***
1. If someone is **lovely,** the person is beautiful to look at or has a very attractive personality. ▸ ***noun*** **loveliness**
2. Enjoyable.
▸ ***adjective*** **lovelier, loveliest**

low (**loh**) ***adjective***
1. Not high or not tall, as in *a low branch.*
2. Below the usual level.
3. Below average, as in *a low grade.*
4. A **low** sound is quiet and soft or deep in pitch.
5. Not having enough.
6. If someone feels **low,** the person is sad or depressed.
▸ ***adjective*** **lower, lowest**

lower (**loh**-er)
1. ***verb*** To move or bring something down, as in *to lower a flag.*
2. ***adjective*** Not as high as something else.
3. ***verb*** To make or become less.
4. ***verb*** To make less loud.
▸ ***verb*** **lowering, lowered**

low•er•case (*loh*-er-**kasse**) ***adjective*** Using letters that are not capitals.
▸ ***noun*** **lowercase** ▸ ***verb*** **lowercase**

low tide ***noun*** The time at which the water level in an ocean, a gulf, or a bay is at its lowest point.

loy•al (**loi**-uhl) ***adjective*** Firm in supporting or faithful to one's country, family, friends, or beliefs. ▸ ***noun*** **loyalty** ▸ ***adverb*** **loyally**

LSD (**el ess dee**) ***noun*** A strong drug that causes people to see frightening, dreamlike things. LSD is illegal in many countries.

lu•bri•cate (**loo**-bruh-*kate*) ***verb*** To add a substance such as oil or grease to the parts of a machine so that it runs more smoothly. ▸ **lubricating, lubricated** ▸ ***noun*** **lubricant,** ***noun*** **lubrication**

luck (**luhk**) ***noun***
1. Something that happens to someone by chance.
2. Good fortune or success.

luck•y (**luhk**-ee) ***adjective***
1. Someone who is **lucky** is fortunate, and good things seem to happen to him or her.
2. Something that is **lucky** happens by chance and is fortunate, as in *a lucky guess.* ▸ ***adverb*** **luckily**
3. A **lucky** number, charm, etc., is one that you think will bring you good luck.
▸ ***adjective*** **luckier, luckiest**

lu•di•crous (**loo**-duh-kruhss) ***adjective*** Ridiculous or foolish. ▸ ***adverb*** **ludicrously**

lug (**luhg**) ***verb*** To carry something with great difficulty or effort. ▸ **lugging, lugged**

luge (**loozh**) ***noun*** A small sled used for racing. ▸ ***verb*** **luge** ▸ ***noun*** **luger**

lug•gage (**luhg**-ij) ***noun*** Suitcases and bags that you take with you when you travel.

luke•warm (**luke**-*worm*) ***adjective***
1. Slightly warm.
2. Not enthusiastic, as in *a lukewarm response.*

lull (**luhl**)
1. ***verb*** To make someone feel peaceful, safe, or sleepy. ▸ **lulling, lulled**
2. ***noun*** A short pause or break during a period of fighting or activity.

lul•la•by (**luhl**-uh-*bye*) ***noun*** A gentle song sung to send a baby to sleep.
▸ ***noun, plural*** **lullabies**

lum•ber (**luhm**-bur)
1. ***noun*** Wood or timber that has been sawed.
2. ***verb*** To move along heavily and clumsily. ▸ **lumbering, lumbered**

lum•ber•jack (**luhm**-bur-*jak*) ***noun*** Someone whose job is to cut down trees and get the logs to a sawmill.

lu•mi•nous (**loo**-muh-nuhss) ***adjective*** Shining or glowing, as in *a luminous campfire.* ▸ ***adverb*** **luminously**

lump (**luhmp**)
1. ***noun*** A shapeless piece of something, as in *a lump of clay.*
2. ***noun*** A swelling or a bump.
3. ***verb*** To put or bring together.
4. ***adjective*** Whole, as in *a lump sum.*
5. ***verb*** To form lumps.
▸ ***verb*** **lumping, lumped**

lu•nar (**loo**-nur) ***adjective*** To do with the moon, as in *a lunar eclipse.*

lunch (**luhnch**) ***noun*** The meal that you eat in the middle of the day. ▸ ***noun, plural*** **lunches** ▸ ***verb*** **lunch**

lung (**luhng**) ***noun*** One of a pair of baglike organs inside your chest that you use to breathe. The lungs supply the blood with oxygen and rid the blood of carbon dioxide.

L

lunge (**luhnj**) ***verb*** To move forward quickly and suddenly. ▸ **lunging, lunged** ▸ ***noun* lunge**

lu•pus (**loo**-puhss) ***noun*** A disease marked by severe skin sores, body aches, shortness of breath, and heart or kidney problems.

lurch (**lurch**)
1. ***verb*** To move in an unsteady, jerky way. ▸ **lurches, lurching, lurched** ▸ ***noun* lurch**
2. If someone **leaves you in the lurch,** you are left in a difficult situation, without any help.

lure (**loor**)
1. ***verb*** To attract and perhaps lead someone or some creature into a trap. ▸ **luring, lured**
2. ***noun*** An attraction.

lurk (**lurk**) ***verb*** To lie hidden, especially for an evil purpose. ▸ **lurking, lurked**

lus•cious (**luhsh**-uhss) ***adjective*** Delicious. ▸ ***adverb* lusciously**

lush (**luhsh**) ***adjective*** Growing thickly and healthily, as in *lush vegetation.* ▸ **lusher, lushest**

lust (**luhst**) ***verb*** If you **lust after** something, you want or desire it very strongly. ▸ **lusting, lusted** ▸ ***noun* lust** ▸ ***adjective* lustful**

lus•ter (**luhss**-tur) ***noun*** A bright shine or glow of soft reflected light.

lute (**loot**) ***noun*** A stringed instrument with a body shaped like a pear, played by plucking the strings. **Lute** sounds like **loot.**

lux•u•ry (**luhk**-shuh-ree *or* **luhg**-zhuh-ree) ***noun***
1. Something that you do not really need but that is enjoyable to have. ▸ ***adjective* luxury**
2. If you live **in luxury,** you are surrounded by expensive and beautiful things that make your life very comfortable and pleasant. ▸ ***adjective* luxurious**

lye (**lye**) ***noun*** A strong substance used in making soap and detergents. Lye is made by soaking wood ashes in water. **Lye** sounds like **lie.**

Lyme disease (**lime**) ***noun*** A bacterial disease transmitted by the bite of a tick. Symptoms include a round, red sore where the tick was attached, fever, chills, and weakness. If it is not treated early, it can lead to joint pain, arthritis, and heart and nerve problems.

lymph (**limf**) ***noun*** A clear liquid that carries nourishment and oxygen to body cells and carries away waste products.

lynx (**lingks**) ***noun*** A wildcat with long legs, a short tail, light brown or orange fur, and tufts of hair on its ears. ▸ ***noun, plural* lynx** *or* **lynxes**

lyre (**lire**) ***noun*** A small, stringed, harplike instrument played mostly in ancient Egypt, Israel, and Greece.

lyr•ic (**lihr**-ik)
1. **lyrics *noun, plural*** The words of a song.
2. ***noun*** A short poem that expresses strong feelings, especially love.

lyr•i•cal (**lihr**-uh-kuhl) ***adjective***
1. Expressing a strong, personal emotion.
2. Like a song, or fit for singing, as in *the lyrical sounds of a nightingale.*

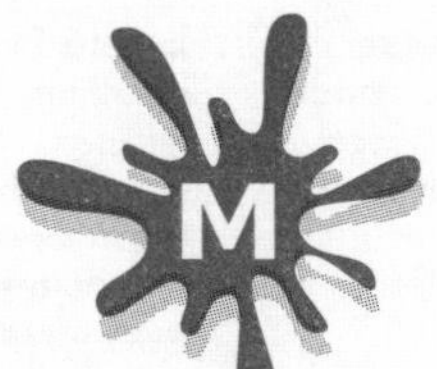

ma'am (**mam**) ***noun*** *(informal)* Short for **madam**.

ma•ca•bre (muh-**kahb** *or* muh-**kah**-bruh) ***adjective*** Gruesome and frightening.

mac•a•ro•ni (mak-uh-**roh**-nee) ***noun*** A food made from dough, usually in the shape of short, hollow tubes.

Mach (**mahk**) ***noun*** A unit for measuring an aircraft's speed. Mach 1 is the speed of sound, 762 miles per hour at sea level.

ma•chet•e (muh-**shet**-ee) ***noun*** A long, heavy knife with a broad blade, used as a tool and weapon.

ma•chine (muh-**sheen**) ***noun***
1. A piece of equipment made up of moving parts that is used to do a job.
2. A simple device that makes it easier to move something. Levers, screws, and pulleys are simple **machines**.
3. machine gun A gun that can fire bullets very quickly without needing to be reloaded.

ma•chin•er•y (muh-**shee**-nuh-ree) ***noun*** A group of machines, or the parts of a machine.

ma•chin•ist (muh-**shee**-nist) ***noun*** A person who is skilled in running machines that make tools and parts.

mack•er•el (**mak**-uh-ruhl) ***noun*** A shiny, dark blue saltwater fish that can be eaten. ▸ ***noun, plural*** **mackerel** *or* **mackerels**

mad (**mad**) ***adjective***
1. Insane. ▸ ***noun*** **madness**
2. Very angry.
3. Very foolish, as in *a mad romance.*
4. Having the disease rabies, as in *a mad dog.*
5. *(informal)* If you are **mad about** someone, you like the person very much.
▸ ***adjective*** **madder, maddest**
▸ ***adverb*** **madly**

mad•am (**mad**-uhm) ***noun*** A formal title for a woman, used in speaking and writing.

mag•a•zine (**mag**-uh-zeen) ***noun***
1. A publication that contains news, articles, photographs, advertisements, etc. Most magazines are issued on a regular basis, such as weekly or monthly, throughout the year.
2. A room or building for storing ammunition or weapons.
3. The part of a gun that holds the bullets.

mag•got (**mag**-uht) ***noun*** The larva of certain flies. Maggots are found in decaying animal matter.

Ma•gi (**may**-*jye*) ***noun, plural*** In the New Testament, the three wise kings who visited the baby Jesus, bringing gifts.

mag•ic (**maj**-ik) ***noun***
1. The power that some people believe exists to make impossible things happen by using charms or spells. ▸ ***adjective*** **magical** ▸ ***adverb*** **magically**
2. Clever tricks done to entertain people.
▸ ***adjective*** **magic** ▸ ***noun*** **magician** (muh-**jish**-uhn)

mag•is•trate (**maj**-uh-strate) ***noun***
1. A government official who has the power to enforce the law.
2. A judge who has limited power, such as a justice of the peace.

mag•lev (**mag**-lev) ***noun*** A short form of *magnetic levitation,* a system of high-speed train transportation in which the train uses powerful magnets to float above its track.

M

mag•ma (**mag**-muh) ***noun*** Melted rock found beneath the earth's surface. Magma flows as lava out of volcanoes and becomes igneous rock when it cools. *See* **volcano.**

mag•ne•si•um (mag-**nee**-zee-uhm) ***noun*** A light, silver-white metal that burns with a dazzling white light. It is often used in making fireworks and is also combined with other metals to make alloys.

mag•net (**mag**-nit) ***noun*** A piece of metal that attracts iron or steel. Magnets have two ends or poles, a north pole and a south pole. ▸ ***noun*** **magnetism** ▸ ***adjective*** **magnetic**

magnetic field ***noun*** The area around a magnet or electric coil that has the power to attract other metals, usually iron or steel.

magnetic pole ***noun***
1. Either of the two points of a magnet where its magnetic force seems to be strongest.
2. Either of the two points of the earth's surface where the earth's magnetic pull is strongest. One of these points is near the North Pole; the other is near the South Pole.

magnetic tape ***noun*** A thin ribbon of plastic coated with a magnetic material on which sound, television images, and other information can be stored.

mag•net•ize (**mag**-nuh-tize) ***verb*** To make a piece of material magnetic, either by exposing it to an electric coil or by attaching a magnet to it.
▸ **magnetizing, magnetized** ▸ ***noun*** **magnetization**

mag•nif•i•cent (mag-**nif**-i-sent) ***adjective*** Very impressive or beautiful.
▸ ***adverb*** **magnificently**

mag•ni•fy (**mag**-nuh-fye)
1. ***verb*** To make something appear larger so that it can be seen more easily.
▸ ***noun*** **magnification** ▸ ***adjective*** **magnified**
2. ***verb*** To make something seem greater or more important than it really is.
3. magnifying glass *noun* A glass lens that makes things look bigger.
▸ ***verb*** **magnifies, magnifying, magnified**

mag•ni•tude (**mag**-nuh-tood) ***noun*** The size or importance of something.

mag•no•li•a (mag-**nohl**-yuh) ***noun*** A tree or tall shrub that has large, fragrant, white, pink, purple, or yellow flowers.

mag•pie (**mag**-*pye*) ***noun*** A noisy, black and white bird with a large beak and long tail feathers. Magpies often collect shiny objects. They are related to crows.

ma•hog•a•ny (muh-**hog**-uh-nee) ***noun***
1. A tropical tree with hard, dark, reddish-brown wood that is used for making furniture.
2. The wood from this tree.
3. A dark, reddish brown color.

maid (**mayd**) ***noun***
1. A female servant who is paid to do housework.
2. A young, unmarried woman.
3. maid of honor An unmarried bridesmaid who is given special honor at a wedding.

maid•en (**mayd**-uhn)
1. ***noun*** A young, unmarried woman.
2. ***adjective*** A **maiden** voyage or flight is the first one made by a particular ship or plane.

maiden name ***noun*** The surname that a married woman used before she was married. Some women continue to use their maiden names after they marry, and some use their husbands' names instead.

mail (**mayl**) ***noun***
1. Letters, cards, and packages sent through a post office. ▸ ***verb*** **mail**
2. Armor made by joining together small metal rings.

3. If you buy something by **mail order,** you order it and pay for it and then the item is sent to you.
Mail sounds like **male.**

mail•box (**mayl**-*boks*) ***noun***
1. A box in which letters are put so that they can be picked up by a mail carrier.
2. A private box for letters and packages delivered to a home or business.

mail car•ri•er (**ka**-ree-ur) ***noun*** A person who delivers the mail to a house or office or picks it up from mailboxes. Also called a **letter carrier.**

mail•man (**mayl**-*man*) ***noun*** A mail carrier. ▸ ***noun, plural*** **mailmen**

maim (**maym**) ***verb*** To injure someone so badly that part of the person's body is damaged for life. ▸ **maiming, maimed**

main (**mayn**)
1. ***adjective*** Largest, or most important, as in *the main reason.*
2. ***noun*** A large pipe or wire that supplies water, gas, or electricity to a building.
Main sounds like **mane.**

main•frame (**mayn**-*fraym*) ***noun*** A large and very powerful computer.

main•land (**mayn**-luhnd) ***noun*** The chief or largest landmass of a country, territory, or continent, as opposed to its islands or peninsulas.

main•ly (**mayn**-lee) ***adverb*** For the most part.

main•stay (**mayn**-*stay*) ***noun***
1. A heavy rope or cable that supports or steadies the mast of a sailing ship.
2. Something or someone who acts as the chief support of something.

main•stream (**mayn**-*streem*)
1. ***noun*** The most common direction or trend of a movement.
2. ***verb*** To place a child with disabilities in a regular classroom.
▸ **mainstreaming, mainstreamed**

main•tain (mayn-**tayn**) ***verb***
1. To keep a machine or building in good condition.
2. To continue to say that something is so.
3. To continue something and not let it come to an end.
4. To give money to support somebody, as in *to maintain a family.*
▸ ***verb*** **maintaining, maintained**
▸ ***noun*** **maintenance** (**mayn**-tuh-nuhnss)

maize (**mayz**) ***noun*** Corn. **Maize** sounds like **maze.**

ma•jes•tic (muh-**jess**-tik) ***adjective***
1. Having great dignity; royal.
2. Having great power and beauty.
▸ ***adverb*** **majestically**

maj•es•ty (**maj**-uh-stee) ***noun***
1. Greatness and dignity.
2. The highest power or authority, as in *the majesty of the law.*
3. The formal title for a king or a queen is *His Majesty* or *Her Majesty.*

ma•jor (**may**-jur)
1. ***adjective*** Larger, greater, or more important.
2. ***noun*** An officer in the army and other branches of the armed forces who ranks above a captain.
3. ***adjective*** A **major** scale in music has a semitone between the third and fourth and the seventh and eighth notes.
4. ***noun*** The main subject studied at a college or university.

ma•jor•ette (*may*-jur-**et**) ***noun*** A girl or woman who leads a band or twirls a baton in a parade.

ma•jor•i•ty (muh-**jor**-uh-tee) ***noun***
1. More than half of a group of people or things.
2. The number of votes by which someone wins an election.
3. When someone reaches his or her **majority,** the person becomes an adult by law.
▸ ***noun, plural*** **majorities**

M

make (**make**)
1. ***verb*** To build or produce something.
2. ***verb*** To do something.
3. ***verb*** To cause something to happen.
4. ***verb*** To add up to.
5. ***verb*** To earn.
6. ***noun*** A particular brand or type of product.
7. ***verb*** To turn out to be.
8. ***verb*** To cause to become.
9. ***verb*** To win a place or spot on a team.
10. ***verb*** To **make believe** is to pretend or imagine.
11. ***verb*** If you can **make** something **out,** you can see it, but just barely.
12. ***verb*** If you **make up** with someone, you go back to being friends after a quarrel.
13. ***verb*** If you **make up** a test, you take it later because you could not take it on time.
▸ ***verb*** **making, made** (**made**)

make-believe
1. ***noun*** Playful pretense or imagination.
2. ***adjective*** Imaginary, or not real.

make•shift (**make**-*shift*) ***adjective*** A **makeshift** object is made from whatever is available and is only meant to be used for a short time.

make•up (**make**-*uhp*) ***noun***
1. Lipstick, powder, eyeshadow, and other cosmetics.
2. The way something is put together.
3. Personality.

ma•lar•i•a (muh-**lair**-ee-uh) ***noun*** A serious tropical disease that people get from mosquito bites. Symptoms include chills, fever, and sweating.

male (**male**) ***noun*** A person or animal of the sex that can father young. **Male** sounds like **mail.** ▸ ***adjective*** **male**

mal•ice (**mal**-iss) ***noun*** A desire or intent to hurt someone; spite.

ma•li•cious (muh-**lish**-uhss) ***adjective*** Showing or done from malice, as in *malicious gossip.* ▸ ***adverb*** **maliciously**

ma•lign (muh-**line**) ***verb*** To say mean, untrue things about someone.
▸ **maligning, maligned**

ma•lig•nan•cy (muh-**lig**-nuhn-see) ***noun*** A malignant tumor. ▸ ***noun, plural*** **malignancies**

ma•lig•nant (muh-**lig**-nuhnt) ***adjective***
1. A **malignant** growth or disease is dangerous because it tends to spread and eventually causes death.
2. Nasty and evil. ▸ ***adverb*** **malignantly**

mall (**mawl**) ***noun***
1. A large, enclosed shopping center.
2. A shaded, public walk.
Mall sounds like **maul.**

mal•lard (**mal**-urd) ***noun*** A common wild duck of North America, Europe, and northern Asia. The male has a green head, a white band around the neck, and a dark body.

mal•le•a•ble (**mal**-ee-uh-buhl) ***adjective*** If a substance is **malleable,** it is easily molded into a different shape.

mal•let (**mal**-it) ***noun***
1. A hammer with a short handle and a heavy wooden head.
2. A wooden club with a long handle, used to hit the ball in croquet or polo.

mal•nu•tri•tion (*mal*-noo-**trish**-uhn) ***noun*** A harmful condition caused by not having enough food or by eating the wrong kinds of food.

malt (**mawlt**) ***noun*** Grain, usually barley, that has been soaked in warm water, allowed to sprout, and then dried.
▸ ***adjective*** **malted**

malted milk ***noun*** A sweetened drink of milk, malted flavoring, and sometimes ice cream.

mal•treat (mal-**treet**) ***verb*** To treat a person or an animal cruelly.
▸ **maltreating, maltreated** ▸ ***noun*** **maltreatment**

mam•mal (**mam**-uhl) ***noun*** A warm-blooded animal with a backbone. Female mammals produce milk to feed their young.

mam•moth (**mam**-uhth)
1. ***noun*** An extinct animal like a large elephant, with long, curved tusks and shaggy hair. Mammoths lived during the Ice Age.
2. ***adjective*** Huge.

man (**man**)
1. ***noun*** An adult male human being.
▸ ***noun* manhood, *noun* manliness**
▸ ***adjective* manly**
2. ***noun*** The human race.
3. ***noun*** A piece used in games such as chess and checkers.
4. ***verb*** To be in charge of a piece of equipment. ▸ **manning, manned**
▸ ***noun, plural* men (men)**

man•age (**man**-ij) ***verb***
1. To be in charge of a store, business, etc. ▸ ***noun* management**
2. To be able to do something that is difficult or awkward.
▸ ***verb* managing, managed**

man•a•ger (**man**-uh-jur) ***noun*** Someone in charge of a store, business, etc., or in charge of a group of people at work. ▸ ***adjective* managerial** (man-uh-**jeer**-ee-uhl)

man•a•tee (**man**-uh-tee) ***noun*** A large mammal with flippers and a flat tail that lives in warm waters and eats plants.

man•da•rin (**man**-dur-in) ***noun***
1. A high official in ancient China.
2. **Mandarin** The official language of the People's Republic of China.
3. A small, sweet orange with a thin rind that is easy to peel. It is also called a **mandarin orange.**

man•date (**man**-date) ***noun***
1. Instructions or support given by voters to their government representatives through the votes cast in an election.
2. An order given by an authority, as in *the king's mandate.*
▸ ***verb* mandate**

man•do•lin (**man**-duh-lin *or man*-duh-**lin**) ***noun*** A small, guitarlike instrument with metal strings and a body that is shaped like a pear.

mane (**mayn**) ***noun*** The long, thick hair on the head and neck of a male lion or a horse. **Mane** sounds like **main.**

ma•neu•ver (muh-**noo**-ver)
1. ***noun*** A difficult movement that needs planning and skill.
2. ***verb*** To move something carefully into a particular position. ▸ **maneuvering, maneuvered**
3. When an army is **on maneuvers,** a large number of soldiers, tanks, etc., are moved around an area in order to train for battle.

man•ger (**mayn**-jur) ***noun*** A large, open box that holds food for cattle and horses.

man•gle (**mang**-guhl) ***verb*** To spoil or destroy something by cutting, tearing, or crushing it. ▸ **mangling, mangled**
▸ ***adjective* mangled**

man•go (**mang**-goh) ***noun*** A yellow-red tropical fruit with a sweet taste. ▸ ***noun, plural* mangoes** *or* **mangos**

man•hole (**man**-*hohl*) ***noun*** A covered hole in the street that leads to sewers or underground pipes or wires.

man•hood (**man**-hud) ***noun***
1. The time or state of being an adult man.
2. Men as a group.

ma•ni•ac (**may**-nee-ak) ***noun***
1. Someone who is insane or acts in a wild or violent manner. ▸ ***adjective* maniacal** (muh-**nye**-uh-kuhl)
2. A person who is very enthusiastic about something, as in *a sports maniac.*

man•i•cure (**man**-uh-kyur) ***noun*** The cleaning, shaping, and polishing of the fingernails. ▸ ***verb* manicure**

ma•nip•u•late (muh-**nip**-yuh-late) ***verb***
1. To influence people in a clever way so that they do what you want them to do.
▸ ***adjective* manipulative**
2. To use your hands in a skillful way.
▸ ***verb* manipulating, manipulated**
▸ ***noun* manipulation**

M

man•kind (**man**-*kinde*) ***noun*** The human race, or human beings as a group.

man-made ***adjective*** Something that is **man-made** is made by people and not produced naturally.

man•ner (**man**-ur) ***noun***
1. The way in which you do something.
2. The way that someone behaves.
3. Kind.
4. manners *noun, plural* Polite behavior.
Manner sounds like **manor.**

man•or (**man**-ur) ***noun***
1. A lord's estate in the Middle Ages.
2. A mansion.
Manor sounds like **manner.**

man•sion (**man**-shuhn) ***noun*** A very large and grand house.

man•slaught•er (**man**-*slaw*-tur) ***noun*** The crime of killing someone without intending to do so.

man•tel (**man**-tuhl) ***noun*** A wooden or stone shelf above a fireplace. **Mantel** sounds like **mantle.**

man•tle (**man**-tuhl) ***noun***
1. A loose cloak without sleeves.
2. Something that covers or hides like a mantle.
3. The part of the earth between the crust and the core. The mantle is about 1,800 miles thick.
Mantle sounds like **mantel.**

man•u•al (**man**-yoo-uhl)
1. *adjective* Operated or done by hand rather than automatically, as in *a manual typewriter.* ▸ ***adverb* manually**
2. *noun* A book of instructions that tells you how to do something.
3. *adjective* If you do **manual** labor, you work hard physically.

man•u•fac•ture (man-yuh-**fak**-chur) ***verb***
1. To make something, often with machines. ▸ ***noun* manufacturing, *noun* manufacturer**
2. To invent something or to make something up.
▸ ***verb* manufacturing, manufactured**

ma•nure (muh-**noo**-ur) ***noun*** Animal waste put on land to improve the quality of the soil and to make crops grow better.

man•u•script (**man**-yuh-skript) ***noun***
1. The original handwritten or typed pages of a book, poem, piece of music, etc., before it is printed.
2. A handwritten document, as in *a medieval manuscript.*

man•y (**men**-ee)
1. *adjective* Numerous. ▸ **more, most**
2. *pronoun* A large number of people or things.
3. *noun* A large number.
▸ ***noun* more, *noun* most**

map (**map**)
1. *noun* A detailed plan of an area, showing features such as towns, roads, rivers, mountains, etc.
2. *verb* To make a map of a place.
3. *verb* If you **map** something **out,** you plan it.
▸ ***verb* mapping, mapped**

ma•ple (**may**-puhl) ***noun*** A tree with large leaves having five points. Maples are grown for their hard wood and their sap, which is used to make syrup and sugar.

mar•a•thon (**mar**-uh-thon) ***noun***
1. A race for runners over a distance of 26 miles and 385 yards.
2. Any long race or competition that tests the participants' ability to hold up under pain, stress, and fatigue.

mar•ble (**mar**-buhl) ***noun***
1. A hard stone with colored patterns in it, used for buildings and sculptures.
2. A small, hard glass ball used in a children's game.
3. marbles A children's game in which these balls are rolled along the ground.

march (**march**)
1. *verb* When soldiers **march,** they walk together with uniform steps. ▸ ***noun* march**
2. *noun* A piece of music with a strong beat to which you can march.

3. ***verb*** To walk somewhere quickly and in a determined way.
4. ***noun*** A large group of people walking together in order to protest or express their opinion about something. ▸ ***verb*** **march**
▸ ***noun, plural*** **marches** ▸ ***verb*** **marches, marching, marched**

March ***noun*** The third month on the calendar, after February and before April. March has 31 days.

mare (**mair**) ***noun*** The female of certain animals, such as the horse, donkey, and zebra.

mar•ga•rine (**mar**-juh-ruhn) ***noun*** A yellow spread similar to butter that is usually made from vegetable oil.

mar•gin (**mar**-juhn) ***noun***
1. The long, blank space that runs down the edge of a page.
2. An amount, especially of time, in addition to what is needed.
3. A difference between two amounts, especially a small one.
▸ ***adjective*** **marginal**

mar•i•gold (**ma**-ruh-*gohld*) ***noun*** A garden plant that has orange, yellow, or red flowers.

mar•i•juan•a (ma-ruh-**wah**-nuh) ***noun*** A drug made from the dried leaves and flowering tops of the hemp plant. Marijuana is illegal in the United States and many other countries.

ma•ri•na (muh-**ree**-nuh) ***noun*** A small harbor where boats, yachts, etc., are kept.

mar•i•na•ra (*mair*-uh-**nair**-uh) ***adjective*** Made with tomatoes, as in *marinara sauce.* Marinara comes from an Italian word that means "in sailor style."
▸ ***noun*** **marinara**

ma•rine (muh-**reen**)
1. ***adjective*** To do with the sea, as in *marine life.*
2. ***adjective*** To do with ships or navigation.
3. ***noun*** A soldier trained to fight on land and water.
4. **Marine** ***noun*** A member of the U.S. Marine Corps.

Marine Corps ***noun*** One of the armed forces of the United States. Marines are trained to fight on both land and water.

mar•i•o•nette (ma-ree-uh-**net**) ***noun*** A puppet that is moved by pulling strings or wires attached to various parts of its body. A marionette is usually made of wood.

mar•i•time (**ma**-ruh-*time*) ***adjective***
1. To do with the sea, ships, or navigation.
2. Of, relating to, or near the sea.

mark (**mark**)
1. ***noun*** A small scratch or stain on something.
2. ***noun*** A written sign or symbol, as in *a question mark.*
3. ***noun*** A line or an object that shows position.
4. ***noun*** A number or letter put on a piece of work to show how good it is.
5. ***verb*** To show something clearly.
▸ **marking, marked**
6. ***noun*** Something that shows clearly.
7. If you **make your mark,** you become successful.
▸ ***verb*** **mark**

mar•ket (**mar**-kit) ***noun***
1. A place where people buy and sell food or goods. ▸ ***verb*** **market**
2. A store where specific kinds of goods are sold, as in *a fish market.*
3. A demand for something.
4. If a product is **on the market,** it is available and can be bought.

market research ***noun*** When people or companies do **market research,** they collect information about the products that customers buy and what customers want and need.

marks•man (**marks**-muhn) ***noun*** Someone who is expert at shooting a gun. ▸ ***noun, plural*** **marksmen**

mar•ma•lade (**mar**-muh-lade) ***noun*** A jam made from oranges or other citrus fruit.

M

M

ma•roon (muh-**roon**)
1. ***noun*** A dark reddish brown color.
▸ ***adjective* maroon**
2. ***verb*** If someone is **marooned** on a desert island, the person is stuck there and cannot leave. ▸ **marooning, marooned**

mar•quee (mar-**kee**) ***noun*** A large awning or rooflike structure over a theater entrance. It displays the name of the current play or movie.

mar•riage (**ma**-rij) ***noun***
1. The state of being married, or the relationship between husband and wife.
2. The wedding ceremony.

mar•ried (**ma**-reed) ***adjective*** Someone who is **married** has a spouse.

mar•row (**ma**-roh) ***noun*** The soft substance inside bones that is used to make blood cells.

mar•ry (**ma**-ree) ***verb***
1. When people **marry,** they go through a ceremony in which they promise to spend their lives together.
2. To perform a marriage ceremony.
▸ ***verb* marries, marrying, married**

Mars (**marz**) ***noun*** The fourth planet in distance from the sun. Mars is the seventh-largest planet in our solar system. It has two moons.

marsh (**marsh**) ***noun*** An area of wet, low land. ▸ ***adjective* marshy**

marshal (**mar**-shuhl)
1. ***noun*** An officer of a federal court who has duties similar to those of a sheriff.
2. ***noun*** An official who investigates suspicious fires.
3. ***noun*** A person who helps organize a public event such as a parade.
4. ***verb*** To gather together a group of people or things and arrange them in a sensible order. ▸ **marshaling, marshaled**
Marshal sounds like **martial.**

marsh•mal•low (**marsh**-*mal*-loh) ***noun*** A soft, spongy kind of white candy.

mar•su•pi•al (mar-**soo**-pee-uhl) ***noun*** The name for a large group of animals that includes the kangaroo, the koala, and the opossum. Female marsupials carry their young in pouches at their abdomens.

mar•tial (**mar**-shuhl)
1. ***adjective*** To do with war or soldiers.
2. martial art *noun* A style of fighting or self-defense that comes mostly from the Far East; for example, judo or karate.
3. martial law *noun* Rule by the army in time of war or disaster.
Martial sounds like **marshal.**

mar•tin (**mart**-uhn) ***noun*** A swallow with a forked tail and long wings.

Martin Lu•ther King Day (**looth**-ur) ***noun*** A national holiday celebrated on the third Monday of January to honor the birth of Dr. Martin Luther King, Jr., the African-American civil rights leader who was assassinated in 1968.

mar•tyr (**mar**-tur) ***noun*** Someone who is killed or made to suffer because of his or her beliefs. ▸ ***noun* martyrdom**

mar•vel (**mar**-vuhl) ***verb*** If you **marvel** at something, you are filled with surprise and wonder. ▸ **marveling, marveled**
▸ ***noun* marvel**

mar•vel•ous (**mar**-vuh-luhss) ***adjective***
1. Causing surprise, wonder, or amazement.
2. Very good or outstanding.
▸ ***adverb* marvelously**

mas•car•a (mass-**ka**-ruh) ***noun*** A substance put on eyelashes to color them and make them look thicker.

mas•cot (**mass**-kot) ***noun*** Something that is supposed to bring good luck, especially an animal kept by a sports team.

mas•cu•line (**mass**-kyuh-lin) ***adjective***
1. To do with men.
2. Someone who is **masculine** has qualities that are supposed to be typical of men. ▸ ***noun* masculinity**

mash (**mash**)
1. ***verb*** To crush food into a soft mixture.
▸ **mashes, mashing, mashed** ▸ ***noun* mash**
2. ***noun*** A mixture of crushed grain and

water that is fed to livestock and poultry.
▸ ***noun, plural* mashes**

mask (**mask**)
1. ***noun*** A covering worn over the face to hide, protect, or disguise it.
▸ ***adjective* masked**
2. ***verb*** To cover up or disguise something.
▸ **masking, masked** ▸ ***noun* mask**

ma•son (**may**-suhn) ***noun*** Someone who builds or works with stone, cement, or bricks.

ma•son•ry (**may**-suhn-ree) ***noun*** Something that is made of stone, cement, or bricks.

mas•quer•ade (*mass*-kuh-**rade**)
1. ***noun*** A party or event at which all the people dress up in costumes.
2. ***verb*** To dress up in order to disguise yourself at a party or other event.
3. ***verb*** To pretend to be something you are not. ▸ ***noun* masquerade**
▸ ***verb* masquerading, masqueraded**

mass (**mass**) ***noun***
1. A lump or pile of matter that has no particular shape, as in *a mass of snow.*
2. A large number of people or things together. ▸ ***verb* mass** ▸ ***adjective* mass**
3. In physics, the **mass** of an object is the amount of physical matter that it contains.
4. the masses *noun, plural* The ordinary people.

Mass *noun* The main religious service in the Roman Catholic Church and certain other churches.

mas•sa•cre (**mass**-uh-kur) ***noun*** The brutal killing of a very large number of people, often in battle. ▸ ***verb* massacre**

mas•sage (**muh**-sahzh) ***verb*** To rub someone's body with the fingers and hands in order to loosen the muscles or to help the person relax. ▸ **massaging, massaged** ▸ ***noun* massage**

mas•sive (**mass**-iv) ***adjective*** Large, heavy, and solid. ▸ ***adverb* massively**

mass media *noun, plural* Different forms of communication that reach a large number of people. Television, radio, and newspapers are all mass media.

mass production *noun* The method of making identical things in a factory. Items that are mass-produced are usually made in large quantities by people or machines on an assembly line.
▸ ***verb* mass-produce**

mass transit *noun* A system of subways, buses, and trains that carry people in large numbers into and around major cities.

mast (**mast**) ***noun*** A tall pole that stands on the deck of a boat or ship and supports its sails.

mas•ter (**mass**-tur)
1. ***noun*** A person with power, rule, or authority over another.
2. ***noun*** An expert.
3. ***verb*** If you **master** a subject or skill, you become very good at it.
4. ***verb*** If you **master** a fear, you overcome it.
5. ***noun*** A male teacher, especially in a private school.
6. ***adjective*** Most important or largest, as in *the master bedroom.*
▸ ***verb* mastering, mastered**

mas•ter•mind (**mass**-tur-*minde*) ***verb*** If you **mastermind** a course of action, you plan it and control the way that it is carried out. ▸ **masterminding, masterminded**

mas•ter•piece (**mass**-tur-*peess*) ***noun***
1. An outstanding piece of work, especially in the areas of art, literature, music, etc.
2. A person's finest achievement.

mat (**mat**) ***noun***
1. A thick pad of material used for covering a floor, wiping your feet, protecting a table, etc.
2. A large, thick floor pad used to protect wrestlers, gymnasts, and other athletes.
3. A thick, tangled mass, especially of hair. ▸ ***verb* mat**
Mat sounds like **matte.**

mat•a•dor (**mat**-uh-dor) ***noun*** A bullfighter.

M

M

match (**mach**)
1. ***noun*** A small, thin piece of wood or cardboard with a chemical tip that is struck to produce a flame.
2. ***noun*** Someone or something that is similar to or goes well with another.
3. ***verb*** To go well with.
4. ***noun*** Someone or something that is equal to another.
5. ***verb*** To equal.
6. ***noun*** A game or a sporting competition, as in *a tennis match.*
7. ***verb*** To put into competition.
▸ ***noun, plural*** **matches** ▸ ***verb*** **matches, matching, matched**

mate (**mate**)
1. ***noun*** One of a pair.
2. ***noun*** A husband or a wife.
3. ***noun*** The male or female partner of a pair of animals.
4. ***verb*** To join together for breeding.
▸ **mating, mated** ▸ ***noun*** **mating**
5. ***noun*** A ship's officer.
6. ***noun*** A friend.

ma•te•ri•al (muh-**tihr**-ee-uhl)
1. ***noun*** Cloth or fabric.
2. ***noun*** The substances from which something is made.
3. ***adjective*** Made from or having to do with matter, as in *the material world.*
4. ***adjective*** To do with the well-being of the body.

ma•te•ri•al•is•tic (muh-*tihr*-ee-uh-**liss**-tik) ***adjective*** People who are **materialistic** are overly concerned with money and possessions. ▸ ***noun*** **materialism**

ma•te•ri•al•ize (muh-**tihr**-ee-uh-*lize*) ***verb*** To appear, or to become real.
▸ **materializing, materialized**

ma•ter•nal (muh-**tur**-nuhl) ***adjective*** To do with being a mother, as in *maternal feelings.*

ma•ter•ni•ty (muh-**tur**-nuh-tee) ***noun***
1. Motherhood.
2. maternity leave Time that a woman is allowed away from her job to have a baby.
3. maternity ward The part of a hospital for women who have just had or are about to have a baby.

math (**math**) ***noun*** Short for **mathematics.**

math•e•ma•ti•cian (*math*-uh-muh-**tish**-uhn) ***noun*** A person who is very good at or specializes in mathematics.

math•e•mat•ics (math-uh-**mat**-iks) ***noun*** The study of numbers, quantities, shapes, and measurements and how they relate to each other. ▸ ***adjective*** **mathematical**

mat•i•nee (mat-uhn-**ay**) ***noun*** An afternoon performance of a play or showing of a movie.

mat•ri•mo•ny (**mat**-ruh-*moh*-nee) ***noun*** Marriage. ▸ ***adjective*** **matrimonial**

ma•trix (**may**-triks) ***noun*** In math, a **matrix** is an arrangement of numbers or other items in columns and rows. A chart showing the standings of major league baseball teams is a type of matrix.
▸ ***noun, plural*** **matrices** (**may**-tri-*seez*)

ma•tron (**may**-truhn) ***noun***
1. An older woman who is married or widowed.
2. A woman who has some authority in an institution.
3. matron of honor A married bridesmaid who is given special honor at a wedding.

matte (**mat**) ***adjective*** Not shiny, as in *a matte finish.* **Matte** sounds like **mat.**

mat•ter (**mat**-ur)
1. ***noun*** Anything that has weight and takes up space, as a solid, liquid, or gas.
2. ***noun*** Content, or material, as in *undigested matter.*
3. ***noun*** A subject of discussion, interest, or concern, as in *a legal matter* or *a business matter.*
4. ***noun*** Something that needs to be dealt with.
5. ***noun*** Written or printed material, as in *reading matter.*
6. ***verb*** If something **matters,** it is important. ▸ **mattering, mattered**

mat•tress (**mat**-riss) ***noun*** A thick pad made of strong cloth filled with soft material and often coiled springs. A mattress is used on or as a bed. ▸ ***noun, plural*** **mattresses**

ma•ture (muh-**chur** *or* muh-**tyur**) ***adjective***
1. Adult or fully grown.
2. Ripe, as in *mature fruit.*
3. Behaving in a sensible, adult way.
▸ ***adverb*** **maturely**
▸ ***noun*** **maturity** ▸ ***verb*** **mature**

maul (**mawl**) ***verb*** To handle someone or something in a rough and possibly damaging way. **Maul** sounds like **mall.**
▸ **mauling, mauled**

mau•so•le•um (maw-suh-**lee**-uhm *or* maw-zuh-**lee**-uhm) ***noun*** A large building that houses a tomb or tombs.

mauve (**mohv**) ***noun*** A light purple color. ▸ ***adjective*** **mauve**

max•i•mum (**mak**-suh-muhm) ***noun*** The greatest possible amount, or the upper limit. ▸ ***adjective*** **maximum**

may (**may**) ***verb*** A helping verb that is used in the following ways:
1. To say that something is possible or likely.
2. To ask or give permission.
3. To express hope or a wish.

May (**may**) ***noun*** The fifth month on the calendar, after April and before June. May has 31 days.

Ma•ya (**mye**-uh) ***noun*** A member of a group of American Indian tribes that live in southern Mexico and Central America. The Maya had a highly structured civilization that flourished until about A.D. 1000. They were conquered by the Spanish during the 16th century. ▸ ***noun, plural*** **Maya** *or* **Mayas** ▸ ***adjective*** **Mayan**

may•be (**may**-bee) ***adverb*** Perhaps.

May•day (**may**-*day*) ***noun*** **Mayday** is a word used all over the world to ask for help or rescue.

may•hem (**may**-hem) ***noun***
1. The crime of deliberately injuring someone seriously.
2. A situation of confusion or violent destruction.

may•on•naise (**may**-uh-naze *or* may-uh-**naze**) ***noun*** A salad dressing or creamy sauce made from egg yolks, oil, and vinegar or lemon juice.

may•or (**may**-ur) ***noun*** The leader of a town or city government.

maze (**mayz**) ***noun*** A complicated network of paths or lines, made as a puzzle to find your way through. **Maze** sounds like **maize.**

me (**mee**) ***pronoun*** The form of **I** used as a grammatical object.

mead•ow (**med**-oh) ***noun*** A field of grass, often used for animals to graze in.

mead•ow•lark (**med**-oh-*lark*) ***noun*** A North American songbird with a pointed bill and a yellow chest with a black crescent across it.

mea•ger (**mee**-gur) ***adjective*** Very little, or barely enough, as in *a meager meal of broth and toast.*

meal (**meel**) ***noun***
1. Food that is served and eaten, usually at a particular time of day. Breakfast, lunch, and dinner are meals.
2. Grain that has been ground.

mean (**meen**)
1. ***verb*** To try to express.
2. ***verb*** To intend to do something.
3. ***verb*** To be defined as.
4. ***verb*** To matter.
5. ***adjective*** Not kind, or not nice.
▸ ***noun*** **meanness**
6. ***noun*** In mathematics, an average.
7. ***adjective*** *(slang)* Good and skillful.
▸ ***verb*** **meaning, meant** ▸ ***adjective*** **meaner, meanest**

me•an•der (mee-**an**-dur) ***verb*** When a river **meanders,** it winds or turns, usually through a flat part of a valley.
▸ **meandering, meandered**

mean•ing (**mee**-ning) ***noun***
1. The idea behind something spoken or written.
2. The importance or significance of something.

M

mean•time (**meen**-*time*) ***noun*** The time in between.

mean•while (**meen**-*wile*) ***adverb***
1. In or during the time between.
2. At the same time.

mea•sles (**mee**-zuhlz) ***noun, plural*** An infectious disease causing fever and a rash. Measles is caused by a virus. The word measles can be used with a singular or a plural verb.

mea•sly (**mee**-zlee) ***adjective*** *(informal)* Inadequate, or not very generous, as in *a measly amount of soup.* ▸ **measlier, measliest**

meas•ure (**mezh**-ur)
1. ***verb*** To find out the size, capacity, weight, etc., of something. ▸ ***noun*** **measurement**
2. ***verb*** To have as a measurement.
3. ***noun*** A unit of measurement.
4. ***noun*** An action intended to achieve a result.
5. ***noun*** An amount or an extent, as in *a measure of truthfulness.*
6. ***noun*** A bar of music.
▸ ***verb*** **measuring, measured**

meat (**meet**) ***noun***
1. The flesh of an animal that can be eaten.
2. The edible part of a fruit or nut.
3. The most important part of something, as in *the meat of a book.*
Meat sounds like **meet.**
▸ ***adjective*** **meaty**

me•chan•ic (muh-**kan**-ik) ***noun*** Someone who is skilled at operating or repairing machinery.

me•chan•i•cal (muh-**kan**-uh-kuhl) ***adjective***
1. To do with machines or tools, as in *mechanical skill.*
2. Operated by machinery, as in *a mechanical toy.*
3. Acting or done as if by a machine, without thought or feeling, as in *a mechanical task.*
▸ ***adverb*** **mechanically**

me•chan•ics (muh-**kan**-iks) ***noun*** A part of physics that deals with the way forces affect still or moving objects.

mech•a•nism (**mek**-uh-*niz*-uhm) ***noun*** A system of moving parts inside a machine.

med•al (**med**-uhl) ***noun*** A piece of metal shaped like a coin, star, or cross that is given to someone for being brave or for service to his or her country or as a prize for some sporting achievement. **Medal** sounds like **meddle.**

med•dle (**med**-uhl) ***verb*** To interfere in someone else's business. **Meddle** sounds like **medal.** ▸ **meddling, meddled** ▸ ***noun*** **meddler**

med•dle•some (**med**-uhl-suhm) ***adjective*** A **meddlesome** person interferes in other people's business.

me•di•a (**mee**-dee-uh) ***noun, plural*** A plural of **medium.**

me•di•an (**mee**-dee-uhn) ***noun***
1. The middle number in a set of numbers listed in order from smallest to largest.
2. A strip of land dividing two or more lanes of traffic going in opposite directions.
▸ ***adjective*** **median**

med•ic (**med**-ik) ***noun*** Someone trained to give medical help in an emergency or during a battle.

Med•i•caid (**med**-uh-*kade*) ***noun*** A system for providing medical aid for those unable to afford it. Medicaid is paid for by state and federal governments.

med•i•cal (**med**-uh-kuhl) ***adjective*** To do with doctors or medicine, as in *medical school.* ▸ ***adverb*** **medically**

Med•i•care (**med**-uh-*kair*) ***noun*** A system for providing medical care to citizens over the age of 65 under the federal Social Security program.

med•i•cine (**med**-uh-suhn) ***noun***
1. A drug or other substance used in treating illness. ▸ ***adjective*** **medicinal**
2. The study of diseases and how to discover, treat, and prevent them.

me•di•e•val (mee-**dee**-vuhl *or* med-ee-**ee**-vuhl) ***adjective*** To do with the Middle Ages, the period of history between approximately A.D. 500 and 1450.

me•di•o•cre (me-dee-**oh**-kur) ***adjective*** Of average or less than average quality.
▸ ***noun*** **mediocrity** (*mee*-dee-**ok**-ri-tee)

med•i•tate (**med**-i-tayt) ***verb***
1. To think very deeply about something.
2. To relax the mind and body by a regular program of mental exercise.
▸ ***verb*** **meditating, meditated** ▸ ***noun*** **meditation**

me•di•um (**mee**-dee-uhm)
1. ***adjective*** Average or middle.
2. ***noun*** The substance or surroundings in which something lives.
3. ***noun*** A means for communicating information to large numbers of people.
4. ***noun*** A substance or means through which something acts or is carried.
5. ***noun*** Someone who claims to make contact with spirits of the dead. ▸ ***noun, plural*** **mediums**
▸ ***noun, plural*** **media** (**mee**-dee-uh) *or* **mediums**

med•ley (**med**-lee) ***noun***
1. A musical piece that consists of bits and pieces of different songs.
2. A mixture or assortment of things.

meek (**meek**) ***adjective*** Quiet, humble, and obedient, as in *a meek servant.*
▸ **meeker, meekest** ▸ ***adverb*** **meekly**

meet (**meet**)
1. ***verb*** To come face to face with someone or something.
2. ***verb*** To come together.
3. ***verb*** To be introduced to.
4. ***verb*** To keep an appointment with.
5. ***verb*** To come together.
6. ***verb*** To satisfy, or to be equal to.
7. ***noun*** A sports contest, as in *a track meet.*
Meet sounds like **meat.**
▸ ***verb*** **meeting, met** (**met**)

meet•ing (**mee**-ting) ***noun*** An arranged event in which people come together, often to discuss something.

meg•a•byte (**meg**-uh-*bite*) ***noun*** A unit used to measure the capacity of a computer's memory. A megabyte is 1 million bytes.

meg•a•phone (**meg**-uh-*fone*) ***noun*** A device shaped like a cone that is used to make the voice sound louder.

mel•an•cho•ly (**mel**-uhn-*kol*-ee) ***adjective*** Very sad. ▸ ***noun*** **melancholy**
▸ ***adjective*** **melancholic**

mel•low (**mel**-oh)
1. ***adjective*** Soft, full, and soothing, as in *mellow music* or *a mellow color.*
2. ***verb*** If someone **mellows,** she or he becomes gentler and more relaxed.
▸ **mellowing, mellowed**
3. ***adjective*** Soft, sweet, and fully ripe, as in *a mellow peach.*
▸ ***adjective*** **mellower, mellowest**

me•lo•di•ous (muh-**loh**-dee-uhss) ***adjective*** Pleasant to hear. ▸ ***noun*** **melodiousness** ▸ ***adverb*** **melodiously**

mel•o•dra•mat•ic (*mel*-uh-druh-**mat**-ik) ***adjective*** Overly dramatic, sentimental, or emotional, as in *a melodramatic play.* ▸ ***noun*** **melodrama**

mel•o•dy (**mel**-uh-dee) ***noun*** A tune.
▸ ***noun, plural*** **melodies** ▸ ***adjective*** **melodic** (muh-**lod**-ik)

mel•on (**mel**-uhn) ***noun*** A large, round, juicy fruit. Melons grow on vines.

melt (**melt**) ***verb***
1. When a substance **melts,** it changes from a solid to a liquid because of heat.
2. To dissolve.
3. To disappear or fade slowly.
4. To soften and become more gentle and more understanding.
▸ ***verb*** **melting, melted**

melt•down (**melt**-*doun*) ***noun*** The melting of the heated core of a nuclear reactor, resulting in the release of radiation into the atmosphere.

M

mem•ber (**mem**-bur) ***noun***
1. A person, animal, or thing that belongs to a group. ▸ ***noun*** **membership**
2. A part of a human or animal body, especially an arm or a leg.

mem•brane (**mem**-brayn) ***noun*** A very thin layer of tissue or skin that lines or covers certain organs or cells.

me•men•to (muh-**men**-toh) ***noun*** A small item kept to remember a place, an experience, or a person.

mem•o (**mem**-oh) ***noun*** Short for **memorandum.**

mem•o•ra•ble (**mem**-ur-uh-buhl) ***adjective*** Easily remembered or worth remembering. ▸ ***adverb*** **memorably**

mem•o•ran•dum (*mem*-uh-**ran**-duhm) ***noun***
1. A brief written reminder.
2. A short letter written to people who work in the same office or organization.
▸ ***noun, plural*** **memorandums** *or* **memoranda** (*mem*-uh-**ran**-duh)

me•mo•ri•al (muh-**mor**-ee-uhl)
1. ***noun*** Something that is built or done to help people continue to remember a person or an event. Monuments, statues, and plaques often are used as memorials.
2. ***adjective*** Meant to help people remember someone or something, as in *a memorial service.*

Memorial Day ***noun*** A holiday celebrated in the United States on the last Monday of May to honor Americans who have died in wars.

mem•o•rize (**mem**-uh-rize) ***verb*** To learn something by heart.
▸ **memorizing, memorized**

mem•o•ry (**mem**-uh-ree) ***noun***
1. The power to remember things.
2. Something that you remember from the past.
3. Honor and respect for someone or something in the past.
4. The part of a computer in which information is stored.
▸ ***noun, plural*** **memories**

men•ace (**men**-iss) ***noun*** A threat or a danger. ▸ ***adjective*** **menacing**

mend (**mend**) ***verb***
1. To fix or repair something, as in *to mend a sock.*
2. To heal or to improve.
▸ ***verb*** **mending, mended**

me•no•rah (muh-**nor**-uh) ***noun*** A special holder for seven or nine candles, used in the Jewish religion. Menorahs for nine candles are used during Hanukkah, the Jewish "Festival of Lights."

men•tal (**men**-tuhl) ***adjective*** To do with or done by the mind, as in *mental health* or *mental calculations.* ▸ ***adverb*** **mentally**

men•tion (**men**-shuhn) ***verb*** To speak or write about something briefly.
▸ **mentioning, mentioned** ▸ ***noun*** **mention**

men•u (**men**-yoo) ***noun***
1. A list of foods served in a restaurant.
2. A list of choices shown on a computer screen.

me•ow (mee-**ou**) ***verb*** To make a noise like a cat. ▸ **meowing, meowed**
▸ ***noun*** **meow**

mer•ce•nar•y (**mur**-suh-ner-ee)
1. ***noun*** A soldier who is paid to fight for a foreign army. ▸ ***noun, plural*** **mercenaries**
2. ***adjective*** If someone is **mercenary,** the person is mainly interested in making money.

mer•chan•dise (**mur**-chuhn-dize *or* **mur**-chuhn-disse) ***noun*** Goods that are bought or sold.

mer•chant (**mur**-chuhnt) ***noun***
1. Someone who sells goods for profit.
2. Someone who owns or manages a store.
3. A country's **merchant marine** is made up of ships and crews that carry goods for trade.

mer•cu•ry (**mur**-kyuh-ree) ***noun*** A poisonous, silvery, liquid metal. Mercury is used in thermometers and barometers.

Mer•cu•ry (**mur**-kyuh-ree) ***noun*** The second-smallest planet in our solar system and the closest planet to the sun.

mer•cy (**mur**-see) ***noun***
1. If you show **mercy** to someone, you do not treat or punish the person as severely as he or she may deserve.
2. Something to be thankful for.
▸ ***noun, plural* mercies** ▸ ***adjective* merciful** ▸ ***adverb* mercifully**

mere (**mihr**) ***adjective*** Nothing more than. ▸ ***adjective* merest**

mere•ly (**mihr**-lee) ***adverb*** Only or simply.

merge (**murj**) ***verb*** When two things **merge,** they join together to form a whole. ▸ **merging, merged**

merg•er (**mur**-jur) ***noun*** The act of making two businesses, teams, etc., into one.

me•rid•i•an (muh-**rid**-ee-uhn) ***noun*** An imaginary circle on the earth's surface, passing through the North and South poles.

mer•it (**mer**-it)
1. ***noun*** If something has **merit,** it is very good or valuable.
2. ***noun*** A good point or quality in a person or thing.
3. ***verb*** To deserve or to be worthy of.
▸ **meriting, merited**
4. merits *noun, plural* The actual facts of a matter.

mer•maid (**mur**-mayd) ***noun*** An imaginary sea creature with the upper body of a woman and the tail of a fish.

mer•ry (**mer**-ee) ***adjective*** Cheerful or joyful, as in *a merry song.* ▸ **merrier, merriest**

me•sa (**may**-suh) ***noun*** A hill or mountain with steep sides and a flat top.

mesh (**mesh**)
1. ***noun*** A net made of threads, wires, or lines woven together with open spaces between them. ▸ ***noun, plural* meshes**
2. ***verb*** To fit together.
▸ **meshes, meshing, meshed**

mess (**mess**)
1. ***noun*** A dirty or untidy state or thing.
▸ ***adjective* messy** ▸ ***adverb* messily**
2. ***noun*** An unpleasant, difficult, or confusing state or thing.
3. ***verb*** If you **mess** something **up**, you make it dirty or untidy or you make it go wrong. ▸ **messes, messing, messed**
4. ***noun*** A meal served to a group of soldiers, sailors, or campers.
5. ***noun*** A group of soldiers, sailors, or campers who eat together.
▸ ***noun, plural* messes**

mes•sage (**mess**-ij) ***noun***
1. Information sent to someone.
2. The meaning of something.

mes•sen•ger (**mess**-uhn-jur) ***noun*** Someone who carries messages or does errands.

me•tab•o•lism (muh-**tab**-uh-*liz*-uhm) ***noun*** The process by which our bodies change the fuel we eat into the energy we need to breathe, digest, and carry on all other important life functions.

met•al (**met**-uhl) ***noun*** A chemical substance, such as iron, copper, or silver, that is usually hard and shiny, is a good conductor of heat and electricity, and can be melted and formed into shapes.
▸ ***adjective* metallic** (muh-**tal**-ik)

met•a•mor•phic (*met*-uh-**mor**-fik) ***adjective*** Resulting from or having to do with metamorphosis.

met•a•mor•pho•sis (*met*-uh-**mor**-fuh-siss) ***noun***
1. The series of changes certain animals go through as they develop from eggs to adults.
2. Any complete or great change in appearance, form, or character.
▸ ***noun, plural* metamorphoses** (*met*-uh-**mor**-fuh-seez)

met•a•phor (**met**-uh-*for or* **met**-uh-*fur*) ***noun*** A way of describing something by calling it something else; for example, "The princess is a shining jewel, and her father is a raging bull."

M

me•te•or (**mee**-tee-ur) ***noun*** A piece of rock or metal from space that enters the earth's atmosphere at high speed, burns, and forms a streak of light as it falls to the earth.

me•te•or•ite (**mee**-tee-ur-*rite*) ***noun*** A remaining part of a meteor that falls to earth before it has burned up.

me•te•o•rol•o•gist (*mee*-tee-ur-**ol**-oh-jist) ***noun*** Someone who specializes in meteorology.

me•te•or•ol•o•gy (mee-tee-uh-**rol**-uh-jee) ***noun*** The study of the earth's atmosphere and, in particular, its climate and weather. ▸ ***adjective*** **meteorological**

me•ter (**mee**-tur) ***noun***
1. The basic unit of length in the metric system. A meter is equal to 39.37 inches, or about 3¼ feet. A meter is about the length of a baseball bat.
2. An instrument for measuring the quantity of something, especially the amount of something that has been used, as in *a gas meter* or *a parking meter.* ▸ ***verb*** **meter**
3. The pattern of rhythm in a line of poetry formed by stressing some syllables and not stressing others.

meth•ane (**meth**-ane) ***noun*** A colorless, odorless gas that burns easily and is used for fuel.

meth•od (**meth**-uhd) ***noun*** A way of doing something.

me•thod•i•cal (muh-**thod**-uh-kuhl) ***adjective*** Careful, logical, and following an orderly system. ▸ ***adverb*** **methodically**

me•tic•u•lous (muh-**tik**-yuh-luhss) ***adjective*** Very careful and precise. ▸ ***adverb*** **meticulously**

met•ric (**met**-rik) ***adjective*** To do with a measuring system based on units of 10. Meters, liters, kilograms, and degrees Celsius are basic metric measurements.

metric system ***noun*** A system of measurement based on counting by 10s. In the metric system, the meter is the basic unit of length, the kilogram is the basic unit of mass or weight, and the liter is the basic unit of liquid volume.

met•ro•nome (**met**-ruh-*nome*) ***noun*** A device that produces a regular beat that helps musicians keep time as they play.

met•ro•pol•i•tan (*met*-ruh-**pol**-uh-tuhn) ***adjective***
1. To do with a large city, as in *a metropolitan police force.*
2. To do with a large city and its surrounding communities, as in *the Los Angeles metropolitan area.*

mi•crobe (**mye**-krobe) ***noun*** A germ or other living thing that is too small to be seen without a microscope; a microorganism.

mi•cro•chip (**mye**-kroh-*chip*) ***noun*** A very thin piece of silicon with electronic circuits printed on it, used in computers and other electronic equipment.

mi•cro•com•pu•ter (**mye**-kroh-kuhm-*pyoo*-tur) ***noun*** A computer that sits on a desk or can be carried in a case.

mi•cro•or•gan•ism (*mye*-kroh-**or**-guh-niz-uhm) ***noun*** A living thing that is too small to be seen without a microscope. Bacteria and viruses are microorganisms.

mi•cro•phone (**mye**-kruh-*fone*) ***noun*** An instrument that changes sound into an electric current to make the sound louder, record it, or transmit it to radio or television stations.

mi•cro•scope (**mye**-kruh-*skope*) ***noun*** An instrument with powerful lenses. A microscope magnifies very small things so that they look large enough to be seen and studied.

mi•cro•scop•ic (mye-kruh-**skop**-ik) ***adjective*** Too small to be seen without a microscope. ▸ ***adverb*** **microscopically**

mi•cro•wave (**mye**-kroh-*wave*) ***noun***
1. An electromagnetic wave that can pass through solid objects. Microwaves are used in radar. They are also used to send messages over long distances and to cook food in microwave ovens.
2. microwave oven An oven that cooks food very quickly by beaming

microwaves into it. The microwaves make the moisture in the food vibrate and get hot. This heat is passed through the food so that it cooks from the inside.

mid•day (**mid**-day) ***noun*** Noon, or 12 o'clock in the middle of the day.
▸ ***adjective*** **midday**

mid•dle (**mid**-uhl)
1. ***adjective*** Half of the way between two things, sides, or outer points. ▸ ***noun*** **middle**
2. If you are **in the middle** of doing something, you are involved in doing it.

middle-aged ***adjective*** Someone who is **middle-aged** is between 40 and 60 years old.

Middle Ages ***noun*** The period of European history from approximately A.D. 500 to 1450.

middle class ***noun*** The group of people whose income level places them between the upper class (wealthy) and the lower class (poor). ▸ ***adjective*** **middle-class**

Middle East ***noun*** A region made up of Egypt, Iran, Iraq, Israel, Saudi Arabia, Syria, Turkey, and other countries. The Middle East overlaps parts of two continents, Asia and Africa. ▸ ***adjective*** **Middle Eastern**

Middle English ***noun*** The English language that was spoken from around A.D. 1150 to 1475.

middle school ***noun*** A school between elementary school and high school. It usually includes the seventh and eighth grades and sometimes the fifth and sixth grades.

mid•get (**mij**-it) ***noun*** A very small thing or person.

mid•night (**mid**-*nite*) ***noun*** Twelve o'clock in the middle of the night.
▸ ***adjective*** **midnight**

mid•way
1. (**mid-way**) ***adverb and adjective*** Half of the way.
2. (**mid**-*way*) ***noun*** The area of a circus, carnival, or fair in which games, rides, and other amusements are located.

Mid•west (**mid-west**) ***noun*** The north-central region of the United States bordered by the Appalachian Mountains on the east; the Rocky Mountains on the west; Canada on the north; and Missouri, Oklahoma, and the Ohio River on the south.

mid•wife (**mid**-*wife*) ***noun*** A person who assists women in childbirth. ▸ ***noun, plural*** **midwives** ▸ ***noun*** **midwifery** (mid-**wif**-uh-ree)

might (**mite**)
1. ***noun*** Strength or force. ▸ ***adjective*** **mighty** ▸ ***adverb*** **mightily**
2. ***verb*** The past tense of **may.**
Might sounds like **mite.**

mi•graine (**mye**-grayn) ***noun*** A very bad headache that can cause nausea and vomiting. Migraines usually cause pain on only one side of the head.

mi•grant (**mye**-gruhnt)
1. ***noun*** Someone or something that migrates.
2. ***adjective*** To do with someone who moves around doing seasonal work, as in *a migrant laborer.*

mi•grate (**mye**-grate) ***verb***
1. To move from one country or region to another.
2. When birds **migrate,** they fly away at a particular time of year to live in another region or climate.
▸ ***verb*** **migrating, migrated** ▸ ***noun*** **migration** ▸ ***adjective*** **migratory**

mild (**milde**) ***adjective***
1. Moderate and not too harsh, as in *mild weather.*
2. Someone who is **mild** is gentle and not aggressive.
▸ ***adjective*** **milder, mildest** ▸ ***noun*** **mildness** ▸ ***adverb*** **mildly**

mil•dew (**mil**-doo) ***noun*** A thin coating of white, powdery fungus that can grow on damp cloth, paper, etc. ▸ ***verb*** **mildew** ▸ ***adjective*** **mildewed,** ***adjective*** **mildewy**

mile (**mile**) ***noun*** A unit of length equal to 5,280 feet. It takes about 20 minutes to walk one mile.

M

mile•stone (**mile**-*stone*) ***noun***
1. A stone marker found at the side of a road that tells the distance in miles to a certain point or points.
2. An important event or development.

mil•i•tant (**mil**-uh-tuhnt) ***adjective*** Someone who is **militant** is prepared to fight or to be very aggressive in support of a cause in which he or she believes.
▸ ***noun*** **militancy** ▸ ***adverb*** **militantly**

mil•i•tar•y (**mil**-uh-*ter*-ee)
1. ***adjective*** To do with soldiers, the armed forces, or war, as in *a military career.*
2. ***noun*** The armed forces of a country.

mi•li•tia (muh-**lish**-uh) ***noun*** A group of citizens who are trained to fight but who only serve in time of emergency, as in the National Guard.

milk (**milk**)
1. ***noun*** The white liquid produced by female mammals to feed their young. People drink milk from cows and sometimes goats or other animals.
▸ ***adjective*** **milky**
2. ***verb*** To take milk from a cow or other animal. ▸ **milking, milked**
3. ***noun*** A white liquid that is made in plants, as in *coconut milk.*
4. **milk teeth** ***noun, plural*** Your first set of teeth, which fall out and are replaced by your permanent teeth.

Milky Way ***noun*** The galaxy that includes the earth and our solar system. The Milky Way is made up of more than 100 billion stars and can be seen as a hazy white streak across the night sky.

mill (**mil**) ***noun***
1. A building containing machinery for grinding grain into flour or meal.
2. A large factory with machinery for processing textiles, wood, paper, steel, etc.
3. A small machine used for grinding something into powder, as in *a pepper mill.*
▸ ***verb*** **mill**

mil•len•ni•um (muh-**len**-ee-uhm) ***noun*** A period of a thousand years. ▸ ***noun, plural*** **millenniums** *or* **millennia** (muh-**len**-ee-uh) ▸ ***adjective*** **millennial**

mil•let (**mil**-it) ***noun*** A grass like wheat that is raised for its small, edible seeds.

mil•li•gram (**mil**-i-*gram*) ***noun*** In the metric system, a measure equal to $\frac{1}{1000}$ gram.

mil•li•me•ter (**mil**-i-*mee*-tur) ***noun*** In the metric system, a measure equal to $\frac{1}{1000}$ meter.

mil•lion (**mil**-yuhn) ***noun***
1. A thousand thousands (1,000,000).
2. A very large number.

mil•lion•aire (*mil*-yuhn-**air**) ***noun*** Someone whose money and property are worth at least a million dollars.

mime (**mime**) ***noun***
1. A form of acting in which actions are used instead of words.
2. A performer who expresses himself or herself without words.
▸ ***verb*** **mime**

mim•ic (**mim**-ik) ***verb*** To imitate someone else's speech or actions, especially to make fun of the person.
▸ **mimicking, mimicked** ▸ ***noun*** **mimic**

min•a•ret (*min*-uh-**ret** *or* **min**-uh-ret) ***noun*** The tall, thin tower of a mosque, from which Muslims are called to prayer.

mince (**minss**) ***verb*** To cut or chop into very small pieces. ▸ **mincing, minced**

mince•meat (**minss**-*meet*) ***noun*** A sweet mixture of finely chopped dried fruit, spices, etc., used in pies.

mind (**minde**)
1. ***noun*** The part of you that thinks, feels, understands, reasons, and remembers.
2. ***verb*** To look after something or someone.
3. ***verb*** To care or to be bothered about something.
4. ***noun*** An opinion or a point of view.
5. ***noun*** Attention.
6. ***noun*** Memory.
7. ***verb*** To watch out for something.
▸ ***verb*** **minding, minded**

mine (**mine**)
1. ***pronoun*** The one or ones belonging

to or having to do with me.
2. ***verb*** To dig up minerals that are underground.
▸ **mining, mined** ▸ ***noun*** **mine,** ***noun*** **miner**
3. ***noun*** A bomb placed underground or underwater.
4. ***noun*** A rich supply.

min•er•al (**min**-ur-uhl) ***noun*** A substance found in nature that is not an animal or a plant. Gold, salt, and copper are all minerals. ▸ ***adjective*** **mineral**

min•gle (**ming**-guhl) ***verb*** To mix together. ▸ **mingling, mingled**

min•i•a•ture (**min**-ee-uh-chur) ***adjective*** Smaller than the usual size, as in *a miniature golf course.* ▸ ***noun*** **miniature**

min•i•mize (**min**-uh-mize) ***verb***
1. To make something as small as possible.
2. To make something seem as unimportant or insignificant as possible.
▸ ***verb*** **minimizing, minimized**

min•i•mum (**min**-uh-muhm) ***noun*** The smallest possible amount, or the lowest limit. ▸ ***adjective*** **minimum**

min•i•ser•ies (**min**-ee-*sihr*-eez) ***noun*** A television production of a story presented as a series of daily or weekly programs.

min•i•skirt (**min**-ee-*skurt*) ***noun*** A very short skirt.

min•is•ter (**min**-uh-stur)
1. ***noun*** A person who is authorized to lead religious ceremonies in a church, especially a Protestant church.
2. ***noun*** Someone sent by a government to represent it overseas.
3. ***verb*** To help or serve someone.
▸ **ministering, ministered**
▸ ***noun*** **ministry** ▸ ***adjective*** **ministerial**

mink (**mingk**) ***noun***
1. A small animal with dark brown, luxurious fur, often raised for its pelt.
2. A coat made from this animal's fur.
▸ ***noun, plural*** **mink** *or* **minks**

min•now (**min**-oh) ***noun*** A tiny freshwater fish.

mi•nor (**mye**-nur)
1. ***adjective*** Less important or less serious.
2. ***noun*** Someone under adult age.
3. ***adjective*** A **minor** scale in music has a semitone between the second and third notes.

mi•nor•i•ty (muh-**nor**-uh-tee *or* mye-**nor**-uh-tee) ***noun***
1. A small number or part within a bigger group.
2. A group of people of a particular race, ethnic group, or religion living among a larger group of a different race, ethnic group, or religion.
▸ ***noun, plural*** **minorities**

min•strel (**min**-struhl) ***noun*** A medieval musician and poet.

mint (**mint**) ***noun***
1. A plant whose leaves have a strong scent and are used for flavoring.
2. A candy flavored with mint.
3. A place where coins are manufactured. ▸ ***verb*** **mint**
4. *(informal)* A very large amount of money.

min•u•end (**min**-yoo-*end*) ***noun*** The number from which another number is subtracted.

mi•nus (**mye**-nuhss)
1. ***adjective*** In math, a **minus** sign (–) is used in a subtraction problem. ▸ ***noun*** **minus**
2. ***preposition*** Without.
3. ***adjective*** Less than zero.
4. ***adjective*** Slightly less or lower than.

min•ute
1. (**min**-it) ***noun*** A unit of time equal to 60 seconds.
2. (**min**-it) ***noun*** A short period of time.
3. (mye-**noot**) ***adjective*** Very small.
4. (mye-**noot**) ***adjective*** Careful and complete.
5. **minutes** (**min**-its) ***noun, plural*** The written record of what is said at a meeting.
▸ ***adjective*** **minuter, minutest**
▸ ***adverb*** **minutely**

M

M

min•ute•man (**min**-it-*man*) ***noun*** A volunteer soldier in the American Revolution who was ready to fight at a minute's notice. ▸ ***noun, plural*** **minutemen**

mir•a•cle (**mihr**-uh-kuhl) ***noun***
1. An amazing event that cannot be explained by the laws of nature.
2. A remarkable and unexpected event.
▸ ***adjective*** **miraculous** (mi-**rak**-yuh-luhss) ▸ ***adverb*** **miraculously**

mi•rage (muh-**razh**) ***noun*** Something that you think you see in the distance, such as water, that is not really there. Mirages are caused by the bending of light rays by layers of air at different temperatures.

mir•ror (**mihr**-ur) ***noun***
1. A metal or glass surface that reflects the image of whatever is in front of it.
2. Something that gives a true picture.
▸ ***verb*** **mirror**

mis•be•have (*miss*-bee-**hayv**) ***verb*** To behave badly. ▸ **misbehaving, misbehaved** ▸ ***noun*** **misbehavior**

mis•cal•cu•late (miss-**kal**-kyuh-*late*) ***verb*** To figure something out incorrectly, or to judge a situation wrongly.
▸ **miscalculating, miscalculated**
▸ ***noun*** **miscalculation**

mis•car•riage (miss-**ka**-rij *or* **miss**-ka-rij) ***noun***
1. When a pregnant woman has a **miscarriage,** she gives birth to a fetus that is not sufficiently formed to live.
▸ ***verb*** **miscarry**
2. A **miscarriage of justice** occurs when the legal system fails to come to the right decision.

mis•cel•la•ne•ous (miss-uh-**lay**-nee-uhss) ***adjective*** Assorted or of different types. ▸ ***noun*** **miscellany**

mis•chief (**miss**-chif) ***noun*** Playful behavior that may cause annoyance or harm to others. ▸ ***adjective*** **mischievous** (**miss**-chuh-vuhss *or* miss-**chee**-vee-uhss) ▸ ***adverb*** **mischievously**

mis•con•duct (miss-**kon**-duhkt) ***noun*** Dishonest, irresponsible, or immoral action, especially by someone in a position of responsibility.

mis•count (miss-**kount**) ***verb*** To make a mistake in counting. ▸ **miscounting, miscounted** ▸ ***noun*** **miscount** (**miss**-*kount*)

mi•ser (**mye**-zur) ***noun*** A very stingy person who spends as little as possible in order to hoard money. ▸ ***noun*** **miserliness** ▸ ***adjective*** **miserly**

mis•er•a•ble (**miz**-ur-uh-buhl) ***adjective***
1. Sad, unhappy, or dejected.
2. Causing great discomfort or unhappiness, as in *a miserable cold* or *miserable weather.* ▸ ***noun*** **misery**
▸ ***adverb*** **miserably**

mis•for•tune (miss-**for**-chuhn) ***noun***
1. An unlucky event.
2. Bad luck.

mis•giv•ing (miss-**giv**-ing) ***noun*** A feeling of worry or doubt.

mis•guid•ed (miss-**gye**-did) ***adjective*** If you are **misguided,** you have the wrong idea about something. ▸ ***adverb*** **misguidedly**

mis•hap (**miss**-*hap*) ***noun*** An unfortunate accident.

mis•lay (miss-**lay**) ***verb*** To lose something for a short while because you have put it in a place where you cannot find it. ▸ **mislaying, mislaid**

mis•lead (miss-**leed**) ***verb*** To give someone the wrong idea about something. ▸ **misleading, misled**
▸ ***adjective*** **misleading** ▸ ***adverb*** **misleadingly**

mis•place (miss-**playss**) ***verb*** To put something down somewhere and then forget where it is. ▸ **misplacing, misplaced** ▸ ***noun*** **misplacement**

mis•print (**miss**-*print*) ***noun*** A mistake in a book, newspaper, etc., where the letters have been printed incorrectly.
▸ ***verb*** **misprint** (*miss*-**print**)

M

mis•pro•nounce (*miss*-proh-**nounss**) ***verb*** To say a word incorrectly.
▸ **mispronouncing, mispronounced**

miss (**miss**)
1. ***verb*** To fail to hit or reach something.
▸ ***noun*** **miss**
2. ***verb*** To fail to catch, see, meet, or do something.
3. ***verb*** To fail to attend or be present for.
4. ***verb*** To be unhappy because something or someone is not with you.
5. ***verb*** To avoid or to escape.
6. ***noun*** A title given to a girl or an unmarried woman. It is written **Miss** before a name, as in *Miss Smith.* ▸ ***noun, plural*** **misses** *or* **Misses**
▸ ***verb*** **misses, missing, missed**

mis•shap•en (miss-**shape**-uhn) ***adjective*** Twisted or bent out of shape.

mis•sile (**miss**-uhl) ***noun*** A weapon that is thrown or shot at a target, as in *an atomic missile.*

missing (**miss**-ing) ***adjective***
1. Lacking, as in *missing information.*
2. Lost, as in *a missing child.*

mis•sion (**mish**-uhn) ***noun***
1. A special job or task.
2. A group of people who are sent to do a special job.
3. A church or other place where missionaries live and work.

mis•sion•ar•y (**mish**-uh-*ner*-ee) ***noun*** Someone who is sent by a church or religious group to teach that group's faith and do good works, especially in a foreign country. ▸ ***noun, plural*** **missionaries**

mis•spell (miss-**spel**) ***verb*** To spell something incorrectly. ▸ **misspelling, misspelled** ▸ ***noun*** **misspelling**

mist (**mist**) ***noun*** A cloud of tiny water droplets in the air. ▸ ***verb*** **mist**
▸ ***adjective*** **misty**

mis•take (muh-**stake**)
1. ***noun*** An error or a misunderstanding.
2. ***verb*** To believe that someone or something is another.
▸ **mistaking, mistook, mistaken**
▸ ***adjective*** **mistaken** ▸ ***adverb*** **mistakenly**

mis•ter (**miss**-tur) ***noun*** A title for a man. It is written **Mister** or **Mr.** before a name.

mis•tle•toe (**miss**-uhl-*toh*) ***noun*** An evergreen plant that grows as a parasite on trees. Mistletoe has white berries and is often used as a Christmas decoration.

mis•treat (miss-**treet**) ***verb*** To treat roughly, cruelly, or badly.
▸ **mistreating, mistreated** ▸ ***noun*** **mistreatment**

mis•tress (**miss**-triss) ***noun*** A woman with power, responsibility, or control over something. ▸ ***noun, plural*** **mistresses**

mis•trust (miss-**truhst**) ***verb*** To be suspicious of someone. ▸ **mistrusting, mistrusted** ▸ ***noun*** **mistrust**

mis•un•der•stand (*miss*-uhn-dur-**stand**) ***verb*** To understand incorrectly.
▸ **misunderstanding, misunderstood**

misunderstanding ***noun***
1. A failure to understand.
2. A disagreement between people.

mis•use (miss-**yooz**) ***verb*** To use something in the wrong way.
▸ **misusing, misused** ▸ ***noun*** **misuse** (miss-**yooss**)

mite (**mite**) ***noun***
1. A tiny animal with eight legs that is related to the spider. A mite lives off plants, animals, or stored food.
2. A small person or thing.
3. A small amount of anything.
Mite sounds like **might.**

mitt (**mit**) ***noun*** A padded leather glove that protects a person's hand when he or she catches a baseball or softball.

mit•ten (**mit**-uhn) ***noun*** A warm covering for the hand with one part for the thumb and another for the rest of the fingers.

mix (**miks**) ***verb***
1. To combine or blend different things.
2. If something **mixes** you **up,** it confuses you. ▸ ***adjective*** **mixed-up**
▸ ***verb*** **mixes, mixing, mixed** ▸ ***noun*** **mix**

mixed number ***noun*** A number made up of a whole number and a fraction, such as 6½.

mix•ture (**miks**-chur) ***noun*** Something consisting of different things mixed together.

mix-up ***noun*** A confused situation.
▸ ***noun, plural*** **mix-ups**

moan (**mohn**) ***verb***
1. To make a low, sad sound, usually because you are in pain or are unhappy.
2. To complain in a sad way.
▸ ***verb*** **moaning, moaned** ▸ ***noun*** **moan**

moat (**moht**) ***noun*** A deep, wide ditch dug all around a castle, fort, or town and filled with water to prevent attacks. Moats were used in the Middle Ages.

mob (**mob**)
1. ***noun*** A large and dangerous crowd of people, as in *an angry mob.*
2. ***noun*** Any large crowd.
3. ***verb*** To crowd around excitedly.
▸ **mobbing, mobbed**

mo•bile
1. (**moh**-buhl *or* **moh**-beel *or* **moh**-bile) ***adjective*** Able to move, as in *a mobile home.* ▸ ***noun*** **mobility**
2. (**moh**-beel) ***noun*** A sculpture made of several items balanced at different heights and hanging from a central wire or thread.

mobile home ***noun*** A large trailer people can live in.

mobile phone ***noun*** A telephone that you can carry around with you.

moc•ca•sin (**mok**-uh-suhn) ***noun*** A soft leather shoe or slipper without a heel. Moccasins originally were worn by American Indians.

mock (**mok**)
1. ***verb*** To make fun of someone in an unpleasant way. ▸ **mocking, mocked** ▸ ***noun*** **mockery**
2. ***adjective*** False or imitation, as in *a mock battle.*

mock•ing•bird (**mok**-ing-*burd*) ***noun*** A gray and white songbird of North and South America that can imitate the calls of other birds.

mode (**mohd**) ***noun***
1. A way of doing something.
2. In mathematics, the most frequent number in a set of numbers.

mod•el (**mod**-uhl)
1. ***adjective*** Small or miniature, as in *a model railroad.* ▸ ***noun*** **model**
2. ***adjective*** Perfect or ideal, as in *a model child.*
3. ***noun*** Someone who poses for an artist or a photographer or who wears clothing in order to show how the clothing looks. ▸ ***noun*** **modeling** ▸ ***verb*** **model**
4. ***noun*** A thing or person who is a good example.
5. ***noun*** A particular type or design of product.
▸ ***adjective*** **model**

mo•dem (**moh**-duhm) ***noun*** A piece of electronic equipment used to send information between computers by telephone lines.

mod•er•ate
1. (**mod**-ur-it) ***adjective*** Not extreme, as in *moderate speed.* ▸ ***adverb*** **moderately**
2. (**mod**-uh-*rate*) ***verb*** To make or become less extreme. ▸ ***noun*** **moderation**
3. (**mod**-ur-it) ***noun*** A person with moderate opinions.
4. (**mod**-uh-*rate*) ***verb*** To lead or preside over a meeting. ▸ ***noun*** **moderator**
▸ ***verb*** **moderating, moderated**

mod•ern (**mod**-urn) ***adjective***
1. To do with the present or the recent past, as in *modern art.*
2. Up-to-date or new in style, as in *modern appliances.*

mod•ern•ize (**mod**-ur-nize) ***verb*** To make something more modern or up-to-date.
▸ **modernizing, modernized** ▸ ***noun*** **modernization**

mod•est (**mod**-ist) ***adjective***
1. People who are **modest** are not boastful about their abilities, possessions, or achievements. ▸ ***noun*** **modesty**
2. Not large or extreme, as in *a modest salary.* ▸ ***adverb*** **modestly**

mod•i•fy (**mod**-uh-fye) ***verb***
1. To change something slightly. ▸ ***noun*** **modification**
2. To limit the meaning of a word or phrase. ▸ ***noun*** **modifier**
▸ ***verb*** **modifies, modifying, modified**

mod•ule (**moj**-ool) ***noun*** A separate, independent section that can be linked to other parts to make something larger, as in *a space module.*

Mohammed *See* **Muhammad.**

Mo•hawk (**moh**-hawk) ***noun*** A member of a group of American Indians that lives primarily in eastern New York, in the Mohawk River valley. The Mohawk are part of the Iroquois Confederation.

Mo•he•gan (moh-**hee**-guhn) *or* **Mo•hi•can** (moh-**hee**-kuhn) ***noun*** A member of a group of American Indians that originally lived in southeastern Connecticut. ▸ ***noun, plural*** **Mohegan, Mohegans** *or* **Mohican, Mohicans**

moist (**moist**) ***adjective*** Slightly wet.
▸ **moister, moistest** ▸ ***noun*** **moisture**
▸ ***verb*** **moisten**

mo•lar (**moh**-lur) ***noun*** A broad, flat tooth at the back of the mouth used for grinding food.

mo•las•ses (muh-**lass**-iz) ***noun*** A thick, sweet syrup made when sugarcane is processed into sugar.

mold (**mohld**)
1. ***noun*** A furry fungus that grows on old food or damp surfaces. ▸ ***noun*** **moldiness** ▸ ***adjective*** **moldy**
2. ***verb*** To model or shape something.
▸ **molding, molded**
3. ***noun*** A hollow container that you can pour liquid into so that it sets in that shape, as in *a gelatin mold.*

mold•ing (**mohl**-ding) ***noun*** A strip of wood or other material used to decorate walls or the edges of windows, doorways, tables, etc.

mole (**mohl**) ***noun***
1. A small, furry mammal that digs tunnels and lives underground.
2. A small growth on the skin.

mol•e•cule (**mol**-uh-kyool) ***noun*** The smallest part of a substance that displays all the chemical properties of that substance. A molecule is made up of more than one atom. ▸ ***adjective*** **molecular** (muh-**lek**-yuh-lur)

mol•lusk (**mol**-uhsk) ***noun*** An animal with a soft body and no spine. A mollusk is usually protected by a hard shell.

molt (**mohlt**) ***verb*** When a bird or an animal **molts,** its outer covering of fur, feathers, or skin comes off so that a new covering can grow. ▸ **molting, molted**

mol•ten (**mohlt**-uhn) ***adjective*** Melted by heat.

mom (**mom**) ***noun*** *(informal)* Mother.

mo•ment (**moh**-muhnt) ***noun***
1. A very brief period of time.
▸ ***adjective*** **momentary** ▸ ***adverb*** **momentarily**
2. If something is happening **at this moment,** it is happening now.

mo•men•tum (moh-**men**-tuhm) ***noun*** The force or speed that an object has when it is moving.

mon•arch (**mon**-urk) ***noun***
1. A ruler, such as a king or queen, who often inherits his or her position. ▸ ***noun*** **monarchy**
2. A large, orange and black butterfly.

mon•as•ter•y (**mon**-uh-*ster*-ee) ***noun*** A group of buildings where monks live and work. ▸ ***noun, plural*** **monasteries**
▸ ***adjective*** **monastic** (muh-**nass**-tik)

Mon•day (**muhn**-day *or* **muhn**-dee) ***noun*** The second day of the week, after Sunday and before Tuesday.

mon•ey (**muhn**-ee) ***noun*** The coins and bills that people use to buy things.
▸ ***noun, plural*** **moneys** *or* **monies**
▸ ***adjective*** **monetary** (**mon**-i-*ter*-ee)

M

mon•goose (**mon**-*gooss*) ***noun*** An animal that resembles a ferret, having a slender body, a long tail, and brown or black fur. Mongooses are known for their ability to kill poisonous snakes. ▸ ***noun, plural*** **mongooses** *or* **mongeese**

mon•grel (**muhng**-gruhl *or* **mong**-gruhl) ***noun*** An animal, especially a dog, that is a mixture of different breeds.

mon•i•tor (**mon**-uh-tur)
1. *noun* A student who is given a special job to do in the classroom, as in *a chalkboard monitor.*
2. *verb* To keep a check on something over a period of time. ▸ **monitoring, monitored**
3. *noun* A person or a device that keeps track of or monitors people, machines, or a situation.
4. *noun* The visual display unit of a computer.
5. *noun* A television screen used in a studio to show what is being recorded or transmitted.

monk (**muhngk**) ***noun*** A man who lives in a religious community and has promised to devote his life to God.

mon•key (**muhng**-kee)
1. *noun* An animal like a small ape, usually with a tail. Monkeys have hands and feet that are adapted for climbing and for grasping objects.
2. *verb* To play in a silly or mischievous way. ▸ **monkeying, monkeyed**

monkey wrench ***noun*** A tool with a grip that adjusts to fit different sizes of nuts and bolts.

mon•o•cle (**mon**-uh-kuhl) ***noun*** A glass lens worn to improve the eyesight of one eye.

mon•o•gram (**mon**-uh-*gram*) ***noun*** A design made from two or more letters, usually someone's initials. ▸ ***verb*** **monogram** ▸ ***adjective*** **monogrammed**

mon•o•lin•gual (*mon*-uh-**ling**-gwuhl) ***adjective*** Able to speak only one language.

mon•o•logue (**mon**-uh-*log*) ***noun*** A long speech by one person.

mon•o•nu•cle•o•sis (*mon*-oh-noo-klee-**oh**-siss) ***noun*** An infectious illness that gives you a sore throat, swollen glands, and a high temperature.

mo•nop•o•lize (muh-**nop**-uh-lize) ***verb*** To keep something all to yourself. ▸ **monopolizing, monopolized**

mo•nop•o•ly (muh-**nop**-uh-lee) ***noun***
1. The complete control of something, especially a service or the supply of a product. ▸ ***adjective*** **monopolistic** (muh-*nop*-uh-**liss**-tik)
2. A group or company that has such control. ▸ ***noun, plural*** **monopolies**

mono•rail (**mon**-uh-*rayl*) ***noun***
1. A railroad that runs on one rail, usually high off the ground.
2. A railroad track that has only one rail.

mo•not•o•nous (muh-**not**-uh-nuhss) ***adjective*** If something is **monotonous,** it goes on and on in a dull and boring way, as in *a monotonous job.* ▸ ***noun*** **monotony** ▸ ***adverb*** **monotonously**

mon•soon (mon-**soon**) ***noun***
1. A very strong wind that blows across the Indian Ocean and southern Asia. In the summer it blows from the ocean toward the land and brings very heavy rains. In the winter it blows from the land toward the ocean, bringing hot, dry weather.
2. The rainy summer season brought on by the monsoon.

mon•ster (**mon**-stur)
1. *noun* A large, fierce, or horrible creature.
2. *noun* A very evil or cruel person.
3. *adjective* Huge, as in *a monster whale.* ▸ ***noun*** **monster**

mon•strous (**mon**-struhss) ***adjective***
1. Horrible or frightening, as in *a monstrous creature.*
2. Huge.
3. Evil and shocking, as in *a monstrous crime.*
▸ ***noun*** **monstrosity** (mon-**stross**-i-tee) ▸ ***adverb*** **monstrously**

month (**muhnth**) ***noun*** One of the 12 parts that make up a year. ▸ ***adjective*** **monthly** ▸ ***adverb*** **monthly**

mon•u•ment (**mon**-yuh-muhnt) ***noun***
1. A statue, building, etc., that is meant to remind people of an event or a person, as in *a war monument.*
2. An important work or achievement.

mon•u•men•tal (mon-yuh-**men**-tuhl) ***adjective*** Very large or very important, as in *a monumental mistake* or *a monumental decision.* ▸ ***adverb*** **monumentally**

mood (**mood**) ***noun*** Your **mood** is the way that you are feeling.

mood•y (**moo**-dee) ***adjective***
1. Gloomy or unhappy. ▸ ***adverb*** **moodily**
2. A **moody** person has frequent changes of mood or feelings.
▸ ***adjective*** **moodier, moodiest** ▸ ***noun*** **moodiness**

moon (**moon**) ***noun***
1. The satellite that moves around the earth once each month and reflects light from the sun.
2. A satellite of a planet.

moon•light (**moon**-*lite*)
1. ***noun*** The light of the moon that you can see at night. ▸ ***adjective*** **moonlit**
2. ***verb*** *(informal)* Someone who **moonlights** holds two jobs, one during the day and one at night.
▸ **moonlighting, moonlighted**

moor (**mor**)
1. ***verb*** If you **moor** a boat, you tie it up or anchor it. ▸ **mooring, moored**
▸ ***noun, plural*** **moorings**
2. ***noun*** An open, grassy area, often covered with heather and marshes.

moose (**mooss**) ***noun*** A large, heavy animal of the deer family that lives in the cold forests of North America, Europe, and Asia. The male has very large, broad antlers. **Moose** sounds like **mousse.**
▸ ***noun, plural*** **moose**

mop (**mop**)
1. ***noun*** A long stick with a sponge or bundle of cloth or string at one end, used to clean floors.
2. ***verb*** To clean a floor or soak up liquid with a mop, cloth, or sponge.
▸ **mopping, mopped**
3. ***noun*** A thick, tangled mass, as in *a mop of hair.*

mope (**mope**) ***verb*** To be gloomy and depressed. ▸ **moping, moped**

mo•ped (**moh**-ped) ***noun*** A heavy bicycle with a small engine.

mor•al (**mor**-uhl)
1. ***adjective*** To do with right and wrong.
2. ***adjective*** Good and honest.
3. ***noun, plural*** Your **morals** are your beliefs about what is right and wrong.
4. ***noun*** The lesson taught by a story.
▸ ***noun*** **morality** ▸ ***adverb*** **morally**

mo•rale (muh-**ral**) ***noun*** The state of mind or spirit of a person or group.

mor•bid (**mor**-bid) ***adjective*** Someone who is **morbid** is very interested in death and gruesome things. ▸ ***adverb*** **morbidly**

more (**mor**)
1. ***adjective*** Greater in number, size, extent, or degree.
2. ***adjective*** Additional or further.
3. ***adverb*** To a greater extent or degree.
4. ***adverb*** In addition or again.
5. ***noun*** An extra amount.
6. ***pronoun*** A greater number.
7. **more or less** Roughly or nearly.

more•o•ver (mor-**oh**-vur) ***adverb*** Beyond what has already been said.

Mor•mon (**mor**-muhn) ***noun*** A member of the Church of Jesus Christ of Latter-day Saints, a religion founded in 1830 by Joseph Smith at Fayette, New York.

morn•ing (**mor**-ning) ***noun*** The time of day between midnight and noon or sunrise and noon. **Morning** sounds like **mourning.**

morning glory ***noun*** A climbing vine with flowers of different colors. The flowers open early in the morning and close in the afternoon. ▸ ***noun, plural*** **morning glories**

mo•rose (muh-**rohss**) ***adjective*** Gloomy or depressed. ▸ ***adverb*** **morosely**

M

morph (**morf**) ***verb*** To change in shape, especially as done by computer animation. ▸ **morphing, morphed**

Morse code (**morss**) ***noun*** A way of signaling that uses light or sound in a pattern of dots and dashes to represent letters.

mor•sel (**mor**-suhl) ***noun*** A small piece of food, as in *a morsel of bread.*

mor•tal (**mor**-tuhl)
1. ***adjective*** Unable to live forever. ▸ ***noun*** **mortality**
2. ***adjective*** Causing death, as in *a mortal wound.* ▸ ***adverb*** **mortally**
3. ***adjective*** Very hostile, as in *mortal enemies.*
4. ***adjective*** Very great or intense.
5. ***noun*** A human being.

mor•tar (**mor**-tur) ***noun***
1. A mixture of lime, sand, water, and cement that is used for building.
2. A deep bowl used with a pestle for crushing things.
3. A very short cannon that fires shells or rockets high in the air.

mort•gage (**mor**-gij) ***noun*** A loan from a bank to buy a house. ▸ ***verb*** **mortgage**

mor•tu•ar•y (**mor**-choo-er-ee) ***noun*** A room or building where dead bodies are kept until burial. ▸ ***noun, plural*** **mortuaries**

mo•sa•ic (moh-**zay**-ik) ***noun*** A pattern or picture made up of small pieces of colored stone, tile, or glass.

Mo•ses (**moh**-ziss *or* moh-**ziz**) ***noun*** In the Old Testament, a Hebrew prophet and giver of laws who led the ancient Jews out of Egypt.

mo•sey (**moh**-zee) ***verb*** *(informal)* To walk slowly or aimlessly. ▸ **moseying, moseyed**

mosh•ing (**mosh**-ing) ***noun*** At rock music concerts, the activity of swaying, dancing, and flinging yourself around while banging into other people.

Moslem (**moz**-luhm) *See* **Muslim.**

mosque (**mosk**) ***noun*** A building used by Muslims for worship.

mos•qui•to (muh-**skee**-toh) ***noun*** A small insect, the female of which bites and sucks blood from animals and humans. Mosquitoes can spread diseases such as malaria and yellow fever. ▸ ***noun, plural*** **mosquitoes** *or* **mosquitos**

moss (**mawss** *or* **moss**) ***noun*** A small, furry, green plant that grows on damp soil, rocks, and tree trunks. Mosses do not have roots, flowers, or fruit but reproduce from spores. ▸ ***noun, plural*** **mosses** ▸ ***adjective*** **mossy**

most (**mohst**)
1. ***adjective*** Greatest in number, amount, or degree.
2. ***adjective*** The majority of.
3. ***noun*** The greatest number, amount, or degree.
4. ***adverb*** Very.
5. ***adverb*** To the greatest degree or extent.

most•ly (**mohst**-lee) ***adverb*** Mainly or usually.

mo•tel (moh-**tel**) ***noun*** A roadside hotel that provides parking spaces adjacent to the rooms.

moth (**mawth**) ***noun*** An insect similar to a butterfly but having a thicker body, a duller color, and antennae shaped like feathers. Unlike butterflies, moths usually fly at night.

moth•er (**muhTH**-ur)
1. ***noun*** A female parent. ▸ ***noun*** **motherhood** ▸ ***verb*** **mother** ▸ ***adjective*** **motherly**
2. ***noun*** The source or origin of something.
3. ***adjective*** Native, as in *mother country.*

mother-in-law ***noun*** Someone's **mother-in-law** is the mother of his or her spouse. ▸ ***noun, plural*** **mothers-in-law**

M

Mother's Day ***noun*** A day set aside for honoring mothers, observed every year on the second Sunday in May.

mo•tion (**moh**-shuhn)
1. ***noun*** Movement.
2. ***verb*** To tell someone something through a movement. ▸ **motioning, motioned**
3. ***noun*** A formal suggestion made at a meeting or in a court of law. ▸ ***verb*** **motion**

mo•tion•less (**moh**-shun-liss) ***adjective*** Not moving. ▸ ***adverb*** **motionlessly**

motion picture ***noun*** A series of still pictures on a strip of film. When the film is run at high speed through a projector, the individual pictures blend into one another so that the people and things in the pictures appear to move.

mo•ti•vate (**moh**-tuh-*vate*) ***verb*** To encourage someone to do something. ▸ **motivating, motivated** ▸ ***noun*** **motivation** ▸ ***adjective*** **motivated**

mo•tive (**moh**-tiv) ***noun*** A reason for doing something.

mo•to•cross (**moh**-tuh-*kross*) ***noun*** A cross-country motorcycle race.

mo•tor (**moh**-tur)
1. ***noun*** A machine that provides the power to make something run or work.
2. ***adjective*** To do with a motor or something run by a motor, as in *motor vehicles* or *motor oil.*
3. ***verb*** To drive. ▸ **motoring, motored** ▸ ***noun*** **motoring**

mo•tor•bike (**moh**-tur-*bike*) ***noun***
1. A bicycle powered by a small motor.
2. A small or light motorcycle.

mo•tor•cy•cle (**moh**-tur-*sye*-kuhl) ***noun*** A heavy vehicle with two wheels and an engine.

mo•tor•ist (**moh**-tur-ist) ***noun*** Someone who travels by car.

mot•tled (**mot**-uhld) ***adjective*** If something is **mottled,** it is covered with patches of different colors.

mot•to (**mot**-oh) ***noun*** A short sentence that is meant to guide behavior or state what someone believes or stands for. ▸ ***noun, plural*** **mottoes** *or* **mottos**

mound (**mound**) ***noun***
1. A hill or a pile, as in *a mound of garbage.* ▸ ***verb*** **mound**
2. A slightly raised area for the pitcher in the center of a baseball diamond.

mount (**mount**)
1. ***verb*** To get on or to climb up.
2. ***verb*** To rise or to increase.
3. ***verb*** To set in place for display.
4. ***noun*** A horse or other animal used for riding.
5. ***noun*** Mountain. This word is usually used as part of a name, as in *Mount Everest.*
▸ ***verb*** **mounting, mounted**

moun•tain (**moun**-tuhn) ***noun***
1. A very high piece of land.
2. A large amount of something, as in *a mountain of work.*

mountain bike ***noun*** A strong bicycle with many gears and heavy tire treads that can be ridden on rough or hilly ground.

moun•tain•eer (*moun*-tuh-**nihr**) ***noun*** Someone who climbs mountains for sport. ▸ ***noun*** **mountaineering**

mountain lion ***noun*** A large, powerful wildcat, found in the mountains of North, Central, and South America. The mountain lion is also known as a **cougar, puma,** or **panther.**

mourn (**morn**) ***verb*** To be very sad and grieve for someone who has died. ▸ **mourning, mourned** ▸ ***noun*** **mourner,** ***noun*** **mourning**

mourn•ful (**morn**-fuhl) ***adjective*** Feeling, showing, or filled with grief, as in *a mournful song.* ▸ ***adverb*** **mournfully**

mouse (**mouss**) ***noun***
1. A small, furry animal with a pointed nose, small ears, and a long tail.
2. A small control box that you use to move the cursor on your computer screen.
▸ ***noun, plural*** **mice** (**misse**)

M

mousse (**mooss**) ***noun***
1. A cold dessert containing beaten egg whites or whipped cream and gelatin. Mousse is like a light and fluffy pudding.
2. A substance that you use to style your hair. **Mousse** sounds like **moose.**

moustache *See* **mustache.**

mous•y (**mou**-see) ***adjective***
1. Mousy hair is light brown.
2. Quiet and shy. ▸ ***noun*** **mousiness** ▸ ***adverb*** **mousily**

mouth
1. (**mouth**) ***noun*** The opening in the body through which people and animals take in foods.
2. (**mouth**) ***noun*** An opening that looks like a mouth, as in *the mouth of a jar* or *the mouth of a cave.*
3. (**mouth**) ***noun*** The part of a river where it empties into another body of water.
4. (**mouTH**) ***verb*** If you **mouth** words, you say them, sometimes insincerely, and sometimes by only moving your lips. ▸ **mouthing, mouthed**

mouth organ ***noun*** A harmonica.

mouth•piece (**mouth**-peess) ***noun***
1. The part of a telephone that you talk into.
2. The part of a musical instrument that you blow over or into.
3. *(informal)* Someone who acts as a spokesperson for an individual or a group.

move (**moov**)
1. *verb* To change place or position.
2. *verb* To change where you live or work.
3. *noun* A step or a movement.
4. *verb* If you are **moved** by something such as a movie or a piece of music, it makes you feel emotional.
5. *verb* To put or keep in motion.
6. *verb* To cause someone to do something.
7. *noun* An action planned to bring about a result.
8. *noun* A person's turn to change the position of a playing piece in games such as chess or checkers.
▸ ***noun*** **move** ▸ ***verb*** **moving, moved** ▸ ***adjective*** **moving,** ***adjective*** **movable** *or* **moveable**

move•ment (**moov**-muhnt) ***noun***
1. The act of moving from one place to another.
2. A group of people who have joined together to support a cause, as in *the civil rights movement.*
3. One of the main parts of a long piece of classical music.

mov•ie (**moo**-vee) ***noun*** A motion picture.

mow (**moh**) ***verb*** To cut grass, grain, hay, etc. ▸ **mowing, mowed, mown** (**mohn**) ▸ ***noun*** **mower**

MP3 (*em-pee-***three**) ***noun*** A type of computer file that records sound accurately. MP3 files can be played by a computer program or a device called an **MP3 player.**

mph *or* **m.p.h.** (**em-pee-aych**) An abbreviation for *miles per hour.*

Mr. (**miss**-ter) ***noun*** A title put in front of a man's name, as in *Mr. James Brown.*

Mrs. (**miss**-iz) ***noun*** A title put in front of a married woman's name, as in *Mrs. Clare White.*

Ms. (**miz**) ***noun*** A title put in front of a woman's name that does not indicate whether she is married or unmarried, as in *Ms. Anna Black.*

much (**muhch**)
1. *adjective* Great in amount or degree.
2. *adverb* Very.
3. *noun* A large amount of something.

mu•ci•lage (**myoo**-suh-lij) ***noun*** A kind of glue.

muck (**muhk**) ***noun*** Anything that is dirty, wet, sticky, or slimy, such as mud or manure.

mu•cus (**myoo**-kuhss) ***noun*** A slimy fluid that coats and protects the inside of your mouth, nose, throat, and other breathing passages. ▸ ***adjective*** **mucous** (**myoo**-kuhss)

mud (**muhd**) ***noun*** Earth that is wet, soft, and sticky.

mud•dle (**muh**-duhl)
1. ***verb*** To mix things up or confuse them. ▸ **muddling, muddled**
2. ***noun*** A mess or confusion.
▸ ***adjective*** **muddled**

mud•dy (**muhd**-ee)
1. ***adjective*** If something is **muddy,** it is covered with wet, sticky earth.
▸ **muddier, muddiest**
2. ***verb*** To make something muddy or unclear.
▸ **muddies, muddying, muddied**

muf•fin (**muhf**-uhn) ***noun*** A small cake or bread shaped like a cupcake.

muf•fle (**muhf**-uhl) ***verb*** To make a sound quieter or duller. ▸ **muffling, muffled**

muf•fler (**muhf**-lur) ***noun***
1. A device that reduces the noise made by an engine.
2. A warm scarf.

mug (**muhg**)
1. ***noun*** A large, heavy cup with a handle.
2. ***verb*** *(informal)* To attack someone and try to steal the person's money.
▸ **mugging, mugged** ▸ ***noun*** **mugger**

mug•gy (**muh**-gee) ***adjective*** If the weather is **muggy,** it is warm and damp. ▸ **muggier, muggiest** ▸ ***noun*** **mugginess**

Mu•ham•mad (moo-**ham**-id) *or* **Mo•ham•mad** (moh-**ham**-id) ***noun*** The founder of the Islamic religion. Muslims believe that Muhammad is God's main prophet.

mul•ber•ry (**muhl**-*ber*-ee) ***noun*** A tree with edible, dark purple berries. Mulberry leaves are sometimes used as food for silkworms.

mule (**myool**) ***noun***
1. An animal produced by mating a female horse with a male donkey.
2. A stubborn person.

mul•ti•cul•tur•al (*muhl*-ti-**kuhl**-chuh-ruhl) ***adjective*** Involving or made up of people from different races or religions, as in *a multicultural community.* ▸ ***adverb*** **multiculturally**

mul•ti•lin•gual (*muhl*-ti-**ling**-gwuhl) ***adjective*** Using or able to use several different languages.

mul•ti•me•di•a (*muhl*-ti-**mee**-dee-uh) ***adjective*** Using or combining different kinds of communication technologies, such as video and printed text. ▸ ***noun*** **multimedia**

mul•ti•na•tion•al (*muhl*-tee-**nash**-uhn-uhl) ***noun*** A company that has factories or offices in more than one country.
▸ ***adjective*** **multinational**

mul•ti•ple (**muhl**-tuh-puhl)
1. ***adjective*** Involving many parts or many things.
2. ***noun*** A number into which a smaller number can go an exact number of times.
3. ***adjective*** A **multiple-choice** test gives you a number of answers for each question, from which you have to choose one.

multiple scle•ro•sis (skluh-**roh**-suhss) ***noun*** A serious disease in which small areas of the brain and spinal cord are destroyed. It causes paralysis and muscle tremors.

mul•ti•pli•cand (*muhl*-tuh-pluh-**kand**) ***noun*** A number that is to be multiplied by another number.

mul•ti•pli•er (**mul**-tuh-*plye*-ur) ***noun*** The number by which you multiply another.

mul•ti•ply (**muhl**-tuh-*plye*) ***verb***
1. To add the same number to itself several times.
2. To grow in number or amount.
▸ ***verb*** **multiplies, multiplying, multiplied** ▸ ***noun*** **multiplication**

mul•ti•ra•cial (*muhl*-tee-**ray**-shuhl) ***adjective*** Involving people of different races, as in *a multiracial community.*
▸ ***adverb*** **multiracially**

M

mul•ti•tude (**muhl**-ti-tood) ***noun***
1. A crowd of people.
2. A large number of things.
▸ ***adjective*** **multitudinous**

mul•ti•vi•ta•min (*muhl*-tee-**vye**-tuh-min) ***noun*** A tablet containing several different vitamins.

mum•ble (**muhm**-buhl) ***verb*** To speak quietly and unclearly. ▸ **mumbling, mumbled**

mum•my (**muh**-mee) ***noun*** A dead body that has been preserved with special salts and resins and wrapped in cloth to make it last for a very long time. The ancient Egyptians placed the mummies of their rulers in elaborate coffins. ▸ ***noun, plural*** **mummies** ▸ ***verb*** **mummify** ▸ ***adjective*** **mummified**

mumps (**muhmps**) ***noun, plural*** An infectious illness caused by a virus that makes the glands at the sides of your face swell up and become sore.

munch (**muhnch**) ***verb*** To chew with a crunching sound. ▸ **munches, munching, munched**

mun•dane (muhn-**dayn**) ***adjective*** Boring and ordinary.

mu•nic•i•pal (myoo-**niss**-uh-puhl) ***adjective*** To do with a city or town and its services.

mu•ral (**myu**-ruhl) ***noun*** A painting on a wall.

mur•der (**mur**-dur) ***verb*** To kill someone deliberately. ▸ **murdering, murdered** ▸ ***noun*** **murder,** ***noun*** **murderer**

murk•y (**mur**-kee) ***adjective*** Dark, cloudy, or gloomy. ▸ **murkier, murkiest**

mur•mur (**mur**-mur) ***verb***
1. To talk very quietly.
2. To make a quiet, low, continuous sound.
▸ ***verb*** **murmuring, murmured** ▸ ***noun*** **murmur**

mus•cle (**muhss**-uhl) ***noun***
1. One of the parts of your body that produces movement. Your muscles are attached to your skeleton and pull on your bones to make them move.
2. Strength or power. *This job requires muscle.* **Muscle** sounds like **mussel.**

muse (**myooz**) ***verb*** To think deeply or to reflect. ▸ **musing, mused** ▸ ***noun*** **musing**

mu•se•um (myoo-**zee**-uhm) ***noun*** A place where interesting objects of art, history, or science are displayed.

mush (**muhsh**) ***noun***
1. A thick cereal made with cornmeal boiled in water or milk.
2. A thick, soft mass.

mush•room (**muhsh**-room *or* **muhsh**-rum)
1. ***noun*** A small fungus that is usually shaped like an umbrella. Many mushrooms can be eaten, but some are poisonous.
2. ***verb*** To grow or spread quickly.
▸ **mushrooming, mushroomed**

mu•sic (**myoo**-zik) ***noun***
1. A pleasant arrangement of sounds, such as in a song.
2. The art of combining sounds in a pleasing way.
3. Printed or written signs or notes that represent musical sounds.

mu•si•cal (**myoo**-zuh-kuhl)
1. ***adjective*** If you are **musical,** you are very interested in music or you can play an instrument well. ▸ ***adverb*** **musically**
2. ***adjective*** To do with music, as in *musical instruments.*
3. ***noun*** A play or movie that includes singing and dancing.
4. ***adjective*** Pleasing to the ear.

musical instrument ***noun*** An instrument on which you can play music.

mu•si•cian (**myoo**-zish-uhn) ***noun*** Someone who plays, sings, or composes music.

musk (**muhsk**) ***noun*** A substance with a strong odor, produced by some male deer, that is used in perfume, medicine, and soap.

mus•ket (**muhss**-kit) ***noun*** A gun with a long barrel that was used before the rifle was invented.

mus•ket•eer (*muhss*-kuh-**tihr**) ***noun*** A soldier who carried a musket.

musk•rat (**muhsk**-*rat*) ***noun*** A small, North American rodent with webbed hind feet, a flat tail, and thick, brown fur. Muskrats live in and around water.
▸ ***noun, plural*** **muskrat** *or* **muskrats**

Mus•lim (**muhz**-luhm) *or* **Mos•lem** (**moz**-luhm) ***noun*** Someone who follows the religion of Islam. ▸ ***adjective*** **Muslim** *or* **Moslem**

mus•lin (**muhz**-luhn) ***noun*** A cotton fabric used to make sheets, curtains, and clothing.

mus•sel (**muhss**-uhl) ***noun*** A type of shellfish that you can eat. **Mussel** sounds like **muscle.**

must (**muhst**)
1. ***verb*** To have to do something.
2. ***verb*** To be forced or required to do something.
3. ***verb*** To be definitely doing something.
4. ***noun*** Something that you need.

mus•tache *or* **mous•tache** (muh-**stash** *or* **muhss**-*tash*) ***noun*** The hair that grows on a person's upper lip.

mus•tang (**muhss**-tang) ***noun*** A wild horse found mostly on the western plains of the United States. Mustangs are descended from horses brought to America by the Spaniards.

mus•tard (**muhss**-turd) ***noun*** A spicy paste or powder made from the pungent seeds of the mustard plant.

mus•ter (**muhss**-tur) ***verb***
1. To assemble in a group.
2. To gather something together.
▸ ***verb*** **mustering, mustered**

must•n't (**muhss**-uhnt) ***contraction*** A short form of *must not.*

must•y (**muhss**-tee) ***adjective*** If something or someplace is **musty,** it smells of dampness, decay, or mold.
▸ **mustier, mustiest** ▸ ***noun*** **mustiness**

mu•tant (**myoot**-uhnt) ***noun*** A living thing that has developed different characteristics because of a change in its parents' genes. ▸ ***noun*** **mutation** ▸ ***verb*** **mutate**

mute (**myoot**)
1. ***adjective*** Silent, or unable to speak.
▸ ***adverb*** **mutely**
2. ***noun*** Someone who cannot speak.
3. ***noun*** Something that can be fitted to a musical instrument to make it play more softly.
▸ ***verb*** **mute**

mu•ti•late (**myoo**-tuh-*late*) ***verb*** To injure or damage something or someone seriously.
▸ **mutilating, mutilated** ▸ ***noun*** **mutilation**

mu•ti•ny (**myoot**-uh-nee) ***noun*** A revolt against someone in charge, especially in the navy. ▸ ***noun, plural*** **mutinies**
▸ ***noun*** **mutineer**
▸ ***verb*** **mutiny** ▸ ***adjective*** **mutinous**

mutt (**muht**) ***noun*** A dog of mixed breed.

mut•ter (**muht**-ur) ***verb*** To speak in a low, unclear way with the mouth nearly closed. ▸ **muttering, muttered** ▸ ***noun*** **mutter**

mut•ton (**muht**-uhn) ***noun*** Meat from a sheep.

mu•tu•al (**myoo**-choo-uhl) ***adjective*** Shared or joint, as in *a mutual friend.*
▸ ***adverb*** **mutually**

muz•zle (**muhz**-uhl) ***noun***
1. An animal's nose, mouth, and jaws.
2. A cover for an animal's mouth to keep it from biting. ▸ ***verb*** **muzzle**
3. The open end of a gun barrel.

my (**mye**) ***adjective*** Belonging to or having to do with me.

my•nah *or* **my•na** (**mye**-nuh) ***noun*** A dark brown bird originally found in Asia that is known for its ability to imitate the human voice.

my•ri•ad (**mihr**-ee-uhd) ***noun*** A large number. ▸ ***adjective*** **myriad**

my•self (*mye*-**self**) ***pronoun*** Me and no one else.

mys•te•ri•ous (miss-**tihr**-ee-uhss) ***adjective*** Very hard to explain or understand, as in *a mysterious stranger.*
▸ ***adverb*** **mysteriously**

N

mys•ter•y (**miss**-tur-ee) ***noun***
1. Something that is hard to explain or understand.
2. A story containing a puzzling crime that has to be solved, as in *a murder mystery.*
▸ ***noun, plural*** **mysteries**

mys•ti•fy (**miss**-tuh-fye) ***verb*** To puzzle or confuse someone. ▸ **mystifies, mystifying, mystified** ▸ ***noun*** **mystification**

myth (**mith**) ***noun***
1. A story that expresses the beliefs of a group of people, tells about gods or goddesses, or gives reasons for something that happens in nature, such as thunder.
2. A false idea that many people believe.

myth•i•cal (**mith**-i-kuhl) ***adjective***
1. To do with myths.
2. Imaginary or not real, as in *a mythical community of aliens.*

my•thol•o•gy (mi-**thol**-uh-jee) ***noun*** A collection of myths. ▸ ***noun, plural*** **mythologies** ▸ ***adjective*** **mythological**

nag (**nag**)
1. ***verb*** To annoy by scolding, complaining, or criticizing all the time. ▸ **nagging, nagged**
2. ***noun*** A horse, especially one that is old or worn-out.

nail (**nayl**) ***noun***
1. A small, pointed piece of metal that you hammer into something. ▸ ***verb*** **nail**
2. The hard covering at the ends of your fingers and toes.

na•ive *or* **na•ïve** (nah-**eev**) ***adjective*** If you are **naive,** you are not very experienced and may believe or trust people too much. ▸ **naiver, naivest** ▸ ***noun*** **naiveté** *or* **naïveté** (nah-*eev*-**tay**) ▸ ***adverb*** **naively**

na•ked (**nay**-kid) ***adjective***
1. Wearing no clothing. ▸ ***noun*** **nakedness** ▸ ***adverb*** **nakedly**
2. Bare or without the usual covering, as in *a naked branch.*
3. Without anything added, as in *the naked truth.*
4. Without the aid of a telescope or other optical instrument.

name (**naym**)
1. ***noun*** What a person, an animal, a place, or a thing is called. ▸ ***verb*** **name**
2. ***noun*** A bad or insulting word or phrase used to describe a person or thing.
3. ***noun*** Reputation.
4. ***verb*** To speak of or to mention.
5. ***verb*** To choose or to appoint.
▸ ***verb*** **naming, named**

nan•ny (**nan**-ee) ***noun***
1. Someone trained to look after young children in the children's home.
2. A female goat.
3. *(informal)* Grandmother.
▸ ***noun, plural*** **nannies**

nap (**nap**)
1. ***verb*** To sleep for a short time. ▸ **napping, napped** ▸ ***noun*** **nap**
2. ***noun*** The soft, fuzzy surface on certain kinds of cloth.

nape (**nape**) ***noun*** The back of your neck.

nap•kin (**nap**-kin) ***noun*** A square piece of paper or cloth used to protect clothes while eating and to wipe hands and lips.

nar•cis•sist (**nar**-si-sist) ***noun*** Someone who is overly interested in his or her own looks or body. ▸ ***noun*** **narcissism** ▸ ***adjective*** **narcissistic**

nar•cis•sus (nar-**siss**-uhss) ***noun*** A plant that grows from a bulb and has yellow or white flowers and long, thin leaves. The daffodil is a kind of narcissus. ▸ ***noun, plural*** **narcissuses** *or* **narcissus**

nar•cot•ic (nar-**kot**-ik) ***noun*** An often addictive drug that can be prescribed by a doctor to relieve pain. ▸ ***adjective*** **narcotic**

nar•rate (**na**-rate *or* na-**rate**) ***verb*** To tell a story. ▸ **narrating, narrated** ▸ ***noun*** **narration,** ***noun*** **narrator**

nar•ra•tive (**na**-ruh-tiv)
1. ***noun*** A story, or an account of something that has happened.
2. ***adjective*** Telling a story, as in *a narrative poem.*

nar•row (**na**-roh) ***adjective***
1. Not broad or wide, as in *a narrow street.* ▸ ***verb*** **narrow**
2. Limited, or small.
3. If you have a **narrow** escape, you only just get away.
4. If you are **narrow-minded,** you stick to your own ideas and do not want to listen to new ones.
▸ ***adjective*** **narrower, narrowest** ▸ ***noun*** **narrowness** ▸ ***adverb*** **narrowly**

na•sal (**nay**-zuhl) ***adjective***
1. To do with your nose, as in *nasal congestion.*
2. Spoken through the nose rather than the mouth.

nas•tur•tium (nuh-**stur**-shuhm) ***noun*** A plant with yellow, red, or orange flowers that are sometimes eaten in salads.

nas•ty (**nass**-tee) ***adjective***
1. Cruel or unkind. ▸ ***adverb*** **nastily**
2. Very unpleasant, as in *cold, nasty weather.*
3. Harmful or severe, as in *a nasty fall.*
▸ ***noun*** **nastiness** ▸ ***adjective*** **nastier, nastiest**

na•tion (**nay**-shuhn) ***noun*** A large group of people who live in the same part of the world and often share the same language, customs, and government.

na•tion•al (**nash**-uh-nuhl) ***adjective*** To do with, belonging to, or characteristic of a nation as a whole, as in *a national library* or *a national costume.* ▸ ***adverb*** **nationally**

National Guard ***noun*** A volunteer military organization with units in each state of the United States. Each National Guard unit is under the control of the governor of the state. However, the president can take command of the National Guard during a state of war or emergency.

na•tion•al•ist (**nash**-uh-nuh-list) ***noun*** Someone who is proud of his or her country or who fights for its independence. ▸ ***noun*** **nationalism** ▸ ***adjective*** **nationalistic**

na•tion•al•i•ty (nash-uh-**nal**-uh-tee) ***noun***
1. Your **nationality** is the status you have in a country by having been born there or by becoming a citizen.
2. A group of people who share a common language, culture, and history.
▸ ***noun, plural*** **nationalities**

na•tion•al•ize (**nash**-uh-nuh-*lize*) ***verb*** If an industry is **nationalized,** its ownership is transferred from a private company to the government. ▸ **nationalizing, nationalized** ▸ ***noun*** **nationalization**

national park ***noun*** A large section of land set aside by the government for public use.

N

na•tive (**nay**-tiv)
1. ***noun*** Someone born in a particular place.
2. ***noun*** A person, an animal, or a plant that originally lived or grew in a certain place.
3. ***adjective*** Belonging to a person because of where he or she was born.
4. Your **native country** is the country where you were born.
▸ ***adjective*** **native**

Native American ***noun*** One of the original inhabitants of North, Central, or South America or a descendant of these. Native Americans are sometimes called **American Indians.** ▸ ***adjective*** **Native American**

Na•tiv•i•ty (nuh-**tiv**-uh-tee *or* nay-**tiv**-uh-tee) ***noun*** The birth of Jesus, or a display or scene commemorating it.

NATO (**nay**-toh) ***noun*** A group of countries, including the United States and Britain, that help each other defend themselves. NATO stands for *North Atlantic Treaty Organization.*

nat•u•ral (**nach**-ur-uhl)
1. ***adjective*** Found in or produced by nature rather than being artificial or made by people, as in *natural rock formations.*
2. ***adjective*** Normal or usual.
3. ***adjective*** Present from birth rather than being learned.
4. ***adjective*** Lifelike or closely following nature.
5. ***adjective*** Not faked or not forced.
6. ***noun*** A person who is good at something because of a special talent or ability.
7. ***adjective*** In music, a **natural** note is one that is not sharp or flat.
8. ***adjective*** In a musical score, a **natural** sign shows that the next note is natural.
▸ ***noun*** **natural** ▸ ***adverb*** **naturally**

natural gas ***noun*** A gas that is found beneath the earth's surface. It consists mainly of methane and is used for heating and cooling.

natural history ***noun*** The study of animals and plants.

na•tu•ral•ist (**nach**-ur-uh-list) ***noun*** Someone who studies animals and plants.

nat•u•ral•ize (**nach**-ur-uh-*lize*) ***verb*** To give citizenship to someone who was born in another country. ▸ **naturalizing, naturalized**

natural resource ***noun*** A material found in nature that is necessary or useful to people. Forests, water, and minerals are some natural resources.

na•ture (**nay**-chur) ***noun***
1. Everything in the world that is not made by people, such as plants, animals, the weather, etc.
2. The character of someone or something.

naught (**nawt**) ***noun***
1. Nothing.
2. Zero.

naught•y (**naw**-tee) ***adjective*** Badly behaved, or disobedient. ▸ **naughtier, naughtiest** ▸ ***noun*** **naughtiness** ▸ ***adverb*** **naughtily**

nau•se•a (**naw**-zee-uh *or* **naw**-zhuh) ***noun*** A feeling of being sick to your stomach. ▸ ***adjective*** **nauseous** (**naw**-shuhss)**,** ***adjective*** **nauseated**

nau•ti•cal (**naw**-tuh-kuhl)
1. ***adjective*** To do with ships, sailing, or navigation.
2. nautical mile ***noun*** A unit for measuring distance at sea or in the air. One nautical mile equals 6,076 feet.

Na•va•jo *or* **Na•va•ho** (**nav**-uh-*hoh*) ***noun*** One of a group of American Indians that lives primarily in New Mexico, Arizona, and Utah. ▸ ***noun, plural*** **Navajo, Navajos** *or* **Navaho, Navahos**

na•val (**nay**-vuhl) ***adjective*** To do with a navy or warships. **Naval** sounds like **navel.**

na•vel (**nay**-vuhl) ***noun*** The small, round hollow in your stomach where your umbilical cord was attached when you were born. **Navel** sounds like **naval.**

nav•i•gate (**nav**-uh-gate) ***verb***
1. To travel in a ship, an aircraft, or other vehicle using maps, compasses, the stars, etc., to guide you.
2. To sail on or across.
▸ ***verb*** **navigating, navigated** ▸ ***noun*** **navigation,** ***noun*** **navigator**

na•vy (**nay**-vee) ***noun*** The entire military sea force of a country, including ships, aircraft, weapons, land bases, and people. ▸ ***noun, plural*** **navies**

navy blue ***noun*** A very dark blue color. ▸ ***adjective*** **navy blue**

Na•zi (**not**-see *or* **nat**-see) ***noun***
1. A member of the group, led by Adolf Hitler, that ruled Germany from 1933 to 1945. Nazis attempted to rid the human race of people they considered "impure" by killing millions of Jews, Gypsies, and other peoples from eastern Europe. They fought World War II to try to spread their beliefs around the world.
2. nazi *or* **Nazi** A person with beliefs similar to those of the Nazis, especially a cruel, violently racist person.
▸ ***adjective*** **Nazi** *or* **nazi**

near (**nihr**)
1. ***preposition*** Close to.
2. ***adverb*** Close. ▸ ***adjective*** **near**
3. ***verb*** To come closer to something.
▸ **nearing, neared**
4. ***adjective*** Narrow or close.
5. ***adjective*** Closely related or associated.
▸ ***noun*** **nearness** ▸ ***adjective and adverb*** **nearer, nearest**

near•by (**nihr-bye**) ***adjective*** Not far away. ▸ ***adverb*** **nearby**

near•ly (**nihr**-lee) ***adverb*** Almost or not quite.

near•sight•ed (**nihr-sye**-tid) ***adjective*** Able to see nearby objects more clearly than faraway ones.

neat (**neet**) ***adjective***
1. Orderly and clean. ▸ ***noun*** **neatness**
2. Done in a clever or skillful way.
▸ ***adjective*** **neater, neatest** ▸ ***adverb*** **neatly**

neb•u•la (**neb**-yuh-luh) ***noun*** A bright, cloudlike mass that can be seen in the night sky. Nebulae are made up of stars or gases and dust. ▸ ***noun, plural*** **nebulae** (**neb**-yuh-*lee or* **neb**-yuh-*lye*) *or* **nebulas**

nec•es•sar•y (**ness**-uh-*ser*-ee) ***adjective*** If something is **necessary,** you have to do it or have it. ▸ ***adverb*** **necessarily**

ne•ces•si•ty (nuh-**sess**-uh-tee) ***noun***
1. A very strong need or requirement.
2. Necessities are the things you cannot live without, such as food and shelter.

neck (**nek**) ***noun***
1. The part of your body that joins your head to your shoulders.
2. The narrow part of a garment that fits around your neck.
3. A narrow part of something, as in *the neck of a bottle.*

neck•er•chief (**nek**-ur-*cheef or* **nek**-ur-chif) ***noun*** A scarf or square of cloth worn around the neck.

neck•lace (**nek**-liss) ***noun*** A piece of jewelry worn around the neck.

neck•tie (**nek**-*tye*) ***noun*** A long, narrow strip of cloth that is tied around the neck and knotted. A necktie is worn under a shirt collar, usually with suits or jackets.

nec•tar (**nek**-tur) ***noun*** A sweet liquid that bees collect from flowers and turn into honey.

nec•tar•ine (*nek*-tuh-**reen**) ***noun*** A fruit similar to a peach but with a smooth skin.

need (**need**)
1. ***verb*** To want or require something urgently.
2. ***noun*** Something that you have to have.
3. ***verb*** To have to do something.
4. ***noun*** A necessity or an obligation.
5. ***noun*** Poverty or hardship.
Need sounds like **knead.**
▸ ***verb*** **needing, needed**

N

nee•dle (**nee**-duhl)
1. ***noun*** A thin, pointed piece of metal with a hole for thread at one end, used for sewing.
2. ***noun*** A long, thin, pointed rod used for knitting.
3. ***noun*** A thin, hollow tube with a sharp point that doctors use for injections or taking blood.
4. ***noun*** A pointer on an instrument such as a compass.
5. ***noun*** A very thin, pointed leaf on a fir tree or pine tree.
6. ***verb*** *(informal)* If someone **needles** you, the person annoys you. ▸ **needling, needled**

need•less (**need**-liss) ***adjective*** If something is **needless,** it is not necessary. ▸ ***adverb*** **needlessly**

nee•dle•work (**need**-uhl-*wurk*) ***noun*** Work that is done with a needle, such as embroidery or lace.

need•n't (**need**-uhnt) ***contraction*** A short form of *need not.*

need•y (**nee**-dee) ***adjective*** Very poor or in need. ▸ **needier, neediest**

neg•a•tive (**neg**-uh-tiv)
1. ***adjective*** Giving the answer "no."
2. ***adjective*** If someone has a **negative** attitude, that person is not optimistic or helpful. ▸ ***adverb*** **negatively**
3. ***noun*** A photographic film used to make prints. A negative shows light areas as dark and dark areas as light.
4. ***adjective*** A **negative** number is less than zero.
5. ***adjective*** Having one of two opposite kinds of electrical charge.
6. ***adjective*** Showing that a disease or condition is not present.
▸ ***noun*** **negative**

neg•lect (ni-**glekt**)
1. ***verb*** To fail to take care of someone or something. ▸ ***adjective*** **neglectful**
2. ***verb*** To fail to do something, especially from carelessness.
3. ***noun*** If a person, building, etc., is suffering from **neglect,** it has not been looked after properly.
▸ ***verb*** **neglecting, neglected**

neg•li•gent (**neg**-luh-juhnt) ***adjective*** Careless or not attentive to one's duties.
▸ ***noun*** **negligence**

ne•go•ti•ate (ni-**goh**-shee-ate *or* ni-**goh**-see-ate) ***verb*** To bargain or discuss something so that you can come to an agreement. ▸ **negotiating, negotiated**
▸ ***noun*** **negotiation,** ***noun*** **negotiator**

Ne•gro (**nee**-groh) ***noun*** A member of a race of people with dark skin, hair, and eyes, thought to have come originally from central and southern Africa. *See* **African American.** ▸ ***noun, plural*** **Negroes**

neigh (**nay**) ***noun*** The sound that a horse makes. ▸ ***verb*** **neigh**

neigh•bor (**nay**-bur) ***noun***
1. Someone who lives next door to you or near to you.
2. A person, place, or thing that is next to or near another.
3. Another human being.

neigh•bor•hood (**nay**-bur-*hud*) ***noun***
1. Your **neighborhood** is the local area around your house.
2. In a city or town, a small area or section where people live.

nei•ther (**nee**-THur *or* **nye**-THur)
1. ***adjective*** Not either.
2. ***pronoun*** Not either one.
3. ***conjunction*** Nor.
4. ***conjunction*** Used with **nor** to show two negative choices or possibilities.

ne•on (**nee**-on) ***noun*** A colorless, odorless gas that glows when an electric current is passed through it. Neon is used in lights and signs.

neph•ew (**nef**-yoo) ***noun*** Someone's **nephew** is the son of his or her brother, sister, brother-in-law, or sister-in-law.

Nep•tune (**nep**-toon) ***noun*** The eighth planet in distance from the sun. Neptune is the fourth-largest planet in our solar system.

nerd (**nurd**) ***noun*** *(slang)* A person who is considered unattractive or clumsy but who also has the reputation of being very smart or expert at something, as in *a computer nerd.* ▸ ***adjective* nerdy**

nerve (**nurv**) ***noun***

1. A **nerve** is one of the thin fibers that send messages between your brain or spinal cord and other parts of your body so that you can move and feel.

2. Courage.

3. *(informal)* Boldness or rudeness.

4. ***noun, plural*** *(informal)* If someone suffers from **nerves,** he or she is worried or frightened.

nerv•ous (**nur**-vuhss)

1. ***adjective*** Easily upset or tense.

2. ***adjective*** Fearful or timid.

3. ***adjective*** To do with the nerves, as in *nervous energy.*

4. ***noun*** If someone has a **nervous breakdown,** the person becomes very depressed and feels unable to cope with his or her problems.

▸ ***noun* nervousness** ▸ ***adverb* nervously**

nervous system ***noun*** A system in the body that includes the brain, spinal cord, and nerves. In vertebrates, the nervous system controls all the actions of the body.

nest (**nest**)

1. ***noun*** A place built by birds and many other animals to lay their eggs and/or bring up their young.

2. ***verb*** To make or settle in a nest or home. ▸ **nesting, nested**

3. ***noun*** A cozy place or shelter.

nes•tle (**ness**-uhl) ***verb*** To settle into a comfortable position. ▸ **nestling, nestled**

net (**net**)

1. ***noun*** Material made from fine threads or ropes that are knotted together with holes in between them.

2. ***noun*** A bag made from such material that is attached to a pole and used to catch fish, butterflies, etc.

3. ***verb*** To catch with or as if with a net.

4. ***noun*** A **net amount** of money is the amount left after everything necessary, such as taxes and expenses, has been taken away.

5. ***noun*** The **net weight** of something is its weight without packaging.

6. ***noun*** The **Net** is short for the **Internet.**

net•tle (**net**-uhl) ***noun*** A weed with sharp hairs that sting you if you touch them.

net•work (**net**-*wurk*)

1. ***noun*** A large number of lines forming a crisscross pattern, as in *a network of railroad tracks.*

2. ***noun*** A system of things that are connected to each other, as in *a television network.*

3. ***verb*** To connect computers so that they can work together. ▸ **networking, networked** ▸ ***noun* network**

4. ***noun*** A group of people who exchange professional or social information with each other. ▸ ***verb* network** ▸ ***noun* networking**

neu•rot•ic (nu-**rot**-ik) ***adjective*** If someone is **neurotic,** the person is very scared or worried, usually about something imaginary. ▸ ***adverb* neurotically**

neu•ter (**noo**-tur)

1. ***adjective*** Neither masculine nor feminine.

2. ***adjective*** In some languages, nouns that are neither masculine nor feminine in gender are **neuter.** In English, the pronoun *it* refers to neuter nouns, such as *table.*

neu•tral (**noo**-truhl)

1. ***adjective*** If a country or a person is **neutral** in a war or an argument, it does not support either side. ▸ ***noun* neutrality** ▸ ***adverb* neutrally**

2. ***noun*** When a car is in **neutral,** the gears are arranged so that they cannot pass on power to the wheels.

3. ***adjective*** **Neutral** colors are pale and not colorful.

4. ***adjective*** In chemistry, a **neutral** substance is neither an acid nor a base.

N

neu·tral·ize (**noo**-truh-*lize*) ***verb*** To stop something from working or from having an effect. ▸ **neutralizing, neutralized**

neu·tron (**noo**-tron) ***noun*** One of the extremely small parts in the nucleus of an atom. The neutron has no electrical charge.

nev·er (**nev**-ur) ***adverb*** At no time or not ever.

nev·er·the·less (*nev*-ur-THuh-**less**) ***adverb*** In spite of that; yet.

new (**noo**) ***adjective***
1. Just made or begun.
2. Seen, known, or thought of for the first time.
3. Unfamiliar or strange.
4. Not yet used to or experienced at.
5. Recently arrived or established in a place, position, relationship, or role.
6. Not yet worn or used, as in *new clothes.*
7. Repeating or beginning again, as in *a new year.*
8. Taking the place of one that came before.

New sounds like **gnu** and **knew.**
▸ ***adjective*** **newer, newest**

new·born (**noo**-*born*) ***adjective***
1. Recently born, as in *a newborn baby.* ▸ ***noun*** **newborn**
2. Fresh or renewed.

new·com·er (**noo**-*kuhm*-ur) ***noun*** Someone who has just come to a place.

New Eng·land (**ing**-gluhnd) ***noun*** A region of the northeastern United States made up of six states: Maine, New Hampshire, Vermont, Massachusetts, Rhode Island, and Connecticut.

new moon ***noun*** The phase of the moon when the side turned toward the earth is entirely dark.

news (**nooz**) ***noun*** Fresh or recent information or facts.

news·cast (**nooz**-*kast*) ***noun*** A television or radio program that presents the news. ▸ ***noun*** **newscaster**

news·pa·per (**nooz**-*pay*-pur) ***noun*** A publication made up of several pages of paper containing news reports, articles, letters, etc. Newspapers are usually published daily.

news·stand (**nooz**-*stand*) ***noun*** A place where newspapers and magazines and sometimes books and snacks are sold.

newt (**noot**) ***noun*** A small salamander with short legs and a long tail that lives on land but lays its eggs in water.

New Testament ***noun*** A collection of writings that makes up the second section of the Christian Bible. It deals with the life and teachings of Jesus Christ and his disciples.

new·ton (**noot**-uhn) ***noun*** A unit used by physicists for measuring force.

New Year's Day ***noun*** January 1, a holiday celebrating the first day of the new year.

next (**nekst**)
1. ***adjective*** Immediately following.
2. ***adjective*** Nearest or closest.
3. ***adverb*** Immediately after.

next door ***adverb*** In or at the nearest house, building, etc. ▸ ***adjective*** **next-door**

Nez Percé (**nez purss**) ***noun*** One of a group of American Indians that lives primarily in Washington, Oregon, and Idaho. French explorers called them Nez Percé, or "pierced nose," because they wore nose pendants. ▸ ***noun, plural*** **Nez Percé** *or* **Nez Percés**

nib·ble (**nib**-uhl) ***verb*** To bite something gently, or to take small bites of something. ▸ **nibbling, nibbled** ▸ ***noun*** **nibble**

nice (**nisse**) ***adjective***
1. Pleasant.
2. Kind.
3. Polite.

▸ ***adjective*** **nicer, nicest** ▸ ***adverb*** **nicely**

niche (**nich**) ***noun***
1. A hollow place in a wall that is often used to hold or display a statue.

N

2. A place, position, or situation for which someone is especially suited.

nick (**nik**)
1. ***noun*** A small cut or chip on a surface or an edge. ▸ ***verb*** **nick**
2. If something happens **in the nick of time,** it happens at the last moment or just in time.

nick•el (**nik**-uhl) ***noun***
1. A hard, silver-gray metal that is added to alloys to make them strong.
2. A coin of the United States equal to five cents.

nick•name (**nik**-*name*) ***noun***
1. A descriptive name used with or instead of a person's real name.
2. A familiar or shortened form of a name.
▸ ***verb*** **nickname**

nic•o•tine (**nik**-uh-teen) ***noun*** A poisonous and addictive substance found in tobacco.

niece (**neess**) ***noun*** Someone's **niece** is the daughter of his or her brother, sister, brother-in-law, or sister-in-law.

night (**nite**) ***noun*** The time between sunset and sunrise, when it is dark.

night•fall (**nite**-*fawl*) ***noun*** The period of time at dusk when the light of day is ending and night begins.

night•gown (**nite**-*goun*) ***noun*** A loose dress that girls or women wear in bed.

night•in•gale (**nite**-uhn-*gale*) ***noun*** A small, brown and white bird that lives in Europe and Asia. The male is known for its beautiful song.

night•ly (**nite**-lee) ***adverb*** Done or happening every night. ▸ ***adjective*** **nightly**

night•mare (**nite**-*mair*) ***noun*** A frightening or unpleasant dream or experience.

night•time (**nite**-*time*) ***noun*** The hours of darkness, from dusk until dawn.

nim•ble (**nim**-buhl) ***adjective*** If you are **nimble,** you move quickly and lightly.
▸ **nimbler, nimblest** ▸ ***adverb*** **nimbly**

nine (**nine**) ***noun*** The whole number, written 9, that comes after 8 and before 10. ▸ ***adjective*** **nine**

nin•ja (**nin**-juh) ***noun*** A person who is highly trained in ancient Japanese martial arts, especially one hired as a spy or an assassin.

nip (**nip**) ***verb***
1. To bite or pinch sharply but not hard.
2. To cut off by pinching.
3. To sting, or to chill. ▸ ***adjective*** **nippy**
▸ ***verb*** **nipping, nipped** ▸ ***noun*** **nip**

nip•ple (**nip**-uhl) ***noun***
1. The small, raised part at the center of a breast or an udder.
2. A small rubber cap with a hole, attached to the top of a baby's bottle.

ni•tro•gen (**nye**-truh-juhn) ***noun*** A colorless, odorless gas that makes up about four-fifths of the earth's air.

nits (**nits**) ***noun, plural*** Eggs laid by lice.

no (**noh**)
1. ***adverb*** Not so; a negative response to a question.
2. ***adverb*** Not at all.
3. ***interjection*** A word used to show surprise, wonder, or disbelief.
4. ***adjective*** Not any.
5. ***adjective*** Not a.
6. ***noun*** A word used to show refusal or denial.
7. ***noun*** A negative vote or voter.
No sounds like **know.**
▸ ***noun, plural*** **noes**

no•ble (**noh**-buhl) ***adjective***
1. If someone is **noble,** the person acts in a way that is idealistic and considerate. ▸ ***adverb*** **nobly**
2. A **noble** family is aristocratic and of high rank. ▸ ***noun*** **noble,** ***noun*** **nobleman,** ***noun*** **noblewoman**
3. Impressive or magnificent in appearance, as in *a noble redwood tree.*
▸ ***adjective*** **nobler, noblest** ▸ ***noun*** **nobility** (noh-**bil**-i-tee)

N

no·bod·y (**noh**-*bod*-ee *or* **noh**-*buh*-dee)
1. ***pronoun*** Not a single person.
2. ***noun*** If someone is a **nobody,** he or she is not considered to be important.
▸ ***noun, plural*** **nobodies**

noc·tur·nal (nok-**tur**-nuhl) ***adjective***
1. To do with the night, or happening at night, as in *a nocturnal journey.* ▸ ***adverb*** **nocturnally**
2. A **nocturnal** animal is active at night.

nod (**nod**) ***verb***
1. To move your head up and down, especially to say yes.
2. To let the head fall forward with a quick motion, especially when you are sleepy.
3. To show or say something by nodding.
4. To bend or to sway.
▸ ***verb*** **nodding, nodded** ▸ ***noun*** **nod**

noise (**noiz**) ***noun*** A sound, especially a loud or unpleasant one. ▸ ***noun*** **noisiness**

nois·y (**noi**-zee) ***adjective*** Loud.
▸ **noisier, noisiest** ▸ ***adverb*** **noisily**

no·mad (**noh**-mad) ***noun***
1. A member of a tribe that wanders around instead of living in one place.
2. A person who wanders from place to place. ▸ ***adjective*** **nomadic**

nom·i·nate (**nom**-uh-nate) ***verb*** To suggest that someone would be the right person to do a job or to receive an honor. ▸ **nominating, nominated**
▸ ***noun*** **nomination**

nom·i·nee (nom-uh-**nee**) ***noun*** Someone who is chosen to run in an election, to fill a position, or to be considered for an award or an honor.

none (**nuhn**)
1. ***pronoun*** No one or not one.
2. ***pronoun*** Not any or no part.
3. ***adverb*** Not at all.
None sounds like **nun.**

none·the·less (*nuhn*-THuh-**less**) ***adverb*** In spite of that.

non·fic·tion (non-**fik**-shuhn) ***noun*** Writing that is not fiction, especially information about real things, people, and events.

non·sense (**non**-senss) ***noun***
1. If something is **nonsense,** it is silly or has no meaning.
2. Talk, writing, or behavior that is silly or annoying.
▸ ***adjective*** **nonsensical**

non·stop (**non-stop**) ***adjective*** Without any stops or breaks, as in *a nonstop flight from New York to Los Angeles.* ▸ ***adverb*** **nonstop**

noo·dle (**noo**-duhl) ***noun*** A flat strip of dried dough, usually made from flour, water, and eggs.

noon (**noon**) ***noun*** Twelve o'clock in the middle of the day.

no one ***pronoun*** Not a single person.

noose (**nooss**) ***noun*** A large loop at the end of a piece of rope that closes up as the rope is pulled.

nor (**nor**) ***conjunction*** And not. Nor is often used with **neither.**

nor·mal (**nor**-muhl)
1. ***adjective*** Usual or regular.
2. ***adjective*** Healthy.
3. ***noun*** The usual condition.
▸ ***noun*** **normality,** ***noun*** **normalcy**
▸ ***adverb*** **normally**

north (**north**)
1. ***noun*** One of the four main points of the compass. North is to your right when you face the direction where the sun sets. ▸ ***adverb*** **north**
2. North ***noun*** Any area or region lying in this direction.
3. the North ***noun*** In the United States, the region that is north of Maryland, the Ohio River, and Missouri, especially the states that fought against the Confederacy in the Civil War.
4. ***adjective*** To do with or existing in the north, as in *the north shore of the lake.*
▸ ***adjective*** **northern**

North A·mer·ic·a (uh-**mer**-i-kuh) ***noun*** The continent in the Western Hemisphere that includes the United States, Canada, Mexico, and Central

America. ▸ ***noun*** **North American** ▸ ***adjective*** **North American**

North•east (*north*-**eest**) ***noun*** The area of the United States to the north and east, including New England, New York, and sometimes New Jersey and Pennsylvania.

Northern Hemisphere ***noun*** The half of the earth that is north of the equator.

northern lights ***noun, plural*** Colorful streams of light that appear at night in the far northern sky. Northern lights are also called the **aurora borealis.**

North Pole ***noun*** The most northern point on Earth, located at the upper tip of the earth's axis. The North Pole is in the Arctic.

North Star ***noun*** A bright star in the northern sky located directly over the North Pole.

north•ward (**north**-wurd) ***adverb*** To or toward the north. ▸ ***adjective*** **northward**

North•west (*north*-**west**) ***noun*** The area of the United States to the north and west that includes Washington, Oregon, and Idaho.

nose (**nohz**)

1. ***noun*** The part of your face that you use when you smell and breathe.

2. ***noun*** The pointed part at the front of some aircraft. *See* **aircraft.**

3. ***verb*** To move forward slowly and carefully. ▸ **nosing, nosed**

nose cone ***noun*** The front section of a missile, rocket, or jet engine that is shaped like a cone to reduce friction with the air. *See* **aircraft, jet engine.**

nosh (**nosh**)

1. ***noun*** A snack or a light meal.▸ ***noun, plural*** **noshes**

2. ***verb*** To eat a snack. ▸ **noshes, noshing, noshed** ▸ ***noun*** **nosher**

nos•tal•gic (noss-**tal**-jik) ***adjective*** People who are **nostalgic** like to think about the past and are sad because things have changed since then. ▸ ***noun*** **nostalgia** (noss-**tal**-juh) ▸ ***adverb*** **nostalgically**

nos•tril (**noss**-truhl) ***noun*** Your **nostrils** are the two openings in your nose through which you breathe and smell.

nos•y (**noh**-zee) ***adjective*** Someone who is **nosy** is too interested in things that do not concern him or her. ▸ **nosier, nosiest** ▸ ***adverb*** **nosily**

not (**not**) ***adverb*** At no time or in no way. *Not* is used to make a statement negative. **Not** sounds like **knot.**

no•ta•ble (**noh**-tuh-buhl)

1. ***adjective*** Important, remarkable, or worthy of notice. ▸ ***adverb*** **notably**

2. ***noun*** An important or well-known person.

no•ta•tion (noh-**tay**-shuhn) ***noun***

1. A series of signs or symbols used to represent elements in a system such as music or math.

2. A short note.

notch (**noch**) ***noun***

1. A cut or nick shaped like a *V*. ▸ ***verb*** **notch**

2. A narrow opening between mountains.

note (**noht**)

1. ***noun*** A short letter or message.

2. ***noun*** A word, phrase, or short sentence written down to remind you of something.

3. ***noun*** A piece of paper money.

4. ***noun*** A musical sound, or the symbol that represents it. *See* **notation.**

5. ***verb*** To notice a fact and pay attention to it.

6. ***verb*** To write something down. ▸ ***verb*** **noting, noted**

note•book (**noht**-*buk*) ***noun***

1. A small pad or book of paper used for writing notes.

2. A very small portable computer.

noth•ing (**nuhth**-ing)

1. ***pronoun*** Not anything at all.

2. ***pronoun*** Not anything important.

3. ***noun*** Zero.

N

N

no•tice (**noh**-tiss)
1. ***verb*** To see something, or to become aware of it. ▸ **noticing, noticed** ▸ ***adjective*** **noticeable** ▸ ***adverb*** **noticeably**
2. ***noun*** Attention or observation.
3. ***noun*** A written message put in a public place to tell people about something.
4. ***noun*** A warning or an announcement.
5. If someone **gives notice,** the person notifies his or her employer that he or she will be leaving that job shortly.

no•ti•fy (**noh**-tuh-fye) ***verb*** To tell someone about something officially or formally. ▸ **notifies, notifying, notified** ▸ ***noun*** **notification**

no•tion (**noh**-shun) ***noun***
1. An idea.
2. A desire or a whim.
3. notions ***noun, plural*** Small, useful items such as needles, pins, buttons, thread, and ribbons.

no•to•ri•ous (noh-**tor**-ee-uhss) ***adjective*** If someone is **notorious,** the person is well known for something bad.

noun (**noun**) ***noun*** A word that names a person, place, or thing.

nour•ish (**nur**-ish) ***verb*** To give a person or an animal enough food to keep him or her strong and healthy. ▸ **nourishes, nourishing, nourished** ▸ ***noun*** **nourishment** ▸ ***adjective*** **nourishing**

nov•el (**nov**-uhl)
1. ***noun*** A book that tells a long story about made-up people and events. ▸ ***noun*** **novelist**
2. ***adjective*** New and unusual, as in *a novel idea.*

nov•el•ty (**nov**-uhl-tee) ***noun*** Something new, interesting, and unusual. ▸ ***noun, plural*** **novelties** ▸ ***adjective*** **novelty**

No•vem•ber (noh-**vem**-bur) ***noun*** The 11th month on the calendar, after October and before December. November has 30 days.

nov•ice (**nov**-iss) ***noun***
1. A beginner or someone who is not very experienced.
2. Someone who joins a religious order for a trial period before taking vows.

now (**nou**)
1. ***adverb*** At present.
2. ***adverb*** At once.
3. ***adverb*** In the recent past.
4. ***noun*** The present time.
5. ***conjunction*** Since.

now•a•days (**nou**-uh-*daze*) ***adverb*** At the present time.

no•where (**no**-*wair*)
1. ***adverb*** Not any place.
2. ***noun*** An unknown or unimportant place or state of being.

noz•zle (**noz**-uhl) ***noun*** A spout that directs the flow of liquid from the end of a hose or tube.

nu•cle•ar (**noo**-klee-ur)
1. ***adjective*** To do with a nucleus.
2. ***adjective*** To do with the energy created by splitting atoms.
3. nuclear power ***noun*** Power created by splitting atoms.
4. nuclear weapon ***noun*** A weapon that uses the power created by splitting atoms.
5. nuclear reactor ***noun*** A large machine that produces nuclear power in a power station.

nu•cle•us (**noo**-klee-uhss) ***noun***
1. A central or core part around which other parts are grouped.
2. The central part of an atom, made up of neutrons and protons.
3. The central part of a cell, containing the chromosomes.
▸ ***noun, plural*** **nuclei** (**noo**-klee-*eye*)

nude (**nood**)
1. ***adjective*** Naked. ▸ ***noun*** **nudist,** ***noun*** **nudity**
2. ***noun*** A naked human figure, especially one in a painting or sculpture.

nudge (**nuhj**) ***verb*** To give someone or something a small push, often with the elbow. ▸ **nudging, nudged** ▸ ***noun*** **nudge**

nug•get (**nuhg**-it) ***noun***
1. A small lump or chunk of something,

especially precious metal, as in *a nugget of gold.*
2. A tiny bit or a tidbit, as in *a nugget of wisdom.*

nui•sance (**noo**-suhnss) ***noun*** Someone or something that annoys you and causes problems for you.

numb (**nuhm**) ***adjective***
1. Unable to feel anything, or unable to move.
2. Stunned.
▸ ***noun*** **numbness** ▸ ***verb*** **numb**

num•ber (**nuhm**-bur)
1. ***noun*** A word or symbol used for counting and for adding and subtracting.
2. ***verb*** To give a number to something.
3. ***verb*** To amount to a number.
4. ***noun*** A number that identifies someone or something, as in *a telephone number.*
5. ***noun*** A large quantity or group.
▸ ***verb*** **numbering, numbered**

nu•mer•al (**noo**-mur-uhl) ***noun*** A written symbol that represents a number, such as 8 or VIII.

nu•mer•a•tor (**noo**-muh-*ray*-tur) ***noun*** In fractions, the **numerator** is the number above the line. The numerator shows how many parts of the denominator are taken.

nu•mer•i•cal (noo-**mer**-uh-kuhl) ***adjective*** To do with numbers, as in *numerical order.* ▸ ***adverb*** **numerically**

nu•mer•ous (**noo**-mur-uhss) ***adjective*** Many, or made up of a large number.

nun (**nuhn**) ***noun*** A woman who lives in a religious community and has promised to devote her life to God. **Nun** sounds like **none.**

nurse (**nurss**)
1. ***noun*** Someone who looks after people who are ill, usually in a hospital.
2. ***verb*** To look after someone who is ill.
3. ***noun*** A woman hired to take care of children.
4. ***verb*** To feed offspring milk from a breast.
5. ***verb*** To treat with care.
▸ ***verb*** **nursing, nursed**

nurs•er•y (**nur**-sur-ee) ***noun***
1. A baby's bedroom.
2. A place where babies and very young children are looked after while their parents are at work.
3. A place where you can buy trees and plants.
4. nursery rhyme A short poem for very young children.
5. nursery school A school for children aged three to five years old, before they go to kindergarten.
▸ ***noun, plural*** **nurseries**

nur•ture (**nur**-chur) ***verb*** To tend to the needs of someone, especially a child.
▸ **nurturing, nurtured** ▸ ***noun*** **nurturer**

nut (**nuht**) ***noun***
1. A fruit or seed with a hard shell called a hull and one or more softer kernels inside that can usually be eaten.
2. The edible kernel of a nut.
3. A small metal piece with a hole in the middle that screws on to a bolt and holds it in place.
4. A strange or silly person.
▸ ***adjective*** **nutty**

nut•crack•er (**nuht**-*krak*-ur) ***noun*** A tool for cracking nuts.

nut•hatch (**nuht**-*hach*) ***noun*** A small bird that eats insects and can climb down trees headfirst.

nut•meg (**nuht**-meg) ***noun*** An aromatic spice made by grinding up the seeds of an evergreen tree that grows in Indonesia and elsewhere in the tropics.

nu•tri•ent (**noo**-tree-uhnt) ***noun*** Something that is needed by people, animals, and plants to stay strong and healthy. Proteins, minerals, and vitamins are all nutrients.

nu•tri•tious (noo-**trish**-uhss) ***adjective*** Food that is **nutritious** contains substances that your body can use to help you stay healthy and strong.
▸ ***noun*** **nutrition** ▸ ***adverb*** **nutritiously**

N

O

nuz•zle (**nuhz**-uhl) ***verb***
1. To rub or touch with the nose as an animal does.
2. To cuddle or lie close to someone or something.
▸ ***verb* nuzzling, nuzzled**

ny•lon (**nye**-lon) ***noun***
1. A strong synthetic fiber used to make clothing, carpets, fishing lines, etc.
2. nylons *noun, plural* Women's stockings made from nylon.

nymph (**nimf**) ***noun***
1. In ancient Greek and Roman stories, a beautiful female spirit or goddess who lived in a forest, a meadow, a mountain, or a stream.
2. A young form of an insect, such as a grasshopper, that changes into an adult by repeatedly shedding its skin.

oak (**ohk**) ***noun*** A large hardwood tree that produces acorns.

oar (**or**) ***noun*** A wooden pole with a flat blade at one end, used for rowing a boat. **Oar** sounds like **or** and **ore.**

oar•lock (**or**-*lok*) ***noun*** A curved piece of metal on the side of a rowboat, used for holding the oar in place while you row.

o•a•sis (oh-**ay**-siss) ***noun*** A place in a desert where there is water and plants and trees grow. ▸ ***noun, plural* oases** (oh-**ay**-seez)

oat (**oht**) ***noun*** The grain of a kind of grass plant used as food for humans and feed for animals.

oath (**ohth**) ***noun***
1. A serious, formal promise.
2. A swear word.

oat•meal (**oht**-*meel*) ***noun***
1. Meal made from oats that have been ground or pressed flat by a roller.
2. A cereal made from this meal.

o•be•di•ent (oh-**bee**-dee-uhnt) ***adjective*** If you are **obedient,** you do what you are told to do. ▸ ***noun* obedience** ▸ ***adverb* obediently**

o•bese (oh-**beess**) ***adjective*** Very fat. ▸ ***noun* obesity**

o•bey (oh-**bay**) ***verb***
1. To do what someone tells you to do.
2. To carry out, or to follow, as in *to obey the law* or *to obey orders.*
▸ ***verb* obeying, obeyed**

o•bi (**oh**-bee) ***noun*** A Japanese sash worn with a kimono.

ob•ject
1. (**ob**-jikt) ***noun*** Something that you can see and touch but is not alive.
2. (**ob**-jikt) ***noun*** A person or thing toward which attention, discussion, feeling, thought, or action is directed.
3. (**ob**-jikt) ***noun*** The thing that you are trying to achieve.
4. (**ob**-jikt) ***noun*** The **object** or **direct object** of a verb is the noun that receives the action of the verb. In *"Heather liked Hannah," Hannah* is the object of the verb *liked.* Prepositions are also followed by objects, as *him* after the preposition *to* in *"Give the book to him."* The **indirect object** of a verb is the noun to which something is given or for which something is done. In *"We gave her a watch," her* is the indirect object.
5. (uhb-**jekt**) ***verb*** If you **object** to something, you dislike it or disagree with

it. ▸ **objecting, objected** ▸ ***noun*** **objection,** ***noun*** **objector**

ob•jec•tion•a•ble (uhb-**jek**-shuh-nuh-buhl) ***adjective*** Unpleasant and likely to offend people, as in *objectionable behavior.*

ob•jec•tive (uhb-**jek**-tiv)
1. ***noun*** An aim that you are working toward.
2. ***adjective*** Influenced by or based on facts, not feelings; fair. ▸ ***noun*** **objectivity** ▸ ***adverb*** **objectively**

ob•li•gate (**ob**-li-gate) ***verb*** To make someone do something because of a law, promise, contract, or sense of duty. ▸ **obligating, obligated**

ob•li•ga•tion (ob-luh-**gay**-shuhn) ***noun*** Something that it is your duty to do. ▸ ***adjective*** **obligatory** (uh-**blig**-uh-*tor*-ee)

o•blige (uh-**blije**) ***verb***
1. If you are **obliged** to do something, you have to do it.
2. To do someone a favor. ▸ ***adjective*** **obliging** ▸ ***adverb*** **obligingly** ▸ ***verb*** **obliging, obliged**

o•blit•er•ate (uh-**blit**-uh-rate) ***verb*** To destroy something completely. ▸ **obliterating, obliterated**

ob•long (**ob**-*lawng*)
1. ***adjective*** Greater in length than in width.
2. ***noun*** A shape with four straight sides and four right angles. An oblong is longer than it is wide.

ob•nox•ious (uhb-**nok**-shuhss) ***adjective*** Very unpleasant, annoying, or offensive. ▸ ***adverb*** **obnoxiously**

o•boe (**oh**-boh) ***noun*** A woodwind instrument with a thin body and a double-reed mouthpiece. An oboe makes a high sound. ▸ ***noun*** **oboist**

ob•scene (uhb-**seen**) ***adjective*** Indecent and shocking, as in *obscene language.* ▸ **obscener, obscenest** ▸ ***noun*** **obscenity** (uhb-**sen**-i-tee) ▸ ***adverb*** **obscenely**

ob•scure (uhb-**skyoor**)
1. ***adjective*** Not well known. ▸ ***noun*** **obscurity**
2. ***adjective*** Not easy to understand.
3. ***verb*** To make it difficult to see something. ▸ **obscuring, obscured** ▸ ***adjective*** **obscurer, obscurest**

ob•serv•ant (uhb-**zur**-vuhnt) ***adjective*** If you are **observant,** you are good at noticing things. ▸ ***adverb*** **observantly**

ob•ser•va•tion (*ob*-zur-**vay**-shuhn) ***noun***
1. The careful watching of someone or something.
2. Something that you have noticed by watching carefully.
3. A remark.

ob•serv•a•to•ry (uhb-**zur**-vuh-tor-ee) ***noun*** A building containing telescopes and other scientific instruments for studying the sky and the stars. ▸ ***noun, plural*** **observatories**

ob•serve (uhb-**zurv**) ***verb***
1. To watch someone or something carefully.
2. To notice something by looking or watching.
3. To make a remark.
4. To follow or to obey.
5. To celebrate.
▸ ***verb*** **observing, observed** ▸ ***noun*** **observer,** ***noun*** **observance**

ob•sess (uhb-**sess**) ***verb*** If something **obsesses** you, you think about it all the time. ▸ **obsesses, obsessing, obsessed** ▸ ***noun*** **obsession** ▸ ***adjective*** **obsessive**

ob•so•lete (**ob**-suh-*leet or ob*-suh-**leet**) ***adjective*** Out-of-date and no longer used.

ob•sta•cle (**ob**-stuh-kuhl) ***noun*** Something that gets in your way or prevents you from doing something.

ob•sti•nate (**ob**-stuh-nit) ***adjective*** If someone is **obstinate,** the person is stubborn and unwilling to change his or her mind. ▸ ***noun*** **obstinacy** ▸ ***adverb*** **obstinately**

O

ob•struct (uhb-**struhkt**) ***verb***
1. To block a road or path.
2. To stand or be in the way of.
3. To prevent something from happening, or to make something difficult.
▸ ***verb*** **obstructing, obstructed**
▸ ***noun*** **obstruction** ▸ ***adjective*** **obstructive**

obtain (uhb-**tayn**) ***verb*** To get or be given something. ▸ **obtaining, obtained**

ob•tuse (uhb-**tooss**) ***adjective***
1. If someone is **obtuse,** he or she is slow to understand things.
2. An **obtuse** angle is an angle of between 90 and 180 degrees.

ob•vi•ous (**ob**-vee-uhss) ***adjective*** If something is **obvious,** it is easy to see or understand. ▸ ***adverb*** **obviously**

oc•ca•sion (uh-**kay**-zhuhn) ***noun***
1. A time when something happens.
2. A special or important event.

oc•ca•sion•al (uh-**kay**-zhuh-nuhl) ***adjective*** Happening from time to time.
▸ ***adverb*** **occasionally**

oc•cu•pa•tion (*ok*-yuh-**pay**-shuhn) ***noun***
1. A job. ▸ ***adjective*** **occupational**
2. The taking over and controlling of a country or an area by an army.

oc•cu•py (**ok**-yuh-pye) ***verb***
1. To live in a building, room, etc. ▸ ***noun*** **occupant,** ***noun*** **occupier**
2. To take up or to fill.
3. If an army **occupies** a country or an area, it captures it and takes control of it.
4. To keep someone busy and happy.
▸ ***verb*** **occupies, occupying, occupied**

oc•cur (uh-**kur**) ***verb***
1. To happen. ▸ ***noun*** **occurrence**
2. If something **occurs to you,** you suddenly think of it.
▸ ***verb*** **occurring, occurred**

o•cean (**oh**-shuhn) ***noun***
1. The entire body of salt water that covers about 71 percent of Earth's surface.
2. One of the four main parts of this vast body of water.

o•cean•og•ra•phy (*oh*-shuh-**nog**-ruh-fee) ***noun*** The science that deals with the oceans and the plants and animals that live in them. ▸ ***noun*** **oceanographer**

oce•lot (**oss**-uh-lot) ***noun*** A wildcat of medium size with spotted fur. The ocelot lives mostly in the southwestern United States, Central America, and parts of South America.

o'clock (uh-**klok**) ***adverb*** A word used when saying what the time is. *O'clock* is short for "of the clock."

oc•ta•gon (**ok**-tuh-*gon or* **ok**-tuh-guhn) ***noun*** A shape with eight sides and eight angles. ▸ ***adjective*** **octagonal** (ok-**tag**-uh-nuhl)

oc•ta•he•dron (*ok*-tuh-**hee**-druhn) ***noun*** A solid shape with eight faces that are usually triangular.

oc•tave (**ok**-tiv *or* **ok**-tave) ***noun*** The eight-note gap in a musical scale between a note and the next note of the same name above or below it.

Oc•to•ber (ok-**toh**-bur) ***noun*** The 10th month on the calendar, after September and before November. October has 31 days.

oc•to•pus (**ok**-tuh-puhss) ***noun*** A sea animal with a soft body and eight long tentacles that it uses to catch its prey. The tentacles have suckers that help the octopus move along the ocean bottom and grasp prey. ▸ ***noun, plural*** **octopuses** *or* **octopi** (**ok**-tuh-pye)

odd (od) ***adjective***
1. Strange, or difficult to explain and understand. ▸ ***adjective*** **odder, oddest**
▸ ***adverb*** **oddly**
2. An **odd** number cannot be divided exactly by two; it does not have two as a factor.
3. Not matching, as in *odd socks.*
4. Occasional.

odd•i•ty (**od**-uh-tee) ***noun*** Someone or something that seems unusual or strange.

odds (**odz**) ***noun, plural*** The probability of something happening.

ode (**ohd**) ***noun*** A long poem, usually rhymed and often written to praise some person or thing.

o•di•ous (**oh**-dee-uhss) ***adjective*** Hateful or disgusting, as in *an odious crime.*

o•dor (**oh**-dur) ***noun*** A smell.

of (**uhv** *or* **ov**) ***preposition***
1. Belonging to.
2. Made with, as in *a ring of gold.*
3. Named or called, as in *the city of Baltimore.*
4. Containing or holding.
5. Before or until.
6. About or concerning.

off (**of** *or* **awf**)
1. ***preposition*** Away from.
2. ***adverb*** Away from a place.
3. ***adverb*** Not turned on or not working.
4. ***adverb*** In the future.
5. ***adjective*** Not at work.
6. ***adjective*** Not as good as usual.
7. ***adjective*** Wrong.

of•fend (uh-**fend**) ***verb*** To make someone feel hurt or angry.
▸ **offending, offended**

of•fend•er (uh-**fen**-dur) ***noun*** Someone who commits a crime or causes offense.

of•fense
1. (uh-**fenss**) ***noun*** A crime.
2. (uh-**fenss**) If you **cause offense,** you upset someone.
3. (uh-**fenss**) If you **take offense,** you feel upset by something that someone has done or said.
4. (**aw**-fenss) ***noun*** In sports, the team that is attacking or trying to score.

of•fen•sive (uh-**fen**-siv)
1. ***adjective*** Causing anger or hurt feelings, as in *an offensive remark.*
2. ***adjective*** Unpleasant, as in *an offensive odor.*
3. ***noun*** An attack, usually a military one.
4. ***adjective*** Attacking.

of•fer (**of**-ur) ***verb***
1. To ask someone if he or she would like something.
2. To say that you are willing to do something for someone.
3. To put forward or suggest something.
▸ ***verb*** **offering, offered** ▸ ***noun*** **offer**

of•fer•ing (**of**-ur-ing) ***noun*** A contribution.

off•hand (**of**-**hand**) ***adjective*** Done, made, or said without much thought or preparation, as in *offhand remarks.*
▸ ***adverb*** **offhand**

of•fice (**of**-iss) ***noun***
1. A room or building in which people work, usually sitting at desks.
2. An important and usually powerful position.
3. The people who work in an office.

of•fi•cer (**of**-uh-sur) ***noun***
1. Someone who is in charge of other people, especially in the armed forces or the police.
2. Someone who has a responsible position in a club or similar group.

of•fi•cial (uh-**fish**-uhl)
1. ***adjective*** If something is **official,** it has been approved by someone in authority. ▸ ***adverb*** **officially**
2. ***noun*** Someone who holds an important position in an organization, as in *a government official.*
3. ***noun*** In sports, the person who enforces the rules of the game.

off-peak ***adjective*** Happening when there is less activity or demand, as in *off-peak travel.*

off-putting ***adjective*** Discouraging or disturbing, as in *an off-putting announcement.*

off-road ***adjective*** Suited for or involving travel on rough ground away from public roads.

off•set (*of*-**set**) ***verb*** To balance, or to make up for. ▸ **offsetting, offset**

O

off•shoot (**of**-*shoot*) ***noun***
1. A stem that grows from the main stalk of a plant.
2. Something that develops or grows from something else.

off•side (**of-side**) ***adjective*** If a player is **offside** in football or hockey, he or she has broken the rules of the game by moving forward, ahead of the ball or puck.

off•spring (**of**-*spring*) ***noun*** An animal's or a human's young. ▸ ***noun, plural*** **offspring**

of•ten (**of**-uhn) ***adverb*** Many times.

o•gre (**oh**-gur) ***noun***
1. A fierce, cruel giant or monster in fairy tales and folktales.
2. Any person who is cruel or frightening.

oh (**oh**) ***interjection*** A word used to express happiness, surprise, disappointment, or pain. **Oh** sounds like **owe.**

ohm (**ohm**) ***noun*** A unit for measuring how much resistance a substance gives to the flow of electricity running through it.

oil (**oil**)
1. ***noun*** A thick, greasy liquid that burns easily and does not mix with water. Different types of oil are used for heating buildings, for cooking, and for making machines run smoothly. ▸ ***adjective*** **oily**
2. ***verb*** To cover or fill something with oil. ▸ **oiling, oiled**
3. ***noun*** A paint that is used by an artist and contains oil.

oil rig ***noun*** A large platform used as a base for drilling for oil under the sea or under the ground.

oil well ***noun*** A deep hole that is dug or drilled in the ground to get crude oil.

oint•ment (**oint**-muhnt) ***noun*** A thick, often greasy substance put on the skin to heal or protect it.

O•jib•wa (oh-**jib**-way) ***noun*** A member of a group of American Indians that lives primarily near Lake Superior in the United States and Canada. The Ojibwa are also called **Chippewa.** ▸ ***noun, plural*** **Ojibwa** *or* **Ojibwas**

o•kay *or* **OK** (**oh-kay**)
1. ***adjective*** All right.
2. ***verb*** If you **okay** something, you agree to it or approve it. ▸ **okaying, okayed**
3. ***noun*** Agreement or approval.

ok•ra (**oh**-kruh) ***noun*** The sticky, green pods of a tall plant. Okra is used in soups and stews and eaten as a vegetable.

old (**ohld**) ***adjective***
1. Someone who is **old** has lived for a long time.
2. Something that is **old** has existed or been used for a long time.
3. Of a certain age.
4. Worn out by a lot of use, as in *old clothing.*
5. Former, or from an earlier time.
▸ ***adjective*** **older, oldest**

old age ***noun*** The time when a person is old.

old•en (**ohl**-din) ***adjective*** Very old or ancient.

Old English ***noun*** The English language that was spoken before A.D. 1150.

old-fash•ioned (**fash**-uhnd) ***adjective***
1. No longer fashionable or popular.
2. Attached to or keeping the ways, ideas, or customs of an earlier time, as in *an old-fashioned wedding.*

Old Testament ***noun*** A collection of writings that makes up the Jewish Bible and the first part of the Christian Bible. It is the story of Jewish history and religion.

ol•ive (**ol**-iv) ***noun*** A small, black or green fruit that is eaten whole or crushed for its oil. ▸ ***noun*** **olive oil**

O•lym•pic Games (oh-**lim**-pik) ***noun, plural*** A competition in summer and winter sports held every four years for athletes from all over the world. Also known as the *Olympics.*

om•e•let *or* **om•e•lette** (**om**-lit) ***noun*** Eggs that have been beaten, cooked in a pan without stirring, and folded over.

Omelets can be filled with vegetables, meat, or cheese.

o•men (**oh**-muhn) ***noun*** A sign or warning about something that will happen in the future.

om•i•nous (**om**-uh-nuhss) ***adjective*** If something is **ominous,** it makes you feel that something bad is going to happen, as in *an ominous black cloud* or *an ominous silence.* ▸ ***adverb* ominously**

omit (oh-**mit**) ***verb*** To leave something out. ▸ **omitting, omitted** ▸ ***noun* omission**

om•ni•vore (**om**-nuh-vor) ***noun*** An animal that eats both plants and meat. Bears are omnivores. ▸ ***adjective* omnivorous** (om-**niv**-ur-uhss)

on (**on**)

1. ***preposition*** Over and supported by.
2. ***preposition*** Next to and touching.
3. ***preposition*** During.
4. ***preposition*** In the direction of.
5. ***preposition*** In a state of.
6. ***preposition*** Using.
7. ***preposition*** About.
8. ***adverb*** In or into contact with something.
9. ***adverb*** Into use.
10. ***adverb*** Forward in time or space.
11. ***adjective*** In operation.

once (**wuhnss**)

1. ***adverb*** One time.
2. ***adverb*** In the past.
3. ***conjunction*** After something has happened.
4. at once *adverb* Immediately.

on•com•ing (**on**-*kuhm*-ing) ***adjective*** Coming nearer or approaching, as *an oncoming car.*

one (**wuhn**)

1. ***noun*** The whole number, written 1, that comes after 0 and before 2.
2. ***noun*** A singular thing.
3. ***adjective*** Single or alone.
4. ***adjective*** Some.
5. ***pronoun*** A certain person or thing.
6. ***pronoun*** Any person.
One sounds like **won.**

one-sid•ed (**sye**-did) ***adjective***

1. Favoring one group, or showing one side.
2. Not equal or even.

one-way ***adjective***

1. A **one-way** street allows traffic to travel in only one direction.
2. A **one-way** ticket allows you to travel to a place but not back again.

on•go•ing (**on**-*goh*-ing) ***adjective*** If something is **ongoing,** it continues to happen or develop, as in *an ongoing argument.*

on•ion (**uhn**-yuhn) ***noun*** A round vegetable with a strong smell and taste. Onions are the edible bulbs of a plant.

on-line ***adjective*** Connected to, or available from a central computer or a system of computers and modems, as in *on-line information.* ▸ ***adverb* on-line**

on•ly (**ohn**-lee)

1. ***adverb*** Not more than; just.
2. ***adjective*** With nothing or no one else.
3. ***conjunction*** But.
4. ***noun*** An **only child** has no brothers or sisters.

on•o•mat•o•poe•ia (*on*-uh-*mat*-uh-**pee**-uh) ***noun*** The use of a word that sounds like the thing it stands for, as in *"Buzz" and "sizzle."* ▸ ***adjective* onomatopoeic** (*on*-uh-*mat*-uh-**pee**-ik) *or* **onomatopoetic** (*on*-uh-*mat*-uh-poh-**et**-ik)

on•set (**on**-*set*) ***noun***

1. The beginning.
2. An attack or an assault.

on•to (**on**-*too or* **on**-tuh) ***preposition*** To a position on or upon.

on•ward (**on**-wurd) *or* **on•wards** (**on**-wurdz) ***adverb*** Forward, as in *from 1987 onward.* ▸ ***adjective* onward**

ooze (**ooz**)

1. ***verb*** To flow out slowly. ▸ **oozing, oozed**
2. ***noun*** Very soft mud, usually found underwater in a pond or stream.

O

o•pal (**oh**-puhl) ***noun*** A mineral used as a gem that shows different colors, depending on how it is held to the light.

o•paque (oh-**pake**) ***adjective*** Not letting light through, or not transparent.

o•pen (**oh**-puhn)
1. ***adjective*** Not shut, closed, or sealed. ▸ ***verb* open**
2. ***adjective*** Not covered or enclosed, as in *open land* or *open air.*
3. ***adjective*** If you are **open** about something, you are honest about it. ▸ ***noun* openness** ▸ ***adverb* openly**
4. ***adjective*** Not limited or restricted, as in *an open discussion.*
5. ***verb*** To start or begin something.
6. ***noun*** If you have an **open mind,** you are able to accept new ideas.
7. ***verb*** To begin working hours. ▸ ***adjective* open** ▸ ***verb* opening, opened**

o•pen•ing (**oh**-puh-ning)
1. ***noun*** A hole or space in something.
2. ***adjective*** Coming at the beginning, as in *the opening lines of a play.* ▸ ***noun* opening**
3. ***noun*** A chance or opportunity, as in *a job opening.*
4. ***noun*** The first time a play is performed.

op•er•a (**op**-ur-uh) ***noun*** A play in which all or most of the words are sung and the singers are accompanied by an orchestra. ▸ ***adjective* operatic** (*op*-uh-**rat**-ik)

op•er•ate (**op**-uh-rate) ***verb***
1. To work or to run.
2. To make something work.
3. To cut open someone's body to repair a damaged part or remove a diseased part. ▸ ***verb* operating, operated**

op•er•a•tion (*op*-uh-**ray**-shuhn) ***noun***
1. The cutting open of someone's body to repair a damaged part or remove a diseased part.
2. An event that has been carefully planned and involves a lot of people, as in *a massive security operation.*
3. If something is **in operation,** it is working. ▸ ***adjective* operational**

op•er•a•tor (**op**-uh-*ray*-tur) ***noun***
1. Someone who helps people make telephone calls.
2. Someone who works a machine or device, as in *an elevator operator.*

op•er•et•ta (*op*-uh-**ret**-uh) ***noun*** A short opera in which some of the lines are spoken.

oph•thal•mol•o•gist (*of*-thuhl-**mol**-uh-jist *or op*-thuhl-**mol**-uh-jist) ***noun*** A medical doctor who specializes in the structure, function, and diseases of the eye. ▸ ***noun* ophthalmology**

o•pin•ion (uh-**pin**-yuhn) ***noun***
1. The ideas and beliefs that you have about something.
2. An expert's judgment, as in *a doctor's opinion.*
3. opinion poll A way of finding out what people think about something by questioning a selection of people.

o•pos•sum (uh-**poss**-uhm) ***noun*** A gray, furry animal that lives mostly in trees and carries its young in a pouch. When threatened, the opossum lies very still and seems to be dead. It is also called a *possum.*

op•po•nent (uh-**poh**-nuhnt) ***noun*** Someone who is against you in a fight, contest, debate, or election.

op•por•tu•ni•ty (op-ur-**too**-nuh-tee) ***noun*** A chance to do something. ▸ ***noun, plural* opportunities**

op•pose (uh-**poze**) ***verb*** To be against something and try to prevent it from happening. ▸ **opposing, opposed**

op•po•site (**op**-uh-zit)
1. ***preposition*** If something is **opposite** you, it is facing you.
2. ***adjective*** Located or facing directly across.

3. ***adjective*** Facing or moving the other way.
4. ***adjective*** Completely different.
5. ***noun*** A person, thing, or idea that is completely different from another.

op•po•si•tion (op-uh-**zish**-uhn) ***noun***
1. When there is **opposition** to something, people are against it.
2. The person or team that you play against in a match or competition.

op•press (uh-**press**) ***verb***
1. To treat people in a cruel, unjust, and hard way. ▸ ***noun* oppression, *noun* oppressor**
2. If something **oppresses** you, it makes you feel worried or weighed down.
▸ ***verb* oppresses, oppressing, oppressed** ▸ ***adjective* oppressive**

opt (**opt**) ***verb***
1. To choose to have or do something.
2. **opt out** To choose not to take part in something.
▸ ***verb* opting, opted**

op•ti•cal (**op**-tuh-kuhl)
1. ***adjective*** To do with eyes or eyesight.
2. ***adjective*** Designed to aid sight.
3. **optical illusion *noun*** Something that you think you see that is not really there.

op•ti•cian (op-**tish**-uhn) ***noun*** Someone who makes or sells glasses and contact lenses.

op•ti•mis•tic (op-tuh-**miss**-tik) ***adjective*** People who are **optimistic** always believe that things will turn out successfully or for the best. ▸ ***noun* optimism, *noun* optimist**

op•tion (**op**-shuhn) ***noun*** Something that you can choose to do.

op•tion•al (**op**-shuh-nuhl) ***adjective*** If something is **optional,** you can choose whether or not to have it or do it.
▸ ***adverb* optionally**

op•tom•e•trist (op-**tom**-i-*trist*) ***noun*** A person who is licensed to test your vision and prescribe glasses or contact lenses.

or (**or**) ***conjunction***
1. A word used to introduce choices or alternatives.
2. A word used to indicate that words or phrases have the same meaning.
3. A word used with *either* or *whether* to show choices.
Or sounds like **oar** and **ore.**

o•ral (**or**-uhl) ***adjective***
1. Spoken, not written, as in *an oral report.*
2. To do with your mouth, as in *oral hygiene.*
▸ ***adverb* orally**

or•ange (**or**-inj) ***noun***
1. The color of carrots, or a mixture of red and yellow. ▸ ***adjective* orange**
2. A round citrus fruit with a thick, orange skin and sweet, juicy flesh.

o•rang•u•tan (uh-**rang**-uh-*tan*) ***noun*** A large ape with long, reddish brown hair and very long, strong arms. Orangutans live in Borneo and Sumatra.

or•bit (**or**-bit)
1. ***noun*** The invisible path followed by an object circling a planet, the sun, etc.
▸ ***adjective* orbital**
2. ***verb*** To travel around a planet, the sun, etc.
▸ **orbiting, orbited**

or•chard (**or**-churd) ***noun*** A field or farm where fruit trees are grown.

or•ches•tra (**or**-kuh-struh) ***noun*** A large group of musicians who play their instruments together. ▸ ***adjective* orchestral** (or-**kess**-truhl)

or•chid (**or**-kid) ***noun*** A plant with colorful and often unusually shaped flowers.

or•dain (or-**dane**) ***verb***
1. To bring someone into the priesthood or ministry. ▸ ***noun* ordination**
2. To order by law.
▸ ***verb* ordaining, ordained**

or•deal (or-**deel**) ***noun*** A very difficult or painful experience.

O

O

or•der (**or**-dur)
1. ***verb*** To tell someone that he or she has to do something.
2. ***verb*** To ask for something in a restaurant.
3. ***verb*** To ask a manufacturer or store to send you something.
4. ***noun*** Arrangement, as in *alphabetical order* or *numerical order.*
5. ***noun*** Neatness.
6. ***noun*** Good behavior.
7. ***noun*** A written request to pay money to someone, as in *a postal money order.*
8. ***noun*** A community of people living under the same religious rules, as in *an order of monks.*
9. If you put things **in order,** you arrange them so that each thing is in the right place.
10. If an object is **out of order,** it is broken and does not work.
11. If a person is **out of order,** he or she is behaving badly.
▸ ***verb*** **ordering, ordered** ▸ ***noun*** **order**

or•der•ly (**or**-dur-lee)
1. ***adjective*** Neat, with everything in its place.
2. ***adjective*** Well behaved, as in *an orderly crowd.*
3. ***noun*** A hospital attendant who cleans and does other jobs.
▸ ***noun*** **orderliness**

or•di•nal number (**ord**-uhn-uhl) ***noun*** A number, such as first, second, third, fourth, etc., used to show the position of something in a series.

or•di•nar•y (**ord**-uh-*ner*-ee) ***adjective***
1. Commonly used or usual. ▸ ***adverb*** **ordinarily**
2. Average, or not distinguished in any way.

ore (**or**) ***noun*** A rock that contains metal, as in *iron ore.* **Ore** sounds like **oar** and **or.**

or•gan (**or**-guhn) ***noun***
1. A large musical instrument with one or more keyboards and pipes of different lengths. ▸ ***noun*** **organist**
2. A part of the body that does a particular job.

or•gan•ic (or-**gan**-ik) ***adjective***
1. Using only natural products and no chemicals, pesticides, etc., as in *organic farming.* ▸ ***adverb*** **organically**
2. To do with or coming from living things.

or•gan•ism (**or**-guh-*niz*-uhm) ***noun*** A living plant or animal.

or•gan•i•za•tion (*or*-guh-nuh-**zay**-shuhn) ***noun***
1. A number of people joined together for a particular purpose.
2. The task of planning and running something.
3. The way something is planned or arranged.

or•gan•ize (**or**-guh-nize) ***verb***
1. To plan and run an event. ▸ ***noun*** **organizer**
2. To arrange things neatly and in order.
▸ ***verb*** **organizing, organized**

O•ri•ent (**or**-ee-uhnt) ***noun*** The countries of the Far East, especially Japan and China. ▸ ***adjective*** **Oriental**

o•ri•en•teer•ing (or-ee-uhn-**tihr**-ing) ***noun*** A sport in which people have to find their way across rough country as fast as they can, using a map and compass.

o•ri•ga•mi (or-uh-**gah**-mee) ***noun*** The Japanese art of paper folding.

or•i•gin (**or**-uh-jin) ***noun***
1. The cause or source of something, or the point where something began.
2. Ancestry, or birth.

o•rig•i•nal (uh-**rij**-uh-nuhl)
1. ***adjective*** First, or earliest. ▸ ***adverb*** **originally**
2. ***adjective*** New, or unusual. ▸ ***noun*** **originality**
3. ***noun*** A work of art that is not a copy.
▸ ***adjective*** **original**

o•rig•i•nate (uh-**rij**-uh-nate) ***verb*** To begin from somewhere or something.
▸ **originating, originated** ▸ ***noun*** **origination**

O

o•ri•ole (**or**-ee-*ohl*) ***noun*** A songbird that is found all over the world. The male is usually bright orange or yellow with black markings.

or•na•ment (**or**-nuh-muhnt) ***noun*** A small, attractive object used as a decoration, as in *a Christmas tree ornament.* ▸ ***adjective*** **ornamental**

or•nate (or-**nayt**) ***adjective*** Richly decorated. ▸ ***adverb*** **ornately**

or•ner•y (**or**-nur-ee) ***adjective*** Stubborn and mean.

or•ni•thol•o•gy (*or*-nuh-**thol**-uh-jee) ***noun*** The study of birds. ▸ ***noun*** **ornithologist**

or•phan (**or**-fuhn) ***noun*** A child whose parents are dead. ▸ ***adjective*** **orphaned**

or•phan•age (**or**-fuh-nij) ***noun*** A place where orphans live and are looked after.

or•tho•don•tist (or-thuh-**don**-tist) ***noun*** A dentist who straightens uneven teeth.

or•tho•dox (**or**-thuh-doks) ***adjective***
1. Members of a religion are described as **orthodox** if they believe in its older, more traditional teachings.
2. **Orthodox** views and beliefs are ones that are accepted by most people.
▸ ***noun*** **orthodoxy**

or•tho•pe•dic (or-thuh-**pee**-dik) ***adjective*** To do with the branch of medicine that deals with bones and joints. ▸ ***noun*** **orthopedics**

os•mo•sis (oz-**moh**-siss *or* oss-**moh**-siss) ***noun*** The process by which a fluid passes through a membrane from a less concentrated solution to a more concentrated solution until the solutions reach the same level of concentration.

os•trich (**oss**-trich) ***noun*** A large African bird that can run very fast but cannot fly. The ostrich is the largest of all living birds and often weighs as much as 300 pounds (140 kilograms). ▸ ***noun, plural*** **ostriches**

oth•er (**uhTH**-ur)
1. ***adjective*** Different; not the same as mentioned. ▸ ***pronoun*** **other**
2. ***adjective*** Remaining.
3. ***adjective*** More or extra.
4. ***adjective*** In the recent past.
5. **others** ***pronoun*** The rest.

oth•er•wise (**uhTH**-ur-*wize*)
1. ***conjunction*** Or else.
2. ***adverb*** In a different way.

ot•ter (**ot**-ur) ***noun*** A furry mammal with webbed feet that lives in or near water and eats fish. Otters are related to weasels and minks.

ouch (**ouch**) ***interjection*** A cry of pain.

ought (**awt**) ***verb*** A helping verb used in the following ways:
1. To show an obligation or a duty.
2. To show what is expected or likely.
3. To offer advice.

ounce (**ounss**) ***noun***
1. A unit of weight equal to 1/16 of a pound. A mouse weighs a little less than one ounce, and a tennis ball weighs two ounces.
2. A **fluid ounce** is a unit used in liquid measurement. There are 16 fluid ounces in a pint and 32 fluid ounces in a quart.
3. A small amount.

our (**our** *or* **ar**) ***pronoun*** Belonging to or to do with us.

ours (**ourz** *or* **arz**) ***pronoun*** The one or ones belonging to or to do with us.

our•selves (our-**selvz** *or* ar-**selvz**) ***pronoun*** Us and no one else.

oust (**oust**) ***verb*** To force someone out of a position or job. ▸ **ousting, ousted**

out (**out**)
1. ***adverb*** Away from the inside or center.
2. ***adverb*** Away from home or work.
3. ***adverb*** Into the open, or into public view.
4. ***adverb*** No longer burning or lit.
5. ***adverb*** No longer taking part in a game.
6. ***adverb*** Aloud.
7. ***adjective*** In baseball, no longer a batter or base runner. ▸ ***noun*** **out**

out•board motor (**out**-*bord*) ***noun*** A motor with a propeller that can be attached to the rear of a small boat.

O

out•break (**out**-*brake*) ***noun*** A sudden start of something such as disease or war.

out•burst (**out**-*burst*) ***noun*** A sudden pouring out of strong emotion, as in *an outburst of anger.*

out•cast (**out**-*kast*) ***noun*** Someone who is not accepted by other people.

out•come (**out**-*kuhm*) ***noun*** The result of something.

out•cry (**out**-*krye*) ***noun*** If there is an **outcry** about something, a lot of people complain loudly about it. ▸ ***noun, plural*** **outcries**

out•dat•ed (*out*-**day**-tid) ***adjective*** Old-fashioned or out-of-date.

out•do (*out*-**doo**) ***verb*** If you **outdo** someone, you do something better than he or she does. ▸ **outdoes, outdoing, outdid, outdone**

out•doors (*out*-**dorz**) ***adverb*** Outside in the open air. ▸ ***noun*** **outdoors** ▸ ***adjective*** **outdoor**

out•er (**ou**-tur) ***adjective*** On the outside or furthest from the middle, as in *the outer edge.*

outer space ***noun*** Space beyond the earth's atmosphere.

out•fit (**out**-fit)
1. ***noun*** A set of clothes.
2. ***noun*** A group of people who work together or form a unit, as in *a commercial outfit* or *a military outfit.*
3. ***verb*** To furnish someone with all the equipment he or she needs to do something. ▸ **outfitting, outfitted**

out•go•ing (**out**-**goh**-ing) ***adjective*** Someone who is **outgoing** is very sociable and friendly.

out•grow (*out*-**groh**) ***verb*** To grow too big or too old for something. ▸ **outgrowing, outgrew, outgrown**

out•ing (**out**-ing) ***noun*** A short trip taken for pleasure.

out•law (**out**-*law*)
1. ***noun*** A criminal, especially one who is running away from the law.
2. ***verb*** To forbid something by law. ▸ **outlawing, outlawed**

out•let (**out**-let) ***noun***
1. A pipe or hole that lets out liquid or gas.
2. A place where appliances can be plugged in and connected to a supply of electrical current.
3. A store where a company's products can be bought at a discount.
4. An activity that lets you express your feelings.

out•line (**out**-*line*) ***noun***
1. A line that shows the edge of something.
2. The basic points or ideas about something.
▸ ***verb*** **outline**

out•look (**out**-*luk*) ***noun***
1. Your general attitude toward things.
2. A situation that seems likely to happen.

out•num•ber (*out*-**nuhm**-bur) ***verb*** To be larger in number than another group. ▸ **outnumbering, outnumbered**

out-of-date ***adjective*** Old-fashioned or obsolete.

out•pa•tient (**out**-*pay*-shuhnt) ***noun*** Someone who goes to a hospital for treatment but does not stay there overnight.

out•post (**out**-*pohst*) ***noun***
1. A military camp set up away from the main group of soldiers to guard against a surprise attack.
2. A remote settlement.

out•put (**out**-*put*) ***noun***
1. The amount produced by a person, machine, or business.
2. Information produced by a computer.
▸ ***verb*** **output**

out•rage (**out**-*raje*) ***noun***
1. An act of violence or cruelty.
2. Extreme anger.
▸ ***verb*** **outrage**

out•ra•geous (*out*-**ray**-juhss) ***adjective*** Very shocking or offensive. ▸ ***adverb*** **outrageously**

out•right (**out**-*rite*)
1. ***adjective*** Total or complete, as in *an*

outright lie.
2. ***adverb*** Instantly.
out•run (out-**ruhn**) ***verb*** To run or go faster than someone or something. ▸ **outrunning, outran** (out-**ran**), **outrun**
out•set (**out**-*set*) ***noun*** The start or the beginning.
out•side
1. (*out*-**side**) ***adverb*** Out of a building, or in the open air.
2. (**out**-*side*) ***noun*** The outer surface, side, or part. ▸ ***adjective*** **outside**
3. (*out*-**side**) ***preposition*** Beyond the limits or boundaries of.
out•skirts (**out**-*skurts*) ***noun, plural*** The outer edges of an area, as in *the outskirts of town.*
out•smart (*out*-**smart**) ***verb*** To be more clever than someone else. ▸ **outsmarting, outsmarted**
out•spo•ken (**out**-**spoh**-kuhn) ***adjective*** If you are **outspoken,** you express your views strongly and clearly, especially when you are criticizing someone.
out•stand•ing (*out*-**stand**-ing) ***adjective***
1. Extremely good, as in *an outstanding performance.*
2. Not yet paid or dealt with, as in *an outstanding bill.*
out•ward (**out**-wurd) *or* **out•wards** (**out**-wurdz)
1. ***adjective*** Appearing on the surface. ▸ ***adverb*** **outwardly**
2. ***adverb*** Toward the outside. ▸ ***adjective*** **outward**
out•wit (*out*-**wit**) ***verb*** To fool or get the better of someone by being more clever than the person. ▸ **outwitting, outwitted**
o•val (**oh**-vuhl) ***noun*** A shape like an egg. ▸ ***adjective*** **oval**
o•va•ry (**oh**-vur-ee) ***noun***
1. The part of a flowering plant in which seeds are formed.
2. The female organ that produces eggs. ▸ ***noun, plural*** **ovaries**
o•va•tion (oh-**vay**-shuhn) ***noun*** A response with loud applause and cheering.
ov•en (**uhv**-uhn) ***noun*** An enclosed space, as in a stove, where food is baked or roasted.
o•ver (**oh**-vur)
1. ***preposition*** Above or on top of something.
2. ***preposition*** More than.
3. ***adjective*** Finished.
4. ***preposition*** Across.
5. ***adverb*** Remaining or surplus.
6. ***adverb*** Again.
7. ***adverb*** Leaning or falling downward.
8. If you **get over** an illness or experience, you recover from it and are no longer ill or upset.
o•ver•all (**oh**-vur-**awl**) ***adverb*** Generally, or considering everything. ▸ ***adjective*** **overall** (**oh**-vur-*awl*)
o•ver•alls (**oh**-vur-*awlz*) ***noun, plural*** Loose pants with shoulder straps and a panel covering the chest.
o•ver•bear•ing (*oh*-vur-**bair**-ing) ***adjective*** Very domineering or bossy.
o•ver•board (**oh**-vur-*bord*) ***adverb***
1. Over the side of a boat.
2. If you **go overboard** about something, you are overly enthusiastic about it.
o•ver•cast (**oh**-vur-*kast*) ***adjective*** An **overcast** sky is covered with clouds.
o•ver•coat (**oh**-vur-*kote*) ***noun*** A heavy coat worn in cold weather.
o•ver•come (*oh*-vur-**kuhm**) ***verb***
1. To defeat or deal with something such as a feeling or a problem.
2. If someone is **overcome** by smoke, emotion, guilt, etc., the person is so strongly affected by it that he or she is made unconscious or helpless. ▸ ***verb*** **overcoming, overcame, overcome**
o•ver•do (*oh*-vur-**doo**) ***verb*** To do too much. ▸ **overdoes, overdoing, overdid, overdone** ▸ ***adjective*** **overdone**

O

O

o•ver•dose (**oh**-vur-*dohss*) ***noun*** A quantity of a drug so large that it can kill you or make you seriously ill. ▸ ***verb*** **overdose** (*oh*-vur-**dohss**)

o•ver•draft (**oh**-vur-*draft*) ***noun*** An amount of money taken out of the bank when there is not enough money in the account. ▸ ***adjective*** **overdrawn**

o•ver•dress (*oh*-vur-**dress**) ***verb*** To wear clothes that are too warm or too formal for an occasion. ▸ **overdresses, overdressing, overdressed**

o•ver•due (**oh**-vur-**doo**) ***adjective*** Late.

o•ver•eat (*oh*-vur-**eet**) ***verb*** To eat too much food. ▸ **overeating, overate**

o•ver•flow (**oh**-vur-*floh*) ***verb***
1. To flow over the edges of something.
2. To flood.
▸ ***verb*** **overflowing, overflowed**

o•ver•grown (*oh*-vur-**grohn**) ***adjective*** An **overgrown** garden is covered with weeds because it has not been looked after.

o•ver•hand (**oh**-vur-*hand*) ***adjective*** Done with your arm raised above your shoulder, as in *an overhand pitch.*

o•ver•haul (*oh*-vur-**hawl**) ***verb*** To examine carefully all the parts of a piece of equipment and make any repairs that are needed. ▸ **overhauling, overhauled** ▸ ***noun*** **overhaul** (**oh**-vur-*hawl*)

o•ver•head
1. (*oh*-vur-**hed**) ***adverb*** Above your head. ▸ ***adjective*** **overhead** (**oh**-vur-hed)
2. (**oh**-vur-*hed*) ***noun*** Regular business expenses such as wages, rent, telephone, heating, and lighting.

o•ver•hear (*oh*-vur-**hihr**) ***verb*** To hear what someone else is saying when the person does not know that you are listening. ▸ **overhearing, overheard**

o•ver•joyed (*oh*-vur-**joid**) ***adjective*** If you are **overjoyed,** you are extremely happy.

o•ver•lap (*oh*-vur-**lap**) ***verb*** To cover part of something. ▸ **overlapping, overlapped** ▸ ***noun*** **overlap** (**oh**-vur-*lap*)

o•ver•load (*oh*-vur-**lode**) ***verb***
1. To give something or someone too much to carry or too much work to do.
2. To send too much electricity through a circuit or device so that it burns out.
▸ ***verb*** **overloading, overloaded**
▸ ***noun*** **overload** (**oh**-vur-*lode*)

o•ver•look (*oh*-vur-**luk**) ***verb***
1. To be able to look down on something from a window or room.
2. To fail to notice something.
3. To choose to ignore something wrong that someone has done.
▸ ***verb*** **overlooking, overlooked**

o•ver•ly (**oh**-vur-lee) ***adverb*** Very or excessively.

o•ver•night
1. (*oh*-vur-**nite**) ***adverb*** During or through the night.
2. (*oh*-vur-**nite) *adverb*** Suddenly.
3. (**oh**-vur-*nite*) ***adjective*** For one night.
4. (**oh**-vur-*nite*) ***adjective*** Used for short trips.

o•ver•pass (**oh**-vur-*pass*) ***noun*** A road or bridge that crosses over another road or a railroad. ▸ ***noun, plural*** **overpasses**

o•ver•pop•u•la•tion (*oh*-vur-*pop*-yuh-**lay**-shuhn) ***noun*** The condition in which the large population of humans or other animals is too great to be sustained by the natural resources available in the area.

o•ver•pow•er (*oh*-vur-**pou**-ur) ***verb***
1. To defeat someone because you are stronger than he or she is.
2. If something **overpowers** you, it affects you very strongly.
▸ ***verb*** **overpowering, overpowered**

o•ver•rat•ed (*oh*-vur-**ray**-tid) ***adjective*** If you think that something is **overrated,** you do not think that it is as good as many other people think it is.

o•ver•rule (*oh*-vur-**rool**) ***verb*** If someone in authority **overrules** a decision, the person says that the decision was wrong and has to be changed. ▸ **overruling, overruled**

o•ver•run (*oh*-vur-**ruhn**) ***verb***
1. To spread all over a place in large numbers.
2. To flood beyond.
3. To go beyond.
▸ ***verb*** **overrunning, overran, overrun**

o•ver•seas (**oh**-vur-*seez*)
1. ***adverb*** Abroad or across the seas.
2. ***adjective*** To do with foreign countries or countries across the sea, as in *overseas trade.*

o•ver•sight (**oh**-vur-*site*) ***noun*** A careless mistake.

o•ver•sleep (*oh*-vur-**sleep**) ***verb*** To sleep for longer than intended.
▸ **oversleeping, overslept**

o•ver•take (*oh*-vur-**take**) ***verb***
1. To catch up to someone.
2. To come upon suddenly or by surprise.
▸ ***verb*** **overtaking, overtook, overtaken**

o•ver•throw (*oh*-vur-**throh**) ***verb***
1. To defeat a leader or ruler and remove the person from power by force.
2. To throw a ball too far, past where it should go.
▸ ***verb*** **overthrowing, overthrew, overthrown** ▸ ***noun*** **overthrow**

o•ver•time (**oh**-vur-*time*) ***noun*** Time spent working beyond normal working hours. ▸ ***adjective*** **overtime** ▸ ***adverb*** **overtime**

o•ver•ture (**oh**-vur-chur) ***noun*** A piece of music played at the start of a musical, an opera, or a ballet.

o•ver•turn (*oh*-vur-**turn**) ***verb***
1. To turn something over so that it is upside down or on its side.
2. To reverse a decision that someone else has made.
▸ ***verb*** **overturning, overturned**

o•ver•weight (**oh**-vur-*wate*) ***adjective*** Weighing more than is normal, desirable, or allowed.

o•ver•whelm (*oh*-vur-**welm**) ***verb***
1. To defeat or overcome completely.
2. To have a very strong effect.
▸ ***verb*** **overwhelming, overwhelmed**
▸ ***adjective*** **overwhelming**

o•ver•work (*oh*-vur-**wurk**) ***verb*** To work too hard. ▸ **overworking, overworked**

owe (**oh**) ***verb***
1. To have to pay money to someone, especially money that you have borrowed.
2. To have a duty to do something for someone in return for something the person has done for you.
3. To be grateful to someone for giving you something.
Owe sounds like **oh.**
▸ ***verb*** **owing, owed**

owl (**oul**) ***noun*** A bird that has a round head, large eyes, and a hooked bill. Owls hunt at night and live mainly on mice and other small animals.

own (**ohn**)
1. ***adjective*** Belonging to oneself or itself.
2. ***verb*** To possess or have something.
▸ ***noun*** **owner**
3. ***verb*** If you **own up** to something, you confess that you have done something wrong.
4. on your own Alone or by yourself.
▸ ***verb*** **owning, owned**

ox (**oks**) ***noun***
1. The adult male of domestic cattle, used as a work animal or for beef.
2. Any of several animals that are related to cattle, such as the buffalo, bison, or yak.
▸ ***noun, plural*** **oxen** (**oks**-in)

ox•ford (**oks**-furd) ***noun***
1. A low shoe with laces over the top of the foot.
2. A cotton cloth used to make lightweight clothing.

P

ox•i•dize (**ok**-suh-*dize*) ***verb*** To combine with oxygen. When something oxidizes, it burns or rusts. ▸ **oxidizing, oxidized** ▸ ***noun*** **oxidizer,** ***noun*** **oxidation**

ox•y•gen (**ok**-suh-juhn) ***noun*** A colorless gas found in the air. Humans and animals need oxygen to breathe, and fires need it to burn. Oxygen makes up 21 percent of the earth's atmosphere.

ox•y•mo•ron (*ok*-si-**mor**-on) ***noun*** A short phrase in which the words seem to contradict each other; for example, "a wise fool."

oy•ster (**oi**-stur) ***noun*** A flat, edible shellfish that lives in shallow coastal waters and has a shell made up of two hinged parts.

o•zone (**oh**-zone) ***noun***
1. A form of oxygen that has a pale blue color and a strong smell. This gas is formed when an electrical discharge passes through the air. It can be poisonous in large quantities.
2. ozone layer A layer of ozone high above the earth's surface that blocks out some of the sun's harmful rays.

pace (**payss**)
1. ***noun*** A step or a stride.
2. ***noun*** The average length of a step when you are walking, about 2 feet for an adult.
3. ***verb*** To measure distance in paces.
4. ***noun*** A rate of speed.
5. ***verb*** To walk back and forth.
▸ ***verb*** **pacing, paced**

pace•mak•er (**payss**-*may*-kur) ***noun*** An electronic device put into someone's body to help the heart beat more regularly.

pac•i•fist (**pass**-uh-fist) ***noun*** Someone who strongly believes that war and violence are wrong and who refuses to fight. ▸ ***noun*** **pacifism**

pac•i•fy (**pass**-uh-fye) ***verb*** If you **pacify** someone, you make the person feel calmer. ▸ **pacifies, pacifying, pacified**

pack (**pak**)
1. ***verb*** To put objects into a box, case, bag, etc. ▸ ***noun*** **packing**
2. ***verb*** To fill a space tightly.
3. ***noun*** A group of something such as animals, people, or things, as in *a pack of wolves* or *a pack of cards.*
4. ***noun*** A bundle of things tied or wrapped together for carrying.
5. ***noun*** A sturdy bag for carrying things on the back.
6. ***noun*** A large quantity or amount, as in *a pack of lies.*
▸ ***verb*** **packing, packed**

pack•age (**pak**-ij) ***noun***
1. A parcel, or a bundle of something that is packed, wrapped, or put into a box.
2. A carton, box, or case that can be packed with something.
▸ ***verb*** **package**

pack•ag•ing (**pak**-uh-jing) ***noun*** The wrapping on something, especially something that you buy.

pack animal ***noun*** An animal, usually a horse or mule, that can carry heavy supplies.

pack•et (**pak**-it) ***noun*** A small container or package, as in *a packet of seeds.*

pact (**pakt**) ***noun*** An agreement, often between two countries, as in *a peace pact.*

pad (**pad**)
1. ***verb*** To walk around softly.
2. ***noun*** A wad or cushion of soft material, usually used to absorb liquid, give comfort, or provide protection.
▸ ***verb* pad**
3. ***noun*** Sheets of paper fastened together, as in *a memo pad.*
4. ***noun*** The soft part on the bottom of the feet of dogs and many other animals.
5. ***noun*** A platform from which a rocket is fired, as in *a launching pad.*
6. ***verb*** To add words to a speech or piece of writing just to make it longer.
7. ***verb*** If you **pad a bill,** you charge someone for more work than you really did.
▸ ***verb* padding, padded**

padding ***noun*** Cotton, foam rubber, or any other material used to make or stuff a pad.

pad•dle (**pad**-uhl)
1. ***noun*** A short, wide oar used to move and steer some boats. ▸ ***verb* paddle**
2. ***noun*** A small board with a short handle used to strike a ball in table tennis and other games.
3. ***noun*** A flat, wooden tool used for stirring, mixing, or beating.
4. ***verb*** To spank with a paddle or the hand.
▸ **paddling, paddled**

paddle wheel ***noun*** A large wheel with paddles arranged around it.

pad•dock (**pad**-uhk) ***noun*** An enclosed field or area where horses can graze or exercise.

pad•dy (**pad**-ee) ***noun*** A wet field where rice is grown. ▸ ***noun, plural* paddies**

pad•lock (**pad**-*lok*) ***noun*** A lock with a metal bar shaped like a U that can be put through an opening or link and snapped shut.

pa•gan (**pay**-guhn) ***noun*** Someone who is not a member of the Christian, Jewish, or Muslim religion. A pagan may worship many gods or have no religion at all. ▸ ***adjective* pagan**

page (**payj**)
1. ***noun*** One side of a sheet of paper in a book, newspaper, or magazine.
2. ***noun*** In the past, a **page** was a boy servant. Today, a page assists someone, such as a senator, by running errands or by being a messenger. A page can also be a boy attendant at a wedding.
3. ***verb*** To find someone by calling out or announcing the person's name or by using a pager. ▸ **paging, paged**

pag•eant (**paj**-uhnt) ***noun*** A public show where people walk in processions or act out historical scenes, as in *a beauty pageant* or *a Thanksgiving pageant.* ▸ ***noun* pageantry**

pag•er (**pay**-jur) ***noun*** A small, electronic beeping device that people such as doctors wear so that they can be reached in emergencies.

pa•go•da (puh-**goh**-duh) ***noun*** A shrine or temple in eastern religions. A pagoda is shaped like a tower with many roofs that curve upward.

pail (**payl**) ***noun*** A bucket. **Pail** sounds like **pale.**

pain (**payn**) ***noun***
1. A feeling of physical hurt or great unhappiness. ▸ ***verb* pain**
2. pains *noun, plural* Efforts or trouble.
Pain sounds like **pane.**

pain•ful (**payn**-fuhl) ***adjective*** If something is **painful**, it hurts you physically or makes you very unhappy.
▸ ***adverb* painfully**

pain•kill•er (**payn**-*kil*-ur) ***noun*** A pill or other medicine taken to stop pain.

pain•less (**payn**-liss) ***adjective*** Free from pain. ▸ ***adverb* painlessly**

pains•tak•ing (**paynz**-*tay*-king) ***adjective*** Careful and thorough, as in *a painstaking worker* or *painstaking research.* ▸ ***adverb* painstakingly**

P

paint (**paynt**)
1. ***noun*** A liquid that you use to color surfaces such as walls or to make pictures.
2. ***verb*** To use paint to make a picture or cover a surface. ▸ **painting, painted** ▸ ***noun*** **painter,** ***noun*** **painting**

paint•brush (**paynt**-*bruhsh*) ***noun*** A brush for spreading paint. ▸ ***noun, plural*** **paintbrushes**

pair (**pair**)
1. ***noun*** Two things that match or go together, as in *a pair of socks.* ▸ ***verb*** **pair**
2. ***noun*** One thing that is made up of two parts, as in *a pair of scissors* or *a pair of glasses.*
3. ***noun*** Two persons or animals that are alike or that work together, as in *a pair of dancers* or *a pair of horses.*
4. pair off ***verb*** To form a pair or into pairs.
Pair sounds like **pare** and **pear.**

pa•ja•mas (puh-**jam**-uhz *or* puh-**jahm**-uhz) ***noun, plural*** A set of clothes to sleep in consisting of a loose shirt and pants or shorts.

pal (**pal**) ***noun*** A good friend or a buddy.

pal•ace (**pal**-iss) ***noun*** A large, grand residence for a king, queen, or other ruler.

pal•ate (**pal**-it) ***noun***
1. The roof of your mouth.
2. A person's sense of taste.
Palate sounds like **palette.**

pale (**payl**)
1. ***adjective*** Having a light skin color, often because of an illness. ▸ ***noun*** **pallor** (**pal**-ur)
2. ***adjective*** Not bright in color.
3. ***verb*** To become pale. ▸ **paling, paled**
Pale sounds like **pail.**
▸ ***noun*** **paleness** ▸ ***adjective*** **paler, palest**

pa•le•on•tol•o•gy (*pale*-ee-uhn-**tol**-uh-jee) ***noun*** The science that deals with fossils and other ancient life forms. Someone who studies paleontology is called a *paleontologist.*

Pa•le•o•zo•ic (*pay*-lee-uh-**zoh**-ik) ***noun*** An era in the earth's history that began about 600 million years ago and ended about 200 million years ago. During this time, land plants, fish, amphibians, and reptiles began to appear. ▸ ***adjective*** **Paleozoic**

pal•ette (**pal**-it) ***noun*** A flat board with a hole for the thumb. A palette is used to mix paints on. **Palette** sounds like **palate.**

pal•in•drome (**pal**-in-*drohm*) ***noun*** A word, sentence, or number that reads the same backward as forward.

pal•i•sade (*pal*-uh-**sayd**) ***noun*** A line of steep cliffs, often bordering a river.

pal•lid (**pal**-id) ***adjective*** If you are **pallid,** your skin looks pale.

palm (**pahm**)
1. ***noun*** The flat surface on the inside of your hand.
2. ***noun*** A tall, tropical tree with large leaves shaped like feathers or fans at the top.
3. ***verb*** To hide something in your palm. ▸ **palming, palmed**

pal•met•to (pal-**met**-oh) ***noun*** A kind of palm tree with leaves shaped like fans. Palmettos grow in the southern United States. ▸ ***noun, plural*** **palmettos** *or* **palmettoes**

palm•ist•ry (**pah**-muh-stree) ***noun*** The practice of telling people's fortunes by looking at the lines in the palms of their hands. ▸ ***noun*** **palmist**

pal•o•mi•no (*pal*-uh-**mee**-noh) ***noun*** A golden-tan or cream horse with a white mane and tail. ▸ ***noun, plural*** **palominos**

pam•pas (**pam**-puhz) ***noun, plural*** Large, treeless plains in South America. The pampas are mainly in central Argentina and Uruguay.

pam•per (**pam**-pur) ***verb*** To take very good care of yourself or someone else

with food, kindness, or anything special.
▸ **pampering, pampered**

pam•phlet (**pam**-flit) ***noun*** A small, thin booklet that usually contains an essay or information on one particular topic.

pan (**pan**)
1. ***noun*** A wide, shallow metal container that is used for cooking.
2. ***verb*** To look for gold by washing earth in a pan or sieve.
3. ***verb*** To move a movie or television camera over a wide area in order to follow an action.
4. ***verb*** *(informal)* To criticize someone or something harshly.
▸ ***verb*** **panning, panned**

pan•cake (**pan**-*kake*) ***noun*** A thin, flat cake made from batter and cooked in a pan or on a griddle.

pan•cre•as (**pan**-kree-uhss) ***noun*** A gland near your stomach that makes a fluid that helps you digest food. The pancreas also makes insulin, a hormone that helps your body use glucose.

pan•da (**pan**-duh) ***noun***
1. An animal found in China that looks like a bear and has thick, black and white fur. It is also called a *giant panda.*
2. A small, reddish brown animal that is found in Asia. It looks like a raccoon and has short legs; a long, bushy tail with rings; and a white face. It is also called a *lesser panda.*

pan•de•mo•ni•um (*pan*-duh-**moh**-nee-uhm) ***noun*** Chaos or confusion.

pane (**payn**) ***noun*** A sheet of glass or plastic in a window or door. **Pane** sounds like **pain.**

pan•el (**pan**-uhl) ***noun***
1. A flat piece of wood or other material made to form part of a surface such as a wall. ▸ ***noun*** **paneling** ▸ ***verb*** **panel**
2. A board with controls or instruments on it.
3. A group of people chosen to do something such as judge a competition, discuss a topic, or serve on a jury.
▸ ***noun*** **panelist**

pang (**pang**) ***noun*** A sudden, brief pain or emotion, as in *hunger pangs* or *a pang of regret.*

pan•ic (**pan**-ik)
1. ***noun*** A sudden feeling of great terror or fright, often affecting many people at once. ▸ ***verb*** **panic** ▸ ***adjective*** **panicky**
2. panic-stricken ***adjective*** Struck with a sudden fear.

pan•o•ram•a (*pan*-uh-**ram**-uh) ***noun*** A wide or complete view of an area.
▸ ***adjective*** **panoramic**

pan•sy (**pan**-zee) ***noun*** A small garden flower with five rounded petals that are often purple, yellow, or white. ▸ ***noun, plural*** **pansies**

pant (**pant**) ***verb*** To breathe quickly and loudly because you are exhausted.
▸ **panting, panted**

pan•ther (**pan**-thur) ***noun***
1. A large leopard with a black coat.
2. Another name for a **cougar, mountain lion,** and **puma.**

pan•to•mime (**pan**-tuh-mime) ***noun***
1. The telling of a story with gestures, body movements, and facial expressions rather than words. ▸ ***verb*** **pantomime**
2. A play or scene acted out with gestures instead of words.

pan•try (**pan**-tree) ***noun*** A small room or a closet in or near a kitchen where food, plates, pans, and other kitchen supplies are kept. ▸ ***noun, plural*** **pantries**

pants (**pants**) ***noun, plural*** A piece of clothing with two legs that covers the lower part of your body.

pan•ty hose (**pan**-tee) ***noun, plural*** An undergarment, similar to tights, that covers the hips, legs, and feet and is often made of nylon.

pa•pa•ya (puh-**pah**-yuh) ***noun*** The yellow or orange sweet fruit that grows on a tropical American tree. It looks like a melon.

P

pa•per (**pay**-pur)
1. ***noun*** A thin piece or sheet of material made from wood pulp and rags. Paper is used for writing, printing, drawing, wrapping, and covering walls.
2. ***noun*** A single sheet of paper.
3. ***noun*** A document, or a sheet of paper with something printed or written on it.
4. ***noun*** A written report or essay for school.
5. ***noun*** A newspaper.
6. ***verb*** To put wallpaper up, or to cover something with paper. ▸ **papering, papered**

pa•per•back (**pay**-pur-*bak*) ***noun*** A book with a paper cover.

paper clip ***noun*** A bent piece of thin wire that is used to hold sheets of paper together.

pa•per•weight (**pay**-pur-*wate*) ***noun*** A heavy, often decorative object used to hold down papers on a desk or other flat surface.

pa•per•work (**pay**-pur-*wurk*) ***noun*** Work that includes writing reports and keeping records.

pa•pier-mâ•ché (**pay**-pur muh-**shay**) ***noun*** Paper that has been soaked in glue. Before hardening, this material can be molded into dolls, toys, furniture, etc. ▸ ***adjective*** **papier-mâché**

pa•poose (pa-**pooss**) ***noun*** An American Indian baby or young child.

pap•ri•ka (pa-**preek**-uh *or* **pap**-ruh-kuh) ***noun*** A reddish orange spice made from powdered sweet red peppers.

pa•py•rus (puh-**pye**-ruhss) ***noun***
1. A tall water plant that grows in northern Africa and southern Europe.
2. Paper made from the stems of this plant. The ancient Egyptians wrote on papyrus. ▸ ***noun, plural*** **papyri** (puh-**pye**-ree) *or* **papyruses**

par (**par**) ***noun***
1. An equal level.
2. An accepted or normal level.
3. In golf, the number of strokes it should take a player to get the ball into the hole or finish a particular course.

par•a•ble (**pa**-ruh-buhl) ***noun*** A fable or story that has a moral or religious lesson.

par•a•chute (**pa**-ruh-*shoot*) ***noun*** A large piece of strong but lightweight fabric attached to thin ropes. A parachute is used to drop people or loads safely from airplanes. ▸ ***noun*** **parachutist** ▸ ***verb*** **parachute**

pa•rade (puh-**rade**)
1. ***noun*** A procession of people and vehicles as part of a ceremony or festivity. ▸ ***verb*** **parade**
2. ***verb*** If you **parade** something, you show it off. ▸ **parading, paraded**

par•a•dise (**pa**-ruh-*dise*) ***noun***
1. A place that is considered extremely beautiful and that makes people feel happy and contented, as in *a vacation paradise.*
2. In some religions, **paradise** is another word for heaven.

par•a•dox (**pa**-ruh-*doks*) ***noun***
1. A statement that seems to contradict itself but in fact may be true.
2. A person or thing that seems to contradict itself.
▸ ***noun, plural*** **paradoxes** ▸ ***adjective*** **paradoxical**

par•af•fin (**pa**-ruh-fin) ***noun*** A white, waxy substance used in making candles and for sealing jars.

par•a•graph (**pa**-ruh-*graf*) ***noun*** A short passage in a piece of writing that begins on a new line and usually is indented. A paragraph is made up of one or more sentences about a single subject or idea.

par•a•keet (**pa**-ruh-*keet*) ***noun*** A small parrot with brightly colored feathers and a long, pointed tail. Parakeets often are kept as pets.

par•a•le•gal (*pa*-ruh-**lee**-guhl) ***noun*** Someone who is trained and paid to assist a lawyer. ▸ ***adjective*** **paralegal**

par•al•lel (**pa**-ruh-*lel*)
1. ***adjective*** If two straight lines are **parallel,** they stay the same distance

from each other, and they never cross or meet.
2. ***noun*** If a situation has a **parallel,** there is another situation very similar to it. ▸ ***verb* parallel**
3. ***noun*** Any of the imaginary lines that circle the earth parallel to the equator. On a map, parallels represent degrees of latitude.
4. If electrical parts are connected **in parallel,** each one can receive power even when the others are not being used.

parallel bars ***noun, plural*** A pair of horizontal wooden bars at the same or different heights used for doing exercises in gymnastics.

par•al•lel•o•gram (*pa*-ruh-**lel**-uh-*gram*) ***noun*** A quadrilateral with opposite sides that are equal in length and parallel.

pa•ral•y•sis (puh-**ral**-uh-siss) ***noun*** A loss of the power to move or feel a part of the body.

par•a•lyze (**pa**-ruh-lize) ***verb***
1. To cause paralysis in.
2. To make someone or something helpless or unable to function.
▸ ***verb* paralyzing, paralyzed**

par•a•me•ci•um (*pa*-ruh-**mee**-see-uhm *or pa*-ruh-**mee**-shee-uhm) ***noun*** A microscopic organism with only one cell that lives in fresh water. It is shaped like a slipper. ▸ ***noun, plural* paramecia** (*pa*-ruh-**mee**-see-uh *or pa*-ruh-**mee**-shee-uh)

par•a•med•ic (*pa*-ruh-**med**-ik) ***noun*** A person trained to give emergency medical treatment but who is not a doctor or a nurse.

par•a•mount (**pa**-ruh-mount) ***adjective*** Above all others in rank, power, or importance.

par•a•pher•na•lia (*pa*-ruh-fur-**nay**-lyuh) ***noun*** Numerous pieces of equipment, belongings, and other personal items.

par•a•phrase (**pa**-ruh-*fraze*) ***verb*** If you **paraphrase** speech or writing, you say or write it again in a different way.
▸ **paraphrasing, paraphrased** ▸ ***noun*** **paraphrase**

par•a•ple•gic (pa-ruh-**plee**-jik) ***noun*** Someone who has no feeling or movement in the lower part of his or her body, usually because of an injury or a disease of the spinal cord. ▸ ***adjective*** **paraplegic**

par•a•site (**pa**-ruh-*site*) ***noun***
1. An animal or plant that gets its food by living on or inside another animal or plant.
2. A person who gets money, food, and shelter from another without doing anything in return. ▸ ***adjective* parasitic** (pa-ruh-**sit**-ik)

par•a•sol (**pa**-ruh-sol) ***noun*** A small, light umbrella that shades you from the sun.

par•a•troops (**pa**-ruh-*troops*) ***noun, plural*** Soldiers who are trained to jump by parachute into battle. ▸ ***noun*** **paratrooper**

par•cel (**par**-suhl)
1. ***noun*** A package, or something that is packed, wrapped, or put into a box.
2. ***noun*** A section or plot of land.
3. ***verb*** To divide into parts and give out.
▸ **parceling, parceled**

parch (**parch**) ***verb***
1. To make very dry.
2. To make very thirsty.
▸ ***verb* parches, parching, parched**
▸ ***adjective* parched**

parch•ment (**parch**-muhnt) ***noun*** Heavy, paperlike material made from the skin of sheep or goats and used for writing on.

par•don (**pard**-uhn)
1. ***verb*** To forgive or excuse someone, or to release the person from punishment.
▸ **pardoning, pardoned** ▸ ***noun*** **pardon**
2. ***interjection*** You say **I beg your pardon** as a polite way of asking someone to repeat what he or she has said or asking someone for forgiveness.

P

pare (**pair**) ***verb***
1. To cut off the outer layer.
2. To reduce or make less step by step, as if by cutting.
Pare sounds like **pair** and **pear.**
▸ ***verb*** **paring, pared**

par•ent (**pa**-ruhnt *or* **pair**-uhnt) ***noun***
1. A mother or a father.
2. A plant or an animal that produces offspring. ▸ ***noun*** **parenthood** ▸ ***verb*** **parent** ▸ ***adjective*** **parental**

pa•ren•the•sis (puh-**ren**-thuh-siss) ***noun*** One of the curved lines ( ) used to enclose a word or phrase in a sentence or to enclose symbols or numbers in a mathematical expression. ▸ ***noun, plural*** **parentheses** (puh-**ren**-thuh-seez)

par•ish (**pa**-rish) ***noun***
1. An area that has its own church and minister or priest.
2. The people who live in a parish.
3. In Louisiana, a county.

pa•rish•ion•er (puh-**rish**-uh-nur) ***noun*** Someone who lives in the parish of a church.

park (**park**)
1. ***noun*** An area of land with trees, benches, and sometimes playgrounds, used by the public for recreation.
2. ***noun*** An area of land set aside by the government so that it can be kept in its natural state.
3. ***verb*** To leave a car or other vehicle in a space in a garage or lot or at the curb of a street. ▸ **parking, parked**

par•ka (**par**-kuh) ***noun*** A large, heavy jacket suitable for winter weather. It has a hood and is usually made of fur or filled with down.

parking meter ***noun*** A machine that you put money into in order to pay for parking. The meter allows you a certain amount of time for each coin you put into it.

park•way (**park**-*way*) ***noun*** A wide highway or road that has grass, bushes, trees, and flowers planted down the middle or along the sides.

par•lia•ment (**par**-luh-muhnt) ***noun*** The group of people who have been elected to make the laws in some countries, such as Canada, the United Kingdom, and Israel. ▸ ***adjective*** **parliamentary**

par•lor (**par**-lur) ***noun***
1. A formal living room, especially in an old house, that is used for receiving guests.
2. A room or rooms used for a business, as in *an ice-cream parlor.*

pa•ro•chi•al (puh-**roh**-kee-uhl) ***adjective***
1. To do with a church parish, as in *a parochial school.*
2. Having a narrow, short-sighted point of view.

par•o•dy (**pa**-ruh-dee) ***noun*** An imitation of a serious piece of writing or song that makes fun of the original work. ▸ ***noun, plural*** **parodies** ▸ ***verb*** **parody**

pa•role (puh-**role**) ***noun*** The early release of a prisoner, usually for good behavior, on the condition that the person behave according to the law. ▸ ***verb*** **parole**

par•ox•ysm (**pa**-ruhk-*siz*-uhm) ***noun*** A sudden outburst or fit, as in *a paroxysm of laughter.*

par•rot (**pa**-ruht) ***noun***
1. A tropical bird with a curved beak and brightly colored feathers. Some parrots can learn to repeat things that are said to them.
2. Someone who repeats or imitates words without understanding what they mean. ▸ ***verb*** **parrot**

parse (**parss**) ***verb*** When you **parse** a sentence, you identify its subject and object and the parts of speech of its words. ▸ **parsing, parsed**

pars•ley (**par**-slee) ***noun*** A leafy, green herb with small leaves, used as food decoration or as seasoning.

pars•nip (**par**-snip) ***noun*** A plant with a pale yellow root eaten as a vegetable.

Parsnips resemble carrots. *See* **vegetable.**

par•son (**par**-suhn) ***noun*** A minister, especially a Protestant minister.

part (**part**)
1. ***noun*** A portion or division of a whole.
2. ***noun*** A piece in a machine or device.
3. ***noun*** An expected share of responsibility or work.
4. ***noun*** A character or role in a play or film.
5. ***noun*** A line in your hair where the hair is combed in two directions. ▸ ***verb*** **part**
6. ***verb*** To separate or to divide.
7. ***adjective*** Not completely or entirely.
8. ***verb*** If you **part with** something, you give it away or give it up.
9. If you **take part,** you participate or join with others in an activity.
▸ ***verb*** **parting, parted**

par•tial (**par**-shuhl) ***adjective***
1. Not complete. ▸ ***adverb*** **partially**
2. Someone who is **partial** favors one person or side more than another.
3. If you are **partial to** a particular food or drink, you are especially fond of it.
▸ ***noun*** **partiality** (*par*-shee-**al**-uh-tee)

par•tic•i•pate (par-**tiss**-uh-*pate*) ***verb*** To join with others in an activity or event. ▸ **participating, participated** ▸ ***noun*** **participant,** ***noun*** **participation**

par•ti•ci•ple (**par**-tuh-*sip*-uhl) ***noun*** A form of a verb that is used with a helping verb or that can be used as an adjective. English has two participles: the **present participle,** ending in -ing, as in "walking" or "singing" and a **past participle,** ending in -ed or sometimes -en, as in "finished" or "swollen."

par•ti•cle (**par**-tuh-kuhl) ***noun*** An extremely small piece or amount of something.

particle physics ***noun*** The study of the behavior of the minute parts of atoms.

par•tic•u•lar (pur-**tik**-yuh-lur)
1. ***adjective*** Individual or special.
2. ***adjective*** Very careful about details.
3. ***adjective*** Special or unusual.
4. ***noun*** A fact or a detail.
5. **in particular** Especially. ▸ ***adverb*** **particularly**

part•ing (**part**-ing)
1. ***noun*** A departure or a separation, as in *an emotional parting.*
2. ***adjective*** To do with a departure or separation, as in *a parting handshake.*

par•ti•tion (par-**tish**-uhn)
1. ***noun*** A movable wall or panel used to divide an area or a room.
2. ***verb*** To section something off or to separate something.
3. ***verb*** To divide into sections or parts.
▸ ***verb*** **partitioning, partitioned**

part•ly (**part**-lee) ***adverb*** In part or to some extent.

part•ner (**part**-nur) ***noun***
1. One of two or more people who do something together, as in *business partners* or *dancing partners.* ▸ ***noun*** **partnership**
2. Someone on your side in a game, as in *a tennis partner.*

part of speech ***noun*** A grammatical class into which a word can be placed according to the way it is used in a phrase or sentence, such as **noun, verb, adjective**, etc. ▸ ***noun, plural*** **parts of speech**

par•tridge (**par**-trij) ***noun*** A plump game bird that has gray, brown, and white feathers.

part-time ***adjective*** If you have a **part-time** job, you work at it for a few hours or a few days each week. ▸ ***noun*** **part-timer** ▸ ***adverb*** **part time**

par•ty (**par**-tee) ***noun***
1. An organized occasion when people enjoy themselves in a group. ▸ ***verb*** **party**
2. A group of people working together.
3. An organized group of people with similar political beliefs who try to win elections. ▸ ***noun, plural*** **parties**
▸ ***adjective*** **party**

P

pass (**pass**)
1. ***verb*** To go by someone or something.
2. ***verb*** To give something to somebody.
3. ***verb*** To kick, throw, or hit a ball to someone on your team in a sport or game. ▸ ***noun*** **pass,** ***noun*** **passer**
4. ***verb*** To succeed in a test or course. ▸ ***noun*** **pass**
5. ***verb*** To move on or to go by.
6. ***verb*** To approve or to make into law.
7. ***noun*** A narrow passage in a mountain range.
8. ***noun*** Written permission.
9. ***noun*** A free ticket.
10. pass away ***verb*** To die.
11. pass out ***verb*** To faint.
12. ***verb*** If you **pass** something **up,** you give up the opportunity to have or do it.
▸ ***noun, plural*** **passes** ▸ ***verb*** **passes, passing, passed**

pas•sage (**pass**-ij) ***noun***
1. A hall or a corridor.
2. A short section in a book or piece of music.
3. A journey by ship or airplane.
4. Approval of a bill into law by a legislature.

pas•sage•way (**pass**-ij-*way*) ***noun*** An alley, a hallway, a tunnel, or anything that allows you to pass from one place to another.

pas•sen•ger (**pass**-uhn-jur) ***noun*** Someone besides the driver who travels in a car or other vehicle.

pass•er•by (**pass**-ur-*bye*) ***noun*** Someone who happens to be passing.
▸ ***noun, plural*** **passersby**

pas•sion (**pash**-uhn) ***noun***
1. A very strong feeling, such as anger, love, or hatred.
2. Great love or enthusiasm.

pas•sion•ate (**pash**-uh-nit) ***adjective*** Having or showing very strong feelings, as in *a passionate speech.* ▸ ***adverb*** **passionately**

pas•sive (**pass**-iv) ***adjective***
1. If you are **passive,** you let things happen to you and do not fight back or resist. ▸ ***adverb*** **passively**
2. A **passive** verb's subject has something done to it rather than doing the action itself. In the sentence "The ball was kicked by the football player," the verb is passive, but in the sentence "The football player kicked the ball," the verb is active.

passive smoking ***noun*** The breathing in of smoke from other people's cigarettes, cigars, or pipes.

Pass•o•ver (**pass**-*oh*-vur) ***noun*** An important Jewish holiday celebrated in the spring. It celebrates the Jews' escape from slavery in Egypt.

pass•port (**pass**-*port*) ***noun*** An official booklet that proves that you are a citizen of a certain country and allows you to travel abroad.

pass•word (**pass**-*wurd*) ***noun*** A secret word, code, or phrase that you need to know to get into a guarded area or a computer system.

past (**past**)
1. ***noun*** The period of time before the present. ▸ ***adjective*** **past**
2. ***adjective*** Just finished or ended.
3. ***preposition*** By, after, or beyond.
▸ ***adverb*** **past**
4. ***adjective*** Former.
5. ***noun*** The **past tense.**

pas•ta (**pah**-stuh) ***noun*** A food made from flour and water. Pasta is made into shapes and dried.

paste (**payst**)
1. ***noun*** A soft, sticky mixture used to stick things together.
2. ***noun*** Any soft, creamy mixture, as in *tomato paste.*
3. ***verb*** To stick with paste.
4. ***verb*** On a computer, to insert at the cursor text or graphics copied or cut from another location.
▸ ***verb*** **pasting, pasted**

pas•tel (pa-**stel**) ***noun***
1. A chalky crayon that is used in drawing.
2. A picture made with pastels.

3. A light, soft shade of a color.
▸ ***adjective*** **pastel**

pas•teur•ize (**pass**-chuh-rize *or* **pass**-tuh-rize) ***verb*** To heat milk or another liquid to a temperature that is high enough to kill harmful bacteria. ▸ ***noun*** **pasteurization** ▸ ***adjective*** **pasteurized**

pas•time (**pass**-*time*) ***noun*** A hobby, a sports activity, or an entertainment that makes the time pass in an enjoyable way.

pas•tor (**pass**-tur) ***noun*** A minister or priest in charge of a church or parish.

pas•tor•al (**pass**-tur-uhl) ***adjective***
1. To do with the countryside.
2. To do with or from a pastor, as in *pastoral guidance.*

past participle ***noun*** A form of a verb that ends in -ed or -en and can be used with a helping verb to show that an action or a condition is completed. In the sentence "I have wrapped his gift," the word "wrapped" is a past participle. A past participle is also used to help form a passive verb, such as "kicked" in the sentence "The ball was kicked." Past participles may also be used as adjectives, such as "swollen" in "a swollen ankle."

pas•try (**pay**-stree) ***noun***
1. A dough that is rolled out and used for pie crusts.
2. Pies, tarts, and other baked goods made with pastry. ▸ ***noun, plural*** **pastries**

past tense ***noun*** A form of a verb that is used to indicate past time, as "went" in "She went to school late yesterday."

pas•ture (**pass**-chur) ***noun*** Grazing land for animals.

pas•ty (**pay**-stee) ***adjective*** If you look **pasty,** you have a pale and sickly complexion. ▸ **pastier, pastiest**

pat (**pat**)
1. ***verb*** To tap or stroke something gently with your hand. ▸ **patting, patted** ▸ ***noun*** **pat**
2. ***noun*** A small, flat piece, as in *a pat of butter.*
3. ***noun*** If you give someone a **pat on the back,** you praise the person and say that he or she has done well.

patch (**pach**)
1. ***verb*** To put a small piece of material on a hole, rip, or worn place in order to mend it. ▸ ***noun*** **patch**
2. ***noun*** A small part or area of something.
3. ***noun*** A small piece of ground.
4. patch up ***verb*** To settle or to smooth over.
▸ ***noun, plural*** **patches** ▸ ***verb*** **patches, patching, patched**

patch•work (**pach**-*wurk*) ***noun*** Fabric with a pattern made by sewing small patches of different material together. Some quilts are patchwork.

patch•y (**pach**-ee) ***adjective*** Uneven; made up of or similar to patches, as in *patchy fog.* ▸ **patchier, patchiest**

pâ•té (pah-**tay**) ***noun*** A spread made of meat, fish, or vegetables that is usually eaten on toast or crackers.

pat•ent (**pat**-uhnt)
1. ***noun*** A legal document giving the inventor of some item sole rights to manufacture or sell the item.
2. ***verb*** To obtain a patent for.
▸ **patenting, patented**
3. ***adjective*** Obvious or open. ▸ ***adverb*** **patently**
4. patent leather ***noun*** Very shiny leather used for shoes, belts, handbags, and other accessories.

pat•er•nal (puh-**tur**-nuhl) ***adjective***
1. To do with or like a father.
2. Related through your father.
▸ ***adverb*** **paternally**

path (**path**) ***noun***
1. A trail or track for walking.
2. The line or route along which a person or thing moves.

pa•thet•ic (puh-**thet**-ik) ***adjective***
1. Causing pity, sorrow, or sympathy.
2. Feeble or useless, as in *a pathetic attempt.* ▸ ***adverb*** **pathetically**

P

pa•tience (**pay**-shuhnss) ***noun*** If you have **patience,** you can put up with problems and delays without getting angry or upset.

pa•tient (**pay**-shuhnt)
1. ***adjective*** If you are **patient,** you are good at putting up with problems and delays and don't get angry or upset.
▸ ***adverb* patiently**
2. ***noun*** Someone who is receiving treatment from a doctor or other health-care provider.

pat•i•o (**pat**-ee-oh) ***noun*** A paved area next to a house, used for relaxing or eating outdoors. ▸ ***noun, plural* patios**

pa•tri•arch (**pay**-tree-ark) ***noun***
1. The male head of a family or tribe.
2. An older man in a group, tribe, or village who is respected and who holds a place of honor.

pa•tri•ot (**pay**-tree-uht) ***noun*** Someone who loves his or her country and is prepared to fight for it. ▸ ***noun* patriotism** ▸ ***adjective* patriotic**

pa•trol (puh-**trohl**)
1. ***verb*** To walk or travel around an area to protect it or to keep watch on people.
▸ **patrolling, patrolled**
2. ***noun*** A group of people who protect and watch an area, as in *a highway patrol.*
3. ***noun*** A group of soldiers, sometimes aboard ships or airplanes, sent out to find or learn about the enemy.

pa•tron (**pay**-truhn) ***noun***
1. A regular customer, as in *a restaurant patron.*
2. Someone who gives money to or helps another person, an activity, or a cause, as in *a patron of the arts.* ▸ ***noun* patronage**

pa•tron•ize (**pay**-truh-*nize or* **pat**-ruh-*nize*) ***verb***
1. To talk or act as though you are better than another person or persons.
2. If you **patronize** a store, restaurant, or other business, you go there regularly.
▸ ***verb* patronizing, patronized**

patron saint ***noun*** A saint who is believed to look after a particular country or group of people.

pat•ter (**pat**-ur)
1. ***verb*** To make light, quick sounds.
▸ **pattering, pattered** ▸ ***noun* patter**
2. ***noun*** Fast talk.

pat•tern (**pat**-urn) ***noun***
1. A repeating arrangement of colors, shapes, and figures. ▸ ***adjective* patterned**
2. A sample or model that you can copy from.
3. A repeated set of actions or characteristics.
▸ ***verb* pattern**

pat•ty (**pat**-ee) ***noun***
1. A round, flat piece of chopped or ground food, as in *a hamburger patty.*
2. A round, flat piece of candy, as in *a mint patty.*
▸ ***noun, plural* patties**

pau•per (**paw**-pur) ***noun*** A very poor person who receives most of his or her money through charity or welfare.

pause (**pawz**) ***verb*** To stop for a short time. ▸ **pausing, paused** ▸ ***noun* pause**

pave (**payv**) ***verb***
1. To cover a road or other surface with a hard material such as concrete or asphalt.
2. pave the way To lead the way, or to make progress easier.
▸ ***verb* paving, paved**

pave•ment (**payv**-muhnt) ***noun***
1. A hard material, such as concrete or asphalt, that is used to cover roads or sidewalks.
2. A paved road, or a sidewalk.

pa•vil•ion (puh-**vil**-yuhn) ***noun***
1. An open building that is used for shelter or recreation or for a show or an exhibit, as in a park or at a fair.
2. One of a group of buildings, especially a building that is part of a hospital.

paw (**paw**) ***noun*** The foot of an animal having four feet and claws.

pawn (**pawn**)
1. ***verb*** To leave a valuable item at a pawnbroker's in return for a loan. The item is returned to you if you repay your debt or may be sold if you fail to do so.
▸ **pawning, pawned**
2. ***noun*** The smallest piece in the game of chess having the lowest value.
3. ***noun*** A person or thing that is used to get something or gain an advantage.

pawn•brok•er (**pawn**-*broh*-kur) ***noun*** A person whose business is to make loans to people who leave valuable objects as security for the loans.

pay (**pay**)
1. ***verb*** To give money for something.
▸ ***noun*** **payment**
2. ***verb*** To be worthwhile or advantageous.
3. ***verb*** To give or offer something.
4. ***verb*** To suffer.
5. ***noun*** Wages or salary.
▸ ***verb*** **pays, paying, paid**

pay-per-view ***noun*** A service for cable television viewers in which customers order and view a single movie or televised event for a fee.

pay•roll (**pay**-*rohl*) ***noun***
1. A list of workers who are paid by a company, along with the amount each is to be paid.
2. The total of all money paid to workers.

PC (**pee see**)
1. ***noun*** Short for **personal computer.**
2. ***adjective*** *(informal)* Someone who is **PC** makes a great effort to be sensitive to the needs and wishes of all groups, including minorities, women, and the disabled, for example. PC stands for *Politically Correct.*

PE (**pee ee**) ***noun*** A period in school during which you play sports or do any kind of physical exercise. PE stands for *Physical Education.*

pea (**pee**) ***noun*** A small, round, green vegetable that grows as a seed in a pod.

peace (**peess**) ***noun***
1. A period without war or fighting.
▸ ***noun*** **peacetime**
2. Calmness of mind or environment.
3. Public security, or law and order.
Peace sounds like **piece.**
▸ ***adjective*** **peaceful** ▸ ***adverb*** **peacefully**

peach (**peech**) ***noun***
1. A soft, round, sweet fruit with a fuzzy, reddish yellow skin and a pit at the center. ▸ ***noun, plural*** **peaches**
2. A pink-yellow color. ▸ ***adjective*** **peach**

pea•cock (**pee**-*kok*) ***noun*** A large bird that is related to the pheasant. The male peacock has brilliant blue and green feathers that spread out in a fan shape when the peacock raises its tail.

peak (**peek**) ***noun***
1. The pointed top of a high mountain.
2. A mountain with a pointed top.
3. The highest or best point. ▸ ***verb*** **peak**
4. The brim, or the curved front part of a cap. **Peak** sounds like **peek.**

peal (**peel**)
1. ***verb*** When bells **peal,** they ring out loudly. ▸ **pealing, pealed**
2. ***noun*** A loud sound or series of sounds, as in *a peal of bells* or *peals of laughter.*
Peal sounds like **peel.**

pea•nut (**pee**-nuht) ***noun*** A nutlike seed that grows in underground pods. Peanuts are eaten roasted or made into peanut butter and cooking oil.

peanut butter ***noun*** A thick, light brown spread made from ground, roasted peanuts.

pear (**pair**) ***noun*** A juicy, sweet, yellow, green, red, or brown fruit with a smooth skin. **Pear** sounds like **pair** and **pare.**

pearl (**purl**) ***noun***
1. A small, round object that grows inside oysters and is used to make valuable jewelry.
2. A valuable person, thing, or idea, as in *pearls of wisdom.*

P

peas•ant (**pez**-uhnt) ***noun*** Someone who owns a small farm or works on a farm, especially in Europe and some Asian nations.

peat (**peet**) ***noun*** Dark brown, partly decayed plant matter that is found in bogs and swamps. Peat can be used as fuel or compost.

peb•ble (**peb**-uhl) ***noun*** A small, round stone. ▸ ***adjective*** **pebbly**

pe•can (**pee**-kan *or* pi-**kahn**) ***noun*** A sweet nut with a thin, smooth shell. Pecans grow on large trees.

peck (**pek**)
1. ***verb*** When a bird **pecks** at something, it strikes it or picks it up with its beak. ▸ **pecking, pecked** ▸ ***noun*** **peck**
2. ***noun*** *(informal)* A quick kiss. ▸ ***verb*** **peck**
3. ***noun*** A unit of measure for dry things, such as fruit, vegetables, and grain. A peck is equal to eight quarts or ¼ of a bushel.

pe•cu•liar (pi-**kyoo**-lyur) ***adjective***
1. Strange or odd.
2. peculiar to Belonging to or having to do with a certain person, group, place, or thing.
▸ ***noun*** **peculiarity** ▸ ***adverb*** **peculiarly**

ped•al (**ped**-uhl)
1. ***noun*** A lever on a bicycle, car, piano, etc., that you push with your foot.
2. ***verb*** To make something work or move by using a pedal or pedals.
▸ **pedaling, pedaled Pedal** sounds like **peddle.**

ped•dle (**ped**-uhl) ***verb*** To travel around selling things. **Peddle** sounds like **pedal.**
▸ **peddling, peddled** ▸ ***noun*** **peddler**

ped•es•tal (**ped**-i-stuhl) ***noun***
1. A base for a statue.
2. Any base or support, as for a large vase.
3. If you put someone **on a pedestal,** you admire and respect the person excessively.

pe•des•tri•an (puh-**dess**-tree-uhn) ***noun*** Someone who travels on foot.

pe•di•a•tric•ian (*pee*-dee-uh-**tri**-shuhn) ***noun*** A doctor who specializes in the care and treatment of babies and children. ▸ ***noun*** **pediatrics**

ped•i•gree (**ped**-uh-gree) ***noun*** A line or list of ancestors, especially of an animal.

peek (**peek**) ***verb*** To look at something secretly or quickly. **Peek** sounds like **peak.** ▸ **peeking, peeked** ▸ ***noun*** **peek**

peel (**peel**)
1. ***noun*** The tough outer skin of a fruit.
2. ***verb*** To remove the skin of a vegetable or a fruit.
3. ***verb*** To remove or to pull off.
4. ***verb*** To come off in pieces or strips.
Peel sounds like **peal.**
▸ ***verb*** **peeling, peeled**

peep (**peep**)
1. ***verb*** To peek or look secretly at something. ▸ **peeping, peeped** ▸ ***noun*** **peep**
2. ***noun*** The sharp sound that a young bird or chicken makes. ▸ ***verb*** **peep**

peer (**pihr**)
1. ***verb*** To look hard at something that is difficult to see. ▸ **peering, peered**
2. ***noun*** An equal, or a person of the same age, rank, or standing as another, as in *a jury of one's peers.*
3. ***noun*** A member of the British nobility, such as a duke or an earl. ▸ ***noun*** **peerage**
Peer sounds like **pier.**

peg (**peg**) ***noun*** A thin piece of wood, metal, or plastic, used to hold things down or hang things up. ▸ ***verb*** **peg**

Pe•king•ese (*peek*-uhn-**eez**) ***noun*** A breed of small dog originally from China. A Pekingese has a long, silky coat and a flat face. ▸ ***noun, plural*** **Pekingese**

pel•i•can (**pel**-uh-kuhn) ***noun*** A large water bird with a pouch below its beak where it holds the fish that it catches.

pel•let (**pel**-it) ***noun*** A small, hard ball of something, such as food or ice.

pell-mell (**pel-mel**) ***adverb*** In a confused or disorderly way.

pelt (**pelt**)
1. ***verb*** To strike or beat again and again. ▸ **pelting, pelted**
2. ***noun*** An animal's skin with the hair or fur still on it.

pen (**pen**)
1. ***noun*** An instrument used for writing or drawing with ink. ▸ ***verb*** **pen**
2. ***noun*** A small, enclosed area for sheep, cattle, pigs, or other animals.
3. ***verb*** To keep or shut up in a pen. ▸ **penning, penned**

pe•nal•ize (**pee**-nuh-*lize or* **pen**-uh-*lize*) ***verb*** To make someone suffer a penalty or punishment for something the person has done wrong. ▸ **penalizing, penalized**

pen•al•ty (**pen**-uhl-tee) ***noun***
1. A punishment.
2. In sports, a disadvantage or punishment that a team or player suffers for breaking the rules.

pen•cil (**pen**-suhl) ***noun*** An instrument used for drawing and writing. A pencil is made from a stick of graphite in a covering usually made of wood. ▸ ***verb*** **pencil**

pen•dant (**pen**-duhnt) ***noun*** A hanging ornament, especially one worn on a necklace.

pen•du•lum (**pen**-juh-luhm *or* **pen**-dyuh-luhm) ***noun*** A weight in a large clock that moves from side to side and helps keep the clock ticking regularly.

pen•e•trate (**pen**-uh-trate) ***verb***
1. To go inside or through something.
2. To understand or to solve, as in *to penetrate a mystery.*
▸ ***verb*** **penetrating, penetrated**
▸ ***noun*** **penetration**

pen•guin (**pen**-gwin *or* **peng**-gwin) ***noun*** A water bird of the Antarctic region that cannot fly. The penguin uses its wings as flippers for underwater swimming.

pen•i•cil•lin (pen-uh-**sil**-uhn) ***noun*** A drug made from a mold called *penicillium* that kills bacteria and helps fight some diseases. Penicillin was the first antibiotic. It was discovered in 1928 by Sir Alexander Fleming, a British scientist.

pen•in•su•la (puh-**nin**-suh-luh) ***noun*** A piece of land that sticks out from a larger land mass and is almost completely surrounded by water. ▸ ***adjective*** **peninsular**

pe•nis (**pee**-niss) ***noun*** The male organ for urinating. ▸ ***noun, plural*** **penises** *or* **penes** (**pee**-neez)

pen•i•tent (**pen**-uh-tuhnt) ***adjective*** If you are **penitent,** you are extremely sorry for what you have done wrong. ▸ ***noun*** **penitent,** ***noun*** **penitence**

pen•i•ten•tia•ry (pen-uh-**ten**-chur-ee) ***noun*** A state or federal prison for people found guilty of serious crimes. ▸ ***noun, plural*** **penitentiaries**

pen•knife (**pen**-*nife*) ***noun*** A small knife with blades that fold into a case. ▸ ***noun, plural*** **penknives**

pen•man•ship (**pen**-muhn-*ship*) ***noun***
1. The art of writing with a pen.
2. The style or quality of handwriting.

pen name ***noun*** A made-up name used by an author instead of his or her real name.

pen•nant (**pen**-uhnt) ***noun***
1. A long, triangular flag, often with the name of a school or team on it.
2. A triangular flag that symbolizes a championship, especially in professional baseball.

pen•ni•less (**pen**-ee-liss) ***adjective*** If you are **penniless,** you have absolutely no money.

pen•ny (**pen**-ee) ***noun*** The coin that is the smallest unit of money in the United States and Canada. A penny equals one cent. One hundred pennies equal one dollar. ▸ ***noun, plural*** **pennies**

pen pal ***noun*** Someone, often from another country, who exchanges letters with you.

P

P

pen•sion (**pen**-shuhn) ***noun*** An amount of money paid regularly to someone who has retired from work. ▸ ***noun*** **pensioner**

pen•ta•gon (**pen**-tuh-gon) ***noun***
1. A flat shape with five sides. ▸ ***adjective*** **pentagonal** (pen-**tag**-uh-nuhl)
2. **the Pentagon** A building with five sides in Arlington, Virginia, that is the headquarters of the U.S. Department of Defense.

pent•house (**pent**-houss) ***noun*** An apartment located on the top floor of a tall building.

pe•o•ny (**pee**-uh-nee) ***noun*** A garden plant with large flowers that may be red, pink, or white. ▸ ***noun, plural*** **peonies**

peo•ple (**pee**-puhl) ***noun***
1. Persons or human beings.
2. A collection of human beings who make up a nation, race, tribe, or group, as in *the American people.* ▸ ***noun, plural*** **peoples**
3. Family or relatives.

pep (**pep**)
1. ***noun*** Great energy and high spirits. ▸ ***adjective*** **pep**
2. ***verb*** If something **peps** you **up,** it fills you with energy. ▸ **pepping, pepped**

pep•per (**pep**-ur) ***noun***
1. A spicy powder made from the dried berries of a tropical climbing plant. ▸ ***verb*** **pepper** ▸ ***adjective*** **peppery**
2. A hollow vegetable that is usually red, green, or yellow.

pep•per•mint (**pep**-ur-*mint*) ***noun***
1. A kind of mint plant. The oil from peppermint leaves is used as a flavoring, especially in candy and toothpaste.
2. A candy flavored with peppermint oil. ▸ ***adjective*** **peppermint**

per (**pur**) ***preposition*** In each or for each. **Per** sounds like **purr.**

per•ceive (pur-**seev**) ***verb***
1. To become aware of through the senses, especially through sight or hearing.
2. To understand. ▸ ***verb*** **perceiving, perceived** ▸ ***noun*** **perception**

per•cent (pur-**sent**) ***noun*** A part that is one one-hundredth. A quarter is 25 percent of one dollar. Percent is also written using the percent symbol %.

per•cent•age (pur-**sen**-tij) ***noun***
1. A fraction or proportion of something expressed as a number out of a hundred.
2. A part considered in relation to the whole; a proportion.

per•cep•ti•ble (pur-**sep**-tuh-buhl) ***adjective*** Noticeable and clear. ▸ ***adverb*** **perceptibly**

per•cep•tive (pur-**sep**-tiv) ***adjective*** If you are **perceptive,** you are quick to notice things or to understand situations.

perch (**purch**)
1. ***noun*** A bar or branch on which a bird can rest. ▸ ***verb*** **perch**
2. ***noun*** Any raised place where a person can sit or stand.
3. ***verb*** To sit or stand on the edge of something, often high up. ▸ **perches, perching, perched**
4. ***noun*** An edible freshwater fish. ▸ ***noun, plural*** **perches** *or* **perch** *(fish only)*

per•chance (pur-**chanss**) ***adverb*** Perhaps or possibly.

per•cus•sion instrument (pur-**kuhsh**-uhn) ***noun*** A musical instrument, such as a drum, that is played by being hit or shaken. ▸ ***noun*** **percussionist**

per•en•ni•al (puh-**ren**-ee-uhl)
1. ***noun*** A plant that lives and flowers for more than two years.
2. ***adjective*** Lasting for a long time, or never–ending. ▸ ***adverb*** **perennially**

per•e•stroi•ka (per-uh-**stroi**-kuh) ***noun*** The policy of economic and governmental reform begun in the former Soviet Union during the mid-1980s.

per•fect
1. (**pur**-fikt) ***adjective*** Without any flaws or mistakes, as in *a perfect apple* or *a perfect copy.* ▸ ***noun*** **perfection** ▸ ***adverb*** **perfectly**

2. (pur-**fekt**) ***verb*** To succeed with effort in making something work well.
▸ **perfecting, perfected**

per•fo•rate (**pur**-fuh-*rayt*) ***verb***
1. To make a hole in.
2. To make a row of small holes through.
▸ ***verb*** **perforating, perforated**
▸ ***noun*** **perforation** ▸ ***adjective*** **perforated**

per•form (pur-**form**) ***verb***
1. To do something or carry something out.
2. To give a show in public.
▸ ***verb*** **performing, performed**

per•form•ance (pur-**for**-muhnss) ***noun***
1. The public presentation of a play, movie, or piece of music.
2. The way something works.

per•form•er (pur-**for**-mur) ***noun*** Someone who entertains an audience in public.

per•fume (**pur**-fyoom *or* pur-**fyoom**) ***noun***
1. A liquid you put on your skin to make yourself smell pleasant.
2. Any pleasing smell or odor.
▸ ***verb*** **perfume** ▸ ***adjective*** **perfumed**

per•haps (pur-**haps**) ***adverb*** Maybe or possibly.

per•il (**per**-uhl) ***noun***
1. Danger.
2. Something dangerous.
▸ ***adjective*** **perilous** ▸ ***adverb*** **perilously**

pe•rim•e•ter (puh-**rim**-uh-tur) ***noun***
1. The outside edge of an area.
2. The distance around the edge of a shape or an area.

pe•ri•od (**pihr**-ee-uhd) ***noun***
1. A length of time.
2. A part of a school day.
3. The punctuation mark (.) used to show that a sentence has ended or that a word has been abbreviated.

pe•ri•od•ic (*pihr*-ee-**od**-ik) ***adjective*** Happening or repeating at regular intervals. ▸ ***adverb*** **periodically**

pe•ri•od•i•cal (*pihr*-ee-**od**-uh-kuhl) ***noun*** A journal or magazine that is published at regular intervals, most often once a week or once a month.

pe•riph•er•al (puh-**rif**-ur-uhl)
1. ***noun*** An external device, such as a printer or modem, that is connected to and controlled by a computer.
2. ***adjective*** To do with the outer part or edge of something, as in *peripheral vision.*
▸ ***adverb*** **peripherally**

pe•riph•er•y (puh-**rif**-ur-ee) ***noun*** The outside edge of something. ▸ ***noun, plural*** **peripheries**

per•i•scope (**per**-uh-*skope*) ***noun*** A vertical tube with prisms or mirrors at each end that allows you to see something from a position a long way below it. Periscopes are often used in submarines.

per•ish (**per**-ish) ***verb*** To die, or to be destroyed. ▸ **perishes, perishing, perished**

per•ish•a•ble (**per**-ish-uh-buhl) ***adjective*** Likely to spoil or decay quickly. ▸ ***noun*** **perishable**

per•ju•ry (**pur**-jur-ee) ***noun*** The act of lying in a court of law while under oath to tell the truth. Perjury is a crime.
▸ ***noun, plural*** **perjuries** ▸ ***verb*** **perjure**

perk (**purk**)
1. ***verb*** To lift up briskly or alertly.
2. ***verb*** If you **perk up,** you become more cheerful. ▸ ***adjective*** **perky**
3. ***noun*** *(informal)* An extra advantage that comes from doing a particular job.
▸ ***verb*** **perking, perked**

perm (**purm**) ***noun*** *(informal)* A process in which hair is treated with chemicals to give it curls or waves that last for several months. Perm is short for *permanent wave.*

per•ma•nent (**pur**-muh-nuhnt) ***adjective*** Lasting or meant to last for a long time, as in *a permanent job.* ▸ ***noun*** **permanence** ▸ ***adverb*** **permanently**

per•me•ate (**pur**-mee-*ate*) ***verb*** To spread or pass through something.
▸ **permeating, permeated**

P

per•mis•si•ble (pur-**miss**-uh-buhl) ***adjective*** If something is **permissible,** it is allowed.

per•mis•sion (pur-**mish**-uhn) ***noun*** If you give **permission** for something, you say that you will allow it to happen.

per•mis•sive (pur-**miss**-iv) ***adjective*** Someone who is **permissive** is not strict and allows freedom where others would not. ▸ ***noun*** **permissiveness**

per•mit
1. (pur-**mit**) ***verb*** To allow something.
▸ **permitting, permitted**
2. (**pur**-mit) ***noun*** A written statement giving permission for something, as in *a hunting permit.*

per•mu•ta•tion (pur-myuh-**tay**-shuhn) ***noun*** One of the ways in which a series of things can be arranged or put in order.

per•pen•dic•u•lar (pur-puhn-**dik**-yuh-lur)
1. ***noun*** A line that is at right angles to another line or to a surface. ▸ ***adjective*** **perpendicular**
2. ***adjective*** Straight up and down or extremely steep, as in *the perpendicular face of a mountain.*

per•pet•u•al (pur-**pech**-oo-uhl) ***adjective*** Without ending or changing, as in *perpetual motion.* ▸ ***adverb*** **perpetually**

per•pet•u•ate (pur-**pech**-oo-ate) ***verb*** To make something last or continue for a very long time. ▸ **perpetuating, perpetuated** ▸ ***noun*** **perpetuation**

per•plex (pur-**pleks**) ***verb*** To make someone puzzled or unsure.
▸ **perplexes, perplexing, perplexed** ▸ ***noun*** **perplexity** ▸ ***adjective*** **perplexed**

per•se•cute (**pur**-suh-kyoot) ***verb*** To continually treat someone cruelly and unfairly, especially because of that person's ideas or political beliefs.
▸ **persecuting, persecuted** ▸ ***noun*** **persecution**

per•se•vere (pur-suh-**veer**) ***verb*** If you **persevere** at something, you keep on trying and do not give up, even if you are faced with obstacles or difficulties.
▸ **persevering, persevered** ▸ ***noun*** **perseverance**

per•sim•mon (pur-**sim**-uhn) ***noun*** An orange-red fruit that is shaped like a plum and is sweet and soft when ripe.

per•sist (pur-**sist** *or* pur-**zist**) ***verb***
1. To last or to continue steadily.
2. To keep on doing something in spite of obstacles or warnings.
▸ ***verb*** **persisting, persisted** ▸ ***noun*** **persistence** ▸ ***adjective*** **persistent** ▸ ***adverb*** **persistently**

per•son (**pur**-suhn) ***noun***
1. An individual human being.
2. In grammar, the *first person* refers to "I" or "we"; the *second person* refers to "you"; the *third person* refers to "he," "she," "it," or "they."
3. in person Physically present.

per•son•al (**pur**-suh-nuhl) ***adjective***
1. Private, or to do with one person only, as in *personal property.*
2. Done or made in person, as in *a personal appearance.*

personal computer ***noun*** A small desktop or portable computer that can be used by an individual at home, at school, or in an office.

per•son•al•i•ty (*pur*-suh-**nal**-uh-tee) ***noun***
1. All of the qualities or traits that make one person different from others.
2. A famous person, as in *a show business personality.*
▸ ***noun, plural*** **personalities**

per•son•al•ly (**pur**-suhn-uh-lee) ***adverb***
1. Without assistance; directly.
2. For oneself.
3. As an individual.

per•son•nel (purss-uh-**nel**) ***noun*** The group of people who work for a company or an organization. ▸ ***noun, plural*** **personnel** ▸ ***adjective*** **personnel**

P

per•spec•tive (pur-**spek**-tiv) ***noun***
1. A particular way of looking at a situation.
2. The way things or events relate to each other in size or importance.
3. If a picture is **in perspective,** distant objects are drawn smaller than nearer ones so that the view looks as someone would see it.

per•spire (pur-**spire**) ***verb*** To sweat. ▸ **perspiring, perspired** ▸ ***noun*** **perspiration**

per•suade (pur-**swade**) ***verb*** To succeed in making someone do or believe something by giving the person good reasons. ▸ **persuading, persuaded** ▸ ***noun*** **persuasion** ▸ ***adjective*** **persuasive**

per•tain (pur-**tane**) ***verb*** To be connected or related. ▸ **pertaining, pertained**

per•ti•nent (**purt**-uh-nuhnt) ***adjective*** To do with what is being discussed or considered.

per•turb (pur-**turb**) ***verb*** To make someone uncomfortable or anxious. ▸ **perturbing, perturbed**

per•verse (pur-**vurss**) ***adjective*** Deliberately unreasonable and stubborn. ▸ ***noun*** **perversity**

pe•so (**pay**-soh) ***noun*** The main unit of money in Mexico, the Philippines, and several South and Central American countries. ▸ ***noun, plural*** **pesos**

pes•si•mis•tic (pess-uh-**miss**-tik) ***adjective*** People who are **pessimistic** are gloomy and always think that the worst will happen. ▸ ***noun*** **pessimism,** ***noun*** **pessimist** ▸ ***adverb*** **pessimistically**

pest (**pest**) ***noun***
1. An insect that destroys or damages flowers, fruits, or vegetables.
2. Any creature that causes serious interference with human activity.
3. A persistently annoying person.

pes•ter (**pess**-tur) ***verb*** To keep annoying other people, often by asking or telling them something over and over again. ▸ **pestering, pestered**

pes•ti•cide (**pess**-tuh-*side*) ***noun*** A chemical used to kill pests, such as insects.

pes•tle (**pess**-uhl *or* **pess**-tuhl) ***noun*** A short stick with a thick, rounded end used to crush things such as herbs and medicine in a bowl called a mortar.

pet (**pet**)
1. ***noun*** A tame animal kept for company or pleasure.
2. ***noun*** Somebody's favorite person or thing, as in *teacher's pet.*
3. ***verb*** To stroke or pat an animal in a gentle, loving way. ▸ **petting, petted** ▸ ***adjective*** **pet**

pet•al (**pet**-uhl) ***noun*** One of the colored outer parts of a flower.

pe•ti•tion (puh-**tish**-uhn) ***noun*** A letter signed by many people asking those in power to change their policy or actions or telling them how the signers feel about a certain issue or situation. ▸ ***verb*** **petition**

pet•ri•fied (**pet**-ruh-fide) ***adjective***
1. If you are **petrified,** you are unable to move because you are so frightened.
2. Petrified wood is dead wood that has turned into stone because minerals have seeped into its cells.
▸ ***verb*** **petrify**

pe•tro•le•um (puh-**troh**-lee-uhm) ***noun*** A thick, oily liquid found below the earth's surface. It is used to make gasoline, kerosene, heating oil, and many other products.

pet•ti•coat (**pet**-ee-*kote*) ***noun*** A thin garment worn underneath a skirt or dress.

pet•ty (**pet**-ee) ***adjective***
1. Trivial and unimportant, as in *petty complaints.*
2. Mean or spiteful, as in *petty gossip.*
▸ ***adjective*** **pettier, pettiest**

P

pe•tu•nia (puh-**too**-nyuh) ***noun*** A garden plant with colorful flowers shaped like trumpets.

pew (**pyoo**) ***noun*** A long, wooden bench with a high back that people sit on in church.

pew•ter (**pyoo**-tur) ***noun***
1. A metal made of tin mixed with lead or copper. Pewter is used to make plates, pitchers, and other utensils.
2. Utensils made of pewter.
▸ ***adjective*** **pewter**

pH (**pee aych**) ***noun*** A measure of how acidic or alkaline a substance is. The initials pH stand for *Potential of Hydrogen.* Acids have pH values under 7, and alkalis have pH values over 7. If a substance has a pH value of 7, it is neutral.

phan•tom (**fan**-tuhm) ***noun*** A ghost.

phar•aoh (**fair**-oh) ***noun*** The title of kings of ancient Egypt.

phar•ma•cist (**far**-muh-sist) ***noun*** A trained person who prepares and sells drugs and medicines.

phar•ma•cy (**far**-muh-see) ***noun*** A drugstore. ▸ ***noun, plural*** **pharmacies**

phase (**faze**)
1. ***noun*** A stage in something or someone's growth or development.
2. ***noun*** A stage of the moon's change in shape as it appears from earth.
3. ***noun*** One part or side of something.
4. phase in ***verb*** To start something gradually.
5. phase out ***verb*** To stop something gradually.
▸ ***verb*** **phasing, phased**

pheas•ant (**fez**-uhnt) ***noun*** A large, brightly colored bird with a long tail that is hunted for sport and for food. Peacocks, partridges, grouse, and quail are types of pheasant.

phe•nom•e•nal (fuh-**nom**-uh-nuhl) ***adjective*** Amazing or astonishing.
▸ ***adverb*** **phenomenally**

phe•nom•e•non (fe-**nom**-uh-non) ***noun***
1. An event or a fact that can be seen or felt.
2. Something very unusual and remarkable. ▸ ***noun, plural*** **phenomena** *or* **phenomenons**

phil•an•thro•pist (fuh-**lan**-thruh-pist) ***noun*** A person who helps others by giving time or money to causes and charities.

phil•o•den•dron (fil-uh-**den**-druhn) ***noun*** A tropical American climbing vine with leaves that are shaped like hearts. The philodendron is a popular indoor plant.

phil•o•soph•i•cal (fil-uh-**sof**-uh-kuhl) ***adjective***
1. To do with philosophy.
2. If you are **philosophical,** you accept difficulties and problems calmly.
▸ ***adverb*** **philosophically**

phi•los•o•phy (fuh-**loss**-uh-fee) ***noun***
1. The study of truth, wisdom, the nature of reality, and knowledge.
2. The systematic study of the basic ideas in any field, as in *the philosophy of science.*
3. A person's **philosophy** is his or her basic ideas and beliefs on how life should be lived.
▸ ***noun*** **philosopher**

phlegm (**flem**) ***noun*** The thick substance that you cough up when you have a cold.

pho•bi•a (**foh**-bee-uh) ***noun*** An extremely strong fear. ▸ ***adjective*** **phobic**

phone (**fohn**) ***noun*** Short for **telephone.** ▸ ***verb*** **phone**

pho•net•i•cal•ly (fuh-**net**-ik-lee) ***adverb*** If something is spelled **phonetically,** it is spelled as it is pronounced, sometimes by using special symbols to represent sounds. The words in this dictionary are spelled phonetically in parentheses.

pho•net•ics (fuh-**net**-iks) ***noun*** The study of the sounds that are used in speaking.

pho•no•graph (**foh**-nuh-*graf*) ***noun*** A machine that picks up and reproduces the sounds that have been recorded in the grooves cut into a record.

phos•pho•res•cence (*foss*-fuh-**ress**-uhnss) ***noun***
1. Light that is given off from a substance after the source of energy has been removed.
2. The light that is given off by a living thing, such as a fish or an insect.
▸ ***adjective*** **phosphorescent**

phos•pho•rus (**foss**-fur-uhss) ***noun*** A chemical element that glows in the dark. It is used in making matches, fertilizers, glass, and steel.

pho•to (**foh**-toh) ***noun*** Short for **photograph.**

pho•to•cop•i•er (**foh**-toh-*kop*-ee-ur) ***noun*** A machine that copies documents using a special lens and ink called *toner.*

pho•to•cop•y (**foh**-toh-*kop*-ee) ***noun*** A copy of a document made by a photocopier. ▸ ***verb*** **photocopy**

photo finish ***noun*** A very close end to a race, where a photograph has to be studied to decide which racer has won.
▸ ***noun, plural*** **photo finishes**

pho•to•gen•ic (*foh*-tuh-**jen**-ik) ***adjective*** If someone is **photogenic,** he or she looks very good in photographs.

pho•to•graph (**foh**-tuh-*graf*) ***noun*** A picture taken by a camera on film and then developed on paper. ▸ ***verb*** **photograph**

pho•to•gra•phy (fuh-**tog**-ruh-fee) ***noun*** The creation of pictures by exposing film inside a camera to light.
▸ ***noun*** **photographer** ▸ ***adjective*** **photographic**

pho•to•jour•nal•ist (*foh*-toh-**jurn**-uh-list) ***noun*** A photographer who takes photographs of news events and tells the story of what has happened through the photos. ▸ ***noun*** **photojournalism**

pho•to•syn•the•sis (*foh*-toh-**sin**-thuh-siss) ***noun*** A chemical process by which green plants make their food. Plants use energy from the sun to turn water and carbon dioxide into food, and they give off oxygen as a by-product.

phrase (**fraze**)
1. ***noun*** A group of words that have a meaning but do not form a sentence.
2. ***verb*** To put into words in a particular way. ▸ **phrasing, phrased**

phys•i•cal (**fiz**-uh-kuhl) ***adjective***
1. To do with the body, as in *physical education.*
2. To do with matter and energy.
3. To do with nature or natural objects.

physical fitness ***noun*** The state of being in good health as a result of exercising and eating nutritious foods.

physical therapy ***noun*** The treatment of diseased or injured muscles and joints by physical and mechanical means, such as exercise, massage, and heat. ▸ ***noun*** **physical therapist**

phy•si•cian (fuh-**zish**-uhn) ***noun*** Someone with a medical degree who has been trained and licensed to treat injured and sick people; a doctor. Physicians are also authorized to write prescriptions for medicine.

phys•ics (**fiz**-iks) ***noun*** The science that deals with matter and energy. It includes the study of light, heat, sound, electricity, motion, and force. ▸ ***noun*** **physicist**

pi (**pye**) ***noun*** In math, a symbol (π) for the ratio of the circumference of a circle to its diameter. Pi equals about 3.1416. **Pi** sounds like **pie.**

pi•an•o (pee-**an**-oh *or* **pyan**-oh)
1. ***noun*** A large keyboard instrument that produces musical sounds when padded hammers inside the piano strike tuned metal strings. ▸ ***noun*** **pianist**
▸ ***noun, plural*** **pianos**
2. ***adverb*** Softly. This word is used in music.

pic•co•lo (**pik**-uh-loh) ***noun*** An instrument that looks like a flute but is smaller and has a higher pitch. ▸ ***noun, plural*** **piccolos**

P

P

pick (**pik**)
1. ***verb*** To choose or to select. ▸ ***noun*** **pick**
2. ***verb*** To collect or to gather.
▸ ***noun*** **picker**
3. ***noun*** A tool with pointed metal ends, used for breaking up soil or rocks.
4. ***noun*** A small piece of plastic or metal used to strum or pluck banjo or guitar strings. ▸ ***verb*** **pick**
5. ***verb*** To cause on purpose.
6. ***verb*** If you **pick on** someone, you tease the person or treat him or her in a mean way.
7. ***verb*** If you **pick at** something, you take bits off it.
▸ ***verb*** **picking, picked**

pick•ax *or* **pick•axe** (**pik**-*aks*) ***noun*** A tool with a long handle and a metal head. One end of the head is a sharp blade, and the other is a pick. A pickax can be used to cut through roots, loosen soil, and break up rocks. ▸ ***noun, plural*** **pickaxes**

pick•er•el (**pik**-ur-uhl) ***noun*** A freshwater fish found in the waters of North America. The pickerel has a long, pointed head and is used for food.
▸ ***noun, plural*** **pickerel** *or* **pickerels**

pick•et (**pik**-it)
1. ***verb*** To stand outside a place to make a protest and sometimes to try to prevent people from entering.
▸ **picketing, picketed** ▸ ***noun*** **picket,** ***noun*** **picketer**
2. ***noun*** A pointed stake that is driven into the ground to hold something in place or to build a fence.

pick•le (**pik**-uhl)
1. ***verb*** To preserve food in vinegar or salt water. ▸ **pickling, pickled**
2. ***noun*** Any food, such as a cucumber, that has been pickled.
3. ***noun*** *(informal)* A difficult situation.

pick•pock•et (**pik**-*pok*-it) ***noun*** Someone who steals from people's pockets or handbags.

pick•up (**pik**-*uhp*) ***noun***
1. An increase in speed.
2. A small truck with a driver's cab and an open back.

pick•y (**pik**-ee) ***adjective*** *(informal)* Fussy or choosy. ▸ **pickier, pickiest**

pic•nic (**pik**-nik) ***noun*** A party or trip that includes a meal eaten out of doors.
▸ ***noun*** **picnicker** ▸ ***verb*** **picnic**

pic•to•graph (**pik**-toh-*graf*) ***noun***
1. A picture used as a symbol in ancient writing systems.
2. Another name for **picture graph.**

pic•to•ri•al (pik-**tor**-ee-uhl) ***adjective*** Using pictures. ▸ ***adverb*** **pictorially**

pic•ture (**pik**-chur)
1. ***noun*** An image of something, such as a painting, photograph, or drawing.
▸ ***verb*** **picture**
2. ***noun*** An image on a television screen.
3. ***noun*** A movie or a motion picture.
4. ***verb*** To imagine something.
5. ***verb*** To describe something in words.
▸ ***noun*** **picture**
▸ ***verb*** **picturing, pictured**

picture graph ***noun*** A graph that shows information by means of picture symbols instead of lines or bars. Another name for picture graph is **pictograph.**

pic•tur•esque (pik-chuh-**resk**) ***adjective*** If a place or view is **picturesque,** it is beautiful to look at.

pie (**pye**) ***noun*** Pastry filled with fruit, custard, meat, or vegetables and baked in an oven. **Pie** sounds like **pi.**

piece (**peess**) ***noun***
1. A bit or section of something larger.
2. A part that has been broken, torn, or cut from a whole, as in *a piece of broken glass* or *a piece of pie.*
3. Something written or made, as in *a musical piece* or *a piece of pottery.*
4. A coin.
5. A small object used in playing checkers, chess, and other board games.
Piece sounds like **peace.**

piece•work (**peess**-*wurk*) ***noun*** Work completed and paid for by the piece, not by the time it takes to do it.

P

pier (**pihr**) ***noun***
1. A platform of metal, stone, concrete, or wood that extends over a body of water. A pier can be used as a landing place for ships and boats.
2. A pillar supporting a bridge.
Pier sounds like **peer.**

pierce (**pihrss**) ***verb***
1. To make a hole in something.
2. To pass into or through, as if with a sharp instrument.
▸ ***verb*** **piercing, pierced**

pierc•ing (**pihr**-sing) ***adjective*** Very loud and shrill.

pig (**pig**) ***noun***
1. A farm animal with a blunt snout that is raised for its meat.
2. *(informal)* A greedy, messy, or disgusting person.

pi•geon (**pij**-uhn) ***noun*** A plump bird sometimes used for racing or for carrying messages. Pigeons are often found in cities. They are related to doves.

pig•gy•back (**pig**-ee-*bak*) ***adverb*** If someone carries you **piggyback,** the person carries you on his or her shoulders or back.

pig•gy bank (**pig**-ee) ***noun*** A small bank, often in the shape of a pig, used mainly by children for saving coins.

pig•ment (**pig**-muhnt) ***noun*** A substance that gives color to something. There is pigment in paints and in your skin.

pig•pen (**pig**-*pen*) ***noun*** An enclosed area where pigs are kept. It is also called a **sty** or a **pigsty.**

pig•sty (**pig**-*stye*) ***noun***
1. A pigpen.
2. *(informal)* A very messy and often dirty place.
▸ ***noun, plural*** **pigsties**

pig•tail (**pig**-*tayl*) ***noun*** A length of hair that has been divided into three sections and braided.

pike (**pike**) ***noun***
1. A large, thin freshwater fish with a flat snout and very sharp teeth.
2. A type of dive in which the diver bends at the waist to touch the toes while in midair, then enters the water with the body fully extended.

pile (**pile**) ***noun***
1. A heap or mound of something, as in *a pile of old newspapers.* ▸ ***verb*** **pile**
2. A very great amount of something.
3. A heavy wood or steel beam that is driven into the ground to support a bridge or pier.
4. The raised loops or pieces of yarn that form the surface of a carpet.

pil•fer (**pil**-fur) ***verb*** To steal small amounts of something or small things.
▸ **pilfering, pilfered** ▸ ***noun*** **pilferer,** ***noun*** **pilferage**

pil•grim (**pil**-gruhm) ***noun***
1. Someone who goes on a journey to worship at a holy place. ▸ ***noun*** **pilgrimage**
2. the Pilgrims ***noun, plural*** The group of people who left England because of religious persecution, came to America, and founded Plymouth Colony in 1620.

pill (**pil**) ***noun*** A small, solid tablet of medicine, such as aspirin.

pil•lar (**pil**-ur) ***noun*** A column that supports part of a building or that stands alone as a monument.

pil•low (**pil**-oh) ***noun*** A large, soft cushion on which you put your head when you are sleeping. Some pillows are used to support the back or to sit on.

pil•low•case (**pil**-oh-*kayss*) ***noun*** A cloth cover that you put over a pillow on a bed to keep it clean.

pi•lot (**pye**-luht)
1. ***noun*** Someone who flies an aircraft.
2. ***noun*** Someone who steers a ship in and out of port.
3. ***verb*** To control or guide something.
▸ **piloting, piloted**
4. ***adjective*** Done as an experiment, as in *a pilot television program.* ▸ ***noun*** **pilot**

pim•ple (**pim**-puhl) ***noun*** A small, raised spot on the skin that is sometimes painful and filled with pus. ▸ ***adjective*** **pimply**

P

pin (**pin**)
1. ***noun*** A thin, pointed piece of metal, usually used to fasten material together.
2. ***noun*** A piece of jewelry or a badge fastened to clothing with a pin or clasp.
3. ***verb*** To fasten things together with a pin.
4. ***verb*** To hold something or someone firmly in position.
5. ***noun*** One of 10 pieces of wood shaped like bottles that are knocked over in bowling.
6. ***noun*** In golf, the flag that indicates where the hole is on the green.
▸ ***verb*** **pinning, pinned**

pi•ña•ta (peen-**yah**-tuh) ***noun*** A decorated container filled with candies and gifts. It is hung from the ceiling to be broken with sticks by blindfolded children. Piñatas are popular at Latin American parties and celebrations.

pin•ball (**pin**-*bawl*) ***noun*** A game in which you shoot small balls around a number of obstacles and targets on a slanted table.

pin•cer (**pin**-sur)
1. ***noun*** The pinching claw of a crustacean such as a crab.
2. **pincers** ***noun, plural*** A tool with jaws for gripping and pulling things.

pinch (**pinch**)
1. ***verb*** To squeeze someone's skin painfully between the thumb and index finger. ▸ ***noun*** **pinch**
2. ***noun*** A small amount of something, as in *a pinch of salt.*
3. ***verb*** To make thin or wrinkled.
4. ***noun*** An emergency or time of need.
▸ ***verb*** **pinches, pinching, pinched**
▸ ***noun, plural*** **pinches**

pin•cush•ion (**pin**-*kush*-uhn) ***noun*** A small cushion used to stick pins in when they are not being used.

pine (**pine**)
1. ***noun*** A tall evergreen tree that produces cones and leaves that look like needles.
2. ***verb*** If you **pine for** someone, you feel very sad because the person has gone away and you miss him or her.
▸ **pining, pined**

pine•ap•ple (**pine**-*ap*-uhl) ***noun*** A large, tropical fruit with yellow flesh and a tough, prickly skin. Pineapples grow on plants with long, stiff leaves.

Ping-Pong (**ping**-*pong*) ***noun*** Another word for table tennis. Ping-Pong is a trademark. *See* **table tennis.**

pink (**pingk**) ***noun*** A pale red color made by mixing red and white. ▸ ***adjective*** **pink,** ***adjective*** **pinkish**

pink•eye (**pingk**-*eye*) ***noun*** A highly contagious disease that causes the surface of the eyeball and the inside of the eyelid to become red, sore, and itchy.

pin•point (**pin**-*point*)
1. ***adjective*** Very exact or precise.
2. ***verb*** If you **pinpoint** something, you locate it exactly. ▸ **pinpointing, pinpointed**

pins and needles ***noun, plural***
1. A prickly, tingling feeling that you get when some of the blood supply to part of your body has been cut off.
2. If you are **on pins and needles,** you are very nervous about something that is going to happen soon.

pin•stripe (**pin**-*stripe*) ***noun*** A fabric with a very narrow stripe woven into it.

pint (**pinte**) ***noun*** A unit of measure equal to half a quart or 16 fluid ounces.

pin•to (**pin**-toh) ***noun***
1. A horse or pony that has spots or patches of two or more colors.
2. A type of kidney bean that is spotted. It is grown mainly in the southwestern part of the United States and is used for food.
▸ ***noun, plural*** **pintos**

pin•wheel (**pin**-*weel*) ***noun*** A toy wheel that spins in the wind. It is made of colored paper or plastic that is pinned to a stick.

pi•o•neer (*pye*-uh-**neer**) ***noun***
1. One of the first people to work in a new and unknown area.
2. Someone who explores unknown

territory and settles there.
▸ ***verb*** **pioneer**

pi•ous (**pye**-uhss) ***adjective*** Someone who is **pious** practices his or her religion faithfully and seriously. ▸ ***adverb*** **piously**

pipe (**pipe**)
1. ***noun*** A tube, usually used to carry a liquid or gas.
2. ***verb*** To send something along pipes, tubes, or wires. ▸ **piping, piped**
3. ***noun*** A tube with a bowl on the end of it, used for smoking tobacco. Pipes are usually made of wood.
4. ***noun*** A tube with holes in it, used as a musical instrument or as part of an instrument.
5. piped music ***noun*** Music that can be heard through speakers all over a building.

pipe•line (**pipe**-*line*) ***noun***
1. A line of large pipes that carry water, gas, or oil over long distances.
2. A direct route for sending information or supplies.

pip•ing (**pye**-ping)
1. ***noun*** A system of pipes.
2. ***noun*** A shrill sound or call, as in *the piping of tiny frogs.*
3. ***noun*** A thin, pipelike line of decoration on a cake, piece of clothing, or furniture.
4. ***adjective*** If food is **piping hot,** it is very, very hot.

pi•rate (**pye**-rit)
1. ***noun*** Someone who attacks and steals from ships at sea. ▸ ***noun*** **piracy**
2. ***verb*** If someone **pirates** a tape, computer game, or anything that has been created by someone else, the person makes copies from the original and sells them illegally. ▸ **pirating, pirated**
▸ ***adjective*** **pirated**

pis•ta•chi•o (pi-**stash**-ee-oh) ***noun***
1. A small, green nut with a hard shell that is sometimes dyed red.
2. A light green color.
▸ ***noun, plural*** **pistachios**

pis•til (**piss**-tuhl) ***noun*** The female part of a flower that is shaped like a stalk. It is the place where the seeds are produced. The pistil includes the ovule, the style, and the stigma of a flower. **Pistil** sounds like **pistol.**

pis•tol (**piss**-tuhl) ***noun*** A small gun designed to be held in the hand. **Pistol** sounds like **pistil.**

pis•ton (**piss**-tuhn) ***noun*** A disk or cylinder that moves back and forth in a large cylinder. Automobile engines have pistons. Their back-and-forth movement is converted to rotational motion.

pit (**pit**)
1. ***noun*** A hole in the ground.
2. ***noun*** The large, hard seed in the middle of some fruits, such as peaches and plums.
3. ***verb*** If two people are **pitted against** each other, they are made to compete with each other. ▸ **pitting, pitted**
4. ***noun*** When a race car makes a **pit stop,** it pulls to the side of the racecourse for fuel and repairs.

pi•ta (**pee**-tuh) ***noun*** A thin, flat bread that can be separated into two layers to form a pocket for meat, vegetables, or another filling.

pitch (**pich**)
1. ***verb*** To throw or toss something, such as a baseball or horseshoe. ▸ ***noun*** **pitch**
2. ***verb*** To fall or plunge forward.
3. ***verb*** When you **pitch** a tent, you put it up.
4. ***noun*** A dark, sticky substance that is made from tar or petroleum. Pitch is used to waterproof roofs and pave streets.
5. ***noun*** A high point or degree, as in *a high pitch of excitement.*
6. ***noun*** The highness or lowness of a musical sound.
7. ***noun*** *(informal)* A talk meant to persuade you to do or buy something, as in *a sales pitch.*
▸ ***noun, plural*** **pitches** ▸ ***verb*** **pitches, pitching, pitched**

P

pitc•her (**pich**-ur) ***noun***
1. A container with an open top for liquids. Pitchers usually have a handle and a lip or spout.
2. A baseball player who throws the ball to the batter.

pitch•fork (**pich**-*fork*) ***noun*** A large fork with a long handle and two or three prongs, used for lifting and throwing hay.

pit•fall (**pit**-*fawl*) ***noun*** A hidden danger or difficulty.

pit•i•ful (**pit**-i-fuhl) ***adjective***
1. Causing or deserving pity.
2. Useless or worthless.
▸ ***adverb*** **pitifully**

pit•i•less (**pit**-ee-liss) ***adjective*** If someone is **pitiless,** he or she shows no pity or sympathy for anyone. ▸ ***adverb*** **pitilessly**

pit•y (**pit**-ee)
1. ***verb*** If you **pity** someone, you feel sorry for the person. ▸ **pities, pitying, pitied** ▸ ***adverb*** **pityingly**
2. ***noun*** A feeling of sorrow or sympathy for the suffering of another. ▸ ***noun, plural*** **pities**

piv•ot (**piv**-uht)
1. ***noun*** A central point on which something turns or balances.
2. ***verb*** To turn suddenly as if on a pivot.
▸ **pivoting, pivoted** ▸ ***adjective*** **pivotal**

pix•el (**piks**-uhl) ***noun*** One of the tiny dots on a video screen or computer monitor that make up the visual image.

pix•ie *or* **pix•y** (**pik**-see) ***noun*** A small elf or fairy in legends and fairy tales.
▸ ***noun, plural*** **pixies**

piz•za (**peet**-suh) ***noun*** A flat pie that is baked with toppings of tomato sauce, cheese, etc.

piz•ze•ri•a (*peet*-suh-**ree**-uh) ***noun*** A place where pizza is made and sold.

plac•ard (**plak**-ard) ***noun*** A poster, sign, or notice that is put up in a public place.

pla•cate (**play**-kate) ***verb*** To make someone calm or less angry, often by giving the person something that he or she wants. ▸ **placating, placated**

place (**playss**)
1. ***noun*** A particular area or location.
2. ***noun*** A particular position or rank.
3. ***noun*** A space for a person or thing.
4. ***verb*** To put something somewhere deliberately and carefully.
5. ***verb*** To identify by putting in context.
6. If something is **in place,** it is in its proper spot or location.
▸ ***verb*** **placing, placed**

plac•id (**plass**-id) ***adjective*** Calm or peaceful, as in *a placid disposition* or *a placid lake.* ▸ ***adverb*** **placidly**

pla•gia•rize (**play**-juh-*rize*) ***verb*** To steal and pass off the ideas or words of another as one's own. ▸ **plagiarizing, plagiarized** ▸ ***noun*** **plagiarism,** ***noun*** **plagiarist**

plague (**playg**)
1. ***noun*** A very serious disease that spreads quickly to many people and often causes death.
2. ***verb*** If something **plagues** you, it troubles and annoys you. ▸ **plaguing, plagued**

plaid (**plad**) ***noun*** A pattern of squares in cloth formed by weaving stripes of different widths and colors that cross each other.

plain (**plane**)
1. ***adjective*** Easy to see or hear.
2. ***adjective*** Easy to understand.
3. ***adjective*** Simple or not fancy, as in *plain food* or *plain dress.*
4. ***adjective*** Simple and straightforward.
5. ***adjective*** Not beautiful or handsome, as in *a plain face.*
6. ***noun*** A large, flat area of land.
Plain sounds like **plane.**
▸ ***adjective*** **plainer, plainest**

plain•tive (**playn**-tiv) ***adjective*** Sad and mournful. ▸ ***adverb*** **plaintively**

plait (**playt** *or* **plat**) ***noun*** A length of hair that has been divided into three sections and braided. ▸ ***verb*** **plait**
▸ ***adjective*** **plaited**

plan (**plan**)
1. ***verb*** To work out ahead of time how you will do something.
2. ***noun*** An idea about how you intend to do something, as in *plans for the future.*
3. ***verb*** If you **plan** to do something, you intend to do it.
4. ***noun*** A diagram or drawing that shows how the parts of something are arranged or put together, as in *plans for a new building.*
▸ ***verb*** **planning, planned**

plane (**plane**) ***noun***
1. A machine with wings that flies through the air. Plane is short for **airplane.**
2. A hand tool with a sharp blade used for smoothing wood. ▸ ***verb*** **plane**
3. A level of difficulty or achievement.
4. In geometry, a flat surface.
Plane sounds like **plain.**

plan•et (**plan**-it) ***noun*** One of the nine large heavenly bodies circling the sun.
▸ ***adjective*** **planetary**

plan•e•tar•i•um (*plan*-uh-**tair**-ee-uhm) ***noun*** A building with equipment for reproducing the positions and movements of the sun, moon, planets, and stars by projecting their images onto a curved ceiling.

plank (**plangk**) ***noun*** A long, flat piece of wood used, for example, for flooring in a house.

plank•ton (**plangk**-tuhn) ***noun*** Animals and plants, usually tiny, that drift or float in oceans and lakes.

plant (**plant**)
1. ***noun*** A living organism with a green pigment called chlorophyll that allows the organism to make food from the energy of the sun. Many land plants have stems, roots, and leaves.
2. ***verb*** To put a plant or seed in the ground so that it can grow.
3. ***verb*** To put something firmly in place.
4. ***noun*** The buildings and equipment used to make a product, such as cars, chemicals, or electricity; a factory.
▸ ***verb*** **planting, planted**

plan•tain (**plan**-tuhn) ***noun*** A tropical fruit that looks like a banana but is eaten cooked.

plan•ta•tion (plan-**tay**-shuhn) ***noun*** A large farm found in warm climates where crops such as coffee, tea, rubber, and cotton are grown.

plaque (plak) ***noun***
1. A plate with words inscribed on it, usually placed on a wall in a public place.
2. The coating made from food, bacteria, and saliva that forms on your teeth and can cause tooth decay.

plas•ma (**plaz**-muh) ***noun*** The clear, yellow, liquid part of the blood. Red and white blood cells float in the watery plasma.

plas•ter (**plass**-tur)
1. ***noun*** A substance made of lime, sand, and water, used by builders to put a smooth finish on walls and ceilings.
▸ ***noun*** **plasterer** ▸ ***verb*** **plaster**
2. ***verb*** To cover or coat something as if you were using plaster. ▸ **plastering, plastered**
3. **plaster cast** ***noun*** A hard, white case that holds broken bones together so that they can heal properly.

plas•tic (**plass**-tik) ***noun*** A synthetic substance that is light and strong and can be molded into different shapes and thicknesses. Cellophane and vinyl are plastics.

plastic surgery ***noun*** Operations on skin and body tissue. Plastic surgery can be used to repair damage or to improve someone's appearance.

plate (**playt**) ***noun***
1. A flat dish used for food.
2. A flat sheet of metal, as in *a license plate* or *plates of armor.*
3. A color illustration in a book.
4. Home base in baseball.
5. One of the sheets of rock that make up the earth's outer crust.

P

pla•teau (pla-**toh**) ***noun*** An area of high, flat land.

plate•let (**plate**-lit) ***noun*** A tiny, flat body in the blood that helps the blood clot.

plate tec•ton•ics (**playt** tek-**ton**-iks) ***noun*** The theory that the earth's crust is made up of huge rigid sections or "plates," that move very slowly.

plat•form (**plat**-*form*) ***noun***
1. A flat, raised structure where people can stand, as in *a train platform* or *a speaker's platform.*
2. A statement of beliefs of a group.

plat•ing (**play**-ting) ***noun*** A thin coating or layer of metal, usually gold or silver.

plat•i•num (**plat**-uhn-uhm) ***noun*** A very valuable silvery-white metal that is often used in jewelry.

pla•toon (pluh-**toon**) ***noun*** A group of soldiers made up of two or more squads. A platoon is usually commanded by a lieutenant.

plat•ter (**plat**-ur) ***noun*** A large, shallow plate used to serve food.

plat•y•pus (**plat**-uh-puhss *or* **plat**-uh-puss) ***noun*** An Australian mammal with webbed feet and a broad bill. The platypus is one of the few mammals that lay eggs. ▸ ***noun, plural*** **platypuses**

plau•si•ble (**plaw**-zuh-buhl) ***adjective*** Believable. ▸ ***adverb*** **plausibly**

play (**play**)
1. ***verb*** To take part in a game or other enjoyable activity.
2. ***noun*** Fun or recreation.
3. ***noun*** A story that is acted, usually on a stage or in a theater.
4. ***noun*** A move, a turn, or an action in a game.
5. ***verb*** To make music on.
6. ***verb*** To take part in a sport or game.
7. ***verb*** To act a part in a play.
8. ***verb*** To act or to behave.
▸ ***noun*** **player** ▸ ***verb*** **playing, played**

play•ful (**play**-fuhl) ***adjective***
1. Frisky and willing to play.
2. Humorous, or meant to amuse or tease.

play•ground (**play**-*ground*) ***noun*** An outdoor area, often with swings, slides, seesaws, and other equipment where children can play.

playing card ***noun*** A card used in a game. The most common group of playing cards has 52 cards divided into four suits called spades, clubs, hearts, and diamonds.

play•mate (**play**-*mate*) ***noun*** A child who plays with another child or children.

play•pen (**play**-*pen*) ***noun*** A usually square folding structure that is a safe place for a baby to play in.

play•room (**play**-*room*) ***noun*** A room in which children can play.

play•wright (**play**-*rite*) ***noun*** Someone who writes plays.

pla•za (**plaz**-uh *or* **plah**-zuh) ***noun***
1. A public square.
2. An open area near large city buildings that often has walkways, trees, shrubs, and benches.

plea (**plee**) ***noun***
1. An extremely emotional request, as in *a plea for mercy.*
2. A defendant's answer to a charge in a court of law.

plead (**pleed**) ***verb***
1. If you **plead** with someone, you beg the person to do something.
2. To say whether you are guilty or not guilty in a court of law.
▸ ***verb*** **pleading, pleaded** *or* **pled (pled)**

pleas•ant (**plez**-uhnt) ***adjective***
1. Enjoyable or giving pleasure.
2. Likeable or friendly, as in *a pleasant personality.*
▸ ***adverb*** **pleasantly**

please (**pleez**)
1. ***verb*** To satisfy or to give pleasure.
▸ ***adjective*** **pleased,** ***adjective*** **pleasing**
2. ***adverb*** A polite word used when you ask for something. It means "be so kind as to."
3. ***verb*** To choose or to prefer.
▸ ***verb*** **pleases, pleasing, pleased**

P

pleas•ure (**plezh**-ur) ***noun***
1. A feeling of enjoyment or satisfaction.
2. Something that gives you a feeling of enjoyment or satisfaction. ▸ ***adjective*** **pleasurable**

pleat (**pleet**) ***noun*** One of a series of parallel folds in a piece of clothing such as a skirt. ▸ ***adjective*** **pleated**

pledge (**plej**) ***verb*** To make a sincere promise. ▸ **pledging, pledged** ▸ ***noun*** **pledge**

plen•ti•ful (**plen**-ti-fuhl) ***adjective*** Existing in large amounts. ▸ ***adverb*** **plentifully**

plen•ty (**plen**-tee) ***noun*** A great number or amount that is more than enough.

pli•a•ble (**plye**-uh-buhl) ***adjective***
1. If an object or material is **pliable,** it can be easily bent or shaped.
2. If a person is **pliable,** he or she can be influenced easily.

pli•ers (**plye**-urz) ***noun, plural*** A tool with two handles and jaws that can grip and bend objects or cut wire.

plight (**plite**) ***noun*** A situation of great danger or hardship.

plod (**plod**) ***verb***
1. To walk in a slow and heavy way.
2. To work in a dull, slow way. ▸ ***verb*** **plodding, plodded** ▸ ***noun*** **plodder**

plot (**plot**)
1. ***verb*** To make a secret plan, usually to do something wrong or illegal. ▸ ***noun*** **plot**
2. ***noun*** A small area of land, as in *a vegetable plot.*
3. ***noun*** The main story of a novel, movie, play, or any work of fiction.
4. ***verb*** To mark out something, such as a graph or a route on a map.
▸ ***verb*** **plotting, plotted**

plo•ver (**pluhv**-ur *or* **ploh**-vur) ***noun*** A bird with long, pointed wings and a short bill that runs along the shore to find food.

plow (**plou**)
1. ***noun*** A piece of farm equipment pulled by an animal or a tractor and used to turn over soil before seeds are planted.
2. ***noun*** A device used to remove or push aside matter, such as snow from roads and sidewalks.
3. ***verb*** To turn over soil using a plow.
4. ***verb*** If you **plow through** something, you work hard to get through it.
▸ ***verb*** **plowing, plowed**

pluck (**pluhk**)
1. ***verb*** To pull feathers out of a bird.
2. ***verb*** To play notes on a stringed instrument by pulling on the strings with your fingers or by using a pick.
3. ***noun*** Courage and bravery.
▸ ***adjective*** **plucky** ▸ ***adverb*** **pluckily**
4. ***verb*** To pick fruit or flowers.
▸ ***verb*** **plucking, plucked** ▸ ***adjective*** **plucked**

plug (**pluhg**)
1. ***noun*** An object pushed into a hole to block it. ▸ ***verb*** **plug**
2. ***noun*** A device at the end of a wire that is put into an electrical outlet to make a connection with a source of electricity. Plugs have metal prongs.
3. ***noun*** Short for **spark plug.**
4. ***verb*** *(informal)* To gain publicity for something by talking about it, usually on radio or television.
5. ***verb*** To work in a steady way.
▸ ***verb*** **plugging, plugged**

plum (**pluhm**) ***noun*** A fruit that is soft when ripe and has a purple or yellow skin.

plum•age (**ploo**-mij) ***noun*** A bird's feathers.

plumb•er (**pluhm**-ur) ***noun*** Someone who puts in and repairs water and sewage systems, from pipes to sinks to toilets.

plumb•ing (**pluhm**-ing) ***noun*** The system of water pipes in a building.

plume (**ploom**) ***noun***
1. A long, fluffy feather often used as an ornament on clothing.
2. Something that looks like a feathery plume. ▸ ***verb*** **plume**

P

plump (**pluhmp**) ***adjective*** Somewhat fat or round in shape, as in *a plump baby* or *a plump cushion.* ▸ **plumper, plumpest**

plun•der (**pluhn**-dur) ***verb*** To steal things by force, often during a battle. ▸ **plundering, plundered** ▸ ***noun*** **plunder**

plunge (**pluhnj**) ***verb***
1. To dive into water.
2. To put or push something in suddenly or with force.
3. To fall steeply or sharply.
4. To do something suddenly, or to make something happen suddenly.
▸ ***verb*** **plunging, plunged** ▸ ***noun*** **plunge**

plu•ral (**ploor**-uhl) ***noun*** The form of a word used for two or more of something. The plural of *child* is *children.* ▸ ***adjective*** **plural**

plus (**pluhss**)
1. ***noun*** In math, a sign (+) used in addition. Also called a *plus sign.* ▸ ***noun, plural*** **pluses**
2. ***preposition*** Added to.
3. ***preposition*** In addition to.
4. ***adjective*** Slightly higher than, as in *a grade of B plus.*

Plu•to (**ploo**-toh) ***noun*** The ninth and smallest planet in our solar system. Pluto is the farthest planet from the sun and can be seen only through a telescope.

plu•to•ni•um (ploo-**toh**-nee-uhm) ***noun*** A radioactive metallic element that is made artificially from uranium. Plutonium is used as a fuel in nuclear reactors. It is also used to make atomic bombs.

ply•wood (**plye**-*wud*) ***noun*** Board made from several thin sheets of wood that have been glued together. Plywood is used for building and carpentry.

P.M. (**pee em**) The initials of the Latin phrase *post meridiem,* which means "after midday." It is used to indicate the time between noon and 11:59 in the evening.

pneu•mat•ic (noo-**mat**-ik) ***adjective***
1. Filled with air.
2. Operated by compressed air.

pneu•mo•nia (noo-**moh**-nyuh) ***noun*** A serious disease that causes the lungs to become inflamed and filled with a thick fluid that makes breathing difficult.

poach (**pohch**) ***verb***
1. To catch fish or animals illegally on someone else's land.
2. To cook food, such as eggs or fish, by heating it in gently boiling liquid.
▸ ***verb*** **poaches, poaching, poached**

poach•er (**pohch-ur**) ***noun***
1. A person who hunts or fishes illegally on someone else's land.
2. A pot designed to poach eggs or fish.

pock•et (**pok**-it)
1. ***noun*** A small cloth pouch that is sewn into clothing and used for carrying small items.
2. ***verb*** To take something secretly. ▸ **pocketing, pocketed**
3. ***noun*** A small area or an isolated group.
4. ***adjective*** Small enough to be carried in your pocket, as in *a pocket calculator.*

pock•et•book (**pok**-it-*buk*) ***noun*** A woman's purse or handbag that is used to carry personal items such as a wallet and keys.

pock•et•knife (**pok**-it-*nife*) ***noun*** A small knife with a blade or blades that fold into the handle. A small pocketknife is called a **penknife.** ▸ ***noun, plural*** **pocketknives**

pocket money ***noun*** Money for minor expenses, such as bus fare or snacks.

pod (**pod**) ***noun*** A long case that holds the seeds of certain plants, as in *a pea pod.*

po•em (**poh**-uhm) ***noun*** A piece of writing set out in short lines, often with a noticeable rhythm and some words that rhyme. Many poems are written to help the reader or listener share an experience or feel a strong emotion. In a poem, words are often chosen for their sounds as well as their meanings.

po•et (**poh**-uht) ***noun*** Someone who writes poetry.

po•et•ry (**poh**-i-tree) ***noun***
1. Literary work in the form of poems.
2. Anything that has the effect of a poem.
▸ ***adjective* poetic**

poin•set•ti•a (poin-**set**-uh *or* poin-**set**-ee-uh) ***noun*** A decorative plant with large red, white, or pink leaves that look like flower petals.

point (**point**)
1. ***verb*** To show where something is by using your index finger.
2. ***noun*** The sharp end of something, as in *a pencil point.* ▸ ***adjective* pointed**
3. ***noun*** A dot in writing, as in *a decimal point.*
4. ***noun*** The main purpose behind something that is said or done.
5. ***noun*** A specific place or stage.
6. ***noun*** A unit for scoring in a game.
7. ***noun*** In geometry, a location in space with no dimension.
8. ***noun*** A particular time or moment.
9. ***noun*** A quality or a trait.
10. ***verb*** To aim at someone or something.
▸ ***verb* pointing, pointed**

point-blank ***adjective***
1. Very close.
2. Plain and blunt, as in *point-blank questions.*

point•less (**point**-liss) ***adjective*** If something is **pointless**, it is useless.
▸ ***adverb* pointlessly**

point of view ***noun*** An attitude, a viewpoint, or a way of looking at or thinking about something.

poise (**poiz**)
1. ***verb*** To balance. ▸ **poising, poised**
2. ***noun*** Composure or self-confidence.

poised (**poizd**) ***adjective*** If you are **poised,** you are self-confident and do not lose your composure.

poi•son (**poi**-zuhn) ***noun*** A substance that can kill or harm someone if it is swallowed, inhaled, or sometimes even touched. ▸ ***verb* poison** ▸ ***adjective* poisonous**

poison ivy ***noun*** A shrub or climbing vine with clusters of three shiny, green leaves. Poison ivy causes an itchy rash on most people who touch it.

poison sumac ***noun*** A variety of sumac that can cause a rash similar to that from poison ivy.

poke (**pohk**) ***verb***
1. To jab sharply with a finger or pointed object. ▸ ***noun* poke**
2. To stick out or thrust quickly.
3. To move slowly. ▸ ***adjective* poky** *or* **pokey**
▸ ***verb* poking, poked**

pok•er (**poh**-kur) ***noun***
1. A long, metal tool used for stirring up a fire.
2. A card game in which a player bets that the value of his or her cards is greater than that of the cards held by the other players.

po•lar (**poh**-lur) ***adjective*** To do with or near the icy regions around the North or South Pole.

polar bear ***noun*** A large bear with thick, white fur that lives in Arctic regions.

pole (**pohl**) ***noun***
1. A long, smooth piece of wood, metal, or plastic, as in *a telephone pole.*
2. One of the two geographical points that are farthest away from the equator, the North Pole or the South Pole.
3. One of the two opposite ends of a magnet.
4. If two people or things are **poles apart,** they are very different or have very different ideas. **Pole** sounds like **poll.**

pole•cat (**pohl**-*kat*) ***noun***
1. A European animal of the weasel family that has brown or black fur. A polecat gives off a strong, unpleasant odor when attacked or frightened.
2. Any of a group of North American skunks.

P

pole vault ***noun*** A jump over a high bar using a flexible pole. ▸ ***noun*** **pole-vaulter** ▸ ***verb*** **pole-vault**

po•lice (puh-**leess**)
1. ***noun, plural*** The people whose job is to keep order, make sure that the law is obeyed, and stop any crimes that are being committed. ▸ ***noun*** **policeman,** ***noun*** **policewoman**
2. ***verb*** To guard or patrol an area and keep order. ▸ **policing, policed**

police officer ***noun*** A member of a police department. A police officer can be a man or a woman.

pol•i•cy (**pol**-uh-see) ***noun***
1. A general plan or principle that people use to help them make decisions or take action.
2. An insurance contract.
▸ ***noun, plural*** **policies**

po•li•o (**poh**-lee-oh) ***noun*** An infectious viral disease that attacks the brain and spinal chord. Polio occurs mainly in children. In serious cases, it can cause paralysis. This disease is now easily prevented with a vaccine. Polio is short for *poliomyelitis.*

pol•ish (**pol**-ish)
1. ***verb*** To rub something to make it shine. ▸ **polishes, polishing, polished** ▸ ***noun*** **polish**
2. ***noun*** A cleaning substance used to make things shine, as in *shoe polish.*
▸ ***noun, plural*** **polishes**

pol•ished (**pol**-isht) ***adjective***
1. Smooth and shiny.
2. If you give a **polished** performance, you are well rehearsed and perform confidently.

po•lite (puh-**lite**) ***adjective*** Having good manners; being well behaved and courteous to others. ▸ **politer, politest** ▸ ***noun*** **politeness** ▸ ***adverb*** **politely**

pol•i•ti•cian (pol-uh-**tish**-uhn) ***noun*** Someone who runs for or holds a government office, such as a senator.

pol•i•tics (**pol**-uh-tiks) ***noun***
1. The debate and activity involved in governing a country.
2. ***noun, plural*** The activities of politicians and political parties.
3. ***noun, plural*** An individual's beliefs about how the government should be run.
▸ ***adjective*** **political** ▸ ***adverb*** **politically**

pol•ka (**pole**-kuh *or* **poke**-uh) ***noun*** A fast dance in which couples swirl around the floor in a circular pattern. The polka came from central Europe.

polka dot ***noun*** One of many round dots that are repeated to form a regular pattern on fabric or other materials.

poll (**pohl**) ***noun***
1. A survey of people's opinions or beliefs. ▸ ***verb*** **poll**
2. **polls** ***noun, plural*** The place where votes are cast and recorded during an election.
Poll sounds like **pole.**

pol•len (**pol**-uhn) ***noun***
1. Tiny yellow grains produced in the anthers of flowers. Pollen grains are the male cells of flowering plants.
2. **pollen count** A measurement of the level of pollen in the air, which indicates how badly people with pollen allergies will be affected.

pol•li•nate (**pol**-uh-nate) ***verb*** To carry or transfer pollen from the stamen to the pistil of the same flower or another flower where female cells can be fertilized to produce seed. ▸ **pollinating, pollinated** ▸ ***noun*** **pollination**

pol•lut•ant (puh-**loot**-uhnt) ***noun*** Anything that pollutes or contaminates is a **pollutant.**

pol•lute (puh-**loot**) ***verb*** To contaminate or make dirty or impure, especially with industrial waste or other products produced by humans. ▸ **polluting, polluted**

pol•lu•tion (puh-**loo**-shuhn) ***noun***
1. Harmful materials that damage or contaminate the air, water, and soil, such

as chemicals, gasoline exhaust, and industrial waste.
2. The act of polluting or the state of being polluted.

po·lo (**poh**-loh) ***noun*** A game played on horseback by two teams of four players. The players try to hit a small ball using long, wooden mallets.

pol·y·es·ter (*pol*-ee-**ess**-tur) ***noun*** A synthetic substance used to make plastic products and fabric.

pol·y·gon (**pol**-ee-gon) ***noun*** A flat, closed figure with three or more straight sides. Triangles, squares, pentagons, and hexagons are all polygons.

pol·y·mer (**pol**-uh-mur) ***noun*** A natural or synthetic compound made up of small, simple molecules linked together in long chains of repeating units.

pol·yp (**pol**-ip) ***noun***
1. A small sea animal with a tubular body and a round mouth surrounded by tentacles. Coral is an example of a polyp.
2. A tumor or mass on the lining of the nose, mouth, or other body passage open to the outside.

pol·y·sty·rene (*pol*-ee-**stye**-reen) ***noun*** A light, stiff plastic often used to make disposable cups, foams, and packing materials. Styrofoam is one form of polystyrene.

pol·y·un·sat·u·rates (*pol*-ee-uhn-**sach**-uh-ruhts) ***noun, plural*** Vegetable fats and oils thought to be healthier for you than other fats. ▸ ***adjective*** **polyunsaturated**

pome·gran·ate (**pom**-uh-*gran*-it) ***noun*** A round, reddish yellow fruit that has a tough skin, red flesh, and many seeds. Pomegranates have a tart flavor.

pomp (**pomp**) ***noun*** Elaborate and stately ceremony or display.

pomp·ous (**pom**-puhss) ***adjective*** Conceited and haughty or arrogant. A pompous person thinks that he or she is better than others. ▸ ***adverb*** **pompously**

pon·cho (**pon**-choh) ***noun***
1. A cloak that looks like a blanket with a hole in the center for the head. Ponchos were originally worn in South America.
2. A similar waterproof garment with a hood. ▸ ***noun, plural*** **ponchos**

pond (**pond**) ***noun*** An enclosed body of fresh water that is smaller than a lake.

pon·der (**pon**-dur) ***verb*** To think about things carefully. ▸ **pondering, pondered**

pon·der·ous (**pon**-dur-uhss) ***adjective***
1. Heavy and slow or clumsy.
2. Hard to understand and dull.
▸ ***adverb*** **ponderously**

po·ny (**poh**-nee) ***noun***
1. A breed of horse that stays small when fully grown.
2. Any horse, especially a small one.
▸ ***noun, plural*** **ponies**

Pony Express ***noun*** A mail service in which a series of riders carried the mail on horseback from Missouri to California. Pony Express service started in April 1860 and ended in October 1861.

po·ny·tail (**poh**-nee-*tayl*) ***noun*** A hairdo that looks like a pony's tail, in which the hair is tied with a band and hangs behind the head.

poo·dle (**poo**-duhl) ***noun*** A breed of dog with thick, curly hair that is usually cut in a fancy style. Poodles range in size from the fairly large standard poodle to the very small toy poodle.

pool (**pool**)
1. ***noun*** A small area of still water.
2. ***noun*** A swimming pool.
3. ***noun*** A game in which players use a stick called a cue to hit colored balls into pockets on a table.
4. ***noun*** A group of people who share something, as in *a car pool.*
5. ***verb*** If people **pool** their money or ideas, they put them together to be shared. ▸ **pooling, pooled**

P

poor (**poor** *or* **por**) ***adjective***
1. If someone is **poor,** he or she does not have much money.
2. Low in quality or standard, as in *poor eyesight* or *a poor crop.*
3. Unfortunate and deserving sympathy or pity.
▸ ***adjective*** **poorer, poorest**

poor•ly (**poor**-lee) ***adverb*** Badly.

pop (**pop**)
1. ***verb*** To explode with a small bang or bursting sound. ▸ ***noun*** **pop**
2. ***noun*** A sweet, carbonated soft drink. Also called *soda pop.*
3. ***verb*** To move or appear quickly or unexpectedly.
4. ***noun*** *(informal)* Father.
5. ***verb*** If you **pop out** in baseball, you hit a fly ball that is caught by a player on the other team.
▸ ***verb*** **popping, popped**

pop•corn (**pop**-*korn*) ***noun*** Kernels of corn that are heated until they swell up and burst open with a popping sound. The kernels become fluffy and can be eaten as a snack.

pope *or* **Pope** (**pohp**) ***noun*** The head of the Roman Catholic church.

pop•lar (**pop**-lur) ***noun*** A tall tree with wide leaves. The aspen and the cottonwood are both poplar trees.

pop music ***noun*** *(informal)* Modern popular music with a strong, and usually fast, beat. ▸ ***noun*** **pop**

pop•py (**pop**-ee) ***noun*** A garden plant with large, usually red, showy flowers. Poppies produce cases through which its seeds may escape when shaken by the wind. ▸ ***noun, plural*** **poppies**

pop•u•lar (**pop**-yuh-lur) ***adjective***
1. Liked or enjoyed by many people.
▸ ***noun*** **popularity** ▸ ***adverb*** **popularly**
2. Having many friends, or liked by many people.
3. Of or for the people.

pop•u•lat•ed (**pop**-yuh-*lay*-tid) ***adjective*** If a place is **populated,** it has people living there.

pop•u•la•tion (*pop*-yuh-**lay**-shuhn) ***noun***
1. The total number of people who live in a place.
2. All of the people living in a certain place.

por•ce•lain (**por**-suh-lin) ***noun*** Very fine china, often used to make ornaments or cups and saucers.

porch (**porch**) ***noun*** A structure with a roof that is attached to the outside of a house, usually near a door. ▸ ***noun, plural*** **porches**

por•cu•pine (**por**-kyuh-*pine*) ***noun*** A large rodent covered with long, sharp quills that are used for protection.

pore (**por**)
1. ***noun*** One of the tiny holes in your skin through which you sweat.
2. ***verb*** To read or study something carefully. ▸ **poring, pored**
Pore sounds like **pour.**

pork (**pork**) ***noun*** The meat from a pig.

po•rous (**por**-uhss) ***adjective*** Something that is **porous** is full of tiny holes and lets liquid or gas through it.

por•poise (**por**-puhss) ***noun*** An ocean mammal with a rounded head and a short, blunt snout. The porpoise is related to but is usually smaller than the dolphin and the whale.

por•ridge (**por**-ij *or* **par**-ij) ***noun*** A breakfast food made by boiling oats or other grains in milk or water until the mixture is thick.

port (**port**) ***noun***
1. A harbor or place where boats and ships can dock or anchor safely.
2. A town or city with a harbor where ships can dock and load and unload cargo.
3. The left side of a ship or an aircraft as one faces forward. ▸ ***adjective*** **port**
4. A strong, sweet red wine.

port•a•ble (**por**-tuh-buhl) ***adjective*** Able to be carried or moved easily, as in *a portable radio.*

port•cul•lis (port-**kuhl**-iss) ***noun*** A heavy grating in the entrance to a castle that was used as an extra defense.
▸ ***noun, plural*** **portcullises**

por•ter (**por**-tur) ***noun***
1. Someone who carries luggage for people at a railroad station or hotel.
2. A person who waits on train passengers.

port•hole (**port**-*hohl*) ***noun*** A small, round window in the side of a ship or boat.

por•ti•co (**por**-tuh-koh) ***noun*** A porch or walkway with a roof that is supported by columns. ▸ ***noun, plural*** **porticos** *or* **porticoes**

por•tion (**por**-shuhn) ***noun***
1. A part or piece of something.
2. An amount of food that is served to someone.
▸ ***verb*** **portion**

port•ly (**port**-lee) ***adjective*** Heavy or stout. ▸ ***noun*** **portliness**

por•trait (**por**-trit *or* **por**-trayt) ***noun***
1. A drawing, painting, or photograph of a person.
2. A written description.

por•tray (por-**tray**) ***verb***
1. To describe in words.
2. To make a picture of something or someone.
3. To act a part in a play or movie.
▸ ***verb*** **portraying, portrayed** ▸ ***noun*** **portrayal**

pose (**pohz**) ***verb***
1. To keep your body in a particular position so that you can be photographed, painted, or drawn.
▸ ***noun*** **pose**
2. To pretend to be someone else in order to deceive people.
3. If you **pose a question,** you ask it.
▸ ***verb*** **posing, posed**

posh (**posh**) ***adjective*** *(informal)* Very stylish or expensive. ▸ **posher, poshest**

po•si•tion (puh-**zish**-uhn)
1. ***noun*** The place where someone or something is.
2. ***verb*** To put something in a particular place. ▸ **positioning, positioned**
3. ***noun*** A person's opinion or point of view on a particular issue or subject.
4. ***noun*** The way in which someone is standing, sitting, or lying, as in *an upright position.*
5. ***noun*** The right place to be.
6. ***noun*** A particular job.

pos•i•tive (**poz**-uh-tiv) ***adjective***
1. Sure or certain.
2. Helpful or constructive.
3. Showing approval or acceptance.
4. A **positive** number is more than zero.
5. Having one of two opposite kinds of electrical charge.
6. If a medical test is **positive,** it shows that a particular disease or organism is present. ▸ ***adverb*** **positively**

pos•se (**poss**-ee) ***noun*** A group of people gathered together by a sheriff to help capture a criminal.

pos•ses•sion (puh-**zesh**-uhn) ***noun***
1. Something that you own. ▸ ***verb*** **possess**
2. If something is **in your possession,** you own it or have it.

pos•ses•sive (puh-**zess**-iv)
1. ***adjective*** If someone is **possessive,** the person wants to keep someone or something for him- or herself and does not want to share it.
2. ***noun*** The form of a noun or pronoun that shows that something belongs to the one referred to. ▸ ***adjective*** **possessive**

pos•si•ble (**poss**-uh-buhl) ***adjective*** If something is **possible,** it might happen or it might be true. ▸ ***noun*** **possibility** ▸ ***adverb*** **possibly**

pos•sum (**poss**-uhm) ***noun***
1. An opossum.
2. When a person or an animal **plays possum,** he, she, or it pretends to be asleep or dead.

P

post (**pohst**)
1. *noun* A long, thick piece of wood, concrete, or metal that is fixed in the ground to support or mark something, as in *a fence post.*
2. *verb* To put up a notice or an announcement of information.
3. *noun* A place where someone on duty is supposed to be.
4. *noun* A military base where soldiers are stationed or trained, as in *an army post.*
5. *noun* A particular job that someone has.
6. *verb* To assign someone to a post.
7. *verb* To mail a letter or package.
▸ ***noun* post**
8. keep posted *verb* *(informal)* To give someone information or the latest news.
▸ ***verb* posting, posted**

post•age (**poh**-stij) ***noun*** The cost of sending a letter or package by mail.

postage stamp ***noun*** A small printed piece of paper issued by a government and attached to mail to show that postage has been paid.

Post•al Service (**pohst**-uhl) ***noun*** The agency that is in charge of selling stamps and delivering the mail. Though the Postal Service is run by the U.S. government, it is an independent agency.

post•card (**pohst**-*kard*) ***noun*** A card, sometimes with a picture on one side, that you send by mail. A postcard does not require an envelope to be mailed.

post•er (**poh**-stur) ***noun*** A large, printed sign that often has a picture. A poster can be put up as an advertisement, a notice, or a decoration.

post•hu•mous (**pohst**-chuh-muhss) ***adjective*** Coming or happening after death. ▸ ***adverb* posthumously**

post•man (**pohst**-muhn) ***noun*** A mail carrier. ▸ ***noun, plural* postmen**

post•mark (**pohst**-*mark*) ***noun*** An official stamp on a piece of mail that cancels the postage stamp and shows the place and date of mailing.

post•mast•er (**pohst**-*mass*-tur) ***noun*** The head of a post office, if the person is a man.

post•mis•tress (**pohst**-*miss*-triss) ***noun*** The head of a post office, if the person is a woman.

post office ***noun*** The place where people go to buy stamps and to send letters and packages.

post•pone (pohst-**pone**) ***verb*** To put something off until later or another time.
▸ **postponing, postponed** ▸ ***noun* postponement**

post•script (**pohst**-*skript*) ***noun*** A short message beginning "P.S." that is added to the end of a letter, after the writer's signature.

pos•ture (**poss**-chur) ***noun*** The position of your body when you stand, sit, or walk.

post•war (**pohst**-**war**) ***adjective*** After or later in time than a war, as in *the postwar period.*

pot (**pot**) ***noun***
1. A deep, round container used for cooking or storing food.
2. A container made of clay or plastic that is used for growing plants.
▸ ***verb* pot**

po•tas•si•um (puh-**tass**-ee-uhm) ***noun*** A silvery-white, metallic chemical element. It is used in making fertilizers, explosives, and soap, and is found in foods such as bananas and potatoes. Potassium is necessary for good nutrition.

po•ta•to (puh-**tay**-toh) ***noun*** The thick underground tuber of a leafy plant. This vegetable was originally grown in South America. ▸ ***noun, plural* potatoes**

po•tent (**poht**-uhnt) ***adjective*** Powerful or strong, as in *a potent drug.* ▸ ***noun* potency** ▸ ***adverb* potently**

po•ten•tial (puh-**ten**-shuhl)
1. *noun* Your **potential** is what you are capable of achieving in the future.
2. *noun* If an idea or a place has **potential,** you think that it has promise

and that you can develop it into something better.
3. ***adjective*** Possible but not yet actual or real, as in *a potential danger* or *a potential customer.* ▸ ***adverb*** **potentially**

pot•hole (**pot**-*hohl*) ***noun*** A hole in the surface of a road.

pot•ter (**pot**-ur) ***noun*** Someone who makes objects out of clay, such as bowls, plates, or vases.

pot•ter•y (**pot**-ur-ee) ***noun***
1. Objects made of baked clay, such as bowls, plates, or vases. Pottery can be used for decorative or practical purposes.
2. A place where clay objects are made.
▸ ***noun, plural*** **potteries**

pouch (**pouch**) ***noun***
1. A leather or fabric bag.
2. A flap of skin in which kangaroos and other marsupials carry their young.
▸ ***noun, plural*** **pouches**

poul•try (**pohl**-tree) ***noun*** Farm birds raised for their eggs and meat. Chickens, turkeys, ducks, and geese are poultry.

pounce (**pounss**) ***verb*** To jump on something suddenly and grab hold of it.
▸ **pouncing, pounced**

pound (**pound**)
1. ***noun*** A unit of weight equal to 16 ounces. A soccer ball weighs about one pound.
2. ***noun*** A unit of money used in England and several other countries.
3. ***verb*** To keep hitting something noisily and with force.
4. ***verb*** To beat quickly or heavily.
5. ***noun*** A place where stray dogs and other animals are kept.
▸ ***verb*** **pounding, pounded**

pour (**por**) ***verb***
1. To make something flow in a steady stream.
2. To rain heavily.
3. To move somewhere quickly and in large numbers.
Pour sounds like **pore.**
▸ ***verb*** **pouring, poured**

pout (**pout**) ***verb*** To push out your lips when you are angry or disappointed about something.
▸ **pouting, pouted** ▸ ***noun*** **pout**

pov•er•ty (**pov**-ur-tee) ***noun*** The state of being poor.

pow•der (**pou**-dur)
1. ***noun*** Tiny particles made by grinding, crushing, or pounding a solid substance.
▸ ***adjective*** **powdery,** ***adjective*** **powdered**
2. ***noun*** A cosmetic or other preparation made from powder.
3. ***verb*** To make or turn something into powder.
4. ***verb*** To cover something with powder.
▸ ***verb*** **powdering, powdered**

pow•er (**pou**-ur) ***noun***
1. The strength or ability to do something.
2. The authority or right to command, control, or make decisions.
3. A person, group, or nation that has great strength, influence, or control over others.
4. Electricity or other forms of energy.
5. In mathematics, the number of times you use a number as a factor in multiplication. Three to the fifth power means 3 as a factor 5 times and equals $3 \times 3 \times 3 \times 3 \times 3$, or 243.

pow•er•ful (**pou**-ur-fuhl) ***adjective*** Having great power, strength, or authority, as in *a powerful punch* or *a powerful king.*

pow•er•less (**pou**-ur-liss) ***adjective*** Having no power, strength, or authority.

prac•ti•cal (**prak**-tuh-kuhl) ***adjective***
1. To do with experience or practice rather than theory and ideas.
2. Useful.
3. Sensible, or showing good judgment.

practical joke ***noun*** A mischievous trick often done to make someone look or feel foolish.

prac•ti•cal•ly (**prak**-tik-lee) ***adverb***
1. Almost or nearly.
2. In a sensible way.

P

P

prac•tice (**prak**-tiss)
1. ***noun*** The repetition of an action regularly in order to improve a skill.
2. ***noun*** A custom or a habit.
3. ***noun*** The business of a doctor, lawyer, or other professional.
4. ***verb*** If someone **practices** a religion, he or she follows its teachings and attends its services or ceremonies.
5. ***verb*** To put something into action.
6. in practice ***adverb*** What really happens rather than what is meant to happen.
▸ ***verb*** **practicing, practiced**

prai•rie (**prair**-ee) ***noun*** A large area of flat or rolling grassland with few or no trees.

prairie dog ***noun*** A small burrowing mammal that is related to the squirrel. Prairie dogs live mainly in the plains of west-central North America. They dig elaborate underground burrows and live in large colonies. Their call sounds like a dog's bark.

prairie schooner ***noun*** A large covered wagon used by pioneers to journey westward to the Pacific coast over the flat, grassy prairies of central North America.

praise (**praze**)
1. ***noun*** Words of approval or admiration.
2. ***verb*** To express praise to someone.
3. ***verb*** To worship and express thanks to.
▸ ***verb*** **praising, praised**

prance (**pranss**) ***verb***
1. To walk or move in a lively or proud way.
2. When a horse **prances,** it springs forward on its hind legs.
▸ ***verb*** **prancing, pranced**

prank (**prangk**) ***noun*** A playful or mischievous trick.

pray (**pray**) ***verb***
1. To talk to God to give thanks or ask for help.
2. To hope very much that something happens.
Pray sounds like **prey.**
▸ ***verb*** **praying, prayed**

pray•er (**pray**-ur) ***noun***
1. The act of praying.
2. An expression of appeal or thanks to God.
3. A set of words used in praying.
4. Something requested or prayed for.

praying man•tis (**man**-tiss) ***noun*** An insect that is related to the grasshopper. When it rests, the praying mantis folds its front legs, which then look like hands folded in prayer. ▸ ***noun, plural*** **praying mantises** *or* **praying mantes** (**man**-teez)

preach (**preech**) ***verb***
1. To give a religious talk to people, especially during a church service.
▸ ***noun*** **preacher**
2. To tell other people what you think they should do, often in a boring or annoying way.
▸ ***verb*** **preaches, preaching, preached**

pre•car•i•ous (pri-**kair**-ee-uhss) ***adjective*** Unsafe and risky. ▸ ***adverb*** **precariously**

pre•cau•tion (pri-**kaw**-shuhn) ***noun*** Something you do in order to prevent something dangerous or unpleasant from happening. ▸ ***adjective*** **precautionary**

pre•cede (pree-**seed**) ***verb*** If one thing **precedes** something else, it comes before it. ▸ **preceding, preceded**
▸ ***adjective*** **preceding**

pre•ce•dent (**press**-uh-duhnt) ***noun*** Something done, said, or written that becomes an example to be followed in the future.

pre•cinct (**pree**-singkt) ***noun***
1. An area or a district in a city or town, as in *a police precinct* or *an election precinct.*
2. A police station in such a district.

pre•cious (**presh**-uhss) ***adjective***
1. Rare and valuable, as in *a precious gem.*

2. Very special or dear, as in *precious memories.*

prec•i•pice (**press**-uh-piss) ***noun*** A steep cliff.

pre•cip•i•tate (pri-**sip**-i-*tate*) ***verb***
1. To rain, sleet, hail, or snow.
2. To make something happen suddenly or sooner than expected.
▸ ***verb*** **precipitating, precipitated**

pre•cip•i•ta•tion (*pri*-sip-i-**tay**-shuhn) ***noun*** The falling of water from the sky in the form of rain, sleet, hail, or snow.

pre•cise (pri-**sisse**) ***adjective*** Very accurate or exact. ▸ ***noun*** **precision** ▸ ***adverb*** **precisely**

pre•co•cious (pri-**koh**-shuhss) ***adjective*** If a child is **precocious,** he or she is very advanced in intelligence for his or her age.

pred•a•tor (**pred**-uh-tur) ***noun*** An animal that lives by hunting other animals for food. Lions, sharks, and hawks are predators. ▸ ***adjective*** **predatory**

pred•e•ces•sor (**pred**-uh-sess-ur) ***noun*** Someone who held an office or a job before another person.

pre•dic•a•ment (pri-**dik**-uh-muhnt) ***noun*** An awkward or difficult situation.

pred•i•cate (**pred**-i-kit) ***noun*** The part of a sentence or clause that tells what the subject does or what is done to the subject. In the sentence "The kitten purred softly," the predicate is "purred softly."

pre•dict (pri-**dikt**) ***verb*** To say what you think will happen in the future. ▸ **predicting, predicted** ▸ ***noun*** **prediction**

pre•dom•i•nate (pri-**dom**-uh-*nate*) ***verb*** To be greater in power or number than others. ▸ **predominating, predominated** ▸ ***noun*** **predominance** ▸ ***adjective*** **predominant**

preen (**preen**) ***verb*** When birds **preen** themselves, they clean and arrange their feathers with their beaks. ▸ **preening, preened**

pref•ace (**pref**-iss) ***noun*** An introduction to a book or speech.

pre•fer (pri-**fur**) ***verb*** To like one thing better than another. ▸ **preferring, preferred** ▸ ***noun*** **preference**

pre•fix (**pree**-fiks) ***noun*** A word part added to the beginning of a word or root to change the meaning. *Sub-, un-,* and *re-* are all prefixes. ▸ ***noun, plural*** **prefixes**

preg•nant (**preg**-nuhnt) ***adjective*** A woman who is **pregnant** has an embryo or a fetus growing in her uterus. ▸ ***noun*** **pregnancy**

pre•his•tor•ic (*pree*-hi-**stor**-ik) ***adjective*** Belonging to a time before history was recorded in written form. ▸ ***noun*** **prehistory**

prej•u•dice (**prej**-uh-diss) ***noun***
1. An opinion or a judgment formed unfairly or without knowing all the facts.
2. A fixed, unreasonable, or unfair opinion about someone based on the person's race, religion, or other characteristic.
3. Hatred or unfair treatment that results from having fixed opinions about some group of people.
▸ ***verb*** **prejudice** ▸ ***adjective*** **prejudiced,** ***adjective*** **prejudicial**

pre•lim•i•nar•y (pri-**lim**-uh-ner-ee) ***adjective*** Preparing the way for something important that comes later. ▸ ***noun*** **preliminary**

pre•ma•ture (*pree*-muh-**choor** *or pree*-muh-**toor**) ***adjective*** Happening, appearing, or done too soon, as in *a premature baby* or *a premature decision.* ▸ ***adverb*** **prematurely**

pre•med•i•tat•ed (pree-**med**-uh-*tay*-tid) ***adjective*** Planned in advance, as in *a premeditated attack.* ▸ ***verb*** **premeditate**

pre•mier (pri-**mihr**)
1. ***adjective*** Leading or top, as in *America's premier rock group.*
2. ***noun*** A prime minister.

P

pre•miere (pri-**mihr** *or* pruh-**myair**) ***noun*** The first public performance of a film, play, or work of music or dance.

prem•ise (**prem**-iss) ***noun***
1. A statement or principle that is accepted as true or taken for granted.
2. premises *noun, plural* Land and the buildings on it.

pre•mi•um (**pree**-mee-uhm) ***noun***
1. Something that is free or less expensive than usual when you buy something else.
2. Money that is paid to take out and maintain an insurance policy.
3. If something is **at a premium,** it is rare and valued very highly.

pre•mo•ni•tion (*pree*-muh-**nish**-uhn *or* prem-uh-**nish**-uhn) ***noun*** A feeling that something is going to happen, especially something bad or harmful.

pre•oc•cu•pied (pree-**ok**-yuh-pide) ***adjective*** If you are **preoccupied,** your thoughts are completely taken up with something, and you can't keep your attention on anything else. ▸ ***noun*** **preoccupation**

pre•pare (pri-**pair**) ***verb***
1. To make or to get ready.
2. To put together various parts or ingredients.
▸ ***verb*** **preparing, prepared** ▸ ***noun*** **preparation**

prep•o•si•tion (prep-uh-**zish**-uhn) ***noun*** A word such as "with" or "on" that shows the relation of a noun or pronoun to other items in a sentence, as in the sentence "The book with a red cover is on the table."

pre•pos•ter•ous (pri-**poss**-tur-uhss) ***adjective*** Ridiculous and absurd, as in *a preposterous idea.* ▸ ***adverb*** **preposterously**

prep school (**prep**) ***noun*** A private school that prepares students for college. Prep school is short for *preparatory school.*

pre•school (**pree-skool**)
1. *adjective* To do with children who are younger than elementary-school age.
2. *noun* A school for children who are too young for elementary school, such as a child care center or a nursery school.

pre•scribe (pri-**skribe**) ***verb***
1. To say what should be done.
2. When doctors **prescribe** medicine for a patient, they write a prescription.
▸ ***verb*** **prescribing, prescribed**

pre•scrip•tion (pri-**skrip**-shuhn) ***noun*** An order for drugs or medicine written by a doctor to a pharmacist. A prescription specifies what type and quantity of medicine to give.

pres•ence (**prez**-uhnss) ***noun***
1. Being in a place at a certain time.
2. The area immediately near a person or thing.

pre•sent
1. (pri-**zent**) ***verb*** To give someone a gift or a prize in a formal way.
2. (**prez**-uhnt) ***noun*** Something that you give to somebody, as in *a birthday present.*
3. (**prez**-uhnt) ***noun*** The time that is happening now.
4. (**prez**-uhnt) ***noun*** The **present tense.**
5. (**prez**-uhnt) ***adjective*** If someone is **present** in a place, he or she is there.
6. (pri-**zent**) ***verb*** To introduce something, such as a television program.
▸ ***verb*** **presenting, presented** ▸ ***noun*** **presenter**

pres•en•ta•tion (*prez*-uhn-**tay**-shuhn *or pree*-zen-**tay**-shuhn) ***noun***
1. The act of giving a prize or present, as in *the presentation of awards.*
2. The way that something is produced and the way it looks.

pres•ent•ly (**prez**-uhnt-lee) ***adverb***
1. Soon or shortly.
2. Now or at the present time.

present participle ***noun*** A form of a verb that ends in "ing" and can be used with a helping verb to form certain tenses and to show that an action or condition is not completed. In the sentence "I am working," the word "working" is a present participle. Present participles may also be used as adjectives, as "thinking" in "A thinking man."

present tense ***noun*** A form of the verb that is used to indicate present time, as "likes" in "He likes cereal for breakfast."

pre•serv•a•tive (pri-**zur**-vuh-tiv) ***noun*** Something used to preserve an item, especially a chemical used to keep food from spoiling. ▸ ***adjective*** **preservative**

pre•serve (pri-**zurv**)
1. ***verb*** To protect something so that it stays in its original state. ▸ ***noun*** **preserve,** ***noun*** **preservation** (*prez*-ur-**va**-shuhn)
2. ***verb*** To treat food so that it does not become spoiled.
3. preserves ***noun, plural*** Jam.
▸ ***verb*** **preserving, preserved**

pre•side (pri-**zide**) ***verb*** To be in charge of something. ▸ **presiding, presided**

pres•i•dent *or* **President** (**prez**-uh-duhnt) ***noun***
1. The elected leader or chief executive of a republic.
2. The head of a company, society, college, club, or organization.
▸ ***noun*** **presidency** ▸ ***adjective*** **presidential**

president-elect ***noun*** The person who has won the election for president but has not yet been sworn into office.

Presidents' Day ***noun*** A holiday observed in most of the United States on the third Monday in February, celebrating the birthdays of George Washington and Abraham Lincoln.

press (**press**)
1. ***verb*** To push firmly.
2. ***verb*** To persuade strongly.
3. ***verb*** To smooth out the creases in clothes with an iron. ▸ ***noun*** **presser**
4. ***noun*** A machine for printing.
5. the press ***noun*** The news media and the people who produce them.
▸ ***noun, plural*** **presses** ▸ ***verb*** **presses, pressing, pressed**

pressing ***adjective*** Urgent and needing immediate attention.

pres•sure (**presh**-ur) ***noun***
1. The force produced by pressing on something, as in *blood pressure* or *water pressure.*
2. Strong influence, force, or persuasion.
▸ ***verb*** **pressure**
3. A burden or a strain.

pres•sur•ize (**presh**-uh-*rize*) ***verb*** To seal off an aircraft cabin, a spacecraft, or a diving chamber so that the air pressure inside is the same as the pressure at the earth's surface.
▸ **pressurizing, pressurized**
▸ ***adjective*** **pressurized**

pres•tige (pre-**steezh** *or* pre-**steej**) ***noun*** The great respect and high status that come from being successful, powerful, rich, or famous. ▸ ***adjective*** **prestigious**

pre•sum•a•bly (pri-**zoo**-muh-blee) ***adverb*** Probably.

pre•sume (pri-**zoom**) ***verb***
1. To think that something is true without being certain or having all the facts.
2. To dare.
▸ ***verb*** **presuming, presumed** ▸ ***noun*** **presumption**

pre•tend (pri-**tend**) ***verb***
1. To make believe.
2. To claim falsely.
3. To give a false show in order to trick or deceive.
▸ ***verb*** **pretending, pretended** ▸ ***noun*** **pretense**

pre•text (**pree**-tekst) ***noun*** A false reason or excuse given to hide a real reason

pret•ty (**prit**-ee)
1. ***adjective*** Attractive and pleasing to look at. ▸ ***noun*** **prettiness** ▸ ***adverb*** **prettily**
2. ***adverb*** Quite, as in *a pretty bad movie.*

P

pret•zel (**pret**-suhl) ***noun*** Dough that has been shaped into a stick or a knot and baked until it is crisp. Pretzels are usually salted on the outside.

pre•vail (pri-**vayl**) ***verb***
1. To succeed in spite of difficulties.
2. To be common or usual. ▸ ***adjective*** **prevalent**
▸ ***verb*** **prevailing, prevailed**

pre•vent (pri-**vent**) ***verb***
1. To stop something from happening.
2. To keep someone from doing something.
▸ ***verb*** **preventing, prevented** ▸ ***noun*** **prevention**

pre•ven•tive (pri-**ven**-tiv)
1. ***adjective*** Meant to prevent or stop something, as in *preventive medicine.*
2. ***noun*** Something that prevents, especially something that prevents a disease.

pre•view (**pree**-vyoo) ***noun*** A showing of a play or a screening of a movie before it is released to the general public. ▸ ***verb*** **preview**

pre•vi•ous (**pree**-vee-uhss) ***adjective*** Former, or happening before. ▸ ***adverb*** **previously**

prey (**pray**)
1. ***noun*** An animal that is hunted by another animal for food.
2. ***verb*** When an animal **preys on** another animal, it hunts it and then eats it.
3. ***verb*** To rob, attack, or take advantage of someone who is helpless or unable to fight back.
4. ***noun*** The victim of an attack or robbery.
Prey sounds like **pray.**
▸ ***verb*** **preying, preyed**

price (**prisse**)
1. ***noun*** The amount that you have to pay for something.
2. ***verb*** To give something a price.
▸ **pricing, priced**
3. ***noun*** The cost at which something is gained.

price•less (**prisse**-liss) ***adjective*** If something is **priceless,** it is too precious for anyone to put a value on it.

prick (**prik**) ***verb***
1. To make a small hole in something with a sharp point. ▸ ***noun*** **prick**
2. To raise up.
▸ ***verb*** **pricking, pricked**

prick•le (**prik**-uhl) ***noun*** A small, sharp point, such as a thorn. ▸ ***adjective*** **prickly**

prickly pear ***noun*** A cactus with yellow flowers and fruit shaped like a pear.

pride (**pride**) ***noun***
1. Self-respect, or a sense of your own importance or worth.
2. A feeling of satisfaction in something that you or someone else has achieved.
▸ ***verb*** **pride**
3. A too-high opinion of your own importance and cleverness.

priest (**preest**) ***noun*** In certain Christian and other religions, a member of the clergy who can lead services and perform rites. ▸ ***noun*** **priesthood**
▸ ***adjective*** **priestly**

prim (**prim**) ***adjective*** Someone who is **prim** is stiffly formal and proper.
▸ **primmer, primmest**

pri•ma don•na (**pree**-muh **don**-uh) ***noun***
1. A female opera or concert star.
2. *(informal)* Someone who is demanding, mean, or conceited.
▸ ***noun, plural*** **prima donnas**

pri•mar•i•ly (prye-**mair**-uh-lee) ***adverb*** Chiefly or mainly.

pri•mar•y (**prye**-mair-ee *or* **prye**-muh-ree)
1. ***adjective*** Most important, chief, or main, as in *a primary concern.*
2. ***adjective*** First or earliest, as in *primary education.*
3. ***noun*** An election to choose a party candidate who will run in the general election.

P

primary colors ***noun, plural*** In painting, the **primary colors** are red, yellow, and blue, which can be mixed to make all the other colors.

primary school ***noun*** A school that includes the first three or four grades and sometimes kindergarten.

pri•mate (**prye**-mate) ***noun*** Any member of the group of intelligent mammals that includes humans, apes, and monkeys.

prime (**prime**)
1. ***adjective*** Of first importance or quality, as in *prime beef.*
2. ***verb*** To prepare a surface to be painted.
3. ***verb*** To pour water into a dry pump in order to start it working properly.
▸ ***verb*** **priming, primed**

prime minister ***noun*** The person in charge of a government in some countries. Both Great Britain and Canada have prime ministers.

prime number ***noun*** A number that has exactly two factors.

pri•me•val (prye-**mee**-vuhl) ***adjective*** Belonging to the earliest period of the earth, as in *primeval oceans.*

prim•i•tive (**prim**-uh-tiv) ***adjective***
1. Very simple or crude.
2. Uncivilized, basic, and crude.
3. To do with an early stage of development.

prim•rose (**prim**-*rohz*) ***noun*** A small garden plant with clusters of brightly colored flowers.

prince (**prinss**) ***noun***
1. The son of a king or queen.
2. The husband of a queen.
3. A nobleman of high rank.

prin•cess (**prin**-suhss *or* **prin**-sess) ***noun***
1. The daughter of a king or queen.
2. The wife of a prince.
3. A noblewoman of high rank.
▸ ***noun, plural*** **princesses**

prin•ci•pal (**prin**-suh-puhl)
1. ***adjective*** Most important, chief, or main. ▸ ***adverb*** **principally**
2. ***noun*** The head of a public school.
Principal sounds like **principle.**

prin•ci•ple (**prin**-suh-puhl)
1. ***noun*** A basic truth, law, or belief.
2. ***noun*** A basic rule that governs a person's behavior.
3. If you agree to someone's plan **in principle,** you are happy with the general idea but not necessarily with the details.
Principle sounds like **principal.**

print (**print**)
1. ***verb*** To produce words or pictures on a page with a machine that uses ink.
▸ ***noun*** **printer**
2. ***verb*** To write using letters that are separate.
3. ***noun*** A photograph or a printed copy of a painting or drawing.
4. ***verb*** To publish.
▸ ***verb*** **printing, printed** ▸ ***adjective*** **printed**

printing press ***noun*** A large machine that prints words and designs by pressing sheets of paper against a surface, such as a metal plate, that has ink on it.

print•out (**print**-*out*) ***noun*** A printed copy of information stored in a computer.

pri•or (**prye**-ur) ***adjective*** Earlier.

pri•or•i•ty (prye-**or**-uh-tee) ***noun*** Something that is more important or more urgent than other things.

prism (**priz**-uhm) ***noun*** A clear glass or plastic shape that bends light or breaks it up into the colors of the spectrum. Prisms usually have a triangular base.

pris•on (**priz**-uhn) ***noun*** A building where people are made to live as punishment for a crime.

pris•on•er (**priz**-uhn-ur) ***noun***
1. Someone who is in prison.
2. Any person who has been captured or is held by force, as in *a prisoner of war.*

P

pri•vate (**prye**-vit)
1. ***adjective*** If something is **private,** it belongs to or concerns one person or group and no one else. ▸ ***noun*** **privacy**
2. ***adjective*** Not meant to be shared, as in *a private conversation* or *a private telephone number.* ▸ ***adverb*** **privately**
3. ***adjective*** Not holding a public office, as in *a private citizen.*
4. ***noun*** A soldier of the lowest rank.

private school ***noun*** A school where parents pay for their children's education, as opposed to a public school, which is supported by tax dollars.

priv•i•lege (**priv**-uh-lij) ***noun*** A special right or advantage given to a person or a group of people. ▸ ***adjective*** **privileged**

prize (**prize**)
1. ***noun*** A reward for winning a game or competition.
2. ***verb*** To value something very much. ▸ **prizing, prized** ▸ ***adjective*** **prized**

pro (**proh**)
1. ***preposition*** If you are **pro** something, you are in favor of it.
2. ***noun*** A shortened form of **professional,** often used in sports, as in *a golf pro.*
3. **pros and cons** (**konz**) Advantages and disadvantages.

prob•a•ble (**prob**-uh-buhl) ***adjective*** Likely to happen or be true. ▸ ***noun*** **probability** ▸ ***adverb*** **probably**

pro•ba•tion (proh-**bay**-shuhn) ***noun***
1. A period of time for testing a person's behavior or job qualifications.
2. If someone who has committed a crime is put on **probation,** he or she is not sent to prison but is allowed to go free under the close supervision of a probation officer.

probe (**prohb**) ***noun***
1. A thorough examination or investigation.
2. A tool or device used to explore or examine something, as in *a space probe.* ▸ ***verb*** **probe**

prob•lem (**prob**-luhm) ***noun***
1. A difficult situation that needs to be figured out or overcome.
2. A puzzle or question to be solved, as in *a math problem.*

pro•ce•dure (pruh-**see**-jur) ***noun*** A way of doing something, especially by a series of steps.

pro•ceed
1. (pruh-**seed**) ***verb*** To move forward or continue. ▸ **proceeding, proceeded**
2. **proceeds** (**proh**-seedz) ***noun, plural*** The **proceeds** of an event are the sum of money that it raises.

proc•ess (**pross**-ess *or* **proh**-sess)
1. ***noun*** An organized series of actions that produce a result. ▸ ***noun, plural*** **processes**
2. ***verb*** To prepare or change by a series of steps. ▸ **processes, processing, processed** ▸ ***noun*** **processing,** ***noun*** **processor** ▸ ***adjective*** **processed**

pro•ces•sion (pruh-**sesh**-uhn) ***noun*** A number of people walking or driving along a route as part of a public festival, a religious service, or a parade.

pro•claim (pruh-**klaym**) ***verb*** If someone **proclaims** something, the person announces it publicly. ▸ **proclaiming, proclaimed** ▸ ***noun*** **proclamation**

pro•cras•ti•nate (proh-**krass**-tuh-*nate*) ***verb*** To put off doing something that you have to do simply because you don't want to do it. ▸ **procrastinating, procrastinated** ▸ ***noun*** **procrastination,** ***noun*** **procrastinator**

prod (**prod**) ***verb***
1. To poke or jab something or someone.
2. To push or urge someone into action. ▸ ***verb*** **prodding, prodded** ▸ ***noun*** **prod**

prod•i•gy (**prod**-uh-jee) ***noun*** A **prodigy** is an extremely smart or talented child or young person. ▸ ***noun, plural*** **prodigies**

P

pro•duce
1. (pruh-**dooss**) ***verb*** To make something.
2. (**prod**-ooss *or* **proh**-dooss) ***noun*** Things that are produced or grown for eating, especially fruits and vegetables.
3. (pruh-**dooss**) ***verb*** To bring something out for people to see.
4. (pruh-**dooss**) ***verb*** To be in charge of putting on a play or making a movie or TV program.
▸ ***noun*** **producer** ▸ ***verb*** **producing, produced**

prod•uct (**prod**-uhkt) ***noun***
1. Something that is manufactured or made by a natural process, as in *a dairy product.*
2. The result you get when you multiply two numbers.

pro•duc•tion (pruh-**duhk**-shuhn) ***noun***
1. The process of manufacturing or growing something.
2. The total amount produced.
3. A play, an opera, a show, or any form of entertainment that is presented to others.
4. production line A system of manufacturing in which the product moves along slowly while different things are added or done to it.

pro•duc•tive (pruh-**duhk**-tiv) ***adjective*** Making a lot of products or producing good results. ▸ ***noun*** **productivity**

pro•fess (pruh-**fess**) ***verb***
1. To state openly or to make known.
2. To say something insincerely, or to pretend that something is true.
▸ ***verb*** **professes, professing, professed**

pro•fes•sion (pruh-**fesh**-uhn) ***noun***
1. An occupation for which you need special training or study.
2. The whole group of people in a profession, as in *the medical profession.*
3. Something that you state openly.

pro•fes•sion•al (pruh-**fesh**-uh-nuhl)
1. ***noun*** A member of a profession, such as a doctor, teacher, nurse, or lawyer.
▸ ***adjective*** **professional**
2. ***adjective*** Making money for doing something others do for fun, as in *a professional athlete.* ▸ ***noun*** **professional**

pro•fes•sor (pruh-**fess**-ur) ***noun*** A teacher of the highest teaching rank at a college or university.

pro•fi•cient (pruh-**fish**-uhnt) ***adjective*** If you are **proficient** at doing something, you are able to do it properly and skillfully. ▸ ***noun*** **proficiency** ▸ ***adverb*** **proficiently**

pro•file (**proh**-file) ***noun***
1. A side view or drawing of someone's head.
2. A brief account of someone's life.
▸ ***verb*** **profile**

prof•it (**prof**-it)
1. ***noun*** The amount of money left after all the costs of running a business have been subtracted from all the money earned.
2. ***noun*** A gain or a benefit.
3. ***verb*** To gain or benefit in some way.
▸ **profiting, profited**
Profit sounds like **prophet.**

prof•it•a•ble (**prof**-i-tuh-buhl) ***adjective*** Producing a profit.

pro•found (pruh-**found**) ***adjective*** Very deeply felt or thought, as in *profound sadness.* ▸ ***adverb*** **profoundly**

pro•fuse (pruh-**fyooss**) ***adjective*** Plentiful or more than enough. ▸ ***noun*** **profusion** (pruh-**fyoo**-zhuhn), ***noun*** **profuseness**

pro•gram (**proh**-gram *or* **proh**-gruhm)
1. ***noun*** A television or radio show.
2. ***noun*** A theater or concert **program** is a booklet that gives you information about the performance.
3. ***noun*** A schedule or plan for doing something.
4. ***noun*** A series of instructions, written in a computer language, that control the way a computer works.
5. ***verb*** To give a computer or other machine instructions to make it work in a certain way. ▸ **programming, programmed**
▸ ***noun*** **programming**

P

pro•gram•mer (**proh**-gram-ur) ***noun*** Someone whose job is to program a computer.

prog•ress
1. (pruh-**gress**) ***verb*** To move forward or to improve. ▸ **progresses, progressing, progressed**
2. (**prog**-ruhss) ***noun*** A forward movement or improvement.
3. (**prog**-ruhss) If something is **in progress,** it is happening.

pro•gress•ive (pruh-**gress**-iv)
1. ***adjective*** Moving forward or happening steadily.
2. ***adjective*** In favor of improvement, progress, or reform, especially in political or social matters.
3. ***noun*** Someone who favors improvement or reform, especially in political, social, or educational matters.

pro•hib•it (proh-**hib**-it) ***verb*** To stop or ban something officially. ▸ **prohibiting, prohibited** ▸ ***noun*** **prohibition**

proj•ect
1. (**proj**-ekt) ***noun*** A plan or a proposal.
2. (**proj**-ekt) ***noun*** A school assignment worked on over a period of time.
3. (pruh-**jekt**) ***verb*** To stick out.
▸ ***adjective*** **projecting**
4. (pruh-**jekt**) ***verb*** To show an image on a screen.
5. (pruh-**jekt**) ***verb*** To look ahead or to forecast.
6. (pruh-**jekt**) ***verb*** If you **project** your voice, you make it carry very far.
7. (**proj**-ekt) ***noun*** A group of apartment buildings planned and built as a unit.
▸ ***verb*** **projecting, projected**

pro•jec•tile (pruh-**jek**-tuhl) ***noun*** An object, such as a bullet or missile, that is thrown or shot through the air.

pro•jec•tion (pruh-**jek**-shuhn) ***noun***
1. Something that sticks out, as in *a rock projection.*
2. A forecast or a prediction.
3. A **map projection** is a way of representing the globe on a flat page.

pro•jec•tor (pruh-**jek**-tur) ***noun*** A machine that shows slides or movies on a screen.

pro•li•fic (pruh-**lif**-ik) ***adjective*** Very productive or producing a large quantity.

pro•logue (**proh**-lawg) ***noun*** A short speech or piece of writing that introduces a play, story, or poem.

pro•long (pruh-**lawng**) ***verb*** To make something last longer. ▸ **prolonging, prolonged**

prom•e•nade (*prom*-uh-**nade** *or prom*-uh-**nahd**)
1. ***noun*** A walk taken for pleasure.
2. ***verb*** To walk for pleasure.
▸ **promenading, promenaded**
3. ***noun*** A place for taking a leisurely walk.

prom•i•nent (**prom**-uh-nuhnt) ***adjective***
1. Very easily seen, as in *a prominent landmark.*
2. Famous or important.
▸ ***noun*** **prominence**

prom•ise (**prom**-iss)
1. ***verb*** If you **promise** to do something, you give your word that you will do it. ▸ **promising, promised**
2. ***noun*** A pledge given by someone that he or she will do something.
3. ***noun*** Someone who shows **promise** seems likely to do well in the future.
▸ ***adjective*** **promising**

prom•on•tor•y (**prom**-uhn-*tor*-ee) ***noun*** A high point of land or rock that sticks out into a body of water.

pro•mote (pruh-**mote**) ***verb***
1. To move someone to a more important job or to a higher grade in school.
2. To help with the growth or development of something.
3. To make the public aware of something or someone.
▸ ***verb*** **promoting, promoted**

pro•mo•tion (pruh-**moh**-shuhn) ***noun***
1. Advancement to a more important job or a higher grade in school.
2. Encouragement.

prompt (**prompt**)
1. ***adjective*** Very quick and without delay.
2. ***adjective*** On time.
3. ***verb*** To move someone to action.
4. ***verb*** To remind actors of their lines when they have forgotten them during a play. ▸ ***noun*** **prompter** ▸ ***verb*** **prompting, prompted** ▸ ***adjective*** **prompter, promptest** ▸ ***adverb*** **promptly**

prone (**prohn**) ***adjective***
1. Likely to act, feel, or be a certain way.
2. Lying flat or face down, as in *a prone position.*

prong (**prong**) ***noun*** One of the sharp points of a fork or other tool.

pro•noun (**proh**-*noun*) ***noun*** A word that is used in place of a noun. "I," "me," "he," and "it" are all pronouns.

pro•nounce (pruh-**nounss**) ***verb***
1. To say words in a particular way.
2. To make a formal announcement. ▸ ***noun*** **pronouncement** ▸ ***verb*** **pronouncing, pronounced**

pro•nun•ci•a•tion (pruh-*nuhn*-see-**ay**-shuhn) ***noun*** The way in which a word is pronounced.

proof (**proof**) ***noun*** Facts or evidence that something is true.

proof•read (**proof**-*reed*) ***verb*** If you **proofread** something, you read it carefully and correct any mistakes in spelling, punctuation, and grammar that you find. ▸ **proofreading, proofread** ▸ ***noun*** **proofreader**

prop (**prop**)
1. ***verb*** To support something that would otherwise fall down. ▸ **propping, propped**
2. ***noun*** Something used as a support.
3. ***noun*** In the theater, movies, or television a **prop** is any item that an actor needs to carry or use. Prop is short for **property**.

prop•a•gan•da (prop-uh-**gan**-duh) ***noun*** Information that is spread to influence the way people think, gain supporters, or damage an opposing group. Propaganda is often incomplete or biased information.

pro•pel (pruh-**pel**) ***verb*** To drive or push something forward. ▸ **propelling, propelled** ▸ ***noun*** **propulsion**

pro•pel•lant (pruh-**pel**-uhnt) ***noun***
1. A chemical or fuel that when burned propels something.
2. A compressed gas or a liquid that releases the contents of an aerosol can.

pro•pel•ler (pruh-**pel**-ur) ***noun*** A set of rotating blades that provide force to move a vehicle through water or air.

prop•er (**prop**-ur) ***adjective***
1. Right or suitable for a given purpose or occasion.
2. Stiffly formal.

prop•er•ly (**prop**-ur-lee) ***adverb***
1. In a correct, appropriate, or suitable way.
2. In an exact or strict sense.

proper noun ***noun*** A **proper noun** is the name of a particular person, place, or thing, such as *Jane, New York,* and *Washington Monument.* A proper noun starts with a capital letter.

prop•er•ty (**prop**-ur-tee) ***noun***
1. Anything that is owned by an individual.
2. Buildings and land belonging to someone.
3. A special quality or characteristic of something, as in *the properties of a liquid.* ▸ ***noun, plural*** **properties**

proph•e•cy (**prof**-uh-see) ***noun*** A prediction. ▸ ***noun, plural*** **prophecies** ▸ ***verb*** **prophesy** (**prof**-uh-sye)

proph•et (**prof**-it) ***noun***
1. A person who speaks or claims to speak for God.
2. Someone who predicts what will happen in the future.
Prophet sounds like **profit.**

pro•por•tion (pruh-**por**-shuhn) ***noun***
1. A part of something.
2. The size, number, or amount of something in relation to another thing.
3. In mathematics, a statement that two ratios are equal.
4. If something is **in proportion** to something else, it is the correct size in relation to it.
5. proportions *noun, plural* The **proportions** of something are its measurements or size. ▸ ***adjective*** **proportional** ▸ ***adverb*** **proportionally**

pro•pose (pruh-**poze**) ***verb***
1. To suggest a plan or an idea.
2. To ask someone to marry you.
▸ ***verb*** **proposing, proposed** ▸ ***noun*** **proposal**

pro•po•si•tion (*prop*-uh-**zi**-shuhn) ***noun***
1. An offer, or a suggestion.
2. Anything brought up for discussion.

pro•pul•sion (pruh-**puhl**-shuhn) ***noun*** The force by which a plane, rocket, etc., is pushed along, as in *jet propulsion.*

prose (**proze**) ***noun*** Ordinary written or spoken language, as opposed to verse or poetry. Short stories and essays are examples of prose.

pros•e•cute (**pross**-uh-kyoot) ***verb*** To begin and carry out a legal action in a court of law against a person accused of a crime. ▸ ***noun*** **prosecution**

pros•e•cu•tor (**pross**-uh-*kyoo*-tur) ***noun*** A lawyer who represents the government in criminal trials.

pros•pect (**pross**-pekt)
1. *noun* Something that is looked forward to or expected.
2. *noun* A view or a scene.
3. *verb* To explore or search for something, especially gold or silver.
▸ **prospecting, prospected** ▸ ***noun*** **prospector**
4. *noun* A possible customer or winner in a political or athletic contest.

pro•spec•tive (pruh-**spek**-tiv) ***adjective***
1. Possible or likely.
2. Future or likely to become, as in *a prospective buyer* or *a prospective bride.*

pro•spec•tus (pruh-**spek**-tuhss) ***noun*** A brochure giving information about a company or any organization. ▸ ***noun, plural*** **prospectuses**

pros•per (**pross**-pur) ***verb*** To be successful or to thrive. ▸ **prospering, prospered** ▸ ***noun*** **prosperity** ▸ ***adjective*** **prosperous**

pros•the•sis (pross-**thee**-siss) ***noun*** An artificial device that replaces a missing part of a body. ▸ ***noun, plural*** **prostheses** (pross-**thee**-seez)

pro•tect (pruh-**tekt**) ***verb*** To guard or keep something safe from harm, attack, or injury. ▸ **protecting, protected** ▸ ***noun*** **protection,** ***noun*** **protector** ▸ ***adjective*** **protective**

pro•tein (**proh**-teen) ***noun*** A substance found in all living plant and animal cells. Foods such as meat, cheese, eggs, beans, and fish are sources of dietary protein.

pro•test
1. (pruh-**test**) ***verb*** To object to something strongly and publicly.
▸ **protesting, protested**
2. (**proh**-test) ***noun*** A demonstration or statement against something, as in *a protest against war.*

Prot•es•tant (**prot**-uh-stuhnt) ***noun*** A Christian who does not belong to the Roman Catholic or the Orthodox church. ▸ ***adjective*** **Protestant**

pro•tist (**proh**-tist) ***noun*** Any organism from the kingdom *Protista.* Protists include amoebas, paramecia, and some algae.

pro•ton (**proh**-ton) ***noun*** One of the very small parts in the nucleus of an atom. A proton carries a positive electrical charge.

pro•to•plasm (**proh**-tuh-*plaz*-uhm) ***noun*** A jellylike substance that makes up the living matter of all cells.

P

pro•to•type (**proh**-tuh-*tipe*) ***noun*** The first version of an invention that tests an idea to see if it will work.

pro•to•zo•an (*proh*-tuh-**zoh**-uhn) ***noun*** A microscopic animal with one cell that reproduces by dividing. Paramecia and amoebas are protozoans. ▸ ***noun, plural*** **protozoans** *or* **protozoa** (*proh*-tuh-**zoh**-uh)

pro•trac•tor (proh-**trak**-tur) ***noun*** A semicircular instrument used for measuring and drawing angles. Protractors are marked off in degrees. They are usually made of transparent plastic.

pro•trude (proh-**trood**) ***verb*** To stick or jut out. ▸ **protruding, protruded** ▸ ***noun*** **protrusion**

proud (**proud**) ***adjective***
1. If you are **proud,** you are pleased and satisfied with what you or someone else has achieved.
2. If you are **proud,** you have self-respect and a sense of your own importance.
3. If you are **proud,** you think too highly of your own value or abilities.
▸ ***adjective*** **prouder, proudest**

prove (**proov**) ***verb*** To show that something is true. ▸ **proving, proved**

prov•erb (**prov**-urb) ***noun*** A wise old saying that tells a common truth, as in *"A stitch in time saves nine."*

pro•vide (pruh-**vide**)
1. ***verb*** To supply the things that someone needs. ▸ ***noun*** **provider,** ***noun*** **provision**
2. ***verb*** To set down as a rule or condition.
3. **provided** ***conjunction*** On condition that or as long as.
▸ ***verb*** **providing, provided**

prov•ince (**prov**-uhnss) ***noun*** A district or a region of some countries. Canada is made up of provinces.

pro•vin•cial (pruh-**vin**-shuhl) ***adjective***
1. To do with a province, as in *a provincial government.*
2. Narrow-minded or having a limited or prejudiced point of view.

pro•vi•sion (pruh-**vizh**-uhn) ***noun***
1. The act of providing something.
2. Something that is named as a condition in an agreement, a law, or a document.
3. **provisions** ***noun, plural*** A supply of groceries or food.

pro•vi•sion•al (pruh-**vizh**-uh-nuhl) ***adjective*** If something is **provisional,** it is temporary or not yet final, as in *a provisional government* or *provisional plans.* ▸ ***adverb*** **provisionally**

pro•voke (pruh-**voke**) ***verb***
1. To annoy someone and make the person angry.
2. To bring on or to arouse.
▸ ***verb*** **provoking, provoked** ▸ ***noun*** **provocation** ▸ ***adjective*** **provocative**

prow (**prou**) ***noun*** The bow or front part of a boat or ship.

prow•ess (**prou**-iss) ***noun*** Skill or bravery.

prowl (**proul**) ***verb*** To move around quietly and secretly, like an animal looking for prey. ▸ **prowling, prowled** ▸ ***noun*** **prowler**

prox•im•i•ty (prok-**sim**-uh-tee) ***noun*** Nearness.

pru•dent (**prood**-uhnt) ***adjective*** If you are **prudent,** you are cautious and think carefully before you do something. ▸ ***noun*** **prudence** ▸ ***adverb*** **prudently**

prune (**proon**)
1. ***noun*** A dried plum.
2. ***verb*** To cut off branches from a tree or bush in order to make it grow more strongly. ▸ **pruning, pruned**

pry (**prye**) ***verb***
1. If you **pry,** you ask someone personal or nosy questions about things he or she does not want to discuss.
2. To remove, raise, or pull apart with force, as with a lever.
3. To get with difficulty or much effort.
▸ ***verb*** **pries, prying, pried**

P

P.S. (**pee ess**) Short for **postscript** or **public school.**

psalm (**sahm**) ***noun*** A sacred song or poem, especially one from the Book of Psalms in the Bible.

pseu•do•nym (**sood**-uh-nim) ***noun*** A false name, especially one used by an author instead of his or her real name.

psy•chi•a•trist (sye-**kye**-uh-trist) ***noun*** A medical doctor who is trained to treat emotional and mental illness. ▸ ***noun*** **psychiatry** ▸ ***adjective*** **psychiatric** (*sye*-kee-**at**-rik)

psy•chic (**sye**-kik) ***adjective*** Someone who is **psychic** claims to be able to tell what people are thinking or to predict the future. ▸ ***noun*** **psychic**

psy•cho•log•i•cal (*sye*-kuh-**loj**-uh-kuhl) ***adjective***
1. To do with psychology.
2. To do with or arising from the mind.

psy•chol•o•gist (sye-**kol**-uh-jist) ***noun*** Someone who studies people's minds and emotions and the ways that people behave.

psy•chol•o•gy (sye-**koh**-luh-jee) ***noun*** The study of the mind, the emotions, and human behavior.

psy•cho•path (**sye**-kuh-*path*) ***noun*** Someone who is mentally unbalanced, especially a person who is violent or dangerous. ▸ ***adjective*** **psychopathic**

pter•o•dac•tyl (*ter*-uh-**dak**-til) ***noun*** A prehistoric flying reptile with wide wings supported by very large fourth fingers.

pub (**puhb**) ***noun*** A bar where adults can go to drink alcohol.

pu•ber•ty (**pyoo**-bur-tee) ***noun*** The time when a person's body changes from a child's to an adult's.

pub•lic (**puhb**-lik)
1. ***adjective*** To do with the people or the community, as in *public safety* or *public opinion.*
2. ***adjective*** If something is **public,** it belongs to or can be used by everybody, as in *public transportation* or *a public beach.*
3. ***adjective*** Working for the government of a town, city, or country, as in *a public official* or *a public servant.*
4. the public *noun* People in general.
▸ ***adjective*** **publicly**

pub•li•ca•tion (puhb-luh-**kay**-shuhn) ***noun***
1. A book, magazine, or newspaper.
2. The production and distribution of a book, magazine, or newspaper.

pub•lic•i•ty (puh-**bliss**-uh-tee) ***noun*** Information about a person or an event that is given out to get the public's attention or approval.

pub•li•cize (**puhb**-luh-*size*) ***verb*** If you **publicize** an event, you make it known to as many people as possible.
▸ **publicizing, publicized**

public opinion ***noun*** The views or beliefs of most of the people in a town, city, or country, usually found out through a public opinion poll.

public relations ***noun, plural*** The methods or activities an organization or a business uses to promote goodwill or a good image with the public.

public school ***noun*** A school that provides free education. Public schools are supported by taxes.

pub•lish (**puhb**-lish) ***verb*** To produce and distribute a book, magazine, newspaper, or any other printed material so that people can buy it.
▸ **publishes, publishing, published**
▸ ***noun*** **publisher,** ***noun*** **publishing**

puck (**puhk**) ***noun*** A hard, round, flat piece of rubber used in ice hockey.

puck•er (**puhk**-ur) ***verb*** To wrinkle or to fold. ▸ **puckering, puckered** ▸ ***noun*** **pucker**

pud•ding (**pud**-ing) ***noun*** A sweet, soft dessert, as in *rice pudding* or *chocolate pudding.*

pud•dle (**puhd**-uhl) ***noun*** A small pool of water or other liquid, as in *a puddle of spilled milk.*

pueb•lo (**pweb**-loh) ***noun***
1. A village consisting of stone and adobe buildings built next to and on

top of each other. Pueblos were built by American Indian tribes in the southwestern United States. ▸ ***noun, plural* pueblos**

2. Pueblo A member of an American Indian tribe of New Mexico and Arizona.

▸ ***noun, plural* Pueblo** *or* **Pueblos**

puff (**puhf**)

1. ***noun*** A short, sudden burst of air, breath, or smoke.

2. ***noun*** Anything that looks soft, light, and fluffy, as in *puffs of clouds.*

3. ***verb*** To blow or come out in puffs.

4. ***verb*** If something **puffs up,** it swells.

▸ ***verb* puffing, puffed** ▸ ***adjective* puffy**

puf•fin (**puf**-uhn) ***noun*** A seabird of northern regions that has black and white feathers, a short neck, and a colorful beak.

pug (**puhg**) ***noun*** A dog with short hair, a flat nose, a wrinkled face, and a curled tail.

pug•na•cious (puhg-**nay**-shuhss) ***adjective*** If someone is **pugnacious,** he or she often picks fights. ▸ ***adverb* pugnaciously**

pull (**pul**)

1. ***verb*** To move something forward or toward you.

2. ***verb*** To tug or pluck something, as in *to pull weeds.*

3. ***noun*** The act of pulling something, or the effort required to pull something, as in *a big pull.*

4. ***noun*** Attraction or influence, as in *the pull of a magnet.*

5. ***verb*** To stretch or strain a part of the body.

6. ***verb*** If you **pull** something **off,** you do it with great success.

7. ***verb*** If you **pull through,** you get through a hard, painful, or dangerous time.

▸ ***verb* pulling, pulled**

pul•ley (**pul**-ee) ***noun***

1. A wheel with a grooved rim in which a rope or chain can run. A pulley is used to lift loads more easily.

2. A lifting machine made from a rope or chain and a set of pulleys linked together.

pull•o•ver (**pul**-*oh*-vur) ***noun*** A shirt or sweater that you can pull over your head.

pulp (**puhlp**) ***noun***

1. The soft, juicy, or fleshy part of fruits and vegetables.

2. Any soft, wet mixture, as in *wood pulp.*

3. The soft inner part of a tooth.

▸ ***verb* pulp**

pul•pit (**puhl**-pit) ***noun*** A raised, enclosed platform in a church where a minister stands to speak to a congregation.

pul•sate (**puhl**-sate) ***verb*** To beat or vibrate regularly. ▸ **pulsating, pulsated**

pulse (**puhlss**) ***noun*** A steady beat or throb, especially the feeling of the heart moving blood through your body.

▸ ***verb* pulse**

pu•ma (**pyoo**-muh *or* **poo**-muh) ***noun*** Another name for a **cougar, mountain lion,** and **panther.**

pum•ice (**puhm**-iss) ***noun*** A light, grayish volcanic rock that is used for cleaning, smoothing, or polishing.

pum•mel (**puhm**-uhl) ***verb*** To punch someone or something repeatedly.

▸ **pummeling, pummeled**

pump (**puhmp**)

1. ***noun*** A machine that forces liquids or gases from one place or container into another, as in *a bicycle pump* or *a water pump.*

2. ***verb*** To empty or fill using a pump.

3. pumps *noun, plural* Formal women's shoes with a medium to high heel.

4. ***verb*** If you **pump** someone for information, you keep asking the person questions.

▸ ***verb* pumping, pumped**

pump•kin (**puhmp**-kin) ***noun*** A big, round, orange fruit that grows on a vine along the ground. People often carve faces in pumpkins at Halloween.

P

pun (**puhn**) ***noun*** A joke based on one word that has two meanings or two words that sound the same but have different meanings. ▸ ***verb*** **pun**

punch (**puhnch**)
1. ***verb*** To hit something or someone with your fist. ▸ ***noun*** **punch,** ***noun*** **puncher**
2. ***noun*** A drink made by mixing fruit juices, often with soda and spices.
3. ***noun*** A metal tool used for making holes.
4. ***verb*** To make a hole in something.
5. punch line ***noun*** The last line of a joke or story that makes it funny or surprising.
▸ ***verb*** **punches, punching, punched**

punc·tu·al (**puhngk**-choo-uhl) ***adjective*** If you are **punctual,** you arrive right on time. ▸ ***noun*** **punctuality** ▸ ***adverb*** **punctually**

punc·tu·a·tion (*puhngk*-choo-**ay**-shuhn) ***noun***
1. The use of periods, commas, and other marks to make the meaning of written material clear. ▸ ***verb*** **punctuate**
2. One or more punctuation marks.

punctuation mark ***noun*** A written mark, such as a comma, period, colon, semicolon, question mark, or exclamation point, used in punctuating.

punc·ture (**puhngk**-chur) ***noun*** A hole made by a sharp object. ▸ ***verb*** **puncture**

pun·gent (**puhn**-juhnt) ***adjective*** If something is **pungent,** it tastes or smells strong or sharp, as in *a pungent odor.*

pun·ish (**puhn**-ish) ***verb*** If you **punish** someone, you make the person suffer for committing a crime or for behaving badly. ▸ **punishes, punishing, punished** ▸ ***noun*** **punishment**

punk (**puhngk**) ***noun***
1. *(slang)* A young person who is inexperienced or always getting into trouble.
2. A style of music and dress that became popular in the late 1970s. People who dressed in this style wore black clothes, used safety pins for decoration, and had brightly colored hair.
3. punk rock Loud, hard rock music that became popular in the late 1970s.

punt (**puhnt**)
1. ***noun*** A boat with a flat bottom that you push along with a long pole. ▸ ***verb*** **punt**
2. ***verb*** To kick a football or soccer ball dropped from the hands before it strikes the ground. ▸ **punting, punted** ▸ ***noun*** **punt,** ***noun*** **punter**

pu·ny (**pyoo**-nee) ***adjective*** Small and weak, or unimportant. ▸ **punier, puniest** ▸ ***noun*** **puniness** ▸ ***adverb*** **punily**

pu·pa (**pyoo**-puh) ***noun*** An insect at the stage of development between a larva and an adult. ▸ ***noun, plural*** **pupas** *or* **pupae** (**pyoo**-pee)

pu·pil (**pyoo**-puhl) ***noun***
1. Someone who is being taught, especially in school.
2. The round, black part of your eye that lets light travel through it.

pup·pet (**puhp**-it) ***noun*** A toy in the shape of a person or an animal that you control by pulling strings that are attached to it or by moving your hand inside it.

pup·py (**puhp**-ee) ***noun*** A young dog. ▸ ***noun, plural*** **puppies**

pur·chase (**pur**-chuhss)
1. ***verb*** To buy something. ▸ **purchasing, purchased** ▸ ***noun*** **purchaser**
2. ***noun*** Something that has been bought.
3. ***noun*** The act of purchasing.

pure (**pyoor**) ***adjective***
1. Not mixed with anything else, as in *pure gold.*
2. Not dirty or not polluted, as in *pure water.*

3. Innocent or free from evil or guilt, as in *a pure heart* or *a pure mind.*
4. Complete or nothing but, as in *pure luck* or *pure nonsense.*
▸ ***adjective*** **purer, purest** ▸ ***noun*** **purity**

pure•bred (**pyoor-bred**) ***adjective*** Having ancestors of the same breed or kind of animal.

pu•ree *or* **pu•rée** (pyoo-**ray**) ***noun*** A thick paste made from food that has been put through a sieve or blender, as in *tomato puree.* ▸ ***verb*** **puree** *or* **purée**

purge (**purj**) ***verb*** To clean something out by getting rid of unwanted things.
▸ **purging, purged** ▸ ***noun*** **purge**

pu•ri•fy (**pyoor**-uh-fye) ***verb*** To make something pure or clean. ▸ **purifies, purifying, purified** ▸ ***noun*** **purification**

Pur•i•tan (**pyoor**-uh-tuhn) ***noun*** One of a group of Protestants in 16th- and 17th-century England who sought simple church services and a strict moral code. Many Puritans fled England and settled in America.

pur•ple (**pur**-puhl) ***noun*** The color that is made by mixing red and blue.
▸ ***adjective*** **purple**

pur•pose (**pur**-puhss) ***noun***
1. A goal or an aim.
2. The reason why something is made or done, or an object's function.
3. on purpose Deliberately rather than by accident.
▸ ***adjective*** **purposeful** ▸ ***adverb*** **purposely**

purr (**pur**) ***verb***
1. When a cat **purrs,** it makes a low, soft sound in its throat.
2. To make a low sound like a cat.
Purr sounds like **per.**
▸ ***verb*** **purring, purred** ▸ ***noun*** **purr**

purse (**purss**)
1. *noun* A handbag or a pocketbook.
2. *noun* A small container in which people keep their money.
3. *noun* A sum of money given as a prize in an athletic contest.
4. *verb* If you **purse** your lips, you press them together into wrinkles. ▸ **pursing, pursed**

pur•sue (pur-**soo**) ***verb***
1. To follow or chase someone in order to catch him or her. ▸ ***noun*** **pursuer**
2. To continue something.
▸ ***verb*** **pursuing, pursued**

pur•suit (pur-**soot**) ***noun***
1. If you are in **pursuit** of someone, you are trying to catch the person.
2. An activity, hobby, or interest.

pus (**puhss**) ***noun*** A thick, yellow liquid that comes out of an infected wound or sore.

push (**push**)
1. *verb* To make something move by pressing on or against it.
2. *verb* To shove or press roughly.
3. *verb* To press yourself forward.
4. *noun* An act of pushing or shoving.
5. *verb* To try very hard to sell or do something.
6. *noun* A great effort or drive, as in *a final push to victory.*
▸ ***noun, plural*** **pushes** ▸ ***noun*** **pusher**
▸ ***verb*** **pushes, pushing, pushed**

push-up ***noun*** An exercise in which you raise your body off the floor from a lying position by pushing with your arms.

pus•sy willow (**puss**-ee) ***noun*** A shrub with soft, gray, furry flowers on long, thin branches.

put (**put**) ***verb***
1. To place, lay, or move something.
2. To express in words.
3. To cause someone to undergo or experience something.
4. If you **put** something **off,** you delay doing it.
5. If you **put** someone **up,** you let the person sleep overnight at your house.
6. If you **put up with** something, you allow it to continue.
▸ ***verb*** **putting, put**

Q

putt (**puht**) ***verb*** To hit a golf ball lightly into the hole on a green. ▸ **putting, putted** ▸ ***noun*** **putt,** ***noun*** **putter**

put·ter (**puht**-ur) ***verb*** To work aimlessly without getting much done. ▸ **puttering, puttered**

put·ty (**puht**-ee) ***noun*** A kind of soft cement made of powdered chalk and linseed oil. It dries hard and is used to fasten windows into frames and to fill holes in wood.

puz·zle (**puhz**-uhl)
1. ***noun*** A game or an activity in which you have to think hard in order to solve problems.
2. ***noun*** Someone or something that is hard to understand.
3. ***verb*** If something **puzzles** you, it makes you confused or unsure. ▸ **puzzling, puzzled** ▸ ***adjective*** **puzzled,** ***adjective*** **puzzling**

py·lon (**pye**-lon) ***noun*** A tall, metal tower that supports electrical cables.

pyr·a·mid (**pihr**-uh-mid) ***noun***
1. A solid shape with a polygon as a base and triangular sides that meet at a point on top. Most pyramids have a square base and four triangular sides.
2. An ancient Egyptian stone monument where pharaohs and their treasures were buried.

py·thon (**pye**-*thon*) ***noun*** A large, powerful snake that wraps itself around its prey and crushes it.

quack (**kwak**)
1. ***verb*** When ducks **quack,** they make a sharp, loud sound. ▸ **quacking, quacked** ▸ ***noun*** **quack**
2. ***noun*** A dishonest person who pretends to be a doctor or an expert. ▸ ***adjective*** **quack**

quad (**kwahd**) ***noun*** A rectangular yard with buildings around it, especially at a college. Quad is short for **quadrangle.**

quad·ran·gle (**kwahd**-*rang*-guhl) ***noun***
1. A closed shape with four sides and four angles; a quadrilateral.
2. A quad, as at a college.

quad·rant (**kwahd**-ruhnt) ***noun*** A quarter of a circle, or a quarter of the circumference of a circle.

quad·ri·lat·er·al (*kwahd*-ruh-**lat**-ur-uhl) ***noun*** A closed shape with four sides and four angles. Squares and rectangles are quadrilaterals. ▸ ***adjective*** **quadrilateral**

quad·ru·ped (**kwahd**-ruh-ped) ***noun*** An animal with four feet. Horses are quadrupeds.

qua·dru·ple (kwah-**droo**-puhl *or* **kwahd**-ruh-puhl)
1. ***verb*** To multiply something by four. ▸ **quadrupling, quadrupled**
2. ***adjective*** Four times as big, or four times as many.

qua·dru·plet (kwah-**droo**-plit) ***noun*** One of four babies born at the same time to one mother.

quag·mire (**kwag**-mire *or* **kwahg**-mire) ***noun*** A soggy area of ground.

qua·hog (**kwaw**-*hawg or* **kwaw**-*hog*) ***noun*** A round, edible clam with a thick, heavy shell found on the eastern coast of North America. Quahog is an American Indian word.

quail (**kwayl**) ***noun*** A small, plump bird with gray or brown feathers that are often speckled with white.

quaint (**kwaynt**) ***adjective*** Charming and old-fashioned, as in *a quaint little fishing village.* ▸ **quainter, quaintest** ▸ ***noun*** **quaintness** ▸ ***adverb*** **quaintly**

quake (**kwake**)
1. ***verb*** To shake and to tremble with fear.
2. ***verb*** To shake or to tremble.
3. ***noun*** An earthquake, or a trembling of the ground.
4. ***noun*** Any trembling or shaking.
▸ ***verb*** **quaking, quaked**

Quak•er (**kway**-kur) ***noun*** A member of the Society of Friends, a Christian group founded in 1650 that prefers simple religious services and opposes war.

qual•i•fi•ca•tion (*kwahl*-uh-fuh-**kay**-shuhn) ***noun*** A skill or an ability that makes you able to do a job or a task or carry out an office.

qual•i•fy (**kwahl**-uh-fye) ***verb***
1. To reach a level or standard that allows you to do something. ▸ ***adjective*** **qualified**
2. To limit or restrict something.
3. To limit or modify the meaning of a word or phrase.
▸ ***verb*** **qualifies, qualifying, qualified**

qual•i•ty (**kwahl**-uh-tee) ***noun***
1. Grade or degree of fineness.
2. A special characteristic of someone or something.
▸ ***noun, plural*** **qualities**

qualm (**kwahm** *or* **kwahlm**) ***noun*** A feeling of worry or uneasiness.

quan•da•ry (**kwahn**-duh-ree) ***noun*** If you are **in a quandary** about something, you are confused and do not know what to do about it. ▸ ***noun, plural*** **quandaries**

quan•ti•ty (**kwahn**-tuh-tee) ***noun***
1. An amount or a number.
2. A large number or amount.
▸ ***noun, plural*** **quantities**

quar•an•tine (**kwor**-uhn-teen) ***noun*** When a person, animal, plant, etc., is put in **quarantine,** it is kept away from others to stop a disease from spreading. ▸ ***verb*** **quarantine**

quark (**kwork**) ***noun*** In physics, any of several particles that are believed to come in pairs. A quark is smaller than an atom.

quar•rel (**kwor**-uhl)
1. ***verb*** To argue or to disagree.
2. ***noun*** An argument.
3. ***verb*** To find fault.
▸ ***verb*** **quarreling, quarreled**

quar•rel•some (**kwor**-uhl-suhm) ***adjective*** A person who is **quarrelsome** argues with others a lot.

quar•ry (**kwor**-ee) ***noun***
1. A place where stone, slate, etc., is dug from the ground. ▸ ***verb*** **quarry**
2. A person or an animal that is being chased or hunted.
▸ ***noun, plural*** **quarries**

quart (**kwort**) ***noun*** A unit of liquid measure equal to 32 ounces, or two pints. Milk is commonly sold in quarts.

quar•ter (**kwor**-tur)
1. ***noun*** One of four equal parts. ▸ ***verb*** **quarter**
2. ***noun*** A coin of the United States and Canada equal to 25 cents, or ¼ of a dollar.
3. ***noun*** One of four periods, usually 15 minutes each, that make up a game of football, basketball, soccer, etc.
4. ***noun*** A part of a town.
5. **quarters** ***noun, plural*** Lodgings, or rooms where people live.
6. ***verb*** To provide people, usually soldiers, with food and lodging.
▸ **quartering, quartered**

quar•ter•back (**kwor**-tur-*bak*) ***noun*** In football, the player who leads the offense by passing the ball or handing it off to a runner.

quart•er•ly (**kwor**-tur-lee)
1. ***adjective*** Happening once every three months.
2. ***adverb*** Once every three months.

Q

quar•tet (kwor-**tet**) ***noun***
1. A piece of music that is played or sung by four people.
2. Four people who play music or sing together.

quartz (**kworts**) ***noun*** A hard mineral that comes in many different forms and colors. Quartz is used to make very accurate clocks, watches, and electronic equipment.

qua•sar (**kway**-zar *or* **kway**-sar) ***noun*** A heavenly body that is larger than a star but smaller than a galaxy. Quasars give off powerful radio waves and huge amounts of light and radioactivity.

quash (**kwahsh**) ***verb***
1. To crush or to stop by force, as in *to quash a rebellion.*
2. To reject an idea or a decision.
▸ ***verb*** **quashes, quashing, quashed**

qua•ver (**kway**-vur)
1. ***verb*** To shake or to tremble.
▸ **quavering, quavered** ▸ ***noun*** **quaver**
2. ***noun*** A musical note representing half of one beat.

quay (**kee**) ***noun*** A place where boats can stop to load or unload. **Quay** sounds like **key.**

quea•sy (**kwee**-zee) ***adjective***
1. Sick to your stomach, or nauseated.
2. Uneasy or troubled.
▸ ***adjective*** **queasier, queasiest**
▸ ***noun*** **queasiness**

queen (**kween**) ***noun***
1. A woman from a royal family who is the ruler of her country.
2. The wife of a king.
3. A playing card that has a picture of a queen on it.
4. The most powerful chess piece. It can move in any direction.
5. A female bee, wasp, or ant that can lay eggs.

queer (**kwihr**) ***adjective*** Odd or strange. ▸ **queerer, queerest** ▸ ***adverb*** **queerly**

quell (**kwel**) ***verb*** To stop or crush by force, as in *to quell a disturbance.*
▸ **quelling, quelled**

quench (**kwench**) ***verb***
1. If you **quench** a fire, you put it out.
2. If you **quench** your thirst, you drink until you are no longer thirsty.
▸ ***verb*** **quenches, quenching, quenched**

que•ry (**kwihr**-ee)
1. ***noun*** A question or doubt about something. ▸ ***noun, plural*** **queries**
2. ***verb*** To ask a question to.
3. ***verb*** To express doubt about something.
▸ ***verb*** **queries, querying, queried**

quest (**kwest**) ***noun***
1. A long search. ▸ ***verb*** **quest**
2. In the Middle Ages, a journey taken by a knight to perform a feat or to find something.

ques•tion (**kwess**-chuhn)
1. ***noun*** A sentence that asks something.
2. ***noun*** A problem, or something that needs to be asked about.
3. ***verb*** To ask questions.
4. ***verb*** To be doubtful about something.
5. ***noun*** Doubt.
▸ ***verb*** **questioning, questioned**

question mark ***noun*** The punctuation mark (?) used in writing to show that a sentence is a question.

ques•tion•naire (*kwess*-chuh-**nair**) ***noun*** A list of questions used to get information or to find out about people's opinions.

quet•zal (ket-**sal**) ***noun*** A bird of Mexico and Central America with crimson and green feathers. The male has long, flowing tail feathers.

queue (**kyoo**)
1. ***noun*** A line of people waiting for something.
2. ***verb*** To wait in a line of people.
▸ **queuing, queued**
Queue sounds like **cue.**

Q

quib•ble (**kwib**-uhl) ***verb*** To argue about unimportant things. ▸ **quibbling, quibbled** ▸ ***noun*** **quibble**

quiche (**keesh**) ***noun*** A food made up of a pastry crust and a filling of eggs, cream or milk, cheese, vegetables, etc.

quick (**kwik**) ***adjective***
1. Fast, as in *a quick lunch.* ▸ ***verb*** **quicken** ▸ ***adverb*** **quick,** ***adverb*** **quickly**
2. Clever and lively, as in *a quick sense of humor* or *a quick mind.*
▸ ***adjective*** **quicker, quickest**

quick•sand (**kwik**-*sand*) ***noun*** Loose, wet sand that you can sink into.

qui•et (**kwye**-uht)
1. ***adjective*** Not loud.
2. ***adjective*** Peaceful and calm.
3. ***noun*** The state of being quiet.
▸ ***noun*** **quietness** ▸ ***verb*** **quiet**
▸ ***adjective*** **quieter, quietest** ▸ ***adverb*** **quietly**

quill (**kwil**) ***noun***
1. The long, hollow central part of a bird's feather.
2. One of the long, pointed spines on a porcupine.
3. quill pen A pen made from a bird's feather, with its quill carved to form a point.

quilt (**kwilt**) ***noun*** A warm, usually padded, covering for a bed. ▸ ***verb*** **quilt**

quilt•ed (**kwil**-tid) ***adjective*** If material is **quilted,** it is padded and sewn in lines or patterns.

quin•tet (kwin-**tet**) ***noun***
1. A piece of music that is played or sung by five people.
2. Five people who play music or sing together.

quin•tup•let (kwin-**tuhp**-lit) ***noun*** One of five babies born at the same time to one mother.

quip (**kwip**) ***noun*** A witty or clever remark.

quirk (**kwerk**) ***noun***
1. A peculiar trait or a strange way of acting. ▸ ***noun*** **quirkiness** ▸ ***adjective*** **quirky**
2. A sudden twist or turn.

quit (**kwit**) ***verb***
1. To stop doing something.
2. To leave something.
▸ ***verb*** **quitting, quit** *or* **quitted**
▸ ***noun*** **quitter**

quite (**kwite**) ***adverb***
1. Completely.
2. Actually or really.
3. Rather or very.

quiv•er (**kwiv**-ur)
1. ***verb*** To tremble or to vibrate.
▸ **quivering, quivered** ▸ ***noun*** **quiver**
2. ***noun*** A case for arrows.

quix•ot•ic (kwik-**sot**-ik) ***adjective*** If a person is **quixotic,** he or she is caught up in doing noble deeds or in trying to achieve goals that are impractical.

quiz (**kwiz**)
1. ***noun*** A short test. ▸ ***noun, plural*** **quizzes**
2. ***verb*** To question someone closely.
▸ **quizzes, quizzing, quizzed**

quo•ta (**kwoh**-tuh) ***noun*** A fixed amount or share of something.

quo•ta•tion (kwoh-**tay**-shuhn) ***noun***
1. A sentence or short passage from a book, play, speech, etc., that is repeated by someone else.
2. The act of repeating another person's words.

quotation mark ***noun*** The punctuation mark (“ or ‘) used in writing to show where speech begins and ends.

quote (**kwote**)
1. ***verb*** To repeat words that were spoken or written by someone else.
▸ **quoting, quoted**
2. ***noun*** A quotation.

quo•tient (**kwoh**-shuhnt) ***noun*** The number that you get when you divide one number by another. In the problem 12 divided by 4, the quotient is 3.

R

rab·bi (**rab**-eye) ***noun*** A Jewish religious leader and teacher.

rab·bit (**rab**-it) ***noun*** A small, furry mammal with long ears that lives in a hole that it digs in the ground.

rab·ble (**rab**-uhl) ***noun*** A noisy crowd of people.

ra·bies (**ray**-beez) ***noun*** An often fatal disease that can affect humans, dogs, bats, and other warm-blooded animals. Rabies is caused by a virus that attacks the brain and spinal cord and is spread by the bite of an infected animal.
▸ ***adjective*** **rabid** (**rab**-id)

rac·coon (ra-**koon**) ***noun*** A mammal with rings on its tail and black and white face markings that look like a mask.

race (**rayss**)
1. ***noun*** A test of speed. ▸ ***verb*** **race**
2. ***noun*** One of the major groups into which human beings can be divided. People of the same race share the same physical characteristics, such as skin color, which are passed on from generation to generation.
3. ***verb*** To run or move very fast.
▸ **racing, raced**

race car ***noun*** A car designed to race at very high speeds.

race relations ***noun, plural*** The way that people of different races get along with each other when they live in the same community.

race·track (**rayss**-*trak*) ***noun*** A round or oval course that is used for racing.

ra·cial (**ray**-shuhl) ***adjective***
1. To do with a person's race, as in *racial characteristics.*
2. Between races, as in *racial prejudice* or *racial harmony.*

rac·ist (**ray**-sist) ***adjective*** Someone who is **racist** thinks that a particular race is better than others or treats people unfairly or cruelly because of their race. ▸ ***noun*** **racism,** ***noun*** **racist**

rack (**rak**)
1. ***noun*** A framework for holding or hanging things, as in *a clothes rack.*
2. ***noun*** An instrument of torture used in the past to stretch the body of a victim.
3. ***verb*** If you **rack your brains,** you think very hard.
▸ **racking, racked**

rack·et (**rak**-it) ***noun***
1. racket *or* **racquet** A stringed frame with a handle that you use in games such as tennis, squash, and badminton.
2. A very loud noise.
3. A dishonest activity.

rac·quet (**rak**-it) *See* **racket.**

rac·quet·ball (**rak**-it-*bawl*) ***noun*** A game played by two or four players who use short rackets to hit a small rubber ball against the walls, floor, and ceiling of an enclosed court.

ra·dar (**ray**-dar) ***noun***
1. Planes and ships use **radar** to find solid objects by reflecting radio waves off them and by receiving the reflected waves. Radar stands for *RAdio Detecting And Ranging.*
2. radar trap A system using radar equipment that is set up by the police to catch speeding drivers.

ra·di·al (**ray**-dee-uhl) ***adjective***
1. Spreading out from the center or arranged like rays.
2. To do with a kind of automobile or truck tire whose design makes it grip the

road better than traditional tires. ▸ ***noun*** **radial**

ra·di·ant (**ray**-dee-uhnt) ***adjective***
1. Bright and shining.
2. Someone who is **radiant** looks very healthy and happy.
▸ ***noun*** **radiance**

ra·di·ate (**ray**-dee-*ate*) ***verb***
1. To give off rays of light or heat.
2. To spread out from the center.
3. To send out something strongly.
▸ ***verb*** **radiating, radiated**

ra·di·a·tion (*ray*-dee-**ay**-shuhn) ***noun***
1. The sending out of rays of light, heat, etc.
2. Particles that are sent out from a radioactive substance.

ra·di·a·tor (**ray**-dee-*ay*-tur) ***noun***
1. A metal container through which hot liquid or steam circulates, sending heat into a room.
2. A metal device through which a liquid, usually water, circulates to cool a vehicle's engine.

rad·i·cal (**rad**-i-kuhl) ***adjective***
1. If a change is **radical,** it is thorough and has a wide range of important effects. ▸ ***adverb*** **radically**
2. Someone who is **radical** believes in extreme political change. ▸ ***noun*** **radical**

ra·di·o (**ray**-dee-oh)
1. ***noun*** A way of communicating using electromagnetic waves broadcast from a central antenna.
2. ***noun*** A device that sends or receives these broadcasts and converts them into sound.
3. ***verb*** To send a message using a radio.
▸ **radios, radioing, radioed**
▸ ***noun, plural*** **radios** ▸ ***adjective*** **radio**

ra·di·o·ac·tive (*ray*-dee-oh-**ak**-tiv) ***adjective*** **Radioactive** materials are made up of atoms whose nuclei break down, giving off harmful radiation.
▸ ***noun*** **radioactivity**

ra·di·og·ra·phy (*ray*-dee-**og**-ruh-fee) ***noun*** The process of taking X-ray photographs of people's bones, organs, etc. ▸ ***noun*** **radiographer**

rad·ish (**rad**-ish) ***noun*** A small, red and white root vegetable that you eat in salads. ▸ ***noun, plural*** **radishes**

ra·di·um (**ray**-dee-uhm) ***noun*** A radioactive element sometimes used to treat cancer.

ra·di·us (**ray**-dee-uhss) ***noun***
1. A straight line segment drawn from the center of a circle to its outer edge.
2. The outer bone in your lower arm.
3. A circular area around a thing or a place.
▸ ***noun, plural*** **radii** (**ray**-dee-eye)

ra·don (**ray**-don) ***noun*** An odorless, colorless, radioactive gas that can seep up from the earth and rocks. Radon is a chemical element produced by radium.

raf·fle (**raf**-uhl) ***noun*** A way of raising money by selling tickets and then giving prizes to people with winning tickets.
▸ ***verb*** **raffle**

raft (**raft**)
1. ***noun*** A floating platform often made from logs tied together.
2. ***verb*** To travel by raft. ▸ **rafting, rafted** ▸ ***noun*** **rafting**
3. ***noun*** An inflatable rubber craft with a flat bottom.

rag (**rag**)
1. ***noun*** A piece of old cloth.
2. **rags** ***noun, plural*** Very old, worn-out clothing.

rage (**rayj**)
1. ***noun*** Violent anger.
2. ***verb*** To be violent or noisy. ▸ **raging, raged**

rag·ged (**rag**-id) ***adjective*** Old, torn, and worn-out. ▸ ***adjective*** **raggedy**
▸ ***adverb*** **raggedly**

rag·time (**rag**-*time*) ***noun*** An early style of jazz having a strong, syncopated rhythm.

R

R

rag•weed (**rag**-*weed*) ***noun*** A weed whose pollen is a cause of hay fever in the fall.

raid (**rayd**) ***noun***
1. A sudden, surprise attack on a place.
▸ ***noun* raider**
2. A sudden visit by the police to search for criminals, drugs, etc.
▸ ***verb* raid**

rail (**rayl**) ***noun***
1. A fixed bar supported by posts.
2. Railroad. ▸ ***adjective* rail**

rail•ing (**ray**-ling) ***noun*** A wooden or metal bar that is a part of a fence or a staircase.

rail•road (**rayl**-*rohd*) ***noun***
1. A track of double rails for a train.
2. A system of transport using trains.

rail•way (**rayl**-*way*) ***noun*** A railroad, or the tracks of a railroad.

rain (**rayn**)
1. ***noun*** Water that falls in drops from clouds.
2. ***noun*** A falling of rain.
3. ***verb*** To fall in rain.
4. ***verb*** To fall or pour like rain.
Rain sounds like **reign** and **rein.**
▸ ***verb* raining, rained** ▸ ***adjective* rainy**

rain•bow (**rayn**-*boh*) ***noun*** An arc of different colors caused by the bending of sunlight as it shines through water vapor.

rain•coat (**rayn**-*koht*) ***noun*** A waterproof coat that keeps you dry when it is raining.

rain•drop (**rayn**-*drop*) ***noun*** A drop of rain.

rain•fall (**rayn**-*fawl*) ***noun*** The amount of rain that falls in one place in a certain time.

rain forest ***noun*** A dense, tropical forest where a lot of rain falls.

raise (**rayz**)
1. ***verb*** To lift something up.
2. ***verb*** If you **raise** money, you collect it for a particular cause or charity.
3. ***verb*** To look after children or young animals until they are grown.
4. ***noun*** An increase in salary. ▸ ***verb* raise**
5. ***verb*** To ask or to bring up, as in *to raise an objection.*
▸ ***verb* raising, raised**

rai•sin (**ray**-zuhn) ***noun*** A dried grape.

rake (**rayk**)
1. ***noun*** A garden tool with metal teeth used to level soil or to collect leaves, grass cuttings, etc.
2. ***verb*** To use a rake.
3. ***verb*** *(informal)* If you **rake it in,** you make a lot of money.
▸ ***verb* raking, raked**

ral•ly (**ral**-ee)
1. ***verb*** To bring together again.
2. ***verb*** To join together to help or support a person or thing.
3. ***verb*** To regain strength, energy, or health.
4. ***noun*** A large meeting, as in *a political rally.*
5. ***noun*** In racket games such as tennis, a **rally** is a long exchange of shots.
▸ ***noun, plural* rallies** ▸ ***verb* rallies, rallying, rallied**

ram (**ram**)
1. ***noun*** A male sheep.
2. ***verb*** To crash into something with great force.
3. ***verb*** To push something into a space.
▸ ***verb* ramming, rammed**

RAM (**ram**) ***noun*** The part of a computer's memory that is lost when you turn the computer off. RAM stands for *Random Access Memory.*

Ram•a•dan (**rahm**-i-*dahn*) ***noun*** The ninth month of the Muslim year, when Muslims fast each day from sunrise to sunset.

ram•ble (**ram**-buhl) ***verb***
1. To wander about without direction or purpose.
2. To go on a long walk for pleasure.
3. To speak or write extensively without sticking to the point.
▸ ***verb* rambling, rambled** ▸ ***noun* ramble, *noun* rambler**

R

ram•bling (**ram**-bling) ***adjective*** Going or growing in many directions, as in *a rambling speech* or *a rambling rose.*

ramp (**ramp**) ***noun*** A sloping passageway or roadway linking one level with another.

ram•page (**ram**-payj) ***noun*** If someone goes **on a rampage,** the person rushes around in a noisy and destructive way. ▸ ***verb*** **rampage**

ram•pant (**ram**-puhnt) ***adjective*** Wild and without restraint, as in *a rampant growth of weeds.*

ram•part (**ram**-part) ***noun*** The surrounding wall or embankment of a fort or castle built to protect against attack.

ram•shack•le (**ram**-*shak*-uhl) ***adjective*** Rickety or likely to fall apart, as in *a ramshackle cottage.*

ranch (**ranch**) ***noun*** A large farm for cattle, sheep, or horses. ▸ ***noun, plural*** **ranches** ▸ ***noun*** **rancher** ▸ ***verb*** **ranch**

ran•cid (**ran**-sid) ***adjective*** **Rancid** food is food that has spoiled.

ran•dom (**ran**-duhm) ***adjective***
1. Without any order or purpose. ▸ ***adverb*** **randomly**
2. If you make a **random** selection from a group of items, each item in the group has the same chance of being chosen.
3. If you do something **at random,** you do it without any plan or method.

range (**raynj**)
1. ***verb*** To vary between one extreme and the other. ▸ ***noun*** **range**
2. ***noun*** The distance that a bullet or rocket can travel or a person can see.
3. ***noun*** A place for shooting at targets or testing rockets.
4. ***noun*** An area of open land used for a special purpose, as in *a cattle range.*
5. ***noun*** A long chain of mountains.
6. ***verb*** To wander over a large area.
7. ***noun*** A cooking stove.
▸ ***verb*** **ranging, ranged**

rang•er (**rayn**-jur) ***noun*** Someone in charge of a park or forest.

rank (**rangk**)
1. ***noun*** An official position or job level.
2. ***verb*** To assign a position to. ▸ **ranking, ranked** ▸ ***noun*** **rank**
3. ***noun*** Social class.
4. ***adjective*** Having a strong and unpleasant odor or taste.
5. ***adjective*** Complete or absolute, as in *a rank amateur.*
▸ ***adjective*** **ranker, rankest**

ran•sack (**ran**-sak) ***verb*** To search a place wildly, usually looking for things to steal. ▸ **ransacking, ransacked**

ran•som (**ran**-suhm) ***noun*** Money that is demanded before someone who is being held captive can be set free. ▸ ***verb*** **ransom**

rant (**rant**) ***verb*** To talk or shout in a loud and angry manner. ▸ **ranting, ranted**

rap (**rap**)
1. ***verb*** To hit something sharply and quickly. ▸ ***noun*** **rap**
2. ***noun*** A type of song in which the words are spoken in a rhythmical way to a musical background. ▸ ***noun*** **rapper** ▸ ***verb*** **rap**
3. ***verb*** *(slang)* To talk.
Rap sounds like **wrap.**
▸ ***verb*** **rapping, rapped**

rap•id (**rap**-id) ***adjective*** Very fast or quick, as in *a rapid heartbeat.* ▸ ***noun*** **rapidity** ▸ ***adverb*** **rapidly**

rap•ids (**rap**-idz) ***noun, plural*** A place in a river where the water flows very fast.

ra•pi•er (**ray**-pee-ur) ***noun*** A long sword with two edges, often used in duels in the 16th and 17th centuries.

rap•ture (**rap**-chur) ***noun*** Great happiness, joy, or delight.

rare (**rair**) ***adjective***
1. Not often seen, found, or happening. ▸ ***noun*** **rarity** ▸ ***adverb*** **rarely**
2. **Rare** meat is very lightly cooked.
3. Unusually good or excellent, as in *a rare beauty* or *a rare gift.*
▸ ***adjective*** **rarer, rarest**

R

ras•cal (**rass**-kuhl) ***noun***
1. Someone who is very mischievous.
2. A dishonest person.

rash (**rash**)
1. ***noun*** An occurrence of spots or red patches on the skin caused by an allergy or illness. ▸ ***noun, plural* rashes**
2. ***adjective*** If you are **rash,** you act quickly, without thinking first. ▸ **rasher, rashest** ▸ ***adverb* rashly**

rasp (**rasp**)
1. ***verb*** To speak in a harsh voice. ▸ **rasping, rasped**
2. ***noun*** A harsh, grating sound.
3. ***noun*** A coarse file used for smoothing metal or wood.

rasp•ber•ry (**raz**-*ber*-ee) ***noun***
1. A small, sweet, black or red berry with very small seeds. Raspberries grow on prickly bushes.
2. A dark purple-red color.
▸ ***noun, plural* raspberries**

rat (**rat**) ***noun***
1. A rodent that looks like a large mouse and has a long tail. Rats sometimes spread disease.
2. *(informal)* A disloyal or treacherous person.
3. rat race A very stressful routine or competition at work.

rate (**rayt**)
1. ***noun*** A degree of speed.
2. ***noun*** A charge or a fee.
3. ***noun*** A standard amount used to calculate a total.
4. ***verb*** To judge the quality or worth of a person or thing.
5. ***verb*** To place in a particular position or rank.
▸ ***noun* rating** ▸ ***verb* rating, rated**

rath•er (**ra**-THur) ***adverb***
1. Fairly or quite.
2. More willingly.
3. More correctly.

rat•i•fy (**rat**-uh-fye) ***verb*** To agree to or approve officially. ▸ **ratifies, ratifying, ratified** ▸ ***noun* ratification**

ra•ti•o (**ray**-shee-oh *or* **ray**-shoh) ***noun*** A comparison of two quantities or numbers using division. Ratios are usually expressed as fractions, or using the word "to."

ra•tion (**rash**-uhn *or* **ray**-shuhn)
1. ***noun*** A limited amount or share, especially of food. ▸ ***noun* rationing**
2. ***verb*** To give out in limited amounts. ▸ **rationing, rationed**

ra•tion•al (**ra**-shuh-nuhl) ***adjective***
1. Sensible and logical.
2. Calm, reasonable, and sane, as in *rational behavior.*
▸ ***adverb* rationally**

rat•tle (**rat**-uhl)
1. ***verb*** To make a rapid series of short, sharp noises. ▸ ***noun* rattle**
2. ***verb*** To talk or say quickly.
3. ***verb*** To upset or embarrass.
4. ***noun*** A baby's toy that makes a rattling sound.
5. ***noun*** The end part of a rattlesnake's tail that produces a rattling sound.
▸ ***verb* rattling, rattled**

rat•tle•snake (**rat**-uhl-*snayk*) ***noun*** A poisonous snake of North and South America with a tail that rattles as it shakes.

rau•cous (**raw**-kuhss) ***adjective***
1. Harsh or loud, as in *a raucous voice.*
2. Loud and rowdy, as in *a raucous party.*
▸ ***adverb* raucously**

rave (**rayv**) ***verb***
1. To speak in a wild, uncontrolled way.
2. *(informal)* To praise something enthusiastically.
▸ ***verb* raving, raved**

ra•vel (**rav**-uhl) ***verb*** To fray, or separate into single loose threads; to unravel. ▸ **raveling, raveled**

ra•ven (**ray**-vuhn) ***noun*** A large, black bird of the crow family.

rav•en•ous (**rav**-uh-nuhss) ***adjective*** Very hungry.

ra•vine (ruh-**veen**) ***noun*** A deep, narrow valley with steep sides.

rav•i•o•li (rav-ee-**oh**-lee) ***noun*** Square pockets of pasta that can be filled with meat, vegetables, or cheese.

raw (**raw**) ***adjective***
1. Food that is **raw** has not been cooked.
2. Not treated, processed, or refined.
3. Not trained or inexperienced, as in *a raw recruit.*
4. Having the skin rubbed off, as in *a raw wound.*
5. Unpleasantly damp and chilly, as in *raw weather.*
▸ ***adjective* rawer, rawest**

raw•hide (**raw**-*hide*) ***noun*** The skin of cattle or other animals before it has been soaked in a special solution and made into leather.

raw material ***noun*** A substance that is treated or processed and made into a useful finished product. Crude oil is the raw material from which we get gasoline.

ray (**ray**) ***noun***
1. A narrow beam of light or other radiation, as in *the rays of the sun.*
2. A type of fish with a flat body; large, winglike fins; and a small, whiplike tail.
3. A tiny amount, as in *a ray of hope.*
4. Part of a line that extends on and on in one direction from a single point.

ray•on (**ray**-on) ***noun*** A synthetic fabric made from cellulose that has the look and feel of silk.

ra•zor (**ray**-zur) ***noun*** An instrument with a sharp blade used to shave hair from the skin.

reach (**reech**)
1. ***verb*** To stretch out to something with your hand.
2. ***verb*** To extend, or to go as far as.
3. ***noun*** The distance a person or thing can reach.
4. ***noun*** An expanse, as in *vast reaches of the sea.*
5. ***verb*** To arrive somewhere.
6. ***verb*** To contact.
7. ***noun*** The act of reaching.
▸ ***verb* reaches, reaching, reached**
▸ ***noun, plural* reaches**

re•act (ree-**akt**) ***verb***
1. To respond to something that happens.
2. If a substance **reacts** with another, a chemical change takes place in one or both of the substances as they are mixed together.
▸ ***verb* reacting, reacted**

re•act•ion (ree-**ak**-shuhn) ***noun*** An action in response to something; a response.

re•ac•tion•ar•y (ree-**ak**-shuh-ner-ee) ***adjective*** If someone is **reactionary,** the person is against change and wants to return things to the way they were in the past. ▸ ***noun* reactionary**

re•ac•tor (ree-**ak**-tur) ***noun*** A large machine in which nuclear energy is produced by splitting atoms under controlled conditions.

read (**reed**) ***verb***
1. To look at written or printed words and understand what they mean.
2. To say aloud something that is written.
3. To learn by reading.
4. To understand some form of communication.
5. To show or to register.
▸ ***verb* reading, read (red)**

read•i•ly (**red**-uhl-ee) ***adverb*** Easily or willingly.

read•y (**red**-ee) ***adjective***
1. Prepared.
2. Willing.
3. Likely or about to do something.
4. Quick, as in *a ready answer.*
▸ ***adjective* readier, readiest**

real (**ree**-uhl *or* **reel**) ***adjective***
1. True and not imaginary.
2. Genuine and not artificial.

real estate ***noun*** Land and the buildings that are on it.

re•al•is•tic (ree-uh-**liss**-tik) ***adjective***
1. Very much like the real thing, as in *a realistic painting.*
2. If you are **realistic,** you view things as they really are.
▸ ***noun* realism** ▸ ***adverb* realistically**

R

R

re•al•i•ty (ree-**al**-uh-tee) ***noun***
1. Truth, or the actual situation.
2. The facts of life that must be faced.
▸ ***noun, plural*** **realities**

re•al•ize (**ree**-uh-lize) ***verb***
1. To become aware that something is true.
2. To make real or to achieve.
▸ ***verb*** **realizing, realized** ▸ ***noun*** **realization**

re•al•ly (**ree**-uh-lee *or* **ree**-lee) ***adverb***
1. Actually, or in reality.
2. Very.

realm (**relm**) ***noun***
1. An area or field of knowledge or interest, as in *the realm of science.*
2. A kingdom.

reap (**reep**) ***verb***
1. To cut grain or to gather a crop by hand or machine.
2. To get as a reward.
▸ ***verb*** **reaping, reaped**

re•ap•pear (ree-uh-**pihr**) ***verb*** To come into sight again. ▸ **reappearing, reappeared** ▸ ***noun*** **reappearance**

rear (**rihr**)
1. ***verb*** To breed and bring up young animals.
2. ***verb*** To care for and raise.
3. ***noun*** The back of something.
▸ ***adjective*** **rear**
4. ***verb*** If a horse **rears,** it rises up on its back legs.
5. ***verb*** To lift up.
▸ ***verb*** **rearing, reared**

re•ar•range (ree-uh-**raynj**) ***verb*** To arrange things differently. ▸ **rearranging, rearranged**

rea•son (**ree**-zuhn)
1. ***noun*** The cause of something, or the motive behind someone's action.
2. ***noun*** An explanation or an excuse.
3. ***verb*** To think in a logical way. ▸ ***noun*** **reason**
4. ***verb*** If you **reason** with someone, you try to persuade the person that what you suggest is sensible.
▸ ***verb*** **reasoning, reasoned**

rea•son•a•ble (**ree**-zuhn-uh-buhl) ***adjective***
1. Fair.
2. Sensible.
3. Costing a fair price. ▸ ***adverb*** **reasonably**

rea•son•ing (**ree**-zuhn-ing) ***noun***
1. The process of thinking in an orderly fashion, drawing conclusions from facts.
2. The reasons used in this process.

re•as•sure (ree-uh-**shur**) ***verb*** To calm someone and give the person confidence or courage. ▸ **reassuring, reassured** ▸ ***noun*** **reassurance** ▸ ***adjective*** **reassuring**

re•bel (**reb**-uhl) ***noun*** Someone who fights against a government or against the people in charge of something.
▸ ***verb*** **rebel** (ri-**bel**) ▸ ***adjective*** **rebellious** (ri-**bel**-yuhss)

re•bel•lion (ri-**bel**-yuhn) ***noun***
1. Armed fight against a government.
2. Any struggle against the people in charge of something.

re•boot (ree-**boot**) ***verb*** To start a computer again.▸ **rebooting, rebooted**

re•buke (ri-**byook**) ***verb*** To scold someone because he or she has done something wrong. ▸ **rebuking, rebuked** ▸ ***noun*** **rebuke**

re•call (ri-**kawl**) ***verb***
1. To remember something.
2. To order someone to return.
3. To call back a purchased product that has a defect.
▸ ***verb*** **recalling, recalled** ▸ ***noun*** **recall** (ri-**kawl** *or* **ree**-kawl)

re•cap (**ree**-kap) ***verb*** *(informal)* To repeat the main points of what has been said. *Recap* is short for *recapitulate.*
▸ **recapping, recapped** ▸ ***noun*** **recap**

re•cede (ri-**seed**) ***verb***
1. To move back.
2. To fade gradually.
▸ ***verb*** **receding, receded** ▸ ***adjective*** **receding**

re•ceipt (ri-**seet**) ***noun*** A piece of paper showing that money, goods, mail, or a service has been received.

R

re•ceive (ri-**seev**) ***verb***
1. To get or accept something.
2. To experience.
3. To greet or to welcome.
▸ ***verb*** **receiving, received**

re•ceiv•er (ri-**see**-vur) ***noun***
1. The part of a telephone that you hold in your hand.
2. A piece of equipment that receives radio or television signals and changes them into sounds or pictures.
3. A person who receives something.

re•cent (**ree**-suhnt) ***adjective***
Happening, made, or done a short time ago. ▸ ***adverb*** **recently**

re•cep•ta•cle (ri-**cep**-ti-kuhl) ***noun***
A container.

re•cep•tion (ri-**sep**-shuhn) ***noun***
1. The way in which someone or something is received.
2. A formal party.

re•cep•tion•ist (ri-**sep**-shuh-nist) ***noun***
A person whose job is to greet people in an office, clinic, etc., or when they call on the telephone.

re•cess (**ree**-sess *or* ri-**sess**) ***noun***
1. A break from work for rest or relaxation. ▸ ***verb*** **recess**
2. A part of a room set back from the main area.
▸ ***noun, plural*** **recesses** ▸ ***adjective*** **recessed**

re•ces•sion (ri-**sesh**-uhn) ***noun*** A time when business slows down and more workers than usual are unemployed.

rec•i•pe (**ress**-i-pee) ***noun*** Instructions for preparing and cooking food.

re•cip•i•ent (ri-**sip**-ee-uhnt) ***noun***
A person who receives something.

re•cit•al (ri-**sye**-tuhl) ***noun***
1. A musical performance by a single performer or by a small group of musicians or dancers.
2. A detailed account or report.

re•cite (ri-**site**) ***verb***
1. To say aloud something that you have learned by heart.
2. To tell about in detail.
▸ ***verb*** **reciting, recited** ▸ ***noun*** **recitation** (*ress*-i-**tay**-shuhn)

reck•less (**rek**-liss) ***adjective*** If you are **reckless,** you are careless about your own or other people's safety. ▸ ***adverb*** **recklessly**

reck•on (**rek**-uhn) ***verb***
1. To calculate or to count up. ▸ ***noun*** **reckoning**
2. To think or to have an opinion.
▸ ***verb*** **reckoning, reckoned**

re•claim (ri-**klaym**) ***verb***
1. To get back something that is yours.
2. To make land suitable for farming, etc., by clearing it or draining it. ▸ ***noun*** **reclamation** (*rek*-luh-**may**-shuhn)
▸ ***verb*** **reclaiming, reclaimed**

re•cline (ri-**kline**) ***verb*** To lean or lie back. ▸ **reclining, reclined**

rec•og•nize (**rek**-uhg-*nize*) ***verb***
1. To see someone and know who the person is. ▸ ***adjective*** **recognizable** ▸ ***adverb*** **recognizably**
2. To understand a situation and accept it as true or right.
▸ ***verb*** **recognizing, recognized**
▸ ***noun*** **recognition** (*rek*-uhg-**ni**-shuhn)

rec•ol•lect (rek-uh-**lekt**) ***verb*** To remember or to recall. ▸ **recollecting, recollected** ▸ ***noun*** **recollection**

rec•om•mend (rek-uh-**mend**) ***verb***
1. To suggest as being good or worthy.
2. To advise.
▸ ***verb*** **recommending, recommended** ▸ ***noun*** **recommendation**

rec•on•cile (**rek**-uhn-*sile*) ***verb***
1. To make up or become friendly again after an argument or a fight. ▸ ***noun*** **reconciliation**
2. If you **reconcile yourself** to something, you decide to put up with it.
▸ ***verb*** **reconciling, reconciled**

re•con•sid•er (*ree*-kuhn-**sid**-ur) ***verb***
To think again about a previous decision, especially with the idea of making a change. ▸ **reconsidering, reconsidered**

R

re•con•struct (*ree*-kuhn-**struhkt**) ***verb***
1. To rebuild something that has been destroyed.
2. To carefully piece together past events.
▸ ***verb*** **reconstructed, reconstructing**
▸ ***noun*** **reconstruction**

rec•ord
1. (ri-**kord**) ***verb*** To write down information so that it can be kept.
▸ ***noun*** **record (rek**-urd)
2. (**rek**-urd) ***noun*** The facts about what a person or group has done.
3. (**rek**-urd) ***noun*** A disk with grooves on which sound, especially music, is recorded to be played by a phonograph. Also called *a phonograph record.*
4. (ri-**kord**) ***verb*** To put music or other sounds onto a tape, compact disk, or record.
5. (**rek**-urd) ***noun*** If you set a **record** in something such as a sport, you do it better than anyone has ever done it before.
▸ ***verb*** **recording, recorded**

re•cord•er (ri-**kor**-dur) ***noun***
1. A machine for recording sounds on magnetic tape.
2. A woodwind musical instrument that is a form of flute. You play the recorder by blowing into the mouthpiece and covering holes with your fingers to make different notes.

re•cord•ing (ri-**kor**-ding) ***noun***
1. A tape, compact disk, or record.
2. The sounds on a tape, compact disk, or record.

re•count
1. (ri-**kount**) ***verb*** To narrate or tell about.
2. (ree-**kount**) ***verb*** To count again. Also spelled **re-count.**
▸ ***verb*** **recounting, recounted**
3. (**ree**-*kount*) ***noun*** An instance of recounting. Also spelled **re-count.**

re•cov•er (ri-**kuhv**-ur) ***verb***
1. To get better after an illness or a difficulty.
2. To get back something that has been lost or stolen.
3. To make up for.
▸ ***verb*** **recovering, recovered** ▸ ***noun*** **recovery**

re-cov•er (ree-**kov**-ur) ***verb*** To cover again. ▸ **re-covering, re-covered**

rec•re•a•tion (rek-ree-**ay**-shuhn) ***noun*** The games, sports, hobbies, etc., that people enjoy in their spare time.
▸ ***adjective*** **recreational**

re•cruit (ri-**kroot**)
1. ***noun*** Someone who has recently joined the armed forces or any group or organization.
2. ***verb*** To get a person to join.
▸ **recruiting, recruited** ▸ ***noun*** **recruitment**

rec•tan•gle (**rek**-*tang*-guhl) ***noun*** A shape with four sides and four right angles. ▸ ***adjective*** **rectangular**

rec•ti•fy (**rek**-tuh-*fye*) ***verb*** To make right or correct, as in *to rectify a mistake.*
▸ **rectifies, rectifying, rectified**

rec•tum (**rek**-tuhm) ***noun*** The lowest portion of the large intestine, ending at the anus. ▸ ***adjective*** **rectal**

re•cu•per•ate (ri-**koo**-puh-*rate*) ***verb*** To recover slowly from an illness or injury. ▸ **recuperating, recuperated**
▸ ***noun*** **recuperation**

re•cur (ri-**kur**) ***verb*** To appear or happen again. ▸ **recurring, recurred**
▸ ***noun*** **recurrence** ▸ ***adjective*** **recurrent**

re•cy•cle (ree-**sye**-kuhl) ***verb*** To process old items such as glass, plastic, newspapers, and aluminum cans so that they can be used to make new products.
▸ **recycling, recycled** ▸ ***adjective*** **recyclable**

red (**red**) ***noun*** One of the three primary colors, along with blue and yellow. Red is the color of beets and blood.
▸ ***adjective*** **red, reddish**

red blood cell ***noun*** A cell in your blood that carries oxygen from your lungs to all the tissues and cells of your body.

red•coat (**red**-*koht*) ***noun*** A British soldier during the time of the Revolutionary War and later wars. These soldiers' uniforms included bright red coats.

Red Cross ***noun*** An international organization that helps victims of disasters of all kinds, from floods and earthquakes to war and famine.

re•deem (ri-**deem**) ***verb***
1. To exchange something for money or merchandise.
2. To save, or to make up for.
▸ ***verb*** **redeeming, redeemed** ▸ ***noun*** **redemption** (ri-**demp**-shuhn)

red-hand•ed (**han**-did) ***adjective*** If you catch someone **red-handed,** you catch the person in the act of doing something wrong.

red herring ***noun*** Something that distracts a person's attention from the real issue.

red tape ***noun*** Rules, regulations, and paperwork that make it difficult to get things done.

re•duce (ri-**dooss** *or* ri-**dyooss**) ***verb***
1. To make something smaller or less.
▸ ***noun*** **reduction** (ri-**duhk**-shuhn)
2. To lose body weight by dieting.
▸ ***verb*** **reducing, reduced**

re•dun•dant (ri-**duhn**-duhnt) ***adjective*** Using too many words for what you mean to say or write. ▸ ***noun*** **redundancy**

red•wood (**red**-*wood*) ***noun*** An evergreen tree found along the western coast of the United States, especially in northern California. The world's tallest redwood, found in Humboldt County, California, is 362 feet (110 meters) tall.

reed (**reed**) ***noun***
1. A tall grass with long, thin, hollow stems that grows in or near water.
2. A piece of thin wood, metal, or plastic in the mouthpieces of some musical instruments, such as the clarinet, oboe, and saxophone. When you blow over the reed, it vibrates and makes a sound.

reef (**reef**) ***noun***
1. A strip of rock, sand, or coral close to the surface of the ocean or another body of water.
2. reef knot A square knot.

reek (**reek**) ***verb*** To smell strongly of something unpleasant. **Reek** sounds like **wreak.** ▸ **reeking, reeked**

reel (**reel**)
1. ***verb*** To stagger around unsteadily.
2. ***noun*** A spool on which thread, film, etc., is wound. ▸ ***verb*** **reel**
3. ***noun*** A type of folk dance that is lively and spirited.
4. ***verb*** If you **reel** something **off,** you say it very fast.
▸ ***verb*** **reeling, reeled**

re•e•lect (*ree*-ee-**lekt**) ***verb*** To elect for another term, as in *to reelect the president.* ▸ **reelecting, reelected** ▸ ***noun*** **reelection**

re•en•try (ree-**en**-tree) ***noun*** The return of a spacecraft or missile to the earth's atmosphere. ▸ ***noun, plural*** **reentries** ▸ ***verb*** **reenter**

ref (**ref**) Short for **referee.**

re•fer (ri-**fur**) ***verb***
1. If you **refer** to a book, you look in it for information.
2. If you **refer** to something while talking or writing, you mention it.
3. To send someone for additional or more detailed information, advice, etc.
▸ ***noun*** **referral**
▸ ***verb*** **referring, referred**

ref•er•ee (*ref*-uh-**ree**) ***noun*** Someone who supervises a sports match or a game and makes sure that the players obey the rules. ▸ ***verb*** **referee**

ref•er•ence (**ref**-uh-renss) ***noun***
1. A mention of someone or something.
2. A written statement about someone's character and abilities.
3. A book, magazine, etc., that you use in order to produce a piece of work.

R

reference book ***noun*** A book that you use to find information quickly and easily.

ref•er•en•dum (*ref*-uh-**ren**-duhm) ***noun*** A vote by the people on a public measure. ▸ ***noun, plural*** **referendums** *or* **referenda**

re•fill (ree-**fil**) ***verb*** To fill something again. ▸ **refilling, refilled** ▸ ***noun*** **refill** (**ree**-fil)

re•fine (ri-**fine**) ***verb*** To purify, or to remove unwanted matter from a substance such as oil or sugar. ▸ **refining, refined**

re•fined (ri-**fined**) ***adjective***
1. A **refined** person is very polite and has elegant manners and tastes.
2. Purified or processed, as in *refined sugar.*

re•fin•er•y (ri-**fye**-nuh-ree) ***noun*** A factory where raw materials are purified and made into finished products. ▸ ***noun, plural*** **refineries**

re•fit (ree-**fit**) ***verb*** To repair something, or to supply it with new parts or equipment. ▸ **refitting, refitted**

re•flect (ri-**flekt**) ***verb***
1. To show an image of something on a shiny surface such as a mirror.
2. When rays of light or heat are **reflected,** they bounce off an object.
3. To think carefully.
4. To bring blame or discredit.
5. To show or to express.
▸ ***verb*** **reflecting, reflected** ▸ ***noun*** **reflection**

re•flec•tive (ri-**flek**-tiv) ***adjective***
1. Acting like a mirror.
2. Serious and thoughtful. ▸ ***adverb*** **reflectively**

re•flec•tor (ri-**flek**-tur) ***noun*** A shiny surface or device that bounces back light or heat.

re•flex (**ree**-fleks) ***noun*** An automatic action that happens without a person's control or effort. ▸ ***noun, plural*** **reflexes** ▸ ***adjective*** **reflex**

reflex angle ***noun*** An angle between 180 degrees and 360 degrees.

re•for•est (ree-**for**-est) ***verb*** To replant trees where all the original trees were cut down or destroyed by fire or disaster. ▸ **reforesting, reforested** ▸ ***noun*** **reforestation**

re•form (ri-**form**)
1. ***verb*** To improve something that is unsatisfactory, or to correct something that is wrong.
2. ***verb*** To change for the better.
3. ***noun*** An improvement, or the correcting of something unsatisfactory, as in *health care reform.*
▸ ***verb*** **reforming, reformed**

re•for•ma•to•ry (ri-**for**-muh-*tor*-ee) ***noun*** A special school or institution for young people who have broken the law. ▸ ***noun, plural*** **reformatories**

re•fract (ri-**frakt**) ***verb*** When a light ray or a sound wave is **refracted,** it changes direction because it has traveled from one medium into another. ▸ **refracting, refracted** ▸ ***noun*** **refraction**

re•frain (ri-**frayn**)
1. ***verb*** To stop yourself from doing something. ▸ **refraining, refrained**
2. ***noun*** A regularly repeated part of a song or poem.

re•fresh (ri-**fresh**) ***verb*** If something **refreshes** you, it makes you feel fresh and strong again. ▸ **refreshes, refreshing, refreshed** ▸ ***adjective*** **refreshing**

re•fresh•ments (ri-**fresh**-muhnts) ***noun, plural*** Drink and food.

re•frig•er•a•tor (ri-**frij**-uh-*ray*-tur) ***noun*** A cabinet with a very cold interior, used for storing food and drink. ▸ ***noun*** **refrigeration** ▸ ***verb*** **refrigerate**

re•fu•el (ree-**fyoo**-uhl) ***verb*** To take on more fuel. ▸ **refueling, refueled**

ref•uge (**ref**-yooj) ***noun***
1. Protection or shelter from danger or trouble.
2. A place that provides protection or shelter, as in *a wildlife refuge.*

ref•u•gee (*ref*-yuh-**jee** *or* **ref**-yuh-jee) ***noun*** A person who is forced to leave his or her home because of war, persecution, or a natural disaster.

re•fund (ri-**fuhnd**) ***verb*** To give money back to the person who paid it. ▸ **refunding, refunded** ▸ ***noun*** **refund** (**ree**-fuhnd)

re•fuse
1. (ri-**fyooz**) ***verb*** To say you will not do something or accept something. ▸ **refusing, refused** ▸ ***noun*** **refusal**
2. (**ref**-yooss) ***noun*** Rubbish or trash.

re•gal (**ree**-guhl) ***adjective*** To do with or fit for a king or queen, as in *a regal manner.* ▸ ***adverb*** **regally**

re•gale (ri-**gale**) ***verb***
1. To give great pleasure, delight, or entertainment.
2. To entertain lavishly with a lot of food and drink.
▸ ***verb*** **regaling, regaled**

re•gard (ri-**gard**)
1. ***verb*** To have an opinion about something.
2. ***noun*** A good opinion; esteem.
3. ***verb*** To look at closely.
4. ***verb*** To respect or to consider.
5. ***noun*** Respect or consideration, as in *no regard for danger.*
6. **regards** ***noun, plural*** If someone sends you his or her **regards,** the person sends you best wishes.
▸ ***verb*** **regarding, regarded**

re•gard•ing (ri-**gar**-ding) ***preposition*** About or concerning.

re•gard•less (ri-**gard**-liss)
1. ***adjective*** Without considering anything or anyone else.
2. ***adverb*** In spite of everything.

re•gat•ta (ri-**gat**-uh) ***noun*** A boat race, or a series of boat races.

reg•gae (**reg**-ay) ***noun*** A type of rhythmic popular music that comes from the West Indies.

re•gime (ri-**zheem**) ***noun*** A government that rules a people during a specific period of time.

reg•i•ment (**rej**-uh-muhnt) ***noun*** A military unit made up of two or more battalions.

re•gion (**ree**-juhn) ***noun*** An area or a district. ▸ ***adjective*** **regional** ▸ ***adverb*** **regionally**

reg•is•ter (**rej**-uh-stur)
1. ***noun*** A book in which names or official records are kept, as in *a class register.*
2. ***verb*** To enter something on an official list.
3. ***noun*** The range of notes produced by a musical instrument or a voice.
4. ***verb*** To show an emotion.
5. ***noun*** A machine that automatically records and counts, as in *a cash register.*
6. ***verb*** To show on a scale or other device.
▸ ***verb*** **registering, registered** ▸ ***noun*** **registration**

registered nurse ***noun*** A nurse who has completed certain training and is licensed by the state in which he or she practices.

re•gret (ri-**gret**) ***verb*** To be sad or sorry about something. ▸ **regretting, regretted** ▸ ***noun*** **regret** ▸ ***adjective*** **regretful**

re•gret•ta•ble (ri-**gret**-uh-buhl) ***adjective*** If something is **regrettable,** it is unfortunate and you wish that it had not happened. ▸ ***adverb*** **regrettably**

reg•u•lar (**reg**-yuh-lur) ***adjective***
1. Usual or normal.
2. According to habit or usual behavior, as in *a regular customer.*
3. Always happening or occurring at the same time, as in *regular meals.*
4. Even or steady, as in *a regular heartbeat.*
5. A **regular** verb is one whose main parts are formed according to a regular pattern. *Love* is a regular verb because its past tense is *loved.* ▸ ***noun*** **regularity** (*reg*-yuh-**la**-ri-tee) ▸ ***adverb*** **regularly**

reg•u•late (**reg**-yuh-late) ***verb***
1. To control or to manage.
2. To adjust or to keep at some standard.
▸ ***verb*** **regulating, regulated**

R

reg•u•la•tion (reg-yuh-**lay**-shuhn) ***noun***
1. An official rule or order, as in *the regulations of a sport.*
2. The act of controlling or adjusting something, as in *government regulation of the banking industry.*

re•gur•gi•tate (ree-**gur**-juh-*tate*) ***verb*** To bring food from the stomach back into the mouth. ▸ **regurgitating, regurgitated**

re•hearse (ri-**hurss**) ***verb***
1. To practice for a public performance.
2. To review or recount something in order.
▸ ***verb*** **rehearsing, rehearsed** ▸ ***noun*** **rehearsal**

reign (**rayn**) ***verb***
1. To rule as a king or queen. ▸ ***noun*** **reign**
2. To be widespread.
Reign sounds like **rain** and **rein.**
▸ ***verb*** **reigning, reigned**

re•im•burse (*ree*-im-**burss**) ***verb*** To pay someone back the money the person has had to spend on your behalf. ▸ **reimbursing, reimbursed** ▸ ***noun*** **reimbursement**

rein (**rayn**) ***noun***
1. reins *noun, plural* Straps attached to a bridle to control or guide a horse.
2. Any method or device for controlling.
Rein sounds like **rain** and **reign.**

rein•deer (**rayn**-*dihr*) ***noun*** A deer that lives in the earth's far north regions. Both male and female reindeer have large, branching antlers. ▸ ***noun, plural*** **reindeer**

re•in•force (*ree*-in-**forss**) ***verb*** To strengthen something. ▸ **reinforcing, reinforced**

re•in•force•ment (*ree*-in-**forss**-muhnt) ***noun***
1. Something that strengthens.
2. reinforcements *noun, plural* Extra troops sent to strengthen a fighting force.

re•ject
1. (ri-**jekt**) ***verb*** To refuse to accept something. ▸ **rejecting, rejected** ▸ ***noun*** **rejection**
2. (**ree**-jekt) ***noun*** Something that has been discarded.

re•joice (ri-**joiss**) ***verb*** To be very happy about something. ▸ **rejoicing, rejoiced**

re•lapse (ri-**laps** *or* **ree**-laps) ***noun*** The act of falling back to a former condition, especially the return of an illness after you were feeling better. ▸ ***verb*** **relapse** (ri-**laps**)

re•late (ri-**late**) ***verb***
1. To narrate, or to tell the story of.
2. If things **relate** to each other, there is a connection between them.
3. If people **relate** to each other, they get along well together or understand each other.
▸ ***verb*** **relating, related**

re•lat•ed (ri-**lay**-tid) ***adjective***
1. If you are **related** to someone, you are both part of the same family.
2. Having some connection, as in *related events.*

re•la•tion (ri-**lay**-shuhn) ***noun***
1. A connection between two or more things.
2. A member of your family.

re•la•tion•ship (ri-**lay**-shuhn-ship) ***noun***
1. The way in which people get along together.
2. The way in which things are connected.

rel•a•tive (**rel**-uh-tiv)
1. *noun* A member of your family.
2. *adjective* Compared with others.

rel•a•tive•ly (**rel**-uh-tiv-lee) ***adverb*** Compared with others.

re•lax (ri-**laks**) ***verb***
1. To rest and take things easy.
2. To become less tense and anxious.
3. To make less strict.
▸ ***verb*** **relaxes, relaxing, relaxed**
▸ ***noun*** **relaxation** (*ree*-lak-**say**-shuhn)

re•lay (**ree**-lay)
1. *noun* A team race in which members

of the team take turns running and passing a baton from one runner to the next.
2. ***verb*** To pass a message on to someone else. ▸ **relaying, relayed**

re•lease (ri-**leess**) ***verb***
1. To free something or someone.
2. If a CD, film, etc., is **released,** it is made available to the public for the first time.
▸ ***verb*** **releasing, released** ▸ ***noun*** **release**

rel•e•gate (**rel**-uh-gate) ***verb***
1. To send to a place or position of less importance.
2. To turn over or assign a task to another person.
▸ ***verb*** **relegating, relegated**

re•lent (ri-**lent**) ***verb*** To become less strict or more merciful. ▸ **relenting, relented**

re•lent•less (ri-**lent**-liss) ***adjective*** Endless and determined. ▸ ***adverb*** **relentlessly**

rel•e•vant (**rel**-uh-vuhnt) ***adjective*** If something is **relevant,** it is directly concerned with what is being discussed or dealt with. ▸ ***noun*** **relevance**

re•li•a•ble (ri-**lye**-uh-buhl) ***adjective*** Trustworthy or dependable. ▸ ***noun*** **reliability** ▸ ***adverb*** **reliably**

rel•ic (**rel**-ik) ***noun***
1. Something that has survived from the past.
2. Some object belonging to a saint or other holy person.

re•lief (ri-**leef**) ***noun***
1. A feeling of freedom from pain or worry.
2. Aid given to people in special need, as in *flood relief.*
3. Freedom from a job or duty, especially when one person takes over for another.
4. Figures or details that are raised from a surface.
5. relief map A map that uses shading or a model that uses relief to show areas of high and low ground.

re•lieve (ri-**leev**) ***verb***
1. To ease someone's trouble or pain.
2. If you **relieve** someone, you take over a duty from the person.
▸ ***verb*** **relieving, relieved**

re•lig•ion (ri-**lij**-uhn) ***noun***
1. Belief in God or gods.
2. A specific system of belief, faith, and worship. Some world religions are Buddhism, Christianity, Hinduism, Islam, and Judaism.
3. The practice of your belief through worship, obedience, and prayer.
▸ ***adjective*** **religious**

rel•ish (**rel**-ish)
1. ***verb*** To enjoy something greatly.
▸ **relishes, relishing, relished** ▸ ***noun*** **relish**
2. ***noun*** A mixture of spices and chopped vegetables, such as olives or pickles, used to flavor food. ▸ ***noun, plural*** **relishes**

re•luc•tant (ri-**luhk**-tuhnt) ***adjective*** If you are **reluctant,** you do not want to do something. ▸ ***noun*** **reluctance** ▸ ***adverb*** **reluctantly**

re•ly (ri-**lye**) ***verb*** If you **rely on** something or someone, you need and trust the thing or person. ▸ **relies, relying, relied** ▸ ***noun*** **reliance** ▸ ***adjective*** **reliant**

re•main (ri-**mayn**) ***verb***
1. To stay in the same place.
2. To be left behind or left over.
3. To continue being.
▸ ***verb*** **remaining, remained**

re•main•der (ri-**mayn**-dur) ***noun***
1. The amount left over.
2. The number found when one number is subtracted from another.
3. The number left over when one number cannot be divided evenly by another.

re•mains (ri-**maynz**) ***noun, plural***
1. Things left over.
2. Parts of something that was once alive.
3. A dead body.

R

re•mark (ri-**mark**) ***verb***
1. To make a comment about something.
2. To notice or to observe.
▸ ***verb*** **remarking, remarked** ▸ ***noun*** **remark**

re•mark•a•ble (ri-**mar**-kuh-buhl) ***adjective*** Worth noticing; extraordinary. ▸ ***adverb*** **remarkably**

re•me•di•al (ri-**mee**-dee-uhl) ***adjective*** Intended to help or correct something, as in *a remedial reading program.*

rem•e•dy (**rem**-uh-dee) ***noun*** Something that relieves pain, cures a disease, or corrects a disorder. ▸ ***noun, plural*** **remedies** ▸ ***verb*** **remedy**

re•mem•ber (ri-**mem**-bur) ***verb***
1. To recall or to bring back to mind.
2. To keep in mind carefully.
▸ ***verb*** **remembering, remembered**

re•mind (ri-**minde**) ***verb*** To make someone remember something. ▸ **reminding, reminded**

re•mind•er (ri-**minde**-ur) ***noun*** Something that helps a person remember.

rem•i•nisce (*rem*-uh-**niss**) ***verb*** To think or talk about the past and things that you remember. ▸ **reminiscing, reminisced** ▸ ***noun*** **reminiscence**

re•mis•sion (ri-**mish**-uhn) ***noun*** If a person with a disease starts to have less pain or the symptoms of the disease start to disappear, the disease is in **remission.**

rem•nant (**rem**-nuhnt) ***noun*** A piece or part of something that is left over, as in *a remnant of material.*

re•mod•el (ree-**mod**-uhl) ***verb*** To make a major change to the structure or design of something. ▸ **remodeling, remodeled**

re•morse (ri-**morss**) ***noun*** A strong feeling of guilt and regret about something wrong that you have done. ▸ ***adjective*** **remorseful** ▸ ***adverb*** **remorsefully**

re•mote (ri-**moht**) ***adjective***
1. Far away, isolated, or distant, as in *a remote island.*
2. Extremely small or slight, as in *a remote possibility.*
▸ ***adjective*** **remoter, remotest** ▸ ***noun*** **remoteness** ▸ ***adverb*** **remotely**

remote control ***noun*** A system for operating machines from a distance, usually by radio signals or by a light beam. ▸ ***adjective*** **remote-controlled**

re•move (ri-**moov**) ***verb***
1. To take something away.
2. To take off or away.
▸ ***verb*** **removing, removed** ▸ ***noun*** **removal**

Re•nais•sance (**ren**-uh-sahnss) ***noun*** The revival of art and learning in Europe between the 14th and 16th centuries. The Renaissance was inspired by an interest in the ancient Greeks and Romans.

ren•der (**ren**-dur) ***verb***
1. To make or cause to become.
2. To give or to deliver.
▸ ***verb*** **rendering, rendered**

ren•dez•vous (**ron**-duh-*voo or* **ron**-*day*-voo) ***noun***
1. An appointment to meet at a certain time or place.
2. The place chosen for a meeting.
▸ ***verb*** **rendezvous**

re•new (ri-**noo** *or* ri-**nyoo**) ***verb***
1. To replace something old with something new.
2. To start something again after a break.
3. To extend the period of a library loan, club membership, magazine subscription, etc.
▸ ***verb*** **renewing, renewed** ▸ ***noun*** **renewal** ▸ ***adjective*** **renewable,** ***adjective*** **renewed**

renewable energy ***noun*** Power from sources that can never be used up, such as wind, waves, and the sun.

ren•o•vate (**ren**-uh-*vate*) ***verb*** To restore something to good condition, or to make it more modern. ▸ **renovating, renovated** ▸ ***noun*** **renovation**

re•nowned (ri-**nound**) ***adjective*** Famous or well-known. ▸ ***noun*** **renown**

rent (**rent**)
1. ***noun*** Money paid by a tenant to the owner of a property in return for living in it or using it.
2. ***verb*** To get or give the right to use something in return for payment.
▸ **renting, rented**

rent•al (**ren**-tuhl) ***noun***
1. The amount paid to rent something.
2. Something that is hired or rented, such as a car or property.
▸ ***adjective*** **rental**

re•pair (ri-**pair**) ***verb*** To make something work again, or to put back together something that is broken.
▸ **repairing, repaired** ▸ ***noun*** **repair**

re•pa•tri•a•tion (ree-*pay*-tree-**ay**-shuhn) ***noun*** The return of someone to the country where he or she was born or where he or she is a citizen, as in *the repatriation of the prisoners of war.* ▸ ***verb*** **repatriate**

re•pay (ri-**pay**) ***verb***
1. To pay or give something back.
2. To give or do something in return.
▸ ***verb*** **repaying, repaid** ▸ ***noun*** **repayment**

re•peal (ri-**peel**) ***verb*** To do away with something officially, such as a law.
▸ **repealing, repealed** ▸ ***noun*** **repeal**

re•peat (ri-**peet**) ***verb*** To say or do something again. ▸ **repeating, repeated** ▸ ***noun*** **repeat** (ri-**peet** *or* **ree**-peet)

re•pel (ri-**pel**) ***verb***
1. To drive away.
2. To disgust someone.
▸ ***verb*** **repelling, repelled**

re•pel•lent (ri-**pel**-uhnt)
1. ***noun*** A chemical that keeps insects and other pests away, as in *a mosquito repellent.*
2. ***adjective*** Disgusting, as in *a repellent smell.*

re•pent (ri-**pent**) ***verb*** To be deeply sorry for the bad things that you have done. ▸ **repenting, repented** ▸ ***noun*** **repentance** ▸ ***adjective*** **repentant**

rep•er•toire (**rep**-ur-*twar*) ***noun*** The collection of songs, jokes, stories, etc., that an entertainer is prepared to perform in public.

rep•e•ti•tion (rep-uh-**tish**-uhn) ***noun*** The repeating of words or actions.
▸ ***adjective*** **repetitious,** ***adjective*** **repetitive** (ri-**pet**-i-tiv)

re•place (ri-**playss**) ***verb***
1. To put one thing or person in place of another.
2. To put something back where it was.
3. To provide substitutes for.
▸ ***verb*** **replacing, replaced** ▸ ***noun*** **replacement**

re•play
1. (ri-**play**) ***verb*** To play back a tape in order to see or hear something again.
▸ **replaying, replayed** ▸ ***noun*** **replay** (**ree**-play)
2. (**ree**-play) ***noun*** A second contest between two teams or players when the first contest has ended in a tie. ▸ ***verb*** **replay** (ri-**play**)

rep•li•ca (**rep**-luh-kuh) ***noun*** An exact copy of something, especially a copy made on a smaller scale than the original. ▸ ***verb*** **replicate**

re•ply (ri-**plye**) ***verb*** To give an answer or a response. ▸ **replies, replying, replied** ▸ ***noun*** **reply**

re•port (ri-**port**)
1. ***noun*** A written or spoken account of something that has happened.
2. ***verb*** To give a report.
3. ***verb*** If you **report** someone, you make an official complaint about the person.
4. ***verb*** To appear for duty.
5. ***verb*** If you **report to** someone, you work for him or her.
▸ ***verb*** **reporting, reported**

report card ***noun*** A listing of a student's grades that is compiled and sent home several times a year. A report card can also include comments from a teacher about a student's behavior.

R

R

re•port•er (ri-**por**-tur) ***noun*** Someone who gathers and reports the news for radio, television, or a newspaper or magazine.

rep•re•sent (*rep*-ri-**zent**) ***verb***
1. To speak or act for someone else.
2. To stand for something.
▸ ***verb* representing, represented**
▸ ***noun* representation**

rep•re•sen•ta•tive (*rep*-ri-**zen**-tuh-tiv) ***noun***
1. Someone who is chosen to speak or act for others.
2. A person or thing that is typical of a group. ▸ ***adjective* representative**

re•press (ri-**press**) ***verb***
1. If you **repress** an emotion, such as anger, you keep it under control and do not show it.
2. To keep people under very strict control.
▸ ***verb* represses, repressing, repressed** ▸ ***noun* repression**
▸ ***adjective* repressed**

re•prieve (ri-**preev**) ***verb*** To postpone a punishment, especially a death sentence.
▸ **reprieving, reprieved** ▸ ***noun*** **reprieve**

rep•ri•mand (**rep**-ruh-*mand*) ***verb*** To criticize someone sharply or formally.
▸ **reprimanding, reprimanded** ▸ ***noun*** **reprimand**

re•pri•sal (ri-**prye**-zuhl) ***noun*** An act of revenge.

re•proach (ri-**prohch**) ***verb*** To blame someone, or to show that you disapprove of something the person has done or said. ▸ **reproaches, reproaching, reproached** ▸ ***noun*** **reproach**

re•pro•duce (*ree*-pruh-**dooss**) ***verb***
1. To make a copy of something.
2. When animals **reproduce,** they breed and produce offspring.
▸ ***verb* reproducing, reproduced**
▸ ***noun* reproduction** (*ree*-pruh-**duhk**-shuhn)

rep•tile (**rep**-tile *or* **rep**-tuhl) ***noun*** A cold-blooded animal that crawls across the ground or creeps on short legs. Reptiles have backbones and reproduce by laying eggs. ▸ ***adjective* reptilian** (rep-**til**-ee-uhn *or* rep-**til**-yuhn)

re•pub•lic (ri-**puhb**-lik) ***noun***
1. A form of government in which the people have the power to elect representatives who manage the government. Republics often have presidents.
2. A country that has such a form of government. The United States is a republic.

re•pub•li•can (ri-**puhb**-li-kuhn) ***adjective*** To do with a republic or in favor of a republic, as in *a republican government.*

Republican Party ***noun*** One of the main political parties in the United States.

re•pug•nant (ri-**puhg**-nuhnt) ***adjective*** Very unpleasant and disgusting.

re•pulse (ri-**puhlss**) ***verb***
1. To drive or force back.
2. To reject something, as in *to repulse an offer.*
▸ ***verb* repulsing, repulsed**

re•pul•sive (ri-**puhl**-siv) ***adjective*** Very distasteful or disgusting. ▸ ***noun*** **repulsion** ▸ ***adverb* repulsively**

rep•u•ta•ble (**rep**-yuh-tuh-buhl) ***adjective*** Reliable and trustworthy.
▸ ***adverb* reputably**

rep•u•ta•tion (*rep*-yuh-**tay**-shuhn) ***noun*** Your worth or character, as judged by other people.

re•pute (ri-**pyoot**) ***noun*** Fame; reputation.

re•put•ed (ri-**pyoo**-tid) ***adjective*** Supposed to be or thought to be.
▸ ***adverb* reputedly**

re•quest (ri-**kwest**)
1. ***verb*** To ask for something politely.
▸ **requesting, requested**
2. ***noun*** Something that you ask for.

R

re•qui•em (**rek**-wee-uhm) ***noun***
1. A church service in which prayers are said for someone who has died.
2. A piece of music composed in memory of a dead person, often a musical setting of the requiem service.

re•quire (ri-**kwire**) ***verb***
1. To need something.
2. If you are **required** to do something, you must do it.
▸ ***verb*** **requiring, required**

re•quire•ment (ri-**kwire**-muhnt) ***noun*** Something that you need to do or have.

re•read (ree-**reed**) ***verb*** To read something again. ▸ **rereading, reread** (ree-**red**)

re•run
1. (ree-**ruhn**) ***verb*** To run again.
▸ **rerunning, reran**
2. (**ree**-*ruhn*) ***noun*** A television program that has been shown before.

res•cue (**ress**-kyoo)
1. ***verb*** To save someone who is in danger or is trapped somewhere.
▸ **rescuing, rescued** ▸ ***noun*** **rescue,** ***noun*** **rescuer**
2. rescue helicopter ***noun*** A specially equipped helicopter used to search for and rescue people on land and at sea.

re•search (ri-**surch** *or* **ree**-surch)
1. ***verb*** To study and find out about a subject, usually by reading a lot of books about it or by doing experiments.
▸ **researches, researching, researched**
2. ***noun*** A study or an investigation in a particular field, usually to learn new facts or solve a problem, as in *medical research.* ▸ ***noun*** **researcher**

re•sem•ble (ri-**zem**-buhl) ***verb*** To be or look like something or someone.
▸ **resembling, resembled** ▸ ***noun*** **resemblance**

re•sent (ri-**zent**) ***verb*** To feel hurt or angry about something that has been done or said to you. ▸ **resenting, resented** ▸ ***noun*** **resentment**
▸ ***adjective*** **resentful**

res•er•va•tion (*rez*-ur-**vay**-shuhn)
1. ***noun*** An arrangement to save space or a seat for someone.
2. ***noun*** An area of land set aside by the government for a special purpose, as in *a tribal reservation.*
3. ***noun, plural*** If you have **reservations** about something, you feel doubtful about it.

re•serve (ri-**zurv**)
1. ***verb*** To arrange for something to be kept for later use.
2. ***verb*** To save for a special purpose or later use.
3. ***verb*** To keep for oneself.
4. ***noun*** A protected place where animals can live and breed safely, as in *a nature reserve.*
5. reserves ***noun, plural*** The part of the armed forces that is kept ready to serve in an emergency.
▸ ***verb*** **reserving, reserved**

re•served (ri-**zurvd**) ***adjective***
1. If a seat, table, or room is **reserved,** it is kept for someone to use later.
2. A **reserved** person behaves in a quiet, shy way and does not show his or her feelings much.

res•er•voir (**rez**-ur-*vwar* *or* **rez**-ur-*vor*) ***noun*** A natural or artificial holding area for storing a large amount of water.

res•i•dence (**rez**-uh-duhnss) ***noun*** The place where somebody lives.

res•i•dent (**rez**-uh-duhnt) ***noun*** Someone who lives in a particular place, as in *the residents of a community.*

res•i•den•tial (rez-i-**den**-shuhl) ***adjective*** To do with a neighborhood or an area where people live, as in *a residential section of the city.*

res•i•due (**rez**-uh-doo *or* **rez**-uh-dyoo) ***noun***
1. What is left after something burns up or evaporates.
2. Anything that remains after the main part has been taken away.
▸ ***adjective*** **residual** (re-**zid**-yoo-uhl)

R

re•sign (ri-**zine**) ***verb***
1. To give up a job, a position, or an office voluntarily.
2. If you **resign yourself** to something, you accept it without complaining or worrying about it. ▸ ***adjective* resigned** ▸ ***verb* resigning, resigned** ▸ ***noun* resignation** (*rez*-ig-**nay**-shuhn)

res•in (**rez**-in) ***noun*** A yellow or brown, sticky substance that oozes from pine, balsam, and other trees and plants. Resin is used to make varnishes, lacquers, plastics, glue, and rubber.

re•sist (ri-**zist**) ***verb***
1. To refuse to accept; to oppose.
2. To fight back.
3. To stop yourself from doing something that you would like to do, as in *to resist temptation.*
▸ ***verb* resisting, resisted**

re•sis•tance (ri-**ziss**-tuhnss) ***noun***
1. Fighting back.
2. The ability to fight off or overcome something.
3. A force that opposes the motion of an object.
4. The ability of a substance or an electrical circuit to oppose an electrical current passing through it because the electricity is turned into heat.

res•o•lute (**rez**-uh-*loot*) ***adjective*** Someone who is **resolute** is strongly determined to do something. ▸ ***adverb* resolutely**

res•o•lu•tion (*rez*-uh-**loo**-shuhn) ***noun***
1. A promise to yourself that you will try hard to do something, as in *New Year's resolutions.*
2. The state of being very determined.

re•solve (ri-**zolv**) ***verb***
1. To decide that you will try hard to do something. ▸ ***noun* resolve**
2. To deal with a problem or difficulty successfully.
▸ ***verb* resolving, resolved**

res•o•nant (**rez**-uh-nuhnt) ***adjective***
1. Having a full, deep sound.
2. Able to amplify sounds or make them last longer.
▸ ***noun* resonance** ▸ ***verb* resonate**

re•sort (ri-**zort**)
1. *noun* A place where people go for rest and relaxation, as in *a ski resort.*
2. *verb* If you **resort to** something, you turn to it because you do not have any other choices. ▸ **resorting, resorted**
3. *noun* If you do something as **a last resort,** you do it because everything else has failed.

re•sound (ri-**zound**) ***verb***
1. To be filled with sound.
2. To make a long, loud, echoing sound.
▸ ***verb* resounding, resounded**

re•source (ri-**sorss** *or* **ree**-sorss) ***noun***
1. Something valuable or useful to a place or a person.
2. Something that you can go to for help or support.

re•source•ful (ri-**sorss**-fuhl *or* ri-**zorss**-fuhl) ***adjective*** If you are **resourceful,** you are good at knowing what to do or where to get help in any situation.

re•spect (ri-**spekt**)
1. *verb* To admire and have a high opinion of someone. ▸ **respecting, respected**
2. *noun* A feeling of admiration or consideration for someone that makes you take the person seriously.
3. *noun* A detail or particular part of something.
4. respects *noun, plural* Regards or greetings.

re•spect•a•ble (ri-**spek**-tuh-buhl) ***adjective***
1. If someone is **respectable,** he or she behaves honestly and decently.
2. Reasonably good.
▸ ***adverb* respectably**

re•spect•ful (ri-**spekt**-fuhl) ***adjective*** Showing proper respect, consideration, or courtesy. ▸ ***adverb* respectfully**

re•spec•tive (ri-**spek**-tiv) ***adjective*** Belonging to or having to do with each one. ▸ ***adverb*** **respectively**

res•pi•ra•tion (*ress*-puh-**ray**-shuhn) ***noun*** The process of taking in oxygen and sending out carbon dioxide, beginning with breathing in and ending with breathing out. ▸ ***adjective*** **respiratory** (**ress**-pi-ruh-*taw*-ree)

re•spond (ri-**spond**) ***verb***
1. To reply or to give an answer.
2. To react to something.
▸ ***verb*** **responding, responded** ▸ ***noun*** **response**

re•spon•si•bil•i•ty (ri-*spon*-suh-**bil**-uh-tee) ***noun***
1. A duty or a job.
2. If you **take responsibility** for something bad that has happened, you agree that you are to blame for it.
▸ ***noun, plural*** **responsibilities**

re•spon•si•ble (ri-**spon**-suh-buhl) ***adjective***
1. If someone is **responsible** for something, he or she has to do it, and it is the person's fault if it goes wrong.
2. If a person is **responsible,** he or she is sensible and can be trusted.
3. Being the cause.
4. Having or involving important duties, as in *a responsible job.*
▸ ***adverb*** **responsibly**

rest (**rest**)
1. ***verb*** To relax, or to sleep.
2. ***noun*** A stopping of work or some activity.
3. ***noun*** Sleep.
4. ***noun*** The others, or the remaining part of something.
5. ***verb*** To lean on something.
6. ***verb*** To stop and stay in one place.
7. ***noun*** The state or fact of not moving.
8. ***noun*** A period of silence in a piece of music.
9. ***verb*** To finish presenting evidence in a court of law.

Rest sounds like **wrest**.
▸ ***verb*** **resting, rested**

res•tau•rant (**ress**-tuh-ruhnt *or* **ress**-tuh-*rahnt*) ***noun*** A place where people pay to eat meals.

rest•less (**rest**-liss) ***adjective*** If someone is **restless,** the person finds it hard to keep still or to concentrate on anything. ▸ ***adverb*** **restlessly**

re•store (ri-**stor**) ***verb***
1. To bring back or to establish again.
2. To bring back to an original condition. ▸ ***noun*** **restorer**
3. To give or bring something back.
▸ ***verb*** **restoring, restored** ▸ ***noun*** **restoration**

re•strain (ri-**strayn**) ***verb***
1. To prevent someone from doing something.
2. To hold back.
▸ ***verb*** **restraining, restrained** ▸ ***noun*** **restraint**

re•strained (ri-**straynd**) ***adjective*** If someone is **restrained,** the person is very quiet and controlled.

re•strict (ri-**strikt**) ***verb*** To confine or keep within limits. ▸ **restricting, restricted** ▸ ***noun*** **restriction** ▸ ***adjective*** **restricted**

rest room ***noun*** A bathroom, especially in a public building.

re•sult (ri-**zuhlt**)
1. ***noun*** Something that happens because of something else.
2. ***verb*** If one thing **results in** something else, it causes it. ▸ **resulting, resulted**

re•sume (ri-**zoom**) ***verb*** To start doing something again after a break. ▸ **resuming, resumed**

re•su•mé (**re**-zuh-*may*) ***noun*** A brief list of all the jobs, education, and awards a person has had.

re•sus•ci•tate (ri-**suhss**-uh-*tate*) ***verb*** To make conscious again, or to bring back from a near-death condition. ▸ **resuscitating, resuscitated** ▸ ***noun*** **resuscitation**

R

re•tail (**ree**-tayl)
1. ***adjective*** To do with the sale of goods directly to customers, as in *a retail store.* ▸ ***noun*** **retail** ▸ ***verb*** **retail**
2. ***noun*** The **retail price** of goods is the price at which they are sold in stores.

re•tail•er (**ree**-tay-lur) ***noun*** Someone who sells goods to the public, usually in a store.

re•tain (ri-**tayn**) ***verb***
1. To keep something.
2. To hold in or to contain. ▸ ***noun*** **retention**
3. If you **retain** a lawyer, you pay him or her a fee to represent you.
▸ ***verb*** **retaining, retained**

re•tal•i•ate (ri-**tal**-ee-*ate*) ***verb*** To do something unpleasant to someone because the person has done something unpleasant to you. ▸ **retaliating, retaliated** ▸ ***noun*** **retaliation** ▸ ***adjective*** **retaliatory**

re•tard (ri-**tard**) ***verb*** To slow down. ▸ **retarding, retarded**

retarded ***adjective*** Slow in mental abilities. ▸ ***noun*** **retardation**

retch (**rech**) ***verb*** When you **retch,** you feel your throat and stomach move as if you are going to vomit. ▸ **retches, retching, retched** ▸ ***noun*** **retch**

ret•i•cent (**ret**-uh-suhnt) ***adjective*** If someone is **reticent,** he or she is unwilling to tell people what he or she knows, thinks, or feels. ▸ ***noun*** **reticence**

ret•i•na (**ret**-uhn-uh) ***noun*** The lining at the back of the eyeball. The retina is sensitive to light and sends images of the things you see to the brain.

re•tire (ri-**tire**) ***verb***
1. To give up work, usually because of your age. ▸ ***noun*** **retirement** ▸ ***adjective*** **retired**
2. To go to bed.
3. To go to a private place.
4. To put out in baseball.
▸ ***verb*** **retiring, retired**

retiring ***adjective*** Shy and reserved.

re•tort
1. (ri-**tort**) ***verb*** To answer someone quickly or sharply. ▸ **retorting, retorted** ▸ ***noun*** **retort**
2. (ri-**tort** *or* **ree**-tort) ***noun*** A glass container with a round body and a long neck. Retorts are used in laboratories.

re•trace (ri-**trayss**) ***verb*** To go back over something. ▸ **retracing, retraced**

re•treat (ri-**treet**)
1. ***verb*** To move back or withdraw from a difficult situation. ▸ **retreating, retreated** ▸ ***noun*** **retreat**
2. ***noun*** A quiet place where you can go to relax, to think, or to be alone.

re•trieve (ri-**treev**) ***verb***
1. To get or bring something back.
2. To locate information in storage, especially by using a computer.
▸ ***verb*** **retrieving, retrieved** ▸ ***noun*** **retrieval**

re•triev•er (ri-**tree**-vur) ***noun*** Any of several popular breeds of large dogs. Retrievers can be trained to find and bring back game shot by hunters.

re•tro•rock•et (**ret**-roh-*rok*-it) ***noun*** A small rocket that fires out of the front of a spacecraft to slow it down or turn it.

ret•ro•vi•rus (**ret**-roh-*vye*-ruhss) ***noun*** Any of a group of viruses that contain RNA instead of the usual DNA. When retroviruses enter the cells of their hosts, they make copies of themselves and attach themselves permanently to the chromosomes of the cells that they attack. ▸ ***noun, plural*** **retroviruses**

re•turn (ri-**turn**)
1. ***verb*** To go back.
2. ***verb*** To take or send something back.
3. ***verb*** To appear or happen again.
4. ***verb*** To give back in the same way, as in *to return a compliment.*
5. ***noun*** The act of returning.
6. ***noun*** Money made as a profit.
7. ***noun*** An official form, as in *a tax return.*

R

8. in return In exchange for something, or as a payment for something.
9. return ticket *noun* A ticket that allows you to travel to a place and back again.
▸ ***verb* returning, returned**

re•un•ion (ree-**yoon**-yuhn) ***noun*** A meeting between people who have not seen each other for a long time.

re•us•a•ble (ree-**yoo**-zuh-buhl) ***adjective*** If something is **reusable,** it can be used again rather than thrown away.

rev (**rev**)
1. *verb* *(informal)* To make an engine run quickly and noisily. ▸ **revving, revved**
2. *noun* *(informal)* A revolution of an engine that is running. *Rev* is short for *revolution.*

re•veal (ri-**veel**) ***verb***
1. To make known.
2. To show or bring into view.
▸ ***verb* revealing, revealed** ▸ ***adjective* revealing**

rev•el (**rev**-uhl) ***verb*** If you **revel in** something, you enjoy it very much.
▸ **reveling, reveled**

rev•e•la•tion (*rev*-uh-**lay**-shuhn) ***noun*** A very surprising fact that is made known.

re•venge (ri-**venj**) ***noun*** Action that you take to pay someone back for harm that the person has done to you or to someone you care about. ▸ ***verb* revenge**

rev•e•nue (**rev**-uh-*noo* or **rev**-uh-*nyoo*) ***noun***
1. The money that a government gets from taxes and other sources.
2. The money that is made from property or other investments.

re•ver•ber•ate (ri-**vur**-buh-*rate*) ***verb*** To echo loudly and repeatedly.
▸ **reverberating, reverberated**
▸ ***noun* reverberation**

rev•er•ence (**rev**-ur-uhnss) ***noun*** Great respect and love. ▸ ***verb* revere** (ri-**veer**) ▸ ***adjective* reverent** ▸ ***adverb* reverently**

re•verse (ri-**vurss**)
1. *verb* To turn something around, upside down, or inside out. ▸ ***adjective* reversible**
2. *noun* The opposite.
3. *adjective* Opposite in position, order, or direction.
4. *noun* The back or rear side of something, as in *the reverse of a record album.*
5. *verb* To transfer telephone fees to someone receiving the call.
6. *verb* To change to the opposite position.
7. *noun* A position of gears that allows a motor vehicle to move backward.
▸ ***verb* reversing, reversed** ▸ ***adjective* reversal**

re•vert (ri-**vurt**) ***verb*** To go back to the way things were. ▸ **reverting, reverted**
▸ ***noun* reversion** (ri-**vur**-zhuhn)

re•view (ri-**vyoo**)
1. *noun* A piece of writing that gives an opinion about a new book, play, movie, etc. ▸ ***noun* reviewer** ▸ ***verb* review**
2. *verb* To study something carefully in order to see whether changes are necessary.
3. *verb* To study or go over again.
4. *verb* To make a formal inspection of.
▸ ***verb* reviewing, reviewed** ▸ ***noun* review**

re•vise (ri-**vize**) ***verb***
1. To change and correct something, often to bring it up-to-date.
2. To change or to make different.
▸ ***verb* revising, revised** ▸ ***noun* revision** (ri-**vi**-zhuhn)

re•vive (ri-**vive**) ***verb***
1. To bring someone back to consciousness after he or she has been unconscious.
2. To bring something back into use.
3. To give new strength or freshness to.
▸ ***verb* reviving, revived** ▸ ***noun* revival**

R

re•voke (ri-**voke**) ***verb*** To take away or to cancel. ▸ **revoking, revoked** ▸ ***noun*** **revocation** (*re*-vuh-**kay**-shuhn)

re•volt (ri-**vohlt**)
1. ***verb*** To fight against authority.
2. ***noun*** A rebellion against a government or an authority.
3. ***verb*** If something **revolts** you, you find it horrible and disgusting.
▸ ***verb*** **revolting, revolted**

revolting ***adjective*** Disgusting, as in *a revolting smell.*

rev•o•lu•tion (*rev*-uh-**loo**-shuhn) ***noun***
1. A violent uprising by the people of a country that changes its system of government.
2. A very large, important change.
3. Movement of one object around another.
▸ ***adjective*** **revolutionary**

Revolutionary War ***noun*** The war in which the 13 American colonies won their independence from Great Britain. The war lasted from 1775 to 1783 and is also known as the *American Revolution.*

rev•o•lu•tion•ize (rev-uh-**loo**-shuh-*nize*) ***verb*** To change something totally.
▸ **revolutionizing, revolutionized**

re•volve (ri-**volv**) ***verb***
1. To keep turning in a circle or orbit around a central point or object.
2. To spin around or to rotate.
3. **revolve around** To center or focus on.
▸ ***verb*** **revolving, revolved**

re•volv•er (ri-**vol**-vur) ***noun*** A small firearm that stores bullets in a cylinder and can fire several shots before it needs to be loaded again.

re•ward (ri-**word**) ***noun*** Something that you receive for doing something good or useful. ▸ ***verb*** **reward**

re•ward•ing (ri-**wor**-ding) ***adjective*** If something is **rewarding,** it gives you pleasure and satisfaction, as in *a rewarding job.*

re•word (ree-**wurd**) ***verb*** To say or write something using different words.
▸ **rewording, reworded**

Reye's syndrome (**rize** *or* **raze**) ***noun*** A rare children's disease with symptoms of high fever, vomiting, and swelling of the liver and brain.

rheumatic fever ***noun*** A serious disease, especially in children, that causes fever, joint pain, and possible heart damage.

rheu•ma•tism (**roo**-muh-*tiz*-uhm) ***noun*** A disease that causes the joints and muscles to become swollen, stiff, and painful. ▸ ***adjective*** **rheumatic** (roo-**ma**-tik)

rhi•noc•er•os (rye-**noss**-ur-uhss) ***noun*** A large mammal from Africa and Asia that has thick skin and one or two large horns on its nose.

rho•do•den•dron (roh-duh-**den**-druhn) ***noun*** A large evergreen shrub with showy clusters of flowers that have a shape like a bell.

rhom•bus (**rom**-buhss) ***noun*** A shape that has four straight sides of equal length but usually does not have right angles. ▸ ***noun, plural*** **rhombuses** *or* **rhombi** (**rom**-*bye*)

rhu•barb (**roo**-barb) ***noun*** A plant with long, red or green stems that can be cooked and eaten and leaves that are poisonous.

rhyme (**rime**)
1. ***verb*** If words **rhyme,** they end with the same sounds. The word *seat* rhymes with *beet* and *feet.* ▸ **rhyming, rhymed**
▸ ***noun*** **rhyme**
2. ***noun*** A short poem.

rhythm (**riTH**-uhm) ***noun*** A regular beat in music, poetry, or dance.

rhyth•mic (**riTH**-mik) ***adjective*** To do with or having a rhythm. ▸ ***adjective*** **rhythmical** ▸ ***adverb*** **rhythmically**

rib (**rib**) ***noun***
1. One of the curved bones that enclose your chest and protect your heart and lungs.

2. Something that looks or functions like a rib, as in *the ribs of an umbrella.*

rib•bon (**rib**-uhn) ***noun***
1. A long, thin band of material used for tying up hair or for decorating a present.
2. A long, thin band of material used for something other than decoration, as in *a typewriter ribbon.*

rice (**risse**) ***noun*** The seeds of a tall grass that is grown in flooded fields. Rice is cooked and eaten.

rich (**rich**) ***adjective***
1. Someone who is **rich** has a lot of money and possessions.
2. If something is **rich** in a particular thing, it contains a lot of it.
3. Food that is **rich** contains a lot of fat or sugar and makes you feel full very quickly.
4. Fertile, as in *rich soil.*
5. riches *noun, plural* Great wealth.
▸ ***adjective* richer, richest** ▸ ***adverb* richly**

rick•et•y (**rik**-uh-tee) ***adjective*** Old, weak, and likely to break.

rick•sha *or* **rick•shaw** (**rik**-*shaw*) ***noun*** A small carriage with two wheels and a cover that usually is pulled by one person. Rickshas originally were used in Asia.

ric•o•chet (**rik**-uh-*shay*) ***verb*** If a stone or bullet **ricochets,** it hits a wall or another hard surface and bounces off in a different direction. ▸ **ricocheting, ricocheted**

rid (**rid**)
1. *verb* To remove something that is unwanted. ▸ **ridding, rid**
2. If you **get rid of** something, you throw it away or otherwise remove it.
3. If you **get rid of** a cold, you overcome it.

rid•dle (**rid**-uhl) ***noun*** A question that seems to make no sense but that has a clever answer. For example: *What has four wheels and flies?* Answer: *A garbage truck.*

ride (**ride**)
1. *verb* To travel on an animal or in a vehicle. ▸ ***noun* rider**
2. *noun* A journey on an animal or in a vehicle.
3. *noun* A device or machine such as a merry-go-round that people ride for fun.
4. *verb* To be supported or carried along.
▸ ***verb* riding, rode** (**rohd**)**, ridden** (**rid**-in)

ridge (**rij**) ***noun***
1. A narrow raised strip on something.
2. A long, narrow chain of mountains or hills.
▸ ***adjective* ridged**

rid•i•cule (**rid**-uh-kyool) ***verb*** To make fun of someone or something.
▸ **ridiculing, ridiculed** ▸ ***noun* ridicule**

ri•dic•u•lous (ri-**dik**-yuh-luhss) ***adjective*** Extremely silly or foolish, as in *a ridiculous hat* or *a ridiculous idea.*
▸ ***adverb* ridiculously**

ri•fle (**rye**-fuhl)
1. *noun* A gun with a long barrel that is fired from the shoulder.
2. *verb* To search through and rob.
▸ **rifling, rifled**

rig (**rig**)
1. *verb* To provide or to equip.
2. *verb* To equip a ship with the necessary masts, sails, ropes, etc.
3. *noun* The arrangement of masts, sails, ropes, etc., on a boat or ship.
4. *noun* A large structure on land or in the sea, used to drill for oil or gas under the ground.
5. *noun* A carriage led by a horse or horses that is used for moving people or goods.
6. *noun* A truck that has a small cab for the driver and a larger trailer in back, used for hauling commercial goods.
7. *noun* Equipment or gear used for a special purpose.
8. *verb* To control something dishonestly.
9. *verb* If you **rig up** something, you make it quickly from whatever you can find.
▸ ***verb* rigging, rigged**

R

rigging ***noun*** The ropes and wires on a boat or ship that support and control the sails.

right (**rite**)
1. ***adjective*** On the side opposite the left. ▸ ***noun* right** ▸ ***adverb* right**
2. ***adjective*** Correct.
3. ***adverb*** Correctly.
4. ***adjective*** Good, fair, and acceptable.
5. ***adjective*** Suitable.
6. ***adverb*** Exactly.
7. ***adverb*** Immediately.
8. ***adverb*** Toward the right.
9. ***adverb*** In a straight line.
10. ***noun*** Something that the law says you can have or do, as in *the right to vote.*
11. In politics, people **on the right** have conservative views.
Right sounds like **write.**
▸ ***adverb* rightly**

right angle ***noun*** An angle of 90 degrees, such as one of the angles of a square.

righ·teous (**rye**-chuhss) ***adjective***
1. Someone who is **righteous** does not do anything that is bad or against the law. ▸ ***noun* righteousness** ▸ ***adverb* righteously**
2. With good reason.

right-hand·ed (**hand**-id) ***adjective*** If you are **right-handed,** you use your right hand more easily than your left hand. ▸ ***noun* right-hander**

right triangle ***noun*** A triangle that includes one right angle.

rig·id (**rij**-id) ***adjective***
1. Stiff and difficult to bend.
2. Very strict and difficult to change, as in *a rigid rule.*
▸ ***noun* rigidity** ▸ ***adverb* rigidly**

rile (**rile**) ***verb*** To annoy or to irritate.
▸ **riling, riled** ▸ ***adjective* riled**

rim (**rim**) ***noun*** The outside or top edge of something.

rind (**rinde**) ***noun*** The tough outer layer on melons, citrus fruits, and some cheeses.

ring (**ring**)
1. ***noun*** A circle.
2. ***verb*** To make or form a ring around.
3. ***noun*** A thin band worn on your finger as a piece of jewelry.
4. ***verb*** To make or cause to make a clear, musical sound. ▸ ***noun* ring**
5. ***noun*** A telephone call.
6. ***noun*** The area in which a boxing or wrestling match takes place.
7. ***noun*** A group of people working together for some unlawful purpose, as in *a smuggling ring.* **Ring** sounds like **wring.**
▸ ***verb* ringing, rang** (**rang**), **rung** (ruhng)

ring·lead·er (**ring**-*lee*-dur) ***noun*** The leader of a group of people who commit crimes or do things that are wrong.

ring·let (**ring**-lit) ***noun*** A long, spiral curl of hair.

rink (**ringk**) ***noun*** An area with a specially prepared surface that is used for ice-skating, roller-skating, or hockey.

rinse (**rinss**)
1. ***verb*** To wash something in clean water without using any soap. ▸ ***noun* rinse**
2. ***verb*** To wash lightly.
3. ***noun*** A special liquid that you can put on hair to color it slightly.
▸ ***verb* rinsing, rinsed**

ri·ot (**rye**-uht)
1. ***verb*** If people **riot,** they behave in a noisy, violent, and usually uncontrollable way. ▸ **rioting, rioted** ▸ ***noun* riot, *noun* rioter, *noun* rioting** ▸ ***adjective* riotous**
2. ***noun*** *(informal)* A person or thing that is extremely funny.

rip (**rip**) ***verb***
1. To tear something. ▸ ***noun* rip**
2. *(slang)* If someone **rips** you **off,** the person sells you a faulty product or charges you an unfair amount of money for something. ▸ ***noun* rip-off**
▸ ***verb* ripping, ripped**

ripe (**ripe**) ***adjective*** Ready to be harvested, picked, or eaten, as in *ripe fruit.* ▸ **riper, ripest** ▸ ***noun* ripeness** ▸ ***verb* ripen**

rip•ple (**rip**-uhl) ***noun***
1. A very small wave on the surface of a lake, pond, etc.
2. Anything that looks like a ripple.
3. A small wave of sound, as in *a ripple of laughter.*
▸ ***verb* ripple**

rise (**rize**)
1. ***verb*** To go or move upward.
2. ***verb*** To stand up.
3. ***verb*** To get out of bed.
4. ***verb*** To increase. ▸ ***noun* rise**
5. ***verb*** To move up in position, rank, or importance.
6. ***verb*** To rebel.
7. ***noun*** An upward slope, as in *the rise of a hill.*
8. ***noun*** The beginning of something.
▸ ***verb* rising, rose** (**rohz**), **risen** (**riz**-in)

risk (**risk**)
1. ***noun*** The possibility of loss or harm; danger. ▸ ***adjective* risky**
2. ***verb*** To expose to risk.
3. ***verb*** To take the risk or chance of.
▸ ***verb* risking, risked**

rit•u•al (**rich**-oo-uhl) ***noun***
1. A set of actions that is always performed in the same way as part of a religious ceremony or social custom.
2. An action or set of actions that you repeat often.
▸ ***adjective* ritual** ▸ ***adverb* ritually**

ri•val (**rye**-vuhl)
1. ***noun*** Someone whom you are competing against. ▸ ***noun* rivalry** ▸ ***adjective* rival**
2. ***verb*** To be as good as something or someone else. ▸ **rivaling, rivaled**

riv•er (**riv**-ur) ***noun*** A large natural stream of fresh water that flows into a lake or an ocean.

riv•et (**riv**-it)
1. ***noun*** A strong metal bolt that is used to fasten pieces of metal together.
▸ ***noun* riveter** ▸ ***verb* rivet**
2. ***verb*** If you are **riveted** by something, you find it so interesting that you cannot stop watching it or listening to it.
▸ **riveting, riveted** ▸ ***adjective* riveting**

RNA (**ar en ay**) ***noun*** The complex molecule produced by living cells and viruses that is responsible for manufacturing the protein in a cell. RNA stands for *RiboNucleic Acid.*

road (**rohd**) ***noun***
1. A wide path with a smooth surface on which vehicles and people travel.
2. The route or path a person takes to achieve a goal, as in *the road to success.*
Road sounds like **rode.**

road map ***noun*** A map for motorists that shows the streets and highways of an area.

road•run•ner (**rohd**-*ruhn*-ur) ***noun*** A small bird with brown-black feathers and a long tail found mainly in the southwestern United States. It gets around by running very fast instead of flying.

road•side (**rohd**-*side*) ***noun*** The area beside a road. ▸ ***adjective* roadside**

roam (**rohm**) ***verb*** To wander around without any particular purpose.
▸ **roaming, roamed**

roar (**ror**) ***verb***
1. To make a loud, deep noise.
2. To laugh very loudly.
▸ ***verb* roaring, roared** ▸ ***noun* roar**

roast (**rohst**)
1. ***verb*** To cook meat or vegetables in a hot oven.
2. ***noun*** A piece of meat that has been cooked in a hot oven, as in *a rib roast.*
3. ***adjective*** Roasted.
4. ***verb*** To be very hot. ▸ ***adjective* roasting**
▸ ***verb* roasting, roasted** ▸ ***adjective* roasted**

R

rob (**rob**) ***verb*** To steal something from somebody. ▸ **robbing, robbed** ▸ ***noun*** **robber**

rob•ber•y (**rob**-uh-ree) ***noun*** The act or crime of stealing money or goods.
▸ ***noun, plural*** **robberies**

robe (**rohb**) ***noun***
1. A piece of clothing like a long, loose coat.
2. A bathrobe.

rob•in (**rob**-in) ***noun*** A songbird that has a reddish orange chest.

ro•bot (**roh**-bot *or* **roh**-buht) ***noun*** A machine that is programmed to do jobs that are usually performed by a person.
▸ ***adjective*** **robotic**

robotic arm ***noun*** A mechanical arm that works like a human arm to control tools or to operate machines.

ro•bot•ics (roh-**bot**-iks) ***noun*** The study of making and using robots.

ro•bust (roh-**buhst**) ***adjective***
1. Strong and healthy, as in *a robust child.*
2. Powerfully built, as in *a robust athlete.*
3. Rich; strong in flavor, as in *robust coffee.*
▸ ***adverb*** **robustly**

rock (**rok**)
1. ***noun*** A large stone.
2. ***noun*** The very hard mineral matter that forms an important part of the earth's crust.
3. ***verb*** To move gently backward and forward or from side to side.
4. ***verb*** To shake or move violently.
5. ***noun*** Popular music with a very strong beat and a simple tune; rock 'n' roll. Also called *rock music.*
▸ ***verb*** **rocking, rocked**

rock climbing ***noun*** The sport of climbing steep rock faces, usually with the help of ropes and other equipment.

rock•et (**rok**-it)
1. ***noun*** A vehicle shaped like a long tube with a pointed end that can travel very fast. Rockets are used for space travel and for carrying missiles.
2. ***verb*** To go up very quickly.
▸ **rocketing, rocketed**

rocking chair ***noun*** A chair mounted on curved runners that allow the sitter to rock back and forth.

rocking horse ***noun*** A toy horse mounted on curved runners so that it can rock back and forth.

rock 'n' roll (**rok**-uhn-**rohl**) ***noun*** A kind of popular music with a strong beat and a simple tune. ▸ ***adjective*** **rock 'n' roll**

rod (**rod**) ***noun***
1. A long, thin pole or stick.
2. A unit of length equal to 5½ yards or 16½ feet.

ro•dent (**rohd**-uhnt) ***noun*** A mammal with large, sharp front teeth that it uses for gnawing things.

ro•de•o (**roh**-dee-oh *or* roh-**day**-oh) ***noun*** A contest in which cowboys and cowgirls compete at riding wild horses and bulls and catching cattle with lassos.

roe (**roh**) ***noun*** The eggs of a fish.

rogue (**rohg**) ***noun***
1. A dishonest person.
2. A vicious and dangerous animal, especially an elephant, that lives apart from the herd.

role (**rohl**) ***noun***
1. The part that a person acts in a play.
2. The job or purpose of a person or thing.
Role sounds like **roll.**

roll (**rohl**)
1. ***verb*** To move along by turning over and over.
2. ***verb*** To make something into the shape of a ball or tube.
3. ***noun*** Something that is in the shape of a tube, as in *a roll of film.*
4. ***verb*** To flatten something by pushing a rounded object over it.
5. ***noun*** A small, round piece of baked bread dough.

R

6. ***noun*** A list of names.
7. ***verb*** To move in a side-to-side or up-and-down way.
8. ***verb*** To make a deep, loud sound.
Roll sounds like **role.**
▸ ***verb*** **rolling, rolled** ▸ ***noun*** **roll**

roll•er (**roh**-lur) ***noun***
1. A cylinder or rod that has something rolled around it, such as a window shade.
2. A cylinder that is used to spread, squeeze, smooth, or crush something, as in *a paint roller.*

Rol•ler•blade (**roh**-lur-*blade*) ***noun*** A trademark for an in-line skate.

roller coast•er (**kohss**-tur) ***noun*** An amusement park ride consisting of a train of cars that travels fast over a track that rises, falls, and curves.

roller-skating ***noun*** The sport of moving about on shoes or boots with wheels attached to them. ▸ ***noun*** **roller skate** ▸ ***verb*** **roller-skate**

rolling pin ***noun*** A cylinder, often made of wood, that is used to flatten out dough.

Rom (**rohm**) ***noun*** A member of a group of people who originated in India and who now live mainly in Europe and North America. The Roma are sometimes called *Gypsies.* ▸ ***noun, plural*** **Roma** (**roh**-muh) ▸ ***adjective*** **Romany** *or* **Romani** (**rom**-uh-nee *or* **roh**-muh-nee)

ROM (**rom**) ***noun*** Memory in a computer with data that can be used but not changed. ROM stands for *Read-Only Memory.*

Ro•man (**roh**-muhn)
1. ***noun*** A person who lived in ancient Rome.
2. ***noun*** A person who was born or is living in modern Rome, Italy.
3. ***adjective*** To do with the people or culture of ancient or modern Rome.
4. **roman** ***noun*** A style of type with upright letters. This sentence is printed in roman.

Roman Catholic
1. ***noun*** A member of the Roman Catholic church.
2. ***adjective*** To do with the Roman Catholic church and its beliefs.

Roman Catholic church ***noun*** A Christian church that has the pope as its leader.

ro•mance (roh-**manss** *or* **roh**-manss) ***noun***
1. An affectionate relationship between people who are in love.
2. A poem or story about the loves and adventures of heroes and heroines.
3. A quality of mystery, excitement, and adventure.

Romance language ***noun*** One of a group of languages that developed from Latin. The Romance languages include Spanish, Italian, French, Portuguese, and Romanian.

Roman numerals ***noun, plural*** Letters used by the ancient Romans to represent numbers. Roman numerals are sometimes used today; for example, on some clocks.

ro•man•tic (roh-**man**-tik) ***adjective***
1. To do with love.
2. Imaginative but not practical, as in *romantic ideas.*

romp (**romp**) ***verb*** To play in a noisy, carefree, and energetic way. ▸ **romping, romped** ▸ ***noun*** **romp**

roof (**roof** *or* **ruf**) ***noun***
1. The covering on the top of a house, building, or vehicle.
2. The top part of something, as in *the roof of your mouth.*

rook (**ruk**)
1. ***noun*** A chess piece, also known as a castle, that can move in straight lines but not diagonally across the board.
2. ***verb*** *(informal)* To cheat someone.
▸ **rooking, rooked**

R

rook•ie (**ruk**-ee) ***noun***
1. Someone who has just joined a group and lacks experience and training, especially an inexperienced police officer.
2. An athlete who is in his or her first season with a professional sports team.

room (**room** *or* **rum**)
1. ***noun*** One of the separate parts of a house or building with its own doorway and walls.
2. ***noun*** Enough space for something.
3. ***noun*** An opportunity or a chance.
4. ***verb*** To share a room or living space with one or more people. ▸ **rooming, roomed**

room•mate (**room**-*mate*) ***noun*** Someone who shares a room or living space with one or more people.

room•y (**roo**-mee) ***adjective*** Large, or having a lot of space. ▸ **roomier, roomiest**

roost (**roost**)
1. ***noun*** A place where birds rest or build nests.
2. ***verb*** When birds **roost,** they settle somewhere for the night. ▸ **roosting, roosted**

roost•er (**roo**-stur) ***noun*** A fully grown male chicken.

root (**root** *or* **rut**)
1. ***noun*** The part of a plant or tree that grows under the ground.
2. ***verb*** To form roots.
3. ***noun*** A part that functions like a root or resembles one, as in *the root of a tooth.*
4. ***noun*** The source, origin, or cause of something.
5. ***noun*** A word to which a prefix or suffix is added to make another word. *Hungry* is the root of *hungriest.*
6. ***verb*** To cheer.
7. ***noun, plural*** Your **roots** are where your family comes from or where you grew up. Many Americans have their roots in Europe, Africa, or Asia.
▸ ***verb*** **rooting, rooted**

root canal ***noun***
1. A groove in a tooth's root through which the nerve passes.
2. A dental procedure to replace the pulp in a tooth's root with another substance in order to save the tooth.

rope (**rohp**)
1. ***noun*** A strong, thick cord made from twisted or woven fibers.
2. ***verb*** To fasten with a cord.
3. ***verb*** To catch with a lasso or rope.
4. ***verb*** To separate an area or object with ropes.
▸ ***verb*** **roping, roped**

rose (**roze**) ***noun***
1. A garden flower that usually has a sweet smell and grows on a bush with thorns. Roses may be red, pink, yellow, or white.
2. A light pink color. ▸ ***adjective*** **rose**

rose•bud (**roze**-*buhd*) ***noun*** The bud from which the rose flower blooms.

Rosh Ha•sha•na (**rohsh** huh-**shah**-nuh) ***noun*** The Jewish New Year, occurring in September or October.

ros•y (**roh**-zee) ***adjective***
1. Pink, as in *rosy cheeks.*
2. Hopeful, as in *a rosy future.*
▸ ***adjective*** **rosier, rosiest**

rot (**rot**) ***verb*** To make or become rotten; to decay. ▸ **rotting, rotted** ▸ ***noun*** **rot**

ro•ta•ry (**roh**-tuh-ree) ***adjective*** Having a part or parts that turn around and around or rotate, as in *a rotary telephone dial* or *a rotary engine.*

ro•tate (**roh**-tate) ***verb***
1. To turn around and around like a wheel.
2. To take turns doing or using things in a fixed order that is repeated.
▸ ***verb*** **rotating, rotated** ▸ ***noun*** **rotation** ▸ ***adjective*** **rotational**

ro•ta•tor cuff (**roh**-tay-tur *or* roh-**tay**-tur) ***noun*** The muscles and tendons that attach the upper arm to the shoulder and allow the arm to rotate in the socket.

ro•tor (**roh**-tur) ***noun***
1. The part of an engine or other machine that turns or rotates.
2. The blades of a helicopter that turn and lift the helicopter into the air.

rot•ten (**rot**-uhn) ***adjective***
1. Food that is **rotten** has gone bad or started to decay from the action of bacteria or fungi.
2. Wood that is **rotten** is weak and likely to crack, break, or give way.
3. *(informal)* Very bad or unpleasant, as in *a rotten trick* or *rotten weather.*

Rott•wei•ler (**rot**-wye-lur) ***noun*** One of a breed of powerful black and brown dogs with short hair and a short tail, often used as guard dogs.

rouge (**roozh**) ***noun*** Red or pink makeup put on the cheeks to make them look less pale.

rough (**ruhf**)
1. ***adjective*** A **rough** surface is not smooth but has dents or bumps in it.
2. ***adjective*** Someone who is **rough** is not gentle or polite and may fight with people or use violence.
3. ***adjective*** *(informal)* Difficult and unpleasant.
4. ***adjective*** Vague or not exact.
5. ***adjective*** **Rough** work is work that you do as preparation for the final piece, as in *a rough sketch.*
6. ***verb*** *(informal)* If you **rough it,** you manage without the usual comforts of home. ▸ **roughing, roughed**
Rough sounds like **ruff.**
▸ ***adjective*** **rougher, roughest**
▸ ***adverb*** **roughly**

rough•age (**ruhf**-ij) ***noun*** The fiber found in cereals, vegetables, and other foods, which passes through the body but is not digested. Roughage helps food move through the intestines.

round (**round**)
1. ***adjective*** Shaped like a circle or a ball.
2. ***adjective*** Having a curved surface or outline.
3. ***noun*** Something round in shape.
4. rounds *noun, plural* A regular route or course of action followed by a mail carrier, doctor, guard, etc.
5. ***noun*** A long burst, as in *a round of applause.*
6. ***noun*** A series of repeated actions or events, as in *the latest round of talks.*
7. ***noun*** A period of play in a sport or contest.
8. ***noun*** A complete game, as in *a round of golf.*
9. ***noun*** A simple song in which people start singing one after another so that they are singing different parts of the song at the same time.
10. ***noun*** One shot fired by a weapon or by each person in a military unit.
11. ***verb*** To make or become round.
12. ***verb*** To go around.
13. ***preposition*** Around.
14. ***adverb*** Around.
15. round off *verb* To make into a round number.
16. round up *verb* To gather together.
▸ ***verb*** **rounding, rounded** ▸ ***adjective*** **rounder, roundest, *adjective* rounded**

round•a•bout (**round**-uh-*bout*) ***adjective*** Indirect in travel, thought, or conversation.

round•house (**round**-*houss*) ***noun*** A circular building with a large turntable in the center, used for storing, repairing, and switching locomotive engines.

round number ***noun*** A number rounded off to the nearest whole number or to the nearest ten, hundred, thousand, etc. Rounding off 158 to the nearest ten gives you a round number of 160. Rounding off 158 to the nearest hundred gives you a round number of 200.

round trip ***noun*** A trip to a place and back again.

round•up (**round**-*uhp*) ***noun***
1. The gathering together of cattle for branding or shipping to market.
2. A gathering together of people, things, or facts, as in *a news roundup.*

R

R

rouse (**rouz**) ***verb***
1. To wake someone up.
2. To make someone feel interested or excited. ▸ ***adjective* rousing**
▸ ***verb* rousing, roused**

rout (**rout**)
1. ***noun*** A complete or overwhelming defeat.
2. ***verb*** To defeat or beat totally.
3. ***verb*** To drive or force out.
▸ ***verb* routing, routed**

route (**root** *or* **rout**) ***noun***
1. The road or course that you follow to get from one place to another.
2. A series of places or customers visited regularly by a person who delivers or sells something, as in *a newspaper route.*

rou•tine (roo-**teen**)
1. ***noun*** A regular way or pattern of doing things.
2. ***adjective*** Something that is **routine** is normal and not at all difficult or unusual, as in *routine chores* or *a routine checkup.*

row
1. (**roh**) ***noun*** A line of people or things side by side, as in *a row of chairs.*
2. (**roh**) ***verb*** To use oars in order to move a boat through water. ▸ **rowing, rowed** ▸ ***noun* rower**
3. (**roh**) ***noun*** A trip made by rowboat.
4. (**rou**) ***noun*** A noisy fight or quarrel.

row•boat (**roh**-*boht*) ***noun*** A small boat that is moved through the water by using oars.

row•dy (**rou**-dee) ***adjective*** Wild and noisy. ▸ **rowdier, rowdiest** ▸ ***noun* rowdiness** ▸ ***adverb* rowdily**

roy•al (**roi**-uhl) ***adjective***
1. To do with or belonging to a king or queen or a member of his or her family.
▸ ***noun* royalty**
2. Magnificent or fit for a king or queen, as in *a royal welcome.*

RSVP (**ar ess vee pee**) The initials of the French phrase *Répondez S'il Vous Plaît,* which means "please reply." RSVP is often written at the bottom of an invitation.

rub (**ruhb**) ***verb***
1. To press one thing against another and move one or both backward and forward.
2. To put or spread on by using pressure.
3. To clean, polish, or make smooth by pressing something against a surface and moving it back and forth. ▸ ***noun* rub**
4. *(informal)* If you **rub it in,** you keep telling someone about his or her mistakes.
▸ ***verb* rubbing, rubbed**

rub•ber (**ruhb**-ur) ***noun***
1. A substance made from the milky sap of a rubber tree or produced artificially. Rubber is strong, elastic, and waterproof and is used for making tires, balls, boots, etc.
2. rubbers *noun, plural* Low boots that protect shoes from water.

rubber band ***noun*** A loop of thin rubber that can be stretched and used to hold things together.

rubber stamp
1. ***noun*** A stamp with a rubber end. Raised letters or a design in the rubber can be inked to print something over and over.
2. rubber-stamp *verb* *(informal)* To approve or vote for without question.

rub•bish (**ruhb**-ish) ***noun***
1. Things that you throw away because they are not useful or valuable.
2. Nonsense.

rub•ble (**ruhb**-uhl) ***noun*** Broken bricks and stones.

ru•ble (**roo**-buhl) ***noun*** The main unit of money in Russia and some of the other countries formed from the Soviet Union in 1989.

ru•by (**roo**-bee) ***noun***
1. A dark red precious stone. ▸ ***noun, plural* rubies**
2. A dark red color.
▸ ***adjective* ruby**

rud•der (**ruhd**-ur) ***noun*** A hinged wood or metal plate attached to the back of a boat, ship, or airplane. A rudder is used for steering.

rude (**rood**) ***adjective***
1. Not polite, as in *rude behavior* or *a rude answer.* ▸ ***noun*** **rudeness**
2. Roughly or crudely made.
▸ ***adjective*** **ruder, rudest** ▸ ***adverb*** **rudely**

ruff (**ruhf**) ***noun***
1. A tall, pleated collar formerly worn by men and women.
2. A collar of feathers or hair on certain birds or animals.
Ruff sounds like **rough.**

ruf•fi•an (**ruhf**-ee-uhn) ***noun*** A rough or violent person.

ruf•fle (**ruhf**-uhl)
1. ***verb*** To disturb something that was smooth so that it becomes uneven or messy.
2. ***verb*** To make someone feel annoyed, worried, or unsettled.
3. ***noun*** A strip of gathered material such as lace or ribbon used as a decoration or trimming.
▸ ***verb*** **ruffling, ruffled**

rug (**ruhg**) ***noun*** A thick mat made from wool or other fibers that is used to cover part of a floor.

rug•by (**ruhg**-bee) ***noun*** A form of football played by two teams that kick, pass, or carry an oval ball.

rug•ged (**ruhg**-id) ***adjective***
1. Rough and uneven, or having a jagged outline, as in *rugged mountain peaks.*
2. Tough and strong.
3. Harsh or difficult.

ru•in (**roo**-in)
1. ***verb*** To spoil or destroy something completely.
2. ***noun*** The destruction of something.
3. ***verb*** To make someone lose all of his or her money.
4. ***noun*** Loss of wealth or social position.
5. ruins *noun, plural* The remains of something that has collapsed or been destroyed.
▸ ***verb*** **ruining, ruined**

rule (**rool**)
1. ***noun*** An official instruction that tells you what you must or must not do.
2. ***verb*** To govern or have power and authority over something, usually a country.
3. ***noun*** Control, or government, as in *rule of the dictator.*
4. ***verb*** To make an official decision or judgment. ▸ ***noun*** **ruling**
5. ***noun*** Something that is usually done.
6. If you do something **as a rule,** you usually do it.
7. ***verb*** If you **rule** something **out,** you decide that it is not possible or not wanted.
▸ ***verb*** **ruling, ruled**

rul•er (**roo**-lur) ***noun***
1. A long, flat piece of wood, plastic, or metal that you use for measuring and drawing straight lines.
2. Someone who rules a country.

rum (**ruhm**) ***noun*** A strong alcoholic drink made from sugarcane.

rum•ble (**ruhm**-buhl) ***verb*** To make a low, rolling noise like the sound of thunder. ▸ **rumbling, rumbled** ▸ ***noun*** **rumble**

rum•mage (**ruhm**-ij) ***verb*** To look for something by moving things around in an untidy or careless way.
▸ **rummaging, rummaged**

ru•mor (**roo**-mur) ***noun*** Something said by many people although it may not be true. ▸ ***verb*** **rumor** ▸ ***adjective*** **rumored**

rump (**ruhmp**) ***noun*** The back part of an animal, above its hind legs.

rum•ple (**ruhm**-puhl) ***verb*** To wrinkle or to crease. ▸ **rumpling, rumpled**
▸ ***adjective*** **rumpled**

R

run (**ruhn**)
1. ***verb*** To move along quickly using your legs.
2. ***noun*** The act of running, as in *to take a run.*
3. ***noun*** A pace of running.
4. ***verb*** To function or to work.
5. ***verb*** To be in charge of something.
6. ***verb*** To travel a regular route.
7. ***verb*** To take part in an election.
8. ***verb*** To continue.
9. ***verb*** To flow in a steady stream.
10. ***verb*** To do something as if by running.
11. ***verb*** To operate a computer program.
12. ***noun*** A small enclosure for animals, as in *a dog run.*
13. ***noun*** Freedom to move about or use something.
14. ***noun*** A series of actions that continue to happen.
15. ***noun*** A length of torn stitches.
▸ ***verb*** **run**
16. ***noun*** In baseball, a score made by touching home plate after touching all three bases.
17. ***verb*** If you **run away,** you escape from a place or leave it secretly.
18. ***verb*** If you have **run out of** something, you have used it all and have none left.
19. ***verb*** If you **run into** or **run across** someone or something, you meet the person or find the thing by chance.
▸ ***verb*** **running, ran** (**ran**), **run**

run•a•way (**ruhn**-uh-*way*)
1. ***noun*** A child who has run away from home.
2. ***adjective*** Out of control, as in *a runaway train.*
3. ***adjective*** Very easy, as in *a runaway victory.*

run-down ***adjective***
1. Old and in need of repair.
2. Tired or weak.

rung (**ruhng**) ***noun*** One of the horizontal bars on a ladder. **Rung** sounds like **wrung.**

run•ner (**ruhn**-ur) ***noun***
1. Someone who runs in a race.
2. The long, narrow part of an object that enables it to move or slide, as the blade on an ice skate or a sled.
3. A long, narrow carpet, often used on stairs.

runner-up ***noun*** The person or team that comes in second in a race or competition. ▸ ***noun, plural*** **runners-up**

running mate ***noun*** A person who runs for public office on another candidate's ticket.

run•ny (**ruhn**-ee) ***adjective***
1. If something is **runny,** it flows or moves like a liquid, as in *runny custard.*
2. If you have a **runny** nose, it tends to drip mucus.
▸ ***adjective*** **runnier, runniest**

run•way (**ruhn**-*way*) ***noun*** A strip of level land that aircraft use for taking off and landing.

rup•ture (**ruhp**-chur) ***verb*** To break open or to burst. ▸ **rupturing, ruptured**
▸ ***noun*** **rupture**

ru•ral (**rur**-uhl) ***adjective*** To do with the countryside or farming, as in *a rural area* or *a rural economy.*

ruse (**rooz**) ***noun*** A clever trick meant to confuse or mislead someone.

rush (**ruhsh**)
1. ***verb*** To go somewhere quickly, or to do something quickly. ▸ **rushes, rushing, rushed**
2. ***noun*** The act of rushing.
3. ***noun*** A sudden burst of speed or activity.
4. ***adjective*** Requiring or done with speed or urgency.
5. **rushes** ***noun, plural*** Tall plants with hollow stems that grow in damp places.
▸ ***noun, plural*** **rushes**

rust (**ruhst**)
1. ***noun*** The reddish brown substance that can form on iron and steel when they are exposed to moisture and air.
▸ ***adjective*** **rusty**
2. ***noun*** A reddish brown color.

S

3. ***verb*** To become covered with rust.
▸ **rusting, rusted**
4. ***noun*** Red or brown disease spots on plants, caused by a fungus.

rus•tic (**ruhss**-tik) ***adjective*** To do with the country.

rus•tle (**ruhss**-uhl) ***verb***
1. When leaves, papers, etc., **rustle,** they make a soft, crackling sound as they move together gently. ▸ ***noun*** **rustle**
2. To steal horses or cattle. ▸ ***noun*** **rustler,** ***noun*** **rustling**
▸ ***verb*** **rustling, rustled**

rust•y (**ruhss**-tee) ***adjective***
1. Covered with rust or having rust spots on it.
2. Not as good as before, especially because of a lack of practice or use.

rut (**ruht**) ***noun***
1. A deep, narrow track made in the ground by wheels or by continuous use.
2. If someone is **in a rut,** he or she keeps doing things in the same dull, boring way.

ruth•less (**rooth**-liss) ***adjective*** Someone who is **ruthless** is cruel and has no pity. ▸ ***noun*** **ruthlessness**
▸ ***adverb*** **ruthlessly**

rye (**rye**) ***noun***
1. A cereal grass grown and used to make flour and whiskey.
2. A dark brown bread made from rye flour.

Sab•bath (**sab**-uhth) ***noun*** The day of rest and worship in some religions. The Jewish Sabbath is from sundown Friday to sundown Saturday, while for most Christians the Sabbath is Sunday.

sa•ber (**say**-bur) ***noun*** A heavy sword with a curved blade and one cutting edge.

saber-toothed tiger (**tootht**) A prehistoric animal related to the lion and tiger that had long, curved teeth in its upper jaw.

sa•ble (**say**-buhl) ***noun***
1. A small animal that looks like a weasel. Sable are found in northern Europe and northern Asia. Their soft, brown fur is very valuable. ▸ ***noun, plural*** **sable** *or* **sables**
2. The color of a sable, either black or dark brown. ▸ ***adjective*** **sable**

sab•o•tage (**sab**-uh-*tahzh*) ***noun*** The deliberate damage or destruction of property, or an act that interferes with work or another activity. ▸ ***verb*** **sabotage**

sab•o•teur (*sab*-uh-**tur**) ***noun*** A person who deliberately damages or destroys property in order to hinder the enemy's war efforts.

sac (**sak**) ***noun*** An animal or plant part that is shaped like a bag or pouch. It often contains a liquid. **Sac** sounds like **sack.**

sac•cha•rin (**sak**-uh-rin *or* **sak**-rin) ***noun*** A very sweet artificial compound with no calories that is used instead of sugar to sweeten food.

sac•cha•rine (**sak**-uh-rin) ***adjective***
1. Overly or sickeningly sweet.
2. To do with or related to sugar.

S

sack (**sak**)
1. ***noun*** A large bag that is made of strong material and is used for storing or carrying potatoes, flour, etc.
2. ***verb*** If an employer **sacks** someone, the employer fires the person from a job.
3. ***verb*** To steal things from a place that has been captured in a war or battle. Sack is another word for **loot** or **plunder.**
Sack sounds like **sac.**
▸ ***verb*** **sacking, sacked**

sa•cred (**say**-krid) ***adjective***
1. Holy, or to do with religion, as in *sacred music* or *sacred ground.*
2. Very important and deserving great respect, as in *a sacred promise.*

sac•ri•fice (**sak**-ruh-fisse)
1. ***verb*** To give up something important or enjoyable for a good reason.
▸ **sacrificing, sacrificed** ▸ ***noun*** **sacrifice**
2. ***noun*** The offering of something to God or a god. ▸ ***adjective*** **sacrificial**
3. ***noun*** In baseball, a **sacrifice hit** is a bunt that advances a base runner but results in the batter being put out.
4. ***noun*** In baseball, a **sacrifice fly** is a fly ball to the outfield that is caught but still allows a base runner to advance.
▸ ***verb*** **sacrifice**

sac•ri•lege (**sak**-ruh-lij) ***noun*** An action that shows disrespect for something holy or very important. ▸ ***adjective*** **sacrilegious** (*sak*-ruh-**lij**-uhss) ▸ ***adverb*** **sacreligiously**

sad (**sad**) ***adjective***
1. Unhappy or sorrowful. ▸ ***noun*** **sadness** ▸ ***verb*** **sadden** ▸ ***adverb*** **sadly**
2. Something that is **sad** makes you feel unhappy, as in *sad news* or *a sad sight.*
▸ ***adjective*** **sadder, saddest**

sad•dle (**sad**-uhl)
1. ***noun*** A leather seat for a rider on the back of a horse. ▸ ***verb*** **saddle**
2. ***noun*** A seat on a bicycle or motorcycle.
3. ***verb*** If someone **saddles** you with an unpleasant job or responsibility, the person leaves you to deal with it.
▸ **saddling, saddled**

sa•fa•ri (suh-**fah**-ree) ***noun*** A trip taken, especially in Africa, to see or hunt large wild animals.

safe (**sayf**)
1. ***adjective*** If something is **safe**, it is not in danger of being harmed or stolen.
▸ ***noun*** **safety** ▸ ***adverb*** **safely**
2. ***adjective*** Not dangerous or not risky.
3. ***adjective*** Careful.
4. ***adjective*** In baseball, a hitter is **safe** if he or she reaches a base without being tagged by an opposing player or called out by the umpire.
5. ***noun*** A strong box in which you can lock away money or valuables.
▸ ***adjective*** **safer, safest**

safe•guard (**sayf**-*gard*)
1. ***verb*** To protect someone or something. ▸ **safeguarding, safeguarded**
2. ***noun*** Something that protects.

safety belt ***noun***
1. A belt or harness that fastens a person who works at great heights to a fixed object. Safety belts prevent falls.
2. Another word for **seat belt.**

safety pin ***noun*** A pin that is bent into the shape of a clasp. It has a guard at one end that covers and holds the point.

sag (**sag**) ***verb***
1. To hang or sink downward.
2. To lose strength.
▸ ***verb*** **sagging, sagged**

sage (**sayj**)
1. ***noun*** An herb with leaves that are often used in cooking.
2. ***adjective*** Wise, as in *sage advice.*
3. ***noun*** A very wise person.

sage•brush (**sayj**-bruhsh) ***noun*** A shrub that grows on the dry plains of the western United States. Sagebrush has silver-green leaves and large clusters of yellow or white flowers.

sail (**sayl**)

1. ***noun*** A large sheet of strong cloth such as canvas that makes a boat or ship move when it catches the wind.

2. ***verb*** To travel in a boat or ship.
▸ ***noun*** **sailing**

3. ***verb*** When a boat or ship **sails,** it starts out on a voyage.

4. ***verb*** To glide or move smoothly.

5. ***noun*** An arm of a windmill.

Sail sounds like **sale.**
▸ ***verb*** **sailing, sailed**

sail•board (**sayl**-*bord*) ***noun*** A flat board with a mast and sail fixed to it, used for windsurfing.

sail•boat (**sayl**-*boht*) ***noun*** A boat that is moved through the water by the wind blowing against its sail or sails.

sail•or (**say**-lur) ***noun***

1. Someone who works on a ship as a member of the crew.

2. A member of a country's navy.

saint (**saynt**) ***noun***

1. A man or woman honored by the Christian church because of his or her very holy life.

2. A very kind and patient person.
▸ ***adjective*** **saintly,** ***adjective*** **sainted**

Saint Ber•nard (bur-**nard**) ***noun*** A large, powerful dog with a big head and fur that is white and reddish brown. The Saint Bernard was originally used to locate lost travelers in the snowy mountains of Switzerland.

sake (**sayk**) ***noun***

1. A benefit or an advantage.

2. A reason or a purpose.

sal•ad (**sal**-uhd) ***noun***

1. A mixture of raw vegetables usually served with a dressing.

2. A mixture of cold foods, as in *a fruit salad.*

sal•a•man•der (**sal**-uh-*man*-dur) ***noun*** An animal that looks like a small lizard. Salamanders are amphibians. They live in or near fresh water and have smooth, moist skin.

sal•a•ry (**sal**-uh-ree) ***noun*** The fixed amount of money someone is paid for his or her work. ▸ ***noun, plural*** **salaries**
▸ ***adjective*** **salaried**

sale (**sayl**) ***noun***

1. The act of selling something.

2. A period of time when items are sold at lower-than-usual prices.

3. sales ***noun, plural*** The number or amount of things sold.

4. for sale Available for people to buy.

5. on sale For sale at reduced prices.

Sale sounds like **sail.**

sales•man (**saylz**-muhn) ***noun*** A man who sells goods or services. ▸ ***noun, plural*** **salesmen**

sales•per•son (**saylz**-*pur*-suhn) ***noun*** A man or woman who sells goods or services. ▸ ***noun, plural*** **salespeople**

sales•wom•an (**saylz**-*wum*-uhn) ***noun*** A woman who sells goods or services.
▸ ***noun, plural*** **saleswomen**

sa•lin•i•ty (suh-**lin**-uh-tee) ***noun*** Saltiness, or the amount of salt in something. ▸ ***adjective*** **saline** (**say**-leen *or* **say**-line)

sa•li•va (suh-**lye**-vuh) ***noun*** The clear liquid in your mouth that keeps it moist and helps you swallow and begin to digest food.

salm•on (**sam**-uhn) ***noun***

1. A large fish with a silvery skin and pink flesh. Most salmon live in salt water but swim to fresh water to lay their eggs. ▸ ***noun, plural*** **salmon**

2. A yellow-pink color.

sal•mo•nel•la (*sal*-muh-**nel**-uh) ***noun*** Any of a group of bacteria that are shaped like rods and that can cause food poisoning, stomach inflammation, and typhoid fever in humans and other warm-blooded animals. ▸ ***noun, plural*** **salmonellas** *or* **salmonellae** (*sal*-muh-**nel**-ee)

S

sa•loon (suh-**loon**) ***noun*** A bar where people can buy and drink alcoholic beverages.

sal•sa (**sahl**-suh) ***noun***
1. A hot, spicy tomato sauce that can be flavored with onions and hot peppers.
2. A popular style of music that originated in Puerto Rico. It has been influenced by jazz and rock.

salt (**sawlt**) ***noun***
1. A common white substance found in seawater and under the ground. Salt is used to season and preserve food.
▸ ***noun* saltiness** ▸ ***verb* salt**
▸ ***adjective* salt, *adjective* salty**
2. In chemistry, a compound formed from an acid and a base.
3. If you take something with **a grain of salt,** you do not believe that it is absolutely true.

salt•wa•ter (**sawlt**-*wah*-tur) ***adjective*** To do with water that is very salty, such as that found in the oceans and in certain inland bodies of water.

sa•lute (suh-**loot**) ***verb***
1. When soldiers **salute,** they raise their right hands to their foreheads as a sign of respect.
2. To praise or honor someone for something that the person has done.
▸ ***verb* saluting, saluted** ▸ ***noun* salute**

sal•vage (**sal**-vij) ***verb*** To rescue property from a shipwreck, fire, or any disaster. ▸ **salvaging, salvaged** ▸ ***noun* salvage, *noun* salvager**

sal•va•tion (sal-**vay**-shuhn) ***noun***
1. The state of being saved from sin, evil, harm, or destruction.
2. Someone or something that saves or rescues.

salve (**sav**) ***noun*** An ointment or a cream that relieves pain and helps heal wounds, burns, or sores.

same (**saym**)
1. ***adjective*** Exactly alike, or identical in every way.
2. ***adjective*** Being the very one and not another.
3. ***adjective*** Not changed or different.
4. ***pronoun*** The identical person or thing.
5. the same In an identical manner.

sam•ple (**sam**-puhl)
1. ***noun*** A small amount of something that shows what the whole of it is like.
2. ***verb*** To try a small amount of something to see if you like it.
▸ **sampling, sampled**

sam•u•rai (**sam**-oo-*rye*) ***noun*** A Japanese warrior who lived in medieval times. ▸ ***noun, plural* samurai**
▸ ***adjective* samurai**

sanc•tion (**sangk**-shuhn)
1. ***verb*** To permit or to give approval.
▸ **sanctioning, sanctioned**
2. ***noun*** Permission or approval.
3. sanctions *noun, plural* Punishment for breaking the law or for unacceptable behavior.

sanc•tu•ar•y (**sangk**-choo-er-ee) ***noun***
1. Safety or protection.
2. A natural area where birds or animals are protected from hunters.
3. A holy or sacred place, such as a church, temple, or mosque.
▸ ***noun, plural* sanctuaries**

sand (**sand**)
1. ***noun*** The tiny grains of rock that make up beaches and deserts.
▸ ***adjective* sandy**
2. ***verb*** To sprinkle or cover with sand.
3. ***verb*** To smooth or polish a surface with sandpaper or a sanding machine.
▸ ***verb* sanding, sanded**

san•dal (**san**-duhl) ***noun*** A light, open shoe with straps that go over the foot.

sand•bag (**sand**-*bag*) ***noun*** A sturdy bag filled with sand and used as a protection against floods, bullets, or explosives. ▸ ***verb* sandbag**

sand•bar (**sand**-*bar*) ***noun*** A ridge of sand in a river or bay or along an ocean's shore. Sandbars are built up by the action of waves or currents.

sand•box (**sand**-*boks*) ***noun*** A large, wooden box with low sides that is filled with sand and used by children to play in.

S

sand•pa•per (**sand**-*pay*-pur) ***noun*** Paper coated with grains of sand and used for rubbing against surfaces to make them smooth. ▸ ***verb*** **sandpaper**

sand•pip•er (**sand**-*pye*-pur) ***noun*** A small bird with a long bill; long, slender legs; and brown or gray feathers. Sandpipers feed in flocks along the seashore.

sand•stone (**sand**-*stohn*) ***noun*** A kind of rock made up mostly of sandlike grains of quartz cemented together by lime or other materials.

sand•wich (**sand**-wich) ***noun*** Two or more pieces of bread around a filling of cheese, meat, or some other food.
▸ ***noun, plural*** **sandwiches**

sane (**sayn**) ***adjective***
1. Someone who is **sane** has a healthy mind.
2. Sensible, or showing good judgment.
▸ ***adjective*** **saner, sanest** ▸ ***noun*** **sanity** ▸ ***adverb*** **sanely**

san•i•tar•y (**san**-uh-*ter*-ee) ***adjective*** Clean and free from germs.

san•i•ta•tion (san-uh-**tay**-shuhn) ***noun*** Systems for cleaning the water supply and disposing of sewage. Sanitation protects people from dirt and disease.

sap (**sap**)
1. ***noun*** The liquid that flows through a plant, carrying water and food from one part of the plant to another.
2. ***verb*** To gradually weaken something.
▸ **sapping, sapped**

sap•ling (**sap**-ling) ***noun*** A young tree.

sap•phire (**sa**-fire) ***noun*** A clear, deep-blue precious stone.

sar•cas•tic (sar-**kass**-tik) ***adjective*** If you are **sarcastic,** you use bitter or mocking words that are meant to hurt or make fun of someone or something.
▸ ***noun*** **sarcasm** ▸ ***adverb*** **sarcastically**

sar•dine (sar-**deen**) ***noun*** A small saltwater fish, often sold in cans as food.

sa•ri (**sah**-ree) ***noun*** A long piece of light material worn wrapped around the body and over one shoulder. Saris are worn mainly by Indian and Pakistani women and girls.

sa•rong (suh-**rong**) ***noun*** A piece of cloth wrapped around the body like a skirt or dress. Sarongs were originally worn by Malaysian men and women.

sash (**sash**) ***noun***
1. A wide strip of material worn around the waist or over one shoulder as an ornament or as part of a uniform.
2. A frame that holds the glass in a window or door.
▸ ***noun, plural*** **sashes**

sa•shi•mi (sah-**shee**-mee *or* **sah**-shuh-mee) ***noun*** A Japanese dish made up of thinly sliced raw fish served with a sauce for dipping.

Sa•tan (**say**-tuhn) ***noun*** The Devil in the Old Testament. Satan is described as an evil spirit that has permanently been sent away from the presence of God and confined to hell.

satch•el (**sach**-uhl) ***noun*** A bag or small suitcase sometimes carried over the shoulder.

sat•el•lite (**sat**-uh-*lite*) ***noun***
1. A spacecraft that is sent into orbit around the earth, the moon, or another heavenly body.
2. A moon or other heavenly body that travels in an orbit around a larger heavenly body.

satellite dish ***noun*** A receiver for radio or television signals sent by satellite. Satellite dishes are shaped like a dish and are often attached to walls outside a home or building. ▸ ***noun, plural*** **satellite dishes**

sat•in (**sat**-uhn) ***noun*** A very smooth fabric that is shiny on one side and dull on the other. Satin is made of silk or a synthetic material.

sat•ire (**sat**-ire) ***noun*** A type of clever, mocking humor that points out the faults in certain people or ideas. ▸ ***noun*** **satirist** ▸ ***adjective*** **satirical** (suh-**tihr**-i-kuhl)

S

sat•is•fac•tion (sat-iss-**fak**-shuhn) ***noun*** A feeling of being content because you have accomplished something that you wanted to do or have done something well.

sat•is•fac•to•ry (sat-iss-**fak**-tuh-ree) ***adjective*** Good enough but not outstanding. ▸ ***adverb*** **satisfactorily**

sat•is•fy (**sat**-iss-*fye*) ***verb***
1. To please someone by doing enough or giving the person enough.
2. To convince or to free from doubt.
▸ ***verb*** **satisfies, satisfying, satisfied**
▸ ***adjective*** **satisfied**

sat•u•rate (**sach**-uh-rate) ***verb*** To soak thoroughly or to fill completely.
▸ **saturating, saturated** ▸ ***noun*** **saturation** ▸ ***adjective*** **saturated**

saturation point ***noun*** The level at which an object is filled to its greatest capacity.

Sat•ur•day (**sat**-ur-dee *or* **sat**-ur-*day*) ***noun*** The seventh day of the week, after Friday and before Sunday.

Sat•urn (**sat**-urn) ***noun*** The sixth planet in distance from the sun. Saturn is the second-largest planet in our solar system. It has 10 moons and is surrounded by rings that are thought to be made of ice, rock, and frozen gases.

sauce (**sawss**) ***noun***
1. A thick liquid served with food to make it taste better.
2. Stewed fruit eaten as dessert or as a side dish, as in *cranberry sauce.*

sauce•pan (**sawss**-*pan*) ***noun*** A metal or glass cooking pot with a handle and sometimes a lid.

sau•cer (**saw**-sur) ***noun*** A small, shallow plate that is placed under a cup.

sau•na (**saw**-nuh *or* **sou**-nuh) ***noun***
1. A bath using dry heat, or a steam bath in which the steam is made by throwing water on hot stones. Saunas originated in Finland.
2. A room for such a bath.

saun•ter (**sawn**-tur) ***verb*** To walk in a slow, leisurely, or casual way.
▸ **sauntering, sauntered**

sau•sage (**saw**-sij) ***noun*** Chopped and seasoned meat stuffed into a thin case shaped like a tube.

sav•age (**sav**-ij)
1. ***adjective*** Not tamed, or not under human control, as in *a savage beast.*
2. ***adjective*** Fierce, dangerous, or violent, as in *a savage battle.* ▸ ***adverb*** **savagely**
3. ***adjective*** Not civilized, as in *a savage society.*
4. ***noun*** A person who lives in a way that is not civilized.
5. ***noun*** A fierce or violent person.

sa•van•na *or* **sa•van•nah** (suh-**van**-uh) ***noun*** A flat, grassy plain with few or no trees. Savannas are found in tropical areas.

save (**sayv**) ***verb***
1. To rescue someone or something from danger.
2. If you **save** time, space, energy, etc., you make the best use of it and do not waste it.
3. To keep money to use in the future rather than spend it now.
4. To stop a ball or puck from going into a goal in soccer or hockey. ▸ ***noun*** **save**
5. To copy a file from a computer's RAM (random access memory) onto a disk or other storage device in order to keep it or protect it from being erased.
▸ ***verb*** **saving, saved** ▸ ***noun*** **saver**

sav•ings (**say**-vingz) ***noun, plural*** Money that you have saved.

sa•vor•y (**say**-vuh-ree) ***adjective*** Pleasing to the taste or smell, as in *savory cooking odors.*

saw (**saw**)
1. ***noun*** A tool used for cutting wood with sharp teeth on its blade.
2. ***verb*** To cut something with a saw.
▸ **sawing, sawed, sawn** (**sawn**)
3. ***verb*** Past tense of **see.**

saw•dust (**saw**-*duhst*) ***noun*** Tiny particles of wood that fall off when you saw wood.

saw•mill (**saw**-*mil*) ***noun*** A place where people use machines to saw logs into lumber.

sax•o•phone (**sak**-suh-*fone*) ***noun*** A wind instrument made of brass, with a mouthpiece, keys for the fingers, and a body that is usually curved. ▸ ***noun*** **saxophonist**

say (**say**)
1. ***verb*** To speak.
2. ***verb*** To state, or to express in words.
3. ***verb*** To repeat or to recite, as in *to say one's prayers.*
4. ***noun*** The chance to speak.
▸ ***verb*** **saying, said (sed)**

say•ing (**say**-ing) ***noun*** A well-known phrase or proverb that gives advice. "Don't cry over spilt milk" is a saying.

sa•yo•na•ra (*sah*-yoh-**nar**-uh) ***interjection*** A Japanese word meaning "good-bye."

scab (**skab**) ***noun***
1. The hard covering that forms over a wound when it is healing.
2. *(informal)* Someone who takes the job of a union worker who is on strike.

scab•bard (**skab**-urd) ***noun*** A case that holds a sword, dagger, or bayonet when it is not in use.

scaf•fold (**skaf**-uhld) ***noun*** The structure made of wooden planks and ropes or metal poles that workers stand on when they are working above the ground on a building.

scald (**skawld**) ***verb*** To burn with very hot liquid or steam. ▸ **scalding, scalded** ▸ ***noun*** **scald** ▸ ***adjective*** **scalding**

scale (**skale**)
1. ***noun*** One of the small pieces of hard skin that cover the body of a fish, snake, or other reptile. ▸ ***adjective*** **scaly**
2. ***verb*** To remove all the scales from.
3. ***noun*** A series of musical notes going up or down in order.
4. ***noun*** A series of numbers, units, etc., that is used to measure something, as in *a scale for measuring the strength of earthquakes.*
5. ***noun*** The ratio between the measurements on a map or model and the actual measurements, as in *a scale of one inch represents 100 miles.*
6. ***noun*** An instrument used for weighing things.
7. ***verb*** To climb up something.
8. ***noun*** A series of stages or steps.
▸ ***verb*** **scaling, scaled**

sca•lene triangle (skay-**leen**) ***noun*** In geometry, a triangle whose three sides each have different lengths.

scal•lion (**skal**-yuhn) ***noun*** An onion with long, grasslike leaves and a small bulb.

scal•lop (**skol**-uhp *or* **skal**-uhp) ***noun***
1. A shellfish with two hinged shells or valves. Scallops move around by opening and closing their valves rapidly.
2. One of a series of curves in a border that looks like the edge of a scallop shell.
▸ ***verb*** **scallop** ▸ ***adjective*** **scalloped**

scalp (**skalp**) ***noun*** The skin covering the top of your head where your hair grows.

scal•pel (**skal**-puhl) ***noun*** A small, sharp knife used by surgeons.

scam•per (**skam**-pur) ***verb*** To run lightly and quickly. ▸ **scampering, scampered**

scan (**skan**) ***verb***
1. To read quickly, without looking for details.
2. To look at closely and carefully, or to examine.
3. If a machine **scans** something, it moves a beam of light over the object in order to examine it or search for something. ▸ ***noun*** **scanner**
▸ ***verb*** **scanning, scanned** ▸ ***noun*** **scan**

scan•dal (**skan**-duhl) ***noun***
1. A dishonest or immoral act that shocks people and disgraces those involved.
2. Harmful gossip.
▸ ***adjective*** **scandalous**

S

Scan•di•na•vi•an (*skan*-duh-**nay**-vee-uhn) ***noun***
1. Someone who was born in or is a citizen of Norway, Denmark, or Sweden. Iceland and Finland also are sometimes considered Scandinavian countries.
2. The languages spoken by people in these countries.
▸ ***adjective*** **Scandinavian**

scan•ner (**skan**-ur) ***noun***
1. A machine or person that scans.
2. A machine that scans an image to be converted into a computer graphics file.

scant (**skant**) ***adjective***
1. Barely enough, or not enough.
2. Not quite the full amount, as in *a scant teaspoonful of salt.*

scant•y (**skan**-tee) ***adjective*** Not enough, or not big enough. ▸ **scantier, scantiest**

scape•goat (**skape**-*goht*) ***noun*** Someone who is unfairly made to take all the blame for something.

scar (**skar**) ***noun*** A mark left on your skin by a cut or wound that has healed.
▸ ***verb*** **scar**

scarce (**skairss**) ***adjective*** Something that is **scarce** is hard to find because there is so little of it. ▸ ***noun*** **scarcity**

scarce•ly (**skairss**-lee) ***adverb***
1. Hardly.
2. Certainly not, as in *scarcely forgive them.*

scare (**skair**)
1. ***verb*** To frighten a person or an animal. ▸ **scaring, scared**
2. ***noun*** Widespread fear or panic, as in *a bomb scare.*
▸ ***adjective*** **scared,** ***adjective*** **scary**

scare•crow (**skair**-*kroh*) ***noun*** A figure made of straw that is shaped and dressed to look like a person and put in a field to frighten birds away from crops.

scarf (**skarf**) ***noun*** A strip of material worn around the neck or head for decoration or warmth. ▸ ***noun, plural*** **scarfs** *or* **scarves** (**skarvz**)

scar•let (**skar**-lit) ***noun*** A bright red color. ▸ ***adjective*** **scarlet**

scarlet fever ***noun*** A highly contagious disease that occurs mostly in children. It causes a bright red rash, a sore throat, and high fever.

scat•ter (**skat**-ur) ***verb***
1. To throw things over a wide area.
2. To hurry away in different directions.
▸ ***verb*** **scattering, scattered**

scav•enge (**skav**-uhnj) ***verb*** To search among garbage for food or something useful. ▸ **scavenging, scavenged**
▸ ***noun*** **scavenger**

sce•nar•i•o (suh-**nair**-ee-*oh* *or* suh-**nah**-ree-*oh*) ***noun***
1. An outline of a movie, a play, or an opera that summarizes the story.
2. An outline of a series of events that might happen in a particular situation.
▸ ***noun, plural*** **scenarios**

scene (**seen**) ***noun***
1. A view or a picture.
2. A part of a story, play, movie, etc., that shows what is happening in one particular place and time.
3. The place where something happens.
4. If you **make a scene,** you get very angry with someone or behave badly in public.

scen•er•y (**see**-nur-ee) ***noun***
1. The natural countryside of an area, such as trees, hills, mountains, and lakes.
2. The painted boards and screens that are used on stage as the background to a play, an opera, or a ballet.

sce•nic (**see**-nik) ***adjective*** A **scenic** place has beautiful natural surroundings.

scent (**sent**)
1. ***noun*** A pleasant smell, as in *the scent of roses.* ▸ ***adjective*** **scented**
2. ***noun*** A liquid that you put on your skin to make you smell pleasant.
3. ***noun*** The odor or trail of a hunted animal or person.
4. ***noun*** The sense of smell.
5. ***verb*** If you **scent** danger or victory, you start to feel that it is near.

▸ **scenting, scented**
Scent sounds like **cent** and **sent.**

scep•ter (**sep**-tur) ***noun*** A rod or staff carried by a king or queen as a symbol of authority.

sched•ule (**skej**-ool *or* **skej**-ul)
1. ***noun*** A plan, program, or timetable.
2. ***verb*** If you **schedule** an event, you plan it for a particular time.
▸ **scheduling, scheduled**

scheme (**skeem**)
1. ***noun*** A plan or plot for doing something.
2. ***verb*** To plan or plot something, especially something secret or dishonest.
▸ **scheming, schemed** ▸ ***noun*** **schemer** ▸ ***adjective*** **scheming**

schol•ar (**skol**-ur) ***noun***
1. A person who has a great deal of knowledge.
2. A serious student. ▸ ***adjective*** **scholarly**

schol•ar•ship (**skol**-ur-ship) ***noun***
1. A grant or prize that pays for you to go to college or to follow a course of study.
2. Knowledge achieved from studying hard.

school (**skool**) ***noun***
1. A place where people go to be taught.
2. Learning that takes place in school.
▸ ***noun*** **schooling** ▸ ***verb*** **school**
3. All the people in a school.
4. A part of a university, as in *a medical school.*
5. A group of fish or other sea creatures, as in *a school of porpoises.*

schoon•er (**skoo**-nur) ***noun*** A fast ship with two masts, a narrow hull, and sails that run lengthwise.

sci•ence (**sye**-uhnss) ***noun***
1. The study of nature and the physical world by testing, experimenting, and measuring.
2. Any of the branches or fields of such study, as biology, physics, or geology.
▸ ***noun*** **scientist** ▸ ***adjective*** **scientific**
▸ ***adverb*** **scientifically**

science fiction ***noun*** Stories about life in the future or life on other planets.

scis•sors (**siz**-urz) ***noun, plural*** A sharp tool with two blades used for cutting paper, fabric, etc.

scoff (**skof** *or* **skawf**) ***verb*** To be scornful and mocking about someone or something.
▸ **scoffing, scoffed**

scold (**skohld**) ***verb*** To tell someone in an angry way that he or she has done something wrong or done a bad job.
▸ **scolding, scolded**

sco•li•o•sis (*skoh*-lee-**oh**-siss) ***noun*** An abnormal curving of the spine to the side. Scoliosis usually occurs during adolescence.

scone (**skohn**) ***noun*** A round biscuit often eaten with butter.

scoop (**skoop**)
1. ***verb*** To lift or pick up something.
▸ **scooping, scooped**
2. ***noun*** A utensil shaped like a spoon with a short handle and a deep hollow to pick things up with, as in *an ice-cream scoop.*
3. ***noun*** A story reported in a newspaper before other papers have a chance to report it.
▸ ***verb*** **scoop**

scoot•er (**skoo**-tur) ***noun***
1. A child's vehicle with a handle, two wheels, and a board that you stand on with one foot while pushing against the ground with the other.
2. A small motorcycle.

scope (**skohp**) ***noun***
1. A range of opportunity.
2. The area or range of operation.

scorch (**skorch**)
1. ***verb*** To burn something slightly, usually with an iron. ▸ ***noun*** **scorch**
2. ***verb*** To dry up something.
3. ***adjective*** If the weather is **scorching,** it is extremely hot.
▸ ***verb*** **scorches, scorching, scorched**

S

score (**skor**)
1. ***verb*** To make a point or points in a game, contest, or test. ▸ ***noun*** **scorer**
2. ***noun*** The number of points made by each person or team in a game, contest, or test.
3. ***noun*** A written piece of music.
4. ***verb*** To arrange a piece of music so that it can be played by different instruments.
5. ***verb*** To cut a line or lines in a surface.
6. ***noun*** Twenty.
7. scores ***noun, plural*** A large number.
8. *(informal)* If you **know the score,** you are well informed about the situation.
▸ ***verb*** **scoring, scored**

scorn (**skorn**)
1. ***noun*** A feeling of hatred or contempt for someone or something thought of as bad, worthless, or low.
2. ***verb*** To treat with scorn.
3. ***verb*** If you **scorn** an offer, you refuse it because you think it is not worth your while.
▸ ***verb*** **scorning, scorned** ▸ ***adjective*** **scornful**

scor·pi·on (**skor**-pee-uhn) ***noun*** An animal related to the spider that has a poisonous sting in its tail.

scoun·drel (**skoun**-druhl) ***noun*** A wicked person, especially someone who cheats and lies.

scour (**skour**) ***verb***
1. To clean or polish something by rubbing it hard. ▸ ***noun*** **scourer**
2. To search an area thoroughly.
▸ ***verb*** **scouring, scoured**

scourge (**skurj**) ***noun*** A cause of great harm and suffering.

scout (**skout**)
1. ***noun*** Someone sent to find out and bring back information.
2. ***verb*** To look or search for something.
▸ **scouting, scouted**

scowl (**skoul**) ***verb*** To make an angry frown. ▸ **scowling, scowled** ▸ ***noun*** **scowl**

scrag·gy (**skrag**-ee) ***adjective*** Thin and bony. ▸ **scraggier, scraggiest** ▸ ***noun*** **scragginess**

scram·ble (**skram**-buhl) ***verb***
1. To climb over rocks or hills.
2. To rush or struggle to get somewhere or something.
3. To mix up or mix together.
4. To alter an electronic signal so that it requires a special receiver to decode the message. ▸ ***noun*** **scrambler**
5. scrambled eggs Egg yolks and whites mixed together and cooked in a pan.
▸ ***verb*** **scrambling, scrambled** ▸ ***noun*** **scramble** ▸ ***adjective*** **scrambled**

scrap (**skrap**)
1. ***noun*** A small piece of paper, food, etc.
2. ***noun*** Metal salvaged from old cars or machines.
3. ***verb*** To get rid of something.
4. ***verb*** *(informal)* To fight or to quarrel.
▸ ***noun*** **scrap,** ***noun*** **scrapper**
▸ ***verb*** **scrapping, scrapped**

scrap·book (**skrap**-*buk*) ***noun*** A book with blank pages on which you mount pictures, newspaper clippings, and other items you wish to keep.

scrape (**skrape**)
1. ***verb*** To clean, peel, or scratch something with a sharp object. ▸ ***noun*** **scrape,** ***noun*** **scraper**
2. ***noun*** *(informal)* An awkward situation.
3. scrape together ***verb*** To gather or collect with great difficulty.
4. scrape by ***verb*** To manage or make your way with difficulty.
▸ ***verb*** **scraping, scraped**

scratch (**skrach**) ***verb***
1. To scrape lightly a part of you that itches.
2. To make a mark or cut.
3. To scrape with the fingernails or claws.
4. *(informal)* To erase or cancel something.
5. *(informal)* If you do something **from**

S

scratch, you start from the beginning.
6. *(informal)* If something is not **up to scratch,** it is not good enough.
▸ ***verb*** **scratches, scratching, scratched** ▸ ***noun*** **scratch**

scratch•y (**skrach**-ee) ***adjective***
1. Causing an itch, as in *a scratchy fabric.*
2. Rough and itchy, as in *a scratchy throat.*
▸ ***adjective*** **scratchier, scratchiest**

scrawl (**skrawl**)
1. ***verb*** To write in a quick, sloppy way.
▸ **scrawling, scrawled**
2. ***noun*** A sloppy handwriting that is difficult to read.

scream (**skreem**)
1. ***verb*** To make a loud, shrill, piercing cry or sound. ▸ **screaming, screamed** ▸ ***noun*** **scream**
2. ***noun*** *(informal)* A very funny thing or person.

screech (**skreech**) ***verb*** To make a high, unpleasant sound. ▸ **screeches, screeching, screeched** ▸ ***noun*** **screech**

screen (**skreen**)
1. ***noun*** Wire or plastic netting in a frame.
2. ***noun*** A light, movable partition used to hide or divide a room. ▸ ***verb*** **screen**
3. ***noun*** The front of a television set or computer monitor.
4. ***noun*** The white surface that movies or slides are projected onto.
5. ***verb*** To show on a screen.
6. ***verb*** To examine carefully in order to make a selection, or to separate into groups.
▸ ***verb*** **screening, screened**

screen saver ***noun*** A computer program that prolongs the life of a monitor by providing a changing or fading image when the machine is on but not in use.

screw (**skroo**)
1. ***noun*** A metal fastener like a nail with a groove in its head and a spiral thread.
2. ***verb*** To fasten something with screws.
3. ***verb*** If you **screw on** a lid, you turn or twist it.
4. ***verb*** To twist into an unnatural position.
5. ***verb*** *(informal)* If you **screw up,** you make a really bad mistake.
▸ ***verb*** **screwing, screwed**

screw•driv•er (**skroo**-*drye*-vur) ***noun*** A tool with a tip that fits into the groove in the head of a screw so that you can turn it.

scrib•ble (**skrib**-uhl) ***verb***
1. To write or draw carelessly or quickly.
2. To make meaningless marks with a pencil, pen, or crayon.
▸ ***verb*** **scribbling, scribbled** ▸ ***noun*** **scribble**

scribe (**skribe**) ***noun*** A person who copies books, letters, contracts, and other documents by hand.

scrim•mage (**skrim**-ij) ***noun***
1. In football, the rough contact that occurs as soon as the ball is picked up off the ground and snapped to another player.
2. A game played for practice in football and other sports.
▸ ***verb*** **scrimmage**

script (**skript**) ***noun***
1. The written text of a play, a movie, or a television or radio show. ▸ ***verb*** **script**
2. Writing in which the letters are joined together.

scrip•ture (**skrip**-chur) ***noun***
1. A sacred book.
2. Scripture The Bible.

scroll (**skrohl**)
1. ***noun*** A piece of paper or parchment with writing on it that is rolled up into the shape of a tube.
2. ***verb*** To move the text on a computer screen up and down so that you can see more of it. ▸ **scrolling, scrolled**

scrounge (**skrounj**) ***verb***
1. To get things from people without paying.
2. To get or collect things with difficulty.
▸ ***verb*** **scrounging, scrounged** ▸ ***noun*** **scrounger**

S

scrub (**skruhb**)
1. ***verb*** To clean something by rubbing it hard.
▸ **scrubbing, scrubbed** ▸ ***noun*** **scrub**
2. ***noun*** Low bushes or short trees that cover a piece of ground.

scruff•y (**skruhf**-ee) ***adjective*** Shabby and messy. ▸ **scruffier, scruffiest** ▸ ***adverb*** **scruffily**

scru•ple (**skroo**-puhl) ***noun*** A strong feeling about what is right that keeps you from doing something wrong.

scru•pu•lous (**skroo**-pyuh-luhss) ***adjective***
1. Having strict beliefs about what is right and proper.
2. Careful and exact.
▸ ***adverb*** **scrupulously**

scru•ti•nize (**skroot**-uh-*nize*) ***verb*** To examine or study something closely.
▸ **scrutinizing, scrutinized** ▸ ***noun*** **scrutiny**

scu•ba diving (**skoo**-buh) ***noun*** Underwater swimming with an air tank on your back that is connected to your mouth by a hose. Scuba stands for *Self-Contained Underwater Breathing Apparatus.* ▸ ***noun*** **scuba diver**

scuff (**skuhf**) ***verb*** To scratch or scrape something and leave a mark. ▸ **scuffing, scuffed**

scuf•fle (**skuhf**-uhl) ***noun*** A confused and disorderly struggle or fight. ▸ ***verb*** **scuffle**

scull (**skuhl**) ***noun***
1. One of a pair of lightweight oars used to propel a boat through water.
2. A small, light boat that is propelled by oars, often used for racing.
Scull sounds like **skull.**
▸ ***verb*** **scull**

sculp•ture (**skuhlp**-chur) ***noun***
1. Something carved or shaped out of stone, wood, metal, marble, or clay or cast in bronze or another metal.
2. The art or work of making sculpture.
▸ ***noun*** **sculptor** ▸ ***verb*** **sculpt**

scum (**skuhm**) ***noun*** A filmy layer that forms on the surface of a liquid or body of water, especially stagnant water.

scur•ry (**skur**-ee) ***verb*** To hurry, or to run with short, quick steps. ▸ **scurries, scurrying, scurried**

scur•vy (**skur**-vee) ***noun*** A disease characterized by bleeding gums and great weakness. Scurvy is caused by a lack of *vitamin C* in the diet. Vitamin C is found in citrus fruits and other fruits and vegetables.

scuz•zy (**skuhz**-ee) ***adjective*** *(slang)* Dirty, grimy, or disgusting in some way.
▸ **scuzzier, scuzziest**

scythe (**siTHe**) ***noun*** A tool with a large, curved blade used for cutting grass or crops by hand.

sea (**see**) ***noun***
1. The body of salt water that covers nearly three-fourths of the earth's surface; the ocean.
2. A body of salt water that is a part of an ocean yet is partly enclosed by land, such as the Caribbean Sea.
3. An overwhelming amount or number, as in *a sea of troubles.*
Sea sounds like **see.**

sea anemone ***noun*** A sea animal with a body shaped like a tube and a mouth opening that is surrounded by brightly colored tentacles.

sea•board (**see**-bord) ***noun*** The land along or near the ocean shore.

sea•far•er (**see**-*fair*-ur) ***noun*** A sailor or someone who travels by sea.

sea•far•ing (**see**-*fair*-ing) ***adjective***
1. Earning one's living by working at sea, as in *a seafaring merchant.*
2. To do with sailors or the sea, as in *a seafaring vessel* or *seafaring tales.*

sea•food (**see**-*food*) ***noun*** Edible fish and shellfish.

sea•gull (**see**-*guhl*) ***noun*** A gray and white bird that is commonly found near the sea.

sea horse ***noun*** A small ocean fish with a head shaped like that of a horse and a long, curling tail.

seal (**seel**)
1. *noun* A sea mammal that lives in coastal waters and has thick fur and flippers.
2. *verb* To close something up.
▸ **sealing, sealed** ▸ ***noun* seal, *noun* sealant**
3. *noun* A design pressed into wax and made into a stamp. A seal is used to make a document official or to close up a letter or an envelope. ▸ ***verb* seal**

sea level ***noun*** The average level of the surface of the ocean, used as a starting point from which to measure the height or depth of any place.

sea lion ***noun*** A large seal found mostly in the Pacific Ocean. It has ears that stick out and large flippers.

seam (**seem**) ***noun***
1. A line of sewing that joins two pieces of material.
2. A band of mineral or metal in the earth, as in *a seam of coal.*
Seam sounds like **seem.**

seam•stress (**seem**-struhss) ***noun*** A woman who sews for a living. ▸ ***noun, plural* seamstresses**

sea•plane (**see**-*plane*) ***noun*** An airplane that can take off from and land on water. A seaplane has floats attached to its underside.

sea•port (**see**-*port*) ***noun***
1. A port or harbor for seafaring ships.
2. A city or town with such a port or harbor.

search (**surch**)
1. *verb* To explore or examine something carefully and thoroughly.
▸ **searches, searching, searched**
▸ ***noun* search, *noun* searcher**
2. search warrant *noun* An order from a court that allows the police to go into a building to look for certain items or people.
3. search engine *noun* A computer program that will search for the words or data you request.

search•ing (**sur**-ching) ***adjective*** Deep and thorough; probing.

search•light (**surch**-*lite*) ***noun*** A large, powerful lamp that can be turned to focus in a particular direction.

sea•shell (**see**-*shel*) ***noun*** The shell of a sea animal such as an oyster or a clam.

sea•shore (**see**-*shor*) ***noun*** The sandy or rocky land next to the sea.

sea•sick (**see**-*sik*) ***adjective*** If you are **seasick,** you feel nauseous and dizzy because of the rolling or tossing movement of a boat or ship.

sea•son (**see**-zuhn)
1. *noun* One of the four natural parts of the year. The four seasons are spring, summer, autumn or fall, and winter.
▸ ***adjective* seasonal** ▸ ***adverb* seasonally**
2. *noun* A part of the year when a certain activity or event takes place, as in *the rainy season* or *the football season.*
3. *verb* To add flavor to food with herbs, salt, or spices. ▸ **seasoning, seasoned**
4. If a food is **in season,** it is fresh and easily available.
5. season ticket *noun* A ticket for a series of events in a season, such as to all the home games of a sports team or performances of a ballet or an opera company.

sea•son•ing (**see**-zuhn-ing) ***noun*** An herb or spice that is added to food to give it more flavor.

seat (**seet**)
1. *noun* Something such as a chair or bench that you can sit on.
2. *noun* Anyplace where you can sit.
3. *verb* To cause to sit.
4. *noun* The part of the body you sit on, or the fabric that covers it.
5. *noun* The central location of something.
6. *verb* To have room for people to sit down.
▸ ***verb* seating, seated**

seat belt ***noun*** A strap or harness that holds a person securely in the seat of a car, a truck, or an airplane for protection in case of an accident.

S

S

sea ur•chin (**ur**-chin) ***noun*** A sea creature with a hard, spiny shell. The spines are used for protection and also help the sea urchin move around.

sea•weed (**see**-*weed*) ***noun*** Any of various types of algae that grow in the sea and need sunlight to make their own food. ▸ ***noun, plural*** **seaweed**

se•cede (si-**seed**) ***verb*** To formally withdraw from a group or an organization, often to form another organization. ▸ **seceding, seceded** ▸ ***noun*** **secession**

se•clud•ed (si-**kloo**-did) ***adjective*** Quiet and private. ▸ ***noun*** **seclusion**

sec•ond (**sek**-uhnd)
1. ***noun*** A unit of time equal to 1/60 of a minute.
2. ***noun*** Any very short period of time.
3. ***adjective*** Next after the first. ▸ ***noun*** **second** ▸ ***adverb*** **second,** ***adverb*** **secondly**
4. seconds ***noun, plural*** Another, or a second, helping of food.
5. ***verb*** If you **second** a motion at a meeting, you formally support it. ▸ **seconding, seconded** ▸ ***noun*** **seconder**

sec•on•dar•y (**sek**-uhn-der-ee) ***adjective***
1. Less important, as in *a secondary problem* or *a secondary cause.* ▸ ***adverb*** **secondarily**
2. Based on something that is not original.
3. To do with the second stage of something, as in *secondary education.*

secondary school ***noun*** A school between elementary school and college.

sec•ond•hand (**sek**-uhnd-*hand*) ***adjective***
1. If something is **secondhand,** it belonged to another person first.
2. Selling used goods, as in *a secondhand furniture store.*

second-rate ***adjective*** Not very good, as in *second-rate merchandise.*

se•cret (**see**-krit)
1. ***noun*** Something that is kept hidden or that only a few people know.
2. ***adjective*** Not known by many people.
3. in secret Privately.
▸ ***noun*** **secrecy** ▸ ***adverb*** **secretly**

secret agent ***noun*** A spy or someone who obtains secret information, usually from another government.

sec•re•tar•y (**sek**-ruh-ter-ee) ***noun***
1. Someone whose job is to prepare letters, answer the telephone, keep records, make appointments, and do other office work for an employer. ▸ ***adjective*** **secretarial**
2. A person in charge of a cabinet department in a government, as in *the secretary of defense.*
▸ ***noun, plural*** **secretaries**

se•crete (si-**kreet**) ***verb***
1. To produce a liquid. ▸ ***noun*** **secretion**
2. To hide.
▸ ***verb*** **secreting, secreted**

se•cre•tive (**see**-kri-tiv *or* si-**kree**-tiv) ***adjective*** Tending to be silent about some matter, as in *a secretive man.*

sect (**sekt**) ***noun*** A group whose members share the same beliefs and practices or follow the same leader. A sect is often a religious group that has broken away from a larger church.

sec•tion (**sek**-shuhn) ***noun***
1. A part or division of something, as in *the tail section of an airplane.*
2. A part of an area.
3. A **cross section.**

sec•tor (**sek**-tur) ***noun***
1. A part of a circle made by drawing two straight lines from the center to different places on the circumference.
2. A part or division of a city or group of people, as in *the public and private sectors.*

se•cure (si-**kyoor**)
1. ***adjective*** If you feel **secure,** you feel safe and sure of yourself.
2. ***adjective*** Safe, firmly closed, or well protected.

S

3. ***verb*** If you **secure** something, you make it safe, especially by closing it tightly.
4. ***adjective*** Firm and steady, or strong, as in *a secure ladder* or *a secure lock.*
5. ***adjective*** Certain or guaranteed, as in *a secure job.*
6. ***verb*** To get.
▸ ***noun*** **security** ▸ ***verb*** **securing, secured** ▸ ***adverb*** **securely**

se•dan (si-**dan**) ***noun*** An enclosed car for four or more people.

se•date (si-**date**)
1. ***adjective*** Calm and not hurried.
2. ***adjective*** Serious or dignified, as in *a sedate judge.*
3. ***verb*** To make someone calm or sleepy, especially by giving the person medicine. ▸ **sedating, sedated** ▸ ***noun*** **sedation**
▸ ***adverb*** **sedately**

sed•a•tive (**sed**-uh-tiv) ***noun*** A drug that makes you quiet and calm.

sed•i•ment (**sed**-uh-muhnt) ***noun***
1. Solid pieces of matter that settle at the bottom of a liquid. ▸ ***noun*** **sedimentation**
2. Rocks, sand, or dirt that has been carried to a place by water, wind, or a glacier.

sed•i•men•tar•y (*sed*-uh-**men**-tuh-ree) ***adjective*** **Sedimentary** rock is formed by layers of sediment in the ground being pressed together.

see (**see**) ***verb***
1. To use your eyes, to look at, or to notice something or someone.
2. To understand or to recognize.
3. To find out or to discover.
4. To visit and spend some time with someone.
5. To date someone regularly.
6. If you **see about** something, you deal with it.
7. If you **see through** someone or something, you are not deceived or tricked by the person or thing.
8. If you **see** a job **through,** you continue doing it right to the end.
See sounds like **sea.**
▸ ***verb*** **seeing, saw, seen** (**seen**)

seed (**seed**) ***noun***
1. ***noun*** The part of a flowering plant from which a new plant can grow, especially a grain, nut, or kernel.
2. ***noun*** The source or beginning of something, as in *the seeds of hope.*
3. ***verb*** To plant land with seeds.
4. ***verb*** To remove seeds from.
▸ ***verb*** **seeding, seeded**

seed•ling (**seed**-ling) ***noun*** A young plant that has been grown from a seed.

seek (**seek**) ***verb***
1. To look or search for something.
▸ ***noun*** **seeker**
2. To try.
3. To ask for.
▸ ***verb*** **seeking, sought** (**sawt**)

seem (**seem**) ***verb***
1. To appear to be, or to give the impression of being.
2. To appear to oneself.
Seem sounds like **seam.**
▸ ***verb*** **seeming, seemed**

seep (**seep**) ***verb*** To flow or trickle slowly. ▸ **seeping, seeped** ▸ ***noun*** **seepage**

see•saw (**see**-*saw*)
1. ***noun*** A long board balanced on a support in the middle. When people sit on opposite sides, one end goes up as the other goes down.
2. ***verb*** To ride on a seesaw.
3. ***verb*** To move up and down or back and forth.
▸ ***verb*** **seesawing, seesawed**

seethe (**seeTH**) ***verb***
1. To be very angry or excited.
2. If a liquid **seethes,** it bubbles or boils.
▸ ***verb*** **seething, seethed** ▸ ***adjective*** **seething**

see-through ***adjective*** Able to be seen through; transparent, as in *a see-through material.*

S

seg•ment (**seg**-muhnt) ***noun***
1. A part or section of something.
2. In geometry, the straight path that connects two points.
▸ ***verb*** **segment** ▸ ***adjective*** **segmental**

seg•re•gate (**seg**-ruh-gate) ***verb*** To separate or keep people or things apart from the main group. ▸ **segregating, segregated** ▸ ***adjective*** **segregated**

seg•re•ga•tion (seg-ruh-**gay**-shuhn) ***noun*** The act or practice of keeping people or groups apart.

seis•mo•graph (**size**-muh-*graf*) ***noun*** An instrument that detects earthquakes and measures their power. ▸ ***noun*** **seismography** (size-**mo**-gruh-fee)

seize (**seez**) ***verb***
1. To grab or take hold of something suddenly.
2. To arrest or capture someone or something.
▸ ***verb*** **seizing, seized**

sei•zure (**see**-zhur) ***noun***
1. A **seizure** is a sudden attack of illness, or a spasm.
2. The act of seizing something or someone.

sel•dom (**sel**-duhm) ***adverb*** Rarely.

se•lect (si-**lekt**)
1. ***verb*** To pick out or to choose. ▸ **selecting, selected** ▸ ***noun*** **selector**
2. ***adjective*** Carefully chosen as the best.

se•lec•tion (suh-**lek**-shuhn) ***noun***
1. The act of picking or choosing something.
2. A person or thing that has been chosen.

se•lec•tive (si-**lek**-tiv) ***adjective*** If you are **selective,** you choose carefully.

self (**self**) ***noun*** One's individual nature or personality. ▸ ***noun, plural*** **selves**

self-centered ***adjective*** Thinking only about yourself; selfish.

self-confident ***adjective*** If you are **self-confident,** you are sure of your own abilities or worth. ▸ ***noun*** **self-confidence** ▸ ***adverb*** **self-confidently**

self-conscious ***adjective*** If you are **self-conscious,** you think that people are looking at you, and you worry about what they are thinking. ▸ ***adverb*** **self-consciously**

self-control ***noun*** Control of your feelings and behavior. ▸ ***adjective*** **self-controlled**

self-defense ***noun*** The act of protecting yourself against attacks or threats.

self-de•struct (di-**struhkt**) ***verb*** To destroy itself or oneself.
▸ **self-destructing, self-destructed**
▸ ***noun*** **self-destruction** ▸ ***adjective*** **self-destructive**

self-employed ***adjective*** If you are **self-employed,** you work for yourself, not an employer. You are your own boss.

self-esteem ***noun*** A feeling of personal pride and of respect for yourself.

self-explanatory ***adjective*** If something is **self-explanatory,** it does not need any further explanation.

self•ish (**sel**-fish) ***adjective*** Someone who is **selfish** puts his or her own feelings and needs first and does not think of others. ▸ ***noun*** **selfishness** ▸ ***adverb*** **selfishly**

self-respect ***noun*** Pride in yourself and your abilities. ▸ ***adjective*** **self-respecting**

self-rising flour ***noun*** Flour containing baking powder, which makes cakes or breads rise.

self-service ***adjective*** If a store or gas station is **self-service**, you help yourself to what you want and then pay a cashier.

self-start•er (**star**-tur) ***noun*** Someone who has the ability or willingness to take a first step in doing or learning something.

self-sufficient ***adjective*** Able to take care of one's own needs without help from others. ▸ ***noun*** **self-sufficiency**

S

sell (sel) ***verb***
1. To give something in exchange for money. ▸ ***noun* seller**
2. To offer for sale.
3. To be sold or to be on sale.
4. To help the sale of something.
5. *(informal)* To make someone believe or want something.
Sell sounds like **cell.**
▸ ***verb* selling, sold (sohld)**

sem•a•phore (**sem**-uh-*for*) ***noun*** A system of making signals by means of flags or your arms. ▸ ***verb* semaphore**

se•mes•ter (suh-**mess**-tur) ***noun*** One of two terms that make up a school year.

sem•i•cir•cle (**sem**-i-*sur*-kuhl) ***noun*** A half of a circle. ▸ ***adjective* semicircular**

sem•i•co•lon (**sem**-i-*koh*-luhn) ***noun*** The punctuation mark (;) used to separate parts of a sentence. A semicolon shows a greater separation of thoughts or ideas than a comma does.

sem•i•con•duc•tor (*sem*-ee-kuhn-**duhk**-tur) ***noun*** A substance, such as silicon, whose ability to conduct electricity is not as good as a conductor, such as copper, but is better than an insulator, such as plastic. Semiconductors are used in electronic devices, including personal computers.

sem•i•fi•nal (**sem**-ee-*fye*-nuhl *or* **sem**-eye-*fye*-nuhl) ***noun*** A match or game to decide who will play in the final. ▸ ***noun* semifinalist** ▸ ***adjective* semifinal**

sem•i•nar•y (**sem**-uh-*ner*-ee) ***noun*** A school that trains students to become priests, ministers, or rabbis. ▸ ***noun, plural* seminaries**

Sem•i•nole (**sem**-uh-nole) ***noun*** A member of a tribe of American Indians that originally lived in Florida. After the United States acquired Florida in 1819, the government attempted to force the Seminoles to move to the Indian Territory in Oklahoma. They resisted, but after fighting three wars, many were sent west. Today, the Seminoles largely live in Oklahoma, but some still live in Florida. ▸ ***noun, plural* Seminoles** *or* **Seminole**

sen•ate (**sen**-it) ***noun***
1. A body of officials elected to make laws.
2. Senate One of the two houses of the U.S. Congress that make laws. Each state has two senators. Senators are elected every six years. Most states have similar legislative bodies. ▸ ***noun* senator** *or* **Senator**

send (**send**) ***verb***
1. To make someone or something go somewhere, as in *to send a letter,* or *to send someone on an errand.* ▸ ***noun* sender**
2. To write to ask for something.
3. If you **send for** something or someone, you make it come to you.
▸ ***verb* sending, sent**

send-off ***noun*** *(informal)* If you are given a **send-off,** people gather to wish you well for a journey, new job, etc.

se•nile (**see**-nile *or* **sen**-ile) ***adjective*** Weak in mind and body because of old age. ▸ ***noun* senility** (si-**nil**-i-tee)

sen•ior (**see**-nyur)
1. *adjective* When a father and son have identical names, **senior** is placed after the surname to indicate the father, as in *John Doe, Senior.*
2. *adjective* Someone who is **senior** to you is older or has a higher rank.
▸ ***noun* seniority**
3. *noun* A student in the fourth year of high school or college. ▸ ***adjective* senior**

senior citizen ***noun*** An elderly person, especially someone who is older than 65 and has retired.

sen•sa•tion (sen-**say**-shuhn) ***noun***
1. The ability to feel or be aware of something through one of the senses, as in *the sensation of touch.*
2. A feeling or an awareness.
3. Something that causes a lot of excitement and interest. ▸ ***adjective* sensational** ▸ ***adverb* sensationally**

S

sense (**senss**)
1. ***noun*** One of the powers a living being uses to learn about its surroundings. Sight, hearing, touch, taste, and smell are the five senses.
2. ***noun*** A feeling, as in *a sense of pride* or *a sense of failure.*
3. ***noun*** An understanding or an appreciation, as in *a good sense of humor.*
4. ***noun*** Good judgment.
5. ***noun*** Meaning, as in *sense of the word.*
6. ***verb*** To feel or be aware of something. ▸ **sensing, sensed**
7. If something **makes sense,** it is understandable or logical.

sense•less (**senss**-liss) ***adjective***
1. Pointless or without meaning. ▸ ***adverb*** **senselessly**
2. Unconscious.

sense organ ***noun*** An organ in the body that receives information, or stimuli, from its surroundings. The human sense organs include the eyes, ears, nose, taste buds, and skin.

sen•si•ble (**sen**-suh-buhl) ***adjective*** If you are **sensible,** you think carefully and do not do stupid or dangerous things. ▸ ***adverb*** **sensibly**

sen•si•tive (**sen**-suh-tiv) ***adjective***
1. Easily offended or hurt.
2. Painful.
3. Aware of other people's feelings.
4. Able to react to the slightest change, as in *a sensitive measuring device.*
▸ ***noun*** **sensitivity** ▸ ***adverb*** **sensitively**

sen•sor (**sen**-sur) ***noun*** An instrument that can detect changes in heat, sound, pressure, etc., and send the information to a controlling device.

sen•tence (**sen**-tuhnss) ***noun***
1. A group of words that expresses a complete thought, having a subject and a verb. A written sentence begins with a capital letter and ends with a period, a question mark, or an exclamation point.
2. A punishment given to a guilty person in court. ▸ ***verb*** **sentence**

sen•ti•ment (**sen**-tuh-muhnt) ***noun***
1. An opinion about a specific matter.
2. A thought or an attitude that is based on feeling or emotion instead of reason.
3. Tender or sensitive feeling.

sen•ti•ment•al (sen-tuh-**men**-tuhl) ***adjective*** To do with emotion, romance, or feelings. ▸ ***noun*** **sentimentality** ▸ ***adverb*** **sentimentally**

sen•try (**sen**-tree) ***noun*** A person who stands guard and warns others of danger. ▸ ***noun, plural*** **sentries**

se•pal (**see**-puhl) ***noun*** The green outer covering of a flower bud. The sepal opens to allow the flower to bloom and remains to protect the petals.

sep•a•rate
1. (**sep**-uh-rate) ***verb*** To part or divide something or some people.
2. (**sep**-ur-it) ***adjective*** Different, individual, or not together. ▸ ***adverb*** **separately**
3. (**sep**-uh-rate) ***verb*** If a husband and wife **separate,** they stop living together.
4. **separates** (**sep**-ur-its) ***noun, plural*** Clothes, such as a skirt and blouse, that you can wear together or with other clothes.
▸ ***verb*** **separating, separated** ▸ ***noun*** **separation**

Sep•tem•ber (sep-**tem**-bur) ***noun*** The ninth month on the calendar, after August and before October. September has 30 days.

se•quel (**see**-kwuhl) ***noun*** A book or movie that continues the story of an earlier work.

se•quence (**see**-kwuhnss) ***noun***
1. The following of one thing after another in a regular or fixed order.
2. A series or collection of things that follow in order. ▸ ***adjective*** **sequential** (see-**kwen**-shuhl)

se•quoi•a (suh-**kwoi**-uh) ***noun*** A giant evergreen tree that can reach a height of over 300 feet (90 meters). Sequoias have thick, reddish brown bark and grow mostly in California.

ser•en•dip•i•ty (*ser*-uhn-**dip**-uh-tee) ***noun*** A fortunate accident in which you find something valuable or pleasing when you were not looking for it.
▸ ***adjective*** **serendipitous**

se•rene (suh-**reen**) ***adjective*** Calm and peaceful, as in *a serene setting.* ▸ ***noun*** **serenity** (suh-**ren**-i-tee) ▸ ***adverb*** **serenely**

serf (**surf**) ***noun*** In medieval times, a farm worker who was owned by a lord and treated as a slave. **Serf** sounds like **surf.** ▸ ***noun*** **serfdom**

ser•geant (**sar**-juhnt) ***noun*** An officer in the army or Marine Corps who is appointed from among the enlisted personnel. A sergeant ranks above a corporal and is in charge of enlisted troops.

se•ri•al (**sihr**-ee-uhl) ***noun*** A story that is told in several parts. The parts are presented one at a time on television or radio or in a magazine. **Serial** sounds like **cereal.** ▸ ***noun*** **serialization**
▸ ***verb*** **serialize**

serial number ***noun*** A number that identifies a member of the armed forces or a vehicle, an appliance, or another product.

se•ries (**sihr**-eez) ***noun***
1. A group of related things that follow in order.
2. A number of television or radio programs that are linked in some way.
3. Electrical parts that are connected **in series** allow electricity to pass through them one after the other.
▸ ***noun, plural*** **series**

se•ri•ous (**sihr**-ee-uhss) ***adjective***
1. Solemn and thoughtful.
2. Sincere or not joking.
3. Very bad, or dangerous.
4. Important and requiring a lot of thought.
▸ ***noun*** **seriousness** ▸ ***adverb*** **seriously**

ser•mon (**sur**-muhn) ***noun***
1. A speech given during a religious service.
2. Any serious talk, especially one that deals with morals or correct behavior.
▸ ***verb*** **sermonize**

ser•pent (**sur**-puhnt) ***noun*** A snake.

ser•rat•ed (**ser**-ay-tid) ***adjective*** A **serrated** knife has teeth like a saw.

se•rum (**sihr**-uhm) ***noun***
1. The clear, thin, liquid part of the blood. It separates from blood when a clot forms.
2. A liquid used to prevent or cure a disease. Serum is taken from the blood of an animal that has had the disease and is already immune to it.
▸ ***noun, plural*** **serums** *or* **sera** (**sihr**-uh)

serv•ant (**sur**-vuhnt) ***noun*** Someone who works in another person's house doing housework, cooking, or other chores.

serve (**surv**)
1. ***verb*** To work for someone as a servant.
2. ***verb*** To give someone food, or to help someone find items in a store.
3. ***verb*** To do your duty in some form of service.
4. ***verb*** To supply.
5. ***verb*** To spend.
6. ***verb*** In games such as tennis and volleyball, to begin play by hitting the ball.
7. ***noun*** The act of hitting a ball over a net to begin play in games such as tennis and volleyball.
▸ ***verb*** **serving, served** ▸ ***noun*** **server**

serv•er (**sur**-vur) ***noun***
1. Someone who serves others, such as a waiter or waitress.
2. The player who serves the ball in tennis, volleyball, or other games.
3. A computer shared by two or more users in a network.

S

S

serv•ice (**sur**-viss) ***noun***
1. The **service** in a store, restaurant, etc., is the way that the staff helps and takes care of you.
2. Work that helps others.
3. Employment as a servant.
4. A system or way of providing something useful or necessary.
5. A branch of the armed forces.
6. A religious ceremony or meeting.
7. A branch of the government, as in *the postal service* or *the foreign service.*
8. The repairing of a car or an appliance.
9. A complete set of matched dishes, as in *a dinner service.*
10. A serve in tennis, volleyball, or any game in which a ball is hit over a net.
▸ ***verb*** **service**

service station ***noun*** Another term for **gas station.**

ses•a•me (**sess**-uh-mee) ***noun*** A small oval seed, or the tropical plant from which this seed comes. Sesame seeds and their oil are used in cooking and baking.

ses•sion (**sesh**-uhn) ***noun***
1. A formal meeting, as in *a session of the Supreme Court.*
2. A series of meetings of a court or legislature.
3. A period of time used for an activity.

set (**set**)
1. ***noun*** A group of things that go together, as in *a chess set.*
2. ***noun*** The stage or scenery for a play or movie.
3. ***adjective*** Ready.
4. ***adjective*** Fixed.
5. ***verb*** To put or to place.
6. ***verb*** To lay out, arrange, or put in order.
7. ***verb*** To begin or to start.
8. ***verb*** To decide on.
9. ***verb*** To model for other people to follow.
10. ***verb*** If a liquid **sets,** it becomes hard or solid.
11. ***verb*** When the sun **sets,** it goes below the horizon.
12. ***noun*** A device for sending out or receiving electronic signals, as in *a television set.*
13. ***noun*** In math, a collection of items that are grouped together or have something in common.
14. If you **set** something **up,** you get it ready for use or arrange it.
15. If you **set aside** something, you save it for another time.
16. If you **set out** for a place, you begin your trip.
17. If you are **set on** something, you want it very much and are determined to get or achieve it.
▸ ***verb*** **setting, set**

set•back (**set**-*bak*) ***noun*** Something that delays you or keeps you from making progress.

set•tee (se-**tee**) ***noun*** A small sofa.

set•tle (**set**-uhl) ***verb***
1. To decide or agree on something.
2. To make yourself comfortable.
3. To make a home or to live in a new place. ▸ ***noun*** **settler**
4. To sink.
5. To calm.
6. If you **settle in,** you get used to your new house, school, etc.
7. If you **settle up,** you pay a bill or an account.
▸ ***verb*** **settling, settled**

set•tle•ment (**set**-uhl-muhnt) ***noun***
1. An agreement or a decision about something that was in doubt.
2. A small village or group of houses.
3. A colony or group of people who have left one place to make a home in another.

set•up (**set**-*uhp*) ***noun*** The way that something is organized or arranged.

sev•en (**sev**-uhn) ***noun*** The whole number, written 7, that comes after six and before eight. ▸ ***adjective*** **seven**

sev•enth (**sev**-uhnth)
1. ***adjective*** That which comes after sixth and before eighth.

2. *noun* One part of something that has been divided into seven equal parts, written $^1/_7$.

sev•er (**sev**-ur) ***verb***
1. To cut off or apart, as in *to sever a limb.*
2. To end or to break off.
▸ ***verb* severing, severed**

sev•er•al (**sev**-ur-uhl)
1. *adjective* More than two, but not many.
2. *noun* More than two, or a few, people or things.

se•vere (suh-**veer**) ***adjective***
1. Strict, harsh, or demanding, as in *severe punishment* or *severe criticism.*
2. Painful or dangerous, as in *a severe burn* or *a severe illness.*
3. Violent, or causing great discomfort or difficulty, as in *a severe storm.*
▸ ***adjective* severer, severest** ▸ ***noun* severity** (suh-**ver**-i-tee) ▸ ***adverb* severely**

sew (**soh**) ***verb*** To make, repair, or fasten something with stitches made by a needle and thread. **Sew** sounds like **so.**
▸ **sewing, sewed, sewn (sohn)** ▸ ***noun* sewing**

sew•age (**soo**-ij) ***noun*** Liquid and solid waste that is carried away in sewers and drains.

sewage plant ***noun*** A place where sewage is treated to make it safe and not poisonous.

sew•er (**soo**-ur) ***noun*** An underground pipe that carries away liquid and solid waste.

sewing machine ***noun*** A machine for sewing very fast or making special stitches.

sex (**seks**) ***noun***
1. One of the two classes of most living things, male or female, into which people and many other living things are divided.
2. The fact or condition of being male or female.
▸ ***noun, plural* sexes**

sex•ist (**sek**-sist) ***adjective*** Someone who is **sexist** discriminates against members of one or the other sex.
▸ ***noun* sexism, *noun* sexist**

shab•by (**shab**-ee) ***adjective***
1. Worn, neglected, or in need of repair.
▸ ***noun* shabbiness**
2. Unfair or mean.
▸ ***adjective* shabbier, shabbiest**
▸ ***adverb* shabbily**

shack (**shak**) ***noun*** A small, roughly built hut or house.

shack•les (**shak**-uhlz) ***noun, plural*** A pair of metal rings locked around the wrists or ankles of a prisoner or a slave.

shad (**shad**) ***noun*** A food fish related to the herring. Shad live along the coasts of Europe and North America and swim up freshwater rivers to lay their eggs, or roe. ▸ ***noun, plural* shad**

shade (**shayd**)
1. *verb* To shelter something from the light.
2. *noun* A device that provides shelter from light, as in *a lamp shade* or *a window shade.*
3. *noun* An area that is sheltered from the light. ▸ ***adjective* shady**
4. *noun* The degree of darkness of a color.
5. *verb* To make part of a drawing darker than the rest.
6. *noun* A small amount or difference.
7. shades *noun, plural* *(slang)* Sunglasses.
▸ ***noun* shading** ▸ ***verb* shading, shaded**

shad•ow (**shad**-oh)
1. *noun* A dark shape made by something blocking out light. ▸ ***adjective* shadowy**
2. *noun* A faint trace or suggestion, as in *a shadow of a doubt.*
3. *verb* To follow someone closely and watch the person carefully and usually secretly. ▸ **shadowing, shadowed**

S

S

shaft (**shaft**) ***noun***
1. The long, narrow rod of a spear, an arrow, or a paddle.
2. A rotating rod that transmits power to wheels or propellers.
3. A thin beam of light.
4. A long, narrow passage that goes straight down, as in *a mine shaft* or *an elevator shaft.*
5. The central stem of a feather.

shag•gy (**shag**-ee) ***adjective*** Having long, rough hair or wool, as in *a shaggy dog* or *a shaggy carpet.* ▸ **shaggier, shaggiest**

shake (**shayk**) ***verb***
1. To move quickly up and down or back and forth.
2. To remove or scatter something by making short, quick movements.
3. To tremble, or to cause to tremble.
4. To upset.
5. To clasp someone's hand as a way of greeting or agreeing with the person.
▸ ***verb*** **shaking, shook (shuk), shaken** (**shay**-kin) ▸ ***noun*** **shake**

shak•y (**shay**-kee) ***adjective***
1. Unsteady and wobbly.
2. Trembling or shaking.
▸ ***adjective*** **shakier, shakiest**

shale (**shayl**) ***noun*** A rock that is formed from hardened clay or mud. It has many thin layers that separate easily.

shall (**shal**) ***verb*** A helping verb that is used in the following ways:
1. To show an action that will take place in the future.
2. To show that an action is required.
3. To ask a question, or to offer a suggestion.

shal•low (**shal**-oh) ***adjective***
1. Not deep.
2. Lacking depth of thought, feeling, or knowledge, as in *a shallow mind.*
▸ ***adjective*** **shallower, shallowest**

sham (**sham**) ***noun*** Something that is false and not what it seems to be.
▸ ***adjective*** **sham**

sham•bles (**sham**-buhlz) ***noun*** If something is a **shambles,** it is very badly organized and chaotic.

shame (**shame**) ***noun***
1. A feeling of guilt and sadness about something wrong or foolish that you have done.
2. Dishonor or disgrace. ▸ ***verb*** **shame**
3. A pity, or a sad thing to have happened.

sham•poo (sham-**poo**) ***noun*** A soapy liquid used for washing hair, carpets, or upholstery. ▸ ***verb*** **shampoo**

sham•rock (**sham**-*rok*) ***noun*** A small, green plant with three leaves. The shamrock is the national emblem of Ireland.

shan•ty (**shan**-tee) ***noun***
1. A roughly built hut or cabin. A shanty is usually made of wood.
2. A **sea shanty** is a song sung by sailors in rhythm with their work.
▸ ***noun, plural*** **shanties**

shape (**shayp**)
1. ***noun*** The form or outline of an object or a figure.
2. ***verb*** To mold something into a shape.
3. ***noun*** Good or fit condition.
4. **shape up** ***verb*** *(informal)* To develop.
▸ ***verb*** **shaping, shaped**

shape•less (**shape**-liss) ***adjective*** Having no clearly defined shape, or having an unattractive shape.

share (**shair**)
1. ***verb*** To divide something between two or more people.
2. ***noun*** The portion of something that someone receives or that is assigned to someone.
3. ***verb*** To use together.
4. ***verb*** To take part.
5. ***noun*** One of many equal parts into which the ownership of a business is divided.
▸ ***verb*** **sharing, shared**

share•ware (**shair**-*wair*) ***noun*** Computer software that has a copyright but is provided free on a trial basis. If a person decides to continue using the software, he or she is expected to pay a fee to the author. ▸ ***noun, plural*** **shareware**

shark (**shark**) ***noun***
1. A large and often fierce fish that feeds on meat and has very sharp teeth.
2. Someone who cheats people.

sharp (**sharp**) ***adjective***
1. Having an edge or a point that cuts or pierces easily, as in *a sharp knife* or *a sharp needle.*
2. Pointed, as in *a sharp mountain peak.*
3. Able to think or notice things quickly, as in *a sharp mind* or *sharp eyes.*
4. Sudden and dramatic.
5. Strong, biting, or harsh, as in *a sharp cheese, sharp words,* or *a sharp wind.*
6. Clearly outlined, as in *a sharp picture.*
7. Exactly.
8. In music, a **sharp** note is one that is higher in pitch than the usual note.
▸ ***noun*** **sharp**
9. *(slang)* Very attractive.
▸ ***adjective*** **sharper, sharpest**

shat•ter (**shat**-ur) ***verb***
1. To break into tiny pieces.
2. To destroy completely or to ruin.
▸ ***verb*** **shattering, shattered**

shave (**shayv**)
1. ***verb*** To remove hair with a razor or an electric shaver. ▸ ***noun*** **shave**
2. ***verb*** To cut off or slice in thin layers.
3. *(informal)* If you have **a close shave,** you only just manage to escape from something.
▸ ***verb*** **shaving, shaved**

shawl (**shawl**) ***noun*** A piece of soft material that is worn over the shoulders or around the head.

Shaw•nee (shaw-**nee**) ***noun*** A member of an American Indian tribe that once lived in the central Ohio valley. The Shawnee now live mainly in Oklahoma.
▸ ***noun, plural*** **Shawnee** *or* **Shawnees**

she (**shee**) ***pronoun*** The female person or animal mentioned before.

sheaf (**sheef**) ***noun*** A bundle, as in *a sheaf of papers.* ▸ ***noun, plural*** **sheaves**

shear (**shihr**) ***verb***
1. To clip or cut with scissors or shears.
2. To cut the fleece off a sheep. **Shear** sounds like **sheer.**
▸ ***verb*** **shearing, sheared** *or* **shorn** (**shorn**)

shears (**shihrz**) ***noun, plural*** A large cutting tool with two blades. Shears are used for cutting hedges, trimming grass, etc.

sheath (**sheeth**) ***noun*** A holder for a knife, sword, or dagger.

shed (**shed**)
1. ***noun*** A small building used for storing things.
2. ***verb*** To let something fall or drop off.
3. ***verb*** To give off or to supply.
▸ ***verb*** **shedding, shed**

she'd (**sheed**) ***contraction*** A short form of *she had* or *she would.*

sheen (**sheen**) ***noun*** A shine on a surface.

sheep (**sheep**) ***noun*** A farm animal raised for its wool and meat. ▸ ***noun, plural*** **sheep**

sheep•dog (**sheep**-*dog*) ***noun*** A working farm dog that guards and rounds up sheep.

sheep•ish (**sheep**-ish) ***adjective*** If someone looks **sheepish,** the person looks embarrassed or ashamed, often because he or she has done something foolish. ▸ ***adverb*** **sheepishly**

sheer (**shihr**) ***adjective***
1. Extremely thin and transparent, as in *sheer stockings.*
2. Total and complete, as in *sheer nonsense* or *sheer exhaustion.*
3. Extremely steep.
Sheer sounds like **shear.**
▸ ***adjective*** **sheerer, sheerest**

sheet (**sheet**) ***noun***
1. A large, thin, rectangular piece of cloth used to cover a bed.
2. A thin, flat piece of paper, glass, metal, or other material.

S

sheik (**sheek** *or* **shake**) ***noun*** The head of an Arab tribe, village, or family.

shelf (**shelf**) ***noun***
1. A horizontal board on a wall or in a cupboard, used for holding or storing things.
2. Something flat that looks like a shelf, such as a ledge of rock.
▸ ***noun, plural*** **shelves** (**shelvz**)

shell (**shel**)
1. ***noun*** A hard outer covering or case. Nuts, tortoises, shellfish, and eggs all have shells.
2. ***noun*** A type of small bomb that is fired from a cannon.
3. ***noun*** A metal or paper case that holds a bullet and its explosive. It is fired from a gun.
4. ***verb*** To remove something from its shell.
5. ***verb*** To bombard, or attack with shells.
▸ ***verb*** **shelling, shelled**

she'll (**sheel**) ***contraction*** A short form of *she will* or *she shall.*

shel•lac (shuh-**lak**) ***noun*** A hard varnish used on wooden floors and furniture to protect them and give them a shiny finish.

shell•fish (**shel**-*fish*) ***noun*** A sea creature with a shell, such as a shrimp, crab, lobster, or mussel. Many shellfish are edible. ▸ ***noun, plural*** **shellfish** *or* **shellfishes**

shel•ter (**shel**-tur) ***noun***
1. A place where you can keep covered in bad weather or stay safe and protected from danger, as in *a bus shelter* or *a bomb shelter.*
2. Protection.
3. A place where a homeless person, a victim of a disaster, or an animal that is not wanted can stay.
▸ ***verb*** **shelter**

shelve (**shelv**) ***verb***
1. To put something off for a while.
2. To put something on a shelf or shelves.
▸ ***verb*** **shelving, shelved**

shep•herd (**shep**-urd)
1. ***noun*** Someone whose job is to look after sheep.
2. ***verb*** To watch over or to guide.
▸ **shepherding, shepherded**

sher•bet (**shur**-buht) *or* **sher•bert** (**shur**-burt) ***noun*** A frozen dessert made of fruit juices, water, sugar, and milk, egg white, or gelatin.

sher•iff (**sher**-if) ***noun*** The chief person in charge of enforcing the law in a county.

sher•ry (**sher**-ee) ***noun*** A strong, sweet wine. ▸ ***noun, plural*** **sherries**

she's (**sheez**) ***contraction*** A short form of *she is* or *she has.*

Shet•land pony (**shet**-luhnd) ***noun*** A small horse with a long mane and tail and a rough coat, originally bred in Scotland's Shetland Islands.

shield (**sheeld**)
1. ***noun*** A piece of armor carried to protect the body from attack.
2. ***noun*** A protective barrier, as in *a heat shield.*
3. ***verb*** To protect something or someone. ▸ **shielding, shielded**
4. ***noun*** A police officer's badge.

shift (**shift**)
1. ***verb*** To change or move something.
2. ***noun*** A movement or a change.
3. ***noun*** A set period of several hours' continuous work, as in *the night shift.*
4. ***verb*** To change the gears in a motor vehicle that does not have an automatic transmission. ▸ ***noun*** **shift**
▸ ***verb*** **shifting, shifted**

shii•ta•ke (shee-**tah**-kee) ***noun*** A dark brown, edible Asian mushroom.

shil•ling (**shil**-ing) ***noun***
1. A coin that was used in Great Britain until 1971. Twenty shillings equaled one pound.

S

2. A coin that is used in several African countries, including Kenya, Somalia, Tanzania, and Uganda. One shilling equals 100 cents.

shim•mer (**shim**-ur) ***verb*** To shine with a faint, unsteady light. ▸ **shimmering, shimmered**

shin (**shin**)
1. ***noun*** The front part of your leg between your knee and your ankle.
2. ***verb*** To climb by using your hands and legs to pull you up, as in *to shin up a tree.* ▸ **shinning, shinned**

shine (**shine**) ***verb***
1. To give off a bright light.
2. To be bright; to make bright or polish.
3. If someone **shines** at something, the person is very good at it.
▸ ***verb*** **shining, shone** (**shohn**) *or* **shined** ▸ ***noun*** **shine**

shin•gle (**shing**-guhl) ***noun*** A thin, flat piece of wood or other material used to cover roofs or outside walls. Shingles are put on in overlapping rows so that water runs off them. ▸ ***verb*** **shingle**

Shin•to (**shin**-toh) ***noun*** The main religion of Japan, which involves the worship of ancestors and the spirits of nature.

ship (**ship**)
1. ***noun*** A large boat that can travel across deep water.
2. ***noun*** An airplane, an airship, or a spacecraft.
3. ***verb*** To send on a ship, a truck, a train, or an airplane.
4. ***verb*** To go on a ship, usually to work.
▸ ***verb*** **shipping, shipped**

ship•ment (**ship**-muhnt) ***noun***
1. A package or a group of packages that is sent from one place to another.
2. The act of shipping.

ship•shape (**ship**-*shayp*) ***adjective*** Clean, neat, and in good order.

ship•wreck (**ship**-*rek*) ***noun***
1. The wrecking or destruction of a ship at sea. ▸ ***verb*** **shipwreck**
2. The remains of a wrecked ship.
▸ ***adjective*** **shipwrecked**

ship•yard (**ship**-*yard*) ***noun*** A place where ships are built or repaired.

shirk (**shurk**) ***verb*** To avoid doing something that should be done.
▸ **shirking, shirked** ▸ ***noun*** **shirker**

shirt (**shurt**) ***noun*** A piece of clothing that you wear on the top half of your body. Shirts usually have a collar and sleeves.

shish ka•bob *or* **shish ke•bob** (**shish** kuh-bob) ***noun*** Small pieces of meat and vegetables cooked on a skewer.

shiv•er (**shiv**-ur) ***verb*** To shake with cold or fear. ▸ **shivering, shivered**
▸ ***noun*** **shiver** ▸ ***adjective*** **shivery**

shoal (**shole**) ***noun***
1. A stretch of shallow water.
2. A large group of fish swimming together.

shock (**shok**)
1. ***noun*** A sudden, violent event, such as an accident or a death, that upsets or disturbs you greatly.
2. ***noun*** The mental or emotional upset caused by such an event.
3. ***noun*** If a person goes into **shock,** he or she suffers a serious lowering of blood pressure and may lose consciousness. Shock may be caused by severe injury or great emotional upset.
4. ***verb*** To surprise, horrify, or disgust someone. ▸ **shocking, shocked**
▸ ***adjective*** **shocking**
5. ***noun*** A sudden, violent impact.
6. ***noun*** The violent effect of an electric current passing through someone's body. ▸ ***verb*** **shock**
7. ***noun*** A thick, bushy mass.

shod•dy (**shod**-ee) ***adjective*** Carelessly produced and of poor quality, as in *shoddy goods.* ▸ **shoddier, shoddiest**
▸ ***noun*** **shoddiness**

S

shoe (**shoo**)
1. ***noun*** An outer covering for the foot. Shoes are usually made of leather or vinyl.
2. ***noun*** A horseshoe.
3. ***noun*** The part of a brake that presses against a wheel to slow or stop it.
4. ***verb*** To fit a shoe or shoes on a horse. ▸ **shoeing, shod** (**shod**) *or* **shoed**

shoe•horn (**shoo**-*horn*) ***noun*** A narrow piece of plastic or metal that you use to help your heel slip easily into a shoe.

shoe•lace (**shoo**-*layss*) ***noun*** A cord or string used for fastening a shoe.

shoot (**shoot**)
1. ***verb*** To wound or kill a person or an animal with a bullet or an arrow.
2. ***verb*** To fire a gun.
3. ***verb*** To make a movie or video.
4. ***verb*** To move very fast.
5. ***noun*** A young plant that has just appeared above the soil, or a new part of a plant that is just beginning to grow.
6. ***verb*** To aim and drive a ball, puck, etc., toward a goal or net.
7. ***verb*** To strive for.
▸ ***verb*** **shooting, shot**

shooting star ***noun*** A meteor, or piece of rock from space that burns up as it enters the earth's atmosphere.

shop (**shop**)
1. ***noun*** A place where goods are displayed and sold, as in *a hat shop* or *a pet shop.*
2. ***noun*** A place where a particular kind of work is done, as in *a flower shop* or *a repair shop.*
3. ***verb*** To go to stores in order to buy goods. ▸ **shopping, shopped** ▸ ***noun*** **shopper,** ***noun*** **shopping**

shop•keep•er (**shop**-*kee*-pur) ***noun*** Someone who owns or runs a small shop or store.

shop•lift•er (**shop**-*lif*-tur) ***noun*** Someone who takes something from a store without paying for it. ▸ ***noun*** **shoplifting** ▸ ***verb*** **shoplift**

shopping center ***noun*** A group of stores with one central parking lot.

shore (**shor**) ***noun*** The land along the edge of an ocean, a river, or a lake.

short (**short**)
1. ***adjective*** Less than the average length, height, distance, time, etc., as in *a short book, a short girl, a short walk, a short wait.* ▸ ***noun*** **shortness** ▸ ***adverb*** **short**
2. ***adjective*** If you are **short of** something, you have less of it than you need.
3. ***adjective*** Brief in a rude or unfriendly way; curt.
4. ***adverb*** Suddenly.
5. ***noun*** A **short circuit.**
6. **shorts** ***noun, plural*** Pants that reach to or above the knees.
7. **shorts** ***noun, plural*** A man's or boy's underwear.
8. **short for** ***adjective*** Shortened from something longer.
▸ ***adjective and adverb*** **shorter, shortest**

short•age (**shor**-tij) ***noun*** When there is a **shortage** of something, there is not enough of it.

short•bread (**short**-*bred*) ***noun*** A rich cookie made with flour, sugar, and shortening.

short circuit ***noun*** An electric circuit that bypasses a device that was designed to be included in the circuit. Sometimes a short circuit can cause a fire or blow a fuse. ▸ ***verb*** **short-circuit**

short•com•ing (**short**-*kuhm*-ing) ***noun*** A failing or weak point in something or someone.

short•en (**short**-uhn) ***verb*** To make short or shorter. ▸ **shortening, shortened**

short•en•ing (**short**-uhn-ing) ***noun*** Butter, lard, or other fat used in baking.

short•hand (**short**-*hand*) ***noun*** A system of writing symbols instead of words. Shorthand is used for taking notes quickly.

short-hand•ed (**han**-did) ***adjective*** If you are **short-handed,** you do not have enough people to do a job.

short•ly (**short**-lee) ***adverb*** Soon or presently.

short-range ***adjective*** Not reaching far in time or distance.

short•sight•ed (**short**-**sye**-tid) ***adjective***
1. Not aware of future consequences.
2. Nearsighted.
▸ ***noun*** **shortsightedness**

short•stop (**short**-*stop*) ***noun*** In baseball or softball, the player whose position is between second and third base.

short-tem•pered (**tem**-purd) ***adjective*** Someone who is **short-tempered** becomes angry very quickly and easily.

shot (**shot**)
1. ***verb*** The past tense and past participle of **shoot.**
2. ***noun*** The firing of a gun.
3. ***noun*** A person who shoots.
4. ***noun*** A single bullet fired from a gun.
5. ***noun*** A single metal ball or pellet fired from a gun or cannon. ▸ ***noun, plural*** **shots** *or* **shot**
6. ***noun*** A throw or thrust of a ball or puck toward a net or other goal in sports such as basketball, hockey, soccer, and golf.
7. ***noun*** The distance or range over which something such as a missile or bullet can travel.
8. ***noun*** A photograph.
9. ***noun*** *(informal)* An injection.
10. ***noun*** A heavy metal ball thrown at a track-and-field event.
11. ***noun*** *(informal)* An attempt.

shot•gun (**shot**-*guhn*) ***noun*** A gun with a long barrel that fires cartridges filled with pellets.

shot put ***noun*** A track-and-field event in which a heavy metal ball is thrown as far as possible.

should (**shud**) ***verb*** A helping verb that is used in the following ways:
1. To show a duty or an obligation.
2. To show that something is likely or expected.
3. To show that something might happen.

shoul•der (**shohl**-dur)
1. ***noun*** The part of your body between your neck and your upper arm.
2. ***noun*** A similar part on an animal's body.
3. ***noun*** The sloping side or edge of a road or highway.
4. ***verb*** To push with your shoulder or shoulders.
5. ***verb*** To take on a burden, as in *to shoulder the blame* or *to shoulder a responsibility.*
▸ ***verb*** **shouldering, shouldered**

shoulder blade ***noun*** One of two large, flat bones in the upper back, just below the shoulder.

should•n't (**shud**-uhnt) ***contraction*** A short form of *should not.*

shout (**shout**) ***verb*** To call out loudly.
▸ **shouting, shouted** ▸ ***noun*** **shout**

shove (**shuhv**) ***verb*** To push hard or roughly. ▸ **shoving, shoved** ▸ ***noun*** **shove**

shov•el (**shuhv**-uhl)
1. ***noun*** A tool with a long handle and a flattened scoop, used for moving material.
2. ***verb*** To move things with a shovel.
▸ **shoveling, shoveled**

show (**shoh**)
1. ***verb*** To let see or be seen.
2. ***verb*** To explain or demonstrate to someone.
3. ***verb*** To make known or clear.
4. ***verb*** To guide or lead someone.
5. ***verb*** To be visible.
6. ***noun*** A public performance or exhibition.
7. ***verb*** If someone **shows up,** the person comes to a place.
▸ ***verb*** **showing, showed, shown** (**shohn**)

S

show business ***noun*** The world of the theater, movies, television, and other forms of entertainment.

show•er (**shou**-er)
1. ***noun*** A piece of equipment that produces a fine spray of water for washing your body.
2. ***verb*** To wash yourself under a shower.
3. ***noun*** A brief rainfall. ▸ ***adjective*** **showery**
4. ***verb*** To fall in large numbers. ▸ ***noun*** **shower**
5. ***verb*** To give someone lots of things.
6. ***noun*** A party at which a woman who is about to marry or give birth is honored and receives presents.
▸ ***verb*** **showering, showered**

show-off ***noun*** Someone who behaves in a bragging way about his or her possessions or abilities. ▸ ***verb*** **show off**

show•room (**shoh**-*room*) ***noun*** A room used to display goods for sale, as in *a car showroom.*

show•y (**shoh**-ee) ***adjective***
1. Striking, or attracting attention because of color or size, as in *showy flowers.*
2. Flashy, or too bright and colorful, as in *a showy dress.*

shrap•nel (**shrap**-nuhl) ***noun*** Small pieces of metal scattered by an exploding shell or bomb.

shred (**shred**) ***noun***
1. A long, thin strip of cloth or paper that has been torn off something. ▸ ***verb*** **shred**
2. A small amount; a bit, as in *a shred of truth* or *a shred of evidence.*

shred•der (**shred**-ur) ***noun*** A machine for cutting documents into tiny pieces so that no one can read them.

shrew (**shroo**) ***noun***
1. A small mammal with a long nose and small eyes.
2. A nagging, scolding woman.

shrewd (**shrood**) ***adjective*** Clever, experienced, and sharp in dealing with practical situations, as in *a shrewd businessman* or *a shrewd shopper.*
▸ **shrewder, shrewdest** ▸ ***adverb*** **shrewdly**

shriek (**shreek**) ***verb*** To cry out or scream in a shrill, piercing way.
▸ **shrieking, shrieked** ▸ ***noun*** **shriek**

shrill (**shril**) ***adjective*** Having a high, sharp sound. ▸ **shriller, shrillest**

shrimp (**shrimp**) ***noun*** A small, edible shellfish with a pair of claws and a long tail.

shrine (**shrine**) ***noun***
1. A holy building that often contains sacred objects.
2. A place that is honored for its history or because it is connected to something important.

shrink (**shringk**)
1. ***verb*** If something **shrinks,** it becomes smaller, often after being wet.
2. ***verb*** To draw back because you are frightened or disgusted.
3. ***noun*** *(slang)* A psychiatrist or a psychologist.
▸ ***verb*** **shrinking, shrank** (**shrangk**) *or* **shrunk** (**shruhngk**)**, shrunk** *or* **shrunken**

shriv•el (**shriv**-uhl) ***verb*** If something **shrivels,** it shrinks and becomes wrinkled, often after drying in heat or sunlight. ▸ **shriveling, shriveled**
▸ ***adjective*** **shriveled**

shroud (**shroud**)
1. ***noun*** A cloth used to wrap a dead body for burial.
2. ***noun*** Something that covers or hides.
3. ***verb*** To cover or hide with a thin veil or haze. ▸ **shrouding, shrouded**

shrub (**shruhb**) ***noun*** A plant or bush with woody stems that branch out at or near the ground.

shrub•ber•y (**shruhb**-ur-ee) ***noun*** A number of shrubs planted together.

shrug (**shruhg**) ***verb*** To raise your shoulders in order to show doubt or lack of interest. ▸ **shrugging, shrugged**
▸ ***noun*** **shrug**

S

shrunk•en (**shruhngk**-uhn)
1. ***verb*** A past participle of **shrink.**
2. ***adjective*** Made smaller.

shud•der (**shuhd**-ur) ***verb*** To shake violently from cold or fear.
▸ **shuddering, shuddered** ▸ ***noun*** **shudder**

shuf•fle (**shuhf**-uhl) ***verb***
1. To walk slowly, hardly raising your feet from the floor or ground.
2. To mix playing cards so that they are in a different order.
3. To move something from one place to another, as in *to shuffle papers.*
▸ ***verb*** **shuffling, shuffled** ▸ ***noun*** **shuffle**

shun (**shuhn**) ***verb*** To avoid someone or something on purpose. ▸ **shunning, shunned**

shunt (**shuhnt**) ***verb*** To move something off to one side. ▸ **shunting, shunted**
▸ ***noun*** **shunt**

shut (**shuht**) ***verb***
1. To block an opening or close something with a door, lid, cover, etc.
▸ ***adjective*** **shut**
2. To confine or to enclose.
3. **shut down** To stop operating or to close down.
4. **shut out** To stop the opposing team from scoring any points.
5. **shut up** To stop talking or to make someone stop talking.
▸ ***verb*** **shutting, shut**

shut•ter (**shuht**-ur) ***noun***
1. A movable cover that protects the outside of a window and keeps out the light.
2. The part of a camera that opens to expose the film to light when a picture is taken.

shut•tle (**shuht**-uhl) ***noun***
1. The part of a loom that carries the thread from side to side.
2. A bus, a subway, a train, or an aircraft that travels frequently between two places. ▸ ***verb*** **shuttle**
3. *See* **space shuttle.**

shy (**shye**)
1. ***adjective*** If someone is **shy,** he or she is bashful and does not feel comfortable around people or with strangers. ▸ ***noun*** **shyness** ▸ ***adverb*** **shyly**
2. ***adjective*** Easily frightened or startled; timid.
3. ***adjective*** Lacking, or short.
4. ***verb*** If a horse **shies,** it moves backward or sideways suddenly because it is frightened or startled. ▸ **shying, shied**
▸ ***adjective*** **shier, shiest**

Si•a•mese cat (sye-uh-**meez**) ***noun*** A slender breed of cat that has blue eyes, short hair, and a pale brown or gray coat. Its ears, paws, and tail are often dark.

sib•ling (**sib**-ling) ***noun*** A brother or a sister.

sick (**sik**) ***adjective***
1. Suffering from a disease; ill. ▸ ***noun*** **sickness**
2. Nauseated, or feeling as though you are going to vomit.
3. Tired or disgusted.
4. Upset or very unhappy.
▸ ***adjective*** **sicker, sickest**

sick•en (**sik**-uhn) ***verb*** If something **sickens** you, it makes you feel nauseated or disgusted. ▸ **sickening, sickened** ▸ ***adjective*** **sickening**
▸ ***adverb*** **sickeningly**

sick•le (**sik**-uhl) ***noun*** A tool with a short handle and a curved blade that is used for cutting grain, grass, or weeds.

sickle-cell anemia ***noun*** A form of anemia in which many normal red blood cells take on a sickle shape and cannot carry oxygen. Sickle-cell anemia is an inherited disease occurring mainly in people of African ancestry.

sick•ly (**sik**-lee) ***adjective***
1. Weak and often ill.
2. Caused by or showing sickness, as in *a sickly complexion.*
▸ ***adjective*** **sicklier, sickliest**

S

side (**side**)
1. ***noun*** A line segment in a figure, or a surface of a shape or an object.
2. ***noun*** An outer part of something that is not the front or the back.
3. ***noun*** The right or left part of the body.
4. ***noun*** One of two opposing individuals, groups, teams, or positions.
5. ***noun*** The area next to someone.
6. ***noun*** A line of ancestors.
7. ***verb*** If you **side** with someone, you support the person in an argument. ▸ **siding, sided**
8. ***adjective*** At or near one side, as in *a side door.*

side•board (**side**-*bord*) ***noun*** A piece of dining room furniture with a large, flat surface and drawers or cabinets below.

side•burns (**side**-*burnz*) ***noun, plural*** The hair that grows down the sides of a man's face.

side effect ***noun*** A usually negative effect of taking a medicine besides the intended effect.

side•line (**side**-*line*) ***noun***
1. A line that marks the side boundary of the playing area in sports such as football, basketball, and soccer.
2. An activity or work done in addition to a regular job.

side•show (**side**-*shoh*) ***noun*** A small show in addition to the main attraction at a fair or circus.

side•step (**side**-*step*) ***verb***
1. To step to one side.
2. To avoid a problem or decision.
▸ ***verb*** **sidestepping, sidestepped**

side•track (**side**-*trak*) ***verb*** To distract someone from what he or she is doing or saying. ▸ **sidetracking, sidetracked**

side•walk (**side**-*wawk*) ***noun*** A paved path beside a street.

side•ways (**side**-*wayz*)
1. ***adjective*** To or from one side.
2. ***adverb*** With one side forward.
3. ***adjective*** Moving or directed toward one side, as in *a sideways glance.*

sid•ing (**sye**-ding) ***noun***
1. A section of railroad track used for storing or shunting cars.
2. Material that covers the outside of a house.

siege (**seej**) ***noun*** The surrounding of a place such as a castle or city to cut off supplies and then wait for those inside to surrender.

si•er•ra (see-**er**-uh) ***noun*** A chain of hills or mountains with peaks that look like sharp, jagged teeth.

si•es•ta (see-**ess**-tuh) ***noun*** An afternoon nap or rest, usually taken after a midday meal.

sieve (**siv**) ***noun*** A container with lots of small holes in it, used for separating large pieces from small pieces or liquids from solids. ▸ ***verb*** **sieve**

sift (**sift**) ***verb***
1. To put a substance through a sieve to get rid of lumps or large chunks.
2. To examine something carefully.
▸ ***verb*** **sifting, sifted**

sigh (**sye**) ***verb*** To breathe out deeply, often to express sadness or relief.
▸ **sighing, sighed** ▸ ***noun*** **sigh**

sight (**site**)
1. ***noun*** The ability to see.
2. ***noun*** The act of seeing.
3. ***noun*** The range or distance a person can see.
4. ***noun*** A view or a scene.
5. ***verb*** To see or to spot. ▸ **sighting, sighted**
6. ***noun*** A small metal device on a rifle that helps in aiming. ▸ ***verb*** **sight**
7. ***noun*** Something funny or odd to look at.
Sight sounds like **cite** and **site.**

sight•se•er (**site**-*see*-ur) ***noun*** Someone who travels for pleasure to see interesting places. ▸ ***noun*** **sightseeing**
▸ ***verb*** **sightsee**

sign (**sine**)
1. ***noun*** A symbol that stands for something, as in *a dollar sign* or *a minus sign.*
2. ***noun*** A public notice giving

information, as in *a road sign.*
3. ***verb*** To write your name in your own way. ▸ **signing, signed**
4. ***noun*** A trace, or evidence left by someone.
5. ***noun*** Something that points out what is to come.

sig•nal (**sig**-nuhl) ***noun***
1. Anything agreed upon to send a message or warning, as in *a traffic signal.* ▸ ***verb*** **signal**
2. One of many electrical pulses transmitted for radio, television, or telephone communications.

sig•na•ture (**sig**-nuh-chur) ***noun*** The individual way that you write your name, usually in script.

sig•nif•i•cant (sig-**nif**-uh-kuhnt) ***adjective*** Important, or meaning a great deal, as in *a significant event.* ▸ ***noun*** **significance** ▸ ***adverb*** **significantly**

sign language ***noun*** A language in which hand gestures, in combination with facial expressions and larger body movements, are used instead of speech. Sign language often is used by people with hearing impairments.

sign•post (**sine**-*pohst*) ***noun*** A post with signs on it to direct travelers.

Sikh (**seek**) ***noun*** A member of a religious sect of India that believes in a single god. ▸ ***noun*** **Sikhism**

si•lage (**sye**-lij) ***noun*** Cut grass or hay that is stored in a silo and used as animal feed.

si•lenc•er (**sye**-luhn-sur) ***noun*** An attachment that reduces noise from a gun.

si•lent (**sye**-luhnt) ***adjective*** Absolutely quiet. ▸ ***noun*** **silence** ▸ ***adverb*** **silently**

sil•hou•ette (sil-oo-**et**) ***noun***
1. A drawing made by filling in the outline of a figure with a solid color, usually black.
2. A dark outline seen against a light background. ▸ ***verb*** **silhouette**

sil•i•con (**sil**-uh-kuhn) ***noun*** A chemical element found in sand and rocks and used to make glass, microchips, and transistors.

silk (**silk**) ***noun*** A soft, shiny fabric made from fibers produced by a silkworm.

silk•worm (**silk**-*wurm*) ***noun*** A caterpillar that spins a cocoon of silk threads.

sil•ky (**sil**-kee) ***adjective*** Made of silk or like silk in texture; smooth, as in *silky hair.*

sill (**sil**) ***noun*** A piece of wood or stone that runs across the bottom of a door or window.

sil•ly (**sil**-ee) ***adjective***
1. Stupid or not sensible, as in *a silly mistake.*
2. Ridiculous or laughable, as in *a silly idea.*
▸ ***adjective*** **sillier, silliest** ▸ ***noun*** **silliness**

si•lo (**sye**-loh) ***noun***
1. A tall, round tower used to store food for farm animals.
2. An underground shelter for a guided missile.
▸ ***noun, plural*** **silos**

silt (**silt**) ***noun*** The fine particles of soil that are carried along by flowing water and eventually settle to the bottom of a river or lake.

sil•ver (**sil**-vur) ***noun***
1. A soft, shiny, white metal that is used to make jewelry, coins, bowls, and utensils.
2. Coins made from silver or metal with a silver color.
3. Forks, spoons, and other items made of or coated with silver; silverware.
4. The color of silver.
▸ ***adjective*** **silver,** ***adjective*** **silvery**

sil•ver•smith (**sil**-vur-*smith*) ***noun*** Someone who makes or repairs silver objects.

sil•ver•ware (**sil**-vur-*wair*) ***noun*** Objects made of or coated with silver, especially forks, spoons, and knives.

sim•i•lar (**sim**-uh-lur) ***adjective*** Alike, or of the same type. ▸ ***noun*** **similarity** (sim-uh-**lair**-i-tee) ▸ ***adverb*** **similarly**

S

S

sim•i•le (**sim**-uh-lee) ***noun*** A way of describing something by comparing it with something else. A simile uses the word *like* or *as.*

sim•mer (**sim**-ur) ***verb***
1. To boil very gently. ▸ ***noun*** **simmer**
2. simmer down *(informal)* To calm down.
▸ ***verb*** **simmering, simmered**

sim•ple (**sim**-puhl) ***adjective***
1. Easy, or not hard to understand or do, as in *a simple test* or *a simple task.*
2. With nothing added, as in *the simple truth.*
3. Plain, or not fancy, as in *a simple meal.*
▸ ***adjective*** **simpler, simplest** ▸ ***noun*** **simplicity** (sim-**pliss**-i-tee)

sim•pli•fy (**sim**-pluh-fye) ***verb*** To make something easier or less complicated.
▸ **simplifies, simplifying, simplified**
▸ ***noun*** **simplification**

sim•ply (**sim**-plee) ***adverb***
1. In a simple way, or plainly.
2. Merely, or just.
3. Very.

sim•u•la•tion (sim-yuh-**lay**-shuhn) ***noun***
1. The act of pretending.
2. A copy or an imitation.
▸ ***verb*** **simulate**

sim•u•la•tor (**sim**-yuh-*lay*-tur) ***noun*** A machine that allows you to experience what it is like to fly a plane, drive a car, etc., by using computer technology, film, and mechanical movement.

si•mul•ta•ne•ous (*sye*-muhl-**tay**-nee-uhss) ***adjective*** Happening at the same time. ▸ ***adverb*** **simultaneously**

sin (**sin**) ***noun*** Bad or evil behavior that goes against moral and religious laws.
▸ ***noun*** **sinner** ▸ ***verb*** **sin** ▸ ***adjective*** **sinful** ▸ ***adverb*** **sinfully**

since (**sinss**)
1. ***conjunction*** From the time that.
2. ***conjunction*** As, or because.
3. ***adverb*** Ago; before now.
4. ***adverb*** From the past until now.
5. ***preposition*** From or during the time after.

sin•cere (sin-**sihr**) ***adjective*** If you are **sincere,** you are honest and truthful in what you say and do. ▸ **sincerer, sincerest** ▸ ***noun*** **sincerity** (sin-**ser**-i-tee) ▸ ***adverb*** **sincerely**

sin•ew (**sin**-yoo) ***noun*** A strong fiber or band of tissue that connects a muscle to a bone; a tendon.

sing (**sing**) ***verb***
1. To produce words and musical sounds with your voice.
2. To perform by singing, as in *to sing a song.*
3. To produce musical sounds. ▸ ***verb*** **singing, sang** (**sang**), **sung** (**suhng**)
▸ ***noun*** **singer**

singe (**sinj**) ***verb*** To burn something slightly. ▸ **singeing, singed**

sin•gle (**sing**-guhl)
1. ***adjective*** One and no more than one.
2. ***adjective*** Intended for one person or family, as in *a single room.*
3. ***adjective*** Not married.
4. single out ***verb*** To choose.
▸ **singling, singled**
5. ***noun*** A recording with one song on each side.
6. ***noun*** A hit in baseball that allows the runner to get to first base. ▸ ***verb*** **single**

single-hand•ed (**han**-did) ***adjective*** Done alone or without help from others, as in *a single-handed rescue.* ▸ ***adverb*** **single-handedly**

single-mind•ed (**mine**-did) ***adjective*** If you are **single-minded,** you concentrate on achieving one aim.

sin•gu•lar (**sing**-gyuh-lur) ***noun*** The form of a word used for one thing or one person. *Chair* and *singer* are singulars. ▸ ***adjective*** **singular**

sin•is•ter (**sin**-uh-stur) ***adjective*** Seeming evil and threatening.

sink (**singk**)
1. ***noun*** A basin used for washing. A sink has faucets for hot and cold water and a drain.
2. ***verb*** To go down slowly.

S

3. ***verb*** To make go under the surface. ▸ ***noun*** **sinking**
4. ***verb*** To fall or drop into a certain state.
5. ***verb*** To become lower in amount.
6. ***verb*** To fall in pitch or volume.
7. ***verb*** To penetrate or go through or into deeply.
▸ ***verb*** **sinking, sank** (**sangk**), **sunk** (**suhngk**)

si•nus (**sye**-nuhss) ***noun*** One of the eight hollow spaces above the eyes and on either side of the nose that lead to the nose. ▸ ***noun, plural*** **sinuses**

Sioux (**soo**) ***noun*** A member of a tribe of American Indians of Minnesota, North and South Dakota, and Wyoming.

sip (**sip**) ***verb*** To drink slowly, taking in small amounts. ▸ **sipping, sipped** ▸ ***noun*** **sip**

si•phon (**sye**-fuhn) ***noun*** A bent tube through which liquid can drain upward and then down to a lower level. Air pressure causes this to happen. ▸ ***verb*** **siphon**

sir (**sur**) ***noun***
1. A formal term for a man used in speaking and writing, as in *Dear Sir* and *Can I help you, sir?*
2. **Sir** The title of someone who has been made a knight, as in *Sir Lancelot.*

si•ren (**sye**-ruhn) ***noun*** A device that makes a loud, shrill sound. A siren is often used as a signal or warning, as in *a police car siren.*

sis•ter (**siss**-tur) ***noun***
1. A girl or woman who has the same parents as another person. ▸ ***adjective*** **sisterly**
2. A nun.
3. A woman who shares an interest or cause with another.

sis•ter•hood (**siss**-tur-hud) ***noun***
1. The warm, close feeling between sisters or any women.
2. A group of women who share a common interest, aim, or cause.

sister-in-law ***noun*** Someone's **sister-in-law** is the sister of his or her spouse or the wife of his or her brother. ▸ ***noun, plural*** **sisters-in-law**

sit (**sit**) ***verb***
1. To rest on your buttocks.
2. To be in a place or on a surface.
3. To pose.
4. To take a place as an official member of a club or legislature.
5. To hold a session or meeting.
6. To baby-sit.
7. If you **sit in** for someone, you take the person's place temporarily.
▸ ***verb*** **sitting, sat** (**sat**)

sit•com (**sit**-*kom*) ***noun*** *(informal)* A humorous television program that features the same group of characters each week. Sitcom is short for *situation comedy.*

site (**site**) ***noun*** The place where something is or happens, as in *the site of the battle.* **Site** sounds like **cite** and **sight.**

sitting room ***noun*** A room in a home or hotel in which people can sit and relax or talk with others.

sit•u•ate (**sich**-oo-ate) ***verb*** To place something in a particular spot or location. ▸ **situating, situated**

sit•u•a•tion (*sich*-oo-**ay**-shuhn) ***noun*** The circumstances that exist at a particular time.

sit-up ***noun*** An exercise for stomach muscles that is done by lying and moving to a sitting position without lifting the feet or legs.

six (**siks**) ***noun*** The whole number, written 6, that comes after five and before seven. ▸ ***adjective*** **six**

sixth (**siksth**)
1. ***adjective*** That which comes after fifth and before seventh.
2. ***noun*** One part of something that has been divided into six equal parts, written $\frac{1}{6}$.

siz•a•ble *or* **size•a•ble** (**size**-uh-buhl) ***adjective*** Fairly large.

S

size (**size**) ***noun***
1. The measurement of how large or small something is.
2. One in a series of standard measurements for clothing, shoes, etc.

siz•zle (**siz**-uhl) ***verb*** To make a hissing noise, especially when frying. ▸ **sizzling, sizzled**

skate (**skayt**)
1. *noun* A boot with a blade on the bottom. Skates are used for gliding over ice.
2. *noun* A roller skate.
3. *verb* To glide or move along on skates. ▸ **skating, skated**
4. *noun* A large, flat, saltwater fish with a long, narrow tail and two wide side fins that are shaped like wings. Skates are related to sharks and rays.

skate•board (**skate**-*bord*) ***noun*** A small board with wheels that you stand on and ride. ▸ ***verb*** **skateboard** ▸ ***noun*** **skateboarding**

ske•dad•dle (ski-**dad**-uhl) ***verb*** *(informal)* To move along quickly or to run away from something that scares you. ▸ **skedaddling, skedaddled**

skel•e•ton (**skel**-uh-tuhn) ***noun*** The framework of bones that supports and protects the body of an animal with a backbone.

skep•ti•cal (**skep**-tuh-kuhl) ***adjective*** If you are **skeptical** about something, you doubt that it is really true. ▸ ***noun*** **skeptic, *noun* skepticism** ▸ ***adverb*** **skeptically**

sketch (**skech**) ***noun***
1. A quick, rough drawing of something. ▸ ***verb*** **sketch**
2. A short essay, especially one that describes a person.
3. A short play that is usually humorous.
▸ ***noun, plural*** **sketches**

sketch•y (**skech**-ee) ***adjective***
1. Roughly drawn or done without detail.
2. Incomplete and not very clear.
▸ ***adjective*** **sketchier, sketchiest**

skew•er (**skyoo**-ur) ***noun*** A long, metal pin for holding pieces of meat or vegetables while they are cooking.
▸ ***verb*** **skewer**

ski (**skee**) ***noun***
1. One of a pair of long, narrow runners that you fasten to boots and use for gliding over snow.
2. A water ski.
▸ ***noun*** **skiing** ▸ ***verb*** **ski**

skid (**skid**)
1. *verb* To slide out of control on a slippery surface. ▸ **skidding, skidded** ▸ ***noun*** **skid**
2. *noun* A runner on the bottom of a helicopter.

skiff (**skif**) ***noun*** A boat small enough to be sailed or rowed by one person.

skill (**skil**) ***noun*** The ability to do something well. ▸ ***adjective*** **skillful, *adjective* skilled**

skil•let (**skil**-it) ***noun*** A frying pan.

skim (**skim**) ***verb***
1. To take something off the top of a liquid. ▸ ***adjective*** **skimmed**
2. To read through something quickly, just to get the main ideas.
3. To glide across a surface.
▸ ***verb*** **skimming, skimmed**

skim milk ***noun*** Milk from which the cream has been removed. It is also called *skimmed milk*.

skin (**skin**)
1. *noun* The outer covering of tissue on the bodies of humans and animals.
2. *noun* The outer layer of a fruit or vegetable, as in *a banana skin*.
3. *verb* To scrape your skin.
4. *verb* To remove the skin from a killed animal.
▸ ***verb*** **skinning, skinned**

skin diving ***noun*** Underwater swimming with a face mask, flippers, and a snorkel. ▸ ***verb*** **skin dive** ▸ ***noun*** **skin diver**

skin•ny (**skin**-ee) ***adjective*** Very thin.
▸ **skinnier, skinniest**

skip (**skip**) ***verb***
1. To move along in a bouncy way,

hopping on each foot in turn. ▸ ***noun*** **skip**
2. To jump over, as in *to skip rope.*
3. To leave something out or to pass over.
4. *(informal)* To leave a place quickly or secretly.
5. To go past one grade in school by going to the next one.
▸ ***verb*** **skipping, skipped**

skirt (**skurt**)
1. ***noun*** A piece of clothing worn by women and girls that hangs from the waist.
2. ***verb*** To pass around a place or to lie around its border or edge.
3. ***verb*** To avoid a question, a discussion, or an issue because it is difficult or because you are afraid that others might disagree with you.
▸ ***verb*** **skirting, skirted**

skit (**skit**) ***noun*** A short, usually funny play.

skit•tish (**skit**-ish) ***adjective*** Easily frightened or excited, as in *a skittish horse.*

skull (**skuhl**) ***noun*** The bony framework of the head that protects the brain. **Skull** sounds like **scull.**

skunk (**skuhngk**) ***noun***
1. A black and white mammal with a bushy tail. Skunks spray liquid with a foul smell when they are threatened.
2. *(informal)* A really mean person.

sky (**skye**) ***noun*** The upper atmosphere, or the area of space that seems to arch over the earth. ▸ ***noun, plural*** **skies**

sky•box (**skye**-*boks*) ***noun*** An elevated, enclosed room at a sports stadium where spectators can watch the action in privacy and luxury.

sky•div•ing (**skye**-*div*-ing) ***noun*** The sport of jumping from an airplane and falling as far as safely possible before opening a parachute. Skydiving often involves stunts or formation work.
▸ ***noun*** **skydiver** ▸ ***verb*** **skydive**

sky•lark (**skye**-*lark*) ***noun*** A brown and white European bird that sings while flying.

sky•light (**skye**-*lite*) ***noun*** A window in a roof or ceiling.

sky•line (**skye**-*line*) ***noun***
1. The outline of buildings, mountains, or other objects seen against the sky from a distance.
2. The horizon, or the line at which the earth and sky seem to meet.

sky•rock•et (**skye**-*rok*-it)
1. ***noun*** A type of firework that shoots into the air and explodes in a shower of sparks of many colors.
2. ***verb*** To rise suddenly and quickly.
▸ **skyrocketing, skyrocketed**

sky•scrap•er (**skye**-*skray*-pur) ***noun*** A very tall building.

slab (**slab**) ***noun*** A broad, flat, thick piece of something, as in *a slab of concrete* or *a slab of bread.*

slack (**slak**) ***adjective***
1. Not tight or not firm; loose.
2. Not busy.
3. If you are **slack** in your work, you do not try very hard at it.
▸ ***adjective*** **slacker, slackest** ▸ ***verb*** **slacken**

slacks (**slaks**) ***noun, plural*** Pants for casual wear.

sla•lom (**slah**-luhm *or* **slal**-uhm) ***noun*** An athletic event in which competitors ski down a hill, zigzagging between gates.

slam (**slam**) ***verb***
1. To close something heavily and loudly.
2. To strike something with great force.
▸ ***verb*** **slamming, slammed** ▸ ***noun*** **slam**

slan•der (**slan**-dur) ***noun*** An untrue spoken statement that damages someone's reputation. ▸ ***verb*** **slander**
▸ ***adjective*** **slanderous**

slang (**slang**) ***noun*** Colorful or lively words and phrases used in ordinary conversation but not in formal speech or writing. Slang often gives new and different meanings to old words.

S

slant (**slant**)
1. ***verb*** To slope, or to be at an angle.
▸ **slanting, slanted** ▸ ***noun*** **slant**
2. ***noun*** A point of view. ▸ ***verb*** **slant**

slap (**slap**) ***verb***
1. To hit someone or something with the palm of your hand. ▸ ***noun*** **slap**
2. To throw down or put on with great force.
▸ ***verb*** **slapping, slapped**

slap•dash (**slap**-*dash*) ***adjective*** **Slapdash** work is done carelessly and in a hurry.

slap•stick (**slap**-*stik*) ***noun*** Comedy that stresses loud, rough action or horseplay, such as a clown slipping on a banana peel.

slash (**slash**) ***verb***
1. To use a knife or blade to make a sharp, sweeping cut in something.
▸ ***noun*** **slash**
2. To reduce something dramatically.
▸ ***verb*** **slashes, slashing, slashed**

slat (**slat**) ***noun*** A long, narrow strip of wood or metal.

slate (**slayt**) ***noun***
1. A blue-gray rock that can be split into thin layers. Slate is sometimes used to make roofs.
2. A tile for roofs or floors made from slate.
3. A dark blue-gray color.
4. A complete list of candidates who are running for office.

slaugh•ter (**slaw**-tur)
1. ***verb*** To kill animals for their meat.
▸ **slaughtering, slaughtered** ▸ ***noun*** **slaughter**
2. ***noun*** The brutal killing of large numbers of people. ▸ ***verb*** **slaughter**

slave (**slayv**)
1. ***noun*** Someone who is owned by another person and thought of as property. ▸ ***noun*** **slavery**
2. ***noun*** A person who is controlled by a habit or by influence.
3. ***verb*** To work very hard. ▸ **slaving, slaved**
4. ***noun*** A person who works as hard as a slave.

slay (**slay**) ***verb*** To kill in a violent way. **Slay** sounds like **sleigh.** ▸ **slaying, slayed, slew** (**sloo**), **slain** (**slayn**)

sled (**sled**) ***noun*** A vehicle with wooden or metal runners used for traveling over snow and ice. ▸ ***verb*** **sled**

sledge•ham•mer (**slej**-*ham*-ur) ***noun*** A heavy hammer with a long handle. A sledgehammer is usually held with both hands.

sleek (**sleek**) ***adjective*** Smooth and shiny. ▸ **sleeker, sleekest**

sleep (**sleep**) ***verb*** To rest in an unconscious state. ▸ **sleeping, slept** (**slept**) ▸ ***noun*** **sleep**

sleeping bag ***noun*** A padded bag in which you sleep, especially when you are camping.

sleep•walk•er (**sleep**-*wawk*-ur) ***noun*** Someone who walks in his or her sleep.
▸ ***verb*** **sleepwalk**

sleep•y (**slee**-pee) ***adjective*** Drowsy, or ready for sleep. ▸ **sleepier, sleepiest**
▸ ***noun*** **sleepiness**

sleet (**sleet**) ***noun*** Partly frozen rain.
▸ ***verb*** **sleet**

sleeve (**sleev**) ***noun*** The part of a shirt, coat, or other garment that covers your arm.

sleigh (**slay**) ***noun*** A sled, usually pulled by horses or other animals. **Sleigh** sounds like **slay.**

slen•der (**slen**-dur) ***adjective***
1. Slim or thin.
2. Small and inadequate in amount.
▸ ***adjective*** **slenderer, slenderest**

sleuth (**slooth**) ***noun*** A detective, or anyone good at finding out facts. ▸ ***verb*** **sleuth**

slice (**slisse**) ***noun*** A thin, flat piece cut from something larger, as in *a slice of bread.* ▸ ***verb*** **slice**

slick (**slik**)
1. ***adjective*** Very smooth or slippery.
▸ ***verb*** **slick**
2. ***noun*** A pool of oil covering an area of water or road.

3. ***adjective*** Very fast, efficient, and professional, as in *a slick performance.*
▸ ***adjective*** **slicker, slickest**

slide (**slide**)
1. ***verb*** To move smoothly over a surface.
2. ***noun*** A smooth surface on which people can slide.
3. ***verb*** To move or fall suddenly.
4. ***noun*** A transparency inside a frame that you view by projecting the image onto a screen.
5. ***noun*** A small piece of glass on which you place a specimen in order to view it under a microscope.
6. ***noun*** A large mass of snow, earth, or rock that slides down suddenly from a great height.
▸ ***verb*** **sliding, slid** (**slid**) ▸ ***noun*** **slide**

slight (**slite**)
1. ***adjective*** Small or not very important, as in *a slight delay.* ▸ ***adverb*** **slightly**
2. ***adjective*** Slender.
3. ***verb*** To treat something as unimportant or to do something carelessly.
4. ***verb*** To insult someone or to treat a person coldly. ▸ ***noun*** **slight**
▸ ***verb*** **slighting, slighted** ▸ ***adjective*** **slighter, slightest**

slim (**slim**)
1. ***adjective*** Thin and graceful.
2. ***adjective*** Very small.
3. ***verb*** To try to reduce your weight.
▸ **slimming, slimmed**
▸ ***adjective*** **slimmer, slimmest**

slime (**slime**) ***noun*** A soft, slippery substance, such as mud. ▸ ***adjective*** **slimy**

sling (**sling**)
1. ***noun*** A loop of cloth used to support a broken arm.
2. ***noun*** A loop of leather used for throwing stones.
3. ***noun*** A strong loop of cable, chain, or rope used to raise heavy objects.
4. ***verb*** To hang or throw something loosely or in a rough way. ▸ **slinging, slung** (**sluhng**)

sling•shot (**sling**-*shot*) ***noun*** A piece of metal or wood shaped like a Y with an elastic band attached. Slingshots are used for shooting small stones.

slip (**slip**)
1. ***verb*** To lose your balance on a slippery surface. ▸ ***noun*** **slip**
2. ***verb*** To move quickly and quietly.
3. ***verb*** To put on or take off quickly and easily.
4. ***verb*** To escape.
5. ***verb*** To move or slide from a place.
6. ***noun*** A small mistake. ▸ ***verb*** **slip**
7. ***noun*** A light garment worn under a skirt or dress.
8. ***noun*** A small piece, as in *a slip of paper.*
9. ***noun*** A small shoot or twig cut from a plant for grafting or planting.
▸ ***verb*** **slipping, slipped**

slip•per (**slip**-ur) ***noun*** A soft, light shoe that you wear indoors, as in *bedroom slippers.*

slip•per•y (**slip**-ur-ee) ***adjective*** Smooth, oily, or wet and very hard to grip onto.

slip•shod (**slip**-*shod*) ***adjective*** Careless and untidy.

slit (**slit**) ***verb*** To make a long, narrow cut in something. ▸ **slitting, slit** ▸ ***noun*** **slit**

slith•er (**sliTH**-ur) ***verb*** To slip and slide along like a snake. ▸ **slithering, slithered**

sliv•er (**sliv**-ur) ***noun*** A very thin and sometimes pointed piece of something, as in *a sliver of cake* or *a sliver of wood.*

slo•gan (**sloh**-guhn) ***noun*** A phrase or motto used by a business, a group, or an individual to express a goal or belief.

sloop (**sloop**) ***noun*** A sailboat with one mast and sails that are set from front to back.

slop (**slop**) ***verb*** To splash or spill liquid.
▸ **slopping, slopped**

S

slope (**slohp**) ***verb*** To be at an angle. ▸ **sloping, sloped** ▸ ***noun*** **slope** ▸ ***adjective*** **sloping**

slop•py (**slop**-ee) ***adjective***
1. Messy, as in *sloppy clothes.*
2. Carelessly done.
3. Wet or slushy, as in *sloppy weather.*
▸ ***adjective*** **sloppier, sloppiest** ▸ ***noun*** **sloppiness** ▸ ***adverb*** **sloppily**

slot (**slot**) ***noun*** A small, narrow opening or groove.

sloth (**slawth** *or* **sloth**) ***noun***
1. A mammal with long arms and legs, curved claws, and a shaggy coat. Sloths move very slowly and hang upside down in trees. They live in Central and South America.
2. Laziness. ▸ ***adjective*** **slothful**

slouch (**slouch**)
1. ***verb*** To sit, stand, or walk in a lazy way, with your shoulders and head drooping. ▸ **slouches, slouching, slouched** ▸ ***noun*** **slouch**
2. ***noun*** An awkward, lazy, or incompetent person. ▸ ***noun, plural*** **slouches**

slov•en•ly (**sluhv**-uhn-lee) ***adjective*** Careless, untidy, and dirty, as in *a slovenly appearance.* ▸ ***noun*** **slovenliness**

slow (**sloh**)
1. ***adjective*** Not fast. ▸ ***noun*** **slowness** ▸ ***adverb*** **slowly**
2. ***adjective*** Behind the right time.
3. ***verb*** To cut down your speed. ▸ **slowing, slowed**
4. ***adjective*** Not busy.
5. ***adjective*** Not able to learn or understand quickly.
6. ***adverb*** In a slow way.
▸ ***adjective and adverb*** **slower, slowest**

sludge (**sluhj**) ***noun*** Soft, thick mud.

slug (**sluhg**)
1. ***noun*** A soft, slimy creature that is similar to a snail but has no shell.
2. ***noun*** A bullet.
3. ***noun*** A metal disk that is used in place of a coin, often illegally.
4. ***verb*** To hit with force. ▸ **slugging, slugged** ▸ ***noun*** **slug**

slug•gish (**sluhg**-ish) ***adjective*** Moving slowly and lacking in energy. ▸ ***noun*** **sluggishness**

slum (**sluhm**) ***noun*** An overcrowded, poor, and neglected area of housing in a town or city.

slum•ber (**sluhm**-bur)
1. ***verb*** To sleep. ▸ **slumbering, slumbered**
2. ***noun*** Sleep.

slump (**sluhmp**)
1. ***verb*** To sink down heavily and suddenly. ▸ **slumping, slumped**
2. ***noun*** A sudden drop or decline, as in *a slump in sales* or *a batting slump.* ▸ ***verb*** **slump**

slur (**slur**)
1. ***verb*** To pronounce words unclearly by running sounds into one another. ▸ **slurring, slurred**
2. ***noun*** If something is a **slur** on your character, it is insulting or damaging.

slurp (**slurp**) ***verb*** To drink or eat something noisily. ▸ **slurping, slurped**

slush (**sluhsh**) ***noun*** Snow or ice that has partly melted. ▸ ***adjective*** **slushy**

sly (**slye**) ***adjective*** Crafty, cunning, and secretive. ▸ **slier, sliest** ▸ ***adverb*** **slyly**

smack (**smak**)
1. ***verb*** To hit someone or something with the palm of your hand.
2. ***verb*** To strike or hit something noisily and with force.
3. ***verb*** To close and open the lips quickly, making a sharp sound.
4. ***noun*** A loud kiss.
▸ ***verb*** **smacking, smacked** ▸ ***noun*** **smack**

small (**smawl**)
1. ***adjective*** Little.
2. ***adjective*** Not important.
3. ***adjective*** Low, soft, or weak, as in *a small voice.*
4. **small talk** ***noun*** Conversation about unimportant things.
▸ ***adjective*** **smaller, smallest**

small intestine ***noun*** The long, coiled part of the digestive system between the stomach and the large intestine, where most nutrients are removed from food and passed into the bloodstream.

small·pox (**smawl**-*poks*) ***noun*** A very contagious disease that causes chills, high fever, and pimples that can leave permanent scars.

smart (**smart**)
1. ***adjective*** Clever and quick in thinking; bright.
2. ***verb*** To sting or to hurt. ▸ **smarting, smarted**
3. ***adjective*** Nicely dressed, tidy, and clean.
4. ***adjective*** Fashionable or stylish.
▸ ***noun*** **smartness** ▸ ***adjective*** **smarter, smartest** ▸ ***adverb*** **smartly**

smash (**smash**)
1. ***verb*** To break something into a lot of pieces by hitting or dropping it.
2. ***verb*** To collide violently with something.
3. ***verb*** To destroy or defeat completely.
4. **smash hit** ***noun*** *(informal)* A recording, movie, or show that is very successful.
▸ ***verb*** **smashes, smashing, smashed**

smear (**smihr**) ***verb***
1. To rub something sticky or greasy over a surface.
2. To become messy or blurred.
3. To try to damage someone's reputation by telling untrue stories about the person.
▸ ***verb*** **smearing, smeared** ▸ ***noun*** **smear**

smell (**smel**)
1. ***verb*** To sense an odor with your nose.
2. ***noun*** An odor or a scent.
3. ***verb*** To give off a smell or odor.
4. ***verb*** To give off an unpleasant odor.
▸ ***adjective*** **smelly**
5. ***verb*** To sniff.
6. ***noun*** The ability to notice smells.
▸ ***verb*** **smelling, smelled** *or* **smelt**

smelt (**smelt**)
1. ***verb*** To melt ore so that the metal can be removed. ▸ **smelting, smelted**
2. ***noun*** A thin, silvery food fish that lives in cold ocean waters and swims up rivers to lay its eggs.

S

smile (**smile**) ***verb*** To widen your mouth and turn it up at the corners to show that you are happy or amused.
▸ **smiling, smiled** ▸ ***noun*** **smile**

smirk (**smurk**) ***verb*** To smile in a smug, knowing, or annoying way. ▸ **smirking, smirked** ▸ ***noun*** **smirk**

smock (**smok**) ***noun*** A garment that looks like a long, loose shirt. Smocks are worn over other clothes to keep them from getting dirty.

smog (**smog**) ***noun*** A mixture of fog and smoke that sometimes hangs in the air over cities and industrial areas.

smoke (**smohk**)
1. ***noun*** The mixture of gas and tiny carbon particles that is given off when something burns. ▸ ***adjective*** **smoky**
2. ***verb*** To give off smoke.
3. ***verb*** To hold a cigarette or cigar in your mouth and inhale its smoke.
▸ ***noun*** **smoker,** ***noun*** **smoking**
4. ***verb*** To preserve food by hanging it in smoke. ▸ ***adjective*** **smoked**
▸ ***verb*** **smoking, smoked**

smoke alarm ***noun*** Another name for a **smoke detector.**

smoke detector ***noun*** A device that warns people of smoke or fire by letting out a loud, piercing sound.

smoke·stack (**smoke**-*stak*) ***noun*** A chimney that allows smoke or gases to escape from a factory, a ship, or a locomotive.

smol·der (**smohl**-dur) ***verb***
1. To burn and smoke slowly with no flames.
2. To show hidden anger, hate, or jealousy.
3. To exist or continue in a hidden state.
▸ ***verb*** **smoldering, smoldered**

S

smooth (**smooTH**)
1. ***adjective*** A **smooth** surface is even and flat, not rough or bumpy, as in *a smooth road.*
2. ***adjective*** Happening easily, with no problems or difficulties, as in *a smooth landing.* ▸ ***adverb*** **smoothly**
3. ***verb*** To make things more even and flat. ▸ **smoothing, smoothed**
4. ***adjective*** Able or skillful, as in *a smooth dancer.*
▸ ***noun*** **smoothness** ▸ ***adjective*** **smoother, smoothest**

smoth•er (**smuTH**-ur) ***verb***
1. To cover someone's nose and mouth so that the person cannot breathe.
2. To cover something thickly.
3. To hide or to hold back, as in *to smother a yawn.*
▸ ***verb*** **smothering, smothered**

smudge (**smuhj**) ***verb*** To make a messy mark by rubbing something.
▸ **smudging, smudged** ▸ ***noun*** **smudge** ▸ ***adjective*** **smudged**

smug (**smuhg**) ***adjective*** If you are **smug,** you are so pleased with yourself that you annoy other people.
▸ **smugger, smuggest** ▸ ***noun*** **smugness** ▸ ***adverb*** **smugly**

smug•gle (**smuhg**-uhl) ***verb***
1. To bring goods into a country illegally.
▸ ***noun*** **smuggler**
2. To take something into or out of a place secretly.
▸ ***verb*** **smuggling, smuggled**

snack (**snak**) ***noun*** A small, light meal.
▸ ***verb*** **snack**

snag (**snag**)
1. ***noun*** A small, unexpected problem or difficulty.
2. ***verb*** To catch on something.
▸ **snagging, snagged** ▸ ***noun*** **snag**

snail (**snayl**) ***noun***
1. A small animal with no legs; a soft, slimy body; and a shell on its back.
2. A person who moves slowly.

snake (**snayk**) ***noun*** A long, thin reptile that has no legs and slithers along the ground. In the United States, only rattlesnakes, copperheads, water moccasins, and coral snakes have poisonous bites.

snap (**snap**)
1. ***verb*** To break with a sudden loud, cracking sound.
2. ***noun*** A sudden cracking sound.
3. ***verb*** To bite or grab suddenly with the mouth or teeth.
4. ***verb*** To speak sharply and angrily.
5. ***verb*** To open or close with a click or snapping sound.
6. **cold snap** ***noun*** A brief period of cold weather.
7. ***noun*** *(informal)* A snapshot.
8. ***verb*** In football, to pick the ball up off the ground and pass it to another player.
9. ***noun*** A **snap decision** is a decision that is made very quickly.
▸ ***noun*** **snap** ▸ ***verb*** **snapping, snapped** ▸ ***adjective*** **snappy**

snap•drag•on (**snap**-*dra*-guhn) ***noun*** A garden plant with brightly colored flowers that grow on spikes. Each flower has two petals that look like lips. The petals open and close when pressed.

snap•shot (**snap**-*shot*) ***noun*** A photograph taken with a simple camera.

snare (**snair**)
1. ***noun*** A trap for catching birds or animals.
2. ***verb*** To catch a bird or an animal in a snare. ▸ **snaring, snared**

snare drum ***noun*** A small drum with strings or wires stretched across its base that produce a rattling sound when hit.

snarl (**snarl**) ***verb***
1. If an animal **snarls,** it shows its teeth and makes a growling sound.
2. To say something angrily.
▸ ***verb*** **snarling, snarled** ▸ ***noun*** **snarl**

snatch (**snach**)
1. ***verb*** To take or grab something quickly. ▸ **snatches, snatching,**

snatched ▸ ***noun*** **snatch**
2. ***noun*** A small part. ▸ ***noun, plural*** **snatches**

sneak (**sneek**)
1. ***verb*** To move quietly and secretly. ▸ ***adjective*** **sneaky** ▸ ***adverb*** **sneakily**
2. ***verb*** To bring someone or something in where it is not supposed to be.
3. ***adjective*** Done secretly or with no warning, as in *a sneak attack.*
4. ***noun*** Someone who is tricky and dishonest.
▸ ***verb*** **sneaking, sneaked** *or* **snuck** (**snuhk**)

sneak•ers (**snee**-kurz) ***noun, plural*** Athletic shoes with rubber soles.

sneer (**snihr**) ***verb*** To smile in a hateful, mocking way. ▸ **sneering, sneered** ▸ ***noun*** **sneer**

sneeze (**sneez**) ***verb*** To push air out through your nose and mouth suddenly, often because you have a cold.
▸ **sneezing, sneezed** ▸ ***noun*** **sneeze**

snick•er (**snik**-ur)
1. ***noun*** A mean or disrespectful little laugh.
2. ***verb*** To laugh in such a way.
▸ **snickering, snickered**

sniff (**snif**) ***verb***
1. To breathe in strongly through your nose.
2. To smell something.
▸ ***verb*** **sniffing, sniffed** ▸ ***noun*** **sniff**

snif•fle (**snif**-uhl) ***verb*** To breathe noisily through your nose, usually because you have a cold. ▸ **sniffling, sniffled** ▸ ***noun*** **sniffle**

snip (**snip**) ***verb*** To cut something using small, quick cuts of shears or scissors.
▸ **snipping, snipped** ▸ ***noun*** **snip**

snipe (**snipe**)
1. ***verb*** To shoot at a person or persons from a hidden place. ▸ **sniping, sniped** ▸ ***noun*** **sniper**
2. ***noun*** A marsh bird with a long bill and brown feathers spotted with black and white.

sniv•el (**sniv**-uhl) ***verb*** To cry or complain in a noisy, whining way.
▸ **sniveling, sniveled**

snob (**snob**) ***noun***
1. Someone who looks down on people who are not rich, successful, or intelligent.
2. A person who thinks that he or she is better than or superior to others.
▸ ***noun*** **snobbery**

snoop (**snoop**)
1. ***verb*** *(informal)* To pry or look around in a sly or sneaky way. ▸ **snooping, snooped**
2. ***noun*** A nosy person who pries into other people's business. ▸ ***adjective*** **snoopy**

snooze (**snooz**) ***verb*** *(informal)* To sleep lightly for a short time, usually during the day. ▸ **snoozing, snoozed** ▸ ***noun*** **snooze**

snore (**snor**) ***verb*** To breathe noisily through your mouth while you are asleep. ▸ **snoring, snored** ▸ ***noun*** **snore**

snor•kel (**snor**-kuhl) ***noun*** A tube that you use to breathe through when you are swimming underwater. ▸ ***noun*** **snorkeling**

snort (**snort**) ***verb***
1. To breathe out noisily through your nose.
2. To show scorn, anger, or disbelief by snorting.
▸ ***verb*** **snorting, snorted** ▸ ***noun*** **snort**

snout (**snout**) ***noun*** The long front part of an animal's head. It includes the nose, mouth, and jaws.

snow (**snoh**)
1. ***noun*** White crystals of ice that form when water vapor freezes in the air.
2. ***verb*** When it **snows,** snow falls from the sky.
▸ **snowing, snowed** ▸ ***adjective*** **snowy**

S

S

snow•ball (**snoh**-*bawl*)
1. ***noun*** Snow pressed into a ball.
2. ***verb*** If something **snowballs,** it grows rapidly. ▸ **snowballing, snowballed**

snow•board (**snoh**-*bord*) ***noun*** A board like a wide ski for riding downhill on snow. ▸ ***verb*** **snowboard** ▸ ***noun*** **snowboarding**

snow•fall (**snoh**-*fawl*) ***noun*** The amount of snow that falls in one place in a certain time.

snow•flake (**snoh**-*flake*) ***noun*** A single flake or crystal of snow.

snow•man (**snoh**-*man*) ***noun*** A figure built to resemble a person by stacking large balls of snow. ▸ ***noun, plural*** **snowmen**

snow•mo•bile (**snoh**-moh-*beel*) ***noun*** A vehicle with an engine and skis or runners, used to travel over snow.

snow•plow (**snoh**-*plou*)
1. ***noun*** A device or vehicle used to push snow off a road, sidewalk, or other surface.
2. ***verb*** When you **snowplow** in skiing, you go down the slope slowly with the tips of your skis pointing inward and the ends pointing out.
▸ **snowplowing, snowplowed** ▸ ***noun*** **snowplow**

snow•shoe (**snoh**-*shoo*) ***noun*** A webbed frame that is shaped like a racket and attached to a boot to keep the foot from sinking into the snow.

snow•storm (**snoh**-*storm*) ***noun*** A storm with strong winds and heavy snow.

snub (**snuhb**) ***verb*** To treat someone coldly or with disrespect; to ignore a person. ▸ **snubbing, snubbed** ▸ ***noun*** **snub**

snuff (**snuhf**)
1. ***noun*** Powdered tobacco used for sniffing. Snuff was very popular in the 18th century.
2. snuff out ***verb*** To extinguish, as in *to snuff out a candle.* ▸ **snuffing, snuffed**

snug (**snuhg**) ***adjective***
1. Cozy and comfortable.
2. Fitting closely or tightly.
▸ ***adjective*** **snugger, snuggest**
▸ ***adverb*** **snugly**

snug•gle (**snuhg**-uhl) ***verb*** To lie close to someone, or to hold something close for warmth or protection or to show affection. ▸ **snuggling, snuggled**
▸ ***adjective*** **snuggly**

so (**soh**)
1. ***adverb*** In this or that way.
2. ***adverb*** To that extent.
3. ***adverb*** Very.
4. ***adverb*** Very much.
5. ***conjunction*** Therefore.
6. ***adverb*** Too or also.
7. ***adjective*** True.
8. ***conjunction*** In order that.
9. ***pronoun*** More or less.
10. ***pronoun*** That way, or the same.
11. ***interjection*** A word that shows surprise, shock, or annoyance.
So sounds like **sew.**

soak (**sohk**) ***verb***
1. To make something completely wet.
2. To put something in water and leave it there.
3. When something **soaks up** liquid, it absorbs it or takes it in.
▸ ***verb*** **soaking, soaked**

soak•ing (**soh**-king) ***adjective*** Very wet.

soap (**sohp**) ***noun*** A substance used for washing and cleaning. Soap is usually made from fat and lye. ▸ ***verb*** **soap**
▸ ***adjective*** **soapy**

soap opera ***noun*** A television series about the tangled loves and lives of a group of people. Soap operas stress suspense and exaggerated emotions.

soar (**sor**) ***verb***
1. To fly very high in the air.
2. To rise or increase very quickly.
Soar sounds like **sore.**
▸ ***verb*** **soaring, soared**

sob (**sob**) ***verb*** To breathe in short bursts or gasps because you have been crying a lot. ▸ **sobbing, sobbed** ▸ ***noun*** **sob**

so•ber (**soh**-bur)
1. ***adjective*** Not drunk.
2. ***adjective*** Serious or solemn.
3. ***verb*** To make someone more serious, solemn, or sober. ▸ **sobering, sobered**
4. ***adjective*** **Sober** colors are dark and dull.
▸ ***adjective*** **soberer, soberest**
▸ ***adverb*** **soberly**

sob story ***noun*** A sad tale intended to evoke sympathy. ▸ ***noun, plural*** **sob stories**

soc•cer (**sok**-ur) ***noun*** A game played by two teams of 11 players who try to score by kicking a ball into goals at each end of a field.

so•cia•ble (**soh**-shuh-buhl) ***adjective*** A **sociable** person is friendly and enjoys talking to people and spending time with them. ▸ ***noun*** **sociability** ▸ ***adverb*** **sociably**

so•cial (**soh**-shuhl)
1. ***adjective*** To do with the way that people live together as a society, as in *social problems.*
2. ***adjective*** To do with people getting together in a friendly way or for companionship, as in *a social visit* or *a social club.*
3. ***adjective*** Friendly or sociable.
4. ***adjective*** **Social** animals live in groups rather than on their own.
5. ***noun*** A party or a gathering of people.
▸ ***adverb*** **socially**

so•cial•ism (**soh**-shuh-*liz*-uhm) ***noun*** An economic system in which the production of goods by factories, businesses, and farms is controlled to a high degree by a government instead of by the owners of the factories, businesses, and farms. ▸ ***noun*** **socialist** ▸ ***adjective*** **socialist**

Social Security ***noun*** A U.S. government program that pays money to people who are elderly, retired, unemployed, or disabled. Workers and employers also contribute funding. Also spelled **social security.**

social studies ***noun*** A subject in school that includes geography, history, and government.

so•ci•e•ty (suh-**sye**-uh-tee) ***noun***
1. All people, or people as a group.
2. All the people who live in the same country or area and share the same laws and customs.
3. An organization for people who share the same interests.
4. The wealthiest part of society that often sets or follows current fashions and style.
▸ ***noun, plural*** **societies**

so•ci•ol•o•gy (*soh*-see-**ol**-uh-jee) ***noun*** The study of the ways in which people live together in different societies. ▸ ***noun*** **sociologist** ▸ ***adjective*** **sociological**

sock (**sok**)
1. ***noun*** A piece of clothing that you wear on your foot.
2. ***verb*** *(informal)* To hit someone very hard. ▸ **socking, socked**

sock•et (**sok**-it) ***noun*** A hole or hollow place where something fits in, as in *an electric socket* or *an eye socket.*

sod (**sod**)
1. ***noun*** The top layer of soil and the grass attached to it.
2. ***noun*** A piece of sod that is held together by matted roots and cut in a square or strip.
3. ***verb*** To cover with pieces of sod.
▸ **sodding, sodded**

so•da (**soh**-duh) ***noun***
1. A soft drink made with soda water.
2. A drink made with soda water, flavoring, and ice cream.
3. Soda water.
4. Baking soda.

soda fountain ***noun*** A counter where ice cream, soft drinks, and light meals are served.

soda water ***noun*** A drink with bubbles, made by mixing water with carbon dioxide gas.

S

sod•den (**sod**-uhn) ***adjective*** Soaking wet.

so•di•um (**soh**-dee-uhm) ***noun*** A chemical found in salt.

sodium bi•car•bon•ate (*bye*-**kar**-buh-nit) ***noun*** A white substance used in baking powder, fire extinguishers, and medicines. Also called **baking soda.**

so•fa (**soh**-fuh) ***noun*** A long, soft seat with arms and a back and room for two or more people; a couch.

soft (**sawft**) ***adjective***
1. Something that is **soft** is not stiff or hard and is easily pressed or bent into a different shape, as in *a soft pillow.* ▸ ***noun*** **softness**
2. Smooth and gentle to touch.
3. Pleasantly quiet and gentle, as in *soft music* or *a soft breeze.* ▸ ***adverb*** **softly**
4. Kind, as in *a soft heart.*
▸ ***adjective*** **softer, softest** ▸ ***verb*** **soften**

soft•ball (**sawft**-*bawl*) ***noun*** A sport, similar to baseball, that is played on a smaller field with a larger, softer ball that is pitched underhand.

soft drink ***noun*** A beverage, made with soda water, that contains no alcohol.

soft•heart•ed (**sawft**-*har*-tid) ***adjective*** If someone is **softhearted,** he or she is very kind, sympathetic, and generous to others.

soft•ware (**sawft**-*wair*) ***noun*** Computer programs that control the workings of the equipment, or hardware, and direct it to do specific tasks.

sog•gy (**sog**-ee) ***adjective*** Very wet; soaked, as in *soggy ground.* ▸ **soggier, soggiest**

soil (**soyl**)
1. ***noun*** Dirt or earth in which plants grow.
2. ***noun*** A land or a country.
3. ***verb*** If you **soil** something, you make it dirty or stain it. ▸ **soiling, soiled**

so•lace (**sol**-iss)
1. ***noun*** Comfort, or relief from sorrow or grief.
2. ***noun*** Something that gives such comfort.
3. ***verb*** To comfort or console someone who is sad or grieving. ▸ **solacing, solaced**

so•lar (**soh**-lur) ***adjective***
1. To do with the sun, as in *a solar eclipse.*
2. Powered by energy from the sun.

solar energy ***noun*** Energy from the sun that can be used for heating and generating electricity.

solar heating ***noun*** Heating powered by energy from the sun.

solar system ***noun*** The sun and the bodies that move in orbit around it. In our solar system there are nine planets, many moons, and also asteroids and comets.

sol•der (**sod**-ur) ***verb*** To join pieces of metal by putting a small amount of hot, liquid metal between them. The liquid metal hardens as it cools. ▸ **soldering, soldered** ▸ ***noun*** **solder**

sol•dier (**sole**-jur) ***noun*** Someone who is in the army.

sole (**sole**)
1. ***noun*** The bottom part of the foot.
2. ***noun*** The bottom part of a shoe, boot, or sock. ▸ ***verb*** **sole**
3. ***noun*** A kind of edible ocean flatfish.
4. ***adjective*** Only. ▸ ***adverb*** **solely**
Sole sounds like **soul.**

sol•emn (**sol**-uhm) ***adjective*** Grave or very serious, as in *a solemn occasion* or *a solemn promise.* ▸ ***noun*** **solemnness,** ***noun*** **solemnity** (suh-**lem**-ni-tee) ▸ ***adverb*** **solemnly**

sol•id (**sol**-id)
1. ***adjective*** Hard and firm; not a liquid or gas. ▸ ***noun*** **solidity**
2. ***adjective*** Not mixed with anything else, as in *solid gold.*
3. ***adjective*** Not hollow, as in *a solid block of ice.*
4. ***adjective*** Dependable, as in *solid citizens.*

5. ***adjective*** Not interrupted.
6. ***noun*** A three-dimensional geometric figure that encloses a part of space.
▸ ***adjective*** **solid**

sol•i•dar•i•ty (*sol*-uh-**da**-ruh-tee) ***noun*** Unity; agreement among a group of people that they will work or fight together to achieve their goal.

so•lid•i•fy (suh-**lid**-uh-fye) ***verb*** To become hard and firm. ▸ **solidifies, solidifying, solidified**

sol•id•ly (**sol**-id-lee) ***adverb***
1. Firmly and strongly.
2. Without stopping.

sol•i•tar•y (**sol**-uh-*ter*-ee) ***adjective***
1. If someone is **solitary,** the person spends a lot of time alone.
2. Single.

solitary con•fine•ment (kuhn-**fine**-muhnt) ***noun*** A punishment in which a prisoner is put in a cell alone and is not allowed to see or talk to anybody.

so•lo (**soh**-loh)
1. ***noun*** A piece of music that is played or sung by one person, with or without accompaniment. ▸ ***noun, plural*** **solos** ▸ ***noun*** **soloist**
2. ***adjective*** Done by one person. ▸ ***adverb*** **solo**
3. ***verb*** To fly a plane alone, especially for the first time. ▸ **soloing, soloed**

sol•u•ble (**sol**-yuh-buhl) ***adjective*** A substance that is **soluble** can be dissolved in liquid.

so•lu•tion (suh-**loo**-shuhn) ***noun***
1. The answer to a problem; an explanation.
2. A mixture made up of a substance that has been dissolved in a liquid.

solve (**solv**) ***verb*** To find the answer to a problem. ▸ **solving, solved** ▸ ***noun*** **solver**

sol•vent (**sol**-vuhnt)
1. ***noun*** A liquid that makes other substances dissolve.
2. ***adjective*** Having enough money to pay one's debts.

som•ber (**som**-bur) ***adjective***
1. Dark and gloomy, as in *a rainy, chilly, somber day.*
2. Very sad or depressed.

som•bre•ro (som-**brer**-oh) ***noun*** A tall straw or felt hat with a wide brim that is worn in Mexico and the southwestern United States. ▸ ***noun, plural*** **sombreros**

some (**suhm**)
1. ***adjective*** A number of things, or an amount of something that is not named or known.
2. ***pronoun*** A certain number of people or things.
3. ***adjective*** *(informal)* Remarkable.
Some sounds like **sum.**

some•bod•y (**suhm**-*bod*-ee *or* **suhm**-buh-dee)
1. ***pronoun*** A person who is not specified or known.
2. ***noun*** An important or famous person.

some•day (**suhm**-*day*) ***adverb*** At some future time.

some•how (**suhm**-*hou*) ***adverb*** In some way.

some•one (**suhm**-*wuhn*) ***pronoun*** Somebody; some person.

som•er•sault (**suhm**-ur-*sawlt*) ***noun*** When you do a **somersault,** you tuck your head into your chest and roll in a complete circle forward or backward. ▸ ***verb*** **somersault**

some•thing (**suhm**-*thing*)
1. ***pronoun*** A thing that is not specified or known.
2. ***adverb*** A little bit.

some•time (**suhm**-*time*) **adverb** At a time that is not specified or known.

some•times (**suhm**-*timez*) ***adverb*** Now and then; at some times but not at others.

some•what (**suhm**-*waht*)
1. ***adverb*** Rather. *My idea is somewhat like yours.*
2. ***pronoun*** Something.

S

some•where (**suhm**-*wair*) ***adverb***
1. To, in, or at a place that is not specified or known. ▸ ***noun* somewhere**
2. At some time, or in some amount.

son (**suhn**) ***noun*** Someone's **son** is his or her male child. **Son** sounds like **sun.**

so•nar (**soh**-nar) ***noun*** An instrument that is used to calculate how deep the water is or where underwater objects are. It works by sending sound waves through the water and listening for when they bounce back off something. Sonar stands for *SOund Navigation And Ranging.*

so•na•ta (suh-**nah**-tuh) ***noun*** A piece of music for one or two instruments that is in three or four movements, or sections.

song (**sawng** *or* **song**) ***noun***
1. A piece of music with words for singing.
2. The musical sounds made by a whale, a bird, or an insect.
3. If you buy something **for a song,** you get it at a very cheap price.

song•bird (**sawng**-*burd*) ***noun*** A bird that has a musical call or song. Larks, finches, and orioles are songbirds.

son•ic (**son**-ik) ***adjective***
1. To do with sound waves.
2. To do with the speed of sound in air, or about 741 miles per hour at sea level.

sonic boom ***noun*** The loud noise produced by a vehicle when it travels faster than the speed of sound and breaks through the sound barrier.

son-in-law ***noun*** Someone's **son-in-law** is the husband of his or her daughter. ▸ ***noun, plural* sons-in-law**

son•net (**son**-it) ***noun*** A poem with 14 lines and a fixed pattern of rhymes.

soon (**soon**) ***adverb***
1. In a short time.
2. Too early.
3. Quickly; without delay.
4. sooner If you would **sooner** do something, you would prefer to do that thing.
▸ ***adverb* sooner, soonest**

soot (**sut**) ***noun*** Black powder that is produced when a fuel such as coal, wood, or oil is burned. Soot often collects in chimneys. ▸ ***adjective* sooty**

soothe (**sooTH**) ***verb***
1. To calm someone who is angry or upset.
2. To relieve something that is painful.
▸ ***verb* soothing, soothed** ▸ ***adjective* soothing**

so•phis•ti•ca•ted (suh-**fiss**-tuh-*kay*-tid) ***adjective***
1. People who are **sophisticated** have a lot of knowledge about the world.
2. A **sophisticated** machine is cleverly designed and able to do difficult or complicated things.
▸ ***noun* sophistication**

soph•o•more (**sof**-*mor or* **sof**-uh-*mor*) ***noun*** A student in the second year of high school or college.

sop•ping (**sop**-ing) ***adjective*** Extremely wet.

so•pran•o (suh-**pran**-oh) ***noun***
1. The highest singing voice. ▸ ***adjective* soprano**
2. Someone who sings in a soprano voice.
▸ ***noun, plural* sopranos**

sor•bet (sor-**bay** *or* **sor**-buht) ***noun*** A frozen dessert made with fruit juice.

sor•cer•er (**sor**-sur-er) ***noun*** Someone who performs magic by controlling evil spirits; a wizard. ▸ ***noun* sorcery**

sor•did (**sor**-did) ***adjective***
1. Dirty or filthy, as in *a sordid slum.*
2. Evil and disgusting, as in *a sordid murder.*
▸ ***noun* sordidness** ▸ ***adverb* sordidly**

sore (**sor**)
1. ***adjective*** Painful, as in *sore muscles.*
▸ ***noun* soreness**
2. ***noun*** An area of painful skin on your body.
3. ***adjective*** Angry.
▸ ***adjective* sorer, sorest**
Sore sounds like **soar.**

S

sor•rel (**sor**-uhl *or* **so**-ruhl) ***noun***
1. A reddish brown color.
2. A horse of this color with a mane and tail of a lighter color.
3. A plant with long clusters of small flowers and edible leaves that are shaped like hearts.

sor•row (**so**-roh) ***noun*** Great sadness or grief. ▸ ***adjective* sorrowful** ▸ ***adverb* sorrowfully**

sor•ry (**so**-ree) ***adjective***
1. Feeling sadness, sympathy, or regret because you have done something wrong or because someone is suffering.
2. If someone or something is **in a sorry state,** it is in very bad condition.
▸ ***adjective* sorrier, sorriest**

sort (**sort**)
1. ***noun*** A type or a kind.
2. ***verb*** To arrange or separate things into groups. ▸ **sorting, sorted**

SOS (**ess oh ess**) ***noun*** A signal sent out by a ship or plane to say that it is in need of urgent help. The initials SOS stand for Save Our Ship.

soul (**sole**)
1. ***noun*** The spiritual part of a person that is often thought to control the ability to think, feel, and act.
2. ***noun*** A person.
3. ***adjective*** To do with African Americans or black culture, as in *soul music* and *soul food.*
Soul sounds like **sole.**

sound (**sound**)
1. ***noun*** Something that you hear.
2. ***noun*** One of the noises that make up human speech.
3. ***verb*** If a horn or bell **sounds,** it makes a noise.
4. ***verb*** To give an impression.
5. ***verb*** To be said or pronounced. The word *sore* sounds like *soar.*
6. ***adjective*** Healthy, as in *a sound mind.*
7. ***adjective*** Sensible, as in *sound advice.*
8. ***adjective*** Deep.
9. ***noun*** A long, narrow arm of water between two bodies of water or between the mainland and an island.
▸ ***verb* sounding, sounded**

sound barrier ***noun*** When a vehicle goes through the **sound barrier,** the sound waves produced by that vehicle are moving more slowly than the vehicle itself. As a result, all of the sound waves that people on the ground usually hear as a roar get bunched together into a single boom.

sound bite ***noun*** A statement or a small portion of a political speech that is recorded and played on a newscast or other program.

sound effects ***noun, plural*** Noises that are used to make a play, a movie, or a radio or television program seem more realistic.

sound•proof (**sound**-*proof*) ***adjective*** A **soundproof** room does not let any sound in or out of it. ▸ ***verb* soundproof**

sound track ***noun***
1. A recording of music from a movie or play.
2. The narrow strip on a motion-picture film or videotape that carries the sound recording.

sound wave ***noun*** A wave or series of vibrations in the air, in a solid, or in a liquid that can be heard.

soup (**soop**)
1. ***noun*** A liquid food made with vegetables, meat, or fish. ▸ ***adjective* soupy**
2. ***verb*** *(slang)* If you **soup up** an engine or motor vehicle, you increase its power.
▸ **souping, souped**

sour (**sour**)
1. ***adjective*** Something that is **sour** has a sharp, acid taste, such as a lemon.
2. ***adjective*** Disagreeable.
3. ***verb*** To make or become acid through spoiling. ▸ **souring, soured**
▸ ***noun* sourness**

S

source (**sorss**) ***noun***
1. The place, person, or thing from which something comes, as in *the source of the problem.*
2. The place where a stream or river starts.
3. Someone or something that provides information.

sour•dough (**sour**-*doh*) ***noun*** A fermented dough used in making breads and rolls.

south (**south**)
1. ***noun*** One of the four main points of the compass. South is to your left when you face the direction where the sun sets. ▸ ***adjective* south** ▸ ***adverb* south**
2. South *noun* Any area or region that is lying in this direction.
3. ***adjective*** To do with or existing in the south, as in *the south side of the city.*
4. the South *noun* In the United States, the states lying south of Pennsylvania and the Ohio River and east of the Mississippi River. The South includes those states that fought for the Confederacy against the Union (or North) in the Civil War.

South•east (*south*-**eest**) ***noun*** The area of the United States to the south and east that stretches from Virginia to Florida and Louisiana.

south•ern (**suhTH**-urn) ***adjective***
1. In or toward the south.
2. Coming from the south, as in *a southern wind.*
3. Southern To do with the part of the United States that is in the South.

Southern Hemisphere ***noun*** The half of the earth that is south of the equator.

South Pole ***noun*** The most southern part of the earth, located at the bottom tip of the earth's axis. The South Pole is in Antarctica.

south•ward (**south**-wurd) ***adverb*** To or toward the south. ▸ ***adjective* southward**

South•west (*south*-**west**) ***noun*** The area of the United States that includes the states west of the Mississippi River and south of Missouri and Kansas.

sou•ve•nir (*soo*-vuh-**nihr** *or* **soo**-vuh-*nihr*) ***noun*** An object that you keep to remind you of a place, a person, or an event.

sov•er•eign (**sov**-ruhn)
1. ***noun*** A king or queen.
2. ***adjective*** Having the highest power, as in *a sovereign ruler.*
3. ***adjective*** Independent, as in *a sovereign nation.*

So•vi•et Union (**soh**-vee-*et*) ***noun*** A former federation of 15 republics that included Russia, Ukraine, and other nations of eastern Europe and northern Asia. Also called *Union of Soviet Socialist Republics.*

sow
1. (**soh**) ***verb*** To scatter seeds over the ground so that they will grow; to plant. ▸ **sowing, sowed, sown** (**sohn**) *or* **sowed**
2. (**sou**) ***noun*** An adult female pig.

soy•bean (**soi**-*been*) ***noun*** A seed that grows in pods on bushy plants. Soybeans are a good source of protein and oil.

soy sauce (**soi**) ***noun*** A dark liquid that is made from soaked and fermented soybeans. It is used as a sauce to flavor food.

space (**spayss**)
1. ***verb*** To leave an empty area between things. ▸ **spacing, spaced**
2. ***noun*** The universe beyond the earth's atmosphere. Also called **outer space.**
3. ***noun*** An empty or available area.
4. ***noun*** A period of time.
5. ***noun*** The open area in which all objects are located. Space has height, width, and depth.

space bar ***noun*** A bar at the bottom of a computer or typewriter keyboard that adds a space to the right of a character when pressed.

space•craft (**spayss**-*kraft*) ***noun*** A vehicle that travels or is used in space.

space•ship (**spayss**-*ship*) ***noun*** A spacecraft designed and built to break free of Earth's atmosphere and travel into space.

space shuttle ***noun*** A spacecraft designed to carry astronauts into space and back to Earth. A space shuttle is made up of four parts (the orbiter, the external fuel tank, and two booster rockets) that separate after the launch. The orbiter returns to Earth.

space station ***noun*** A spacecraft large enough to house a crew for long periods of time. Space stations are placed in orbit and are used for scientific observation and as a launching site for other spacecraft.

space•suit (**spayss**-*soot*) ***noun*** The protective clothing that an astronaut wears in space.

space•walk (**spayss**-*wawk*) ***noun*** A period of time during which an astronaut leaves his or her spacecraft and moves around in space. ▸ ***noun* spacewalker** ▸ ***verb* spacewalk**

spa•cious (**spay**-shuhss) ***adjective*** If something is **spacious,** it is very large and roomy.

spade (**spayd**) ***noun***
1. A tool with a flat blade and a long handle. Spades are used for digging. ▸ ***verb* spade**
2. spades *noun, plural* One of the four suits in a deck of cards. Spades have a black symbol that looks like a heart with a stalk.

spa•ghet•ti (spuh-**get**-ee) ***noun*** Long, thin strands of pasta made of flour and water and cooked by boiling.

span (**span**)
1. *noun* The distance between two points. The span of a bridge is its length from one end to the other.
2. *noun* The full reach or length of something, as in *the wing span of an airplane* or *a person's life span.*
3. *noun* A length of time.
4. *verb* To reach over or stretch across something. ▸ **spanning, spanned**

spank (**spangk**) ***verb*** To hit someone with an open hand or a flat object, especially on the buttocks, as a punishment. ▸ **spanking, spanked**

spare (**spair**)
1. *adjective* Kept for use when needed, as in *a spare tire.* ▸ ***noun* spare**
2. *adjective* Not taken up by work; free, as in *spare time.*
3. *adjective* Lean and thin.
4. *verb* To give or make something available.
5. *verb* To show mercy, or to not hurt someone, as in *to spare a life* or *to spare someone's feelings.*
6. *verb* To free from the need to do something.
7. *noun* The knocking down of all 10 pins in bowling with two rolls of the ball. ▸ ***verb* sparing, spared**

spark (**spark**)
1. *noun* A small bit of burning material thrown off by a fire.
2. *noun* A quick flash of light, as in *an electrical spark.*
3. *noun* A small bit or trace, as in *a spark of enthusiasm.*
4. *verb* To make something happen. ▸ **sparking, sparked** ▸ ***verb* spark**

spar•kle (**spar**-kuhl) ***verb***
1. To shine with many flashing points of light; to glitter.
2. To bubble.
3. To accomplish something in a brilliant or lively way.
▸ ***verb* sparkling, sparkled** ▸ ***noun* sparkle**

spark plug ***noun*** One of the parts of a gasoline engine that supplies an electrical spark to ignite the fuel-and-air mixture in a cylinder. Spark plugs are screwed into the cylinders and connected to the distributor, which supplies the current to create the spark.

S

spar•row (**spa**-roh) ***noun*** A small, common songbird with brown, white, and gray feathers and a short bill.

sparse (**sparss**) ***adjective*** Thinly spread; not crowded or dense, as in *sparse vegetation.* ▸ ***adverb* sparsely**

spasm (**spaz**-uhm) ***noun***
1. A sudden tightening of a muscle that cannot be controlled.
2. A short, sudden burst of energy, activity, or emotion, as in *a spasm of laughter.*

spat (**spat**) ***noun*** A short, unimportant argument or quarrel.

spat•ter (**spat**-ur) ***verb*** To scatter or splash in drops or small bits.
▸ **spattering, spattered**

spat•u•la (**spach**-uh-luh) ***noun***
1. A tool with a broad, flat blade that bends easily. It is used to mix, spread, or lift food or to mix paint.
2. An instrument with a flat blade used by doctors and scientists.

spawn (**spawn**)
1. *noun* The eggs produced by fish and amphibians.
2. *verb* To produce a large number of eggs. ▸ **spawning, spawned**

speak (**speek**) ***verb***
1. To talk, or to say words out loud.
2. To tell or make known your ideas, opinions, or feelings.
3. To deliver a speech.
4. To talk in a certain language.
5. If you **speak out** or **speak up,** you speak loudly or you speak openly and honestly about what you really believe.
▸ ***verb* speaking, spoke (spohk), spoken (spoh**-kin)

speak•er (**spee**-kur) ***noun***
1. The one who is speaking.
2. Somebody who gives a speech in public.
3. A loudspeaker, especially one attached to a sound system.

spear (**spihr**)
1. *noun* A weapon with a long handle and a pointed head.
2. *noun* A long blade, shoot, or stalk of a plant, as in *asparagus spears.*
3. *verb* To pick up with something sharp. ▸ **spearing, speared**

spear•mint (**speer**-*mint*) ***noun*** A mint plant with leaves that are shaped like spears and are used to flavor candy and food.

spe•cial (**spesh**-uhl)
1. *adjective* Different or unusual, as in *a special occasion* or *a special request.*
▸ ***adverb* specially**
2. *adjective* Particular.
3. *noun* A television program intended as a single show rather than as one in a series.

spe•cial•ist (**spesh**-uh-list) ***noun*** An expert at one particular job or area.

spe•cial•ize (**spesh**-uh-*lize*) ***verb*** To focus on one area of work, or to learn a lot about one subject. ▸ **specializing, specialized** ▸ ***noun* specialization**

spe•cial•ty (**spesh**-uhl-tee) ***noun***
1. The thing that you are particularly good at.
2. A particular product or service.
▸ ***noun, plural* specialties**

spe•cies (**spee**-sheez *or* **spee**-seez) ***noun*** One of the groups into which animals and plants of the same genus are divided according to their shared characteristics. Members of the same species can mate and have offspring.
▸ ***noun, plural* species**

spe•ci•fic (spi-**sif**-ik) ***adjective*** Particular, definite, or individually named. ▸ ***adverb* specifically**

spec•i•fi•ca•tions (*spess*-uh-fuh-**kay**-shuhnz) ***noun, plural*** Detailed information and instructions about something that is to be built or made.

spec•i•fy (**spess**-uh-*fye*) ***verb*** To mention something in an exact way.
▸ **specifies, specifying, specified**

spec•i•men (**spess**-uh-muhn) ***noun*** A sample, or an example used to stand for a whole group, as in *a butterfly specimen* or *a blood specimen.* ▸ ***adjective*** **specimen**

speck (**spek**) ***noun***
1. A small spot or mark.
2. A tiny particle or bit, as in *a speck of dust.*

speck•led (**spek**-uhld) ***adjective*** Covered with small, irregular spots or marks, as in *a speckled egg.*

spec•ta•cle (**spek**-tuh-kuhl) ***noun*** A remarkable and dramatic sight.

spec•ta•cles (**spek**-tuh-kuhlz) ***noun, plural*** Eyeglasses.

spec•tac•u•lar (spek-**tak**-yuh-lur) ***adjective*** Remarkable or dramatic, as in *a spectacular sunset.* ▸ ***adverb*** **spectacularly**

spec•ta•tor (**spek**-tay-tur) ***noun*** Someone who watches an event and does not participate in it. ▸ ***adjective*** **spectator**

spec•ter (**spek**-tur) ***noun*** A ghost. ▸ ***adjective*** **spectral**

spec•trum (**spek**-truhm) ***noun***
1. The range of colors that is revealed when light shines through a prism or through drops of water, as in a rainbow.
2. A wide range of things or ideas.
▸ ***noun, plural*** **spectrums** *or* **spectra** (**spek**-truh)

spec•u•late (**spek**-yuh-late) ***verb***
1. To wonder or guess about something without knowing all the facts.
2. To invest in something that is risky, such as a business or a stock.
▸ ***verb*** **speculating, speculated**
▸ ***noun*** **speculation,** ***noun*** **speculator**

speech (**speech**) ***noun***
1. The ability to speak.
2. A talk given to a group of people.
▸ ***noun, plural*** **speeches**
3. The way in which someone speaks.

speech•less (**speech**-liss) ***adjective*** Unable to speak.

speed (**speed**)
1. ***noun*** The rate at which something moves.
2. ***noun*** The rate of any action.
3. ***verb*** To travel very fast or faster than is allowed. ▸ **speeding, sped** (**sped**) *or* **speeded**
4. ***noun*** Quickness of movement.

speed bump ***noun*** A ridge of asphalt or hard rubber that has been laid across a road or parking lot to make drivers slow down.

speed•om•e•ter (spi-**dom**-uh-tur) ***noun*** An instrument in a vehicle that shows how fast you are traveling.

spell (**spel**)
1. ***verb*** To write or say the letters of a word in their correct order.
2. ***verb*** To mean.
3. ***verb*** To take someone's place for a time.
4. ***noun*** A period of time, usually a short one, as in *a spell of rainy weather.*
5. ***noun*** A word or words supposed to have magical powers.
6. ***verb*** If you **spell out** an idea or a plan, you explain it clearly and in detail.
▸ ***verb*** **spelling, spelled**

spell checker ***noun*** A computer program that searches for misspelled words by comparing each word in a document to correctly spelled words.

spe•lunk•ing (spi-**luhng**-king) ***noun*** If you go **spelunking,** you explore caves. ▸ ***noun*** **spelunker**

spend (**spend**) ***verb***
1. To use money to buy things.
2. To pass time.
3. If you **spend** time or energy, you use it.
▸ ***verb*** **spending, spent** (**spent**)

sperm (**spurm**) ***noun*** One of the reproductive cells from a male that is capable of fertilizing eggs in a female.

S

sphere (**sfihr**) ***noun***
1. A solid shape like a basketball or globe, with all points of the shape the same distance from the center of the shape. ▸ ***adjective* spherical** (**sfihr**-uh-kuhl *or* **sfer**-uh-kuhl)
2. An area of activity, interest, or knowledge.

sphinx (**sfingks**) ***noun***
1. In Egyptian mythology, a creature with the body of a lion and the head of a woman, ram, or hawk.
2. the Sphinx A large statue of this creature in Giza, Egypt.
▸ ***noun, plural* sphinxes**

spice (**spisse**) ***noun***
1. A substance with a distinctive smell or taste used to flavor foods.
2. Anything that adds excitement or interest. ▸ ***verb* spice**

spi•cy (**spye**-see) ***adjective*** Containing lots of spices; having a pungent taste.
▸ **spicier, spiciest**

spi•der (**spye**-dur) ***noun*** A small animal with eight legs, a body divided into two parts, and no wings. Spiders spin webs to trap insects for food.

spig•ot (**spig**-uht) ***noun*** A device used to control the flow of liquid in a pipe; a faucet.

spike (**spike**)
1. *noun* A large, heavy nail often used to fasten rails to railroad ties. ▸ ***verb* spike**
2. *noun* A pointed piece of metal attached to the sole of a shoe to help athletes get and keep firm footing.
3. *noun* An ear of wheat or grain, such as corn.
4. *noun* A long cluster of flowers on one stem.
5. *verb* To hit a volleyball down and over the net with force so that it is difficult to return. ▸ **spiking, spiked**
▸ ***noun* spike** ▸ ***adjective* spiked**

spill (**spil**)
1. *verb* If you **spill** something, you let the contents of a container fall out, often accidentally.
2. *verb* To run out or flow over.
3. *noun* A serious fall.
▸ ***verb* spilling, spilled** *or* **spilt** (**spilt**)

spin (**spin**)
1. *verb* To make thread by twisting fine fibers together.
2. *verb* To make a web or cocoon by giving off a liquid that hardens into thread.
3. *verb* To rotate or to whirl around.
4. *verb* To tell or to relate.
5. *verb* To feel dizzy, or as if your head is whirling around.
6. *noun* A short ride.
7. *noun* A special interpretation or point of view.
▸ ***verb* spinning, spun** (**spuhn**)

spin•ach (**spin**-ich) ***noun*** A dark green, leafy vegetable.

spinal column ***noun*** A series of connected bones in your back that support and protect the spinal cord. Spinal column is another term for **backbone.**

spinal cord ***noun*** A thick cord of nerve tissue that starts at the brain and runs through the center of the spinal column. The spinal cord carries impulses to and from the brain and links the brain to the rest of the nerves in the body.

spin•dle (**spin**-duhl) ***noun*** The round stick or rod on a spinning wheel that holds and winds thread.

spin•dly (**spind**-lee) ***adjective*** Long, thin, and rather weak. ▸ **spindlier, spindliest**

spine (**spine**) ***noun***
1. The backbone. ▸ ***adjective* spinal**
2. A hard, sharp, pointed growth, such as a thorn or quill, on some plants and animals. ▸ ***adjective* spiny**
3. The central, vertical piece of a book's cover.

spinning wheel ***noun*** A device worked by hand consisting of a large wheel and a spindle. A spinning wheel is used to spin fibers into thread or yarn.

spin-off ***noun***
1. An object or product that was first used in a different or unrelated way.
2. A television show starring a character who had a popular but less important role on an earlier program. ▸ ***verb*** **spin off**

spin•ster (**spin**-stur) ***noun*** A woman who has never been married.

spi•ral (**spye**-ruhl) ***adjective*** A **spiral** pattern winds around in circles like a spring. ▸ ***noun*** **spiral** ▸ ***verb*** **spiral**

spire (**spire**) ***noun*** A structure that comes to a point at the top. Spires are often built on top of church steeples.

spir•it (**spihr**-it)
1. ***noun*** The part of a person that is believed to control thoughts and feelings; the soul.
2. ***noun*** Enthusiasm and determination in a person or group of people.
▸ ***adjective*** **spirited**
3. ***noun*** A ghost.
4. ***noun, plural*** **spirits** A person's mood or state of mind.
5. ***noun*** The real meaning or intent, as in *the spirit of the law.*
6. ***verb*** To carry off mysteriously or secretly. ▸ **spiriting, spirited**

spir•i•tu•al (**spihr**-uh-choo-uhl)
1. ***adjective*** To do with the soul and not with physical things. ▸ ***adverb*** **spiritually**
2. ***adjective*** To do with religion.
3. ***noun*** A type of religious folk song that was originated by African Americans in the South.

spit (**spit**)
1. ***verb*** To force saliva out of your mouth.
2. ***noun*** Saliva.
3. ***verb*** To make an angry, hissing sound.
4. ***noun*** A long, pointed rod that holds meat over a fire for cooking.
5. ***noun*** A narrow point of land that sticks out into water.
▸ ***verb*** **spitting, spat** (**spat**) *or* **spit**

spite (**spite**)
1. ***noun*** Deliberate nastiness.
▸ ***adjective*** **spiteful** ▸ ***adverb*** **spitefully**
2. ***verb*** To be mean or nasty to.
▸ **spiting, spited**
3. in spite of Without being hindered by; regardless, or in defiance of.

splash (**splash**) ***verb***
1. To throw a liquid.
2. To make wet by splashing.
▸ ***verb*** **splashes, splashing, splashed**
▸ ***noun*** **splash**

splash•down (**splash**-*doun*) ***noun*** The landing of a spacecraft in the ocean.

splen•did (**splen**-did) ***adjective***
1. Very beautiful or impressive; brilliant, as in *a splendid performance.*
2. Very good; excellent, as in *a splendid idea.*
▸ ***adverb*** **splendidly**

splen•dor (**splen**-dur) ***noun*** Great or magnificent beauty.

splint (**splint**) ***noun*** A piece of wood, plastic, or metal used to support an injured limb.

splin•ter (**splin**-tur)
1. ***noun*** A thin, sharp piece of wood, glass, metal, etc.
2. ***verb*** To break into thin, sharp pieces.
▸ **splintering, splintered**

split (**split**)
1. ***verb*** To break along the grain, as in *to split logs.*
2. ***verb*** To divide.
3. ***verb*** To burst or break apart by force.
4. ***noun*** A crack or a break.
5. ***noun*** An acrobatic or dance move in which you slide to the floor with your legs spread in opposite directions.
▸ ***verb*** **splitting, split**

S

spoil (**spoil**)
1. ***verb*** To ruin or wreck something.
2. ***verb*** To become rotten or unfit for eating.
3. ***adjective*** If children are **spoiled,** their parents have pampered them and allowed them to have their own way too often.
▸ ***verb*** **spoiling, spoiled** *or* **spoilt**

spoke (**spoke**)
1. ***verb*** The past tense of **speak.**
2. ***noun*** One of the thin rods that connect the rim of a wheel to the hub.

sponge (**spuhnj**) ***noun***
1. A sea animal that has a rubbery skeleton with many holes that absorb water. The dried skeletons of sponges are often used for washing and cleaning.
2. A cleaning pad made of plastic or another artificial material that absorbs water.
▸ ***verb*** **sponge** ▸ ***adjective*** **spongy**

spon•sor (**spon**-sur)
1. ***verb*** To give money and support to people who are doing something worthwhile, often for charity. ▸ ***noun*** **sponsorship**
2. ***verb*** To pay the costs of a radio or television broadcast in return for having your products advertised. ▸ ***noun*** **sponsor**
3. ***noun*** A person who is responsible for someone or something.
▸ ***verb*** **sponsoring, sponsored**

spon•ta•ne•ous (spon-**tay**-nee-uhss) ***adjective***
1. Without previous thought or planning, as in *spontaneous applause.*
2. Happening by itself, without any apparent outside cause, as in *a spontaneous explosion.* ▸ ***noun*** **spontaneity** (spon-tuh-**nee**-uh-tee *or* spon-tuh-**nay**-uh-tee) ▸ ***adverb*** **spontaneously**

spool (**spool**) ***noun*** A reel on which film, tape, thread, etc., is wound.

spoon (**spoon**) ***noun*** A utensil with a handle on one end and a surface shaped like a shallow bowl on the other. Spoons are used for eating, stirring, and measuring. ▸ ***verb*** **spoon**

spore (**spor**) ***noun*** A plant cell that develops into a new plant. Spores are produced by plants that do not flower, such as fungi, mosses, and ferns.

sport (**sport**) ***noun***
1. A game involving physical activity. A sport can be played professionally or for pleasure.
2. A person who plays fair and accepts losing with good grace, as in *a good sport.*

sports•man•ship (**sports**-muhn-ship) ***noun*** Fair and reasonable behavior, especially in playing a sport.

spot (**spot**)
1. ***noun*** A small mark or stain.
2. ***noun*** An area on the skin or fur that is different from the area around it.
▸ ***adjective*** **spotted**
3. ***noun*** A place or a location.
4. ***noun*** A small amount of something.
5. ***verb*** To notice something or someone. ▸ **spotting, spotted**
6. If something **hits the spot,** it is satisfying and is exactly the right thing to have at that moment.
7. If you are **in a tight spot,** you are in a lot of trouble and will not get out of it easily.

spot•less (**spot**-liss) ***adjective***
1. Absolutely clean.
2. Without a flaw or weak part, as in *a spotless reputation.*
▸ ***adverb*** **spotlessly**

spot•light (**spot**-*lite*) ***noun***
1. A powerful beam of light used to light up a small area.
2. A lamp that sends a strong beam of light. A spotlight is used in a reading area, on a theater stage, or in an exhibit to highlight items on display.
3. If someone is **in the spotlight,** he or she is in the news or is the focus of a lot of public attention.
▸ ***verb*** **spotlight**

spouse (**spouss**) ***noun*** A husband or a wife.

spout (**spout**)
1. ***noun*** A pipe, a tube, or an opening through which liquid flows or is poured.
2. ***verb*** To shoot or pour out with force.
▸ **spouting, spouted**

sprain (**sprayn**) ***verb*** To injure a joint by twisting or tearing its muscles or ligaments. ▸ **spraining, sprained**
▸ ***noun*** **sprain**

sprawl (**sprawl**) ***verb***
1. To sit or lie with your arms and legs spread out carelessly.
2. To spread out in all directions. ▸ ***noun*** **sprawl**
▸ ***verb*** **sprawling, sprawled**

spray (**spray**) ***verb*** To scatter liquid in very fine drops. ▸ **spraying, sprayed**
▸ ***noun*** **spray**

spread (**spred**)
1. ***verb*** To unfold or to stretch out.
2. ***verb*** To cover a surface with something. ▸ ***noun*** **spread**
3. ***verb*** To reach out or extend over an area.
4. ***verb*** To scatter or make known.
5. ***noun*** *(informal)* An elaborate meal put on a table.
▸ ***verb*** **spreading, spread**

spread·sheet (**spred**-*sheet*) ***noun***
1. A wide sheet of paper that is divided into rows and columns. Spreadsheets are used for organizing financial records.
2. A computer program that allows you to keep track of budgets and other financial records in a spreadsheet format.

spree (**spree**) ***noun*** A period of eating, drinking, shopping, etc., without restraint and usually to excess.

spring (**spring**)
1. ***noun*** The season between winter and summer, when the weather becomes warmer and plants and flowers begin to grow.
2. ***verb*** To jump suddenly. ▸ ***noun*** **spring**
3. ***verb*** To appear suddenly.
4. ***verb*** To make known suddenly.
5. ***noun*** A coil of metal that moves back to its original shape or position after being stretched or pushed down.
6. ***noun*** A place where water rises up from underground and becomes a stream.
▸ ***verb*** **springing, sprang** (**sprang**), **sprung** (**spruhng**)

spring·board (**spring**-*bord*) ***noun*** A flexible board used in diving or gymnastics to help a person jump high in the air.

spring-cleaning ***noun*** A thorough cleaning of a place, usually done once a year.

spring fever ***noun*** A lazy or restless feeling that often is associated with the coming of spring.

sprin·kle (**spring**-kuhl) ***verb***
1. To scatter something in small drops or bits.
2. To rain in small amounts.
▸ ***verb*** **sprinkling, sprinkled** ▸ ***noun*** **sprinkle**

sprin·kler (**springk**-lur) ***noun*** A device that attaches to a hose and sprays water over a lawn or garden.

sprint (**sprint**)
1. ***verb*** To run fast for a short distance.
▸ **sprinting, sprinted**
2. ***noun*** A very fast race run over a short distance.
▸ ***noun*** **sprinter** ▸ ***adjective*** **sprint**

sprock·et (**sprok**-it) ***noun*** A wheel with a rim made of toothlike points that fit into the holes of a chain. The chain then drives the wheel.

sprout (**sprout**)
1. ***verb*** When a plant **sprouts,** it starts to grow and produce shoots or buds.
2. ***noun*** A new or young plant growth, such as a bud or shoot.
3. **sprouts** ***noun, plural*** The young edible shoots of various plants that are often eaten raw.
4. ***verb*** To grow, appear, or develop suddenly or quickly.
▸ ***verb*** **sprouting, sprouted**

S

spruce (**sprooss**) ***noun*** An evergreen tree with short leaves shaped like needles, drooping cones, and wood that is often used in making pulp for paper.

spur (**spur**)
1. ***noun*** A spike or spiked wheel on the heel of a rider's boot. Spurs are used to make a horse go faster or obey commands.
2. ***verb*** If something **spurs** you **on,** it encourages or motivates you.
▸ **spurring, spurred** ▸ ***noun*** **spur**

spurt (**spurt**)
1. ***verb*** When liquid **spurts,** it flows or gushes suddenly in short bursts.
▸ **spurting, spurted** ▸ ***noun*** **spurt**
2. ***noun*** A sudden burst of energy, growth, or speed. ▸ ***verb*** **spurt**

sput•ter (**spuht**-ur) ***verb***
1. To make popping, spitting, or coughing noises.
2. To speak quickly and in a confused way.
3. To spit out small bits of food or saliva, especially when you are talking in an excited way.
▸ ***verb*** **sputtering, sputtered**

spy (**spye**)
1. ***verb*** To watch something closely from a hidden place.
2. ***verb*** To sight.
3. ***noun*** Someone, especially a government agent, who secretly collects information about an enemy. ▸ ***noun, plural*** **spies** ▸ ***verb*** **spy**
▸ ***verb*** **spies, spying, spied**

squab•ble (**skwahb**-uhl) ***noun*** A noisy argument or quarrel, usually over something unimportant. ▸ ***verb*** **squabble**

squad (**skwahd**) ***noun*** A small group of people involved in the same activity, such as soldiers, football players, or police officers.

squad•ron (**skwahd**-ruhn) ***noun*** A group of ships, cavalry troops, or other military units.

squal•id (**skwahl**-id) ***adjective*** Filthy and gloomy, usually because of neglect or poverty.

squall (**skwawl**) ***noun*** A sudden, violent wind that usually brings rain, snow, or sleet with it.

squa•lor (**skwah**-lur) ***noun*** The condition of being dirty, gloomy, and very poor.

squan•der (**skwahn**-dur) ***verb*** To spend money wastefully and use it up.
▸ **squandering, squandered**

square (**skwair**)
1. ***noun*** A shape with four equal sides and four right angles. ▸ ***adjective*** **square**
2. ***verb*** To multiply a number by itself.
▸ **squaring, squared**
3. ***noun*** A number is a **square** is if it can be expressed as the product of the same two numbers. Four is the square of 2 because $2 \times 2 = 4$.
4. ***noun*** An open area in a town or city with streets on all four sides. Squares are often used as parks.
5. ***adjective*** Honest or fair, especially in business affairs.
6. ***adjective*** Nutritious and filling, as in *a square meal.*
7. ***adjective*** *(slang)* Not cool or not hip; old-fashioned, as in *square ideas.* ▸ ***noun*** **square**
▸ ***adjective*** **squarer, squarest**

square dance ***noun*** A dance in which sets of four couples form the sides of a square and move to the commands called out by the leader, or caller.

square root ***noun*** A number that, when multiplied by itself, gives a particular number. The square root of 25 is 5, because $5 \times 5 = 25$. The symbol for a square root is $\sqrt{\ }$; $\sqrt{25} = 5$

squash (**skwahsh**)
1. ***verb*** To crush or to flatten.
▸ **squashes, squashing, squashed**
2. ***noun*** A game played by two people who hit a small rubber ball against the

walls of an enclosed court with rackets.
3. ***noun*** A fleshy fruit that grows on a vine in many shapes, sizes, and colors. Squash are related to pumpkins and gourds. They are cooked and eaten as vegetables. ▸ ***noun, plural*** **squash** *or* **squashes**

squat (**skwaht**)
1. ***verb*** To crouch, or sit on your heels with your knees bent. ▸ ***noun*** **squat**
2. ***verb*** To live without permission on empty land or in an empty house that does not belong to you. ▸ ***noun*** **squatter**
3. ***adjective*** Short and broad.
▸ **squatter, squattest**
▸ ***verb*** **squatting, squatted**

squawk (**skwawk**)
1. ***noun*** A loud, harsh screech like the sound made by some parrots.
2. ***verb*** To make this sound.
3. ***verb*** *(informal)* To complain loudly.
4. ***noun*** *(informal)* Any loud complaint or protest. ▸ ***noun*** **squawker** ▸ ***verb*** **squawking, squawked**

squeak (**skweek**) ***verb*** To make a short, high sound like the noise of a mouse. ▸ **squeaking, squeaked** ▸ ***noun*** **squeak** ▸ ***adjective*** **squeaky**

squeal (**skweel**) ***verb***
1. To make a shrill, high sound or cry.
2. *(informal)* To betray a friend or secret; to turn informer.
▸ ***verb*** **squealing, squealed** ▸ ***noun*** **squeal**

squea•mish (**skwee**-mish) ***adjective*** Easily sickened or nauseated. ▸ ***adverb*** **squeamishly**

squeeze (**skweez**) ***verb***
1. To press something firmly together from opposite sides. ▸ ***noun*** **squeezer**
2. To force something into or through a space.
3. To hug someone.
▸ ***verb*** **squeezing, squeezed** ▸ ***noun*** **squeeze**

squid (**skwid**) ***noun*** A sea animal with a long, soft body and 10 tentacles. Squid swim by squirting water out of their bodies with great force. ▸ ***noun, plural*** **squid** *or* **squids**

squint (**skwint**) ***verb*** If you **squint** at something, you nearly close your eyes in order to see it more clearly.
▸ **squinting, squinted** ▸ ***noun*** **squint**

squire (**skwire**) ***noun***
1. In medieval times, a **squire** was a young nobleman who accompanied and helped a knight.
2. An English country gentleman.

squirm (**skwurm**) ***verb***
1. To wriggle about uncomfortably.
2. To feel uncomfortable because you are embarrassed or ashamed.
▸ ***verb*** **squirming, squirmed**

squir•rel (**skwurl**) ***noun*** A rodent that climbs trees and has a bushy tail.

squirt (**skwurt**) ***verb*** To send out a stream of liquid. ▸ **squirting, squirted** ▸ ***noun*** **squirt**

squish•y (**skwish**-ee) ***adjective*** *(informal)* Soft and soggy.

stab (**stab**)
1. ***verb*** To wound someone by piercing the person with a knife or other sharp instrument. ▸ ***noun*** **stab**
2. ***verb*** To stick or drive a pointed object into something.
3. ***noun*** A sharp, brief feeling or pang, as in *a stab of pain* or *a stab of guilt.*
4. *(informal)* If you **make a stab** at something, you make an attempt at doing it.
▸ ***verb*** **stabbing, stabbed**

sta•ble (**stay**-buhl)
1. ***noun*** A building or a part of a building where horses or cattle are kept.
▸ ***verb*** **stable**
2. ***adjective*** Firm and steady. ▸ ***verb*** **stabilize**
3. ***adjective*** Safe and secure.
▸ ***adjective*** **stabler, stablest**

S

stac•ca•to (stuh-**kah**-toh) ***adverb*** In music, when you play notes **staccato,** you make them short, sharp, and separate from each other.

stack (**stak**)
1. ***verb*** To pile things up, one on top of another. ▸ **stacking, stacked**
2. ***noun*** A large, neat pile of hay, straw, or grain.
3. ***noun*** A neat pile of something arranged in layers, as in *a stack of books.*
4. ***noun*** A chimney or a smokestack.

sta•di•um (**stay**-dee-uhm) ***noun*** A large structure in which sports events and concerts are held. It usually has an open field surrounded by rows of rising seats. ▸ ***noun, plural*** **stadiums** *or* **stadia** (**stay**-dee-uh)

staff (**staf**)
1. ***noun*** A group of people who work for a company, an institution, or a person, as in *a newspaper staff.* ▸ ***noun, plural*** **staffs**
2. ***verb*** To provide an organization with employees. ▸ **staffing, staffed**
3. ***noun*** A stick or pole used as a support in walking or as a weapon, as in *a shepherd's staff.*
4. ***noun*** A flagpole.
5. ***noun*** The set of lines and spaces on which music is written.
▸ ***noun, plural*** **staffs** *or* **staves**

stag (**stag**) ***noun*** An adult male deer.

stage (**stayj**)
1. ***noun*** A raised platform on which actors and other entertainers perform.
2. ***noun*** The profession of acting.
3. ***noun*** A level of progress.
4. ***noun*** A period of development.
5. ***noun*** A stagecoach.
6. ***verb*** To organize a public performance or event. ▸ **staging, staged**

stage•coach (**stayj**-*kohch*) ***noun*** A coach pulled by a horse or horses and used in the past to carry passengers and mail over long distances. ▸ ***noun, plural*** **stagecoaches**

stag•ger (**stag**-ur) ***verb***
1. To walk or stand unsteadily.
2. If you are **staggered** by something, you are astonished and overwhelmed.
3. When you **stagger** events, you time them so that they do not happen at the same time. ▸ ***adjective*** **staggered**
▸ ***verb*** **staggering, staggered**

stag•ger•ing (**stag**-ur-ing) ***adjective*** Amazing or astonishing.

stag•nant (**stag**-nuhnt) ***adjective***
1. Not moving or not flowing; still.
2. Foul or polluted as a result of not moving.
3. Not active or not growing, as in *a stagnant economy.*

stag•nate (**stag**-nayt) ***verb***
1. When water **stagnates,** it becomes dirty or polluted, changes color, and often gives off a foul odor.
2. If situations or persons **stagnate,** they remain the same for a long time, when they should be changing.
▸ ***verb*** **stagnating, stagnated** ▸ ***noun*** **stagnation**

staid (**stayd**) ***adjective*** If you are **staid,** you are sedate, proper, and serious.
▸ **staider, staidest** ▸ ***noun*** **staidness**
▸ ***adverb*** **staidly**

stain (**stayn**)
1. ***noun*** A mark or spot that is hard to remove, as in *a grass stain.*
2. ***verb*** To make a mark that is hard to remove. ▸ **staining, stained**
3. ***noun*** A dye used to color wood.

stained glass ***noun*** Colored pieces of glass held together by lead strips, forming a picture, pattern, or design. Stained glass is often used in church windows. ▸ ***adjective*** **stained-glass**

stain•less steel (**stayn**-liss) ***noun*** A type of steel that does not rust or tarnish.

stair (**stair**) ***noun***
1. One of a group of steps that allows you to walk from one level of a building to another.

2. **stairs** ***noun, plural*** Another word for **stairway. Stair** sounds like **stare.**

stair•way (**stair**-*way*) ***noun*** A flight of steps with a railing and a structure that supports it.

stake (**stayk**)
1. ***noun*** A thick, pointed post that can be driven into the ground. ▸ ***verb*** **stake**
2. ***verb*** To bet. ▸ **staking, staked**
3. ***noun*** Something, especially money, that is bet or risked, as in *high stakes.*
4. ***noun*** If you have **a stake** in something, you are involved in it or you have put money, time, or effort into it.
5. If something is **at stake,** it is at risk.
6. If you **pull up stakes,** you leave a place.

Stake sounds like **steak.**

sta•lac•tite (stuh-**lak**-*tite*) ***noun*** A thin piece of rock shaped like an icicle that hangs from the roof of a cave. Stalactites are made from calcium minerals dissolved in drops of water that have slowly solidified.

sta•lag•mite (stuh-**lag**-*mite*) ***noun*** A thin piece of rock shaped like an icicle that sticks up from the floor of a cave. Stalagmites are made from calcium minerals dissolved in drops of water that have slowly solidified.

stale (**stayl**) ***adjective***
1. No longer fresh, as in *stale bread* or *stale air.*
2. No longer new or interesting, as in *a stale joke* or *stale news.*

▸ ***adjective*** **staler, stalest**

stale•mate (**stayl**-*mayt*) ***noun***
1. A situation in an argument or game of chess in which neither side can win or make any more moves.
2. Any position or situation that results in a deadlock, with no progress possible.

stalk (**stawk**)
1. ***noun*** The long main part or stem of a plant from which the leaves and flowers grow.
2. ***verb*** To hunt or track a person or an animal in a quiet, secret way. ▸ ***noun*** **stalker**
3. ***verb*** To walk in an angry, stiff way.

▸ ***verb*** **stalking, stalked**

stall (**stawl**)
1. ***verb*** When a car **stalls,** its engine stops running.
2. ***noun*** A counter or booth where things are displayed for sale at a market.
3. ***noun*** A section in a stable or barn where a single animal is kept, as in *a horse stall.*
4. ***verb*** To delay doing something on purpose. ▸ ***noun*** **stall**

▸ ***verb*** **stalling, stalled**

stal•lion (**stal**-yuhn) ***noun*** An adult male horse.

sta•men (**stay**-muhn) ***noun*** The part of a flower that produces pollen. It consists of a thin stalk, called the filament, and a tip, called the anther, that has pollen on it.

stam•i•na (**stam**-uh-nuh) ***noun*** The energy and strength to keep doing something for a long time.

stam•mer (**stam**-ur) ***verb*** To speak in an unsure way, stopping often and repeating certain sounds. People sometimes stammer when they are nervous or excited. ▸ **stammering, stammered** ▸ ***noun*** **stammer**

stamp (**stamp**)
1. ***noun*** A small piece of paper that you stick onto a letter or package to show that you have paid for it to be sent; a postage stamp.
2. ***noun*** An object used to print a mark by pressing it against a pad of ink and then transferring the ink onto paper.
3. ***verb*** To bang your foot down.

▸ **stamping, stamped**

▸ ***noun*** **stamp**

stam•pede (stam-**peed**) ***verb*** When people or animals **stampede,** they make a sudden, wild rush in one direction, usually because something has frightened them. ▸ **stampeding, stampeded** ▸ ***noun*** **stampede**

S

stand (**stand**)
1. ***verb*** To be on or get on your feet with your body upright.
2. ***verb*** To put something in an upright position.
3. ***verb*** To be located.
4. ***verb*** To be in a certain rank or order.
5. ***verb*** To have an opinion or to take a position. ▸ ***noun* stand**
6. ***verb*** To continue without any change.
7. ***noun*** An object on which you put things, as in *a music stand.*
8. stands *noun, plural* A covered area for spectators at a ballpark or stadium.
9. ***noun*** A small booth, counter, or stall where goods are sold, as in *a hot dog stand.*
10. stand for *verb* To represent.
11. ***verb*** If you cannot **stand** something, you hate it or are unable to bear it.
12. ***verb*** If you **stand by** someone, you support the person when he or she is in trouble.
13. ***verb*** If something **stands out,** it can be seen or noticed easily.
14. If you **take a stand** on an issue, you state your opinion in a clear and forceful way.
▸ ***verb* standing, stood** (**stud**)

stan•dard (**stan**-durd)
1. ***noun*** A rule or model that is used to judge or measure how good something is.
2. ***noun*** The flag or banner of a nation or military group.
3. ***adjective*** Usual or average.
4. ***adjective*** Used or accepted as a standard, rule, or model.
5. ***adjective*** Widely used or accepted as correct, as in *standard spelling* or *standard English.*

stand•by (**stand**-*bye*) ***noun*** Someone or something that is ready to be used if needed.

stand-in ***noun*** Someone who takes the place of another person when that person cannot be there or cannot do something. ▸ ***verb* stand in**

stand•ing (**stan**-ding) ***noun***
1. Position, rank, or reputation.
2. If you are **in good standing** with a group of people, you are respected by them and accepted within that group.
3. standings *noun, plural* The positions or rankings of all the teams within a sport during a regular season of play.

stand•still (**stand**-*stil*) ***noun*** If something is at a **standstill,** it has come to a complete halt.

stand-up ***adjective*** A **stand-up** comic or comedian performs while standing alone on a stage or in front of a camera.
▸ ***noun* stand-up**

stan•za (**stan**-zuh) ***noun*** One of the groups of lines into which a poem or song is divided; a verse.

sta•ple (**stay**-puhl) ***noun***
1. A thin piece of wire that is shaped like a U and punched through sheets of paper to hold them together. ▸ ***noun* stapler** ▸ ***verb* staple**
2. Any food or product that is used regularly and kept in large amounts, as in *flour, salt, and sugar.*
3. A main product that is grown or produced in a country or region.

star (**star**)
1. ***noun*** A ball of burning gases in space. A star is seen from the earth as a tiny point of light in the night sky.
▸ ***adjective* starry**
2. ***noun*** A shape with five or more points.
3. ***noun*** A person who plays a leading role in a movie, television program, or play.
4. ***noun*** A person who is outstanding in some field, as in *a basketball star.*
5. ***verb*** To take the leading role in a movie, television program, or play.
▸ **starring, starred**

star•board (**star**-burd) ***noun*** The right-hand side of a ship or an aircraft.
▸ ***adjective* starboard**

starch (**starch**) ***noun***
1. A white substance found in such foods as potatoes, bread, and rice. Starch is very filling and gives you energy.
2. A substance used for making cloth stiff. ▸ ***verb*** **starch**

stare (**stair**) ***verb*** To look directly at someone or something for a long time without moving your eyes. **Stare** sounds like **stair.** ▸ **staring, stared** ▸ ***noun*** **stare**

star•fish (**star**-*fish*) ***noun*** A sea animal with five or more arms. A starfish is shaped like a star. ▸ ***noun, plural*** **starfish**

stark (**stark**) ***adjective***
1. Bare and grim; having little or no plant life.
2. Complete or extreme, as in *stark poverty.*
▸ ***adjective*** **starker, starkest**

star•ling (**star**-ling) ***noun*** A plump bird with pointed wings, a yellow bill, a short tail, and brown or green-black feathers. Starlings are found in most parts of the world.

Stars and Stripes ***noun*** The flag of the United States. The red and white stripes represent the 13 original colonies. The white stars represent the 50 states.

start (**start**)
1. ***verb*** To begin to move, act, or happen.
2. ***verb*** To make something move, act, or happen.
3. ***noun*** The beginning of something.
4. ***verb*** To jump in surprise. ▸ ***noun*** **start**
5. ***noun*** An advantage at the beginning of a race.
▸ ***verb*** **starting, started**

star•tle (**star**-tuhl) ***verb*** To surprise or frighten someone and make the person jump. ▸ **startling, startled** ▸ ***adjective*** **startled,** ***adjective*** **startling**

starve (**starv**) ***verb***
1. To suffer or die from lack of food.
▸ ***noun*** **starvation**
2. To need or want something very much.
▸ ***verb*** **starving, starved**

starv•ing (**starv**-ing) ***adjective***
1. Suffering or dying from lack of food.
2. *(informal)* Very hungry.

state (**state**)
1. ***verb*** To say something in words; to tell or explain. ▸ **stating, stated**
2. ***noun*** A group of people united under one government; a nation.
3. ***noun*** Any of the political and geographical units that make up a country such as the United States.
▸ ***noun*** **statehood**
4. ***noun*** The way that something is, or the condition it is in.

state•ly (**state**-lee) ***adjective*** Grand, dignified, or majestic, as in *a stately mansion.*

state•ment (**state**-muhnt) ***noun***
1. Something that is said in words.
2. A list of all the amounts paid into and out of a bank account.

state-of-the-art ***adjective*** Very advanced and up-to-date, as in *state-of-the-art technology.*

states•man (**statess**-muhn) ***noun*** A person respected for great experience and leadership in government. ▸ ***noun, plural*** **statesmen**

states•wom•an (**statess**-*wum*-uhn) ***noun*** A woman respected for great experience and leadership in government. ▸ ***noun, plural*** **stateswomen**

stat•ic (**stat**-ik)
1. ***adjective*** Not moving, changing, or growing, as in *a static situation* or *a static population.*
2. ***noun*** The crackling noises that you hear when static electricity in the air interferes with a radio or television signal.

static electricity ***noun*** Electricity that builds up in an object and stays there. Static electricity can be produced when one object rubs against another.

S

sta•tion (**stay**-shuhn) ***noun***
1. A place where tickets for trains, buses, or other vehicles are sold and where passengers are let on and off.
2. A building where a service is provided, as in *a fire station, a police station,* or *a gas station.*
3. A place with equipment to send out television or radio signals.
4. A place where a person or thing stands or is supposed to stand.

sta•tion•ar•y (**stay**-shuh-*ner*-ee) ***adjective***
1. Not moving or not able to be moved.
2. Not changing, as in *stationary prices.*
Stationary sounds like **stationery.**

sta•tion•er•y (**stay**-shuh-*ner*-ee) ***noun***
1. Writing materials, such as paper, envelopes, pens, and notebooks.
2. Paper and envelopes used to write letters. **Stationery** sounds like **stationary.**

station wagon ***noun*** A motor vehicle with a large, enclosed cargo area behind the rear seats, where the trunk would ordinarily be. The rear seats can be folded down for extra storage space.

sta•tis•tic (stuh-**tiss**-tik) ***noun*** A fact or piece of information expressed as a number or percentage. ▸ ***adjective*** **statistical** ▸ ***adverb*** **statistically**

stat•ue (**stach**-oo) ***noun*** A model of a person or an animal made from metal, stone, wood, or any solid material.

sta•tus (**stay**-tuhss *or* **stat**-uhss) ***noun***
1. A person's rank or position in a group, an organization, or a society.
2. The state of affairs or condition of a situation.

stat•ute (**stach**-oot) ***noun*** A rule or a law.

stave (**stayv**)
1. ***noun*** One of the long, thin strips of wood that form the sides of a barrel.
2. ***noun*** The set of lines and spaces on which music is written; a staff.
3. ***verb*** To break or smash a hole in something.
4. ***verb*** If you **stave** something **off**, you manage to keep it away.
▸ ***verb*** **staving, staved** *or* **stove** (**stohv**)

stay (**stay**)
1. ***verb*** To remain in one place or condition.
2. ***verb*** To spend time somewhere.
3. ***noun*** A period of time spent somewhere as a visitor.
▸ ***verb*** **staying, stayed**

stead•fast (**sted**-*fast*) ***adjective*** Firm and steady or not changing, as in *steadfast loyalty* or *a steadfast gaze.*

stead•y (**sted**-ee)
1. ***adjective*** Continuous and not changing much, as in *a steady rain.*
▸ ***adverb*** **steadily**
2. ***adjective*** Firm or stable; not shaky, as in *a steady hand* or *a steady chair.*
3. ***verb*** To stop something from moving about or shaking. ▸ **steadies, steadying, steadied**
4. ***adjective*** Sensible and dependable, as in *a steady worker.*
5. ***adjective*** Regular, as in *a steady customer.* ▸ ***adjective*** **steadier, steadiest**

steak (**stayk**) ***noun*** A thick slice of meat or fish. **Steak** sounds like **stake.**

steal (**steel**)
1. ***verb*** To take something that does not belong to you.
2. ***verb*** To do something in a secret or tricky way.
3. ***verb*** To get to the next base in baseball without a hit or an error.
▸ ***noun*** **steal**
4. ***noun*** Something bought at a very low price; a bargain.
Steal sounds like **steel.**
▸ ***verb*** **stealing, stole** (**stohl**), **stolen** (**stohl**-in)

stealth•y (**stel**-thee) ***adjective*** Secret and quiet. ▸ **stealthier, stealthiest**
▸ ***noun*** **stealth** ▸ ***adverb*** **stealthily**

steam (**steem**)
1. ***noun*** The vapor that is formed when water boils. ▸ ***verb*** **steam**

S

2. ***verb*** To cook using steam, as in *to steam vegetables.*
3. ***noun*** The mist formed when water vapor condenses.
4. ***verb*** When glass **steams up,** it becomes covered with condensation.
5. *(informal)* If you **let off steam** or **blow off steam,** you release the energy or angry feelings that you have stored up.
6. *(informal)* If you **run out of steam,** you have no more energy left.
▸ ***verb*** **steaming, steamed**

steam•boat (**steem**-*boht*) ***noun*** A boat powered by a steam engine.

steam engine ***noun*** An engine powered by steam. Coal or wood burned in a boiler heats the water in a tank. As the water in the tank boils, it creates steam. This steam is forced into cylinders where it pushes pistons to operate machinery.

steam•er (**stee**-mur) ***noun***
1. A boat powered by steam.
2. A large, covered pot used to cook foods with steam.

steam locomotive ***noun*** An engine powered by steam and used for pulling trains. Steam locomotives were used on most trains in the United States until about 1940. Today, most trains are powered by diesel engines.

steam•roll•er (**steem**-*roh*-lur) ***noun*** A heavy vehicle that is used to flatten road surfaces.

steam•ship (**steem**-*ship*) ***noun*** A ship powered by a steam engine.

steed (**steed**) ***noun*** A horse, especially one that is spirited.

steel (**steel**)
1. ***noun*** A hard, strong metal made chiefly from iron.
2. ***verb*** To prepare oneself by becoming determined and hard, like steel.
▸ **steeling, steeled**
Steel sounds like **steal.**

steel band ***noun*** A group that plays music on drums made from oil barrels.

steel wool ***noun*** A mass of very fine threads of steel. Steel wool is used for cleaning, smoothing, and polishing things.

steep (**steep**)
1. ***adjective*** Sharply sloping up or down, as in *a steep hill.* ▸ ***adverb*** **steeply**
2. ***adjective*** Sharp or rapid.
3. ***verb*** To soak something in a liquid.
4. ***verb*** To be full of something.
5. ***adjective*** Very high, as in *steep prices.*
▸ ***verb*** **steeping, steeped** ▸ ***adjective*** **steeper, steepest**

stee•ple (**stee**-puhl) ***noun*** A high tower on a church or other building. It usually has a spire on top.

stee•ple•chase (**stee**-puhl-*chayss*) ***noun*** A long horse race with fences and water jumps.

steer (**stihr**)
1. ***verb*** To make a vehicle go in a particular direction.
2. ***verb*** To be guided.
3. ***verb*** To guide or to direct.
4. ***noun*** A young male of the domestic cattle family raised especially for its beef.
▸ ***verb*** **steering, steered**

steering wheel ***noun*** The wheel in a vehicle used to control its direction.

steg•o•sau•rus (*steg*-uh-**sor**-uhss) ***noun*** A dinosaur that fed on plants and had bony plates along its back, a small head, and a long tail with spikes.

stem (**stem**)
1. ***noun*** The long main part of a plant from which the leaves and flowers grow.
2. **stem from** ***verb*** To originate or come from.
3. ***verb*** To stop something from flowing or spreading.
▸ ***verb*** **stemming, stemmed**

stench (**stench**) ***noun*** A strong, unpleasant smell, as in *the stench at the garbage dump.* ▸ ***noun, plural*** **stenches**

sten•cil (**sten**-suhl) ***noun*** A piece of paper, plastic, or metal with a design cut out of it. A stencil can be painted over to transfer the design onto a surface.
▸ ***verb*** **stencil**

S

step (**step**)
1. ***noun*** One of the flat surfaces on a stairway.
2. steps *noun, plural* A set of stairs.
3. *verb* To move your foot forward and put it down in walking, climbing, or dancing. ▸ **stepping, stepped** ▸ ***noun*** **step**
4. *noun* The distance covered by a step.
5. *noun* The sound of someone walking.
6. *noun* One of the things that you need to do in order to make or achieve something.
7. *noun* If you do something **step by step,** you do it in a gradual and steady way.
8. *noun* *(informal)* If someone says that you should **watch your step,** the person is telling you to be careful.
Step sounds like **steppe.**

step•fam•i•ly (**step**-*fam*-lee) ***noun*** The family of your stepfather or stepmother.

step•fa•ther (**step**-*faTH*-ur) ***noun*** Someone's **stepfather** is the man who married that person's mother after the death or divorce of the person's father.

step•moth•er (**step**-*muhTH*-ur) ***noun*** Someone's **stepmother** is the woman who married that person's father after the death or divorce of the person's mother.

steppe (**step**) ***noun*** Any of the vast, treeless plains found in southeastern Europe and Asia. **Steppe** sounds like **step.**

ste•re•o (**ster**-ee-oh *or* **stirh**-ee-oh) ***noun*** A phonograph, radio, or other sound system that uses two or more channels of sound so that the listener hears sounds in a more natural way.
▸ ***adjective*** **stereo**

ste•re•o•type (**ster**-ee-oh-*tipe* *or* **stirh**-ee-oh-*tipe*) ***noun*** An overly simple picture or opinion of a person, group, or thing. ▸ ***verb*** **stereotype** ▸ ***adjective*** **stereotypical** (*ster*-ee-oh-**tip**-i-kuhl)

ster•ile (**ster**-uhl) ***adjective*** Free from germs and dirt.

ster•i•lize (**ster**-uh-*lize*) ***verb*** To clean something so thoroughly that you make it free from germs and dirt.
▸ **sterilizing, sterilized** ▸ ***noun*** **sterilization** (*ster*-uh-li-**zay**-shuhn)

ster•ling silver (**stur**-ling) ***noun*** A metal that is made of 92.5 percent pure silver.

stern (**stern**)
1. *adjective* Strict or harsh, as in *a stern teacher* or *a stern lecture.* ▸ **sterner, sternest**
2. *noun* The back end of a ship or boat.

ste•roid (**stihr**-oid *or* **ster**-oid) ***noun*** A chemical substance found naturally in plants and animals, including humans. The use of steroids by athletes to enhance their strength and performance is banned in most sports competitions.

steth•o•scope (**steth**-uh-*skope*) ***noun*** A medical instrument used by doctors and nurses to listen to the sounds from a patient's heart, lungs, and other areas.

stew (**stoo**)
1. *noun* A dish made of meat or fish and vegetables cooked slowly in liquid.
2. *verb* To cook something for a long time over low heat. ▸ ***adjective*** **stewed**
3. *noun* If you are **in a stew** about something, you are upset and worried about it.
4. *verb* If you **stew** about something, you worry about it.
▸ **stewing, stewed**

stew•ard (**stoo**-urd) ***noun***
1. A man who serves passengers on an airplane or a ship.
2. Someone who serves food and drink at a hotel, club, or restaurant, as in *a wine steward.*

stew•ard•ess (**stoo**-ur-diss) ***noun*** A woman who serves passengers, especially on an airplane.

stick (**stik**)
1. *noun* A long, thin piece of wood.
2. *noun* Something shaped like a stick, as in *a stick of gum, a stick of dynamite,* or *carrot sticks.*

S

3. ***verb*** To glue or fasten one thing to another. ▸ ***adjective* sticky**
4. ***verb*** To push something with a point into something else.
5. ***verb*** To remain attached, as if glued.
6. ***verb*** If something **sticks,** it becomes fixed in a particular position.
7. ***verb*** If something **sticks out,** it is prominent, often because it is higher or longer than other things nearby.
8. ***verb*** *(informal)* If you **stick up for** someone, you support or defend the person.
9. ***verb*** If you **stick to** something, you keep at it.
▸ ***verb* sticking, stuck (stuhk)**

stick•er (**stik**-ur) ***noun*** A paper or plastic label with glue on the back.

stiff (**stif**) ***adjective***
1. Difficult to bend or turn.
2. If you feel **stiff,** your muscles hurt, often because you have overworked them.
3. Not flowing easily; thick.
4. Difficult or severe, as in *stiff competition* or *stiff punishment.*
5. Not natural or easy in manner; formal.
6. Strong and steady; powerful, as in *a stiff wind.*
▸ ***verb* stiffen** ▸ ***adjective* stiffer, stiffest** ▸ ***adverb* stiffly**

sti•fle (**stye**-fuhl) ***verb***
1. To hold back or to stop, as in *to stifle a yawn* or *to stifle someone's creativity.*
2. To feel smothered because of a lack of fresh or cool air.
▸ ***verb* stifling, stifled** ▸ ***adjective* stifling**

stig•ma (**stig**-ma) ***noun***
1. A mark of shame or embarrassment.
2. The part of a flower that receives the pollen in pollination.
▸ ***noun, plural* stigmata** (stig-**mat**-uh) *or* **stigmas**

still (**stil**)
1. ***adjective*** Without sound; quiet; silent.
2. ***adjective*** Without motion; quiet and calm. ▸ ***noun* still** ▸ ***verb* still**
3. ***adverb*** Without moving.
4. ***adverb*** Even now.
5. ***adverb*** All the same; nevertheless.
6. ***adverb*** Even; yet.
▸ ***noun* stillness** ▸ ***adjective* stiller, stillest**

stilt (**stilt**) ***noun***
1. One of two poles, each with a rest or strap for the foot, used to raise the wearer above the ground in walking.
2. One of the posts that holds a building, pier, or other structure above the ground or water level.

stim•u•lant (**stim**-yuh-luhnt) ***noun*** A substance that stimulates activity in a part of the body. ▸ ***adjective* stimulant**

stim•u•late (**stim**-yuh-late) ***verb***
1. To encourage something to grow or develop.
2. If someone or something **stimulates** you, it fills you with exciting new ideas.
▸ ***verb* stimulating, stimulated**
▸ ***noun* stimulation** ▸ ***adjective* stimulating**

stim•u•lus (**stim**-yuh-luhss) ***noun***
1. Anything that excites or causes an action.
2. Something that causes or speeds up a reaction in a person, an animal, or a plant. Your eyes, ears, and nose receive stimuli from your surroundings.
▸ ***noun, plural* stimuli** (**stim**-yuh-lye)

sting (**sting**)
1. ***verb*** To pierce or wound with a small, sharp point.
2. ***verb*** To hurt with or as if with a sharp or throbbing pain.
3. ***noun*** A stinger.
▸ ***noun* sting** ▸ ***verb* stinging, stung (stuhng)**

sting•er (**sting**-ur) ***noun*** A sharp, pointed part of an insect or animal that can be used to sting.

sting•ray (**sting**-*ray*) ***noun*** A fish with a flat body; large, winglike fins; and a long tail with poisonous spines that can cause a painful wound.

S

stin•gy (**stin**-jee) ***adjective*** Not willing to give or spend money; not generous.
▸ **stingier, stingiest** ▸ ***adverb*** **stingily**

stink (**stingk**) ***verb***
1. To give off a strong, unpleasant smell.
▸ ***noun*** **stink**
2. *(slang)* To be very bad or worthless.
▸ ***verb*** **stinking, stank** (**stangk**), **stunk** (**stuhngk**) ▸ ***adjective*** **stinky**

stir (**stur**)
1. ***verb*** To mix a liquid by moving a spoon or stick around and around in it.
2. ***verb*** To move or cause to move slightly.
3. ***verb*** To excite or cause strong feelings in.
4. ***noun*** If you cause **a stir,** you make people excited about something.
▸ ***noun*** **stir** ▸ ***verb*** **stirring, stirred**

stir-fry ***verb*** To fry food quickly over high heat in a lightly oiled pan or wok while stirring continuously. ▸ **stir-fries, stir-frying, stir-fried**

stir•rup (**stur**-uhp) ***noun***
1. A ring or loop that hangs down from a saddle and holds a rider's foot.
2. One of the three small bones in the middle ear. It looks somewhat like a stirrup.

stitch (**stich**)
1. ***noun*** A complete movement of a needle with thread on it, used in sewing and embroidery and to close wounds.
2. ***noun*** A loop of yarn produced in knitting or crocheting.
3. ***verb*** To make stitches in sewing or knitting.
4. ***verb*** To close up a wound with stitches.
5. ***noun*** A sudden, sharp pain in your side caused by running.
▸ ***noun, plural*** **stitches** ▸ ***verb*** **stitches, stitching, stitched**

stock (**stok**)
1. ***verb*** If a store **stocks** a product, it keeps a supply of the product to sell.
2. ***noun*** All the products that a factory, warehouse, or store has to sell.
3. ***noun*** Cattle, sheep, pigs, and other animals raised on a ranch or farm; livestock.
4. ***noun*** A liquid used in cooking, made from the juices of meat or vegetables, as in *chicken stock.*
5. ***noun*** If you own **stock** in a company, you have invested money in it and own a part of the company.
6. ***noun*** Ancestors.
7. ***verb*** If you **stock up** on something, you buy a large supply of it.
▸ ***verb*** **stocking, stocked**

stock•ade (stok-**ade**) ***noun***
1. A fence or enclosure made of strong posts set firmly in the ground to protect against attacks.
2. A jail for people in the military.

stock•bro•ker (**stok**-*broh*-kur) ***noun*** Someone whose job is buying and selling stocks and shares in companies for other people.

stock car ***noun*** A car for racing, made from a regular model sold to the public.

stock•hold•er (**stok**-*hohl*-dur) ***noun*** Someone who owns shares, or stock, in a company.

stock•ing (**stok**-ing) ***noun*** A tight, knitted covering for the foot and leg.

stock market *or* **stock exchange** ***noun*** A place where stocks and shares in companies are bought and sold.

stock•pile (**stok**-*pile*) ***verb*** To build up a large supply of food or weapons that you can use in the future. ▸ **stockpiling, stockpiled** ▸ ***noun*** **stockpile**

stocks (**stoks**) ***noun, plural*** A heavy, wooden frame with holes in it used to hold people by their ankles and sometimes their wrists. Stocks were once used to punish people publicly for minor offenses such as drunkenness.

stock•y (**stok**-ee) ***adjective*** A **stocky** person has a short, heavy build.
▸ **stockier, stockiest**

stock•yard (**stok**-*yard*) ***noun*** An enclosed area where livestock are kept before being shipped or slaughtered.

stodg•y (**stoj**-ee) ***adjective***
1. Very dull or boring, as in *a stodgy speech.*
2. Very old-fashioned and stuffy.
▸ ***adjective*** **stodgier, stodgiest**

sto•ic (**stoh**-ik) ***noun*** A person who is not moved or affected by pain or pleasure. ▸ ***adjective*** **stoic,** ***adjective*** **stoical** ▸ ***adverb*** **stoically**

stoke (**stohk**) ***verb*** To put more fuel on a fire in order to keep it burning.
▸ **stoking, stoked**

stom•ach (**stuhm**-uhk)
1. ***noun*** The muscular, pouchlike organ of your body where chewed food begins to be digested.
2. ***noun*** The front part of your body, between your chest and thighs, containing this organ; the belly or abdomen.
3. ***verb*** If you cannot **stomach** something, you cannot bear it.
▸ **stomaching, stomached**

stomp (**stomp**) ***verb***
1. To walk heavily or loudly across a floor.
2. To bang your foot down, especially in anger. ▸ ***noun*** **stomp**
▸ ***verb*** **stomping, stomped**

stone (**stone**)
1. ***noun*** Naturally hardened mineral matter that is found in the earth; rock.
▸ ***adjective*** **stony**
2. ***noun*** A small piece of this material.
3. ***verb*** To hit with stones. ▸ **stoning, stoned**
4. ***noun*** A valuable jewel or gem.
5. ***noun*** A hard seed found in the middle of a fruit such as a cherry or peach.

Stone Age ***noun*** A period in history when stone was commonly used to make tools and weapons. Different parts of the world experienced a Stone Age at different times.

stone•wall (**stone**-*wawl*) ***verb*** To ignore a question, or to stand in the way of an investigation by refusing to give information. ▸ **stonewalling, stonewalled**

stone•washed (**stone**-*washt*) ***adjective*** **Stonewashed** jeans are washed with stones that soften and fade the fabric.

stool (**stool**) ***noun*** A seat with no back or arms.

stoop (**stoop**)
1. ***verb*** To bend forward and down, often with the knees bent.
2. ***verb*** To walk, sit, or stand with your head and shoulders bent forward.
3. ***verb*** To lower yourself to do something; to condescend or degrade yourself.
4. ***noun*** A small porch with steps outside a doorway.
▸ ***verb*** **stooping, stooped** ▸ ***noun*** **stoop**

stop (**stop**)
1. ***verb*** When something **stops,** it comes to an end.
2. ***verb*** If you **stop** something, you put an end to it or prevent it from continuing or moving.
3. ***verb*** To be no longer moving or working.
4. ***verb*** To close up or block an opening.
5. ***noun*** The act of stopping.
6. ***noun*** One of the regular places on a route where someone pauses, such as the place where a bus or train picks up and drops off passengers.
7. ***noun*** A brief stay or visit.
▸ ***verb*** **stopping, stopped**

stop•light (**stop**-*lite*) ***noun***
1. Another word for **traffic light.**
2. A light on the rear part of a motor vehicle that comes on when the driver steps on the brakes.

stop•per (**stop**-ur) ***noun*** A piece of cork or plastic that fits into the top of a container such as a test tube, jar, or bottle in order to close it.

stop•watch (**stop**-*wahch*) ***noun*** A watch that you can start and stop at any time. A stopwatch is used to measure the exact time of a race, contest, or other event.

S

stor•age (**stor**-ij) ***noun*** If you put something **in storage,** you put it away in a place where it can be kept until it is needed.

store (**stor**)
1. ***noun*** A place where things are sold, as in *a grocery store, a toy store,* or *a department store.*
2. ***noun*** A supply or stock of something kept for future use, as in *a store of wood* or *a store of weapons.*
3. ***verb*** To put things away until they are needed.
4. ***verb*** To copy data into the memory of a computer or onto a floppy disk or other storage device.
▸ ***verb*** **storing, stored**

store•keep•er (**stor**-*kee*-pur) ***noun*** Someone who owns or runs a store.

stork (**stork**) ***noun*** A large bird with long, thin legs; a long neck; and a long, straight bill. The stork is a wading bird that lives in marshes, swamps, and grasslands.

storm (**storm**)
1. ***noun*** Heavy rain, snow, sleet, or hail accompanied by strong winds. Some storms also can have thunder and lightning. ▸ ***verb*** **storm**
2. ***noun*** A sudden, strong outburst, as in *a storm of applause* or *a storm of protest.*
3. ***verb*** To attack suddenly or violently.
4. ***verb*** If you **storm out** of a place, you rush out angrily or violently.
▸ ***verb*** **storming, stormed** ▸ ***adjective*** **stormy**

sto•ry (**stor**-ee) ***noun***
1. A spoken or written account of something that happened, as in *a news story* or *the story of the first Thanksgiving.*
2. A tale made up to entertain people, as in *a science fiction story.*
3. A lie.
4. A floor or level of a building.
▸ ***noun, plural*** **stories**

stout (**stout**) ***adjective***
1. Quite fat; large and heavily built.
2. Strong and sturdy.
3. Brave or determined.
▸ ***adjective*** **stouter, stoutest**

stove (**stohv**) ***noun*** A piece of equipment used for cooking or for heating a room. A stove can be fueled by gas, electricity, wood, or oil.

stow (**stoh**) ***verb*** To put away or to store. ▸ **stowing, stowed** ▸ ***noun*** **stowage**

stow•a•way (**stoh**-uh-*way*) ***noun*** Someone who hides in a plane, ship, or other vehicle to avoid paying a fare.
▸ ***verb*** **stow away**

strag•gle (**strag**-uhl) ***verb*** To follow slowly behind a group of people; to wander or stray. ▸ **straggling, straggled** ▸ ***noun*** **straggler**

straight (**strayt**)
1. ***adjective*** Not bent or not curved.
2. ***adjective*** Not curly or not wavy, as in *straight hair.*
3. ***adjective*** Not crooked or not stooping, as in *straight posture.*
4. ***adjective*** Level or even, as in *a straight hem.*
5. ***adjective*** Honest, sincere, or correct.
6. ***adverb*** Immediately or directly.
Straight sounds like **strait.**
▸ ***verb*** **straighten** ▸ ***adjective*** **straighter, straightest** ▸ ***adverb*** **straight**

straight•a•way (**strayt**-uh-*way*) ***adverb*** At once.

straight•for•ward (*strayt*-**for**-wurd) ***adjective*** Honest and open, as in *a straightforward answer.*

strain (**strayn**)
1. ***verb*** To draw or pull tight; to stretch.
2. ***noun*** Stress or tension.
3. ***verb*** If you **strain** a mixture, you pour it through a sieve or colander to separate the solids from the liquid.
▸ ***noun*** **strainer**
4. ***verb*** If you **strain** a muscle in your body, you damage it by pulling it or overusing it.
5. ***verb*** If you **strain** to do something, you try very hard to do it.

▸ ***verb*** **straining, strained** ▸ ***adjective*** **strained**

strait (**strayt**) ***noun***
1. A narrow strip of water that connects two larger bodies of water.
2. ***noun, plural*** If you are in **dire straits,** you are in a very difficult situation.
Strait sounds like **straight.**

strand (**strand**)
1. ***noun*** One of the threads or wires that are twisted together to form a rope, string, or cable.
2. ***noun*** Something that looks like a thread, as in *a strand of hair* or *a strand of spaghetti.*
3. ***noun*** Something made up of objects strung or twisted together, as in *a strand of pearls.*
4. ***verb*** To force onto the shore; to drive onto a beach, reef, or sandbar.
5. ***verb*** To leave in a strange or unpleasant place, especially without any money or way to depart.
▸ ***verb*** **stranding, stranded**

strange (**straynj**) ***adjective***
1. Different from the usual; odd or peculiar.
2. Not known, heard, or seen before; not familiar.
3. Ill at ease; not comfortable.
▸ ***adjective*** **stranger, strangest**
▸ ***noun*** **strangeness** ▸ ***adverb*** **strangely**

strang•er (**strayn**-jur) ***noun***
1. Someone you do not know.
2. Someone who is in a place where he or she has not been before.

stran•gle (**strang**-guhl) ***verb***
1. To kill someone by squeezing the person's throat so that he or she cannot breathe.
2. To be unable to breathe; to choke.
▸ ***verb*** **strangling, strangled** ▸ ***noun*** **strangler,** ***noun*** **strangulation**

strap (**strap**)
1. ***noun*** A strip of leather or other material used to fasten things together.
2. ***verb*** To fasten things or hold things in place with straps. ▸ **strapping, strapped**

strat•e•gy (**strat**-uh-jee) ***noun*** A clever plan for winning a military battle or achieving a goal. ▸ ***noun, plural*** **strategies** ▸ ***noun*** **strategist**
▸ ***adjective*** **strategic** (struh-**tee**-jik)
▸ ***adverb*** **strategically**

strat•o•sphere (**strat**-uh-sfihr) ***noun*** The layer of the earth's atmosphere that begins about 7 miles (11 kilometers) above the earth and ends about 31 miles (50 kilometers) above the earth. Clouds rarely form here, and the air is very cold and thin.

straw (**straw**) ***noun***
1. The dried stalks of wheat, barley, oats, or other cereal plants that are left after the grain has been removed.
2. A thin, hollow plastic or paper tube through which you can drink.

straw•ber•ry (**straw**-*ber*-ee) ***noun*** The red, juicy fruit of a small, low plant of the rose family. ▸ ***noun, plural*** **strawberries**

stray (**stray**)
1. ***verb*** To wander away or to get lost.
▸ **straying, strayed** ▸ ***adjective*** **stray**
2. ***noun*** A lost cat or dog.

streak (**streek**)
1. ***noun*** A long, thin mark or stripe, as in *a streak of gray in her hair* or *a streak of lightning.* ▸ ***adjective*** **streaky**
2. ***noun*** A character trait.
3. ***noun*** A small series.
4. ***verb*** To move very fast. ▸ **streaking, streaked**

stream (**streem**)
1. ***noun*** A body of flowing water, especially a brook or a small river.
2. ***noun*** A steady flow of anything, as in *a stream of cars* or *a stream of light.*
3. ***verb*** To move or flow steadily.
4. ***verb*** To float or to wave.
▸ ***verb*** **streaming, streamed**

stream•er (**stree**-mur) ***noun*** A long, thin strip of colored paper or material used as a decoration.

S

stream•lined (**streem**-*lined*) ***adjective***
1. If a car, plane, or boat is **streamlined,** it is designed so that it can move through air or water very quickly and easily.
2. If a government or system for doing something is **streamlined,** it is made simpler or more efficient.

street (**street**) ***noun***
1. A road in a city or town, often with sidewalks, houses, or other buildings along it.
2. Everyone who lives or works on a street.

street•car (**street**-*kar*) ***noun*** A vehicle that holds many passengers and runs on rails through city streets. Streetcars are powered by electricity.

street•light (**street**-*lite*) ***noun*** A light mounted on a pole by the side of a street to help drivers and pedestrians see at night.

street•wise (**street**-*wize*) ***adjective*** If you are **streetwise,** you know how to survive in towns or cities without getting into trouble.

strength (**strengkth** *or* **strenth**) ***noun***
1. The quality of being strong; force; power.
2. The power to resist or hold up under strain or stress; toughness.
3. A person's good point, or the thing that the person can do well.

stren•u•ous (**stren**-yoo-uhss) ***adjective***
1. Needing great energy or effort, as in *strenuous exercise.*
2. Very active or energetic, as in *strenuous opposition.*
▸ ***adverb*** **strenuously**

stress (**stress**)
1. ***noun*** Worry, strain, or pressure.
▸ ***noun, plural*** **stresses** ▸ ***adjective*** **stressful**
2. ***verb*** To pronounce a word with more loudness or emphasis on a certain syllable.
3. ***verb*** If you **stress** something, you claim that it is important.
▸ ***noun*** **stress** ▸ ***verb*** **stresses, stressing, stressed**

stretch (**strech**)
1. ***verb*** To spread out your arms, legs, or body to full length.
2. ***verb*** To extend or to spread out.
3. ***verb*** To make something bigger, longer, or greater.
4. ***noun*** *(slang)* An unbroken space of time, especially time spent in a prison.
5. ***noun*** An unbroken length or distance.
6. stretch out *verb* To lie at full length.
▸ ***noun*** **stretch** ▸ ***noun, plural*** **stretches** ▸ ***verb*** **stretches, stretching, stretched**

stretch•er (**strech**-ur) ***noun*** A piece of canvas attached to two poles, used for carrying an injured or sick person.

strew (**stroo**) ***verb***
1. To scatter, sprinkle, or throw here and there.
2. To cover a surface with things that have been scattered or sprinkled.
▸ ***verb*** **strewing, strewed, strewn** (**stroon**)

strict (**strikt**) ***adjective***
1. If someone is **strict,** the person makes you obey rules exactly and behave properly.
2. If a rule is **strict,** it is enforced all the time.
3. Complete or total.
▸ ***adjective*** **stricter, strictest** ▸ ***noun*** **strictness** ▸ ***adverb*** **strictly**

stride (**stride**) ***verb*** To walk with long steps. ▸ **striding, strode** (**strode**), **stridden** (**strid**-uhn) ▸ ***noun*** **stride**

strife (**strife**) ***noun*** A bitter conflict between enemies; a fight or a struggle.

strike (**strike**)
1. ***verb*** To hit or attack someone or something.
2. ***verb*** When a clock **strikes,** it indicates the time with a ring or another sound.
3. ***verb*** To make an impression on someone.
4. ***verb*** To find or discover suddenly.

5. *verb* If you **strike** a match, you light it.
6. *verb* When people **strike,** they refuse to work because of an argument or a disagreement with their employer over wages or working conditions. ▸ ***noun*** **striker**
7. *noun* In baseball, a ball pitched over the plate between the batter's chest and knees, or any pitch that is swung at and missed.
8. *noun* In bowling, the act of knocking down all 10 pins with the first ball.
▸ ***noun* strike** ▸ ***verb* striking, struck (struhk)**

strik•ing ***adjective*** Unusual or noticeable in some way. ▸ ***adverb*** **strikingly**

string (**string**)
1. *noun* A thin cord or rope.
2. *noun* A thin wire on a musical instrument such as a guitar or violin.
▸ ***verb* string** ▸ ***adjective* stringed**
3. *verb* To put a row of objects on a piece of string or wire.
4. *noun* A number of things of the same or similar kind all in a row.
5. string out *verb* If you **string** something **out,** you stretch or lengthen it.
▸ ***verb* stringing, strung (struhng)**

string bean ***noun*** A long, thin, green pod that is eaten as a vegetable.

strings (**stringz**) ***noun, plural*** Stringed instruments that are played with a bow or plucked.

strip (**strip**)
1. *verb* To take off clothing; to undress.
2. *verb* To pull, tear, or take something off.
3. *noun* A long, narrow piece of something, as in *a strip of paper* or *a strip of land.*
▸ ***verb* stripping, stripped**

stripe (**stripe**) ***noun*** A narrow band of color. ▸ ***verb* stripe** ▸ ***adjective* striped**

strive (**strive**) ***verb*** To make a great effort to do something. ▸ **striving, strove (strohv), striven (striv**-in)

strobe (**strohb**) ***noun*** A light that flashes on and off very quickly.

stroke (**strohk**)
1. *verb* To pass your hand gently over something. ▸ **stroking, stroked** ▸ ***noun*** **stroke**
2. *noun* An unexpected action or event that has a powerful effect, as in *a stroke of lightning* or *a stroke of good luck.*
3. *noun* A hit or a blow, as in *the stroke of an ax.*
4. *noun* A line drawn by a pen, pencil, or brush.
5. *noun* When someone has a **stroke,** there is a sudden lack of oxygen in part of the brain caused by the blocking or breaking of a blood vessel.
6. *noun* A method of moving in swimming or rowing, or a method of hitting the ball in tennis.

stroll (**strohl**) ***noun*** A slow, relaxed walk. ▸ ***verb* stroll**

strol•ler (**stroh**-lur) ***noun*** A small, folding carriage for a baby or small child to sit in and be pushed around.

strong (**strong**) ***adjective***
1. Powerful or having great force, as in *strong arms* or *a strong wind.*
2. Hard to break; firm, as in *a strong rope* or *strong beliefs.*
3. Having a sharp or bitter taste or odor, as in *a strong cheese* or *a strong smell.*
▸ ***adjective* stronger, strongest**
▸ ***adverb* strongly**

strong•hold (**strong**-*hohld*) ***noun*** A fortress, or a place that is well protected against attack or danger.

struc•ture (**struhk**-chur) ***noun***
1. Something that has been built, such as a house, an office building, a bridge, or a dam.
2. The organization of something or the way that it is put together, as in *the structure of government* or *the structure of a cell.*
▸ ***verb* structure** ▸ ***adjective*** **structural**

S

strug•gle (**struhg**-uhl) ***verb***
1. If you **struggle** with something, you try very hard, or make a great effort, to do it.
2. If you **struggle** with someone, you fight or battle the person.
▸ ***verb*** **struggling, struggled** ▸ ***noun*** **struggle**

strum (**struhm**) ***verb*** To play a musical instrument such as a guitar or harp by brushing your fingers over the strings.
▸ **strumming, strummed** ▸ ***noun*** **strum**

strut (**struht**)
1. ***verb*** To walk with a swagger or in an arrogant manner. ▸ **strutting, strutted**
2. ***noun*** A wooden or metal supporting bar.

stub (**stuhb**)
1. ***noun*** A short part of something that remains after the rest has been used or torn off, as in *a pencil stub* or *a check stub.* ▸ ***adjective*** **stubby**
2. ***verb*** To hurt your toe or foot by banging it against something.
▸ **stubbing, stubbed**

stub•ble (**stuhb**-uhl) ***noun***
1. Short, spiky stalks of grain that are left in a field after harvesting.
2. The short, rough hairs that grow on a man's face if he does not shave.
▸ ***adjective*** **stubbly**

stub•born (**stuhb**-urn) ***adjective***
1. Not willing to give in or change; set on having your own way.
2. Hard to treat or deal with, as in *a stubborn cold.*
▸ ***noun*** **stubbornness** ▸ ***adverb*** **stubbornly**

stu•dent (**stood**-uhnt) ***noun***
1. Someone who studies at a school.
2. Someone who studies or observes something on his or her own, as in *a student of human nature.*

stu•di•o (**stoo**-dee-oh) ***noun***
1. A room or building in which an artist or a photographer works.
2. A place where movies, television and radio shows, or recordings are made.
3. A place that transmits radio or television programs.
4. A one-room apartment.

stu•di•ous (**stoo**-dee-uhss) ***adjective***
If you are **studious,** you like or tend to study very hard. ▸ ***noun*** **studiousness**
▸ ***adverb*** **studiously**

stud•y (**stuhd**-ee)
1. ***verb*** To spend time learning a subject or skill by reading about it or by practicing it.
2. ***noun*** A room used for studying or reading. ▸ ***noun, plural*** **studies**
3. ***verb*** To examine something carefully.
▸ ***verb*** **studies, studying, studied**
▸ ***noun*** **study**

stuff (**stuhf**)
1. ***noun*** The material or ingredients something is made of.
2. ***noun*** Personal belongings.
3. ***noun*** Useless or worthless things; junk.
4. ***verb*** To fill something tightly.
5. ***verb*** To put something into something else.
6. ***verb*** To fill yourself with too much food.
7. If you are **stuffed up,** you have a cold or an allergy and cannot breathe through your nose.
▸ ***verb*** **stuffing, stuffed**

stuff•ing (**stuhf**-ing) ***noun***
1. Soft material used to fill pillows, cushions, and other articles made of or covered with cloth.
2. A mixture of chopped food that is cooked inside poultry and other food.

stuf•fy (**stuhf**-ee) ***adjective***
1. A **stuffy** room is hard to breathe in because it lacks fresh air.
2. A **stuffy** person is dull, old-fashioned, and easily shocked. ▸ ***adverb*** **stuffily**
▸ ***adjective*** **stuffier, stuffiest** ▸ ***noun*** **stuffiness**

S

stum•ble (**stuhm**-buhl) ***verb***
1. To trip, or to walk in an unsteady way.
2. To make mistakes when you are talking or reading aloud; to speak or act in a confused way.
3. To come upon or discover something unexpectedly.
▸ ***verb*** **stumbling, stumbled**

stump (**stuhmp**)
1. ***noun*** The part of a tree trunk that is left when a tree is cut down.
2. ***noun*** A short or broken-off piece of anything, as in *a pencil stump.*
3. ***verb*** *(informal)* To puzzle or to confuse. ▸ **stumping, stumped**

stump•y (**stuhm**-pee) ***adjective*** Short and thick. ▸ **stumpier, stumpiest**

stun (**stuhn**) ***verb*** If something **stuns** you, it shocks or dazes you or knocks you out. ▸ **stunning, stunned**

stun•ning (**stuhn**-ing) ***adjective***
1. *(informal)* Extremely beautiful.
2. Amazing or remarkable, as in *a stunning victory.*
3. Hard enough to knock you out, as in *a stunning blow.*
▸ ***adverb*** **stunningly**

stunt (**stuhnt**)
1. ***noun*** An act that shows great skill or daring.
2. ***noun*** Something that is done to show off or attract attention.
3. ***verb*** To stop the proper growth of something. ▸ **stunting, stunted**
▸ ***adjective*** **stunted**
4. ***noun*** A **stunt person** takes the place of an actress or actor in an action scene or when a special skill or great risk is called for.

stu•pen•dous (stoo-**pen**-duhss) ***adjective*** Amazing or awesome.
▸ ***adverb*** **stupendously**

stu•pid (**stoo**-pid) ***adjective***
1. Slow to learn or understand; not intelligent.
2. Lacking common sense; foolish or silly.
▸ ***adjective*** **stupider, stupidest** ▸ ***noun*** **stupidity** ▸ ***adverb*** **stupidly**

stur•dy (**stur**-dee) ***adjective*** Strong and firm; solidly made or built. ▸ **sturdier, sturdiest**

stur•geon (**stur**-juhn) ***noun*** A large fish covered with rows of bony, pointed scales. It is used for food and prized for its eggs, known as *caviar.*

stut•ter (**stuht**-ur) ***verb*** If you **stutter** when you speak, you repeat the first sound of a word before you are able to say the whole word. ▸ **stuttering, stuttered** ▸ ***noun*** **stutter,** ***noun*** **stutterer**

sty (**stye**) ***noun***
1. A pen in which pigs live. ▸ ***noun, plural*** **sties**
2. A red, painful swelling on the eyelid.
▸ ***noun, plural*** **sties** *or* **styes**

style (**stile**)
1. ***noun*** The way in which something is written, spoken, made, or done.
2. ***noun*** The way in which people act and dress in a particular time period, especially the most recent one; fashion.
3. ***noun*** If you have **style,** you have an elegant manner.
4. ***verb*** To arrange or design something.
▸ **styling, styled** ▸ ***noun*** **style,** ***noun*** **stylist**
5. ***noun*** The part of a flower that extends from the ovary and supports the stigma.

sty•lish (**stile**-ish) ***adjective*** To do with the latest style; fashionable. ▸ ***adverb*** **stylishly**

Sty•ro•foam (**stye**-ruh-fohm) ***noun*** The trademark for a very lightweight, rigid plastic that is used in many items, from building insulation to drinking cups.

sub•con•scious (suhb-**kon**-shuhss) ***noun*** The part of the mind where hidden thoughts are as well as the feelings you are not aware of. ▸ ***adjective*** **subconscious** ▸ ***adverb*** **subconsciously**

S

sub•con•ti•nent (suhb-**kon**-tuh-nuhnt) ***noun*** A large area of land that is part of a continent but is considered a separate geographical or political unit.

sub•di•vide (*suhb*-duh-**vide** *or* **suhb**-duh-*vide*) ***verb***
1. To divide into smaller, even parts something that has already been divided.
2. To divide an area of land into lots for building homes.
▸ ***verb*** **subdividing, subdivided**
▸ ***noun*** **subdivision**

sub•due (suhb-**doo**) ***verb***
1. To defeat in battle; to conquer.
2. To control.
▸ ***verb*** **subduing, subdued**

sub•dued (suhb-**dood**) ***adjective***
1. Unusually quiet and controlled.
2. Not harsh or not strong, as in *subdued lighting.*

sub•ject
1. (**suhb**-jikt) ***noun*** The person or thing that is discussed or thought about in a book, newspaper article, conversation, etc.
2. (**suhb**-jikt) ***noun*** An area of study, such as geography or mathematics.
3. (**suhb**-jikt) ***noun*** A word or group of words in a sentence that tells whom or what the sentence is about. The subject of a sentence usually precedes the verb.
4. (**suhb**-jikt) ***noun*** A person or thing that is studied or examined.
5. (**suhb**-jikt) ***noun*** A person who lives in a kingdom or under the authority of a king or queen.
6. (**suhb**-jikt) If you are **subject to** something, you are likely to be affected by it.
7. (suhb-**jekt**) ***verb*** If you **subject** someone to something, you force the person to go through it. ▸ **subjecting, subjected**

sub•jec•tive (suhb-**jek**-tiv) ***adjective*** To do with your feelings or opinions rather than with actual facts. ▸ ***adverb*** **subjectively**

sub•ma•rine (**suhb**-muh-reen *or suhb*-muh-**reen**) ***noun*** A ship that can travel both on the surface and under the water.

sub•merge (suhb-**murj**) ***verb***
1. To sink or plunge beneath the surface of a liquid, especially water.
2. To cover with water or another liquid.
▸ ***verb*** **submerging, submerged**

sub•mit (suhb-**mit**) ***verb***
1. To hand in or to put something forward.
2. To agree to obey something.
▸ ***verb*** **submitting, submitted** ▸ ***noun*** **submission**

sub•or•di•nate (suh-**bord**-uhn-it)
1. ***adjective*** Less important; lower in rank.
2. ***noun*** Someone who is lower in rank or importance and can be told what to do.
▸ ***verb*** **subordinate** (suh-**bord**-uh-nate)

sub•scribe (suhb-**skribe**) ***verb***
1. To pay money regularly for a product or service such as a newspaper, magazine, or cable television. ▸ ***noun*** **subscriber,** ***noun*** **subscription**
2. To agree with or go along with a belief or an idea.
▸ ***verb*** **subscribing, subscribed**

sub•se•quent (**suhb**-suh-kwuhnt) ***adjective*** Coming after, or following.
▸ ***adverb*** **subsequently**

sub•set (**suhb**-*set*) ***noun*** In math, a **subset** is a set of items that are all members within another set. For example, the numbers 1 through 10 are a subset of the numbers 1 through 1,000.

sub•side (suhb-**side**) ***verb***
1. To sink to a lower or more normal level.
2. To become less intense or active.
▸ ***verb*** **subsiding, subsided**

sub•sid•i•ar•y (suhb-**sid**-ee-*er*-ee) ***adjective*** Minor, or less important, as in *a subsidiary role.* ▸ ***noun*** **subsidiary**

sub•si•dy (**suhb**-suh-dee) ***noun*** Money that a government or person contributes to help a worthy enterprise or in order to make goods or services cheaper. ▸ ***noun, plural*** **subsidies** ▸ ***verb*** **subsidize**

sub•stance (**suhb**-stuhnss) ***noun***
1. Something that has weight and takes up space; matter.
2. The material that something is made of.
3. The important part of something.

sub•stan•tial (suhb-**stan**-shuhl) ***adjective***
1. Large.
2. Solidly built; strong or firm, as in *a substantial bridge.*
3. Not imaginary; real.
▸ ***adverb*** **substantially**

sub•sti•tute (**suhb**-stuh-toot) ***noun*** Something or someone used in place of another, such as a teammate who plays when another player is injured. ▸ ***noun*** **substitution** ▸ ***verb*** **substitute**

sub•ti•tle (**suhb**-*tye*-tuhl) ***noun***
1. The second, less important title of a book, a movie, an essay, a song, etc. The subtitle usually explains a bit about the title.
2. subtitles ***noun, plural*** The translated words that appear on the screen when a movie in another language is shown.

sub•tle (**suht**-uhl) ***adjective***
1. Not strong; faint or delicate, as in *a subtle flavor.*
2. Clever or disguised, as in *a subtle plan.*
▸ ***adjective*** **subtler, subtlest** ▸ ***noun*** **subtlety,** ***noun*** **subtleness** ▸ ***adverb*** **subtly**

sub•tract (suhb-**trakt**) ***verb*** To take one number away from another.
▸ **subtracting, subtracted** ▸ ***noun*** **subtraction**

sub•tra•hend (**suhb**-truh-*hend*) ***noun*** In math, a number that is subtracted from another number.

sub•urb (**suhb**-urb) ***noun*** An area or a district on or close to the outer edge of a city. A suburb is made up mostly of homes, with few businesses. ▸ ***noun*** **suburbia** (suh-**bur**-bee-uh), ***noun*** **suburbanite** ▸ ***adjective*** **suburban**

sub•way (**suhb**-*way*) ***noun*** An electric train or a system of trains that runs underground in a city.

suc•ceed (suhk-**seed**) ***verb***
1. To manage to do something.
2. To do well or to get what you want.
3. To take over from someone in an important position.
▸ ***verb*** **succeeding, succeeded**

suc•cess (suhk-**sess**) ***noun***
1. A good or favorable outcome; desired results.
2. A person or thing that has achieved success.
▸ ***noun, plural*** **successes** ▸ ***adjective*** **successful** ▸ ***adverb*** **successfully**

suc•ces•sion (suhk-**sesh**-uhn) ***noun***
1. A number of persons or things that follow one after another in order; a series.
2. The coming of one person or thing after another.
3. The order in which one person after another takes over a title, a throne, or an estate.

suc•cess•ive (suhk-**sess**-iv) ***adjective*** Following in a logical or sequential order.
▸ ***adverb*** **successively**

suc•ces•sor (suhk-**sess**-ur) ***noun*** One who follows another in a position or sequence.

suc•cu•lent (**suhk**-yuh-luhnt) ***adjective*** Juicy, as in *a succulent peach.* ▸ ***noun*** **succulence**

such (**suhch**)
1. ***adjective*** Of the same or that kind.
2. ***adjective*** Like, or similar.
3. ***adjective*** So much, or so great.
4. ***pronoun*** Others of that kind.

suck (**suhk**) ***verb***
1. To draw something into your mouth using your tongue and lips.
2. To pull strongly or draw in.
3. To hold in the mouth and lick.
▸ ***verb*** **sucking, sucked** ▸ ***noun*** **suck**

S

S

suck•er (**suhk**-ur) ***noun***
1. A body part of certain animals that is used to stick to surfaces.
2. *(slang)* Someone who is easily cheated or fooled.
3. A piece of candy, such as a lollipop, that is held in the mouth and licked.

suc•tion (**suhk**-shuhn) ***noun*** The act of drawing air out of a space to create a vacuum. This causes the surrounding air or liquid to be sucked into the empty space. Vacuum cleaners and drinking straws work by suction.

sud•den (**suhd**-uhn) ***adjective***
1. Happening without warning; unexpected, as in *a sudden storm.*
2. Quick, hasty, or abrupt, as in *a sudden decision* or *a sudden stop.*
▸ ***noun*** **suddenness** ▸ ***adverb*** **suddenly**

sudden infant death syndrome ***noun*** The death, usually during sleep, of a seemingly healthy infant for no known cause. Also known as *SIDS* or *crib death.*

suds (**suhdz**) ***noun, plural*** The bubbles that form on top of a substance such as water containing soap.

sue (**soo**) ***verb*** To start a suit or case against someone in a court of law.
▸ **suing, sued**

suede (**swayd**) ***noun*** Soft leather with a velvetlike surface.

su•et (**soo**-it) ***noun*** A hard fat from cattle and sheep that is used in cooking.

suf•fer (**suhf**-ur) ***verb***
1. To have pain, discomfort, or sorrow.
2. To experience or undergo something unpleasant.
3. To be damaged, or to become worse.
▸ ***verb*** **suffering, suffered** ▸ ***noun*** **suffering**

suf•fi•cient (suh-**fish**-uhnt) ***adjective*** If something is **sufficient,** it is enough or adequate. ▸ ***adverb*** **sufficiently**

suf•fix (**suhf**-iks) ***noun*** A syllable or syllables added at the end of a word or root that change its meaning. ▸ ***noun, plural*** **suffixes**

suf•fo•cate (**suhf**-uh-kate) ***verb***
1. To kill by cutting off the supply of air or oxygen.
2. To die from lack of oxygen.
3. To have difficulty breathing.
▸ ***verb*** **suffocating, suffocated** ▸ ***noun*** **suffocation**

suf•frage (**suhf**-rij) ***noun*** The right to vote.

sug•ar (**shug**-ur) ***noun*** A sweet substance that comes from sugar beets and sugarcane and is used in foods and drinks. ▸ ***adjective*** **sugary**

sugar beet ***noun*** A root vegetable from which sugar is produced.

sugar•cane (**shug**-ur-*kayn*) ***noun*** A tall, tropical grass that has sugar in its woody stems.

sug•gest (suhg-**jest**) ***verb***
1. To put something forward as an idea or a possibility.
2. To bring or call to mind.
3. To hint or show indirectly.
▸ ***verb*** **suggesting, suggested** ▸ ***noun*** **suggestion**

su•i•cide (**soo**-uh-*side*) ***noun*** If someone commits **suicide,** the person kills him- or herself on purpose. ▸ ***adjective*** **suicidal** ▸ ***adverb*** **suicidally**

suit (**soot**)
1. ***noun*** A set of matching clothes, usually a man's jacket and pants or a woman's jacket and skirt.
2. ***noun*** One of the four types of playing cards in a deck of cards. The four suits are clubs, diamonds, hearts, and spades.
3. ***noun*** A case that is brought before a court of law; a lawsuit.
4. ***verb*** To be acceptable and convenient.
5. ***verb*** If a haircut or an outfit **suits** you, it makes you look good.
▸ ***verb*** **suiting, suited**

suit•a•ble (**soo**-tuh-buhl) ***adjective*** If something is **suitable,** it is right for a particular purpose. ▸ ***noun*** **suitability** ▸ ***adverb*** **suitably**

S

suit•case (**soot**-*kayss*) ***noun*** A flat bag used for carrying clothes and belongings when you travel.

suite ***noun***
1. (**sweet**) A group of rooms that are connected, as in *a hotel suite.*
2. (**sweet** *or* **soot**) A set of matching items, as in *a bedroom suite.*
3. (**sweet**) A piece of music made up of several parts.

suit•or (**soo**-tur) ***noun*** A man who courts a woman.

sul•fur (**suhl**-fur) ***noun*** A yellow chemical element used in gunpowder, matches, and fertilizer.

sulfur di•ox•ide (dye-**ok**-side) ***noun*** A poisonous gas found in some industrial waste. Sulfur dioxide causes air pollution.

sulk (**suhlk**) ***verb*** If you **sulk,** you are angry and silent. ▸ **sulking, sulked** ▸ ***noun*** **sulk** ▸ ***adjective*** **sulky**

sul•len (**suhl**-uhn) ***adjective*** Gloomy and silent because you feel angry, bitter, or hurt. ▸ ***adverb*** **sullenly**

sul•tan (**suhlt**-uhn) ***noun*** An emperor or ruler of some Muslim countries.

sul•try (**suhl**-tree) ***adjective*** If the weather is **sultry,** it is hot and humid. ▸ **sultrier, sultriest** ▸ ***noun*** **sultriness**

sum (**suhm**)
1. ***noun*** An amount of money.
2. ***noun*** A number that you get from adding two or more numbers together.
3. ***verb*** If you **sum up,** you go through the main points of what has been said. ▸ **summing, summed**
4. **sum** *or* **sum total** ***noun*** The whole or final amount.
Sum sounds like **some.**

su•mac (**soo**-mak) ***noun*** A bush or tree with pointed leaves and clusters of flowers or red berries.

sum•ma•ry (**suhm**-ur-ee) ***noun*** A short statement that gives the main points or ideas of something that has been said or written. ▸ ***noun, plural*** **summaries** ▸ ***verb*** **summarize**

sum•mer (**suhm**-ur) ***noun*** The season between spring and autumn, when the weather is warmest. ▸ ***adjective*** **summery**

sum•mit (**suhm**-it) ***noun***
1. The highest point; the top, as in *the summit of a mountain.*
2. A meeting of important leaders from different countries.

sum•mon (**suhm**-uhn) ***verb***
1. To call or request someone to come.
2. If you **summon up** courage, you make a great effort to be brave.
▸ ***verb*** **summoning, summoned**

sum•mons (**suhm**-uhnz) ***noun*** An order to appear in court. ▸ ***noun, plural*** **summonses** ▸ ***verb*** **summons**

su•mo wrestling (**soo**-moh) ***noun*** A Japanese form of wrestling. ▸ ***noun*** **sumo wrestler**

sun (**suhn**)
1. ***noun*** The star that the earth and other planets revolve around and that gives us light and warmth. Sometimes written **Sun.**
2. ***noun*** Any star that is the center of a system of planets.
3. ***noun*** Light and warmth from the sun.
4. ***verb*** If you **sun** yourself, you sit or lie in the sun. ▸ **sunning, sunned**
Sun sounds like **son.**

sun•bathe (**suhn**-*bayTH*) ***verb*** To sit or lie in sunlight in order to make your body suntanned. ▸ **sunbathing, sunbathed** ▸ ***noun*** **sunbath**

sun•burn (**suhn**-burn) ***noun*** Sore, red skin caused by staying in sunlight too long. ▸ ***adjective*** **sunburned** *or* **sunburnt**

sun•dae (**suhn**-dee *or* **suhn**-*day*) ***noun*** Ice cream served with one or more toppings, such as syrup, whipped cream, nuts, or fruit.

Sun•day (**suhn**-dee *or* **suhn**-*day*) ***noun*** The first day of the week, after Saturday and before Monday.

S

sun·dial (**suhn**-*dye*-uhl) ***noun*** An instrument that shows the time by using the sun's light. A pointer casts a shadow that moves slowly around a flat, marked dial.

sun·down (**suhn**-*doun*) ***noun*** Sunset, the time of day just before nightfall, when the sun dips below the horizon.

sun·flow·er (**suhn**-*flou*-ur) ***noun*** A large flower with yellow petals and a dark center. Sunflower plants can grow as large as 12 feet high.

sun·glass·es (**suhn**-*glass*-iz) ***noun, plural*** Dark glasses that protect your eyes from the glare of sunlight.

sunk·en (**suhng**-kuhn) ***adjective***
1. Below the surface, as in *sunken treasure.*
2. Below the other areas nearby.
3. Very hollow, as in *sunken cheeks.*

sun·light (**suhn**-*lite*) ***noun*** The light of the sun.

sun·rise (**suhn**-*rize*) ***noun*** The time in the morning when the sun appears above the horizon.

sun·screen (**suhn**-*skreen*) ***noun*** A cream or lotion containing a chemical that protects the skin from the harmful rays of the sun.

sun·set (**suhn**-*set*) ***noun*** The time in the evening when the sun sinks below the horizon.

sun·shine (**suhn**-*shine*) ***noun*** The light from the sun.

sun·stroke (**suhn**-*strohk*) ***noun*** An illness caused by staying in hot sunlight too long. Symptoms of sunstroke include fever, dizziness, and headaches.

sun·tan (**suhn**-*tan*) ***noun*** If you have a **suntan,** your skin is brown because you have been in the rays of strong sunlight.
▸ ***adjective*** **suntanned**

su·per (**soo**-pur)
1. ***adjective*** Very good; excellent.
2. ***noun*** *(informal)* Short for **superintendent.**

su·perb (su-**purb**) ***adjective*** Excellent or outstanding, as in *a superb meal* or *a superb performance.* ▸ ***adverb*** **superbly**

su·per·fi·cial (*soo*-pur-**fish**-uhl) ***adjective***
1. On the surface, as in *a superficial cut.*
2. Not deep, or not thorough.
▸ ***adverb*** **superficially**

su·per·flu·ous (suh-**pur**-floo-uhss) ***adjective*** More than is needed or wanted; not necessary, as in *a superfluous remark.*

su·per·her·o (**soo**-pur-*hihr*-oh) ***noun*** A fictional character with superhuman powers such as extraordinary strength or the ability to fly. ▸ ***noun, plural*** **superheroes**

su·per·hu·man (*soo*-pur-**hyoo**-muhn) ***adjective*** Having or requiring characteristics or abilities beyond those of an ordinary human.

su·per·in·ten·dent (*soo*-pur-in-**ten**-duhnt) ***noun***
1. An official who directs or manages an organization, as in *superintendent of schools.*
2. A person in charge of a building; a janitor.

su·pe·ri·or (suh-**pihr**-ee-ur *or* soo-**pihr**-ee-ur)
1. ***adjective*** Higher in rank or position, as in *a superior officer.*
2. ***adjective*** Above average in quality or ability; excellent, as in *a superior piece of writing* or *a superior team.*
3. ***noun*** A person who has a higher rank or position than others.
4. ***adjective*** If someone acts in a **superior** way, the person behaves as if he or she were better than other people.
▸ ***noun*** **superiority**

su·per·la·tive (suh-**pur**-luh-tiv) ***adjective***
1. Superlative adjectives and adverbs are used to describe the greatest or highest degree of things or actions.
▸ ***noun*** **superlative**
2. The very best, as in *a superlative performance.* ▸ ***adverb*** **superlatively**

su·per·mar·ket (**soo**-pur-*mar*-kit) ***noun*** A large store that sells food and household items.

su•per•nat•u•ral (*soo*-pur-**nach**-ur-uhl) ***noun*** If something is **supernatural,** it involves things that natural laws cannot explain, as in *supernatural forces.* ▸ ***adverb*** **supernaturally**

su•per•no•va (*soo*-pur-**noh**-vuh) ***noun*** An extremely bright exploding star that can give off millions of times more light than the sun. ▸ ***noun, plural*** **supernovas** *or* **supernovae** (*soo*-pur-**noh**-vee)

su•per•son•ic (*soo*-pur-**son**-ik) ***adjective*** Faster than the speed of sound.

su•per•sti•tion (*soo*-pur-**sti**-shuhn) ***noun*** A belief that some action not connected to a future event can influence the outcome of the event. A common superstition is that if you walk under a ladder you will have bad luck. ▸ ***adjective*** **superstitious**

su•per•tank•er (**soo**-pur-*tang*-kur) ***noun*** A very large oil tanker used to transport large amounts of crude oil to refineries.

su•per•vise (**soo**-pur-*vize*) ***verb*** To watch over or direct a group of people; to be in charge of. ▸ **supervising, supervised** ▸ ***noun*** **supervision**

su•per•vi•sor (**soo**-pur-*vye*-zur) ***noun*** Someone who watches over and directs the work of other people.

sup•per (**suhp**-ur) ***noun*** An evening meal.

sup•ple (**suhp**-uhl) ***adjective*** If you are **supple,** you can move or bend your body easily. ▸ **suppler, supplest** ▸ ***noun*** **suppleness**

sup•ple•ment (**suhp**-luh-muhnt)
1. ***noun*** Something added to complete another thing or to make up for what is missing.
2. ***verb*** To add to something.
▸ **supplementing, supplemented**
▸ ***adjective*** **supplementary**

sup•ply (suh-**plye**)
1. ***verb*** To provide something that is needed or wanted. ▸ **supplies, supplying, supplied** ▸ ***noun*** **supplier**
2. ***noun*** An amount of something that is available for use. ▸ ***noun, plural*** **supplies**
3. supplies ***noun, plural*** Materials needed to do something.

sup•port (suh-**port**) ***verb***
1. To hold something up in order to keep it from falling.
2. To earn a living for; to provide for.
3. To help and encourage someone.
▸ ***adjective*** **supportive**
4. To believe in someone or favor something.
5. To show to be true.
▸ ***verb*** **supporting, supported** ▸ ***noun*** **support,** ***noun*** **supporter**

sup•pose (suh-**poze**) ***verb***
1. To imagine or assume that something is true or possible.
2. To believe or to guess.
3. To expect.
▸ ***verb*** **supposing, supposed**
▸ ***adjective*** **supposed**

sup•press (suh-**press**) ***verb***
1. To stop something from happening.
2. To hide or control something.
▸ ***verb*** **suppresses, suppressing, suppressed** ▸ ***noun*** **suppression**

su•preme (suh-**preem**) ***adjective*** Greatest, best, or most powerful. ▸ ***noun*** **supremacy** ▸ ***adverb*** **supremely**

Supreme Court ***noun*** The highest and most powerful court in the United States. It has the power to overturn decisions made in lower courts and also to declare laws unconstitutional. The Supreme Court consists of nine justices.

sure (**shoor**)
1. ***adjective*** Having no doubt; certain; confident.
2. ***adjective*** Certain to happen; impossible to avoid, as in *a sure defeat.*
3. ***adjective*** Firm or steady, as in *sure footing* or *a sure grip.*
4. ***adverb*** Without a doubt; certainly.
▸ ***adjective*** **surer, surest**

sure•ly (**shoor**-lee) ***adverb*** With certainty; absolutely; without a doubt.

S

S

surf (**surf**)
1. ***noun*** Waves as they break on the shore.
2. ***verb*** To ride on breaking waves using a surfboard. ▸ **surfing, surfed** ▸ ***noun*** **surfer,** ***noun*** **surfing**
3. ***verb*** To search through the Internet or the World Wide Web.
Surf sounds like **serf.**

sur•face (**sur**-fiss)
1. ***noun*** The outside or outermost layer of something, as in *the surface of the earth.*
2. ***noun*** One of the sides of something that has several sides.
3. ***noun*** Outward appearance.
4. ***verb*** To come to the surface or to appear. ▸ **surfacing, surfaced**

surf•board (**surf**-*bord*) ***noun*** A narrow board that surfers stand on to ride breaking waves.

surge (**surj**)
1. ***verb*** To rush or sweep forward with force, like a wave. ▸ **surging, surged**
2. ***noun*** A sudden, strong rush.
3. ***noun*** A sudden increase, as in *a surge in prices* or *a surge of interest.* ▸ ***verb*** **surge**

sur•geon (**sur**-juhn) ***noun*** A doctor who performs operations.

sur•ger•y (**sur**-jer-ee) ***noun***
1. Medical treatment that involves repairing, removing, or replacing injured or diseased parts of the body. Surgery is done by cutting the patient open or by using lasers. ▸ ***adjective*** **surgical**
2. The branch of medicine that deals with injury and disease in this way.
3. An operation performed by a surgeon.

sur•ly (**sur**-lee) ***adjective*** If someone is **surly,** he or she is mean, rude, and unfriendly. ▸ **surlier, surliest**

sur•name (**sur**-*name*) ***noun*** A person's last name or family name.

sur•pass (sur-**pass**) ***verb***
1. To be better, greater, or stronger than another person or thing.
2. To go beyond the limits or powers of.
▸ ***verb*** **surpasses, surpassing, surpassed**

sur•plus (**sur**-pluhss) ***noun*** An amount greater than what is used or needed; excess, as in *a surplus of grain.*
▸ ***adjective*** **surplus**

sur•prise (sur-**prize**) ***verb***
1. To amaze or astonish someone by doing or saying something unexpected.
2. To come upon suddenly and without warning.
▸ ***verb*** **surprising, surprised** ▸ ***noun*** **surprise** ▸ ***adjective*** **surprising**

sur•ren•der (suh-**ren**-dur) ***verb*** To give up, or to admit that you are beaten in a fight or battle. ▸ **surrendering, surrendered** ▸ ***noun*** **surrender**

sur•round (suh-**round**) ***verb*** To be on every side of something. ▸ **surrounding, surrounded**

sur•round•ings (suh-**roun**-dingz) ***noun, plural*** The things or conditions around something or someone.

sur•vey
1. (**sur**-vay) ***noun*** A report or study on what people think about something.
▸ ***verb*** **survey** (sur-**vay** *or* **sur**-vay)
2. (sur-**vay**) ***verb*** To look at the whole of a scene or situation.
3. (sur-**vay**) ***verb*** To measure an area in order to make a map or plan. ▸ ***noun*** **survey** (**sur**-vay), ***noun*** **surveyor**
▸ ***verb*** **surveying, surveyed**

sur•vive (sur-**vive**) ***verb***
1. To stay alive through or after some dangerous event.
2. To continue to live or exist.
▸ ***verb*** **surviving, survived** ▸ ***noun*** **survival**

sur•vi•vor (sur-**vye**-vur) ***noun*** Someone who lives through a disaster or horrible event.

su•shi (**soo**-shee) ***noun*** A Japanese dish made of raw fish or seafood pressed into rice.

sus•pect
1. (suh-**spekt**) ***verb*** To think that something may be true; to guess or

suppose. ▸ ***adjective* suspect** (**suhss**-pekt *or* suh-**spekt**)
2. (suh-**spekt**) ***verb*** To think that someone is guilty with little or no proof.
3. (suh-**spekt**) ***verb*** To have doubts about; to distrust.
4. (**suhss**-pekt) ***noun*** Someone thought to be responsible for a crime.
▸ ***verb* suspecting, suspected**

sus•pend (suh-**spend**) ***verb***
1. To attach something to a support so that it hangs downward.
2. To keep from falling as if attached from above.
3. To stop something for a short time.
4. To punish someone by stopping the person from taking part in an activity for a short while.
▸ ***verb* suspending, suspended**
▸ ***noun* suspension**

sus•pend•ers (suh-**spen**-durz) ***noun, plural*** A pair of elastic straps worn over the shoulders and attached to pants or a skirt to hold up the garment.

sus•pense (suh-**spenss**) ***noun*** An anxious and uncertain feeling caused by having to wait to see what happens.

sus•pen•sion bridge (suh-**spen**-shuhn) ***noun*** A bridge hung from cables or chains strung from towers.

sus•pi•cion (suh-**spish**-uhn) ***noun***
1. A thought, based more on feeling than on fact, that something is wrong or bad.
2. If you are **under suspicion,** people think that you may have done something wrong.

sus•pi•cious (suh-**spish**-uhss) ***adjective***
1. If you feel **suspicious,** you think that something is wrong or bad, but you have little or no proof to back up your feelings.
2. If you think that someone seems or looks **suspicious,** you have a feeling that the person has done something wrong and cannot be believed or trusted.

sus•tain (suh-**stayn**) ***verb***
1. To keep something going.
2. If something **sustains** you, it gives you the energy and strength to keep going.
3. To suffer something.
▸ ***verb* sustaining, sustained**

SUV (ess-yoo-**vee**) ***noun*** A large car that is built like a truck and that can be driven where there are no roads. SUV stands for *Sport Utility Vehicle.*

swag•ger (**swag**-ur) ***verb*** To walk or act in a bold, conceited way.
▸ **swaggering, swaggered** ▸ ***noun* swagger**

swal•low (**swahl**-oh)
1. ***verb*** To make food or drink travel down from your mouth to your stomach. ▸ ***noun* swallow**
2. ***verb*** To cause to disappear as if by swallowing.
3. ***verb*** To keep back.
4. ***noun*** A migrating bird with long wings and a forked tail.
5. ***verb*** *(informal)* To accept or believe without question.
▸ ***verb* swallowing, swallowed**

swamp (**swahmp**)
1. ***noun*** An area of wet, spongy ground; a marsh. ▸ ***adjective* swampy**
2. ***verb*** To fill with or sink in water.
3. ***verb*** To overwhelm.
▸ ***verb* swamping, swamped**

swan (**swahn**) ***noun*** A large water bird with white feathers, webbed feet, and a long, graceful neck.

swap (**swahp**) ***verb*** *(informal)* To trade or exchange one thing for another.
▸ **swapping, swapped** ▸ ***noun* swap**

swarm (**sworm**)
1. ***noun*** A group of people or insects that gather or move in large numbers.
2. ***verb*** When bees **swarm,** they fly together in a thick mass.
3. ***verb*** If a place **is swarming** with people or animals, it is filled with them.
▸ ***verb* swarming, swarmed**

swar•thy (**swor**-THee) ***adjective*** A **swarthy** person has dark skin.
▸ **swarthier, swarthiest**

S

swas•ti•ka (**swahss**-tuh-kuh) ***noun*** An ancient symbol consisting of a cross with the arms bent at right angles. During the 20th century, the swastika became a symbol of aggression and hatred when it was adopted as the emblem of the Nazi party in Germany.

swat (**swaht**) ***verb*** To hit with a quick, sharp blow. ▸ **swatting, swatted** ▸ ***noun*** **swat**

sway (**sway**) ***verb***
1. To move or swing from side to side.
2. To change or influence the way someone thinks or acts.
▸ ***verb*** **swaying, swayed** ▸ ***noun*** **sway**

swear (**swair**) ***verb***
1. To make a formal, solemn promise.
2. To use rude or bad language; to curse.
▸ ***verb*** **swearing, swore** (**swor**), **sworn** (**sworn**)

sweat (**swet**) ***verb*** When you **sweat,** a salty liquid comes out through the pores in your skin because you are hot or nervous. Sweat is another word for **perspire.** ▸ **sweating, sweat** *or* **sweated** ▸ ***noun*** **sweat**

sweat•er (**swet**-ur) ***noun*** A knitted piece of clothing that you wear on the top half of your body.

sweat•shirt (**swet**-*shurt*) ***noun*** A heavy, collarless, casual top with long sleeves.

sweep (**sweep**) ***verb***
1. To clean or clear away with a brush or broom.
2. To move or carry rapidly and forcefully.
3. To touch or brush lightly.
4. To move or pass over a wide area quickly and steadily.
▸ ***verb*** **sweeping, swept** (**swept**) ▸ ***noun*** **sweep**

sweep•ing (**sweep**-ing) ***adjective*** Something that is **sweeping** affects many things or people.

sweet (**sweet**)
1. ***adjective*** Food that is **sweet** has a taste like that of sugar or honey, as in *a sweet peach.*
2. ***adjective*** Pleasant in taste, smell, or sound, as in *the sweet smell of roses* or *sweet music.*
3. ***adjective*** Gentle and kind; good-natured, as in *a sweet disposition.*
4. ***noun*** A piece of candy or other food that tastes sweet.
▸ ***adjective*** **sweeter, sweetest**
▸ ***adverb*** **sweetly**

sweet•en (**sweet**-uhn) ***verb*** To make something sweet or sweeter, usually by adding sugar. ▸ **sweetening, sweetened**

sweet•heart (**sweet**-*hart*) ***noun***
1. Either person of a loving couple.
2. A lovable person.

sweet potato ***noun*** The thick, sweet, orange root of a vine. Sweet potatoes are eaten as vegetables. ▸ ***noun, plural*** **sweet potatoes**

swell (**swel**)
1. ***verb*** To grow larger, greater, or stronger. ▸ ***noun*** **swelling** ▸ **swelling, swelled, swollen**
2. ***noun*** A long, rolling wave or waves.
3. ***adjective*** *(slang)* Wonderful.

swel•ter•ing (**swel**-tur-ing) ***adjective*** **Sweltering** weather is very hot. ▸ ***verb*** **swelter**

swerve (**swurv**) ***verb*** To change direction quickly, usually to avoid something. ▸ **swerving, swerved** ▸ ***noun*** **swerve**

swift (**swift**)
1. ***adjective*** Moving or able to move very fast, as in *a swift runner.* ▸ ***noun*** **swiftness** ▸ ***adverb*** **swiftly**
2. ***adjective*** Happening or done quickly, as in *a swift reply.*
3. ***noun*** A migrating bird with long, narrow wings. A swift is similar to a swallow.
▸ ***adjective*** **swifter, swiftest**

swig (**swig**) ***verb*** To drink in large gulps, usually from a bottle or other container. ▸ **swigging, swigged** ▸ ***noun*** **swig**

swim (**swim**) ***verb***
1. To move through the water using the arms and legs or the fins, flippers, or tail. ▸ ***noun*** **swim,** ***noun*** **swimmer**
2. To float on or be covered by liquid.
▸ ***verb*** **swimming, swam (swam), swum (swuhm)**

swim•suit (**swim**-*soot*) ***noun*** Clothing worn for swimming; a bathing suit.

swin•dle (**swin**-duhl) ***verb*** To cheat someone out of money, property, etc. ▸ **swindling, swindled** ▸ ***noun*** **swindle,** ***noun*** **swindler**

swine (**swine**) ***noun***
1. A pig or a hog.
2. A hateful, vicious, or greedy person.

swing (**swing**)
1. ***verb*** To move back and forth.
2. ***verb*** To move on a hinge or pivot.
3. ***verb*** To move or turn with a curved, sweeping motion. ▸ ***noun*** **swing**
4. ***noun*** A piece of play equipment on which you can sit and move back and forth.
5. ***noun*** A style of lively jazz music originally played by large dance bands in the 1930s.
▸ ***verb*** **swinging, swung (swuhng)**

swipe (**swipe**) ***verb***
1. *(informal)* To hit something or somebody with a hard, sweeping blow. ▸ ***noun*** **swipe**
2. *(slang)* To steal something.
▸ ***verb*** **swiping, swiped**

swirl (**swurl**) ***verb*** To move in circles; to whirl. ▸ **swirling, swirled** ▸ ***noun*** **swirl**

swish (**swish**)
1. ***verb*** To move with a soft, rustling sound. ▸ **swishes, swishing, swished**
2. ***noun*** A soft, rustling sound. ▸ ***noun, plural*** **swishes**

switch (**swich**)
1. ***verb*** To trade one thing for another.
2. ***verb*** To change from one thing to another.
3. ***noun*** A change or a trade.
4. ***verb*** To turn a piece of electrical equipment on or off.
5. ***noun*** A device that interrupts the flow of electricity in a circuit, as in *a light switch.*
6. ***noun*** A long, thin stick or rod used for whipping.
7. ***noun*** A quick, jerking motion.
8. ***noun*** A section of railroad track used to move a train from one track to another. ▸ ***verb*** **switch**
▸ ***verb*** **switches, switching, switched**
▸ ***noun, plural*** **switches**

switch•board (**swich**-*bord*) ***noun*** The control center or panel for connecting the lines of a telephone system.

swiv•el (**swiv**-uhl) ***verb*** To turn or rotate on the spot. ▸ **swiveling, swiveled**

swol•len (**swohl**-in)
1. ***verb*** The past participle of **swell.**
2. ***adjective*** Made large by swelling, as in *a swollen gland.*

swoon (**swoon**) ***verb*** To faint, often from excitement. ▸ **swooning, swooned**

swoop (**swoop**) ***verb*** To rush down or pounce upon suddenly. ▸ **swooping, swooped** ▸ ***noun*** **swoop**

sword (**sord**) ***noun*** A weapon with a handle and a long, sharp blade.

sword•fish (**sord**-*fish*) ***noun*** A large saltwater food fish with a swordlike bone sticking out from its upper jaw. ▸ ***noun, plural*** **swordfish**

syc•a•more (**sik**-uh-*mor*) ***noun*** A North American tree with smooth, brown bark that peels off in layers.

syl•la•ble (**sil**-uh-buhl) ***noun*** A unit of sound in a word. A syllable contains a vowel and possibly one or more consonants.

syl•la•bus (**sil**-uh-buhss) ***noun*** An outline or a summary of work that must be covered for a particular course of study. ▸ ***noun, plural*** **syllabuses** *or* **syllabi** (**sil**-uh-bye)

S

S

sym•bol (**sim**-buhl) ***noun*** A design or an object that represents something else. **Symbol** sounds like **cymbal.**

sym•bol•ize (**sim**-buh-lize) ***verb*** To stand for or represent something else. ▸ **symbolizing, symbolized**

sym•met•ri•cal (si-**met**-ruh-kuhl) ***adjective*** Having matching points, parts, or shapes on both sides of a dividing line. The capital letters *M* and *X* are symmetrical because you can draw a line dividing them into two matching halves. ▸ ***adverb*** **symmetrically**

sym•me•try (**sim**-uh-tree) ***noun*** A balanced arrangement of parts on either side of a line or around a central point.

sym•pa•thize (**sim**-puh-*thize*) ***verb***
1. To understand or appreciate other people's troubles.
2. To be in agreement.
▸ ***verb*** **sympathizing, sympathized**

sym•pa•thy (**sim**-puh-thee) ***noun***
1. The understanding and sharing of other people's troubles.
2. If you are **in sympathy** with somebody's aims or actions, you agree with the person and support him or her.
▸ ***adjective*** **sympathetic** (sim-puh-**thet**-ik)

sym•pho•ny (**sim**-fuh-nee) ***noun***
1. A long piece of music for an orchestra. A symphony is usually in four parts called movements.
2. A large orchestra that usually plays classical music.
▸ ***noun, plural*** **symphonies** ▸ ***adjective*** **symphonic** (sim-**fon**-ic)

symp•tom (**simp**-tuhm) ***noun***
1. Something that shows that you have an illness.
2. An indication of something.

syn•a•gogue (**sin**-a-gog) ***noun*** A building used by Jewish people for worship and religious study.

syn•chro•nize (**sing**-kruh-*nize*) ***verb*** To arrange events so that they happen at the same time or in a certain order. ▸ **synchronizing, synchronized** ▸ ***noun*** **synchronization**

synchronized swimming ***noun*** Swimming that is synchronized to a musical accompaniment and that uses movements to form dancelike patterns.

syn•co•pate (**sing**-kuh-*pate*) ***verb*** To stress beats in a piece of music that are not normally stressed. ▸ **syncopating, syncopated** ▸ ***noun*** **syncopation** ▸ ***adjective*** **syncopated**

syn•drome (**sin**-*drohm*) ***noun*** A group of signs and symptoms that occur together and are characteristic of a particular disease or disorder.

syn•o•nym (**sin**-uh-nim) ***noun*** A word that means the same or nearly the same as another word.

syn•on•y•mous (si-**non**-uh-muhss) ***adjective***
1. Having the same or almost the same meaning.
2. Having the same implication or reference.

syn•op•sis (si-**nop**-siss) ***noun*** A brief summary of a longer piece of writing. ▸ ***noun, plural*** **synopses** (si-**nop**-seez)

syn•tax (**sin**-taks) ***noun*** The rules of grammar that govern the way words are put together to make phrases and sentences. ▸ ***adjective*** **syntactic** (sin-**tak**-tik)

syn•the•siz•er (**sin**-thuh-*sye*-zur) ***noun*** An electronic keyboard instrument that can make a variety of sounds and imitate other musical instruments.

syn•thet•ic (sin-**thet**-ik) ***adjective*** Something that is **synthetic** is manufactured or artificial rather than found in nature. ▸ ***noun*** **synthetic** ▸ ***adverb*** **synthetically**

sy•phon (**sye**-fuhn) Another spelling of **siphon.**

sy•ringe (suh-**rinj**) ***noun*** A tube with a plunger and a hollow needle, used for giving injections.

syr•up (**sihr**-uhp *or* **sur**-uhp) ***noun***
1. A sweet, thick liquid made by boiling sugar and water, usually with some flavoring, as in *chocolate syrup.*
2. A sweet, thick liquid made by boiling down the sap of a tree or plant, as in *maple syrup.* ▸ ***adjective* syrupy**

sys•tem (**siss**-tuhm) ***noun***
1. A group of things or parts that exist or work together in an organized way, as in *the solar system* or *a computer system.*
2. A way of organizing or arranging things, as in *the educational system* or *a system of government.*
3. An orderly way of doing something; a method. ▸ ***adjective* systematic** ▸ ***adverb* systematically**

T

tab (**tab**) ***noun***
1. A small flap or loop that is attached to something. Tabs are used for labeling, pulling, or opening.
2. *(informal)* If you **keep tabs on** someone, you watch the person closely to see what he or she is doing.
3. *(informal)* If you **pick up the tab,** you pay the bill in a restaurant.

tab•by (**tab**-ee) ***noun***
1. A cat with a striped coat.
2. Any domestic cat, especially a female.

tab•er•na•cle (**tab**-ur-*nak*-uhl) ***noun***
1. A building used for worship.
2. A case or box for holy objects.

ta•ble (**tay**-buhl) ***noun***
1. A piece of furniture with a flat top resting on legs.
2. A chart that lists facts and figures, usually in columns.
3. Food put on a table.
4. If you **turn the tables** on someone, you reverse the situation so that things are in your favor.
5. If something is done **under the table,** it is done in secret or illegally.

ta•ble•cloth (**tay**-buhl-*klawth*) ***noun*** A piece of material used to protect or decorate a table.

table manners ***noun, plural*** The way you behave when you are eating.

ta•ble•spoon (**tay**-buhl-*spoon*) ***noun*** A large spoon that you use to serve food or as a measure in cooking. A tablespoon is equal to three teaspoons. ▸ ***noun* tablespoonful**

tab•let (**tab**-lit) ***noun***
1. A pad of writing paper glued together at one end.
2. A small, solid piece of medicine that you swallow.
3. A piece of stone with writing carved on it.

table tennis ***noun*** A game for two or four players who use wooden paddles to hit a small, light ball over a low net on a table. Table tennis is also known as **Ping-Pong.**

tab•loid (**tab**-loid) ***noun*** A newspaper that contains brief articles and many pictures. The pictures and articles are often intended to stir up interest or excitement. ▸ ***adjective* tabloid**

ta•boo (tuh-**boo** *or* **ta**-boo) ***adjective*** If a subject is **taboo,** you may upset or offend people if you talk about it. ▸ ***noun* taboo**

T

tab•u•lar (**tab**-yuh-lur) ***adjective*** Set out in the form of a table or chart. ▸ ***verb*** **tabulate**

tac•it (**tass**-it) ***adjective*** If something is **tacit,** it is understood or agreed to without being stated. ▸ ***adverb*** **tacitly**

tac•i•turn (**tass**-uh-turn) ***adjective*** If someone is **taciturn,** the person is quiet and shy and does not talk much. ▸ ***adverb*** **taciturnly**

tack (**tak**)
1. ***noun*** A small nail with a sharp point and a large, flat head.
2. ***noun*** A course of action.
3. ***verb*** To add or attach something extra or different.
4. ***verb*** If you **tack** material, you sew it loosely before doing it neatly. ▸ ***noun*** **tack**
5. ***verb*** To sail in a zigzag course against the wind.
6. ***noun*** Equipment that you need to ride a horse, such as a saddle and bridle.
▸ ***verb*** **tacking, tacked**

tack•le (**tak**-uhl)
1. ***verb*** In football, if you **tackle** someone, you knock or throw the person to the ground in order to stop forward progress. ▸ ***noun*** **tackle,** ***noun*** **tackler**
2. ***verb*** To deal with a problem or difficulty.
3. ***noun*** The equipment that you need for a particular activity, as in *fishing tackle.*
4. ***noun*** A system of ropes and pulleys used to raise, lower, or move heavy loads.
▸ ***verb*** **tackling, tackled**

ta•co (**tah**-koh) ***noun*** A Mexican food consisting of a fried tortilla that is folded around one or more fillings such as beef, chicken, or cheese. ▸ ***noun, plural*** **tacos**

tact (**takt**) ***noun*** If you handle a person or situation with **tact,** you are sensitive and do not upset or hurt anyone.
▸ ***adjective*** **tactful** ▸ ***adverb*** **tactfully**

tac•tics (**tak**-tiks) ***noun, plural*** Plans or methods to win a game or battle or achieve a goal. ▸ ***adjective*** **tactical** ▸ ***adverb*** **tactically**

tad•pole (**tad**-*pole*) ***noun*** A young frog or toad that is in the larva stage of development. It lives in water, breathes through gills, and has a long tail but no legs.

taf•fy (**taf**-ee) ***noun*** A thick, sweet, chewy candy that is made of brown sugar or molasses and butter. The ingredients are boiled together, then stretched and folded over and over until the mixture holds its shape. ▸ ***noun, plural*** **taffies**

tag (**tag**)
1. ***noun*** A label, as in *a price tag* or *a name tag.*
2. ***noun*** A children's game in which the player called "It" has to chase the other players and touch one of them. ▸ ***verb*** **tag**
3. ***verb*** In baseball, to put a runner out by touching him or her with the ball.
▸ ***noun*** **tag**
4. ***verb*** If you **tag along** with someone, you follow the person.
▸ ***verb*** **tagging, tagged**

tail (**tayl**)
1. ***noun*** A part that sticks out at the back end of an animal's body and is often long and slender.
2. ***noun*** Something that is shaped like a tail, as in *the tail of a kite* or *the tail of a comet.*
3. ***noun*** The rear part or end of something.
4. **tails** ***noun*** The side of a coin opposite the head, or main side.
5. ***verb*** *(informal)* If you **tail** someone, you follow the person closely. ▸ **tailing, tailed** ▸ ***noun*** **tail** **Tail** sounds like **tale.**

tail•gate (**tale**-*gayt*)
1. ***noun*** A board or gate at the rear of a station wagon or truck that can be folded down or removed for loading and unloading.

T

2. ***verb*** To drive so closely behind another vehicle that you do not have room to stop in an emergency.
3. ***verb*** To set up a picnic on the tailgate of a vehicle, especially in the parking lot of a sports stadium.
▸ ***verb*** **tailgating, tailgated**

tai•lor (**tay**-lur)
1. ***noun*** Someone who makes or alters clothes. ▸ ***verb*** **tailor**
2. ***verb*** To design or alter something so that it suits someone perfectly.
▸ **tailoring, tailored**

take (**tayk**) ***verb***
1. To get, seize, or capture something with the hands.
2. To move, carry, or remove something.
3. To accept something.
4. To use something.
5. To receive or to accept.
6. To do or perform an action.
7. To tolerate, or to permit.
8. To win something.
9. To lead.
10. To understand or believe something.
11. If you **take after** someone in your family, you look or act like the person.
12. *(informal)* If you are **taken in** by someone, you believe the lies that the person tells you.
13. If you **take off** something, you remove it.
14. If you **take up** something, you begin it, as in *I am taking up French;* or you shorten it, as in *I will take up the hem of my skirt before the party.*
15. If you **take to** something or someone, you like the thing or person.
▸ ***verb*** **taking, took** (**tuk**), **taken** (**tayk**-in)

take•off (**tayk**-*awf*) ***noun*** The beginning of a flight, when an aircraft leaves the ground. ▸ ***verb*** **take off**

take•out (**tayk**-*out*) ***noun***
1. A restaurant selling meals that you take and eat somewhere else.
▸ ***adjective*** **take-out**
2. Food that you buy from a take-out restaurant.

take•o•ver (**tayk**-*oh*-vur) ***noun***
1. If there is a **takeover** of a company, one company buys enough shares of stock in another to control it.
2. If there is a **takeover** of a country, a new group or individual seizes possession or control.
▸ ***verb*** **take over**

talc (**talk**) ***noun*** A soft mineral that is ground up to make talcum powder, face powder, paint, and plastics.

tal•cum powder (**tal**-kuhm) ***noun*** A fine, white powder made from talc. You can use talcum powder to dry your body or to make it smell nice.

tale (**tayl**) ***noun***
1. A story, as in *a fairy tale.*
2. A story that is not true; a lie.
Tale sounds like **tail.**

tal•ent (**tal**-uhnt) ***noun***
1. A natural ability or skill.
2. A person with talent.
▸ ***adjective*** **talented**

talk (**tawk**)
1. ***verb*** To say words; to speak. ▸ ***noun*** **talker**
2. ***verb*** To discuss.
3. ***verb*** To speak to a person or group in a persuasive way.
4. ***noun*** A conversation.
5. ***noun*** A speech or a lecture.
▸ ***verb*** **talking, talked**

talk•a•tive (**taw**-kuh-tiv) ***adjective*** If you are **talkative,** you talk a lot.

talk show ***noun*** A television or radio program in which a host interviews or has discussions with guests, audience members, and callers.

tall (**tawl**) ***adjective***
1. Higher than usual; not short or low, as in *a tall building.*
2. Having a certain height.
3. Hard to believe; exaggerated, as in *a tall tale.*
▸ ***adjective*** **taller, tallest**

T

tal·low (**tal**-oh) ***noun*** Fat from cattle and sheep that is used mainly to make candles and soap.

tal·ly (**tal**-ee)
1. ***noun*** An account, a record, or a score.
2. ***verb*** To add up an account, record, or score.
3. ***verb*** To match, or to agree.
▸ ***verb*** **tallies, tallying, tallied**

Tal·mud (**tal**-muhd *or* **tal**-mud) ***noun*** The collection of Jewish civil and religious laws.

tal·on (**tal**-uhn) ***noun*** A sharp claw of a bird of prey such as an eagle, a hawk, or a falcon.

ta·ma·le (tuh-**mah**-lee) ***noun*** A Mexican dish consisting of seasoned chopped meat rolled in cornmeal dough. The mixture is wrapped in husks of corn and steamed.

tam·bou·rine (tam-bur-**een**) ***noun*** A small, round musical instrument that is similar to a drum. It has jingling metal disks around the rim and is played by shaking or striking it with the hand.

tame (**taym**) ***adjective***
1. Taken from a wild or natural state and trained to live with or be useful to people. ▸ ***verb*** **tame** ▸ ***noun*** **tamer**
2. Gentle or not afraid; not shy.
3. Not very exciting; dull.
▸ ***adjective*** **tamer, tamest** ▸ ***adverb*** **tamely**

tam·per (**tam**-pur) ***verb*** To interfere with something so that it becomes damaged or broken. ▸ **tampering, tampered**

tan (**tan**)
1. ***noun*** A light yellow-brown color.
▸ ***adjective*** **tan**
2. ***noun*** If you have a **tan,** your skin has become darker because you have been out in the sun a lot. ▸ ***verb*** **tan**
3. ***verb*** To make animal hide into leather by soaking it in a solution containing chemicals found in the bark and wood of many trees. ▸ **tanning, tanned** ▸ ***noun*** **tannery**

tan·dem (**tan**-duhm) ***noun*** A bicycle for two people, with one seat behind the other.

tan·door·i (tan-**door**-ee) ***noun*** An Indian method of cooking meat, bread, or any food by baking it in a clay pot.

tan·gent (**tan**-juhnt) ***noun***
1. In geometry, a straight line that touches the edge of a curve in one place.
2. If you **go off on a tangent,** you suddenly start talking about something other than the main topic of discussion.

tan·ger·ine (*tan*-juh-**reen**) ***noun*** A sweet, orange citrus fruit that is smaller than an orange and easier to peel.

tan·gle (**tang**-guhl) ***verb*** To twist together in a confused mass; to snarl.
▸ **tangling, tangled** ▸ ***noun*** **tangle**

tan·gram (**tang**-gram) ***noun*** A Chinese puzzle made of a square cut into various shapes that you can put together to make a number of different patterns.

tang·y (**tang**-ee) ***adjective*** Having a strong, sharp flavor or odor. ▸ **tangier, tangiest** ▸ ***noun*** **tang**

tank (**tangk**) ***noun***
1. A large container for liquid or gas.
2. An armored combat vehicle equipped with heavy guns. Most tanks can travel over rough ground because they move on two continuous belts of metal treads.

tank·er (**tang**-kur) ***noun*** A ship, a truck, or an airplane that is equipped with tanks for carrying liquids.

tan·trum (**tan**-truhm) ***noun*** An outburst of anger or bad temper.

tap (**tap**)
1. ***verb*** To hit something gently or lightly. ▸ ***noun*** **tap**
2. ***noun*** A small metal plate attached to the soles of shoes.
3. ***verb*** To make or do by tapping again and again.
4. ***verb*** To make a hole in order to draw off a liquid, as in *to tap a maple tree for its sap.*
5. ***verb*** To listen in on a telephone

T

conversation using a secret device.
▸ ***noun*** **tap**
6. ***noun*** A device used to control the flow of a liquid in a pipe; a faucet.
▸ ***verb*** **tapping, tapped**

tap dancing ***noun*** Dancing in which shoes with taps are worn to make rhythmical clicking sounds with the feet.
▸ ***noun*** **tap dancer** ▸ ***verb*** **tap-dance**

tape (**tayp**)
1. ***noun*** A thin strip of material, paper, or plastic, as in *adhesive tape.*
2. ***verb*** To fasten together, wrap, or bind with tape.
3. ***noun*** A long piece of magnetic ribbon used for recording sound or pictures. Tape is usually contained in a plastic case, or cassette.
4. ***verb*** To record sound and/or pictures on tape.
▸ ***verb*** **taping, taped**

tape measure ***noun*** A long, thin piece of ribbon or steel marked in inches or centimeters so that you can measure things easily.

ta•per (**tay**-pur)
1. ***verb*** To make or become narrower at one end.
2. ***verb*** To become smaller or less; to diminish.
3. ***noun*** A slender candle.
Taper sounds like **tapir.**
▸ ***verb*** **tapering, tapered**

tape recorder ***noun*** A machine that you use to play back or record music and sound on magnetic tape. ▸ ***noun*** **tape recording** ▸ ***verb*** **tape-record**

tap•es•try (**tap**-uh-stree) ***noun*** A heavy piece of cloth with pictures or patterns woven into it. ▸ ***noun, plural*** **tapestries**

ta•pir (**tay**-pur) ***noun*** A large animal that has hoofs and a long, flexible snout. The tapir looks like a pig. It is found in Central America, South America, and southern Asia and is distantly related to the horse and rhinoceros. **Tapir** sounds like **taper.**

taps (**taps**) ***noun*** A bugle call played at the end of the day in military camps as a signal that all lights must be put out. Taps is also played at military funerals.

tar (**tar**) ***noun*** A thick, black, sticky substance used for paving roads and patching roofs. Tar is made from coal or wood. ▸ ***verb*** **tar**

ta•ran•tu•la (tuh-**ran**-chuh-luh) ***noun*** A large, hairy spider found mainly in warm regions. Its bite is painful but not seriously poisonous to people.

tar•dy (**tar**-dee) ***adjective*** Not on time; late. ▸ **tardier, tardiest** ▸ ***noun*** **tardiness**

tar•get (**tar**-git)
1. ***noun*** A mark, a circle, or an object that is aimed or shot at. ▸ ***verb*** **target**
2. ***noun*** Someone or something that is criticized or made fun of.
3. ***noun*** A goal or an aim.
4. ***verb*** If you **target** something, you concentrate on it. ▸ **targeting, targeted**

tar•iff (**ta**-rif) ***noun*** A tax charged on goods that are imported or exported.

tar•nish (**tar**-nish) ***verb*** If something **tarnishes,** it becomes duller or less bright. ▸ **tarnishes, tarnishing, tarnished** ▸ ***noun*** **tarnish**

tar•pau•lin (**tar**-puh-lin) ***noun*** A heavy, waterproof covering, usually made of canvas, that is used to protect playing fields, boats, or any outdoor item from wet weather. A tarpaulin is also called a *tarp.*

tart (**tart**)
1. ***noun*** A small pie or pastry that usually contains fruit.
2. ***adjective*** If food is **tart,** it tastes sour or sharp.
3. ***adjective*** A **tart** remark is mean, sharp, or bitter in tone. ▸ ***adverb*** **tartly** ▸ ***adjective*** **tarter, tartest** ▸ ***noun*** **tartness**

tar•tan (**tart**-uhn) ***noun*** A type of plaid, or a woolen cloth with a plaid pattern. Tartan is used especially for Scottish kilts.

T

tar•tar (**tar**-tur) ***noun***
1. A yellow substance that forms on the teeth. Tartar consists of food particles, saliva, and calcium. If not removed, it becomes hard.
2. tartar sauce A sauce made with mayonnaise and chopped pickles, often served with fish.

task (**task**) ***noun*** A piece of work to be done, especially work assigned by another person; a job or duty.

task force ***noun*** A group formed for a limited period of time to deal with a specific problem.

tas•sel (**tass**-uhl) ***noun***
1. A bunch of threads tied at one end and used as a decoration on shoes, clothing, graduation caps, furniture, or rugs.
2. Something that is like a **tassel**, such as the **tassel** of silk on an ear of corn. ▸ ***adjective*** **tasseled**

taste (**tayst**)
1. ***noun*** Your sense of **taste** allows you to identify a food by its taste, or flavor.
2. ***noun*** The **taste** of a food is its flavor; for example, sweet, sour, salty, or bitter. ▸ ***adjective*** **tasty**
3. ***noun*** If you have good **taste,** you make good choices of furnishings, clothes, etc. ▸ ***adjective*** **tasteful**
4. ***verb*** To have a certain flavor. *Sugar tastes sweet.*
5. ***verb*** To try a bit of food or drink to see if you like it. ▸ ***noun*** **taste** ▸ ***verb*** **tasting, tasted**

taste bud ***noun*** One of the clusters of cells in the tongue that sense whether something is sweet, sour, salty, or bitter.

taste•less (**tayst**-liss) ***adjective***
1. Having little or no flavor; bland.
2. Showing little sense of what is appropriate; lacking tact; rude, as in *a tasteless remark.*

tat•tered (**tat**-urd) ***adjective*** Old and torn, as in *a tattered jacket.*

tat•tle (**tat**-uhl) ***verb*** To tell someone in authority that someone else is doing something wrong. ▸ **tattling, tattled** ▸ ***noun*** **tattler**

tat•tle•tale (**tat**-uhl-*tale*) ***noun*** A **tattletale** is someone who tells other people's secrets.

tat•too (ta-**too**) ***noun*** A picture or phrase that has been printed onto somebody's skin with pigments and needles. ▸ ***verb*** **tattoo**

taunt (**tawnt**) ***verb*** To try to make someone angry or upset by teasing him or her. ▸ **taunting, taunted** ▸ ***noun*** **taunt**

taut (**tawt**) ***adjective*** Stretched tight, as in *a taut rope.* ▸ **tauter, tautest**

tav•ern (**tav**-urn) ***noun***
1. A place where people can sit and drink alcoholic beverages; a bar.
2. An inn.

taw•ny (**taw**-nee) ***adjective*** Having a light, sandy-brown color, as in *a tawny lion.* ▸ **tawnier, tawniest**

tax (**taks**)
1. ***noun*** Money that people and businesses must pay in order to support a government, as in *a sales tax* or *an income tax.* ▸ ***noun, plural*** **taxes** ▸ ***noun*** **taxation** ▸ ***verb*** **tax**
2. ***verb*** To make heavy demands on; to strain. ▸ **taxes, taxing, taxed** ▸ ***adjective*** **taxing**

tax•i (**tak**-see)
1. ***noun*** A car with a driver whom you pay to take you where you want to go.
2. ***verb*** When planes **taxi,** they move along the ground before taking off or after landing. ▸ **taxies, taxiing, taxied**

T cell (**tee**) ***noun*** Any of a group of cells found in the lymph glands that help protect the body against disease.

tea (**tee**) ***noun***
1. A drink made from the leaves of a shrub that is grown in China, Japan, and India.
2. This shrub or its dried leaves.
3. A similar drink made from the leaves of other plants, as in *herb tea.*

4. A light afternoon meal.
5. A late-afternoon social gathering at which tea and other refreshments are served.

teach (**teech**) ***verb*** To give a lesson, or to show someone how to do something. ▸ **teaches, teaching, taught** (tawt) ▸ ***noun*** **teacher**

tea•ket•tle (**tee**-*ket*-uhl) ***noun*** A kettle with a handle and a spout. A teakettle is used for boiling water.

teal (**teel**) ***noun***
1. Any of several small ducks with short necks. Teal live in rivers and marshes. The males often have brightly colored feathers.
2. A dark color between green and blue.
▸ ***adjective*** **teal**
▸ ***noun, plural*** **teal** *or* **teals**

team (**teem**)
1. ***noun*** A group of people who work together or play a sport together, as in *a team of doctors* or *a hockey team.*
▸ ***noun*** **teamwork**
2. ***noun*** Two or more horses or oxen that are harnessed together to do work.
3. ***verb*** If two or more people **team up,** they join together to do something.
▸ **teaming, teamed**
Team sounds like **teem.**

team•mate (**teem**-*mate*) ***noun*** A fellow member of a team.

tear
1. (**tihr**) ***noun*** A drop of clear, salty liquid that comes from your eye.
▸ ***adjective*** **tearful**
2. (**tair**) ***noun*** A rip in a piece of paper or other substance.
3. (**tair**) ***verb*** To pull or be pulled apart by force.
4. (**tair**) ***verb*** To make a hole in by pulling; to rip.
5. (**tair**) ***verb*** To move very quickly.
▸ ***verb*** **tearing, tore** (**tor**), **torn** (**torn**)

tease (**teez**) ***verb*** To mock someone by playfully saying unkind and hurtful things to the person; to kid. ▸ **teasing, teased** ▸ ***noun*** **tease,** ***noun*** **teaser**

tea•spoon (**tee**-*spoon*) ***noun*** A small spoon that you use for stirring liquids or as a measure in cooking. A teaspoon equals ⅓ tablespoon. ▸ ***noun*** **teaspoonful**

tech•ni•cal (**tek**-nuh-kuhl) ***adjective***
1. To do with science, engineering, or the mechanical or industrial arts.
2. Using words that only experts in a particular field or subject understand.
▸ ***adverb*** **technically**

tech•ni•cian (tek-**nish**-uhn) ***noun*** Someone who works with specialized equipment or does practical laboratory work, as in *a lighting technician* or *a dental technician.*

tech•nique (tek-**neek**) ***noun*** A method or way of doing something that requires skill, as in the arts, sports, or the sciences.

tech•nol•o•gy (tek-**nol**-uh-jee) ***noun*** The use of science and engineering to do practical things, such as make businesses and factories more efficient. ▸ ***noun, plural*** **technologies** ▸ ***adjective*** **technological** (*tek*-noh-**log**-i-kuhl)

ted•dy bear (**ted**-ee) ***noun*** A stuffed toy bear made from soft, furry material.

te•di•ous (**tee**-dee-uhss *or* **tee**-juhss) ***adjective*** Tiring and boring. ▸ ***adverb*** **tediously**

teem (**teem**) ***verb***
1. To be very full; to swarm.
2. To rain very hard; to pour.
Teem sounds like **team.**

teen•ag•er (**teen**-*ayj*-ur) ***noun*** A person who is between the ages of 13 and 19. ▸ ***adjective*** **teenage** *or* **teenaged**

teens (**teenz**) ***noun, plural*** The years of a person's life between 13 and 19.

tee•pee (**tee**-*pee*) Another spelling of **tepee.**

teeth (**teeth**) ***noun, plural*** The white, bony parts of the mouth that are used for biting and chewing food.

T

teethe (**teeTH**) ***verb*** If a baby is **teething,** new teeth are coming through his or her gums. ▸ **teething, teethed**

Tef·lon (**tef**-lon) ***noun*** The trademark for a synthetic coating used on cooking utensils to prevent sticking.

tel·e·cast (**tel**-uh-*kast*) ***noun*** A program broadcast by television. ▸ ***verb*** **telecast**

tel·e·com·mu·ni·ca·tion (*tel*-uh-kuh-myoo-nuh-**kay**-shuhn) ***noun***
1. The science that deals with the sending of messages over long distances by telephone, satellite, radio, and other electronic means. Also called *telecommunications.*
2. Any message sent this way.

tel·e·com·mute (*tel*-uh-kuh-**myoot**) ***verb*** To do your work by staying at home and communicating with your office by means of a computer with a modem, a fax machine, or any other form of electronic communication.
▸ **telecommuting, telecommuted**
▸ ***noun*** **telecommuter**

tel·e·gram (**tel**-uh-*gram*) ***noun*** A message that is sent by telegraph.
▸ ***verb*** **telegram**

tel·e·graph (**tel**-uh-*graf*) ***noun*** A device or system for sending messages over long distances. It uses a code of electrical signals sent by wire or radio. The telegraph was invented by Samuel Morse in 1837. ▸ ***noun*** **telegrapher** (tuh-**leg**-ruh-fur) ▸ ***verb*** **telegraph**

tel·e·mar·ket·ing (*tel*-uh-**mar**-kuh-ting) ***noun*** The selling of goods and services by telephone.

te·lem·e·try (tuh-**lem**-uh-tree) ***noun*** The use of radio waves to transmit and record information about pressure, speed, or temperature from a measuring instrument.

tel·e·phone (**tel**-uh-*fone*) ***noun***
1. A system for sending sounds over distances by changing them into electrical signals. The signals are sent by wires or radio waves and then changed back into sounds.
2. A device for sending and receiving sounds, especially speech, in this way. The telephone was invented by Alexander Graham Bell in 1876.
▸ ***verb*** **telephone**

tel·e·pho·to lens (*tel*-uh-**foh**-toh) ***noun*** A camera lens that makes distant objects seem larger and closer.

tel·e·scope (**tel**-uh-*skope*) ***noun*** An instrument that makes distant objects seem larger and closer. Telescopes are used especially for studying the stars and other heavenly bodies. ▸ ***adjective*** **telescopic** (*tel*-uh-**skop**-ik)

tel·e·vise (**tel**-uh-vize) ***verb*** To broadcast by television. ▸ **televising, televised**

tel·e·vi·sion (**tel**-uh-vizh-uhn) ***noun***
1. A piece of equipment with a screen that receives and shows moving pictures with sound.
2. The sending of sounds and moving pictures along radio waves to be picked up by a television set.

tell (**tel**) ***verb***
1. To put into words; to say.
2. To give the story; to report or describe.
3. To show something.
4. To order or to command.
5. To recognize or to identify.
6. If you **tell** someone **off,** you scold the person because he or she has done something wrong.
7. If you **tell on** someone, you report to someone else what that person has done.
▸ ***verb*** **telling, told (tohld)**

tel·ler (**tel**-ur) ***noun***
1. Someone who tells or relates stories.
2. A bank employee who gives out and receives money.

tem·per (**tem**-pur)
1. ***noun*** A tendency to get angry.
2. ***noun*** A person's usual state of mind; disposition.

3. ***noun*** A calm state of mind; self-control.
4. ***verb*** To make less harsh; to moderate.
5. ***verb*** To make hard or strong, as in *to temper steel.*
▸ ***verb*** **tempering, tempered**

tem•per•a•ment (**tem**-pur-uh-muhnt) ***noun*** Your nature or personality; the way you usually think, act, or respond to other people or to situations.

tem•per•a•men•tal (tem-pur-uh-**men**-tuhl) ***adjective*** Moody, unpredictable, or too sensitive. ▸ ***adverb*** **temperamentally**

tem•per•ate (**tem**-pur-it) ***adjective*** If an area has a **temperate** climate, it has neither very high nor very low temperatures.

tem•per•a•ture (**tem**-pur-uh-chur) ***noun***
1. The degree of heat or cold in something, usually measured by a thermometer.
2. If you have a **temperature,** your body is hotter than normal because you are ill. Normal human body temperature is generally around 98.6 degrees Fahrenheit.

tem•pest (**tem**-pist) ***noun***
1. A violent storm.
2. A violent or noisy commotion; an uproar.

tem•plate (**tem**-plate) ***noun***
1. A shape or pattern that you draw or cut around to make the same shape in paper, metal, material, etc.
2. In computers, a document or pattern that is used to create similar documents. For example, a magazine designer could use a template for a page that follows the same general format from issue to issue.

tem•ple (**tem**-puhl) ***noun***
1. The flat area on either side of the forehead, above the cheek and in front of the ear.
2. A building used for worship.

tem•po (**tem**-poh) ***noun*** The speed or timing of a piece of music. ▸ ***noun, plural*** **tempos** *or* **tempi** (**tem**-pee)

tem•po•rar•y (**tem**-puh-*rer*-ee) ***adjective*** If something is **temporary,** it lasts for only a short time. ▸ ***adverb*** **temporarily**

tempt (**tempt**) ***verb***
1. If you **tempt** someone, you try to get the person to do or want something that is wrong or foolish. ▸ ***noun*** **tempter** ▸ ***adjective*** **tempting**
2. To appeal strongly to; to attract.
▸ ***verb*** **tempting, tempted**

temp•ta•tion (temp-**tay**-shuhn) ***noun***
1. Something that you want to have or do, although you know it is wrong.
2. The act of being tempted.

ten (**ten**) ***noun*** The whole number, written 10, that comes after 9 and before 11. ▸ ***adjective*** **ten**

ten•ant (**ten**-uhnt) ***noun*** Someone who rents a room, a house, an apartment, an office, or land that belongs to someone else.

tend (**tend**) ***verb***
1. If something **tends** to happen, it often or usually happens.
2. If you **tend** a person, an animal, or a plant, you take care of it.
▸ ***verb*** **tending, tended**

ten•den•cy (**ten**-duhn-see) ***noun*** If you have a **tendency** to do something, you often or usually do it. ▸ ***noun, plural*** **tendencies**

ten•der (**ten**-dur) ***adjective***
1. Sore or painful.
2. Soft.
3. Gentle and kind. ▸ ***adverb*** **tenderly** ▸ ***noun*** **tenderness**

ten•don (**ten**-duhn) ***noun*** A strong, thick cord or band of tissue that joins a muscle to a bone or other body part.

ten•e•ment (**ten**-uh-muhnt) ***noun*** A run-down apartment building, especially one that is crowded and in a poor part of a city.

ten•nis (**ten**-iss) ***noun*** A game played on a court by two or four players who use rackets to hit a ball over a net.

ten•or (**ten**-ur) ***noun***
1. A male singing voice that is quite high. ▸ ***adjective* tenor**
2. A singer with a tenor voice.

T

tense (**tenss**)
1. ***adjective*** If you are **tense,** you are nervous or worried. ▸ ***adverb* tensely**
2. ***adjective*** Stretched tight and stiff.
3. ***noun*** A form of a verb that shows whether an action happened in the past, is happening in the present, or will happen in the future. *I was, I am,* and *I will be* are examples of the past, present, and future tenses of the verb *to be.*
▸ ***noun* tenseness** ▸ ***verb* tense**
▸ ***adjective* tenser, tensest**

ten•sion (**ten**-shuhn) ***noun***
1. A feeling of worry, nervousness, or suspense.
2. The tightness or stiffness of a rope, wire, etc.
3. If there is **tension** between two people, there is difficulty or strain in their relationship.

tent (**tent**) ***noun*** A portable shelter made of nylon or canvas supported by poles and ropes.

ten•ta•cle (**ten**-tuh-kuhl) ***noun*** One of the long, flexible limbs of some animals, such as the octopus and squid. Tentacles are used for moving, feeling, and grasping.

ten•ta•tive (**ten**-tuh-tiv) ***adjective*** Hesitant or unsure. ▸ ***adverb* tentatively**

ten•ter•hooks (**ten**-tur-*huks*) ***noun, plural*** If you are **on tenterhooks,** you are in suspense waiting for something to happen.

tenth (**tenth**)
1. ***noun*** One part of something that has been divided into 10 equal parts, written $^1/_{10}$.
2. ***adjective*** That which comes after ninth and before eleventh.
3. ***noun*** In decimal notation, the position to the right of the decimal point is known as **tenths place.** In the number 4.0129, the digit 0 is in tenths place.

ten•u•ous (**ten**-yoo-uhss) ***adjective*** Not very strong or substantial; shaky.
▸ ***adverb* tenuously**

te•pee (**tee**-*pee*) ***noun*** A tent shaped like a cone and made from animal skins by North American Indians.

tep•id (**tep**-id) ***adjective*** Slightly warm; lukewarm.

ter•i•ya•ki (ter-ee-**yah**-kee) ***noun*** A Japanese dish of chicken, meat, or fish that has been soaked in soy sauce and broiled or grilled.

term (**turm**) ***noun***
1. A word with a specific meaning in some particular field, as in *musical terms* or *computer terms.*
2. A definite or limited period of time.
3. A part of the school year.
4. terms *noun, plural* The conditions of an agreement, a contract, a will, or a sale.
5. terms *noun, plural* A relationship between people.

ter•mi•nal (**tur**-muh-nuhl)
1. ***noun*** A station at either end of a transportation line, as in *an airport terminal.*
2. ***noun*** A computer keyboard and screen linked to a network.
3. ***adjective*** If someone has a **terminal** illness, he or she cannot be cured and will die from it.
4. Terminal velocity is the maximum speed an object can reach falling through the air.
▸ ***adverb* terminally**

ter•mi•nate (**tur**-muh-nate) ***verb*** To stop or to end. *The train terminates here.*
▸ **terminating, terminated**

ter•mite (**tur**-mite) ***noun*** An antlike insect that eats wood. Termites build large mounds, where they live together in colonies.

ter•race (**ter**-iss) ***noun***
1. A paved, open area next to a house; a patio.
2. A balcony of an apartment building.
3. A raised, flat platform of land with sloping sides.
▸ ***adjective*** **terraced**

ter•ra-cot•ta (**ter**-uh **kot**-uh) ***noun*** A hard, waterproof clay used in making pottery and roofs. ▸ ***adjective*** **terra cotta**

ter•rain (tuh-**rayn**) ***noun*** Ground, or land.

ter•ra•pin (**ter**-uh-pin) ***noun*** A North American turtle that lives in or near fresh water or along seashores.

ter•rar•i•um (tuh-**rer**-ee-uhm) ***noun*** A glass or plastic container for growing small plants or raising small land animals. ▸ ***noun, plural*** **terrariums** *or* **terraria** (tuh-**rer**-ee-uh)

ter•res•tri•al (tuh-**ress**-tree-uhl) ***adjective*** To do with the earth, or living on the earth.

ter•ri•ble (**ter**-uh-buhl) ***adjective***
1. Causing great fear or terror, as in *a terrible flood* or *a terrible roar.*
2. Very great; extreme or severe, as in *terrible suffering* or *terrible heat.*
3. Very bad or unpleasant, as in *a terrible movie.*
▸ ***adverb*** **terribly**

ter•ri•er (**ter**-ee-ur) ***noun*** Any of several breeds of small, lively dogs that were originally bred for hunting small animals that live in burrows.

ter•ri•fic (tuh-**rif**-ik) ***adjective***
1. Very good or excellent; wonderful, as in *a terrific idea.*
2. Very great; extreme or severe.
3. Causing great fear or terror.
▸ ***adverb*** **terrifically**

ter•ri•fy (**ter**-uh-fye) ***verb*** To frighten greatly; to fill someone with terror.
▸ **terrifies, terrifying, terrified**
▸ ***adjective*** **terrifying** ▸ ***adverb*** **terrifyingly**

ter•ri•to•ry (**ter**-uh-tor-ee) ***noun***
1. Any large area of land; a region, as in *enemy territory.*
2. The land and waters under the control of a state, nation, or ruler.
3. A part of the United States not admitted as a state.
▸ ***noun, plural*** **territories** ▸ ***adjective*** **territorial**

ter•ror (**ter**-ur) ***noun***
1. Very great fear.
2. A person or thing that causes very great fear.

ter•ror•ist (**ter**-ur-ist) ***noun*** Someone who uses violence and threats to frighten people into obeying. ▸ ***noun*** **terrorism**

ter•ror•ize (**ter**-uh-*rize*) ***verb*** To frighten someone a great deal.
▸ **terrorizing, terrorized**

terse (**turss**) ***adjective*** Brief and abrupt.
▸ **terser, tersest**

tes•sel•late (**tess**-uh-late) ***verb*** When shapes **tessellate,** they fit together exactly on a flat surface, without leaving gaps. ▸ **tessellating, tessellated**
▸ ***noun*** **tessellation** ▸ ***adjective*** **tessellated**

test (**test**)
1. ***noun*** A set of questions, problems, or tasks used to measure your knowledge or skill.
2. ***noun*** A way of studying something to find out what it is like, what it contains, or how good it is, as in *a road test, a blood test,* or *an eye test.*
3. ***verb*** To try something out. ▸ **testing, tested**

tes•ta•ment (**tess**-tuh-muhnt) ***noun***
1. A written statement of what you believe.
2. Testament Either of the two main divisions of the Christian Bible, the New Testament or the Old Testament.

tes•ti•fy (**tess**-tuh-fye) ***verb*** To state the truth, or to give evidence in a court of law. ▸ **testifies, testifying, testified**

tes•ti•mo•ny (**tess**-tuh-*moh*-nee) ***noun*** A statement given by a witness who is under oath in a court of law. ▸ ***noun, plural*** **testimonies**

T

test pilot ***noun*** A pilot who flies new airplanes in order to test them for safety and strength.

test tube ***noun*** A narrow glass tube that is closed at one end. Test tubes are used in laboratory tests and experiments.

tet·a·nus (**tet**-nuhss) ***noun*** A serious disease caused by bacteria getting into a cut or wound. Tetanus makes your muscles, especially those in your jaw, become very stiff. It can be fatal. Another word for tetanus is **lockjaw.**

teth·er (**teTH**-ur) ***noun***
1. A rope or chain that is used to tie up an animal so that it cannot move far.
▸ ***verb*** **tether**
2. If you are **at the end of your tether,** you have run out of patience or energy.

Tex-Mex (**teks meks**) ***adjective*** To do with a style of cooking or music that originated in southern Texas and combines Mexican and American culture.

text (**tekst**) ***noun***
1. The main section of writing in a book, other than the pictures or index.
2. The original or exact words of a speaker or writer.
3. The topic or theme of a piece of writing or a speech.
4. A textbook.
5. In a computer word-processing program, data in the form of words and sentences, as opposed to art, graphs, and so on.

text·book (**tekst**-*buk*) ***noun*** A book used to teach and study a subject.

tex·tile (**tek**-stuhl *or* **tek**-stile) ***noun*** A fabric or cloth that has been woven or knitted.

tex·ture (**teks**-chur) ***noun*** The look and feel of something, especially its roughness or smoothness.

than (**THan**) ***conjunction***
1. In comparison with.
2. Except; besides.

thank (**thangk**)
1. ***verb*** To tell someone that you are grateful.
2. ***verb*** To blame or to hold responsible.
3. thanks *interjection* An expression showing that you are grateful.
4. thanks *noun, plural* Gratitude.
▸ ***verb*** **thanking, thanked**

thank·ful (**thangk**-fuhl) ***adjective*** Glad, or grateful. ▸ ***adverb*** **thankfully**

thank·less (**thangk**-liss) ***adjective***
1. Not appreciated.
2. Not likely to give thanks or show gratitude, as in *a thankless child.*

Thanks·giv·ing Day (*thangks*-**giv**-ing) ***noun***
1. A holiday observed in the United States on the fourth Thursday in November. It commemorates the first Pilgrims' harvest feast, which was held in 1621. This holiday is set apart for giving thanks and feasting.
2. A similar holiday observed in Canada on the second Monday in October.

that (**THat**)
1. ***pronoun*** A person or thing mentioned or indicated. *That was a delicious cake.*
2. ***pronoun*** A thing farther away than or contrasted with another thing. *This is a chocolate cake, and that is a carrot cake.*
3. ***pronoun*** Used to introduce a clause that defines a word before it. In the sentence *I took a bite of the cake that he baked,* "that he baked" defines which cake is meant.
4. ***adjective*** Used to indicate a person, place, or thing present or already mentioned. *He made that cake yesterday.*
5. ***adjective*** Used to indicate a person or thing farther away than or contrasted with another thing. *This cake is his, and that one is mine.*
6. ***conjunction*** Used to show reason or cause, as in *I'm sorry that you can't try the chocolate cake.*
7. ***conjunction*** Used to introduce a clause in a sentence. *She thinks that she will try every cake on the table.*

T

8. ***conjunction*** Used to indicate a result, as in *I ate so much cake that I couldn't even think about eating dinner.*
9. ***adverb*** To that extent; so.
▸ ***pronoun, plural*** **those** ▸ ***adjective, plural*** **those**

thatch (**thach**) ***noun*** A roof covering made from straw or reeds. ▸ ***noun, plural*** **thatches** ▸ ***verb*** **thatch** ▸ ***adjective*** **thatched**

that's (**THats**) ***contraction*** A short form of *that is.*

thaw (**thaw**)
1. ***verb*** To melt.
2. ***verb*** To become room temperature after being frozen.
3. ***noun*** A time when snow and ice melt because the weather has become warmer.
▸ ***verb*** **thawing, thawed**

the (THuh *or* **THee**)
1. ***definite article*** Used before a noun or noun phrase that stands for a particular or previously mentioned person or thing.
2. ***definite article*** Used to show that a thing is the only one of it there is, as in *the Colosseum* or *the Mississippi River.*
3. ***definite article*** Used to show that a person or thing is thought of as the best, most important, or greatest, and therefore one of a kind.
4. ***definite article*** Used to make a singular noun general.
5. ***adverb*** To that degree; that much; by that much.

the·a·ter *or* **the·a·tre** (**thee**-uh-tur) ***noun***
1. A building where plays or movies are shown.
2. The work of writing, producing, or acting in plays.

the·at·ri·cal (thee-**at**-ruh-kuhl) ***adjective***
1. To do with the theater, as in *theatrical costumes.*
2. If something is **theatrical,** it is done in an exaggerated way to create a dramatic effect.

thee (**THee**) ***pronoun*** An old word for **you.**

theft (**theft**) ***noun*** The act of stealing.

their (**THair**) ***adjective*** Belonging to or to do with them. **Their** sounds like **there** and **they're.**

theirs (**THairz**) ***pronoun*** The one or ones belonging to or to do with them.

them (**THem**) ***pronoun*** **Them** is the form of **they** that is used as the object of a verb or preposition.

theme (**theem**) ***noun***
1. The main subject or idea of a piece of writing or a talk.
2. A short essay or piece of writing on one subject.
3. The main melody in a piece of music.
4. theme park A park with rides and attractions based on a subject, such as space travel.

them·selves (*THuhm*-**selvz**) ***pronoun***
1. Them and no one else; their own selves.
2. Their usual or true selves.

then (**THen**)
1. ***adverb*** At that time.
2. ***adverb*** After that; next.
3. ***adverb*** In that case; therefore.
4. ***noun*** That time.

the·ol·o·gy (thee-**ol**-uh-jee) ***noun*** The study of religion and religious beliefs.
▸ ***adjective*** **theological**

the·o·rem (**thee**-ur-uhm *or* **thihr**-uhm) ***noun*** A statement, especially in mathematics, that can be proved to be true.

the·o·ry (**thee**-ur-ee *or* **thihr**-ee) ***noun***
1. An idea or a statement that explains how or why something happens, as in *the theory of evolution.*
2. An idea or opinion based on some facts or evidence but not proved.
3. The rules and principles of an art or a science, rather than its practice.
4. If something should happen **in theory,** you expect it to happen but it may not.
▸ ***adjective*** **theoretical** ▸ ***adverb*** **theoretically**

T

ther•a•py (**ther**-uh-pee) ***noun*** A treatment for an illness, an injury, or a disability, as in *art therapy* or *speech therapy*. ▸ ***noun, plural* therapies** ▸ ***noun* therapist**

there (**THair**)
1. ***adverb*** To, in, or at that place.
2. ***pronoun*** A word used to introduce a sentence in which the verb comes before the subject.
3. ***noun*** That place.
There sounds like **their** and **they're.**

there•af•ter (*THair*-**af**-tur) ***adverb*** Afterward; after that; from that time on.

there•by (**THair**-*bye or THair*-**bye**) ***adverb*** In that way; by that means.

there•fore (**THair**-*for*) ***adverb*** As a result; for that reason.

therm (**thurm**) ***noun*** A unit for measuring heat.

ther•mal (**thur**-muhl)
1. ***adjective*** To do with heat or holding in heat.
2. ***noun*** A rising current of warm air.

ther•mom•e•ter (thur-**mom**-uh-tur) ***noun*** An instrument used to measure temperature.

ther•mos bottle (**thur**-muhss) ***noun*** A container that keeps liquids hot or cold for many hours. The vacuum between its two glass walls prevents heat or cold from escaping.

ther•mo•stat (**thur**-muh-*stat*) ***noun*** A device that senses temperature changes and turns on switches that control furnaces, refrigerators, air conditioners, and other heating and cooling systems.

the•sau•rus (thi-**sor**-uhss) ***noun*** A book containing lists of synonyms and antonyms. ▸ ***noun, plural* thesauri** (thi-**sor**-eye) *or* **thesauruses**

these (**THeez**) ***pronoun, plural*** The plural of **this.** ▸ ***adjective, plural* these**

the•sis (**thee**-siss) ***noun*** An idea or argument that is to be debated or proved. ▸ ***noun, plural* theses** (**thee**-seez)

they (**THay**) ***pronoun***
1. The people, animals, or things mentioned before.
2. People in general.

they'd (**THayd**) ***contraction*** A short form of *they had* or *they would.*

they'll (**THay**-uhl) ***contraction*** A short form of *they will* or *they shall.*

they're (**THair**) ***contraction*** A short form of *they are.* **They're** sounds like **their** and **there.**

they've (**THayv**) ***contraction*** A short form of *they have.*

thick (**thik**) ***adjective***
1. Great in width or depth; not thin, as in *a thick wall.*
2. As measured from one side or surface to the other.
3. Growing, being, or having parts that are close together; dense, as in *thick hair* or *a thick forest.*
4. Not flowing or pouring easily, as in *thick soup.*
▸ ***adjective* thicker, thickest** ▸ ***noun* thickness** ▸ ***verb* thicken** ▸ ***adverb* thick, *adverb* thickly**

thick•et (**thik**-it) ***noun*** A thick growth of plants, bushes, or small trees.

thief (**theef**) ***noun*** Someone who steals things. ▸ ***noun, plural* thieves** (**theevz**) ▸ ***verb* thieve** (**theev**) ▸ ***adjective* thieving**

thigh (**thye**) ***noun*** Your **thigh** is the top part of your leg, between your knee and your hip.

thim•ble (**thim**-buhl) ***noun*** A small cap made of metal, wood, plastic, or porcelain. It is worn while sewing to protect the finger that pushes the needle through the cloth.

thin (**thin**) ***adjective***
1. Small in width or depth; not thick, as in *a thin sheet of paper.*
2. Not fat; lean; slender, as in *a thin waist.*
3. Not close together; not dense, as in *thin hair.*
4. Flowing or pouring easily, as in *thin soup.*

5. Not deep or firm; weak, as in *a thin voice.*

6. Easily seen through; flimsy, as in *a thin excuse.*

▸ ***adjective*** **thinner, thinnest** ▸ ***noun*** **thinness** ▸ ***verb*** **thin** ▸ ***adverb*** **thinly**

thing (**thing**)

1. ***noun*** An object, idea, or event.

2. things ***noun, plural*** Belongings.

3. things ***noun, plural*** The general state of affairs.

think (**thingk**) ***verb***

1. To use your mind; to form ideas or to make decisions. ▸ ***noun*** **thinker**

2. To have an idea or opinion.

3. To have as a thought; to imagine.

4. To remember.

5. To be thoughtful or considerate.

▸ ***verb*** **thinking, thought**

third (**thurd**)

1. ***adjective*** That which comes after second and before fourth.

2. ***noun*** One part of something that has been divided into three equal parts, written $\frac{1}{3}$. ▸ ***adverb*** **thirdly**

Third World ***noun*** The poorer, developing countries of the world.

thirst (**thurst**) ***noun***

1. A dry feeling in the mouth, caused by a need to drink liquids.

2. A need or desire for liquid.

3. A longing for something.

▸ ***verb*** **thirst**

thirst•y (**thur**-stee) ***adjective*** If you are **thirsty,** you need or want to drink something. ▸ **thirstier, thirstiest** ▸ ***adverb*** **thirstily**

this (**THiss**)

1. ***pronoun*** A person or thing present, nearby, or just mentioned.

2. ***pronoun*** Something that is nearer or is being compared.

3. ***pronoun*** Something about to be said.

4. ***adjective*** Used to indicate a person or thing present, nearby, or just mentioned.

5. ***adjective*** Used to indicate a person or thing nearer than or contrasted with another thing.

6. ***adverb*** To this extent; so. *Are they always this late?*

▸ ***pronoun, plural*** **these** ▸ ***adjective, plural*** **these**

this•tle (**thiss**-uhl) ***noun*** A wild plant that has prickly leaves and purple, pink, white, blue, or yellow flowers.

thong (**thong**) ***noun***

1. A narrow strip of leather used to fasten things together.

2. A sandal held to the foot with a piece of leather or plastic that goes between the first two toes.

tho•rax (**thor**-aks) ***noun***

1. The part of your body between your neck and your abdomen.

2. The part of an insect's body between its head and its abdomen.

thorn (**thorn**) ***noun*** A sharp point on the branch or stem of a plant such as a rose.

thorn•y (**thor**-nee) ***adjective***

1. Covered with thorns, as in *a thorny plant.*

2. Difficult.

▸ ***adjective*** **thornier, thorniest**

thor•ough (**thur**-oh) ***adjective*** If you are **thorough,** you do a job carefully and completely. ▸ ***noun*** **thoroughness** ▸ ***adverb*** **thoroughly**

thor•ough•fare (**thur**-oh-*fair*) ***noun*** A main road.

those (**THoze**) ***pronoun, plural*** The plural of **that.** ▸ ***adjective, plural*** **those**

thou (**THou**) ***pronoun*** An old word for **you.**

though (**THoh**)

1. ***conjunction*** In spite of the fact that; although.

2. ***conjunction*** Yet; but; however.

3. ***adverb*** However; nevertheless.

thought (**thawt**)

1. ***verb*** Past tense and past participle of **think.**

2. ***noun*** The act of thinking.

3. ***noun*** An idea or an opinion.

4. ***noun*** Close attention to something.

T

thought•ful (**thawt**-fuhl) ***adjective***
1. Serious and involving a lot of thought.
2. A **thoughtful** person considers other people's feelings and needs.
▸ ***adverb*** **thoughtfully**

thought•less (**thawt**-liss) ***adjective***
1. Careless.
2. A **thoughtless** person does not consider other people's feelings and needs.
▸ ***adverb*** **thoughtlessly**

thou•sand (**thou**-zuhnd) ***noun*** The whole number, written 1,000, that is equal to 10 times 100. ▸ ***adjective*** **thousand**

thou•sandth (**thou**-zuhndth)
1. ***noun*** One of a thousand equal parts, also written $1/1000$ or 0.001.
2. ***adjective*** Having to do with the last in a sequence of 1,000 items.
3. ***noun*** In decimal notation, the position of the third number to the right of the decimal point is known as the *thousandths place.* In the number 4.0129, the digit 2 is in the thousandths place.

thrash (**thrash**) ***verb***
1. To give someone a severe beating.
2. To move wildly or violently.
3. To beat someone thoroughly in a game.
4. If you **thrash out** an idea or a problem, you talk about it until something is decided.
▸ ***verb*** **thrashes, thrashing, thrashed**
▸ ***noun*** **thrashing**

thread (**thred**)
1. ***noun*** A strand of cotton, silk, etc., used for sewing.
2. ***verb*** To pass a thread through something such as the eye of a needle or a set of beads.
3. ***verb*** To make one's way by following a winding or twisting course.
4. ***noun*** The theme or main idea that connects different ideas or events.
5. ***noun*** The raised, spiral ridge around a screw or nut.
▸ ***verb*** **threading, threaded**

thread•bare (**thred**-*bair*) ***adjective*** If your clothes are **threadbare,** they are old and worn out.

threat (**thret**) ***noun***
1. A warning that punishment or harm will follow if a certain thing is done or not done.
2. A sign or possibility that something harmful or dangerous might happen.
3. A person or thing regarded as a danger.

threat•en (**thret**-uhn) ***verb*** If someone or something **threatens** you, it frightens you or puts you in danger.
▸ **threatening, threatened**

three (**three**) ***noun*** The whole number, written 3, that comes after 2 and before 4. ▸ ***adjective*** **three**

three-dimensional *or* **3-D** (**three dee**) ***adjective***
1. Having three dimensions, such as length, width, and height; solid; not flat.
2. Having or seeming to have depth, as in *a three-dimensional drawing.*

thresh (**thresh**) ***verb*** To separate the grain or seed from a cereal plant such as wheat by beating. Today most farmers use combine harvesters to thresh their crops. ▸ **threshes, threshing, threshed**

thresh•old (**thresh**-ohld) ***noun***
1. The bottom of a door frame. A threshold is usually made of a piece of wood, metal, or stone.
2. The beginning of something.

thrift•y (**thrif**-tee) ***adjective*** Someone who is **thrifty** does not waste money, food, supplies, or anything. ▸ **thriftier, thriftiest** ▸ ***noun*** **thrift**

thrill (**thril**) ***noun*** A strong feeling of excitement and pleasure. ▸ ***verb*** **thrill**
▸ ***adjective*** **thrilling**

thril•ler (**thril**-ur) ***noun*** An exciting story that is filled with action, mystery, or suspense.

thrive (**thrive**) ***verb*** To do well and flourish. ▸ **thriving, thrived** ▸ ***adjective*** **thriving**

T

throat (**throht**) ***noun***
1. The front of your neck.
2. The passage that runs from your mouth into your stomach or lungs.

throb (**throb**) ***verb*** To beat loudly or rapidly; to pound. ▸ **throbbing, throbbed** ▸ ***noun*** **throb**

throne (**throhn**) ***noun***
1. An elaborate chair for a king or queen.
2. The power or authority of a king or queen.

throng (**throng**) ***noun*** A large crowd of people. ▸ ***verb*** **throng**

throt•tle (**throt**-uhl)
1. ***verb*** If you **throttle** someone, you squeeze the person's throat so that he or she cannot breathe. ▸ **throttling, throttled** ▸ ***noun*** **throttle**
2. ***noun*** A valve in a vehicle's engine that opens to let steam, fuel, or fuel and air flow into it, thereby controlling the speed. ▸ ***verb*** **throttle**

through (**throo**)
1. ***preposition*** In one side and out the other.
2. ***preposition*** To many places in; around.
3. ***preposition*** By way of; because of.
4. ***preposition*** As a result of.
5. ***preposition*** From the beginning to the end of.
6. ***preposition*** In the midst of; among or between.
7. ***preposition*** Finished with.
8. ***adverb*** From one side or end to the other.
9. ***adverb*** Completely.
10. ***adverb*** From beginning to end.
11. ***adjective*** Allowing passage from one end or side to the other.
12. ***adjective*** Finished.

through•out (*throo*-**out**)
1. ***preposition*** All the way through.
2. ***adverb*** In every part; everywhere.

through•way (**throo**-*way*) ***noun*** Another spelling of **thruway.**

throw (**throh**) ***verb***
1. To send through the air; to fling, hurl, or toss. ▸ ***noun*** **throw**
2. To make someone or something fall to the ground.
3. To put on or take off quickly or carelessly.
4. To put in a certain condition or place.
5. *(informal)* If something **throws** you, it confuses you.
6. **throw away** To get rid of something.
7. **throw up** *(informal)* To vomit.

▸ ***verb*** **throwing, threw** (**throo**), **thrown** (**throhn**)

thrush (**thruhsh**) ***noun*** Any of several songbirds. Robins, bluebirds, and nightingales are types of thrushes. ▸ ***noun, plural*** **thrushes**

thrust (**thruhst**)
1. ***verb*** To push something suddenly and hard. ▸ **thrusting, thrust** ▸ ***noun*** **thrust**
2. ***noun*** The forward force produced by the engine of a jet or rocket.
3. ***noun*** The **thrust** of an argument is its main point.

thru•way (**throo**-*way*) ***noun*** A wide highway used for high-speed, long-distance travel. A thruway usually has four or more lanes.

thud (**thuhd**) ***noun*** The dull thump made when a heavy object falls to the ground. ▸ ***verb*** **thud**

thug (**thuhg**) ***noun*** A rough, violent person.

thumb (**thuhm**)
1. ***noun*** The short, thick finger that you have on each hand.
2. ***verb*** To turn over the pages of a book. ▸ **thumbing, thumbed**
3. If someone is **all thumbs,** the person is very clumsy.

thumb•tack (**thuhm**-*tak*) ***noun*** A small pin with a flat, round head, used for fastening paper on bulletin boards, walls, and other surfaces.

T

thump (**thuhmp**)
1. ***noun*** A blow with a blunt, heavy object.
2. ***noun*** A dull, heavy sound made by such a blow.
3. ***verb*** To beat heavily and rapidly; to pound or throb. ▸ **thumping, thumped**

thun•der (**thuhn**-dur)
1. ***noun*** The loud, rumbling sound that comes after a flash of lightning. Thunder is caused by the expansion of air that has been heated by lightning.
2. ***verb*** To make a loud noise like thunder. ▸ **thundering, thundered**
▸ ***noun*** **thunder**

thun•der•cloud (**thuhn**-dur-*kloud*) ***noun*** A large cloud charged with static electricity so that it produces lightning and thunder.

thun•der•storm (**thuhn**-dur-*storm*) ***noun*** A rainstorm with thunder and lightning.

Thurs•day (**thurz**-dee *or* **thurz**-*day*) ***noun*** The fifth day of the week, after Wednesday and before Friday.

thus (**THuhss**) ***adverb***
1. In this way.
2. As a result.

thwart (**thwort**) ***verb*** If you **thwart** somebody's plans, you prevent them from happening or succeeding.
▸ **thwarting, thwarted**

thy (**THye**) ***pronoun*** An old word for **your.**

thyme (**time**) ***noun*** An herb related to mint. Its aromatic leaves are used to flavor food. **Thyme** sounds like **time.**

ti•ar•a (tee-**er**-uh *or* tee-**ah**-ruh) ***noun*** A piece of jewelry like a small crown.

tick (**tik**)
1. ***noun*** The light clicking sound that a clock or watch makes.
2. ***verb*** To make such a sound.
3. ***verb*** To mark by ticking.
4. ***noun*** A mark that someone makes to show that an answer is correct or that something has been done.
5. ***verb*** To mark with a tick.
6. ***noun*** A very small insect that looks like a spider. Ticks suck blood from under the skin of animals and people.
7. ***verb*** If you **tick** someone **off,** you make the person extremely angry.
▸ ***verb*** **ticking, ticked**

tick•et (**tik**-it) ***noun***
1. A printed piece of paper or card that proves you have paid to do something, such as ride on a train or sit in a movie theater.
2. A written order to pay a fine or appear in court for breaking a traffic law.
3. A price tag or a label.
4. The list of candidates belonging to a particular political party to be voted on in an election.
▸ ***verb*** **ticket**

tick•le (**tik**-uhl) ***verb***
1. To keep touching or poking someone gently, often causing the person to laugh.
2. To have a tingling or scratching feeling.
3. To please, delight, or amuse.
▸ ***verb*** **tickling, tickled** ▸ ***noun*** **tickle**

tick•lish (**tik**-lish) ***adjective***
1. Easily tickled.
2. Requiring sensitivity or delicate treatment, as in *a ticklish situation.*

tick-tack-toe *or* **tic-tac-toe** (**tik tak toh**) ***noun*** A game played on a grid of nine squares. Two players take turns putting an X or an O in an empty square. The winner is the first person to get three X's or O's in a row.

tidal wave ***noun*** A huge, forceful ocean wave set into motion by an underwater earthquake, a volcanic eruption, or very strong winds.

tid•bit (**tid**-bit) ***noun*** A choice or pleasing bit of food or gossip.

tide (**tide**) ***noun***
1. The constant change in sea level that is caused by the pull of the sun and the moon on the earth. ▸ ***adjective*** **tidal**
2. Something that changes like the tides of the sea.

T

tid•ings (**tye**-dingz) ***noun, plural*** News or information.

ti•dy (**tye**-dee) ***adjective*** Neat, or in proper order. ▸ **tidier, tidiest** ▸ ***noun*** **tidiness** ▸ ***verb*** **tidy**

tie (**tye**)
1. ***verb*** To join two pieces of string or cord together with a knot or bow.
▸ **ties, tying, tied** ▸ ***noun*** **tie**
2. ***noun*** A long piece of fabric that is worn knotted around the collar of a shirt; a necktie.
3. ***noun*** Something that holds or bonds people together, as in *strong family ties.*
4. ***noun*** A situation in which two people or teams have exactly the same score in a competition. ▸ ***verb*** **tie**

tie•break•er (**tye**-*bray*-kur) ***noun*** A special or extra game played to decide a tie game.

tier (**tihr**) ***noun*** One of several rows or layers placed one above the other. A tier can be found in a large structure such as a concert hall or stadium, or on something smaller, like a wedding cake.

ti•ger (**tye**-gur) ***noun*** A large, striped, wild cat that lives in Asia. The tiger is the largest member of the cat family.

tiger lily ***noun*** A type of lily that is shaped like a trumpet and has red or orange flowers and black spots.

tight (**tite**) ***adjective***
1. Fitting closely, as in *tight shoes* or *a tight belt.*
2. Fastened or held firmly; secure, as in *a tight knot* or *a tight grip.*
3. Fully stretched; not loose, as in *a tight rope.*
4. Not letting water or air pass through, as in *a tight seal.*
5. *(informal)* Stingy with money.
6. Having little time to spare.
7. Difficult.
8. Even or almost even in score; close, as in *a tight game.*
▸ ***adjective*** **tighter, tightest** ▸ ***verb*** **tighten** ▸ ***adverb*** **tightly**

tight•rope (**tite**-*rope*) ***noun*** A stretched high wire on which circus performers balance.

tights (**titess**) ***noun, plural*** A garment that fits closely and covers the hips, legs, and feet.

tile (**tile**) ***noun***
A square of stone, plastic, or baked and glazed clay. Tiles are often used for covering floors or walls.

till (**til**)
1. ***preposition and conjunction*** Another word for **until.**
2. ***noun*** A drawer or box in a store, used to hold money; part of a cash register.
3. ***verb*** To prepare land for growing crops. ▸ **tilling, tilled**

till•er (**til**-ur) ***noun*** A handle attached to the rudder of a boat. The tiller is used to steer the boat.

tilt (**tilt**) ***verb*** To lean, tip, or slant to one side. ▸ **tilting, tilted** ▸ ***noun*** **tilt**

tim•ber (**tim**-bur) ***noun***
1. Cut wood used for building; lumber.
2. A long, heavy piece of wood; a beam.
3. Trees; forest, as in *an acre of timber.*

tim•ber•line (**tim**-bur-*line*) ***noun*** The highest point at which trees can grow on a mountain, or the farthest northern point in the arctic regions where trees can grow. The timberline on a mountain is also known as the *tree line.*

time (**time**)
1. ***noun*** The past, present, and future measured in seconds, minutes, hours, and so on.
2. ***noun*** A particular moment shown on a clock or watch. ▸ ***noun*** **timer**
3. ***noun*** A particular period.
4. ***verb*** To measure how long something takes.
5. ***verb*** To choose the moment for something. ▸ ***adjective*** **timely**
6. ***noun*** One in a series of repeated actions.
7. ***noun*** The beat in a piece of music.
Time sounds like **thyme.**
▸ ***verb*** **timing, timed**

T

time•less (**time**-liss) ***adjective***
1. Not affected, changed, or weakened by time, as in *timeless beauty.*
2. Not referring to a particular time or date, as in *a timeless story of good versus evil.*
▸ ***adverb* timelessly**

time•ta•ble (**time**-*tay*-buhl) ***noun*** A printed chart of the times when buses, trains, planes, or boats arrive and depart; a schedule.

time zone ***noun*** A region in which the same time is used. The earth is divided into 24 time zones. Each zone is 15 degrees of longitude in width and usually observes a clock time one hour earlier than the zone immediately to its east.

tim•id (**tim**-id) ***adjective*** Shy and easily frightened. ▸ ***noun* timidity** (ti-**mid**-i-tee) ▸ ***adverb* timidly**

tin (**tin**) ***noun***
1. A soft, silvery metal that does not rust easily. It is used to coat steel cans and can be mixed with other metals to make pewter and bronze. Tin is a chemical element.
2. A container that is made of or coated with tin.

tin•foil (**tin**-*foil*) ***noun*** A paper-thin, flexible sheet of tin or aluminum used for wrapping food.

tinge (**tinj**) ***noun***
1. A very small amount of added color.
2. A slight trace.
▸ ***verb* tinge**

tin•gle (**ting**-guhl) ***verb*** To sting, prick, or tickle. ▸ **tingling, tingled** ▸ ***noun* tingle**

tin•ker (**ting**-kur)
1. ***verb*** To make repairs in a clumsy or unskilled way. ▸ **tinkering, tinkered**
2. ***noun*** A person who travels from place to place mending pots, pans, and other metal kitchen utensils.

tin•kle (**ting**-kuhl) ***verb*** To make a light, ringing sound such as that made by a small bell. ▸ **tinkling, tinkled** ▸ ***noun* tinkle**

tint (**tint**)
1. ***noun*** A variety of a color, often one with white added.
2. ***noun*** A pale, delicate color.
3. ***verb*** To give a slight color to.
▸ **tinting, tinted**
▸ ***adjective* tinted**

ti•ny (**tye**-nee) ***adjective*** Very small; minute. ▸ **tinier, tiniest**

tip (**tip**)
1. ***verb*** To make something lean or fall over. ▸ ***noun* tip**
2. ***verb*** To lean or to fall over.
3. ***noun*** The end part or point of something, as in *the tips of the fingers* or *the tip of a spear.*
4. ***noun*** A useful hint, as in *a sewing tip.*
5. ***noun*** A sum of money given in addition to the bill to a taxi driver, waitress, etc., as thanks for his or her services. ▸ ***verb* tip**
6. ***verb*** To raise or touch your hat as a greeting to someone.
▸ ***verb* tipping, tipped**

tip•toe (**tip**-*toh*) ***verb*** To walk very quietly on or as if you were on the tips of your toes. ▸ **tiptoeing, tiptoed**

tire (**tire**)
1. ***noun*** A band of rubber that fits around the rim of a wheel and usually is filled with air.
2. ***verb*** To make or become weak or unable to continue because of a need for rest. ▸ ***adjective* tired**
3. ***verb*** To bore or to become bored.
▸ ***verb* tiring, tired** ▸ ***noun* tiredness**

tire•some (**tire**-suhm) ***adjective*** Tiring, boring, or annoying, as in *tiresome behavior.*

tis•sue (**tish**-oo) ***noun***
1. Soft, thin paper used for wiping, wrapping, etc.
2. A mass of similar cells that form a particular part or organ of an animal or a plant, as in *muscle tissue.*

ti•tle (**tye**-tuhl) ***noun***
1. The name of a book, movie, song, painting, or other work. ▸ ***verb* title**

2. A word used to show a person's status, rank, or occupation. *Ms., Dr., Lord,* and *Senator* are titles.
3. Legal ownership, or a document that shows legal ownership.
4. A championship.

Tlin•git (**tling**-kuht *or* **kling**-kuht) ***noun*** One of a group of American Indians that lives on the islands and coast of southern Alaska. ▸ ***noun, plural*** **Tlingit** *or* **Tlingits**

to (**too**) ***preposition***
1. Toward; in the direction of.
2. As far as.
3. On, against, or in contact with.
4. In or for each.
5. Until.
6. Compared with.
7. For the attention, benefit, or purpose of.
8. Concerning or regarding.
9. Before.
10. Used before a verb to form an infinitive.
11. Used to show the receiver of an action.
12. In agreement with.
To sounds like **too** and **two.**

toad (**tohd**) ***noun*** An amphibian that looks like a frog but has a rougher, drier skin. Toads live mainly on land.

toad•stool (**tohd**-*stool*) ***noun*** A mushroom, especially one that is poisonous.

toast (**tohst**)
1. ***noun*** Bread browned by heat. ▸ ***verb*** **toast**
2. ***verb*** To warm thoroughly.
3. ***verb*** To drink in honor of someone.
▸ ***noun*** **toast**
▸ ***verb*** **toasting, toasted**

toast•er (**tohss**-tur) ***noun*** An electrical appliance that toasts bread.

to•bac•co (tuh-**bak**-oh) ***noun*** The chopped, dried leaves of the tobacco plant. Tobacco is used for smoking or chewing. ▸ ***noun, plural*** **tobaccos**

to•bog•gan (tuh-**bog**-uhn)
1. ***noun*** A long, flat sled with a front edge that turns up. A toboggan has no runners.
2. ***verb*** To travel by toboggan, especially downhill. ▸ **tobogganing, tobogganed**

to•day (tuh-**day**)
1. ***noun*** This present day or time.
2. ***adverb*** On or during this day.
3. ***adverb*** Nowadays, or at the present time.

tod•dler (**tod**-lur) ***noun*** A young child who has just learned to walk.

toe (**toh**) ***noun***
1. One of the five slender parts at the end of your foot.
2. The part of a shoe, boot, sock, or stocking that covers the toes.
Toe sounds like **tow.**

tof•fee (**tof**-ee) ***noun*** A hard, chewy candy made by boiling sugar and butter together.

to•fu (**toh**-foo) ***noun*** A soft, cheeselike food made from soybeans. Tofu is also called *bean curd.*

to•ga (**toh**-guh) ***noun*** A piece of clothing worn by men in ancient Rome. It was wrapped around the body and draped over the left shoulder.

to•geth•er (tuh-**geTH**-ur) ***adverb***
1. With one another.
2. Into one group, mass, or place.
3. At the same time.
4. In agreement or cooperation.

toil (**toil**)
1. ***verb*** To work very hard for a long time.
2. ***verb*** To move slowly with pain or effort.
3. ***noun*** Hard, exhausting work.
▸ ***verb*** **toiling, toiled** ▸ ***noun*** **toiler**

toi•let (**toi**-lit) ***noun***
1. A large bowl that can be flushed with water. A toilet is used for disposing of human wastes.
2. A room containing a toilet; a bathroom.

T

to•ken (**toh**-kuhn) ***noun***
1. Something that stands for something else; a sign or symbol.
2. A piece of stamped metal that can be used in place of money.

tol•er•ance (**tol**-ur-uhnss) ***noun***
1. The willingness to respect or accept the customs, beliefs, or opinions of others.
2. The ability to put up with or endure something such as pain or hardship.
▸ ***adjective* tolerant**

tol•er•ate (**tol**-uh-*rate*) ***verb*** If you **tolerate** something, you put up with it or endure it. ▸ **tolerating, tolerated** ▸ ***noun* toleration**

toll (**tohl**)
1. ***verb*** To ring a bell slowly and regularly. ▸ **tolling, tolled** ▸ ***noun* toll**
2. ***noun*** A charge or tax paid for using a highway, bridge, or tunnel.
3. ***noun*** A charge for a service such as a long-distance telephone call.
4. If something **takes its toll,** it results in serious damage or suffering.

tom•a•hawk (**tom**-uh-*hawk*) ***noun*** A small ax once used by some North American Indians as a tool or weapon.

to•ma•to (tuh-**may**-toh *or* tuh-**mat**-oh) ***noun*** A red, juicy fruit eaten as a vegetable either raw or cooked. ▸ ***noun, plural* tomatoes**

tomb (**toom**) ***noun*** A grave, room, or building for holding a dead body.

tom•boy (**tom**-*boi*) ***noun*** A girl who enjoys activities that were once associated with boys, such as climbing trees or playing football.

tomb•stone (**toom**-*stone*) ***noun*** A carved block of stone that marks the place where someone is buried. It usually gives the dead person's name and dates of birth and death.

tom•cat (**tom**-*kat*) ***noun*** A male cat.

to•mor•row (tuh-**mor**-oh) ***noun***
1. The day after today.
2. The future, as in *the world of tomorrow.*
▸ ***adverb* tomorrow**

ton (**tuhn**) ***noun*** A unit of weight equal to 2,000 pounds in the United States and Canada and 2,240 pounds in Great Britain. A small automobile weighs about one ton.

tone (**tohn**) ***noun***
1. A single sound, especially one that is musical, thought of in terms of its pitch, length, quality, or loudness, as in *the deep tones of an organ.*
2. A way of speaking or writing that shows a certain feeling or attitude.
3. The general quality, feeling, or style of something.
4. In music, a **tone** is the difference in pitch between two musical notes.
5. A tint or shade of a color.
6. The normal, healthy firmness of the muscles.

tongs (**tongz** *or* **tawngz**) ***noun, plural*** A tool with two connected arms used for picking up things.

tongue (**tuhng**) ***noun***
1. The movable muscle in your mouth that is used for tasting, swallowing, and talking.
2. The tongue of an animal such as a cow, cooked and used as food.
3. A language.
4. The ability to speak.
5. The flap of material under the laces of a shoe.
6. When you **hold your tongue,** you stop yourself from saying something.

tongue twister ***noun*** A sentence or verse that is very hard to say or repeat quickly, such as "red leather, yellow leather."

ton•ic (**ton**-ik) ***noun*** Something that makes you feel stronger or refreshed.

to•night (tuh-**nite**) ***noun*** This evening or night. ▸ ***adverb* tonight**

ton•sil•li•tis (*ton*-suh-**lye**-tiss) ***noun*** An illness that makes your tonsils infected and painful.

ton•sils (**ton**-suhlz) ***noun, plural*** Two flaps of soft tissue that lie one on each side of the throat.

too (**too**) ***adverb***
1. As well; also; in addition.
2. More than enough.
3. Very; extremely.
Too sounds like **to** and **two.**

tool (**tool**) ***noun***
1. A piece of equipment that you use to do a particular job.
2. Anything that helps you accomplish something.

tool•box (**tool**-*boks*) ***noun*** A box designed for storing or carrying hand tools.

toot (**toot**) ***verb*** To sound a horn or whistle in short blasts. ▸ **tooting, tooted** ▸ ***noun*** **toot**

tooth (**tooth**) ***noun***
1. One of the white, bony parts of your mouth that you use for biting and chewing food.
2. One of a row of parts that stick out on a saw, comb, or gear.
▸ ***noun, plural*** **teeth**

tooth•ache (**tooth**-*ake*) ***noun*** A pain in or near a tooth.

tooth•brush (**tooth**-*bruhsh*) ***noun*** A small brush that is used to clean the teeth.

tooth•paste (**tooth**-*payst*) ***noun*** A paste that is put on a toothbrush and used to clean the teeth.

tooth•pick (**tooth**-*pik*) ***noun*** A small, thin piece of wood or plastic that is used to remove food from between the teeth.

top (**top**)
1. ***noun*** The highest point or part of something, as in *the top of a hill* or *the top of a page.*
2. ***noun*** A cover or a lid, as in *a bottle top.*
3. ***noun*** The highest rank or position.
4. ***noun*** A piece of clothing for the upper part of your body.
5. ***noun*** The highest or greatest degree or pitch.
6. ***verb*** To do better than. ▸ **topping, topped**
7. ***noun*** A toy that is shaped like a cone and spins on a pointed end.
▸ ***verb*** **top** ▸ ***adjective*** **top**

to•paz (**toh**-paz) ***noun*** A clear mineral that is used as a gem. It is usually a color ranging from yellow to brown.

top•ic (**top**-ik) ***noun*** The subject of a discussion, study, lesson, speech, or piece of writing.

top•i•cal (**top**-uh-kuhl) ***adjective***
1. Of interest now; in the news at present.
2. A **topical** anesthetic is used to make a specific part of the body numb.

to•pog•ra•phy (tuh-**pog**-ruh-fee) ***noun*** The detailed description of the physical features of an area, including hills, valleys, mountains, plains, and rivers.
▸ ***noun*** **topographer**

top•ple (**top**-uhl) ***verb***
1. To fall over, usually from a height.
2. To make something fall, as in *to topple a government.*
▸ ***verb*** **toppling, toppled**

top•soil (**top**-*soil*) ***noun*** The top or surface layer of soil. Topsoil is good for planting because it contains decaying leaves, grass, and other organic matter.

top•sy-tur•vy (**top**-see **tur**-vee) ***adjective*** Upside down, mixed-up, or confused. ▸ ***adverb*** **topsy-turvy**

To•rah (**tor**-uh *or* **toh**-ruh) ***noun*** The sacred scroll kept in a Jewish synagogue on which is written in Hebrew the first five books of the Bible: Genesis, Exodus, Leviticus, Numbers, and Deuteronomy.

torch (**torch**)
1. ***noun*** A flaming light that can be carried in the hand.
2. ***noun*** A tool that gives off a very hot flame used to weld or cut metals; a blowtorch.
3. ***verb*** If you **torch** somethng, you set fire to it.
▸ **torches, torching, torched**
▸ ***noun, plural*** **torches**

to•re•a•dor (**tor**-ee-uh-*dor*) ***noun*** A bullfighter.

T

T

tor•ment
1. (tor-**ment**) ***verb*** To upset or annoy someone deliberately. ▸ **tormenting, tormented** ▸ ***noun*** **tormentor**
2. (**tor**-ment) ***noun*** Great pain or suffering.

tor•na•do (tor-**nay**-doh) ***noun*** A violent, whirling column of air that appears as a dark cloud shaped like a funnel. A tornado travels rapidly and usually destroys everything in its narrow path. ▸ ***noun, plural*** **tornadoes** *or* **tornados**

tor•pe•do (tor-**pee**-doh) ***noun*** An underwater missile that explodes when it hits a target, such as a ship. ▸ ***noun, plural*** **torpedoes** ▸ ***verb*** **torpedo**

tor•rent (**tor**-uhnt) ***noun*** A violent, swiftly flowing stream of water or any liquid. ▸ ***adjective*** **torrential**

tor•rid (**tor**-id) ***adjective*** Extremely hot; burning; scorching, as in *a torrid climate.* ▸ ***noun*** **torridness** ▸ ***adverb*** **torridly**

tor•so (**tor**-soh) ***noun*** The part of your body between your neck and your waist, not including your arms; the trunk. ▸ ***noun, plural*** **torsos**

tor•til•la (tor-**tee**-yuh) ***noun*** A round, flat bread made from cornmeal or flour. Tortillas are often served with a topping or filling.

tor•toise (**tor**-tuhss) ***noun*** A turtle, especially one that lives on land.

tor•ture (**tor**-chur)
1. ***verb*** To cause someone extreme pain or mental suffering. ▸ **torturing, tortured**
2. ***noun*** The act of causing extreme pain as a punishment or as a way of forcing someone to do or say something against his or her will.
3. ***noun*** Extreme pain or mental suffering; torment.

toss (**tawss**) ***verb***
1. To throw something with little force.
2. To move, fling, or rock back and forth.
3. To mix a salad lightly.
4. To throw a coin into the air to decide something according to which side lands face up.
▸ ***verb*** **tosses, tossing, tossed** ▸ ***noun*** **toss** ▸ ***adjective*** **tossed**

tot (**tot**) ***noun*** A small child.

to•tal (**toh**-tuhl)
1. ***adjective*** Making up the whole amount; entire.
2. ***adjective*** Complete; utter. ▸ ***adverb*** **totally**
3. ***noun*** A number gotten by adding; a sum. ▸ ***verb*** **total**
4. ***verb*** *(informal)* To completely demolish. ▸ **totaling, totaled**

tote (**toht**) ***verb*** To carry or haul something. ▸ **toting, toted**

to•tem pole (**toh**-tuhm) ***noun*** A pole carved and painted with animals, plants, and other natural objects that represent a family or clan. Certain North American Indians placed totem poles in front of their homes.

tot•ter (**tot**-ur) ***verb***
1. To walk in an unsteady way.
2. To tremble or rock as if about to fall; to sway.
▸ ***verb*** **tottering, tottered**

tou•can (**too**-kan) ***noun*** A brightly colored tropical American bird that has a very large beak.

touch (**tuhch**)
1. ***verb*** To make contact with your hand or another area of your body.
2. ***verb*** To make gentle contact with another object.
3. ***noun*** The act of touching.
4. ***verb*** To affect emotionally.
5. ***noun*** Your sense of **touch** is your ability to feel things with your fingers or other parts of your body.
6. ***noun*** A very small amount.
7. If you **keep in touch** with someone, you contact the person regularly by telephone, letter, E-mail, etc.
▸ ***noun, plural*** **touches** ▸ ***verb*** **touches, touching, touched**

touch•down (**tuhch**-*doun*) ***noun***
1. In football, a play in which the ball is

carried over the opponent's goal line, scoring six points.
2. The moment when an aircraft or a spacecraft lands.

touch•ing (**tuhch**-ing) ***adjective*** Something that is **touching** makes you feel compassion, sympathy, or other tender emotions. ▸ ***adverb*** **touchingly**

touch•y (**tuhch**-ee) ***adjective*** Irritable and easily annoyed; sensitive.
▸ **touchier, touchiest** ▸ ***noun*** **touchiness**

tough (**tuhf**) ***adjective***
1. Strong and difficult to damage, as in *tough boots.*
2. Hard to cut or chew, as in *tough meat.*
3. Difficult to deal with or do, as in *a tough decision.*
4. Able to stand strain or hardship; rugged.
5. Stubborn, as in *a tough stain.*
6. Rough or violent, as in *a tough neighborhood.*
7. Unhappy or unlucky, as in *a tough life.*
▸ ***adjective*** **tougher, toughest**

tou•pee (too-**pay**) ***noun*** A wig used to cover a man's baldness.

tour (**toor**) ***noun***
1. A trip around a set route, often for sightseeing. ▸ ***verb*** **tour**
2. When a band, team, or theater group goes **on tour,** it travels to different places to play or perform.

tour•ist (**toor**-ist) ***noun*** Someone who travels and visits places for pleasure.
▸ ***noun*** **tourism**

tour•na•ment (**tur**-nuh-muhnt) ***noun***
1. A series of contests in which a number of people or teams try to win the championship, as in *a tennis tournament* or *a chess tournament.*
2. In the Middle Ages, **tournaments** were events in which knights jousted against each other.

tour•ni•quet (**tur**-nuh-ket) ***noun*** A bandage or band twisted tightly around a limb to prevent a wound or cut from bleeding too much.

tout (**tout**) ***verb*** To praise or publicize in a loud or exaggerated way. ▸ **touting, touted**

tow (**toh**) ***verb*** To pull something behind you, usually with a rope or chain. **Tow** sounds like **toe.** ▸ **towing, towed**
▸ ***noun*** **tow**

to•ward (**tord** *or* tuh-**word**) *or* **to•wards** (**tordz** *or* tuh-**wordz**) ***preposition***
1. In the direction of.
2. With regard to; concerning.
3. Just before; near.
4. In order to buy; for.

tow•el (**tou**-uhl) ***noun*** A piece of soft cloth or paper that is used for drying or wiping. ▸ ***verb*** **towel**

tow•er (**tou**-ur)
1. ***noun*** A tall structure that is thin in relation to its height.
2. ***verb*** To be very tall and dominant.
▸ **towering, towered** ▸ ***adjective*** **towering**

town (**toun**) ***noun*** A place that has houses, stores, offices, schools, etc. A town is larger than a village but smaller than a city.

tox•ic (**tok**-sik) ***adjective*** Poisonous, as in *toxic waste.* ▸ ***noun*** **toxin,** ***noun*** **toxicity** (tok-**si**-si-tee)

toy (**toi**)
1. ***noun*** An object that children play with.
2. ***verb*** If you **toy** with something, you handle or treat it in a halfhearted, careless way. ▸ **toying, toyed**

trace (**trayss**)
1. ***verb*** To follow the trail, path, or course of someone or something; to track.
2. ***verb*** To copy a picture or shape by following lines visible through a piece of thin paper. ▸ ***noun*** **tracing**
3. ***verb*** To follow, study, or describe the history or development of something.
4. ***noun*** A visible mark or sign that something has happened or that someone has been somewhere.
▸ ***verb*** **tracing, traced**

T

T

track (**trak**)
1. ***noun*** The marks left behind by a moving animal or person.
2. ***noun*** A path or a trail.
3. ***noun*** A prepared path or course for runners or racing animals.
4. ***noun*** A rail or set of rails for vehicles such as trains and trolleys to run on.
5. ***verb*** To follow someone or something. ▸ **tracking, tracked** ▸ ***noun*** **tracking,** ***noun*** **tracker**

track and field ***noun*** A group of sports events that includes running, jumping, and throwing contests such as the hurdles, pole vault, and shot put.
▸ ***adjective*** **track-and-field**

tract (**trakt**) ***noun***
1. An area or expanse of land.
2. A group of parts or organs in the body that perform a specific function, as in *the digestive tract.*
3. A booklet or pamphlet, especially one on a religious or political subject.

trac•tion (**trak**-shuhn) ***noun*** The friction or gripping power that keeps a moving body from slipping on a surface.

trac•tor (**trak**-tur) ***noun***
1. A powerful vehicle with either large tires that have deep treads or continuous belts of metal treads. Tractors are often used to pull farm machinery or heavy loads.
2. A truck that has a cab and no body. It is used for pulling a trailer.

trade (**trade**)
1. ***noun*** The business of buying and selling goods; commerce. ▸ ***noun*** **trader** ▸ ***verb*** **trade**
2. ***noun*** A particular job or craft, especially one that requires working with the hands or with machines.
3. ***verb*** To exchange one thing for another. ▸ **trading, traded** ▸ ***noun*** **trade**

trade•mark (**trade**-*mark*) ***noun*** A word, picture, or design that shows that a product is made by a particular company. A trademark is usually registered with the government. It can legally be used only by the owner.
▸ ***verb*** **trademark**

trading post ***noun*** A store in a wilderness area where people can exchange local products such as furs or hides for food and supplies.

tra•di•tion (truh-**dish**-uhn) ***noun***
1. The handing down of customs, ideas, and beliefs from one generation to the next.
2. A custom, an idea, or a belief that is handed down in this way.
▸ ***adjective*** **traditional**

traf•fic (**traf**-ik)
1. ***noun*** Moving vehicles.
2. ***verb*** To buy and sell goods, especially illegally. ▸ **trafficking, trafficked** ▸ ***noun*** **trafficking**

traffic light ***noun*** A set of lights that control traffic. Traffic lights are usually placed where streets intersect.

trag•e•dy (**traj**-uh-dee) ***noun***
1. A serious play with a sad ending.
2. A very sad event.
▸ ***noun, plural*** **tragedies**

trag•ic (**traj**-ik) ***adjective***
1. To do with or in the style of a tragedy or sad story.
2. Extremely unfortunate, or disastrous, as in *a tragic accident.*
▸ ***adverb*** **tragically**

trail (**trayl**)
1. ***noun*** A track or path for people to follow, especially in the woods.
2. ***noun*** A mark, scent, or path left behind by an animal or a person.
3. ***noun*** Something that follows along behind, as in *a trail of dust.*
4. ***verb*** To follow the scent or trail of an animal or a person; to track.
5. ***verb*** To follow slowly behind others.
▸ ***verb*** **trailing, trailed**

trail bike ***noun*** A light, strong motorcycle built for cross-country racing and riding.

trail•er (**trayl**-ur) ***noun***
1. A vehicle that is towed by a car or

truck and used to carry things.
2. A mobile home.
3. A short piece of film used to advertise a movie or television program to be shown in the future.

train (**trane**)
1. ***noun*** A string of railroad cars powered by steam, diesel fuel, or electricity.
2. ***noun*** A group of people, animals, or vehicles traveling in a line, as in *a mule train* or *a wagon train.*
3. ***verb*** To prepare oneself by practicing, learning, or drilling.
4. ***verb*** To teach a person or an animal how to do something.
5. ***verb*** To bring up children a certain way.
6. ***verb*** To make a plant grow in a certain direction or shape.
7. ***noun*** The long piece of fabric that trails behind a bride's dress.
▸ ***noun*** **training** ▸ ***verb*** **training, trained**

train•er (**tray**-nur) ***noun***
1. A person who trains circus animals, show animals, or pets.
2. A person who helps athletes get in the best condition to compete in a sports event or exhibition.

traipse (**trayps**) ***verb*** To walk or travel about without a plan or purpose.
▸ **traipsing, traipsed**

trait (**trate**) ***noun*** A quality or characteristic that makes one person or thing different from another.

trai•tor (**tray**-tur) ***noun***
1. Someone who aids the enemy of his or her country; a person who betrays his or her country or commits treason.
2. Someone who is unfaithful or false to a friend, cause, or trust.

tramp (**tramp**)
1. ***verb*** To walk or tread with heavy steps.
2. ***verb*** To go for a long walk or hike.
▸ ***noun*** **tramp**
3. ***noun*** Someone who wanders from place to place and does not have a permanent home.
4. ***noun*** The sound made by heavy steps.
▸ ***verb*** **tramping, tramped**

tram•ple (**tram**-puhl) ***verb*** To damage or crush something by walking heavily all over it. ▸ **trampling, trampled**

tram•po•line (*tram*-puh-**leen** *or* **tram**-puh-*leen*) ***noun*** A piece of canvas attached to a frame by elastic ropes or springs. Trampolines are used for jumping, either as a sport or for pleasure.

trance (**transs**) ***noun*** If you are **in a trance,** you are in a conscious state but not really aware of what is happening around you.

tran•quil (**trang**-kwuhl) ***adjective*** Calm and peaceful. ▸ ***noun*** **tranquillity** *or* **tranquility**

trans•ac•tion (tran-**zak**-shuhn) ***noun*** An exchange of goods, services, or money. ▸ ***verb*** **transact**

trans•at•lan•tic (*tran*-suht-**lan**-tik *or* *tran*-zuht-**lan**-tik) ***adjective***
1. Crossing the Atlantic Ocean.
2. On or from the other side of the Atlantic.

trans•con•ti•nen•tal (*transs*-kon-tuh-**nen**-tuhl) ***adjective*** Crossing a continent.

trans•fer
1. (transs-**fur** *or* **transs**-fur) ***verb*** To move from one person or place to another. ▸ ***noun*** **transfer** (**transs**-fur)
2. (**transs**-fur) ***verb*** To change from one vehicle or method of transportation to another.
3. (**transs**-fur) ***noun*** A printed ticket that permits you to change from one vehicle or route to another without paying more money.
4. (**transs**-fur) ***noun*** A small picture or design that can be stuck to another surface by rubbing or ironing.
▸ ***noun*** **transferal** ▸ ***verb*** **transferring, transferred**

T

trans•form (transs-**form**) ***verb*** To make a great change in something. ▸ **transforming, transformed** ▸ ***noun*** **transformation**

trans•form•er (transs-**for**-mur) ***noun*** A piece of equipment that changes the voltage of an electric current.

trans•fu•sion (transs-**fyoo**-zhuhn) ***noun*** The injection of blood from one person into the body of someone else who is injured or ill.

tran•sient (**tran**-shuhnt)
1. ***adjective*** Lasting for only a short time, as in *a transient illness.*
2. ***noun*** A person without a permanent home who moves from place to place.

tran•sis•tor (tran-**ziss**-tur) ***noun*** A small electronic device that controls the flow of electric current in radios, television sets, computers, etc.

tran•sit (**tran**-sit *or* **tran**-zit) ***noun***
1. A system for carrying people or goods from one place to another on trains, buses, and other vehicles; a public transportation system.
2. If people or goods are **in transit,** they are in the process of going from one place to another.

tran•si•tion (tran-**zish**-uhn) ***noun*** A change from one form, condition, or place to another.

tran•si•tive (**tran**-suh-tiv) ***adjective*** A **transitive** verb needs an object in order to complete its meaning. *See* **intransitive.**

trans•late (transs-**late** *or* **transs**-late) ***verb*** To express in a different language. ▸ **translating, translated** ▸ ***noun*** **translation,** ***noun*** **translator**

trans•lu•cent (transs-**loo**-suhnt) ***adjective*** A **translucent** substance is not completely clear like glass but will let some light through. ▸ ***noun*** **translucence**

trans•mis•sion (transs-**mish**-uhn) ***noun***
1. The act of transmitting or sending something from one person or place to another.
2. Something that is transmitted, such as a telegram.
3. In an automobile, a series of gears that send power from the engine to the wheels.

trans•mit (transs-**mit**) ***verb***
1. To send or pass something from one place or person to another, as in *to transmit a message* or *to transmit a disease.*
2. To send out radio or television signals. ▸ ***noun*** **transmitter**
3. To cause or allow something such as light, heat, or sound to pass through a material or substance.
▸ ***verb*** **transmitting, transmitted**

tran•som (**tran**-suhm) ***noun***
1. A small window over a door or another window.
2. If something comes **over the transom,** you did not request it or arrange to receive it.

trans•par•en•cy (transs-**pair**-uhn-see *or* transs-**pa**-ruhn-see) ***noun*** Something transparent, especially a photographic slide. ▸ ***noun, plural*** **transparencies**

trans•par•ent (transs-**pair**-uhnt *or* transs-**pa**-ruhnt) ***adjective***
1. A **transparent** substance is clear like glass and lets light through so that objects on the other side can be seen clearly.
2. Obvious or clear, as in *a transparent lie.*

tran•spi•ra•tion (*transs*-puh-**ray**-shuhn) ***noun*** The process by which plants give off moisture into the atmosphere. ▸ ***verb*** **transpire**

trans•plant
1. (transs-**plant**) ***verb*** To dig up a plant and plant it somewhere else. ▸ **transplanting, transplanted** ▸ ***noun*** **transplant** (**transs**-plant)
2. (**transs**-plant) ***noun*** A surgical operation in which a diseased organ such as a kidney is replaced by a healthy one. ▸ ***verb*** **transplant** (transs-**plant**)

trans•port
1. (transs-**port**) ***verb*** To move people and freight from one place to another.
▸ ***noun*** **transport** (**transs**-port)
2. (**transs**-port) ***noun*** A vehicle that carries people or freight, such as a ship or plane.
3. (transs-**port**) ***verb*** To fill or overwhelm with strong emotion.
▸ ***verb*** **transporting, transported**

trans•por•ta•tion (*transs*-pur-**tay**-shuhn) ***noun*** A means or system for moving people and freight from one place to another.

trap (**trap**)
1. ***noun*** A device for capturing an animal.
2. ***noun*** Anything used to trick or catch someone.
3. ***verb*** To capture a person or an animal in a trap. ▸ **trapping, trapped**
▸ ***noun*** **trapper**

trap•door (**trap-dor**) ***noun*** A door in a floor, ceiling, or roof.

tra•peze (tra-**peez** *or* truh-**peez**) ***noun*** A horizontal bar hanging from two ropes. A trapeze is used by circus performers and gymnasts.

tra•pe•zi•um (truh-**pee**-zee-uhm) ***noun*** A shape with four sides, none of which is parallel to another. ▸ ***noun, plural*** **trapeziums** *or* **trapezia** (truh-**pee**-zee-uh)

trap•e•zoid (**trap**-uh-zoid) ***noun*** A shape with four sides of which only two are parallel.

trap•per (**trap**-ur) ***noun*** Someone who makes a living by trapping wild animals, usually for their fur.

trash (**trash**) ***noun***
1. Things that you have thrown away because they are worthless; garbage.
2. Nonsense.

trau•ma (**traw**-muh *or* **trou**-muh) ***noun***
1. A severe and painful emotional shock.
2. A severe physical wound or injury.

trau•mat•ic (traw-**mat**-ik) ***adjective*** If something is **traumatic,** it is shocking and very upsetting.

trav•el (**trav**-uhl) ***verb***
1. To go from one place to another; to take a trip. ▸ ***noun*** **travel** ▸ ***adjective*** **traveling**
2. To pass or to move; to be transmitted.
3. In basketball, to move illegally by failing to dribble the ball while walking or running.
▸ ***verb*** **traveling, traveled**

travel agent ***noun*** A person or company that organizes travel and vacations for its customers. ▸ ***noun*** **travel agency**

trav•el•er (**trav**-uh-lur) ***noun*** Someone who travels.

trawl•er (**traw**-lur) ***noun*** A fishing boat that drags a large net shaped like a bag through the water. ▸ ***verb*** **trawl**

tray (**tray**) ***noun*** A flat, shallow container with a low rim. Trays are used for carrying, holding, or displaying things.

treach•er•ous (**trech**-ur-uhss) ***adjective***
1. Not to be trusted; disloyal, as in *a treacherous spy.* ▸ ***noun*** **treachery**
2. Dangerous; hazardous.
▸ ***adverb*** **treacherously**

tread (**tred**)
1. ***verb*** To walk on, over, or along.
2. ***verb*** To press or crush with the feet; to trample.
3. ***noun*** The flat, horizontal part of a step.
4. ***noun*** The ridges on a car tire or the sole of a shoe that help prevent slipping.
5. If you **tread water,** you swim in one place with your body in a vertical position.
▸ ***verb*** **treading, trod** (**trod**), **trodden** (**trod**-in)

tread•mill (**tred**-*mil*) ***noun*** A device that is worked by a continuously moving belt or the moving steps of a wheel. Some treadmills are used for exercise.

T

trea•son (**tree**-zuhn) ***noun*** The crime of betraying your country by spying for another country or by helping an enemy during a war.

treas•ure (**trezh**-ur)
1. ***noun*** Gold, jewels, money, or other valuable things that have been collected or hidden, as in *buried treasure.*
2. ***verb*** To love and value very highly something that you have or own.
▸ **treasuring, treasured** ▸ ***noun*** **treasure** ▸ ***adjective*** **treasured**

treas•ur•er (**trezh**-ur-ur) ***noun*** The person in charge of the money of a government, company, or club.

treas•ur•y (**trezh**-ur-ee) ***noun***
1. The funds of a government, company, or club.
2. Treasury A government department that is in charge of collecting taxes and managing the public's money.
3. A place where money or treasure is stored.
▸ ***noun, plural*** **treasuries**

treat (**treet**) ***verb***
1. To deal with or act toward people or things in a certain way.
2. To try to cure or heal; to give medical attention to.
3. To process something in order to change it in some way.
4. To give someone a special gift or take someone someplace special. ▸ ***noun*** **treat**
▸ ***verb*** **treating, treated** ▸ ***noun*** **treatment**

trea•ty (**tree**-tee) ***noun*** A formal agreement between two or more countries. ▸ ***noun, plural*** **treaties**

treb•le (**treb**-uhl)
1. ***adjective*** Three times as big or three times as many; triple.
2. ***adjective*** High in pitch, as in *a treble recorder.*
3. ***verb*** To increase to three times the original amount; to triple. ▸ **trebling, trebled**
4. ***noun*** The highest musical part, voice, or instrument.

tree (**tree**)
1. ***noun*** A large, woody plant with a long trunk, roots, branches, and leaves.
2. ***verb*** To pursue and chase up a tree.
▸ **treeing, treed**
3. ***noun*** Something that looks like a tree, such as the branching diagram used to show family relationships or a pole for hanging up clothes.

trek (**trek**) ***verb*** To make a slow, difficult journey. ▸ **trekking, trekked** ▸ ***noun*** **trek**

trel•lis (**trel**-iss) ***noun*** A crisscross framework of thin strips of wood. Trellises are used to support growing plants. ▸ ***noun, plural*** **trellises**

trem•ble (**trem**-buhl) ***verb***
1. To shake, especially from cold, fear, or excitement.
2. To vibrate; to quiver or quake.
▸ ***verb*** **trembling, trembled**

tre•men•dous (tri-**men**-duhss) ***adjective***
1. Huge or enormous.
2. Very good or excellent.
▸ ***adverb*** **tremendously**

trem•or (**trem**-ur) ***noun*** A shaking or trembling movement.

trench (**trench**) ***noun*** A long, narrow ditch, especially one used to protect soldiers in battle. ▸ ***noun, plural*** **trenches**

trend (**trend**) ***noun***
1. The general direction in which things are changing. ▸ ***verb*** **trend**
2. The latest fashion. ▸ ***adjective*** **trendy**

tres•pass (**tress**-puhss *or* **tress**-pass)
1. ***verb*** To enter someone's private property without permission.
▸ **trespasses, trespassing, trespassed** ▸ ***noun*** **trespasser**
2. ***noun*** A sin. ▸ ***noun, plural*** **trespasses** ▸ ***verb*** **trespass**

tress (**tress**) ***noun***
1. A lock of long hair. ▸ ***noun, plural*** **tresses**

2. tresses *noun, plural* A woman's or girl's hair, especially when it is worn long and loose.

tres•tle (**tress**-uhl) ***noun*** A framework that supports a bridge or railroad track.

tri•al (**trye**-uhl) ***noun***
1. The examination of evidence in a court of law to decide if a charge or claim is true.
2. The act of trying or testing something; a test.
3. A frustrating or difficult experience that tests a person's faith, strength, or patience.

tri•an•gle (**trye**-ang-guhl) ***noun***
1. A closed shape with three straight sides and three angles. ▸ ***adjective* triangular**
2. A triangular percussion instrument made of steel. You play the triangle by striking it with a small metal rod.

tri•ath•lon (trye-**ath**-lon) ***noun*** A long-distance race made up of three parts—usually, but not always, swimming, bicycling, and running. ▸ ***noun* triathlete** (trye-**ath**-leet)

tribe (**tribe**) ***noun*** A group of people who share the same ancestors, customs, and laws. ▸ ***adjective* tribal**

trib•u•la•tion (*trib*-yuh-**lay**-shuhn) ***noun***
1. Severe distress or suffering.
2. A trying experience.

tri•bu•nal (tri-**byoo**-nuhl *or* trye-**byoo**-nuhl) ***noun*** A court of law.

trib•u•tar•y (**trib**-yuh-*ter*-ee) ***noun*** A stream or river that flows into a larger stream or river. ▸ ***noun, plural* tributaries**

trib•ute (**trib**-yoot) ***noun*** Something done, given, or said to show thanks or respect.

tri•cer•a•tops (trye-**ser**-uh-*tops*) ***noun*** A large dinosaur that fed on plants and had three horns and a bony collar in the shape of a fan at the back of its head. ▸ ***noun, plural* triceratops** *or* **triceratopses**

trich•i•no•sis (*trik*-uh-**noh**-siss) ***noun*** A disease caused by tiny worms often found in pork that has not been fully cooked. The symptoms include fever, diarrhea, and painful muscles.

trick (**trik**)
1. ***verb*** To fool or cheat someone; to make someone believe something that is not true. ▸ **tricking, tricked** ▸ ***noun* trick, *noun* trickery**
2. ***noun*** A clever or skillful act, as in *a magic trick.*
3. ***noun*** A prank or a practical joke.

trick•le (**trik**-uhl) ***verb*** To flow very slowly in a thin stream, or to fall in drops. ▸ **trickling, trickled** ▸ ***noun* trickle**

trick or treat ***noun*** A Halloween custom in which children go from house to house asking for treats and threatening to play tricks if something is not given. ▸ ***verb* trick-or-treat**

trick•y (**trik**-ee) ***adjective***
1. Likely to use tricks; crafty.
2. Difficult in an unexpected way; requiring careful thought or handling, as in *a tricky question* or *a tricky situation.* ▸ ***adjective* trickier, trickiest**

tri•cy•cle (**trye**-suh-kuhl *or* **trye**-sik-uhl) ***noun*** A children's vehicle that has three wheels.

tri•fle (**trye**-fuhl)
1. ***noun*** Something that is not very valuable or important. ▸ ***adjective* trifling**
2. ***noun*** A small amount; a bit.
3. ***verb*** To play with or not take seriously. ▸ **trifling, trifled**

trig•ger (**trig**-ur)
1. ***noun*** The lever on a gun that you pull to fire it.
2. ***verb*** To cause something to happen as a reaction. ▸ **triggering, triggered**

tril•o•gy (**tril**-uh-jee) ***noun*** A group of three related plays, novels, programs, etc., that together make a series. ▸ ***noun, plural* trilogies**

T

trim (**trim**)
1. ***verb*** To cut small pieces off something in order to improve its shape or to get rid of excess.
2. ***adjective*** Neat, tidy, or in good condition. ▸ **trimmer, trimmest**
3. ***verb*** To add ornaments or decorations to something, as in *to trim a tree* or *to trim a gown.*
▸ ***noun*** **trim**
▸ ***verb*** **trimming, trimmed**

trim·ming (**trim**-ing)
1. ***noun*** Something used as a decoration.
2. trimmings ***noun, plural*** The things that are added to or that go with something.

tri·o (**tree**-oh) ***noun***
1. A group of three things or people.
2. A piece of music that is played or sung by three people.
▸ ***noun, plural*** **trios**

trip (**trip**)
1. ***verb*** To stumble and/or fall.
2. ***verb*** To cause someone to stumble and/or fall.
3. ***noun*** A journey and/or a visit, as in *a trip to the zoo.*
4. ***verb*** To make a mistake.
▸ ***verb*** **tripping, tripped**

tripe (**tripe**) ***noun***
1. The lining of the stomach of an ox or a cow. Tripe is eaten as food.
2. *(informal)* Anything that is useless or worthless.

trip·le (**trip**-uhl)
1. ***adjective*** Three times as big, or three times as many. ▸ ***verb*** **triple**
2. ***adjective*** Made up of three parts.
3. ***verb*** In baseball, to get a hit that allows you to reach third base.
▸ **tripling, tripled** ▸ ***noun*** **triple**

trip·let (**trip**-lit) ***noun*** One of three children born at the same birth.

tri·pod (**trye**-*pod*) ***noun*** A stand with three legs that is used to steady a camera or other piece of equipment.

tri·umph (**trye**-uhmf) ***noun*** A great victory, success, or achievement. ▸ ***verb*** **triumph** ▸ ***adjective*** **triumphant** (trye-**uhm**-fuhnt)

triv·i·al (**triv**-ee-uhl) ***adjective*** If something is **trivial,** it is not very important. ▸ ***noun, plural*** **trivia**

troll (**trohl**)
1. ***verb*** To fish by trailing a line with bait from behind a slowly moving boat.
▸ **trolling, trolled** ▸ ***noun*** **troller**
2. ***noun*** In fairy tales, a dwarf or giant that lives in a cave, in the hills, or under a bridge.

trol·ley (**trol**-ee) ***noun*** An electric streetcar that runs on tracks and gets its power from an overhead wire.

trom·bone (trom-**bone**) ***noun*** A brass musical instrument with a long, bent tube that can be slid back and forth to change the pitch of the tones.

troop (**troop**)
1. ***noun*** An organized group of soldiers, scouts, etc.
2. ***verb*** To move in a group. ▸ **trooping, trooped**

troop·er (**troo**-pur) ***noun*** A state police officer.

tro·phy (**troh**-fee) ***noun*** A prize or an award such as a silver cup or plaque given to a winning athlete or team or to someone who has done something outstanding. ▸ ***noun, plural*** **trophies**

trop·i·cal (**trop**-uh-kuhl) ***adjective*** To do with or living in the hot, rainy area of the tropics.

tropical fish ***noun*** Any of various small or brightly colored fish that originally come from the tropics. Tropical fish are often kept as pets in aquariums. ▸ ***noun, plural*** **tropical fish** *or* **tropical fishes**

trop·ics (**trop**-iks) ***noun, plural*** The extremely hot area of the earth near the equator.

T

trot (**trot**) ***verb***
1. When a horse **trots,** it moves briskly at a gait between a walk and a canter.
▸ ***noun* trot, *noun* trotter**
2. When a person **trots,** he or she runs slowly or jogs.
▸ ***verb* trotting, trotted**

trou•ble (**truh**-buhl)
1. ***noun*** A difficult, dangerous, or upsetting situation. ▸ ***adjective* troublesome**
2. ***verb*** To disturb or worry someone.
▸ ***adjective* troubling, *adjective* troubled**
3. ***noun*** A cause of difficulty, worry, or annoyance.
4. If you **take the trouble** to do something, you make an extra effort to do it.
5. ***verb*** To ask someone for help, or to make an extra effort.
▸ ***verb* troubling, troubled**

trough (**trawf**) ***noun*** A long, narrow container from which animals can drink or eat.

trou•sers (**trou**-zurz) ***noun, plural*** Another word for **pants.** ▸ ***adjective* trouser**

trout (**trout**) ***noun*** An edible freshwater fish that is related to the salmon.

trow•el (**trou**-uhl) ***noun***
1. A hand tool with a flat blade shaped like a diamond. Trowels are used for laying cement, filling holes in plaster, etc.
2. A hand tool with a small, curved blade, used for planting and other light garden work.

tru•ant (**troo**-uhnt) ***noun*** A student who stays away from school without permission. ▸ ***noun* truancy** ▸ ***adjective* truant**

truce (**trooss**) ***noun*** A temporary agreement to stop fighting.

truck (**truhk**) ***noun*** A large motor vehicle used for carrying goods by road.

trudge (**truhj**) ***verb*** To walk slowly and with effort; to plod. ▸ **trudging, trudged**

true (**troo**) ***adjective***
1. Agreeing with the facts; not false; accurate, as in *a true story.*
2. Loyal or faithful, as in *a true friend.*
3. Real or genuine.
▸ ***adjective* truer, truest** ▸ ***adverb* truly**

trum•pet (**truhm**-pit) ***noun***
1. A brass wind instrument that makes a loud, blaring sound. It has a long, looped tube that flares into a funnel shape and three valves that can be used to change the tones.
2. A loud, blaring sound, such as the cry of an elephant. ▸ ***verb* trumpet**

trunk (**truhngk**) ***noun***
1. The main stem of a tree. Tree trunks contain xylem and phloem vessels, which transport fluids up and down the tree.
2. A large case or box used for storage or for carrying clothes on a long journey.
3. The upper part of your body, not including your head and arms.
4. The long nose of an elephant.
5. An enclosed compartment in a car, usually at the rear, where luggage and a spare tire can be stored.
6. trunks *noun, plural* Shorts worn by men or boys for swimming or boxing.

trust (**truhst**) ***verb*** If you **trust** someone, you believe that he or she is honest and reliable. ▸ **trusting, trusted** ▸ ***noun* trust** ▸ ***adjective* trusting**

trust•wor•thy (**truhst**-*wur*-THee) ***adjective*** Honest, reliable, and able to be trusted, as in *a trustworthy friend.*

trust•y (**truhss**-tee) ***adjective*** Capable of being trusted; reliable; dependable.

truth (**trooth**) ***noun***
1. The real facts. *Is he telling the truth?*
2. The quality of being true, real, honest, or accurate.
▸ ***adjective* truthful** ▸ ***adverb* truthfully**

T

try (**trye**) ***verb***
1. To attempt to do something, or to do the best you can. ▸ ***noun* try**
2. To examine in a court of law someone accused of a criminal offense.
3. To test the quality, strength, or effect of something.
4. To put a strain on; to tax, as in *to try someone's patience.*
▸ ***verb* tries, trying, tried**

try·ing (**trye**-ing) ***adjective*** If a person is very **trying,** he or she is difficult or annoying.

try·out (**trye**-*out*) ***noun*** A trial or test to see if a person is qualified to do something such as perform a role in a play or play on a team; an audition.
▸ ***verb* try out**

tsar (**zar**) *See* **czar.**

tsa·ri·na (za-**ree**-nuh) *See* **czarina.**

T-shirt *or* **tee shirt** (**tee**-*shurt*) ***noun*** A light cotton shirt or undershirt with short sleeves and no collar.

tsu·na·mi (tsoo-**nah**-mee) ***noun*** A very large, destructive wave caused by an underwater earthquake or volcano.

tub (**tuhb**) ***noun***
1. A bathtub.
2. A round, open container used for packing or storing foods, as in *a tub of ice cream.*
3. A large, wide container used for bathing or for washing clothes.

tu·ba (**too**-buh) ***noun*** A large, brass wind instrument with several valves. Tubas have a full, deep tone.

tube (**toob**) ***noun***
1. A long, hollow cylinder, especially one used to carry or hold liquids, as in *a test tube.*
2. A long container made of soft metal or plastic with a cap that screws on, as in *a tube of toothpaste.*
3. The hollow rubber ring that is put inside some bicycle tires and filled with air.
4. the tube *(informal)* Television.

tu·ber (**too**-bur) ***noun*** The thick underground stem of a plant such as a potato.

tu·ber·cu·lo·sis (tu-*bur*-kyuh-**loh**-siss) ***noun*** A highly contagious bacterial disease that usually affects the lungs.

tu·bu·lar (**too**-byuh-lur) ***adjective*** Shaped like a tube.

tuck (**tuhk**)
1. *verb* To fold or push the ends of something into place.
2. *verb* To put to bed and cover snugly.
3. *verb* To put into a snug or hidden place.
4. *noun* A small fold sewn in material.
▸ ***verb* tuck**
▸ ***verb* tucking, tucked**

Tues·day (**tooz**-dee *or* **tooz**-*day*) ***noun*** The third day of the week, after Monday and before Wednesday.

tuft (**tuhft**) ***noun*** A bunch of hair, grass, feathers, etc., attached together at the base. ▸ ***adjective* tufted**

tug (**tuhg**)
1. *verb* To pull hard. ▸ **tugging, tugged**
▸ ***noun* tug**
2. tug *or* **tugboat** (**tuhg**-*boht*) ***noun*** A small, powerful boat that tows or pushes ships and barges.

tug-of-war ***noun*** A contest between two teams, each holding onto opposite ends of a rope, who try to pull each other over a center line.

tu·i·tion (too-**ish**-uhn) ***noun*** Money paid to a private school or college in order for a student to receive instruction there.

tu·lip (**too**-lip) ***noun*** A plant with a tall stem topped with a colorful flower shaped like a cup. Tulips grow from bulbs.

tum·ble (**tuhm**-buhl) ***verb***
1. To fall suddenly and helplessly.
2. To do somersaults, handsprings, or other acrobatic feats. ▸ ***noun* tumbler**
3. To roll or toss about.
4. To move in a hurried, disorderly way.

▸ ***verb*** **tumbling, tumbled** ▸ ***noun*** **tumble**

tum•bler (**tuhm**-blur) ***noun*** A tall drinking glass with straight sides.

tum•ble•weed (**tum**-buhl-*weed*) ***noun*** A bushy plant of western North America that dries up in autumn, breaks off from its roots, and blows around in the wind.

tum•my (**tuhm**-ee) ***noun*** *(informal)* The stomach. ▸ ***noun, plural*** **tummies**

tu•mor (**too**-mur) ***noun*** An abnormal lump or mass of tissue in the body.

tu•mult (**too**-muhlt) ***noun*** Loud noise and confusion. ▸ ***adjective*** **tumultuous** (too-**muhl**-choo-uhss) ▸ ***adverb*** **tumultuously**

tu•na (**too**-nuh) ***noun*** A large, edible fish found in warm seas throughout the world. ▸ ***noun, plural*** **tuna** *or* **tunas**

tun•dra (**tuhn**-druh) ***noun*** A cold area of northern Europe and Asia where there are no trees and the soil under the surface of the ground is permanently frozen.

tune (**toon** *or* **tyoon**)

1. ***noun*** A series of musical notes arranged in a pattern; a simple melody that is easy to remember. ▸ ***adjective*** **tuneful**

2. ***verb*** To adjust the pitch of a musical instrument. ▸ ***noun*** **tuner**

3. ***noun*** The condition of having the correct musical pitch.

4. ***noun*** Harmony; agreement.

5. ***verb*** If you **tune in** a radio or television program or station, you adjust the dial to receive it.

6. ***verb*** If you **tune** a car engine **up,** you put it in good working order by adjusting the parts.

▸ ***verb*** **tuning, tuned**

tu•nic (**too**-nik *or* **tyoo**-nik) ***noun*** A loose, sleeveless garment.

tuning fork ***noun*** A piece of metal with two prongs used for tuning musical instruments. When struck, it vibrates to produce a particular tone.

tun•nel (**tuhn**-uhl) ***noun***

1. A passage built beneath the ground or water or through a mountain for use by cars, trains, or other vehicles.

2. An animal's burrow. ▸ ***verb*** **tunnel**

tunnel vision ***noun***

1. The condition in which the eye has no peripheral vision but sees things as if through a tunnel.

2. An extremely narrow outlook on things, without consideration of possible alternatives.

tur•ban (**tur**-buhn) ***noun*** A head covering made by winding a long scarf around the head or around a cap. Turbans are worn especially by men in Arab countries and India.

tur•bine (**tur**-buhn *or* **tur**-bine) ***noun*** An engine driven by water, steam, or gas passing through the blades of a wheel and making it revolve.

tur•bo (**tur**-boh) ***adjective*** A **turbo** or **turbo-charged** engine has high-pressure air forced into its cylinders by a turbine, producing extra power.

tur•bo•fan (**tur**-boh-*fan*) ***noun*** A type of aircraft engine in which a large fan, driven by a turbine, pushes air into the hot exhaust at the rear of the engine, giving extra power.

tur•bu•lent (**tur**-byuh-luhnt) ***adjective*** Wild, confused, or violent; not calm or smooth, as in *turbulent rapids* or *a turbulent time in history.*

turf (**turf**) ***noun*** The surface layer of grass and earth on a lawn or playing field.

tur•key (**tur**-kee) ***noun***

1. A large North American bird with red-brown feathers and a tail that spreads out like a fan.

2. *(slang)* A hopeless or useless person or thing.

tur•moil (**tur**-moil) ***noun*** Great confusion.

T

turn (**turn**)
1. ***verb*** To change direction.
2. ***noun*** A change in direction or position, or the point where such a change takes place.
3. ***verb*** To spin or to rotate.
4. ***noun*** The act of turning; a rotation, as in *one turn of the wheel.*
5. ***verb*** To change appearance or state.
6. ***noun*** A change in events or time, as in *a turn for the worse* or *the turn of the century.*
7. ***verb*** To become.
8. ***verb*** To move a switch, faucet, etc., in order to control the supply of something.
9. ***verb*** To unsettle, or to make sick.
10. ***noun*** If it is your **turn** to do something, it is your chance or duty to do it.
11. ***noun*** A **good turn** is a helpful action.
12. ***verb*** If you **turn** something **down,** you refuse it.
13. ***verb*** If someone **turns in,** the person goes to bed.
14. ***verb*** If someone **turns up,** he or she appears.
15. ***verb*** *(slang)* If something **turns** you **on,** it makes you enthusiastic or excited.
▸ ***noun*** **turn-on**
▸ ***verb*** **turning, turned** ▸ ***noun*** **turn**

tur•nip (**tur**-nuhp) ***noun*** A round, white or yellow root vegetable.

turn•out (**turn**-*out*) ***noun*** The number of people at a gathering or an event.

turn•pike (**turn**-*pike*) ***noun*** An expressway on which tolls are paid.

turn•stile (**turn**-*stile*) ***noun*** A revolving gate or movable bar at an exit or entrance. A turnstile lets people pass through one at a time.

turn•ta•ble (**turn**-*tay*-buhl) ***noun*** A circular, revolving surface. A turntable can be used for playing phonograph records.

tur•pen•tine (**tur**-puhn-tine) ***noun*** A clear liquid made from the sap of certain pine trees. Turpentine is often used to thin paints.

tur•quoise (**tur**-koiz *or* **tur**-kwoiz) ***noun***
1. A valuable, blue-green stone used in making jewelry.
2. A blue-green color.
▸ ***adjective*** **turquoise**

tur•ret (**tur**-it) ***noun***
1. A round tower on a building, usually on a corner. Many castles have turrets.
2. A structure on a tank, warship, or fighter plane that holds one or more guns. It usually rotates so that the gun can be fired in different directions.

tur•tle (**tur**-tuhl) ***noun*** A reptile that can pull its head, legs, and tail into its hard shell for protection. Turtles live on land and in water.

tur•tle•neck (**tur**-tuhl-*nek*) ***noun***
1. A high collar that turns down and fits snugly around the neck.
2. A sweater or shirt with such a collar.

tusk (**tuhsk**) ***noun*** One of the pair of long, curved, pointed teeth of an elephant, a walrus, a wild boar, and some other animals.

tus•sle (**tuhss**-uhl) ***verb*** To fight or wrestle vigorously; to scuffle. ▸ **tussling, tussled** ▸ ***noun*** **tussle**

tu•tor (**too**-tur) ***noun*** A teacher who gives private lessons to one student at a time. ▸ ***verb*** **tutor**

tu•tu (**too**-too) ***noun*** A short ballet skirt made of several layers of stiff net.

tux•e•do (tuhk-**see**-doh) ***noun*** A man's jacket, usually black with satin lapels, worn with a bow tie for formal occasions. ▸ ***noun, plural*** **tuxedos**

TV (*tee*-**vee**) ***noun*** Short for **television.**

tweed (**tweed**) ***noun*** A rough wool cloth woven with yarns of two or more colors.

twee•zers (**twee**-zurz) ***noun, plural*** A small pincers used for pulling out hairs or for picking up very small objects.

twelfth (**twelfth**)
1. ***adjective*** That which comes after eleventh and before thirteenth.

T

2. ***noun*** One part of something that has been divided into 12 equal parts, written 1/12.

twelve (**twelv**) ***noun*** The whole number, written 12, that comes after 11 and before 13. ▸ ***adjective* twelve**

twen•ty (**twen**-tee) ***noun*** The whole number, written 20, that is equal to 2 times 10. ▸ ***adjective* twenty**

twice (**twisse**) ***adverb*** Two times.

twig (**twig**) ***noun*** A small, thin branch of a tree or other woody plant.

twi•light (**twye**-*lite*) ***noun*** The time of day when the sun has just set and it is beginning to get dark.

twin (**twin**)

1. ***noun*** One of two children born at the same birth. ▸ ***adjective* twin**

2. ***adjective*** Belonging to a pair that are exactly the same, as in *twin beds.* ▸ ***noun* twin**

twine (**twine**)

1. ***noun*** A very strong string made of two or more strands twisted together.

2. ***verb*** To wind or grow in a coil. ▸ **twining, twined**

twinge (**twinj**) ***noun*** A sudden pain or unpleasant feeling.

twin•kle (**twing**-kuhl)

1. ***verb*** To shine with quick flashes of light; to sparkle. ▸ **twinkling, twinkled**

2. ***noun*** A flash of light.

twirl (**twurl**) ***verb*** To turn or spin around quickly. ▸ **twirling, twirled** ▸ ***noun* twirl**

twist (**twist**) ***verb***

1. To turn, wind, or bend.

2. To wind two strands of something together.

3. To sprain.

4. When you **twist** someone's words, you purposely change the meaning of what he or she said.

▸ ***verb* twisting, twisted** ▸ ***noun* twist**

twis•ter (**twiss**-tur) ***noun*** *(informal)* A tornado.

twitch (**twich**) ***verb*** To make small, jerky movements. ▸ **twitches, twitching, twitched** ▸ ***noun* twitch** ▸ ***adjective* twitchy**

twit•ter (**twit**-ur) ***noun***

1. The short, high, chirping sounds that a bird makes. ▸ ***verb* twitter**

2. A state of nervous excitement.

two (**too**) ***noun*** The whole number, written 2, that comes after 1 and before 3. **Two** sounds like **to** and **too.** ▸ ***adjective* two**

ty•coon (tye-**koon**) ***noun*** A very wealthy, powerful businessperson.

type (**tipe**)

1. ***noun*** A kind or a sort.

2. ***noun*** Small pieces of metal with raised letters, numbers, punctuation marks, etc., on their surfaces. Type is used in printing.

3. ***verb*** To write something with a typewriter or computer. ▸ **typing, typed**

4. ***noun*** Printed letters and numbers.

type•set (**tipe**-*set*) ***verb*** To put a piece of writing into a typed form that can be used in printing. ▸ **typesetting, typeset** ▸ ***noun* typesetter** ▸ ***adjective* typeset**

type•writ•er (**tipe**-*rye*-tur) ***noun*** A machine that prints letters, numbers, and punctuation marks when you press keys with your fingers.

ty•phoid (**tye**-foid) ***noun*** A serious infectious disease with symptoms of high fever and diarrhea that sometimes leads to death. It is caused by germs in food or water.

ty•phoon (tye-**foon**) ***noun*** A violent tropical storm. Typhoons occur in the western Pacific Ocean.

typ•i•cal (**tip**-uh-kuhl) ***adjective***

1. Having traits or qualities that are normal for a type or class; conforming to a type or class.

2. If someone does something that is **typical,** the person behaves in his or her usual way.

▸ ***adverb* typically**

U

typ•ist (**tye**-pist) ***noun*** Someone who uses a typewriter or computer to write things.

ty•ran•no•saur (ti-**ran**-uh-*sor*) ***noun*** A huge dinosaur that fed on meat and walked upright on its hind legs.

ty•rant (**tye**-ruhnt) ***noun*** Someone who rules other people in a cruel or unjust way. ▸ ***noun* tyranny** (**tihr**-uh-nee) ▸ ***adjective* tyrannical** (ti-**ran**-i-kuhl)

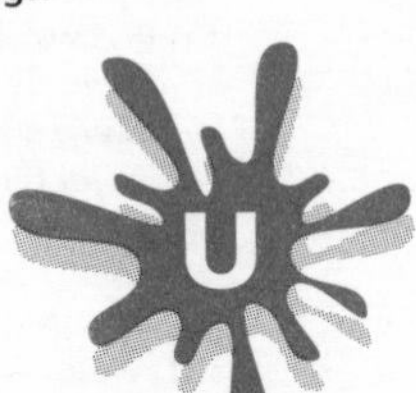

ud•der (**uhd**-ur) ***noun*** The baglike part of a female cow, sheep, etc., that hangs down near its back legs. The udder contains the glands that produce milk.

UFO (**yoo ef oh**) ***noun*** An object that is seen or is thought to be seen flying in the sky, believed by some people to be a spaceship from another planet. UFO is short for *Unidentified Flying Object.*

ug•ly (**uhg**-lee) ***adjective***
1. If someone or something is **ugly,** it is not attractive or pleasant to look at.
2. Disgusting or unpleasant.
3. Nasty or mean, as in *an ugly mood.*
▸ ***adjective* uglier, ugliest**

u•ku•le•le (yoo-kuh-**lay**-lee) ***noun*** A small, four-stringed guitar originally made popular in Hawaii.

ul•cer (**uhl**-sur) ***noun*** An open, painful sore on the skin or on the lining of the stomach.

ul•ti•mate (**uhl**-tuh-mit) ***adjective***
1. Last or final.
2. Original or basic.
3. Greatest or best.
▸ ***noun* ultimate** ▸ ***adverb* ultimately**

ul•ti•ma•tum (uhl-tuh-**may**-tuhm) ***noun*** A final offer or demand, especially one that carries with it the threat of punishment or the use of force if rejected. ▸ ***noun, plural* ultimatums** *or* **ultimata** (uhl-tuh-**may**-tuh)

ul•tra•light (**uhl**-truh-*lite*) ***noun*** A very light aircraft, usually for one person, which is powered by a small engine.

ul•tra•sound (**uhl**-truh-*sound*) ***noun*** Sound whose frequency is too high for the human ear to hear. Ultrasound waves are used in medical scans.

ul•tra•vi•o•let light (*uhl*-truh-**vye**-uh-lit) ***noun*** Light that cannot be seen by the human eye. It is given off by the sun and causes the skin to get darker.

um•bil•i•cal cord (uhm-**bil**-uh-kuhl) ***noun*** The tube that connects an unborn baby to its mother's body and through which it gets oxygen and food.

um•brel•la (uhm-**brel**-uh) ***noun*** A folding frame with a circular cloth stretched over it that you hold over your head to protect you from the rain or the sun.

um•pire (**uhm**-pire) ***noun*** An official who rules on plays in baseball, tennis, and certain other sports. ▸ ***verb* umpire**

un•a•ble (uhn-**ay**-buhl) ***adjective*** If you are **unable** to do something, you cannot do it.

un•ac•cept•a•ble (uhn-uhk-**sep**-tuh-buhl) ***adjective*** If something is **unacceptable,** it is not good enough to be allowed or accepted. ▸ ***adverb* unacceptably**

U

un•ac•cus•tomed (uhn-uh-**kuhss**-tuhmd) ***adjective*** If you are **unaccustomed** to something, you are not used to it.

un•adul•ter•at•ed (uhn-uh-**duhl**-tuh-*ray*-tid) ***adjective*** If a substance is **unadulterated,** it is pure; it has not had anything extra or artificial added to it.

un•aid•ed (uhn-**ay**-did) ***adjective*** If you do something **unaided,** you do it on your own without any help.

u•nan•i•mous (yoo-**nan**-uh-muhss) ***adjective*** Agreed on by everyone, as in *a unanimous decision.* ▸ ***adverb*** **unanimously**

un•ap•proach•a•ble (*uhn*-uh-**proh**-chuh-buhl) ***adjective***
1. Someone who is **unapproachable** is not friendly or easy to get to know.
2. If a place is **unapproachable,** you cannot get to it.

un•armed (uhn-**armd**) ***adjective*** Someone who is **unarmed** is not carrying any weapons.

un•au•tho•rized (uhn-**aw**-thuh-rized) ***adjective*** If something is **unauthorized,** it is done without official permission.

un•a•void•a•ble (*uhn*-uh-**voi**-duh-buhl) ***adjective*** If something is **unavoidable,** it is impossible to prevent. ▸ ***adverb*** **unavoidably**

un•a•ware (*uhn*-uh-**wair**) ***adjective*** If you are **unaware** of something, you do not know that it exists or is happening.

un•bear•a•ble (uhn-**bair**-uh-buhl) ***adjective*** If something is **unbearable,** it is so bad or unpleasant that you cannot stand it. ▸ ***adverb*** **unbearably**

un•be•com•ing (*uhn*-bi-**kuhm**-ing) ***adjective***
1. Not attractive or not flattering, as in *an unbecoming outfit.*
2. Not in good taste; not proper, as in *unbecoming behavior.*

un•be•liev•a•ble (*uhn*-bi-**leev**-uh-buhl) ***adjective*** If something is **unbelievable,** it is so strange, amazing, surprising, or wonderful that you find it hard to accept that it is true.

un•bend•ing (uhn-**ben**-ding) ***adjective*** If someone is **unbending,** the person is very firm or stubborn and will not change his or her mind.

un•break•a•ble (uhn-**bray**-kuh-buhl) ***adjective*** Not able to be broken, or not likely to be broken, as in *unbreakable dishes.*

un•bro•ken (uhn-**broh**-kuhn) ***adjective***
1. Not broken; whole.
2. Not interrupted; without a stop or break; continuous.
3. Not tamed or trained for use with a harness.
4. Not bettered or topped, as in *an unbroken sports record.*

un•bur•den (uhn-**bur**-duhn) ***verb*** If you **unburden** yourself, you tell another person about your troubles, fears, or worries. ▸ **unburdening, unburdened**

un•can•ny (uhn-**kan**-ee) ***adjective***
1. Very strange and difficult to explain or understand; mysterious; eerie, as in *uncanny sounds.*
2. Remarkable or extraordinary, as in *an uncanny sense of direction.*
▸ ***adverb*** **uncannily**

un•cer•tain (uhn-**sur**-tuhn) ***adjective***
1. If you are **uncertain** about something, you are not sure about it.
2. If the weather is **uncertain,** it is likely to change.
▸ ***noun*** **uncertainty**

un•civ•i•lized (uhn-**siv**-uh-lized) ***adjective***
1. Not yet civilized or educated, as in *an uncivilized people.*
2. **Uncivilized** behavior is rude and wild.

un•cle (**uhng**-kuhl) ***noun*** The brother of your mother or father, or the husband of your aunt.

un•com•fort•a•ble (uhn-**kuhm**-fur-tuh-buhl *or* uhn-**kuhmf**-tuh-buhl) ***adjective***
1. If you are **uncomfortable,** you do not feel relaxed in your body or your mind. ▸ ***adverb*** **uncomfortably**
2. Something that is **uncomfortable** makes you worry or feel pain, as in *an uncomfortable situation* or *uncomfortable shoes.*

un•com•mon (uhn-**kom**-uhn) ***adjective*** Rare or unusual; out of the ordinary.

un•com•pli•men•ta•ry (uhn-*kom*-pluh-**men**-tuh-ree) ***adjective*** If someone says **uncomplimentary** things about you, the words are insulting, rude, or negative.

un•com•pro•mis•ing (uhn-**kom**-pruh-*mye*-zing) ***adjective*** If you are **uncompromising,** you refuse to give in or change your ideas or accept something that is not exactly what you wanted. ▸ ***adverb*** **uncompromisingly**

un•con•cerned (*uhn*-kuhn-**surnd**) ***adjective***
1. Not interested; indifferent.
2. Not worried, anxious, or upset.

un•con•di•tion•al (*uhn*-kuhn-**dish**-uh-nuhl) ***adjective*** Not limited by any conditions; without limitations, as in *unconditional surrender.* ▸ ***adverb*** **unconditionally**

un•con•firmed (*uhn*-kuhn-**furmd**) ***adjective*** Not yet known to be true, as in *unconfirmed rumors.*

un•con•scious (uhn-**kon**-shuhss) ***adjective***
1. Not awake; not able to see, feel, or think.
2. Unaware of something.
3. Not done on purpose.

un•con•sti•tu•tion•al (uhn-*kon*-stuh-**too**-shuh-nuhl) ***adjective*** Not in keeping with the basic principles or laws set forth in the constitution of a state or country, especially the Constitution of the United States.

un•con•trol•la•ble (*uhn*-kuhn-**troh**-luh-buhl) ***adjective*** Something that is **uncontrollable** cannot be stopped, held in, or restrained, as in *uncontrollable laughter.* ▸ ***adverb*** **uncontrollably**

un•co•op•er•a•tive (*uhn*-koh-**op**-uh-ruh-tiv) ***adjective*** If you are **uncooperative,** you refuse to help people or do what they ask.

un•couth (uhn-**kooth**) ***adjective*** Rough and rude.

un•cov•er (uhn-**kuhv**-ur) ***verb***
1. To take a cover off something.
2. To reveal something; to make something known.
▸ ***verb*** **uncovering, uncovered**

un•daunt•ed (uhn-**dawn**-tid) ***adjective*** If you are **undaunted,** you are not discouraged or frightened by dangers or difficulties.

un•de•cid•ed (*uhn*-di-**sye**-did) ***adjective***
1. If you are **undecided** about something, you have not made up your mind about it.
2. Not yet settled.

un•de•ni•a•ble (*uhn*-di-**nye**-uh-buhl) ***adjective*** Something that is **undeniable** is clearly true. ▸ ***adverb*** **undeniably**

un•der (**uhn**-dur) ***preposition***
1. Below or beneath. ▸ ***adverb*** **under**
2. Less than a number or amount.
3. According to.
4. Controlled or bound by, as in *under oath.*

un•der•arm (**uhn**-dur-*arm*)
1. ***adverb*** Underhand.
2. ***noun*** The armpit, or the part of the body that is under the arm.
▸ ***adjective*** **underarm**

un•der•brush (**uhn**-dur-*bruhsh*) ***noun*** Bushes, shrubs, and other plants that grow beneath the large trees in the forest or woods.

un•der•clothes (**uhn**-dur-*kloze*) ***noun, plural*** Underwear.

un•der•de•vel•oped (*uhn*-dur-di-**vel**-uhpt) ***adjective*** Not completely or normally developed, as in *underdeveloped film* or *underdeveloped muscles.*

un•der•dog (**uhn**-dur-*dawg*) ***noun*** A person, team, or group that is expected to be the loser in a game, a race, an election, or other contest.

un•der•es•ti•mate (uhn-dur-**ess**-tuh-*mate*) ***verb***
1. To think that something is not as good or as great as it really is.
2. To make a guess that is too low.
▸ ***verb* underestimating, underestimated** ▸ ***noun* underestimate** (uhn-dur-**ess**-tuh-muht), ***noun* underestimation**

un•der•foot (*uhn*-der-**fut**) ***adverb***
1. Under your feet; on the ground.
2. In the way.

un•der•go (*uhn*-dur-**goh**) ***verb*** To experience or have to go through something. ▸ **undergoes, undergoing, underwent, undergone**

un•der•ground (**uhn**-dur-*ground*) ***adjective***
1. Below the ground, as in *an underground stream.*
2. Secret or hidden, as in *an underground organization.*
▸ ***noun* underground** ▸ ***adverb* underground** (*uhn*-dur-**ground**)

Underground Railroad ***noun*** A network of people who secretly helped slaves from the South escape to free states in the North or to Canada before the American Civil War.

un•der•growth (**uhn**-dur-*grohth*) ***noun*** The saplings, seedlings, shrubs, and other plants that grow beneath the tall, mature trees in a forest.

un•der•hand (**uhn**-dur-*hand*) ***adjective*** Thrown or pitched with the hand below the shoulder or elbow level. ▸ ***adverb* underhand**

un•der•hand•ed (**uhn**-dur-*han*-did) ***adjective*** Sneaky or dishonest; done in secret; unfair.

un•der•line (**uhn**-dur-*line*) ***verb***
1. To draw a line under a word or sentence.
2. To stress how important something is.
▸ ***verb* underlining, underlined**

un•der•mine (**uhn**-dur-mine) ***verb*** To weaken or destroy something slowly.
▸ **undermining, undermined**

un•der•neath (*uhn*-dur-**neeth**) ***preposition*** Under or below. ▸ ***adverb* underneath**

un•der•nour•ished (*uhn*-dur-**nur**-isht) ***adjective*** Someone who is **undernourished** is weak and unhealthy from lack of nutritious food.

un•der•pants (**uhn**-dur-*pants*) ***noun, plural*** Short pants worn as underwear.

un•der•pass (**uhn**-dur-*pass*) ***noun*** A road or passage that goes underneath another road or a bridge.

un•der•priv•i•leged (*uhn*-dur-**priv**-uh-lijd) ***adjective*** Someone who is **underprivileged** is usually poor and does not have the advantages or opportunities that richer people have.

un•der•sea (*uhn*-dur-**see**) ***adjective*** Located, done, or used below the surface of the ocean, as in *undersea plants* or *undersea exploration.*

un•der•shirt (**uhn**-dur-*shurt*) ***noun*** A shirt with short sleeves or no sleeves worn as underwear.

un•der•side (**uhn**-dur-*side*) ***noun*** The bottom side or surface of something, as in *the underside of a boat* or *the underside of a rock.*

un•der•stand (*uhn*-dur-**stand**) ***verb***
1. To know what something means or how something works.
2. To know very well.
3. To have sympathy for someone.
4. To believe that something is true; to gather from indirect information.
▸ ***verb* understanding, understood**
▸ ***noun* understanding** ▸ ***adjective* understanding**

un•der•stand•a•ble (*uhn*-dur-**stan**-duh-buhl) ***adjective*** Easy to grasp or understand. ▸ ***adverb* understandably**

U

U

un·der·take (*uhn*-dur-**take**) ***verb***
1. To agree to do a job or task; to accept a responsibility.
2. To set about; to try or attempt.
▸ ***verb*** **undertaking, undertook, undertaken** ▸ ***noun*** **undertaking**

un·der·tak·er (**uhn**-dur-*tay*-kur) ***noun*** Someone whose job is to arrange funerals and prepare dead bodies to be buried or cremated.

un·der·tow (**uhn**-dur-*toh*) ***noun*** A strong current below the surface of a body of water that usually flows in a direction opposite to that of the surface current. An undertow can pull swimmers away from the shore.

un·der·wa·ter (**uhn**-dur-*waw*-tur) ***adjective*** Located, used, or done under the surface of the water. ▸ ***adverb*** **underwater**

un·der·wear (**uhn**-dur-*wair*) ***noun*** Clothes that you wear next to your skin, under your outer clothes; underclothes.

un·der·weight (*uhn*-dur-**wate**) ***adjective*** Having less than the normal or required weight; weighing too little.

un·der·world (**uhn**-dur-*wurld*) ***noun***
1. The part of society that is involved in organized crime.
2. In Greek and Roman mythology, the **underworld** is the place under the ground where the spirits of dead people go.

un·de·sir·a·ble (*uhn*-di-**zye**-ruh-buhl) ***adjective*** Not wanted or not pleasant.

un·dis·turbed (uhn-diss-**turbd**) ***adjective*** Not bothered, or not interrupted; peaceful and calm.

un·do (uhn-**doo**) ***verb***
1. To untie, unfasten, or open something.
2. To remove or reverse the effects of something.
▸ ***verb*** **undoes, undoing, undid, undone**

un·done (uhn-**duhn**) ***adjective*** Not finished or not completed.

un·dress (uhn-**dress**) ***verb*** To take clothes off. ▸ **undresses, undressing, undressed**

un·dy·ing (uhn-**dye**-ing) ***adjective*** Lasting forever.

un·earth (uhn-**urth**) ***verb***
1. To dig something up.
2. To find, discover, or uncover something after searching for it.
▸ ***verb*** **unearthing, unearthed**

un·eas·y (uhn-**ee**-zee) ***adjective***
1. Worried, nervous, or anxious.
2. Awkward, uncomfortable, or embarrassed, as in *an uneasy silence.*
▸ ***noun*** **uneasiness** ▸ ***adverb*** **uneasily**

un·em·ployed (*uhn*-em-**ploid**) ***adjective*** Someone who is **unemployed** does not have a job or work of any kind. ▸ ***noun*** **unemployment**

un·e·qual (uhn-**ee**-kwuhl) ***adjective***
1. Not the same in size, value, or amount, as in *an unequal division of property.*
2. Not well matched or not well balanced.
▸ ***adverb*** **unequally**

un·e·ven (uhn-**ee**-vuhn) ***adjective***
1. Not flat, smooth, or straight, as in *uneven ground.*
2. Not regular, or not consistent.
3. In mathematics, an **uneven number** is a whole number that does not have two as a factor. ▸ ***adverb*** **unevenly**

un·e·vent·ful (*uhn*-i-**vent**-fuhl) ***adjective*** Not interesting, or not exciting, as in *an uneventful afternoon.*
▸ ***adverb*** **uneventfully**

un·ex·pect·ed (*uhn*-ek-**spek**-tid) ***adjective*** Something that is **unexpected** is surprising because you did not think it would happen. ▸ ***adverb*** **unexpectedly**

un·fair (uhn-**fair**) ***adjective*** Not fair, right, or just. ▸ **unfairer, unfairest**
▸ ***noun*** **unfairness** ▸ ***adverb*** **unfairly**

un·faith·ful (uhn-**fayth**-fuhl) ***adjective*** Not loyal, or not trustworthy. ▸ ***adverb*** **unfaithfully**

un·fa·mil·iar (*uhn*-fuh-**mil**-yur) ***adjective***

U

1. Not well known or not easily recognized; strange.
2. If you are **unfamiliar** with something, you do not know about it, or you do not have any experience using it.

un•fas•ten (uhn-**fass**-uhn) ***verb***
1. To release or to detach.
2. To open something that has been fastened.
▸ ***verb*** **unfastening, unfastened**

un•feel•ing (uhn-**fee**-ling) ***adjective*** Without kindness or sympathy; cruel.

un•fit (uhn-**fit**) ***adjective***
1. Not suitable, or not good enough.
2. Not healthy, or not strong.

un•fold (uhn-**fohld**) ***verb***
1. To open and spread out something that was folded.
2. When a story or plan **unfolds,** more of it becomes known.
▸ ***verb*** **unfolding, unfolded**

un•fore•seen (*uhn*-for-**seen**) ***adjective*** Not expected or not planned.

un•for•get•ta•ble (*uhn*-fur-**get**-uh-buhl) ***adjective*** So good, bad, etc., that you will not forget it, as in *an unforgettable experience.* ▸ ***adverb*** **unforgettably**

un•for•giv•a•ble (*uhn*-fur-**giv**-uh-buhl) ***adjective*** If someone does something **unforgivable,** he or she does something so bad or mean that you cannot forgive the person. ▸ ***adverb*** **unforgivably**

un•for•tu•nate (uhn-**for**-chuh-nit) ***adjective***
1. Unlucky, as in *an unfortunate accident.* ▸ ***adverb*** **unfortunately**
2. Not wise, proper, or suitable.

un•friend•ly (uhn-**frend**-lee) ***adjective***
1. Not friendly; feeling or showing dislike.
2. Not pleasant or not favorable.
▸ ***adjective*** **unfriendlier, unfriendliest**
▸ ***noun*** **unfriendliness**

un•grate•ful (uhn-**grate**-fuhl) ***adjective*** If you are **ungrateful** for something, you are not thankful for it and do not show or feel appreciation for it. ▸ ***adverb*** **ungratefully**

un•hap•py (uhn-**hap**-ee) ***adjective***
1. Without joy; sad, as in *an unhappy child.*
2. Not lucky or fortunate, as in *an unhappy incident.*
3. Not suitable, as in *an unhappy choice.*
▸ ***adjective*** **unhappier, unhappiest**
▸ ***noun*** **unhappiness** ▸ ***adverb*** **unhappily**

un•health•y (uhn-**hel**-thee) ***adjective***
1. Not healthy; in poor health; not well.
2. Resulting from poor health.
3. Harmful to one's health.

un•heard-of (uhn-**hurd**) ***adjective*** Not known or done before, as in *an unheard-of artist* or *an unheard-of athletic feat.*

u•ni•corn (**yoo**-nuh-*korn*) ***noun*** An imaginary animal that looks like a horse with one straight horn growing from its forehead.

u•ni•cy•cle (**yoo**-nuh-*sye*-kuhl) ***noun*** A vehicle that has pedals like a bicycle but only one wheel and no handlebars.

un•i•den•ti•fied (*uhn*-eye-**den**-tuh-*fide*) ***adjective*** Not identified; not known or recognized. ▸ ***adjective*** **unidentifiable**

u•ni•form (**yoo**-nuh-*form*)
1. ***noun*** A special set of clothes worn by all the members of a particular group or organization. Nurses, soldiers, police officers, and mail carriers wear uniforms. ▸ ***adjective*** **uniformed**
2. ***adjective*** Always the same; never changing.
3. ***adjective*** All alike; not different in any way, as in *a uniform row of houses.*
▸ ***noun*** **uniformity** ▸ ***adverb*** **uniformly**

u•ni•fy (**yoo**-nuh-fye) ***verb*** To bring or join together into a whole or a unit; to unite. ▸ **unifies, unifying, unified**
▸ ***noun*** **unification** (*yoo*-nuh-fi-**kay**-shuhn)

un•im•por•tant (*uhn*-im-**port**-uhnt) ***adjective*** Not important; of no special value or interest; minor.

U

un•in•hab•it•ed (*uhn*-in-**hab**-uh-tid) ***adjective*** If a place is **uninhabited,** no one lives there.

un•in•tel•li•gi•ble (*uhn*-in-**tel**-uh-juh-buhl) ***adjective*** If something is **unintelligible,** it cannot be understood. ▸ ***adverb* unintelligibly**

un•in•ten•tion•al (*uhn*-in-**ten**-shuh-nuhl) ***adjective*** Something that is **unintentional** is done by accident, not on purpose. ▸ ***adverb* unintentionally**

un•in•ter•est•ed (uhn-**in**-truh-stid) ***adjective*** If you are **uninterested** in something, you do not want to know about it.

un•ion (**yoon**-yuhn) ***noun***
1. An organized group of workers set up to help improve such things as working conditions, wages, and health benefits.
2. The joining together of two or more things or people to form a larger group.
3. **the Union** The United States of America.
4. **the Union** The states that remained loyal to the federal government during the Civil War; the North.

u•nique (yoo-**neek**) ***adjective*** If something is **unique,** it is the only one of its kind. ▸ ***adverb* uniquely**

u•ni•sex (**yoo**-nuh-*seks*) ***adjective*** Able to be used by both men and women, as in *unisex clothing.*

u•ni•son (**yoo**-nuh-suhn) ***noun*** If people say, sing, or do something **in unison,** they say, sing, or do it together.

u•nit (**yoo**-nit) ***noun***
1. A single person, thing, or group that is part of a larger group or whole, as in *an apartment unit* or *an army unit.*
2. An amount used as a standard of measurement.
3. A machine or piece of equipment that has a special purpose, as in *an air-conditioning unit.*
4. The number one.

u•nite (yoo-**nite**) ***verb***
1. If people **unite,** they join together or work together to achieve something.
2. To put or join together in order to make a whole.
▸ ***verb* uniting, united** ▸ ***noun* unity**
▸ ***adjective* united**

u•ni•ver•sal (*yoo*-nuh-**vur**-suhl) ***adjective***
1. Something that is **universal** is shared by everyone or everything.
2. Something that is **universal** is found everywhere.
▸ ***adverb* universally**

u•ni•verse (**yoo**-nuh-vurss) ***noun*** The earth, the planets, the stars, and all things that exist in space.

u•ni•ver•si•ty (*yoo*-nuh-**vur**-suh-tee) ***noun*** A school for higher learning after high school where people can study for degrees, do research, or learn a profession such as law or medicine. A university is usually made up of colleges.
▸ ***noun, plural* universities**

un•just (uhn-**juhst**) ***adjective*** Not just, fair, or right, as in *an unjust accusation.*
▸ ***adverb* unjustly**

un•kempt (uhn-**kempt**) ***adjective***
1. Not combed, as in *unkempt hair.*
2. Not tidy or neat in appearance, as in *an unkempt room* or *an unkempt lawn.*

un•kind (uhn-**kinde**) ***adjective*** Not kind; harsh or cruel, as in *unkind words.*
▸ **unkinder, unkindest** ▸ ***adverb* unkindly**

un•known (uhn-**nohn**) ***adjective*** Not familiar or not known about, as in *unknown territory.* ▸ ***noun* unknown**

un•less (uhn-**less**) ***conjunction*** Except on the condition that.

un•like (uhn-**like**)
1. ***adjective*** Not alike; different.
2. ***preposition*** Different from; not like.
3. ***preposition*** Not typical of.
4. ***adjective*** In a pair of magnets, **unlike** poles attract each other while like poles repel each other.

un•like•ly (uhn-**like**-lee) ***adjective***
1. Not probable.
2. Not likely to succeed, as in *an unlikely plan.*

U

un•lim•it•ed (uhn-**lim**-uh-tid) ***adjective*** Having no limits, bounds, or restrictions.

un•load (uhn-**lohd**) ***verb***
1. To remove things from a container or vehicle.
2. To remove ammunition from a gun.
▸ ***verb*** **unloading, unloaded**

un•lock (uhn-**lok**) ***verb***
1. To open something with a key.
2. To solve, or to provide a key to, as in *to unlock a mystery.*
▸ ***verb*** **unlocking, unlocked**

un•luck•y (uhn-**luhk**-ee) ***adjective***
1. Someone who is **unlucky** is unfortunate, and bad things seem to happen to him or her.
2. Something that is **unlucky** happens by chance and is unfortunate. ▸ ***adverb*** **unluckily**
3. An **unlucky** number, date, etc., is one that you think will bring you bad luck.
▸ ***adjective*** **unluckier, unluckiest**

un•mis•tak•a•ble (*uhn*-muh-**stay**-kuh-buhl) ***adjective*** Something that is **unmistakable** is very obvious and cannot be confused with anything else.
▸ ***adverb*** **unmistakably**

un•nat•u•ral (uhn-**nach**-ur-uhl) ***adjective***
1. Not usual or not normal; not happening in nature.
2. False, or not sincere.
▸ ***adverb*** **unnaturally**

un•nec•es•sar•y (uhn-**ness**-uh-*ser*-ee) ***adjective*** If something is **unnecessary,** you do not need to do it or have it.
▸ ***adverb*** **unnecessarily**

un•ob•served (*uhn*-uhb-**zurvd**) ***adjective*** Not seen or not noticed.

un•oc•cu•pied (uhn-**ok**-yuh-pide) ***adjective***
1. Having no occupants; vacant, as in *an unoccupied apartment.*
2. Not held by enemy forces, as in *unoccupied territory.*

un•of•fi•cial (*uhn*-uh-**fish**-uhl) ***adjective***
1. Not approved by someone in authority, as in *an unofficial report.*
2. Informal, as in *an unofficial visit.*
▸ ***adverb*** **unofficially**

un•pack (uhn-**pak**) ***verb*** To take objects out of a box, suitcase, trunk, vehicle, or container of any kind. ▸ **unpacking, unpacked**

un•pleas•ant (uhn-**plez**-uhnt) ***adjective*** Not pleasing; offensive; disagreeable, as in *an unpleasant odor.*
▸ ***adverb*** **unpleasantly**

un•plug (uhn-**pluhg**) ***verb***
1. To remove a plug from an electric socket.
2. To remove a stopper or something that blocks an opening.
▸ ***verb*** **unplugging, unplugged**

un•pop•u•lar (uhn-**pop**-yuh-lur) ***adjective*** Not liked or approved of by many people.

un•prec•e•dent•ed (un-**press**-uh-*den*-tid) ***adjective*** Not known or done before; without a previous example.

un•pre•dict•a•ble (*uhn*-pri-**dik**-tuh-buhl) ***adjective*** If someone or something is **unpredictable,** you do not know what the person will do or what will happen next. ▸ ***adverb*** **unpredictably**

un•pre•pared (*uhn*-pri-**paird**) ***adjective*** Not ready for something.

un•pro•voked (*uhn*-pruh-**vohkt**) ***adjective*** If an action is **unprovoked,** no one has done anything to cause it or encourage it.

un•rav•el (uhn-**rav**-uhl) ***verb***
1. To unwind a tangled mass of string, wool, or strands of any kind.
2. To undo or pull apart a woven or knitted fabric.
3. To search for and discover the truth about a complex situation.
▸ ***verb*** **unraveling, unraveled**

un•rea•son•a•ble (uhn-**ree**-zuhn-uh-buhl) ***adjective***
1. Not showing reason or good sense.
2. Too great; excessive, as in *an unreasonable price.*
▸ ***adverb*** **unreasonably**

U

un•rec•og•niz•a•ble (uhn-*rek*-uhg-**nye**-zuh-buhl) ***adjective*** Something or someone that is **unrecognizable** has totally changed so that you do not immediately know what or who it is.

un•re•li•a•ble (*uhn*-ri-**lye**-uh-buhl) ***adjective*** Something or someone that is **unreliable** cannot be depended upon or trusted.

un•rest (uhn-**rest**) ***noun*** Disturbance and trouble; a lack of calm; dissatisfaction, as in *political unrest.*

un•re•strict•ed (*uhn*-ri-**strik**-tid) ***adjective*** Without rules or limitations.

un•ripe (uhn-**ripe**) ***adjective*** Not yet ready to be harvested, picked, or eaten, as in *unripe fruit.*

un•ri•valed (uhn-**rye**-vuhld) ***adjective*** Better than anything else; having no equal.

un•roll (uhn-**role**) ***verb*** To open or spread out something that is rolled up. ▸ **unrolling, unrolled**

un•ruf•fled (un-**ruhf**-uhld) ***adjective*** Completely calm, especially after a disturbing incident.

un•rul•y (uhn-**roo**-lee) ***adjective*** Hard to control or discipline, as in *unruly hair* or *an unruly mob.* ▸ **unrulier, unruliest**

un•sat•is•fac•to•ry (*uhn*-sat-iss-**fak**-tuh-ree) ***adjective*** Not good enough to meet a certain need or standard. ▸ ***adverb*** **unsatisfactorily**

un•scathed (uhn-**skayTHd**) ***adjective*** Not hurt.

un•scru•pu•lous (uhn-**skroo**-pyuh-luhss) ***adjective*** **Unscrupulous** people have few principles or scruples and are not concerned whether their actions are right or wrong. ▸ ***adverb*** **unscrupulously**

un•seen (uhn-**seen**) ***adjective*** Hidden or not able to be seen.

un•set•tle (uhn-**set**-uhl) ***verb*** To upset or to disturb. ▸ **unsettling, unsettled**

un•set•tled (uhn-**set**-uhld) ***adjective***
1. Not calm or not orderly; disturbed, as in *unsettled political conditions.*
2. Not decided or not determined; doubtful, as in *an unsettled question.*
3. Not inhabited.
4. Likely to change; uncertain, as in *unsettled weather.*
5. Not paid, as in *an unsettled bill.*

un•sight•ly (uhn-**site**-lee) ***adjective*** Ugly and unpleasant to look at, as in *an unsightly scar* or *unsightly litter.*

un•skilled (uhn-**skild**) ***adjective*** An **unskilled** worker has no particular skill, training, or experience.

un•sound (uhn-**sound**) ***adjective***
1. Not strong or not solid; weak; unsafe, as in *an old, unsound bridge.*
2. Not based on good judgment or clear thinking; not sensible, as in *unsound advice.*
3. Not healthy, as in *an unsound mind.*

un•sta•ble (uhn-**stay**-buhl) ***adjective***
1. Not firm or not steady; shaky, as in *an unstable ladder.*
2. Likely to change, as in *an unstable government.*
3. An **unstable** person has rapid changes of mood and behavior.

un•stead•y (uhn-**sted**-ee) ***adjective*** Shaky or wobbly; not firm, as in *an unsteady voice.* ▸ ***adverb*** **unsteadily**

un•suc•cess•ful (*uhn*-suhk-**sess**-fuhl) ***adjective*** If someone is **unsuccessful,** the person does not do well or get what he or she wants. ▸ ***adverb*** **unsuccessfully**

un•suit•a•ble (uhn-**soo**-tuh-buhl) ***adjective*** Not right for a particular purpose or occasion. ▸ ***noun*** **unsuitability** ▸ ***adverb*** **unsuitably**

un•sure (uhn-**shoor**) ***adjective*** Not certain or not definite.

un•tan•gle (uhn-**tang**-guhl) ***verb***
1. To remove knots or tangles, as in *to untangle a necklace.*
2. To clear up or explain, as in *to untangle a mystery.*
▸ ***verb*** **untangling, untangled**

un•think•a•ble (uhn-**thingk**-uh-buhl) ***adjective*** If something is **unthinkable,**

it is out of the question and cannot be considered.

un•ti•dy (uhn-**tye**-dee) ***adjective*** Not neat; messy. ▸ ***noun*** **untidiness** ▸ ***adverb*** **untidily**

un•tie (uhn-**tye**) ***verb***
1. To loosen or undo something that has been tied or fastened.
2. To free from something that ties, fastens, or restrains.
▸ ***verb*** **untying, untied**

un•til (uhn-**til**)
1. ***preposition*** Up to the time of.
2. ***preposition*** Before.
3. ***conjunction*** Up to the time that.
4. ***conjunction*** Before.
5. ***conjunction*** To the point, degree, or place that.

un•to (**uhn**-too) ***preposition*** An old word for **to.**

un•told (uhn-**tohld**) ***adjective***
1. Too great to be counted or measured.
2. Not told or not revealed.

un•touched (uhn-**tuhcht**) ***adjective***
1. Not handled or touched by anyone.
2. Left alone or ignored.
3. Not moved or not affected.

un•true (uhn-**troo**) ***adjective***
1. False or incorrect, as in *an untrue story.*
2. Not faithful or not loyal.

un•used (uhn-**yoozd**) ***adjective***
1. An **unused** item has never been used.
2. Not accustomed.

un•u•su•al (uhn-**yoo**-zhoo-uhl) ***adjective*** Not usual, common, or ordinary; rare. ▸ ***adverb*** **unusually**

un•wel•come (uhn-**wel**-kuhm) ***adjective*** If someone or something is **unwelcome,** it is not gladly received or accepted.

un•well (uhn-**wel**) ***adjective*** Sick or ill.

un•wield•y (uhn-**weel**-dee) ***adjective*** Difficult to hold or hard to manage because of its shape, size, weight, or complexity, as in *an unwieldy package.*

un•will•ing (uhn-**wil**-ing) ***adjective*** Reluctant or not eager to do something. ▸ ***adverb*** **unwillingly**

un•wind (uhn-**winde**) ***verb***
1. To undo something that has been rolled or wound up.
2. To relax and become less worried or tense.
▸ ***verb*** **unwinding, unwound**

un•wor•thy (uhn-**wur**-THee) ***adjective***
1. Not deserving.
2. Not fitting, proper, or appropriate.
▸ ***adverb*** **unworthily**

un•wrap (uhn-**rap**) ***verb*** To take the packaging or outer layer off something. ▸ **unwrapping, unwrapped**

up (**uhp**)
1. ***adverb*** From a lower to a higher place.
2. ***adverb*** In, at, or to a higher place or position.
3. ***adverb*** To a higher point or degree.
4. ***adverb*** On one's feet; in an upright position.
5. ***adverb*** Entirely.
6. ***adverb*** To a higher volume.
7. ***adjective*** Moving upward.
8. ***adverb*** Out of bed.
9. ***adjective*** Above the horizon.
10. ***preposition*** From a lower to a higher position or place in or on.
11. ***preposition*** At or to a farther point in or on.
12. ***preposition*** Toward the source or inner part of.
13. up against Faced with.
14. If you are **up to** a job, you are capable of performing or dealing with it.
15. If something is left **up to** a person, it depends on that person or is his or her responsibility.
16. If you are **up to** something, you are doing it.

up•beat (**uhp**-*beet*) ***adjective*** *(informal)* Optimistic and cheerful, as in *an upbeat personality.*

up•bring•ing (**uhp**-*bring*-ing) ***noun*** The care and training a person receives while growing up.

U

up•date (*uhp*-**date**) ***verb***
1. To give someone the latest information. ▸ ***noun*** **update** (**uhp**-*date*)
2. To change something in order to include the latest style or information.
▸ ***verb*** **updating, updated**

up•grade (**uhp**-*grade or uhp*-**grade**)
1. ***verb*** To promote someone to a better or more important job or status.
2. ***verb*** To improve something.
3. ***verb*** To replace a computer part or a piece of software with a better, more powerful, or more recently released version. ▸ ***noun*** **upgrade**
4. ***noun*** (**uhp**-*grade*) The upward slope of a hill or road.
▸ ***verb*** **upgrading, upgraded**

up•heav•al (*uhp*-**hee**-vuhl) ***noun***
1. A sudden and violent upset or disturbance, as in *the emotional upheaval caused by war.*
2. A forceful lifting up of part of the earth's crust, especially during an earthquake.

up•hill (**uhp-hil**)
1. ***adjective*** Sloping upward. ▸ ***adverb*** **uphill**
2. If something is an **uphill battle,** it is very tiring or difficult to do.

up•hold (*uhp*-**hohld**) ***verb*** To support something that you believe to be right.
▸ **upholding, upheld**

up•hol•ster (uhp-**hohl**-stur) ***verb*** To put new upholstery on a piece of furniture. ▸ **upholstering, upholstered**
▸ ***noun*** **upholsterer** ▸ ***adjective*** **upholstered**

up•hol•ster•y (uhp-**hohl**-stur-ee) ***noun*** The stuffing, springs, cushions, and covering that are put on furniture.
▸ ***noun, plural*** **upholsteries**

up•keep (**uhp**-*keep*) ***noun*** The work or cost of keeping something in good condition.

up•load (**uhp**-*lohd*) ***verb*** To send information to another computer over a network. ▸ **uploading, uploaded**

up•on (uh-**pon**) ***preposition*** On.

up•per (**uhp**-ur) ***adjective*** Higher in position or rank, as in *an upper floor* or *the upper house of a legislature.*

up•per•case (**uhp**-ur-*kayss*) ***adjective*** **Uppercase** letters are capital letters.
▸ ***noun*** **uppercase** ▸ ***verb*** **uppercase**

upper hand ***noun*** A position of advantage or control.

up•per•most (**uhp**-ur-*mohst*)
1. ***adjective*** Highest in place, rank, or importance.
2. ***adverb*** In the highest or most important place or rank.

up•right (**uhp**-*rite*)
1. ***adjective*** Standing straight up; vertical. ▸ ***noun*** **upright** ▸ ***adverb*** **upright**
2. ***adjective*** Honest and fair; moral.
3. ***noun*** An **upright piano** has strings that are arranged vertically, or up and down.

up•ris•ing (**uhp**-*rye*-zing) ***noun*** A rebellion or a revolt.

up•roar (**uhp**-*ror*) ***noun*** Shouting, noise, and confusion.

up•roar•i•ous (uhp-**ror**-ee-uhss) ***adjective***
1. Noisy or confused; full of uproar.
2. Extremely funny, as in *an uproarious joke.*

up•root (*uhp*-**root**) ***verb***
1. To tear or pull out by the roots.
2. To force someone to leave.
▸ ***verb*** **uprooting, uprooted**

up•set (*uhp*-**set**) ***verb***
1. To make someone nervous or worried.
2. To tip, turn, or knock something over.
3. To make someone feel ill.
4. To interfere with.
5. To defeat unexpectedly.
▸ ***verb*** **upsetting, upset** ▸ ***noun*** **upset** (**uhp**-*set*) ▸ ***adjective*** **upset** (*uhp*-**set**)

up•side down (**uhp**-*side*) ***adverb***
1. With the top at the bottom.
▸ ***adjective*** **upside-down**
2. In a confused or messy condition.

U

up•stairs (**uhp-stairz**)
1. ***adverb*** Up the stairs.
2. ***adverb*** To or on a higher floor.
3. ***adjective*** On an upper floor.
4. ***noun*** The upper floor or floors of a building.

up•stream (**uhp-streem**) ***adverb*** Toward the source of a stream; against the current. ▸ ***adjective* upstream**

up•tight (**uhp-tite**) ***adjective*** *(slang)* Tense, nervous, or anxious.

up-to-date ***adjective*** If something is **up-to-date,** it contains the most recent information or is in the latest style.

up•ward (**uhp**-wurd) *or* **up•wards** (**uhp**-wurdz)
1. ***adverb*** Toward a higher place or position.
2. ***adjective*** Moving or rising toward a higher place or position, as in *an upward slope.*

ur•a•ni•um (yu-**ray**-nee-uhm) ***noun*** A silver-white radioactive metal that is the main source of nuclear energy. Uranium is a chemical element.

Ur•a•nus (**yur**-uh-nuhss *or* yu-**ray**-nuhss) ***noun*** The seventh planet in distance from the sun. Uranus is the third-largest planet in our solar system. It has 15 known moons as well as nine rings circling its equator.

ur•ban (**ur**-buhn) ***adjective*** To do with or living in a city, as in *urban problems* or *the urban population.*

urge (**urj**)
1. ***verb*** To encourage or persuade someone strongly. ▸ **urging, urged**
2. ***noun*** A strong wish or need to do something.

ur•gent (**ur**-juhnt) ***adjective*** If something is **urgent,** it needs very quick or immediate attention. ▸ ***noun* urgency** ▸ ***adverb* urgently**

u•rin•ar•y system (**yoor**-uh-*nar*-ee) ***noun*** The organs and body parts that produce, store, and release urine. In humans and other mammals, it includes the kidneys, bladder, and tubes that carry urine.

u•ri•nate (**yoor**-uh-nate) ***verb*** To pass urine from the body. ▸ **urinating, urinated** ▸ ***noun* urination**

u•rine (**yoor**-uhn) ***noun*** The liquid waste that people and animals pass out of their bodies. Urine consists of water and wastes taken out of the blood by the kidneys. It is stored in the bladder.

URL (*yoo-ar*-**el**) ***noun*** The address of a file on the Internet or the World Wide Web. URL stands for *Uniform Resource Locator* or *Universal Resource Locator.*

urn (**urn**) ***noun***
1. A vase with a base or pedestal. An urn is used as an ornament or a container.
2. A large metal container with a faucet used for making and serving coffee or tea.

Urn sounds like **earn.**

us (**uhss**) ***pronoun*** The form of **we** that is used after a verb or preposition.

us•age (**yoo**-sij *or* **yoo**-zij) ***noun***
1. The way that something is used or treated.
2. The way that a language is usually spoken and written.

use
1. (**yooz**) ***verb*** To do a job with something.
2. (**yooz**) ***verb*** To spend or consume by using.
3. (**yooss**) ***noun*** The action of using something.
4. (**yooss**) ***noun*** The right or ability to use something.
5. (**yooss**) ***noun*** A purpose for which something can be used.
6. (**yooss**) ***noun*** Advantage or benefit.
7. (**yooss**) ***noun*** The need to use something.
8. (**yooz**) ***verb*** If you **use** someone, you take advantage of the person in order to get something that you want.

▸ ***noun* user** ▸ ***verb* using, used**

V

used
1. (**yoozd**) ***adjective*** Already made use of, as in *a used car.*
2. (**yoost**) ***adjective*** If you are **used to** something, you know it well.
3. (**yoost**) ***verb*** If you **used to do** something, you did it in the past.

use•ful (**yooss**-fuhl) ***adjective*** Something that is **useful** is helpful and can be used a lot. ▸ ***noun*** **usefulness**

use•less (**yooss**-liss) ***adjective***
1. Something that is **useless** has no use or value or is not helpful.
2. Hopeless; not capable of producing any result.
3. *(informal)* Not very good.

user-friendly ***adjective*** If something such as a computer is **user-friendly,** it is easy for people without experience to learn and operate.

ush•er (**uhsh**-ur) ***noun*** Someone who shows people to their seats in a church, theater, or stadium. ▸ ***verb*** **usher**

u•su•al (**yoo**-zhoo-uhl) ***adjective*** Normal, common, or expected. ▸ ***adverb*** **usually**

u•ten•sil (yoo-**ten**-suhl) ***noun*** A tool or container, often used in the kitchen, that has a special purpose.

u•ter•us (**yoo**-tur-uhss) ***noun*** The hollow organ in women and other female mammals that holds and nourishes a fetus; the womb. ▸ ***noun, plural*** **uteri** (**yoo**-ter-eye) *or* **uteruses**

u•til•i•ty (yoo-**til**-uh-tee) ***noun***
1. A basic service supplied to a community, such as telephone, water, gas, or electric.
2. A company that supplies a basic utility.
3. Usefulness.
4. A **utility program** on a computer is one that performs a specific task that allows the computer to run more efficiently. One kind of utility program, for example, manages computer files. ▸ ***noun, plural*** **utilities**

ut•most (**uht**-*mohst*) ***noun*** The most, or the greatest possible. ▸ ***adjective*** **utmost**

ut•ter (**uht**-ur)
1. ***verb*** To speak or to make some sort of sound from your mouth. ▸ **uttering, uttered** ▸ ***noun*** **utterance**
2. ***adjective*** Complete or total. ▸ ***adverb*** **utterly**

U-turn (**yoo**) ***noun***
1. A turn in the shape of a U made by a vehicle in order to go in the opposite direction.
2. A complete reversal of policy or attitude.

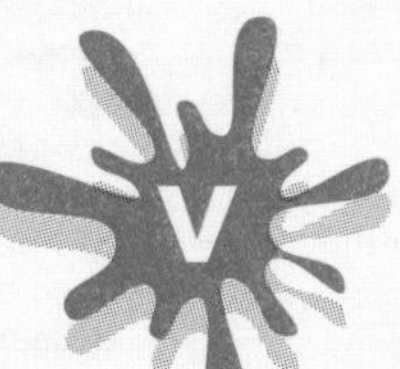

va•cant (**vay**-kuhnt) ***adjective***
1. Empty or not occupied, as in *a vacant house* or *a vacant lot.*
2. Available. ▸ ***noun*** **vacancy**
3. If someone looks **vacant,** the person has a blank expression on his or her face.

va•cate (**vay**-kate) ***verb*** To leave, or to leave something empty. ▸ **vacating, vacated**

va•ca•tion (vay-**kay**-shuhn) ***noun*** A time of rest from school, work, and other regular duties; especially a pleasure trip away from home. ▸ ***verb*** **vacation**

vac•ci•nate (**vak**-suh-nate) ***verb*** To protect someone against a disease by giving the person an injection or a dose of a vaccine. ▸ **vaccinating, vaccinated** ▸ ***noun*** **vaccination**

vac•cine (vak-**seen** *or* **vak**-seen) ***noun*** A substance containing dead, weakened, or living organisms that can be injected or taken orally. A vaccine causes a person to produce antibodies that protect him or her from the disease caused by the organisms.

vac•u•um (**vak**-yuhm *or* **vak**-yoom) ***noun***
1. A sealed space from which all air or gas has been emptied.
2. A vacuum cleaner. ▸ ***verb*** **vacuum**

vacuum cleaner ***noun*** A machine that picks up dirt from carpets, furniture, etc. To work, a vacuum cleaner reduces the air pressure inside itself. Then dirt is carried into it by outside air rushing to fill the partial vacuum.

va•gi•na (vuh-**jye**-nuh) ***noun*** The passage in women and other female mammals that leads from the uterus, through which babies are born.

vague (**vayg**) ***adjective*** Not clear or not definite. ▸ **vaguer, vaguest**

vain (**vayn**) ***adjective***
1. If you are **vain,** you are conceited or too proud of yourself, especially of the way you look.
2. Unsuccessful or futile.
Vain sounds like **vane** and **vein.**
▸ ***adjective*** **vainer, vainest**

val•en•tine (**val**-uhn-*tine*) ***noun***
1. A gift or greeting card sent to a friend, relative, or loved one on Valentine's Day.
2. A sweetheart or loved one chosen on Valentine's Day.

Valentine's Day ***noun*** February 14, a day named in honor of Saint Valentine, a Christian martyr of the third century A.D. It is celebrated by sending valentines.

val•iant (**val**-yuhnt) ***adjective*** Brave or courageous, as in *valiant soldiers* or *a valiant effort.* ▸ ***adverb*** **valiantly**

val•id (**val**-id) ***adjective***
1. Sensible; based on facts or evidence.
2. Acceptable or legal.
▸ ***noun*** **validity** ▸ ***verb*** **validate**

val•ley (**val**-ee) ***noun***
1. An area of low ground between two hills, usually containing a river.
2. An area of land drained by a river system.

val•or (**val**-ur) ***noun*** Great bravery or courage, especially in battle.

val•u•a•ble (**val**-yoo-uh-buhl *or* **val**-yuh-buhl)
1. ***adjective*** Something that is **valuable** is worth a lot of money or is very important in some other way, as in *a valuable jewel* or *valuable information.*
2. valuables ***noun, plural*** Possessions that are worth a lot of money.

val•ue (**val**-yoo)
1. ***noun*** What something is worth.
2. ***verb*** To think that something is important.
3. ***verb*** To assess how much something is worth.
4. ***noun*** In mathematics, an assigned or calculated number or quantity.
5. ***noun, plural*** People's **values** are their beliefs and ideas about what is most important in their lives.
▸ ***verb*** **valuing, valued**

valve (**valv**) ***noun*** A movable part that controls the flow of a liquid or gas through a pipe or other channel.

vam•pire (**vam**-pire) ***noun***
1. Any of the bats of Central and South America that feed on the blood of birds and mammals, especially livestock.
2. In folktales and horror stories, a **vampire** is a dead person who rises from the grave to feed on the blood of humans.

V

van (**van**) ***noun***
1. A large, enclosed truck used for moving animals or household goods from place to place.
2. A smaller motor vehicle that is shaped like a box. A van has rear or side doors and side panels that often have windows.

van·dal (**van**-duhl) ***noun*** Someone who needlessly damages or destroys other people's property. ▸ ***noun*** **vandalism** ▸ ***verb*** **vandalize**

vane (**vayn**) ***noun***
1. A **weather vane** is a pointer that swings around to show the direction of the wind.
2. The flat part of a bird's feather.
Vane sounds like **vain** and **vein.**

va·nil·la (vuh-**nil**-uh) ***noun*** A flavoring made from the seed pods of a tropical orchid. It is used in ice cream, candies, cookies, and other foods.

van·ish (**van**-ish) ***verb***
1. To disappear suddenly.
2. To cease to exist.
▸ ***verb*** **vanishes, vanishing, vanished**

van·i·ty (**van**-uh-tee) ***noun*** A feeling of extreme pride and conceit. ▸ ***noun, plural*** **vanities**

vanity plate ***noun*** A motor vehicle license plate with letters or numbers selected by the owner. A vanity plate often spells out a clever slogan or the owner's name.

van·quish (**vang**-kwish) ***verb***
1. To defeat or conquer an enemy in battle.
2. To defeat an opponent in a contest or competition.
3. To overcome an emotion or a fear.
▸ ***verb*** **vanquishes, vanquishing, vanquished**

va·por (**vay**-pur) ***noun***
1. Fine particles of mist, steam, or smoke that can be seen hanging in the air.
2. A gas formed from something that is usually a liquid or solid at normal temperatures.

var·i·a·ble (**vair**-ee-uh-buhl)
1. ***adjective*** Likely to change, as in *variable weather.* ▸ ***noun*** **variable**
2. ***noun*** In mathematics, a **variable** is a symbol, such as *x*, *y*, or □, that stands for a number.

var·i·a·tion (vair-ee-**ay**-shuhn) ***noun***
1. A change from the usual.
2. Something that is slightly different from another thing of the same type.

va·ri·e·ty (vuh-**rye**-uh-tee) ***noun***
1. Difference, or change.
2. A selection of different things.
3. A different type of the same thing, as in *a new variety of rose.*
▸ ***noun, plural*** **varieties**

var·i·ous (**vair**-ee-uhss) ***adjective***
1. Different.
2. Several.

var·mint (**var**-muhnt) ***noun*** *(informal)*
1. An undesirable animal, such as one that kills a rancher's livestock.
2. A person who is undesirable, obnoxious, or troublesome.

var·nish (**var**-nish) ***noun*** A clear coating that you put on wood to protect it and give it a shiny finish. ▸ ***noun, plural*** **varnishes** ▸ ***verb*** **varnish**

var·y (**vair**-ee) ***verb***
1. To change or to be different.
2. If you **vary** something, you make changes in it.
▸ ***verb*** **varies, varying, varied** ▸ ***noun*** **variant**

vase (**vayss** *or* **vayz**) ***noun*** An ornamental container often used for flowers.

vas·sal (**vass**-uhl) ***noun*** In the Middle Ages, a person who was given land and protection by a lord in return for loyalty and military service.

vast (**vast**) ***adjective*** Huge in area or extent. ▸ **vaster, vastest** ▸ ***noun*** **vastness** ▸ ***adverb*** **vastly**

vat (**vat**) ***noun*** A large tank or container used for storing liquids.

vault (**vawlt**)
1. ***verb*** To leap over something using your hands or other support.
▸ **vaulting, vaulted** ▸ ***noun*** **vault**
2. ***noun*** A room or compartment for keeping money and other valuables safe, as in *a bank vault.*
3. ***noun*** An underground burial chamber.

V-chip ***noun*** A device that can be installed in a television set to allow parents to block certain programs so that children cannot watch them.

VCR (**vee see ar**) ***noun*** An electronic machine that is connected to a television set. It uses magnetic tape to record or play back movies and television programs. VCR is short for *VideoCassette Recorder.*

veal (**veel**) ***noun*** The meat from a calf.

vee•jay (**vee**-*jay*) ***noun*** An announcer on a television program that features music videos.

veer (**vihr**) ***verb*** To change direction or turn suddenly. ▸ **veering, veered**

veg•an (**vee**-guhn *or* **vej**-uhn) ***noun*** A vegetarian who does not eat any animal or dairy products. ▸ ***noun*** **veganism** ▸ ***adjective*** **vegan**

veg•e•ta•ble (**vej**-tuh-buhl) ***noun*** A plant grown to be used as food. Vegetables are usually eaten as side dishes to entrees or in salads.

veg•e•tar•i•an (*vej*-uh-**ter**-ee-uhn) ***noun*** Someone who eats only plants and plant products and sometimes eggs or dairy products. ▸ ***noun*** **vegetarianism** ▸ ***adjective*** **vegetarian**

veg•e•ta•tion (*vej*-uh-**tay**-shuhn) ***noun*** Plant life or the plants that cover an area.

ve•he•ment (**vee**-uh-muhnt) ***adjective*** If you are **vehement** about something, you express your feelings about it very strongly. ▸ ***noun*** **vehemence** ▸ ***adverb*** **vehemently**

ve•hi•cle (**vee**-uh-kuhl) ***noun*** Something in which people or goods are carried from one place to another. Vehicles can range in size and power from a sled or tricycle to an express train.

veil (**vayl**) ***noun***
1. A piece of material worn by women as a covering for the head or face.
2. Something that hides like a veil or curtain, as in *a veil of mist* or *a veil of secrecy.*
▸ ***verb*** **veil**

vein (**vayn**) ***noun***
1. One of the vessels through which blood is carried back to the heart from other parts of the body.
2. One of the stiff, narrow tubes that form the framework of a leaf or an insect's wing.
3. A narrow band of mineral in rock.
Vein sounds like **vain** and **vane.**

Vel•cro (**vel**-*kroh*) ***noun*** The trademark for a fastener that consists of two pieces of fabric. One piece is covered with tiny hooks that stick to the tiny loops on the second piece.

vel•lum (**vel**-uhm) ***noun***
1. Fine parchment paper made from the skin of a calf, lamb, or baby goat.
2. Very high quality writing paper.

ve•loc•i•ty (vuh-**loss**-uh-tee) ***noun*** Speed. ▸ ***noun, plural*** **velocities**

vel•vet (**vel**-vit)
1. ***noun*** A soft, thick fabric made from cotton, silk, or other materials.
2. ***adjective*** Made of velvet, or covered in velvet.
3. ***adjective*** Smooth and soft like velvet, as in *velvet fur.*
4. ***noun*** The soft skin on the growing antlers of a deer.

ven•det•ta (ven-**det**-uh) ***noun*** A long-lasting feud between two families, gangs, etc.

vend•ing machine (**vend**-ing) ***noun*** A machine in which you insert money to buy food items, beverages, or other products.

ven•dor (**ven**-dur) ***noun*** A person who sells something, as in *a fruit vendor.*

ve•ne•tian blind (vuh-**nee**-shuhn) ***noun*** An indoor window covering made from thin strips that can be raised or tilted to vary the amount of light coming in.

ven•geance (**ven**-juhnss) ***noun*** Action that you take to pay someone back for harm that he or she has done to you or someone you care about.

ven•i•son (**ven**-uh-suhn) ***noun*** The meat of a deer.

ven•om (**ven**-uhm) ***noun***
1. Poison produced by some snakes and spiders. Venom is usually passed into a victim's body through a bite or sting.
2. Ill will; spite or malice.

vent (**vent**)
1. ***noun*** An opening through which smoke or fumes can escape.
2. ***noun*** The shaft of a volcano through which smoke and lava escape.
3. ***verb*** If you **vent** your feelings, you show them in an obvious way.
▸ **venting, vented**

ven•ti•late (**ven**-tuh-*late*) ***verb*** To allow fresh air into a place and to send stale air out. ▸ **ventilating, ventilated**
▸ ***noun*** **ventilation,** ***noun*** **ventilator**

ven•tri•cle (**ven**-truh-kuhl) ***noun*** Either one of the two lower chambers of the heart. The ventricles receive blood from the atria and pump it to the arteries.

ven•tril•o•quism (ven-**tril**-uh-*kwiz*-uhm) ***noun*** The art of throwing your voice so that your words seem to come from a source other than yourself.
▸ ***noun*** **ventriloquist**

ven•ture (**ven**-chur)
1. ***noun*** A project that is somewhat risky, as in *a business venture.*
2. ***verb*** To put yourself at risk by doing something daring or dangerous.
▸ **venturing, ventured**

ven•ue (**ven**-yoo) ***noun*** A place where an event is held.

Ve•nus (**vee**-nuhss) ***noun*** The second planet in distance from the sun. Venus is the sixth-largest planet in our solar system and is brighter in our sky than any other heavenly body except the sun and moon.

ve•ran•da *or* **ve•ran•dah** (vuh-**ran**-duh) ***noun*** An open porch around the outside of a house, often with a roof.

verb (**vurb**) ***noun*** A word that expresses an action or a state of being.

ver•bal (**vur**-buhl) ***adjective***
1. To do with words, as in *a verbal aptitude test.*
2. Spoken, as in *a verbal agreement.*

ver•dict (**vur**-dikt) ***noun***
1. The decision of a jury on whether an accused person is guilty or not guilty.
2. A decision or an opinion.

verge (**vurj**)
1. If you are **on the verge** of doing something, you will do it soon.
2. ***verb*** To be very near to something.
▸ **verging, verged**

ver•i•fy (**ver**-uh-fye) ***verb***
1. To prove that something is true.
2. To test or check the accuracy of something.
▸ ***verb*** **verifies, verifying, verified**
▸ ***noun*** **verification** ▸ ***adjective*** **verifiable**

ver•min (**vur**-min) ***noun***
1. Any of various small, common insects or animals that are harmful pests. Fleas, rats, and lice are vermin.
2. A mean or offensive person.
▸ ***noun, plural*** **vermin**

ver•sa•tile (**vur**-suh-tuhl) ***adjective*** Talented or useful in many ways, as in *a versatile entertainer* or *a versatile tool.*
▸ ***noun*** **versatility**

verse (**vurss**) ***noun***
1. One part of a poem or song. A verse is made up of several lines.
2. Poetry.

ver•sion (**vur**-zhuhn) ***noun***
1. One description or account given from a particular point of view.
2. A different or changed form of something such as a book or car.

ver•sus (**vur**-suhss) ***preposition*** Against. In general, versus is abbreviated *vs.* When referring to court cases, however, it is abbreviated *v.*, as in the 1954 Supreme Court decision *Brown v. Board of Education of Topeka (Kansas).*

ver•te•bra (**vur**-tuh-bruh) ***noun*** One of the small bones that make up the backbone. ▸ ***noun, plural*** **vertebrae** (**vur**-tuh-*bree* *or* **vur**-tuh-*bray*)

ver•te•brate (**vur**-tuh-brit *or* **vur**-tuh-brate) ***noun*** Any animal that has a backbone. ▸ ***adjective*** **vertebrate**

ver•tex (**vur**-teks) ***noun***
1. The highest point of something, as in *the vertex of the mountain.*
2. The point where two lines meet to form an angle.
▸ ***noun, plural*** **vertices** (**vur**-tuh-*seez*)

ver•ti•cal (**vur**-tuh-kuhl) ***adjective*** Upright, or straight up and down.
▸ ***adverb*** **vertically**

ver•y (**ver**-ee)
1. ***adverb*** To a great extent, much, or most.
2. ***adjective*** Exact.

ves•sel (**vess**-uhl) ***noun***
1. A ship or a large boat.
2. A tube in the body that fluids pass through. Arteries and veins are blood vessels.
3. A hollow container for holding liquids, such as a bowl, vase, or jar.

vest (**vest**)
1. ***noun*** A short, sleeveless piece of clothing that is worn over a blouse or shirt.
2. ***verb*** To give power or authority to some person or group. ▸ **vesting, vested**

ves•tige (**vess**-tij) ***noun*** A trace or sign of something that no longer exists.

vet (**vet**) ***noun***
1. *(informal)* A veterinarian.
2. *(informal)* A veteran, as in *a Vietnam vet.*

vet•er•an (**vet**-ur-uhn) ***noun***
1. Someone with a lot of experience in a profession, a position, or an activity.
2. Someone who has served in the armed forces, especially during a war.
▸ ***adjective*** **veteran**

Veterans Day ***noun*** November 11, a day honoring men and women who served in the armed services and fought in wars for the United States. Formerly known as *Armistice Day,* this national holiday was first observed to celebrate the armistice, or truce, that ended World War I on November 11, 1918.

vet•er•i•nar•i•an (*vet*-ur-uh-**ner**-ee-uhn) ***noun*** A doctor who is trained to diagnose and treat sick or injured animals.

vet•er•i•nar•y (**vet**-ur-uh-*ner*-ee) ***adjective*** To do with the treatment of animals, as in *veterinary studies.*

ve•to (**vee**-toh)
1. ***noun*** The right or power of a president, a governor, or an official group to reject a bill that has been passed by a legislature and to keep it from becoming a law. ▸ ***noun, plural*** **vetoes**
2. ***verb*** To stop a bill from becoming a law.
3. ***verb*** To forbid, or to refuse to approve.
▸ ***verb*** **vetoes, vetoing, vetoed**

vex (**veks**) ***verb*** To annoy or irritate somebody. ▸ **vexes, vexing, vexed**
▸ ***noun*** **vexation** ▸ ***adjective*** **vexatious,** ***adjective*** **vexed**

vi•a (**vye**-uh *or* **vee**-uh) ***preposition*** By way of.

vi•a•ble (**vye**-uh-buhl) ***adjective*** Workable or capable of succeeding, as in *a viable plan.* ▸ ***noun*** **viability**

vi•a•duct (**vye**-uh-duhkt) ***noun*** A large bridge that carries a railroad track, road, or pipeline across a valley or over a city street.

vi•brant (**vye**-bruhnt) ***adjective*** Bright or lively, as in *vibrant colors* or *a vibrant personality.* ▸ ***noun*** **vibrancy** ▸ ***adverb*** **vibrantly**

vi•brate (**vye**-brate) ***verb*** To move back and forth rapidly. ▸ **vibrating, vibrated** ▸ ***noun*** **vibration**

vice (**visse**) ***noun*** Immoral or harmful behavior. **Vice** sounds like **vise.**

vice president ***noun*** An officer who ranks second to a president and acts for the president when necessary.

vice ver•sa (**visse vur**-suh *or* **vye**-suh **vur**-suh) ***adverb*** A Latin phrase meaning "the other way around."

vi•cin•i•ty (vuh-**sin**-uh-tee) ***noun*** The area near a particular place. ▸ ***noun, plural*** **vicinities**

vi•cious (**vish**-uhss) ***adjective***
1. Cruel and mean, as in *vicious lies.*
2. Evil or wicked, as in *a vicious crime.*
3. Fierce or dangerous, as in *a vicious dog.* ▸ ***noun*** **viciousness** ▸ ***adverb*** **viciously**

vic•tim (**vik**-tuhm) ***noun***
1. A person who is hurt, killed, or made to suffer, as in *an accident victim* or *a murder victim.*
2. A person who is cheated or tricked, as in *a swindler's victim.*

vic•tim•ize (**vik**-tuh-*mize*) ***verb*** To pick someone out for unfair treatment. ▸ **victimizing, victimized** ▸ ***noun*** **victimization**

vic•tor (**vik**-tur) ***noun*** The winner in a battle or contest.

vic•to•ry (**vik**-tuh-ree) ***noun*** A win in a battle or contest. ▸ ***noun, plural*** **victories** ▸ ***adjective*** **victorious** (vik-**tor**-ee-uhss) ▸ ***adverb*** **victoriously**

vid•e•o (**vid**-ee-oh)
1. ***adjective*** To do with the visual part of a television program or with a computer display.
2. ***noun*** The visual part of television.
3. ***noun*** A recording of a movie or television show that can be played on a VCR.
4. ***noun*** A videotaped performance of a song, as in *a rock video.*
▸ ***noun, plural*** **videos**

vid•e•o•cas•sette (*vid*-ee-oh-kuh-**set**) ***noun*** A plastic case that contains videotape. It can be inserted into a VCR and used to record or play back movies and television programs.

videocassette recorder *See* **VCR.**

video display terminal ***noun*** The monitor or display screen of a computer. A video display terminal is also known as a *VDT.*

video game ***noun*** An electronic or computerized game played by using buttons or levers to move images around on a television or computer screen. Video games often emphasize fast action.

vid•e•o•tape (**vid**-ee-oh-*tape*) ***noun***
1. Magnetic tape on which sound and pictures are recorded.
2. A recording on this kind of tape.
▸ ***verb*** **videotape**

vie (**vye**) ***verb*** To compete. ▸ **vying, vied**

view (**vyoo**)
1. ***noun*** The act of looking or seeing; sight.
2. ***noun*** What you can see from a certain place.
3. ***noun*** The range or field of sight.
4. ***noun*** What you think about something, or your opinion. ▸ ***verb*** **view**
5. ***verb*** To look at something.
▸ **viewing, viewed**

view•point (**vyoo**-*point*) ***noun***
1. The place or position from which a person views a situation, an event, etc.
2. An attitude or a way of thinking.

vig•i•lant (**vij**-uh-luhnt) ***adjective*** Watchful and alert. ▸ ***noun*** **vigilance** ▸ ***adverb*** **vigilantly**

vig•or (**vig**-ur) ***noun***
1. Great force or energy.
2. Physical energy or strength.

vig•or•ous (**vig**-ur-uhss) ***adjective*** Energetic, lively, or forceful, as in *vigorous exercise* or *a vigorous protest.* ▸ ***noun*** **vigor** ▸ ***adverb*** **vigorously**

Vi•king (**vye**-king) ***noun*** A member of one of the Scandinavian peoples who invaded the coasts of Europe between the 8th and 11th centuries.

vile (**vile**) ***adjective***
1. Evil or immoral, as in *a vile crime.*
2. Disgusting or repulsive, as in *vile language.*
▸ ***adjective*** **viler, vilest** ▸ ***noun*** **vileness**

vil•la (**vil**-uh) ***noun*** A large, luxurious house, especially one in the country.

vil•lage (**vil**-ij) ***noun*** A small group of houses that make up a community. A village is usually smaller than a town.
▸ ***noun*** **villager**

vil•lain (**vil**-uhn) ***noun*** A wicked person, often an evil character in a play.
▸ ***adjective*** **villainous**

vin•dic•tive (vin-**dik**-tiv) ***adjective*** Someone who is **vindictive** does not forgive and wants revenge. ▸ ***noun*** **vindictiveness** ▸ ***adverb*** **vindictively**

vine (**vine**) ***noun*** A plant with a long, twining stem that grows along the ground or climbs on trees, fences, or other supports. Melons, cucumbers, and pumpkins grow on vines.

vin•e•gar (**vin**-uh-gur) ***noun*** A sour liquid made from fermented wine, cider, etc., and used to flavor and preserve food.

vine•yard (**vin**-yurd) ***noun*** An area of land where grapes are grown.

vin•tage (**vin**-tij)
1. ***noun*** The wine produced in a particular year.
2. ***adjective*** Very good, or the best of its kind.

vi•nyl (**vye**-nuhl) ***noun*** A flexible, waterproof, shiny plastic that is used to make floor coverings, raincoats, and other products.

vi•o•la (vee-**oh**-luh) ***noun*** A stringed musical instrument that looks like a violin but is slightly larger and has a deeper tone.

vi•o•late (**vye**-uh-*late*) ***verb***
1. To break a promise, a rule, or a law.
2. To treat a person or place with no respect.
3. To disturb rudely or without any right, as in *to violate someone's privacy.*
▸ ***verb*** **violating, violated** ▸ ***noun*** **violation,** ***noun*** **violator**

vi•o•lence (**vye**-uh-luhnss) ***noun***
1. The use of physical force.
2. Great force or strength.

vi•o•lent (**vye**-uh-luhnt) ***adjective***
1. Showing or caused by great physical force.
2. Showing or caused by strong feeling or emotion, as in *a violent temper.*

vi•o•let (**vye**-uh-lit) ***noun***
1. A small, low plant with small flowers that are usually purple, yellow, or white. Pansies are a type of violet.
2. A blue-purple color. ▸ ***adjective*** **violet**

vi•o•lin (vye-uh-**lin**) ***noun*** A musical instrument with four strings, played with a bow. ▸ ***noun*** **violinist**

VIP (**vee eye pee**) ***noun*** The initials **VIP** stand for *Very Important Person.*

vi•per (**vye**-pur) ***noun***
1. Any poisonous snake.
2. An adder.

vir•gin (**vur**-jin) ***adjective*** Untouched, or in its natural state, as in *virgin snow* or *virgin forests.*

vir•tu•al•ly (**vur**-choo-uh-lee) ***adverb*** Nearly or almost. ▸ ***adjective*** **virtual**

virtual reality ***noun*** An environment that looks three-dimensional, created through a computer. Virtual reality seems real to the person who experiences it.

vir•tue (**vur**-choo) ***noun***
1. Moral goodness. ▸ ***adjective*** **virtuous** ▸ ***adverb*** **virtuously**
2. An example of moral goodness.
3. Any good quality or trait.

vir•tu•o•so (vur-choo-**oh**-soh) ***noun*** A highly skilled performer, especially a musician. ▸ ***noun, plural*** **virtuosos** *or* **virtuosi** (vur-choo-**oh**-see)

V

vir•u•lent (**vihr**-yuh-luhnt) ***adjective***
1. If a disease is **virulent,** it is very severe or harmful, as in *a virulent virus.*
2. Bitter, spiteful, or full of hate, as in *virulent criticism* or *a virulent speech.*
▸ ***noun*** **virulence** ▸ ***adverb*** **virulently**

vi•rus (**vye**-ruhss) ***noun***
1. A very tiny organism that can reproduce and grow only when inside living cells. Viruses are smaller than bacteria. They cause diseases such as polio, measles, the common cold, and AIDS. *See* **AIDS.**
2. The disease caused by a virus.
3. Hidden instructions within a computer program designed to destroy a computer system or damage data.
▸ ***noun, plural*** **viruses**

vi•sa (**vee**-zuh) ***noun*** A document giving permission for someone to enter a foreign country.

vise (**visse**) ***noun*** A device with two jaws that open and close with a screw or lever. A vise is used to hold an object firmly in place while it is being worked on. **Vise** sounds like **vice.**

vis•i•ble (**viz**-uh-buhl) ***noun*** Something that is **visible** is able to be seen. ▸ ***noun*** **visibility** ▸ ***adverb*** **visibly**

vi•sion (**vizh**-uhn) ***noun***
1. The sense of sight.
2. A lovely or beautiful sight.
3. The ability to think ahead and plan, as in *a leader of great vision.* ▸ ***noun*** **visionary**
4. Something that you imagine or dream about.

vis•it (**viz**-it) ***verb*** To go to see people or places. ▸ **visiting, visited** ▸ ***noun*** **visit,** ***noun*** **visitor**

vi•sor (**vye**-zur) ***noun***
1. A brim that sticks out of the front of a cap to shade the eyes from the sun.
2. A movable shade inside a car, above the windshield, that protects the eyes from glare.
3. The movable, see-through shield on the front of a helmet that protects the face.

vis•u•al (**vizh**-oo-uhl) ***adjective***
1. To do with seeing, as in *a visual nerve.*
▸ ***adverb*** **visually**
2. Designed or able to be seen.

vi•su•al•ize (**vizh**-oo-uh-*lize*) ***verb*** To picture something or to see something in your mind. ▸ **visualizing, visualized**
▸ ***noun*** **visualization**

vi•tal (**vye**-tuhl) ***adjective***
1. Very important or essential. ▸ ***adverb*** **vitally**
2. To do with life.
3. Necessary for life.
4. Full of life or energetic, as in *a vital personality.*

vi•tal•i•ty (vye-**tal**-uh-tee) ***noun*** Energy and liveliness.

vi•ta•min (**vye**-tuh-min) ***noun*** One of the substances in food that is necessary for good health.

vi•va•cious (vye-**vay**-shuhss *or* vi-**vay**-shuhss) ***adjective*** A **vivacious** person has a lively personality. ▸ ***noun*** **vivacity** (vi-**vass**-i-tee) ▸ ***adverb*** **vivaciously**

viv•id (**viv**-id) ***adjective***
1. Bright and strong, as in *vivid colors.*
2. Lively or active, as in *a vivid imagination.*
3. Sharp and clear, as in *vivid memories.*
▸ ***noun*** **vividness** ▸ ***adverb*** **vividly**

viv•i•sec•tion (*viv*-uh-**sek**-shuhn) ***noun*** The use of live animals for scientific and medical research.

vo•cab•u•lar•y (voh-**kab**-yuh-ler-ee) ***noun*** The range of words that a person uses and understands. ▸ ***noun, plural*** **vocabularies**

vo•cal (**voh**-kuhl)
1. ***adjective*** To do with the voice.
2. ***adjective*** If someone is **vocal,** the person is outspoken and often expresses his or her opinions.
3. ***noun, plural*** In music, the **vocals** are the parts that are sung.
▸ ***adverb*** **vocally**

vocal cords ***noun, plural*** Either of two pairs of bands or folds of membranes in the larynx. When air from the lungs passes through the lower pair, it causes them to vibrate and produce sound.

vo•cal•ist (**voh**-kuh-list) ***noun*** A singer.

vo•ca•tion (voh-**kay**-shuhn) ***noun***
1. A job or profession, especially one that needs special training. ▸ ***adjective*** **vocational**
2. A strong feeling for a particular job, especially a religious career.

vo•cif•er•ous (voh-**sif**-ur-uhss) ***adjective*** If someone is **vociferous,** the person is noisy and talkative and insists on being heard. ▸ ***adverb*** **vociferously**

vod•ka (**vod**-kuh) ***noun*** A strong alcoholic drink that is clear in color and is made from grain or potatoes.

vogue (**vohg**) ***noun*** If something is **in vogue,** it is the current fashion.

voice (**voiss**)
1. ***noun*** The power to speak and sing.
2. ***noun*** The sound produced when you speak or sing.
3. ***verb*** When you **voice** an opinion, you express it. ▸ **voicing, voiced**
4. ***noun*** The right to express your opinion.

voice mail ***noun*** A system that allows you to leave and play back spoken messages by telephone.

voice•print (**voiss**-*print*) ***noun*** A graph that shows the special patterns and characteristics of an individual speaker's voice.

void (**void**)
1. ***noun*** An empty space. ▸ ***adjective*** **void**
2. ***adjective*** If a result is declared **void,** it does not count anymore. ▸ ***verb*** **void**

vol•a•tile (**vol**-uh-tuhl) ***adjective***
1. A **volatile** chemical will evaporate very easily or is unstable in some other way. ▸ ***noun*** **volatility**
2. Someone who is **volatile** has rapid mood changes.

vol•ca•no (vol-**kay**-noh) ***noun*** A mountain with vents through which molten lava, ash, cinders, and gas erupt, sometimes violently. Volcanoes occur along the boundaries of the earth's plates, where molten rock is forced upward from magma reservoirs. ▸ ***noun, plural*** **volcanoes** *or* **volcanos**

vol•ley (**vol**-ee) ***noun***
1. A shot in games such as tennis and soccer where the ball is hit or kicked before it can bounce. ▸ ***verb*** **volley**
2. The firing of a number of bullets, missiles, etc., at the same time.
3. A burst or outburst of many things at the same time, as in *a volley of protests.*

vol•ley•ball (**vol**-ee-*bawl*) ***noun***
1. A game in which team members use their forearms and hands to hit a large ball over a net and try to make the ball hit the ground on their opponent's side. Volleyball can be played on a court or on the beach.
2. The ball used in this game.

volt (**vohlt**) ***noun*** A unit for measuring the force of an electrical current or the stored power of a battery. Volts are used to measure **voltage**.

volt•age (**vohl**-tij) ***noun*** The force of an electrical current, expressed in volts.

vol•ume (**vol**-yuhm) ***noun***
1. A book.
2. One book of a set.
3. The amount of space taken up by a three-dimensional shape such as a box or a room. To figure out the volume of a rectangular object, you multiply its length by its height by its width.
4. Loudness.

vol•un•tar•y (**vol**-uhn-*ter*-ee) ***adjective***
1. Willing; not forced, as in *a voluntary decision.*
2. Controlled by the will.
3. Done on purpose and not by accident, as in *voluntary manslaughter.*

vol•un•teer (*vol*-uhn-**tihr**)
1. ***verb*** To offer to do a job, usually without pay. ▸ **volunteering, volunteered** ▸ ***noun*** **volunteer**
2. ***adjective*** Formed or made up of volunteers, as in *volunteer firefighters.*

W

vom•it (**vom**-it) ***verb*** When you **vomit,** you bring up food and other substances from your stomach and expel them from your mouth. ▸ **vomiting, vomited** ▸ ***noun* vomit**

vote (**voht**) ***verb*** To make a choice in an election or other poll. ▸ **voting, voted** ▸ ***noun* vote, *noun* voter**

vouch (**vouch**) ***verb*** If you **vouch for** something or someone, you say that the thing or person is true, good, reliable, etc. ▸ **vouching, vouched**

vow (**vou**) ***verb*** To make a serious and important promise. ▸ **vowing, vowed** ▸ ***noun* vow**

vow•el (**vou**-uhl) ***noun*** A speech sound made with a free flow of air through the mouth. Vowels are represented by the letters *a, e, i, o, u,* and sometimes *y.*

voy•age (**voi**-ij) ***noun*** A long journey, as in *the immigrants' ocean voyage to the United States.* ▸ ***noun* voyager** ▸ ***verb* voyage**

vul•gar (**vuhl**-gur) ***adjective*** Rude or in bad taste, as in *vulgar language* or *a vulgar joke.* ▸ ***noun* vulgarity** (vuhl-**ga**-ri-tee)

vul•ner•a•ble (**vuhl**-nur-uh-buhl) ***adjective*** If someone or something is **vulnerable,** it is in a weak position and likely to be hurt or damaged in some way. ▸ ***noun* vulnerability** ▸ ***adverb* vulnerably**

vul•ture (**vuhl**-chur) ***noun*** A large bird of prey that has dark feathers and a bald head and neck. Vultures are related to hawks, eagles, and falcons. They feed mainly on the meat of dead animals.

wack•y (**wak**-ee) ***adjective*** *(slang)* Odd or crazy in a silly or amusing way. ▸ **wackier, wackiest** ▸ ***noun* wackiness** ▸ ***adverb* wackily**

wad (**wahd**)
1. ***noun*** A small, tightly packed ball or piece of something soft, as in *a wad of cotton* or *a wad of chewing gum.*
2. ***noun*** A tight, thick roll, as in *a wad of dollar bills.*
3. ***verb*** To press or roll something into a wad. ▸ **wadding, wadded**

wad•dle (**wahd**-uhl) ***verb*** To walk awkwardly, taking short steps and swaying from side to side. ▸ **waddling, waddled** ▸ ***noun* waddle**

wade (**wayd**) ***verb***
1. To walk through water.
2. To move through something slowly and with difficulty.

▸ ***verb* wading, waded**

wad•er (**way**-dur) ***noun***
1. A bird such as the crane or heron that wades in shallow water looking for food.
2. **waders *noun, plural*** Thigh-high, waterproof boots used for fishing in deep water.

wa•fer (**way**-fur) ***noun***
1. A thin, light, crisp cookie or cracker.
2. A thin, flat piece of candy.

waf•fle (**wahf**-uhl)
1. ***noun*** A type of cake baked in an appliance that presses a crisscross pattern into it.
2. ***verb*** *(informal)* To avoid giving a direct answer to a question; to keep changing your mind or position.

▸ **waffling, waffled** ▸ ***noun* waffle, *noun* waffler**

waft (**wahft**) ***verb*** To float or be carried through the air, as if by a breeze. ▸ **wafting, wafted** ▸ ***noun* waft**

wag (**wag**) ***verb*** To move something quickly from side to side or up and down. ▸ **wagging, wagged** ▸ ***noun*** **wag**

wage (**waje**)
1. wage *noun* *or* **wages *noun, plural*** The money someone is paid for his or her work.
2. *verb* If you **wage** a campaign or a war, you start it and carry on with it.
▸ **waging, waged**

wa•ger (**way**-jur) ***noun*** A bet. ▸ ***verb*** **wager**

wag•on (**wag**-uhn) ***noun***
1. A vehicle with four wheels that is used to carry heavy loads and is pulled by a horse or horses.
2. A child's toy vehicle or cart with four wheels and a long handle that is used for pulling.

wagon train ***noun*** In frontier times, a line or group of covered wagons that traveled west together for safety.

waif (**wafe**) ***noun***
1. A homeless, lost, or abandoned person, especially a young child.
2. A stray animal.

wail (**wale**) ***verb*** To let out a long cry of sadness or distress. **Wail** sounds like **whale.** ▸ **wailing, wailed** ▸ ***noun*** **wail**

waist (**wayst**) ***noun***
1. The middle part of your body between your ribs and your hips.
2. The part of a garment that covers the body around the waist area.
Waist sounds like **waste.**

wait (**wate**) ***verb***
1. To stay in a place or do nothing for a period of time until someone comes or something happens. ▸ ***noun*** **wait**
2. To look forward to something.
3. To be delayed or put off.
4. If you **wait on** someone, you serve as the person's waiter, waitress, salesperson, or servant.
Wait sounds like **weight.**
▸ ***verb*** **waiting, waited**

wait•er (**way**-tur) ***noun*** A man who serves people food and beverages in a restaurant.

waiting room ***noun*** A room or an area where people sit and wait for something such as a train, an airplane, or a doctor's appointment.

wait•ress (**way**-triss) ***noun*** A woman who serves people food and beverages in a restaurant.

waive (**wayv**) ***verb***
1. To give up something by choice.
▸ ***noun*** **waiver**
2. To postpone, or to set aside.
Waive sounds like **wave.**
▸ ***verb*** **waiving, waived**

wake (**wayk**)
1. *verb* To become fully conscious after being asleep.
2. *verb* To rouse someone from his or her sleep.
3. *noun* A watch kept over the body of a dead person before the funeral.
4. *noun* The trail of ripples in the water left by a moving boat.
5. *noun* The trail left by something passing through.
▸ ***verb*** **waking, woke** (**wohk**) *or* **waked, waked** *or* **woken** (**wohk**-in)

walk (**wawk**)
1. *verb* To move along by placing one foot on the ground before lifting the other. ▸ ***noun*** **walk,** ***noun*** **walker**
2. *noun* A journey on foot.
3. *verb* To accompany or to go with.
4. *noun* A path or other area that is set apart or designed for walking.
5. *verb* To make or help walk.
6. *noun* In baseball, the right of the batter to go to first base after the pitcher has thrown four pitches that are not swung at and are not called strikes by the umpire. ▸ ***verb*** **walk**
7. *(informal)* If you **walk all over** somebody, you take advantage of the person.
▸ ***verb*** **walking, walked**

walk•ie-talk•ie (**waw**-kee **taw**-kee) ***noun*** A radio that is held in the hand, powered by batteries, and is used to communicate over short distances.

walk•o•ver (**wawk**-*oh*-vur) ***noun*** *(informal)* A very easy victory.

walk•way (**wawk**-*way*) ***noun*** A path or passage for walking.

wall (**wawl**) ***noun***
1. A solid structure that separates two areas or supports a roof. ▸ ***verb*** **wall**
2. Anything that blocks the way, shuts something in, or divides one thing from another; a barrier, as in *a wall of marchers, a wall of fire,* or *a wall of secrecy.*

wal•la•by (**wol**-uh-*bee*) ***noun*** A small marsupial of the kangaroo family. Wallabies are found in Australia, New Zealand, and New Guinea. Many wallabies are about the size of a rabbit.
▸ ***noun, plural*** **wallabies**

wal•let (**wol**-it) ***noun*** A small, flat case for holding money, photographs, and/or cards.

wal•lop (**wol**-uhp) ***verb*** *(informal)* To hit someone or something very hard.
▸ **walloping, walloped** ▸ ***noun*** **wallop**

wal•low (**wol**-oh) ***verb***
1. To roll around in mud or water.
2. To enjoy something greatly, or to get completely involved in something.
▸ ***verb*** **wallowing, wallowed**

wall•pa•per (**wawl**-*pay*-pur) ***noun*** Patterned or colored paper that is pasted in sections to a wall in order to decorate a room. ▸ ***verb*** **wallpaper**

wal•nut (**wawl**-*nuht*) ***noun*** A sweet nut that grows on a tall tree and has a hard, wrinkled shell. The wood of the walnut tree is often used to make furniture.

wal•rus (**wawl**-ruhss) ***noun*** A large sea animal that lives in the Arctic. Walruses have tusks, flippers, tough skin, and a thick layer of blubber. They are related to seals and sea lions. ▸ ***noun, plural*** **walruses** *or* **walrus**

waltz (**wawlts**) ***noun***
1. A smooth, gliding ballroom dance with a regular 1-2-3 beat. ▸ ***verb*** **waltz** ▸ ***noun*** **waltzer**
2. A piece of music that accompanies a waltz.
▸ ***noun, plural*** **waltzes**

wam•pum (**wahm**-puhm) ***noun*** Beads made from polished shells strung together or woven to make belts, collars, and necklaces. Wampum was used by some American Indian tribes as money.

wand (**wond**) ***noun*** A thin rod or stick, especially one used by magicians.

wan•der (**won**-dur) ***verb***
1. To move about without a particular purpose or place to go; to roam; to ramble. ▸ ***noun*** **wanderer**
2. To get lost; to stray.
3. To stray from a particular subject; to become easily distracted.
▸ ***verb*** **wandering, wandered**

wane (**wayn**) ***verb***
1. To become less or smaller in size, importance, or strength.
2. When the moon **wanes,** it appears to get smaller.
▸ ***verb*** **waning, waned**

wan•gle (**wang**-guhl) ***verb*** *(informal)* To gain something by clever, tricky, or dishonest methods. ▸ **wangling, wangled**

want (**wont**)
1. ***verb*** To feel that you would like to have, do, or get something; to wish for; to desire.
2. ***verb*** To need or require something.
3. ***noun*** A lack.
4. ***noun*** A need, desire, or requirement.
5. ***noun*** The condition of being very poor or needy; poverty, as in *a family in want.*
▸ ***verb*** **wanting, wanted**

war (**wor**) ***noun***
1. Fighting between opposing forces.
2. A struggle or fight against something.
▸ ***verb*** **war**

war•bler (**warb**-lur) ***noun*** Any of several small, lively American songbirds.

Many warblers have brightly colored feathers.

ward (**word**)

1. ***noun*** A large room or section in a hospital where many patients are taken care of.

2. ***noun*** A person who is under the care of a guardian or the court.

3. ***noun*** For voting purposes, a district of a town or city.

4. ward off *verb* To prevent something from attacking or hurting you.

▸ **warding, warded**

war•den (**word**-uhn) ***noun***

1. Someone in charge of a prison.

2. An official who is responsible for enforcing certain laws, as in *a game warden.*

ward•robe (**word**-*robe*) ***noun***

1. A collection of clothes, especially all the clothes belonging to one person.

2. A tall piece of furniture or a closet used for storing clothes.

ware (**wair**) ***noun***

1. wares *noun, plural* Things that are for sale; goods.

2. Items of the same general kind, as in *silverware, hardware,* or *software.*

Ware sounds like **wear** and **where.**

ware•house (**wair**-*hous*) ***noun*** A large building used for storing goods or merchandise. ▸ ***verb*** **warehouse**

war•fare (**wor**-*fair*) ***noun*** The fighting of wars, or armed combat, as in *jungle warfare.*

war•like (**wor**-*like*) ***adjective*** Hostile, aggressive, or likely to start a war, as in *warlike behavior.*

warm (**worm**)

1. ***adjective*** A bit hot; not cold.

2. ***verb*** To increase the temperature of something.

3. ***adjective*** Holding in body heat, as in *a warm sweater.*

4. ***adjective*** Very friendly. ▸ ***adverb*** **warmly**

5. ***verb*** If you **warm up** before a sports match or athletic activity, you stretch or exercise gently in preparation. ▸ ***noun*** **warm-up**

6. ***verb*** When an engine **warms up,** it starts to run smoothly.

▸ ***noun*** **warmth** ▸ ***verb*** **warming, warmed** ▸ ***adjective*** **warmer, warmest**

warm-blood•ed (**bluhd**-id) ***adjective*** **Warm-blooded** animals have a body temperature that remains approximately the same, whatever their surroundings.

warn (**worn**) ***verb***

1. If you **warn** someone, you tell the person about a danger or a bad thing that might happen.

2. To give advice.

Warn sounds like **worn.**

▸ ***verb*** **warning, warned** ▸ ***noun*** **warning**

warp (**worp**) ***verb*** If an object **warps,** it gets twisted, curved, or bent out of shape. ▸ **warping, warped**

war•rant (**wor**-uhnt)

1. ***noun*** An official piece of paper that gives permission for something, as in *a search warrant.*

2. ***verb*** To guarantee. ▸ ***noun*** **warranty**

3. ***verb*** To deserve.

▸ ***verb*** **warranting, warranted**

war•ren (**wor**-uhn) ***noun*** A group of underground tunnels where rabbits breed and live.

war•ri•or (**wor**-ee-ur) ***noun*** A soldier, or someone who is experienced in fighting battles.

war•ship (**wor**-*ship*) ***noun*** A ship with heavy guns that is used in war.

wart (**wort**) ***noun***

1. A small, hard lump on the skin. Warts are caused by a virus.

2. A small lump or bump that grows on a plant. ▸ ***adjective*** **warty**

war•y (**wair**-ee) ***adjective*** Cautious and careful. ▸ **warier, wariest** ▸ ***noun*** **wariness** ▸ ***adverb*** **warily**

was (**wuhz**) ***verb*** The form of **be** used with *I, he, she,* or *it* or with singular nouns in the past tense.

W

wash (**wosh**)
1. ***verb*** To clean with water or soap and water. ▸ ***noun*** **wash,** ***noun*** **washing**
2. ***noun*** Clothing that needs to be or has been washed. ▸ ***noun, plural*** **washes**
3. ***verb*** To wear away by the action of moving water.
4. ***verb*** If the sea **washes** something **up,** it leaves it on the shore.
▸ ***verb*** **washes, washing, washed**

wash•a•ble (**wosh**-uh-buhl) ***adjective*** If a material is **washable,** you can wash it without causing any damage to it.

wash•er (**wosh**-ur) ***noun***
1. A washing machine.
2. A ring that fits between a nut and a bolt to give a tighter fit or prevent a leak.

washing machine ***noun*** A machine that washes clothes, linens, and similar items.

Wash•ing•ton's Birthday (**wosh**-ing-tuhnz) ***noun*** A holiday that honors the birthday of George Washington, the first president of the United States. Originally celebrated on February 22, Washington's actual birthday, this holiday is now observed on the third Monday in February as part of **Presidents' Day.**

was•n't (**wuhz**-uhnt) ***contraction*** A short form of *was not.*

wasp (**wosp**) ***noun*** A flying insect that has a slender body. Female wasps can give a painful sting.

waste (**wayst**)
1. ***verb*** If you **waste** something, you use or spend it foolishly or carelessly. ▸ ***noun*** **waste**
2. ***verb*** If someone **wastes away,** the person gets thinner and weaker because of illness.
3. ***noun*** Garbage, or something left over and not needed, as in *chemical waste.*
4. ***noun*** What the body does not use or need after food has been digested.
Waste sounds like **waist.**
▸ ***verb*** **wasting, wasted** ▸ ***adjective*** **waste**

waste•bas•ket (**wayst**-*bass*-kit) ***noun*** A small basket or open container used for scraps of paper or other small items of trash.

waste•ful (**wayst**-fuhl) ***adjective*** If you are **wasteful,** you use things up needlessly or carelessly and do not think about saving them. ▸ ***noun*** **wastefulness** ▸ ***adverb*** **wastefully**

waste•land (**wayst**-*land*) ***noun*** An area of land that is barren or empty; land where few plants or animals can live.

watch (**woch**)
1. ***noun*** A small clock usually worn on the wrist.
2. ***verb*** To look at something.
3. ***verb*** To be alert or careful about something.
4. ***verb*** To keep guard over. ▸ ***noun*** **watch**
5. ***noun*** A person or group that guards or protects.
6. ***noun*** The time that a guard is on duty.
▸ ***noun, plural*** **watches** ▸ ***verb*** **watches, watching, watched**

watch•dog (**woch**-*dawg*) ***noun***
1. A dog trained to guard a house, property, or people.
2. Someone who guards against theft, waste, or illegal practices.

watch•ful (**woch**-fuhl) ***adjective*** Observing carefully; alert. ▸ ***noun*** **watchfulness** ▸ ***adverb*** **watchfully**

wa•ter (**waw**-tur)
1. ***noun*** The colorless liquid that falls as rain and fills oceans, rivers, and lakes.
2. **waters** ***noun, plural*** The water in an ocean, a river, or a lake.
3. ***verb*** To pour water on something.
4. ***verb*** If your mouth **waters,** it produces saliva in response to the sight, smell, or thought of food.
5. ***verb*** If your eyes **water,** tears fill them.
6. ***verb*** If you **water** something **down,**

you make it weaker, usually by adding water.
▸ ***verb*** **watering, watered**

water buffalo ***noun*** A black buffalo with long horns that curve upward and outward. Found in Asia, it is often used to pull or carry heavy loads. ▸ ***noun, plural*** **water buffalo, water buffalos,** *or* **water buffaloes**

wa•ter•col•or (**waw**-tur-*kuhl*-ur) ***noun***
1. Paint that is mixed with water, not oil.
2. A picture painted with watercolors.
▸ ***noun*** **watercolorist**

wa•ter•cress (**waw**-tur-*kress*) ***noun*** A plant found in wet soil or running water. It has pungent leaves and is used mostly in salads.

water cycle ***noun*** The constant movement of the earth's water. Plants give off moisture, and water from rivers and oceans evaporates, making water vapor. This vapor rises, forms clouds, and then falls as rain, hail, or snow.

wa•ter•fall (**waw**-tur-*fawl*) ***noun*** Water from a stream or river that falls from a high place to a lower place.

wa•ter•front (**waw**-tur-*fruhnt*) ***noun*** Any land or area of a city or town that is located beside a body of water.
▸ ***adjective*** **waterfront**

watering can ***noun*** A metal or plastic container with a handle and a long spout used for watering plants.

water lily ***noun*** A plant that grows in freshwater ponds and lakes. Its wide, flat leaves float on the water, and it has fragrant, colorful flowers. ▸ ***noun, plural*** **water lilies**

wa•ter•logged (**waw**-tur-*logd*) ***adjective*** If something is **waterlogged,** it is so filled or soaked with water that it becomes heavy or hard to manage.

water main ***noun*** A large, main pipe in a system of pipes that carry water.

wa•ter•mark (**waw**-tur-*mark*) ***noun***
1. A mark or design in paper that you can see when you hold the paper up to the light.
2. A mark on a wall or other surface that shows how high the water in a river, a lake, or an ocean has risen.

wa•ter•mel•on (**waw**-tur-*mel*-uhn) ***noun*** A large, juicy fruit that grows on vines. It usually has a thick, green rind, many seeds, and sweet, watery pulp that is pink, red, or yellow.

water moccasin ***noun*** A poisonous snake that lives near water and in swamps in the southeastern part of the United States. It is also called a cottonmouth.

wa•ter•proof (**waw**-tur-*proof*) ***adjective*** If something is **waterproof,** it keeps water out, as in *a waterproof raincoat.* ▸ ***verb*** **waterproof**

wa•ter•shed (**waw**-tur-*shed*) ***noun***
1. A ridge or area of high land that separates two river basins.
2. The region or land area that drains into a river or lake.
3. An important factor; a turning point.

water-ski ***verb*** To travel on skis over water, towed by a boat. ▸ **water-skiing, water-skied** ▸ ***noun*** **water-skier,** ***noun*** **waterskiing**

wa•ter•tight (**waw**-tur-*tite*) ***adjective***
1. If something is **watertight,** it is completely sealed so that water cannot enter or leave it.
2. If an argument is **watertight,** it has no faults and can be clearly understood.

water vapor ***noun*** The gas produced when water evaporates.

wa•ter•way (**waw**-tur-*way*) ***noun*** A river, canal, or other body of water on which ships and boats travel.

wa•ter•wheel (**waw**-tur-*weel*) ***noun*** A large wheel that is turned by water flowing over or under it. Waterwheels are used to provide power.

wa•ter•works (**waw**-tur-*wurks*) ***noun, plural*** The system that provides water to a community or town, including reservoirs, pipes, machinery, and buildings. Waterworks can be used with a singular or a plural verb.

W

watt (**wot**) ***noun*** A unit for measuring electrical power. ▸ ***noun* wattage**

wat•tle and daub (**wot**-uhl **and daub**) ***noun*** A mixture of woven sticks and mud or clay that people once used to build houses.

wave (**wayv**)

1. ***verb*** To move your hand back and forth to get someone's attention or to say hello or good-bye. ▸ ***noun* wave**

2. ***verb*** To move or sway back and forth or up and down.

3. ***noun*** A moving ridge on the surface of water, especially the ocean.

4. ***noun*** A curl in your hair. ▸ ***verb* wave**

5. ***noun*** A vibration of energy that travels through air or water, as in *sound waves* or *radio waves.*

6. ***noun*** A sudden change or increase, as in *a heat wave* or *a crime wave.*

Wave sounds like **waive.**

▸ ***verb* waving, waved** ▸ ***adjective* wavy**

wave•length (**wayv**-*length*) ***noun***

1. The distance between one crest of a wave of light or sound and the next.

2. *(informal)* If you are **on the same wavelength** as someone, you have similar thoughts.

wa•ver (**way**-vur) ***verb***

1. To be uncertain or unsteady.

2. To quiver or to tremble.

▸ ***verb* wavering, wavered** ▸ ***noun* waver**

wax (**waks**)

1. ***noun*** A yellow substance that is secreted by bees and is used for building honeycombs.

2. ***noun*** A substance made from fats or oils and used to make crayons, polish, and candles.

3. ***verb*** To put wax or polish on something such as a car or furniture.

4. ***verb*** When the moon **waxes,** it appears to get larger.

5. ***verb*** To grow, or to become.

▸ ***verb* waxes, waxing, waxed**

▸ ***adjective* waxy**

way (**way**) ***noun***

1. A direction.

2. A road or a route.

3. A method or style of doing something.

4. A manner or a style.

5. Distance.

6. The opportunity to do or get what one wishes.

7. A point or a detail.

8. Space or a path.

9. ways *noun, plural* Habits or customs.

Way sounds like **weigh** and **whey.**

we (**wee**) ***pronoun, plural*** The people who are speaking or writing. **We** sounds like **wee.**

weak (**week**) ***adjective***

1. Having little strength, force, or power, as in *a weak person, a weak argument,* or *a weak light.* ▸ ***adverb* weakly**

2. Likely to break, fall, or collapse.

3. Lacking flavor.

4. Lacking in skill or knowledge.

5. Your **weak** points are the things that you are not very good at.

Weak sounds like **week.**

▸ ***adjective* weaker, weakest** ▸ ***noun* weakness** ▸ ***verb* weaken**

weak•ling (**week**-ling) ***noun*** A person without physical or moral strength.

wealth (**welth**) ***noun***

1. A great amount of money, property, or valuable possessions; riches.

2. A great amount of anything, as in *a wealth of ideas* or *a wealth of information.*

wealth•y (**wel**-thee) ***adjective*** Someone who is **wealthy** has a lot of money or property. ▸ **wealthier, wealthiest**

wean (**ween**) ***verb***

1. When you **wean** babies, you start giving them other food instead of their mothers' milk.

2. If you **wean** someone **from** something, you help him or her give it up gradually.

▸ ***verb* weaning, weaned**

weap•on (**wep**-uhn) ***noun***
1. Something that can be used in a fight to attack or defend, such as a sword, gun, knife, or bomb. ▸ ***noun*** **weaponry**
2. Anything that can be used to win a fight, struggle, or contest.

wear (**wair**)
1. ***verb*** To be dressed in something, or to carry or have something on your body. ▸ ***noun*** **wearer**
2. ***verb*** To have, or to show.
3. ***noun*** Clothes.
4. ***noun*** The gradual damage done to something by constant use.
5. ***verb*** To last a long time.
6. ***verb*** If an activity **wears** you **out,** it makes you very tired.
7. ***verb*** If you **wear out** your clothes, you make them ragged and useless.
8. wear away ***verb*** To destroy something slowly, bit by bit.
9. wear off ***verb*** To become less.
Wear sounds like **ware** and **where.**
▸ ***verb*** **wearing, wore** (**wor**), **worn**

wea•ry (**wihr**-ee) ***adjective***
1. Very tired, or exhausted.
2. Having little patience or interest; bored.
▸ ***adjective*** **wearier, weariest** ▸ ***noun*** **weariness** ▸ ***adverb*** **wearily**

wea•sel (**wee**-zuhl) ***noun*** A small animal with a long, slender body; short legs; and soft, thick, reddish brown fur. It feeds on rats, mice, rabbits, small birds, and snakes.

weath•er (**weTH**-ur)
1. ***noun*** The condition of the outside air or atmosphere at a particular time and place. Weather can be described as hot or cold, wet or dry, calm or windy, clear or cloudy.
2. ***verb*** If wood, stone, or another material **weathers,** it changes after being outside for a long time.
3. ***verb*** If you **weather** a storm or crisis, you get through it.
4. If you are **under the weather,** you aren't feeling very well.
Weather sounds like **whether.**
▸ ***verb*** **weathering, weathered**

weather-beaten ***adjective*** Something that is **weather-beaten** is damaged or worn by the weather.

weather forecast ***noun*** A prediction about the weather for the next day or the next few days. ▸ ***noun*** **weather forecaster**

weather vane ***noun*** A device placed on the ground or on the roof of a building that turns freely to show which way the wind is blowing.

weave (**weev**)
1. ***verb*** To make cloth, baskets, and other objects by passing threads or strips over and under each other. ▸ ***noun*** **weaver**
2. ***verb*** To spin a web or cocoon.
3. ***verb*** To move from side to side or in and out in order to get through something.
4. ***noun*** A method or pattern of weaving.
Weave sounds like **we've.**
▸ ***verb*** **weaving, wove** (**wohv**) *or* **weaved, woven** (**woh**-vin) *or* **weaved**

web (**web**) ***noun***
1. A very fine net of sticky threads made by a spider to catch flies and other insects.
2. Anything put together in a careful or complicated way; something that snares or traps, as in *a web of city streets* or *a web of lies.*
3. The fold of skin or tissue that connects the toes of a duck, frog, or other animal that swims.
4. The Web is short for the World Wide Web.

web-foot•ed (**fut**-id) ***adjective*** Having toes that are connected by a web or fold of skin.

Web page ***noun*** A computer file linked to the World Wide Web. It may contain text, pictures, video, or other information.

Web site ***noun*** A group of linked computer files on the World Wide Web.

W

wed (**wed**) ***verb***
1. To get married to someone.
2. To perform a marriage ceremony.
▸ ***verb*** **wedding, wedded** *or* **wed**

we'd (**weed**) ***contraction*** A short form of *we would, we had,* or *we should.* **We'd** sounds like **weed.**

wed·ding (**wed**-ing) ***noun*** A marriage ceremony.

wedge (**wej**)
1. ***noun*** A piece of food, wood, metal, or plastic that is thin at one end and thick at the other.
2. ***verb*** To split, force apart, or hold in place with a wedge.
3. ***verb*** To squeeze or crowd into a limited space.
▸ ***verb*** **wedging, wedged**

Wed·nes·day (**wenz**-dee *or* **wenz**-*day*) ***noun*** The fourth day of the week, after Tuesday and before Thursday.

wee (**wee**) ***adjective*** Very small; tiny. **Wee** sounds like **we.**

weed (**weed**)
1. ***noun*** A plant that is seen as useless or harmful and growing where it is not wanted.
2. ***verb*** If you **weed** your garden, you pull the weeds out.
3. ***verb*** If you **weed** something **out,** you remove it because it is useless or harmful.
Weed sounds like **we'd.**
▸ ***verb*** **weeding, weeded**

week (**week**) ***noun***
1. A period of seven days, usually from Sunday to Saturday.
2. The hours or days that a person works or spends in school each week.
Week sounds like **weak.**

week·day (**week**-*day*) ***noun*** Any day of the week except Saturday or Sunday.

week·end (**week**-*end*) ***noun*** The period of time from Friday night through Sunday night.

week·ly (**week**-lee)
1. ***adjective*** Done, happening, or appearing once a week or every week, as in *a weekly visit* or *a weekly newspaper.*
2. ***adverb*** Once a week, or every week.
3. ***noun*** A newspaper or magazine that is published once a week. ▸ ***noun, plural*** **weeklies**

weep (**weep**) ***verb*** To cry because you feel very sad or very emotional.
▸ **weeping, wept** (**wept**) ▸ ***adjective*** **weepy**

wee·vil (**wee**-vuhl) ***noun*** A beetle with a snout that curves downward. The weevil is a pest to farmers because its larvae eat grain, cotton, fruit, and other plants and crops.

weigh (**way**) ***verb***
1. To measure how heavy or light someone or something is by using a scale.
2. To have a particular weight.
3. To consider something carefully before deciding.
4. If you are **weighed down,** you have too much to carry, do, or think about.
Weigh sounds like **way** and **whey.**
▸ ***verb*** **weighing, weighed**

weight (**wate**) ***noun***
1. Someone or something's **weight** is the measure of how heavy the person or thing is.
2. A unit, such as the ounce, pound, or ton, that is used for measuring weight.
3. A heavy object used to hold things down, as in *a paperweight.*
4. weights ***noun, plural*** Heavy objects that people lift as an exercise to make their muscles stronger.
5. A heavy load or burden; pressure.
Weight sounds like **wait.**

weight·less (**wate**-liss) ***adjective***
1. Having little or no weight.
2. Free of the pull of gravity.
▸ ***noun*** **weightlessness** ▸ ***adverb*** **weightlessly**

weight lift·er (**lift**-ur) ***noun*** A person who lifts weights in competitions or for pleasure. ▸ ***noun*** **weight lifting**

weird (**wihrd**) ***adjective*** Strange or mysterious. ▸ **weirder, weirdest**
▸ ***noun*** **weirdness** ▸ ***adverb*** **weirdly**

W

wel•come (**wel**-kuhm)
1. ***verb*** If you **welcome** someone, you greet the person in a friendly way.
▸ ***interjection* welcome**
2. ***adjective*** If something is **welcome,** you like it or are glad to have it.
3. ***verb*** If you **welcome** something, you are glad to have it.
4. ***adjective*** "You're **welcome**" is the polite response when someone says, "Thank you."
▸ ***verb* welcoming, welcomed** ▸ ***noun* welcome** ▸ ***adjective* welcoming**

weld (**weld**) ***verb***
1. To join two pieces of metal or plastic by heating them until they are soft enough to be joined together. ▸ ***noun* weld, *noun* welder**
2. To bring together; to unite.
▸ ***verb* welding, welded**

wel•fare (**wel**-fair) ***noun***
1. Someone's **welfare** is the person's state of health, happiness, and comfort.
2. Money or other help given by a government to people who are in need.

well (**wel**)
1. ***adverb*** If you do something **well,** you do it in a good, skillful, or satisfactory way.
2. ***adverb*** Thoroughly.
3. ***adverb*** Much; to a great extent.
4. ***adverb*** In a close or familiar way.
5. ***adjective*** Healthy.
6. ***noun*** A deep hole from which you can draw water, oil, or natural gas from under the ground.
7. ***interjection*** You say **well** to show surprise or doubt.

we'll (**weel**) ***contraction*** A short form of *we will* or *we shall.* **We'll** sounds like **wheel.**

well-balanced ***adjective***
1. Nicely or evenly balanced, as in *a well-balanced diet.*
2. Sane or sensible.

well-behaved ***adjective*** Acting properly and with good manners, as in *well-behaved students.*

well-being ***noun*** Health and happiness.

well-known ***adjective*** Known by many people; famous, as in *a well-known actor.*

well-off ***adjective***
1. If someone is **well-off,** he or she is wealthy or rich.
2. If someone is **well-off,** everything is going well for him or her.

well-round•ed (**wel-round**-id) ***adjective*** A **well-rounded** person has experience or interests in many different areas.

were (**wur**) ***verb*** The form of **be** used with *we, you,* or *they* or with plural nouns in the past tense. **Were** sounds like **whir.**

we're (**wihr**) ***contraction*** A short form of *we are.*

weren't (**wurnt** *or* **wur**-uhnt) ***contraction*** A short form of *were not.*

west (**west**)
1. ***noun*** One of the four main points of the compass. West is the direction in which the sun sets. ▸ ***adverb* west**
2. West *noun* Any area or region lying in this direction.
3. the West *noun* In the United States, the region that is west of the Mississippi River.
4. ***adjective*** To do with or existing in the west, as in *the west side of the street.*
▸ ***adverb* westerly, *adverb* westward**

west•ern (**wess**-turn)
1. ***adjective*** In, of, toward, or from the west.
2. ***adjective*** To do with a western region, as in *western Canada.*
3. Western *adjective* To do with the West, as in *Western ranches.*
4. Western *or* **western *noun*** A cowboy movie or television show set in the western part of the United States, especially during the last half of the 19th century.

Western Hemisphere ***noun*** The half of the world west of the Atlantic Ocean. It includes North, Central, and South America and surrounding waters.

West In•dies (**in**-deez) ***noun, plural*** A string of islands in the Western Hemisphere that separates the Caribbean Sea from the Atlantic Ocean.

west•ward (**west**-wurd) ***adverb*** To or toward the west. ▸ ***adjective*** **westward**

wet (**wet**)
1. ***adjective*** Covered with or full of liquid, as in *a wet cloth.*
2. ***adjective*** Not yet set or dry, as in *wet cement* or *wet paint.*
3. ***adjective*** Rainy.
4. ***verb*** To make something wet.
▸ **wetting, wet** *or* **wetted**
▸ ***adjective*** **wetter, wettest**

wet•land (**wet**-*land* or **wet**-luhnd) *or* **wet•lands** (**wet**-*landz* or **wet**-luhndz) ***noun*** Marshy land; land where there is much moisture in the soil.

we've (**weev**) ***contraction*** A short form of *we have.* **We've** sounds like **weave.**

whack (**wak**) ***noun***
1. *(informal)* A hard, sharp hit or slap.
▸ ***verb*** **whack**
2. *(slang)* An attempt.

whale (**wale**)
1. ***noun*** A large sea animal that looks like a fish but is actually a mammal that breathes air. Dolphins and porpoises are members of the whale family.
2. ***verb*** To hunt for whales. ▸ **whaling, whaled**
Whale sounds like **wail.**

whal•er (**way**-lur) ***noun***
1. Someone who hunts whales for their meat, oil, and bones. ▸ ***noun*** **whaling**
2. A boat used to catch whales.

wharf (**worf**) ***noun*** A long platform, built along a shore, where boats and ships can load and unload; a dock.
▸ ***noun, plural*** **wharves** (worvz) *or* **wharfs**

what (**wot** *or* **wuht**)
1. ***pronoun*** The word **what** is used in questions to discover more about something or someone.
2. ***pronoun*** The thing or things that.
3. ***adjective*** The word **what** is used to emphasize how great, small, strange, etc., something or someone is.
4. ***adverb*** In which way; how.
5. ***interjection*** The word **what** is used to show surprise or anger.

what•ev•er (wot-**ev**-ur *or* wuht-**ev**-ur)
1. ***pronoun*** Anything that. ▸ ***adjective*** **whatever**
2. ***pronoun*** No matter what.
3. ***pronoun*** Which thing or things; what.
4. ***adjective*** Any that.
5. ***adjective*** Of any kind or type; at all.

what's (**wots** *or* **wuhts**) ***contraction*** A short form of *what is* or *what has.*

wheat (**weet**) ***noun*** A cereal grass whose grain is used for making flour, pasta, and breakfast foods.

wheel (**weel**)
1. ***noun*** A round frame or object that turns on an axle. Wheels are used to work machinery or move a vehicle.
2. ***noun*** Anything that uses or is shaped like a wheel, as in *a spinning wheel* or *a steering wheel.*
3. ***verb*** To push something on wheels.
4. ***verb*** To turn.
5. **wheels *noun, plural*** *(slang)* An automobile.
Wheel sounds like **we'll.**
▸ ***verb*** **wheeling, wheeled**

wheel•bar•row (**weel**-*ba*-roh) ***noun*** A small cart with one wheel at the front, often used to carry things around in yards or gardens.

wheel•chair (**weel**-*chair*) ***noun*** A chair on wheels for people who are ill, injured, or disabled.

wheel•ie (**wee**-lee) ***noun*** *(informal)* If you do a **wheelie** on a bicycle or motorcycle, you ride with the front wheel off the ground.

wheeze (**weez**) ***verb*** To breathe with difficulty, making a whistling noise in your chest. People sometimes wheeze when they have asthma or a bad cold.
▸ **wheezing, wheezed** ▸ ***noun*** **wheeziness** ▸ ***adjective*** **wheezy**

whelk (**welk**) ***noun*** A large snail that lives in salt water and has a spiral shell.

when (**wen**)
1. ***adverb*** The word **when** is used to ask about the time of an event.
2. ***conjunction*** At the time that.
3. ***conjunction*** At any time; whenever.
4. ***conjunction*** Although; but.
5. ***conjunction*** Considering the fact that.

when•ev•er (*wen*-**ev**-ur) ***conjunction*** At any time.

where (**wair**)
1. ***adverb*** The word **where** is used to ask about the place or position of someone or something.
2. ***conjunction*** In, at, or to the place that or in which.
3. ***conjunction*** In or at which place.
4. ***pronoun*** What place.
Where sounds like **ware** and **wear.**

where•a•bouts (**wair**-uh-*bouts*)
1. ***adverb*** Roughly where.
2. ***noun*** The place where someone or something is. Whereabouts can be used with a singular or plural verb.

where•as (*wair*-**az**) ***conjunction*** On the other hand.

where•up•on (**wair**-uh-**pon**) ***conjunction*** After which; at which time; and then.

wher•ev•er (*wair*-**ev**-ur) ***conjunction*** In, at, or to any place. ▸ ***adverb*** **wherever**

wheth•er (**weTH**-ur) ***conjunction***
1. If.
2. The word **whether** is used to show a choice between two things.
Whether sounds like **weather.**

whew (**hyoo**) ***interjection*** A word used to show relief, discomfort, or surprise.

whey (**way**) ***noun*** The watery part of milk that separates when milk sours or when you make cheese. **Whey** sounds like **way** and **weigh.**

which (**wich**)
1. ***adjective*** The word **which** is used to ask about a choice of things.
2. ***pronoun*** What one or ones.
3. ***pronoun*** The one or ones that.
4. ***conjunction*** The one or ones mentioned; that.
Which sounds like **witch.**

which•ev•er (*wich*-**ev**-ur)
1. ***pronoun*** Any one or ones. *Buy whichever you want.*
2. ***pronoun*** No matter which. *Whichever you buy is fine with me.*
3. ***adjective*** Any one or ones. *Read whichever book seems the most fun.*
4. ***adjective*** No matter which. *Whichever book you read, you'll like it.*

whiff (**wif**) ***noun***
1. A light puff of air or smoke.
2. A faint smell in the air.
▸ ***verb*** **whiff**

while (**wile**)
1. ***noun*** A period of time.
2. ***conjunction*** During the time that.
3. ***conjunction*** Although.
4. ***verb*** To pass or spend time in a pleasant or relaxed way. ▸ **whiling, whiled**

whim (**wim**) ***noun*** A sudden idea or wish.

whim•per (**wim**-pur) ***verb*** To make weak, crying noises. ▸ **whimpering, whimpered** ▸ ***noun*** **whimper**

whine (**wine**) ***verb***
1. To make a shrill, drawn-out sound that is sad or unpleasant.
2. To complain or moan about something in an annoying way. ▸ ***noun*** **whiner**
Whine sounds like **wine.**
▸ ***verb*** **whining, whined**

whin•ny (**win**-ee) ***noun*** A horse's low, gentle neigh. ▸ ***noun, plural*** **whinnies** ▸ ***verb*** **whinny**

whip (**wip**)
1. ***noun*** A long piece of leather on a handle, used especially for driving horses and cattle. ▸ ***verb*** **whip**
2. ***verb*** To move, pull, or take something suddenly.
3. ***verb*** *(informal)* To defeat badly.
4. ***verb*** To beat something such as eggs or cream into a foam.
▸ ***verb*** **whipping, whipped**

W

whip•poor•will (**wip**-uhr-*wil*) ***noun*** A plump bird with brown, gray, and black spots on its brown feathers. It is found in eastern North America and feeds and sings at night. Its call sounds very much like its name.

whir (**wur**)
1. ***verb*** To move, fly, or operate with a buzzing or humming sound. ▸ **whirring, whirred**
2. ***noun*** A buzzing or humming sound.

whirl (**wurl**)
1. ***verb*** If something **whirls,** it moves around quickly in a circle. ▸ **whirling, whirled**
2. ***noun*** A fast or confused movement. ▸ ***verb*** **whirl**
3. *(informal)* If you **give** something **a whirl,** you try it out.

whirl•pool (**wurl**-*pool*) ***noun***
1. A current of water that moves quickly in a circle and pulls floating objects toward its center.
2. A soothing bath in which all or part of the body is covered by whirling currents of hot water. Also called a *whirlpool bath.*

whirl•wind (**wurl**-*wind*)
1. ***noun*** A wind like a cyclone that moves in a tall column and goes around and around rapidly and often violently.
2. ***adjective*** Very quick and sudden.

whisk (**wisk**)
1. ***noun*** A metal tool that you use for beating eggs or cream. ▸ ***verb*** **whisk**
2. ***verb*** To move something quickly or suddenly.
3. ***verb*** To brush or remove with a quick, sweeping motion.
▸ ***verb*** **whisking, whisked**

whisk•er (**wiss**-kur) ***noun***
1. **whiskers** ***noun, plural*** The hairs that grow on a man's face; a beard.
2. One of the hairs that grows on a man's face, especially on the cheeks and jaw.
3. One of the long, stiff hairs near the mouth of some animals such as cats and rabbits.

whis•key (**wiss**-kee) ***noun*** A strong, alcoholic drink made from barley, corn, or rye. ▸ ***noun, plural*** **whiskeys**

whis•per (**wiss**-pur)
1. ***verb*** To talk very quietly or softly. ▸ **whispering, whispered** ▸ ***noun*** **whisper**
2. ***noun*** A soft, rustling sound, as in *the whisper of leaves in the breeze.* ▸ ***verb*** **whisper**

whis•tle (**wiss**-uhl)
1. ***noun*** An instrument that makes a high, shrill, loud sound when you blow it.
2. ***verb*** To make a high, shrill sound by blowing air through your lips.
3. ***verb*** To make a whistling sound.
4. ***noun*** A whistling sound made by the lips or by a whistle.
5. ***verb*** To move very fast with a whistling sound.
▸ ***verb*** **whistling, whistled**

white (**wite**)
1. ***noun*** The lightest color; the color of snow or milk. ▸ ***adjective*** **white**
2. ***noun*** The **white** of an egg is the part around the yolk.
3. ***adjective*** Light in color, as in *white meat of a chicken.*
4. ***adjective*** Pale or pallid.
5. ***adjective*** Pale gray or silver.
▸ ***adjective*** **whiter, whitest**

white blood cell ***noun*** A colorless blood cell that is part of the body's immune system. It protects the body against infection by destroying diseased cells and germs.

White House ***noun***
1. The official home of the president of the United States, located on 1600 Pennsylvania Avenue in Washington, D.C.
2. The office or power of the president of the United States.

whit•en (**wite**-uhn) ***verb*** To make white or become white. ▸ **whitening, whitened**

white noise ***noun***
1. A mixture of sound waves that creates a noise used to mask annoying or distracting sounds.
2. Background noise from appliances such as air conditioners and fans.

white•wash (**wite**-*wosh*)
1. ***noun*** A mixture of lime and water used for painting walls and wood fences white. ▸ ***noun, plural*** **whitewashes** ▸ ***verb*** **whitewash**
2. ***verb*** To cover up someone's mistakes, crimes, or wrongdoings.
▸ **whitewashes, whitewashing, whitewashed**

whit•tle (**wit**-uhl) ***verb***
1. To cut or shave small pieces from wood or soap with a knife.
2. To make or carve something by doing this.
3. To reduce bit by bit.
▸ ***verb*** **whittling, whittled** ▸ ***noun*** **whittling**

whiz *or* **whizz** (**wiz**)
1. ***verb*** To move very fast, often with a buzzing sound. ▸ **whizzes, whizzing, whizzed**
2. ***noun*** *(slang)* A person who has great skill or ability in a particular field or activity. ▸ ***noun, plural*** **whizzes**

who (**hoo**) ***pronoun***
1. The word **who** is used to ask questions about people.
2. The word **who** is used to show which person you are talking about or to give more information about someone.

who'd (**hood**) ***contraction*** A short form of *who would* or *who had.*

who•ev•er (*hoo*-**ev**-ur) ***pronoun***
1. Anyone at all, or no matter who.
2. Who.

whole (**hole**)
1. ***adjective*** Entire or total; all of.
2. ***adjective*** Complete, with nothing missing.
3. ***noun*** The entire thing; all the parts of something.
Whole sounds like **hole.**

whole number ***noun*** Any of the set of numbers beginning with 0 and continuing with each number being one more than the number before it. The whole numbers are 0, 1, 2, 3, 4, . . . They go on and on without end. Numbers such as –5, 2½ and 5.3 are not whole numbers.

whole•sale (**hole**-*sale*) ***adverb*** When storekeepers buy things **wholesale,** they buy them cheaply in large quantities in order to sell them at a profit. ▸ ***noun*** **wholesaler** ▸ ***adjective*** **wholesale**

whole•some (**hole**-suhm) ***adjective***
1. Healthy, or good for you, as in *a wholesome diet.*
2. Suggesting good health, a sound mind, or good or moral behavior.

whole wheat ***adjective*** Made from the entire kernel of wheat, as in *whole wheat bread.*

who'll (**hool**) ***contraction*** A short form of *who will* or *who shall.*

whol•ly (**hoh**-lee) ***adverb*** Completely. **Wholly** sounds like **holy.**

whom (**hoom**) ***pronoun*** What or which person or people. **Whom** is the form of **who** that functions as the object of a verb or preposition. It is often used in formal speech and writing.

whom•ev•er (*hoom*-**ev**-ur) ***pronoun*** The form of **whoever** used as the object of a verb or preposition.

whoop (**hoop** *or* **hup** *or* **wup**) ***noun*** A loud cry or shout. ▸ ***verb*** **whoop**

whooping cough ***noun*** An infectious disease that makes children and babies cough violently and breathe noisily.

whooping crane ***noun*** A large, white crane with black wing tips and a red face. Its call sounds like a trumpet. Whooping cranes live in Canada and the United States, but today there are only about 200 of them in all.

who's (**hooz**) ***contraction*** A short form of *who is* or *who has.* **Who's** sounds like **whose.**

W

W

whose (**hooz**) ***pronoun***
1. The word **whose** is used to ask who something belongs to.
2. The word **whose** is used to indicate the person or thing that you are talking about.
Whose sounds like **who's.**

why (**wye**)
1. ***adverb*** The word **why** is used to ask about the reason for something.
2. ***conjunction*** The reason for which.
3. ***interjection*** The word **why** is used to show mild surprise or to show that a person is pausing to think.

wick (**wik**) ***noun*** The twisted cord running through a candle, an oil lamp, or a lighter that soaks up the fuel and burns when lit.

wick•ed (**wik**-id) ***adjective*** Very bad, cruel, or evil. ▸ ***noun*** **wickedness** ▸ ***adverb*** **wickedly**

wick•er (**wik**-ur) ***noun*** Thin, flexible twigs or branches, usually from a willow tree, that are woven to make baskets and furniture. ▸ ***adjective*** **wicker**

wick•et (**wik**-it) ***noun*** One of several small wire arches through which balls are hit in croquet.

wide (**wide**)
1. ***adjective*** Having a certain distance from one side to the other or from edge to edge.
2. ***adjective*** Large from side to side; broad. ▸ ***verb*** **widen**
3. ***adjective*** Covering a large number of things.
4. ***adjective*** Completely open, as in *wide eyes.*
5. ***adverb*** Not close to.
6. ***adverb*** Over a large area.
7. ***adverb*** To the full extent.
▸ ***adjective*** **wider, widest** ▸ ***adverb*** **widely**

wide•spread (**wide**-*spred*) ***adjective***
1. Happening in many places or among many people.
2. Fully open.

wid•ow (**wid**-oh) ***noun*** A woman whose husband has died and who has not married again. ▸ ***adjective*** **widowed**

wid•ow•er (**wid**-oh-ur) ***noun*** A man whose wife has died and who has not married again. ▸ ***adjective*** **widowed**

width (**width**) ***noun*** The distance from one side of something to the other.

wife (**wife**) ***noun*** The female partner in a marriage. ▸ ***noun, plural*** **wives**

wig (**wig**) ***noun*** A covering of real or artificial hair made to fit someone's head.

wig•gle (**wig**-uhl) ***verb*** To make small movements from side to side or up and down. ▸ **wiggling, wiggled** ▸ ***noun*** **wiggle,** ***noun*** **wiggler** ▸ ***adjective*** **wiggly**

wig•wam (**wig**-*wahm*) ***noun*** A hut made of poles and covered with bark or hides. Some American Indian tribes, chiefly in the eastern United States, once lived in wigwams.

wild (**wilde**)
1. ***adjective*** Natural and not tamed by humans, as in *wild animals.*
2. ***adjective*** Not controlled, or not disciplined, as in *wild children.*
3. ***adjective*** Overcome with an emotion such as grief, anger, or happiness.
4. ***adjective*** Crazy, fantastic, or reckless.
5. ***noun*** An area that has been left in its natural state; wilderness.
▸ ***noun*** **wildness** ▸ ***adjective*** **wilder, wildest** ▸ ***adverb*** **wildly**

wild•cat (**wilde**-*kat*) ***noun*** Any of several wild members of the cat family that are small or medium in size, including the bobcat, ocelot, and lynx. Wildcats are distantly related to the domestic cat.

wil•der•ness (**wil**-dur-niss) ***noun*** An area of wild land where no people live, such as a dense forest. ▸ ***noun, plural*** **wildernesses**

wild•flow•er (**wilde**-*flou*-ur) ***noun*** Any flower of a plant that grows in a field, woods, or any wild area without the help of human beings.

wild•life (**wilde**-*life*) ***noun*** Wild animals living in their natural environment.

W

will (**wil**)
1. ***noun*** Written instructions stating what should happen to someone's property and money when the person dies.
2. ***noun*** The power to choose or control what you will and will not do. ▸ ***verb* will**
3. ***noun*** Strong purpose; determination.
4. ***verb* Will** is a helping verb used to show that something is going to take place or exist in the future or to show determination. ▸ ***verb* would**

will•ful (**wil**-fuhl) ***adjective***
1. Deliberate, as in *willful damage.* ▸ ***adjective* willfully**
2. Someone who is **willful** is determined to have his or her own way. ▸ ***noun* willfulness**

will•ing (**wil**-ing) ***adjective*** Ready and eager to offer help or do what is asked. ▸ ***noun* willingness** ▸ ***adverb* willingly**

wil•low (**wil**-oh) ***noun*** A tree with narrow leaves and thin branches that bend easily. Willows are often found near water.

wilt (**wilt**) ***verb***
1. If a plant **wilts,** it begins to droop.
2. If a person **wilts,** he or she becomes tired through lack of energy or food. ▸ ***verb* wilting, wilted**

wimp (**wimp**) ***noun*** *(informal)* A weak or cowardly person. ▸ ***adjective* wimpy**

win (**win**) ***verb***
1. To come in first in a contest. ▸ ***noun* win, *noun* winner**
2. To gain or deserve something. ▸ ***verb* winning, won**

wince (**winss**) ***verb*** To flinch or shrink back because you are in pain, embarrassed, or disgusted. ▸ **wincing, winced** ▸ ***noun* wince**

winch (**winch**) ***noun*** A machine that lifts or pulls heavy objects. A winch is made up of cable wound around a rotating drum. A ship's anchor is lifted with a winch. ▸ ***noun, plural* winches** ▸ ***verb* winch**

wind
1. (**wind**) ***noun*** Moving air. ▸ ***adjective* windy**
2. (**wind**) ***noun*** The ability to breathe; breath. ▸ ***verb* wind**
3. (**winde**) ***verb*** To wrap something around something else.
4. (**winde**) ***verb*** To twist and turn.
5. (**winde**) ***verb*** To turn the key of a clock.
6. wind up (**winde**) ***verb*** *(slang)* If you **wind** something **up,** you finish it. ▸ ***noun* windup** ▸ ***verb* winding, wound** (**wound**)

wind-chill factor ***noun*** A measurement given in degrees that reports the combined effect of low temperature and wind speed on the human body. Also called the *chill factor* or the *wind-chill index.*

wind•ed (**win**-did) ***adjective*** If you are **winded,** you are out of breath because of exercise or a sudden blow to the stomach.

wind•fall (**wind**-*fawl*) ***noun***
1. Fruit that has been blown off a tree.
2. A sudden piece of good news or good luck, usually an unexpected gain of money.

wind instrument ***noun*** A musical instrument, such as a flute, trumpet, or harmonica, played by blowing.

wind•mill (**wind**-*mil*) ***noun*** A machine operated by wind power that is used to grind grain into flour, pump water, or generate electricity.

win•dow (**win**-doh) ***noun***
1. An opening, especially in the wall of a building, that lets in air and light. Windows are usually enclosed by a frame that contains panes of glass or clear plastic. They can usually be opened and shut.
2. A single sheet or pane of glass in a window.
3. The viewing space on a computer screen in which you can see information and work with a program.

W

win•dow•pane (**win**-doh-*pane*) ***noun*** A single sheet or section of glass in a window.

window-shop ***verb*** If you **window-shop,** you look at merchandise in store windows but do not buy anything. ▸ **window-shopping, window-shopped**

wind•pipe (**wind**-*pipe*) ***noun*** The tube that links the lungs with the throat and carries air for breathing.

wind•shear (**wind**-*shihr*) ***noun*** A sudden change in wind speed and direction that is caused by a downward flow of cool air. Windshears occur during thunderstorms. They can cause aircraft to lose altitude quickly.

wind•shield (**wind**-*sheeld*) ***noun*** The window of strengthened glass or plastic in the front of a motor vehicle that protects the driver and passengers from the wind.

wind•surf•ing (**wind**-*surf*-ing) ***noun*** The sport of sailing by standing on a board with a flexible mast and a sail and holding onto a curved bar known as a *boom.* ▸ ***noun*** **windsurfer**

wind•swept (**wind**-*swept*) ***adjective*** Exposed to or blown by the wind.

wind turbine ***noun*** An engine that is driven by propellers and uses energy from the wind to make electricity.

wine (**wine**) ***noun*** An alcoholic drink made from the fermented juice of grapes. **Wine** sounds like **whine.**

wing (**wing**) ***noun***
1. One of the feather-covered limbs of a bird that the bird flaps in order to fly.
2. A movable part on an insect or a bat that allows it to fly.
3. A winglike structure on an aircraft that makes it able to fly.
4. An outer part or extension of something.
5. wings *noun, plural* The sides of a theater stage that cannot be seen by the audience.

wing•span (**wing**-*span*) ***noun*** The distance between the outer tips of the wings of a bird or an aircraft.

wink (**wingk**)
1. *verb* To close one eye briefly as a signal or a friendly gesture. ▸ **winking, winked** ▸ ***noun*** **wink**
2. *noun* The time it takes to wink; a very short time; an instant.

win•ner (**win**-ur) ***noun***
1. A person, a team, an animal, or a thing that wins a contest.
2. *(informal)* A person, an idea, or a plan that seems likely to succeed.

win•ning (**win**-ing)
1. *adjective* Successful or victorious.
2. *adjective* Pleasing, attractive, or charming.
3. winnings *noun, plural* Something that is won in a game or competition, especially money.

win•ter (**win**-tur) ***noun*** The season between autumn and spring, when the weather is coldest. ▸ ***adjective*** **wintry**

win•ter•green (**win**-tur-*green*) ***noun*** A low evergreen plant with white flowers and red berries. Its leaves produce a minty oil used in medicines and flavorings. ▸ ***adjective*** **wintergreen**

wipe (**wipe**) ***verb***
1. To clean or dry by rubbing.
2. To clear or remove by rubbing.
3. wipe out To destroy something totally.
▸ ***verb*** **wiping, wiped**

wire (**wire**)
1. *noun* A long, thin, flexible piece of metal. Wire can be used to pull or support things or to conduct an electrical current.
2. *noun* A telegram. ▸ ***verb*** **wire**
3. *verb* To fasten things together with a piece of wire.
4. *verb* To install or put in wires for electricity.
▸ ***verb*** **wiring, wired** ▸ ***noun*** **wiring**

wir•y (**wye**-ree) ***adjective***
1. Tough and stiff, as in *wiry hair.*

2. A **wiry** person is thin but tough.
▸ ***adjective*** **wirier, wiriest**

wis•dom (**wiz**-duhm) ***noun*** Knowledge, experience, and good judgment.

wisdom tooth ***noun*** Any of the four teeth that come in last, usually after adolescence. ▸ ***noun, plural*** **wisdom teeth**

wise (**wize**) ***adjective*** Having or showing good judgment and intelligence.
▸ **wiser, wisest** ▸ ***adverb*** **wisely**

wish (**wish**)
1. ***noun*** A strong desire or longing for something. ▸ ***noun, plural*** **wishes**
2. ***verb*** To want something very much.
3. ***verb*** To hope for something for somebody else.
▸ ***verb*** **wishes, wishing, wished**

wish•bone (**wish**-*bohn*) ***noun*** A bone shaped like a Y in front of the breastbone of most birds. According to superstition, when two people pull a wishbone apart, the one who gets the longer piece will have a wish granted.

wisp (**wisp**) ***noun*** A small and delicate piece, strand, or streak of something, as in *a wisp of hair* or *a wisp of smoke.*
▸ ***adjective*** **wispy**

wis•te•ri•a (wi-**stihr**-ee-uh) ***noun*** A vine plant with woody stems and hanging clusters of blue, white, pink, or purple flowers.

wist•ful (**wist**-fuhl) ***adjective*** Sadly wishful; yearning or longing. ▸ ***adverb*** **wistfully**

wit (**wit**) ***noun***
1. The ability to say clever and funny things.
2. Someone who can say clever and funny things.
3. **wits** ***noun, plural*** The ability to think quickly and clearly.

witch (**wich**) ***noun*** A person, especially a woman, believed by some people to have magic powers. **Witch** sounds like **which.** ▸ ***noun, plural*** **witches**

with (**wiTH** *or* **with**) ***preposition***
1. In the company or care of.
2. Having.
3. In a way that shows.
4. In addition to.
5. In the opinion of.
6. By using.
7. In regard to.
8. Against.
9. In support of.

with•draw (wiTH-**draw** *or* with-**draw**) ***verb***
1. To remove or take away something.
2. To drop out, or to go away.
▸ ***verb*** **withdrawing, withdrew, withdrawn** ▸ ***noun*** **withdrawal**

with•drawn (wiTH-**drawn** *or* with-**drawn**) ***adjective*** A **withdrawn** person is very shy and quiet.

with•er (**wiTH**-ur) ***verb*** When something **withers,** it shrivels up because it has lost moisture.
▸ **withering, withered**

with•hold (with-**hohld** *or* wiTH-**hold**) ***verb*** To keep something back, or to refuse to give something.
▸ **withholding, withheld**

with•in (wiTH-**in** *or* with-**in**) ***preposition***
1. Inside. ▸ ***adverb*** **within**
2. Not beyond the limits of.

with•out (wiTH-**out** *or* with-**out**) ***preposition***
1. Not having; lacking.
2. Not accompanied by.
3. In a way that avoids.

with•stand (with-**stand** *or* wiTH-**stand**) ***verb*** To stand strongly against; to resist. ▸ **withstanding, withstood**

wit•ness (**wit**-niss) ***noun***
1. A person who has seen or heard something.
2. A person who gives evidence in a court of law.
3. A person who signs an official paper to prove that he or she watched a contract, will, or other legal document being signed.
▸ ***noun, plural*** **witnesses** ▸ ***verb*** **witness**

W

who
...us or
...ciest
...noun
...pecially a man, believed
...agic powers; a sorcerer.
...neone who is extremely good at
something.

wob•ble (**wob**-uhl) ***verb*** To move unsteadily from side to side.
▸ **wobbling, wobbled** ▸ ***adjective*** **wobbly**

woe (**woh**) ***noun*** Great sadness or grief; sorrow; suffering. ▸ ***adjective*** **woeful**
▸ ***adverb*** **woefully**

wok (**wok**) ***noun*** A pan shaped like a bowl that is used especially for stir-frying food.

wolf (**wulf**)
1. ***noun*** A wild mammal that is related to the dog and hunts in a pack for prey.
▸ ***noun, plural*** **wolves** (**wulvz**)
2. ***verb*** To eat quickly and greedily.
▸ **wolfing, wolfed**

wol•ver•ine (**wul**-vuh-reen) ***noun*** A powerfully built mammal with dark brown fur and a long, bushy tail. Wolverines are found in northern regions. They are related to weasels.

wom•an (**wum**-uhn) ***noun*** An adult female human being. ▸ ***noun, plural*** **women** (**wi**-min) ▸ ***adverb*** **womanly**

wom•an•hood (**wum**-uhn-hud) ***noun***
1. The time or state of being a female adult.
2. Women as a group.

womb (**woom**) ***noun*** The hollow organ in female mammals that holds and nourishes a fetus; the uterus.

wom•bat (**wom**-bat) ***noun*** An Australian animal that looks like a small bear. Wombats are marsupials. The female carries her young in a pouch.

won (**wuhn**) ***verb*** Past tense and past participle of **win. Won** sounds like **one.**

won•der (**wuhn**-dur)
1. ***noun*** Something so remarkable or impressive that it causes surprise or amazement; a marvel.
2. ***noun*** The feeling caused by something remarkable or impressive; awe.
3. ***verb*** To be curious about something; to want to know or learn more.
4. ***verb*** To be amazed and impressed by something.
▸ ***verb*** **wondering, wondered**

won•der•ful (**wuhn**-dur-fuhl) ***adjective***
1. Causing wonder; remarkable, amazing, or impressive.
2. Very good; excellent.
▸ ***adverb*** **wonderfully**

won't (**wohnt**) ***contraction*** A short form of *will not.*

wood (**wud**) ***noun***
1. The hard substance that forms the trunk and branches of a tree.
▸ ***adjective*** **wooden**
2. woods ***noun, plural*** An area of thickly growing trees; a forest.
▸ ***adjective*** **wooded**
Wood sounds like **would.**

wood•chuck (**wud**-*chuhk*) ***noun*** A North American animal that has a stout body and brown or gray fur. It lives underground and sleeps all winter. The woodchuck is also called a **groundhog.**

wood•land (**wud**-luhnd) ***noun*** Land covered mainly by trees; a forest.

wood•peck•er (**wud**-*pek*-ur) ***noun*** Any of a number of birds that live in forests throughout the world. Woodpeckers have strong, pointed bills, which they use to drill holes in trees to get insects.

wood•wind (**wud**-*wind*) ***adjective*** The **woodwind** section of an orchestra is made up of wind instruments that were originally made of wood, such as the flute, clarinet, and oboe. ▸ ***noun*** **woodwind**

wood•work (**wud**-*wurk*) ***noun***
1. Things made out of wood, especially wooden parts inside a house, such as window frames, doors, and moldings.
2. woodworking The art or craft of making things from wood. ▸ ***noun*** **woodworker**

wool (**wul**) ***noun***
1. The soft, thick, curly hair of sheep and certain other animals such as the llama and alpaca. Wool is spun into yarn, which is used to make fabric.
2. Yarn or fabric made of wool.
3. Anything made of a thick mass of fibers, as in *steel wool.*
▸ ***adjective*** **woolen,** ***adjective*** **woolly**

word (**wurd**)
1. ***noun*** A unit of one or more spoken sounds or written letters that has a meaning in a given language.
2. ***noun*** A brief remark or comment.
3. ***noun*** A short conversation.
4. ***noun*** News, or a message.
5. If you **give your word,** you promise you will do something.
6. ***verb*** To put into words. ▸ **wording, worded**

word•ing (**wur**-ding) ***noun*** The way in which something is said or written; the choice and arrangement of words.

word processing ***noun*** The use of a computer or similar machine to type and print documents. Words are viewed on the screen and can easily be changed, moved, copied, and stored.
▸ ***noun*** **word processor**

word•y (**wur**-dee) ***adjective*** Having or using too many words. ▸ **wordier, wordiest**

work (**wurk**)
1. ***noun*** Effort or labor to get something done.
2. ***verb*** To get something done by using your energy or ability.
3. ***verb*** To function properly.
4. ***verb*** To have a job.
5. ***verb*** To bring about or to cause.
6. ***noun*** A person's job; what someone does to earn a living.
7. ***noun*** A task.
8. ***noun*** A piece of music, a painting, or a sculpture, as in *a work of art.*
9. works ***noun, plural*** The moving parts of a watch or machine.
10. ***verb*** If you **work out** a puzzle, you solve it by thinking hard.
11. ***verb*** When you **work out** in a gym, you do physical exercise. ▸ ***noun*** **workout** ▸ ***verb*** **working, worked**

work•a•ble (**wurk**-uh-buhl) ***adjective*** If a plan is **workable,** it can be carried out.

work•a•hol•ic (*wur*-kuh-**hol**-ik) ***noun*** Someone who feels driven to work hard. A workaholic puts in long hours and rarely takes time off.

work•bench (**wurk**-*bench*) ***noun*** A strong table used by someone who works with tools, such as a carpenter or a mechanic.

work•book (**wurk**-*buk*) ***noun*** A book with problems and exercises to be done by students.

work•er (**wur**-kur) ***noun***
1. Someone who is employed to do a job.
2. A female bee, ant, termite, or other insect that does all the work for the colony but does not reproduce.

work•man (**wurk**-muhn) ***noun*** A man who does manual work or who works with machines. ▸ ***noun, plural*** **workmen**

work•man•ship (**wurk**-muhn-ship) ***noun*** The skill and care with which something is made, usually by hand.

work•shop (**wurk**-*shop*) ***noun***
1. A room, shed, or other building where things are made or fixed.
2. A group of people who meet to discuss, learn about, or practice a particular skill, as in *a writers' workshop.*

W

work•sta•tion (**wurk**-*stay*-shuhn) ***noun***
1. An area with the equipment needed to do a specific job. A workstation is usually used by one person.
2. A computer that runs programs and allows people to gain access to a computer network.

world (**wurld**) ***noun***
1. The earth.
2. A particular part of the earth, as in *the Western world.*
3. Everyone who lives on earth.
4. An area of activity, as in *the world of sports.*
5. A large amount; a great deal.
6. A division of living things, as in *the animal world.*

world-class ***adjective*** Of the highest rank or level in the world.

World War I ***noun*** A war fought from 1914 to 1918, mainly in Europe. The United States, Great Britain, France, Russia, Italy, Japan, and other allied nations defeated Germany, Austria-Hungary, Turkey, and Bulgaria.

World War II ***noun*** A war in which the United States, France, Great Britain, the Soviet Union, and other allied nations defeated Germany, Italy, and Japan. World War II started in 1939 when Germany invaded Poland and ended in 1945 with the surrender of Germany and Japan.

world•wide (**wurld-wide**) ***adjective*** Extending or spreading throughout the world, as in *worldwide fame* or *worldwide concern.*

World Wide Web ***noun*** The linked system of Web pages on the Internet. Also called the **Web.**

worm (**wurm**)
1. ***noun*** A small animal that lives in the soil. Worms have long, thin, soft bodies and no backbones or legs.
2. ***verb*** To move like a worm by wriggling or twisting and turning from side to side. ▸ **worming, wormed**

worn (**worn**)
1. ***verb*** Past participle of **wear.**
2. ***adjective*** Damaged by wear or use.
Worn sounds like **warn.**

worn-out ***adjective***
1. No longer useful or in good condition.
2. Very tired; exhausted.

wor•ry (**wur**-ee)
1. ***verb*** To be anxious or uneasy about something. ▸ **worries, worrying, worried**
2. ***noun*** Anxiety, or nervousness.
3. ***noun*** Something that makes you anxious.
▸ ***noun, plural*** **worries** ▸ ***noun*** **worrier** ▸ ***adjective*** **worrying** ▸ ***adverb*** **worriedly**

worse (**wurss**)
1. ***adjective*** More inferior; less good.
2. ***adjective*** More evil or bad.
3. ***adjective*** More unpleasant, severe, or harmful.
4. ***adjective*** More ill.
5. ***adverb*** In a worse way.
6. ***noun*** Something that is worse.

wor•ship (**wur**-ship)
1. ***verb*** To express love and devotion to God or a god. ▸ ***noun*** **worship**
2. ***noun*** A church service.
3. ***verb*** If you **worship** someone, you think that the person is wonderful.
▸ ***verb*** **worshiping** *or* **worshipping, worshiped** *or* **worshipped**

worst (**wurst**)
1. ***adjective*** Most inferior, harmful, or unpleasant; worse than any other one.
2. ***adverb*** In the worst way.
3. ***noun*** Someone or something that is the worst.

worth (**wurth**)
1. ***adjective*** Having a certain value in money. ▸ ***noun*** **worth**
2. ***adjective*** Deserving, or good enough for.
3. ***noun*** The quality that makes someone or something valuable or important.

W

worth•less (**wurth**-liss) ***adjective*** If something is **worthless,** it has no value or is useless. ▸ ***noun*** **worthlessness**

worth•while (**wurth-wile**) ***adjective*** Useful and valuable.

wor•thy (**wur**-THee) ***adjective***
1. Having value or merit; good or worthwhile.
2. Good enough for; deserving.
▸ ***adjective*** **worthier, worthiest**

would (**wud**) ***verb***
1. Past tense of the helping verb **will.**
2. Would expresses a possibility.
3. Would expresses frequent or habitual action in the past.
4. Would expresses a request.
Would sounds like **wood.**

would•n't (**wud**-uhnt) ***contraction*** A short form of *would not.*

wound
1. (**woond**) ***noun*** An injury in which the skin is cut, usually because of an accident or violence. ▸ ***verb*** **wound**
2. (**woond**) ***verb*** To hurt someone's feelings. ▸ **wounding, wounded**
▸ ***noun*** **wound**
3. (**wound**) ***verb*** Past tense and past participle of **wind.**

wran•gle (**rang**-guhl) ***verb***
1. To argue or debate in a noisy or angry way. ▸ ***noun*** **wrangle**
2. To herd horses and livestock on the range. ▸ ***noun*** **wrangler**
▸ ***verb*** **wrangling, wrangled**

wrap (**rap**)
1. ***verb*** To cover something with paper, material, etc.
2. ***verb*** To hide by covering.
3. ***verb*** To wind or to clasp.
4. ***noun*** An outer garment such as a coat or shawl.
5. If you are **wrapped up** in something, you are totally involved in it.
Wrap sounds like **rap.**
▸ ***verb*** **wrapping, wrapped**

wrap•per (**rap**-ur) ***noun*** The protective material in which something is wrapped, as in *a candy wrapper.*

wrath (**rath**) ***noun*** Great anger; rage.

wreak (**reek**) ***verb*** To cause or to inflict. **Wreak** sounds like **reek.** ▸ **wreaking, wreaked**

wreath (**reeth**) ***noun*** A circle of flowers, leaves, or branches that are twisted together.

wreck (**rek**)
1. ***verb*** To destroy or ruin something.
▸ **wrecking, wrecked**
2. ***noun*** The remains of something that has been destroyed or damaged.

wreck•age (**rek**-ij) ***noun*** The broken parts or pieces lying around at the site of a crash or an explosion.

wren (**ren**) ***noun*** A small songbird with a long, slender bill; brown feathers; and a small tail that sticks up.

wrench (**rench**)
1. ***verb*** To pull something suddenly and forcefully.
2. ***verb*** To injure yourself by twisting a part of your body.
3. ***noun*** A tool with jaws for tightening and loosening nuts. ▸ ***noun, plural*** **wrenches**
▸ ***verb*** **wrenches, wrenching, wrenched**

wrest (**rest**) ***verb***
1. To twist, pull, or tear away.
2. To take by force or violence.
Wrest sounds like **rest.**

wres•tle (**ress**-uhl) ***verb***
1. To fight by gripping or holding your opponent and trying to throw the person to the ground.
2. If you **wrestle** with a problem, you try to solve it by thinking very hard.
▸ ***verb*** **wrestling, wrestled**

wres•tling (**ress**-ling) ***noun*** A sport in which two opponents try to throw or force each other to the ground. ▸ ***noun*** **wrestler**

wretch•ed (**rech**-id) ***adjective***
1. Miserable or unfortunate.
2. Mean or evil.
▸ ***noun*** **wretch**

X

wrig•gle (**rig**-uhl) ***verb*** To twist and turn. ▸ **wriggling, wriggled**

wring (**ring**) ***verb***
1. To squeeze the moisture from wet material by twisting it with both hands.
▸ ***noun*** **wringer**
2. To get by using force or threats.
Wring sounds like **ring.**
▸ ***verb*** **wringing, wrung** (**ruhng**)

wrin•kle (**ring**-kuhl) ***noun*** A crease or line in skin or in material. ▸ ***verb*** **wrinkle**

wrist (**rist**) ***noun*** The joint that connects your hand and your arm.

wrist•watch (**rist**-*woch*) ***noun*** A watch worn on a strap or band that fits around the wrist.

write (**rite**) ***verb***
1. To put down letters, words, or numbers on paper or another surface, using a pen, pencil, etc.
2. To be the author or composer of stories, poems, articles, or music.
3. To send a letter or word of some kind.
Write sounds like **right.**
▸ ***verb*** **writing, wrote** (**rote**), **written** (**rit**-in) ▸ ***noun*** **writer**

writhe (**riTHe**) ***verb*** To twist and turn around, as in pain. ▸ **writhing, writhed**

writ•ing (**rye**-ting) ***noun***
1. The act of putting letters on paper.
2. A written work such as a story, book, or poem.
3. Written form.
4. Handwriting.

wrong (**rawng** *or* **rong**) ***adjective***
1. Not correct or not true, as in *wrong answers.*
2. Bad or immoral.
▸ ***noun*** **wrong** ▸ ***adverb*** **wrongly**

wrong•do•ing (**rawng**-*doo*-ing *or* **rong**-*doo*-ing) ***noun*** Any act or behavior that is wrong, evil, or illegal.

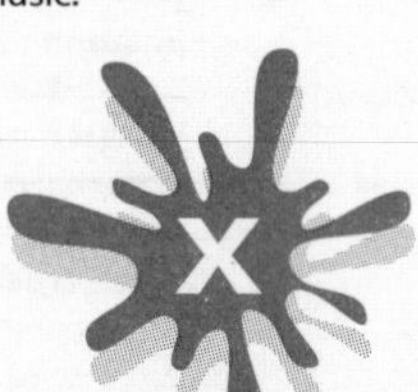

Xe•rox (**zee**-roks) ***noun*** Trademark name for a kind of photocopier. ▸ ***verb*** **Xerox**

X•mas (**kriss**-muhss *or* **eks**-muhss) ***noun*** Christmas.

X ray (**eks**) ***noun***
1. An invisible high-energy beam of light that can pass through solid objects. X rays are used to take pictures of teeth, bones, and organs inside the body.
2. A photograph of the inside of a person's body, taken using X rays.
▸ ***verb*** **X-ray**
▸ ***adjective*** **X-ray**

xy•lo•phone (**zye**-luh-*fone*) ***noun*** A musical instrument with wooden bars of different lengths that are struck to give different notes.

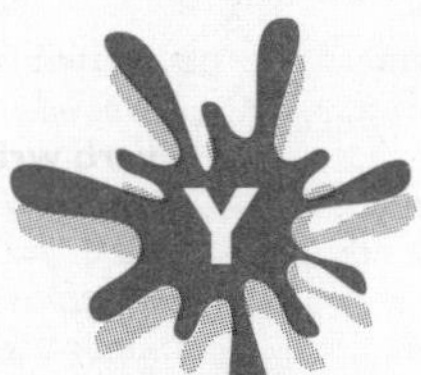

yacht (**yot**) ***noun*** A large boat or small ship used for pleasure or for racing.
▸ ***noun*** **yachting**

yak (**yak**) ***noun*** An ox of Tibet and central Asia that has long, shaggy hair. Yaks are used as work animals.

yam (**yam**) ***noun***
1. The starchy root of a trailing vine that grows in the tropics. It is ground into flour or eaten as a vegetable.
2. A large sweet potato that has reddish flesh.

yank (**yangk**) ***verb*** To give a sudden, sharp pull; to jerk. ▸ **yanking, yanked**
▸ ***noun*** **yank**

Yan•kee (**yang**-kee) ***noun***
1. A person born or living in one of the northern states, especially a state in New England.
2. A person who fought for the Union during the Civil War.
3. Any person born or living in the United States.

yap (**yap**) ***verb***
1. To bark repeatedly with short, high sounds.
2. *(slang)* To talk in a noisy, stupid way.
▸ ***verb*** **yapping, yapped**

yard (**yard**) ***noun***
1. A unit of length equal to 3 feet or 36 inches. A softball bat can be up to 34 inches, just slightly shorter than a yard.
2. An area of ground surrounding or next to a house, school, or other building.
3. An enclosed area used for a certain type of work or business, as in *a navy yard.*
4. An area next to a railroad station where trains are switched, repaired, or stored.

yard•stick (**yard**-*stik*) ***noun***
1. A measuring stick that is one yard long.
2. A standard used to judge or compare things or people.

yar•mul•ke (**yah**-muh-kuh *or* **yar**-muhl-kuh) ***noun*** A small, round cap that Jewish men and boys wear on their heads, especially during religious services.

yarn (**yarn**) ***noun***
1. Fibers such as wool, cotton, silk, or nylon that have been twisted or spun into long strands for use in knitting or weaving.
2. *(informal)* If someone **spins a yarn,** he or she tells a long and exaggerated story.

yawn (**yawn**) ***verb***
1. To open your mouth wide and breathe in deeply, often because you are tired or bored. ▸ ***noun*** **yawn**
2. To open wide.
▸ ***verb*** **yawning, yawned**

year (**yihr**) ***noun***
1. The period of time in which the earth makes one complete trip around the sun, about 365 days and 6 hours.
2. On the calendar that we commonly use today, a **year** is a period of 365 days, or 366 in a leap year, divided into 52 weeks or 12 months. The year begins January 1 and ends December 31.
3. Any period of 12 months.
4. A part of a year spent in a particular activity, as in *the school year.*

year•ly (**yihr**-lee) ***adjective*** Happening or done each year. ▸ ***adverb*** **yearly**

Y

yearn (**yurn**) ***verb*** To wish or long for something very strongly. ▸ **yearning, yearned** ▸ ***noun*** **yearning**

yeast (**yeest**) ***noun*** A yellow fungus used to make bread dough rise and to ferment alcoholic drinks.

yell (**yel**) ***verb*** To shout, cry out, or scream loudly. ▸ **yelling, yelled** ▸ ***noun*** **yell**

yel•low (**yel**-oh)
1. ***noun*** One of the three primary colors, along with red and blue. Yellow is the color of lemons and butter.
2. ***noun*** The yolk of an egg.
3. ***verb*** To become or make yellow.
▸ **yellowing, yellowed**
▸ ***adjective*** **yellow**

yellow jacket ***noun*** A wasp that has black and bright yellow stripes. It usually nests in or near the ground and has a painful sting.

yelp (**yelp**) ***verb*** When a dog **yelps,** it makes a sharp, high, crying sound, showing that it is in pain. ▸ **yelping, yelped** ▸ ***noun*** **yelp**

yen (**yen**) ***noun***
1. The main unit of money in Japan.
2. *(informal)* If you have a **yen** for something, you want it very much.

yes (**yess**)
1. ***adverb*** A word used to show that you agree or that something is true.
2. ***noun*** An answer that shows agreement, approval, or acceptance.
3. ***noun*** A vote or voter in favor of something.
▸ ***noun, plural*** **yeses** *or* **yesses**

yes•ter•day (**yess**-tur-dee *or* **yess**-tur-*day*)
1. ***noun*** The day before today.
2. ***noun*** The recent past.
3. ***adverb*** On the day before today.

yet (**yet**)
1. ***adverb*** Up to now; so far.
2. ***adverb*** At the present time; now.
3. ***adverb*** In addition; even.
4. ***adverb*** At some future time; eventually.
5. ***conjunction*** But.

yew (**yoo**) ***noun*** An evergreen tree or shrub with a red-brown bark; poisonous, dark green needles; and red berries. It is grown widely as a decorative plant or hedge. The wood of the yew is often used to make archery bows. **Yew** sounds like **ewe** and **you.**

yield (**yeeld**) ***verb***
1. To produce something. ▸ ***noun*** **yield**
2. To surrender or to give in.
▸ ***verb*** **yielding, yielded**

yo (**yoh**) ***interjection*** *(slang)* A word used to get someone's attention, say hello, or acknowledge being called.

yo•del (**yoh**-duhl) ***verb*** To sing in a voice that changes rapidly between high and low sounds. ▸ **yodeling, yodeled** ▸ ***noun*** **yodeler**

yo•ga (**yoh**-guh) ***noun*** A system of exercises and meditation that helps people become mentally relaxed and physically fit. Yoga came originally from Hindu teachings.

yo•gurt (**yoh**-gurt) ***noun*** A slightly sour food prepared from milk fermented by bacteria.

yoke (**yoke**) ***noun***
1. A wooden frame attached to the necks of oxen or other work animals to link them together for plowing. ▸ ***verb*** **yoke**
2. The part of a shirt, blouse, or dress that fits around the shoulders and neck.
Yoke sounds like **yolk.**

yolk (**yoke**) ***noun*** The yellow part of an egg. If the egg is fertilized, the protein and fat from the yolk nourish the developing embryo. **Yolk** sounds like **yoke.**

Yom Kip•pur (*yom* **kip**-ur *or* **yohm** ki-**poor**) ***noun*** A Jewish holiday that falls 10 days after Rosh Hashanah during September or October. On Yom Kippur, Jewish people fast to atone for sins.

yon•der (**yon**-dur) ***adverb*** Over there. ▸ ***adjective*** **yonder**

you (**yoo**) ***pronoun***
1. The person or people that someone is

speaking or writing to.
2. Anyone, or people in general.
You sounds like **ewe** and **yew.**

you'd (**yood**) ***contraction*** A short form of *you had* or *you would.*

you'll (**yool**) ***contraction*** A short form of *you shall* or *you will.* **You'll** sounds like **Yule.**

young (**yuhng**)
1. ***adjective*** Someone who is **young** has lived for a short time.
2. ***adjective*** Something that is **young** has existed for a short time.
3. ***adjective*** Having the qualities of a young person; fresh; vigorous.
4. ***noun*** The offspring of an animal.
▸ ***noun, plural*** **young**
▸ ***adjective*** **younger, youngest**

young·ster (**yuhng**-stur) ***noun*** A young person.

your (**yur** *or* **yor**) ***adjective*** Belonging to or having to do with you.

you're (**yur** *or* **yer**) ***contraction*** A short form of *you are.*

yours (**yurz** *or* **yorz**) ***pronoun*** The one or ones belonging to or having to do with you.

your·self (yur-**self**) ***pronoun*** Your own self. ▸ ***pronoun, plural*** **yourselves**

youth (**yooth**) ***noun***
1. The time of life when a person is no longer a child but is not yet an adult.
2. The quality or state of being young.
3. A young person, especially a young male between 13 and 18 years of age.
4. Young people in general.

you've (**yoov**) ***contraction*** A short form of *you have.*

yowl (**youl**) ***noun*** A long, mournful cry; a howl. ▸ ***verb*** **yowl**

yo-yo (**yoh yoh**) ***noun*** A toy consisting of a string wound around a flat reel. You loop the string over your finger and flick the reel up and down on the string.

Yule (**yool**) ***noun*** Another word for **Christmas. Yule** sounds like **you'll.**

Yule·tide (**yool**-*tide*) ***noun*** The Christmas season.

yup·py (**yuhp**-ee) ***noun*** A young person with a well-paid job and an expensive lifestyle. ▸ ***noun, plural*** **yuppies**

za·ny (**zay**-nee) ***adjective*** Humorous in an unusual, crazy way. ▸ **zanier, zaniest** ▸ ***adverb*** **zanily**

zap (**zap**) ***verb*** *(slang)*
1. To shoot or destroy with force, as in an electronic game.
2. To cook with microwaves.
3. To change channels on a television set with a remote control.
▸ ***verb*** **zapping, zapped**

zeal (**zeel**) ***noun*** Enthusiasm and eagerness. ▸ ***noun*** **zealot** (**zel**-uht) ▸ ***adjective*** **zealous** (**zel**-uhss)

ze·bra (**zee**-bruh) ***noun*** A wild animal of southern and eastern Africa. A zebra is similar to a horse except that it is smaller and has black and white stripes on its body. A zebra's stripes help protect it from predators.

ze·nith (**zee**-nith) ***noun***
1. The point in the sky directly overhead.
2. The highest point.

zep·pe·lin (**zep**-uh-lin) ***noun*** An airship, or dirigible, with a rigid frame. A zeppelin is shaped like a cigar.

Z

ze•ro (**zihr**-oh) ***noun***
1. The numeral or figure 0, which indicates the number of objects in an empty set.
2. A point on a thermometer or other scale at which numbering or measurement begins.
3. Nothing.
▸ ***noun, plural*** **zeros** *or* **zeroes**
▸ ***adjective*** **zero**

zest (**zest**) ***noun*** Enthusiasm and liveliness, as in *a zest for life.*

zig•zag (**zig**-*zag*) ***noun*** A line or course that moves in short, sharp turns or angles from one side to the other.
▸ ***verb*** **zigzag**

zilch (**zilch**) ***noun*** *(slang)* Absolutely nothing; zero.

zinc (**zingk**) ***noun*** A blue-white metal that is used in some alloys and for coating metals so that they will not rust. Zinc is a chemical element.

zin•ni•a (**zin**-ee-yuh) ***noun*** A garden plant with round, brightly colored flowers.

zip (**zip**)
1. ***verb*** To fasten clothes with a zipper.
2. ***noun*** A short, hissing sound, as in *the zip of a bullet.* ▸ ***verb*** **zip**
3. ***verb*** *(informal)* To move fast.
▸ ***verb*** **zipping, zipped**

zip code *or* **ZIP code** ***noun*** A number given by the Postal Service to each delivery area in the United States. Zip codes speed the sorting and delivery of mail. ZIP stands for *Zone Improvement Plan.*

zip•per (**zip**-ur) ***noun*** A fastener for clothes or other objects. A zipper consists of two strips of metal or plastic teeth that link up when the strips are pulled together.

zith•er (**zith**-ur *or* **ziTH**-ur) ***noun*** A musical instrument made up of a flat box with strings stretched across it. Instruments in the zither family can have up to 40 strings, which are plucked with a pick or with the fingers.

zo•di•ac (**zoh**-dee-ak) ***noun*** A circular, imaginary belt in the sky that includes the path of the sun, the moon, and the planets. The zodiac is divided into 12 equal parts, each named for a different constellation.

zone (**zohn**) ***noun***
1. An area that is separate from other areas and used for a special purpose, as in *a "No Parking" zone* or *the end zone of a football field.*
2. Any of the five areas of the earth divided according to climate. There are two frigid zones, two temperate zones, and one torrid zone.

zoo (**zoo**) ***noun*** A place where animals are kept for people to see or study them.

zo•ol•o•gy (zoh-**ol**-uh-jee) ***noun*** The science that deals with the study of animal life. ▸ ***noun*** **zoologist**
▸ ***adjective*** **zoological** (*zoh*-uh-**loj**-i-kuhl)

zoom (**zoom**) ***verb***
1. To move quickly with a loud, humming sound.
2. To increase or rise rapidly and suddenly.
▸ ***verb*** **zooming, zoomed**

zuc•chi•ni (zu-**kee**-nee) ***noun*** A long squash that has green skin. ▸ ***noun, plural*** **zucchini** *or* **zucchinis**

Zu•ni (**zoo**-nee) *or* **Zu•ñi** (**zoo**-nyee) ***noun*** A member of a tribe of American Indians that now lives in western New Mexico. ▸ ***noun, plural*** **Zuni** *or* **Zunis,** *or* **Zuñi** *or* **Zuñis**

Measurement Tables

LENGTH

U.S.

1 foot = 12 inches
1 yard = 3 feet
1 mile = 5,280 feet = 1,760 yards

Metric

1 centimeter = 10 millimeters
1 meter = 100 centimeters
1 kilometer = 1,000 meters

Conversion

1 inch = 2.54 centimeters
1 centimeter = 0.394 inch
1 meter = 1.094 yards
1 foot = 30.48 centimeters
1 mile = 1.609 kilometers
1 kilometer = 0.621 mile

WEIGHT

U.S.

1 pound = 16 ounces
1 ton = 2,000 pounds

Metric

1 gram = 1,000 milligrams
1 kilogram = 1,000 grams
1 metric ton = 1,000 kilograms

Conversion

1 ounce = 28.349 grams
1 gram = 0.035 ounce
1 pound = 0.453 kilogram
1 kilogram = 2.204 pounds
1 ton = 0.907 metric ton
1 metric ton = 1.102 tons

TEMPERATURE

Use the following formulas to convert temperatures from Fahrenheit to Celsius or Celsius to Fahrenheit.

If you know the Celsius temperature and want to find out the Fahrenheit, use this formula

$°F = °C \times 9/5 + 32$

If you know the Fahrenheit temperature and want to find out the Celsius, use this formula

$°C = 5/9 \times (°F - 32)$

Facts about the 50 States

State	Postal abbrev.	Nickname	Population	Capital	Year of (order of) admission
Alabama	AL	Heart of Dixie	4,500,752	Montgomery	1819 (22)
Alaska	AK	The Last Frontier (unofficial)	648,818	Juneau	1959 (49)
Arizona	AZ	Grand Canyon State	5,580,811	Phoenix	1912 (48)
Arkansas	AR	Land of Opportunity	2,725,714	Little Rock	1836 (25)
California	CA	Golden State	35,484,453	Sacramento	1850 (31)
Colorado	CO	Centennial State	4,550,688	Denver	1876 (38)
Connecticut	CT	Constitution State	3,483,372	Hartford	1788 (5)
Delaware	DE	First State	817,491	Dover	1787 (1)
Florida	FL	Sunshine State	17,019,068	Tallahassee	1845 (27)
Georgia	GA	Empire State of the South	8,684,715	Atlanta	1788 (4)
Hawaii	HI	Aloha State	1,257,608	Honolulu	1959 (50)
Idaho	ID	Gem State	1,366,332	Boise	1890 (43)
Illinois	IL	Prairie State	12,653,544	Springfield	1818 (21)
Indiana	IN	Hoosier State	6,195,643	Indianapolis	1816 (19)
Iowa	IA	Hawkeye State	2,944,062	Des Moines	1846 (29)
Kansas	KS	Sunflower State	2,723,507	Topeka	1861 (34)
Kentucky	KY	Bluegrass State	4,117,827	Frankfort	1792 (15)
Louisiana	LA	Pelican State	4,496,334	Baton Rouge	1812 (18)
Maine	ME	Pine Tree State	1,305,728	Augusta	1820 (23)
Maryland	MD	Old Line State	5,508,909	Annapolis	1788 (7)
Massachusetts	MA	Bay State	6,433,422	Boston	1788 (6)
Michigan	MI	Wolverine State	10,079,985	Lansing	1837 (26)
Minnesota	MN	Gopher State	5,059,375	St. Paul	1858 (32)
Mississippi	MS	Magnolia State	2,881,281	Jackson	1817 (20)
Missouri	MO	Show Me State	5,704,484	Jefferson City	1821 (24)

These population figures were taken from the U.S. Census Bureau's 2003 population estimates.

State	Postal abbrev.	Nickname	Population	Capital	Year of (order of) admission
Montana	MT	Treasure State	917,621	Helena	1889 (41)
Nebraska	NE	Cornhusker State	1,739,291	Lincoln	1867 (37)
Nevada	NV	Silver State	2,241,154	Carson City	1864 (36)
New Hampshire	NH	Granite State	1,287,687	Concord	1788 (9)
New Jersey	NJ	Garden State	8,638,396	Trenton	1787 (3)
New Mexico	NM	Land of Enchantment	1,874,614	Santa Fe	1912 (47)
New York	NY	Empire State	19,190,115	Albany	1788 (11)
North Carolina	NC	Tar Heel State	8,407,248	Raleigh	1789 (12)
North Dakota	ND	Peace Garden State	633,837	Bismarck	1889 (39)
Ohio	OH	Buckeye State	11,435,798	Columbus	1803 (17)
Oklahoma	OK	Sooner State	3,511,532	Oklahoma City	1907 (46)
Oregon	OR	Beaver State	3,559,596	Salem	1859 (33)
Pennsylvania	PA	Keystone State	12,365,455	Harrisburg	1787 (2)
Rhode Island	RI	Ocean State	1,076,164	Providence	1790 (13)
South Carolina	SC	Palmetto State	4,147,152	Columbia	1788 (8)
South Dakota	SD	Mount Rushmore State	764,309	Pierre	1889 (40)
Tennessee	TN	Volunteer State	5,841,748	Nashville	1796 (16)
Texas	TX	Lone Star State	22,118,509	Austin	1845 (28)
Utah	UT	Beehive State	2,351,467	Salt Lake City	1896 (45)
Vermont	VT	Green Mountain State	619,107	Montpelier	1791 (14)
Virginia	VA	Old Dominion	7,386,330	Richmond	1788 (10)
Washington	WA	Evergreen State	6,131,445	Olympia	1889 (42)
West Virginia	WV	Mountain State	1,810,354	Charleston	1863 (35)
Wisconsin	WI	Badger State	5,472,299	Madison	1848 (30)
Wyoming	WY	Equality State	501,242	Cheyenne	1890 (44)

For the most recent figures, go to www.census.gov